2016 ALMANAC OF
BUSINESS AND INDUSTRIAL FINANCIAL RATIOS

Philip Wilson

 Wolters Kluwer

EDITORIAL STAFF

Production .... Christopher Zwirek
Design.. Craig Arritola

This publication is designed to provide accurate and authoritative information in regard to the subject matter covered. It is sold with the understanding that the publisher is not engaged in rendering legal, accounting, or other professional service and that the author is not offering such advice in this publication. If legal advice or other professional assistance is required, the services of a competent professional person should be sought.

ISBN: 978-0-8080-4109-2

Printed in the United States of America

DEDICATED

Professor Leo Troy, the author of The *Almanac of Business and Financial Ratios*, passed away on November 2, 2013. The *Almanac*, now in its 47th edition, is the product of our beloved father's vision. He recognized early on that the raw data collected by the IRS could be used to sharpen one's understanding of the true value of a business or industry. Dad painstakingly set about creating the Almanac out of that data so that its users could make more informed decisions. The *Almanac* thus reflects his passion for truth, his devotion to education, his curiosity and intellect, his diligence, and his relentless drive to provide a better life for his family. Dad appreciated the work of his colleagues **Ka-Neng Au** and **Phil Wilson**, and we thank them for their invaluable contributions to the *Almanac*. All of us, Dad's children and grandchildren, his relatives, friends and colleagues, seek to follow the example he set for us.

The memory of the righteous is for blessing.

Alexander Troy & Suzannah B. Troy

PREFACE

Now in its 47th Edition, the *Almanac of Business and Industrial Financial Ratios* provides a precise benchmark for evaluating an individual company's financial performance. The performance data is derived from the latest available IRS figures on U.S. and international companies, and tracks 50 operating and financial factors in nearly 200 industries. The *Almanac* provides competitive norms in actual dollar amounts for revenue and capital factors, as well as important average operating costs in percent of net sales. It also provides other critical financial factors in percentage, including debt ratio, return on assets, return on equity, profit margin, and more. Beyond its reliable insights into corporate behavior, the *Almanac* can be used by other countries looking to model their economies on American performance.

Also included with the text is a URL link that contains a special template that allows the reader to add individual company data of interest to compare and contrast with data from the book. This template can be found at *http://www.tax.cchgroup.com/downloads/files/SupplementalData/Almanac_of_Business_&_Industrial_Financial_Ratios_2016_files.zip*

2016 Edition Highlights

The 2016 Edition of the *Almanac of Business and Industrial Financial Ratios* has been updated to include the following:

- **Broad scope:** *2016 Almanac* features the North American Industry Classification System (NAICS), so you can benchmark or analyze results consistently with corporations in the United States, Canada, and Mexico.

- **Most industry types:** *2016 Almanac* highlights most industry types, including industries with advanced technologies and newly emerging industries such as paging and wireless communications.

- **A truer picture** of corporate financial performance, since the data isn't based on a mixed bag of averages that might include partnerships or sole proprietors. *2016 Almanac* features a homogeneous universe of American corporate financial performance.

- **Many classifications:** *2016 Almanac* analyzes 195 industries with 50 financial performance items.

- **Benchmarks:** *2016 Almanac* provides 13 benchmarks, including such critical measures as Receipts to Cash Flow, Debt to Total Assets, and Return on Equity both before and after taxes.

- **Analytical tables:** *Table I, Corporations with and without Net Income (All Corporations), and Table II, Corporations with Net Income.*

- **Easier apples-to-apples comparisons:** Each table is divided into 13 asset sizes.

- **More comprehensive:** Total receipts of all corporations covered by *2016 Almanac* is $29.4 trillion, making the *Almanac* the Anatomy of American Corporate Capitalism.

Philip Wilson

July 2015

INTRODUCTION

QUESTIONS, ANSWERS AND COMMENTS ON THE *ALMANAC*

Some users have requested further information on the use of the *Almanac's* ratios and statistics. This Q & A addition to the *Almanac* is in response to that demand.

1. What are the general purposes of the Almanac?

The goal of the *Almanac* is to provide users with a reliable and comprehensive source of standard financial ratios and financial statistics on all corporations, public and private, including those filing 1120S returns in the United States. Excluded are all individual proprietorships and partnerships. The *Almanac* makes available key business and financial statistics, which are consistent and neutral (unbiased by any commercial publisher or trade association).

2. What is the source and reliability of the Almanac's results?

The *Almanac's* results are computed from the Department of the Treasury, Internal Revenue Service's statistical sampling of the tax returns of all corporations. Dividends received from foreign corporations are included in total receipts of those corporations affected. The statistics apply to the company rather than the establishment.

3. Are international comparisons available?

Yes. Because of the adoption of a common system of industrial classification by the U.S., Canada and Mexico, known as the North American Industrial Classification System of industries (NAICS), under the North American Free Trade Agreement, users in Canada and Mexico can compare and contrast their results with those corporations in the United States.

4. What about comparisons within the U.S?

These are the most important applications of the *Almanac*. Results are available for each and every corporation within the U.S., whether public or private, and include small business corporations, those which file the 1120S tax return. Therefore, users can compare their corporate performance with that of their industry and asset size group of corporate enterprise in the United States.

5. How many corporations are covered in the Almanac?

The *Almanac's* results are derived from more than 5.8 million corporation tax returns. Furthermore, the user can easily determine the number of enterprises for the total of each industry and by each of the 12 asset size groups. This makes for a total of 13 asset size comparisons.

6. What about differences in the size of corporations?

In addition to the results for each industry, the *Almanac* displays 12 columns of performance by the size of assets. Again, this makes for a total of 13 asset size comparisons.

7. Does the Almanac distinguish between the profitability of corporations?

In a word, yes. Each industry is divided between two tables: Table I reports the results of all corporations in an industry, that is, those with and without net income. It is followed by a second table for the same industry, Table II, which reports only those corporations with net income.

8. How many items of information are there for each industry?

There are 50 indicators of corporate performance in each table and each industry and for all asset size groups, except where the IRS' data sample is too small, or it does not supply the necessary information.

9. Who are the users of the Almanac?

Accountants, corporate managers, business consultants, investors evaluating a corporate takeover, entrepreneurs considering new businesses, lawyers, and students of accounting, business, and management.

10. What accounting time period is covered?

The Internal Revenue Service provides the most recent statistics publicly available for the *Almanac*. For the 2016 *Almanac*, these statistics apply to the accounting period from July 2012 through June 2013.

WHAT'S NEW IN THIS EDITION

Beginning with the year 2002, the *Almanac of Business and Industrial Financial Ratios* began using the North American Industry Classification System (NAICS). NAICS replaces the Internal Revenue Service's own system, which it had used for many years, an adaptation of Standard Industrial Classification (SIC); all previous *Almanacs* had used that adaptation.

The new industrial classification system is the product of the North American Free Trade Agreement (NAFTA), and it replaces the existing classification systems not only of the United States but also of Canada and Mexico. Hence, the new system applies uniformly to the three countries, and users of the *Almanac 2016*, utilizing the new international industrial classification system, can now compare their results with corporations in all three nations.

In the United States, the new manual was created by the Office of Management and Budget (OMB). The NAICS system gives special attention to industries producing and furnishing advanced technologies, new and emerging industries, as well as service industries in general. NAICS divides the economy into 21 sectors, five in the predominantly goods-producing area, and 16 in the service producing area.

INDUSTRY SECTORS

In 2010 and 2011, the titles, definitions, and content of numerous NAICS industries were revised to reflect structural changes in the economy. Some related industries in the manufacturing sector have been consolidated, while others (e.g. electric power generation) have been reclassified into new and separate industries.

The 2012 NAICS Manual, which codified these revisions, is the basis for the industry groups and sectors covered by the latest IRS data. However, none of these changes affect the nearly 200 industry categories in the Almanac 2016.

The source of the IRS's data are the tax returns of all *active* public and private corporations. Because the *Almanac's* data are derived only from corporate tax returns, there is a mixture of corporate with the financial performance of partnerships and individual proprietorships; the *Almanac's* information constitutes a **homogeneous universe**. The tax returns are classified by the IRS on the basis of the business activity which accounts for a corporation's largest percentage of total receipts. Large corporations with dissimilar business activities are included in only one industry, despite operations that are unrelated to the industry in which they are grouped.

The data developed by the IRS are derived from a stratified probability sample of corporation income tax returns. Where the sample data from the sample are small and should those numbers be used in a denominator, the result is reported as a dot (·) in the *Almanac*. Returns of the largest corporations are generally in the sample from year to year, but comparability can be affected by consolidations and mergers, changes in the law and the tax forms, and changes in the industrial classification system used over the years.

REPRESENTATIVE INDUSTRIES

The *Almanac* reports on nearly 200 industries. Minor industries are denoted by a six-digit code; major industries are designated by a three-digit industry code; industrial sectors by a two-digit code; and industrial divisions by a two-digit code. When the data are the same for minor, major, sector, and industrial division, the IRS reports only the industrial division, and similarly for other identities applicable to the major and sectoral industries; the *Almanac* follows this procedure.

Almanac 2016 continues the previous coverage of reporting information: for all industries, **Table I, Corporations with and without Net Income** (that is, the entire universe of active reporting corporations), and **Table II, Corporations with Net Income**, a subset of the universe. In the *Almanac 2016*, Table I covers over 5.8 million enterprises (corporations), and Table II covers 3.5 million corporations with net income. This implies that 2.3 million corporations reported deficits. The IRS defines net income (or deficit) as the companies' net profit or loss from taxable sources of income reduced by allowable deductions. Total receipts of the 5.8 million corporations reported in *Almanac 2016* was $29.4 trillion, up by $1.1 trillion.

The *Almanac* continues to report performance results not only by the total for each industry, but by 12 other asset size groups (a total of 13 asset size groups), providing 50 items of data and/or ratios on corporate performance:

TOTAL

Zero

$1 to $500,000

$500,001 to $1,000,000

$1,000,001 to $5,000,000

$5,000,001 to $10,000,000

$10,000,001 to $25,000,000

$25,000,001 to $50,000,000

$50,000,001 to $100,000,000

$100,000,001 to $250,000,000

$250,000,001 to $500,000,000

$500,000,001 to $2,500,000,000

$2,500,000,001 or more

All data in Tables I and II cover an accounting period identified on all tables and are the most recent information available from the IRS. For the *Almanac 2016*, the accounting period is July 2012 through June 2013. The dating of the data is counterbalanced by the most extensive industrial coverage available in any report on financial performance, the number of items of corporate performance, and their availability in thirteen asset size groups. Moreover, the timing of the data are also counterbalanced by the stability of the *Almanac's* values as past trends have indicated. Therefore, the *Almanac's* financial results are reliable in assessing current corporate performance.

Beyond its reliable insights into corporate behavior on a micro basis, its comprehensive and detailed coverage make the *Almanac* the **Anatomy of American Corporate Capitalism**. In this macro sense, it constitutes **the** example to those countries desirous of modeling their economies on the American performance.

HOW TO USE THE ALMANAC

On the micro level, the *Almanac* multiplies manyfold the power of financial analysis to evaluate an individual company's financial performance: In contrast to many standard reports, the *Almanac* gives management, and analysts independent of any company, more of the fundamental analytical tools needed to compare their company with companies in the same industry and of the same asset size. The *Almanac* can enhance the value of any company's annual report because it affords the analyst and the stockholder detailed background of financial information for comparison.

All items and ratios are listed in Both Table I and Table II. No figures are reported in the *Almanac* when the IRS has either suppressed the underlying data, or the sample size, or other reasons affecting a calculated result, and where the ratio/item was not applicable to an industry. The 50 tax-based items that provide that financial analysis are as follows:

1. Number of Enterprises

These are the count of corporate tax returns filed by active corporations on one of the Form 1120-series returns.

> **SPECIAL NOTE:** Net Sales is used to compute the percentage of items 3 to 7 to Net Sales for all industries, except Finance, Insurance, and Real Estate (FIRE). For the FIRE industries, Total Receipts are used to compute the percentage of items 3 to 7.

REVENUES ($ IN THOUSANDS), ITEMS 2 TO 9

2. Operating Income (Net Sales)

This is the IRS item Business Receipts, the gross operating receipts reduced by the cost of returned goods and allowances.

3. Interest

Taxable interest includes interest on U.S. Government obligations, loans, notes, mortgages, arbitrage bonds, nonexempt private activity bonds, corporate bonds, bank deposits, and tax refunds; interest received from tax-exempt state or local municipal bonds and ESOP loans are not included in this item.

4. Rents

These are the gross amounts received from the use or occupancy of property by corporations whose principal activities did not involve operating rental properties.

5. Royalties

These are gross payments received for the use of property rights before taking deductions.

6. Other Portfolio Income

These consist of cash, notes, and accounts receivable, less allowance for bad debts and inventories.

7. Other Receipts

These receipts include such items as income from minor operations, cash discounts, claims, license rights, judgments, and joint ventures.

8. Total Receipts

Total receipts are the sum of ten items: 1. Business receipts; 2. Interest; 3. Interest on government obligations: state and local; 4. Rents; 5. Royalties; 6. Net capital gains (excluding long-term gains from regulated investment companies); 7. Net gain, noncapital assets; 8. Dividends received from domestic corporations; 9. Dividends received from foreign corporations; 10. Other receipts.

9. Average Total Receipts

Total receipts divided by the number of enterprises.

OPERATING COSTS/OPERATING INCOME, ITEMS 10 TO 22

10. Cost of Operations

This is the IRS's Costs of Goods Sold; it consists of the costs incurred in producing the goods or furnishing the services that generated the corporations' business receipts.

11. Salaries and Wages

These include the amount of salaries and wages paid as well as bonuses and director's fees, but no contributions to pension plans (see item 16) nor compensation of officers (see item 20).

12. Taxes Paid

Excludes Federal Income Taxes; they are the amounts paid for ordinary state and local taxes, social security, payroll taxes, unemployment insurance taxes, excise taxes, import and tariff duties, and business license and privilege taxes.

13. Interest Paid

These amounts consist of interest paid on all business indebtedness.

14. Depreciation

The charges allowed are governed principally by the IRS rules in effect in 1997, basically enacted in 1986, but also include other modifications. Hence, depreciation could represent amounts computed by different sets of rules.

15. Amortization and Depletion

Most amortization is calculated on a straight-line basis. Depletion is allowed for the exhaustion of natural deposits and timber.

16. Pensions, Profit-Sharing, Stock Bonus, and Annuity Plans

These are amounts deducted during the current year for qualified pension, profit-sharing, or other funded deferred compensation plans.

17. Employee Benefits

These are employer contributions to death benefit, insurance, health, accident, and sickness, and other welfare plans.

18. Advertising

Amounts include promotion and publicity expenses.

19. Other Expenses

These include expenses for repairs, bad debts, rent paid on business property, domestic production activities, contributions and gifts, and expenses not allocable to specific deductible items.

20. Officers' Compensation

Salaries, wages, stock bonuses, bonds, and other forms of compensation are included in this item.

21. Operating Margin

This is the net income after all operating costs have been deducted.

22. Operating Margin Before Officers' Compensation

This measure takes into account the effect of Officers' Compensation on the operating margin.

SELECTED AVERAGE BALANCE SHEET ITEMS ($ IN THOUSANDS) ITEMS 23 TO 29

23. Average Net Receivables

The total of Notes and Accounts Receivable, less Allowance for Bad Debts, divided by the number of enterprises. Notes and Accounts Receivable are the gross amounts arising from business sales or services to customers on credit in the course of ordinary trade or business. This includes commercial paper, charge accounts, current intercompany receivables, property investment loans, and trade acceptances.

24. Average Inventories

Total inventories are divided by the number of enterprises. Inventories include finished goods, partially finished goods, new materials and supplies acquired for sale, merchandise on hand or in transit, and growing crops reported as assets by agricultural enterprises.

25. Average Net Property, Plant and Equipment

This includes depreciable assets less accumulated depreciation, depletable assets less accumulated depletion, and land; the sum is divided by the number of enterprises. Depreciable assets consist of end-of-year balance sheet tangible property, such as buildings and equipment used in trade or business, or held for the production of income, and that has a useful life of one year or more. The amount of accumulated depreciation represents the portion written off in the current year, as well as in prior years. Depletable assets represent the end-of-year value of mineral property, oil and gas wells, and other natural resources; standing timber; intangible development and drilling costs capitalized; and leases and leaseholds, subject to depletion. Accumulated depletion represents the cumulative adjustment of these assets.

26. Average Total Assets

Total Assets (and Total Liabilities) are amounts reported in the end-of-year balance sheet. Total Assets are net amounts after reduction from accumulated depreciation, accumulated amortization, accumulated depletion, and the reserve for bad debts. Total Liabilities include the claims of creditors and stockholders' equity, and were net after reduction by the cost of treasury stock. The average of total assets was obtained by dividing it by the number of enterprises.

27. Average of Notes and Loans Payable, and Mortgages

These liabilities were separated on the balance sheet according to the time to maturity of the obligations. Time to maturity was based on the date of the balance sheet, rather than the date of issue of the obligations. The total was divided by the number of enterprises.

28. Average of All Other Liabilities

These included accounts payable, and other liabilities including other current liabilities. The total was divided by the number of enterprises.

29. Average Net Worth

Net Worth represents the stockholders' equity in the corporation (total assets minus the claims of creditors). It consists of Capital Stock, Paid-In Capital Surplus, Retained Earnings Appropriated, Retained Earnings Unappropriated, less cost of treasury stock.

SELECTED FINANCIAL RATIOS, NUMBER OF TIMES TO ONE, RATIOS 30 TO 44

30. CURRENT RATIO

The items that used Current Assets for this ratio are Cash; Notes and Accounts Receivable, Less: Allowance for Bad Debts; Inventories; Government Obligations; Tax-Exempt Securities; and Other Current Assets. For Current Liabilities, the following items were included: Accounts Payable; Mortgages and Notes Maturing in Less than 1 Year; and Other Current Liabilities.

This ratio, rated highest by CPAs as a measure of liquidity, gauges the ability of a company to meet its short-term financial obligations should it be compelled to liquidate its assets. However, it is not an absolute measure of the company's ability to meet its obligations. It is obtained by dividing current assets by current liabilities. The standard guideline has been a ratio of 2 to 1; however, some companies have found that in their experience, a ratio less than 2 to 1 is adequate, while others consider a larger one to be necessary. The ratio is affected by the method of valuation of inventory (LIFO or FIFO) and by inflation. The *Almanac* provides measures that can be treated as standards by size of asset.

31. Quick Ratio

This ratio is also known as the "Acid Test Ratio" because it is often used to estimate a company's general liquidity. There is some disagreement about the inclusion of inventory in the numerator because it may be slow moving, obsolete, or pledged to specific creditors, and, therefore, not be readily convertible into cash. The *Almanac* adopts a conservative approach and does not include the item in calculating the ratio. Excluding inventories and other current assets, the numerator is the same as that used in determining current assets. The denominator, current liabilities, is unchanged. The ratio of 1 to 1 has been considered a reasonable standard, but it is jeopardized because accounts and notes receivable may not be convertible into cash at face value and at short notice. The *Almanac* provides measures that can be treated as standards by size of asset.

32. Net Sales to Working Capital

This is an efficiency, or turnover, ratio that measures the rate at which current assets less current liabilities (Working Capital) is used in making sales. (In industries in Finance, Insurance, and Real Estate, total receipts rather than net sales is used.) A low ratio indicates a less efficient (profitable) use of working capital in making sales. The *Almanac* provides measures that can be treated as standards by size of asset. Working Capital is the difference between current assets and current liabilities.

33. Coverage Ratio

This ratio measures the number of times all interest paid by the company is covered by earnings before interest charges and taxes (EBIT). For that reason, the ratio is also known as the "times interest earned ratio." The ratio indicates the company's ability to service its debt based on its income.

34. Total Asset Turnover

The ratio is an efficiency ratio because it indicates the effectiveness of the company's use of its total assets in generating sales. It is measured by dividing net sales by total assets.

35. Inventory Turnover

Inventory turnover measures the liquidity of the inventory. It is computed by dividing the cost of goods sold by the average inventory. The result shows the number of times that the average inventory can be converted into receivables or cash. The ratio reflects both on the quality of the inventory and the efficiency of management. Typically, the higher the turnover rate, the more likely profits will be higher.

> **SPECIAL NOTE:** Inventory turnover is not computed for industries in Finance, Insurance, and Real Estate.

36. Receivables Turnover

This ratio measures the liquidity of accounts receivable. It indicates the average collection period throughout the year. It is obtained by dividing sales average by net receivables. It is not computed in the Finance, Insurance, and Real Estate industries (although it is calculated for all other industries even though conventional analysis typically omits it) for many of the industries in the *Almanac*.

37. Total Liabilities to Net Worth

This ratio indicates the extent to which the company's funds are supplied by short- and long-term creditors compared to its owners. It is an indicator of the company's long-term debt paying ability. The ratio is one of the most important bearing on the company's capital structure. Net worth is defined in ratio 29.

38. Current Assets to Working Capital

The dependence of Working Capital in part on current assets is important to understanding this part of the source of Working Capital. Current Assets are defined in ratio 30 and Working Capital is defined in ratio 32.

39. Current Liabilities to Working Capital

The dependence of Working Capital in part on current liabilities is important to understanding this part of the source of Working Capital. Current Liabilities are defined in ratio 30 and Working Capital is defined in ratio 32.

40. Working Capital to Net Sales or Total Receipts

The purpose of this ratio is to determine the working capital needed in relation to projected sales or receipts. Working Capital is defined in ratio 32.

41. Inventory to Working Capital

This ratio, by showing the proportion of Working Capital invested in Inventory, indicates the part of Current Assets that are least liquid. Inventories which exceed working capital indicate that current liabilities exceed liquid current assets. Working Capital is defined in ratio 32.

42. Total Receipts to Cash Flow

Cash Flow is the difference between cash receipts and cash disbursements. The ratio of total receipts to cash flow could suggest steps which management might take to improve the company's cash position.

43. Cost of Goods to Cash Flow

This ratio can be the basis for projections of cash requirements needed to fund projected costs of production. Cash flow is defined in ratio 42.

44. Cash Flow to Total Debt

This ratio indicates the extent to which a company could service its total debt from cash flow. It is analogous to the coverage ratio; refer to ratio 33. Cash flow is defined in ratio 42.

SELECTED FINANCIAL FACTORS (IN PERCENTAGES), ITEMS 45 TO 50

45. Debt Ratio (Total Liabilities to Total Assets)

This ratio indicates the company's ability to pay all its debts. It measures the creditors' and owners' of the company's ability to withstand losses. It is an indicator of the long-run solvency of the firm.

46. Return on Total Assets

The ratio combines the turnover and profit ratios (Sales/Total Assets x [times] Profit/Sales) and yields the return on investment (Total Assets). The result is the end product of the DuPont System of financial analysis. The system takes into account both operating income and operating assets. In Table I of each industry, the Return on Investment (ROI) is net income less deficit before income taxes divided by total assets. In Table II of each industry, the ROI is net income before income taxes divided by Total Assets. Total Assets are used because management has discretion in the investment of the resources provided by both the creditors and owners.

47. Return on Equity Before Income Taxes

This ratio measures the profitability of the company's operations to owners, before income taxes. For Table I this is net income, less deficit before income taxes and before credits. For Table II this is net income minus income tax before credits.

48. Return on Equity After Income Taxes

This ratio measures the profitability of the company's operations to owners, after income taxes. For Table I this is net income, less deficit and minus income tax before credits. For Table II this is net income minus income tax and before credits.

49. Profit Margin (Before Income Tax)

This is net income before income tax divided by net sales (or total receipts) and indicates the contribution of sales to the profitability of the company. Competition, capital structure, and operating characteristics cause the margin to vary within and among industries. For Table I, net income less deficit and before income taxes is the numerator; for Table II it is net income before tax.

50. Profit Margin (After Income Tax)

This ratio is the same as ratio 49 except that income taxes are taken into account.

TABLE OF CONTENTS

Page references to tables for industries with net income are in italic

PRINCIPAL BUSINESS ACTIVITY (BASED ON NAICS)

47TH
ANNUAL EDITION

2016 ALMANAC OF

BUSINESS AND INDUSTRIAL FINANCIAL RATIOS

Selected Average Balance Sheet ($ in Thousands)

Net Receivables 23	108	0	4	29	70	605	1514	5830	8603	•	•	•	•
Inventories 24	140	0	11	36	151	845	2440	4320	12749	•	•	•	•
Net Property, Plant and Equipment 25	516	0	76	360	1003	4018	6329	12753	26532	•	•	•	•
Total Assets 26	1207	0	169	721	1978	6954	15376	34096	71021	•	•	•	•
Notes and Loans Payable 27	590	0	173	439	939	4208	7640	15466	25536	•	•	•	•
All Other Liabilities 28	182	0	15	56	235	744	2326	5647	12189	•	•	•	•
Net Worth 29	435	0	-18	226	804	2001	5410	12983	33296	•	•	•	•

Selected Financial Ratios (Times to 1)

Current Ratio 30	1.6	•	2.1	2.4	1.4	1.5	1.4	1.4	1.8	•	•	•	•
Quick Ratio 31	0.8	•	1.4	1.7	0.8	0.7	0.6	0.8	0.7	•	•	•	•
Net Sales to Working Capital 32	8.1	•	8.4	4.8	12.8	8.9	9.3	6.5	5.1	•	•	•	•
Coverage Ratio 33	4.2	3.3	4.7	6.0	4.5	3.0	4.0	2.3	2.9	•	•	•	•
Total Asset Turnover 34	1.0	•	1.5	0.8	0.9	0.9	1.1	0.9	1.0	•	•	•	•
Inventory Turnover 35	4.8	•	3.8	4.4	5.2	3.9	4.1	4.3	3.6	•	•	•	•
Receivables Turnover 36	11.9	•	67.2	21.0	24.0	10.7	10.3	5.7	7.4	•	•	•	•
Total Liabilities to Net Worth 37	1.8	•	•	2.2	1.5	2.5	1.8	1.6	1.1	•	•	•	•
Current Assets to Working Capital 38	2.7	•	1.9	1.7	3.6	3.2	3.3	3.2	2.3	•	•	•	•
Current Liabilities to Working Capital 39	1.7	•	0.9	0.7	2.6	2.2	2.3	2.2	1.3	•	•	•	•
Working Capital to Net Sales 40	0.1	•	0.1	0.2	0.1	0.1	0.1	0.2	0.2	•	•	•	•
Inventory to Working Capital 41	0.9	•	0.4	0.3	1.0	1.3	1.4	1.1	1.0	•	•	•	•
Total Receipts to Cash Flow 42	2.8	1.6	1.5	1.5	2.3	2.2	3.9	3.9	4.3	•	•	•	•
Cost of Goods to Cash Flow 43	1.5	0.3	0.3	0.4	1.0	1.2	2.4	2.4	2.9	•	•	•	•
Cash Flow to Total Debt 44	0.6	•	0.9	0.8	0.7	0.6	0.4	0.4	0.4	•	•	•	•

Selected Financial Factors (in Percentages)

Debt Ratio 45	64.0	•	110.9	68.7	59.3	71.2	64.8	61.9	53.1	•	•	•	•
Return on Total Assets 46	7.6	•	14.0	11.6	7.9	6.8	5.4	3.2	3.3	•	•	•	•
Return on Equity Before Income Taxes 47	16.2	•	•	31.0	15.1	15.6	11.5	4.8	4.6	•	•	•	•
Return on Equity After Income Taxes 48	14.2	•	•	29.3	13.5	13.8	9.9	3.8	4.3	•	•	•	•
Profit Margin (Before Income Tax) 49	5.6	10.8	7.5	12.2	6.5	5.2	3.8	2.0	2.2	•	•	•	•
Profit Margin (After Income Tax) 50	4.9	8.2	7.0	11.5	5.9	4.6	3.3	1.6	2.0	•	•	•	•

Table II

Corporations with Net Income

AGRICULTURAL PRODUCTION

MONEY AMOUNTS AND SIZE OF ASSETS IN THOUSANDS OF DOLLARS

Item Description for Accounting Period 7/12 Through 6/13	Total	Zero Assets	Under 500	500 to 1000	1,000 to 5,000	5,000 to 10,000	10,000 to 25,000	25,000 to 50,000	50,000 to 100,000	100,000 to 250,000	250,000 to 500,000	500,000 to 2,500,000	2,500,000 and over
Number of Enterprises 1	61969	4202	31130	12992	12071	904	420	123	60	40	•	•	0

Revenues ($ in Thousands)

	Total	Zero Assets	Under 500	500 to 1000	1,000 to 5,000	5,000 to 10,000	10,000 to 25,000	25,000 to 50,000	50,000 to 100,000	100,000 to 250,000	250,000 to 500,000	500,000 to 2,500,000	2,500,000 and over
Net Sales 2	99900679	1018519	9996638	8359116	26112465	6939416	7071739	4447041	4860103	7591597	•	•	0
Interest 3	116475	2599	8672	12929	38653	9214	4811	5058	2066	12752	•	•	0
Rents 4	987576	25738	171084	128667	451827	72286	22657	14027	20441	40106	•	•	0
Royalties 5	365493	0	5897	9171	50769	18735	5986	53	2403	205936	•	•	0
Other Portfolio Income 6	1597761	133254	216062	197286	517422	108347	106653	76929	35783	141407	•	•	0
Other Receipts 7	16823644	494637	3377394	3797894	5058978	2003154	731062	337967	343778	147984	•	•	0
Total Receipts 8	119791628	1674747	13775747	12505063	32230114	9151152	7942908	4881075	5264574	8139782	•	•	0
Average Total Receipts 9	1933	399	443	963	2670	10123	18912	39684	87743	203495	•	•	•

Operating Costs/Operating Income (%)

	Total	Zero Assets	Under 500	500 to 1000	1,000 to 5,000	5,000 to 10,000	10,000 to 25,000	25,000 to 50,000	50,000 to 100,000	100,000 to 250,000	250,000 to 500,000	500,000 to 2,500,000	2,500,000 and over
Cost of Operations 10	53.7	4.9	14.8	27.7	41.7	56.5	61.5	53.5	63.8	75.2	•	•	•
Salaries and Wages 11	6.5	8.4	7.6	7.9	9.0	7.6	7.0	8.4	6.4	4.1	•	•	•
Taxes Paid 12	2.0	4.1	2.5	3.5	2.3	1.8	1.8	1.5	1.2	1.0	•	•	•
Interest Paid 13	1.5	1.5	1.4	2.1	1.7	2.0	1.2	0.9	0.9	0.9	•	•	•
Depreciation 14	5.7	6.3	8.9	14.2	7.5	5.0	3.5	2.9	3.2	2.2	•	•	•
Amortization and Depletion 15	0.2	0.0	0.1	0.1	0.1	0.1	0.0	0.0	0.3	0.5	•	•	•
Pensions and Other Deferred Comp. 16	0.2	0.0	0.1	0.2	0.1	0.1	0.1	0.2	0.1	0.1	•	•	•
Employee Benefits 17	0.7	1.0	0.9	1.4	0.8	0.7	0.6	0.4	0.7	0.7	•	•	•
Advertising 18	0.3	1.4	0.2	0.1	0.2	0.2	0.3	0.2	0.2	0.1	•	•	•
Other Expenses 19	36.3	91.5	77.1	69.3	46.0	48.6	25.3	32.7	23.5	12.2	•	•	•
Officers' Compensation 20	1.9	4.8	4.5	4.5	2.4	0.8	1.1	1.3	0.7	0.7	•	•	•
Operating Margin 21	•	•	•	•	•	•	•	•	•	2.3	•	•	•
Operating Margin Before Officers' Comp. 22	•	•	•	•	•	•	•	•	•	3.0	•	•	•

Selected Average Balance Sheet ($ in Thousands)

	C1	C2	C3	C4	C5	C6	C7	C8	C9	C10	C11	C12	C13
Net Receivables 23	136	0	5	23	77	763	1602	6800	10111	31793	•	•	•
Inventories 24	148	0	12	33	148	926	2489	3937	12436	27035	•	•	•
Net Property, Plant and Equipment 25	551	0	85	327	979	3609	5666	10499	26499	49054	•	•	•
Total Assets 26	1388	0	202	733	1951	6884	15358	35024	71686	146254	•	•	•
Notes and Loans Payable 27	542	0	107	306	857	3655	5932	10234	21534	40785	•	•	•
All Other Liabilities 28	218	0	19	58	178	825	2288	6100	13331	26998	•	•	•
Net Worth 29	627	0	76	369	916	2404	7137	18690	36821	78470	•	•	•

Selected Financial Ratios (Times to 1)

	C1	C2	C3	C4	C5	C6	C7	C8	C9	C10	C11	C12	C13
Current Ratio 30	1.7	•	3.0	2.2	1.6	1.3	1.7	2.1	1.8	2.4	•	•	•
Quick Ratio 31	1.0	•	2.2	1.6	0.9	0.7	0.8	1.3	0.8	1.3	•	•	•
Net Sales to Working Capital 32	7.5	•	6.2	5.4	10.6	14.6	6.9	4.0	5.5	4.2	•	•	•
Coverage Ratio 33	8.4	28.7	15.2	9.7	7.9	5.3	9.1	9.6	9.4	11.8	•	•	•
Total Asset Turnover 34	1.2	•	1.6	0.9	1.1	1.1	1.1	1.0	1.1	1.3	•	•	•
Inventory Turnover 35	5.9	•	4.1	5.3	6.1	4.7	4.2	4.9	4.2	5.3	•	•	•
Receivables Turnover 36	14.4	•	61.7	30.2	31.2	11.4	10.3	6.3	7.6	•	•	•	•
Total Liabilities to Net Worth 37	1.2	•	1.6	1.0	1.1	1.9	1.2	0.9	0.9	0.9	•	•	•
Current Assets to Working Capital 38	2.4	•	1.5	1.9	2.7	4.4	2.4	1.9	2.3	1.7	•	•	•
Current Liabilities to Working Capital 39	1.4	•	0.5	0.9	1.7	3.4	1.4	0.9	1.3	0.7	•	•	•
Working Capital to Net Sales 40	0.1	•	0.2	0.2	0.1	0.1	0.1	0.3	0.2	0.2	•	•	•
Inventory to Working Capital 41	0.7	•	0.2	0.3	0.7	1.8	1.0	0.5	1.0	0.6	•	•	•
Total Receipts to Cash Flow 42	2.7	1.0	1.3	1.5	2.3	2.1	3.4	2.8	3.6	5.1	•	•	•
Cost of Goods to Cash Flow 43	1.4	0.0	0.2	0.4	1.0	1.2	2.1	1.5	2.3	3.9	•	•	•
Cash Flow to Total Debt 44	0.8	•	1.9	1.2	0.9	0.8	0.6	0.8	0.6	0.5	•	•	•

Selected Financial Factors (in Percentages)

	C1	C2	C3	C4	C5	C6	C7	C8	C9	C10	C11	C12	C13
Debt Ratio 45	54.8	•	62.2	49.6	53.0	65.1	53.5	46.6	48.6	46.3	•	•	•
Return on Total Assets 46	14.6	•	33.4	18.2	14.8	11.7	12.0	9.1	9.3	13.4	•	•	•
Return on Equity Before Income Taxes 47	28.5	•	82.6	32.4	27.6	27.2	23.0	15.3	16.2	22.9	•	•	•
Return on Equity After Income Taxes 48	26.2	•	80.0	31.0	25.7	25.1	21.3	14.2	15.8	17.7	•	•	•
Profit Margin (Before Income Tax) 49	11.1	40.5	19.6	18.6	11.7	8.5	9.8	7.9	7.4	9.5	•	•	•
Profit Margin (After Income Tax) 50	10.2	36.4	19.0	17.8	10.9	7.9	9.0	7.3	7.2	7.3	•	•	•

Table I

Corporations with and without Net Income

FORESTRY AND LOGGING

MONEY AMOUNTS AND SIZE OF ASSETS IN THOUSANDS OF DOLLARS

Item Description for Accounting Period 7/12 Through 6/13	Total	Zero Assets	Under 500	500 to 1,000	1,000 to 5,000	5,000 to 10,000	10,000 to 25,000	25,000 to 50,000	50,000 to 100,000	100,000 to 250,000	250,000 to 500,000	500,000 to 2,500,000	2,500,000 and over
Number of Enterprises 1	8118	710	5509	912	807	63	69	32	12	0	4	0	0

Revenues ($ in Thousands)													
Net Sales 2	11550948	302958	3039562	2061485	3055682	447880	1046617	760890	394241	0	441635	0	0
Interest 3	45575	2278	515	63	1480	15	573	42	5183	0	35426	0	0
Rents 4	24770	1192	12	10374	4458	471	2299	629	272	0	5063	0	0
Royalties 5	6195	2673	0	0	0	0	200	0	0	0	3322	0	0
Other Portfolio Income 6	254263	34417	8945	59879	33651	39198	52904	3249	696	0	21322	0	0
Other Receipts 7	92050	56882	618	16385	11776	5115	6647	1964	6001	0	-13338	0	0
Total Receipts 8	11973801	400400	3049652	2148186	3107047	492679	1109240	766774	406393	0	493430	0	0
Average Total Receipts 9	1475	564	554	2355	3850	7820	16076	23962	33866	•	123358	•	•

Operating Costs/Operating Income (%)													
Cost of Operations 10	52.3	99.4	21.8	49.7	47.7	75.3	83.5	89.4	87.5	•	81.9	•	•
Salaries and Wages 11	7.8	0.6	6.1	9.7	12.3	9.2	4.6	1.1	1.6	•	8.0	•	•
Taxes Paid 12	2.6	1.6	2.5	2.2	3.6	4.8	1.7	2.1	1.9	•	1.7	•	•
Interest Paid 13	1.3	6.5	1.1	1.2	0.9	1.4	0.5	1.3	3.7	•	3.3	•	•
Depreciation 14	6.0	0.1	4.6	8.5	9.7	6.2	3.0	1.2	1.7	•	2.2	•	•
Amortization and Depletion 15	0.6	0.1	0.0	0.1	0.0	3.7	0.2	1.6	2.6	•	5.9	•	•
Pensions and Other Deferred Comp. 16	0.1	•	•	0.0	0.2	0.0	0.2	0.2	0.2	•	0.6	•	•
Employee Benefits 17	0.8	•	0.1	1.3	1.2	0.7	0.7	0.8	1.1	•	1.2	•	•
Advertising 18	0.0	0.0	0.0	0.0	0.0	0.1	0.1	0.0	0.1	•	0.3	•	•
Other Expenses 19	27.8	8.2	56.0	22.4	26.1	5.3	6.8	4.9	7.9	•	13.1	•	•
Officers' Compensation 20	2.0	•	2.3	2.5	2.1	1.7	2.6	0.5	1.1	•	0.8	•	•
Operating Margin 21	•	•	5.5	2.5	•	•	•	•	•	•	•	•	•
Operating Margin Before Officers' Comp. 22	0.6	•	7.8	5.1	•	•	•	•	•	•	•	•	•

Selected Average Balance Sheet ($ in Thousands)

Net Receivables 23	76	0	3	35	101	105	1280	1680	6274	•	65661	•	•
Inventories 24	45	0	2	5	70	43	3382	1135	938	•	2302	•	•
Net Property, Plant and Equipment 25	560	0	73	421	1430	4541	5918	22636	36772	•	185893	•	•
Total Assets 26	1194	0	111	775	2356	5860	16060	37318	77052	•	719120	•	•
Notes and Loans Payable 27	603	0	110	630	1562	2496	2542	10233	27080	•	366861	•	•
All Other Liabilities 28	58	0	3	33	161	889	1094	1808	3107	•	17410	•	•
Net Worth 29	533	0	-2	112	633	2475	12424	25277	46864	•	334849	•	•

Selected Financial Ratios (Times to 1)

Current Ratio 30	2.0	•	2.2	1.1	1.5	0.8	2.7	3.0	4.5	•	4.3	•	•
Quick Ratio 31	1.3	•	1.6	0.4	1.0	0.5	1.3	2.3	3.0	•	3.9	•	•
Net Sales to Working Capital 32	10.9	•	28.4	154.9	20.3	•	4.6	5.9	3.1	•	1.4	•	•
Coverage Ratio 33	2.6	3.4	6.5	6.8	•	2.2	5.2	•	•	•	•	•	•
Total Asset Turnover 34	1.2	•	5.0	2.9	1.6	1.2	0.9	0.6	0.4	•	0.2	•	•
Inventory Turnover 35	16.6	•	69.2	204.6	25.6	123.1	3.7	18.7	30.6	•	39.3	•	•
Receivables Turnover 36	15.8	•	179.6	75.1	28.6	79.8	12.3	11.0	7.7	•	1.2	•	•
Total Liabilities to Net Worth 37	1.2	•	•	5.9	2.7	1.4	0.3	0.5	0.6	•	1.1	•	•
Current Assets to Working Capital 38	2.0	•	1.8	19.9	2.9	•	1.6	1.5	1.3	•	1.3	•	•
Current Liabilities to Working Capital 39	1.0	•	0.8	18.9	1.9	•	0.6	0.5	0.3	•	0.3	•	•
Working Capital to Net Sales 40	0.1	•	0.0	0.0	0.0	•	0.2	0.2	0.3	•	0.7	•	•
Inventory to Working Capital 41	0.3	•	0.1	0.0	0.4	•	0.8	0.2	0.1	•	0.0	•	•
Total Receipts to Cash Flow 42	4.2	8.5	1.8	4.3	6.2	18.4	34.2	58.8	1336.4	•	•	•	•
Cost of Goods to Cash Flow 43	2.2	8.5	0.4	2.1	3.0	13.8	28.5	52.6	1169.0	•	•	•	•
Cash Flow to Total Debt 44	0.5	•	2.7	0.8	0.4	0.1	0.1	0.0	0.0	•	•	•	•

Selected Financial Factors (in Percentages)

Debt Ratio 45	55.4	•	101.7	85.6	73.1	57.8	22.6	32.3	39.2	•	53.4	•	•
Return on Total Assets 46	4.2	•	34.2	23.1	•	3.7	2.3	•	•	•	•	•	•
Return on Equity Before Income Taxes 47	5.8	•	•	136.4	•	4.8	2.4	•	•	•	•	5.8	•
Return on Equity After Income Taxes 48	4.3	•	•	123.4	•	4.4	1.4	•	•	•	•	•	•
Profit Margin (Before Income Tax) 49	2.2	15.7	5.8	6.7	•	1.7	1.9	•	•	•	•	•	•
Profit Margin (After Income Tax) 50	1.6	8.8	5.8	6.1	•	1.5	1.1	•	•	•	•	•	•

Table II
Corporations with Net Income

FORESTRY AND LOGGING

MONEY AMOUNTS AND SIZE OF ASSETS IN THOUSANDS OF DOLLARS

Item Description for Accounting Period 7/12 Through 6/13		Total	Zero Assets	Under 500	500 to 1,000	1,000 to 5,000	5,000 to 10,000	10,000 to 25,000	25,000 to 50,000	50,000 to 100,000	100,000 to 250,000	250,000 to 500,000	500,000 to 2,500,000	2,500,000 and over
Number of Enterprises	1	5761	442	4199	660	368	•	34	6	0	•	•	•	0

Revenues ($ in Thousands)

		Total	Zero Assets	Under 500	500 to 1,000	1,000 to 5,000	5,000 to 10,000	10,000 to 25,000	25,000 to 50,000	50,000 to 100,000	100,000 to 250,000	250,000 to 500,000	500,000 to 2,500,000	2,500,000 and over
Net Sales	2	7637758	115109	2737292	1705266	913232	•	1040167	633354	0	•	•	•	0
Interest	3	42755	2276	515	57	1400	•	158	30	0	•	•	•	0
Rents	4	22608	1192	12	10344	4424	•	1992	0	0	•	•	•	0
Royalties	5	6195	2673	0	0	0	•	200	0	0	•	•	•	0
Other Portfolio Income	6	223104	34417	41	53192	31583	•	47581	1676	0	•	•	•	0
Other Receipts	7	110453	55123	263	16164	4891	•	3646	4953	0	•	•	•	0
Total Receipts	8	8042873	210790	2738123	1785023	955530	•	1093744	640013	0	•	•	•	0
Average Total Receipts	9	1396	477	652	2705	2597	•	32169	106669	•	•	•	•	•

Operating Costs/Operating Income (%)

		Total	Zero Assets	Under 500	500 to 1,000	1,000 to 5,000	5,000 to 10,000	10,000 to 25,000	25,000 to 50,000	50,000 to 100,000	100,000 to 250,000	250,000 to 500,000	500,000 to 2,500,000	2,500,000 and over
Cost of Operations	10	46.6	82.7	19.7	52.9	25.8	•	84.0	90.6	•	•	•	•	•
Salaries and Wages	11	7.7	1.6	6.1	11.4	12.4	•	4.2	0.8	•	•	•	•	•
Taxes Paid	12	2.6	3.2	2.1	2.4	4.7	•	1.4	1.6	•	•	•	•	•
Interest Paid	13	1.1	16.3	0.3	0.8	0.9	•	0.4	0.4	•	•	•	•	•
Depreciation	14	4.1	0.2	3.5	7.1	5.2	•	1.2	0.4	•	•	•	•	•
Amortization and Depletion	15	0.1	0.4	0.0	0.1	0.0	•	0.1	0.1	•	•	•	•	•
Pensions and Other Deferred Comp.	16	0.1	•	•	0.0	0.4	•	0.1	0.2	•	•	•	•	•
Employee Benefits	17	0.7	•	0.1	1.3	1.4	•	0.7	0.8	•	•	•	•	•
Advertising	18	0.0	0.0	0.0	0.0	0.1	•	0.1	0.0	•	•	•	•	•
Other Expenses	19	31.2	5.4	58.3	17.4	40.8	•	5.1	1.0	•	•	•	•	•
Officers' Compensation	20	2.0	•	1.7	2.6	3.7	•	1.9	0.2	•	•	•	•	•
Operating Margin	21	3.9	•	8.0	4.0	4.7	•	0.9	4.0	•	•	•	•	•
Operating Margin Before Officers' Comp.	22	5.8	•	9.7	6.5	8.4	•	2.8	4.2	•	•	•	•	•

Selected Average Balance Sheet ($ in Thousands)													
Net Receivables 23	36	0	4	35	104	•	2252	3759	•	•	•	•	•
Inventories 24	47	0	2	7	128	•	4785	3699	•	•	•	•	•
Net Property, Plant and Equipment 25	284	0	57	341	934	•	5201	6167	•	•	•	•	•
Total Assets 26	836	0	96	801	2211	•	15035	37834	•	•	•	•	•
Notes and Loans Payable 27	476	0	66	538	631	•	3572	14089	•	•	•	•	•
All Other Liabilities 28	41	0	2	34	140	•	1538	6166	•	•	•	•	•
Net Worth 29	319	0	28	228	1440	•	9925	17580	•	•	•	•	•

Selected Financial Ratios (Times to 1)													
Current Ratio 30	1.8	•	1.8	1.2	2.7	•	2.3	2.5	•	•	•	•	•
Quick Ratio 31	1.0	•	1.6	0.5	1.3	•	0.9	1.7	•	•	•	•	•
Net Sales to Working Capital 32	15.3	•	40.2	36.7	5.9	•	7.2	11.6	•	•	•	•	•
Coverage Ratio 33	9.2	5.5	24.4	11.3	11.5	•	17.6	13.1	•	•	•	•	•
Total Asset Turnover 34	1.6	•	6.8	3.2	1.1	•	2.0	2.8	•	•	•	•	•
Inventory Turnover 35	13.2	•	56.5	184.2	5.0	•	5.4	25.8	•	•	•	•	•
Receivables Turnover 36	26.1	•	162.5	74.6	15.6	•	13.9	•	•	•	•	•	•
Total Liabilities to Net Worth 37	1.6	•	2.4	2.5	0.5	•	0.5	1.2	•	•	•	•	•
Current Assets to Working Capital 38	2.2	•	2.2	5.3	1.6	•	1.8	1.7	•	•	•	•	•
Current Liabilities to Working Capital 39	1.2	•	1.2	4.3	0.6	•	0.8	0.7	•	•	•	•	•
Working Capital to Net Sales 40	0.1	•	0.0	0.0	0.2	•	0.1	0.1	•	•	•	•	•
Inventory to Working Capital 41	0.5	•	0.2	•	0.3	•	1.1	0.4	•	•	•	•	•
Total Receipts to Cash Flow 42	3.1	2.1	1.7	4.8	3.6	•	16.8	17.5	•	•	•	•	•
Cost of Goods to Cash Flow 43	1.4	1.7	0.3	2.6	0.9	•	14.1	15.9	•	•	•	•	•
Cash Flow to Total Debt 44	0.8	•	5.6	0.9	0.9	•	0.4	0.3	•	•	•	•	•

Selected Financial Factors (in Percentages)													
Debt Ratio 45	61.9	•	71.0	71.5	34.9	•	34.0	53.5	•	•	•	•	•
Return on Total Assets 46	16.2	•	56.9	30.6	11.4	•	13.0	14.7	•	•	•	•	•
Return on Equity Before Income Taxes 47	38.0	•	187.9	97.9	16.0	•	18.6	29.3	•	•	•	•	•
Return on Equity After Income Taxes 48	34.3	•	187.6	89.2	14.8	•	16.0	25.2	•	•	•	•	•
Profit Margin (Before Income Tax) 49	9.1	73.3	8.1	8.7	9.3	•	6.0	4.9	•	•	•	•	•
Profit Margin (After Income Tax) 50	8.2	55.1	8.1	7.9	8.6	•	5.2	4.2	•	•	•	•	•

Table I

Corporations with and without Net Income

SUPPORT ACTIVITIES AND FISHING, HUNTING AND TRAPPING

MONEY AMOUNTS AND SIZE OF ASSETS IN THOUSANDS OF DOLLARS

Item Description for Accounting Period 7/12 Through 6/13	Total	Zero Assets	Under 500	500 to 1,000	1,000 to 5,000	5,000 to 10,000	10,000 to 25,000	25,000 to 50,000	50,000 to 100,000	100,000 to 250,000	250,000 to 500,000	500,000 to 2,500,000	2,500,000 and over
Number of Enterprises 1	28233	6318	16845	1999	2342	487	150	59	24	•	•	•	0

Revenues ($ in Thousands)													
Net Sales 2	42715026	347922	6908954	2223549	14017241	7270834	4462553	2166801	1981212	•	•	•	0
Interest 3	21784	496	377	350	8202	2745	4178	3297	1539	•	•	•	0
Rents 4	21140	167	591	1568	3274	6169	3251	5444	676	•	•	•	0
Royalties 5	12313	0	0	0	0	2112	667	0	9534	•	•	•	0
Other Portfolio Income 6	175577	14865	60588	4136	50926	8743	18506	4179	9484	•	•	•	0
Other Receipts 7	1787664	262	688170	70492	647197	156760	89883	61440	30609	•	•	•	0
Total Receipts 8	44733504	363712	7658680	2300095	14726840	7447363	4579038	2241161	2033054	•	•	•	0
Average Total Receipts 9	1584	58	455	1151	6288	15292	30527	37986	84711	•	•	•	•

Operating Costs/Operating Income (%)													
Cost of Operations 10	67.9	49.2	26.2	59.7	73.6	88.1	75.0	69.8	78.8	•	•	•	•
Salaries and Wages 11	9.0	2.7	22.6	6.8	7.1	2.9	10.8	5.4	4.4	•	•	•	•
Taxes Paid 12	1.8	2.3	4.6	1.8	1.2	0.6	2.0	1.4	1.3	•	•	•	•
Interest Paid 13	0.5	0.0	0.6	0.5	0.4	0.4	0.6	0.9	0.7	•	•	•	•
Depreciation 14	2.2	2.7	2.4	4.0	2.4	0.9	2.2	2.5	2.2	•	•	•	•
Amortization and Depletion 15	0.1	•	0.1	0.0	0.1	0.1	0.1	0.0	0.1	•	•	•	•
Pensions and Other Deferred Comp. 16	0.2	•	0.4	0.1	0.1	0.0	0.2	0.2	0.1	•	•	•	•
Employee Benefits 17	0.5	0.1	0.5	1.0	0.3	0.2	0.9	0.6	0.6	•	•	•	•
Advertising 18	0.1	0.1	0.2	0.2	0.1	0.1	0.1	0.2	0.1	•	•	•	•
Other Expenses 19	14.4	31.2	33.6	17.8	14.3	5.4	7.0	14.9	5.7	•	•	•	•
Officers' Compensation 20	1.9	5.9	5.2	3.6	1.0	1.0	1.3	1.8	0.8	•	•	•	•
Operating Margin 21	1.3	5.9	3.6	4.4	•	0.3	•	2.3	5.1	•	•	•	•
Operating Margin Before Officers' Comp. 22	3.2	11.7	8.8	8.0	0.4	1.2	1.1	4.1	5.9	•	•	•	•

Selected Average Balance Sheet ($ in Thousands)

Net Receivables 23	103	0	3	33	230	1796	2175	6930	10214	•	•	•	•
Inventories 24	92	0	7	36	166	670	3999	3545	7810	•	•	•	•
Net Property, Plant and Equipment 25	206	0	47	221	739	1358	4876	7884	16843	•	•	•	•
Total Assets 26	709	0	116	662	2058	6480	15936	33098	70016	•	•	•	•
Notes and Loans Payable 27	217	0	42	282	600	1309	7196	11298	16160	•	•	•	•
All Other Liabilities 28	173	0	21	55	439	2146	4770	8871	19382	•	•	•	•
Net Worth 29	319	0	53	325	1019	3025	3970	12929	34474	•	•	•	•

Selected Financial Ratios (Times to 1)

Current Ratio 30	1.8	•	2.4	3.5	1.8	1.6	1.5	1.6	1.6	•	•	•	•
Quick Ratio 31	1.1	•	1.8	2.3	1.1	1.1	0.7	1.1	0.8	•	•	•	•
Net Sales to Working Capital 32	9.3	•	14.8	4.5	15.3	9.2	10.1	5.1	6.5	•	•	•	•
Coverage Ratio 33	12.1	1779.7	26.6	18.1	10.9	7.5	4.7	6.9	12.1	•	•	•	•
Total Asset Turnover 34	2.1	•	3.5	1.7	2.9	2.3	1.9	1.1	1.2	•	•	•	•
Inventory Turnover 35	11.2	•	16.2	18.5	26.6	19.6	5.6	7.2	8.3	•	•	•	•
Receivables Turnover 36	14.9	•	105.4	23.5	24.2	10.0	12.0	5.9	9.5	•	•	•	•
Total Liabilities to Net Worth 37	1.2	•	1.2	1.0	1.0	1.1	3.0	1.6	1.0	•	•	•	•
Current Assets to Working Capital 38	2.3	•	1.7	1.4	2.3	2.6	2.9	2.6	2.8	•	•	•	•
Current Liabilities to Working Capital 39	1.3	•	0.7	0.4	1.3	1.6	1.9	1.6	1.8	•	•	•	•
Working Capital to Net Sales 40	0.1	•	0.1	0.2	0.1	0.1	0.1	0.2	0.2	•	•	•	•
Inventory to Working Capital 41	0.6	•	0.2	0.2	0.5	0.6	1.3	0.6	0.8	•	•	•	•
Total Receipts to Cash Flow 42	6.0	3.0	2.6	5.3	6.5	14.4	13.4	5.6	8.5	•	•	•	•
Cost of Goods to Cash Flow 43	4.1	1.5	0.7	3.2	4.7	12.7	10.0	3.9	6.7	•	•	•	•
Cash Flow to Total Debt 44	0.6	•	2.5	0.6	0.9	0.3	0.2	0.3	0.3	•	•	•	•

Selected Financial Factors (in Percentages)

Debt Ratio 45	55.1	•	54.7	50.9	50.5	53.3	75.1	60.9	50.8	•	•	•	•
Return on Total Assets 46	13.9	•	53.0	13.9	14.1	7.2	5.6	7.3	9.8	•	•	•	•
Return on Equity Before Income Taxes 47	28.4	•	112.6	26.8	25.9	13.3	17.8	16.0	18.2	•	•	•	•
Return on Equity After Income Taxes 48	27.1	•	111.1	25.8	24.6	12.6	14.6	14.5	16.9	•	•	•	•
Profit Margin (Before Income Tax) 49	6.0	10.2	14.4	7.8	4.4	2.7	2.4	5.6	7.6	•	•	•	•
Profit Margin (After Income Tax) 50	5.7	8.8	14.2	7.5	4.2	2.6	2.0	5.1	7.1	•	•	•	•

Table II

Corporations with Net Income

SUPPORT ACTIVITIES AND FISHING, HUNTING AND TRAPPING

MONEY AMOUNTS AND SIZE OF ASSETS IN THOUSANDS OF DOLLARS

Item Description for Accounting Period 7/12 Through 6/13		Total	Zero Assets	Under 500	500 to 1,000	1,000 to 5,000	5,000 to 10,000	10,000 to 25,000	25,000 to 50,000	50,000 to 100,000	100,000 to 250,000	250,000 to 500,000	500,000 to 2,500,000	2,500,000 and over
Number of Enterprises	1	16050	2994	9080	1534	1920	•	107	47	21	•	•	•	0

Revenues ($ in Thousands)

		Total	Zero Assets	Under 500	500 to 1,000	1,000 to 5,000	5,000 to 10,000	10,000 to 25,000	25,000 to 50,000	50,000 to 100,000	100,000 to 250,000	250,000 to 500,000	500,000 to 2,500,000	2,500,000 and over
Net Sales	2	38034142	297026	6163201	1462651	13127398	•	3568586	2117783	1887815	•	•	•	0
Interest	3	20839	496	161	349	8081	•	3645	3297	1539	•	•	•	0
Rents	4	16558	167	529	1568	3239	•	1421	5444	676	•	•	•	0
Royalties	5	9534	0	0	0	0	•	0	0	9534	•	•	•	0
Other Portfolio Income	6	167611	14275	57011	2947	50154	•	17801	3608	9473	•	•	•	0
Other Receipts	7	1244961	434	510783	59832	310867	•	75992	61597	30530	•	•	•	0
Total Receipts	8	39493645	312398	6731685	1527347	13499739	•	3667445	2191729	1939567	•	•	•	0
Average Total Receipts	9	2461	104	741	996	7031	•	34275	46633	92360	•	•	•	

Operating Costs/Operating Income (%)

		Total	Zero Assets	Under 500	500 to 1,000	1,000 to 5,000	5,000 to 10,000	10,000 to 25,000	25,000 to 50,000	50,000 to 100,000	100,000 to 250,000	250,000 to 500,000	500,000 to 2,500,000	2,500,000 and over
Cost of Operations	10	69.9	55.2	26.8	56.6	76.7	•	83.1	70.4	78.7	•	•	•	•
Salaries and Wages	11	8.0	3.2	23.0	8.2	6.2	•	3.5	5.5	3.7	•	•	•	•
Taxes Paid	12	1.6	1.3	4.2	1.9	1.1	•	1.1	1.3	1.2	•	•	•	•
Interest Paid	13	0.4	0.0	0.4	0.6	0.4	•	0.6	0.9	0.6	•	•	•	•
Depreciation	14	1.8	1.0	1.5	4.3	1.9	•	1.9	2.5	2.2	•	•	•	•
Amortization and Depletion	15	0.1	•	0.1	0.0	0.1	•	0.1	0.0	0.2	•	•	•	•
Pensions and Other Deferred Comp.	16	0.1	•	0.3	0.2	0.1	•	0.1	0.2	0.1	•	•	•	•
Employee Benefits	17	0.4	0.1	0.3	1.5	0.2	•	0.4	0.6	0.6	•	•	•	•
Advertising	18	0.1	•	0.2	0.2	0.1	•	0.1	0.2	0.1	•	•	•	•
Other Expenses	19	11.5	22.6	28.8	13.5	9.7	•	6.3	15.1	5.2	•	•	•	•
Officers' Compensation	20	1.6	2.6	4.7	2.9	1.0	•	1.4	0.7	0.8	•	•	•	•
Operating Margin	21	4.2	14.0	9.7	10.1	2.5	•	1.5	2.7	6.5	•	•	•	•
Operating Margin Before Officers' Comp.	22	5.9	16.6	14.4	13.0	3.5	•	2.9	3.4	7.4	•	•	•	•

	Selected Average Balance Sheet ($ in Thousands)												
Net Receivables 23	161	0	6	27	246	•	2580	8588	9611	•	•	•	•
Inventories 24	144	0	8	33	183	•	5220	5658	9589	•	•	•	•
Net Property, Plant and Equipment 25	238	0	30	213	631	•	3844	8059	18047	•	•	•	•
Total Assets 26	986	0	144	653	2141	•	15751	33998	68185	•	•	•	•
Notes and Loans Payable 27	261	0	13	284	638	•	4670	12742	16470	•	•	•	•
All Other Liabilities 28	246	0	28	35	483	•	5606	10452	18320	•	•	•	•
Net Worth 29	478	0	103	334	1021	•	5476	10804	33396	•	•	•	•

	Selected Financial Ratios (Times to 1)												
Current Ratio 30	1.9	•	3.6	4.8	1.8	•	1.5	1.6	1.7	•	•	•	•
Quick Ratio 31	1.2	•	2.9	3.1	1.2	•	0.7	1.1	0.9	•	•	•	•
Net Sales to Working Capital 32	8.7	•	12.5	3.2	14.9	•	10.0	5.3	6.0	•	•	•	•
Coverage Ratio 33	19.1	2833.1	53.7	25.4	15.0	•	7.8	7.6	15.4	•	•	•	•
Total Asset Turnover 34	2.4	•	4.7	1.5	3.2	•	2.1	1.3	1.3	•	•	•	•
Inventory Turnover 35	11.5	•	21.7	16.2	28.7	•	5.3	5.6	7.4	•	•	•	•
Receivables Turnover 36	16.1	•	99.7	17.9	26.2	•	11.5	•	•	•	•	•	•
Total Liabilities to Net Worth 37	1.1	•	0.4	1.0	1.1	•	1.9	2.1	1.0	•	•	•	•
Current Assets to Working Capital 38	2.1	•	1.4	1.3	2.2	•	3.0	2.6	2.4	•	•	•	•
Current Liabilities to Working Capital 39	1.1	•	0.4	0.3	1.2	•	2.0	1.6	1.4	•	•	•	•
Working Capital to Net Sales 40	0.1	•	0.1	0.3	0.1	•	0.1	0.2	0.2	•	•	•	•
Inventory to Working Capital 41	0.6	•	0.2	0.1	0.5	•	1.5	0.7	0.6	•	•	•	•
Total Receipts to Cash Flow 42	6.0	2.8	2.6	4.2	7.6	•	11.6	5.5	7.7	•	•	•	•
Cost of Goods to Cash Flow 43	4.2	1.6	0.7	2.4	5.8	•	9.6	3.8	6.1	•	•	•	•
Cash Flow to Total Debt 44	0.8	•	6.5	0.7	0.8	•	0.3	0.4	0.3	•	•	•	•

	Selected Financial Factors (in Percentages)												
Debt Ratio 45	51.5	•	28.2	48.8	52.3	•	65.2	68.2	51.0	•	•	•	•
Return on Total Assets 46	20.4	•	91.2	22.1	18.4	•	10.3	9.3	12.9	•	•	•	•
Return on Equity Before Income Taxes 47	39.8	•	124.6	41.4	36.0	•	25.7	25.4	24.7	•	•	•	•
Return on Equity After Income Taxes 48	38.3	•	123.2	40.2	34.4	•	22.6	23.2	23.1	•	•	•	•
Profit Margin (Before Income Tax) 49	8.0	19.1	18.9	14.5	5.4	•	4.2	6.1	9.2	•	•	•	•
Profit Margin (After Income Tax) 50	7.7	17.4	18.7	14.1	5.1	•	3.7	5.6	8.6	•	•	•	•

Table I

Corporations with and without Net Income

OIL AND GAS EXTRACTION

MONEY AMOUNTS AND SIZE OF ASSETS IN THOUSANDS OF DOLLARS

Item Description for Accounting Period 7/12 Through 6/13		Total	Zero Assets	Under 500	500 to 1,000	1,000 to 5,000	5,000 to 10,000	10,000 to 25,000	25,000 to 50,000	50,000 to 100,000	100,000 to 250,000	250,000 to 500,000	500,000 to 2,500,000	2,500,000 and over
Number of Enterprises	1	20736	3355	12503	1642	1537	715	436	185	109	90	47	72	46
Revenues ($ in Thousands)														
Net Sales	2	226212165	3097121	4598626	1315977	3832631	2962034	2605446	1975232	1796563	5031978	4087949	21332457	173576150
Interest	3	1323675	9953	1035	4912	9691	3118	11702	3282	7284	13266	15936	204913	1038583
Rents	4	536417	14356	8	16783	38528	56562	44526	4660	13343	4850	1387	6873	334541
Royalties	5	748603	25431	38402	1177	19932	74667	70147	45421	36358	35772	3870	25661	371767
Other Portfolio Income	6	17061254	138818	20409	37868	273335	167135	167017	115803	405552	206299	152892	1193500	14182625
Other Receipts	7	12613491	254726	289320	145848	156248	244605	339837	633461	415673	828971	104749	2087179	7112874
Total Receipts	8	258495605	3540405	4947800	1522565	4330365	3508121	3238675	2777859	2674773	6121136	4366783	24850583	196616540
Average Total Receipts	9	12466	1055	396	927	2817	4906	7428	15015	24539	68013	92910	345147	4274273
Operating Costs/Operating Income (%)														
Cost of Operations	10	48.2	22.6	47.4	28.9	27.7	37.8	18.5	28.3	25.9	37.4	24.7	35.1	52.9
Salaries and Wages	11	5.9	11.9	2.8	15.8	10.6	12.1	11.1	10.9	10.3	9.4	6.4	4.9	5.4
Taxes Paid	12	3.2	1.9	2.1	4.6	4.2	3.3	5.5	5.0	4.8	3.1	3.3	5.2	2.9
Interest Paid	13	5.3	14.4	0.5	1.1	1.4	0.9	2.0	2.6	5.1	2.5	5.6	9.7	5.0
Depreciation	14	10.2	9.4	1.7	9.4	3.7	4.7	7.6	10.7	12.3	10.3	10.3	11.6	10.5
Amortization and Depletion	15	10.0	14.6	1.1	1.4	1.8	3.6	7.2	7.4	18.0	14.0	20.1	22.8	8.5
Pensions and Other Deferred Comp.	16	0.4	0.0	0.2	1.8	0.2	0.5	0.4	0.5	0.6	0.7	0.2	0.2	0.5
Employee Benefits	17	0.8	0.6	0.6	0.7	0.9	1.3	0.8	1.2	1.1	0.6	0.7	0.4	0.8
Advertising	18	0.0	0.0	0.1	0.2	0.4	0.1	0.2	0.2	0.0	0.0	0.0	0.0	0.0
Other Expenses	19	32.1	42.5	25.8	40.9	34.6	27.0	59.0	41.6	60.2	33.7	25.3	40.0	30.4
Officers' Compensation	20	1.1	1.5	5.9	7.5	4.9	4.9	4.0	4.3	3.2	1.9	2.2	1.3	0.5
Operating Margin	21	•	•	11.8	•	9.6	3.9	•	•	•	•	1.3	•	•
Operating Margin Before Officers' Comp.	22	•	•	17.7	•	14.5	8.8	•	•	•	•	3.4	•	•

Selected Average Balance Sheet ($ in Thousands)

Net Receivables 23	2414	0	15	48	641	1044	1761	4207	5511	12141	26264	81872	819482
Inventories 24	277	0	0	15	12	87	141	287	366	1922	2548	9238	98506
Net Property, Plant and Equipment 25	20782	0	25	213	613	1269	4756	11506	30749	67855	170641	786051	7612010
Total Assets 26	32737	0	122	750	2486	7635	16216	34392	70764	151165	334034	1217777	11492605
Notes and Loans Payable 27	9480	0	72	405	878	1136	3529	9857	16463	37516	100495	487041	3142076
All Other Liabilities 28	8888	0	12	247	665	2824	4390	8833	18275	29438	60573	251455	3294724
Net Worth 29	14368	0	38	98	942	3675	8298	15702	36026	84212	172966	479281	5055804

Selected Financial Ratios (Times to 1)

Current Ratio 30	0.9	•	4.1	1.7	2.2	1.7	1.7	1.7	2.0	1.6	1.4	1.0	0.8
Quick Ratio 31	0.7	•	3.9	1.0	2.0	1.3	1.3	1.4	1.5	1.1	1.1	0.7	0.6
Net Sales to Working Capital 32	•	•	8.2	4.7	3.1	2.2	2.1	1.8	1.5	4.6	4.0	53.2	•
Coverage Ratio 33	0.8	0.6	37.7	4.4	17.6	27.2	4.9	11.8	2.5	4.2	2.4	•	0.6
Total Asset Turnover 34	0.3	•	3.0	1.1	1.0	0.5	0.4	0.3	0.2	0.4	0.3	0.2	0.3
Inventory Turnover 35	19.0	•	471.8	15.3	57.3	18.0	7.8	10.5	11.6	10.9	8.4	11.3	20.3
Receivables Turnover 36	4.6	•	18.3	18.3	4.8	3.9	3.3	3.0	2.8	4.4	2.7	4.5	4.6
Total Liabilities to Net Worth 37	1.3	•	2.2	6.6	1.6	1.1	1.0	1.2	1.0	0.8	0.9	1.5	1.3
Current Assets to Working Capital 38	•	•	1.3	2.4	1.8	2.5	2.4	2.4	2.0	2.8	3.7	32.0	•
Current Liabilities to Working Capital 39	•	•	0.3	1.4	0.8	1.5	1.4	1.4	1.0	1.8	2.7	31.0	•
Working Capital to Net Sales 40	•	•	0.1	0.2	0.3	0.5	0.5	0.6	0.7	0.2	0.3	0.0	•
Inventory to Working Capital 41	•	•	0.0	0.1	0.0	0.1	0.0	0.0	0.0	0.1	0.1	1.8	•
Total Receipts to Cash Flow 42	4.1	3.0	2.6	2.6	2.1	2.3	1.7	1.6	2.0	2.6	3.4	4.9	4.6
Cost of Goods to Cash Flow 43	2.0	0.7	1.2	0.7	0.6	0.9	0.3	0.5	0.5	1.0	0.8	1.7	2.4
Cash Flow to Total Debt 44	0.1	•	1.7	0.5	0.8	0.4	0.5	0.4	0.2	0.3	0.2	0.1	0.1

Selected Financial Factors (in Percentages)

Debt Ratio 45	56.1	•	69.0	86.9	62.1	51.9	48.8	54.3	49.1	44.3	48.2	60.6	56.0
Return on Total Assets 46	1.3	•	60.0	5.0	23.9	12.5	3.6	9.4	2.9	3.9	3.5	•	1.0
Return on Equity Before Income Taxes 47	•	•	188.1	29.3	59.5	25.1	5.6	18.9	3.4	5.4	4.0	•	•
Return on Equity After Income Taxes 48	•	•	185.8	25.8	56.8	24.2	3.9	18.4	2.0	3.8	2.1	•	•
Profit Margin (Before Income Tax) 49	•	•	19.3	3.6	22.5	22.2	7.8	27.8	7.4	8.1	7.9	•	•
Profit Margin (After Income Tax) 50	•	•	19.1	3.2	21.4	21.5	5.4	27.1	4.4	5.6	4.3	•	•

Table II

Corporations with Net Income

OIL AND GAS EXTRACTION

MONEY AMOUNTS AND SIZE OF ASSETS IN THOUSANDS OF DOLLARS

Item Description for Accounting Period 7/12 Through 6/13	Total	Zero Assets	Under 500	500 to 1,000	1,000 to 5,000	5,000 to 10,000	10,000 to 25,000	25,000 to 50,000	50,000 to 100,000	100,000 to 250,000	250,000 to 500,000	500,000 to 2,500,000	2,500,000 and over
Number of Enterprises **1**	14758	2755	8839	910	1232	481	286	89	60	47	20	22	16

Revenues ($ in Thousands)

Net Sales **2**	96403508	692374	4036737	723455	3347196	2675947	2170550	1530359	1077132	3703091	2864405	8539693	65042570
Interest **3**	252279	3449	455	239	9099	1981	6075	579	4514	6612	6014	24667	188596
Rents **4**	484200	767	0	15245	38029	52066	39556	1541	13146	806	411	2380	320253
Royalties **5**	421046	13230	37898	873	17277	64833	55280	45335	26798	30128	1	5570	123823
Other Portfolio Income **6**	13902142	123308	20119	35847	253701	161700	147970	88089	330620	153698	90555	536534	11960000
Other Receipts **7**	6479893	245231	288418	154223	99378	233800	283929	594994	335571	622891	47919	962114	2611423
Total Receipts **8**	117943068	1078359	4383627	929882	3764680	3190327	2703360	2260897	1787781	4517226	3009305	10070958	80246665
Average Total Receipts **9**	7992	391	496	1022	3056	6633	9452	25403	29796	96111	150465	457771	5015417

Operating Costs/Operating Income (%)

Cost of Operations **10**	37.6	40.7	46.3	22.0	26.4	39.2	17.9	24.6	26.5	41.6	24.6	37.6	39.1
Salaries and Wages **11**	8.1	4.2	2.3	10.3	7.9	10.1	10.0	8.2	8.2	9.0	4.3	4.4	8.9
Taxes Paid **12**	3.8	3.3	1.7	4.4	3.9	2.9	5.4	4.6	5.5	2.5	3.2	3.5	4.0
Interest Paid **13**	4.0	1.4	0.3	0.5	1.0	0.8	1.1	0.8	1.7	0.9	1.1	4.8	5.0
Depreciation **14**	10.7	3.0	1.0	4.9	3.5	4.2	6.0	8.1	9.1	7.9	7.4	8.9	12.8
Amortization and Depletion **15**	6.7	6.6	0.9	1.7	1.7	2.3	5.1	3.8	11.2	6.2	3.7	14.5	6.7
Pensions and Other Deferred Comp. **16**	0.6	0.2	0.2	3.2	0.2	0.4	0.4	0.4	0.5	0.7	0.1	0.2	0.7
Employee Benefits **17**	1.1	0.3	0.5	1.1	1.0	1.1	0.7	0.9	1.2	0.5	0.6	0.4	1.3
Advertising **18**	0.1	0.0	0.1	0.1	0.1	0.1	0.1	0.2	0.0	0.0	0.0	0.0	0.0
Other Expenses **19**	29.4	36.3	22.3	37.9	26.7	19.4	29.1	27.6	38.3	23.7	20.8	20.4	32.0
Officers' Compensation **20**	1.4	0.4	6.0	7.6	4.7	4.3	3.4	3.4	2.9	1.2	1.7	1.1	0.6
Operating Margin **21**	•	3.5	18.4	6.1	23.0	15.2	20.8	17.3	•	5.6	32.4	4.3	•
Operating Margin Before Officers' Comp. **22**	•	3.9	24.4	13.7	27.7	19.5	24.2	20.7	•	6.8	34.0	5.4	•

Selected Average Balance Sheet ($ in Thousands)

Net Receivables 23	1609	0	15	29	624	1083	1650	4582	5779	15564	42123	70109	1121968
Inventories 24	191	0	1	16	11	96	110	457	495	3021	2293	15984	130838
Net Property, Plant and Equipment 25	10601	0	26	207	411	1092	4260	10017	20847	52155	154182	699781	8169155
Total Assets 26	17372	0	140	752	2422	7964	16250	34337	71313	150311	334622	1192616	12228850
Notes and Loans Payable 27	4547	0	52	202	666	818	2156	4240	10349	25665	45034	436703	3244746
All Other Liabilities 28	4282	0	9	296	325	2868	3818	6782	12593	23078	76280	263415	3137601
Net Worth 29	8543	0	79	254	1431	4278	10276	23315	48371	101568	213308	492498	5846503

Selected Financial Ratios (Times to 1)

Current Ratio 30	1.3	•	5.4	1.4	4.2	1.8	2.9	3.3	2.9	2.1	2.3	1.2	1.0
Quick Ratio 31	1.0	•	5.2	1.1	3.7	1.5	2.2	2.6	2.2	1.6	1.8	0.7	0.8
Net Sales to Working Capital 32	9.1	•	8.3	5.7	2.4	2.4	1.5	1.4	1.0	3.9	2.1	9.5	91.4
Coverage Ratio 33	6.8	43.1	100.0	64.5	36.6	44.7	40.2	83.1	36.3	32.1	34.8	5.7	4.6
Total Asset Turnover 34	0.4	•	3.3	1.1	1.1	0.7	0.5	0.5	0.3	0.5	0.4	0.3	0.3
Inventory Turnover 35	12.9	•	404.9	10.7	66.3	22.7	12.3	9.3	9.6	10.9	15.4	9.1	12.2
Receivables Turnover 36	4.5	•	20.2	22.4	5.3	5.3	4.1	4.1	3.0	4.5	2.7	5.1	4.2
Total Liabilities to Net Worth 37	1.0	•	0.8	2.0	0.7	0.9	0.6	0.5	0.5	0.5	0.6	1.4	1.1
Current Assets to Working Capital 38	4.3	•	1.2	3.2	1.3	2.3	1.5	1.4	1.5	1.9	1.8	5.4	36.7
Current Liabilities to Working Capital 39	3.3	•	0.2	2.2	0.3	1.3	0.5	0.4	0.5	0.9	0.8	4.4	35.7
Working Capital to Net Sales 40	0.1	•	0.1	0.2	0.4	0.4	0.7	0.7	1.0	0.3	0.5	0.1	0.0
Inventory to Working Capital 41	0.3	•	0.0	•	0.0	0.1	0.0	0.0	0.0	0.1	0.0	0.4	3.9
Total Receipts to Cash Flow 42	2.4	1.2	2.2	1.4	1.9	2.0	1.4	1.1	1.2	2.0	1.8	2.6	2.8
Cost of Goods to Cash Flow 43	0.9	0.5	1.0	0.3	0.5	0.8	0.3	0.3	0.3	0.8	0.4	1.0	1.1
Cash Flow to Total Debt 44	0.3	•	3.4	1.1	1.4	0.8	0.9	1.4	0.6	0.8	0.7	0.2	0.2

Selected Financial Factors (in Percentages)

Debt Ratio 45	50.8	•	43.7	66.2	40.9	46.3	36.8	32.1	32.2	32.4	36.3	58.7	52.2
Return on Total Assets 46	10.1	•	88.9	37.2	40.8	24.6	21.6	32.9	15.7	15.0	16.4	8.8	7.6
Return on Equity Before Income Taxes 47	17.6	•	156.4	108.2	67.2	44.7	33.3	47.8	22.5	21.4	25.1	17.5	12.5
Return on Equity After Income Taxes 48	14.8	•	154.8	105.8	65.0	43.6	31.1	47.2	20.6	18.9	21.6	15.8	9.5
Profit Margin (Before Income Tax) 49	23.0	59.2	27.0	34.6	35.4	34.4	45.1	64.9	60.7	27.6	37.3	22.2	18.0
Profit Margin (After Income Tax) 50	19.3	52.6	26.8	33.9	34.2	33.5	42.1	63.9	55.6	24.3	32.2	20.0	13.6

Table I

Corporations with and without Net Income

COAL MINING

MONEY AMOUNTS AND SIZE OF ASSETS IN THOUSANDS OF DOLLARS

Item Description for Accounting Period 7/12 Through 6/13	Total	Zero Assets	Under 500	500 to 1,000	1,000 to 5,000	5,000 to 10,000	10,000 to 25,000	25,000 to 50,000	50,000 to 100,000	100,000 to 250,000	250,000 to 500,000	500,000 to 2,500,000	2,500,000 and over
Number of Enterprises 1	1064	20	681	70	124	42	57	23	18	7	4	10	7

Revenues ($ in Thousands)

Net Sales 2	33057636	142357	0	323543	1003816	286275	918578	886805	1043940	512930	1228184	5590091	21121119
Interest 3	571276	0	791	0	723	0	373	113	156	348	1923	19072	547777
Rents 4	8850	0	0	0	78	0	377	811	2749	0	1044	624	3166
Royalties 5	197068	0	0	0	12062	0	380	1979	13080	5	2	932	168630
Other Portfolio Income 6	572308	32621	0	0	1587	256	20344	1263	61740	3820	1149	59580	389950
Other Receipts 7	2303397	944	0	0	32783	9278	29076	-8851	14426	38156	114353	628929	1444298
Total Receipts 8	36710535	175922	791	323543	1051049	295809	969128	882120	1136091	555259	1346655	6299228	23674940
Average Total Receipts 9	34502	8796	1	4622	8476	7043	17002	38353	63116	79323	336664	629923	3382134

Operating Costs/Operating Income (%)

Cost of Operations 10	61.7	58.1	•	49.3	77.7	59.6	86.7	60.8	71.1	81.7	84.9	67.8	56.2
Salaries and Wages 11	5.5	5.7	•	•	0.6	•	1.4	3.3	2.6	1.5	1.5	3.7	7.1
Taxes Paid 12	5.9	5.9	•	2.1	4.6	5.6	4.2	2.7	3.7	5.0	1.3	5.0	6.9
Interest Paid 13	6.1	0.3	•	•	0.2	•	0.8	0.8	1.8	4.4	2.5	4.0	8.1
Depreciation 14	7.1	4.4	•	0.0	1.4	4.8	3.8	8.0	6.4	10.0	4.1	8.3	7.5
Amortization and Depletion 15	5.3	9.2	•	•	0.8	•	2.3	3.1	5.1	5.6	5.7	4.3	6.1
Pensions and Other Deferred Comp. 16	0.9	•	•	•	0.6	0.4	0.3	0.4	0.2	0.3	0.0	1.0	1.0
Employee Benefits 17	5.2	2.4	•	1.8	0.4	•	1.7	2.5	2.1	2.2	3.1	5.2	6.3
Advertising 18	0.0	•	•	•	0.0	0.0	0.0	0.0	0.1	0.0	0.0	0.0	0.0
Other Expenses 19	12.9	6.6	•	18.2	15.4	42.8	9.6	19.9	9.4	10.1	19.4	7.7	13.4
Officers' Compensation 20	0.4	•	•	1.3	0.2	2.6	1.4	1.0	0.7	1.3	0.3	0.7	0.2
Operating Margin 21	•	7.6	•	27.2	•	•	•	•	•	•	•	•	•
Operating Margin Before Officers' Comp. 22	•	7.6	•	28.5	•	•	•	•	•	•	•	•	•

Selected Average Balance Sheet ($ in Thousands)													
Net Receivables 23	8523	0	0	380	475	344	1791	8900	4943	13632	54092	45635	1115013
Inventories 24	1805	0	0	0	15	138	721	1050	2706	2909	26338	40340	181481
Net Property, Plant and Equipment 25	38261	0	0	17	436	741	3372	10171	27354	69547	132435	425592	4918887
Total Assets 26	75133	0	100	520	2078	5470	16056	33708	74771	170712	304454	996367	9133881
Notes and Loans Payable 27	27129	0	0	0	1365	25	3702	9646	18195	56099	78777	361784	3372706
All Other Liabilities 28	25269	0	191	184	1222	731	5326	11838	11148	30530	125156	383897	3032986
Net Worth 29	22736	0	-91	336	-508	4714	7027	12223	45428	84084	100521	250686	2728189

Selected Financial Ratios (Times to 1)													
Current Ratio 30	1.6	•	0.5	2.7	0.7	4.4	2.5	1.8	1.4	1.8	1.1	0.6	2.0
Quick Ratio 31	1.2	•	0.2	2.7	0.5	4.2	1.9	1.6	1.1	1.6	0.8	0.4	1.5
Net Sales to Working Capital 32	5.4	•	•	14.5	•	2.8	4.1	5.3	13.1	5.3	21.8	•	3.3
Coverage Ratio 33	1.0	118.3	•	•	18.1	•	•	•	4.0	•	•	2.3	0.9
Total Asset Turnover 34	0.4	•	•	8.9	3.9	1.2	1.0	1.1	0.8	0.4	1.0	0.6	0.3
Inventory Turnover 35	10.6	•	•	•	416.1	29.4	19.4	22.3	15.2	20.6	9.9	9.4	9.3
Receivables Turnover 36	3.6	•	•	•	21.4	7.7	9.0	4.6	12.3	5.7	3.3	11.9	2.7
Total Liabilities to Net Worth 37	2.3	•	•	0.5	•	0.2	1.3	1.8	0.6	1.0	2.0	3.0	2.3
Current Assets to Working Capital 38	2.7	•	•	1.6	•	1.3	1.7	2.3	3.4	2.3	8.1	•	2.0
Current Liabilities to Working Capital 39	1.7	•	•	0.6	•	0.3	0.7	1.3	2.4	1.3	7.1	•	1.0
Working Capital to Net Sales 40	0.2	•	•	0.1	•	0.4	0.2	0.2	0.1	0.2	0.0	•	0.3
Inventory to Working Capital 41	0.3	•	•	•	•	0.0	0.3	0.2	0.6	0.2	1.5	•	0.2
Total Receipts to Cash Flow 42	11.4	3.0	•	2.2	5.9	6.3	•	8.2	8.0	•	64.6	9.7	12.3
Cost of Goods to Cash Flow 43	7.0	1.7	•	1.1	4.6	3.7	•	5.0	5.7	•	54.9	6.6	6.9
Cash Flow to Total Debt 44	0.1	•	•	11.4	0.5	1.4	•	0.2	0.2	•	0.0	0.1	0.0

Selected Financial Factors (in Percentages)													
Debt Ratio 45	69.7	•	191.6	35.3	124.5	13.8	56.2	63.7	39.2	50.7	67.0	74.8	70.1
Return on Total Assets 46	2.5	•	•	242.1	12.0	•	•	•	5.7	•	•	5.0	2.5
Return on Equity Before Income Taxes 47	0.0	•	7.1	374.3	•	•	•	•	7.0	•	•	11.1	•
Return on Equity After Income Taxes 48	•	•	7.2	374.3	•	•	•	•	6.9	•	•	10.4	•
Profit Margin (Before Income Tax) 49	0.0	31.1	•	27.2	2.9	•	•	•	5.5	•	•	5.0	•
Profit Margin (After Income Tax) 50	•	27.5	•	27.2	2.4	•	•	•	5.4	•	•	4.7	•

Table II

Corporations with Net Income

COAL MINING

MONEY AMOUNTS AND SIZE OF ASSETS IN THOUSANDS OF DOLLARS

Item Description for Accounting Period 7/12 Through 6/13		Total	Zero Assets	Under 500	500 to 1,000	1,000 to 5,000	5,000 to 10,000	10,000 to 25,000	25,000 to 50,000	50,000 to 100,000	100,000 to 250,000	250,000 to 500,000	500,000 to 2,500,000	2,500,000 and over
Number of Enterprises	1	439	4	•	70	54	0	22	5	12	0	0	3	•
Revenues ($ in Thousands)														
Net Sales	2	16769212	142357	•	323543	437893	0	238515	407101	1148869	0	0	2303658	•
Interest	3	533230	0	•	0	584	0	310	10	69	0	0	15581	•
Rents	4	3750	0	•	0	36	0	377	0	2078	0	0	0	•
Royalties	5	33130	0	•	0	11921	0	81	0	12396	0	0	386	•
Other Portfolio Income	6	455654	32621	•	0	1587	0	20296	208	64995	0	0	808	•
Other Receipts	7	1607627	944	•	0	9981	0	13822	363	26560	0	0	442529	•
Total Receipts	8	19402603	175922	•	323543	462002	0	273401	407682	1254967	0	0	2762962	•
Average Total Receipts	9	44197	43980	•	4622	8556	•	12427	81536	104581	•	•	920987	•
Operating Costs/Operating Income (%)														
Cost of Operations	10	47.2	58.1	•	49.3	60.7	•	69.1	72.2	69.4	•	•	65.1	•
Salaries and Wages	11	10.0	5.7	•	•	1.3	•	3.9	0.6	1.6	•	•	7.6	•
Taxes Paid	12	6.2	5.9	•	2.1	1.3	•	7.0	4.0	4.3	•	•	4.3	•
Interest Paid	13	6.6	0.3	•	•	0.1	•	0.7	0.2	0.5	•	•	0.5	•
Depreciation	14	7.0	4.4	•	0.0	0.7	•	2.7	2.5	5.2	•	•	6.0	•
Amortization and Depletion	15	5.2	9.2	•	•	1.8	•	5.7	4.0	6.2	•	•	3.0	•
Pensions and Other Deferred Comp.	16	1.0	•	•	•	1.4	•	0.5	0.8	0.3	•	•	1.2	•
Employee Benefits	17	5.1	2.4	•	1.8	0.2	•	1.2	2.9	2.2	•	•	3.6	•
Advertising	18	0.1	•	•	•	•	•	0.0	0.0	0.1	•	•	0.0	•
Other Expenses	19	16.5	6.6	•	18.2	17.7	•	14.5	4.5	8.0	•	•	6.1	•
Officers' Compensation	20	0.3	•	•	1.3	0.4	•	3.1	1.3	0.7	•	•	0.1	•
Operating Margin	21	•	7.6	•	27.2	14.5	•	•	7.0	1.6	•	•	2.4	•
Operating Margin Before Officers' Comp.	22	•	7.6	•	28.5	14.9	•	•	8.3	2.3	•	•	2.5	•

Selected Average Balance Sheet ($ in Thousands)

	C1	C2		C3	C4		C5	C6	C7			C8	
Net Receivables 23	16392	0	•	380	1074	•	1368	12438	12680	•	•	66641	•
Inventories 24	2018	0	•	0	0	•	623	1025	2004	•	•	57594	•
Net Property, Plant and Equipment 25	42370	0	•	17	224	•	1792	7939	33649	•	•	272091	•
Total Assets 26	93988	0	•	520	2179	•	15895	34619	92377	•	•	1312386	•
Notes and Loans Payable 27	30193	0	•	0	1975	•	16	4574	12526	•	•	0	•
All Other Liabilities 28	29912	0	•	184	1034	•	8933	7304	21122	•	•	479465	•
Net Worth 29	33884	0	•	336	-830	•	6947	22741	58729	•	•	832922	•

Selected Financial Ratios (Times to 1)

Current Ratio 30	2.4	•	•	2.7	1.4	•	6.6	2.8	2.0	•	•	2.7	•
Quick Ratio 31	1.9	•	•	2.7	1.3	•	5.4	2.6	1.7	•	•	1.9	•
Net Sales to Working Capital 32	2.7	•	•	14.5	22.0	•	1.3	6.0	7.7	•	•	5.0	•
Coverage Ratio 33	2.6	118.3	•	•	371.6	•	9.2	31.6	24.2	•	•	48.5	•
Total Asset Turnover 34	0.4	•	•	8.9	3.7	•	0.7	2.4	1.0	•	•	0.6	•
Inventory Turnover 35	8.9	•	•	•	•	•	12.0	57.3	33.2	•	•	8.7	•
Receivables Turnover 36	2.4	•	•	•	12.3	•	6.5	7.8	10.4	•	•	23.0	•
Total Liabilities to Net Worth 37	1.8	•	•	0.5	•	•	1.3	0.5	0.6	•	•	0.6	•
Current Assets to Working Capital 38	1.7	•	•	1.6	3.8	•	1.2	1.6	2.0	•	•	1.6	•
Current Liabilities to Working Capital 39	0.7	•	•	0.6	2.8	•	0.2	0.6	1.0	•	•	0.6	•
Working Capital to Net Sales 40	0.4	•	•	0.1	0.0	•	0.8	0.2	0.1	•	•	0.2	•
Inventory to Working Capital 41	0.2	•	•	•	•	•	0.1	0.1	0.2	•	•	0.4	•
Total Receipts to Cash Flow 42	4.6	3.0	•	2.2	2.8	•	10.0	9.8	6.2	•	•	3.7	•
Cost of Goods to Cash Flow 43	2.2	1.7	•	1.1	1.7	•	6.9	7.1	4.3	•	•	2.4	•
Cash Flow to Total Debt 44	0.1	•	•	11.4	1.0	•	0.1	0.7	0.5	•	•	0.4	•

Selected Financial Factors (in Percentages)

Debt Ratio 45	63.9	•	•	35.3	138.1	•	56.3	34.3	36.4	•	•	36.5	•
Return on Total Assets 46	7.0	•	•	242.1	74.5	•	4.7	17.3	11.7	•	•	13.3	•
Return on Equity Before Income Taxes 47	11.9	•	•	374.3	•	•	9.5	25.5	17.6	•	•	20.6	•
Return on Equity After Income Taxes 48	9.4	•	•	374.3	•	•	1.6	23.8	16.7	•	•	19.9	•
Profit Margin (Before Income Tax) 49	10.6	31.1	•	27.2	20.0	•	6.1	7.1	10.8	•	•	22.3	•
Profit Margin (After Income Tax) 50	8.4	27.5	•	27.2	18.7	•	1.0	6.7	10.3	•	•	21.6	•

Table I

Corporations with and without Net Income

METAL ORE MINING

MONEY AMOUNTS AND SIZE OF ASSETS IN THOUSANDS OF DOLLARS

Item Description for Accounting Period 7/12 Through 6/13	Total	Zero Assets	Under 500	500 to 1,000	1,000 to 5,000	5,000 to 10,000	10,000 to 25,000	25,000 to 50,000	50,000 to 100,000	100,000 to 250,000	250,000 to 500,000	500,000 to 2,500,000	2,500,000 and over
Number of Enterprises **1**	1249	45	666	205	147	35	55	30	19	18	8	11	11

Revenues ($ in Thousands)

Net Sales **2**	57728873	5399	1221	44344	2567	6187	240102	27622	327182	701056	1472325	5635392	49265475
Interest **3**	586545	27	93	5	100	2870	767	292	915	7298	2423	19486	552269
Rents **4**	48943	752	19432	0	2634	70	296	0	14	33	103	9	25599
Royalties **5**	336931	0	0	0	127	4582	14499	233	371	0	0	939	316181
Other Portfolio Income **6**	2515681	0	238	0	13	13801	9588	2197	2355	2775	7	86132	2398576
Other Receipts **7**	2037767	6393	13	0	4627	4313	14178	2853	34189	55487	10180	261734	1643799
Total Receipts **8**	63254740	12571	20997	44349	10068	31823	279430	33197	365026	766649	1485038	6003692	54201899
Average Total Receipts **9**	50644	279	32	216	68	909	5081	1107	19212	42592	185630	545790	4927445

Operating Costs/Operating Income (%)

Cost of Operations **10**	54.7	•	13.8	•	111.6	43.0	74.1	95.1	41.1	57.2	51.8	66.5	53.4
Salaries and Wages **11**	1.9	0.6	610.1	•	223.5	201.1	16.6	30.1	12.8	12.5	0.5	1.1	1.7
Taxes Paid **12**	1.2	•	403.3	0.9	34.8	2.6	1.7	5.6	4.0	3.3	1.2	0.7	1.2
Interest Paid **13**	3.1	0.8	4.9	•	247.8	24.9	2.2	22.6	5.2	4.2	0.8	1.4	3.4
Depreciation **14**	6.7	1.9	120.8	0.6	147.9	6.7	4.1	79.7	8.4	11.1	9.1	5.4	6.6
Amortization and Depletion **15**	12.2	41.7	•	17.6	664.9	94.3	8.3	76.2	13.3	13.6	12.0	10.9	12.2
Pensions and Other Deferred Comp. **16**	0.5	•	•	•	1.2	4.7	0.1	0.3	0.8	0.7	0.0	0.1	0.5
Employee Benefits **17**	0.8	0.2	270.4	2.3	13.1	0.3	1.9	3.6	2.9	1.4	3.2	0.4	0.8
Advertising **18**	0.0	•	•	•	10.4	•	0.1	1.1	0.1	0.1	0.0	0.1	0.0
Other Expenses **19**	11.7	1049.2	2307.5	105.9	3923.4	513.0	155.6	158.4	35.7	17.0	15.0	8.9	10.3
Officers' Compensation **20**	0.3	•	1441.2	10.0	43.1	9.9	1.7	10.0	3.2	2.0	•	0.6	0.2
Operating Margin **21**	7.0	•	•	•	•	•	•	•	•	•	•	6.4	3.9	9.8
Operating Margin Before Officers' Comp. **22**	7.3	•	•	•	•	•	•	•	•	•	•	6.4	4.6	10.0

Selected Average Balance Sheet ($ in Thousands)

Net Receivables 23	22221	0	2	0	21	149	653	2848	2167	3727	9318	52584	2442034
Inventories 24	7801	0	0	0	21	63	78	710	3066	6884	30208	102016	742411
Net Property, Plant and Equipment 25	43156	0	21	309	578	1431	6061	17074	21201	39574	161340	661578	3923718
Total Assets 26	157822	0	106	757	1895	7993	15292	34989	73017	154415	331673	1352678	15704116
Notes and Loans Payable 27	24927	0	1	406	1751	191	8901	11513	40929	36368	62626	228427	2318650
All Other Liabilities 28	44358	0	101	18	1070	9256	5223	13093	15933	35693	145004	270084	4463165
Net Worth 29	88536	0	3	332	-925	-1453	1168	10383	16155	82354	124043	854167	8922301

Selected Financial Ratios (Times to 1)

Current Ratio 30	2.0	•	0.4	10.1	0.8	0.2	2.1	0.4	1.4	2.0	1.6	1.8	2.1
Quick Ratio 31	1.4	•	0.4	9.7	0.1	0.0	1.2	0.4	1.0	1.1	0.5	1.2	1.4
Net Sales to Working Capital 32	2.1	•	•	1.2	•	•	2.9	•	4.1	1.9	4.6	3.2	2.0
Coverage Ratio 33	6.8	•	•	•	•	•	•	•	•	•	10.0	9.0	7.4
Total Asset Turnover 34	0.3	•	0.0	0.3	0.0	0.0	0.3	0.0	0.2	0.3	0.6	0.4	0.3
Inventory Turnover 35	3.2	•	•	•	0.9	1.2	41.7	1.2	2.3	3.2	3.2	3.3	3.2
Receivables Turnover 36	2.0	•	•	•	0.3	2.1	3.2	0.4	3.9	14.8	26.2	8.6	1.8
Total Liabilities to Net Worth 37	0.8	•	32.7	1.3	•	•	12.1	2.4	3.5	0.9	1.7	0.6	0.8
Current Assets to Working Capital 38	2.0	•	•	1.1	•	•	1.9	•	3.5	2.0	2.6	2.3	1.9
Current Liabilities to Working Capital 39	1.0	•	•	0.1	•	•	0.9	•	2.5	1.0	1.6	1.3	0.9
Working Capital to Net Sales 40	0.5	•	•	0.8	•	•	0.4	•	0.2	0.5	0.2	0.3	0.5
Inventory to Working Capital 41	0.4	•	•	•	•	•	0.1	•	0.7	0.4	0.9	0.5	0.3
Total Receipts to Cash Flow 42	3.8	•	•	2.8	•	•	•	•	6.5	•	4.7	5.6	3.5
Cost of Goods to Cash Flow 43	2.1	•	•	•	•	•	•	•	2.7	•	2.5	3.7	1.9
Cash Flow to Total Debt 44	0.2	•	•	0.2	•	•	•	•	0.0	•	0.2	0.2	0.2

Selected Financial Factors (in Percentages)

Debt Ratio 45	43.9	•	97.0	56.1	148.8	118.2	92.4	70.3	77.9	46.7	62.6	36.9	43.2
Return on Total Assets 46	6.2	•	•	•	•	•	•	•	•	•	4.5	4.6	7.1
Return on Equity Before Income Taxes 47	9.5	•	•	•	94.9	47.7	•	•	•	•	10.8	6.5	10.8
Return on Equity After Income Taxes 48	5.7	•	•	•	94.9	48.8	•	•	•	•	5.0	4.0	6.8
Profit Margin (Before Income Tax) 49	18.2	•	•	•	•	•	•	•	•	•	7.3	10.9	21.6
Profit Margin (After Income Tax) 50	10.9	•	•	•	•	•	•	•	•	•	3.3	6.7	13.6

Table II

Corporations with Net Income

METAL ORE MINING

MONEY AMOUNTS AND SIZE OF ASSETS IN THOUSANDS OF DOLLARS

Item Description for Accounting Period 7/12 Through 6/13		Total	Zero Assets	Under 500	500 to 1,000	1,000 to 5,000	5,000 to 10,000	10,000 to 25,000	25,000 to 50,000	50,000 to 100,000	100,000 to 250,000	250,000 to 500,000	500,000 to 2,500,000	2,500,000 and over
Number of Enterprises	1	520	0	417	59	0	3	14	0	4	3	3	7	11

Revenues ($ in Thousands)

Net Sales	2	54547556	0	1221	44344	0	0	214814	0	215711	372757	1029905	3403328	49265475
Interest	3	564267	0	0	0	0	18	167	0	69	961	481	10302	552269
Rents	4	26038	0	0	0	0	70	252	0	14	0	103	0	25599
Royalties	5	336096	0	0	0	0	4582	14499	0	0	0	0	835	316181
Other Portfolio Income	6	2507036	0	0	0	0	13412	8365	0	518	49	0	86117	2398576
Other Receipts	7	1915997	0	0	0	0	3960	5213	0	21508	3726	8629	229160	1643799
Total Receipts	8	59896990	0	1221	44344	0	22042	243310	0	237820	377493	1039118	3729742	54201899
Average Total Receipts	9	115187	•	3	752	•	7347	17379	•	59455	125831	346373	532820	4927445

Operating Costs/Operating Income (%)

Cost of Operations	10	52.9	•	13.8	•	•	•	76.1	•	28.6	29.2	40.0	53.5	53.4
Salaries and Wages	11	1.8	•	•	•	•	•	1.7	•	13.0	16.3	0.3	1.5	1.7
Taxes Paid	12	1.2	•	2.0	0.0	•	•	0.5	•	2.9	2.2	1.6	1.1	1.2
Interest Paid	13	3.2	•	•	•	•	•	1.0	•	1.9	2.5	0.3	1.5	3.4
Depreciation	14	6.6	•	•	•	•	•	0.6	•	7.9	6.9	6.7	6.1	6.6
Amortization and Depletion	15	12.4	•	•	14.9	•	•	0.7	•	8.8	9.9	14.1	15.4	12.2
Pensions and Other Deferred Comp.	16	0.5	•	•	•	•	•	0.1	•	0.2	0.8	•	0.1	0.5
Employee Benefits	17	0.8	•	•	•	•	•	0.4	•	4.1	1.5	4.5	0.7	0.8
Advertising	18	0.0	•	•	•	•	•	0.0	•	0.0	0.0	•	0.1	0.0
Other Expenses	19	10.6	•	68.3	18.3	•	•	7.9	•	31.1	17.9	17.0	10.8	10.3
Officers' Compensation	20	0.2	•	•	•	•	•	0.3	•	1.1	0.5	•	0.5	0.2
Operating Margin	21	9.8	•	15.8	66.8	•	•	10.7	•	0.4	12.4	15.5	8.6	9.8
Operating Margin Before Officers' Comp.	22	10.0	•	15.8	66.8	•	•	11.0	•	1.5	12.8	15.5	9.1	10.0

Selected Average Balance Sheet ($ in Thousands)

Net Receivables 23	52313	•	0	0	•	1527	2011	•	4427	15045	18255	27141	2442034
Inventories 24	17898	•	0	0	•	0	517	•	8134	28128	69096	120730	742411
Net Property, Plant and Equipment 25	93479	•	0	540	•	50	7429	•	20202	36208	168294	659693	3923718
Total Assets 26	355995	•	66	712	•	6390	15587	•	73546	138113	378542	1460094	15704116
Notes and Loans Payable 27	52670	•	2	6	•	1112	5319	•	48504	20155	22677	211673	2318650
All Other Liabilities 28	99159	•	0	6	•	1384	1269	•	22124	83340	154252	234872	4463165
Net Worth 29	204166	•	64	700	•	3895	8998	•	2918	34618	201613	1013550	8922301

Selected Financial Ratios (Times to 1)

Current Ratio 30	2.1	•	•	1.9	•	0.9	2.8	•	4.2	1.7	1.8	2.4	2.1
Quick Ratio 31	1.4	•	•	1.9	•	0.8	2.3	•	3.3	0.7	0.7	1.6	1.4
Net Sales to Working Capital 32	2.0	•	0.8	70.8	•	•	6.4	•	2.5	4.0	5.4	2.3	2.0
Coverage Ratio 33	7.7	•	•	•	•	14.3	26.7	•	12.3	6.4	55.4	13.3	7.4
Total Asset Turnover 34	0.3	•	0.0	1.1	•	•	1.0	•	0.7	0.9	0.9	0.3	0.3
Inventory Turnover 35	3.1	•	•	•	•	•	22.6	•	1.9	1.3	2.0	2.2	3.2
Receivables Turnover 36	1.9	•	•	•	•	•	7.4	•	4.0	16.5	27.0	15.6	1.8
Total Liabilities to Net Worth 37	0.7	•	0.0	0.0	•	0.6	0.7	•	24.2	3.0	0.9	0.4	0.8
Current Assets to Working Capital 38	1.9	•	1.0	2.1	•	•	1.5	•	1.3	2.4	2.2	1.7	1.9
Current Liabilities to Working Capital 39	0.9	•	•	1.1	•	•	0.5	•	0.3	1.4	1.2	0.7	0.9
Working Capital to Net Sales 40	0.5	•	1.3	0.0	•	•	0.2	•	0.4	0.2	0.2	0.4	0.5
Inventory to Working Capital 41	0.4	•	•	•	•	•	0.2	•	0.2	0.9	1.2	0.5	0.3
Total Receipts to Cash Flow 42	3.5	•	1.2	1.2	•	•	3.3	•	2.7	4.7	3.1	3.7	3.5
Cost of Goods to Cash Flow 43	1.8	•	0.2	•	•	•	2.5	•	0.8	1.4	1.2	2.0	1.9
Cash Flow to Total Debt 44	0.2	•	1.2	53.7	•	0.8	0.7	•	0.3	0.3	0.6	0.3	0.2

Selected Financial Factors (in Percentages)

Debt Ratio 45	42.6	•	3.0	1.7	•	39.1	42.3	•	96.0	74.9	46.7	30.6	43.2
Return on Total Assets 46	7.2	•	0.7	70.5	•	81.3	26.1	•	17.3	14.5	15.2	6.8	7.1
Return on Equity Before Income Taxes 47	11.0	•	0.7	71.7	•	124.1	43.5	•	400.5	49.0	28.0	9.1	10.8
Return on Equity After Income Taxes 48	7.0	•	0.7	71.7	•	119.7	31.5	•	397.4	38.1	18.4	5.8	6.8
Profit Margin (Before Income Tax) 49	21.3	•	15.9	66.8	•	•	25.5	•	21.7	13.6	16.4	18.9	21.6
Profit Margin (After Income Tax) 50	13.6	•	15.9	66.8	•	•	18.5	•	21.5	10.6	10.8	12.2	13.6

Table I

Corporations with and without Net Income

NONMETALLIC MINERAL MINING AND QUARRYING

MONEY AMOUNTS AND SIZE OF ASSETS IN THOUSANDS OF DOLLARS

Item Description for Accounting Period 7/12 Through 6/13		Total	Zero Assets	Under 500	500 to 1,000	1,000 to 5,000	5,000 to 10,000	10,000 to 25,000	25,000 to 50,000	50,000 to 100,000	100,000 to 250,000	250,000 to 500,000	500,000 to 2,500,000	2,500,000 and over
Number of Enterprises	1	3946	523	1995	421	641	138	90	65	29	23	6	13	0
Revenues ($ in Thousands)														
Net Sales	2	25602868	275971	1111184	692073	2113723	1342057	1433177	1675411	1199729	2730191	1708641	11320713	0
Interest	3	23344	438	17	1	628	774	1920	1461	1118	3433	1141	12411	0
Rents	4	83897	4	0	69	3146	131	1335	6267	1382	2726	736	68101	0
Royalties	5	30973	355	0	0	0	5175	0	177	177	533	33	24522	0
Other Portfolio Income	6	314732	42407	0	4373	12203	36902	6403	65840	10698	29958	5482	100467	0
Other Receipts	7	298543	5927	5	15475	16947	6096	45776	-47884	14939	-7220	28249	220231	0
Total Receipts	8	26354357	325102	1111206	711991	2146647	1391135	1488611	1701272	1228043	2759621	1744282	11746445	0
Average Total Receipts	9	6679	622	557	1691	3349	10081	16540	26173	42346	119984	290714	903573	•
Operating Costs/Operating Income (%)														
Cost of Operations	10	63.9	69.8	21.0	67.8	53.2	67.2	65.7	70.0	69.6	67.8	71.4	65.5	•
Salaries and Wages	11	5.0	7.9	20.3	1.7	3.6	2.6	5.7	4.5	5.2	3.4	4.0	4.6	•
Taxes Paid	12	2.3	2.6	1.3	4.1	4.1	3.0	2.7	2.0	1.6	1.7	1.3	2.1	•
Interest Paid	13	3.2	0.9	1.6	1.5	1.2	2.2	1.6	3.2	1.8	2.6	1.6	4.7	•
Depreciation	14	7.1	5.0	11.4	6.3	3.7	8.2	6.0	6.6	9.4	6.1	6.3	7.6	•
Amortization and Depletion	15	3.2	4.4	3.8	1.3	2.4	1.1	2.4	2.6	1.6	2.4	3.0	4.2	•
Pensions and Other Deferred Comp.	16	0.8	0.1	•	0.1	0.7	0.2	0.5	0.6	0.4	1.0	1.8	1.0	•
Employee Benefits	17	2.7	2.1	1.6	2.8	2.1	1.4	2.3	1.8	2.3	2.1	0.9	3.8	•
Advertising	18	0.2	0.1	0.1	0.1	0.5	0.2	0.1	0.2	0.2	0.1	0.1	0.2	•
Other Expenses	19	10.2	6.9	38.7	10.4	18.7	9.4	10.6	10.2	9.8	8.2	4.9	7.3	•
Officers' Compensation	20	1.4	0.7	0.2	3.2	3.6	2.0	2.2	2.5	1.9	1.6	1.1	0.6	•
Operating Margin	21	0.1	•	•	0.8	6.3	2.3	0.2	•	•	2.9	3.6	•	•
Operating Margin Before Officers' Comp.	22	1.5	0.2	0.1	4.0	9.9	4.4	2.3	•	•	4.5	4.7	•	•

Selected Average Balance Sheet ($ in Thousands)													
Net Receivables 23	814	0	0	143	305	1030	2492	3394	6380	17060	29762	124242	•
Inventories 24	796	0	0	27	209	414	2547	2443	7539	16189	32062	135866	•
Net Property, Plant and Equipment 25	4046	0	55	388	1184	4968	6884	14888	28616	64117	155044	724898	•
Total Assets 26	9609	0	91	743	2665	7647	17555	34709	66628	165514	336944	1774162	•
Notes and Loans Payable 27	3344	0	21	523	772	3781	4971	13282	23365	45793	56751	656353	•
All Other Liabilities 28	1929	0	23	71	215	670	3096	5159	13164	31061	70395	397964	•
Net Worth 29	4337	0	47	149	1677	3196	9488	16269	30099	88660	209799	719845	•

Selected Financial Ratios (Times to 1)													
Current Ratio 30	2.1	•	3.7	4.6	4.2	1.8	1.6	1.9	2.1	2.2	3.2	1.9	•
Quick Ratio 31	1.2	•	2.9	4.0	3.2	1.3	1.0	1.2	1.2	1.2	2.1	0.9	•
Net Sales to Working Capital 32	5.1	•	25.4	6.0	3.2	10.9	4.9	5.0	3.6	4.0	3.8	5.6	•
Coverage Ratio 33	1.9	20.7	0.9	3.4	7.7	3.8	3.5	0.2	0.2	2.5	4.6	1.5	•
Total Asset Turnover 34	0.7	•	6.1	2.2	1.2	1.3	0.9	0.7	0.6	0.7	0.8	0.5	•
Inventory Turnover 35	5.2	•	•	41.7	8.4	15.8	4.1	7.4	3.8	5.0	6.3	4.2	•
Receivables Turnover 36	7.9	•	1111184.0	10.9	9.8	8.5	6.0	7.6	5.6	6.4	8.3	7.5	•
Total Liabilities to Net Worth 37	1.2	•	0.9	4.0	0.6	1.4	0.9	1.1	1.2	0.9	0.6	1.5	•
Current Assets to Working Capital 38	1.9	•	1.4	1.3	1.3	2.3	2.6	2.1	1.9	1.9	1.5	2.1	•
Current Liabilities to Working Capital 39	0.9	•	0.4	0.3	0.3	1.3	1.6	1.1	0.9	0.9	0.5	1.1	•
Working Capital to Net Sales 40	0.2	•	0.0	0.2	0.3	0.1	0.2	0.2	0.3	0.2	0.3	0.2	•
Inventory to Working Capital 41	0.6	•	•	0.1	0.3	0.4	0.7	0.5	0.7	0.5	0.4	0.9	•
Total Receipts to Cash Flow 42	11.5	6.1	3.6	9.6	5.5	8.9	8.5	24.4	16.7	11.3	11.3	20.1	•
Cost of Goods to Cash Flow 43	7.3	4.2	0.7	6.5	2.9	6.0	5.6	17.1	11.6	7.7	8.0	13.2	•
Cash Flow to Total Debt 44	0.1	•	3.6	0.3	0.6	0.2	0.2	0.1	0.1	0.1	0.2	0.0	•

Selected Financial Factors (in Percentages)													
Debt Ratio 45	54.9	•	48.4	80.0	37.1	58.2	46.0	53.1	54.8	46.4	37.7	59.4	•
Return on Total Assets 46	4.2	•	9.2	11.4	11.2	10.4	5.1	0.4	0.3	4.7	6.2	3.4	•
Return on Equity Before Income Taxes 47	4.5	•	•	40.2	15.5	18.2	6.7	•	•	5.4	7.8	2.6	•
Return on Equity After Income Taxes 48	3.0	•	•	40.2	15.4	16.7	6.6	•	•	4.0	5.7	0.7	•
Profit Margin (Before Income Tax) 49	3.0	17.3	•	3.6	7.9	6.0	4.0	•	•	4.0	5.7	2.2	•
Profit Margin (After Income Tax) 50	2.0	16.5	•	3.6	7.8	5.5	3.9	•	•	3.0	4.2	0.6	•

Table II

Corporations with Net Income

NONMETALLIC MINERAL MINING AND QUARRYING

MONEY AMOUNTS AND SIZE OF ASSETS IN THOUSANDS OF DOLLARS

Item Description for Accounting Period 7/12 Through 6/13	Total	Zero Assets	Under 500	500 to 1,000	1,000 to 5,000	5,000 to 10,000	10,000 to 25,000	25,000 to 50,000	50,000 to 100,000	100,000 to 250,000	250,000 to 500,000	500,000 to 2,500,000	2,500,000 and over
Number of Enterprises **1**	3110	•	•	307	548	69	65	36	16	18	•	8	0

Revenues ($ in Thousands)

Net Sales **2**	16578637	•	•	508443	1869440	854172	1134316	1063005	747646	2391166	•	5204615	0
Interest **3**	18013	•	•	0	434	523	1694	1456	632	3051	•	8744	0
Rents **4**	47376	•	•	0	1353	56	935	5117	1190	1422	•	37139	0
Royalties **5**	12448	•	•	0	0	5175	0	94	177	516	•	6131	0
Other Portfolio Income **6**	212666	•	•	3996	10157	36902	5356	62991	8694	27893	•	12092	0
Other Receipts **7**	295839	•	•	14235	14774	654	44471	16885	4211	1776	•	165624	0
Total Receipts **8**	17164979	•	•	526674	1896158	897482	1186772	1149548	762550	2425824	•	5434345	0
Average Total Receipts **9**	5519	•	•	1716	3460	13007	18258	31932	47659	134768	•	679293	•

Operating Costs/Operating Income (%)

Cost of Operations **10**	60.4	•	•	66.3	49.8	61.8	66.1	66.0	68.6	68.0	•	61.6	•
Salaries and Wages **11**	4.9	•	•	0.3	3.4	2.4	5.9	4.7	3.8	2.8	•	4.0	•
Taxes Paid **12**	2.0	•	•	3.5	4.0	2.7	2.0	2.0	1.7	1.6	•	1.5	•
Interest Paid **13**	1.8	•	•	1.9	0.9	1.3	0.7	1.0	1.0	2.7	•	2.5	•
Depreciation **14**	6.7	•	•	7.6	3.2	10.8	6.2	6.5	6.2	6.1	•	7.2	•
Amortization and Depletion **15**	3.4	•	•	1.6	2.3	0.7	2.1	1.9	1.6	2.4	•	5.5	•
Pensions and Other Deferred Comp. **16**	0.7	•	•	0.1	0.8	0.3	0.5	0.9	0.5	1.2	•	0.7	•
Employee Benefits **17**	1.9	•	•	3.2	2.2	1.4	1.7	1.8	2.1	1.7	•	2.1	•
Advertising **18**	0.2	•	•	0.1	0.6	0.1	0.1	0.3	0.2	0.1	•	0.2	•
Other Expenses **19**	10.7	•	•	9.0	19.1	9.9	7.2	8.4	6.1	7.3	•	8.2	•
Officers' Compensation **20**	1.6	•	•	2.9	3.8	2.4	1.6	2.6	1.5	1.5	•	1.0	•
Operating Margin **21**	5.6	•	•	3.6	10.0	6.4	5.8	4.0	6.7	4.6	•	5.3	•
Operating Margin Before Officers' Comp. **22**	7.2	•	•	6.5	13.9	8.7	7.5	6.5	8.2	6.2	•	6.3	•

Selected Average Balance Sheet ($ in Thousands)

Net Receivables 23	672	•	•	122	285	1852	2611	4019	7053	17825	•	108366	•
Inventories 24	525	•	•	28	202	225	2108	2786	7066	16055	•	93009	•
Net Property, Plant and Equipment 25	2623	•	•	403	1182	4639	7083	15075	22895	67204	•	446200	•
Total Assets 26	5914	•	•	756	2634	8473	18523	33036	63201	162503	•	986957	•
Notes and Loans Payable 27	1742	•	•	570	602	3524	2791	7055	15716	49890	•	340990	•
All Other Liabilities 28	1028	•	•	58	142	940	2723	4501	9160	29688	•	202458	•
Net Worth 29	3144	•	•	128	1890	4009	13010	21480	38325	82926	•	443508	•

Selected Financial Ratios (Times to 1)

Current Ratio 30	2.6	•	•	6.0	7.4	1.7	3.1	3.0	3.0	2.5	•	2.0	•
Quick Ratio 31	1.7	•	•	5.3	5.7	1.6	2.1	1.8	1.8	1.4	•	1.1	•
Net Sales to Working Capital 32	4.4	•	•	5.6	2.8	9.4	3.0	3.7	2.8	3.6	•	5.5	•
Coverage Ratio 33	6.0	•	•	4.8	14.4	9.7	15.0	12.9	10.0	3.3	•	4.9	•
Total Asset Turnover 34	0.9	•	•	2.2	1.3	1.5	0.9	0.9	0.7	0.8	•	0.7	•
Inventory Turnover 35	6.1	•	•	38.8	8.4	34.0	5.5	7.0	4.5	5.6	•	4.3	•
Receivables Turnover 36	8.4	•	•	22.7	10.5	7.2	7.9	6.7	6.1	9.1	•	6.2	•
Total Liabilities to Net Worth 37	0.9	•	•	4.9	0.4	1.1	0.4	0.5	0.6	1.0	•	1.2	•
Current Assets to Working Capital 38	1.6	•	•	1.2	1.2	2.4	1.5	1.5	1.5	1.7	•	2.0	•
Current Liabilities to Working Capital 39	0.6	•	•	0.2	0.2	1.4	0.5	0.5	0.5	0.7	•	1.0	•
Working Capital to Net Sales 40	0.2	•	•	0.2	0.4	0.1	0.3	0.3	0.4	0.3	•	0.2	•
Inventory to Working Capital 41	0.4	•	•	0.1	0.2	0.1	0.3	0.4	0.5	0.4	•	0.7	•
Total Receipts to Cash Flow 42	6.5	•	•	7.1	4.6	6.4	6.7	5.5	7.9	9.5	•	7.3	•
Cost of Goods to Cash Flow 43	3.9	•	•	4.7	2.3	4.0	4.4	3.6	5.5	6.4	•	4.5	•
Cash Flow to Total Debt 44	0.3	•	•	0.4	1.0	0.4	0.5	0.5	0.2	0.2	•	0.2	•

Selected Financial Factors (in Percentages)

Debt Ratio 45	46.8	•	•	83.0	28.3	52.7	29.8	35.0	39.4	49.0	•	55.1	•
Return on Total Assets 46	9.9	•	•	19.9	16.0	18.6	10.5	11.7	7.1	7.1	•	8.1	•
Return on Equity Before Income Taxes 47	15.5	•	•	93.1	20.7	35.3	14.0	16.6	10.6	9.7	•	14.3	•
Return on Equity After Income Taxes 48	12.9	•	•	93.1	20.6	32.9	13.8	15.2	10.3	7.9	•	9.4	•
Profit Margin (Before Income Tax) 49	9.1	•	•	7.2	11.5	11.4	10.4	12.1	8.7	6.1	•	9.8	•
Profit Margin (After Income Tax) 50	7.6	•	•	7.2	11.4	10.7	10.3	11.0	8.4	4.9	•	6.4	•

Table I

Corporations with and without Net Income

SUPPORT ACTIVITIES FOR MINING

MONEY AMOUNTS AND SIZE OF ASSETS IN THOUSANDS OF DOLLARS

Item Description for Accounting Period 7/12 Through 6/13		Total	Zero Assets	Under 500	500 to 1,000	1,000 to 5,000	5,000 to 10,000	10,000 to 25,000	25,000 to 50,000	50,000 to 100,000	100,000 to 250,000	250,000 to 500,000	500,000 to 2,500,000	2,500,000 and over
Number of Enterprises	1	11920	2118	6085	1239	1816	224	215	74	45	44	19	23	18
Revenues ($ in Thousands)														
Net Sales	2	113277439	1660374	4638459	1814740	9920139	2637327	4999811	3808324	4880854	4892217	3649472	13178397	57197325
Interest	3	733048	1506	46	414	897	1466	6073	1367	2241	3317	9755	41962	664004
Rents	4	1457650	100300	595	0	2844	30284	2278	62	5816	103373	80978	81522	1049599
Royalties	5	354612	0	0	190	0	28691	5602	510	1182	11238	373	277	306549
Other Portfolio Income	6	2356050	54812	59079	77011	53153	43145	44868	46966	6497	138557	46373	157320	1628266
Other Receipts	7	2463305	121996	8077	1188	751227	37668	129068	40600	82166	232460	15303	161072	882481
Total Receipts	8	120642104	1938988	4706256	1893543	10728260	2778581	5187700	3897829	4978756	5381162	3802254	13620550	61728224
Average Total Receipts	9	10121	915	773	1528	5908	12404	24129	52673	110639	122299	200119	592198	3429346
Operating Costs/Operating Income (%)														
Cost of Operations	10	50.3	52.9	4.9	31.4	45.8	42.0	48.3	50.2	66.4	52.1	55.3	54.0	53.2
Salaries and Wages	11	9.9	7.0	51.8	17.0	12.1	13.3	11.3	11.2	8.2	12.2	11.0	8.8	5.8
Taxes Paid	12	2.4	1.5	2.9	3.2	2.2	4.1	2.5	2.6	1.8	2.3	2.4	1.9	2.4
Interest Paid	13	3.0	1.8	0.5	0.2	0.7	0.6	1.0	1.0	1.1	2.6	5.1	4.3	3.9
Depreciation	14	10.6	22.7	2.8	2.3	6.0	7.8	5.2	8.1	3.8	8.5	15.7	16.1	11.8
Amortization and Depletion	15	0.8	0.6	0.1	0.0	0.1	0.1	0.1	0.2	0.4	1.4	1.9	1.3	0.9
Pensions and Other Deferred Comp.	16	0.5	0.3	0.2	0.8	0.2	0.3	0.2	0.3	0.1	0.2	0.3	0.3	0.7
Employee Benefits	17	1.5	1.1	0.9	0.7	1.1	1.1	1.0	1.3	1.1	2.0	1.3	1.6	1.8
Advertising	18	0.1	0.1	0.4	0.3	0.2	0.2	0.2	0.1	0.2	0.2	0.1	0.1	0.1
Other Expenses	19	18.4	24.0	23.0	27.2	27.8	20.1	21.8	18.4	15.1	17.5	21.5	11.0	17.4
Officers' Compensation	20	1.4	3.1	3.9	6.8	3.9	4.0	2.8	1.2	0.5	1.5	0.9	0.8	0.5
Operating Margin	21	1.2	•	8.5	10.0	•	6.6	5.5	5.3	1.3	•	•	•	1.6
Operating Margin Before Officers' Comp.	22	2.6	•	12.4	16.8	3.8	10.6	8.2	6.5	1.8	1.1	•	0.6	2.1

Selected Average Balance Sheet ($ in Thousands)

Net Receivables 23	2497	0	12	181	353	1737	4674	9705	16483	29535	66190	140207	1121817
Inventories 24	479	0	0	57	89	116	415	1828	2521	4151	28198	27004	209613
Net Property, Plant and Equipment 25	4948	0	50	114	645	1967	3924	11712	19988	54631	119286	476555	2148992
Total Assets 26	14224	0	104	686	2090	7197	15302	34476	69592	141703	377275	1049573	6452187
Notes and Loans Payable 27	4540	0	77	257	823	1169	4212	7333	25586	41507	108955	272183	2156667
All Other Liabilities 28	3659	0	9	210	519	1324	4220	10399	19876	40603	124716	281219	1603380
Net Worth 29	6025	0	18	220	748	4704	6870	16744	24130	59594	143605	496171	2692140

Selected Financial Ratios (Times to 1)

Current Ratio 30	2.1	•	2.1	1.8	2.2	2.6	2.0	2.0	1.3	1.8	1.3	1.9	2.3
Quick Ratio 31	1.5	•	2.0	1.4	1.8	2.3	1.7	1.6	1.0	1.4	0.9	1.5	1.6
Net Sales to Working Capital 32	4.0	•	31.9	7.3	10.1	5.6	5.5	6.3	17.0	4.4	6.7	5.3	2.8
Coverage Ratio 33	3.7	2.0	21.8	85.4	12.4	20.8	10.1	8.8	4.1	4.7	•	1.7	3.7
Total Asset Turnover 34	0.7	•	7.3	2.1	2.6	1.6	1.5	1.5	1.6	0.8	0.5	0.5	0.5
Inventory Turnover 35	10.0	•	•	8.1	28.2	42.7	27.1	14.1	28.6	14.0	3.8	11.5	8.1
Receivables Turnover 36	4.0	•	58.6	10.1	19.9	6.3	5.4	5.9	7.0	4.2	3.4	3.4	3.0
Total Liabilities to Net Worth 37	1.4	•	4.9	2.1	1.8	0.5	1.2	1.1	1.9	1.4	1.6	1.1	1.4
Current Assets to Working Capital 38	1.9	•	1.9	2.3	1.9	1.6	2.0	2.0	4.7	2.3	4.3	2.1	1.8
Current Liabilities to Working Capital 39	0.9	•	0.9	1.3	0.9	0.6	1.0	1.0	3.7	1.3	3.3	1.1	0.8
Working Capital to Net Sales 40	0.2	•	0.0	0.1	0.1	0.2	0.2	0.2	0.1	0.2	0.1	0.2	0.4
Inventory to Working Capital 41	0.2	•	•	0.3	0.2	0.1	0.1	0.2	0.4	0.2	1.1	0.3	0.2
Total Receipts to Cash Flow 42	5.1	5.2	3.4	2.6	3.6	3.8	4.2	4.8	6.6	4.8	38.8	11.3	4.9
Cost of Goods to Cash Flow 43	2.5	2.7	0.2	0.8	1.6	1.6	2.0	2.4	4.4	2.5	21.4	6.1	2.6
Cash Flow to Total Debt 44	0.2	•	2.6	1.2	1.1	1.2	0.7	0.6	0.4	0.3	0.0	0.1	0.2

Selected Financial Factors (in Percentages)

Debt Ratio 45	57.6	•	82.9	67.9	64.2	34.6	55.1	51.4	65.3	57.9	61.9	52.7	58.3
Return on Total Assets 46	7.4	•	76.3	31.1	22.9	21.1	15.6	12.9	6.8	9.5	•	4.0	7.0
Return on Equity Before Income Taxes 47	12.8	•	426.6	95.8	58.7	30.7	31.3	23.5	15.0	17.9	•	3.5	12.2
Return on Equity After Income Taxes 48	9.5	•	424.8	95.5	54.9	27.6	26.5	19.4	12.5	13.4	•	1.4	8.8
Profit Margin (Before Income Tax) 49	8.1	1.8	10.0	14.4	8.0	12.3	9.2	7.6	3.3	9.6	•	3.1	10.4
Profit Margin (After Income Tax) 50	6.1	0.1	9.9	14.3	7.5	11.0	7.8	6.3	2.8	7.2	•	1.2	7.4

Table II
Corporations with Net Income

SUPPORT ACTIVITIES FOR MINING

MONEY AMOUNTS AND SIZE OF ASSETS IN THOUSANDS OF DOLLARS

Item Description for Accounting Period 7/12 Through 6/13	Total	Zero Assets	Under 500	500 to 1,000	1,000 to 5,000	5,000 to 10,000	10,000 to 25,000	25,000 to 50,000	50,000 to 100,000	100,000 to 250,000	250,000 to 500,000	500,000 to 2,500,000	2,500,000 and over
Number of Enterprises **1**	8569	•	4107	931	1343	155	159	51	31	30	•	10	•

Revenues ($ in Thousands)

Net Sales **2**	99369580	•	4086856	1638470	8732923	2298250	4519872	2990756	4527791	3772317	•	7546955	•
Interest **3**	682004	•	46	414	795	1306	5839	1333	928	3226	•	5245	•
Rents **4**	1095134	•	0	0	1482	30062	936	50	0	103373	•	68716	•
Royalties **5**	346306	•	0	190	0	26649	31	510	1182	11238	•	0	•
Other Portfolio Income **6**	2153635	•	59079	77011	39644	13821	32662	40608	5199	121349	•	97373	•
Other Receipts **7**	1484477	•	6495	125	106279	33378	81860	31193	38236	233933	•	35618	•
Total Receipts **8**	105131136	•	4152476	1716210	8881123	2403466	4641200	3064450	4573336	4245436	•	7753907	•
Average Total Receipts **9**	12269	•	1011	1843	6613	15506	29190	60087	147527	141515	•	775391	•

Operating Costs/Operating Income (%)

Cost of Operations **10**	50.2	•	5.5	30.1	44.2	40.3	47.6	57.9	68.2	50.1	•	49.7	•
Salaries and Wages **11**	9.5	•	55.9	16.1	11.3	12.1	10.7	7.5	6.0	12.7	•	10.3	•
Taxes Paid **12**	2.4	•	2.9	3.4	2.2	4.3	2.3	2.6	1.7	2.4	•	2.4	•
Interest Paid **13**	2.6	•	0.3	0.1	0.6	0.4	0.7	1.0	0.7	1.5	•	2.5	•
Depreciation **14**	9.2	•	2.6	2.4	5.9	7.7	4.7	6.2	2.6	7.3	•	10.9	•
Amortization and Depletion **15**	0.6	•	0.1	0.0	0.0	0.0	0.1	0.1	0.2	1.0	•	0.5	•
Pensions and Other Deferred Comp. **16**	0.5	•	0.2	0.9	0.2	0.3	0.2	0.4	0.1	0.2	•	0.2	•
Employee Benefits **17**	1.5	•	0.9	0.6	1.1	1.0	1.0	1.5	0.9	2.1	•	1.5	•
Advertising **18**	0.1	•	0.5	0.2	0.3	0.2	0.2	0.1	0.1	0.2	•	0.1	•
Other Expenses **19**	16.6	•	17.5	26.6	21.6	17.9	20.0	12.5	14.2	16.4	•	9.9	•
Officers' Compensation **20**	1.4	•	3.4	7.5	3.4	4.2	2.7	1.4	0.4	1.8	•	1.0	•
Operating Margin **21**	5.4	•	10.1	12.1	9.1	11.6	9.8	8.8	4.9	4.5	•	10.8	•
Operating Margin Before Officers' Comp. **22**	6.7	•	13.5	19.6	12.6	15.9	12.4	10.1	5.3	6.3	•	11.8	•

	Selected Average Balance Sheet ($ in Thousands)											
Net Receivables 23	3120	•	10	184	457	2204	4952	10670	18631	30620	•	226610	•
Inventories 24	557	•	0	23	96	90	483	1837	2428	3707	•	49122	•
Net Property, Plant and Equipment 25	5097	•	53	81	703	2346	3620	11520	16596	51774	•	429173	•
Total Assets 26	15510	•	108	680	2067	7612	15432	35870	69179	145122	•	981360	•
Notes and Loans Payable 27	5094	•	50	118	798	913	3515	7067	21879	26478	•	287615	•
All Other Liabilities 28	3892	•	8	92	254	1151	4045	8258	19654	45444	•	237684	•
Net Worth 29	6524	•	50	470	1015	5548	7871	20545	27647	73201	•	456061	•

	Selected Financial Ratios (Times to 1)											
Current Ratio 30	2.1	•	1.9	4.4	3.0	2.9	2.2	2.0	1.3	2.0	•	2.1	•
Quick Ratio 31	1.6	•	1.9	3.9	2.6	2.6	1.8	1.6	1.0	1.5	•	1.7	•
Net Sales to Working Capital 32	4.3	•	42.0	4.9	8.7	5.9	5.6	6.4	19.5	3.9	•	4.1	•
Coverage Ratio 33	5.5	•	37.3	139.8	19.4	46.9	18.6	12.3	9.9	12.6	•	6.4	•
Total Asset Turnover 34	0.7	•	9.2	2.6	3.1	1.9	1.8	1.6	2.1	0.9	•	0.8	•
Inventory Turnover 35	10.5	•	•	22.6	29.8	66.1	28.0	18.5	41.0	17.0	•	7.6	•
Receivables Turnover 36	4.1	•	147.3	11.1	19.7	6.8	6.4	5.9	8.7	5.3	•	3.0	•
Total Liabilities to Net Worth 37	1.4	•	1.2	0.4	1.0	0.4	1.0	0.7	1.5	1.0	•	1.2	•
Current Assets to Working Capital 38	1.9	•	2.1	1.3	1.5	1.5	1.9	2.0	4.4	2.0	•	1.9	•
Current Liabilities to Working Capital 39	0.9	•	1.1	0.3	0.5	0.5	0.9	1.0	3.4	1.0	•	0.9	•
Working Capital to Net Sales 40	0.2	•	0.0	0.2	0.1	0.2	0.2	0.2	0.1	0.3	•	0.2	•
Inventory to Working Capital 41	0.2	•	•	0.1	0.2	0.0	0.1	0.2	0.3	0.1	•	0.3	•
Total Receipts to Cash Flow 42	4.6	•	4.0	2.4	4.0	3.4	4.0	5.3	5.7	3.6	•	5.6	•
Cost of Goods to Cash Flow 43	2.3	•	0.2	0.7	1.8	1.4	1.9	3.1	3.9	1.8	•	2.8	•
Cash Flow to Total Debt 44	0.3	•	4.3	3.4	1.6	2.1	0.9	0.7	0.6	0.5	•	0.3	•

	Selected Financial Factors (in Percentages)											
Debt Ratio 45	57.9	•	53.7	30.9	50.9	27.1	49.0	42.7	60.0	49.6	•	53.5	•
Return on Total Assets 46	10.7	•	110.8	43.9	36.0	33.0	24.3	19.9	13.8	16.1	•	12.4	•
Return on Equity Before Income Taxes 47	20.7	•	232.9	63.1	69.4	44.4	45.0	32.0	31.0	29.3	•	22.5	•
Return on Equity After Income Taxes 48	16.5	•	232.0	62.9	65.7	40.5	39.4	27.2	27.8	23.9	•	17.2	•
Profit Margin (Before Income Tax) 49	11.7	•	11.7	16.8	10.8	16.6	12.5	11.2	5.9	17.1	•	13.6	•
Profit Margin (After Income Tax) 50	9.3	•	11.6	16.8	10.3	15.2	10.9	9.5	5.3	13.9	•	10.4	•

Table I

Corporations with and without Net Income

ELECTRIC POWER GENERATION, TRANSMISSION AND DISTRIBUTION

MONEY AMOUNTS AND SIZE OF ASSETS IN THOUSANDS OF DOLLARS

Item Description for Accounting Period 7/12 Through 6/13	Total	Zero Assets	Under 500	500 to 1,000	1,000 to 5,000	5,000 to 10,000	10,000 to 25,000	25,000 to 50,000	50,000 to 100,000	100,000 to 250,000	250,000 to 500,000	500,000 to 2,500,000	2,500,000 and over
Number of Enterprises **1**	996	29	284	247	148	30	67	33	20	34	23	35	45

Revenues ($ in Thousands)													
Net Sales **2**	286494195	5125956	0	205538	437735	183022	536531	2131919	864961	2270082	2370413	12699501	259668536
Interest **3**	3263647	2153	206224	1	1183	105	5357	1182	15838	66990	19182	159560	2785870
Rents **4**	1066971	6173	0	0	1151	0	56	0	289	699	10910	8000	1039693
Royalties **5**	41090	0	0	0	0	0	0	1102	141	0	0	1605	38242
Other Portfolio Income **6**	2982430	202	0	0	1305	0	4414	37	228616	109721	207906	182141	2248088
Other Receipts **7**	11217125	-10684	55073	713	33745	8618	371	33303	33798	101114	149205	432287	10379585
Total Receipts **8**	305065458	5123800	261297	206252	475119	191745	546729	2167543	1143643	2548606	2757616	13483094	276160014
Average Total Receipts **9**	306291	176683	920	835	3210	6392	8160	65683	57182	74959	119896	385231	6136889

Operating Costs/Operating Income (%)													
Cost of Operations **10**	51.4	1.1	•	53.0	52.6	55.2	62.8	68.7	72.8	81.1	61.4	58.2	51.5
Salaries and Wages **11**	4.0	3.8	•	8.9	10.1	17.1	6.1	6.5	5.5	4.5	4.0	4.6	3.9
Taxes Paid **12**	4.5	5.9	•	3.8	2.6	3.2	1.4	1.0	3.0	1.1	2.5	2.3	4.6
Interest Paid **13**	7.5	7.4	•	0.4	0.9	2.2	2.5	1.1	3.8	5.0	9.1	7.6	7.6
Depreciation **14**	17.1	24.8	•	0.3	3.6	4.5	6.3	1.7	6.6	8.9	11.8	11.3	17.6
Amortization and Depletion **15**	1.7	1.7	•	0.1	0.3	1.0	6.6	0.0	1.0	0.9	0.6	1.8	1.7
Pensions and Other Deferred Comp. **16**	1.5	3.5	•	•	0.1	•	1.1	0.5	1.0	0.2	1.1	1.0	1.5
Employee Benefits **17**	1.4	2.6	•	0.6	2.7	0.5	1.6	2.2	0.3	0.4	0.9	1.1	1.4
Advertising **18**	0.2	0.0	•	0.1	•	0.1	0.4	0.3	1.1	0.3	0.3	0.1	0.2
Other Expenses **19**	24.3	61.0	•	32.0	13.0	22.3	20.8	18.2	14.9	19.7	35.4	23.0	23.7
Officers' Compensation **20**	0.5	0.4	•	13.6	4.6	22.7	2.1	1.3	1.8	1.9	0.5	0.4	0.4
Operating Margin **21**	•	•	•	•	9.6	•	•	•	•	•	•	•	•
Operating Margin Before Officers' Comp. **22**	•	•	•	0.7	14.2	•	•	•	•	•	•	•	•

Selected Average Balance Sheet ($ in Thousands)

Net Receivables	23	43083	0	0	94	581	157	2564	6199	6497	19477	14260	79183	856203
Inventories	24	17221	0	0	17	9	183	693	254	1163	866	13457	35392	344146
Net Property, Plant and Equipment	25	596546	0	1	123	800	2407	4929	8877	23445	58749	165867	669621	12524378
Total Assets	26	1026538	0	106	783	2661	6343	15743	35385	73873	145639	368327	1220654	21372858
Notes and Loans Payable	27	394229	0	0	293	1136	476	6684	12523	25422	56578	185707	564080	8113103
All Other Liabilities	28	365683	0	22	338	804	2210	4673	29023	37774	26210	113536	289024	7740018
Net Worth	29	266627	0	84	152	721	3657	4386	-6161	10678	62851	69085	367550	5519737

Selected Financial Ratios (Times to 1)

Current Ratio	30	1.0	•	0.6	1.8	1.2	1.1	1.7	0.6	0.7	2.0	1.2	1.3	1.0
Quick Ratio	31	0.5	•	0.6	1.7	1.2	0.4	1.2	0.4	0.4	1.7	0.7	0.9	0.5
Net Sales to Working Capital	32	•	•	•	2.9	16.7	57.8	2.7	•	•	3.5	9.0	5.8	•
Coverage Ratio	33	•	•	1.1	•	21.3	•	•	1.2	6.5	•	•	0.4	•
Total Asset Turnover	34	0.3	•	•	1.1	1.1	1.0	0.5	1.8	0.6	0.5	0.3	0.3	0.3
Inventory Turnover	35	8.6	•	•	26.7	165.1	18.4	7.3	175.1	27.1	62.5	4.7	6.0	8.6
Receivables Turnover	36	6.6	•	•	13.2	8.3	6.0	2.9	12.1	5.6	3.5	9.2	4.7	6.6
Total Liabilities to Net Worth	37	2.9	•	0.3	4.2	2.7	0.7	2.6	•	5.9	1.3	4.3	2.3	2.9
Current Assets to Working Capital	38	•	•	•	2.2	5.7	13.5	2.3	•	•	2.0	5.6	4.2	•
Current Liabilities to Working Capital	39	•	•	•	1.2	4.7	12.5	1.3	•	•	1.0	4.6	3.2	•
Working Capital to Net Sales	40	•	•	•	0.3	0.1	0.0	0.4	•	•	0.3	0.1	0.2	•
Inventory to Working Capital	41	•	•	•	0.1	0.1	1.7	0.3	•	•	0.0	1.4	0.7	•
Total Receipts to Cash Flow	42	9.1	2.6	•	8.9	4.0	•	15.4	6.3	5.7	•	5.6	7.5	9.8
Cost of Goods to Cash Flow	43	4.7	0.0	•	4.7	2.1	•	9.7	4.4	4.1	•	3.5	4.4	5.0
Cash Flow to Total Debt	44	0.0	•	11.2	0.1	0.4	•	0.0	0.2	0.1	•	0.1	0.1	0.0

Selected Financial Factors (in Percentages)

Debt Ratio	45	74.0	•	20.6	80.6	72.9	42.3	72.1	117.4	85.5	56.8	81.2	69.9	74.2
Return on Total Assets	46	•	•	653.2	•	21.1	•	•	2.3	14.3	•	•	0.8	•
Return on Equity Before Income Taxes	47	•	•	51.4	•	74.3	•	•	•	83.6	•	•	•	•
Return on Equity After Income Taxes	48	•	•	50.6	•	74.3	•	•	4.7	52.9	•	•	•	•
Profit Margin (Before Income Tax)	49	•	•	•	•	18.1	•	•	0.2	20.6	•	•	•	•
Profit Margin (After Income Tax)	50	•	•	•	•	18.1	•	•	•	13.1	•	•	•	•

Table II
Corporations with Net Income

ELECTRIC POWER GENERATION, TRANSMISSION AND DISTRIBUTION

MONEY AMOUNTS AND SIZE OF ASSETS IN THOUSANDS OF DOLLARS

Item Description for Accounting Period 7/12 Through 6/13	Total	Zero Assets	Under 500	500 to 1,000	1,000 to 5,000	5,000 to 10,000	10,000 to 25,000	25,000 to 50,000	50,000 to 100,000	100,000 to 250,000	250,000 to 500,000	500,000 to 2,500,000	2,500,000 and over
Number of Enterprises **1**	419	8	•	•	121	0	•	11	9	9	9	11	14
Revenues ($ in Thousands)													
Net Sales **2**	46905229	1926	•	•	511628	0	•	713495	803102	1911552	1241092	3547312	37763552
Interest **3**	536608	0	•	•	1121	0	•	154	7184	415	9879	65830	244703
Rents **4**	131972	0	•	•	0	0	•	0	120	509	119	384	130783
Royalties **5**	7239	0	•	•	0	0	•	1102	0	0	0	306	5831
Other Portfolio Income **6**	1092760	0	•	•	1305	0	•	37	228573	88324	206722	159499	407115
Other Receipts **7**	2068902	0	•	•	33631	0	•	29748	2508	86846	123150	272262	1519757
Total Receipts **8**	50742710	1926	•	•	547685	0	•	744536	1041487	2087646	1580962	4045593	40071741
Average Total Receipts **9**	121104	241	•	•	4526	•	•	67685	115721	231961	175662	367781	2862267
Operating Costs/Operating Income (%)													
Cost of Operations **10**	49.7	•	•	•	57.8	•	•	48.1	75.2	89.1	61.4	47.3	46.9
Salaries and Wages **11**	3.3	•	•	•	8.2	•	•	17.1	5.2	3.2	2.0	7.1	2.7
Taxes Paid **12**	6.7	4.4	•	•	1.8	•	•	2.7	2.7	0.7	2.0	3.4	7.8
Interest Paid **13**	7.9	•	•	•	0.5	•	•	2.3	2.0	3.6	8.9	5.1	8.2
Depreciation **14**	14.5	•	•	•	2.4	•	•	0.5	2.8	2.0	9.0	10.7	16.5
Amortization and Depletion **15**	0.9	•	•	•	0.3	•	•	0.1	1.0	0.3	0.8	2.5	0.8
Pensions and Other Deferred Comp. **16**	2.2	•	•	•	0.0	•	•	1.5	0.3	0.2	0.0	1.3	2.6
Employee Benefits **17**	1.4	•	•	•	2.1	•	•	6.2	0.1	0.4	0.8	1.9	1.3
Advertising **18**	0.1	•	•	•	0.0	•	•	0.8	1.2	0.3	0.1	0.1	0.1
Other Expenses **19**	16.5	33.7	•	•	6.0	•	•	11.8	8.2	4.8	29.3	25.5	16.2
Officers' Compensation **20**	0.6	54.0	•	•	3.6	•	•	3.4	1.7	0.1	0.3	0.4	0.5
Operating Margin **21**	•	7.9	•	•	17.3	•	•	5.3	•	•	•	•	•
Operating Margin Before Officers' Comp. **22**	•	61.9	•	•	20.9	•	•	8.7	1.3	•	•	•	•

Selected Average Balance Sheet ($ in Thousands)

Net Receivables 23	17540	0	•	•	679	•	•	6199	9613	22732	18160	173428	339838
Inventories 24	6511	0	•	•	0	•	•	303	1725	930	21494	23956	160154
Net Property, Plant and Equipment 25	233641	0	•	•	728	•	•	12060	21830	61269	178123	417297	6473398
Total Assets 26	365487	0	•	•	2556	•	•	39913	74753	160209	385718	1164106	9542289
Notes and Loans Payable 27	136815	0	•	•	1123	•	•	5936	18831	79492	193296	318934	3636252
All Other Liabilities 28	121421	0	•	•	908	•	•	21012	25926	52522	154782	361312	3167649
Net Worth 29	107251	0	•	•	525	•	•	12965	29996	28196	37640	483861	2738388

Selected Financial Ratios (Times to 1)

Current Ratio 30	1.2	•	•	•	1.3	•	•	1.4	1.4	1.6	1.5	1.5	1.1
Quick Ratio 31	0.7	•	•	•	1.1	•	•	0.7	0.8	1.2	0.5	1.3	0.6
Net Sales to Working Capital 32	15.0	•	•	•	13.6	•	•	10.1	9.1	10.4	4.4	2.3	47.2
Coverage Ratio 33	1.6	•	•	•	45.2	•	•	5.2	15.4	2.3	2.4	2.9	1.3
Total Asset Turnover 34	0.3	•	•	•	1.7	•	•	1.6	1.2	1.3	0.4	0.3	0.3
Inventory Turnover 35	8.5	•	•	•	•	•	•	103.1	38.9	203.5	3.9	6.4	7.9
Receivables Turnover 36	7.4	•	•	•	10.3	•	•	11.1	11.3	9.9	9.4	2.7	8.7
Total Liabilities to Net Worth 37	2.4	•	•	•	3.9	•	•	2.1	1.5	4.7	9.2	1.4	2.5
Current Assets to Working Capital 38	6.6	•	•	•	3.9	•	•	3.7	3.4	2.8	3.0	2.8	17.3
Current Liabilities to Working Capital 39	5.6	•	•	•	2.9	•	•	2.7	2.4	1.8	2.0	1.8	16.3
Working Capital to Net Sales 40	0.1	•	•	•	0.1	•	•	0.1	0.1	0.1	0.2	0.4	0.0
Inventory to Working Capital 41	0.7	•	•	•	•	•	•	0.1	0.1	0.0	1.1	0.2	2.0
Total Receipts to Cash Flow 42	6.6	3.2	•	•	3.5	•	•	5.1	5.2	22.2	2.8	3.3	7.6
Cost of Goods to Cash Flow 43	3.3	•	•	•	2.0	•	•	2.4	3.9	19.8	1.7	1.5	3.5
Cash Flow to Total Debt 44	0.1	•	•	•	0.6	•	•	0.5	0.4	0.1	0.1	0.1	0.1

Selected Financial Factors (in Percentages)

Debt Ratio 45	70.7	•	•	•	79.5	•	•	67.5	59.9	82.4	90.2	58.4	71.3
Return on Total Assets 46	3.8	•	•	•	41.1	•	•	19.4	37.5	10.9	7.8	4.2	3.1
Return on Equity Before Income Taxes 47	4.7	•	•	•	196.0	•	•	48.3	87.3	34.5	47.0	6.6	2.7
Return on Equity After Income Taxes 48	4.1	•	•	•	187.1	•	•	39.1	63.0	27.9	37.7	5.7	2.5
Profit Margin (Before Income Tax) 49	4.5	7.9	•	•	24.3	•	•	9.6	29.3	4.6	12.8	9.9	2.7
Profit Margin (After Income Tax) 50	4.0	4.5	•	•	23.2	•	•	7.8	21.2	3.7	10.3	8.5	2.5

Table I

Corporations with and without Net Income

NATURAL GAS DISTRIBUTION

MONEY AMOUNTS AND SIZE OF ASSETS IN THOUSANDS OF DOLLARS

Item Description for Accounting Period 7/12 Through 6/13	Total	Zero Assets	Under 500	500 to 1,000	1,000 to 5,000	5,000 to 10,000	10,000 to 25,000	25,000 to 50,000	50,000 to 100,000	100,000 to 250,000	250,000 to 500,000	500,000 to 2,500,000	2,500,000 and over
Number of Enterprises **1**	231	14	93	0	34	18	10	9	13	12	3	9	16

Revenues ($ in Thousands)

	Total	Zero Assets	Under 500	500 to 1,000	1,000 to 5,000	5,000 to 10,000	10,000 to 25,000	25,000 to 50,000	50,000 to 100,000	100,000 to 250,000	250,000 to 500,000	500,000 to 2,500,000	2,500,000 and over
Net Sales **2**	52753906	9776	2757	0	262530	233757	324290	218470	847467	4414352	433090	9069768	36937647
Interest **3**	500501	57	0	0	332	68	36	438	786	405	4565	8886	484929
Rents **4**	47353	0	0	0	0	127	0	0	0	2352	1772	126	42976
Royalties **5**	207	0	0	0	0	0	0	0	11	0	0	79	117
Other Portfolio Income **6**	334421	1394	421	0	445	816	136	129	1018	472	135	102173	227283
Other Receipts **7**	2863755	9	10	0	1026	3226	5715	19502	31404	30425	1599	359634	2411203
Total Receipts **8**	56500143	11236	3188	0	264333	237994	330177	238539	880686	4448006	441161	9540666	40104155
Average Total Receipts **9**	244589	803	34	•	7774	13222	33018	26504	67745	370667	147054	1060074	2506510

Operating Costs/Operating Income (%)

	Total	Zero Assets	Under 500	500 to 1,000	1,000 to 5,000	5,000 to 10,000	10,000 to 25,000	25,000 to 50,000	50,000 to 100,000	100,000 to 250,000	250,000 to 500,000	500,000 to 2,500,000	2,500,000 and over
Cost of Operations **10**	70.8	6.8	0.8	•	83.8	76.6	82.7	72.2	69.2	94.6	51.1	87.4	63.9
Salaries and Wages **11**	4.5	4.3	•	•	2.8	2.6	5.8	6.0	8.0	1.3	5.8	2.1	5.3
Taxes Paid **12**	2.5	4.8	0.1	•	0.2	1.1	0.8	2.3	2.0	0.3	6.0	1.2	3.2
Interest Paid **13**	4.0	0.0	•	•	0.2	0.5	0.0	1.5	0.8	0.2	4.4	2.3	5.1
Depreciation **14**	8.8	10.5	1.1	•	0.8	4.2	0.9	4.2	3.7	1.2	9.9	4.0	11.2
Amortization and Depletion **15**	1.2	•	0.0	•	0.0	0.2	•	0.3	0.5	0.0	0.5	0.4	1.6
Pensions and Other Deferred Comp. **16**	1.0	•	•	•	0.1	•	0.3	0.2	0.8	0.1	1.3	0.7	1.1
Employee Benefits **17**	1.4	2.3	•	•	0.3	2.2	0.4	0.9	1.3	0.2	2.4	0.8	1.8
Advertising **18**	0.1	0.0	•	•	•	0.6	0.0	0.0	1.0	0.0	0.2	0.1	0.1
Other Expenses **19**	13.2	61.1	132.1	•	3.7	5.1	2.2	18.3	9.2	1.7	17.7	7.0	16.3
Officers' Compensation **20**	0.7	8.5	•	•	•	1.7	0.9	2.5	2.0	0.3	0.6	1.0	0.6
Operating Margin **21**	•	1.7	•	•	8.1	5.3	6.1	•	1.4	•	•	•	•
Operating Margin Before Officers' Comp. **22**	•	10.2	•	•	8.1	7.0	7.0	•	3.4	0.2	0.6	•	•

Selected Average Balance Sheet ($ in Thousands)

Net Receivables 23	43198	0	394	•	828	242	2810	4276	15658	35212	16547	95437	519280
Inventories 24	14059	0	0	•	0	386	1142	318	3630	7008	26274	109010	128298
Net Property, Plant and Equipment 25	336396	0	58	•	134	5540	4092	13752	23308	54292	223018	538996	4434913
Total Assets 26	690529	0	456	•	2185	8188	14337	33191	67283	133897	325848	1218793	9023616
Notes and Loans Payable 27	316685	0	49	•	160	1339	159	6868	13311	23648	112959	400003	4291307
All Other Liabilities 28	357982	0	337	•	949	1757	4834	3329768	19199	61731	78130	485548	2936725
Net Worth 29	15863	0	70	•	1076	5092	9344	-3303445	34774	48518	134758	333242	1795584

Selected Financial Ratios (Times to 1)

Current Ratio 30	1.1	•	1.2	•	1.6	1.5	1.9	3.0	1.9	1.2	1.1	1.4	1.0
Quick Ratio 31	0.5	•	1.2	•	1.5	0.8	1.6	2.8	1.3	0.9	0.4	0.7	0.5
Net Sales to Working Capital 32	23.2	•	0.5	•	13.9	31.0	8.1	2.1	4.3	30.1	27.5	12.2	37.0
Coverage Ratio 33	0.7	543.7	•	•	42.7	14.8	279.5	1.6	7.8	4.2	1.4	0.2	0.7
Total Asset Turnover 34	0.3	•	0.1	•	3.5	1.6	2.3	0.7	1.0	2.7	0.4	0.8	0.3
Inventory Turnover 35	11.5	•	•	•	•	25.7	23.5	55.1	12.4	49.7	2.8	8.1	11.5
Receivables Turnover 36	4.8	•	•	•	9.2	41.5	6.9	•	•	•	4.4	6.3	4.2
Total Liabilities to Net Worth 37	42.5	•	5.5	•	1.0	0.6	0.5	•	0.9	1.8	1.4	2.7	4.0
Current Assets to Working Capital 38	14.2	•	6.6	•	2.7	3.0	2.2	1.5	2.2	5.4	11.1	3.4	28.0
Current Liabilities to Working Capital 39	13.2	•	5.6	•	1.7	2.0	1.2	0.5	1.2	4.4	10.1	2.4	27.0
Working Capital to Net Sales 40	0.0	•	2.0	•	0.1	0.0	0.1	0.5	0.2	0.0	0.0	0.1	0.0
Inventory to Working Capital 41	1.4	•	•	•	•	1.1	0.2	0.0	0.2	0.6	3.9	1.2	2.0
Total Receipts to Cash Flow 42	10.8	1.6	3.3	•	8.5	8.8	10.2	5.9	7.4	45.6	6.0	23.2	9.0
Cost of Goods to Cash Flow 43	7.6	0.1	0.0	•	7.1	6.8	8.5	4.3	5.2	43.2	3.1	20.3	5.8
Cash Flow to Total Debt 44	0.0	•	0.0	•	0.8	0.5	0.6	0.0	0.3	0.1	0.1	0.0	0.0

Selected Financial Factors (in Percentages)

Debt Ratio 45	97.7	•	84.6	•	50.8	37.8	34.8	10052.9	48.3	63.8	58.6	72.7	80.1
Return on Total Assets 46	1.0	•	•	•	31.9	12.1	17.9	1.7	5.9	2.5	2.8	0.4	0.9
Return on Equity Before Income Taxes 47	•	•	•	•	63.2	18.1	27.4	•	10.0	5.3	2.0	•	•
Return on Equity After Income Taxes 48	•	•	•	•	42.5	18.1	26.7	0.0	7.9	4.5	1.3	•	•
Profit Margin (Before Income Tax) 49	•	16.7	•	•	8.8	7.1	7.9	0.8	5.3	0.7	1.8	•	•
Profit Margin (After Income Tax) 50	•	15.7	•	•	5.9	7.1	7.7	•	4.2	0.6	1.2	•	•

Table II

Corporations with Net Income

NATURAL GAS DISTRIBUTION

MONEY AMOUNTS AND SIZE OF ASSETS IN THOUSANDS OF DOLLARS

Item Description for Accounting Period 7/12 Through 6/13	Total	Zero Assets	Under 500	500 to 1,000	1,000 to 5,000	5,000 to 10,000	10,000 to 25,000	25,000 to 50,000	50,000 to 100,000	100,000 to 250,000	250,000 to 500,000	500,000 to 2,500,000	2,500,000 and over
Number of Enterprises 1	94	•	•	0	34	5	•	0	8	•	0	4	•
Revenues ($ in Thousands)													
Net Sales 2	21229129	•	•	0	262530	107078	•	0	789341	•	0	6438355	•
Interest 3	113175	•	•	0	332	0	•	0	705	•	0	2903	•
Rents 4	34317	•	•	0	0	0	•	0	0	•	0	35	•
Royalties 5	180	•	•	0	0	0	•	0	11	•	0	67	•
Other Portfolio Income 6	113581	•	•	0	445	0	•	0	898	•	0	101355	•
Other Receipts 7	1438349	•	•	0	1026	2383	•	0	34090	•	0	348544	•
Total Receipts 8	22928731	•	•	0	264333	109461	•	0	825045	•	0	6891259	•
Average Total Receipts 9	243923	•	•	•	7774	21892	•	•	103131	•	•	1722815	•
Operating Costs/Operating Income (%)													
Cost of Operations 10	66.2	•	•	•	83.8	76.6	•	•	72.0	•	•	93.9	•
Salaries and Wages 11	5.6	•	•	•	2.8	•	•	•	6.9	•	•	1.5	•
Taxes Paid 12	2.3	•	•	•	0.2	0.2	•	•	1.7	•	•	0.4	•
Interest Paid 13	4.2	•	•	•	0.2	0.0	•	•	0.7	•	•	1.7	•
Depreciation 14	9.2	•	•	•	0.8	3.5	•	•	3.1	•	•	1.3	•
Amortization and Depletion 15	0.2	•	•	•	0.0	0.0	•	•	0.5	•	•	0.2	•
Pensions and Other Deferred Comp. 16	0.7	•	•	•	0.1	•	•	•	0.7	•	•	0.1	•
Employee Benefits 17	1.9	•	•	•	0.3	0.1	•	•	1.2	•	•	0.1	•
Advertising 18	0.1	•	•	•	•	•	•	•	1.0	•	•	0.0	•
Other Expenses 19	11.6	•	•	•	3.7	1.1	•	•	6.4	•	•	5.5	•
Officers' Compensation 20	0.7	•	•	•	•	•	•	•	1.4	•	•	1.0	•
Operating Margin 21	•	•	•	•	8.1	18.4	•	•	4.4	•	•	•	•
Operating Margin Before Officers' Comp. 22	•	•	•	•	8.1	18.4	•	•	5.8	•	•	•	•

Selected Average Balance Sheet ($ in Thousands)

Net Receivables 23	75088	•	•	•	828	297	•	•	19135	•	•	111548	•
Inventories 24	17841	•	•	•	0	811	•	•	5206	•	•	187582	•
Net Property, Plant and Equipment 25	410301	•	•	•	134	5747	•	•	30861	•	•	264860	•
Total Assets 26	983557	•	•	•	2185	10055	•	•	72182	•	•	1014392	•
Notes and Loans Payable 27	484787	•	•	•	160	0	•	•	12149	•	•	217477	•
All Other Liabilities 28	363837	•	•	•	949	241	•	•	22144	•	•	715732	•
Net Worth 29	134933	•	•	•	1076	9813	•	•	37889	•	•	81182	•

Selected Financial Ratios (Times to 1)

Current Ratio 30	0.9	•	•	•	1.6	5.3	•	•	1.7	•	•	1.4	•
Quick Ratio 31	0.4	•	•	•	1.5	2.3	•	•	1.3	•	•	0.7	•
Net Sales to Working Capital 32	•	•	•	•	13.9	20.5	•	•	7.5	•	•	14.6	•
Coverage Ratio 33	2.3	•	•	•	42.7	1162.7	•	•	14.1	•	•	1.8	•
Total Asset Turnover 34	0.2	•	•	•	3.5	2.1	•	•	1.4	•	•	1.6	•
Inventory Turnover 35	8.4	•	•	•	•	20.2	•	•	13.6	•	•	8.1	•
Receivables Turnover 36	4.1	•	•	•	9.2	25.5	•	•	•	•	•	7.0	•
Total Liabilities to Net Worth 37	6.3	•	•	•	1.0	0.0	•	•	0.9	•	•	11.5	•
Current Assets to Working Capital 38	•	•	•	•	2.7	1.2	•	•	2.5	•	•	3.4	•
Current Liabilities to Working Capital 39	•	•	•	•	1.7	0.2	•	•	1.5	•	•	2.4	•
Working Capital to Net Sales 40	•	•	•	•	0.1	0.0	•	•	0.1	•	•	0.1	•
Inventory to Working Capital 41	•	•	•	•	•	0.5	•	•	0.4	•	•	1.4	•
Total Receipts to Cash Flow 42	6.7	•	•	•	8.5	4.8	•	•	6.9	•	•	15.8	•
Cost of Goods to Cash Flow 43	4.4	•	•	•	7.1	3.6	•	•	5.0	•	•	14.8	•
Cash Flow to Total Debt 44	0.0	•	•	•	0.8	18.6	•	•	0.4	•	•	0.1	•

Selected Financial Factors (in Percentages)

Debt Ratio 45	86.3	•	•	•	50.8	2.4	•	•	47.5	•	•	92.0	•
Return on Total Assets 46	2.2	•	•	•	31.9	43.9	•	•	13.2	•	•	4.7	•
Return on Equity Before Income Taxes 47	9.0	•	•	•	63.2	45.0	•	•	23.3	•	•	26.2	•
Return on Equity After Income Taxes 48	6.9	•	•	•	42.5	45.0	•	•	20.3	•	•	25.1	•
Profit Margin (Before Income Tax) 49	5.4	•	•	•	8.8	20.6	•	•	9.0	•	•	1.3	•
Profit Margin (After Income Tax) 50	4.1	•	•	•	5.9	20.6	•	•	7.8	•	•	1.3	•

Table I

Corporations with and without Net Income

WATER, SEWAGE AND OTHER SYSTEMS

MONEY AMOUNTS AND SIZE OF ASSETS IN THOUSANDS OF DOLLARS

Item Description for Accounting Period 7/12 Through 6/13	Total	Zero Assets	Under 500	500 to 1,000	1,000 to 5,000	5,000 to 10,000	10,000 to 25,000	25,000 to 50,000	50,000 to 100,000	100,000 to 250,000	250,000 to 500,000	500,000 to 2,500,000	2,500,000 and over
Number of Enterprises **1**	4722	453	3225	402	335	178	71	26	10	4	6	11	3

Revenues ($ in Thousands)

	Total	Zero Assets	Under 500	500 to 1,000	1,000 to 5,000	5,000 to 10,000	10,000 to 25,000	25,000 to 50,000	50,000 to 100,000	100,000 to 250,000	250,000 to 500,000	500,000 to 2,500,000	2,500,000 and over
Net Sales **2**	10588742	139739	679105	518316	193602	599212	595014	251572	153063	101096	250033	2423908	4684082
Interest **3**	30401	2	378	106	527	73	524	1048	16	873	1167	5574	20113
Rents **4**	17208	18	379	0	1370	0	383	2320	63	730	1060	9791	1093
Royalties **5**	370	0	0	0	0	0	0	78	0	9	0	0	283
Other Portfolio Income **6**	212513	19017	1983	124	16252	2064	17621	4975	1533	7914	2179	26556	112297
Other Receipts **7**	219659	534	249	247	83331	8048	7678	5836	19216	8220	4195	32878	49227
Total Receipts **8**	11068893	159310	682094	518793	295082	609397	621220	265829	173891	118842	258634	2498707	4867095
Average Total Receipts **9**	2344	352	212	1291	881	3424	8750	10224	17389	29710	43106	227155	1622365

Operating Costs/Operating Income (%)

	Total	Zero Assets	Under 500	500 to 1,000	1,000 to 5,000	5,000 to 10,000	10,000 to 25,000	25,000 to 50,000	50,000 to 100,000	100,000 to 250,000	250,000 to 500,000	500,000 to 2,500,000	2,500,000 and over
Cost of Operations **10**	28.9	•	14.2	43.9	34.6	31.1	41.9	40.5	59.9	34.5	17.3	38.7	21.9
Salaries and Wages **11**	8.3	3.8	3.3	6.4	10.2	8.0	17.4	6.0	12.4	3.0	15.1	5.9	9.1
Taxes Paid **12**	6.5	6.3	1.9	4.7	3.7	5.9	3.3	5.9	4.4	9.0	7.4	5.5	8.6
Interest Paid **13**	7.8	1.0	0.4	0.6	8.5	3.4	2.6	7.3	3.1	8.8	14.3	9.8	9.9
Depreciation **14**	15.0	0.7	5.4	5.4	15.6	11.9	7.1	15.8	6.4	20.5	22.7	16.8	18.1
Amortization and Depletion **15**	1.2	0.0	0.4	•	5.0	0.1	0.6	2.4	1.8	•	8.8	0.9	1.3
Pensions and Other Deferred Comp. **16**	1.8	•	0.7	0.2	1.3	0.3	1.7	1.4	0.2	3.2	3.0	3.0	1.9
Employee Benefits **17**	2.7	0.0	1.9	1.6	1.4	1.9	5.8	3.0	1.6	0.8	3.9	2.9	2.6
Advertising **18**	0.2	0.1	0.7	0.2	0.1	0.1	0.1	0.5	0.4	•	0.1	0.0	0.3
Other Expenses **19**	29.3	36.4	41.3	29.9	81.3	23.3	15.1	22.8	30.8	15.6	17.6	18.9	34.4
Officers' Compensation **20**	2.8	45.2	11.2	4.3	1.9	3.4	6.7	4.9	1.6	3.4	4.6	1.1	0.4
Operating Margin **21**	•	6.5	18.5	3.0	•	10.6	•	•	•	1.2	•	•	•
Operating Margin Before Officers' Comp. **22**	•	51.7	29.8	7.3	•	14.0	4.4	•	•	4.6	•	•	•

Selected Average Balance Sheet ($ in Thousands)

Net Receivables 23	274	0	3	53	91	237	1191	580	6338	3899	3715	29623	220754
Inventories 24	100	0	4	7	16	99	28	436	2041	5043	5096	7874	87359
Net Property, Plant and Equipment 25	6513	0	66	638	1446	3661	8895	20106	42459	124652	223269	714573	5957587
Total Assets 26	9195	0	115	825	2659	6454	16981	34294	71076	158614	301058	1061776	7916329
Notes and Loans Payable 27	3292	0	45	380	1204	2909	5141	8905	35320	30272	110211	346181	2928019
All Other Liabilities 28	3067	0	18	46	295	926	7222	9826	18283	60224	121299	392733	2633532
Net Worth 29	2836	0	51	398	1160	2618	4618	15563	17474	68118	69548	322863	2354779

Selected Financial Ratios (Times to 1)

Current Ratio 30	0.7	•	1.3	1.5	0.6	1.2	1.2	1.8	2.1	0.8	0.4	1.1	0.4
Quick Ratio 31	0.4	•	1.3	1.2	0.6	0.7	0.8	0.9	0.9	0.8	0.2	0.6	0.3
Net Sales to Working Capital 32	•	•	23.3	22.7	•	15.4	11.2	4.8	1.6	•	•	21.8	•
Coverage Ratio 33	1.0	20.9	53.4	6.4	•	4.6	1.8	0.3	•	3.1	0.2	0.9	0.6
Total Asset Turnover 34	0.2	•	1.8	1.6	0.2	0.5	0.5	0.3	0.2	0.2	0.1	0.2	0.2
Inventory Turnover 35	6.5	•	7.9	75.6	12.3	10.6	127.0	9.0	4.5	1.7	1.4	10.8	3.9
Receivables Turnover 36	7.5	•	47.8	24.5	7.5	14.5	7.6	15.0	3.9	3.9	10.5	8.5	5.6
Total Liabilities to Net Worth 37	2.2	•	1.2	1.1	1.3	1.5	2.7	1.2	3.1	1.3	3.3	2.3	2.4
Current Assets to Working Capital 38	•	•	4.0	3.2	•	7.5	6.4	2.3	1.9	•	•	8.7	•
Current Liabilities to Working Capital 39	•	•	3.0	2.2	•	6.5	5.4	1.3	0.9	•	•	7.7	•
Working Capital to Net Sales 40	•	•	0.0	0.0	•	0.1	0.1	0.2	0.6	•	•	0.0	•
Inventory to Working Capital 41	•	•	•	0.1	•	0.9	0.0	0.2	0.4	•	•	1.5	•
Total Receipts to Cash Flow 42	6.2	2.0	1.9	4.0	1.8	3.5	8.4	7.5	5.6	3.3	78.2	8.6	11.1
Cost of Goods to Cash Flow 43	1.8	•	0.3	1.7	0.6	1.1	3.5	3.0	3.4	1.1	13.6	3.3	2.4
Cash Flow to Total Debt 44	0.1	•	1.8	0.8	0.2	0.2	0.1	0.1	0.1	0.1	0.0	0.0	0.0

Selected Financial Factors (in Percentages)

Debt Ratio 45	69.2	•	55.5	51.7	56.4	59.4	72.8	54.6	75.4	57.1	76.9	69.6	70.3
Return on Total Assets 46	1.9	•	35.5	5.7	•	8.2	2.2	0.7	•	4.4	0.4	1.9	1.1
Return on Equity Before Income Taxes 47	•	•	78.1	10.0	•	15.8	3.5	•	•	6.9	•	•	•
Return on Equity After Income Taxes 48	•	•	78.1	9.7	•	15.7	1.5	•	•	5.7	•	•	•
Profit Margin (Before Income Tax) 49	•	20.6	19.0	3.1	•	12.3	1.9	•	•	18.7	•	•	•
Profit Margin (After Income Tax) 50	•	16.9	19.0	3.0	•	12.2	0.8	•	•	15.4	•	•	•

Table II

Corporations with Net Income

WATER, SEWAGE AND OTHER SYSTEMS

MONEY AMOUNTS AND SIZE OF ASSETS IN THOUSANDS OF DOLLARS

Item Description for Accounting Period 7/12 Through 6/13	Total	Zero Assets	Under 500	500 to 1,000	1,000 to 5,000	5,000 to 10,000	10,000 to 25,000	25,000 to 50,000	50,000 to 100,000	100,000 to 250,000	250,000 to 500,000	500,000 to 2,500,000	2,500,000 and over
Number of Enterprises 1	4046	•	2884	•	123	112	42	18	•	•	3	7	0
Revenues ($ in Thousands)													
Net Sales 2	7808541	•	644728	•	56452	493532	469237	147561	•	•	177574	4958215	0
Interest 3	28212	•	289	•	426	70	263	1009	•	•	763	24451	0
Rents 4	12112	•	379	•	0	0	78	2040	•	•	992	7811	0
Royalties 5	283	•	0	•	0	0	0	0	•	•	0	283	0
Other Portfolio Income 6	146897	•	1983	•	0	2064	16325	3774	•	•	190	95509	0
Other Receipts 7	117740	•	170	•	79428	3083	7449	3782	•	•	686	8036	0
Total Receipts 8	8113785	•	647549	•	136306	498749	493352	158166	•	•	180205	5094305	0
Average Total Receipts 9	2005	•	225	•	1108	4453	11746	8787	•	•	60068	727758	•
Operating Costs/Operating Income (%)													
Cost of Operations 10	26.9	•	14.9	•	4.8	35.5	42.6	28.7	•	•	17.0	24.9	•
Salaries and Wages 11	8.7	•	3.5	•	11.8	5.1	20.0	3.9	•	•	11.2	9.2	•
Taxes Paid 12	6.9	•	2.0	•	4.0	5.4	2.6	8.1	•	•	5.4	8.5	•
Interest Paid 13	7.3	•	0.4	•	7.0	1.6	1.3	5.6	•	•	8.8	10.2	•
Depreciation 14	14.0	•	5.3	•	17.4	10.4	5.5	15.7	•	•	22.6	17.3	•
Amortization and Depletion 15	0.9	•	0.5	•	•	0.1	0.2	0.3	•	•	0.3	1.2	•
Pensions and Other Deferred Comp. 16	1.5	•	0.7	•	2.6	0.3	1.9	2.2	•	•	3.2	1.8	•
Employee Benefits 17	2.7	•	1.9	•	2.3	1.6	4.5	3.5	•	•	4.6	2.9	•
Advertising 18	0.2	•	0.8	•	0.0	0.1	0.0	0.0	•	•	0.0	0.2	•
Other Expenses 19	23.4	•	38.2	•	152.6	18.0	11.6	24.3	•	•	13.3	21.5	•
Officers' Compensation 20	3.4	•	11.8	•	3.6	3.8	7.9	5.8	•	•	4.7	0.5	•
Operating Margin 21	4.1	•	20.0	•	•	18.0	1.8	1.8	•	•	8.9	1.8	•
Operating Margin Before Officers' Comp. 22	7.4	•	31.8	•	•	21.8	9.8	7.6	•	•	13.6	2.2	•

Selected Average Balance Sheet ($ in Thousands)

Net Receivables 23	208	•	4	•	40	321	1558	452	•	•	5176	91548	•
Inventories 24	77	•	0	•	23	289	24	64	•	•	777	6025	•
Net Property, Plant and Equipment 25	5005	•	66	•	1518	2323	8158	24242	•	•	262715	2466385	•
Total Assets 26	6916	•	118	•	2373	6309	15275	35745	•	•	322290	3331897	•
Notes and Loans Payable 27	2529	•	51	•	765	3212	4913	7899	•	•	86043	1247039	•
All Other Liabilities 28	2134	•	21	•	428	909	6190	12231	•	•	127753	1042795	•
Net Worth 29	2253	•	46	•	1180	2188	4172	15614	•	•	108495	1042063	•

Selected Financial Ratios (Times to 1)

Current Ratio 30	0.8	•	1.2	•	1.4	2.4	1.4	1.8	•	•	1.3	0.6	•
Quick Ratio 31	0.5	•	1.2	•	1.3	1.4	1.0	0.9	•	•	0.5	0.4	•
Net Sales to Working Capital 32	•	•	35.6	•	4.4	3.1	7.4	3.7	•	•	15.4	•	•
Coverage Ratio 33	2.1	•	54.6	•	6.1	12.8	6.2	2.6	•	•	2.2	1.4	•
Total Asset Turnover 34	0.3	•	1.9	•	0.2	0.7	0.7	0.2	•	•	0.2	0.2	•
Inventory Turnover 35	6.8	•	•	•	0.9	5.4	194.7	36.6	•	•	12.9	29.2	•
Receivables Turnover 36	8.3	•	•	•	7.3	14.2	7.9	13.3	•	•	22.9	•	•
Total Liabilities to Net Worth 37	2.1	•	1.5	•	1.0	1.9	2.7	1.3	•	•	2.0	2.2	•
Current Assets to Working Capital 38	•	•	5.8	•	3.4	1.7	3.3	2.3	•	•	4.9	•	•
Current Liabilities to Working Capital 39	•	•	4.8	•	2.4	0.7	2.3	1.3	•	•	3.9	•	•
Working Capital to Net Sales 40	•	•	0.0	•	0.2	0.3	0.1	0.3	•	•	0.1	•	•
Inventory to Working Capital 41	•	•	•	•	0.1	0.2	0.0	0.0	•	•	0.2	•	•
Total Receipts to Cash Flow 42	4.3	•	1.9	•	0.7	3.3	7.4	3.5	•	•	4.9	5.8	•
Cost of Goods to Cash Flow 43	1.2	•	0.3	•	0.0	1.2	3.2	1.0	•	•	0.8	1.4	•
Cash Flow to Total Debt 44	0.1	•	1.6	•	0.6	0.3	0.1	0.1	•	•	0.1	0.1	•

Selected Financial Factors (in Percentages)

Debt Ratio 45	67.4	•	60.5	•	50.3	65.3	72.7	56.3	•	•	66.3	68.7	•
Return on Total Assets 46	4.2	•	39.5	•	8.2	14.4	6.1	3.3	•	•	3.5	3.1	•
Return on Equity Before Income Taxes 47	6.8	•	98.2	•	13.8	38.3	18.6	4.7	•	•	5.6	3.1	•
Return on Equity After Income Taxes 48	6.1	•	98.2	•	13.5	38.1	14.9	3.1	•	•	4.2	2.6	•
Profit Margin (Before Income Tax) 49	8.0	•	20.4	•	35.4	19.0	7.0	9.0	•	•	10.3	4.5	•
Profit Margin (After Income Tax) 50	7.2	•	20.4	•	34.6	18.9	5.6	5.9	•	•	7.7	3.8	•

Table I

Corporations with and without Net Income

COMBINATION GAS AND ELECTRIC

MONEY AMOUNTS AND SIZE OF ASSETS IN THOUSANDS OF DOLLARS

Item Description for Accounting Period 7/12 Through 6/13	Total	Zero Assets	Under 500	500 to 1,000	1,000 to 5,000	5,000 to 10,000	10,000 to 25,000	25,000 to 50,000	50,000 to 100,000	100,000 to 250,000	250,000 to 500,000	500,000 to 2,500,000	2,500,000 and over
Number of Enterprises 1	436	0	399	0	0	0	3	3	3	0	0	3	25
Revenues ($ in Thousands)													
Net Sales 2	156464261	0	4648	0	0	0	36534	363768	765959	0	0	1333551	153959801
Interest 3	508493	0	0	0	0	0	0	0	948	0	0	5151	502394
Rents 4	620287	0	0	0	0	0	0	0	0	0	0	12910	607377
Royalties 5	14919	0	0	0	0	0	0	0	0	0	0	0	14919
Other Portfolio Income 6	863661	0	0	0	0	0	0	0	0	0	0	2689	860972
Other Receipts 7	2410008	0	0	0	0	0	0	1877	-3953	0	0	28922	2383161
Total Receipts 8	160881629	0	4648	0	0	0	36534	365645	762954	0	0	1383223	158328624
Average Total Receipts 9	368995	•	12	•	•	•	12178	121882	254318	•	•	461074	6333145
Operating Costs/Operating Income (%)													
Cost of Operations 10	41.1	•	•	•	•	•	82.1	86.3	75.6	•	•	52.1	40.7
Salaries and Wages 11	8.7	•	56.7	•	•	•	12.3	4.5	2.7	•	•	2.5	8.7
Taxes Paid 12	4.6	•	12.2	•	•	•	2.0	0.8	1.2	•	•	4.1	4.6
Interest Paid 13	5.3	•	•	•	•	•	2.5	4.2	2.3	•	•	4.9	5.3
Depreciation 14	16.3	•	104.6	•	•	•	4.4	0.1	0.2	•	•	12.0	16.5
Amortization and Depletion 15	0.7	•	•	•	•	•	•	0.2	0.1	•	•	0.3	0.7
Pensions and Other Deferred Comp. 16	1.9	•	•	•	•	•	•	0.1	0.1	•	•	6.0	1.9
Employee Benefits 17	2.2	•	•	•	•	•	1.0	0.7	0.3	•	•	0.9	2.3
Advertising 18	0.2	•	•	•	•	•	0.0	0.1	2.9	•	•	0.1	0.2
Other Expenses 19	23.5	•	65.1	•	•	•	11.6	3.0	14.0	•	•	18.5	23.6
Officers' Compensation 20	0.3	•	•	•	•	•	•	0.7	0.2	•	•	1.3	0.3
Operating Margin 21	•	•	•	•	•	•	•	•	0.5	•	•	•	•
Operating Margin Before Officers' Comp. 22	•	•	•	•	•	•	•	•	0.6	•	•	•	•

Selected Average Balance Sheet ($ in Thousands)

Net Receivables 23	48401	•	0	•	•	•	2432	23389	33499	•	•	60831	829696
Inventories 24	24010	•	0	•	•	•	1414	0	727	•	•	17176	416376
Net Property, Plant and Equipment 25	684326	•	9	•	•	•	4825	217	1320	•	•	846146	11832205
Total Assets 26	1124292	•	18	•	•	•	15933	39234	127872	•	•	1611292	19392057
Notes and Loans Payable 27	375769	•	15	•	•	•	619	81163	4776	•	•	571522	6474204
All Other Liabilities 28	435555	•	-43	•	•	•	4672	2241	75153	•	•	582642	7516997
Net Worth 29	312968	•	46	•	•	•	10642	-44170	47943	•	•	457128	5400856

Selected Financial Ratios (Times to 1)

Current Ratio 30	0.8	•	•	•	•	•	1.0	0.5	1.3	•	•	1.0	0.8
Quick Ratio 31	0.4	•	•	•	•	•	0.8	0.4	0.9	•	•	0.5	0.4
Net Sales to Working Capital 32	•	•	1.3	•	•	•	156.1	•	12.0	•	•	70.4	•
Coverage Ratio 33	0.6	•	•	•	•	•	•	1.0	1.0	•	•	1.2	0.6
Total Asset Turnover 34	0.3	•	0.7	•	•	•	0.8	3.1	2.0	•	•	0.3	0.3
Inventory Turnover 35	6.1	•	•	•	•	•	7.1	•	265.6	•	•	13.5	6.0
Receivables Turnover 36	7.1	•	•	•	•	•	5.1	•	•	•	•	7.3	7.0
Total Liabilities to Net Worth 37	2.6	•	•	•	•	•	0.5	•	1.7	•	•	2.5	2.6
Current Assets to Working Capital 38	•	•	1.0	•	•	•	53.3	•	4.0	•	•	25.6	•
Current Liabilities to Working Capital 39	•	•	•	•	•	•	52.3	•	3.0	•	•	24.6	•
Working Capital to Net Sales 40	•	•	0.8	•	•	•	0.0	•	0.1	•	•	0.0	•
Inventory to Working Capital 41	•	•	•	•	•	•	7.6	•	0.0	•	•	2.3	•
Total Receipts to Cash Flow 42	7.0	•	•	•	•	•	•	39.2	7.2	•	•	7.3	7.0
Cost of Goods to Cash Flow 43	2.9	•	•	•	•	•	•	33.8	5.5	•	•	3.8	2.8
Cash Flow to Total Debt 44	0.1	•	0.3	•	•	•	•	0.0	0.4	•	•	0.1	0.1

Selected Financial Factors (in Percentages)

Debt Ratio 45	72.2	•	•	•	•	•	33.2	212.6	62.5	•	•	71.6	72.1
Return on Total Assets 46	1.0	•	•	•	•	•	•	12.5	4.7	•	•	1.6	1.0
Return on Equity Before Income Taxes 47	•	•	•	•	•	•	•	0.5	0.5	•	•	1.0	•
Return on Equity After Income Taxes 48	•	•	•	•	•	•	•	0.5	•	•	•	1.0	•
Profit Margin (Before Income Tax) 49	•	•	•	•	•	•	•	•	0.1	•	•	1.0	•
Profit Margin (After Income Tax) 50	•	•	•	•	•	•	•	•	•	•	•	1.0	•

Table II

Corporations with Net Income

COMBINATION GAS AND ELECTRIC

MONEY AMOUNTS AND SIZE OF ASSETS IN THOUSANDS OF DOLLARS

Item Description for Accounting Period 7/12 Through 6/13	Total	Zero Assets	Under 500	500 to 1,000	1,000 to 5,000	5,000 to 10,000	10,000 to 25,000	25,000 to 50,000	50,000 to 100,000	100,000 to 250,000	250,000 to 500,000	500,000 to 2,500,000	2,500,000 and over
Number of Enterprises **1**	14	0	0	0	0	0	0	0	•	0	0	0	•

Revenues ($ in Thousands)

Net Sales **2**	58685621	0	0	0	0	0	0	0	•	0	0	0	•
Interest **3**	124612	0	0	0	0	0	0	0	•	0	0	0	•
Rents **4**	123560	0	0	0	0	0	0	0	•	0	0	0	•
Royalties **5**	14844	0	0	0	0	0	0	0	•	0	0	0	•
Other Portfolio Income **6**	348393	0	0	0	0	0	0	0	•	0	0	0	•
Other Receipts **7**	1242410	0	0	0	0	0	0	0	•	0	0	0	•
Total Receipts **8**	60539440	0	0	0	0	0	0	0	•	0	0	0	•
Average Total Receipts **9**	4324246	•	•	•	•	•	•	•	•	•	•	•	•

Operating Costs/Operating Income (%)

Cost of Operations **10**	47.0	•	•	•	•	•	•	•	•	•	•	•	•
Salaries and Wages **11**	6.7	•	•	•	•	•	•	•	•	•	•	•	•
Taxes Paid **12**	4.0	•	•	•	•	•	•	•	•	•	•	•	•
Interest Paid **13**	5.3	•	•	•	•	•	•	•	•	•	•	•	•
Depreciation **14**	12.0	•	•	•	•	•	•	•	•	•	•	•	•
Amortization and Depletion **15**	0.6	•	•	•	•	•	•	•	•	•	•	•	•
Pensions and Other Deferred Comp. **16**	1.1	•	•	•	•	•	•	•	•	•	•	•	•
Employee Benefits **17**	1.3	•	•	•	•	•	•	•	•	•	•	•	•
Advertising **18**	0.3	•	•	•	•	•	•	•	•	•	•	•	•
Other Expenses **19**	19.1	•	•	•	•	•	•	•	•	•	•	•	•
Officers' Compensation **20**	0.4	•	•	•	•	•	•	•	•	•	•	•	•
Operating Margin **21**	2.3	•	•	•	•	•	•	•	•	•	•	•	•
Operating Margin Before Officers' Comp. **22**	2.6	•	•	•	•	•	•	•	•	•	•	•	•

Selected Average Balance Sheet ($ in Thousands)

Net Receivables 23	558180	•	•	•	•	•	•	•	•	•	•	•	•	•	•
Inventories 24	323435	•	•	•	•	•	•	•	•	•	•	•	•	•	•
Net Property, Plant and Equipment 25	6909682	•	•	•	•	•	•	•	•	•	•	•	•	•	•
Total Assets 26	11357078	•	•	•	•	•	•	•	•	•	•	•	•		•
Notes and Loans Payable 27	4048593	•	•	•	•	•	•	•	•	•	•	•	•	•	•
All Other Liabilities 28	4299264	•	•	•	•	•	•	•	•	•	•	•	•	•	•
Net Worth 29	3009221	•	•	•	•	•	•	•	•	•	•	•	•	•	•

Selected Financial Ratios (Times to 1)

Current Ratio 30	1.1	•	•	•	•	•	•	•	•	•	•	1.1	•	•	•
Quick Ratio 31	0.5	•	•	•	•	•	•	•	•	•	•	0.5	•	•	•
Net Sales to Working Capital 32	57.3	•	•	•	•	•	•	•	•	•	•	57.3	•	•	•
Coverage Ratio 33	2.0	•	•	•	•	•	•	•	•	•	•	•	•	•	•
Total Asset Turnover 34	0.4	•	•	•	•	•	•	•	•	•	•	0.4	•	•	•
Inventory Turnover 35	6.1	•	•	•	•	•	•	•	•	•	•	•	•	•	•
Receivables Turnover 36	7.5	•	•	•	•	•	•	•	•	•	•	•	•	•	•
Total Liabilities to Net Worth 37	2.8	•	•	•	•	•	•	•	•	•	•	•	•	•	•
Current Assets to Working Capital 38	19.7	•	•	•	•	•	•	•	•	•	•	19.7	•	•	•
Current Liabilities to Working Capital 39	18.7	•	•	•	•	•	•	•	•	•	•	•	•	•	•
Working Capital to Net Sales 40	0.0	•	•	•	•	•	•	•	•	•	•	0.0	•	•	•
Inventory to Working Capital 41	6.5	•	•	•	•	•	•	•	•	•	•	•	•	•	•
Total Receipts to Cash Flow 42	5.3	•	•	•	•	•	•	•	•	•	•	•	•	•	•
Cost of Goods to Cash Flow 43	2.5	•	•	•	•	•	•	•	•	•	•	•	•	•	•
Cash Flow to Total Debt 44	0.1	•	•	•	•	•	•	•	•	•	•	0.1	•	•	•

Selected Financial Factors (in Percentages)

Debt Ratio 45	73.5	•	•	•	•	•	•	•	•	•	45	•	•	•	•
Return on Total Assets 46	3.9	•	•	•	•	•	•	•	•	•	•	•	•	•	•
Return on Equity Before Income Taxes 47	7.5	•	•	•	•	•	•	•	•	•	47	•	7.5	•	•
Return on Equity After Income Taxes 48	6.5	•	•	•	•	•	•	•	•	•	•	•	•	•	•
Profit Margin (Before Income Tax) 49	5.4	•	•	•	•	•	•	•	•	•	49	•	•	•	•
Profit Margin (After Income Tax) 50	4.6	•	•	•	•	•	•	•	•	•	•	•	•	•	•

Table I
Corporations with and without Net Income

CONSTRUCTION OF BUILDINGS

MONEY AMOUNTS AND SIZE OF ASSETS IN THOUSANDS OF DOLLARS

Item Description for Accounting Period 7/12 Through 6/13		Total	Zero Assets	Under 500	500 to 1,000	1,000 to 5,000	5,000 to 10,000	10,000 to 25,000	25,000 to 50,000	50,000 to 100,000	100,000 to 250,000	250,000 to 500,000	500,000 to 2,500,000	2,500,000 and over
Number of Enterprises	1	204258	43252	125508	13897	16515	2607	1691	420	189	106	•	•	•

Revenues ($ in Thousands)

		Total	Zero Assets	Under 500	500 to 1,000	1,000 to 5,000	5,000 to 10,000	10,000 to 25,000	25,000 to 50,000	50,000 to 100,000	100,000 to 250,000	250,000 to 500,000	500,000 to 2,500,000	2,500,000 and over
Net Sales	2	433527261	4969457	56141436	27892059	78007344	32524170	52645685	27756734	26501215	29444736	•	•	•
Interest	3	461478	44131	7858	8209	24213	10684	14307	7925	13272	22921	•	•	•
Rents	4	488860	6365	49661	19738	64043	43677	36251	36952	17440	60324	•	•	•
Royalties	5	13015	0	691	0	39	1039	631	0	28	10356	•	•	•
Other Portfolio Income	6	1140675	37615	57109	59973	261659	172231	46180	31488	27104	68685	•	•	•
Other Receipts	7	4201701	219727	154548	365493	510412	164124	246620	114229	135472	367732	•	•	•
Total Receipts	8	439832990	5277295	56411303	28345472	78867710	32915925	52989674	27947328	26694531	29974754	•	•	•
Average Total Receipts	9	2153	122	449	2040	4776	12626	31336	66541	141241	282781	•	•	•

Operating Costs/Operating Income (%)

		Total	Zero Assets	Under 500	500 to 1,000	1,000 to 5,000	5,000 to 10,000	10,000 to 25,000	25,000 to 50,000	50,000 to 100,000	100,000 to 250,000	250,000 to 500,000	500,000 to 2,500,000	2,500,000 and over
Cost of Operations	10	84.4	63.4	67.1	79.0	83.9	85.7	88.5	90.6	91.6	90.4	•	•	•
Salaries and Wages	11	3.8	5.1	6.3	4.1	3.7	3.2	2.7	2.5	2.6	2.6	•	•	•
Taxes Paid	12	1.1	1.2	2.0	1.4	1.4	1.0	0.8	0.7	0.8	0.7	•	•	•
Interest Paid	13	0.6	0.4	0.5	0.8	0.4	0.3	0.3	0.4	0.4	0.3	•	•	•
Depreciation	14	0.5	1.3	0.8	0.6	0.5	0.5	0.4	0.4	0.3	0.7	•	•	•
Amortization and Depletion	15	0.1	0.1	0.0	0.0	0.0	0.0	0.0	0.0	0.0	0.2	•	•	•
Pensions and Other Deferred Comp.	16	0.2	0.0	0.1	0.2	0.2	0.2	0.2	0.1	0.2	0.2	•	•	•
Employee Benefits	17	0.8	0.4	0.8	1.4	0.5	0.8	0.7	0.4	0.5	0.6	•	•	•
Advertising	18	0.3	0.6	0.5	0.3	0.2	0.2	0.2	0.1	0.2	0.2	•	•	•
Other Expenses	19	5.7	26.9	13.4	7.5	5.2	4.8	3.4	2.7	2.6	3.1	•	•	•
Officers' Compensation	20	2.2	4.6	5.5	4.0	2.5	2.3	1.5	1.0	1.2	0.7	•	•	•
Operating Margin	21	0.3	•	2.9	0.6	1.5	1.0	1.2	1.0	•	0.3	•	•	•
Operating Margin Before Officers' Comp.	22	2.5	0.6	8.4	4.7	4.0	3.3	2.7	2.1	0.8	1.0	•	•	•

Selected Average Balance Sheet ($ in Thousands)

Net Receivables 23	285	0	11	145	515	2025	5323	11897	25804	51873	•	•	•
Inventories 24	217	0	12	119	352	1286	2035	4097	6657	14656	•	•	•
Net Property, Plant and Equipment 25	135	0	24	171	326	749	1838	3671	5999	19647	•	•	•
Total Assets 26	1250	0	96	728	2125	7037	15261	34556	68278	152781	•	•	•
Notes and Loans Payable 27	379	0	61	419	767	2077	4116	8436	16786	21198	•	•	•
All Other Liabilities 28	509	0	26	191	788	2782	6822	17058	36776	74505	•	•	•
Net Worth 29	362	0	8	118	570	2177	4323	9062	14715	57078	•	•	•

Selected Financial Ratios (Times to 1)

Current Ratio 30	1.6	•	1.8	1.7	1.7	1.6	1.5	1.4	1.4	1.4	•	•	•
Quick Ratio 31	0.9	•	1.1	0.9	0.9	1.0	1.0	1.0	1.0	1.0	•	•	•
Net Sales to Working Capital 32	6.4	•	17.0	9.9	7.5	5.8	7.7	8.4	9.6	8.8	•	•	•
Coverage Ratio 33	3.9	6.0	7.7	4.0	6.9	7.9	8.1	5.5	1.8	8.5	•	•	•
Total Asset Turnover 34	1.7	•	4.7	2.8	2.2	1.8	2.0	1.9	2.1	1.8	•	•	•
Inventory Turnover 35	8.2	•	25.6	13.3	11.2	8.3	13.5	14.6	19.3	17.1	•	•	•
Receivables Turnover 36	7.6	•	40.5	14.3	8.4	6.2	6.1	5.9	5.9	5.5	•	•	•
Total Liabilities to Net Worth 37	2.5	•	10.5	5.2	2.7	2.2	2.5	2.8	3.6	1.7	•	•	•
Current Assets to Working Capital 38	2.7	•	2.2	2.4	2.5	2.6	2.9	3.3	3.7	3.4	•	•	•
Current Liabilities to Working Capital 39	1.7	•	1.2	1.4	1.5	1.6	1.9	2.3	2.7	2.4	•	•	•
Working Capital to Net Sales 40	0.2	•	0.1	0.1	0.1	0.2	0.1	0.1	0.1	0.1	•	•	•
Inventory to Working Capital 41	0.7	•	0.4	0.5	0.6	0.5	0.5	0.5	0.4	0.4	•	•	•
Total Receipts to Cash Flow 42	16.3	3.7	6.8	12.3	16.1	19.5	23.3	29.4	46.9	23.3	•	•	•
Cost of Goods to Cash Flow 43	13.7	2.3	4.5	9.8	13.5	16.7	20.6	26.6	42.9	21.1	•	•	•
Cash Flow to Total Debt 44	0.1	•	0.8	0.3	0.2	0.1	0.1	0.1	0.1	0.1	•	•	•

Selected Financial Factors (in Percentages)

Debt Ratio 45	71.1	•	91.3	83.8	73.2	69.1	71.7	73.8	78.4	62.6	•	•	•
Return on Total Assets 46	4.0	•	17.9	8.4	6.4	4.4	4.4	3.9	1.6	4.2	•	•	•
Return on Equity Before Income Taxes 47	10.3	•	178.5	38.6	20.3	12.4	13.6	12.3	3.2	9.8	•	•	•
Return on Equity After Income Taxes 48	9.6	•	176.3	37.8	19.5	11.8	13.1	11.8	2.8	9.3	•	•	•
Profit Margin (Before Income Tax) 49	1.8	2.2	3.3	2.3	2.4	2.2	1.9	1.7	0.3	2.0	•	•	•
Profit Margin (After Income Tax) 50	1.6	2.1	3.3	2.2	2.4	2.1	1.8	1.6	0.3	1.9	•	•	•

25

Table II

Corporations with Net Income

CONSTRUCTION OF BUILDINGS

MONEY AMOUNTS AND SIZE OF ASSETS IN THOUSANDS OF DOLLARS

Item Description for Accounting Period 7/12 Through 6/13	Total	Zero Assets	Under 500	500 to 1,000	1,000 to 5,000	5,000 to 10,000	10,000 to 25,000	25,000 to 50,000	50,000 to 100,000	100,000 to 250,000	250,000 to 500,000	500,000 to 2,500,000	2,500,000 and over
Number of Enterprises 1	125831	23691	78921	8565	11074	1812	1196	312	•	79	23	•	6

Revenues ($ in Thousands)

Net Sales 2	338176658	2940451	41731211	19957239	62083928	26600593	43954704	24260501	•	26227543	16665497	•	23786338
Interest 3	266263	43011	3330	4159	15315	6826	11064	6659	•	19228	20367	•	72440
Rents 4	336467	5121	4244	4136	50559	28929	23364	29929	•	33358	52348	•	37077
Royalties 5	10804	0	0	0	39	111	70	0	•	10342	0	•	5
Other Portfolio Income 6	811838	24160	39504	53760	205592	26383	35826	22524	•	41998	38051	•	59441
Other Receipts 7	3608937	208118	109202	360692	433660	96467	205622	106998	•	283640	125251	•	1092149
Total Receipts 8	343210967	3220861	41887491	20379986	62789093	26759309	44230650	24426611	•	26616109	16901514	•	25047450
Average Total Receipts 9	2728	136	531	2379	5670	14768	36982	78290	•	336913	734848	•	4174575

Operating Costs/Operating Income (%)

Cost of Operations 10	83.6	49.7	65.0	77.3	82.7	85.4	87.6	90.0	•	90.0	92.0	•	85.3
Salaries and Wages 11	3.4	3.4	5.6	3.9	3.6	2.5	2.7	2.3	•	2.5	2.2	•	5.6
Taxes Paid 12	1.0	1.2	1.9	1.1	1.2	1.0	0.7	0.7	•	0.7	0.5	•	1.3
Interest Paid 13	0.3	0.5	0.4	0.7	0.3	0.2	0.2	0.2	•	0.2	0.3	•	0.8
Depreciation 14	0.4	1.0	0.7	0.5	0.4	0.4	0.3	0.3	•	0.5	0.4	•	0.6
Amortization and Depletion 15	0.1	0.0	0.0	0.0	0.0	0.0	0.0	0.0	•	0.0	0.1	•	0.4
Pensions and Other Deferred Comp. 16	0.2	•	0.1	0.1	0.2	0.2	0.2	0.1	•	0.2	0.1	•	0.4
Employee Benefits 17	0.7	0.2	0.7	1.5	0.5	0.7	0.7	0.4	•	0.5	0.8	•	1.7
Advertising 18	0.2	0.6	0.4	0.2	0.2	0.2	0.2	0.1	•	0.1	0.1	•	0.4
Other Expenses 19	4.9	27.9	12.1	7.6	4.7	3.6	3.0	2.4	•	2.9	1.7	•	4.5
Officers' Compensation 20	2.2	4.3	5.6	3.8	2.4	2.3	1.5	1.0	•	0.7	0.7	•	1.3
Operating Margin 21	2.9	11.1	7.4	3.1	3.9	3.5	3.0	2.4	•	1.7	1.0	•	•
Operating Margin Before Officers' Comp. 22	5.1	15.5	13.1	6.9	6.2	5.8	4.5	3.4	•	2.5	1.7	•	•

Selected Average Balance Sheet ($ in Thousands)

Net Receivables 23	357	0	9	156	597	2298	5976	13611	•	60812	98906	•	733199
Inventories 24	137	0	10	90	333	907	1432	2665	•	5070	19097	•	1561636
Net Property, Plant and Equipment 25	131	0	21	115	276	708	1218	2604	•	16446	30964	•	325800
Total Assets 26	1292	0	88	722	2216	6898	15071	33937	•	149416	342863	•	5326045
Notes and Loans Payable 27	303	0	43	366	653	1545	2813	5063	•	16371	60492	•	1570860
All Other Liabilities 28	540	0	16	191	842	2856	7535	18413	•	82708	164426	•	1621062
Net Worth 29	450	0	29	165	721	2496	4723	10462	•	50336	117945	•	2134123

Selected Financial Ratios (Times to 1)

Current Ratio 30	1.6	•	2.4	2.0	1.7	1.7	1.5	1.4	•	1.3	1.3	•	2.0
Quick Ratio 31	1.0	•	1.6	1.1	1.0	1.1	1.1	1.1	•	1.1	0.9	•	0.9
Net Sales to Working Capital 32	7.7	•	16.7	9.3	7.7	6.4	8.9	9.9	•	13.0	14.3	•	2.3
Coverage Ratio 33	14.4	44.8	21.9	8.4	18.2	22.0	19.4	14.9	•	19.4	9.2	•	4.5
Total Asset Turnover 34	2.1	•	6.0	3.2	2.5	2.1	2.4	2.3	•	2.2	2.1	•	0.7
Inventory Turnover 35	16.5	•	33.0	19.9	13.9	13.8	22.5	26.2	•	58.9	34.9	•	2.2
Receivables Turnover 36	8.1	•	48.3	14.9	9.0	6.7	6.7	6.4	•	6.0	•	•	•
Total Liabilities to Net Worth 37	1.9	•	2.1	3.4	2.1	1.8	2.2	2.2	•	2.0	1.9	•	1.5
Current Assets to Working Capital 38	2.7	•	1.7	2.0	2.4	2.4	3.0	3.5	•	4.3	4.4	•	2.0
Current Liabilities to Working Capital 39	1.7	•	0.7	1.0	1.4	1.4	2.0	2.5	•	3.3	3.4	•	1.0
Working Capital to Net Sales 40	0.1	•	0.1	0.1	0.1	0.2	0.1	0.1	•	0.1	0.1	•	0.4
Inventory to Working Capital 41	0.5	•	0.3	0.3	0.5	0.4	0.4	0.4	•	0.2	0.4	•	0.9
Total Receipts to Cash Flow 42	12.4	2.1	5.5	9.0	12.4	15.0	17.8	22.0	•	19.1	28.7	•	17.4
Cost of Goods to Cash Flow 43	10.4	1.1	3.6	6.9	10.3	12.8	15.6	19.8	•	17.2	26.4	•	14.8
Cash Flow to Total Debt 44	0.3	•	1.6	0.5	0.3	0.2	0.2	0.2	•	0.2	0.1	•	0.1

Selected Financial Factors (in Percentages)

Debt Ratio 45	65.2	•	67.4	77.1	67.5	63.8	68.7	69.2	•	66.3	65.6	•	59.9
Return on Total Assets 46	9.7	•	49.4	19.2	12.8	9.0	9.2	7.6	•	7.4	5.7	•	2.8
Return on Equity Before Income Taxes 47	25.9	•	144.5	73.8	37.2	23.9	27.8	23.0	•	20.8	14.8	•	5.4
Return on Equity After Income Taxes 48	25.1	•	143.6	72.9	36.3	23.1	27.3	22.4	•	19.9	12.5	•	4.6
Profit Margin (Before Income Tax) 49	4.3	20.7	7.8	5.2	4.8	4.1	3.6	3.1	•	3.2	2.4	•	2.9
Profit Margin (After Income Tax) 50	4.2	20.4	7.8	5.2	4.7	3.9	3.5	3.0	•	3.0	2.0	•	2.5

Table I

Corporations with and without Net Income

HEAVY AND CIVIL ENGINEERING CONSTRUCTION

MONEY AMOUNTS AND SIZE OF ASSETS IN THOUSANDS OF DOLLARS

Item Description for Accounting Period 7/12 Through 6/13		Total	Zero Assets	Under 500	500 to 1,000	1,000 to 5,000	5,000 to 10,000	10,000 to 25,000	25,000 to 50,000	50,000 to 100,000	100,000 to 250,000	250,000 to 500,000	500,000 to 2,500,000	2,500,000 and over
Number of Enterprises	1	23330	3698	10694	2231	3989	1422	733	303	140	71	23	18	7
Revenues ($ in Thousands)														
Net Sales	2	200974984	996319	6751955	4487566	21648919	24134080	23478771	20318676	15974203	15327253	10582747	21215107	36059389
Interest	3	194392	963	5829	3360	7916	10083	10039	5681	6191	52576	9680	11946	70129
Rents	4	114701	10503	0	8443	4548	4594	11481	23192	13630	12622	6624	4894	14169
Royalties	5	98776	0	0	0	0	14	2554	246	53	206	12926	25794	56982
Other Portfolio Income	6	1320617	103901	63371	14377	148772	120739	95987	119739	144389	145110	70520	120374	173338
Other Receipts	7	3172424	74421	34415	15982	66831	126838	130207	137146	237419	253786	466649	405310	1223418
Total Receipts	8	205875894	1186107	6855570	4529728	21876986	24396348	23729039	20604680	16375885	15791553	11149146	21783425	37597425
Average Total Receipts	9	8825	321	641	2030	5484	17156	32372	68002	116971	222416	484745	1210190	5371061
Operating Costs/Operating Income (%)														
Cost of Operations	10	78.0	50.1	49.4	57.2	69.9	78.7	80.2	80.9	79.1	79.2	85.2	84.5	81.3
Salaries and Wages	11	4.0	12.4	13.4	3.9	5.4	3.7	3.0	3.0	3.4	4.7	3.0	3.2	3.3
Taxes Paid	12	1.6	5.4	3.2	2.3	2.3	1.7	1.6	1.2	1.5	1.5	1.3	1.5	0.8
Interest Paid	13	0.6	0.9	0.7	0.7	0.5	0.4	0.4	0.5	0.4	0.5	0.5	0.7	1.0
Depreciation	14	2.7	4.5	1.9	2.3	3.1	2.1	2.4	2.8	3.2	2.8	2.7	2.9	2.9
Amortization and Depletion	15	0.3	0.2	0.1	0.0	0.0	0.0	0.0	0.1	0.2	0.2	0.5	0.5	1.2
Pensions and Other Deferred Comp.	16	0.4	0.2	0.1	0.1	0.2	0.7	0.4	0.4	0.5	0.6	0.2	0.2	0.2
Employee Benefits	17	1.1	2.0	1.1	1.1	1.3	1.4	1.1	1.0	1.4	1.1	0.8	1.2	0.6
Advertising	18	0.1	0.1	0.6	0.2	0.2	0.1	0.1	0.1	0.1	0.1	0.1	0.2	0.0
Other Expenses	19	8.1	37.4	22.4	24.7	10.8	6.0	6.3	6.7	7.6	7.5	6.0	5.8	6.8
Officers' Compensation	20	1.9	10.5	7.8	2.8	2.9	2.5	1.8	1.4	1.2	1.1	1.5	0.6	1.4
Operating Margin	21	1.2	•	•	4.7	3.4	2.5	2.7	2.0	1.4	0.7	•	•	0.4
Operating Margin Before Officers' Comp.	22	3.1	•	7.1	7.5	6.3	5.0	4.5	3.4	2.6	1.9	•	•	1.8

Selected Average Balance Sheet ($ in Thousands)

Net Receivables 23	1304	0	27	142	616	2683	5129	11204	19309	33959	80759	203240	823102
Inventories 24	162	0	1	26	100	197	388	1349	2485	7808	10717	38641	69401
Net Property, Plant and Equipment 25	1490	0	49	283	758	1515	3529	9200	19613	35210	91198	231425	1649181
Total Assets 26	5597	0	139	669	2325	7073	14895	34463	71224	157827	352647	826459	6105454
Notes and Loans Payable 27	1257	0	96	248	592	1405	2687	7147	13841	27663	54730	195487	1510616
All Other Liabilities 28	2121	0	25	145	536	2705	5036	10263	23378	48244	120849	304589	3019710
Net Worth 29	2219	0	17	275	1197	2963	7171	17054	34004	81920	177067	326383	1575128

Selected Financial Ratios (Times to 1)

Current Ratio 30	1.3	•	2.2	2.2	2.0	1.7	1.9	1.8	1.7	1.8	1.8	1.5	0.6
Quick Ratio 31	1.0	•	2.0	1.9	1.6	1.4	1.5	1.4	1.3	1.3	1.2	1.0	0.4
Net Sales to Working Capital 32	13.1	•	15.1	11.1	8.1	7.9	6.9	7.3	6.4	5.4	5.4	9.4	•
Coverage Ratio 33	7.2	•	2.2	8.6	10.0	10.0	11.5	8.2	10.7	8.9	7.6	3.3	5.7
Total Asset Turnover 34	1.5	•	4.5	3.0	2.3	2.4	2.2	1.9	1.6	1.4	1.3	1.4	0.8
Inventory Turnover 35	41.6	•	244.5	44.5	37.9	67.8	66.2	40.2	36.3	21.9	36.6	25.8	60.4
Receivables Turnover 36	6.8	•	21.8	13.9	9.1	6.1	6.7	6.0	5.9	6.6	7.1	5.8	6.5
Total Liabilities to Net Worth 37	1.5	•	7.1	1.4	0.9	1.4	1.1	1.0	1.1	0.9	1.0	1.5	2.9
Current Assets to Working Capital 38	4.1	•	1.8	1.8	2.0	2.4	2.1	2.3	2.4	2.2	2.3	3.1	•
Current Liabilities to Working Capital 39	3.1	•	0.8	0.8	1.0	1.4	1.1	1.3	1.4	1.2	1.3	2.1	•
Working Capital to Net Sales 40	0.1	•	0.1	0.1	0.1	0.1	0.1	0.1	0.2	0.2	0.2	0.1	•
Inventory to Working Capital 41	0.2	•	0.0	0.2	0.1	0.1	0.1	0.1	0.1	0.2	0.1	0.3	•
Total Receipts to Cash Flow 42	11.5	3.8	5.7	3.9	8.5	15.3	15.4	14.3	11.9	12.6	13.2	25.0	10.1
Cost of Goods to Cash Flow 43	9.0	1.9	2.8	2.2	6.0	12.0	12.4	11.6	9.4	10.0	11.2	21.1	8.2
Cash Flow to Total Debt 44	0.2	•	0.9	1.3	0.6	0.3	0.3	0.3	0.3	0.2	0.2	0.1	0.1

Selected Financial Factors (in Percentages)

Debt Ratio 45	60.4	•	87.6	58.8	48.5	58.1	51.9	50.5	52.3	48.1	49.8	60.5	74.2
Return on Total Assets 46	6.5	•	7.3	19.0	11.5	9.5	8.7	7.5	6.9	5.7	5.2	3.1	5.0
Return on Equity Before Income Taxes 47	14.0	•	32.6	40.8	20.0	20.3	16.5	13.3	13.0	9.8	9.0	5.5	15.9
Return on Equity After Income Taxes 48	12.7	•	28.6	39.3	19.1	19.2	15.6	12.0	11.9	8.6	6.4	3.0	14.9
Profit Margin (Before Income Tax) 49	3.6	•	0.9	5.6	4.4	3.6	3.7	3.4	3.9	3.7	3.4	1.5	4.8
Profit Margin (After Income Tax) 50	3.3	•	0.8	5.4	4.2	3.4	3.5	3.1	3.5	3.3	2.4	0.8	4.6

Table II

Corporations with Net Income

HEAVY AND CIVIL ENGINEERING CONSTRUCTION

MONEY AMOUNTS AND SIZE OF ASSETS IN THOUSANDS OF DOLLARS

Item Description for Accounting Period 7/12 Through 6/13	Total	Zero Assets	Under 500	500 to 1,000	1,000 to 5,000	5,000 to 10,000	10,000 to 25,000	25,000 to 50,000	50,000 to 100,000	100,000 to 250,000	250,000 to 500,000	500,000 to 2,500,000	2,500,000 and over
Number of Enterprises 1	13054	665	6145	1488	2682	1101	561	227	104	49	18	11	3

Revenues ($ in Thousands)													
Net Sales 2	156280011	414014	4585128	3659941	17505977	19505464	18542975	16019944	12497878	11363781	8612396	18082601	25489911
Interest 3	110724	742	5060	494	3989	8384	8370	4454	4339	49603	8666	9292	7330
Rents 4	68381	5516	0	0	2849	3685	3676	19999	11673	2062	4599	4005	10318
Royalties 5	38205	0	0	0	0	0	2505	224	53	136	12926	22253	108
Other Portfolio Income 6	921579	98273	32908	1656	108292	63900	75033	105405	123640	122117	57640	93458	39258
Other Receipts 7	2625053	87015	31068	13102	54803	92164	98036	116628	217329	234832	389888	218847	1071342
Total Receipts 8	160043953	605560	4654164	3675193	17675910	19673597	18730595	16266654	12854912	11772531	9086115	18430456	26618267
Average Total Receipts 9	12260	911	757	2470	6591	17869	33388	71659	123605	240256	504784	1675496	8872756

Operating Costs/Operating Income (%)													
Cost of Operations 10	77.4	72.3	48.6	55.6	69.4	78.1	78.2	78.9	77.7	77.5	84.7	82.7	83.0
Salaries and Wages 11	3.8	4.7	13.3	3.3	5.0	3.5	3.0	3.2	3.2	5.1	2.8	2.7	3.3
Taxes Paid 12	1.5	3.4	3.2	2.0	2.2	1.7	1.6	1.4	1.6	1.6	1.3	1.6	0.4
Interest Paid 13	0.4	1.3	0.5	0.6	0.4	0.3	0.3	0.4	0.3	0.3	0.5	0.5	0.1
Depreciation 14	2.2	5.1	1.5	1.9	2.9	1.9	2.2	2.7	2.9	2.2	2.3	2.3	1.3
Amortization and Depletion 15	0.2	0.3	0.0	0.0	0.0	0.0	0.0	0.0	0.1	0.2	0.5	0.5	0.4
Pensions and Other Deferred Comp. 16	0.4	0.4	0.1	0.2	0.2	0.9	0.5	0.5	0.6	0.6	0.2	0.2	0.2
Employee Benefits 17	1.0	1.1	0.9	0.9	1.1	1.3	1.1	1.1	1.4	1.1	0.9	1.2	0.3
Advertising 18	0.1	0.2	0.7	0.2	0.2	0.1	0.1	0.1	0.1	0.0	0.1	0.3	0.0
Other Expenses 19	7.2	26.6	19.9	26.0	9.9	4.9	5.9	6.2	7.1	6.5	4.9	5.4	5.6
Officers' Compensation 20	1.9	6.8	6.2	1.9	2.8	2.6	1.8	1.5	1.2	1.1	1.7	0.5	1.6
Operating Margin 21	4.0	•	5.1	7.6	5.8	4.7	5.3	4.0	3.8	3.7	0.3	2.0	3.7
Operating Margin Before Officers' Comp. 22	5.8	•	11.3	9.4	8.6	7.4	7.1	5.5	5.0	4.9	2.0	2.5	5.3

Selected Average Balance Sheet ($ in Thousands)

Net Receivables 23	1713	0	28	142	638	2740	5194	11223	20521	33710	83468	260003	1213956
Inventories 24	189	0	1	28	132	153	313	1108	1977	8254	11621	48764	19513
Net Property, Plant and Equipment 25	1310	0	46	291	724	1425	3422	9131	18971	30368	82952	231304	462567
Total Assets 26	6581	0	146	668	2443	7104	15098	34644	72649	154325	346714	942571	7194199
Notes and Loans Payable 27	984	0	55	248	570	1290	2338	6350	13183	17626	57492	195787	337980
All Other Liabilities 28	2708	0	16	150	511	2664	4838	9649	22694	46262	117343	321564	5182129
Net Worth 29	2889	0	76	270	1362	3150	7921	18644	36772	90437	171878	425220	1674090

Selected Financial Ratios (Times to 1)

Current Ratio 30	1.3	•	4.3	2.6	2.2	1.8	2.0	1.9	1.7	2.1	1.9	1.8	0.5
Quick Ratio 31	1.0	•	4.0	2.2	1.8	1.5	1.6	1.5	1.3	1.6	1.3	1.2	0.4
Net Sales to Working Capital 32	13.3	•	11.4	12.6	8.1	7.5	6.5	6.9	6.5	4.9	5.0	7.9	•
Coverage Ratio 33	19.1	19.6	15.4	14.9	17.0	17.5	22.6	16.1	21.5	28.3	11.8	8.4	56.3
Total Asset Turnover 34	1.8	•	5.1	3.7	2.7	2.5	2.2	2.0	1.7	1.5	1.4	1.7	1.2
Inventory Turnover 35	49.1	•	278.1	48.4	34.3	90.6	82.6	50.3	47.2	21.8	34.9	27.9	361.4
Receivables Turnover 36	7.1	•	23.8	16.3	10.6	6.3	7.3	7.0	6.3	7.1	•	6.5	•
Total Liabilities to Net Worth 37	1.3	•	0.9	1.5	0.8	1.3	0.9	0.9	1.0	0.7	1.0	1.2	3.3
Current Assets to Working Capital 38	4.0	•	1.3	1.6	1.8	2.2	2.0	2.1	2.4	1.9	2.1	2.3	•
Current Liabilities to Working Capital 39	3.0	•	0.3	0.6	0.8	1.2	1.0	1.1	1.4	0.9	1.1	1.3	•
Working Capital to Net Sales 40	0.1	•	0.1	0.1	0.1	0.1	0.2	0.1	0.2	0.2	0.2	0.1	•
Inventory to Working Capital 41	0.2	•	0.0	0.2	0.2	0.1	0.1	0.1	0.1	0.2	0.1	0.2	•
Total Receipts to Cash Flow 42	9.3	2.2	4.7	3.3	7.5	12.4	11.4	11.0	9.4	9.8	11.4	17.0	7.8
Cost of Goods to Cash Flow 43	7.2	1.6	2.3	1.8	5.2	9.7	8.9	8.7	7.3	7.6	9.6	14.1	6.4
Cash Flow to Total Debt 44	0.3	•	2.2	1.9	0.8	0.4	0.4	0.4	0.4	0.4	0.2	0.2	0.2

Selected Financial Factors (in Percentages)

Debt Ratio 45	56.1	•	48.3	59.5	44.2	55.7	47.5	46.2	49.4	41.4	50.4	54.9	76.7
Return on Total Assets 46	12.2	•	36.3	31.5	19.2	14.7	14.5	12.1	11.4	11.4	8.6	7.7	9.8
Return on Equity Before Income Taxes 47	26.4	•	65.6	72.6	32.4	31.3	26.3	21.0	21.6	18.7	15.9	15.0	41.4
Return on Equity After Income Taxes 48	24.6	•	64.0	70.3	31.2	30.0	25.2	19.5	20.2	17.1	12.5	11.9	39.7
Profit Margin (Before Income Tax) 49	6.4	24.1	6.7	8.0	6.8	5.6	6.3	5.6	6.6	7.3	5.7	3.9	8.1
Profit Margin (After Income Tax) 50	5.9	21.8	6.5	7.7	6.5	5.3	6.0	5.1	6.2	6.7	4.5	3.1	7.8

Table I

Corporations with and without Net Income

LAND SUBDIVISION

MONEY AMOUNTS AND SIZE OF ASSETS IN THOUSANDS OF DOLLARS

Item Description for Accounting Period 7/12 Through 6/13	Total	Zero Assets	Under 500	500 to 1,000	1,000 to 5,000	5,000 to 10,000	10,000 to 25,000	25,000 to 50,000	50,000 to 100,000	100,000 to 250,000	250,000 to 500,000	500,000 to 2,500,000	2,500,000 and over
Number of Enterprises **1**	29043	4515	12857	3556	6499	822	521	157	55	39	13	9	0

Revenues ($ in Thousands)

	Total	Zero Assets	Under 500	500 to 1,000	1,000 to 5,000	5,000 to 10,000	10,000 to 25,000	25,000 to 50,000	50,000 to 100,000	100,000 to 250,000	250,000 to 500,000	500,000 to 2,500,000	2,500,000 and over
Net Sales **2**	14718736	233329	926660	504000	1830082	3767503	1303624	1627768	498862	1923734	1012858	1090315	0
Interest **3**	117756	456	5247	894	7450	8091	2863	8070	4626	17559	32565	29934	0
Rents **4**	326600	1515	5543	3936	7586	23257	32220	13587	20126	75463	35200	108167	0
Royalties **5**	31298	0	0	3	439	0	282	3397	0	338	0	26839	0
Other Portfolio Income **6**	390424	28054	6445	2996	27595	7346	18080	13640	21739	64264	61046	139218	0
Other Receipts **7**	482418	-132905	35202	33534	83587	64792	24299	30970	41298	38954	79272	183418	0
Total Receipts **8**	16067232	130449	979097	545363	1956739	3870989	1381368	1697432	586651	2120312	1220941	1577891	0
Average Total Receipts **9**	553	29	76	153	301	4709	2651	10812	10666	54367	93919	175321	•

Operating Costs/Operating Income (%)

	Total	Zero Assets	Under 500	500 to 1,000	1,000 to 5,000	5,000 to 10,000	10,000 to 25,000	25,000 to 50,000	50,000 to 100,000	100,000 to 250,000	250,000 to 500,000	500,000 to 2,500,000	2,500,000 and over
Cost of Operations **10**	79.9	119.7	64.8	70.0	87.4	90.3	80.7	80.1	75.4	61.0	86.1	69.2	•
Salaries and Wages **11**	7.2	8.5	14.8	10.2	5.9	2.6	7.6	8.2	9.5	6.5	8.1	14.1	•
Taxes Paid **12**	2.5	2.2	3.4	2.7	4.2	1.6	2.7	2.0	3.7	2.0	1.5	4.0	•
Interest Paid **13**	4.9	9.8	5.9	5.3	5.9	1.4	6.8	3.8	11.7	4.1	7.4	8.6	•
Depreciation **14**	2.3	1.3	1.8	2.8	2.2	0.8	4.3	1.8	4.2	2.2	2.6	5.3	•
Amortization and Depletion **15**	0.3	0.0	0.0	0.0	0.1	0.0	0.3	0.1	0.3	0.1	0.2	2.2	•
Pensions and Other Deferred Comp. **16**	0.6	0.0	0.3	0.0	0.1	1.4	0.0	0.2	0.1	0.6	1.0	0.5	•
Employee Benefits **17**	0.9	0.7	2.6	0.6	1.2	0.4	0.6	0.4	0.7	1.2	0.7	1.9	•
Advertising **18**	0.6	0.8	0.6	0.1	0.5	0.2	0.7	0.9	1.1	0.6	0.8	1.4	•
Other Expenses **19**	16.1	46.4	32.5	13.8	19.2	5.4	16.1	13.5	23.9	14.0	17.5	31.1	•
Officers' Compensation **20**	2.8	4.0	3.3	0.4	6.9	1.7	2.1	2.1	3.1	2.7	2.0	3.2	•
Operating Margin **21**	•	•	•	•	•	•	•	•	•	4.9	•	•	•
Operating Margin Before Officers' Comp. **22**	•	•	•	•	•	•	•	•	•	7.6	•	•	•

Selected Average Balance Sheet ($ in Thousands)

Net Receivables 23	153	0	5	6	151	670	525	3237	5358	11178	36121	93518	•
Inventories 24	495	0	46	252	463	3066	4025	8413	16757	30479	85515	78959	•
Net Property, Plant and Equipment 25	656	0	37	173	720	1756	4958	10363	19409	42914	78037	429959	•
Total Assets 26	2043	0	142	648	2072	6878	14399	34220	70942	156805	310750	1018469	•
Notes and Loans Payable 27	1240	0	308	458	1308	3863	10265	19089	37514	96631	146827	295811	•
All Other Liabilities 28	293	0	9	51	229	1584	1765	6829	9000	27356	47410	139060	•
Net Worth 29	510	0	-175	139	535	1431	2369	8302	24429	32817	116513	583598	•

Selected Financial Ratios (Times to 1)

Current Ratio 30	2.8	•	3.5	1.8	3.5	2.6	2.4	2.9	4.0	1.8	4.9	2.8	•
Quick Ratio 31	0.8	•	0.9	0.3	0.8	0.7	0.4	1.1	1.4	0.6	2.1	1.5	•
Net Sales to Working Capital 32	0.9	•	1.2	1.0	0.4	1.8	0.6	1.0	0.5	1.5	0.7	0.7	•
Coverage Ratio 33	•	•	•	1.5	•	•	•	•	•	4.7	•	1.4	•
Total Asset Turnover 34	0.2	•	0.5	0.2	0.1	0.7	0.2	0.3	0.1	0.3	0.3	0.1	•
Inventory Turnover 35	0.8	•	1.0	0.4	0.5	1.3	0.5	1.0	0.4	1.0	0.8	1.1	•
Receivables Turnover 36	3.3	•	19.5	16.0	1.8	6.9	3.4	3.2	1.9	4.5	1.5	2.0	•
Total Liabilities to Net Worth 37	3.0	•	•	3.7	2.9	3.8	5.1	3.1	1.9	3.8	1.7	0.7	•
Current Assets to Working Capital 38	1.6	•	1.4	2.2	1.4	1.6	1.7	1.5	1.3	2.2	1.3	1.5	•
Current Liabilities to Working Capital 39	0.6	•	0.4	1.2	0.4	0.6	0.7	0.5	0.3	1.2	0.3	0.5	•
Working Capital to Net Sales 40	1.1	•	0.8	1.0	2.4	0.5	1.7	1.0	2.0	0.7	1.4	1.5	•
Inventory to Working Capital 41	0.8	•	0.7	1.6	0.7	1.0	0.9	0.7	0.7	1.0	0.6	0.6	•
Total Receipts to Cash Flow 42	80.5	•	29.8	7.6	•	73.6	•	139.4	•	4.3	291.5	5.8	•
Cost of Goods to Cash Flow 43	64.3	•	19.3	5.3	•	66.4	•	111.6	•	2.6	251.0	4.0	•
Cash Flow to Total Debt 44	0.0	•	0.0	0.0	•	0.0	•	0.0	•	0.1	0.0	0.0	•

Selected Financial Factors (in Percentages)

Debt Ratio 45	75.0	•	223.7	78.6	74.2	79.2	83.5	75.7	65.6	79.1	62.5	42.7	•
Return on Total Assets 46	•	•	•	1.7	•	•	•	•	•	6.1	•	1.4	•
Return on Equity Before Income Taxes 47	•	•	10.0	2.5	•	•	•	•	•	22.8	•	0.7	•
Return on Equity After Income Taxes 48	•	•	10.0	2.5	•	•	•	•	•	22.5	•	0.4	•
Profit Margin (Before Income Tax) 49	•	•	•	2.5	•	•	•	•	•	15.1	•	3.2	•
Profit Margin (After Income Tax) 50	•	•	•	2.4	•	•	•	•	•	15.0	•	1.9	•

Table II

Corporations with Net Income

LAND SUBDIVISION

MONEY AMOUNTS AND SIZE OF ASSETS IN THOUSANDS OF DOLLARS

Item Description for Accounting Period 7/12 Through 6/13	Total	Zero Assets	Under 500	500 to 1,000	1,000 to 5,000	5,000 to 10,000	10,000 to 25,000	25,000 to 50,000	50,000 to 100,000	100,000 to 250,000	250,000 to 500,000	500,000 to 2,500,000	2,500,000 and over
Number of Enterprises 1	6283	663	2468	565	2113	258	121	57	17	13	3	6	0

Revenues ($ in Thousands)													
Net Sales 2	10295017	150329	596631	243418	1133542	3221165	593908	1209808	204895	1567718	428484	945119	0
Interest 3	74735	0	2420	76	1069	4655	1091	1355	2774	6291	30108	24896	0
Rents 4	219475	0	5543	43	2105	14681	28411	9244	16126	34476	1346	107500	0
Royalties 5	30958	0	0	0	439	0	282	3397	0	0	0	26839	0
Other Portfolio Income 6	280945	27204	6414	1385	2329	6808	14245	1809	20102	61303	134	139210	0
Other Receipts 7	609927	16922	29237	13251	151535	80504	24209	37280	23989	14725	63092	155185	0
Total Receipts 8	11511057	194455	640245	258173	1291019	3327813	662146	1262893	267886	1684513	523164	1398749	0
Average Total Receipts 9	1832	293	259	457	611	12898	5472	22156	15758	129578	174388	233125	•

Operating Costs/Operating Income (%)													
Cost of Operations 10	69.9	84.0	42.6	33.7	61.3	85.9	62.6	79.4	46.6	58.6	71.5	65.9	•
Salaries and Wages 11	6.3	5.5	18.8	16.1	5.2	2.2	3.9	5.4	13.0	4.4	10.9	13.9	•
Taxes Paid 12	2.0	1.0	2.9	1.8	3.4	1.2	2.4	1.3	5.5	1.5	0.7	4.4	•
Interest Paid 13	2.1	0.9	0.6	3.2	2.5	0.4	3.7	1.5	6.7	1.4	2.8	7.5	•
Depreciation 14	1.7	0.9	0.7	0.5	2.1	0.8	2.9	0.9	5.4	1.1	1.3	5.6	•
Amortization and Depletion 15	0.3	•	0.0	•	0.1	0.0	0.3	0.1	0.1	0.1	0.1	2.5	•
Pensions and Other Deferred Comp. 16	0.8	0.0	0.4	0.0	0.0	1.6	0.0	0.2	0.2	0.7	2.2	0.0	•
Employee Benefits 17	0.9	0.1	3.7	0.3	1.5	0.4	0.5	0.1	0.9	1.2	0.0	1.9	•
Advertising 18	0.6	0.0	0.9	0.1	0.4	0.2	0.8	1.0	1.1	0.4	0.4	1.6	•
Other Expenses 19	10.0	7.8	14.0	15.8	7.0	3.3	10.4	6.7	19.1	9.9	16.6	31.7	•
Officers' Compensation 20	2.8	2.3	3.9	0.8	8.6	1.7	2.0	1.7	2.4	2.9	0.2	3.0	•
Operating Margin 21	2.6	•	11.4	27.6	7.9	2.4	10.5	1.7	•	17.8	•	•	•
Operating Margin Before Officers' Comp. 22	5.5	•	15.4	28.4	16.4	4.1	12.5	3.4	1.4	20.7	•	•	•

Selected Average Balance Sheet ($ in Thousands)

Net Receivables 23	375	0	7	0	151	1761	780	4782	7942	24363	56232	95987	•
Inventories 24	515	0	31	348	395	2193	2565	5056	13527	13412	104852	81677	•
Net Property, Plant and Equipment 25	1356	0	30	53	729	2077	5205	14741	20352	40456	78920	626584	•
Total Assets 26	3565	0	175	672	2222	6677	15009	35092	75016	160819	327884	1167602	•
Notes and Loans Payable 27	1511	0	38	856	1061	2389	9210	15138	28507	71868	188768	348602	•
All Other Liabilities 28	497	0	-12	138	185	1694	2081	7683	10008	43767	31465	120704	•
Net Worth 29	1558	0	149	-322	976	2594	3717	12270	36500	45184	107650	698296	•

Selected Financial Ratios (Times to 1)

Current Ratio 30	2.9	•	8.2	0.6	4.9	1.6	3.4	3.2	7.1	2.0	3.6	3.3	•
Quick Ratio 31	1.2	•	3.5	0.1	1.2	1.1	0.8	1.7	2.8	1.0	1.9	1.9	•
Net Sales to Working Capital 32	1.6	•	2.2	•	0.6	8.9	1.0	1.9	0.5	3.0	1.0	0.8	•
Coverage Ratio 33	8.0	32.4	33.9	11.6	9.6	14.3	6.9	4.9	5.4	19.2	6.5	2.3	•
Total Asset Turnover 34	0.5	•	1.4	0.6	0.2	1.9	0.3	0.6	0.2	0.7	0.4	0.1	•
Inventory Turnover 35	2.2	•	3.4	0.4	0.8	4.9	1.2	3.3	0.4	5.3	1.0	1.3	•
Receivables Turnover 36	5.4	•	42.5	2735.0	3.8	6.8	5.5	5.0	2.0	8.0	2.4	3.3	•
Total Liabilities to Net Worth 37	1.3	•	0.2	•	1.3	1.6	3.0	1.9	1.1	2.6	2.0	0.7	•
Current Assets to Working Capital 38	1.5	•	1.1	•	1.3	2.6	1.4	1.4	1.2	2.0	1.4	1.4	•
Current Liabilities to Working Capital 39	0.5	•	0.1	•	0.3	1.6	0.4	0.4	0.2	1.0	0.4	0.4	•
Working Capital to Net Sales 40	0.6	•	0.5	•	1.8	0.1	1.0	0.5	2.2	0.3	1.0	1.2	•
Inventory to Working Capital 41	0.6	•	0.4	•	0.5	0.7	0.8	0.5	0.5	0.7	0.6	0.4	•
Total Receipts to Cash Flow 42	4.9	3.7	3.6	2.1	3.6	11.6	3.5	9.1	2.3	3.4	3.6	4.4	•
Cost of Goods to Cash Flow 43	3.4	3.1	1.5	0.7	2.2	10.0	2.2	7.2	1.1	2.0	2.6	2.9	•
Cash Flow to Total Debt 44	0.2	•	2.6	0.2	0.1	0.3	0.1	0.1	0.1	0.3	0.2	0.1	•

Selected Financial Factors (in Percentages)

Debt Ratio 45	56.3	•	14.9	147.8	56.1	61.1	75.2	65.0	51.3	71.9	67.2	40.2	•
Return on Total Assets 46	7.6	•	26.6	23.6	5.9	11.5	8.4	4.6	5.8	20.0	7.9	2.4	•
Return on Equity Before Income Taxes 47	15.2	•	30.4	•	12.0	27.4	29.0	10.4	9.7	67.4	20.3	2.3	•
Return on Equity After Income Taxes 48	14.7	•	30.0	•	11.8	27.1	26.6	10.3	9.7	66.9	18.0	1.9	•
Profit Margin (Before Income Tax) 49	14.4	26.8	18.7	33.6	21.8	5.7	22.0	6.0	29.5	25.2	15.3	10.0	•
Profit Margin (After Income Tax) 50	14.0	24.6	18.5	33.5	21.4	5.6	20.2	5.9	29.3	25.1	13.5	8.5	•

Table I

Corporations with and without Net Income

ELECTRICAL CONTRACTORS

MONEY AMOUNTS AND SIZE OF ASSETS IN THOUSANDS OF DOLLARS

Item Description for Accounting Period 7/12 Through 6/13	Total	Zero Assets	Under 500	500 to 1,000	1,000 to 5,000	5,000 to 10,000	10,000 to 25,000	25,000 to 50,000	50,000 to 100,000	100,000 to 250,000	250,000 to 500,000	500,000 to 2,500,000	2,500,000 and over
Number of Enterprises 1	58116	11768	38833	2703	3793	580	306	•	34	19	•	•	•
Revenues ($ in Thousands)													
Net Sales 2	87061390	1646940	17684820	6034351	19435772	11090570	10294529	•	5197708	5941289	•	•	•
Interest 3	34814	21	1590	893	13541	2456	1317	•	1152	7866	•	•	•
Rents 4	6128	0	0	1569	2604	807	440	•	360	349	•	•	•
Royalties 5	3	0	0	0	0	0	2	•	0	0	•	•	•
Other Portfolio Income 6	327722	512	41532	20784	65515	19001	6669	•	1355	23071	•	•	•
Other Receipts 7	1316534	35262	41022	3783	32245	57843	42905	•	19929	28361	•	•	•
Total Receipts 8	88746591	1682735	17768964	6061380	19549677	11170677	10345862	•	5220504	6000936	•	•	•
Average Total Receipts 9	1527	143	458	2242	5154	19260	33810	•	153544	315839	•	•	•
Operating Costs/Operating Income (%)													
Cost of Operations 10	69.3	46.8	50.4	64.9	71.7	74.7	76.3	•	80.2	79.8	•	•	•
Salaries and Wages 11	7.3	10.2	10.5	6.5	6.6	7.7	4.9	•	4.9	6.0	•	•	•
Taxes Paid 12	2.6	2.9	3.4	2.7	3.0	2.3	2.1	•	2.2	1.5	•	•	•
Interest Paid 13	0.3	0.3	0.4	0.4	0.3	0.3	0.3	•	0.2	0.3	•	•	•
Depreciation 14	1.2	1.2	1.4	1.0	1.1	0.7	0.8	•	0.8	0.9	•	•	•
Amortization and Depletion 15	0.2	0.0	0.1	0.1	0.1	0.1	0.0	•	0.0	0.2	•	•	•
Pensions and Other Deferred Comp. 16	0.4	0.1	0.3	0.3	0.3	0.5	0.4	•	0.4	0.5	•	•	•
Employee Benefits 17	2.5	3.2	0.9	2.9	2.6	3.4	3.4	•	2.8	1.5	•	•	•
Advertising 18	0.2	0.5	0.6	0.2	0.1	0.1	0.1	•	0.1	0.0	•	•	•
Other Expenses 19	9.2	22.5	17.8	10.3	7.7	6.1	5.3	•	4.3	5.9	•	•	•
Officers' Compensation 20	4.2	5.6	8.0	5.8	3.5	2.8	3.4	•	1.4	1.1	•	•	•
Operating Margin 21	2.6	6.6	6.2	4.8	2.9	1.3	2.8	•	2.7	2.3	•	•	•
Operating Margin Before Officers' Comp. 22	6.8	12.2	14.2	10.7	6.5	4.1	6.2	•	4.1	3.4	•	•	•

Selected Average Balance Sheet ($ in Thousands)

Net Receivables 23	254	0	15	231	880	3726	7819	•	34967	71100	•	•	•
Inventories 24	21	0	8	65	75	186	471	•	1498	3337	•	•	•
Net Property, Plant and Equipment 25	87	0	20	126	246	802	1440	•	6060	12025	•	•	•
Total Assets 26	609	0	88	714	1883	7116	15051	•	66498	136399	•	•	•
Notes and Loans Payable 27	108	0	42	130	373	1296	2123	•	11266	12155	•	•	•
All Other Liabilities 28	231	0	19	172	660	3399	6367	•	30161	75763	•	•	•
Net Worth 29	270	0	27	412	850	2421	6562	•	25072	48481	•	•	•

Selected Financial Ratios (Times to 1)

Current Ratio 30	1.8	•	1.8	2.6	2.0	1.5	1.7	•	1.6	1.5	•	•	•
Quick Ratio 31	1.4	•	1.4	2.0	1.7	1.2	1.4	•	1.3	1.2	•	•	•
Net Sales to Working Capital 32	7.8	•	18.9	7.1	6.7	10.1	6.6	•	7.3	8.8	•	•	•
Coverage Ratio 33	14.3	32.6	17.7	14.1	11.8	7.2	12.2	•	15.9	12.5	•	•	•
Total Asset Turnover 34	2.5	•	5.2	3.1	2.7	2.7	2.2	•	2.3	2.3	•	•	•
Inventory Turnover 35	49.1	•	29.2	22.4	48.8	76.8	54.5	•	81.9	74.8	•	•	•
Receivables Turnover 36	6.0	•	31.4	8.6	5.7	4.5	4.5	•	3.9	5.9	•	•	•
Total Liabilities to Net Worth 37	1.3	•	2.3	0.7	1.2	1.9	1.3	•	1.7	1.8	•	•	•
Current Assets to Working Capital 38	2.3	•	2.2	1.6	2.0	3.0	2.4	•	2.6	3.0	•	•	•
Current Liabilities to Working Capital 39	1.3	•	1.2	0.6	1.0	2.0	1.4	•	1.6	2.0	•	•	•
Working Capital to Net Sales 40	0.1	•	0.1	0.1	0.1	0.1	0.2	•	0.1	0.1	•	•	•
Inventory to Working Capital 41	0.1	•	0.3	0.2	0.1	0.1	0.1	•	0.1	0.1	•	•	•
Total Receipts to Cash Flow 42	8.8	3.4	4.6	7.3	11.1	15.6	14.7	•	17.1	15.6	•	•	•
Cost of Goods to Cash Flow 43	6.1	1.6	2.3	4.7	8.0	11.7	11.3	•	13.7	12.5	•	•	•
Cash Flow to Total Debt 44	0.5	•	1.6	1.0	0.4	0.3	0.3	•	0.2	0.2	•	•	•

Selected Financial Factors (in Percentages)

Debt Ratio 45	55.6	•	69.5	42.3	54.9	66.0	56.4	•	62.3	64.5	•	•	•
Return on Total Assets 46	11.9	•	36.7	17.8	9.9	6.3	8.1	•	7.7	8.2	•	•	•
Return on Equity Before Income Taxes 47	24.8	•	113.8	28.7	20.0	16.1	17.0	•	19.2	21.1	•	•	•
Return on Equity After Income Taxes 48	22.6	•	113.1	28.6	18.0	14.1	16.2	•	18.5	17.7	•	•	•
Profit Margin (Before Income Tax) 49	4.5	8.8	6.7	5.3	3.3	2.0	3.3	•	3.1	3.3	•	•	•
Profit Margin (After Income Tax) 50	4.1	8.7	6.6	5.3	3.0	1.8	3.2	•	3.0	2.8	•	•	•

Table II

Corporations with Net Income

ELECTRICAL CONTRACTORS

MONEY AMOUNTS AND SIZE OF ASSETS IN THOUSANDS OF DOLLARS

Item Description for Accounting Period 7/12 Through 6/13		Total	Zero Assets	Under 500	500 to 1,000	1,000 to 5,000	5,000 to 10,000	10,000 to 25,000	25,000 to 50,000	50,000 to 100,000	100,000 to 250,000	250,000 to 500,000	500,000 to 2,500,000	2,500,000 and over
Number of Enterprises	1	39395	7363	26661	2089	2473	433	275	54	•	16	•	0	0

Revenues ($ in Thousands)

Net Sales	2	68030126	1371882	11940889	4828024	15052623	8801317	9652761	4634876	•	5242312	•	0	0
Interest	3	23483	0	601	647	12804	1470	1020	781	•	835	•	0	0
Rents	4	6109	0	0	1569	2589	807	440	0	•	349	•	0	0
Royalties	5	2	0	0	0	0	0	2	0	•	0	•	0	0
Other Portfolio Income	6	233572	512	38524	10506	13022	14339	6124	2480	•	1571	•	0	0
Other Receipts	7	1308091	14455	23286	3461	81192	52501	39819	31032	•	21397	•	0	0
Total Receipts	8	69601383	1386849	12003300	4844207	15162230	8870434	9700166	4669169	•	5266464	•	0	0
Average Total Receipts	9	1767	188	450	2319	6131	20486	35273	86466	•	329154	•	•	•

Operating Costs/Operating Income (%)

Cost of Operations	10	68.7	47.9	46.5	65.6	68.7	75.5	75.8	79.1	•	79.2	•	•	•
Salaries and Wages	11	6.8	10.7	10.0	4.6	6.7	6.8	4.9	4.3	•	5.8	•	•	•
Taxes Paid	12	2.6	2.9	3.4	2.5	3.0	2.3	2.2	1.5	•	1.4	•	•	•
Interest Paid	13	0.3	0.3	0.4	0.3	0.2	0.3	0.2	0.1	•	0.2	•	•	•
Depreciation	14	1.2	0.7	1.5	1.0	1.1	0.7	0.7	0.7	•	0.9	•	•	•
Amortization and Depletion	15	0.1	0.0	0.0	0.1	0.1	0.1	0.0	0.1	•	0.1	•	•	•
Pensions and Other Deferred Comp.	16	0.4	0.1	0.2	0.3	0.4	0.4	0.4	0.7	•	0.6	•	•	•
Employee Benefits	17	2.5	3.9	1.2	3.1	2.7	2.8	3.6	2.7	•	1.5	•	•	•
Advertising	18	0.2	0.6	0.5	0.2	0.1	0.1	0.1	0.1	•	0.0	•	•	•
Other Expenses	19	8.7	17.3	17.8	9.9	7.8	5.5	5.1	3.1	•	5.0	•	•	•
Officers' Compensation	20	3.8	3.0	7.7	5.6	3.3	2.4	3.4	3.2	•	1.2	•	•	•
Operating Margin	21	4.7	12.5	10.9	6.8	5.8	3.0	3.5	4.4	•	4.0	•	•	•
Operating Margin Before Officers' Comp.	22	8.6	15.5	18.6	12.4	9.1	5.4	6.9	7.5	•	5.2	•	•	•

Selected Average Balance Sheet ($ in Thousands)

Net Receivables 23	292	0	15	219	910	3639	8262	20230	•	74924	•	•	•
Inventories 24	23	0	8	72	78	213	470	537	•	2771	•	•	•
Net Property, Plant and Equipment 25	96	0	22	114	254	898	1317	2365	•	12829	•	•	•
Total Assets 26	693	0	93	719	1978	6902	15284	34715	•	133558	•	•	•
Notes and Loans Payable 27	94	0	35	121	341	1019	2014	2848	•	12551	•	•	•
All Other Liabilities 28	264	0	20	167	682	3747	6406	17064	•	73167	•	•	•
Net Worth 29	334	0	39	431	955	2137	6864	14804	•	47840	•	•	•

Selected Financial Ratios (Times to 1)

Current Ratio 30	1.8	•	2.0	2.6	2.3	1.4	1.8	1.7	•	1.5	•	•	•
Quick Ratio 31	1.5	•	1.6	1.9	1.9	1.2	1.5	1.5	•	1.3	•	•	•
Net Sales to Working Capital 32	7.5	•	15.0	7.0	6.9	12.2	6.5	6.8	•	9.0	•	•	•
Coverage Ratio 33	27.4	43.8	29.9	21.4	30.2	14.4	17.1	45.6	•	22.4	•	•	•
Total Asset Turnover 34	2.5	•	4.8	3.2	3.1	2.9	2.3	2.5	•	2.5	•	•	•
Inventory Turnover 35	50.8	•	27.7	21.2	53.7	72.1	56.6	126.4	•	93.6	•	•	•
Receivables Turnover 36	6.0	•	30.7	10.0	6.6	4.6	4.9	4.5	•	•	•	•	•
Total Liabilities to Net Worth 37	1.1	•	1.4	0.7	1.1	2.2	1.2	1.3	•	1.8	•	•	•
Current Assets to Working Capital 38	2.2	•	2.0	1.6	1.8	3.5	2.3	2.4	•	2.9	•	•	•
Current Liabilities to Working Capital 39	1.2	•	1.0	0.6	0.8	2.5	1.3	1.4	•	1.9	•	•	•
Working Capital to Net Sales 40	0.1	•	0.1	0.1	0.1	0.1	0.2	0.1	•	0.1	•	•	•
Inventory to Working Capital 41	0.1	•	0.3	0.2	0.1	0.1	0.1	0.0	•	0.1	•	•	•
Total Receipts to Cash Flow 42	7.4	3.4	3.8	6.5	8.2	13.2	13.6	14.5	•	14.3	•	•	•
Cost of Goods to Cash Flow 43	5.1	1.6	1.7	4.3	5.6	10.0	10.3	11.4	•	11.3	•	•	•
Cash Flow to Total Debt 44	0.6	•	2.2	1.2	0.7	0.3	0.3	0.3	•	0.3	•	•	•

Selected Financial Factors (in Percentages)

Debt Ratio 45	51.7	•	58.5	40.0	51.7	69.0	55.1	57.4	•	64.2	•	•	•
Return on Total Assets 46	18.2	•	56.6	24.1	20.7	12.1	9.7	12.9	•	11.4	•	•	•
Return on Equity Before Income Taxes 47	36.3	•	131.7	38.3	41.4	36.4	20.4	29.6	•	30.4	•	•	•
Return on Equity After Income Taxes 48	33.7	•	131.1	38.2	38.6	33.4	19.5	28.9	•	26.4	•	•	•
Profit Margin (Before Income Tax) 49	7.0	13.6	11.4	7.1	6.5	3.8	4.0	5.1	•	4.4	•	•	•
Profit Margin (After Income Tax) 50	6.5	13.4	11.4	7.1	6.1	3.5	3.8	5.0	•	3.9	•	•	•

Table I

Corporations with and without Net Income

PLUMBING, HEATING, AND AIR-CONDITIONING CONTRACTORS

MONEY AMOUNTS AND SIZE OF ASSETS IN THOUSANDS OF DOLLARS

Item Description for Accounting Period 7/12 Through 6/13	Total	Zero Assets	Under 500	500 to 1,000	1,000 to 5,000	5,000 to 10,000	10,000 to 25,000	25,000 to 50,000	50,000 to 100,000	100,000 to 250,000	250,000 to 500,000	500,000 to 2,500,000	2,500,000 and over
Number of Enterprises 1	72576	9627	54464	3729	3563	678	405	•	28	7	•	0	•

Revenues ($ in Thousands)

Net Sales 2	116273276	1275381	34220420	9119055	22570673	12937012	15215189	•	4847578	2525153	•	0	•
Interest 3	23279	496	3432	2179	3931	1994	9639	•	280	0	•	0	•
Rents 4	9168	0	986	308	2758	733	2629	•	1695	0	•	0	•
Royalties 5	0	0	0	0	0	0	0	•	0	0	•	0	•
Other Portfolio Income 6	93475	659	31976	3817	32390	8323	12034	•	697	625	•	0	•
Other Receipts 7	338619	12538	21929	19662	119780	58840	26433	•	20535	16311	•	0	•
Total Receipts 8	116737817	1289074	34278743	9145021	22729532	13006902	15265924	•	4870785	2542089	•	0	•
Average Total Receipts 9	1608	134	629	2452	6379	19184	37694	•	173957	363156	•	•	•

Operating Costs/Operating Income (%)

Cost of Operations 10	66.9	51.0	50.4	57.8	69.6	75.4	78.7	•	82.6	85.5	•	•	•
Salaries and Wages 11	8.2	6.8	12.5	8.5	7.5	6.6	5.4	•	3.6	4.2	•	•	•
Taxes Paid 12	2.8	2.6	3.5	3.1	2.9	2.4	2.0	•	1.5	3.9	•	•	•
Interest Paid 13	0.4	0.8	0.5	0.5	0.3	0.2	0.3	•	0.2	0.1	•	•	•
Depreciation 14	0.8	1.2	1.1	1.1	0.8	0.5	0.6	•	0.5	0.5	•	•	•
Amortization and Depletion 15	0.1	0.5	0.0	0.2	0.1	0.0	0.1	•	0.0	0.0	•	•	•
Pensions and Other Deferred Comp. 16	0.4	0.0	0.2	0.5	0.8	0.5	0.5	•	0.2	0.4	•	•	•
Employee Benefits 17	1.9	0.6	1.9	1.9	1.7	2.2	3.1	•	2.2	0.8	•	•	•
Advertising 18	0.7	0.9	0.9	1.5	1.1	0.4	0.2	•	0.1	0.1	•	•	•
Other Expenses 19	9.8	30.0	16.4	12.3	8.6	6.6	4.7	•	3.5	•	•	•	•
Officers' Compensation 20	4.8	3.0	8.6	7.1	3.8	3.2	2.0	•	1.0	1.9	•	•	•
Operating Margin 21	3.3	2.5	4.0	5.6	2.7	2.0	2.5	•	4.7	4.0	•	•	•
Operating Margin Before Officers' Comp. 22	8.1	5.5	12.6	12.8	6.5	5.1	4.5	•	5.7	5.9	•	•	•

Selected Average Balance Sheet ($ in Thousands)

Net Receivables 23	213	0	19	260	939	3533	8341	•	34930	64831	•	•	•
Inventories 24	25	0	6	64	176	278	484	•	2029	908	•	•	•
Net Property, Plant and Equipment 25	59	0	25	84	235	730	1339	•	6992	10927	•	•	•
Total Assets 26	504	0	95	734	2252	7259	15098	•	67832	138468	•	•	•
Notes and Loans Payable 27	104	0	55	226	405	672	1989	•	9292	6127	•	•	•
All Other Liabilities 28	212	0	25	205	856	3443	7385	•	30848	74022	•	•	•
Net Worth 29	188	0	15	303	992	3144	5724	•	27692	58320	•	•	•

Selected Financial Ratios (Times to 1)

Current Ratio 30	1.7	•	1.7	2.4	2.0	1.8	1.6	•	1.6	1.7	•	•	•
Quick Ratio 31	1.4	•	1.4	2.0	1.6	1.4	1.3	•	1.3	1.3	•	•	•
Net Sales to Working Capital 32	9.9	•	26.1	7.4	7.3	7.1	7.8	•	8.8	7.3	•	•	•
Coverage Ratio 33	11.3	5.7	9.8	13.1	10.8	14.7	11.4	•	29.8	84.4	•	•	•
Total Asset Turnover 34	3.2	•	6.6	3.3	2.8	2.6	2.5	•	2.6	2.6	•	•	•
Inventory Turnover 35	43.6	•	49.0	21.9	25.1	51.7	61.1	•	70.5	339.6	•	•	•
Receivables Turnover 36	7.5	•	30.0	9.7	6.5	5.0	4.8	•	•	6.1	•	•	•
Total Liabilities to Net Worth 37	1.7	•	5.2	1.4	1.3	1.3	1.6	•	1.4	1.4	•	•	•
Current Assets to Working Capital 38	2.4	•	2.5	1.7	2.1	2.3	2.6	•	2.7	2.5	•	•	•
Current Liabilities to Working Capital 39	1.4	•	1.5	0.7	1.1	1.3	1.6	•	1.7	1.5	•	•	•
Working Capital to Net Sales 40	0.1	•	0.0	0.1	0.1	0.1	0.1	•	0.1	0.1	•	•	•
Inventory to Working Capital 41	0.2	•	0.3	0.2	0.2	0.1	0.1	•	0.1	0.0	•	•	•
Total Receipts to Cash Flow 42	9.0	3.3	5.8	6.3	10.5	14.0	16.7	•	13.7	40.4	•	•	•
Cost of Goods to Cash Flow 43	6.0	1.7	2.9	3.6	7.3	10.5	13.1	•	11.3	34.5	•	•	•
Cash Flow to Total Debt 44	0.6	•	1.3	0.9	0.5	0.3	0.2	•	0.3	0.1	•	•	•

Selected Financial Factors (in Percentages)

Debt Ratio 45	62.8	•	83.9	58.8	56.0	56.7	62.1	•	59.2	57.9	•	•	•
Return on Total Assets 46	12.9	•	30.3	21.4	10.5	7.1	7.7	•	13.5	12.2	•	•	•
Return on Equity Before Income Taxes 47	31.7	•	169.1	47.9	21.7	15.3	18.5	•	32.0	28.7	•	•	•
Return on Equity After Income Taxes 48	30.5	•	167.7	47.4	20.7	14.7	17.8	•	31.7	28.7	•	•	•
Profit Margin (Before Income Tax) 49	3.7	3.6	4.1	5.9	3.4	2.5	2.8	•	5.1	4.6	•	•	•
Profit Margin (After Income Tax) 50	3.6	3.4	4.1	5.9	3.2	2.4	2.7	•	5.1	4.6	•	•	•

Table II
Corporations with Net Income

PLUMBING, HEATING, AND AIR-CONDITIONING CONTRACTORS

MONEY AMOUNTS AND SIZE OF ASSETS IN THOUSANDS OF DOLLARS

Item Description for Accounting Period 7/12 Through 6/13	Total	Zero Assets	Under 500	500 to 1,000	1,000 to 5,000	5,000 to 10,000	10,000 to 25,000	25,000 to 50,000	50,000 to 100,000	100,000 to 250,000	250,000 to 500,000	500,000 to 2,500,000	2,500,000 and over
Number of Enterprises 1	50413	4505	39287	2787	2807	589	340	61	•	7	•	0	0
Revenues ($ in Thousands)													
Net Sales 2	95944636	727269	23764693	7307785	19314294	11417836	13122961	5265702	•	2525153	•	0	0
Interest 3	13341	427	1253	1843	3131	1709	3394	587	•	0	•	0	0
Rents 4	8143	0	378	308	2340	733	2629	0	•	0	•	0	0
Royalties 5	0	0	0	0	0	0	0	0	•	0	•	0	0
Other Portfolio Income 6	72848	659	21941	3296	25713	6202	11536	1299	•	625	•	0	0
Other Receipts 7	269479	1226	14910	14429	83109	56346	30980	16135	•	16311	•	0	0
Total Receipts 8	96308447	729581	23803175	7327661	19428587	11482826	13171500	5283723	•	2542089	•	0	0
Average Total Receipts 9	1910	162	606	2629	6921	19495	38740	86618	•	363156	•	•	•
Operating Costs/Operating Income (%)													
Cost of Operations 10	68.0	57.0	50.5	54.5	69.9	73.6	77.8	81.4	•	85.5	•	•	•
Salaries and Wages 11	7.1	3.8	9.7	8.6	7.5	6.9	5.5	5.8	•	4.2	•	•	•
Taxes Paid 12	2.6	2.6	3.3	2.9	2.7	2.4	2.0	1.3	•	3.9	•	•	•
Interest Paid 13	0.3	0.2	0.4	0.4	0.3	0.2	0.2	0.1	•	0.1	•	•	•
Depreciation 14	0.7	1.0	1.0	1.1	0.7	0.5	0.6	0.5	•	0.5	•	•	•
Amortization and Depletion 15	0.1	•	0.0	0.2	0.0	0.0	0.1	0.0	•	0.0	•	•	•
Pensions and Other Deferred Comp. 16	0.5	•	0.2	0.5	0.9	0.6	0.5	0.6	•	0.4	•	•	•
Employee Benefits 17	1.8	1.0	1.9	1.7	1.6	2.1	3.0	0.7	•	0.8	•	•	•
Advertising 18	0.6	1.0	0.9	1.7	1.0	0.4	0.2	0.1	•	0.1	•	•	•
Other Expenses 19	8.5	21.6	14.9	12.8	8.0	6.7	4.5	3.4	•	•	•	•	•
Officers' Compensation 20	4.6	2.3	9.4	7.0	3.5	3.3	2.0	1.6	•	1.9	•	•	•
Operating Margin 21	5.2	9.6	7.9	8.6	4.0	3.2	3.8	4.6	•	4.0	•	•	•
Operating Margin Before Officers' Comp. 22	9.8	11.9	17.3	15.6	7.5	6.6	5.7	6.2	•	5.9	•	•	•

Selected Average Balance Sheet ($ in Thousands)

Net Receivables 23	262	0	17	249	1043	3349	8253	18811	•	64831	•	•	•
Inventories 24	28	0	6	65	191	291	388	568	•	803	•	•	•
Net Property, Plant and Equipment 25	65	0	22	83	225	717	1366	3042	•	10927	•	•	•
Total Assets 26	601	0	92	758	2281	7230	14805	35716	•	138468	•	•	•
Notes and Loans Payable 27	95	0	37	197	370	536	1722	1954	•	6127	•	•	•
All Other Liabilities 28	257	0	21	212	928	3221	7093	19973	•	74022	•	•	•
Net Worth 29	250	0	34	349	984	3473	5990	13789	•	58320	•	•	•

Selected Financial Ratios (Times to 1)

Current Ratio 30	1.8	•	2.1	2.6	1.9	1.9	1.7	1.5	•	1.7	•	•	•
Quick Ratio 31	1.5	•	1.7	2.2	1.5	1.5	1.4	1.2	•	1.3	•	•	•
Net Sales to Working Capital 32	9.2	•	19.7	7.2	7.9	6.7	7.6	9.3	•	7.3	•	•	•
Coverage Ratio 33	22.6	40.7	23.9	22.1	17.8	25.9	25.3	37.3	•	84.4	•	•	•
Total Asset Turnover 34	3.2	•	6.6	3.5	3.0	2.7	2.6	2.4	•	2.6	•	•	•
Inventory Turnover 35	46.1	•	49.9	22.0	25.2	49.0	77.3	123.6	•	383.7	•	•	•
Receivables Turnover 36	7.4	•	33.3	11.5	6.5	5.3	5.0	4.5	•	•	•	•	•
Total Liabilities to Net Worth 37	1.4	•	1.7	1.2	1.3	1.1	1.5	1.6	•	1.4	•	•	•
Current Assets to Working Capital 38	2.3	•	1.9	1.6	2.1	2.1	2.5	3.2	•	2.5	•	•	•
Current Liabilities to Working Capital 39	1.3	•	0.9	0.6	1.1	1.1	1.5	2.2	•	1.5	•	•	•
Working Capital to Net Sales 40	0.1	•	0.1	0.1	0.1	0.1	0.1	0.1	•	0.1	•	•	•
Inventory to Working Capital 41	0.1	•	0.2	0.2	0.2	0.1	0.1	0.1	•	0.0	•	•	•
Total Receipts to Cash Flow 42	8.5	3.4	5.1	5.2	9.8	11.9	14.4	15.1	•	40.4	•	•	•
Cost of Goods to Cash Flow 43	5.8	1.9	2.6	2.8	6.8	8.8	11.2	12.3	•	34.5	•	•	•
Cash Flow to Total Debt 44	0.6	•	2.0	1.2	0.5	0.4	0.3	0.3	•	0.1	•	•	•

Selected Financial Factors (in Percentages)

Debt Ratio 45	58.4	•	63.3	53.9	56.9	52.0	59.5	61.4	•	57.9	•	•	•
Return on Total Assets 46	18.4	•	55.4	32.2	14.7	10.6	11.2	12.2	•	12.2	•	•	•
Return on Equity Before Income Taxes 47	42.3	•	144.8	66.8	32.1	21.2	26.5	30.8	•	28.7	•	•	•
Return on Equity After Income Taxes 48	41.0	•	143.8	66.2	30.8	20.5	25.7	30.3	•	28.7	•	•	•
Profit Margin (Before Income Tax) 49	5.6	9.9	8.1	8.9	4.6	3.8	4.1	4.9	•	4.6	•	•	•
Profit Margin (After Income Tax) 50	5.4	9.6	8.0	8.8	4.4	3.7	4.0	4.8	•	4.6	•	•	•

Table I

Corporations with and without Net Income

OTHER SPECIALTY TRADE CONTRACTORS

MONEY AMOUNTS AND SIZE OF ASSETS IN THOUSANDS OF DOLLARS

Item Description for Accounting Period 7/12 Through 6/13		Total	Zero Assets	Under 500	500 to 1,000	1,000 to 5,000	5,000 to 10,000	10,000 to 25,000	25,000 to 50,000	50,000 to 100,000	100,000 to 250,000	250,000 to 500,000	500,000 to 2,500,000	2,500,000 and over
Number of Enterprises	1	299808	59261	210455	12647	14036	2011	1013	239	94	34	10	8	0
Revenues ($ in Thousands)														
Net Sales	2	342180448	6814311	113460989	28811331	75935464	37518334	31634731	15317259	10645741	8769436	4636349	8636505	0
Interest	3	73384	325	7214	3621	15701	7113	10167	7462	6200	4619	6441	4522	0
Rents	4	226444	3008	17726	6749	38253	4660	5889	1852	1321	4604	12	142371	0
Royalties	5	42903	0	54	0	254	0	1396	3759	1206	2	33715	2517	0
Other Portfolio Income	6	941936	75562	299725	129058	112249	40464	81551	66334	34978	27095	41909	33014	0
Other Receipts	7	1169233	96041	250494	28516	215033	99231	188852	102133	101078	38563	112939	-63654	0
Total Receipts	8	344634348	6989247	114036202	28979275	76316954	37669802	31922586	15498799	10790524	8844319	4831365	8755275	0
Average Total Receipts	9	1150	118	542	2291	5437	18732	31513	64849	114793	260127	483136	1094409	•
Operating Costs/Operating Income (%)														
Cost of Operations	10	66.0	41.7	55.1	60.2	69.1	76.1	77.1	78.6	79.4	74.3	81.2	80.8	•
Salaries and Wages	11	7.1	8.7	8.7	9.6	6.8	5.3	4.5	4.6	5.3	5.3	5.1	4.8	•
Taxes Paid	12	2.3	2.3	2.8	3.0	2.3	1.8	2.0	1.8	1.5	1.8	0.7	1.0	•
Interest Paid	13	0.5	0.4	0.4	0.5	0.5	0.3	0.4	0.4	0.4	0.7	0.6	2.2	•
Depreciation	14	1.5	2.3	1.2	1.8	1.4	1.1	1.8	2.1	1.7	2.6	1.4	2.1	•
Amortization and Depletion	15	0.1	0.1	0.0	0.0	0.0	0.0	0.1	0.1	0.1	0.2	0.1	1.1	•
Pensions and Other Deferred Comp.	16	0.3	0.1	0.2	0.2	0.3	0.2	0.5	0.5	0.4	0.2	0.5	0.2	•
Employee Benefits	17	1.5	1.3	1.2	1.3	1.8	1.5	1.9	2.3	1.6	1.4	0.9	0.8	•
Advertising	18	0.4	0.8	0.7	0.5	0.3	0.4	0.2	0.2	0.1	0.1	0.1	0.1	•
Other Expenses	19	12.9	29.8	19.3	15.3	10.3	7.1	6.8	6.0	5.3	8.9	7.2	7.3	•
Officers' Compensation	20	4.0	6.1	6.1	4.8	3.5	2.6	1.9	1.5	1.5	1.4	0.8	0.7	•
Operating Margin	21	3.5	6.4	4.2	2.6	3.7	3.5	3.0	1.9	2.6	3.1	1.3	•	•
Operating Margin Before Officers' Comp.	22	7.4	12.4	10.3	7.4	7.2	6.1	4.8	3.4	4.2	4.5	2.1	•	•

Selected Average Balance Sheet ($ in Thousands)

Net Receivables 23	130	0	13	187	788	3251	6452	12673	24434	57910	88381	214184	•
Inventories 24	16	0	4	47	97	320	350	1246	1843	4459	12359	34178	•
Net Property, Plant and Equipment 25	80	0	25	160	447	1120	2667	6849	10758	34604	35147	171736	•
Total Assets 26	380	0	82	699	2080	7157	15029	33413	69015	158966	294214	765529	•
Notes and Loans Payable 27	121	0	50	226	612	1455	3187	7953	11623	26742	38113	464244	•
All Other Liabilities 28	127	0	25	185	643	2679	5270	12643	28039	63855	89252	247747	•
Net Worth 29	132	0	7	288	826	3023	6572	12816	29353	68370	166850	53538	•

Selected Financial Ratios (Times to 1)

Current Ratio 30	1.7	•	1.5	2.1	1.9	1.7	1.7	1.6	1.6	1.7	1.6	1.1	•
Quick Ratio 31	1.4	•	1.2	1.7	1.5	1.4	1.4	1.3	1.3	1.4	1.3	0.9	•
Net Sales to Working Capital 32	11.1	•	37.7	9.4	7.7	8.5	6.9	8.1	6.9	6.0	7.7	30.5	•
Coverage Ratio 33	9.7	24.9	11.9	7.6	10.1	13.9	10.3	8.0	10.4	6.9	10.2	1.3	•
Total Asset Turnover 34	3.0	•	6.6	3.3	2.6	2.6	2.1	1.9	1.6	1.6	1.6	1.4	•
Inventory Turnover 35	46.0	•	77.4	29.0	38.7	44.4	68.8	40.4	48.8	43.0	30.5	25.5	•
Receivables Turnover 36	9.1	•	44.1	11.7	7.2	6.0	5.1	5.1	•	4.8	4.5	•	•
Total Liabilities to Net Worth 37	1.9	•	10.5	1.4	1.5	1.4	1.3	1.6	1.4	1.3	0.8	13.3	•
Current Assets to Working Capital 38	2.4	•	3.2	1.9	2.1	2.5	2.4	2.7	2.7	2.5	2.6	9.7	•
Current Liabilities to Working Capital 39	1.4	•	2.2	0.9	1.1	1.5	1.4	1.7	1.7	1.5	1.6	8.7	•
Working Capital to Net Sales 40	0.1	•	0.0	0.1	0.1	0.1	0.1	0.1	0.1	0.2	0.1	0.0	•
Inventory to Working Capital 41	0.2	•	0.3	0.2	0.1	0.2	0.1	0.2	0.1	0.1	0.2	1.0	•
Total Receipts to Cash Flow 42	7.3	2.9	4.9	6.9	8.7	12.1	12.8	15.6	15.1	10.0	10.8	21.0	•
Cost of Goods to Cash Flow 43	4.8	1.2	2.7	4.2	6.0	9.2	9.9	12.2	12.0	7.4	8.8	16.9	•
Cash Flow to Total Debt 44	0.6	•	1.5	0.8	0.5	0.4	0.3	0.2	0.2	0.3	0.3	0.1	•

Selected Financial Factors (in Percentages)

Debt Ratio 45	65.1	•	91.3	58.8	60.3	57.8	56.3	61.6	57.5	57.0	43.3	93.0	•
Return on Total Assets 46	14.0	•	33.8	12.1	12.1	11.1	8.9	6.8	7.3	7.5	10.4	4.1	•
Return on Equity Before Income Taxes 47	36.1	•	355.8	25.5	27.4	24.3	18.3	15.6	15.4	14.8	16.5	14.9	•
Return on Equity After Income Taxes 48	34.9	•	352.3	25.0	26.7	23.5	17.0	14.2	14.0	13.3	15.2	4.7	•
Profit Margin (Before Income Tax) 49	4.2	9.0	4.7	3.2	4.2	3.9	3.9	3.1	4.0	3.9	6.0	0.7	•
Profit Margin (After Income Tax) 50	4.0	8.8	4.7	3.2	4.1	3.8	3.6	2.8	3.6	3.5	5.5	0.2	•

Table II

Corporations with Net Income

OTHER SPECIALTY TRADE CONTRACTORS

MONEY AMOUNTS AND SIZE OF ASSETS IN THOUSANDS OF DOLLARS

Item Description for Accounting Period 7/12 Through 6/13	Total	Zero Assets	Under 500	500 to 1,000	1,000 to 5,000	5,000 to 10,000	10,000 to 25,000	25,000 to 50,000	50,000 to 100,000	100,000 to 250,000	250,000 to 500,000	500,000 to 2,500,000	2,500,000 and over
Number of Enterprises 1	207200	37763	147536	8714	10632	1461	800	179	•	28	7	•	0

Revenues ($ in Thousands)

	Total	Zero Assets	Under 500	500 to 1,000	1,000 to 5,000	5,000 to 10,000	10,000 to 25,000	25,000 to 50,000	50,000 to 100,000	100,000 to 250,000	250,000 to 500,000	500,000 to 2,500,000	2,500,000 and over
Net Sales 2	269177658	5029807	86534725	21223250	63071488	28650905	26967390	12398404	•	7787634	2786853	•	0
Interest 3	47167	38	2338	1976	10998	4215	7647	4196	•	1773	6441	•	0
Rents 4	183337	3008	13075	5873	32242	3764	4590	1489	•	429	12	•	0
Royalties 5	42803	0	0	0	254	0	1351	3759	•	2	33715	•	0
Other Portfolio Income 6	789384	59488	264700	92878	85859	30627	68719	60196	•	26507	38856	•	0
Other Receipts 7	998453	58828	152265	40876	179058	73414	166474	86099	•	30926	98640	•	0
Total Receipts 8	271238802	5151169	86967103	21364853	63379899	28762925	27216171	12554143	•	7847271	2964517	•	0
Average Total Receipts 9	1309	136	589	2452	5961	19687	34020	70135	•	280260	423502	•	•

Operating Costs/Operating Income (%)

	Total	Zero Assets	Under 500	500 to 1,000	1,000 to 5,000	5,000 to 10,000	10,000 to 25,000	25,000 to 50,000	50,000 to 100,000	100,000 to 250,000	250,000 to 500,000	500,000 to 2,500,000	2,500,000 and over
Cost of Operations 10	64.2	39.1	52.1	57.1	67.7	74.6	76.1	77.7	•	74.5	74.5	•	•
Salaries and Wages 11	7.1	8.4	8.7	10.5	6.6	5.6	4.4	4.3	•	5.1	7.0	•	•
Taxes Paid 12	2.2	2.3	2.7	2.9	2.1	1.6	1.9	1.8	•	1.6	0.9	•	•
Interest Paid 13	0.4	0.2	0.4	0.5	0.4	0.3	0.3	0.4	•	0.3	0.5	•	•
Depreciation 14	1.3	1.2	1.0	1.4	1.3	1.0	1.6	2.0	•	2.3	1.4	•	•
Amortization and Depletion 15	0.1	0.1	0.0	0.0	0.0	0.0	0.0	0.1	•	0.1	0.1	•	•
Pensions and Other Deferred Comp. 16	0.3	0.1	0.2	0.3	0.4	0.3	0.5	0.5	•	0.3	0.8	•	•
Employee Benefits 17	1.4	1.0	1.1	1.5	1.6	1.4	1.9	2.4	•	1.4	1.4	•	•
Advertising 18	0.4	0.6	0.6	0.5	0.3	0.3	0.2	0.2	•	0.1	0.2	•	•
Other Expenses 19	12.5	26.2	19.5	14.4	10.2	6.5	6.3	5.5	•	8.8	7.5	•	•
Officers' Compensation 20	3.9	6.3	6.0	4.6	3.6	2.8	1.9	1.4	•	1.3	0.9	•	•
Operating Margin 21	6.2	14.7	7.7	6.4	5.8	5.8	4.7	3.7	•	4.3	4.7	•	•
Operating Margin Before Officers' Comp. 22	10.1	20.9	13.7	11.0	9.4	8.6	6.6	5.2	•	5.6	5.6	•	•

Selected Average Balance Sheet ($ in Thousands)

Net Receivables 23	145	0	12	185	815	3301	6839	12997	•	60859	67540	•	•
Inventories 24	16	0	4	52	93	259	348	1131	•	4373	12267	•	•
Net Property, Plant and Equipment 25	84	0	24	147	433	1127	2594	6848	•	34048	34700	•	•
Total Assets 26	414	0	83	704	2089	7112	15361	33412	•	164827	307498	•	•
Notes and Loans Payable 27	110	0	43	230	487	1173	2905	7006	•	18241	35704	•	•
All Other Liabilities 28	134	0	21	187	639	2529	5393	12641	•	68594	63162	•	•
Net Worth 29	170	0	19	287	963	3409	7063	13765	•	77993	208632	•	•

Selected Financial Ratios (Times to 1)

Current Ratio 30	1.8	•	1.7	2.4	2.1	1.9	1.8	1.6	•	1.7	1.7	•	•
Quick Ratio 31	1.5	•	1.4	2.0	1.7	1.6	1.5	1.3	•	1.4	1.3	•	•
Net Sales to Working Capital 32	10.3	•	30.3	8.7	7.6	7.4	6.9	8.2	•	5.8	7.6	•	•
Coverage Ratio 33	18.4	106.1	22.4	16.1	17.0	23.7	17.1	13.3	•	17.4	26.2	•	•
Total Asset Turnover 34	3.1	•	7.1	3.5	2.8	2.8	2.2	2.1	•	1.7	1.3	•	•
Inventory Turnover 35	53.3	•	84.0	26.6	43.2	56.5	73.7	47.6	•	47.4	24.2	•	•
Receivables Turnover 36	10.0	•	50.0	14.1	8.3	6.6	5.5	5.5	•	5.7	4.3	•	•
Total Liabilities to Net Worth 37	1.4	•	3.4	1.5	1.2	1.1	1.2	1.4	•	1.1	0.5	•	•
Current Assets to Working Capital 38	2.2	•	2.4	1.7	1.9	2.1	2.3	2.7	•	2.4	2.5	•	•
Current Liabilities to Working Capital 39	1.2	•	1.4	0.7	0.9	1.1	1.3	1.7	•	1.4	1.5	•	•
Working Capital to Net Sales 40	0.1	•	0.0	0.1	0.1	0.1	0.1	0.1	•	0.2	0.1	•	•
Inventory to Working Capital 41	0.1	•	0.2	0.2	0.1	0.1	0.1	0.2	•	0.1	0.2	•	•
Total Receipts to Cash Flow 42	6.2	2.5	4.2	5.7	7.4	10.0	10.8	12.7	•	9.0	6.4	•	•
Cost of Goods to Cash Flow 43	4.0	1.0	2.2	3.3	5.0	7.5	8.2	9.8	•	6.7	4.8	•	•
Cash Flow to Total Debt 44	0.9	•	2.2	1.0	0.7	0.5	0.4	0.3	•	0.4	0.6	•	•

Selected Financial Factors (in Percentages)

Debt Ratio 45	58.8	•	77.4	59.3	53.9	52.1	54.0	58.8	•	52.7	32.2	•	•
Return on Total Assets 46	23.1	•	60.7	26.1	18.9	17.8	13.1	11.2	•	9.0	15.9	•	•
Return on Equity Before Income Taxes 47	53.1	•	256.7	60.0	38.6	35.6	26.8	25.0	•	17.9	22.6	•	•
Return on Equity After Income Taxes 48	51.8	•	254.8	59.2	37.9	34.7	25.2	23.3	•	16.3	21.0	•	•
Profit Margin (Before Income Tax) 49	7.0	17.1	8.2	7.1	6.3	6.2	5.6	5.0	•	5.0	11.8	•	•
Profit Margin (After Income Tax) 50	6.8	16.9	8.1	7.0	6.2	6.0	5.3	4.6	•	4.6	11.0	•	•

Table I

Corporations with and without Net Income

ANIMAL FOOD AND GRAIN AND OILSEED MILLING

MONEY AMOUNTS AND SIZE OF ASSETS IN THOUSANDS OF DOLLARS

Item Description for Accounting Period 7/12 Through 6/13	Total	Zero Assets	Under 500	500 to 1,000	1,000 to 5,000	5,000 to 10,000	10,000 to 25,000	25,000 to 50,000	50,000 to 100,000	100,000 to 250,000	250,000 to 500,000	500,000 to 2,500,000	2,500,000 and over
Number of Enterprises **1**	1794	12	1081	60	231	171	98	55	32	28	12	8	5

Revenues ($ in Thousands)

Net Sales **2**	150546067	433232	173679	17090	2119323	3260597	4181046	4133846	5522081	10307252	4663289	9425887	106308745
Interest **3**	142462	2	162	0	704	344	1828	1431	1192	3157	16696	6196	110750
Rents **4**	132719	0	0	0	425	378	173	748	161	996	1057	160	128621
Royalties **5**	530610	7	0	0	0	0	0	0	0	246	3005	4145	523208
Other Portfolio Income **6**	452414	35765	0	0	850	1643	27874	14473	2481	11222	60806	37513	259789
Other Receipts **7**	1311899	11110	27365	111	5067	11513	21664	90004	46574	51224	22110	57002	968152
Total Receipts **8**	153116171	480116	201206	17201	2126369	3274475	4232585	4240502	5572489	10374097	4766963	9530903	108299265
Average Total Receipts **9**	85349	40010	186	287	9205	19149	43190	77100	174140	370503	397247	1191363	21659853

Operating Costs/Operating Income (%)

Cost of Operations **10**	82.0	84.9	74.3	92.1	85.3	83.6	85.7	85.0	82.8	85.2	75.9	79.5	81.7
Salaries and Wages **11**	2.5	5.4	3.7	19.3	2.5	5.4	3.2	3.1	4.0	2.3	4.6	3.2	2.2
Taxes Paid **12**	0.5	0.4	6.9	3.8	0.8	1.0	0.5	0.7	0.7	0.7	1.1	0.6	0.4
Interest Paid **13**	1.3	1.6	0.5	5.9	0.5	0.5	0.4	0.3	0.4	0.5	1.9	3.3	1.3
Depreciation **14**	1.8	2.7	2.7	12.6	1.5	1.1	1.1	1.7	1.5	1.6	3.0	3.8	1.7
Amortization and Depletion **15**	0.2	0.7	•	0.0	•	0.0	0.0	0.1	0.1	0.1	0.7	0.9	0.1
Pensions and Other Deferred Comp. **16**	0.4	0.4	•	•	0.1	0.0	0.1	0.3	0.3	0.2	0.3	0.7	0.4
Employee Benefits **17**	0.5	1.2	0.7	0.8	0.5	0.7	0.4	0.7	0.8	0.6	0.6	0.8	0.5
Advertising **18**	5.3	1.0	0.1	•	0.1	0.7	0.4	1.1	0.6	0.6	0.6	0.7	7.3
Other Expenses **19**	3.9	3.9	13.7	76.2	6.8	4.8	4.9	5.0	5.3	3.9	7.5	5.5	3.4
Officers' Compensation **20**	0.3	0.1	9.0	•	1.7	0.6	0.8	0.9	0.5	0.5	1.5	0.2	0.1
Operating Margin **21**	1.2	•	•	•	0.3	1.4	2.5	1.1	2.9	3.7	2.5	0.8	0.9
Operating Margin Before Officers' Comp. **22**	1.5	•	•	•	2.0	2.0	3.3	2.0	3.4	4.2	4.0	1.0	1.0

Selected Average Balance Sheet ($ in Thousands)

Net Receivables 23	3684	0	3	2	802	1832	3975	6990	15553	28469	55088	100543	514454
Inventories 24	7567	0	10	27	1054	1647	3000	7755	18834	35494	40741	140037	1822575
Net Property, Plant and Equipment 25	11820	0	14	460	635	1690	4412	8457	20825	48026	88213	355198	2783429
Total Assets 26	58658	0	39	546	2505	6057	14252	35592	69313	160619	345707	985068	16288794
Notes and Loans Payable 27	25293	0	545	5973	672	2475	3854	6548	16630	42064	160523	570096	6982716
All Other Liabilities 28	14705	0	26	917	1057	2002	4626	11729	21002	36551	84018	265246	3957518
Net Worth 29	18659	0	-533	-6344	776	1580	5772	17316	31681	82004	101166	149727	5348560

Selected Financial Ratios (Times to 1)

Current Ratio 30	1.2	•	0.7	0.0	1.5	1.6	1.4	1.7	1.9	1.9	1.8	2.0	1.1
Quick Ratio 31	0.4	•	0.3	0.0	0.9	0.8	0.8	0.9	0.9	0.9	1.0	0.8	0.3
Net Sales to Working Capital 32	28.0	•	•	•	15.4	11.9	15.8	8.7	8.8	10.0	7.8	8.0	89.7
Coverage Ratio 33	3.6	6.3	8.5	•	2.3	4.8	9.3	12.7	9.7	9.5	4.1	1.6	3.5
Total Asset Turnover 34	1.4	•	4.1	0.5	3.7	3.1	3.0	2.1	2.5	2.3	1.1	1.2	1.3
Inventory Turnover 35	9.1	•	12.0	9.8	7.4	9.7	12.2	8.2	7.6	8.8	7.2	6.7	9.5
Receivables Turnover 36	20.1	•	52.3	356.0	8.9	11.1	12.4	13.3	10.2	12.4	8.9	11.4	29.8
Total Liabilities to Net Worth 37	2.1	•	•	•	2.2	2.8	1.5	1.1	1.2	1.0	2.4	5.6	2.0
Current Assets to Working Capital 38	5.9	•	•	•	3.0	2.6	3.4	2.4	2.1	2.1	2.3	2.0	17.8
Current Liabilities to Working Capital 39	4.9	•	•	•	2.0	1.6	2.4	1.4	1.1	1.1	1.3	1.0	16.8
Working Capital to Net Sales 40	0.0	•	•	•	0.1	0.1	0.1	0.1	0.1	0.1	0.1	0.1	0.0
Inventory to Working Capital 41	2.6	•	•	•	1.2	1.3	1.3	1.1	1.0	1.0	0.9	1.0	8.1
Total Receipts to Cash Flow 42	17.7	27.3	6.0	•	16.2	17.7	12.9	12.9	12.5	13.8	10.1	17.1	20.1
Cost of Goods to Cash Flow 43	14.5	23.2	4.4	•	13.8	14.8	11.1	11.0	10.3	11.7	7.6	13.6	16.4
Cash Flow to Total Debt 44	0.1	•	0.0	•	0.3	0.2	0.4	0.3	0.4	0.3	0.2	0.1	0.1

Selected Financial Factors (in Percentages)

Debt Ratio 45	68.2	•	1475.3	1261.7	69.0	73.9	59.5	51.4	54.3	48.9	70.7	84.8	67.2
Return on Total Assets 46	6.5	•	19.1	•	3.9	7.3	12.4	8.3	10.6	11.2	8.6	6.3	5.8
Return on Equity Before Income Taxes 47	14.7	•	•	4.9	7.1	22.0	27.2	15.8	20.8	19.7	22.3	15.8	12.7
Return on Equity After Income Taxes 48	10.3	•	•	4.9	5.5	20.8	26.5	14.4	19.3	15.6	14.5	13.6	8.2
Profit Margin (Before Income Tax) 49	3.3	8.6	4.1	•	0.6	1.8	3.7	3.6	3.8	4.4	5.8	2.0	3.2
Profit Margin (After Income Tax) 50	2.3	6.0	4.0	•	0.5	1.7	3.6	3.3	3.6	3.5	3.8	1.7	2.1

Table II
Corporations with Net Income

ANIMAL FOOD AND GRAIN AND OILSEED MILLING

MONEY AMOUNTS AND SIZE OF ASSETS IN THOUSANDS OF DOLLARS

Item Description for Accounting Period 7/12 Through 6/13	Total	Zero Assets	Under 500	500 to 1,000	1,000 to 5,000	5,000 to 10,000	10,000 to 25,000	25,000 to 50,000	50,000 to 100,000	100,000 to 250,000	250,000 to 500,000	500,000 to 2,500,000	2,500,000 and over
Number of Enterprises **1**	781	12	305	0	153	111	85	•	•	24	•	5	5
Revenues ($ in Thousands)													
Net Sales **2**	141953733	433232	18746	0	1020954	1998723	3872423	•	•	8973845	•	7402733	106308745
Interest **3**	135665	2	0	0	615	205	1827	•	•	1312	•	2792	110750
Rents **4**	131680	0	0	0	425	291	173	•	•	398	•	160	128621
Royalties **5**	530610	7	0	0	0	0	0	•	•	246	•	4145	523208
Other Portfolio Income **6**	444001	35765	0	0	621	1141	27874	•	•	8942	•	35686	259789
Other Receipts **7**	1274004	11110	27360	0	620	8848	13355	•	•	42915	•	51319	968152
Total Receipts **8**	144469693	480116	46106	0	1023235	2009208	3915652	•	•	9027658	•	7496835	108299265
Average Total Receipts **9**	184980	40010	151	•	6688	18101	46066	•	•	376152	•	1499367	21659853
Operating Costs/Operating Income (%)													
Cost of Operations **10**	81.6	84.9	87.7	•	79.3	79.1	85.4	•	•	84.4	•	77.0	81.7
Salaries and Wages **11**	2.5	5.4	1.0	•	3.0	6.5	3.2	•	•	2.2	•	3.8	2.2
Taxes Paid **12**	0.5	0.4	1.0	•	1.2	0.9	0.5	•	•	0.7	•	0.7	0.4
Interest Paid **13**	1.3	1.6	3.4	•	0.5	0.6	0.4	•	•	0.5	•	3.4	1.3
Depreciation **14**	1.8	2.7	0.2	•	1.5	0.6	0.8	•	•	1.5	•	3.5	1.7
Amortization and Depletion **15**	0.2	0.7	•	•	•	0.0	0.0	•	•	0.1	•	1.1	0.1
Pensions and Other Deferred Comp. **16**	0.4	0.4	•	•	0.1	0.0	0.1	•	•	0.2	•	0.8	0.4
Employee Benefits **17**	0.5	1.2	0.1	•	0.6	0.9	0.4	•	•	0.7	•	0.8	0.5
Advertising **18**	5.6	1.0	•	•	0.2	0.8	0.4	•	•	0.7	•	0.8	7.3
Other Expenses **19**	3.8	3.9	3.4	•	8.6	5.9	4.5	•	•	3.8	•	6.3	3.4
Officers' Compensation **20**	0.3	0.1	•	•	3.0	0.7	0.8	•	•	0.5	•	0.2	0.1
Operating Margin **21**	1.6	•	3.3	•	2.2	3.9	3.4	•	•	4.6	•	1.6	0.9
Operating Margin Before Officers' Comp. **22**	1.8	•	3.3	•	5.2	4.6	4.2	•	•	5.1	•	1.9	1.0

Selected Average Balance Sheet ($ in Thousands)

Net Receivables 23	7534	0	0	•	666	2303	4152	•	•	29458	•	125110	514454
Inventories 24	15675	0	0	•	868	1685	2603	•	•	33822	•	188764	1822575
Net Property, Plant and Equipment 25	25053	0	0	•	428	1140	4136	•	•	48208	•	430700	2783429
Total Assets 26	128729	0	6	•	2085	5957	14233	•	•	163382	•	1249881	16288794
Notes and Loans Payable 27	54561	0	0	•	545	2427	3465	•	•	42038	•	785131	6982716
All Other Liabilities 28	31960	0	1	•	982	1662	4409	•	•	34761	•	359965	3957518
Net Worth 29	42208	0	5	•	558	1868	6358	•	•	86584	•	104784	5348560

Selected Financial Ratios (Times to 1)

Current Ratio 30	1.2	•	8.0	•	1.5	2.0	1.7	•	•	2.1	•	1.8	1.1
Quick Ratio 31	0.4	•	7.3	•	0.9	1.1	1.0	•	•	1.0	•	0.7	0.3
Net Sales to Working Capital 32	27.9	•	13.3	•	12.2	7.9	12.2	•	•	9.3	•	9.2	89.7
Coverage Ratio 33	3.9	6.3	45.5	•	6.2	8.6	11.4	•	•	11.1	•	1.9	3.5
Total Asset Turnover 34	1.4	•	10.7	•	3.2	3.0	3.2	•	•	2.3	•	1.2	1.3
Inventory Turnover 35	9.5	•	•	•	6.1	8.5	15.0	•	•	9.3	•	6.0	9.5
Receivables Turnover 36	22.0	•	•	•	6.7	7.9	13.6	•	•	12.5	•	•	29.8
Total Liabilities to Net Worth 37	2.0	•	0.2	•	2.7	2.2	1.2	•	•	0.9	•	10.9	2.0
Current Assets to Working Capital 38	5.8	•	1.1	•	2.9	2.0	2.5	•	•	2.0	•	2.2	17.8
Current Liabilities to Working Capital 39	4.8	•	0.1	•	1.9	1.0	1.5	•	•	1.0	•	1.2	16.8
Working Capital to Net Sales 40	0.0	•	0.1	•	0.1	0.1	0.1	•	•	0.1	•	0.1	0.0
Inventory to Working Capital 41	2.6	•	•	•	1.0	0.9	0.9	•	•	0.8	•	1.2	8.1
Total Receipts to Cash Flow 42	16.9	27.3	0.7	•	11.1	10.6	12.2	•	•	12.4	•	13.4	20.1
Cost of Goods to Cash Flow 43	13.8	23.2	0.6	•	8.8	8.4	10.5	•	•	10.4	•	10.3	16.4
Cash Flow to Total Debt 44	0.1	•	106.3	•	0.4	0.4	0.5	•	•	0.4	•	0.1	0.1

Selected Financial Factors (in Percentages)

Debt Ratio 45	67.2	•	15.4	•	73.2	68.6	55.3	•	•	47.0	•	91.6	67.2
Return on Total Assets 46	7.0	•	1639.8	•	9.2	15.2	15.8	•	•	13.1	•	7.7	5.8
Return on Equity Before Income Taxes 47	15.8	•	1895.0	•	28.9	42.8	32.2	•	•	22.5	•	43.4	12.7
Return on Equity After Income Taxes 48	11.4	•	1884.8	•	25.5	41.3	31.4	•	•	17.9	•	38.4	8.2
Profit Margin (Before Income Tax) 49	3.7	8.6	149.2	•	2.4	4.4	4.5	•	•	5.2	•	3.1	3.2
Profit Margin (After Income Tax) 50	2.6	6.0	148.4	•	2.1	4.3	4.4	•	•	4.2	•	2.7	2.1

Table I

Corporations with and without Net Income

SUGAR AND CONFECTIONERY PRODUCT

MONEY AMOUNTS AND SIZE OF ASSETS IN THOUSANDS OF DOLLARS

Item Description for Accounting Period 7/12 Through 6/13	Total	Zero Assets	Under 500	500 to 1,000	1,000 to 5,000	5,000 to 10,000	10,000 to 25,000	25,000 to 50,000	50,000 to 100,000	100,000 to 250,000	250,000 to 500,000	500,000 to 2,500,000	2,500,000 and over
Number of Enterprises 1	1242	0	884	145	103	35	21	21	14	7	0	8	3
Revenues ($ in Thousands)													
Net Sales 2	66123442	0	1218880	263104	547231	691229	781069	1979399	2209283	2168734	0	8009325	48255187
Interest 3	111481	0	0	0	29	193	201	32	69	127	0	19841	90990
Rents 4	28189	0	0	0	0	273	66	35	0	5479	0	16601	5734
Royalties 5	334342	0	0	0	0	0	11840	100	10	3873	0	4914	313605
Other Portfolio Income 6	2236804	0	0	240	0	0	1961	2379	4734	321	0	11306	2215862
Other Receipts 7	322330	0	961	0	5809	1362	314	8621	2818	2276	0	20941	279230
Total Receipts 8	69156588	0	1219841	263344	553069	693057	795451	1990566	2216914	2180810	0	8082928	51160608
Average Total Receipts 9	55682	•	1380	1816	5370	19802	37879	94789	158351	311544	•	1010366	17053536
Operating Costs/Operating Income (%)													
Cost of Operations 10	53.8	•	49.9	70.1	72.1	66.4	74.8	80.5	70.2	59.9	•	73.1	47.7
Salaries and Wages 11	5.6	•	17.4	8.9	6.2	8.4	6.2	1.7	6.5	7.5	•	2.2	5.8
Taxes Paid 12	1.1	•	5.1	2.7	2.1	2.2	1.1	0.7	1.2	1.6	•	0.9	1.0
Interest Paid 13	2.6	•	0.2	0.8	2.6	0.6	0.5	0.7	0.9	2.5	•	1.0	3.2
Depreciation 14	2.5	•	0.3	0.9	2.0	3.7	1.1	2.0	2.0	3.5	•	2.9	2.6
Amortization and Depletion 15	1.1	•	•	•	0.0	0.0	0.2	0.5	0.3	0.6	•	0.7	1.3
Pensions and Other Deferred Comp. 16	0.6	•	•	1.7	0.7	0.4	0.1	0.1	0.4	0.3	•	0.5	0.7
Employee Benefits 17	1.2	•	•	0.2	0.9	0.8	1.4	0.5	1.7	0.9	•	1.1	1.3
Advertising 18	6.8	•	0.9	0.3	0.0	2.1	0.9	0.5	3.3	5.5	•	0.4	8.7
Other Expenses 19	18.7	•	16.0	9.8	10.6	12.2	10.0	6.4	8.6	12.9	•	9.4	21.8
Officers' Compensation 20	1.0	•	9.1	3.2	5.1	2.5	1.4	2.6	1.2	1.1	•	1.1	0.6
Operating Margin 21	5.0	•	1.2	1.4	•	0.6	2.2	3.9	3.7	3.6	•	6.8	5.2
Operating Margin Before Officers' Comp. 22	6.0	•	10.2	4.5	2.7	3.1	3.6	6.5	4.9	4.7	•	8.0	5.8

Selected Average Balance Sheet ($ in Thousands)

Net Receivables 23	4732	•	45	251	769	1448	3448	5649	15963	41351	•	69970	1469226
Inventories 24	4639	•	71	389	642	1400	6472	7284	20523	37934	•	169147	1071572
Net Property, Plant and Equipment 25	10144	•	18	125	926	2719	3298	10198	19390	86750	•	267903	3022870
Total Assets 26	74780	•	143	820	2817	7873	14597	35506	68967	231599	•	1009247	26784358
Notes and Loans Payable 27	26667	•	8	547	1906	3196	4457	7537	26065	63617	•	236080	9924800
All Other Liabilities 28	21449	•	104	71	723	1253	3730	8245	19221	97036	•	282774	7652536
Net Worth 29	26664	•	30	202	188	3425	6410	19723	23682	70946	•	490393	9207023

Selected Financial Ratios (Times to 1)

Current Ratio 30	0.7	•	1.2	5.8	1.7	2.4	3.0	2.4	2.1	1.2	•	1.4	0.6
Quick Ratio 31	0.4	•	0.5	2.7	1.0	1.3	1.5	1.3	0.9	0.7	•	0.4	0.3
Net Sales to Working Capital 32	•	•	85.9	3.2	7.4	8.2	5.5	9.0	7.0	14.9	•	10.6	•
Coverage Ratio 33	5.2	•	7.5	2.7	0.5	2.4	8.5	7.7	5.6	4.2	•	8.4	5.1
Total Asset Turnover 34	0.7	•	9.7	2.2	1.9	2.5	2.5	2.7	2.3	1.3	•	1.0	0.6
Inventory Turnover 35	6.2	•	9.7	3.3	6.0	9.4	4.3	10.4	5.4	4.9	•	4.3	7.2
Receivables Turnover 36	11.0	•	•	6.9	•	14.0	10.3	15.5	10.6	9.4	•	14.9	10.6
Total Liabilities to Net Worth 37	1.8	•	3.7	3.1	14.0	1.3	1.3	0.8	1.9	2.3	•	1.1	1.9
Current Assets to Working Capital 38	•	•	7.6	1.2	2.4	1.7	1.5	1.7	1.9	5.7	•	3.8	•
Current Liabilities to Working Capital 39	•	•	6.6	0.2	1.4	0.7	0.5	0.7	0.9	4.7	•	2.8	•
Working Capital to Net Sales 40	•	•	0.0	0.3	0.1	0.1	0.2	0.1	0.1	0.1	•	0.1	•
Inventory to Working Capital 41	•	•	4.4	0.6	0.9	0.7	0.7	0.8	0.9	2.4	•	1.9	•
Total Receipts to Cash Flow 42	3.8	•	8.3	15.5	11.6	11.7	8.6	10.1	9.0	6.6	•	6.8	3.2
Cost of Goods to Cash Flow 43	2.0	•	4.1	10.9	8.4	7.8	6.4	8.1	6.3	4.0	•	5.0	1.5
Cash Flow to Total Debt 44	0.3	•	1.5	0.2	0.2	0.4	0.5	0.6	0.4	0.3	•	0.3	0.3

Selected Financial Factors (in Percentages)

Debt Ratio 45	64.3	•	78.7	75.3	93.3	56.5	56.1	44.5	65.7	69.4	•	51.4	65.6
Return on Total Assets 46	9.8	•	13.8	5.1	2.4	3.8	11.7	13.9	11.2	14.2	•	8.7	9.8
Return on Equity Before Income Taxes 47	22.1	•	56.3	13.0	•	5.0	23.5	21.8	26.7	35.2	•	15.8	22.9
Return on Equity After Income Taxes 48	14.6	•	56.3	10.2	•	0.8	18.2	20.5	23.8	28.2	•	10.0	14.9
Profit Margin (Before Income Tax) 49	11.1	•	1.2	1.4	•	0.9	4.0	4.6	4.0	8.1	•	7.7	13.1
Profit Margin (After Income Tax) 50	7.3	•	1.2	1.1	•	0.1	3.1	4.3	3.6	6.5	•	4.9	8.5

Table II
Corporations with Net Income

SUGAR AND CONFECTIONERY PRODUCT

MONEY AMOUNTS AND SIZE OF ASSETS IN THOUSANDS OF DOLLARS

Item Description for Accounting Period 7/12 Through 6/13	Total	Zero Assets	Under 500	500 to 1,000	1,000 to 5,000	5,000 to 10,000	10,000 to 25,000	25,000 to 50,000	50,000 to 100,000	100,000 to 250,000	250,000 to 500,000	500,000 to 2,500,000	2,500,000 and over
Number of Enterprises **1**	1072	0	827	87	70	28	15	•	•	•	0	•	3

Revenues ($ in Thousands)

Net Sales **2**	63501564	0	1127383	174625	459961	551015	608319	•	•	•	0	•	48255187
Interest **3**	100333	0	0	0	0	193	103	•	•	•	0	•	90990
Rents **4**	28072	0	0	0	0	273	0	•	•	•	0	•	5734
Royalties **5**	328838	0	0	0	0	0	11840	•	•	•	0	•	313605
Other Portfolio Income **6**	2236720	0	0	240	0	0	1877	•	•	•	0	•	2215862
Other Receipts **7**	308512	0	0	0	0	507	163	•	•	•	0	•	279230
Total Receipts **8**	66504039	0	1127383	174865	459961	551988	622302	•	•	•	0	•	51160608
Average Total Receipts **9**	62037	•	1363	2010	6571	19714	41487	•	•	•	•	•	17053536

Operating Costs/Operating Income (%)

Cost of Operations **10**	53.5	•	47.9	61.6	71.6	70.1	72.7	•	•	•	•	•	47.7
Salaries and Wages **11**	5.5	•	17.7	13.4	5.7	6.0	7.3	•	•	•	•	•	5.8
Taxes Paid **12**	1.1	•	5.4	3.9	2.0	1.9	1.3	•	•	•	•	•	1.0
Interest Paid **13**	2.6	•	0.1	1.3	1.8	0.7	0.5	•	•	•	•	•	3.2
Depreciation **14**	2.5	•	0.0	1.3	2.1	3.0	1.0	•	•	•	•	•	2.6
Amortization and Depletion **15**	1.1	•	•	•	0.0	0.0	0.1	•	•	•	•	•	1.3
Pensions and Other Deferred Comp. **16**	0.6	•	•	•	•	0.5	0.0	•	•	•	•	•	0.7
Employee Benefits **17**	1.2	•	•	0.3	0.6	0.7	1.5	•	•	•	•	•	1.3
Advertising **18**	6.8	•	0.9	0.5	•	1.0	1.1	•	•	•	•	•	8.7
Other Expenses **19**	18.7	•	16.4	14.2	9.4	8.2	9.9	•	•	•	•	•	21.8
Officers' Compensation **20**	0.9	•	9.4	1.5	1.6	2.9	1.2	•	•	•	•	•	0.6
Operating Margin **21**	5.5	•	2.1	2.0	5.1	4.9	3.5	•	•	•	•	•	5.2
Operating Margin Before Officers' Comp. **22**	6.4	•	11.5	3.5	6.7	7.8	4.7	•	•	•	•	•	5.8

Selected Average Balance Sheet ($ in Thousands)

Net Receivables 23	5150	•	41	97	1070	1732	3618	•	•	•	•	•	1469226
Inventories 24	4729	•	51	581	876	1102	6190	•	•	•	•	•	1071572
Net Property, Plant and Equipment 25	11237	•	3	208	1230	2310	3290	•	•	•	•	•	3022870
Total Assets 26	84176	•	119	911	3537	7881	15311	•	•	•	•	•	26784358
Notes and Loans Payable 27	29877	•	0	797	2237	3335	3918	•	•	•	•	•	9924800
All Other Liabilities 28	24140	•	94	58	715	1004	3656	•	•	•	•	•	7652536
Net Worth 29	30159	•	24	57	585	3542	7737	•	•	•	•	•	9207023

Selected Financial Ratios (Times to 1)

Current Ratio 30	0.7	•	1.2	5.0	2.3	3.3	3.6	•	•	•	•	•	0.6
Quick Ratio 31	0.4	•	0.5	1.6	1.3	2.0	1.8	•	•	•	•	•	0.3
Net Sales to Working Capital 32	•	•	65.2	3.6	5.6	6.5	5.1	•	•	•	•	•	•
Coverage Ratio 33	5.6	•	15.2	2.7	3.8	8.0	13.4	•	•	•	•	•	5.1
Total Asset Turnover 34	0.7	•	11.5	2.2	1.9	2.5	2.6	•	•	•	•	•	0.6
Inventory Turnover 35	6.7	•	12.9	2.1	5.4	12.5	4.8	•	•	•	•	•	7.2
Receivables Turnover 36	11.2	•	37.8	7.2	6.6	15.3	10.0	•	•	•	•	•	10.6
Total Liabilities to Net Worth 37	1.8	•	3.9	15.1	5.0	1.2	1.0	•	•	•	•	•	1.9
Current Assets to Working Capital 38	•	•	5.5	1.2	1.8	1.4	1.4	•	•	•	•	•	•
Current Liabilities to Working Capital 39	•	•	4.5	0.2	0.8	0.4	0.4	•	•	•	•	•	•
Working Capital to Net Sales 40	•	•	0.0	0.3	0.2	0.2	0.2	•	•	•	•	•	•
Inventory to Working Capital 41	•	•	3.2	0.8	0.7	0.5	0.6	•	•	•	•	•	•
Total Receipts to Cash Flow 42	3.7	•	7.7	10.9	6.9	9.6	7.3	•	•	•	•	•	3.2
Cost of Goods to Cash Flow 43	2.0	•	3.7	6.7	5.0	6.8	5.3	•	•	•	•	•	1.5
Cash Flow to Total Debt 44	0.3	•	1.9	0.2	0.3	0.5	0.7	•	•	•	•	•	0.3

Selected Financial Factors (in Percentages)

Debt Ratio 45	64.2	•	79.4	93.8	83.5	55.1	49.5	•	•	•	•	•	65.6
Return on Total Assets 46	10.1	•	25.9	7.6	12.9	14.6	16.7	•	•	•	•	•	9.8
Return on Equity Before Income Taxes 47	23.1	•	117.5	77.4	57.5	28.4	30.5	•	•	•	•	•	22.9
Return on Equity After Income Taxes 48	15.4	•	117.5	60.6	57.5	23.3	24.4	•	•	•	•	•	14.9
Profit Margin (Before Income Tax) 49	11.8	•	2.1	2.2	5.1	5.1	5.8	•	•	•	•	•	13.1
Profit Margin (After Income Tax) 50	7.9	•	2.1	1.7	5.1	4.2	4.7	•	•	•	•	•	8.5

Table I

Corporations with and without Net Income

FRUIT AND VEGETABLE PRESERVING AND SPECIALTY FOOD

MONEY AMOUNTS AND SIZE OF ASSETS IN THOUSANDS OF DOLLARS

Item Description for Accounting Period 7/12 Through 6/13	Total	Zero Assets	Under 500	500 to 1,000	1,000 to 5,000	5,000 to 10,000	10,000 to 25,000	25,000 to 50,000	50,000 to 100,000	100,000 to 250,000	250,000 to 500,000	500,000 to 2,500,000	2,500,000 and over
Number of Enterprises 1	931	80	414	0	177	21	102	60	29	25	8	8	6

Revenues ($ in Thousands)

	Total	Zero Assets	Under 500	500 to 1,000	1,000 to 5,000	5,000 to 10,000	10,000 to 25,000	25,000 to 50,000	50,000 to 100,000	100,000 to 250,000	250,000 to 500,000	500,000 to 2,500,000	2,500,000 and over
Net Sales 2	55577606	950533	2466	0	1087200	567556	2899042	3594642	3117423	6705977	4135706	10815630	21701431
Interest 3	127399	7995	6	0	740	495	380	974	1918	1043	525	2834	110487
Rents 4	17162	639	0	0	1678	0	177	11	3092	2871	982	1765	5947
Royalties 5	297012	18227	0	0	0	0	0	0	0	0	0	0	278786
Other Portfolio Income 6	125145	55	65	0	10170	356	532	3146	19412	1930	4314	1876	83290
Other Receipts 7	1368478	252629	67	0	1087	644	44031	22420	54872	33578	10251	53618	895278
Total Receipts 8	57512802	1230078	2604	0	1100875	569051	2944162	3621193	3196717	6745399	4151778	10875723	23075219
Average Total Receipts 9	61775	15376	6	•	6220	27098	28864	60353	110232	269816	518972	1359465	3845870

Operating Costs/Operating Income (%)

	Total	Zero Assets	Under 500	500 to 1,000	1,000 to 5,000	5,000 to 10,000	10,000 to 25,000	25,000 to 50,000	50,000 to 100,000	100,000 to 250,000	250,000 to 500,000	500,000 to 2,500,000	2,500,000 and over
Cost of Operations 10	69.9	81.3	53.1	•	84.3	82.2	73.3	74.3	80.9	78.5	76.3	63.0	65.1
Salaries and Wages 11	5.0	25.1	18.8	•	2.6	1.4	4.9	3.8	2.5	3.4	2.4	6.9	5.0
Taxes Paid 12	1.1	1.3	32.8	•	2.1	1.2	1.5	1.1	1.0	1.2	0.9	1.6	0.8
Interest Paid 13	2.4	2.7	1.8	•	1.3	1.2	0.7	0.8	1.4	0.7	2.5	1.7	3.9
Depreciation 14	2.6	0.8	4.1	•	1.2	1.6	2.0	2.2	2.4	2.5	2.1	2.4	3.1
Amortization and Depletion 15	0.9	0.7	0.1	•	0.0	0.0	0.1	0.1	0.4	0.1	0.7	1.3	1.5
Pensions and Other Deferred Comp. 16	0.5	0.2	•	•	•	0.0	0.3	0.2	0.2	0.2	0.1	0.3	0.8
Employee Benefits 17	1.2	0.8	0.8	•	0.4	0.2	1.3	0.9	1.0	0.9	0.9	2.2	1.0
Advertising 18	2.6	0.3	0.1	•	0.3	1.1	1.0	1.8	0.7	0.3	2.2	6.1	2.5
Other Expenses 19	10.6	9.6	919.9	•	5.8	2.7	9.1	9.0	7.1	7.9	8.4	11.1	12.9
Officers' Compensation 20	0.6	0.5	8.3	•	0.7	1.7	1.2	0.9	1.0	0.6	0.7	0.7	0.2
Operating Margin 21	2.7	•	•	•	1.3	6.7	4.6	4.9	1.5	3.7	3.0	2.7	3.2
Operating Margin Before Officers' Comp. 22	3.3	•	•	•	2.0	8.5	5.8	5.8	2.5	4.2	3.7	3.4	3.4

Selected Average Balance Sheet ($ in Thousands)

Net Receivables 23	8074	0	0	•	719	2418	2493	6484	9815	25192	31823	79044	815638
Inventories 24	9242	0	0	•	702	3575	4925	12573	22891	59146	96562	162811	488500
Net Property, Plant and Equipment 25	11800	0	1	•	1193	829	4599	8458	21706	48174	102354	272583	824492
Total Assets 26	91980	0	3	•	3107	6001	15754	36487	67082	161386	377640	1225092	10393033
Notes and Loans Payable 27	24028	0	2	•	1396	874	4216	11582	29087	46687	135283	361715	2498758
All Other Liabilities 28	17486	0	1	•	772	1628	4801	7632	17024	43074	93221	267124	1784587
Net Worth 29	50466	0	1	•	939	3499	6738	17273	20971	71624	149136	596253	6109689

Selected Financial Ratios (Times to 1)

Current Ratio 30	1.6	•	1.5	•	1.8	3.1	1.9	2.1	1.8	1.7	2.0	2.1	1.4
Quick Ratio 31	0.8	•	0.8	•	1.0	2.4	0.8	0.7	0.6	0.5	0.6	0.9	0.9
Net Sales to Working Capital 32	7.1	•	14.9	•	8.6	7.9	6.1	4.7	6.1	6.6	6.3	7.6	7.7
Coverage Ratio 33	3.7	3.2	•	•	2.9	6.7	9.4	7.7	4.0	6.7	2.4	2.9	3.5
Total Asset Turnover 34	0.6	•	2.0	•	2.0	4.5	1.8	1.6	1.6	1.7	1.4	1.1	0.3
Inventory Turnover 35	4.5	•	11.9	•	7.4	6.2	4.2	3.5	3.8	3.6	4.1	5.2	4.8
Receivables Turnover 36	7.8	•	38.8	•	5.4	9.1	9.5	10.0	11.5	11.5	14.1	18.9	4.9
Total Liabilities to Net Worth 37	0.8	•	4.0	•	2.3	0.7	1.3	1.1	2.2	1.3	1.5	1.1	0.7
Current Assets to Working Capital 38	2.6	•	2.9	•	2.3	1.5	2.2	1.9	2.2	2.3	2.0	1.9	3.5
Current Liabilities to Working Capital 39	1.6	•	1.9	•	1.3	0.5	1.2	0.9	1.2	1.3	1.0	0.9	2.5
Working Capital to Net Sales 40	0.1	•	0.1	•	0.1	0.1	0.2	0.2	0.2	0.2	0.2	0.1	0.1
Inventory to Working Capital 41	1.1	•	0.8	•	0.8	0.3	1.1	1.1	1.4	1.5	1.1	1.0	1.0
Total Receipts to Cash Flow 42	7.0	7.8	•	•	15.4	11.8	7.6	8.1	11.4	9.9	9.8	8.6	5.1
Cost of Goods to Cash Flow 43	4.9	6.3	•	•	13.0	9.7	5.6	6.0	9.2	7.7	7.5	5.4	3.3
Cash Flow to Total Debt 44	0.2	•	•	•*	0.2	0.9	0.4	0.4	0.2	0.3	0.2	0.3	0.2

Selected Financial Factors (in Percentages)

Debt Ratio 45	45.1	•	79.8	•	69.8	41.7	57.2	52.7	68.7	55.6	60.5	51.3	41.2
Return on Total Assets 46	5.6	•	•	•	7.6	36.9	12.4	10.6	8.7	8.3	8.0	5.5	4.8
Return on Equity Before Income Taxes 47	7.5	•	•	•	16.5	54.0	25.8	19.6	20.7	15.9	11.7	7.4	5.8
Return on Equity After Income Taxes 48	5.5	•	•	•	15.3	53.3	24.3	17.6	17.7	13.9	7.9	5.6	3.8
Profit Margin (Before Income Tax) 49	6.3	6.1	•	•	2.5	7.0	6.1	5.6	4.0	4.2	3.4	3.2	9.8
Profit Margin (After Income Tax) 50	4.6	6.1	•	•	2.3	6.9	5.8	5.1	3.5	3.7	2.3	2.5	6.4

Table II
Corporations with Net Income

FRUIT AND VEGETABLE PRESERVING AND SPECIALTY FOOD

MONEY AMOUNTS AND SIZE OF ASSETS IN THOUSANDS OF DOLLARS

Item Description for Accounting Period 7/12 Through 6/13	Total	Zero Assets	Under 500	500 to 1,000	1,000 to 5,000	5,000 to 10,000	10,000 to 25,000	25,000 to 50,000	50,000 to 100,000	100,000 to 250,000	250,000 to 500,000	500,000 to 2,500,000	2,500,000 and over
Number of Enterprises 1	440	71	•	0	147	17	83	57	21	22	•	8	6

Revenues ($ in Thousands)

	Total	Zero Assets	Under 500	500 to 1,000	1,000 to 5,000	5,000 to 10,000	10,000 to 25,000	25,000 to 50,000	50,000 to 100,000	100,000 to 250,000	250,000 to 500,000	500,000 to 2,500,000	2,500,000 and over
Net Sales 2	53288732	906419	•	0	1067675	495757	2541946	3442055	2339148	6253772	•	10815630	21701431
Interest 3	117328	0	•	0	229	495	176	789	819	995	•	2834	110487
Rents 4	16329	0	•	0	1678	0	177	11	3092	2871	•	1765	5947
Royalties 5	278786	0	•	0	0	0	0	0	0	0	•	0	278786
Other Portfolio Income 6	118593	0	•	0	10170	11	378	866	19410	1790	•	1876	83290
Other Receipts 7	1076416	2903	•	0	1087	58	34176	21652	31541	32761	•	53618	895278
Total Receipts 8	54896184	909322	•	0	1080839	496321	2576853	3465373	2394010	6292189	•	10875723	23075219
Average Total Receipts 9	124764	12807	•	•	7353	29195	31046	60796	114000	286009	•	1359465	3845870

Operating Costs/Operating Income (%)

	Total	Zero Assets	Under 500	500 to 1,000	1,000 to 5,000	5,000 to 10,000	10,000 to 25,000	25,000 to 50,000	50,000 to 100,000	100,000 to 250,000	250,000 to 500,000	500,000 to 2,500,000	2,500,000 and over
Cost of Operations 10	69.3	81.5	•	•	84.4	82.7	73.0	73.5	80.2	78.3	•	63.0	65.1
Salaries and Wages 11	4.7	1.7	•	•	2.6	1.4	4.8	3.9	2.4	3.4	•	6.9	5.0
Taxes Paid 12	1.1	1.1	•	•	2.1	1.1	1.4	1.1	1.1	1.2	•	1.6	0.8
Interest Paid 13	2.3	0.3	•	•	1.2	0.2	0.5	0.8	1.1	0.7	•	1.7	3.9
Depreciation 14	2.5	0.5	•	•	1.0	0.4	1.5	2.2	2.0	2.6	•	2.4	3.1
Amortization and Depletion 15	1.0	0.7	•	•	0.0	•	0.1	0.1	0.2	0.1	•	1.3	1.5
Pensions and Other Deferred Comp. 16	0.5	0.2	•	•	•	•	0.3	0.2	0.2	0.2	•	0.3	0.8
Employee Benefits 17	1.2	0.6	•	•	0.4	•	1.3	0.9	1.0	0.8	•	2.2	1.0
Advertising 18	2.7	0.2	•	•	0.3	1.2	1.0	1.8	0.6	0.2	•	6.1	2.5
Other Expenses 19	10.5	5.8	•	•	5.8	2.8	8.6	9.2	6.5	7.9	•	11.1	12.9
Officers' Compensation 20	0.5	0.5	•	•	0.7	1.9	1.3	0.9	1.0	0.6	•	0.7	0.2
Operating Margin 21	3.7	6.9	•	•	1.3	8.2	6.0	5.3	3.7	4.1	•	2.7	3.2
Operating Margin Before Officers' Comp. 22	4.2	7.4	•	•	2.0	10.1	7.3	6.2	4.7	4.7	•	3.4	3.4

Selected Average Balance Sheet ($ in Thousands)

Net Receivables 23	16607	0	•	•	828	2987	2495	6215	10398	27229	•	79044	815638
Inventories 24	17564	0	•	•	741	4169	4880	11645	23939	58984	•	162811	490950
Net Property, Plant and Equipment 25	23775	0	•	•	1222	1024	4369	8573	20831	50785	•	272583	824492
Total Assets 26	191034	0	•	•	3340	6352	15972	36699	68716	168356	•	1225092	10393033
Notes and Loans Payable 27	48861	0	•	•	1579	1079	3374	11811	24409	45431	•	361715	2498758
All Other Liabilities 28	35951	0	•	•	877	1989	4187	7436	17117	46337	•	267124	1784587
Net Worth 29	106221	0	•	•	884	3283	8412	17452	27190	76589	•	596253	6109689

Selected Financial Ratios (Times to 1)

Current Ratio 30	1.6	•	•	•	1.8	2.6	2.3	2.1	1.9	1.8	•	2.1	1.4
Quick Ratio 31	0.8	•	•	•	1.0	1.9	1.0	0.7	0.6	0.6	•	0.9	0.9
Net Sales to Working Capital 32	7.0	•	•	•	8.5	9.1	5.2	4.7	5.7	6.4	•	7.6	7.7
Coverage Ratio 33	4.0	28.2	•	•	3.1	45.1	14.5	8.1	6.4	8.2	•	2.9	3.5
Total Asset Turnover 34	0.6	•	•	•	2.2	4.6	1.9	1.6	1.6	1.7	•	1.1	0.3
Inventory Turnover 35	4.8	•	•	•	8.3	5.8	4.6	3.8	3.7	3.8	•	5.2	4.8
Receivables Turnover 36	8.1	•	•	•	9.2	8.3	12.6	12.2	11.9	11.9	•	18.9	•
Total Liabilities to Net Worth 37	0.8	•	•	•	2.8	0.9	0.9	1.1	1.5	1.2	•	1.1	0.7
Current Assets to Working Capital 38	2.5	•	•	•	2.3	1.6	1.8	1.9	2.1	2.3	•	1.9	3.5
Current Liabilities to Working Capital 39	1.5	•	•	•	1.3	0.6	0.8	0.9	1.1	1.3	•	0.9	2.5
Working Capital to Net Sales 40	0.1	•	•	•	0.1	0.1	0.2	0.2	0.2	0.2	•	0.1	0.1
Inventory to Working Capital 41	1.1	•	•	•	0.8	0.5	0.9	1.2	1.3	1.5	•	1.0	1.0
Total Receipts to Cash Flow 42	6.8	9.3	•	•	15.3	10.2	7.1	7.8	10.1	9.5	•	8.6	5.1
Cost of Goods to Cash Flow 43	4.7	7.6	•	•	12.9	8.4	5.2	5.7	8.1	7.4	•	5.4	3.3
Cash Flow to Total Debt 44	0.2	•	•	•	0.2	0.9	0.6	0.4	0.3	0.3	•	0.3	0.2

Selected Financial Factors (in Percentages)

Debt Ratio 45	44.4	•	•	•	73.5	48.3	47.3	52.4	60.4	54.5	•	51.3	41.2
Return on Total Assets 46	5.8	•	•	•	8.2	39.1	15.2	11.3	11.5	9.1	•	5.5	4.8
Return on Equity Before Income Taxes 47	7.8	•	•	•	21.0	74.0	26.9	20.8	24.6	17.5	•	7.4	5.8
Return on Equity After Income Taxes 48	5.7	•	•	•	19.5	73.2	25.4	18.7	21.4	15.4	•	5.6	3.8
Profit Margin (Before Income Tax) 49	6.8	7.2	•	•	2.6	8.3	7.4	6.0	6.0	4.7	•	3.2	9.8
Profit Margin (After Income Tax) 50	5.0	7.2	•	•	2.4	8.2	7.0	5.4	5.2	4.1	•	2.5	6.4

Table I

Corporations with and without Net Income

DAIRY PRODUCT

MONEY AMOUNTS AND SIZE OF ASSETS IN THOUSANDS OF DOLLARS

Item Description for Accounting Period 7/12 Through 6/13	Total	Zero Assets	Under 500	500 to 1,000	1,000 to 5,000	5,000 to 10,000	10,000 to 25,000	25,000 to 50,000	50,000 to 100,000	100,000 to 250,000	250,000 to 500,000	500,000 to 2,500,000	2,500,000 and over
Number of Enterprises 1	1462	5	1119	0	129	78	33	39	20	17	9	10	3

Revenues ($ in Thousands)

	Total	Zero Assets	Under 500	500 to 1,000	1,000 to 5,000	5,000 to 10,000	10,000 to 25,000	25,000 to 50,000	50,000 to 100,000	100,000 to 250,000	250,000 to 500,000	500,000 to 2,500,000	2,500,000 and over
Net Sales 2	58025997	1237584	995044	0	1526702	1617369	1202385	3544691	3131591	4484029	5498710	16260996	18526895
Interest 3	14977	24	4	0	748	222	579	2460	1954	2452	7	1525	5003
Rents 4	19119	1088	0	0	51	624	351	717	3040	10719	0	226	2303
Royalties 5	158300	0	0	0	0	0	0	989	2420	65	0	143506	11321
Other Portfolio Income 6	479620	13150	0	0	4927	768	1524	1252	2713	3873	951	216592	233869
Other Receipts 7	408625	5773	493	0	1374	4777	2550	3053	11665	21120	8474	232559	116786
Total Receipts 8	59106638	1257619	995541	0	1533802	1623760	1207389	3553162	3153383	4522258	5508142	16855404	18896177
Average Total Receipts 9	40429	251524	890	•	11890	20817	36588	91107	157669	266015	612016	1685540	6298726

Operating Costs/Operating Income (%)

	Total	Zero Assets	Under 500	500 to 1,000	1,000 to 5,000	5,000 to 10,000	10,000 to 25,000	25,000 to 50,000	50,000 to 100,000	100,000 to 250,000	250,000 to 500,000	500,000 to 2,500,000	2,500,000 and over
Cost of Operations 10	77.4	78.6	77.9	•	81.3	84.0	88.0	77.8	76.2	82.5	71.7	77.6	76.1
Salaries and Wages 11	4.4	2.5	2.9	•	6.0	3.1	2.5	5.3	4.6	3.0	4.4	4.1	5.0
Taxes Paid 12	1.0	0.7	1.9	•	1.6	1.4	0.8	1.1	1.0	0.9	0.8	0.7	1.1
Interest Paid 13	1.0	0.0	1.4	•	0.4	0.7	0.3	0.4	0.7	0.6	0.7	1.3	1.4
Depreciation 14	2.5	2.0	1.2	•	1.3	1.8	2.4	1.8	2.1	2.5	2.3	3.3	2.3
Amortization and Depletion 15	0.5	0.0	0.1	•	0.0	0.0	0.3	0.0	0.3	0.1	0.2	0.5	0.8
Pensions and Other Deferred Comp. 16	0.5	0.9	0.2	•	0.5	0.1	0.1	0.5	0.2	0.3	0.5	0.5	0.7
Employee Benefits 17	0.8	0.5	0.2	•	1.0	0.5	0.5	1.6	1.0	0.9	1.1	0.7	0.6
Advertising 18	1.5	1.4	0.1	•	0.3	0.4	0.5	0.3	0.6	0.6	2.9	2.4	1.1
Other Expenses 19	7.6	4.5	10.9	•	5.5	6.8	4.4	6.7	10.5	4.8	7.9	7.0	8.8
Officers' Compensation 20	0.6	2.5	•	•	2.3	1.7	0.4	1.4	0.8	0.6	0.5	0.6	0.1
Operating Margin 21	2.4	6.2	3.1	•	•	•	•	3.1	1.8	3.1	7.1	1.3	2.0
Operating Margin Before Officers' Comp. 22	3.0	8.7	3.1	•	2.3	1.2	0.3	4.4	2.7	3.7	7.6	1.9	2.2

Selected Average Balance Sheet ($ in Thousands)

Net Receivables 23	3224	0	43	•	647	1826	4977	11859	12953	17607	36518	145681	489895
Inventories 24	2668	0	45	•	878	2278	2856	4087	7754	31405	67762	149455	330403
Net Property, Plant and Equipment 25	7587	0	14	•	797	2825	4451	12134	22387	42785	120208	357613	1433233
Total Assets 26	21012	0	207	•	3079	7705	15725	35104	67790	152859	325426	995027	3589280
Notes and Loans Payable 27	8809	0	223	•	775	3751	2327	10084	17552	50480	107439	504093	1516701
All Other Liabilities 28	6989	0	51	•	700	2287	4904	13502	19051	31512	92461	418897	1088851
Net Worth 29	5213	0	-66	•	1604	1666	8494	11517	31186	70867	125526	72037	983728

Selected Financial Ratios (Times to 1)

Current Ratio 30	1.5	•	1.2	•	2.0	1.2	1.5	1.4	1.5	2.3	1.9	1.2	1.5
Quick Ratio 31	0.8	•	0.9	•	1.0	0.7	0.9	1.0	0.9	1.1	0.9	0.7	0.9
Net Sales to Working Capital 32	14.2	•	24.5	•	11.4	24.0	11.4	14.8	14.5	7.3	8.1	20.5	15.4
Coverage Ratio 33	5.3	332.5	3.3	•	2.1	0.8	2.0	8.5	4.4	8.1	10.7	5.4	3.9
Total Asset Turnover 34	1.9	•	4.3	•	3.8	2.7	2.3	2.6	2.3	1.7	1.9	1.6	1.7
Inventory Turnover 35	11.5	•	15.5	•	10.9	7.7	11.2	17.3	15.4	6.9	6.5	8.4	14.2
Receivables Turnover 36	13.2	•	•	•	•	10.9	6.8	8.2	13.0	12.4	15.5	8.9	25.2
Total Liabilities to Net Worth 37	3.0	•	•	•	0.9	3.6	0.9	2.0	1.2	1.2	1.6	12.8	2.6
Current Assets to Working Capital 38	3.1	•	5.0	•	2.0	5.1	2.9	3.4	3.0	1.8	2.1	5.3	2.9
Current Liabilities to Working Capital 39	2.1	•	4.0	•	1.0	4.1	1.9	2.4	2.0	0.8	1.1	4.3	1.9
Working Capital to Net Sales 40	0.1	•	0.0	•	0.1	0.0	0.1	0.1	0.1	0.1	0.1	0.0	0.1
Inventory to Working Capital 41	1.0	•	1.2	•	0.8	2.1	1.1	0.6	0.8	0.8	1.0	1.4	0.8
Total Receipts to Cash Flow 42	10.0	8.8	8.7	•	24.8	21.6	25.3	11.8	8.5	12.5	7.2	9.6	9.9
Cost of Goods to Cash Flow 43	7.7	6.9	6.8	•	20.2	18.2	22.3	9.2	6.5	10.3	5.1	7.5	7.5
Cash Flow to Total Debt 44	0.3	•	0.4	•	0.3	0.2	0.2	0.3	0.5	0.3	0.4	0.2	0.2

Selected Financial Factors (in Percentages)

Debt Ratio 45	75.2	•	131.9	•	47.9	78.4	46.0	67.2	54.0	53.6	61.4	92.8	72.6
Return on Total Assets 46	10.3	•	19.5	•	3.0	1.5	1.3	9.7	7.6	7.7	15.0	11.3	9.3
Return on Equity Before Income Taxes 47	33.7	•	•	•	3.0	•	1.3	26.1	12.7	14.6	35.3	127.0	25.3
Return on Equity After Income Taxes 48	26.8	•	•	•	1.2	•	0.1	23.8	9.4	12.4	33.6	100.2	17.1
Profit Margin (Before Income Tax) 49	4.4	7.8	3.2	•	0.4	•	0.3	3.3	2.5	3.9	7.3	5.6	4.0
Profit Margin (After Income Tax) 50	3.5	6.8	3.2	•	0.2	•	0.0	3.0	1.9	3.3	6.9	4.4	2.7

43

Table II
Corporations with Net Income

DAIRY PRODUCT

MONEY AMOUNTS AND SIZE OF ASSETS IN THOUSANDS OF DOLLARS

Item Description for Accounting Period 7/12 Through 6/13	Total	Zero Assets	Under 500	500 to 1,000	1,000 to 5,000	5,000 to 10,000	10,000 to 25,000	25,000 to 50,000	50,000 to 100,000	100,000 to 250,000	250,000 to 500,000	500,000 to 2,500,000	2,500,000 and over
Number of Enterprises **1**	1333	•	•	0	70	63	26	33	15	•	•	7	•

Revenues ($ in Thousands)

Net Sales **2**	53004104	•	•	0	1023434	1414536	1004082	3055129	2505839	•	•	13479861	•
Interest **3**	13456	•	•	0	621	101	579	2287	1416	•	•	1522	•
Rents **4**	15422	•	•	0	0	624	351	80	51	•	•	212	•
Royalties **5**	158164	•	•	0	0	0	0	989	2420	•	•	143370	•
Other Portfolio Income **6**	456383	•	•	0	3413	0	1197	1086	2456	•	•	206409	•
Other Receipts **7**	371127	•	•	0	822	4586	2383	2645	8677	•	•	200588	•
Total Receipts **8**	54018656	•	•	0	1028290	1419847	1008592	3062216	2520859	•	•	14031962	•
Average Total Receipts **9**	40524	•	•	•	14690	22537	38792	92794	168057	•	•	2004566	•

Operating Costs/Operating Income (%)

Cost of Operations **10**	77.5	•	•	•	80.8	83.2	89.3	78.1	75.0	•	•	78.7	•
Salaries and Wages **11**	4.0	•	•	•	5.9	2.7	2.2	4.7	4.6	•	•	3.3	•
Taxes Paid **12**	0.9	•	•	•	1.2	1.2	0.7	1.0	0.9	•	•	0.6	•
Interest Paid **13**	1.1	•	•	•	0.4	0.7	0.2	0.3	0.3	•	•	1.5	•
Depreciation **14**	2.1	•	•	•	1.1	1.4	1.0	1.5	1.8	•	•	2.3	•
Amortization and Depletion **15**	0.4	•	•	•	0.0	0.0	0.3	0.0	0.2	•	•	0.5	•
Pensions and Other Deferred Comp. **16**	0.5	•	•	•	0.6	0.1	0.1	0.4	0.2	•	•	0.6	•
Employee Benefits **17**	0.8	•	•	•	1.2	0.6	0.5	1.5	1.0	•	•	0.7	•
Advertising **18**	1.4	•	•	•	0.4	0.4	0.3	0.3	0.5	•	•	2.4	•
Other Expenses **19**	7.6	•	•	•	6.0	6.9	3.3	6.8	11.5	•	•	6.4	•
Officers' Compensation **20**	0.5	•	•	•	0.8	1.8	0.4	1.4	1.0	•	•	0.7	•
Operating Margin **21**	3.1	•	•	•	1.5	1.0	1.6	4.0	3.1	•	•	2.3	•
Operating Margin Before Officers' Comp. **22**	3.6	•	•	•	2.3	2.8	2.0	5.4	4.1	•	•	3.0	•

Selected Average Balance Sheet ($ in Thousands)

Net Receivables 23	3082	•	•	•	735	2036	5682	12569	13448	•	•	147630	•
Inventories 24	2438	•	•	•	919	2109	3173	4007	9100	•	•	159507	•
Net Property, Plant and Equipment 25	7147	•	•	•	355	2978	2856	10983	21934	•	•	362008	•
Total Assets 26	20305	•	•	•	3090	7751	15743	35830	65988	•	•	1095785	•
Notes and Loans Payable 27	8239	•	•	•	850	3240	2024	9347	11177	•	•	541733	•
All Other Liabilities 28	6742	•	•	•	600	2406	5038	13638	18700	•	•	470299	•
Net Worth 29	5324	•	•	•	1640	2106	8680	12845	36111	•	•	83754	•

Selected Financial Ratios (Times to 1)

Current Ratio 30	1.5	•	•	•	2.8	1.1	1.7	1.5	1.6	•	•	1.4	•
Quick Ratio 31	0.8	•	•	•	1.6	0.6	1.0	1.1	1.0	•	•	0.7	•
Net Sales to Working Capital 32	12.9	•	•	•	9.0	44.1	9.2	12.8	12.3	•	•	14.7	•
Coverage Ratio 33	5.9	•	•	•	5.5	3.1	9.9	14.9	14.9	•	•	5.7	•
Total Asset Turnover 34	2.0	•	•	•	4.7	2.9	2.5	2.6	2.5	•	•	1.8	•
Inventory Turnover 35	12.6	•	•	•	12.9	8.9	10.9	18.1	13.8	•	•	9.5	•
Receivables Turnover 36	15.9	•	•	•	22.2	11.4	7.2	8.2	•	•	•	12.9	•
Total Liabilities to Net Worth 37	2.8	•	•	•	0.9	2.7	0.8	1.8	0.8	•	•	12.1	•
Current Assets to Working Capital 38	2.8	•	•	•	1.6	8.5	2.5	3.1	2.5	•	•	3.8	•
Current Liabilities to Working Capital 39	1.8	•	•	•	0.6	7.5	1.5	2.1	1.5	•	•	2.8	•
Working Capital to Net Sales 40	0.1	•	•	•	0.1	0.0	0.1	0.1	0.1	•	•	0.1	•
Inventory to Working Capital 41	0.9	•	•	•	0.6	3.7	0.9	0.5	0.7	•	•	1.1	•
Total Receipts to Cash Flow 42	9.3	•	•	•	17.0	16.0	22.2	10.5	7.2	•	•	8.7	•
Cost of Goods to Cash Flow 43	7.2	•	•	•	13.8	13.3	19.8	8.2	5.4	•	•	6.9	•
Cash Flow to Total Debt 44	0.3	•	•	•	0.6	0.2	0.2	0.4	0.8	•	•	0.2	•

Selected Financial Factors (in Percentages)

Debt Ratio 45	73.8	•	•	•	46.9	72.8	44.9	64.2	45.3	•	•	92.4	•
Return on Total Assets 46	12.3	•	•	•	11.5	6.0	5.6	11.8	10.1	•	•	15.3	•
Return on Equity Before Income Taxes 47	38.7	•	•	•	17.8	15.0	9.1	30.8	17.2	•	•	165.0	•
Return on Equity After Income Taxes 48	31.3	•	•	•	14.6	14.6	7.6	28.4	13.5	•	•	132.1	•
Profit Margin (Before Income Tax) 49	5.2	•	•	•	2.0	1.4	2.0	4.3	3.7	•	•	7.2	•
Profit Margin (After Income Tax) 50	4.2	•	•	•	1.6	1.4	1.7	3.9	2.9	•	•	5.7	•

Table I

Corporations with and without Net Income

MEAT AND SEAFOOD PROCESSING

MONEY AMOUNTS AND SIZE OF ASSETS IN THOUSANDS OF DOLLARS

Item Description for Accounting Period 7/12 Through 6/13	Total	Zero Assets	Under 500	500 to 1,000	1,000 to 5,000	5,000 to 10,000	10,000 to 25,000	25,000 to 50,000	50,000 to 100,000	100,000 to 250,000	250,000 to 500,000	500,000 to 2,500,000	2,500,000 and over
Number of Enterprises **1**	3621	1097	1500	192	501	24	157	59	33	25	15	13	5

Revenues ($ in Thousands)

Net Sales **2**	145676700	267591	1150389	854106	5352460	1270834	10253881	6337198	7015541	7961564	12419911	21527850	71265375
Interest **3**	109701	4	7	138	284	1634	896	491	286	3304	7273	8347	87038
Rents **4**	37664	0	0	302	1570	112	798	1009	349	6165	11496	2752	13111
Royalties **5**	18610	0	0	0	3	0	0	22	100	0	0	6851	11633
Other Portfolio Income **6**	428779	58	13428	3787	46508	2241	23329	5100	863	14414	14395	171694	132961
Other Receipts **7**	996322	330	286	55230	9920	18346	52474	23732	24390	34674	60	129543	647337
Total Receipts **8**	147267776	267983	1164110	913563	5410745	1293167	10331378	6367552	7041529	8020121	12453135	21847037	72157455
Average Total Receipts **9**	40670	244	776	4758	10800	53882	65805	107925	213380	320805	830209	1680541	14431491

Operating Costs/Operating Income (%)

Cost of Operations **10**	85.7	64.5	78.0	92.5	79.2	87.3	86.3	84.1	83.8	86.9	86.5	75.4	89.4
Salaries and Wages **11**	2.9	4.9	4.1	3.3	3.5	4.6	2.8	3.9	2.6	2.6	2.3	7.1	1.6
Taxes Paid **12**	0.7	1.7	1.0	0.9	1.3	0.8	0.7	0.9	0.8	0.7	0.9	0.7	0.6
Interest Paid **13**	0.9	1.2	0.2	4.8	0.4	0.1	0.4	0.6	0.5	0.7	0.6	1.0	1.0
Depreciation **14**	1.6	1.3	0.1	0.5	1.1	0.4	1.0	1.5	1.7	1.9	2.2	2.0	1.6
Amortization and Depletion **15**	0.3	0.5	0.8	0.0	0.1	0.0	0.1	0.1	0.1	0.2	0.3	1.1	0.2
Pensions and Other Deferred Comp. **16**	0.2	0.0	0.0	0.0	0.5	0.0	0.1	0.2	0.1	0.2	0.1	0.2	0.2
Employee Benefits **17**	0.8	0.4	0.0	0.6	0.8	0.5	0.6	0.5	1.2	0.6	0.7	1.5	0.6
Advertising **18**	0.4	0.0	2.4	0.3	0.3	0.1	0.5	0.5	1.0	0.4	0.9	0.3	0.2
Other Expenses **19**	4.9	18.6	6.2	2.9	7.9	7.2	5.1	5.6	4.8	3.9	3.5	8.9	3.7
Officers' Compensation **20**	0.5	3.9	4.7	1.8	2.3	0.3	0.8	0.6	0.6	0.4	0.3	0.5	0.2
Operating Margin **21**	1.2	3.1	2.5	•	2.6	•	1.6	1.6	2.9	1.5	1.8	1.2	0.8
Operating Margin Before Officers' Comp. **22**	1.7	7.0	7.2	•	4.9	•	2.4	2.2	3.5	1.9	2.1	1.7	1.0

Selected Average Balance Sheet ($ in Thousands)

Net Receivables 23	2582	0	19	79	801	2395	3902	6143	16737	23928	50839	100843	929160
Inventories 24	3573	0	6	199	487	1831	2574	8884	19102	25005	91063	205111	1277254
Net Property, Plant and Equipment 25	4506	0	0	72	982	1530	4504	10336	24102	49710	122596	216182	1554044
Total Assets 26	17774	0	89	814	3338	8609	16046	33135	72252	152308	354422	964738	6733011
Notes and Loans Payable 27	5487	0	5	2034	1441	753	5498	11449	22927	52006	142281	356487	1673527
All Other Liabilities 28	4905	0	1	636	957	1597	3853	7156	17143	37287	70826	254726	2043934
Net Worth 29	7381	0	83	-1857	940	6259	6695	14531	32182	63016	141315	353525	3015549

Selected Financial Ratios (Times to 1)

Current Ratio 30	1.6	•	47.2	0.7	2.9	3.4	1.8	2.1	1.9	1.7	2.0	1.6	1.5
Quick Ratio 31	0.7	•	42.9	0.2	1.7	2.1	1.0	1.2	0.9	0.9	0.9	0.6	0.7
Net Sales to Working Capital 32	13.0	•	21.7	•	8.3	11.6	16.3	10.4	10.3	11.9	10.1	10.9	15.3
Coverage Ratio 33	3.7	3.6	18.2	0.9	9.7	8.2	7.2	4.8	7.2	4.4	4.2	3.6	3.1
Total Asset Turnover 34	2.3	•	8.6	5.5	3.2	6.2	4.1	3.2	2.9	2.1	2.3	1.7	2.1
Inventory Turnover 35	9.6	•	92.6	20.7	17.4	25.3	21.9	10.2	9.3	11.1	7.9	6.1	10.0
Receivables Turnover 36	17.0	•	40.5	59.4	13.2	23.2	19.1	15.8	12.5	13.8	15.1	16.5	18.5
Total Liabilities to Net Worth 37	1.4	•	0.1	•	2.6	0.4	1.4	1.3	1.2	1.4	1.5	1.7	1.2
Current Assets to Working Capital 38	2.6	•	1.0	•	1.5	1.4	2.3	1.9	2.2	2.3	2.0	2.8	3.1
Current Liabilities to Working Capital 39	1.6	•	0.0	•	0.5	0.4	1.3	0.9	1.2	1.3	1.0	1.8	2.1
Working Capital to Net Sales 40	0.1	•	0.0	•	0.1	0.1	0.1	0.1	0.1	0.1	0.1	0.1	0.1
Inventory to Working Capital 41	1.2	•	0.1	•	0.4	0.3	0.8	0.8	0.9	0.9	1.0	1.4	1.4
Total Receipts to Cash Flow 42	16.2	5.5	12.7	128.0	10.4	16.2	15.8	15.0	14.1	19.1	21.6	10.6	19.6
Cost of Goods to Cash Flow 43	13.9	3.6	9.9	118.4	8.3	14.1	13.6	12.6	11.8	16.6	18.7	8.0	17.5
Cash Flow to Total Debt 44	0.2	•	9.4	0.0	0.4	1.4	0.4	0.4	0.4	0.2	0.2	0.3	0.2

Selected Financial Factors (in Percentages)

Debt Ratio 45	58.5	•	7.2	328.2	71.8	27.3	58.3	56.1	55.5	58.6	60.1	63.4	55.2
Return on Total Assets 46	7.2	•	33.9	22.5	13.2	3.5	11.0	8.6	11.2	6.0	6.4	6.5	6.6
Return on Equity Before Income Taxes 47	12.6	•	34.5	1.7	42.1	4.2	22.8	15.6	21.6	11.3	12.2	12.8	9.9
Return on Equity After Income Taxes 48	10.0	•	31.3	1.8	40.9	2.2	21.9	14.4	20.6	9.5	11.4	11.1	6.3
Profit Margin (Before Income Tax) 49	2.3	3.2	3.7	•	3.7	0.5	2.3	2.1	3.3	2.2	2.1	2.7	2.1
Profit Margin (After Income Tax) 50	1.8	3.2	3.4	•	3.6	0.3	2.2	2.0	3.1	1.9	2.0	2.4	1.3

Table II

Corporations with Net Income

MEAT AND SEAFOOD PROCESSING

MONEY AMOUNTS AND SIZE OF ASSETS IN THOUSANDS OF DOLLARS

Item Description for Accounting Period 7/12 Through 6/13	Total	Zero Assets	Under 500	500 to 1,000	1,000 to 5,000	5,000 to 10,000	10,000 to 25,000	25,000 to 50,000	50,000 to 100,000	100,000 to 250,000	250,000 to 500,000	500,000 to 2,500,000	2,500,000 and over
Number of Enterprises 1	2418	•	987	123	364	16	134	42	29	19	11	•	•

Revenues ($ in Thousands)

	Total	Zero Assets	Under 500	500 to 1,000	1,000 to 5,000	5,000 to 10,000	10,000 to 25,000	25,000 to 50,000	50,000 to 100,000	100,000 to 250,000	250,000 to 500,000	500,000 to 2,500,000	2,500,000 and over
Net Sales 2	114063352	•	933926	323483	4727427	344681	9228778	4578959	6297377	6301011	7525768	•	•
Interest 3	76686	•	7	138	283	1464	844	224	286	812	5219	•	•
Rents 4	31882	•	0	302	1570	0	195	1009	349	1097	11496	•	•
Royalties 5	18515	•	0	0	3	0	0	22	100	0	0	•	•
Other Portfolio Income 6	402932	•	13428	3787	46441	2211	23231	4428	863	1981	11385	•	•
Other Receipts 7	859897	•	234	429	9778	16253	29126	22558	19999	15999	38197	•	•
Total Receipts 8	115453264	•	947595	328139	4785502	364609	9282174	4607200	6318974	6320900	7592065	•	•
Average Total Receipts 9	47747	•	960	2668	13147	22788	69270	109695	217896	332679	690188	•	•

Operating Costs/Operating Income (%)

	Total	Zero Assets	Under 500	500 to 1,000	1,000 to 5,000	5,000 to 10,000	10,000 to 25,000	25,000 to 50,000	50,000 to 100,000	100,000 to 250,000	250,000 to 500,000	500,000 to 2,500,000	2,500,000 and over
Cost of Operations 10	83.5	•	84.6	75.6	79.7	82.5	85.5	82.4	82.9	87.0	81.9	•	•
Salaries and Wages 11	3.3	•	0.4	5.6	2.9	4.3	2.9	4.8	2.7	2.1	3.1	•	•
Taxes Paid 12	0.7	•	0.5	2.3	1.3	1.3	0.8	0.9	0.8	0.6	0.8	•	•
Interest Paid 13	0.8	•	0.1	1.0	0.4	0.2	0.4	0.6	0.5	0.4	0.5	•	•
Depreciation 14	1.8	•	0.0	1.2	1.0	0.7	0.8	1.2	1.7	1.9	2.9	•	•
Amortization and Depletion 15	0.3	•	1.0	0.0	0.0	0.0	0.1	0.1	0.1	0.1	0.2	•	•
Pensions and Other Deferred Comp. 16	0.2	•	0.0	0.1	0.5	0.0	0.1	0.3	0.1	0.2	0.1	•	•
Employee Benefits 17	0.9	•	0.0	1.5	0.8	0.3	0.6	0.6	1.3	0.6	1.1	•	•
Advertising 18	0.5	•	3.0	0.8	0.2	0.3	0.6	0.7	1.1	0.5	1.1	•	•
Other Expenses 19	5.5	•	1.1	7.3	7.0	8.2	5.2	5.2	4.8	3.4	4.4	•	•
Officers' Compensation 20	0.5	•	4.8	4.7	2.3	0.8	0.9	0.7	0.6	0.3	0.3	•	•
Operating Margin 21	2.0	•	4.6	•	3.8	1.3	2.2	2.6	3.5	3.0	3.4	•	•
Operating Margin Before Officers' Comp. 22	2.5	•	9.4	4.6	6.1	2.1	3.1	3.3	4.1	3.4	3.7	•	•

Selected Average Balance Sheet ($ in Thousands)

Net Receivables 23	2876	•	0	122	1029	2108	4011	6533	17536	27803	42259	•	•
Inventories 24	4172	•	0	96	582	1866	2426	9787	17090	23494	70415	•	•
Net Property, Plant and Equipment 25	5696	•	0	112	914	1195	4499	9853	23090	54873	130522	•	•
Total Assets 26	21790	•	101	795	3641	8287	16525	34615	72082	149033	346542	•	•
Notes and Loans Payable 27	5636	•	7	60	726	1064	5721	9467	20984	51927	101840	•	•
All Other Liabilities 28	5907	•	2	113	826	1620	3871	6599	15861	40252	69029	•	•
Net Worth 29	10248	•	92	622	2089	5604	6933	18549	35237	56854	175674	•	•

Selected Financial Ratios (Times to 1)

Current Ratio 30	1.7	•	17.6	2.0	4.2	3.4	1.8	2.6	2.2	1.6	2.2	•	•
Quick Ratio 31	0.7	•	16.9	1.3	2.4	2.0	1.0	1.5	1.0	0.9	1.0	•	•
Net Sales to Working Capital 32	12.0	•	50.1	18.7	7.0	4.4	15.8	7.9	8.7	13.3	8.8	•	•
Coverage Ratio 33	5.0	•	115.3	2.2	13.4	36.5	8.2	6.6	8.5	9.1	8.9	•	•
Total Asset Turnover 34	2.2	•	9.4	3.3	3.6	2.6	4.2	3.1	3.0	2.2	2.0	•	•
Inventory Turnover 35	9.4	•	29264.9	20.6	17.8	9.5	24.3	9.2	10.5	12.3	8.0	•	•
Receivables Turnover 36	17.8	•	•	•	13.0	9.4	21.7	14.3	14.0	13.1	15.1	•	•
Total Liabilities to Net Worth 37	1.1	•	0.1	0.3	0.7	0.5	1.4	0.9	1.0	1.6	1.0	•	•
Current Assets to Working Capital 38	2.5	•	1.1	2.0	1.3	1.4	2.2	1.6	1.8	2.6	1.8	•	•
Current Liabilities to Working Capital 39	1.5	•	0.1	1.0	0.3	0.4	1.2	0.6	0.8	1.6	0.8	•	•
Working Capital to Net Sales 40	0.1	•	0.0	0.1	0.1	0.2	0.1	0.1	0.1	0.1	0.1	•	•
Inventory to Working Capital 41	1.2	•	0.0	0.7	0.4	0.3	0.7	0.6	0.8	1.0	0.9	•	•
Total Receipts to Cash Flow 42	13.3	•	17.0	21.0	9.6	7.2	14.6	13.2	13.1	16.3	13.5	•	•
Cost of Goods to Cash Flow 43	11.1	•	14.4	15.9	7.7	5.9	12.5	10.9	10.9	14.1	11.0	•	•
Cash Flow to Total Debt 44	0.3	•	6.0	0.7	0.9	1.1	0.5	0.5	0.4	0.2	0.3	•	•

Selected Financial Factors (in Percentages)

Debt Ratio 45	53.0	•	9.1	21.7	42.6	32.4	58.0	46.4	51.1	61.9	49.3	•	•
Return on Total Assets 46	8.7	•	57.5	7.1	19.4	19.0	13.3	12.0	13.2	8.4	9.4	•	•
Return on Equity Before Income Taxes 47	14.7	•	62.7	5.0	31.3	27.4	27.8	19.0	23.8	19.5	16.5	•	•
Return on Equity After Income Taxes 48	11.9	•	58.3	4.2	30.6	24.0	26.7	17.7	22.7	16.9	15.6	•	•
Profit Margin (Before Income Tax) 49	3.2	•	6.1	1.2	5.0	7.1	2.8	3.2	3.9	3.3	4.2	•	•
Profit Margin (After Income Tax) 50	2.6	•	5.6	1.0	4.9	6.3	2.7	3.0	3.7	2.9	4.0	•	•

Table I

Corporations with and without Net Income

BAKERIES AND TORTILLA

MONEY AMOUNTS AND SIZE OF ASSETS IN THOUSANDS OF DOLLARS

Item Description for Accounting Period 7/12 Through 6/13	Total	Zero Assets	Under 500	500 to 1,000	1,000 to 5,000	5,000 to 10,000	10,000 to 25,000	25,000 to 50,000	50,000 to 100,000	100,000 to 250,000	250,000 to 500,000	500,000 to 2,500,000	2,500,000 and over
Number of Enterprises **1**	3789	689	2311	3	383	201	104	46	21	13	3	15	•

Revenues ($ in Thousands)

Net Sales **2**	50448825	1879072	919763	4913	2288639	4148578	3476952	2999584	2918748	2544676	1557601	27710299	•
Interest **3**	81218	863	1	2	594	349	727	353	102	603	2487	75137	•
Rents **4**	10628	3	14	0	20	217	462	424	30	353	365	8739	•
Royalties **5**	61436	223	0	0	0	0	33	8358	0	0	36376	16447	•
Other Portfolio Income **6**	707126	74900	12976	1	77	249	28495	5129	4124	2359	0	578818	•
Other Receipts **7**	217294	6311	263	2	4879	14205	5751	8290	7985	18142	5494	145970	•
Total Receipts **8**	51526527	1961372	933017	4918	2294209	4163598	3512420	3022138	2930989	2566133	1602323	28535410	•
Average Total Receipts **9**	13599	2847	404	1639	5990	20714	33773	65699	139571	197395	534108	1902361	

Operating Costs/Operating Income (%)

Cost of Operations **10**	64.7	64.5	46.2	63.0	74.8	72.4	70.6	69.7	63.9	67.6	66.4	61.9	•
Salaries and Wages **11**	9.3	18.3	11.1	9.3	5.1	8.2	4.9	6.6	10.4	8.3	3.5	10.3	•
Taxes Paid **12**	1.9	0.6	3.7	3.7	2.5	2.1	1.8	2.0	2.1	1.8	1.3	1.8	•
Interest Paid **13**	1.3	2.5	0.0	0.2	0.2	0.4	1.1	1.4	0.6	1.0	0.3	1.7	•
Depreciation **14**	2.7	2.2	1.7	1.0	1.3	2.0	3.5	3.3	4.3	3.2	1.5	2.7	•
Amortization and Depletion **15**	0.7	1.3	0.0	•	0.2	0.0	0.1	0.6	0.5	0.3	1.1	1.0	•
Pensions and Other Deferred Comp. **16**	0.9	0.3	•	0.1	0.4	0.1	0.2	0.8	1.3	1.6	0.2	1.1	•
Employee Benefits **17**	2.8	2.2	0.0	1.4	1.1	2.1	1.3	2.3	2.7	2.6	1.4	3.5	•
Advertising **18**	1.5	0.9	0.4	0.3	1.1	0.2	0.6	0.5	1.3	1.1	3.9	1.9	•
Other Expenses **19**	12.0	13.7	22.1	13.0	7.8	7.8	8.8	9.6	10.1	9.3	18.7	13.3	•
Officers' Compensation **20**	1.3	1.1	17.3	7.1	2.8	2.0	2.7	1.8	0.9	0.8	1.0	0.3	•
Operating Margin **21**	0.9	•	•	0.9	2.6	2.6	4.4	1.5	1.9	2.4	0.6	0.4	•
Operating Margin Before Officers' Comp. **22**	2.1	•	14.8	8.0	5.4	4.6	7.2	3.3	2.8	3.1	1.6	0.8	•

Selected Average Balance Sheet ($ in Thousands)

Net Receivables 23	1028	0	14	41	468	1541	2670	4909	11857	31423	38084	139964	•
Inventories 24	690	0	10	995	236	1075	1997	3356	6480	14210	33581	103246	•
Net Property, Plant and Equipment 25	2510	0	20	210	639	3642	6304	13264	34700	52988	71040	372664	•
Total Assets 26	9093	0	91	748	2055	7967	15340	35539	73953	154300	334965	1603986	•
Notes and Loans Payable 27	2956	0	24	55	487	2293	5280	17727	19982	29934	41102	546868	•
All Other Liabilities 28	3169	0	26	19	386	3015	3241	6090	18649	44203	109412	618838	•
Net Worth 29	2968	0	41	673	1182	2659	6819	11721	35322	80164	184451	438280	•

Selected Financial Ratios (Times to 1)

Current Ratio 30	1.1	•	1.6	6.4	3.2	1.0	1.7	1.6	1.5	1.6	1.6	0.8	•
Quick Ratio 31	0.6	•	1.1	4.6	1.9	0.6	1.1	1.0	1.0	1.2	0.7	0.5	•
Net Sales to Working Capital 32	98.6	•	18.5	8.0	6.8	446.5	11.2	13.5	16.4	8.0	9.1	•	•
Coverage Ratio 33	3.3	•	•	7.2	13.0	7.9	5.8	2.6	5.0	4.1	14.8	3.0	•
Total Asset Turnover 34	1.5	•	4.4	2.2	2.9	2.6	2.2	1.8	1.9	1.3	1.6	1.2	•
Inventory Turnover 35	12.5	•	18.5	1.0	19.0	13.9	11.8	13.5	13.7	9.3	10.3	11.1	•
Receivables Turnover 36	13.6	•	40.8	4.0	15.4	14.7	13.5	14.6	11.7	6.4	27.3	13.4	•
Total Liabilities to Net Worth 37	2.1	•	1.2	0.1	0.7	2.0	1.2	2.0	1.1	0.9	0.8	2.7	•
Current Assets to Working Capital 38	20.5	•	2.6	1.2	1.4	76.0	2.4	2.8	2.9	2.7	2.6	•	•
Current Liabilities to Working Capital 39	19.5	•	1.6	0.2	0.4	75.0	1.4	1.8	1.9	1.7	1.6	•	•
Working Capital to Net Sales 40	0.0	•	0.1	0.1	0.1	0.0	0.1	0.1	0.1	0.1	0.1	•	•
Inventory to Working Capital 41	5.3	•	0.4	0.3	0.3	24.7	0.7	0.8	0.7	0.6	0.6	•	•
Total Receipts to Cash Flow 42	9.7	12.8	8.9	11.4	13.3	13.0	8.1	10.0	11.0	9.3	5.1	9.6	•
Cost of Goods to Cash Flow 43	6.3	8.3	4.1	7.2	10.0	9.4	5.7	7.0	7.0	6.3	3.4	5.9	•
Cash Flow to Total Debt 44	0.2	•	0.9	1.9	0.5	0.3	0.5	0.3	0.3	0.3	0.7	0.2	•

Selected Financial Factors (in Percentages)

Debt Ratio 45	67.4	•	54.7	10.0	42.5	66.6	55.5	67.0	52.2	48.0	44.9	72.7	•
Return on Total Assets 46	6.4	•	•	2.6	9.0	8.8	14.4	6.6	5.4	5.4	5.9	5.9	•
Return on Equity Before Income Taxes 47	13.7	•	•	2.5	14.5	23.0	26.8	12.4	9.0	7.8	9.9	14.6	•
Return on Equity After Income Taxes 48	10.5	•	•	1.1	13.4	22.6	24.8	10.8	7.3	7.5	8.7	10.0	•
Profit Margin (Before Income Tax) 49	3.0	•	•	1.0	2.9	3.0	5.5	2.2	2.3	3.2	3.5	3.5	•
Profit Margin (After Income Tax) 50	2.3	•	•	0.4	2.7	2.9	5.1	1.9	1.8	3.1	3.1	2.4	•

Table II

Corporations with Net Income

BAKERIES AND TORTILLA

MONEY AMOUNTS AND SIZE OF ASSETS IN THOUSANDS OF DOLLARS

Item Description for Accounting Period 7/12 Through 6/13	Total	Zero Assets	Under 500	500 to 1,000	1,000 to 5,000	5,000 to 10,000	10,000 to 25,000	25,000 to 50,000	50,000 to 100,000	100,000 to 250,000	250,000 to 500,000	500,000 to 2,500,000	2,500,000 and over
Number of Enterprises **1**	1700	9	1193	0	226	109	87	34	17	13	0	11	•

Revenues ($ in Thousands)

Net Sales **2**	36642804	426520	603747	0	1956990	2807078	3176468	2119970	2596714	3047743	0	19907575	•
Interest **3**	32539	0	2	0	303	325	712	330	101	3089	0	27676	•
Rents **4**	10012	0	14	0	0	0	462	111	0	718	0	8707	•
Royalties **5**	48158	0	0	0	0	0	33	345	0	36376	0	11404	•
Other Portfolio Income **6**	672759	74638	1	0	77	32	28495	684	4122	2359	0	562354	•
Other Receipts **7**	195183	1821	2	0	4799	6181	5148	7431	7401	20567	0	141830	•
Total Receipts **8**	37601455	502979	603766	0	1962169	2813616	3211318	2128871	2608338	3110852	0	20659546	•
Average Total Receipts **9**	22119	55887	506	•	8682	25813	36912	62614	153432	239296	•	1878141	•

Operating Costs/Operating Income (%)

Cost of Operations **10**	66.3	69.6	38.2	•	75.3	66.4	70.5	68.6	63.3	60.2	•	66.5	•
Salaries and Wages **11**	6.8	9.8	9.1	•	4.5	10.6	4.7	6.6	10.5	8.2	•	6.1	•
Taxes Paid **12**	1.9	2.4	3.8	•	2.5	2.6	1.7	2.1	2.1	1.8	•	1.7	•
Interest Paid **13**	1.2	1.7	0.0	•	0.2	0.4	0.9	0.6	0.5	0.7	•	1.7	•
Depreciation **14**	2.6	1.7	1.3	•	1.3	1.2	3.0	3.1	3.6	2.2	•	2.8	•
Amortization and Depletion **15**	0.6	0.0	•	•	0.0	0.0	0.1	0.2	0.4	0.7	•	0.8	•
Pensions and Other Deferred Comp. **16**	0.6	0.3	0.0	•	0.5	0.0	0.2	1.1	1.3	1.5	•	0.5	•
Employee Benefits **17**	2.5	2.4	0.0	•	1.0	1.7	1.2	2.2	2.7	2.5	•	3.1	•
Advertising **18**	1.8	1.0	0.2	•	1.2	0.3	0.6	0.3	1.2	2.8	•	2.4	•
Other Expenses **19**	11.6	11.1	20.0	•	7.2	9.7	8.6	8.1	9.5	14.7	•	12.6	•
Officers' Compensation **20**	1.5	4.7	25.6	•	2.5	2.5	2.8	2.1	1.0	1.0	•	0.3	•
Operating Margin **21**	2.6	•	1.8	•	3.8	4.4	5.8	4.8	3.9	3.7	•	1.4	•
Operating Margin Before Officers' Comp. **22**	4.1	•	27.4	•	6.2	6.9	8.5	6.9	4.9	4.7	•	1.8	•

Selected Average Balance Sheet ($ in Thousands)

Net Receivables	23	1743	0	0	•	755	1684	2782	4655	13064	30957	•	144075	•
Inventories	24	1223	0	11	•	307	746	1854	3023	6220	13396	•	124646	•
Net Property, Plant and Equipment	25	4031	0	15	•	764	2787	6451	13977	34761	52606	•	367862	•
Total Assets	26	14347	0	72	•	2454	8042	15712	34937	75411	181888	•	1515700	•
Notes and Loans Payable	27	4081	0	14	•	550	2080	4612	7758	19533	27322	•	474270	•
All Other Liabilities	28	5006	0	1	•	535	1695	3271	4872	19339	44103	•	622777	•
Net Worth	29	5261	0	56	•	1369	4268	7830	22306	36539	110464	•	418653	•

Selected Financial Ratios (Times to 1)

Current Ratio	30	1.5	•	23.8	•	2.9	1.5	1.9	2.2	1.6	2.0	•	1.2	•
Quick Ratio	31	0.9	•	23.0	•	2.2	1.0	1.2	1.5	1.1	1.3	•	0.7	•
Net Sales to Working Capital	32	14.1	•	16.9	•	8.4	19.3	9.8	8.0	14.4	6.2	•	21.7	•
Coverage Ratio	33	5.4	8.5	1064.2	•	17.2	11.7	8.5	9.5	9.0	9.6	•	4.1	•
Total Asset Turnover	34	1.5	•	7.1	•	3.5	3.2	2.3	1.8	2.0	1.3	•	1.2	•
Inventory Turnover	35	11.7	•	18.0	•	21.3	22.9	13.9	14.2	15.5	10.5	•	9.7	•
Receivables Turnover	36	13.0	•	46442.1	•	16.1	17.2	15.4	17.1	13.5	9.6	•	11.7	•
Total Liabilities to Net Worth	37	1.7	•	0.3	•	0.8	0.9	1.0	0.6	1.1	0.6	•	2.6	•
Current Assets to Working Capital	38	3.2	•	1.0	•	1.5	2.8	2.1	1.8	2.6	2.0	•	5.3	•
Current Liabilities to Working Capital	39	2.2	•	0.0	•	0.5	1.8	1.1	0.8	1.6	1.0	•	4.3	•
Working Capital to Net Sales	40	0.1	•	0.1	•	0.1	0.1	0.1	0.1	0.1	0.2	•	0.0	•
Inventory to Working Capital	41	0.8	•	0.0	•	0.3	0.6	0.6	0.5	0.7	0.4	•	1.5	•
Total Receipts to Cash Flow	42	8.6	4.8	9.6	•	12.3	9.6	7.4	8.2	9.3	5.4	•	9.3	•
Cost of Goods to Cash Flow	43	5.7	3.3	3.7	•	9.3	6.4	5.2	5.6	5.9	3.3	•	6.2	•
Cash Flow to Total Debt	44	0.3	•	3.4	•	0.6	0.7	0.6	0.6	0.4	0.6	•	0.2	•

Selected Financial Factors (in Percentages)

Debt Ratio	45	63.3	•	21.5	•	44.2	46.9	50.2	36.2	51.5	39.3	•	72.4	•
Return on Total Assets	46	9.7	•	12.5	•	15.1	16.2	18.1	10.5	10.0	8.3	•	8.2	•
Return on Equity Before Income Taxes	47	21.6	•	15.9	•	25.6	28.0	32.0	14.7	18.3	12.3	•	22.4	•
Return on Equity After Income Taxes	48	17.6	•	13.8	•	24.0	27.5	29.9	13.5	16.3	11.6	•	15.9	•
Profit Margin (Before Income Tax)	49	5.3	13.1	1.8	•	4.0	4.6	6.9	5.3	4.4	5.8	•	5.2	•
Profit Margin (After Income Tax)	50	4.3	13.1	1.5	•	3.8	4.6	6.4	4.8	3.9	5.5	•	3.7	•

Table I

Corporations with and without Net Income

OTHER FOOD

MONEY AMOUNTS AND SIZE OF ASSETS IN THOUSANDS OF DOLLARS

Item Description for Accounting Period 7/12 Through 6/13		Total	Zero Assets	Under 500	500 to 1,000	1,000 to 5,000	5,000 to 10,000	10,000 to 25,000	25,000 to 50,000	50,000 to 100,000	100,000 to 250,000	250,000 to 500,000	500,000 to 2,500,000	2,500,000 and over
Number of Enterprises	1	3215	472	1099	449	700	139	165	82	43	37	16	10	3

Revenues ($ in Thousands)														
Net Sales	2	129914672	4483472	448557	1450636	3488744	2026240	5023137	6839861	5345114	10376778	7987002	14137378	68307753
Interest	3	1982056	4326	1	3	801	941	394	810	2742	5075	2597	48902	1915463
Rents	4	135251	0	0	0	6	70	725	1359	8619	6674	10715	2022	105060
Royalties	5	1072443	23193	0	0	0	0	51	1828	81	924	18746	871	1026749
Other Portfolio Income	6	372880	598	0	0	4420	37759	1504	1926	23785	29914	12909	55982	204083
Other Receipts	7	5358582	-5200	0	4574	15109	7516	40340	29413	11242	77817	16820	492798	4668155
Total Receipts	8	138835884	4506389	448558	1455213	3509080	2072526	5066151	6875197	5391583	10497182	8048789	14737953	76227263
Average Total Receipts	9	43184	9547	408	3241	5013	14910	30704	83844	125386	283708	503049	1473795	25409088

Operating Costs/Operating Income (%)														
Cost of Operations	10	71.4	65.7	42.8	73.5	73.0	67.0	73.7	79.0	78.0	65.7	71.9	75.8	70.4
Salaries and Wages	11	5.7	7.0	20.9	2.4	7.9	7.2	6.1	4.5	4.8	7.7	5.6	3.4	5.7
Taxes Paid	12	1.1	0.9	4.6	2.7	1.9	2.6	1.4	0.9	1.0	1.5	1.0	0.9	0.9
Interest Paid	13	5.1	2.6	0.0	0.5	0.6	0.5	0.5	0.4	1.0	0.9	1.6	2.9	8.4
Depreciation	14	1.8	2.0	0.1	0.9	1.2	1.3	1.8	1.3	2.5	2.6	2.1	2.5	1.5
Amortization and Depletion	15	0.5	0.3	0.0	0.1	0.1	0.1	0.1	0.3	0.5	0.4	0.6	0.9	0.6
Pensions and Other Deferred Comp.	16	0.6	1.4	0.4	0.0	0.2	0.3	0.4	0.2	0.2	0.4	0.2	0.5	0.7
Employee Benefits	17	1.5	0.9	0.0	0.4	1.4	1.3	1.0	0.7	1.0	2.1	0.7	1.3	1.8
Advertising	18	2.8	5.6	0.4	0.2	0.8	0.4	0.6	1.3	1.1	1.8	3.3	0.6	3.8
Other Expenses	19	12.3	7.0	18.6	13.0	9.7	11.3	7.1	5.2	6.4	12.9	7.3	10.3	15.3
Officers' Compensation	20	0.6	1.2	12.8	2.6	3.2	3.6	1.7	0.9	1.3	0.8	0.9	0.4	0.1
Operating Margin	21	•	5.4	•	3.6	0.0	4.4	5.7	5.4	2.3	3.3	4.8	0.5	•
Operating Margin Before Officers' Comp.	22	•	6.7	12.0	6.2	3.2	8.0	7.4	6.3	3.6	4.1	5.7	1.0	•

Selected Average Balance Sheet ($ in Thousands)

Net Receivables 23	74504	0	0	272	349	1608	3084	6413	12690	21218	32844	155994	78162854
Inventories 24	3041	0	3	46	435	1519	3645	8482	15790	32255	51233	168541	1187237
Net Property, Plant and Equipment 25	5004	0	6	91	412	1567	4280	9175	18950	50336	74895	276226	2479916
Total Assets 26	147599	0	16	738	1886	6491	14689	34564	70466	157726	308382	1225019	146883280
Notes and Loans Payable 27	22852	0	12	138	845	2226	3692	7727	22075	38945	111577	538565	20563631
All Other Liabilities 28	88215	0	11	275	582	1153	3419	10665	22308	47747	98680	312128	91347646
Net Worth 29	36532	0	-6	326	459	3112	7579	16173	26083	71034	98125	374326	34972002

Selected Financial Ratios (Times to 1)

Current Ratio 30	0.9	•	0.4	1.3	2.0	3.1	2.0	1.7	1.5	2.0	1.4	2.0	0.9
Quick Ratio 31	0.9	•	0.2	1.0	0.9	1.8	1.1	0.8	0.7	1.0	0.5	0.9	0.9
Net Sales to Working Capital 32	•	•	•	35.4	8.7	5.3	6.8	9.6	9.7	8.0	14.2	6.2	•
Coverage Ratio 33	1.8	3.3	•	9.0	2.0	13.9	14.3	15.8	4.1	6.1	4.5	2.7	1.4
Total Asset Turnover 34	0.3	•	25.3	4.4	2.6	2.2	2.1	2.4	1.8	1.8	1.6	1.2	0.2
Inventory Turnover 35	9.5	•	58.8	51.7	8.4	6.4	6.2	7.8	6.1	5.7	7.0	6.4	13.5
Receivables Turnover 36	0.5	•	380.9	19.5	14.1	9.0	10.2	14.2	10.4	13.7	14.5	8.9	0.3
Total Liabilities to Net Worth 37	3.0	•	•	1.3	3.1	1.1	0.9	1.1	1.7	1.2	2.1	2.3	3.2
Current Assets to Working Capital 38	•	•	•	4.3	2.0	1.5	2.0	2.3	2.9	2.0	3.6	2.0	•
Current Liabilities to Working Capital 39	•	•	•	3.3	1.0	0.5	1.0	1.3	1.9	1.0	2.6	1.0	•
Working Capital to Net Sales 40	•	•	•	0.0	0.1	0.2	0.1	0.1	0.1	0.1	0.1	0.2	•
Inventory to Working Capital 41	•	•	•	0.9	0.8	0.5	0.8	1.1	1.3	0.9	1.9	0.7	•
Total Receipts to Cash Flow 42	7.1	9.7	7.2	7.8	13.7	6.2	8.5	10.1	12.8	6.5	8.9	7.7	6.2
Cost of Goods to Cash Flow 43	5.1	6.4	3.1	5.8	10.0	4.1	6.3	8.0	10.0	4.3	6.4	5.8	4.4
Cash Flow to Total Debt 44	0.1	•	2.5	1.0	0.3	0.7	0.5	0.5	0.2	0.5	0.3	0.2	0.0

Selected Financial Factors (in Percentages)

Debt Ratio 45	75.2	•	139.3	55.8	75.7	52.1	48.4	53.2	63.0	55.0	68.2	69.4	76.2
Return on Total Assets 46	2.5	•	•	19.3	3.3	16.2	14.7	15.2	7.3	9.6	11.5	8.9	1.8
Return on Equity Before Income Taxes 47	4.5	•	49.4	38.9	6.7	31.4	26.4	30.5	14.9	17.8	28.3	18.3	2.2
Return on Equity After Income Taxes 48	3.3	•	49.4	38.7	5.0	30.5	25.4	29.3	13.0	14.8	23.2	11.1	1.4
Profit Margin (Before Income Tax) 49	4.1	5.9	•	3.9	0.6	6.7	6.6	5.9	3.1	4.5	5.6	4.9	3.3
Profit Margin (After Income Tax) 50	3.0	3.4	•	3.9	0.5	6.5	6.3	5.7	2.7	3.8	4.6	3.0	2.1

Table II

Corporations with Net Income

OTHER FOOD

MONEY AMOUNTS AND SIZE OF ASSETS IN THOUSANDS OF DOLLARS

Item Description for Accounting Period 7/12 Through 6/13	Total	Zero Assets	Under 500	500 to 1,000	1,000 to 5,000	5,000 to 10,000	10,000 to 25,000	25,000 to 50,000	50,000 to 100,000	100,000 to 250,000	250,000 to 500,000	500,000 to 2,500,000	2,500,000 and over
Number of Enterprises **1**	2367	8	1082	328	550	106	135	70	32	31	•	•	0

Revenues ($ in Thousands)													
Net Sales **2**	103874897	4014295	448557	1363329	2303378	1606101	4166447	6378099	4404744	9350543	•	•	0
Interest **3**	1968346	4257	1	0	489	844	339	786	2728	5004	•	•	0
Rents **4**	134185	0	0	0	6	0	601	1359	8600	6583	•	•	0
Royalties **5**	728014	23041	0	0	0	0	0	0	81	395	•	•	0
Other Portfolio Income **6**	263308	548	0	0	4333	37759	1504	1685	23675	29839	•	•	0
Other Receipts **7**	5203030	2826	0	4574	12080	5757	39746	28653	9781	76349	•	•	0
Total Receipts **8**	112171780	4044967	448558	1367903	2320286	1650461	4208637	6410582	4449609	9468713	•	•	0
Average Total Receipts **9**	47390	505621	415	4170	4219	15570	31175	91580	139050	305442	•	•	•

Operating Costs/Operating Income (%)													
Cost of Operations **10**	73.4	66.2	42.8	75.1	65.8	64.5	72.7	78.9	79.4	65.4	•	•	•
Salaries and Wages **11**	5.4	5.9	20.3	1.8	8.7	7.0	5.9	4.6	3.8	7.8	•	•	•
Taxes Paid **12**	1.2	0.9	4.5	2.7	2.2	3.0	1.3	0.8	0.9	1.6	•	•	•
Interest Paid **13**	3.6	2.6	0.0	0.5	0.3	0.5	0.4	0.4	0.9	0.7	•	•	•
Depreciation **14**	1.6	2.1	0.1	0.8	1.4	1.4	1.8	1.1	1.9	2.3	•	•	•
Amortization and Depletion **15**	0.3	0.2	0.0	•	0.0	0.1	0.1	0.1	0.4	0.3	•	•	•
Pensions and Other Deferred Comp. **16**	0.6	1.5	0.4	0.0	0.1	0.3	0.4	0.2	0.1	0.4	•	•	•
Employee Benefits **17**	1.0	0.8	0.0	0.4	0.9	1.5	0.9	0.7	0.7	2.2	•	•	•
Advertising **18**	2.3	5.1	0.3	0.1	1.2	0.4	0.5	0.9	0.9	1.9	•	•	•
Other Expenses **19**	12.7	5.8	13.7	11.5	10.6	9.7	6.8	5.1	5.2	12.7	•	•	•
Officers' Compensation **20**	0.6	0.0	12.8	2.1	3.2	3.8	1.8	0.9	1.3	0.8	•	•	•
Operating Margin **21**	•	8.9	5.1	4.9	5.7	7.8	7.3	6.4	4.4	3.9	•	•	•
Operating Margin Before Officers' Comp. **22**	•	8.9	17.9	7.0	8.9	11.6	9.1	7.3	5.7	4.7	•	•	•

	Selected Average Balance Sheet ($ in Thousands)												
Net Receivables 23	98933	0	0	291	285	1712	3087	7024	13989	22947	•	•	•
Inventories 24	3529	0	1	100	400	1250	3384	8884	16810	32520	•	•	•
Net Property, Plant and Equipment 25	5637	0	6	107	440	1728	4398	9097	15735	49913	•	•	•
Total Assets 26	173789	0	14	793	1770	6440	14697	35391	70322	163063	•	•	•
Notes and Loans Payable 27	22058	0	0	97	590	1656	3242	7968	20786	31473	•	•	•
All Other Liabilities 28	115239	0	6	342	358	943	3020	10589	24114	51459	•	•	•
Net Worth 29	36492	0	8	354	822	3841	8435	16834	25423	80132	•	•	•

	Selected Financial Ratios (Times to 1)												
Current Ratio 30	0.9	•	1.2	1.2	3.1	3.3	2.3	1.8	1.6	2.0	•	•	•
Quick Ratio 31	0.9	•	0.8	0.9	1.4	2.2	1.3	0.8	0.7	1.0	•	•	•
Net Sales to Working Capital 32	•	•	319.7	71.6	6.2	6.0	6.3	9.3	9.4	7.8	•	•	•
Coverage Ratio 33	2.6	4.6	3240.1	12.0	24.9	22.3	21.7	19.1	7.0	8.5	•	•	•
Total Asset Turnover 34	0.3	•	29.6	5.2	2.4	2.4	2.1	2.6	2.0	1.8	•	•	•
Inventory Turnover 35	9.1	•	129.8	31.1	6.9	7.8	6.6	8.1	6.5	6.1	•	•	•
Receivables Turnover 36	0.4	•	1937.6	•	11.5	9.2	10.4	15.0	11.2	14.5	•	•	•
Total Liabilities to Net Worth 37	3.8	•	0.8	1.2	1.2	0.7	0.7	1.1	1.8	1.0	•	•	•
Current Assets to Working Capital 38	•	•	5.9	7.1	1.5	1.4	1.8	2.2	2.8	2.0	•	•	•
Current Liabilities to Working Capital 39	•	•	4.9	6.1	0.5	0.4	0.8	1.2	1.8	1.0	•	•	•
Working Capital to Net Sales 40	•	•	0.0	0.0	0.2	0.2	0.2	0.1	0.1	0.1	•	•	•
Inventory to Working Capital 41	•	•	2.1	1.7	0.5	0.4	0.7	1.1	1.3	0.8	•	•	•
Total Receipts to Cash Flow 42	6.2	7.6	6.8	7.7	7.4	5.4	7.6	9.2	11.3	6.3	•	•	•
Cost of Goods to Cash Flow 43	4.6	5.0	2.9	5.8	4.9	3.5	5.5	7.2	9.0	4.1	•	•	•
Cash Flow to Total Debt 44	0.1	•	9.7	1.2	0.6	1.1	0.6	0.5	0.3	0.6	•	•	•

	Selected Financial Factors (in Percentages)												
Debt Ratio 45	79.0	•	45.1	55.4	53.6	40.4	42.6	52.4	63.8	50.9	•	•	•
Return on Total Assets 46	2.4	•	149.6	30.0	16.0	26.1	18.4	18.8	12.3	11.0	•	•	•
Return on Equity Before Income Taxes 47	6.9	•	272.5	61.5	33.0	41.7	30.5	37.5	29.1	19.8	•	•	•
Return on Equity After Income Taxes 48	5.2	•	272.4	61.3	31.8	40.7	29.3	36.2	26.5	16.7	•	•	•
Profit Margin (Before Income Tax) 49	5.7	9.6	5.1	5.2	6.5	10.6	8.3	6.9	5.4	5.3	•	•	•
Profit Margin (After Income Tax) 50	4.3	6.8	5.1	5.2	6.2	10.3	8.0	6.7	4.9	4.4	•	•	•

Table I

Corporations with and without Net Income

SOFT DRINK AND ICE

MONEY AMOUNTS AND SIZE OF ASSETS IN THOUSANDS OF DOLLARS

Item Description for Accounting Period 7/12 Through 6/13		Total	Zero Assets	Under 500	500 to 1,000	1,000 to 5,000	5,000 to 10,000	10,000 to 25,000	25,000 to 50,000	50,000 to 100,000	100,000 to 250,000	250,000 to 500,000	500,000 to 2,500,000	2,500,000 and over
Number of Enterprises	1	491	4	260	65	69	11	18	26	11	14	7	4	3
Revenues ($ in Thousands)														
Net Sales	2	48014181	131037	10849	188608	395107	200068	561230	2143466	1599150	4094696	2517628	4405062	31767280
Interest	3	79445	0	3	3	250	123	3	367	3366	523	4867	3525	66416
Rents	4	53216	20	0	0	263	271	205	0	135	2148	7360	5198	37616
Royalties	5	1242602	0	0	0	0	0	0	0	0	44	194	0	1242365
Other Portfolio Income	6	1732392	6356	0	1	1430	6073	397	342	816	36836	6366	2814	1670960
Other Receipts	7	2653660	29	0	-54	562	9773	15053	4877	9803	35112	33443	484993	2060069
Total Receipts	8	53775496	137442	10852	188558	397612	216308	576888	2149052	1613270	4169359	2569858	4901592	36844706
Average Total Receipts	9	109522	34360	42	2901	5762	19664	32049	82656	146661	297811	367123	1225398	12281569
Operating Costs/Operating Income (%)														
Cost of Operations	10	49.6	62.8	105.6	66.1	65.9	43.9	75.7	71.7	60.3	70.1	59.8	63.1	41.4
Salaries and Wages	11	13.9	17.4	•	3.2	10.0	11.0	5.5	7.1	14.7	6.9	14.1	16.7	15.0
Taxes Paid	12	1.9	0.5	0.4	3.8	2.0	2.7	1.2	1.5	1.3	1.2	2.9	2.3	1.9
Interest Paid	13	2.1	2.0	•	0.1	0.9	1.6	0.5	0.6	0.7	1.6	3.5	4.2	2.0
Depreciation	14	4.4	2.0	3.2	1.0	5.5	2.0	1.4	2.7	1.8	3.3	3.4	4.1	5.0
Amortization and Depletion	15	1.2	0.1	•	0.1	0.0	1.0	0.8	0.1	0.8	0.8	0.9	1.2	1.4
Pensions and Other Deferred Comp.	16	3.3	•	•	0.8	0.0	0.3	0.2	0.4	0.2	0.5	1.5	0.5	4.7
Employee Benefits	17	4.2	7.1	•	4.2	1.2	2.0	0.6	2.1	0.9	1.9	1.9	3.7	5.1
Advertising	18	3.6	0.6	4.7	2.2	0.8	2.4	3.0	1.9	3.1	2.3	1.0	0.8	4.6
Other Expenses	19	18.2	8.2	13.4	21.5	19.1	22.7	6.7	6.4	7.0	9.1	11.4	13.6	22.2
Officers' Compensation	20	0.5	3.9	•	4.6	2.5	2.4	1.3	1.8	1.9	0.5	0.3	0.7	0.2
Operating Margin	21	•	•	•	•	•	8.1	3.0	3.6	7.3	1.7	•	•	•
Operating Margin Before Officers' Comp.	22	•	•	•	•	•	10.5	4.3	5.4	9.2	2.3	•	•	•

	Selected Average Balance Sheet ($ in Thousands)												
Net Receivables 23	8528	0	5	137	378	1493	2214	6592	12509	19241	30059	137184	919002
Inventories 24	5724	0	7	379	94	638	1942	5312	7597	15623	21706	72136	618240
Net Property, Plant and Equipment 25	27419	0	5	53	1453	2103	4157	11784	21136	62563	103220	310284	3293681
Total Assets 26	138011	0	28	634	2800	7539	17617	37224	71471	161982	352065	900469	19011162
Notes and Loans Payable 27	80456	0	1	143	1012	1928	2978	19883	16573	54352	124851	483218	11694292
All Other Liabilities 28	36996	0	11	105	1164	7002	3520	15189	20309	53468	109920	325828	4831667
Net Worth 29	20559	0	16	387	625	-1391	11119	2153	34589	54162	117294	91423	2485204

	Selected Financial Ratios (Times to 1)												
Current Ratio 30	0.4	•	2.1	5.4	0.5	0.4	1.7	1.2	2.0	1.4	1.1	1.3	0.3
Quick Ratio 31	0.2	•	1.4	2.2	0.4	0.2	1.2	0.7	1.1	0.7	0.7	0.9	0.2
Net Sales to Working Capital 32	•	•	3.5	6.3	•	•	12.2	30.7	9.3	21.8	36.2	16.6	•
Coverage Ratio 33	6.7	1.2	•	•	•	11.2	13.5	7.2	13.3	3.3	1.4	1.1	9.4
Total Asset Turnover 34	0.7	•	1.5	4.6	2.0	2.4	1.8	2.2	2.0	1.8	1.0	1.2	0.6
Inventory Turnover 35	8.5	•	6.0	5.1	40.2	12.5	12.2	11.1	11.5	13.1	9.9	9.6	7.1
Receivables Turnover 36	11.4	•	15.9	14.7	21.2	12.6	11.6	12.4	11.0	14.3	11.9	8.4	11.4
Total Liabilities to Net Worth 37	5.7	•	0.7	0.6	3.5	•	0.6	16.3	1.1	2.0	2.0	8.8	6.6
Current Assets to Working Capital 38	•	•	1.9	1.2	•	•	2.3	6.3	2.0	3.7	8.8	3.9	•
Current Liabilities to Working Capital 39	•	•	0.9	0.2	•	•	1.3	5.3	1.0	2.7	7.8	2.9	•
Working Capital to Net Sales 40	•	•	0.3	0.2	•	•	0.1	0.0	0.1	0.0	0.0	0.1	•
Inventory to Working Capital 41	•	•	0.6	0.7	•	•	0.6	2.4	0.5	1.2	2.0	1.1	•
Total Receipts to Cash Flow 42	4.0	15.0	•	13.0	17.2	3.0	8.5	12.0	7.3	9.3	11.2	9.6	3.1
Cost of Goods to Cash Flow 43	2.0	9.4	•	8.6	11.4	1.3	6.5	8.6	4.4	6.5	6.7	6.0	1.3
Cash Flow to Total Debt 44	0.2	•	•	0.9	0.2	0.7	0.6	0.2	0.5	0.3	0.1	0.1	0.2

	Selected Financial Factors (in Percentages)												
Debt Ratio 45	85.1	•	42.3	39.0	77.7	118.5	36.9	94.2	51.6	66.6	66.7	89.8	86.9
Return on Total Assets 46	10.0	•	•	•	•	42.9	11.0	9.9	18.0	9.3	4.9	5.7	10.4
Return on Equity Before Income Taxes 47	57.0	•	•	•	•	•	16.1	147.1	34.4	19.3	4.1	5.1	71.4
Return on Equity After Income Taxes 48	37.7	•	•	•	•	•	15.6	137.7	33.5	14.5	1.2	•	46.5
Profit Margin (Before Income Tax) 49	12.0	0.4	•	•	•	16.2	5.7	3.8	8.2	3.6	1.3	0.4	16.8
Profit Margin (After Income Tax) 50	7.9	0.4	•	•	•	15.6	5.6	3.6	8.0	2.7	0.4	•	10.9

Table II

Corporations with Net Income

SOFT DRINK AND ICE

MONEY AMOUNTS AND SIZE OF ASSETS IN THOUSANDS OF DOLLARS

Item Description for Accounting Period 7/12 Through 6/13	Total	Zero Assets	Under 500	500 to 1000	1,000 to 5,000	5,000 to 10,000	10,000 to 25,000	25,000 to 50,000	50,000 to 100,000	100,000 to 250,000	250,000 to 500,000	500,000 to 2,500,000	2,500,000 and over
Number of Enterprises 1	165	•	0	58	31	11	12	22	•	10	•	0	3

Revenues ($ in Thousands)

Item Description for Accounting Period 7/12 Through 6/13	Total	Zero Assets	Under 500	500 to 1000	1,000 to 5,000	5,000 to 10,000	10,000 to 25,000	25,000 to 50,000	50,000 to 100,000	100,000 to 250,000	250,000 to 500,000	500,000 to 2,500,000	2,500,000 and over
Net Sales 2	43839215	•	0	173123	291849	200068	465989	1698855	•	3425689	•	0	31767280
Interest 3	71088	•	0	2	0	123	0	366	•	410	•	0	66416
Rents 4	48489	•	0	0	0	271	0	0	•	107	•	0	37616
Royalties 5	1242408	•	0	0	0	0	0	0	•	44	•	0	1242365
Other Portfolio Income 6	1692602	•	0	1	1430	6073	396	279	•	886	•	0	1670960
Other Receipts 7	2637628	•	0	294	301	9773	15028	4844	•	29271	•	0	2060069
Total Receipts 8	49531430	•	0	173420	293580	216308	481413	1704344	•	3456407	•	0	36844706
Average Total Receipts 9	300190	•	•	2990	9470	19664	40118	77470	•	345641	•	•	12281569

Operating Costs/Operating Income (%)

Item Description for Accounting Period 7/12 Through 6/13	Total	Zero Assets	Under 500	500 to 1000	1,000 to 5,000	5,000 to 10,000	10,000 to 25,000	25,000 to 50,000	50,000 to 100,000	100,000 to 250,000	250,000 to 500,000	500,000 to 2,500,000	2,500,000 and over
Cost of Operations 10	48.1	•	•	63.9	64.9	43.9	76.4	69.4	•	71.5	•	•	41.4
Salaries and Wages 11	14.1	•	•	0.6	9.7	11.0	4.2	7.8	•	6.1	•	•	15.0
Taxes Paid 12	1.8	•	•	3.8	1.5	2.7	1.1	1.5	•	1.1	•	•	1.9
Interest Paid 13	1.7	•	•	0.1	0.4	1.6	0.2	0.5	•	0.5	•	•	2.0
Depreciation 14	4.3	•	•	1.0	1.3	2.0	1.2	2.3	•	2.4	•	•	5.0
Amortization and Depletion 15	1.1	•	•	0.1	•	1.0	0.6	0.0	•	0.6	•	•	1.4
Pensions and Other Deferred Comp. 16	3.6	•	•	0.8	0.0	0.3	0.2	0.4	•	0.4	•	•	4.7
Employee Benefits 17	4.4	•	•	4.6	1.4	2.0	0.5	2.1	•	1.9	•	•	5.1
Advertising 18	3.9	•	•	2.0	0.8	2.4	3.4	2.1	•	2.6	•	•	4.6
Other Expenses 19	18.9	•	•	19.9	16.2	22.7	5.7	6.3	•	7.9	•	•	22.2
Officers' Compensation 20	0.5	•	•	3.0	2.4	2.4	0.9	2.2	•	0.4	•	•	0.2
Operating Margin 21	•	•	•	0.3	1.3	8.1	5.4	5.3	•	4.4	•	•	•
Operating Margin Before Officers' Comp. 22	•	•	•	3.3	3.7	10.5	6.3	7.5	•	4.9	•	•	•

Selected Average Balance Sheet ($ in Thousands)

Net Receivables **23**	22770	•	•	139	510	1493	2499	6247	•	21941	•	•	919002
Inventories **24**	15112	•	•	321	95	638	2644	5360	•	17651	•	•	618240
Net Property, Plant and Equipment **25**	72126	•	•	52	334	2103	2785	9972	•	55161	•	•	3293681
Total Assets **26**	388158	•	•	637	1473	7539	18364	36715	•	166126	•	•	19011162
Notes and Loans Payable **27**	224780	•	•	156	536	1928	1639	9893	•	45939	•	•	11694292
All Other Liabilities **28**	104559	•	•	72	1173	7002	3373	12626	•	57500	•	•	4831667
Net Worth **29**	58820	•	•	409	-236	-1391	13352	14196	•	62687	•	•	2485204

Selected Financial Ratios (Times to 1)

Current Ratio **30**	0.4	•	•	7.9	0.7	0.4	2.6	1.9	•	1.2	•	•	0.3
Quick Ratio **31**	0.2	•	•	3.2	0.5	0.2	1.9	1.1	•	0.7	•	•	0.2
Net Sales to Working Capital **32**	•	•	•	6.1	•	•	8.6	9.3	•	37.9	•	•	•
Coverage Ratio **33**	9.1	•	•	8.2	5.4	11.2	39.8	13.0	•	11.1	•	•	9.4
Total Asset Turnover **34**	0.7	•	•	4.7	6.4	2.4	2.1	2.1	•	2.1	•	•	0.6
Inventory Turnover **35**	8.5	•	•	5.9	64.6	12.5	11.2	10.0	•	13.9	•	•	7.1
Receivables Turnover **36**	11.6	•	•	22.7	23.0	12.6	10.7	15.6	•	14.9	•	•	11.4
Total Liabilities to Net Worth **37**	5.6	•	•	0.6	•	•	0.4	1.6	•	1.7	•	•	6.6
Current Assets to Working Capital **38**	•	•	•	1.1	•	•	1.6	2.1	•	5.5	•	•	•
Current Liabilities to Working Capital **39**	•	•	•	0.1	•	•	0.6	1.1	•	4.5	•	•	•
Working Capital to Net Sales **40**	•	•	•	0.2	•	•	0.1	0.1	•	0.0	•	•	•
Inventory to Working Capital **41**	•	•	•	0.6	•	•	0.4	0.8	•	2.0	•	•	•
Total Receipts to Cash Flow **42**	3.6	•	•	7.3	7.9	3.0	7.2	9.8	•	8.7	•	•	3.1
Cost of Goods to Cash Flow **43**	1.8	•	•	4.6	5.1	1.3	5.5	6.8	•	6.2	•	•	1.3
Cash Flow to Total Debt **44**	0.2	•	•	1.8	0.7	0.7	1.1	0.3	•	0.4	•	•	0.2

Selected Financial Factors (in Percentages)

Debt Ratio **45**	84.8	•	•	35.8	116.0	118.5	27.3	61.3	•	62.3	•	•	86.9
Return on Total Assets **46**	10.5	•	•	2.4	14.8	42.9	18.9	12.8	•	12.1	•	•	10.4
Return on Equity Before Income Taxes **47**	61.8	•	•	3.3	•	•	25.3	30.5	•	29.2	•	•	71.4
Return on Equity After Income Taxes **48**	41.7	•	•	2.8	•	•	24.7	28.8	•	23.4	•	•	46.5
Profit Margin (Before Income Tax) **49**	13.7	•	•	0.5	1.9	16.2	8.7	5.6	•	5.3	•	•	16.8
Profit Margin (After Income Tax) **50**	9.2	•	•	0.4	1.9	15.6	8.5	5.3	•	4.3	•	•	10.9

Table I

Corporations with and without Net Income

BREWERIES

MONEY AMOUNTS AND SIZE OF ASSETS IN THOUSANDS OF DOLLARS

Item Description for Accounting Period 7/12 Through 6/13	Total	Zero Assets	Under 500	500 to 1,000	1,000 to 5,000	5,000 to 10,000	10,000 to 25,000	25,000 to 50,000	50,000 to 100,000	100,000 to 250,000	250,000 to 500,000	500,000 to 2,500,000	2,500,000 and over
Number of Enterprises 1	402	•	96	201	5	58	•	6	•	4	3	4	0
Revenues ($ in Thousands)													
Net Sales 2	22276261	•	67131	56351	42777	356459	•	248307	•	876863	833439	18386126	0
Interest 3	14941	•	0	0	0	50	•	0	•	4	48	14632	0
Rents 4	3618	•	0	0	0	0	•	0	•	0	0	3618	0
Royalties 5	215571	•	0	0	0	0	•	0	•	0	0	215533	0
Other Portfolio Income 6	36211	•	0	0	0	17028	•	66	•	3239	516	15295	0
Other Receipts 7	360320	•	0	15	162	323	•	9240	•	8953	4781	331407	0
Total Receipts 8	22906922	•	67131	56366	42939	373860	•	257613	•	889059	838784	18966611	0
Average Total Receipts 9	56982	•	699	280	8588	6446	•	42936	•	222265	279595	4741653	•
Operating Costs/Operating Income (%)													
Cost of Operations 10	42.4	•	42.1	20.0	34.3	56.4	•	62.0	•	60.4	40.8	39.8	•
Salaries and Wages 11	7.1	•	3.2	4.2	2.3	6.1	•	7.0	•	4.5	11.8	7.2	•
Taxes Paid 12	11.1	•	0.9	4.7	2.8	3.2	•	2.7	•	10.5	3.9	12.1	•
Interest Paid 13	13.1	•	2.9	3.4	0.4	0.5	•	1.9	•	0.2	0.3	15.7	•
Depreciation 14	2.5	•	18.2	0.4	1.9	9.3	•	3.8	•	2.9	5.6	2.0	•
Amortization and Depletion 15	0.7	•	0.2	0.0	•	0.0	•	0.3	•	0.0	0.4	0.8	•
Pensions and Other Deferred Comp. 16	1.4	•	•	0.9	0.3	0.4	•	0.8	•	1.1	0.3	1.6	•
Employee Benefits 17	1.2	•	•	1.0	0.9	1.6	•	0.5	•	0.6	1.2	1.2	•
Advertising 18	3.8	•	4.2	0.1	2.1	3.0	•	0.8	•	3.9	3.7	4.0	•
Other Expenses 19	10.7	•	31.2	6.2	13.0	7.9	•	15.0	•	5.8	20.7	10.5	•
Officers' Compensation 20	0.5	•	•	2.8	3.3	2.2	•	0.8	•	0.7	0.4	0.4	•
Operating Margin 21	5.6	•	•	56.2	38.7	9.2	•	4.4	•	9.5	10.8	4.8	•
Operating Margin Before Officers' Comp. 22	6.1	•	•	59.0	41.9	11.4	•	5.2	•	10.2	11.2	5.2	•

Selected Average Balance Sheet ($ in Thousands)

Net Receivables 23	5419	•	0	18	151	388	•	6218	•	45795	15115	450660	•
Inventories 24	1953	•	27	1	6387	520	•	7993	•	9586	92894	153271	•
Net Property, Plant and Equipment 25	17707	•	260	310	1515	3826	•	19841	•	58845	108367	1458084	•
Total Assets 26	238930	•	349	975	4380	6524	•	41010	•	175857	295771	23236236	•
Notes and Loans Payable 27	153217	•	497	841	955	3304	•	10646	•	78171	1593	15161826	•
All Other Liabilities 28	29793	•	45	29	474	903	•	10104	•	44310	114523	2803073	•
Net Worth 29	55919	•	-192	105	2951	2317	•	20260	•	53377	179655	5271338	•

Selected Financial Ratios (Times to 1)

Current Ratio 30	1.5	•	0.7	29.5	4.0	3.5	•	1.3	•	2.2	2.0	1.5	•
Quick Ratio 31	1.3	•	0.4	29.4	1.7	2.6	•	0.7	•	2.0	1.3	1.2	•
Net Sales to Working Capital 32	4.8	•	•	0.5	4.0	3.3	•	15.2	•	3.9	7.5	4.7	•
Coverage Ratio 33	1.6	•	•	17.5	98.1	28.1	•	5.2	•	58.7	45.9	1.5	•
Total Asset Turnover 34	0.2	•	2.0	0.3	2.0	0.9	•	1.0	•	1.2	0.9	0.2	•
Inventory Turnover 35	12.0	•	10.8	45.0	0.5	6.7	•	3.2	•	13.8	1.2	11.9	•
Receivables Turnover 36	9.8	•	17.5	15.1	11.3	16.2	•	2.5	•	5.1	0.8	20.4	•
Total Liabilities to Net Worth 37	3.3	•	•	8.3	0.5	1.8	•	1.0	•	2.3	0.6	3.4	•
Current Assets to Working Capital 38	3.0	•	•	1.0	1.3	1.4	•	4.5	•	1.8	2.0	3.2	•
Current Liabilities to Working Capital 39	2.0	•	•	0.0	0.3	0.4	•	3.5	•	0.8	1.0	2.2	•
Working Capital to Net Sales 40	0.2	•	•	2.1	0.3	0.3	•	0.1	•	0.3	0.1	0.2	•
Inventory to Working Capital 41	0.2	•	•	0.0	0.4	0.3	•	1.5	•	0.2	0.6	0.2	•
Total Receipts to Cash Flow 42	6.0	•	4.2	1.7	2.1	5.3	•	5.3	•	6.4	3.3	6.3	•
Cost of Goods to Cash Flow 43	2.5	•	1.8	0.3	0.7	3.0	•	3.3	•	3.8	1.3	2.5	•
Cash Flow to Total Debt 44	0.1	•	0.3	0.2	2.9	0.3	•	0.4	•	0.3	0.7	0.0	•

Selected Financial Factors (in Percentages)

Debt Ratio 45	76.6	•	155.2	89.2	32.6	64.5	•	50.6	•	69.6	39.3	77.3	•
Return on Total Assets 46	5.0	•	•	17.2	77.0	13.8	•	10.1	•	13.5	10.9	4.7	•
Return on Equity Before Income Taxes 47	8.3	•	10.7	149.9	113.2	37.5	•	16.6	•	43.7	17.6	7.0	•
Return on Equity After Income Taxes 48	5.9	•	10.7	149.9	113.2	36.2	•	16.6	•	43.6	13.8	4.5	•
Profit Margin (Before Income Tax) 49	8.4	•	•	56.3	39.0	14.1	•	8.1	•	10.6	11.4	8.0	•
Profit Margin (After Income Tax) 50	6.0	•	•	56.3	39.0	13.7	•	8.1	•	10.6	8.9	5.2	•

Table II

Corporations with Net Income

BREWERIES

MONEY AMOUNTS AND SIZE OF ASSETS IN THOUSANDS OF DOLLARS

Item Description for Accounting Period 7/12 Through 6/13	Total	Zero Assets	Under 500	500 to 1,000	1,000 to 5,000	5,000 to 10,000	10,000 to 25,000	25,000 to 50,000	50,000 to 100,000	100,000 to 250,000	250,000 to 500,000	500,000 to 2,500,000	2,500,000 and over
Number of Enterprises 1	101	0	0	10	5	58	11	•	•	•	0	•	0

Revenues ($ in Thousands)

Net Sales 2	21257739	0	0	56351	42777	356459	224769	•	•	•	0	•	0
Interest 3	14751	0	0	0	0	50	17	•	•	•	0	•	0
Rents 4	3618	0	0	0	0	0	0	•	•	•	0	•	0
Royalties 5	215533	0	0	0	0	0	0	•	•	•	0	•	0
Other Portfolio Income 6	36162	0	0	0	0	17028	19	•	•	•	0	•	0
Other Receipts 7	355043	0	0	15	162	323	852	•	•	•	0	•	0
Total Receipts 8	21882846	0	0	56366	42939	373860	225657	•	•	•	0	•	0
Average Total Receipts 9	216662	•	•	5637	8588	6446	20514	•	•	•	•	•	•

Operating Costs/Operating Income (%)

Cost of Operations 10	41.4	•	•	20.0	34.3	56.4	62.8	•	•	•	•	•	•
Salaries and Wages 11	7.2	•	•	4.2	2.3	6.1	4.2	•	•	•	•	•	•
Taxes Paid 12	11.3	•	•	4.7	2.8	3.2	4.6	•	•	•	•	•	•
Interest Paid 13	13.6	•	•	•	0.4	0.5	0.4	•	•	•	•	•	•
Depreciation 14	2.4	•	•	0.4	1.9	9.3	4.1	•	•	•	•	•	•
Amortization and Depletion 15	0.7	•	•	0.0	•	0.0	0.0	•	•	•	•	•	•
Pensions and Other Deferred Comp. 16	1.5	•	•	0.9	0.3	0.4	0.4	•	•	•	•	•	•
Employee Benefits 17	1.2	•	•	1.0	0.9	1.6	1.2	•	•	•	•	•	•
Advertising 18	3.8	•	•	0.1	2.1	3.0	2.7	•	•	•	•	•	•
Other Expenses 19	10.6	•	•	6.2	13.0	7.9	6.3	•	•	•	•	•	•
Officers' Compensation 20	0.5	•	•	2.8	3.3	2.2	2.6	•	•	•	•	•	•
Operating Margin 21	6.0	•	•	59.7	38.7	9.2	10.7	•	•	•	•	•	•
Operating Margin Before Officers' Comp. 22	6.5	•	•	62.4	41.9	11.4	13.3	•	•	•	•	•	•

Selected Average Balance Sheet ($ in Thousands)

Net Receivables 23	20892	•	•	368	151	388	1567	•	•	•	•	•	•	•	•
Inventories 24	7400	•	•	25	6387	520	2621	•	•	•	•	•	•	•	•
Net Property, Plant and Equipment 25	67477	•	•	42	1515	3826	5524	•	•	•	•	•	•	•	•
Total Assets 26	937981	•	•	663	4380	6524	13550	•	•	•	•	•	•	•	•
Notes and Loans Payable 27	604339	•	•	0	955	3304	1730	•	•	•	•	•	•	•	•
All Other Liabilities 28	114582	•	•	247	474	903	3018	•	•	•	•	•	•	•	•
Net Worth 29	219061	•	•	416	2951	2317	8803	•	•	•	•	•	•	•	•

Selected Financial Ratios (Times to 1)

Current Ratio 30	1.5	•	•	10.2	4.0	3.5	2.7	•	•	•	•	•	•	•	•
Quick Ratio 31	1.3	•	•	9.8	1.7	2.6	1.2	•	•	•	•	•	•	•	•
Net Sales to Working Capital 32	4.7	•	•	10.1	4.0	3.3	4.5	•	•	•	•	•	•	•	•
Coverage Ratio 33	1.7	•	•	•	98.1	28.1	25.9	•	•	•	•	•	•	•	•
Total Asset Turnover 34	0.2	•	•	8.5	2.0	0.9	1.5	•	•	•	•	•	•	•	•
Inventory Turnover 35	11.8	•	•	45.0	0.5	6.7	4.9	•	•	•	•	•	•	•	•
Receivables Turnover 36	9.5	•	•	15.1	11.3	16.2	13.7	•	•	•	•	•	•	•	•
Total Liabilities to Net Worth 37	3.3	•	•	0.6	0.5	1.8	0.5	•	•	•	•	•	•	•	•
Current Assets to Working Capital 38	3.0	•	•	1.1	1.3	1.4	1.6	•	•	•	•	•	•	•	•
Current Liabilities to Working Capital 39	2.0	•	•	0.1	0.3	0.4	0.6	•	•	•	•	•	•	•	•
Working Capital to Net Sales 40	0.2	•	•	0.1	0.3	0.3	0.2	•	•	•	•	•	•	•	•
Inventory to Working Capital 41	0.2	•	•	0.0	0.4	0.3	0.8	•	•	•	•	•	•	•	•
Total Receipts to Cash Flow 42	5.9	•	•	1.6	2.1	5.3	6.5	•	•	•	•	•	•	•	•
Cost of Goods to Cash Flow 43	2.4	•	•	0.3	0.7	3.0	4.1	•	•	•	•	•	•	•	•
Cash Flow to Total Debt 44	0.0	•	•	14.6	2.9	0.3	0.7	•	•	•	•	•	•	•	•

Selected Financial Factors (in Percentages)

Debt Ratio 45	76.6	•	•	37.2	32.6	64.5	35.0	•	•	•	•	•	•	•	•
Return on Total Assets 46	5.1	•	•	507.2	77.0	13.8	17.4	•	•	•	•	•	•	•	•
Return on Equity Before Income Taxes 47	8.6	•	•	807.9	113.2	37.5	25.7	•	•	•	•	•	•	•	•
Return on Equity After Income Taxes 48	6.1	•	•	807.9	113.2	36.2	24.0	•	•	•	•	•	•	•	•
Profit Margin (Before Income Tax) 49	8.9	•	•	59.7	39.0	14.1	11.1	•	•	•	•	•	•	•	•
Profit Margin (After Income Tax) 50	6.4	•	•	59.7	39.0	13.7	10.3	•	•	•	•	•	•	•	•

Table I

Corporations with and without Net Income

WINERIES AND DISTILLERIES

MONEY AMOUNTS AND SIZE OF ASSETS IN THOUSANDS OF DOLLARS

Item Description for Accounting Period 7/12 Through 6/13	Total	Zero Assets	Under 500	500 to 1,000	1,000 to 5,000	5,000 to 10,000	10,000 to 25,000	25,000 to 50,000	50,000 to 100,000	100,000 to 250,000	250,000 to 500,000	500,000 to 2,500,000	2,500,000 and over
Number of Enterprises 1	1848	•	509	352	249	162	65	50	23	•	4	•	5
Revenues ($ in Thousands)													
Net Sales 2	29504973	•	399637	214104	361175	561187	677333	1157621	1035022	•	580496	•	19718400
Interest 3	63848	•	665	1	624	207	657	691	3025	•	1	•	48158
Rents 4	6775	•	0	0	503	348	259	62	1189	•	11	•	3512
Royalties 5	832921	•	0	0	0	0	0	0	0	•	0	•	832777
Other Portfolio Income 6	126236	•	0	8	320	194	11269	12410	13230	•	4634	•	64178
Other Receipts 7	684358	•	0	11189	15886	19396	9767	32149	12318	•	22461	•	455539
Total Receipts 8	31219111	•	400302	225302	378508	581332	699285	1202933	1064784	•	607603	•	21122564
Average Total Receipts 9	16893	•	786	640	1520	3588	10758	24059	46295	•	151901	•	4224513
Operating Costs/Operating Income (%)													
Cost of Operations 10	55.4	•	•	49.4	30.8	31.1	55.5	40.9	67.6	•	51.1	•	57.6
Salaries and Wages 11	7.4	•	•	7.1	18.1	16.9	15.9	10.9	8.8	•	10.2	•	6.9
Taxes Paid 12	9.4	•	0.7	4.5	5.0	4.4	9.0	9.7	2.3	•	4.9	•	10.2
Interest Paid 13	4.2	•	•	5.4	1.1	6.3	2.0	1.6	2.6	•	5.1	•	5.3
Depreciation 14	3.4	•	1.1	2.6	6.4	6.8	4.0	5.3	5.1	•	8.3	•	2.7
Amortization and Depletion 15	2.0	•	•	•	0.1	0.3	0.1	0.6	0.5	•	5.9	•	2.5
Pensions and Other Deferred Comp. 16	0.7	•	•	•	1.2	0.3	0.2	0.3	0.3	•	0.3	•	0.8
Employee Benefits 17	1.1	•	•	0.2	4.3	1.8	0.6	1.4	0.7	•	2.2	•	1.1
Advertising 18	5.5	•	•	3.8	2.0	1.2	2.2	2.4	1.0	•	3.3	•	7.1
Other Expenses 19	9.9	•	97.7	9.1	34.7	23.9	19.3	15.1	9.4	•	5.7	•	6.5
Officers' Compensation 20	1.3	•	0.9	22.8	4.2	2.0	11.1	3.5	1.0	•	0.9	•	0.7
Operating Margin 21	•	•	•	•	•	5.1	•	8.4	0.7	•	2.2	•	•
Operating Margin Before Officers' Comp. 22	1.1	•	0.6	17.8	•	7.0	•	11.9	1.7	•	3.1	•	•

Selected Average Balance Sheet ($ in Thousands)

Net Receivables	23	2361	•	0	31	42	275	1051	4222	5838	•	24586	•	388374
Inventories	24	5706	•	0	256	1254	1889	6475	10208	20299	•	110507	•	1151130
Net Property, Plant and Equipment	25	4497	•	29	344	684	3929	4996	12951	27765	•	112368	•	697633
Total Assets	26	29976	•	95	775	2116	8221	15670	35322	68232	•	323364	•	7871296
Notes and Loans Payable	27	11051	•	28	693	611	6343	7331	9108	28697	•	141690	•	3026142
All Other Liabilities	28	5903	•	-7	58	59	333	4721	6691	11389	•	65051	•	1413277
Net Worth	29	13022	•	73	25	1446	1545	3617	19524	28146	•	116622	•	3431877

Selected Financial Ratios (Times to 1)

Current Ratio	30	2.1	•	•	4.1	9.4	4.1	1.8	2.5	1.3	•	1.6	•	2.2
Quick Ratio	31	0.7	•	•	0.5	1.6	0.5	0.5	1.0	0.3	•	0.3	•	0.6
Net Sales to Working Capital	32	3.2	•	12.0	2.0	1.1	1.4	2.9	2.1	6.8	•	2.7	•	4.1
Coverage Ratio	33	2.6	•	•	1.1	•	2.4	•	8.7	2.3	•	2.3	•	2.4
Total Asset Turnover	34	0.5	•	8.3	0.8	0.7	0.4	0.7	0.7	0.7	•	0.4	•	0.5
Inventory Turnover	35	1.5	•	•	1.2	0.4	0.6	0.9	0.9	1.5	•	0.7	•	2.0
Receivables Turnover	36	4.4	•	55.8	25.1	22.7	10.5	9.9	6.0	7.2	•	6.4	•	4.1
Total Liabilities to Net Worth	37	1.3	•	0.3	30.2	0.5	4.3	3.3	0.8	1.4	•	1.8	•	1.3
Current Assets to Working Capital	38	1.9	•	1.0	1.3	1.1	1.3	2.2	1.7	4.7	•	2.8	•	1.8
Current Liabilities to Working Capital	39	0.9	•	•	0.3	0.1	0.3	1.2	0.7	3.7	•	1.8	•	0.8
Working Capital to Net Sales	40	0.3	•	0.1	0.5	0.9	0.7	0.3	0.5	0.1	•	0.4	•	0.2
Inventory to Working Capital	41	1.2	•	•	1.2	0.8	0.8	1.5	1.0	2.9	•	2.3	•	1.2
Total Receipts to Cash Flow	42	8.0	•	2.5	•	3.9	4.0	•	4.1	9.9	•	9.3	•	9.2
Cost of Goods to Cash Flow	43	4.4	•	•	•	1.2	1.2	•	1.7	6.7	•	4.7	•	5.3
Cash Flow to Total Debt	44	0.1	•	14.6	•	0.5	0.1	•	0.4	0.1	•	0.1	•	0.1

Selected Financial Factors (in Percentages)

Debt Ratio	45	56.6	•	23.1	96.8	31.7	81.2	76.9	44.7	58.7	•	63.9	•	56.4
Return on Total Assets	46	5.7	•	•	4.4	•	6.3	•	9.0	4.0	•	5.4	•	6.3
Return on Equity Before Income Taxes	47	8.0	•	•	6.9	•	19.4	•	14.4	5.6	•	8.5	•	8.4
Return on Equity After Income Taxes	48	5.5	•	•	6.9	•	18.7	•	13.5	4.4	•	8.3	•	5.4
Profit Margin (Before Income Tax)	49	6.5	•	•	0.3	•	8.7	•	12.1	3.5	•	6.9	•	7.3
Profit Margin (After Income Tax)	50	4.5	•	•	0.3	•	8.4	•	11.3	2.7	•	6.6	•	4.7

Table II
Corporations with Net Income

WINERIES AND DISTILLERIES

MONEY AMOUNTS AND SIZE OF ASSETS IN THOUSANDS OF DOLLARS

Item Description for Accounting Period 7/12 Through 6/13	Total	Zero Assets	Under 500	500 to 1,000	1,000 to 5,000	5,000 to 10,000	10,000 to 25,000	25,000 to 50,000	50,000 to 100,000	100,000 to 250,000	250,000 to 500,000	500,000 to 2,500,000	2,500,000 and over
Number of Enterprises **1**	601	•	93	190	95	109	32	37	14	•	•	•	5
Revenues ($ in Thousands)													
Net Sales **2**	27487055	•	399637	108858	203532	547439	336593	992325	738597	•	•	•	19718400
Interest **3**	58899	•	665	0	624	199	228	691	1483	•	•	•	48158
Rents **4**	5376	•	0	0	503	295	101	62	236	•	•	•	3512
Royalties **5**	832921	•	0	0	0	0	0	0	0	•	•	•	832777
Other Portfolio Income **6**	113604	•	0	0	268	0	215	12396	12125	•	•	•	64178
Other Receipts **7**	652755	•	0	0	5863	19234	9343	28567	7801	•	•	•	455539
Total Receipts **8**	29150610	•	400302	108858	210790	567167	346480	1034041	760242	•	•	•	21122564
Average Total Receipts **9**	48504	•	4304	573	2219	5203	10828	27947	54303	•	•	•	4224513
Operating Costs/Operating Income (%)													
Cost of Operations **10**	54.9	•	•	41.5	25.2	29.7	55.1	37.2	66.8	•	•	•	57.6
Salaries and Wages **11**	6.9	•	•	7.2	13.1	16.2	6.3	9.9	7.5	•	•	•	6.9
Taxes Paid **12**	9.7	•	0.7	5.4	3.8	4.3	6.7	10.7	2.0	•	•	•	10.2
Interest Paid **13**	4.3	•	•	7.4	1.0	6.0	1.9	1.3	2.6	•	•	•	5.3
Depreciation **14**	3.1	•	1.1	2.1	3.8	3.8	4.6	4.5	3.8	•	•	•	2.7
Amortization and Depletion **15**	2.1	•	•	•	0.1	0.3	0.0	0.5	0.1	•	•	•	2.5
Pensions and Other Deferred Comp. **16**	0.7	•	•	•	2.2	0.3	0.1	0.4	0.2	•	•	•	0.8
Employee Benefits **17**	1.1	•	•	•	5.1	1.8	0.5	1.6	0.7	•	•	•	1.1
Advertising **18**	5.5	•	•	5.7	0.6	0.8	0.7	2.4	1.2	•	•	•	7.1
Other Expenses **19**	9.3	•	97.1	0.4	34.9	22.0	12.4	14.0	7.1	•	•	•	6.5
Officers' Compensation **20**	1.1	•	0.9	24.8	7.3	1.9	1.5	4.1	1.4	•	•	•	0.7
Operating Margin **21**	1.2	•	0.3	5.4	3.0	12.9	10.2	13.5	6.6	•	•	•	•
Operating Margin Before Officers' Comp. **22**	2.3	•	1.2	30.1	10.3	14.7	11.7	17.6	7.9	•	•	•	•

Selected Average Balance Sheet ($ in Thousands)

Net Receivables 23	6801	•	2	28	64	382	935	5044	6950	•	•	•	388374
Inventories 24	15314	•	0	346	1481	2515	6907	9176	21876	•	•	•	1151130
Net Property, Plant and Equipment 25	10850	•	52	343	256	4176	4302	12456	26677	•	•	•	697633
Total Assets 26	84475	•	394	776	2479	7902	14934	36045	67572	•	•	•	7871296
Notes and Loans Payable 27	30841	•	5	800	440	4703	6182	7236	19757	•	•	•	3026142
All Other Liabilities 28	16516	•	-36	34	208	426	3767	7340	10721	•	•	•	1413277
Net Worth 29	37118	•	424	-58	1831	2773	4985	21470	37093	•	•	•	3431877

Selected Financial Ratios (Times to 1)

Current Ratio 30	2.1	•	•	2.4	9.2	3.5	2.7	2.6	1.8	•	•	•	2.2
Quick Ratio 31	0.7	•	•	0.3	1.6	0.6	0.9	1.2	0.6	•	•	•	0.6
Net Sales to Working Capital 32	3.3	•	12.6	2.5	1.1	2.2	2.1	2.3	3.8	•	•	•	4.1
Coverage Ratio 33	2.9	•	•	1.7	7.8	3.7	7.9	15.0	4.6	•	•	•	2.4
Total Asset Turnover 34	0.5	•	10.9	0.7	0.9	0.6	0.7	0.7	0.8	•	•	•	0.5
Inventory Turnover 35	1.6	•	•	0.7	0.4	0.6	0.8	1.1	1.6	•	•	•	2.0
Receivables Turnover 36	4.3	•	•	40.6	18.4	10.9	8.6	7.0	6.5	•	•	•	4.1
Total Liabilities to Net Worth 37	1.3	•	•	•	0.4	1.9	2.0	0.7	0.8	•	•	•	1.3
Current Assets to Working Capital 38	1.9	•	1.0	1.7	1.1	1.4	1.6	1.6	2.2	•	•	•	1.8
Current Liabilities to Working Capital 39	0.9	•	•	0.7	0.1	0.4	0.6	0.6	1.2	•	•	•	0.8
Working Capital to Net Sales 40	0.3	•	0.1	0.4	0.9	0.5	0.5	0.4	0.3	•	•	•	0.2
Inventory to Working Capital 41	1.2	•	•	1.5	0.6	1.2	1.0	0.8	1.4	•	•	•	1.2
Total Receipts to Cash Flow 42	7.4	•	2.5	•	3.2	3.2	4.5	3.5	6.8	•	•	•	9.2
Cost of Goods to Cash Flow 43	4.0	•	•	•	0.8	0.9	2.5	1.3	4.5	•	•	•	5.3
Cash Flow to Total Debt 44	0.1	•	•	•	1.0	0.3	0.2	0.5	0.3	•	•	•	0.1

Selected Financial Factors (in Percentages)

Debt Ratio 45	56.1	•	•	107.5	26.1	64.9	66.6	40.4	45.1	•	•	•	56.4
Return on Total Assets 46	6.8	•	5.2	9.4	6.5	14.3	10.6	14.0	9.5	•	•	•	6.3
Return on Equity Before Income Taxes 47	10.2	•	4.8	•	7.6	29.8	27.8	21.9	13.5	•	•	•	8.4
Return on Equity After Income Taxes 48	7.5	•	4.1	•	7.2	29.3	21.9	20.8	12.0	•	•	•	5.4
Profit Margin (Before Income Tax) 49	8.3	•	0.5	5.4	6.5	16.5	13.2	17.5	9.5	•	•	•	7.3
Profit Margin (After Income Tax) 50	6.1	•	0.4	5.4	6.2	16.2	10.4	16.6	8.4	•	•	•	4.7

Table I
Corporations with and without Net Income

TOBACCO MANUFACTURING

MONEY AMOUNTS AND SIZE OF ASSETS IN THOUSANDS OF DOLLARS

Item Description for Accounting Period 7/12 Through 6/13	Total	Zero Assets	Under 500	500 to 1,000	1,000 to 5,000	5,000 to 10,000	10,000 to 25,000	25,000 to 50,000	50,000 to 100,000	100,000 to 250,000	250,000 to 500,000	500,000 to 2,500,000	2,500,000 and over
Number of Enterprises 1	31	0	0	0	0	0	•	8	•	•	0	•	4

Revenues ($ in Thousands)

Net Sales 2	47490586	0	0	0	0	0	•	436419	•	•	0	•	44862189
Interest 3	51589	0	0	0	0	0	•	0	•	•	0	•	51589
Rents 4	735863	0	0	0	0	0	•	0	•	•	0	•	735863
Royalties 5	57341	0	0	0	0	0	•	0	•	•	0	•	53834
Other Portfolio Income 6	847735	0	0	0	0	0	•	598	•	•	0	•	841343
Other Receipts 7	407096	0	0	0	0	0	•	24774	•	•	0	•	381057
Total Receipts 8	49590210	0	0	0	0	0	•	461791	•	•	0	•	46925875
Average Total Receipts 9	1599684	•	•	•	•	•	•	57724	•	•	•	•	11731469

Operating Costs/Operating Income (%)

Cost of Operations 10	30.5	•	•	•	•	•	•	81.6	•	•	•	•	29.8
Salaries and Wages 11	3.5	•	•	•	•	•	•	3.3	•	•	•	•	3.5
Taxes Paid 12	27.7	•	•	•	•	•	•	0.6	•	•	•	•	27.2
Interest Paid 13	3.6	•	•	•	•	•	•	0.0	•	•	•	•	3.8
Depreciation 14	0.8	•	•	•	•	•	•	1.8	•	•	•	•	0.8
Amortization and Depletion 15	0.8	•	•	•	•	•	•	0.0	•	•	•	•	0.9
Pensions and Other Deferred Comp. 16	1.2	•	•	•	•	•	•	0.0	•	•	•	•	1.3
Employee Benefits 17	1.3	•	•	•	•	•	•	0.2	•	•	•	•	1.3
Advertising 18	0.5	•	•	•	•	•	•	0.2	•	•	•	•	0.5
Other Expenses 19	16.1	•	•	•	•	•	•	3.7	•	•	•	•	16.5
Officers' Compensation 20	0.4	•	•	•	•	•	•	1.1	•	•	•	•	0.4
Operating Margin 21	13.5	•	•	•	•	•	•	7.5	•	•	•	•	14.1
Operating Margin Before Officers' Comp. 22	14.0	•	•	•	•	•	•	8.6	•	•	•	•	14.4

Net Receivables 23	55038	•	•	•	•	•	•	2231	•	•	•	•	403468
Inventories 24	116486	•	•	•	•	•	•	4192	•	•	•	•	805411
Net Property, Plant and Equipment 25	125569	•	•	•	•	•	•	11228	•	•	•	•	894811
Total Assets 26	1958572	•	•	•	•	•	•	33982	•	•	•	•	14637082
Notes and Loans Payable 27	810003	•	•	•	•	•	•	202	•	•	•	•	6147084
All Other Liabilities 28	851373	•	•	•	•	•	•	2406	•	•	•	•	6480273
Net Worth 29	297196	•	•	•	•	•	•	31373	•	•	•	•	2009726

Current Ratio 30	1.1	•	•	•	•	•	•	7.4	•	•	•	•	1.0
Quick Ratio 31	0.7	•	•	•	•	•	•	2.7	•	•	•	•	0.6
Net Sales to Working Capital 32	49.8	•	•	•	•	•	•	3.3	•	•	•	•	8813.8
Coverage Ratio 33	6.1	•	•	•	•	•	•	633.2	•	•	•	•	6.1
Total Asset Turnover 34	0.8	•	•	•	•	•	•	1.6	•	•	•	•	0.8
Inventory Turnover 35	4.0	•	•	•	•	•	•	10.6	•	•	•	•	4.2
Receivables Turnover 36	42.3	•	•	•	•	•	•	26.5	•	•	•	•	43.9
Total Liabilities to Net Worth 37	5.6	•	•	•	•	•	•	0.1	•	•	•	•	6.3
Current Assets to Working Capital 38	15.5	•	•	•	•	•	•	1.2	•	•	•	•	2626.6
Current Liabilities to Working Capital 39	14.5	•	•	•	•	•	•	0.2	•	•	•	•	2625.6
Working Capital to Net Sales 40	0.0	•	•	•	•	•	•	0.3	•	•	•	•	0.0
Inventory to Working Capital 41	3.9	•	•	•	•	•	•	0.3	•	•	•	•	667.4
Total Receipts to Cash Flow 42	3.1	•	•	•	•	•	•	6.1	•	•	•	•	3.0
Cost of Goods to Cash Flow 43	1.0	•	•	•	•	•	•	5.0	•	•	•	•	0.9
Cash Flow to Total Debt 44	0.3	•	•	•	•	•	•	3.4	•	•	•	•	0.3

Debt Ratio 45	84.8	•	•	•	•	•	•	7.7	•	•	•	•	86.3
Return on Total Assets 46	17.2	•	•	•	•	•	•	21.4	•	•	•	•	17.5
Return on Equity Before Income Taxes 47	94.6	•	•	•	•	•	•	23.2	•	•	•	•	106.5
Return on Equity After Income Taxes 48	62.1	•	•	•	•	•	•	23.2	•	•	•	•	69.4
Profit Margin (Before Income Tax) 49	18.4	•	•	•	•	•	•	13.3	•	•	•	•	19.1
Profit Margin (After Income Tax) 50	12.1	•	•	•	•	•	•	13.3	•	•	•	•	12.4

Table II
Corporations with Net Income

TOBACCO MANUFACTURING

MONEY AMOUNTS AND SIZE OF ASSETS IN THOUSANDS OF DOLLARS

Item Description for Accounting Period 7/12 Through 6/13	Total	Zero Assets	Under 500	500 to 1,000	1,000 to 5,000	5,000 to 10,000	10,000 to 25,000	25,000 to 50,000	50,000 to 100,000	100,000 to 250,000	250,000 to 500,000	500,000 to 2,500,000	2,500,000 and over
Number of Enterprises **1**	23	0	0	0	0	0	8	•	•	0	0	0	4

Revenues ($ in Thousands)

Item	Total	Zero Assets	Under 500	500 to 1,000	1,000 to 5,000	5,000 to 10,000	10,000 to 25,000	25,000 to 50,000	50,000 to 100,000	100,000 to 250,000	250,000 to 500,000	500,000 to 2,500,000	2,500,000 and over
Net Sales **2**	46976879	0	0	0	0	0	650205	•	•	0	0	0	44862189
Interest **3**	51589	0	0	0	0	0	0	•	•	0	0	0	51589
Rents **4**	735863	0	0	0	0	0	0	•	•	0	0	0	735863
Royalties **5**	53834	0	0	0	0	0	0	•	•	0	0	0	53834
Other Portfolio Income **6**	847735	0	0	0	0	0	174	•	•	0	0	0	841343
Other Receipts **7**	406992	0	0	0	0	0	191	•	•	0	0	0	381057
Total Receipts **8**	49072892	0	0	0	0	0	650570	•	•	0	0	0	46925875
Average Total Receipts **9**	2133604	•	•	•	•	•	81321	•	•	•	•	•	11731469

Operating Costs/Operating Income (%)

Item	Total	Zero Assets	Under 500	500 to 1,000	1,000 to 5,000	5,000 to 10,000	10,000 to 25,000	25,000 to 50,000	50,000 to 100,000	100,000 to 250,000	250,000 to 500,000	500,000 to 2,500,000	2,500,000 and over
Cost of Operations **10**	30.4	•	•	•	•	•	36.0	•	•	•	•	•	29.8
Salaries and Wages **11**	3.5	•	•	•	•	•	3.7	•	•	•	•	•	3.5
Taxes Paid **12**	27.6	•	•	•	•	•	42.1	•	•	•	•	•	27.2
Interest Paid **13**	3.6	•	•	•	•	•	0.1	•	•	•	•	•	3.8
Depreciation **14**	0.8	•	•	•	•	•	0.5	•	•	•	•	•	0.8
Amortization and Depletion **15**	0.8	•	•	•	•	•	0.0	•	•	•	•	•	0.9
Pensions and Other Deferred Comp. **16**	1.2	•	•	•	•	•	0.4	•	•	•	•	•	1.3
Employee Benefits **17**	1.3	•	•	•	•	•	0.4	•	•	•	•	•	1.3
Advertising **18**	0.5	•	•	•	•	•	1.0	•	•	•	•	•	0.5
Other Expenses **19**	16.2	•	•	•	•	•	6.9	•	•	•	•	•	16.5
Officers' Compensation **20**	0.4	•	•	•	•	•	2.7	•	•	•	•	•	0.4
Operating Margin **21**	13.7	•	•	•	•	•	6.3	•	•	•	•	•	14.1
Operating Margin Before Officers' Comp. **22**	14.2	•	•	•	•	•	9.0	•	•	•	•	•	14.4

Selected Average Balance Sheet ($ in Thousands)

Net Receivables **23**	73668	•	•	•	•	•	4550	•	•	•	•	•	403468
Inventories **24**	155867	•	•	•	•	•	5511	•	•	•	•	•	805411
Net Property, Plant and Equipment **25**	168466	•	•	•	•	•	1562	•	•	•	•	•	894811
Total Assets **26**	2622813	•	•	•	•	•	16866	•	•	•	•	•	14637082
Notes and Loans Payable **27**	1080387	•	•	•	•	•	503	•	•	•	•	•	6147084
All Other Liabilities **28**	1136089	•	•	•	•	•	4505	•	•	•	•	•	6480273
Net Worth **29**	406338	•	•	•	•	•	11857	•	•	•	•	•	2009726

Selected Financial Ratios (Times to 1)

Current Ratio **30**	1.1	•	•	•	•	•	3.5	•	•	•	•	•	1.0
Quick Ratio **31**	0.7	•	•	•	•	•	2.0	•	•	•	•	•	0.6
Net Sales to Working Capital **32**	44.7	•	•	•	•	•	8.4	•	•	•	•	•	8813.8
Coverage Ratio **33**	6.1	•	•	•	•	•	58.1	•	•	•	•	•	6.1
Total Asset Turnover **34**	0.8	•	•	•	•	•	4.8	•	•	•	•	•	0.8
Inventory Turnover **35**	4.0	•	•	•	•	•	5.3	•	•	•	•	•	4.2
Receivables Turnover **36**	42.2	•	•	•	•	•	18.9	•	•	•	•	•	43.9
Total Liabilities to Net Worth **37**	5.5	•	•	•	•	•	0.4	•	•	•	•	•	6.3
Current Assets to Working Capital **38**	13.9	•	•	•	•	•	1.4	•	•	•	•	•	2626.6
Current Liabilities to Working Capital **39**	12.9	•	•	•	•	•	0.4	•	•	•	•	•	2625.6
Working Capital to Net Sales **40**	0.0	•	•	•	•	•	0.1	•	•	•	•	•	0.0
Inventory to Working Capital **41**	3.5	•	•	•	•	•	0.5	•	•	•	•	•	667.4
Total Receipts to Cash Flow **42**	3.1	•	•	•	•	•	7.8	•	•	•	•	•	3.0
Cost of Goods to Cash Flow **43**	0.9	•	•	•	•	•	2.8	•	•	•	•	•	0.9
Cash Flow to Total Debt **44**	0.3	•	•	•	•	•	2.1	•	•	•	•	•	0.3

Selected Financial Factors (in Percentages)

Debt Ratio **45**	84.5	•	•	•	•	•	29.7	•	•	•	•	•	86.3
Return on Total Assets **46**	17.3	•	•	•	•	•	31.0	•	•	•	•	•	17.5
Return on Equity Before Income Taxes **47**	93.3	•	•	•	•	•	43.4	•	•	•	•	•	106.5
Return on Equity After Income Taxes **48**	61.3	•	•	•	•	•	43.4	•	•	•	•	•	69.4
Profit Margin (Before Income Tax) **49**	18.6	•	•	•	•	•	6.3	•	•	•	•	•	19.1
Profit Margin (After Income Tax) **50**	12.2	•	•	•	•	•	6.3	•	•	•	•	•	12.4

Table I

Corporations with and without Net Income

TEXTILE MILLS

MONEY AMOUNTS AND SIZE OF ASSETS IN THOUSANDS OF DOLLARS

Item Description for Accounting Period 7/12 Through 6/13	Total	Zero Assets	Under 500	500 to 1,000	1,000 to 5,000	5,000 to 10,000	10,000 to 25,000	25,000 to 50,000	50,000 to 100,000	100,000 to 250,000	250,000 to 500,000	500,000 to 2,500,000	2,500,000 and over
Number of Enterprises 1	1727	•	925	•	153	•	67	21	17	10	7	4	0
Revenues ($ in Thousands)													
Net Sales 2	13307115	•	365171	•	376659	•	1837720	904563	1832749	2105482	2855580	1782973	0
Interest 3	32570	•	1	•	1582	•	1099	1150	1303	1963	11058	14370	0
Rents 4	5939	•	0	•	1143	•	2495	185	492	259	956	408	0
Royalties 5	22368	•	0	•	0	•	0	136	35	261	3456	18481	0
Other Portfolio Income 6	89747	•	13603	•	11486	•	4845	2143	6455	323	10939	39951	0
Other Receipts 7	129458	•	0	•	664	•	5626	14596	7971	13974	47671	35787	0
Total Receipts 8	13587197	•	378775	•	391534	•	1851785	922773	1849005	2122262	2929660	1891970	0
Average Total Receipts 9	7868	•	409	•	2559	•	27639	43942	108765	212226	418523	472992	•
Operating Costs/Operating Income (%)													
Cost of Operations 10	75.8	•	40.2	•	84.9	•	77.3	75.9	81.9	74.1	76.9	70.5	•
Salaries and Wages 11	5.5	•	7.8	•	1.1	•	7.0	7.8	3.8	5.0	4.0	8.8	•
Taxes Paid 12	1.5	•	1.6	•	2.5	•	1.5	2.5	1.0	1.0	1.4	2.0	•
Interest Paid 13	1.9	•	1.0	•	0.3	•	0.7	1.9	0.6	1.4	2.2	5.6	•
Depreciation 14	2.4	•	0.5	•	2.3	•	1.6	2.9	2.0	3.7	2.9	2.3	•
Amortization and Depletion 15	0.4	•	0.0	•	•	•	0.0	0.3	0.1	0.6	0.3	1.7	•
Pensions and Other Deferred Comp. 16	0.6	•	0.0	•	0.1	•	0.5	0.3	0.6	0.3	0.7	1.4	•
Employee Benefits 17	1.6	•	2.8	•	2.3	•	1.1	0.8	0.9	2.0	1.6	2.8	•
Advertising 18	0.3	•	0.0	•	0.0	•	0.3	0.2	0.3	0.2	0.5	0.2	•
Other Expenses 19	8.1	•	24.5	•	11.4	•	7.3	6.5	7.0	7.8	8.7	9.0	•
Officers' Compensation 20	1.6	•	9.7	•	3.5	•	1.4	1.2	1.1	0.9	1.8	1.0	•
Operating Margin 21	0.4	•	11.8	•	•	•	1.2	•	0.9	3.0	•	•	•
Operating Margin Before Officers' Comp. 22	2.0	•	21.5	•	•	•	2.6	1.0	2.0	3.9	0.8	•	•

Selected Average Balance Sheet ($ in Thousands)

Net Receivables 23	1204	•	48	•	280	•	4003	7668	14242	27521	86973	91866	•
Inventories 24	1037	•	0	•	412	•	4557	7214	15562	28084	59838	57435	•
Net Property, Plant and Equipment 25	1294	•	3	•	623	•	3050	6493	19386	51525	78234	92040	•
Total Assets 26	6234	•	86	•	2693	•	15630	32622	67575	140142	402193	694064	•
Notes and Loans Payable 27	2190	•	35	•	633	•	5804	14320	10053	44990	138891	323648	•
All Other Liabilities 28	1771	•	47	•	755	•	2062	8087	19704	41001	127758	175430	•
Net Worth 29	2273	•	4	•	1306	•	7765	10214	37818	54151	135544	194986	•

Selected Financial Ratios (Times to 1)

Current Ratio 30	1.8	•	1.5	•	7.6	•	3.4	1.7	2.3	1.5	1.5	1.9	•
Quick Ratio 31	0.9	•	1.5	•	4.5	•	1.7	0.9	1.1	0.8	0.8	1.2	•
Net Sales to Working Capital 32	5.8	•	14.8	•	1.9	•	3.7	5.4	4.9	9.4	6.5	5.2	•
Coverage Ratio 33	2.4	•	16.5	•	•	•	3.6	1.9	4.1	3.7	1.8	1.3	•
Total Asset Turnover 34	1.2	•	4.6	•	0.9	•	1.8	1.3	1.6	1.5	1.0	0.6	•
Inventory Turnover 35	5.6	•	36703.5	•	5.1	•	4.7	4.5	5.7	5.6	5.2	5.5	•
Receivables Turnover 36	6.7	•	•	•	7.9	•	6.7	6.2	8.0	6.8	6.1	4.9	•
Total Liabilities to Net Worth 37	1.7	•	19.3	•	1.1	•	1.0	2.2	0.8	1.6	2.0	2.6	•
Current Assets to Working Capital 38	2.2	•	3.1	•	1.2	•	1.4	2.5	1.7	3.0	2.9	2.1	•
Current Liabilities to Working Capital 39	1.2	•	2.1	•	0.2	•	0.4	1.5	0.7	2.0	1.9	1.1	•
Working Capital to Net Sales 40	0.2	•	0.1	•	0.5	•	0.3	0.2	0.2	0.1	0.2	0.2	•
Inventory to Working Capital 41	0.8	•	0.0	•	0.3	•	0.6	1.0	0.7	1.2	1.0	0.6	•
Total Receipts to Cash Flow 42	11.7	•	3.6	•	36.8	•	13.7	14.0	13.4	11.3	10.8	12.6	•
Cost of Goods to Cash Flow 43	8.9	•	1.4	•	31.3	•	10.6	10.7	10.9	8.4	8.3	8.9	•
Cash Flow to Total Debt 44	0.2	•	1.3	•	0.0	•	0.3	0.1	0.3	0.2	0.1	0.1	•

Selected Financial Factors (in Percentages)

Debt Ratio 45	63.5	•	95.1	•	51.5	•	50.3	68.7	44.0	61.4	66.3	71.9	•
Return on Total Assets 46	5.6	•	75.6	•	•	•	4.7	4.9	4.1	7.9	3.9	4.7	•
Return on Equity Before Income Taxes 47	9.0	•	1439.3	•	•	•	6.9	7.5	5.5	15.0	5.1	3.8	•
Return on Equity After Income Taxes 48	6.9	•	1434.4	•	•	•	5.4	5.7	4.2	11.4	2.5	1.7	•
Profit Margin (Before Income Tax) 49	2.7	•	15.5	•	•	•	2.0	1.8	1.9	3.8	1.7	1.7	•
Profit Margin (After Income Tax) 50	2.0	•	15.5	•	•	•	1.5	1.3	1.5	2.9	0.8	0.8	•

Table II
Corporations with Net Income

TEXTILE MILLS

MONEY AMOUNTS AND SIZE OF ASSETS IN THOUSANDS OF DOLLARS

Item Description for Accounting Period 7/12 Through 6/13	Total	Zero Assets	Under 500	500 to 1,000	1,000 to 5,000	5,000 to 10,000	10,000 to 25,000	25,000 to 50,000	50,000 to 100,000	100,000 to 250,000	250,000 to 500,000	500,000 to 2,500,000	2,500,000 and over
Number of Enterprises 1	1606	•	•	56	77	57	49	17	14	•	7	0	0
Revenues ($ in Thousands)													
Net Sales 2	10746367	•	•	256491	119957	857000	1391783	615639	1600052	•	3415105	0	0
Interest 3	12425	•	•	0	1153	35	815	70	1302	•	7085	0	0
Rents 4	5370	•	•	0	885	0	2495	185	457	•	1089	0	0
Royalties 5	419	•	•	0	0	0	0	136	18	•	5	0	0
Other Portfolio Income 6	46969	•	•	3	4795	0	4147	41	6120	•	17936	0	0
Other Receipts 7	93169	•	•	13	33	508	5969	12262	6736	•	52935	0	0
Total Receipts 8	10904719	•	•	256507	126823	857543	1405209	628333	1614685	•	3494155	0	0
Average Total Receipts 9	6790	•	•	4580	1647	15045	28678	36961	115335	•	499165	•	•
Operating Costs/Operating Income (%)													
Cost of Operations 10	74.5	•	•	74.4	74.3	82.7	77.4	70.9	81.2	•	72.5	•	•
Salaries and Wages 11	5.4	•	•	1.7	0.6	4.2	6.4	7.1	3.7	•	6.2	•	•
Taxes Paid 12	1.3	•	•	3.7	3.1	0.7	1.0	1.2	0.8	•	1.7	•	•
Interest Paid 13	1.1	•	•	0.3	0.4	0.4	0.9	1.6	0.7	•	1.3	•	•
Depreciation 14	2.3	•	•	1.5	1.3	0.3	1.2	4.1	2.0	•	2.5	•	•
Amortization and Depletion 15	0.3	•	•	0.0	•	0.1	0.0	0.4	0.1	•	0.4	•	•
Pensions and Other Deferred Comp. 16	0.5	•	•	0.0	0.1	0.1	0.4	0.1	0.6	•	0.9	•	•
Employee Benefits 17	1.5	•	•	2.0	5.7	0.3	1.3	0.6	0.8	•	1.9	•	•
Advertising 18	0.3	•	•	0.2	0.0	0.0	0.4	0.2	0.3	•	0.4	•	•
Other Expenses 19	7.7	•	•	7.9	14.5	2.6	7.5	7.2	5.6	•	7.9	•	•
Officers' Compensation 20	1.4	•	•	7.6	1.0	0.7	1.3	0.8	0.8	•	1.1	•	•
Operating Margin 21	3.8	•	•	0.8	•	7.8	2.1	5.8	3.4	•	3.2	•	•
Operating Margin Before Officers' Comp. 22	5.2	•	•	8.4	0.1	8.5	3.4	6.6	4.3	•	4.3	•	•

	Selected Average Balance Sheet ($ in Thousands)												
Net Receivables 23	1018	•	•	348	239	800	4107	8356	13822	•	99981	•	•
Inventories 24	825	•	•	106	491	1101	4244	7320	12641	•	73533	•	•
Net Property, Plant and Equipment 25	1017	•	•	202	78	310	2742	7700	21081	•	92352	•	•
Total Assets 26	4490	•	•	692	1628	5528	15459	28569	66121	•	461228	•	•
Notes and Loans Payable 27	1310	•	•	216	399	726	7749	10472	11119	•	137725	•	•
All Other Liabilities 28	1211	•	•	323	48	3854	2145	8324	20797	•	102918	•	•
Net Worth 29	1970	•	•	153	1181	948	5565	9773	34206	•	220585	•	•

	Selected Financial Ratios (Times to 1)												
Current Ratio 30	1.9	•	•	1.1	13.9	1.3	3.0	1.9	2.1	•	2.0	•	•
Quick Ratio 31	1.0	•	•	0.8	9.5	0.3	1.5	1.1	1.0	•	1.0	•	•
Net Sales to Working Capital 32	5.8	•	•	194.0	1.4	14.4	4.2	4.2	6.3	•	4.8	•	•
Coverage Ratio 33	6.0	•	•	4.0	12.5	19.6	4.3	5.8	7.5	•	5.3	•	•
Total Asset Turnover 34	1.5	•	•	6.6	1.0	2.7	1.8	1.3	1.7	•	1.1	•	•
Inventory Turnover 35	6.0	•	•	32.1	2.4	11.3	5.2	3.5	7.3	•	4.8	•	•
Receivables Turnover 36	7.3	•	•	26.3	4.2	13.8	7.8	•	9.9	•	•	•	•
Total Liabilities to Net Worth 37	1.3	•	•	3.5	0.4	4.8	1.8	1.9	0.9	•	1.1	•	•
Current Assets to Working Capital 38	2.1	•	•	19.7	1.1	4.7	1.5	2.1	1.9	•	2.0	•	•
Current Liabilities to Working Capital 39	1.1	•	•	18.7	0.1	3.7	0.5	1.1	0.9	•	1.0	•	•
Working Capital to Net Sales 40	0.2	•	•	0.0	0.7	0.1	0.2	0.2	0.2	•	0.2	•	•
Inventory to Working Capital 41	0.8	•	•	4.5	0.3	0.7	0.6	0.9	0.8	•	0.7	•	•
Total Receipts to Cash Flow 42	9.3	•	•	20.2	6.3	11.1	11.5	7.3	11.6	•	8.4	•	•
Cost of Goods to Cash Flow 43	6.9	•	•	15.1	4.6	9.2	8.9	5.2	9.4	•	6.1	•	•
Cash Flow to Total Debt 44	0.3	•	•	0.4	0.6	0.3	0.2	0.3	0.3	•	0.2	•	•

	Selected Financial Factors (in Percentages)												
Debt Ratio 45	56.1	•	•	77.9	27.4	82.8	64.0	65.8	48.3	•	52.2	•	•
Return on Total Assets 46	9.5	•	•	6.8	4.9	22.5	7.4	12.0	8.9	•	7.4	•	•
Return on Equity Before Income Taxes 47	18.1	•	•	23.2	6.3	124.6	15.7	29.0	14.9	•	12.6	•	•
Return on Equity After Income Taxes 48	15.5	•	•	19.8	5.5	119.5	12.8	26.6	13.2	•	10.0	•	•
Profit Margin (Before Income Tax) 49	5.3	•	•	0.8	4.7	7.9	3.1	7.8	4.4	•	5.7	•	•
Profit Margin (After Income Tax) 50	4.6	•	•	0.7	4.2	7.5	2.5	7.2	4.0	•	4.5	•	•

Table I

Corporations with and without Net Income

TEXTILE PRODUCT MILLS

MONEY AMOUNTS AND SIZE OF ASSETS IN THOUSANDS OF DOLLARS

Item Description for Accounting Period 7/12 Through 6/13	Total	Zero Assets	Under 500	500 to 1,000	1,000 to 5,000	5,000 to 10,000	10,000 to 25,000	25,000 to 50,000	50,000 to 100,000	100,000 to 250,000	250,000 to 500,000	500,000 to 2,500,000	2,500,000 and over
Number of Enterprises **1**	2151	•	1188	•	445	•	44	35	11	10	7	4	0
Revenues ($ in Thousands)													
Net Sales **2**	22281938	•	753971	•	3284748	•	1634896	2331724	1067582	2267614	3199730	6811618	0
Interest **3**	31835	•	1	•	34	•	344	696	221	2255	2677	25235	0
Rents **4**	4231	•	0	•	0	•	0	983	42	2010	6	354	0
Royalties **5**	39485	•	0	•	0	•	0	0	170	86	11728	27495	0
Other Portfolio Income **6**	203127	•	0	•	23620	•	138	7896	76	50530	3321	117482	0
Other Receipts **7**	99410	•	16787	•	14207	•	6284	12453	22992	-8233	-46274	80393	0
Total Receipts **8**	22660026	•	770759	•	3322609	•	1641662	2353752	1091083	2314262	3171188	7062577	0
Average Total Receipts **9**	10535	•	649	•	7467	•	37310	67250	99189	231426	453027	1765644	•
Operating Costs/Operating Income (%)													
Cost of Operations **10**	68.9	•	58.7	•	58.1	•	81.2	79.0	78.0	81.7	74.2	61.2	•
Salaries and Wages **11**	9.2	•	5.9	•	11.8	•	3.6	5.6	5.5	5.5	7.6	13.9	•
Taxes Paid **12**	1.9	•	3.4	•	1.8	•	1.1	1.0	1.6	1.4	1.5	2.4	•
Interest Paid **13**	1.4	•	0.4	•	0.4	•	0.7	1.0	1.4	0.9	2.9	1.7	•
Depreciation **14**	1.7	•	0.2	•	1.2	•	1.0	1.2	1.1	2.4	1.3	2.6	•
Amortization and Depletion **15**	0.3	•	0.0	•	0.0	•	0.1	0.4	0.4	0.4	0.4	0.4	•
Pensions and Other Deferred Comp. **16**	0.8	•	•	•	0.2	•	0.1	0.2	0.1	0.4	0.5	1.9	•
Employee Benefits **17**	1.7	•	0.2	•	1.1	•	1.0	1.1	1.7	1.4	1.2	2.9	•
Advertising **18**	0.5	•	1.1	•	1.3	•	0.3	0.2	0.4	0.3	0.9	0.2	•
Other Expenses **19**	10.5	•	12.8	•	19.1	•	7.1	5.8	7.6	7.3	7.6	11.4	•
Officers' Compensation **20**	2.2	•	18.1	•	3.8	•	1.4	1.3	1.1	0.6	1.1	0.6	•
Operating Margin **21**	0.9	•	•	•	1.2	•	2.2	3.2	1.0	•	0.8	0.8	•
Operating Margin Before Officers' Comp. **22**	3.1	•	17.4	•	5.0	•	3.6	4.5	2.1	•	1.9	1.3	•

Selected Average Balance Sheet ($ in Thousands)

Net Receivables 23	1013	•	38	•	638	•	3866	7069	13899	36736	72575	71080	•
Inventories 24	1711	•	37	•	950	•	5945	11256	17253	39366	81887	291990	•
Net Property, Plant and Equipment 25	1304	•	30	•	661	•	2194	7271	8932	38479	37139	318470	•
Total Assets 26	9004	•	116	•	2566	•	13873	37997	66621	154205	364616	2685766	•
Notes and Loans Payable 27	2314	•	94	•	552	•	3597	11277	43469	60852	170092	389195	•
All Other Liabilities 28	2660	•	66	•	672	•	4563	7988	15558	41289	122517	831175	•
Net Worth 29	4031	•	-44	•	1341	•	5712	18732	7594	52064	72007	1465396	•

Selected Financial Ratios (Times to 1)

Current Ratio 30	1.5	•	1.2	•	2.4	•	1.9	2.4	2.0	1.3	1.4	1.2	•
Quick Ratio 31	0.6	•	0.7	•	1.1	•	0.8	1.1	0.9	0.6	0.7	0.4	•
Net Sales to Working Capital 32	8.4	•	39.4	•	6.9	•	7.5	5.2	5.4	12.0	8.2	16.2	•
Coverage Ratio 33	3.0	•	5.2	•	6.4	•	4.5	5.1	3.3	0.9	1.0	3.9	•
Total Asset Turnover 34	1.2	•	5.5	•	2.9	•	2.7	1.8	1.5	1.5	1.3	0.6	•
Inventory Turnover 35	4.2	•	10.0	•	4.5	•	5.1	4.7	4.4	4.7	4.1	3.6	•
Receivables Turnover 36	8.6	•	•	•	9.9	•	9.7	8.5	7.2	6.1	6.5	10.5	•
Total Liabilities to Net Worth 37	1.2	•	•	•	0.9	•	1.4	1.0	7.8	2.0	4.1	0.8	•
Current Assets to Working Capital 38	3.1	•	5.3	•	1.7	•	2.1	1.7	2.0	4.8	3.3	7.1	•
Current Liabilities to Working Capital 39	2.1	•	4.3	•	0.7	•	1.1	0.7	1.0	3.8	2.3	6.1	•
Working Capital to Net Sales 40	0.1	•	0.0	•	0.1	•	0.1	0.2	0.2	0.1	0.1	0.1	•
Inventory to Working Capital 41	1.3	•	2.3	•	0.9	•	1.1	0.8	1.1	2.0	1.4	2.5	•
Total Receipts to Cash Flow 42	10.2	•	8.0	•	6.8	•	12.3	12.0	11.2	30.5	18.1	8.1	•
Cost of Goods to Cash Flow 43	7.0	•	4.7	•	4.0	•	10.0	9.5	8.8	24.9	13.4	5.0	•
Cash Flow to Total Debt 44	0.2	•	0.5	•	0.9	•	0.4	0.3	0.1	0.1	0.1	0.2	•

Selected Financial Factors (in Percentages)

Debt Ratio 45	55.2	•	137.9	•	47.7	•	58.8	50.7	88.6	66.2	80.3	45.4	•
Return on Total Assets 46	4.8	•	10.6	•	7.9	•	9.0	9.1	6.7	1.2	3.5	4.3	•
Return on Equity Before Income Taxes 47	7.3	•	•	•	12.7	•	17.0	14.8	41.2	•	•	5.8	•
Return on Equity After Income Taxes 48	5.9	•	•	•	11.9	•	13.6	13.3	39.1	•	•	4.5	•
Profit Margin (Before Income Tax) 49	2.8	•	1.6	•	2.3	•	2.6	4.2	3.2	•	•	5.0	•
Profit Margin (After Income Tax) 50	2.3	•	1.6	•	2.2	•	2.1	3.7	3.1	•	•	3.9	•

Table II
Corporations with Net Income

TEXTILE PRODUCT MILLS

MONEY AMOUNTS AND SIZE OF ASSETS IN THOUSANDS OF DOLLARS

Item Description for Accounting Period 7/12 Through 6/13	Total	Zero Assets	Under 500	500 to 1,000	1,000 to 5,000	5,000 to 10,000	10,000 to 25,000	25,000 to 50,000	50,000 to 100,000	100,000 to 250,000	250,000 to 500,000	500,000 to 2,500,000	2,500,000 and over
Number of Enterprises **1**	993	0	•	135	320	25	36	24	8	6	•	4	0

Revenues ($ in Thousands)

Net Sales **2**	17780032	0	•	225712	2624360	340965	1332075	1470762	885982	1302525	•	6811618	0
Interest **3**	30336	0	•	25	12	17	344	690	220	1148	•	25235	0
Rents **4**	2856	0	•	0	0	836	0	686	42	932	•	354	0
Royalties **5**	28583	0	•	0	0	0	0	0	170	22	•	27495	0
Other Portfolio Income **6**	125165	0	•	0	0	63	115	6091	67	1132	•	117482	0
Other Receipts **7**	161515	0	•	43	14037	528	5967	11940	18700	9191	•	80393	0
Total Receipts **8**	18128487	0	•	225780	2638409	342409	1338501	1490169	905181	1314950	•	7062577	0
Average Total Receipts **9**	18256	•	•	1672	8245	13696	37181	62090	113148	219158	•	1765644	•

Operating Costs/Operating Income (%)

Cost of Operations **10**	67.0	•	•	52.0	55.8	69.2	80.6	77.2	77.6	76.4	•	61.2	•
Salaries and Wages **11**	9.8	•	•	8.0	13.7	5.5	3.7	5.0	5.6	6.1	•	13.9	•
Taxes Paid **12**	1.8	•	•	2.3	1.9	3.6	1.1	0.8	1.6	1.6	•	2.4	•
Interest Paid **13**	1.4	•	•	0.3	0.4	2.7	0.4	0.7	1.0	0.8	•	1.7	•
Depreciation **14**	1.8	•	•	2.6	1.0	1.2	0.6	1.0	1.1	3.0	•	2.6	•
Amortization and Depletion **15**	0.3	•	•	0.8	0.0	0.0	0.1	0.1	0.3	0.3	•	0.4	•
Pensions and Other Deferred Comp. **16**	0.9	•	•	0.3	0.3	0.4	0.1	0.2	0.2	0.4	•	1.9	•
Employee Benefits **17**	1.8	•	•	•	1.2	0.4	1.1	1.1	1.8	1.8	•	2.9	•
Advertising **18**	0.5	•	•	0.1	1.5	0.1	0.3	0.3	0.2	0.2	•	0.2	•
Other Expenses **19**	10.8	•	•	9.5	17.5	7.4	7.5	5.1	7.2	6.9	•	11.4	•
Officers' Compensation **20**	1.6	•	•	8.3	4.1	8.4	1.4	1.2	0.8	0.7	•	0.6	•
Operating Margin **21**	2.3	•	•	16.0	2.7	1.0	3.0	7.4	2.7	1.9	•	0.8	•
Operating Margin Before Officers' Comp. **22**	3.8	•	•	24.3	6.8	9.4	4.4	8.6	3.5	2.7	•	1.3	•

Selected Average Balance Sheet ($ in Thousands)

Net Receivables 23	1639	•	•	341	633	1153	3830	7148	16551	29283	•	71080	•
Inventories 24	2388	•	•	49	1157	3677	5432	10758	16391	24068	•	266714	•
Net Property, Plant and Equipment 25	2327	•	•	274	507	1408	1747	6672	9228	49427	•	318470	•
Total Assets 26	17033	•	•	821	2514	7396	13560	36921	69090	167268	•	2685766	•
Notes and Loans Payable 27	3754	•	•	21	370	3334	3081	6765	51030	49198	•	389195	•
All Other Liabilities 28	5112	•	•	181	836	1119	4507	6130	16977	35032	•	831175	•
Net Worth 29	8166	•	•	619	1307	2943	5972	24025	1083	83038	•	1465396	•

Selected Financial Ratios (Times to 1)

Current Ratio 30	1.4	•	•	2.5	2.3	1.9	1.9	3.1	1.8	1.6	•	1.2	•
Quick Ratio 31	0.6	•	•	2.5	1.0	0.6	0.8	1.5	0.8	0.8	•	0.4	•
Net Sales to Working Capital 32	8.9	•	•	6.0	7.5	5.5	7.0	4.3	5.9	7.0	•	16.2	•
Coverage Ratio 33	4.2	•	•	57.6	9.4	1.5	8.7	14.2	5.7	4.6	•	3.9	•
Total Asset Turnover 34	1.1	•	•	2.0	3.3	1.8	2.7	1.7	1.6	1.3	•	0.6	•
Inventory Turnover 35	5.0	•	•	17.6	4.0	2.6	5.5	4.4	5.2	6.9	•	3.9	•
Receivables Turnover 36	9.2	•	•	5.2	9.0	9.8	10.5	7.8	9.3	9.2	•	•	•
Total Liabilities to Net Worth 37	1.1	•	•	0.3	0.9	1.5	1.3	0.5	62.8	1.0	•	0.8	•
Current Assets to Working Capital 38	3.3	•	•	1.6	1.8	2.1	2.1	1.5	2.2	2.7	•	7.1	•
Current Liabilities to Working Capital 39	2.3	•	•	0.6	0.8	1.1	1.1	0.5	1.2	1.7	•	6.1	•
Working Capital to Net Sales 40	0.1	•	•	0.2	0.1	0.2	0.1	0.2	0.2	0.1	•	0.1	•
Inventory to Working Capital 41	1.4	•	•	0.1	0.9	1.3	1.1	0.7	1.2	1.1	•	2.5	•
Total Receipts to Cash Flow 42	8.1	•	•	4.6	6.0	13.9	10.7	8.4	9.6	11.3	•	8.1	•
Cost of Goods to Cash Flow 43	5.4	•	•	2.4	3.3	9.6	8.7	6.5	7.5	8.6	•	5.0	•
Cash Flow to Total Debt 44	0.3	•	•	1.8	1.1	0.2	0.5	0.6	0.2	0.2	•	0.2	•

Selected Financial Factors (in Percentages)

Debt Ratio 45	52.1	•	•	24.6	48.0	60.2	56.0	34.9	98.4	50.4	•	45.4	•
Return on Total Assets 46	6.1	•	•	33.1	11.9	7.7	10.7	15.5	9.4	4.7	•	4.3	•
Return on Equity Before Income Taxes 47	9.7	•	•	43.1	20.4	6.8	21.4	22.2	496.3	7.5	•	5.8	•
Return on Equity After Income Taxes 48	8.2	•	•	43.1	19.2	4.7	17.4	20.4	475.8	5.7	•	4.5	•
Profit Margin (Before Income Tax) 49	4.4	•	•	16.0	3.3	1.5	3.5	8.7	4.9	2.9	•	5.0	•
Profit Margin (After Income Tax) 50	3.8	•	•	16.0	3.1	1.0	2.8	8.0	4.7	2.2	•	3.9	•

Table I
Corporations with and without Net Income

APPAREL KNITTING MILLS

MONEY AMOUNTS AND SIZE OF ASSETS IN THOUSANDS OF DOLLARS

Item Description for Accounting Period 7/12 Through 6/13	Total	Zero Assets	Under 500	500 to 1,000	1,000 to 5,000	5,000 to 10,000	10,000 to 25,000	25,000 to 50,000	50,000 to 100,000	100,000 to 250,000	250,000 to 500,000	500,000 to 2,500,000	2,500,000 and over
Number of Enterprises 1	264	0	•	0	32	13	21	4	•	0	5	0	0
Revenues ($ in Thousands)													
Net Sales 2	7875921	0	•	0	23041	179098	467307	260421	•	0	6542850	0	0
Interest 3	7403	0	•	0	5038	4	756	1148	•	0	222	0	0
Rents 4	421	0	•	0	0	0	6	4	•	0	270	0	0
Royalties 5	45075	0	•	0	0	0	0	0	•	0	37695	0	0
Other Portfolio Income 6	38569	0	•	0	1996	0	3217	2	•	0	27503	0	0
Other Receipts 7	17778	0	•	0	1	8	15257	363	•	0	1923	0	0
Total Receipts 8	7985167	0	•	0	30076	179110	486543	261938	•	0	6610463	0	0
Average Total Receipts 9	30247	•	•	•	940	13778	23169	65484	•	•	1322093	•	•
Operating Costs/Operating Income (%)													
Cost of Operations 10	78.7	•	•	•	50.0	75.8	65.1	75.9	•	•	80.1	•	•
Salaries and Wages 11	6.0	•	•	•	33.9	5.4	8.5	5.0	•	•	5.9	•	•
Taxes Paid 12	1.1	•	•	•	5.7	1.3	1.1	1.7	•	•	0.9	•	•
Interest Paid 13	2.3	•	•	•	0.0	0.7	0.7	0.6	•	•	2.6	•	•
Depreciation 14	0.6	•	•	•	0.2	1.5	0.4	1.0	•	•	0.6	•	•
Amortization and Depletion 15	0.2	•	•	•	•	•	0.0	0.0	•	•	0.2	•	•
Pensions and Other Deferred Comp. 16	0.4	•	•	•	0.1	•	0.4	0.2	•	•	0.4	•	•
Employee Benefits 17	1.3	•	•	•	1.4	1.6	0.7	1.5	•	•	1.4	•	•
Advertising 18	2.3	•	•	•	0.1	1.8	0.2	1.2	•	•	2.6	•	•
Other Expenses 19	8.0	•	•	•	36.3	7.1	8.1	12.5	•	•	7.2	•	•
Officers' Compensation 20	1.0	•	•	•	6.8	4.9	3.2	0.8	•	•	0.6	•	•
Operating Margin 21	•	•	•	•	•	•	11.6	•	•	•	•	•	•
Operating Margin Before Officers' Comp. 22	•	•	•	•	•	4.8	14.8	0.5	•	•	•	•	•

Selected Average Balance Sheet ($ in Thousands)

Net Receivables 23	3246	•	•	•	72	1441	2783	5664	•	•	139458	•	•
Inventories 24	6700	•	•	•	108	2508	1937	10157	•	•	280541	•	•
Net Property, Plant and Equipment 25	1452	•	•	•	9	1022	966	2670	•	•	59730	•	•
Total Assets 26	28310	•	•	•	2129	5717	15086	34051	•	•	1316835	•	•
Notes and Loans Payable 27	8648	•	•	•	0	1870	2601	14900	•	•	415385	•	•
All Other Liabilities 28	19906	•	•	•	282	1092	1529	6795	•	•	1016930	•	•
Net Worth 29	-244	•	•	•	1847	2754	10956	12355	•	•	-115480	•	•

Selected Financial Ratios (Times to 1)

Current Ratio 30	2.1	•	•	•	1.2	2.0	2.8	2.5	•	•	2.2	•	•
Quick Ratio 31	0.7	•	•	•	0.9	0.7	1.7	0.9	•	•	0.7	•	•
Net Sales to Working Capital 32	5.0	•	•	•	10.9	6.5	3.5	3.7	•	•	5.1	•	•
Coverage Ratio 33	0.9	•	•	•	•	0.9	22.8	1.5	•	•	0.5	•	•
Total Asset Turnover 34	1.1	•	•	•	0.3	2.4	1.5	1.9	•	•	1.0	•	•
Inventory Turnover 35	3.5	•	•	•	3.3	4.2	7.5	4.9	•	•	3.7	•	•
Receivables Turnover 36	9.6	•	•	•	9.4	9.9	7.2	9.9	•	•	•	•	•
Total Liabilities to Net Worth 37	•	•	•	•	0.2	1.1	0.4	1.8	•	•	•	•	•
Current Assets to Working Capital 38	1.9	•	•	•	5.2	2.0	1.5	1.6	•	•	1.9	•	•
Current Liabilities to Working Capital 39	0.9	•	•	•	4.2	1.0	0.5	0.6	•	•	0.9	•	•
Working Capital to Net Sales 40	0.2	•	•	•	0.1	0.2	0.3	0.3	•	•	0.2	•	•
Inventory to Working Capital 41	1.0	•	•	•	1.1	1.2	0.3	0.6	•	•	1.1	•	•
Total Receipts to Cash Flow 42	17.9	•	•	•	6.2	23.1	4.6	9.3	•	•	24.7	•	•
Cost of Goods to Cash Flow 43	14.1	•	•	•	3.1	17.5	3.0	7.1	•	•	19.7	•	•
Cash Flow to Total Debt 44	0.1	•	•	•	0.4	0.2	1.2	0.3	•	•	0.0	•	•

Selected Financial Factors (in Percentages)

Debt Ratio 45	100.9	•	•	•	13.3	51.8	27.4	63.7	•	•	108.8	•	•
Return on Total Assets 46	2.1	•	•	•	•	1.5	24.1	1.6	•	•	1.4	•	•
Return on Equity Before Income Taxes 47	37.2	•	•	•	•	•	31.7	1.6	•	•	13.5	•	•
Return on Equity After Income Taxes 48	67.8	•	•	•	•	•	31.7	•	•	•	16.7	•	•
Profit Margin (Before Income Tax) 49	•	•	•	•	•	•	15.6	0.3	•	•	•	•	•
Profit Margin (After Income Tax) 50	•	•	•	•	•	•	15.6	•	•	•	•	•	•

Table II
Corporations with Net Income

APPAREL KNITTING MILLS

MONEY AMOUNTS AND SIZE OF ASSETS IN THOUSANDS OF DOLLARS

Item Description for Accounting Period 7/12 Through 6/13	Total	Zero Assets	Under 500	500 to 1,000	1,000 to 5,000	5,000 to 10,000	10,000 to 25,000	25,000 to 50,000	50,000 to 100,000	100,000 to 250,000	250,000 to 500,000	500,000 to 2,500,000	2,500,000 and over
Number of Enterprises 1	23	0	0	0	•	0	13	4	0	0	•	0	0

Revenues ($ in Thousands)													
Net Sales 2	2612793	0	0	0	•	0	412347	196126	0	0	•	0	0
Interest 3	1139	0	0	0	•	0	728	211	0	0	•	0	0
Rents 4	296	0	0	0	•	0	6	21	0	0	•	0	0
Royalties 5	1751	0	0	0	•	0	0	0	0	0	•	0	0
Other Portfolio Income 6	13613	0	0	0	•	0	1989	110	0	0	•	0	0
Other Receipts 7	19715	0	0	0	•	0	18081	199	0	0	•	0	0
Total Receipts 8	2649307	0	0	0	•	0	433151	196667	0	0	•	0	0
Average Total Receipts 9	115187	•	•	•	•	•	33319	49167	•	•	•	•	•

Operating Costs/Operating Income (%)													
Cost of Operations 10	77.0	•	•	•	•	•	64.8	78.7	•	•	•	•	•
Salaries and Wages 11	4.9	•	•	•	•	•	9.3	4.4	•	•	•	•	•
Taxes Paid 12	1.0	•	•	•	•	•	0.9	2.1	•	•	•	•	•
Interest Paid 13	1.4	•	•	•	•	•	0.6	0.7	•	•	•	•	•
Depreciation 14	0.9	•	•	•	•	•	0.3	1.5	•	•	•	•	•
Amortization and Depletion 15	0.2	•	•	•	•	•	0.0	0.1	•	•	•	•	•
Pensions and Other Deferred Comp. 16	0.3	•	•	•	•	•	0.4	0.5	•	•	•	•	•
Employee Benefits 17	1.0	•	•	•	•	•	0.8	0.6	•	•	•	•	•
Advertising 18	1.7	•	•	•	•	•	0.2	1.4	•	•	•	•	•
Other Expenses 19	7.0	•	•	•	•	•	8.1	6.8	•	•	•	•	•
Officers' Compensation 20	0.8	•	•	•	•	•	1.4	1.4	•	•	•	•	•
Operating Margin 21	3.8	•	•	•	•	•	13.2	1.8	•	•	•	•	•
Operating Margin Before Officers' Comp. 22	4.6	•	•	•	•	•	14.6	3.2	•	•	•	•	•

Selected Average Balance Sheet ($ in Thousands)

Net Receivables **23**	16742	•	•	•	•	•	4012	5957	•	•	•	•	•
Inventories **24**	47360	•	•	•	•	•	2982	16124	•	•	•	•	•
Net Property, Plant and Equipment **25**	8902	•	•	•	•	•	746	8135	•	•	•	•	•
Total Assets **26**	75520	•	•	•	•	•	15208	45493	•	•	•	•	•
Notes and Loans Payable **27**	28378	•	•	•	•	•	3647	5338	•	•	•	•	•
All Other Liabilities **28**	24652	•	•	•	•	•	2076	9406	•	•	•	•	•
Net Worth **29**	22489	•	•	•	•	•	9485	30748	•	•	•	•	•

Selected Financial Ratios (Times to 1)

Current Ratio **30**	2.2	•	•	•	•	•	2.2	3.5	•	•	•	•	•
Quick Ratio **31**	0.8	•	•	•	•	•	1.0	1.5	•	•	•	•	•
Net Sales to Working Capital **32**	3.9	•	•	•	•	•	5.0	2.2	•	•	•	•	•
Coverage Ratio **33**	4.9	•	•	•	•	•	33.7	3.9	•	•	•	•	•
Total Asset Turnover **34**	1.5	•	•	•	•	•	2.1	1.1	•	•	•	•	•
Inventory Turnover **35**	1.8	•	•	•	•	•	6.9	2.4	•	•	•	•	•
Receivables Turnover **36**	5.2	•	•	•	•	•	6.6	•	•	•	•	•	•
Total Liabilities to Net Worth **37**	2.4	•	•	•	•	•	0.6	0.5	•	•	•	•	•
Current Assets to Working Capital **38**	1.8	•	•	•	•	•	1.8	1.4	•	•	•	•	•
Current Liabilities to Working Capital **39**	0.8	•	•	•	•	•	0.8	0.4	•	•	•	•	•
Working Capital to Net Sales **40**	0.3	•	•	•	•	•	0.2	0.5	•	•	•	•	•
Inventory to Working Capital **41**	1.0	•	•	•	•	•	0.5	0.7	•	•	•	•	•
Total Receipts to Cash Flow **42**	9.5	•	•	•	•	•	4.1	13.0	•	•	•	•	•
Cost of Goods to Cash Flow **43**	7.3	•	•	•	•	•	2.6	10.2	•	•	•	•	•
Cash Flow to Total Debt **44**	0.2	•	•	•	•	•	1.4	0.3	•	•	•	•	•

Selected Financial Factors (in Percentages)

Debt Ratio **45**	70.2	•	•	•	•	•	37.6	32.4	•	•	•	•	•
Return on Total Assets **46**	10.1	•	•	•	•	•	39.3	3.0	•	•	•	•	•
Return on Equity Before Income Taxes **47**	27.0	•	•	•	•	•	61.1	3.3	•	•	•	•	•
Return on Equity After Income Taxes **48**	23.2	•	•	•	•	•	61.1	2.2	•	•	•	•	•
Profit Margin (Before Income Tax) **49**	5.4	•	•	•	•	•	18.3	2.0	•	•	•	•	•
Profit Margin (After Income Tax) **50**	4.6	•	•	•	•	•	18.3	1.4	•	•	•	•	•

Table I

Corporations with and without Net Income

CUT AND SEW APPAREL CONTRACTORS AND MFRS.

MONEY AMOUNTS AND SIZE OF ASSETS IN THOUSANDS OF DOLLARS

Item Description for Accounting Period 7/12 Through 6/13	Total	Zero Assets	Under 500	500 to 1,000	1,000 to 5,000	5,000 to 10,000	10,000 to 25,000	25,000 to 50,000	50,000 to 100,000	100,000 to 250,000	250,000 to 500,000	500,000 to 2,500,000	2,500,000 and over
Number of Enterprises 1	5007	2093	1738	365	502	154	84	25	26	10	•	•	0
Revenues ($ in Thousands)													
Net Sales 2	36563918	547421	667866	1327727	3000903	2482710	2741434	2288469	2898530	2182741	•	•	0
Interest 3	17597	243	10	0	2176	53	535	1377	197	921	•	•	0
Rents 4	10888	1	0	0	2	17	12	429	2233	0	•	•	0
Royalties 5	1050842	84	14451	0	185	0	6144	5763	15010	1589	•	•	0
Other Portfolio Income 6	102837	4688	420	0	3	19	30158	10	1575	2283	•	•	0
Other Receipts 7	639036	17092	6	2099	23183	13690	47264	6254	21722	13839	•	•	0
Total Receipts 8	38385118	569529	682753	1329826	3026452	2496489	2825547	2302302	2939267	2201373	•	•	0
Average Total Receipts 9	7666	272	393	3643	6029	16211	33637	92092	113049	220137	•	•	•
Operating Costs/Operating Income (%)													
Cost of Operations 10	63.8	50.9	60.1	79.4	70.6	71.1	69.2	72.1	76.2	58.6	•	•	•
Salaries and Wages 11	10.0	19.6	11.7	7.9	4.9	9.9	7.9	6.7	7.5	11.6	•	•	•
Taxes Paid 12	2.2	3.2	3.4	1.1	5.3	1.5	1.9	3.3	1.6	2.4	•	•	•
Interest Paid 13	1.4	5.1	0.3	0.2	1.0	0.7	0.8	0.6	0.8	1.2	•	•	•
Depreciation 14	1.1	0.9	0.7	0.1	0.2	0.4	0.4	0.5	0.7	1.0	•	•	•
Amortization and Depletion 15	0.5	2.6	0.1	0.4	0.0	0.0	0.1	0.0	0.5	0.2	•	•	•
Pensions and Other Deferred Comp. 16	1.2	0.1	•	0.0	0.4	1.1	0.1	0.5	0.3	0.6	•	•	•
Employee Benefits 17	0.9	0.3	0.7	0.6	0.5	0.4	0.9	0.5	1.1	1.9	•	•	•
Advertising 18	2.8	1.2	0.3	1.5	0.3	2.5	1.3	1.0	1.2	2.3	•	•	•
Other Expenses 19	14.2	34.1	21.7	13.2	6.4	9.3	12.2	9.2	6.2	9.8	•	•	•
Officers' Compensation 20	2.1	3.1	4.9	2.8	5.4	1.8	4.2	2.0	1.4	1.5	•	•	•
Operating Margin 21	•	•	•	•	4.9	1.2	1.0	3.5	2.7	9.0	•	•	•
Operating Margin Before Officers' Comp. 22	1.9	•	1.1	•	10.3	3.1	5.2	5.6	4.1	10.5	•	•	•

Selected Average Balance Sheet ($ in Thousands)

	1	2	3	4	5	6	7	8	9	10	11	12	13
Net Receivables 23	900	0	20	50	430	1971	3114	5735	14067	21460	•	•	•
Inventories 24	1101	0	17	131	925	2899	4828	14980	22269	35836	•	•	•
Net Property, Plant and Equipment 25	497	0	14	8	205	583	941	3300	4993	18913	•	•	•
Total Assets 26	5345	0	108	603	2165	7057	15678	32879	69445	140647	•	•	•
Notes and Loans Payable 27	1506	0	78	647	666	2653	2896	5995	17099	28510	•	•	•
All Other Liabilities 28	2052	0	72	289	670	3209	4487	8923	14521	28301	•	•	•
Net Worth 29	1787	0	-42	-334	829	1195	8295	17960	37825	83836	•	•	•

Selected Financial Ratios (Times to 1)

	1	2	3	4	5	6	7	8	9	10	11	12	13
Current Ratio 30	1.9	•	2.4	0.8	2.4	2.3	2.9	2.4	2.7	3.7	•	•	•
Quick Ratio 31	1.0	•	2.0	0.2	1.1	1.0	1.1	0.8	1.2	1.9	•	•	•
Net Sales to Working Capital 32	5.5	•	8.6	•	5.3	5.0	3.7	5.8	3.3	3.4	•	•	•
Coverage Ratio 33	4.5	•	•	•	7.0	3.6	6.0	7.7	6.5	9.3	•	•	•
Total Asset Turnover 34	1.4	•	3.5	6.0	2.8	2.3	2.1	2.8	1.6	1.6	•	•	•
Inventory Turnover 35	4.2	•	13.4	22.0	4.6	4.0	4.7	4.4	3.8	3.6	•	•	•
Receivables Turnover 36	8.2	•	19.7	49.8	15.1	6.7	9.2	17.2	8.0	•	•	•	•
Total Liabilities to Net Worth 37	2.0	•	•	•	1.6	4.9	0.9	0.8	0.8	0.7	•	•	•
Current Assets to Working Capital 38	2.1	•	1.7	•	1.7	1.8	1.5	1.7	1.6	1.4	•	•	•
Current Liabilities to Working Capital 39	1.1	•	0.7	•	0.7	0.8	0.5	0.7	0.6	0.4	•	•	•
Working Capital to Net Sales 40	0.2	•	0.1	•	0.2	0.2	0.3	0.2	0.3	0.3	•	•	•
Inventory to Working Capital 41	0.8	•	0.3	•	0.8	0.9	0.4	0.9	0.7	0.6	•	•	•
Total Receipts to Cash Flow 42	6.5	7.2	6.9	32.9	9.2	10.6	7.9	8.8	11.6	6.5	•	•	•
Cost of Goods to Cash Flow 43	4.2	3.7	4.2	26.1	6.5	7.5	5.4	6.3	8.9	3.8	•	•	•
Cash Flow to Total Debt 44	0.3	•	0.4	0.1	0.5	0.3	0.6	0.7	0.3	0.6	•	•	•

Selected Financial Factors (in Percentages)

	1	2	3	4	5	6	7	8	9	10	11	12	13
Debt Ratio 45	66.6	•	138.5	155.3	61.7	83.1	47.1	45.4	45.5	40.4	•	•	•
Return on Total Assets 46	8.7	•	•	•	18.6	5.7	10.2	13.3	7.8	17.1	•	•	•
Return on Equity Before Income Taxes 47	20.4	•	14.2	76.4	41.5	24.2	16.1	21.2	12.1	25.7	•	•	•
Return on Equity After Income Taxes 48	15.0	•	14.5	76.4	40.4	20.7	15.1	19.3	11.1	22.7	•	•	•
Profit Margin (Before Income Tax) 49	5.0	•	•	•	5.8	1.8	4.1	4.2	4.1	9.9	•	•	•
Profit Margin (After Income Tax) 50	3.7	•	•	•	5.6	1.5	3.8	3.8	3.8	8.7	•	•	•

Table II

Corporations with Net Income

CUT AND SEW APPAREL CONTRACTORS AND MFRS.

MONEY AMOUNTS AND SIZE OF ASSETS IN THOUSANDS OF DOLLARS

Item Description for Accounting Period 7/12 Through 6/13		Total	Zero Assets	Under 500	500 to 1,000	1,000 to 5,000	5,000 to 10,000	10,000 to 25,000	25,000 to 50,000	50,000 to 100,000	100,000 to 250,000	250,000 to 500,000	500,000 to 2,500,000	2,500,000 and over
Number of Enterprises	1	1980	16	1012	254	472	98	66	•	•	10	•	8	0
Revenues ($ in Thousands)														
Net Sales	2	33514456	131550	357799	1166829	2930740	1857519	2315796	•	•	2182741	•	16312835	0
Interest	3	17490	200	10	0	2176	53	513	•	•	921	•	12057	0
Rents	4	10858	1	0	0	2	17	12	•	•	0	•	8193	0
Royalties	5	1044115	84	14451	0	185	0	0	•	•	1589	•	1007617	0
Other Portfolio Income	6	71412	4685	198	0	3	0	950	•	•	2283	•	62884	0
Other Receipts	7	644958	16499	0	2099	23168	30133	46988	•	•	13839	•	461754	0
Total Receipts	8	35303289	153019	372458	1168928	2956274	1887722	2364259	•	•	2201373	•	17865340	0
Average Total Receipts	9	17830	9564	368	4602	6263	19262	35822	•	•	220137	•	2233168	•
Operating Costs/Operating Income (%)														
Cost of Operations	10	63.6	63.2	52.7	76.1	69.9	69.8	68.9	•	•	58.6	•	58.4	•
Salaries and Wages	11	9.4	11.5	12.2	4.1	5.0	8.1	6.0	•	•	11.6	•	11.6	•
Taxes Paid	12	2.1	5.7	4.7	0.6	5.4	1.5	2.0	•	•	2.4	•	1.5	•
Interest Paid	13	1.3	0.8	0.3	0.2	1.0	0.4	0.6	•	•	1.2	•	1.9	•
Depreciation	14	1.2	0.2	0.9	0.1	0.2	0.5	0.3	•	•	1.0	•	1.7	•
Amortization and Depletion	15	0.5	•	0.1	0.2	0.0	0.0	0.1	•	•	0.2	•	0.9	•
Pensions and Other Deferred Comp.	16	1.2	0.0	•	•	0.4	1.4	0.1	•	•	0.6	•	2.0	•
Employee Benefits	17	1.0	•	1.0	•	0.6	0.6	0.6	•	•	1.9	•	1.1	•
Advertising	18	2.8	0.3	0.1	0.0	0.3	1.5	1.1	•	•	2.3	•	4.0	•
Other Expenses	19	13.6	15.3	19.8	11.8	6.6	10.3	9.9	•	•	9.8	•	18.3	•
Officers' Compensation	20	2.1	3.2	6.2	2.4	5.5	2.4	4.5	•	•	1.5	•	1.3	•
Operating Margin	21	1.3	•	2.2	4.5	5.0	3.5	5.8	•	•	9.0	•	•	•
Operating Margin Before Officers' Comp.	22	3.4	3.0	8.4	7.0	10.5	5.8	10.3	•	•	10.5	•	•	•

Selected Average Balance Sheet ($ in Thousands)

Net Receivables 23	2150	0	13	30	433	2279	3460	•	•	21460	•	334514	•
Inventories 24	2388	0	13	161	792	2800	4104	•	•	35836	•	280775	•
Net Property, Plant and Equipment 25	1200	0	17	10	215	879	1031	•	•	18913	•	192345	•
Total Assets 26	12643	0	88	566	2236	7298	15553	•	•	140647	•	2185809	•
Notes and Loans Payable 27	3369	0	52	144	708	1738	2913	•	•	28510	•	620678	•
All Other Liabilities 28	4935	0	33	248	645	4575	4453	•	•	28301	•	948665	•
Net Worth 29	4339	0	4	174	882	984	8187	•	•	83836	•	616467	•

Selected Financial Ratios (Times to 1)

Current Ratio 30	1.9	•	1.6	2.0	2.5	1.9	2.8	•	•	3.7	•	1.5	•
Quick Ratio 31	1.0	•	1.4	0.3	1.2	0.9	1.2	•	•	1.9	•	0.9	•
Net Sales to Working Capital 32	5.7	•	16.7	18.7	5.2	6.6	4.1	•	•	3.4	•	7.4	•
Coverage Ratio 33	6.5	22.6	25.7	31.9	7.0	15.2	13.3	•	•	9.3	•	4.9	•
Total Asset Turnover 34	1.3	•	4.0	8.1	2.8	2.6	2.3	•	•	1.6	•	0.9	•
Inventory Turnover 35	4.5	•	14.6	21.7	5.5	4.7	5.9	•	•	3.6	•	4.2	•
Receivables Turnover 36	8.0	•	15.8	•	15.8	6.4	8.8	•	•	•	•	6.5	•
Total Liabilities to Net Worth 37	1.9	•	24.1	2.2	1.5	6.4	0.9	•	•	0.7	•	2.5	•
Current Assets to Working Capital 38	2.1	•	2.6	2.0	1.6	2.1	1.6	•	•	1.4	•	2.9	•
Current Liabilities to Working Capital 39	1.1	•	1.6	1.0	0.6	1.1	0.6	•	•	0.4	•	1.9	•
Working Capital to Net Sales 40	0.2	•	0.1	0.1	0.2	0.2	0.2	•	•	0.3	•	0.1	•
Inventory to Working Capital 41	0.8	•	0.4	0.7	0.8	0.9	0.4	•	•	0.6	•	1.0	•
Total Receipts to Cash Flow 42	5.9	3.4	5.4	7.1	9.0	7.2	6.4	•	•	6.5	•	4.8	•
Cost of Goods to Cash Flow 43	3.8	2.2	2.9	5.4	6.3	5.0	4.4	•	•	3.8	•	2.8	•
Cash Flow to Total Debt 44	0.3	•	0.8	1.7	0.5	0.4	0.7	•	•	0.6	•	0.3	•

Selected Financial Factors (in Percentages)

Debt Ratio 45	65.7	•	96.0	69.2	60.5	86.5	47.4	•	•	40.4	•	71.8	•
Return on Total Assets 46	10.9	•	26.0	39.6	19.2	14.2	19.4	•	•	17.1	•	8.5	•
Return on Equity Before Income Taxes 47	26.8	•	627.6	124.7	41.6	98.0	34.0	•	•	25.7	•	24.1	•
Return on Equity After Income Taxes 48	21.2	•	622.2	124.6	40.6	91.2	32.6	•	•	22.7	•	16.0	•
Profit Margin (Before Income Tax) 49	6.9	16.2	6.3	4.7	5.9	5.1	7.9	•	•	9.9	•	7.3	•
Profit Margin (After Income Tax) 50	5.4	13.9	6.2	4.7	5.8	4.7	7.6	•	•	8.7	•	4.8	•

Table I
Corporations with and without Net Income

APPAREL ACCESSORIES AND OTHER APPAREL

MONEY AMOUNTS AND SIZE OF ASSETS IN THOUSANDS OF DOLLARS

Item Description for Accounting Period 7/12 Through 6/13	Total	Zero Assets	Under 500	500 to 1,000	1,000 to 5,000	5,000 to 10,000	10,000 to 25,000	25,000 to 50,000	50,000 to 100,000	100,000 to 250,000	250,000 to 500,000	500,000 to 2,500,000	2,500,000 and over
Number of Enterprises **1**	3618	1172	•	246	162	59	50	15	•	0	•	•	0

Revenues ($ in Thousands)

Net Sales **2**	8627025	181877	•	571107	835023	1157053	1463634	932073	•	0	•	•	0
Interest **3**	3258	6	•	0	35	1723	613	84	•	0	•	•	0
Rents **4**	150	0	•	0	0	0	2	0	•	0	•	•	0
Royalties **5**	1515	923	•	0	0	153	14	0	•	0	•	•	0
Other Portfolio Income **6**	12458	6763	•	0	150	650	1417	1729	•	0	•	•	0
Other Receipts **7**	50454	12125	•	0	4929	190	4134	1061	•	0	•	•	0
Total Receipts **8**	8694860	201694	•	571107	840137	1159769	1469814	934947	•	0	•	•	0
Average Total Receipts **9**	2403	172	•	2322	5186	19657	29396	62330	•	•	•	•	•

Operating Costs/Operating Income (%)

Cost of Operations **10**	65.0	83.7	•	61.3	56.5	74.3	76.7	62.4	•	•	•	•	•
Salaries and Wages **11**	9.7	7.6	•	12.8	9.3	7.8	6.4	12.6	•	•	•	•	•
Taxes Paid **12**	3.3	2.6	•	2.0	2.4	3.6	1.4	2.2	•	•	•	•	•
Interest Paid **13**	1.8	4.0	•	0.9	0.2	0.7	2.3	0.7	•	•	•	•	•
Depreciation **14**	0.7	0.6	•	0.4	0.4	0.3	0.5	1.5	•	•	•	•	•
Amortization and Depletion **15**	0.5	0.9	•	0.0	0.0	0.0	0.2	0.1	•	•	•	•	•
Pensions and Other Deferred Comp. **16**	0.3	0.0	•	0.3	1.7	0.0	0.1	0.1	•	•	•	•	•
Employee Benefits **17**	0.8	0.3	•	0.9	0.9	0.9	0.6	1.2	•	•	•	•	•
Advertising **18**	1.5	1.3	•	0.6	0.4	0.1	1.2	1.8	•	•	•	•	•
Other Expenses **19**	11.9	13.1	•	16.0	9.9	6.0	7.2	12.3	•	•	•	•	•
Officers' Compensation **20**	2.6	4.2	•	2.0	7.8	1.9	2.1	2.1	•	•	•	•	•
Operating Margin **21**	1.8	•	•	2.8	10.4	4.5	1.4	3.1	•	•	•	•	•
Operating Margin Before Officers' Comp. **22**	4.4	•	•	4.8	18.2	6.4	3.5	5.2	•	•	•	•	•

Selected Average Balance Sheet ($ in Thousands)

Net Receivables 23	235	0	•	179	734	1933	2709	6590	•	•	•	•	•
Inventories 24	390	0	•	130	359	3105	6133	17409	•	•	•	•	•
Net Property, Plant and Equipment 25	118	0	•	411	265	176	1305	4289	•	•	•	•	•
Total Assets 26	1138	0	•	897	2057	6747	14334	30981	•	•	•	•	•
Notes and Loans Payable 27	542	0	•	593	170	2034	5207	12222	•	•	•	•	•
All Other Liabilities 28	358	0	•	170	442	3160	3094	6198	•	•	•	•	•
Net Worth 29	238	0	•	134	1445	1554	6033	12561	•	•	•	•	•

Selected Financial Ratios (Times to 1)

Current Ratio 30	1.9	•	•	1.3	3.3	1.5	2.3	1.9	•	•	•	•	•
Quick Ratio 31	0.8	•	•	0.7	2.5	0.6	0.9	0.6	•	•	•	•	•
Net Sales to Working Capital 32	6.1	•	•	26.9	4.3	10.8	4.4	5.1	•	•	•	•	•
Coverage Ratio 33	2.5	•	•	4.1	47.4	7.3	1.8	5.7	•	•	•	•	•
Total Asset Turnover 34	2.1	•	•	2.6	2.5	2.9	2.0	2.0	•	•	•	•	•
Inventory Turnover 35	4.0	•	•	11.0	8.1	4.7	3.7	2.2	•	•	•	•	•
Receivables Turnover 36	9.4	•	•	19.5	7.5	8.0	11.6	8.3	•	•	•	•	•
Total Liabilities to Net Worth 37	3.8	•	•	5.7	0.4	3.3	1.4	1.5	•	•	•	•	•
Current Assets to Working Capital 38	2.1	•	•	4.2	1.4	3.1	1.8	2.1	•	•	•	•	•
Current Liabilities to Working Capital 39	1.1	•	•	3.2	0.4	2.1	0.8	1.1	•	•	•	•	•
Working Capital to Net Sales 40	0.2	•	•	0.0	0.2	0.1	0.2	0.2	•	•	•	•	•
Inventory to Working Capital 41	1.0	•	•	1.7	0.3	1.8	0.9	1.3	•	•	•	•	•
Total Receipts to Cash Flow 42	8.9	•	•	8.6	5.2	11.3	13.7	7.1	•	•	•	•	•
Cost of Goods to Cash Flow 43	5.8	•	•	5.3	3.0	8.4	10.5	4.4	•	•	•	•	•
Cash Flow to Total Debt 44	0.3	•	•	0.4	1.6	0.3	0.3	0.5	•	•	•	•	•

Selected Financial Factors (in Percentages)

Debt Ratio 45	79.1	•	•	85.1	29.7	77.0	57.9	59.5	•	•	•	•	•
Return on Total Assets 46	9.2	•	•	9.6	28.3	15.8	8.3	8.2	•	•	•	•	•
Return on Equity Before Income Taxes 47	26.4	•	•	49.0	39.4	59.4	8.8	16.8	•	•	•	•	•
Return on Equity After Income Taxes 48	24.6	•	•	49.0	38.6	59.3	7.6	14.0	•	•	•	•	•
Profit Margin (Before Income Tax) 49	2.6	•	•	2.8	11.1	4.7	1.8	3.4	•	•	•	•	•
Profit Margin (After Income Tax) 50	2.5	•	•	2.8	10.8	4.7	1.6	2.8	•	•	•	•	•

Table II
Corporations with Net Income

APPAREL ACCESSORIES AND OTHER APPAREL

MONEY AMOUNTS AND SIZE OF ASSETS IN THOUSANDS OF DOLLARS

Item Description for Accounting Period 7/12 Through 6/13	Total	Zero Assets	Under 500	500 to 1,000	1,000 to 5,000	5,000 to 10,000	10,000 to 25,000	25,000 to 50,000	50,000 to 100,000	100,000 to 250,000	250,000 to 500,000	500,000 to 2,500,000	2,500,000 and over
Number of Enterprises 1	1818	259	1079	246	•	55	35	11	•	0	0	0	0

Revenues ($ in Thousands)

	Total	Zero Assets	Under 500	500 to 1,000	1,000 to 5,000	5,000 to 10,000	10,000 to 25,000	25,000 to 50,000	50,000 to 100,000	100,000 to 250,000	250,000 to 500,000	500,000 to 2,500,000	2,500,000 and over
Net Sales 2	6896701	86356	1096276	571107	•	1156720	1222829	668144	•	0	0	0	0
Interest 3	183	6	0	0	•	0	38	84	•	0	0	0	0
Rents 4	18	0	0	0	•	0	2	0	•	0	0	0	0
Royalties 5	426	0	0	0	•	0	0	0	•	0	0	0	0
Other Portfolio Income 6	4462	0	0	0	•	650	185	1729	•	0	0	0	0
Other Receipts 7	21452	10252	0	0	•	190	609	880	•	0	0	0	0
Total Receipts 8	6923242	96614	1096276	571107	•	1157560	1223663	670837	•	0	0	0	0
Average Total Receipts 9	3808	373	1016	2322	•	21047	34962	60985	•	•	•	•	•

Operating Costs/Operating Income (%)

	Total	Zero Assets	Under 500	500 to 1,000	1,000 to 5,000	5,000 to 10,000	10,000 to 25,000	25,000 to 50,000	50,000 to 100,000	100,000 to 250,000	250,000 to 500,000	500,000 to 2,500,000	2,500,000 and over
Cost of Operations 10	66.9	62.9	69.8	61.3	•	74.2	74.8	59.8	•	•	•	•	•
Salaries and Wages 11	8.5	2.0	7.4	12.8	•	7.8	5.8	13.2	•	•	•	•	•
Taxes Paid 12	2.9	1.0	1.4	2.0	•	3.5	1.5	2.2	•	•	•	•	•
Interest Paid 13	0.7	7.3	0.0	0.9	•	0.6	1.5	0.7	•	•	•	•	•
Depreciation 14	0.5	0.2	0.0	0.4	•	0.3	0.4	1.5	•	•	•	•	•
Amortization and Depletion 15	0.1	0.6	0.2	0.0	•	0.0	0.0	0.1	•	•	•	•	•
Pensions and Other Deferred Comp. 16	0.3	0.1	0.2	0.3	•	0.0	0.1	0.1	•	•	•	•	•
Employee Benefits 17	0.7	0.6	0.0	0.9	•	0.9	0.6	0.6	•	•	•	•	•
Advertising 18	1.5	0.3	0.4	0.6	•	0.1	1.2	1.7	•	•	•	•	•
Other Expenses 19	9.1	15.4	10.6	16.0	•	5.1	6.2	12.9	•	•	•	•	•
Officers' Compensation 20	2.9	4.9	3.6	2.0	•	1.8	1.9	2.4	•	•	•	•	•
Operating Margin 21	5.9	4.8	6.2	2.8	•	5.8	5.9	5.0	•	•	•	•	•
Operating Margin Before Officers' Comp. 22	8.8	9.7	9.9	4.8	•	7.6	7.8	7.4	•	•	•	•	•

Selected Average Balance Sheet ($ in Thousands)

	1	2	3	4	5	6	7	8	9	10	11	12	13
Net Receivables 23	342	0	51	179	•	1771	3538	5997	•	•	•	•	•
Inventories 24	574	0	73	144	•	3132	7697	20686	•	•	•	•	•
Net Property, Plant and Equipment 25	161	0	1	411	•	189	1379	4288	•	•	•	•	•
Total Assets 26	1438	0	225	897	•	6418	15020	31204	•	•	•	•	•
Notes and Loans Payable 27	476	0	174	593	•	1081	4452	11149	•	•	•	•	•
All Other Liabilities 28	402	0	67	170	•	3163	3592	5452	•	•	•	•	•
Net Worth 29	561	0	-17	134	•	2174	6976	14603	•	•	•	•	•

Selected Financial Ratios (Times to 1)

	1	2	3	4	5	6	7	8	9	10	11	12	13
Current Ratio 30	2.0	•	3.1	1.3	•	1.5	2.0	2.5	•	•	•	•	•
Quick Ratio 31	0.8	•	2.0	0.7	•	0.5	0.6	0.8	•	•	•	•	•
Net Sales to Working Capital 32	6.4	•	7.1	26.9	•	11.5	5.3	4.1	•	•	•	•	•
Coverage Ratio 33	9.5	3.3	144.7	4.1	•	10.8	5.0	8.5	•	•	•	•	•
Total Asset Turnover 34	2.6	•	4.5	2.6	•	3.3	2.3	1.9	•	•	•	•	•
Inventory Turnover 35	4.4	•	9.7	9.9	•	5.0	3.4	1.8	•	•	•	•	•
Receivables Turnover 36	10.6	•	•	•	•	8.8	11.7	7.0	•	•	•	•	•
Total Liabilities to Net Worth 37	1.6	•	•	5.7	•	2.0	1.2	1.1	•	•	•	•	•
Current Assets to Working Capital 38	2.0	•	1.5	4.2	•	3.1	2.0	1.7	•	•	•	•	•
Current Liabilities to Working Capital 39	1.0	•	0.5	3.2	•	2.1	1.0	0.7	•	•	•	•	•
Working Capital to Net Sales 40	0.2	•	0.1	0.0	•	0.1	0.2	0.2	•	•	•	•	•
Inventory to Working Capital 41	1.0	•	0.5	1.7	•	2.0	1.3	1.1	•	•	•	•	•
Total Receipts to Cash Flow 42	7.6	3.4	7.0	8.6	•	10.9	9.6	6.0	•	•	•	•	•
Cost of Goods to Cash Flow 43	5.1	2.1	4.9	5.3	•	8.1	7.2	3.6	•	•	•	•	•
Cash Flow to Total Debt 44	0.6	•	0.6	0.4	•	0.5	0.5	0.6	•	•	•	•	•

Selected Financial Factors (in Percentages)

	1	2	3	4	5	6	7	8	9	10	11	12	13
Debt Ratio 45	61.0	•	107.4	85.1	•	66.1	53.6	53.2	•	•	•	•	•
Return on Total Assets 46	18.5	•	28.3	9.6	•	21.2	17.2	11.9	•	•	•	•	•
Return on Equity Before Income Taxes 47	42.4	•	•	49.0	•	56.8	29.7	22.4	•	•	•	•	•
Return on Equity After Income Taxes 48	40.9	•	•	49.0	•	56.7	28.3	19.1	•	•	•	•	•
Profit Margin (Before Income Tax) 49	6.3	16.8	6.2	2.8	•	5.9	5.9	5.4	•	•	•	•	•
Profit Margin (After Income Tax) 50	6.0	12.7	6.2	2.8	•	5.9	5.7	4.6	•	•	•	•	•

Table I

Corporations with and without Net Income

MANUFACTURING
316115

LEATHER AND ALLIED PRODUCT MANUFACTURING

MONEY AMOUNTS AND SIZE OF ASSETS IN THOUSANDS OF DOLLARS

Item Description for Accounting Period 7/12 Through 6/13		Total	Zero Assets	Under 500	500 to 1,000	1,000 to 5,000	5,000 to 10,000	10,000 to 25,000	25,000 to 50,000	50,000 to 100,000	100,000 to 250,000	250,000 to 500,000	500,000 to 2,500,000	2,500,000 and over
Number of Enterprises	1	1091	260	•	0	139	5	42	14	5	9	0	•	•
Revenues ($ in Thousands)														
Net Sales	2	9140719	520541	•	0	380020	56409	1106702	1000961	276165	2707948	0	•	•
Interest	3	7692	882	•	0	377	185	213	0	730	4950	0	•	•
Rents	4	873	0	•	0	0	7	3	0	75	0	0	•	•
Royalties	5	107680	0	•	0	0	0	0	0	423	724	0	•	•
Other Portfolio Income	6	45994	0	•	0	1007	27	32	0	34	44885	0	•	•
Other Receipts	7	100285	-9801	•	0	-8865	99	5014	3301	3139	6263	0	•	•
Total Receipts	8	9403243	511622	•	0	372539	56727	1111964	1004262	280566	2764770	0	•	•
Average Total Receipts	9	8619	1968	•	•	2680	11345	26475	71733	56113	307197	•	•	•
Operating Costs/Operating Income (%)														
Cost of Operations	10	63.9	58.8	•	•	64.6	76.2	72.6	72.3	65.1	58.2	•	•	•
Salaries and Wages	11	11.0	7.0	•	•	11.0	7.8	7.4	6.9	10.4	9.6	•	•	•
Taxes Paid	12	1.7	1.5	•	•	3.5	1.0	1.4	1.6	1.5	1.5	•	•	•
Interest Paid	13	0.7	0.1	•	•	0.1	0.4	0.5	0.3	2.0	0.7	•	•	•
Depreciation	14	1.1	1.0	•	•	0.4	0.4	0.7	1.2	1.4	1.4	•	•	•
Amortization and Depletion	15	0.2	0.3	•	•	•	0.0	0.0	0.0	3.1	0.2	•	•	•
Pensions and Other Deferred Comp.	16	0.6	0.0	•	•	0.1	0.1	0.1	0.1	0.1	0.7	•	•	•
Employee Benefits	17	1.5	3.8	•	•	0.4	0.9	0.7	0.7	1.2	1.4	•	•	•
Advertising	18	3.4	5.0	•	•	1.0	0.1	1.8	1.4	2.6	2.0	•	•	•
Other Expenses	19	11.6	15.1	•	•	15.5	9.6	7.9	9.5	12.5	16.1	•	•	•
Officers' Compensation	20	2.0	0.6	•	•	3.4	2.3	2.4	2.2	2.3	2.0	•	•	•
Operating Margin	21	2.3	6.6	•	•	•	1.1	4.5	3.7	•	6.1	•	•	•
Operating Margin Before Officers' Comp.	22	4.3	7.3	•	•	3.4	3.4	6.9	5.9	0.2	8.1	•	•	•

Selected Average Balance Sheet ($ in Thousands)

	1	2	3	4	5	6	7	8	9	10	11	12	13
Net Receivables 23	2036	0	•	•	79	637	3564	10476	10481	37234	•	•	•
Inventories 24	1520	0	•	•	548	2172	4333	14722	16382	45224	•	•	•
Net Property, Plant and Equipment 25	623	0	•	•	160	779	1382	3677	4576	23267	•	•	•
Total Assets 26	7456	0	•	•	1411	7961	14279	33152	62343	199229	•	•	•
Notes and Loans Payable 27	2278	0	•	•	15	799	3371	9030	16933	50507	•	•	•
All Other Liabilities 28	2752	0	•	•	1531	948	2876	6759	9345	108022	•	•	•
Net Worth 29	2427	0	•	•	-135	6214	8032	17363	36065	40701	•	•	•

Selected Financial Ratios (Times to 1)

	1	2	3	4	5	6	7	8	9	10	11	12	13
Current Ratio 30	1.7	•	•	•	0.8	4.8	2.6	2.0	2.4	1.2	•	•	•
Quick Ratio 31	0.9	•	•	•	0.2	3.0	1.3	0.9	1.2	0.4	•	•	•
Net Sales to Working Capital 32	4.6	•	•	•	•	2.2	3.5	5.5	3.2	14.1	•	•	•
Coverage Ratio 33	8.8	43.6	•	•	•	5.3	11.3	14.1	0.7	13.1	•	•	•
Total Asset Turnover 34	1.1	•	•	•	1.9	1.4	1.8	2.2	0.9	1.5	•	•	•
Inventory Turnover 35	3.5	•	•	•	3.2	4.0	4.4	3.5	2.2	3.9	•	•	•
Receivables Turnover 36	4.5	•	•	•	16.1	35.4	10.1	6.6	5.6	10.6	•	•	•
Total Liabilities to Net Worth 37	2.1	•	•	•	•	0.3	0.8	0.9	0.7	3.9	•	•	•
Current Assets to Working Capital 38	2.5	•	•	•	•	1.3	1.6	2.0	1.7	6.3	•	•	•
Current Liabilities to Working Capital 39	1.5	•	•	•	•	0.3	0.6	1.0	0.7	5.3	•	•	•
Working Capital to Net Sales 40	0.2	•	•	•	•	0.5	0.3	0.2	0.3	0.1	•	•	•
Inventory to Working Capital 41	0.9	•	•	•	•	0.4	0.7	1.0	0.8	2.6	•	•	•
Total Receipts to Cash Flow 42	7.0	6.3	•	•	12.5	11.5	8.7	7.9	10.2	4.8	•	•	•
Cost of Goods to Cash Flow 43	4.5	3.7	•	•	8.1	8.7	6.3	5.7	6.6	2.8	•	•	•
Cash Flow to Total Debt 44	0.2	•	•	•	0.1	0.6	0.5	0.6	0.2	0.4	•	•	•

Selected Financial Factors (in Percentages)

	1	2	3	4	5	6	7	8	9	10	11	12	13
Debt Ratio 45	67.5	•	•	•	109.6	21.9	43.7	47.6	42.2	79.6	•	•	•
Return on Total Assets 46	6.7	•	•	•	•	2.9	10.1	9.4	1.3	13.9	•	•	•
Return on Equity Before Income Taxes 47	18.3	•	•	•	46.4	3.1	16.3	16.6	•	62.8	•	•	•
Return on Equity After Income Taxes 48	16.2	•	•	•	47.5	2.2	16.3	16.6	•	54.9	•	•	•
Profit Margin (Before Income Tax) 49	5.3	4.9	•	•	•	1.7	5.0	4.0	•	8.5	•	•	•
Profit Margin (After Income Tax) 50	4.7	3.9	•	•	•	1.2	5.0	4.0	•	7.4	•	•	•

Table II

Corporations with Net Income

LEATHER AND ALLIED PRODUCT MANUFACTURING

MONEY AMOUNTS AND SIZE OF ASSETS IN THOUSANDS OF DOLLARS

Item Description for Accounting Period 7/12 Through 6/13	Total	Zero Assets	Under 500	500 to 1,000	1,000 to 5,000	5,000 to 10,000	10,000 to 25,000	25,000 to 50,000	50,000 to 100,000	100,000 to 250,000	250,000 to 500,000	500,000 to 2,500,000	2,500,000 and over
Number of Enterprises 1	687	•	596	0	30	•	30	14	•	•	0	3	0

Revenues ($ in Thousands)

	Total	Zero Assets	Under 500	500 to 1,000	1,000 to 5,000	5,000 to 10,000	10,000 to 25,000	25,000 to 50,000	50,000 to 100,000	100,000 to 250,000	250,000 to 500,000	500,000 to 2,500,000	2,500,000 and over
Net Sales 2	8401028	•	309938	0	190934	•	850991	1000961	•	•	0	2652585	0
Interest 3	6668	•	0	0	377	•	0	0	•	•	0	354	0
Rents 4	871	•	0	0	0	•	0	0	•	•	0	788	0
Royalties 5	106902	•	0	0	0	•	0	0	•	•	0	106533	0
Other Portfolio Income 6	44952	•	0	0	0	•	32	0	•	•	0	10	0
Other Receipts 7	99686	•	3	0	0	•	2227	3301	•	•	0	101131	0
Total Receipts 8	8660107	•	309941	0	191311	•	853250	1004262	•	•	0	2861401	0
Average Total Receipts 9	12606	•	520	•	6377	•	28442	71733	•	•	•	953800	•

Operating Costs/Operating Income (%)

	Total	Zero Assets	Under 500	500 to 1,000	1,000 to 5,000	5,000 to 10,000	10,000 to 25,000	25,000 to 50,000	50,000 to 100,000	100,000 to 250,000	250,000 to 500,000	500,000 to 2,500,000	2,500,000 and over
Cost of Operations 10	63.2	•	33.2	•	76.4	•	72.1	72.3	•	•	•	65.5	•
Salaries and Wages 11	11.1	•	22.8	•	10.3	•	6.5	6.9	•	•	•	15.5	•
Taxes Paid 12	1.6	•	5.5	•	1.5	•	1.1	1.6	•	•	•	1.5	•
Interest Paid 13	0.6	•	1.6	•	•	•	0.5	0.3	•	•	•	0.8	•
Depreciation 14	1.2	•	0.5	•	0.2	•	0.9	1.2	•	•	•	1.2	•
Amortization and Depletion 15	0.1	•	•	•	•	•	0.0	0.0	•	•	•	0.1	•
Pensions and Other Deferred Comp. 16	0.6	•	•	•	•	•	0.1	0.1	•	•	•	1.2	•
Employee Benefits 17	1.6	•	4.5	•	0.3	•	0.2	0.7	•	•	•	1.7	•
Advertising 18	3.6	•	4.5	•	0.7	•	1.6	1.4	•	•	•	6.5	•
Other Expenses 19	11.2	•	20.1	•	8.7	•	6.3	9.5	•	•	•	7.3	•
Officers' Compensation 20	1.9	•	1.7	•	1.3	•	2.4	2.2	•	•	•	1.9	•
Operating Margin 21	3.4	•	5.6	•	0.6	•	8.4	3.7	•	•	•	•	•
Operating Margin Before Officers' Comp. 22	5.3	•	7.3	•	1.9	•	10.8	5.9	•	•	•	•	•

Selected Average Balance Sheet ($ in Thousands)

Net Receivables	23	3130	•	0	•	0	•	3649	10476	•	•	•	506675	•
Inventories	24	2105	•	31	•	1892	•	4762	13679	•	•	•	194435	•
Net Property, Plant and Equipment	25	917	•	3	•	256	•	1702	3677	•	•	•	103342	•
Total Assets	26	10607	•	176	•	2106	•	14199	33152	•	•	•	1540283	•
Notes and Loans Payable	27	3391	•	172	•	0	•	3758	9030	•	•	•	523140	•
All Other Liabilities	28	3416	•	0	•	716	•	2854	6759	•	•	•	516638	•
Net Worth	29	3800	•	4	•	1390	•	7588	17363	•	•	•	500505	•

Selected Financial Ratios (Times to 1)

Current Ratio	30	2.0	•	12.0	•	2.4	•	2.5	2.0	•	•	•	2.0	•
Quick Ratio	31	1.1	•	4.1	•	0.9	•	1.2	0.9	•	•	•	1.3	•
Net Sales to Working Capital	32	3.9	•	8.0	•	6.1	•	4.0	5.5	•	•	•	2.2	•
Coverage Ratio	33	11.2	•	4.4	•	•	•	18.7	14.1	•	•	•	6.6	•
Total Asset Turnover	34	1.2	•	3.0	•	3.0	•	2.0	2.2	•	•	•	0.6	•
Inventory Turnover	35	3.7	•	5.5	•	2.6	•	4.3	3.8	•	•	•	3.0	•
Receivables Turnover	36	4.5	•	2190.4	•	10.9	•	10.0	6.9	•	•	•	2.0	•
Total Liabilities to Net Worth	37	1.8	•	46.7	•	0.5	•	0.9	0.9	•	•	•	2.1	•
Current Assets to Working Capital	38	2.0	•	1.1	•	1.7	•	1.7	2.0	•	•	•	2.0	•
Current Liabilities to Working Capital	39	1.0	•	0.1	•	0.7	•	0.7	1.0	•	•	•	1.0	•
Working Capital to Net Sales	40	0.3	•	0.1	•	0.2	•	0.2	0.2	•	•	•	0.4	•
Inventory to Working Capital	41	0.8	•	0.7	•	1.0	•	0.8	1.0	•	•	•	0.6	•
Total Receipts to Cash Flow	42	6.6	•	4.3	•	15.9	•	7.2	7.9	•	•	•	10.3	•
Cost of Goods to Cash Flow	43	4.2	•	1.4	•	12.2	•	5.2	5.7	•	•	•	6.7	•
Cash Flow to Total Debt	44	0.3	•	0.7	•	0.6	•	0.6	0.6	•	•	•	0.1	•

Selected Financial Factors (in Percentages)

Debt Ratio	45	64.2	•	97.9	•	34.0	•	46.6	47.6	•	•	•	67.5	•
Return on Total Assets	46	8.3	•	21.5	•	2.4	•	18.3	9.4	•	•	•	3.2	•
Return on Equity Before Income Taxes	47	21.2	•	796.7	•	3.7	•	32.4	16.6	•	•	•	8.3	•
Return on Equity After Income Taxes	48	19.1	•	796.5	•	3.2	•	32.4	16.6	•	•	•	7.1	•
Profit Margin (Before Income Tax)	49	6.6	•	5.6	•	0.8	•	8.7	4.0	•	•	•	4.7	•
Profit Margin (After Income Tax)	50	5.9	•	5.6	•	0.7	•	8.7	4.0	•	•	•	4.0	•

Table I

Corporations with and without Net Income

WOOD PRODUCT MANUFACTURING

MONEY AMOUNTS AND SIZE OF ASSETS IN THOUSANDS OF DOLLARS

Item Description for Accounting Period 7/12 Through 6/13		Total	Zero Assets	Under 500	500 to 1,000	1,000 to 5,000	5,000 to 10,000	10,000 to 25,000	25,000 to 50,000	50,000 to 100,000	100,000 to 250,000	250,000 to 500,000	500,000 to 2,500,000	2,500,000 and over
Number of Enterprises	1	11542	1401	6249	1347	1630	460	261	80	53	36	9	16	0

Revenues ($ in Thousands)														
Net Sales	2	73090409	696863	3930607	2592082	9299664	7553112	7077997	4087481	4353406	7290576	4620612	21588008	0
Interest	3	158450	513	4	103	1480	1895	3203	3787	4316	7528	22850	112772	0
Rents	4	43722	28	0	1758	7147	3792	1315	1713	2474	3852	3230	18412	0
Royalties	5	33642	0	0	0	0	0	42	1679	1478	345	0	30098	0
Other Portfolio Income	6	408436	34992	36507	9490	17896	14147	16375	12978	29900	52071	34452	149634	0
Other Receipts	7	819077	22664	4583	612	56269	28423	41379	18628	50618	193472	21421	381004	0
Total Receipts	8	74553736	755060	3971701	2604045	9382456	7601369	7140311	4126266	4442192	7547844	4702565	22279928	0
Average Total Receipts	9	6459	539	636	1933	5756	16525	27358	51578	83815	209662	522507	1392496	•

Operating Costs/Operating Income (%)														
Cost of Operations	10	75.5	73.5	57.8	74.2	71.1	77.2	75.3	80.1	80.5	79.2	76.2	77.2	•
Salaries and Wages	11	6.0	7.3	14.4	6.5	7.4	5.4	5.5	3.9	4.9	4.4	4.4	5.5	•
Taxes Paid	12	1.7	1.7	2.3	2.6	2.8	1.8	2.0	1.8	1.8	1.4	1.3	1.1	•
Interest Paid	13	1.6	0.9	0.5	1.4	0.6	0.7	0.6	1.1	1.2	1.5	2.1	3.1	•
Depreciation	14	2.6	2.2	1.7	1.7	1.3	1.5	2.4	2.5	2.8	3.7	3.1	3.4	•
Amortization and Depletion	15	0.5	0.2	0.1	0.1	0.0	0.1	0.1	0.5	0.5	0.6	0.2	1.2	•
Pensions and Other Deferred Comp.	16	0.4	0.0	0.0	0.0	0.3	0.1	0.2	0.3	0.3	0.2	0.7	0.9	•
Employee Benefits	17	1.2	0.8	1.1	0.9	1.5	0.7	1.1	0.9	1.4	1.0	0.3	1.6	•
Advertising	18	0.5	0.2	0.7	0.2	0.2	0.5	0.2	0.2	0.3	0.7	0.8	0.7	•
Other Expenses	19	8.1	14.4	16.9	8.2	8.8	8.4	8.3	5.0	6.9	9.1	8.8	6.1	•
Officers' Compensation	20	1.4	0.5	2.4	4.2	3.4	1.9	1.4	0.9	0.8	1.1	0.3	0.4	•
Operating Margin	21	0.5	•	2.3	0.1	2.6	1.8	3.0	3.0	•	•	1.9	•	•
Operating Margin Before Officers' Comp.	22	1.9	•	4.6	4.3	6.0	3.7	4.4	3.9	•	•	2.2	•	•

Selected Average Balance Sheet ($ in Thousands)

Net Receivables 23	548	0	23	143	490	1209	2451	7149	11603	18209	47040	107635	•
Inventories 24	696	0	14	191	603	2467	3876	8897	13269	18930	55681	123026	•
Net Property, Plant and Equipment 25	1506	0	52	194	617	2246	4936	9538	23690	62696	159891	484978	•
Total Assets 26	4576	0	148	699	2374	7087	14819	33101	70248	161693	388955	1516260	•
Notes and Loans Payable 27	1686	0	93	581	991	2648	4045	8698	20297	53435	136055	580522	•
All Other Liabilities 28	1266	0	36	235	494	940	2950	5279	14512	44145	164445	487595	•
Net Worth 29	1624	0	19	-117	889	3499	7824	19124	35439	64113	88455	448143	•

Selected Financial Ratios (Times to 1)

Current Ratio 30	1.5	•	1.4	1.0	2.0	2.0	2.1	3.1	2.2	1.3	1.2	1.2	•
Quick Ratio 31	0.8	•	1.0	0.5	1.1	0.8	1.0	1.7	1.1	0.6	0.6	0.6	•
Net Sales to Working Capital 32	10.4	•	29.5	189.6	7.5	7.6	6.1	3.7	4.7	18.0	21.0	25.0	•
Coverage Ratio 33	2.5	8.6	7.0	1.4	7.0	4.6	7.5	4.7	1.5	1.5	2.7	1.7	•
Total Asset Turnover 34	1.4	•	4.2	2.8	2.4	2.3	1.8	1.5	1.2	1.3	1.3	0.9	•
Inventory Turnover 35	6.9	•	26.5	7.5	6.7	5.1	5.3	4.6	5.0	8.5	7.0	8.5	•
Receivables Turnover 36	11.2	•	29.1	12.2	11.4	12.2	11.4	7.2	7.0	12.2	11.3	11.0	•
Total Liabilities to Net Worth 37	1.8	•	6.9	•	1.7	1.0	0.9	0.7	1.0	1.5	3.4	2.4	•
Current Assets to Working Capital 38	2.9	•	3.6	42.4	2.0	2.0	1.9	1.5	1.9	4.9	6.0	6.9	•
Current Liabilities to Working Capital 39	1.9	•	2.6	41.4	1.0	1.0	0.9	0.5	0.9	3.9	5.0	5.9	•
Working Capital to Net Sales 40	0.1	•	0.0	0.0	0.1	0.1	0.2	0.3	0.2	0.1	0.0	0.0	•
Inventory to Working Capital 41	1.2	•	0.7	16.7	0.8	1.2	0.9	0.6	0.7	1.9	2.3	2.4	•
Total Receipts to Cash Flow 42	12.3	7.4	6.6	17.9	10.6	12.0	9.4	13.6	19.1	15.4	9.7	15.8	•
Cost of Goods to Cash Flow 43	9.3	5.4	3.8	13.3	7.5	9.3	7.1	10.9	15.4	12.2	7.4	12.2	•
Cash Flow to Total Debt 44	0.2	•	0.7	0.1	0.4	0.4	0.4	0.3	0.1	0.1	0.2	0.1	•

Selected Financial Factors (in Percentages)

Debt Ratio 45	64.5	•	87.3	116.7	62.6	50.6	47.2	42.2	49.6	60.3	77.3	70.4	•
Return on Total Assets 46	5.7	•	16.4	5.4	9.7	7.1	8.2	7.7	2.3	2.8	7.6	4.7	•
Return on Equity Before Income Taxes 47	9.8	•	111.3	•	22.3	11.2	13.4	10.4	1.6	2.4	21.2	6.4	•
Return on Equity After Income Taxes 48	8.7	•	108.4	•	21.5	10.4	12.2	9.5	1.0	1.8	19.8	4.9	•
Profit Margin (Before Income Tax) 49	2.5	6.6	3.3	0.6	3.5	2.4	3.9	3.9	0.7	0.7	3.7	2.1	•
Profit Margin (After Income Tax) 50	2.2	5.1	3.2	0.5	3.3	2.2	3.5	3.5	0.4	0.6	3.4	1.6	•

Table II
Corporations with Net Income

WOOD PRODUCT MANUFACTURING

MONEY AMOUNTS AND SIZE OF ASSETS IN THOUSANDS OF DOLLARS

Item Description for Accounting Period 7/12 Through 6/13		Total	Zero Assets	Under 500	500 to 1,000	1,000 to 5,000	5,000 to 10,000	10,000 to 25,000	25,000 to 50,000	50,000 to 100,000	100,000 to 250,000	250,000 to 500,000	500,000 to 2,500,000	2,500,000 and over
Number of Enterprises	1	6172	429	3058	837	1221	309	180	68	•	22	•	11	0

Revenues ($ in Thousands)

		Total	Zero Assets	Under 500	500 to 1,000	1,000 to 5,000	5,000 to 10,000	10,000 to 25,000	25,000 to 50,000	50,000 to 100,000	100,000 to 250,000	250,000 to 500,000	500,000 to 2,500,000	2,500,000 and over
Net Sales	2	58716934	396499	3544503	2243940	7390678	6307403	5662762	3606996	•	4835386	•	18309030	0
Interest	3	148635	204	0	11	1284	1827	2622	3141	•	787	•	112765	0
Rents	4	35589	0	0	140	7147	148	1292	1713	•	2519	•	18412	0
Royalties	5	32083	0	0	0	0	0	2	1679	•	305	•	30098	0
Other Portfolio Income	6	348720	14347	26260	4103	17230	13319	6869	12300	•	46327	•	148844	0
Other Receipts	7	693906	21080	3848	146	30411	21421	27440	12606	•	174816	•	352503	0
Total Receipts	8	59975867	432130	3574611	2248340	7446750	6344118	5700987	3638435	•	5060140	•	18971652	0
Average Total Receipts	9	9717	1007	1169	2686	6099	20531	31672	53506	•	230006	•	1724696	•

Operating Costs/Operating Income (%)

		Total	Zero Assets	Under 500	500 to 1,000	1,000 to 5,000	5,000 to 10,000	10,000 to 25,000	25,000 to 50,000	50,000 to 100,000	100,000 to 250,000	250,000 to 500,000	500,000 to 2,500,000	2,500,000 and over
Cost of Operations	10	74.7	63.0	58.0	74.0	69.9	77.3	74.0	78.9	•	78.9	•	77.7	•
Salaries and Wages	11	5.9	8.4	15.4	6.1	6.1	5.4	5.3	4.1	•	4.7	•	5.4	•
Taxes Paid	12	1.6	1.4	2.2	2.4	2.5	1.7	1.9	1.8	•	1.4	•	1.0	•
Interest Paid	13	1.6	0.5	0.3	1.0	0.4	0.4	0.4	0.7	•	1.4	•	3.4	•
Depreciation	14	2.1	1.6	1.4	1.7	1.3	1.0	2.0	2.1	•	2.7	•	2.7	•
Amortization and Depletion	15	0.3	0.1	0.0	0.0	0.0	0.0	0.0	0.1	•	0.6	•	0.8	•
Pensions and Other Deferred Comp.	16	0.4	0.0	0.0	0.0	0.3	0.1	0.2	0.3	•	0.3	•	0.9	•
Employee Benefits	17	1.2	0.4	1.2	0.6	1.6	0.6	1.1	0.8	•	0.9	•	1.5	•
Advertising	18	0.4	0.1	0.6	0.1	0.2	0.5	0.1	0.2	•	0.7	•	0.6	•
Other Expenses	19	7.4	8.4	12.9	7.6	7.8	7.7	7.8	5.2	•	6.4	•	6.3	•
Officers' Compensation	20	1.4	0.4	1.7	3.7	3.9	1.8	1.4	0.8	•	1.2	•	0.5	•
Operating Margin	21	2.8	15.8	6.3	2.7	6.0	3.7	5.8	5.0	•	0.9	•	•	•
Operating Margin Before Officers' Comp.	22	4.2	16.2	8.1	6.4	9.9	5.5	7.2	5.9	•	2.1	•	•	•

Selected Average Balance Sheet ($ in Thousands)

Net Receivables 23	813	0	46	192	507	1495	2964	7693	•	15360	•	137410	•
Inventories 24	880	0	17	135	509	3031	3783	7313	•	14886	•	136454	•
Net Property, Plant and Equipment 25	1817	0	47	222	633	1942	4094	8984	•	56398	•	448722	•
Total Assets 26	6387	0	202	709	2488	7387	14896	32713	•	154515	•	1771046	•
Notes and Loans Payable 27	2226	0	78	692	637	2040	3040	7311	•	37312	•	727573	•
All Other Liabilities 28	1786	0	50	216	422	1001	2811	5058	•	32612	•	631371	•
Net Worth 29	2375	0	74	-198	1428	4346	9044	20344	•	84590	•	412102	•

Selected Financial Ratios (Times to 1)

Current Ratio 30	1.7	•	2.4	1.0	2.8	2.1	2.5	3.2	•	1.5	•	1.2	•
Quick Ratio 31	0.9	•	1.8	0.6	1.6	0.8	1.3	1.7	•	0.7	•	0.6	•
Net Sales to Working Capital 32	8.9	•	14.3	899.7	5.6	7.7	5.8	3.7	•	12.1	•	23.8	•
Coverage Ratio 33	4.1	53.7	23.8	3.8	16.3	12.6	16.4	9.5	•	5.1	•	1.9	•
Total Asset Turnover 34	1.5	•	5.7	3.8	2.4	2.8	2.1	1.6	•	1.4	•	0.9	•
Inventory Turnover 35	8.1	•	40.5	14.7	8.3	5.2	6.2	5.7	•	11.7	•	9.5	•
Receivables Turnover 36	12.6	•	30.7	13.6	13.4	12.9	11.8	8.3	•	17.0	•	11.9	•
Total Liabilities to Net Worth 37	1.7	•	1.7	•	0.7	0.7	0.6	0.6	•	0.8	•	3.3	•
Current Assets to Working Capital 38	2.4	•	1.7	153.9	1.5	1.9	1.7	1.5	•	2.8	•	7.0	•
Current Liabilities to Working Capital 39	1.4	•	0.7	152.9	0.5	0.9	0.7	0.5	•	1.8	•	6.0	•
Working Capital to Net Sales 40	0.1	•	0.1	0.0	0.2	0.1	0.2	0.3	•	0.1	•	0.0	•
Inventory to Working Capital 41	0.9	•	0.2	45.4	0.6	1.1	0.7	0.6	•	1.1	•	2.3	•
Total Receipts to Cash Flow 42	9.9	3.6	6.5	13.7	8.4	10.3	7.9	10.6	•	9.7	•	13.7	•
Cost of Goods to Cash Flow 43	7.4	2.3	3.8	10.1	5.8	8.0	5.8	8.4	•	7.6	•	10.7	•
Cash Flow to Total Debt 44	0.2	•	1.4	0.2	0.7	0.6	0.7	0.4	•	0.3	•	0.1	•

Selected Financial Factors (in Percentages)

Debt Ratio 45	62.8	•	63.4	127.9	42.6	41.2	39.3	37.8	•	45.3	•	76.7	•
Return on Total Assets 46	9.7	•	43.1	15.1	17.5	12.8	14.5	10.7	•	10.0	•	6.0	•
Return on Equity Before Income Taxes 47	19.8	•	112.7	•	28.5	20.1	22.5	15.4	•	14.6	•	12.1	•
Return on Equity After Income Taxes 48	18.3	•	111.3	•	27.9	19.1	20.9	14.3	•	13.9	•	9.7	•
Profit Margin (Before Income Tax) 49	5.0	24.7	7.2	2.9	6.7	4.3	6.5	5.9	•	5.6	•	3.0	•
Profit Margin (After Income Tax) 50	4.6	22.0	7.1	2.9	6.6	4.1	6.0	5.5	•	5.4	•	2.4	•

Table I

Corporations with and without Net Income

PULP, PAPER, AND PAPERBOARD MILLS

MONEY AMOUNTS AND SIZE OF ASSETS IN THOUSANDS OF DOLLARS

Item Description for Accounting Period 7/12 Through 6/13		Total	Zero Assets	Under 500	500 to 1,000	1,000 to 5,000	5,000 to 10,000	10,000 to 25,000	25,000 to 50,000	50,000 to 100,000	100,000 to 250,000	250,000 to 500,000	500,000 to 2,500,000	2,500,000 and over
Number of Enterprises	1	467	5	198	86	68	29	12	16	12	14	8	15	5
Revenues ($ in Thousands)														
Net Sales	2	65307216	21862	223411	203459	1350973	361181	285881	798029	2166231	3037837	3231865	16018036	37608451
Interest	3	436814	1034	0	31	0	4	6	0	601	9747	7596	12412	405384
Rents	4	13092	0	0	0	0	0	373	0	47	3	3569	1534	7566
Royalties	5	76057	0	0	0	0	0	0	0	0	0	104	36990	38963
Other Portfolio Income	6	904492	3360	69034	0	0	662	13953	4533	243	7923	3873	39101	761809
Other Receipts	7	345289	-108973	141	0	0	3652	1482	4197	21910	14924	18584	246972	142399
Total Receipts	8	67082960	-82717	292586	203490	1350973	365499	301695	806759	2189032	3070434	3265591	16355045	38964572
Average Total Receipts	9	143647	-16543	1478	2366	19867	12603	25141	50422	182419	219317	408199	1090336	7792914
Operating Costs/Operating Income (%)														
Cost of Operations	10	77.2	98.4	39.9	37.0	104.3	76.2	84.8	68.2	83.6	86.2	74.4	77.3	75.8
Salaries and Wages	11	3.8	•	19.6	10.2	0.6	3.3	4.4	7.3	3.7	2.1	4.9	4.4	3.5
Taxes Paid	12	1.2	0.8	2.7	2.1	0.2	1.7	1.3	0.9	0.8	0.6	1.3	1.0	1.4
Interest Paid	13	3.5	5.2	3.4	1.2	0.4	1.4	0.3	0.8	0.7	2.3	3.6	1.7	4.8
Depreciation	14	4.5	•	1.2	0.6	0.0	2.8	11.3	3.3	1.8	3.4	4.3	5.1	4.6
Amortization and Depletion	15	0.5	•	3.2	•	•	0.1	0.3	0.2	0.1	0.5	0.4	0.6	0.5
Pensions and Other Deferred Comp.	16	0.9	•	•	11.4	•	0.0	0.0	1.3	0.4	0.4	1.2	0.8	1.0
Employee Benefits	17	1.8	•	0.4	3.1	•	1.7	1.1	1.7	1.1	2.7	2.1	2.1	1.7
Advertising	18	0.2	•	0.9	0.8	•	0.1	0.4	0.1	0.4	0.2	0.4	0.3	0.1
Other Expenses	19	6.4	2.2	26.7	10.9	0.9	17.5	10.7	7.6	6.6	3.8	4.6	4.9	7.3
Officers' Compensation	20	0.6	•	6.3	20.3	0.5	0.7	1.2	1.7	0.5	0.6	0.9	0.8	0.4
Operating Margin	21	•	•	•	2.4	•	•	•	6.8	0.1	•	1.8	0.9	•
Operating Margin Before Officers' Comp.	22	•	•	1.9	22.8	•	•	•	8.5	0.6	•	2.7	1.8	•

Selected Average Balance Sheet ($ in Thousands)

Net Receivables 23	24803	0	14	230	0	1249	1142	5832	17748	27699	41076	175413	1571312
Inventories 24	14626	0	0	98	0	1943	2897	5263	15158	25143	43838	132161	755913
Net Property, Plant and Equipment 25	65738	0	2	321	5	3236	8798	11278	26902	59073	132223	596978	3825852
Total Assets 26	247767	0	54	788	3310	6649	15600	33290	78008	162877	368344	1270992	17852625
Notes and Loans Payable 27	100687	0	0	330	484	4532	7165	11033	26415	75955	176679	342631	7726421
All Other Liabilities 28	66734	0	13	392	976	2657	2265	20489	22325	48879	138780	429046	4426412
Net Worth 29	80346	0	41	66	1849	-541	6170	1768	29268	38043	52885	499315	5699792

Selected Financial Ratios (Times to 1)

Current Ratio 30	0.8	•	3.9	1.0	0.8	0.8	1.8	1.0	1.8	1.5	1.3	2.1	0.6
Quick Ratio 31	0.5	•	3.9	0.7	0.8	0.4	0.7	0.5	0.9	0.8	0.6	1.1	0.4
Net Sales to Working Capital 32	•	•	29.2	•	•	•	8.4	96.1	9.9	10.0	17.4	5.1	•
Coverage Ratio 33	1.6	•	8.8	3.1	•	•	•	10.5	2.6	0.4	1.8	2.8	1.5
Total Asset Turnover 34	0.6	•	20.8	3.0	6.0	1.9	1.5	1.5	2.3	1.3	1.1	0.8	0.4
Inventory Turnover 35	7.4	•	•	8.9	•	4.9	7.0	6.5	10.0	7.4	6.9	6.2	7.5
Receivables Turnover 36	5.5	•	157.7	7.6	•	9.1	10.6	8.2	12.0	9.4	9.3	6.4	4.5
Total Liabilities to Net Worth 37	2.1	•	0.3	11.0	0.8	•	1.5	17.8	1.7	3.3	6.0	1.5	2.1
Current Assets to Working Capital 38	•	•	1.3	•	•	•	2.3	33.6	2.3	3.0	4.6	1.9	•
Current Liabilities to Working Capital 39	•	•	0.3	•	•	•	1.3	32.6	1.3	2.0	3.6	0.9	•
Working Capital to Net Sales 40	•	•	0.0	•	•	•	0.1	0.0	0.1	0.1	0.1	0.2	•
Inventory to Working Capital 41	•	•	•	•	•	•	0.8	9.5	0.9	1.2	1.9	0.7	•
Total Receipts to Cash Flow 42	14.8	•	2.8	11.0	•	11.8	•	7.1	15.2	84.9	16.8	16.7	12.3
Cost of Goods to Cash Flow 43	11.4	•	1.1	4.1	•	9.0	•	4.9	12.7	73.2	12.5	12.9	9.3
Cash Flow to Total Debt 44	0.1	•	30.5	0.3	•	0.1	•	0.2	0.2	0.0	0.1	0.1	0.1

Selected Financial Factors (in Percentages)

Debt Ratio 45	67.6	•	24.5	91.7	44.1	108.1	60.4	94.7	62.5	76.6	85.6	60.7	68.1
Return on Total Assets 46	3.2	•	623.1	10.8	•	•	•	13.0	4.4	1.1	7.1	4.0	3.1
Return on Equity Before Income Taxes 47	3.7	•	731.6	88.4	•	96.3	•	221.9	7.2	•	22.1	6.5	3.3
Return on Equity After Income Taxes 48	2.8	•	731.6	79.1	•	96.5	•	211.0	4.3	•	16.0	4.9	2.8
Profit Margin (Before Income Tax) 49	2.1	•	26.5	2.5	•	•	•	7.9	1.2	•	2.9	3.0	2.5
Profit Margin (After Income Tax) 50	1.6	•	26.5	2.2	•	•	•	7.5	0.7	•	2.1	2.3	2.1

Table II
Corporations with Net Income

PULP, PAPER, AND PAPERBOARD MILLS

MONEY AMOUNTS AND SIZE OF ASSETS IN THOUSANDS OF DOLLARS

Item Description for Accounting Period 7/12 Through 6/13	Total	Zero Assets	Under 500	500 to 1,000	1,000 to 5,000	5,000 to 10,000	10,000 to 25,000	25,000 to 50,000	50,000 to 100,000	100,000 to 250,000	250,000 to 500,000	500,000 to 2,500,000	2,500,000 and over
Number of Enterprises 1	351	•	•	86	0	•	6	12	9	•	5	11	•

Revenues ($ in Thousands)

Net Sales 2	52067246	•	•	203459	0	•	132160	726790	1738430	•	2251233	13236958	•
Interest 3	428997	•	•	31	0	•	5	0	588	•	4301	10883	•
Rents 4	12688	•	•	0	0	•	373	0	47	•	3401	1468	•
Royalties 5	75953	•	•	0	0	•	0	0	0	•	0	36990	•
Other Portfolio Income 6	877271	•	•	0	0	•	13953	4533	225	•	3830	19536	•
Other Receipts 7	263714	•	•	0	0	•	1364	3774	20131	•	11034	93574	•
Total Receipts 8	53725869	•	•	203490	0	•	147855	735097	1759421	•	2273799	13399409	•
Average Total Receipts 9	153065	•	•	2366	•	•	24642	61258	195491	•	454760	1218128	•

Operating Costs/Operating Income (%)

Cost of Operations 10	73.9	•	•	37.0	•	•	77.4	66.2	81.6	•	73.7	74.1	•
Salaries and Wages 11	4.1	•	•	10.2	•	•	4.0	7.4	3.2	•	5.5	4.2	•
Taxes Paid 12	1.4	•	•	2.1	•	•	1.9	0.9	0.8	•	1.3	1.1	•
Interest Paid 13	3.3	•	•	1.2	•	•	0.3	0.8	0.3	•	3.7	1.2	•
Depreciation 14	4.6	•	•	0.6	•	•	1.3	3.4	1.0	•	4.0	4.9	•
Amortization and Depletion 15	0.5	•	•	•	•	•	0.3	0.2	0.1	•	0.2	0.5	•
Pensions and Other Deferred Comp. 16	1.0	•	•	11.4	•	•	•	1.2	0.5	•	1.5	0.8	•
Employee Benefits 17	1.6	•	•	3.1	•	•	0.6	1.8	1.3	•	2.1	2.3	•
Advertising 18	0.2	•	•	0.8	•	•	0.0	0.1	0.5	•	0.4	0.4	•
Other Expenses 19	7.3	•	•	10.9	•	•	8.5	7.8	7.4	•	3.0	5.2	•
Officers' Compensation 20	0.7	•	•	20.3	•	•	1.2	1.8	0.6	•	1.0	0.9	•
Operating Margin 21	1.6	•	•	2.4	•	•	4.5	8.5	2.6	•	3.6	4.5	•
Operating Margin Before Officers' Comp. 22	2.3	•	•	22.8	•	•	5.6	10.3	3.2	•	4.6	5.3	•

Selected Average Balance Sheet ($ in Thousands)

Net Receivables 23	29231	•	•	230	•	•	1474	4835	19955	•	48367	199509	•
Inventories 24	13968	•	•	103	•	•	2246	5189	15458	•	41784	111036	•
Net Property, Plant and Equipment 25	68002	•	•	321	•	•	5825	14080	21255	•	148578	558075	•
Total Assets 26	284842	•	•	788	•	•	13699	34802	80143	•	383391	1275842	•
Notes and Loans Payable 27	122523	•	•	330	•	•	1123	7063	16773	•	207648	268956	•
All Other Liabilities 28	65481	•	•	392	•	•	1823	8784	25650	•	155664	422076	•
Net Worth 29	96839	•	•	66	•	•	10753	18954	37720	•	20079	584810	•

Selected Financial Ratios (Times to 1)

Current Ratio 30	0.7	•	•	1.0	•	•	3.7	1.9	1.7	•	1.4	2.4	•
Quick Ratio 31	0.4	•	•	0.7	•	•	1.2	1.0	0.9	•	0.6	1.3	•
Net Sales to Working Capital 32	•	•	•	•	•	•	3.8	8.2	9.6	•	11.9	5.1	•
Coverage Ratio 33	2.5	•	•	3.1	•	•	58.7	13.8	12.4	•	2.2	5.7	•
Total Asset Turnover 34	0.5	•	•	3.0	•	•	1.6	1.7	2.4	•	1.2	0.9	•
Inventory Turnover 35	7.9	•	•	8.5	•	•	7.6	7.7	10.2	•	7.9	8.0	•
Receivables Turnover 36	5.0	•	•	•	•	•	7.0	11.5	13.3	•	11.2	6.6	•
Total Liabilities to Net Worth 37	1.9	•	•	11.0	•	•	0.3	0.8	1.1	•	18.1	1.2	•
Current Assets to Working Capital 38	•	•	•	•	•	•	1.4	2.2	2.4	•	3.3	1.7	•
Current Liabilities to Working Capital 39	•	•	•	•	•	•	0.4	1.2	1.4	•	2.3	0.7	•
Working Capital to Net Sales 40	•	•	•	•	•	•	0.3	0.1	0.1	•	0.1	0.2	•
Inventory to Working Capital 41	•	•	•	•	•	•	0.4	0.7	0.8	•	1.3	0.5	•
Total Receipts to Cash Flow 42	9.9	•	•	11.0	•	•	9.6	6.3	10.0	•	16.7	11.3	•
Cost of Goods to Cash Flow 43	7.3	•	•	4.1	•	•	7.4	4.2	8.1	•	12.3	8.3	•
Cash Flow to Total Debt 44	0.1	•	•	0.3	•	•	0.8	0.6	0.5	•	0.1	0.2	•

Selected Financial Factors (in Percentages)

Debt Ratio 45	66.0	•	•	91.7	•	•	21.5	45.5	52.9	•	94.8	54.2	•
Return on Total Assets 46	4.2	•	•	10.8	•	•	26.7	18.1	10.1	•	9.8	6.5	•
Return on Equity Before Income Taxes 47	7.5	•	•	88.4	•	•	33.5	30.8	19.7	•	103.3	11.7	•
Return on Equity After Income Taxes 48	6.4	•	•	79.1	•	•	22.1	29.5	16.6	•	77.5	9.8	•
Profit Margin (Before Income Tax) 49	4.9	•	•	2.5	•	•	16.3	9.6	3.8	•	4.6	5.7	•
Profit Margin (After Income Tax) 50	4.2	•	•	2.2	•	•	10.8	9.2	3.2	•	3.5	4.8	•

Table I

Corporations with and without Net Income

CONVERTED PAPER PRODUCT

MONEY AMOUNTS AND SIZE OF ASSETS IN THOUSANDS OF DOLLARS

Item Description for Accounting Period 7/12 Through 6/13	Total	Zero Assets	Under 500	500 to 1,000	1,000 to 5,000	5,000 to 10,000	10,000 to 25,000	25,000 to 50,000	50,000 to 100,000	100,000 to 250,000	250,000 to 500,000	500,000 to 2,500,000	2,500,000 and over
Number of Enterprises **1**	2198	49	373	234	1060	156	174	68	38	18	10	12	7

Revenues ($ in Thousands)													
Net Sales **2**	99858369	378221	518538	803944	6252240	2634519	5807499	4554832	4037124	4896459	5075744	13470285	51428963
Interest **3**	444813	558	2	4	745	192	628	3148	2186	3113	2614	91734	339890
Rents **4**	39209	8	0	0	12	221	581	3248	1453	124	18	28833	4711
Royalties **5**	2047473	0	0	0	0	0	2023	0	0	1974	4995	3784	2034696
Other Portfolio Income **6**	1184042	3649	0	73	8296	17298	5878	6297	11963	1986	4474	42850	1081276
Other Receipts **7**	868673	-18757	15747	442	7842	33008	42021	23209	23318	15055	11215	36982	678594
Total Receipts **8**	104442579	363679	534287	804463	6269135	2685238	5858630	4590734	4076044	4918711	5099060	13674468	55568130
Average Total Receipts **9**	47517	7422	1432	3438	5914	17213	33670	67511	107264	273262	509906	1139539	7938304

Operating Costs/Operating Income (%)													
Cost of Operations **10**	70.2	73.4	74.0	67.9	66.3	83.6	75.6	77.7	74.6	76.8	75.2	75.3	65.8
Salaries and Wages **11**	8.2	10.8	2.1	4.9	10.1	3.8	5.5	6.2	6.2	4.9	5.5	4.8	10.5
Taxes Paid **12**	1.3	2.2	3.0	1.3	2.4	1.9	1.6	1.4	1.3	1.0	1.1	1.4	1.1
Interest Paid **13**	2.1	0.6	0.3	0.0	0.6	1.0	0.7	0.8	0.8	1.4	1.8	3.7	2.5
Depreciation **14**	3.5	1.9	0.7	0.4	1.2	2.8	2.6	3.2	3.3	2.0	2.5	3.7	4.3
Amortization and Depletion **15**	0.6	0.8	0.0	•	0.1	0.0	0.1	0.1	0.2	0.4	0.6	0.7	0.8
Pensions and Other Deferred Comp. **16**	0.8	0.3	0.0	0.0	0.4	0.2	0.1	0.5	0.5	0.6	0.6	0.6	1.2
Employee Benefits **17**	1.8	2.1	0.0	0.6	2.1	0.7	1.1	1.5	1.5	1.3	1.5	1.4	2.2
Advertising **18**	0.8	0.1	0.2	0.0	0.2	0.1	0.2	0.1	0.2	0.3	0.6	0.1	1.3
Other Expenses **19**	8.0	11.8	13.1	8.7	9.3	7.1	7.7	6.6	6.5	6.6	8.3	6.8	8.6
Officers' Compensation **20**	0.9	7.6	5.2	6.3	2.3	1.7	2.7	1.4	1.2	0.7	0.7	0.4	0.5
Operating Margin **21**	1.7	•	1.4	9.8	4.9	•	2.0	0.5	3.7	4.0	1.7	1.1	1.3
Operating Margin Before Officers' Comp. **22**	2.6	•	6.6	16.1	7.3	•	4.7	1.9	4.9	4.7	2.4	1.5	1.8

Selected Average Balance Sheet ($ in Thousands)

Net Receivables 23	8160	0	188	439	751	1589	3870	7863	10448	36796	62187	134906	1744323
Inventories 24	4269	0	34	46	449	1373	3344	7204	15410	29216	50935	108174	668517
Net Property, Plant and Equipment 25	11948	0	24	34	453	2914	5197	13211	23796	45221	97365	340844	2389363
Total Assets 26	62508	0	382	729	2078	6817	15144	36369	69181	175475	314397	1100488	15224113
Notes and Loans Payable 27	19371	0	120	14	797	3179	5753	10973	18241	52519	111297	514434	4359582
All Other Liabilities 28	16939	0	122	211	418	2767	7142	10839	18089	56596	104842	295172	3998001
Net Worth 29	26198	0	140	504	863	871	2249	14558	32850	66360	98258	290881	6866530

Selected Financial Ratios (Times to 1)

Current Ratio 30	1.1	•	2.0	2.6	2.7	1.1	1.9	1.4	1.8	1.8	1.6	1.4	1.0
Quick Ratio 31	0.7	•	1.7	2.3	1.8	0.6	1.0	0.7	0.9	1.0	0.9	0.8	0.6
Net Sales to Working Capital 32	23.5	•	8.0	10.2	5.9	86.8	8.1	14.0	7.4	8.0	10.3	12.3	•
Coverage Ratio 33	4.6	•	14.1	388.1	9.8	0.0	5.0	2.6	6.9	4.1	2.2	1.7	5.9
Total Asset Turnover 34	0.7	•	3.6	4.7	2.8	2.5	2.2	1.8	1.5	1.6	1.6	1.0	0.5
Inventory Turnover 35	7.5	•	30.4	50.9	8.7	10.3	7.5	7.2	5.1	7.2	7.5	7.8	7.2
Receivables Turnover 36	6.4	•	7.6	8.9	9.2	10.3	9.0	8.4	9.9	7.1	7.2	8.3	5.2
Total Liabilities to Net Worth 37	1.4	•	1.7	0.4	1.4	6.8	5.7	1.5	1.1	1.6	2.2	2.8	1.2
Current Assets to Working Capital 38	7.7	•	2.0	1.6	1.6	18.7	2.2	3.8	2.3	2.2	2.6	3.4	•
Current Liabilities to Working Capital 39	6.7	•	1.0	0.6	0.6	17.7	1.2	2.8	1.3	1.2	1.6	2.4	•
Working Capital to Net Sales 40	0.0	•	0.1	0.1	0.2	0.0	0.1	0.1	0.1	0.1	0.1	0.1	•
Inventory to Working Capital 41	2.2	•	0.2	0.1	0.5	7.0	0.9	1.5	1.1	0.8	0.9	1.1	•
Total Receipts to Cash Flow 42	8.6	•	11.4	6.8	9.4	34.7	12.4	18.3	11.1	10.4	11.5	14.3	6.6
Cost of Goods to Cash Flow 43	6.0	•	8.4	4.6	6.2	29.0	9.4	14.2	8.3	8.0	8.7	10.7	4.3
Cash Flow to Total Debt 44	0.1	•	0.5	2.2	0.5	0.1	0.2	0.2	0.3	0.2	0.2	0.1	0.1

Selected Financial Factors (in Percentages)

Debt Ratio 45	58.1	•	63.3	30.9	58.5	87.2	85.1	60.0	52.5	62.2	68.7	73.6	54.9
Return on Total Assets 46	7.1	•	17.4	46.6	16.5	0.1	7.9	3.8	8.2	9.1	6.4	6.5	7.0
Return on Equity Before Income Taxes 47	13.3	•	44.0	67.3	35.6	•	42.4	5.9	14.7	18.2	11.2	10.4	13.0
Return on Equity After Income Taxes 48	9.3	•	43.9	67.3	35.6	•	37.1	4.4	13.3	16.6	10.1	6.0	8.7
Profit Margin (Before Income Tax) 49	7.7	•	4.4	9.9	5.2	•	2.9	1.3	4.6	4.4	2.2	2.7	12.1
Profit Margin (After Income Tax) 50	5.4	•	4.4	9.9	5.2	•	2.5	1.0	4.1	4.1	2.0	1.5	8.1

Table II
Corporations with Net Income

CONVERTED PAPER PRODUCT

MONEY AMOUNTS AND SIZE OF ASSETS IN THOUSANDS OF DOLLARS

Item Description for Accounting Period 7/12 Through 6/13		Total	Zero Assets	Under 500	500 to 1,000	1,000 to 5,000	5,000 to 10,000	10,000 to 25,000	25,000 to 50,000	50,000 to 100,000	100,000 to 250,000	250,000 to 500,000	500,000 to 2,500,000	2,500,000 and over
Number of Enterprises	1	1571	•	•	180	779	65	121	43	30	•	7	8	7

Revenues ($ in Thousands)

Net Sales	2	87559254	•	•	653205	5133591	995050	4178288	3214371	3346782	•	4136612	9789179	51428963
Interest	3	435901	•	•	0	15	169	282	2724	200	•	1109	88406	339890
Rents	4	36836	•	•	0	12	221	36	3117	0	•	18	28598	4711
Royalties	5	2043594	•	•	0	0	0	2023	0	0	•	1130	3770	2034696
Other Portfolio Income	6	1146573	•	•	2	6858	8509	1436	4179	7482	•	4474	30335	1081276
Other Receipts	7	812912	•	•	178	3552	8284	24373	10708	21577	•	10465	26576	678594
Total Receipts	8	92035070	•	•	653385	5144028	1012233	4206438	3235099	3376041	•	4153808	9966864	55568130
Average Total Receipts	9	58584	•	•	3630	6603	15573	34764	75235	112535	•	593401	1245858	7938304

Operating Costs/Operating Income (%)

Cost of Operations	10	69.1	•	•	67.3	68.1	75.7	73.8	76.1	73.4	•	74.8	75.1	65.8
Salaries and Wages	11	8.5	•	•	6.0	9.0	5.2	5.4	5.6	6.2	•	5.6	4.8	10.5
Taxes Paid	12	1.2	•	•	1.0	2.3	2.0	1.7	1.3	1.4	•	1.2	1.3	1.1
Interest Paid	13	1.9	•	•	0.0	0.5	0.4	0.7	0.7	0.8	•	0.8	2.3	2.5
Depreciation	14	3.6	•	•	0.4	0.8	3.0	2.4	3.3	3.6	•	2.5	4.1	4.3
Amortization and Depletion	15	0.6	•	•	•	0.1	0.0	0.2	0.1	0.2	•	0.6	0.5	0.8
Pensions and Other Deferred Comp.	16	0.9	•	•	•	0.2	0.3	0.2	0.5	0.5	•	0.6	0.4	1.2
Employee Benefits	17	1.8	•	•	0.7	1.9	1.4	1.2	1.4	1.4	•	1.7	0.9	2.2
Advertising	18	0.8	•	•	0.0	0.2	0.1	0.2	0.1	0.2	•	0.6	0.1	1.3
Other Expenses	19	7.9	•	•	7.7	7.2	7.0	7.0	6.3	6.0	•	7.6	7.2	8.6
Officers' Compensation	20	0.9	•	•	4.6	2.6	2.8	2.7	1.5	1.2	•	0.6	0.5	0.5
Operating Margin	21	2.6	•	•	12.2	7.1	2.1	4.5	3.0	5.0	•	3.3	2.8	1.3
Operating Margin Before Officers' Comp.	22	3.5	•	•	16.8	9.7	4.9	7.3	4.5	6.2	•	3.9	3.3	1.8

Selected Average Balance Sheet ($ in Thousands)

Net Receivables	23	10447	•	•	466	741	1686	4036	8481	10273	•	66640	142190	1744323
Inventories	24	4889	•	•	16	387	1203	3209	8031	15443	•	47999	114210	649455
Net Property, Plant and Equipment	25	15247	•	•	25	442	2036	5320	15132	26795	•	103732	413895	2389363
Total Assets	26	82289	•	•	763	1950	6685	15727	37427	69030	•	301506	1263151	15224113
Notes and Loans Payable	27	23833	•	•	8	580	1591	5761	10539	17693	•	73146	421616	4359582
All Other Liabilities	28	21491	•	•	199	365	2224	3646	10113	15488	•	99978	299994	3998001
Net Worth	29	36965	•	•	555	1005	2870	6320	16775	35849	•	128382	541541	6866530

Selected Financial Ratios (Times to 1)

Current Ratio	30	1.1	•	•	2.8	2.9	1.6	2.1	1.6	1.7	•	2.0	1.4	1.0
Quick Ratio	31	0.7	•	•	2.7	2.1	0.9	1.2	0.8	0.8	•	1.1	0.8	0.6
Net Sales to Working Capital	32	25.4	•	•	10.1	7.0	9.6	7.0	10.2	8.2	•	7.9	11.9	•
Coverage Ratio	33	5.8	•	•	806.5	16.2	10.0	8.3	6.4	8.5	•	5.6	3.1	5.9
Total Asset Turnover	34	0.7	•	•	4.8	3.4	2.3	2.2	2.0	1.6	•	2.0	1.0	0.5
Inventory Turnover	35	7.9	•	•	150.9	11.6	9.6	7.9	7.1	5.3	•	9.2	8.1	7.4
Receivables Turnover	36	6.4	•	•	•	10.5	9.3	9.9	9.1	10.4	•	9.5	8.2	•
Total Liabilities to Net Worth	37	1.2	•	•	0.4	0.9	1.3	1.5	1.2	0.9	•	1.3	1.3	1.2
Current Assets to Working Capital	38	8.5	•	•	1.6	1.5	2.6	1.9	2.7	2.4	•	2.0	3.3	•
Current Liabilities to Working Capital	39	7.5	•	•	0.6	0.5	1.6	0.9	1.7	1.4	•	1.0	2.3	•
Working Capital to Net Sales	40	0.0	•	•	0.1	0.1	0.1	0.1	0.1	0.1	•	0.1	0.1	•
Inventory to Working Capital	41	2.3	•	•	0.0	0.4	0.9	0.8	1.1	1.1	•	0.7	1.1	•
Total Receipts to Cash Flow	42	7.7	•	•	5.9	8.7	13.4	10.1	13.0	10.1	•	10.1	11.1	6.6
Cost of Goods to Cash Flow	43	5.3	•	•	4.0	5.9	10.1	7.5	9.9	7.4	•	7.6	8.4	4.3
Cash Flow to Total Debt	44	0.2	•	•	3.0	0.8	0.3	0.4	0.3	0.3	•	0.3	0.2	0.1

Selected Financial Factors (in Percentages)

Debt Ratio	45	55.1	•	•	27.2	48.5	57.1	59.8	55.2	48.1	•	57.4	57.1	54.9
Return on Total Assets	46	7.6	•	•	58.2	26.4	9.7	13.0	8.6	10.8	•	8.9	6.8	7.0
Return on Equity Before Income Taxes	47	14.0	•	•	79.8	48.1	20.3	28.4	16.2	18.4	•	17.1	10.6	13.0
Return on Equity After Income Taxes	48	10.1	•	•	79.8	48.1	18.2	25.6	14.2	16.8	•	15.9	7.0	8.7
Profit Margin (Before Income Tax)	49	9.3	•	•	12.2	7.3	3.8	5.2	3.6	5.9	•	3.7	4.7	12.1
Profit Margin (After Income Tax)	50	6.7	•	•	12.2	7.3	3.4	4.7	3.2	5.4	•	3.4	3.1	8.1

76

Table I

Corporations with and without Net Income

PRINTING AND RELATED SUPPORT ACTIVITIES

MONEY AMOUNTS AND SIZE OF ASSETS IN THOUSANDS OF DOLLARS

Item Description for Accounting Period 7/12 Through 6/13	Total	Zero Assets	Under 500	500 to 1,000	1,000 to 5,000	5,000 to 10,000	10,000 to 25,000	25,000 to 50,000	50,000 to 100,000	100,000 to 250,000	250,000 to 500,000	500,000 to 2,500,000	2,500,000 and over
Number of Enterprises 1	22866	4752	13797	1359	2137	383	263	102	33	15	11	10	3
Revenues ($ in Thousands)													
Net Sales 2	72974952	913461	8467914	2961351	11256662	5012369	7712617	5438459	3128780	2705664	4082419	7301017	13994239
Interest 3	69375	4106	18	133	4620	1097	2654	1347	876	2567	3201	11169	37588
Rents 4	24457	0	87	137	5062	188	486	86	140	336	2792	3134	12009
Royalties 5	94157	0	0	0	0	382	6395	5544	0	27614	5781	47389	1050
Other Portfolio Income 6	241851	22451	3463	34084	19562	13491	26415	11849	15554	8727	13871	48277	24108
Other Receipts 7	1029909	10742	49178	8174	55033	23468	67510	104604	37219	379036	33534	24952	236460
Total Receipts 8	74434701	950760	8520660	3003879	11340939	5050995	7816077	5561889	3182569	3123944	4141598	7435938	14305454
Average Total Receipts 9	3255	200	618	2210	5307	13188	29719	54528	96441	208263	376509	743594	4768485
Operating Costs/Operating Income (%)													
Cost of Operations 10	61.2	47.2	51.4	47.9	59.2	68.4	68.0	69.4	71.0	58.7	63.5	43.1	70.1
Salaries and Wages 11	11.3	3.5	9.8	15.7	12.6	8.3	10.3	9.6	7.8	21.1	12.1	15.8	9.2
Taxes Paid 12	2.2	2.5	2.2	3.1	2.5	2.3	2.0	2.0	2.2	2.3	2.1	2.4	2.1
Interest Paid 13	2.1	3.0	0.7	0.7	0.8	0.5	0.9	1.1	1.6	4.6	2.6	3.9	4.2
Depreciation 14	2.8	2.2	1.4	1.2	1.9	3.3	2.8	3.3	2.9	4.7	3.1	3.1	3.6
Amortization and Depletion 15	0.7	2.4	0.1	0.1	0.1	0.1	0.2	0.3	1.0	1.5	1.8	2.5	0.7
Pensions and Other Deferred Comp. 16	0.6	0.1	0.2	0.2	0.3	1.0	0.2	0.3	0.2	0.2	1.3	0.4	1.5
Employee Benefits 17	1.6	2.0	0.8	0.8	1.2	1.3	1.5	1.6	2.0	2.6	2.9	2.7	1.6
Advertising 18	0.9	1.1	0.5	1.2	0.4	0.2	0.2	0.6	0.4	6.6	0.3	3.2	0.2
Other Expenses 19	12.0	32.7	19.7	15.6	13.0	10.6	8.3	8.6	6.9	8.9	12.0	16.6	7.6
Officers' Compensation 20	2.7	2.7	7.7	7.1	3.4	2.9	2.3	2.1	1.6	1.3	0.5	1.4	0.5
Operating Margin 21	1.9	0.6	5.3	6.5	4.6	1.3	3.3	1.1	2.3	•	•	4.9	•
Operating Margin Before Officers' Comp. 22	4.6	3.3	13.1	13.6	8.0	4.1	5.6	3.2	4.0	•	•	6.3	•

	Selected Average Balance Sheet ($ in Thousands)												
Net Receivables 23	418	0	27	199	524	1846	4719	8096	13665	30558	60611	127135	725840
Inventories 24	168	0	9	67	188	874	1895	4112	10239	12756	34912	39149	219373
Net Property, Plant and Equipment 25	522	0	47	134	523	2309	5070	10609	16803	39151	58234	136244	1180685
Total Assets 26	2326	0	131	647	2094	6872	16442	34236	73612	148243	367076	1107925	5270059
Notes and Loans Payable 27	1053	0	99	200	673	1545	5808	10474	25371	81370	160426	471671	3095029
All Other Liabilities 28	723	0	37	146	485	1834	4366	8765	20255	50568	110658	261582	2263551
Net Worth 29	550	0	-5	300	936	3494	6268	14997	27986	16304	95993	374672	-88521

	Selected Financial Ratios (Times to 1)												
Current Ratio 30	1.4	•	1.7	2.9	1.8	1.7	1.5	1.8	1.6	1.4	2.0	1.6	0.9
Quick Ratio 31	1.0	•	1.4	2.3	1.4	1.2	1.0	1.2	1.0	0.9	1.2	1.2	0.6
Net Sales to Working Capital 32	12.2	•	21.7	7.4	9.8	7.9	9.9	7.1	7.3	10.3	5.7	7.1	•
Coverage Ratio 33	3.0	2.6	9.6	13.0	7.8	4.7	6.2	4.1	3.5	1.7	0.7	3.0	1.2
Total Asset Turnover 34	1.4	•	4.7	3.4	2.5	1.9	1.8	1.6	1.3	1.2	1.0	0.7	0.9
Inventory Turnover 35	11.7	•	35.3	15.6	16.5	10.2	10.5	9.0	6.6	8.3	6.7	8.0	14.9
Receivables Turnover 36	7.7	•	23.0	8.7	10.8	7.4	6.5	6.8	7.0	6.3	6.6	4.7	6.7
Total Liabilities to Net Worth 37	3.2	•	•	1.2	1.2	1.0	1.6	1.3	1.6	8.1	2.8	2.0	•
Current Assets to Working Capital 38	3.2	•	2.5	1.5	2.2	2.4	3.1	2.3	2.6	3.5	2.0	2.6	•
Current Liabilities to Working Capital 39	2.2	•	1.5	0.5	1.2	1.4	2.1	1.3	1.6	2.5	1.0	1.6	•
Working Capital to Net Sales 40	0.1	•	0.0	0.1	0.1	0.1	0.1	0.1	0.1	0.1	0.2	0.1	•
Inventory to Working Capital 41	0.6	•	0.3	0.2	0.4	0.5	0.7	0.6	0.8	0.8	0.6	0.3	•
Total Receipts to Cash Flow 42	8.3	3.3	5.2	6.1	7.7	12.4	9.5	10.9	12.5	10.4	13.3	4.8	15.5
Cost of Goods to Cash Flow 43	5.1	1.6	2.7	2.9	4.6	8.5	6.4	7.6	8.9	6.1	8.5	2.1	10.8
Cash Flow to Total Debt 44	0.2	•	0.9	1.0	0.6	0.3	0.3	0.3	0.2	0.1	0.1	0.2	0.1

	Selected Financial Factors (in Percentages)												
Debt Ratio 45	76.4	•	103.5	53.6	55.3	49.2	61.9	56.2	62.0	89.0	73.8	66.2	101.7
Return on Total Assets 46	8.3	•	31.2	29.0	15.4	4.9	9.9	7.0	7.3	9.7	1.9	7.7	4.6
Return on Equity Before Income Taxes 47	23.3	•	•	57.7	30.1	7.6	21.9	12.0	13.6	37.0	•	15.1	•
Return on Equity After Income Taxes 48	20.4	•	•	57.0	29.8	7.3	20.5	10.9	11.4	29.1	•	9.5	•
Profit Margin (Before Income Tax) 49	4.0	4.7	6.0	7.9	5.3	2.0	4.7	3.4	4.0	3.3	•	7.8	1.0
Profit Margin (After Income Tax) 50	3.5	3.7	6.0	7.9	5.3	2.0	4.4	3.1	3.4	2.6	•	4.9	0.7

77

Table II
Corporations with Net Income

PRINTING AND RELATED SUPPORT ACTIVITIES

MONEY AMOUNTS AND SIZE OF ASSETS IN THOUSANDS OF DOLLARS

Item Description for Accounting Period 7/12 Through 6/13	Total	Zero Assets	Under 500	500 to 1,000	1,000 to 5,000	5,000 to 10,000	10,000 to 25,000	25,000 to 50,000	50,000 to 100,000	100,000 to 250,000	250,000 to 500,000	500,000 to 2,500,000	2,500,000 and over
Number of Enterprises 1	16457	3224	9994	1050	1634	237	198	71	•	11	4	•	3

Revenues ($ in Thousands)

	Total	Zero Assets	Under 500	500 to 1,000	1,000 to 5,000	5,000 to 10,000	10,000 to 25,000	25,000 to 50,000	50,000 to 100,000	100,000 to 250,000	250,000 to 500,000	500,000 to 2,500,000	2,500,000 and over
Net Sales 2	60553961	588658	7223571	2197081	9597913	3342832	6332344	3984306	•	2128983	1843404	•	13994239
Interest 3	56057	0	9	59	3883	679	2171	1056	•	2408	2597	•	37588
Rents 4	21089	0	87	56	3898	188	476	84	•	335	682	•	12009
Royalties 5	92757	0	0	0	0	382	6395	5544	•	27614	5101	•	1050
Other Portfolio Income 6	218449	22451	3169	33820	12771	1998	26140	11788	•	8614	13207	•	24108
Other Receipts 7	922743	9843	46810	7560	38085	5470	49351	101326	•	364130	12368	•	236460
Total Receipts 8	61865056	620952	7273646	2238576	9656550	3351549	6416877	4104104	•	2532084	1877359	•	14305454
Average Total Receipts 9	3759	193	728	2132	5910	14142	32408	57804	•	230189	469340	•	4768485

Operating Costs/Operating Income (%)

	Total	Zero Assets	Under 500	500 to 1,000	1,000 to 5,000	5,000 to 10,000	10,000 to 25,000	25,000 to 50,000	50,000 to 100,000	100,000 to 250,000	250,000 to 500,000	500,000 to 2,500,000	2,500,000 and over
Cost of Operations 10	61.3	42.6	53.5	41.5	60.1	66.3	67.2	70.3	•	55.8	73.6	•	70.1
Salaries and Wages 11	10.9	1.3	8.4	18.4	11.6	9.4	9.6	8.8	•	24.3	7.3	•	9.2
Taxes Paid 12	2.1	2.1	1.9	3.2	2.3	2.2	1.9	2.0	•	2.4	1.5	•	2.1
Interest Paid 13	1.9	0.7	0.6	0.4	0.7	0.5	0.7	0.9	•	5.4	0.7	•	4.2
Depreciation 14	2.7	1.2	1.3	0.7	1.9	3.4	2.4	3.3	•	5.0	1.8	•	3.6
Amortization and Depletion 15	0.5	0.2	0.0	0.1	0.1	0.0	0.2	0.2	•	1.5	0.3	•	0.7
Pensions and Other Deferred Comp. 16	0.6	0.0	0.2	0.2	0.3	0.1	0.2	0.4	•	0.2	1.2	•	1.5
Employee Benefits 17	1.5	0.8	0.6	0.8	1.1	1.2	1.6	1.5	•	3.2	1.2	•	1.6
Advertising 18	1.0	1.6	0.5	1.7	0.3	0.2	0.2	0.7	•	7.1	0.5	•	0.2
Other Expenses 19	11.2	35.2	18.8	15.5	11.9	8.1	8.1	6.8	•	7.7	9.5	•	7.6
Officers' Compensation 20	2.4	2.5	6.1	7.8	2.9	2.7	2.3	2.2	•	1.5	0.6	•	0.5
Operating Margin 21	3.8	11.8	8.1	9.7	6.8	5.8	5.6	2.9	•	•	1.9	•	•
Operating Margin Before Officers' Comp. 22	6.3	14.3	14.1	17.5	9.7	8.5	7.9	5.2	•	•	2.5	•	•

Selected Average Balance Sheet ($ in Thousands)

Net Receivables 23	461	0	26	155	571	1912	4737	7781	•	33854	64594	•	725840
Inventories 24	177	0	10	76	162	1144	1923	4308	•	11659	75245	•	213026
Net Property, Plant and Equipment 25	585	0	53	134	537	2408	5065	10645	•	42154	46660	•	1180685
Total Assets 26	2537	0	150	636	2088	6696	16124	34149	•	155672	377747	•	5270059
Notes and Loans Payable 27	1086	0	79	160	617	1551	5450	8841	•	103060	47863	•	3095029
All Other Liabilities 28	825	0	39	104	530	1876	3720	8610	•	49978	108658	•	2263551
Net Worth 29	626	0	32	373	942	3269	6954	16697	•	2634	221225	•	-88521

Selected Financial Ratios (Times to 1)

Current Ratio 30	1.4	•	1.8	4.3	1.9	1.7	1.6	1.9	•	1.4	2.2	•	0.9
Quick Ratio 31	1.0	•	1.5	3.2	1.5	1.1	1.1	1.2	•	1.0	1.1	•	0.6
Net Sales to Working Capital 32	12.8	•	20.4	6.3	9.8	8.8	9.2	6.9	•	10.8	4.5	•	•
Coverage Ratio 33	4.3	24.4	15.9	27.3	11.4	13.0	10.4	7.7	•	2.0	6.9	•	1.2
Total Asset Turnover 34	1.5	•	4.8	3.3	2.8	2.1	2.0	1.6	•	1.2	1.2	•	0.9
Inventory Turnover 35	12.7	•	37.7	11.4	21.8	8.2	11.2	9.2	•	9.3	4.5	•	15.4
Receivables Turnover 36	8.4	•	29.5	8.1	12.1	6.7	7.4	8.2	•	8.0	•	•	12.9
Total Liabilities to Net Worth 37	3.1	•	3.7	0.7	1.2	1.0	1.3	1.0	•	58.1	0.7	•	•
Current Assets to Working Capital 38	3.3	•	2.3	1.3	2.1	2.5	2.6	2.2	•	3.3	1.9	•	•
Current Liabilities to Working Capital 39	2.3	•	1.3	0.3	1.1	1.5	1.6	1.2	•	2.3	0.9	•	•
Working Capital to Net Sales 40	0.1	•	0.0	0.2	0.1	0.1	0.1	0.1	•	0.1	0.2	•	•
Inventory to Working Capital 41	0.7	•	0.3	0.2	0.3	0.7	0.6	0.6	•	0.8	0.7	•	•
Total Receipts to Cash Flow 42	7.3	2.2	4.6	5.0	7.2	9.5	8.0	9.5	•	9.5	9.0	•	15.5
Cost of Goods to Cash Flow 43	4.5	0.9	2.5	2.1	4.3	6.3	5.4	6.7	•	5.3	6.6	•	10.8
Cash Flow to Total Debt 44	0.3	•	1.3	1.6	0.7	0.4	0.4	0.3	•	0.1	0.3	•	0.1

Selected Financial Factors (in Percentages)

Debt Ratio 45	75.3	•	78.6	41.4	54.9	51.2	56.9	51.1	•	98.3	41.4	•	101.7
Return on Total Assets 46	11.6	•	44.9	39.6	22.8	13.8	15.1	11.2	•	13.4	5.5	•	4.6
Return on Equity Before Income Taxes 47	36.0	•	196.8	65.2	46.1	26.1	31.7	19.9	•	392.5	8.0	•	•
Return on Equity After Income Taxes 48	32.4	•	196.5	64.5	45.7	25.7	30.1	18.5	•	326.2	6.4	•	•
Profit Margin (Before Income Tax) 49	6.1	17.3	8.7	11.6	7.4	6.1	6.9	5.9	•	5.3	3.8	•	1.0
Profit Margin (After Income Tax) 50	5.5	15.8	8.7	11.5	7.3	5.9	6.5	5.5	•	4.4	3.1	•	0.7

Table I

Corporations with and without Net Income

PETROLEUM REFINERIES (INCLUDING INTEGRATED)

MONEY AMOUNTS AND SIZE OF ASSETS IN THOUSANDS OF DOLLARS

Item Description for Accounting Period 7/12 Through 6/13	Total	Zero Assets	Under 500	500 to 1,000	1,000 to 5,000	5,000 to 10,000	10,000 to 25,000	25,000 to 50,000	50,000 to 100,000	100,000 to 250,000	250,000 to 500,000	500,000 to 2,500,000	2,500,000 and over
Number of Enterprises 1	217	4	3	0	139	4	6	11	5	12	4	7	23

Revenues ($ in Thousands)													
Net Sales 2	2282715109	34960529	0	0	157711	76796	73370	752268	759419	2539048	5342660	309388172	2207114493
Interest 3	11734229	32125	183	0	34	0	84	37	981	50	5790	34207	11660739
Rents 4	1066587	52790	20	0	0	0	216	782	0	1638	4706	31663	974773
Royalties 5	1144421	18428	0	0	0	0	0	0	0	25	1	47960	1078008
Other Portfolio Income 6	48852611	6420	0	0	0	0	1129	538	233	5083	5663	50875	48782670
Other Receipts 7	51247634	258793	8448	0	55750	19226	193	38360	-10929	58307	15386	910526	49893569
Total Receipts 8	2396760591	35329085	8651	0	213495	96022	74992	791985	749704	2604151	5374206	320140482	2319504252
Average Total Receipts 9	11044980	8832271	2884	•	1536	24006	12499	71999	149941	217013	1343552	4573435	100848011

Operating Costs/Operating Income (%)													
Cost of Operations 10	90.7	89.0	•	•	108.6	83.5	40.1	86.2	95.8	88.5	92.2	87.2	90.8
Salaries and Wages 11	1.3	0.5	•	•	5.7	6.7	8.7	2.4	1.5	2.4	0.7	2.1	1.3
Taxes Paid 12	1.4	6.2	•	•	0.9	1.1	2.6	0.9	0.6	0.5	0.4	1.3	1.3
Interest Paid 13	1.0	0.2	•	•	1.3	0.3	0.7	0.2	1.2	1.9	0.1	1.1	1.0
Depreciation 14	0.9	0.3	•	•	0.5	1.4	0.3	1.5	2.4	1.9	1.3	1.6	0.9
Amortization and Depletion 15	0.4	0.1	•	•	0.0	0.1	•	0.1	0.3	0.1	0.1	0.5	0.4
Pensions and Other Deferred Comp. 16	0.2	0.5	•	•	•	•	0.4	0.0	0.0	0.1	0.0	0.1	0.2
Employee Benefits 17	0.1	0.1	•	•	0.3	0.5	•	0.5	0.1	0.4	0.1	0.2	0.1
Advertising 18	0.0	0.0	•	•	0.0	0.2	0.1	0.0	0.0	0.0	0.0	0.1	0.0
Other Expenses 19	3.5	2.9	•	•	0.5	11.4	36.6	6.8	5.6	5.2	1.4	3.6	3.5
Officers' Compensation 20	0.1	0.3	•	•	1.2	4.9	7.6	1.3	0.2	1.4	0.1	0.3	0.1
Operating Margin 21	0.3	•	•	•	•	•	2.9	0.1	•	•	3.5	1.8	0.3
Operating Margin Before Officers' Comp. 22	0.4	0.2	•	•	•	•	10.5	1.4	•	•	3.7	2.1	0.4

Selected Average Balance Sheet ($ in Thousands)

Net Receivables 23	3559065	0	9	•	76	283	3051	5652	10505	26399	38915	215865	33486467
Inventories 24	191777	0	0	•	31	279	5131	3115	6386	26086	48355	253197	1705867
Net Property, Plant and Equipment 25	1493012	0	59	•	365	706	981	6312	36432	39302	139225	607078	13843229
Total Assets 26	11089088	0	321	•	2743	7355	12123	27136	72162	147413	391161	1578697	103947993
Notes and Loans Payable 27	2173194	0	26	•	192	1478	5332	4312	23659	47520	16999	346013	20360534
All Other Liabilities 28	3772427	0	4167	•	199	944	2414	8943	14609	40067	87633	613416	35359198
Net Worth 29	5143467	0	-3873	•	2352	4934	4376	13881	33894	59826	286529	619268	48228260

Selected Financial Ratios (Times to 1)

Current Ratio 30	1.4	•	0.8	•	1.4	7.0	1.2	1.6	1.5	1.5	3.3	2.0	1.4
Quick Ratio 31	1.2	•	0.7	•	0.5	2.2	1.0	1.0	1.1	1.0	2.0	1.1	1.2
Net Sales to Working Capital 32	9.9	•	•	•	16.3	3.4	10.9	12.0	14.3	8.7	9.1	12.3	9.7
Coverage Ratio 33	7.6	5.3	•	•	14.0	59.8	8.4	28.2	•	1.0	31.0	5.8	7.6
Total Asset Turnover 34	0.9	•	•	•	0.4	2.6	1.0	2.5	2.1	1.4	3.4	2.8	0.9
Inventory Turnover 35	49.8	•	•	•	39.1	57.5	1.0	18.9	22.8	7.2	25.5	15.2	51.1
Receivables Turnover 36	2.9	•	•	•	28.4	135.7	2.0	18.0	13.5	5.9	27.1	21.9	2.8
Total Liabilities to Net Worth 37	1.2	•	•	•	0.2	0.5	1.8	1.0	1.1	1.5	0.4	1.5	1.2
Current Assets to Working Capital 38	3.8	•	•	•	3.8	1.2	5.6	2.8	2.9	2.9	1.4	2.1	3.8
Current Liabilities to Working Capital 39	2.8	•	•	•	2.8	0.2	4.6	1.8	1.9	1.9	0.4	1.1	2.8
Working Capital to Net Sales 40	0.1	•	•	•	0.1	0.3	0.1	0.1	0.1	0.1	0.1	0.1	0.1
Inventory to Working Capital 41	0.2	•	•	•	0.6	0.0	0.7	0.9	0.1	0.8	0.3	0.7	0.2
Total Receipts to Cash Flow 42	12.6	36.5	•	•	7.9	4.0	2.5	9.4	•	24.8	20.0	13.6	12.4
Cost of Goods to Cash Flow 43	11.4	32.5	•	•	8.6	3.3	1.0	8.1	•	22.0	18.4	11.9	11.3
Cash Flow to Total Debt 44	0.1	•	0.1	•	0.4	2.0	0.6	0.5	•	0.1	0.6	0.3	0.1

Selected Financial Factors (in Percentages)

Debt Ratio 45	53.6	•	1307.7	•	14.3	32.9	63.9	48.8	53.0	59.4	26.7	60.8	53.6
Return on Total Assets 46	7.0	•	•	•	7.3	39.8	5.8	14.1	•	2.7	14.5	18.0	6.9
Return on Equity Before Income Taxes 47	13.0	•	107.7	•	7.9	58.4	14.2	26.6	•	0.0	19.2	38.0	12.9
Return on Equity After Income Taxes 48	8.3	•	107.7	•	7.9	58.4	9.4	24.8	•	•	12.2	26.5	8.2
Profit Margin (Before Income Tax) 49	6.4	0.9	•	•	16.4	15.0	5.1	5.4	•	0.0	4.1	5.3	6.5
Profit Margin (After Income Tax) 50	4.1	0.6	•	•	16.4	15.0	3.4	5.0	•	•	2.6	3.7	4.1

Table II
Corporations with Net Income

PETROLEUM REFINERIES (INCLUDING INTEGRATED)

MONEY AMOUNTS AND SIZE OF ASSETS IN THOUSANDS OF DOLLARS

Item Description for Accounting Period 7/12 Through 6/13		Total	Zero Assets	Under 500	500 to 1,000	1,000 to 5,000	5,000 to 10,000	10,000 to 25,000	25,000 to 50,000	50,000 to 100,000	100,000 to 250,000	250,000 to 500,000	500,000 to 2,500,000	2,500,000 and over
Number of Enterprises	1	159	•	0	0	105	•	3	11	0	6	•	7	19

Revenues ($ in Thousands)

Net Sales	2	2001625757	•	0	0	0	•	73327	752268	0	2140738	•	30938817	1928345527
Interest	3	11307748	•	0	0	0	•	84	37	0	5	•	34207	11235533
Rents	4	906622	•	0	0	0	•	216	782	0	0	•	31663	816696
Royalties	5	1076912	•	0	0	0	•	0	0	0	0	•	47960	1010523
Other Portfolio Income	6	48747253	•	0	0	0	•	1129	538	0	982	•	50875	48681646
Other Receipts	7	49907043	•	0	0	26545	•	194	38360	0	45308	•	910526	48594696
Total Receipts	8	2113571335	•	0	0	26545	•	74950	791985	0	2187033	•	32014048	2038684621
Average Total Receipts	9	13292901	•	•	•	253	•	24983	71999	•	364506	•	4573435	107299191

Operating Costs/Operating Income (%)

Cost of Operations	10	90.3	•	•	•	•	•	40.1	86.2	•	90.1	•	87.2	90.3
Salaries and Wages	11	1.3	•	•	•	•	•	8.7	2.4	•	1.6	•	2.1	1.3
Taxes Paid	12	1.5	•	•	•	•	•	2.6	0.9	•	0.4	•	1.3	1.4
Interest Paid	13	1.0	•	•	•	•	•	0.7	0.2	•	0.3	•	1.1	1.0
Depreciation	14	1.0	•	•	•	•	•	0.3	1.5	•	1.0	•	1.6	1.0
Amortization and Depletion	15	0.4	•	•	•	•	•	•	0.1	•	0.0	•	0.5	0.4
Pensions and Other Deferred Comp.	16	0.2	•	•	•	•	•	0.4	0.0	•	0.1	•	0.1	0.2
Employee Benefits	17	0.1	•	•	•	•	•	•	0.5	•	0.4	•	0.2	0.1
Advertising	18	0.0	•	•	•	•	•	0.1	0.0	•	0.0	•	0.1	0.0
Other Expenses	19	3.3	•	•	•	•	•	36.6	6.8	•	1.9	•	3.6	3.3
Officers' Compensation	20	0.1	•	•	•	•	•	7.6	1.3	•	0.5	•	0.3	0.1
Operating Margin	21	0.8	•	•	•	•	•	2.9	0.1	•	3.6	•	1.8	0.8
Operating Margin Before Officers' Comp.	22	0.9	•	•	•	•	•	10.5	1.4	•	4.1	•	2.1	0.9

Selected Average Balance Sheet ($ in Thousands)

Net Receivables 23	4782312	•	•	•	0	•	3361	5652	•	44370	•	215865 39915793
Inventories 24	233581	•	•	•	0	•	1593	5261	•	48813	•	260573 1838787
Net Property, Plant and Equipment 25	1845779	•	•	•	0	•	1962	6312	•	25996	•	607078 15194022
Total Assets 26	13823271	•	•	•	2253	•	14590	27136	•	152232	•	1578697 114960524
Notes and Loans Payable 27	2740405	•	•	•	0	•	911	4312	•	43951	•	346013 22786608
All Other Liabilities 28	4811671	•	•	•	0	•	2674	8943	•	39851	•	613416 40005914
Net Worth 29	6271194	•	•	•	2253	•	11006	13881	•	68430	•	619268 52168002

Selected Financial Ratios (Times to 1)

Current Ratio 30	1.4	•	•	•	•	•	5.7	1.6	•	1.8	•	2.0 1.4
Quick Ratio 31	1.3	•	•	•	•	•	4.6	1.0	•	1.0	•	1.1 1.3
Net Sales to Working Capital 32	8.5	•	•	•	•	•	3.4	12.0	•	8.1	•	12.3 8.3
Coverage Ratio 33	8.4	•	•	•	•	•	8.4	28.2	•	19.3	•	5.8 8.5
Total Asset Turnover 34	0.9	•	•	•	•	•	1.7	2.5	•	2.3	•	2.8 0.9
Inventory Turnover 35	48.7	•	•	•	•	•	6.2	11.2	•	6.6	•	14.8 49.9
Receivables Turnover 36	2.5	•	•	•	•	•	•	24.2	•	5.8	•	• 2.5
Total Liabilities to Net Worth 37	1.2	•	•	•	•	•	0.3	1.0	•	1.2	•	1.5 1.2
Current Assets to Working Capital 38	3.6	•	•	•	1.0	•	1.2	2.8	•	2.3	•	2.1 3.6
Current Liabilities to Working Capital 39	2.6	•	•	•	•	•	0.2	1.8	•	1.3	•	1.1 2.6
Working Capital to Net Sales 40	0.1	•	•	•	•	•	0.3	0.1	•	0.1	•	0.1 0.1
Inventory to Working Capital 41	0.2	•	•	•	•	•	0.2	0.9	•	0.8	•	0.7 0.2
Total Receipts to Cash Flow 42	11.4	•	•	•	•	•	2.5	9.4	•	14.1	•	13.6 11.3
Cost of Goods to Cash Flow 43	10.3	•	•	•	•	•	1.0	8.1	•	12.7	•	11.9 10.2
Cash Flow to Total Debt 44	0.1	•	•	•	•	•	2.8	0.5	•	0.3	•	0.3 0.1

Selected Financial Factors (in Percentages)

Debt Ratio 45	54.6	•	•	•	•	•	24.6	48.8	•	55.0	•	60.8 54.6
Return on Total Assets 46	7.9	•	•	•	11.2	•	9.7	14.1	•	14.1	•	18.0 7.8
Return on Equity Before Income Taxes 47	15.3	•	•	•	11.2	•	11.3	26.6	•	29.8	•	38.0 15.2
Return on Equity After Income Taxes 48	10.0	•	•	•	11.2	•	7.5	24.8	•	28.6	•	26.5 9.9
Profit Margin (Before Income Tax) 49	7.6	•	•	•	•	•	5.1	5.4	•	5.7	•	5.3 7.8
Profit Margin (After Income Tax) 50	5.0	•	•	•	•	•	3.4	5.0	•	5.5	•	3.7 5.1

Table I

Corporations with and without Net Income

ASPHALT PAVING, ROOFING, OTHER PETROLEUM AND COAL PRODUCTS

MONEY AMOUNTS AND SIZE OF ASSETS IN THOUSANDS OF DOLLARS

Item Description for Accounting Period 7/12 Through 6/13	Total	Zero Assets	Under 500	500 to 1,000	1,000 to 5,000	5,000 to 10,000	10,000 to 25,000	25,000 to 50,000	50,000 to 100,000	100,000 to 250,000	250,000 to 500,000	500,000 to 2,500,000	2,500,000 and over
Number of Enterprises **1**	925	11	463	56	174	114	49	23	11	11	7	6	0

Revenues ($ in Thousands)

	Total	Zero Assets	Under 500	500 to 1,000	1,000 to 5,000	5,000 to 10,000	10,000 to 25,000	25,000 to 50,000	50,000 to 100,000	100,000 to 250,000	250,000 to 500,000	500,000 to 2,500,000	2,500,000 and over
Net Sales **2**	21063571	79353	119347	250939	697708	2532446	1181584	1298236	1277816	2485172	4603169	6537800	0
Interest **3**	21245	0	0	500	18	19	860	720	475	73	6029	12552	0
Rents **4**	12837	187	0	628	0	0	689	0	804	518	191	9821	0
Royalties **5**	17488	0	0	0	0	0	0	0	172	59	149	17108	0
Other Portfolio Income **6**	98226	0	0	42	1772	2578	1663	33528	1137	6508	5230	45767	0
Other Receipts **7**	332295	3239	0	0	2265	1124	3787	3562	4227	51742	137740	124609	0
Total Receipts **8**	21545662	82779	119347	252109	701763	2536167	1188583	1336046	1284631	2544072	4752508	6747657	0
Average Total Receipts **9**	23293	7525	258	4502	4033	22247	24257	58089	116785	231279	678930	1124610	•

Operating Costs/Operating Income (%)

	Total	Zero Assets	Under 500	500 to 1,000	1,000 to 5,000	5,000 to 10,000	10,000 to 25,000	25,000 to 50,000	50,000 to 100,000	100,000 to 250,000	250,000 to 500,000	500,000 to 2,500,000	2,500,000 and over
Cost of Operations **10**	74.2	72.7	30.1	82.6	84.4	76.2	71.5	73.5	82.6	76.7	92.7	58.0	•
Salaries and Wages **11**	4.3	3.5	40.9	1.1	2.6	4.1	6.0	5.7	2.9	4.3	1.8	5.5	•
Taxes Paid **12**	1.1	1.7	3.7	2.8	1.2	1.2	1.6	1.1	0.8	0.9	0.4	1.3	•
Interest Paid **13**	1.6	2.3	1.9	0.3	0.4	0.6	0.8	0.6	1.1	0.4	0.4	3.8	•
Depreciation **14**	2.4	3.5	•	2.5	1.4	2.9	2.3	1.9	1.7	2.3	0.5	4.1	•
Amortization and Depletion **15**	0.1	•	•	0.0	•	0.1	0.1	0.2	0.5	0.1	0.1	0.1	•
Pensions and Other Deferred Comp. **16**	0.3	•	•	0.0	•	0.2	0.3	0.4	0.3	0.2	0.1	0.7	•
Employee Benefits **17**	0.9	1.3	•	2.1	0.1	1.0	2.1	0.6	0.6	0.4	0.5	1.3	•
Advertising **18**	0.7	1.3	0.7	1.8	0.4	1.1	0.2	1.6	0.2	2.3	0.1	0.5	•
Other Expenses **19**	11.3	15.3	32.8	3.8	6.8	3.1	8.3	8.2	4.0	7.2	2.7	25.0	•
Officers' Compensation **20**	1.2	0.3	•	2.5	2.6	2.2	2.4	1.6	1.0	0.9	0.4	0.9	•
Operating Margin **21**	1.8	•	•	0.6	0.1	7.2	4.5	4.6	4.2	4.3	0.3	•	•
Operating Margin Before Officers' Comp. **22**	2.9	•	•	3.1	2.7	9.4	6.9	6.2	5.3	5.2	0.7	•	•

Selected Average Balance Sheet ($ in Thousands)

Net Receivables 23	3058	0	0	24	587	2654	3752	4871	14491	29733	111596	143150	•
Inventories 24	1877	0	0	146	257	607	2400	7022	15163	27121	35056	104056	•
Net Property, Plant and Equipment 25	3481	0	0	611	606	1943	5655	5180	23232	33200	48582	250288	•
Total Assets 26	16335	0	1	921	1766	7363	14670	32678	69755	138420	333831	1302267	•
Notes and Loans Payable 27	5046	0	104	189	4417	2871	5103	8067	18253	21516	60231	369781	•
All Other Liabilities 28	7004	0	17	34	2541	2037	2682	7841	11270	29070	114603	706214	•
Net Worth 29	4284	0	-119	699	-5192	2454	6885	16771	40231	87834	158997	226272	•

Selected Financial Ratios (Times to 1)

Current Ratio 30	2.1	•	0.0	3.5	0.4	2.0	1.7	2.8	2.3	3.5	2.9	2.0	•
Quick Ratio 31	1.3	•	0.0	1.8	0.3	1.5	1.1	1.0	1.4	2.2	1.2	1.4	•
Net Sales to Working Capital 32	5.0	•	•	22.7	•	8.4	7.9	4.4	6.9	4.3	3.4	4.0	•
Coverage Ratio 33	3.6	2.0	•	5.0	2.8	12.7	7.7	13.3	5.2	19.6	8.9	1.6	•
Total Asset Turnover 34	1.4	•	238.2	4.9	2.3	3.0	1.6	1.7	1.7	1.6	2.0	0.8	•
Inventory Turnover 35	9.0	•	•	25.4	13.2	27.9	7.2	5.9	6.3	6.4	17.4	6.1	•
Receivables Turnover 36	8.6	•	•	139.4	8.5	7.1	6.2	12.5	6.5	6.0	10.3	10.0	•
Total Liabilities to Net Worth 37	2.8	•	•	0.3	•	2.0	1.1	0.9	0.7	0.6	1.1	4.8	•
Current Assets to Working Capital 38	1.9	•	•	1.4	•	2.0	2.5	1.6	1.8	1.4	1.5	2.0	•
Current Liabilities to Working Capital 39	0.9	•	•	0.4	•	1.0	1.5	0.6	0.8	0.4	0.5	1.0	•
Working Capital to Net Sales 40	0.2	•	•	0.0	•	0.1	0.1	0.2	0.1	0.2	0.3	0.2	•
Inventory to Working Capital 41	0.4	•	•	0.7	•	0.2	0.7	0.6	0.6	0.4	0.3	0.5	•
Total Receipts to Cash Flow 42	7.4	6.0	4.7	33.4	15.8	11.1	8.2	8.3	14.8	7.8	18.1	4.1	•
Cost of Goods to Cash Flow 43	5.5	4.3	1.4	27.6	13.4	8.4	5.9	6.1	12.2	6.0	16.8	2.4	•
Cash Flow to Total Debt 44	0.3	•	0.5	0.6	0.0	0.4	0.4	0.4	0.3	0.6	0.2	0.2	•

Selected Financial Factors (in Percentages)

Debt Ratio 45	73.8	•	11112.6	24.2	394.0	66.7	53.1	48.7	42.3	36.5	52.4	82.6	•
Return on Total Assets 46	8.0	•	•	6.2	2.5	24.0	9.6	14.0	9.8	11.7	7.8	5.1	•
Return on Equity Before Income Taxes 47	22.2	•	22.1	6.5	•	66.5	17.8	25.2	13.7	17.4	14.6	10.8	•
Return on Equity After Income Taxes 48	17.6	•	22.1	6.5	•	64.1	17.6	21.6	12.0	14.4	10.7	5.4	•
Profit Margin (Before Income Tax) 49	4.2	2.4	•	1.0	0.7	7.3	5.1	7.5	4.8	6.8	3.5	2.2	•
Profit Margin (After Income Tax) 50	3.3	0.3	•	1.0	0.3	7.1	5.0	6.4	4.2	5.6	2.6	1.1	•

Table II

Corporations with Net Income

ASPHALT PAVING, ROOFING, OTHER PETROLEUM AND COAL PRODUCTS

MONEY AMOUNTS AND SIZE OF ASSETS IN THOUSANDS OF DOLLARS

Item Description for Accounting Period 7/12 Through 6/13	Total	Zero Assets	Under 500	500 to 1,000	1,000 to 5,000	5,000 to 10,000	10,000 to 25,000	25,000 to 50,000	50,000 to 100,000	100,000 to 250,000	250,000 to 500,000	500,000 to 2,500,000	2,500,000 and over
Number of Enterprises 1	730	•	406	56	65	•	37	•	11	8	7	•	0

Revenues ($ in Thousands)

	Total	Zero Assets	Under 500	500 to 1,000	1,000 to 5,000	5,000 to 10,000	10,000 to 25,000	25,000 to 50,000	50,000 to 100,000	100,000 to 250,000	250,000 to 500,000	500,000 to 2,500,000	2,500,000 and over
Net Sales 2	17156797	•	119347	250939	403348	•	926476	•	1277816	2096839	4603169	•	0
Interest 3	10928	•	0	500	18	•	22	•	475	28	6029	•	0
Rents 4	11631	•	0	628	0	•	0	•	804	0	191	•	0
Royalties 5	377	•	0	0	0	•	0	•	172	56	149	•	0
Other Portfolio Income 6	53236	•	0	42	1621	•	278	•	1137	6237	5230	•	0
Other Receipts 7	275738	•	0	0	256	•	3644	•	4227	13824	137740	•	0
Total Receipts 8	17508707	•	119347	252109	405243	•	930420	•	1284631	2116984	4752508	•	0
Average Total Receipts 9	23985	•	294	4502	6235	•	25146	•	116785	264623	678930	•	•

Operating Costs/Operating Income (%)

	Total	Zero Assets	Under 500	500 to 1,000	1,000 to 5,000	5,000 to 10,000	10,000 to 25,000	25,000 to 50,000	50,000 to 100,000	100,000 to 250,000	250,000 to 500,000	500,000 to 2,500,000	2,500,000 and over
Cost of Operations 10	77.3	•	30.1	82.6	75.5	•	70.5	•	82.6	76.7	92.7	•	•
Salaries and Wages 11	4.0	•	40.9	1.1	4.5	•	6.2	•	2.9	3.8	1.8	•	•
Taxes Paid 12	1.0	•	3.7	2.8	2.0	•	1.6	•	0.8	0.8	0.4	•	•
Interest Paid 13	0.7	•	1.9	0.3	0.3	•	0.8	•	1.1	0.3	0.4	•	•
Depreciation 14	2.4	•	•	2.5	2.4	•	2.2	•	1.7	1.4	0.5	•	•
Amortization and Depletion 15	0.1	•	•	0.0	•	•	0.1	•	0.5	0.1	0.1	•	•
Pensions and Other Deferred Comp. 16	0.4	•	•	0.0	•	•	0.3	•	0.3	0.2	0.1	•	•
Employee Benefits 17	0.7	•	•	2.1	0.2	•	1.6	•	0.6	0.3	0.5	•	•
Advertising 18	0.8	•	0.7	1.8	0.7	•	0.3	•	0.2	2.7	0.1	•	•
Other Expenses 19	7.4	•	20.6	3.8	7.8	•	7.1	•	4.0	5.4	2.7	•	•
Officers' Compensation 20	1.1	•	•	2.5	4.5	•	2.7	•	1.0	0.8	0.4	•	•
Operating Margin 21	4.0	•	2.1	0.6	2.1	•	6.6	•	4.2	7.4	0.3	•	•
Operating Margin Before Officers' Comp. 22	5.1	•	2.1	3.1	6.6	•	9.3	•	5.3	8.2	0.7	•	•

Selected Average Balance Sheet ($ in Thousands)

Net Receivables 23	3272	•	0	24	659	•	3793	•	14491	30294	111596	• •
Inventories 24	1978	•	0	146	689	•	2469	•	11763	24781	35056	• •
Net Property, Plant and Equipment 25	3226	•	0	611	489	•	6148	•	23232	27122	48582	• •
Total Assets 26	14243	•	1	921	2502	•	15141	•	69755	134116	333831	• •
Notes and Loans Payable 27	4599	•	0	189	1241	•	5766	•	18253	24180	60231	• •
All Other Liabilities 28	3784	•	19	34	368	•	2799	•	11270	24627	114603	• •
Net Worth 29	5860	•	-18	699	893	•	6576	•	40231	85308	158997	• •

Selected Financial Ratios (Times to 1)

Current Ratio 30	2.6	•	0.0	3.5	5.8	•	1.7	•	2.3	4.2	2.9	• •
Quick Ratio 31	1.5	•	0.0	1.8	3.3	•	1.1	•	1.4	2.7	1.2	• •
Net Sales to Working Capital 32	4.4	•	•	22.7	3.7	•	7.7	•	6.9	4.4	3.4	• •
Coverage Ratio 33	9.6	•	2.1	5.0	9.6	•	9.2	•	5.2	26.0	8.9	• •
Total Asset Turnover 34	1.7	•	318.3	4.9	2.5	•	1.7	•	1.7	2.0	2.0	• •
Inventory Turnover 35	9.2	•	•	25.4	6.8	•	7.2	•	8.2	8.1	17.4	• •
Receivables Turnover 36	8.1	•	•	139.4	7.7	•	•	•	7.9	•	10.3	• •
Total Liabilities to Net Worth 37	1.4	•	•	0.3	1.8	•	1.3	•	0.7	0.6	1.1	• •
Current Assets to Working Capital 38	1.6	•	•	1.4	1.2	•	2.5	•	1.8	1.3	1.5	• •
Current Liabilities to Working Capital 39	0.6	•	•	0.4	0.2	•	1.5	•	0.8	0.3	0.5	• •
Working Capital to Net Sales 40	0.2	•	•	0.0	0.3	•	0.1	•	0.1	0.2	0.3	• •
Inventory to Working Capital 41	0.4	•	•	0.7	0.4	•	0.8	•	0.6	0.4	0.3	• •
Total Receipts to Cash Flow 42	8.3	•	4.7	33.4	11.2	•	7.5	•	14.8	7.8	18.1	• •
Cost of Goods to Cash Flow 43	6.4	•	1.4	27.6	8.4	•	5.3	•	12.2	6.0	16.8	• •
Cash Flow to Total Debt 44	0.3	•	3.3	0.6	0.3	•	0.4	•	0.3	0.7	0.2	• •

Selected Financial Factors (in Percentages)

Debt Ratio 45	58.9	•	2050.9	24.2	64.3	•	56.6	•	42.3	36.4	52.4	• •
Return on Total Assets 46	11.3	•	1271.5	6.2	7.2	•	12.9	•	9.8	17.2	7.8	• •
Return on Equity Before Income Taxes 47	24.6	•	•	6.5	18.0	•	26.6	•	13.7	26.1	14.6	• •
Return on Equity After Income Taxes 48	20.4	•	•	6.5	12.5	•	26.3	•	12.0	21.7	10.7	• •
Profit Margin (Before Income Tax) 49	6.1	•	2.1	1.0	2.6	•	7.0	•	4.8	8.5	3.5	• •
Profit Margin (After Income Tax) 50	5.1	•	2.1	1.0	1.8	•	6.9	•	4.2	7.1	2.6	• •

Table I

Corporations with and without Net Income

BASIC CHEMICAL

MONEY AMOUNTS AND SIZE OF ASSETS IN THOUSANDS OF DOLLARS

Item Description for Accounting Period 7/12 Through 6/13	Total	Zero Assets	Under 500	500 to 1,000	1,000 to 5,000	5,000 to 10,000	10,000 to 25,000	25,000 to 50,000	50,000 to 100,000	100,000 to 250,000	250,000 to 500,000	500,000 to 2,500,000	2,500,000 and over
Number of Enterprises 1	771	68	151	59	167	35	91	46	40	25	22	40	26

Revenues ($ in Thousands)

Net Sales 2	199795317	3576790	122692	138282	701757	381254	5421558	2229834	3678814	6403310	5511873	37559039	134070113
Interest 3	1794279	24196	0	0	52	364	1172	787	4329	3811	12727	251993	1494847
Rents 4	227484	754	0	0	0	0	1203	278	962	1091	0	48592	174604
Royalties 5	3609346	42068	0	0	0	0	16	0	3930	9899	37832	77122	3438478
Other Portfolio Income 6	2734985	94631	0	0	4278	206	20058	1249	81493	8905	32378	578173	1913614
Other Receipts 7	4310471	246465	0	6099	6220	-7366	1461	-1843	38901	40851	72581	853765	3053340
Total Receipts 8	212471882	3984904	122692	144381	712307	374458	5445468	2230305	3808429	6467867	5667391	39368684	144144996
Average Total Receipts 9	275580	58602	813	2447	4265	10699	59840	48485	95211	258715	257609	984217	5544038

Operating Costs/Operating Income (%)

Cost of Operations 10	75.1	71.8	71.8	46.7	64.4	85.8	83.2	70.7	73.6	84.0	74.1	76.8	74.2
Salaries and Wages 11	5.4	9.0	3.1	14.9	7.6	5.5	4.0	6.3	4.7	3.7	4.7	4.1	5.8
Taxes Paid 12	0.9	0.7	1.1	2.6	1.2	1.8	0.9	1.6	1.1	0.8	0.8	0.9	0.9
Interest Paid 13	4.0	5.2	•	0.9	0.6	0.4	0.3	1.0	0.8	1.0	4.4	2.3	4.9
Depreciation 14	3.8	2.2	1.8	1.3	3.2	2.8	1.0	2.1	3.7	2.7	9.5	3.4	3.9
Amortization and Depletion 15	0.7	0.6	•	0.1	0.0	0.0	0.2	0.4	0.7	0.7	0.8	1.0	0.7
Pensions and Other Deferred Comp. 16	1.4	0.6	•	0.2	0.3	0.1	0.2	0.3	0.4	0.2	0.4	0.7	1.8
Employee Benefits 17	1.4	2.1	1.2	4.1	1.2	0.9	0.8	1.6	0.9	0.8	1.1	1.3	1.5
Advertising 18	0.4	0.4	0.0	0.0	0.2	0.2	0.2	0.2	0.2	0.1	0.1	0.1	0.5
Other Expenses 19	7.3	9.8	31.0	19.1	12.1	9.6	5.9	9.5	8.1	5.5	9.0	8.1	7.0
Officers' Compensation 20	0.7	1.5	1.5	20.1	2.0	2.8	1.7	2.5	1.1	1.2	0.7	0.6	0.6
Operating Margin 21	•	•	•	•	7.1	•	1.6	3.9	4.7	•	•	0.7	•
Operating Margin Before Officers' Comp. 22	•	•	•	10.1	9.1	•	3.3	6.4	5.8	0.6	•	1.3	•

Selected Average Balance Sheet ($ in Thousands)

Net Receivables 23	133334	0	95	196	465	1362	3507	6161	13809	29859	52390	158637	3586544
Inventories 24	30005	0	87	290	139	1662	3973	7371	9616	24897	38983	126210	592642
Net Property, Plant and Equipment 25	76755	0	6	133	397	1909	4540	9594	23891	49344	144323	296890	1574676
Total Assets 26	537414	0	316	615	1649	7258	16036	35190	73120	159662	364249	1172694	13416030
Notes and Loans Payable 27	235045	0	281	571	97	2531	3717	8837	18779	58031	158150	469796	5993117
All Other Liabilities 28	132187	0	16	103	549	1109	3639	9127	18378	42251	91855	373788	3163947
Net Worth 29	170181	0	19	-59	1003	3618	8680	17226	35963	59380	114244	329110	4258966

Selected Financial Ratios (Times to 1)

Current Ratio 30	1.1	•	18.8	0.9	1.9	2.6	2.7	1.8	2.7	1.8	1.6	1.4	1.0
Quick Ratio 31	0.9	•	12.1	0.4	1.1	1.4	1.5	1.0	1.7	1.1	1.0	0.8	0.9
Net Sales to Working Capital 32	14.6	•	2.9	•	7.3	4.3	9.9	6.0	4.1	8.2	5.5	8.3	24.9
Coverage Ratio 33	2.5	2.5	•	•	16.3	•	8.0	4.8	11.6	1.4	0.5	3.7	2.4
Total Asset Turnover 34	0.5	•	2.6	3.8	2.5	1.5	3.7	1.4	1.3	1.6	0.7	0.8	0.4
Inventory Turnover 35	6.5	•	6.7	3.8	19.5	5.6	12.5	4.6	7.0	8.6	4.8	5.7	6.5
Receivables Turnover 36	2.0	•	11.0	7.8	9.5	6.9	14.8	7.4	7.0	8.2	4.7	6.2	1.5
Total Liabilities to Net Worth 37	2.2	•	15.6	•	0.6	1.0	0.8	1.0	1.0	1.7	2.2	2.6	2.2
Current Assets to Working Capital 38	10.8	•	1.1	•	2.1	1.6	1.6	2.3	1.6	2.3	2.7	3.6	23.1
Current Liabilities to Working Capital 39	9.8	•	0.1	•	1.1	0.6	0.6	1.3	0.6	1.3	1.7	2.6	22.1
Working Capital to Net Sales 40	0.1	•	0.3	•	0.1	0.2	0.1	0.2	0.2	0.1	0.2	0.1	0.0
Inventory to Working Capital 41	1.6	•	0.3	•	0.4	0.5	0.6	0.9	0.5	0.7	0.8	1.3	2.5
Total Receipts to Cash Flow 42	10.2	7.1	5.9	9.9	5.6	•	15.0	8.6	8.2	21.5	28.2	8.8	10.2
Cost of Goods to Cash Flow 43	7.7	5.1	4.2	4.6	3.6	•	12.4	6.1	6.0	18.1	20.9	6.8	7.6
Cash Flow to Total Debt 44	0.1	•	0.5	0.4	1.2	•	0.5	0.3	0.3	0.1	0.0	0.1	0.1

Selected Financial Factors (in Percentages)

Debt Ratio 45	68.3	•	94.0	109.6	39.2	50.1	45.9	51.0	50.8	62.8	68.6	71.9	68.3
Return on Total Assets 46	4.9	•	•	•	23.4	•	8.7	6.9	11.3	2.3	1.7	6.8	4.5
Return on Equity Before Income Taxes 47	9.3	•	•	221.4	36.0	•	14.0	11.1	21.0	1.9	•	17.6	8.3
Return on Equity After Income Taxes 48	6.0	•	•	225.0	33.9	•	12.0	7.4	17.8	•	•	10.9	5.5
Profit Margin (Before Income Tax) 49	6.1	7.6	•	•	8.6	•	2.0	4.0	8.2	0.4	•	6.2	6.8
Profit Margin (After Income Tax) 50	3.9	6.7	•	•	8.1	•	1.7	2.6	7.0	•	•	3.8	4.5

Table II
Corporations with Net Income

BASIC CHEMICAL

MONEY AMOUNTS AND SIZE OF ASSETS IN THOUSANDS OF DOLLARS

Item Description for Accounting Period 7/12 Through 6/13		Total	Zero Assets	Under 500	500 to 1,000	1,000 to 5,000	5,000 to 10,000	10,000 to 25,000	25,000 to 50,000	50,000 to 100,000	100,000 to 250,000	250,000 to 500,000	500,000 to 2,500,000	2,500,000 and over
Number of Enterprises	1	588	65	95	56	•	16	76	32	34	18	7	31	•

Revenues ($ in Thousands)														
Net Sales	2	175865071	3281024	79716	138282	•	350304	2379119	1763498	3033307	4534345	2197967	28316615	•
Interest	3	1658430	23444	0	0	•	336	1079	534	4222	3680	8315	183254	•
Rents	4	226628	621	0	0	•	0	1203	0	811	1091	0	48357	•
Royalties	5	3542558	31325	0	0	•	0	16	0	3930	9899	37584	75124	•
Other Portfolio Income	6	2657221	94631	0	0	•	206	12917	621	77715	8456	30703	526776	•
Other Receipts	7	3947536	244007	0	6099	•	56	11602	6551	36603	29701	18904	671110	•
Total Receipts	8	187897444	3675052	79716	144381	•	350902	2405936	1771204	3156588	4587172	2293473	29821236	•
Average Total Receipts	9	319553	56539	839	2578	•	21931	31657	55350	92841	254843	327639	961975	•

Operating Costs/Operating Income (%)														
Cost of Operations	10	73.7	71.5	71.1	46.7	•	84.0	64.5	70.5	71.5	81.0	66.3	73.4	•
Salaries and Wages	11	5.6	9.0	4.8	13.9	•	3.0	8.0	5.1	5.2	3.6	5.8	4.5	•
Taxes Paid	12	0.9	0.7	1.6	2.5	•	0.8	1.7	1.4	1.2	0.9	1.0	0.9	•
Interest Paid	13	4.3	5.0	•	0.9	•	0.2	0.4	0.5	0.6	0.8	3.9	2.4	•
Depreciation	14	3.6	2.2	2.7	1.2	•	0.9	1.9	1.7	3.2	2.1	2.6	3.1	•
Amortization and Depletion	15	0.7	0.4	•	•	•	0.0	0.2	0.1	0.7	0.5	0.7	1.0	•
Pensions and Other Deferred Comp.	16	1.5	0.7	•	•	•	0.1	0.3	0.3	0.5	0.2	0.4	0.8	•
Employee Benefits	17	1.4	2.2	1.9	4.1	•	0.3	1.6	1.5	1.0	0.8	1.2	1.4	•
Advertising	18	0.4	0.4	0.0	0.0	•	0.1	0.5	0.2	0.2	0.1	0.1	0.1	•
Other Expenses	19	7.1	9.2	11.0	15.1	•	5.6	10.8	7.7	7.6	5.2	9.4	8.4	•
Officers' Compensation	20	0.7	1.4	2.4	19.4	•	2.8	2.3	2.2	1.3	1.4	1.0	0.7	•
Operating Margin	21	•	•	4.6	•	•	2.0	7.6	8.8	7.0	3.4	7.5	3.3	•
Operating Margin Before Officers' Comp.	22	0.7	•	6.9	15.6	•	4.8	9.9	11.0	8.3	4.8	8.5	4.0	•

Selected Average Balance Sheet ($ in Thousands)

Net Receivables 23	170002	0	88	207	•	2350	3878	6921	14204	33853	112690	176240	•
Inventories 24	32663	0	123	292	•	3096	4486	8081	9192	24317	58048	104204	•
Net Property, Plant and Equipment 25	85093	0	9	135	•	983	4294	7708	22508	40202	68053	259713	•
Total Assets 26	651078	0	363	614	•	7915	16247	33472	72065	158719	367786	1085034	•
Notes and Loans Payable 27	285218	0	2	351	•	788	3312	6015	17345	51032	122289	402780	•
All Other Liabilities 28	155279	0	16	72	•	1763	3583	7656	17794	47694	103776	336407	•
Net Worth 29	210581	0	345	191	•	5364	9352	19801	36927	59993	141720	345847	•

Selected Financial Ratios (Times to 1)

Current Ratio 30	1.1	•	20.6	1.8	•	3.9	3.0	2.6	2.9	1.6	2.1	1.6	•
Quick Ratio 31	0.9	•	12.7	0.8	•	2.1	1.6	1.6	1.8	1.0	1.5	1.0	•
Net Sales to Working Capital 32	15.5	•	2.6	11.8	•	4.3	4.6	4.2	3.7	8.4	3.2	6.4	•
Coverage Ratio 33	2.8	2.9	•	1.7	•	10.8	22.4	19.7	19.4	7.0	4.5	4.9	•
Total Asset Turnover 34	0.5	•	2.3	4.0	•	2.8	1.9	1.6	1.2	1.6	0.9	0.8	•
Inventory Turnover 35	6.8	•	4.9	3.9	•	5.9	4.5	4.8	6.9	8.4	3.6	6.4	•
Receivables Turnover 36	1.8	•	19.1	7.8	•	7.0	7.1	7.5	7.3	7.9	2.6	5.6	•
Total Liabilities to Net Worth 37	2.1	•	0.1	2.2	•	0.5	0.7	0.7	1.0	1.6	1.6	2.1	•
Current Assets to Working Capital 38	12.1	•	1.1	2.2	•	1.3	1.5	1.6	1.5	2.6	1.9	2.6	•
Current Liabilities to Working Capital 39	11.1	•	0.1	1.2	•	0.3	0.5	0.6	0.5	1.6	0.9	1.6	•
Working Capital to Net Sales 40	0.1	•	0.4	0.1	•	0.2	0.2	0.2	0.3	0.1	0.3	0.2	•
Inventory to Working Capital 41	1.6	•	0.4	1.1	•	0.3	0.6	0.6	0.4	0.8	0.4	0.7	•
Total Receipts to Cash Flow 42	9.0	6.6	8.5	7.8	•	16.5	5.8	6.5	7.1	11.9	5.6	7.0	•
Cost of Goods to Cash Flow 43	6.7	4.7	6.0	3.7	•	13.8	3.7	4.6	5.1	9.6	3.7	5.1	•
Cash Flow to Total Debt 44	0.1	•	5.4	0.7	•	0.5	0.8	0.6	0.4	0.2	0.2	0.2	•

Selected Financial Factors (in Percentages)

Debt Ratio 45	67.7	•	5.0	68.9	•	32.2	42.4	40.8	48.8	62.2	61.5	68.1	•
Return on Total Assets 46	5.6	•	10.5	5.9	•	6.7	17.6	16.0	14.5	8.5	14.9	9.9	•
Return on Equity Before Income Taxes 47	11.1	•	11.1	7.7	•	9.0	29.3	25.7	26.9	19.2	30.2	24.8	•
Return on Equity After Income Taxes 48	7.7	•	9.9	6.5	•	6.1	27.1	21.1	23.2	14.8	19.9	16.6	•
Profit Margin (Before Income Tax) 49	7.8	9.5	4.6	0.6	•	2.2	8.8	9.2	11.1	4.6	13.6	9.4	•
Profit Margin (After Income Tax) 50	5.4	8.5	4.1	0.5	•	1.5	8.1	7.6	9.6	3.5	9.0	6.3	•

Table I

Corporations with and without Net Income

RESIN, SYNTHETIC RUBBER AND FIBERS AND FILAMENTS

MONEY AMOUNTS AND SIZE OF ASSETS IN THOUSANDS OF DOLLARS

Item Description for Accounting Period 7/12 Through 6/13	Total	Zero Assets	Under 500	500 to 1,000	1,000 to 5,000	5,000 to 10,000	10,000 to 25,000	25,000 to 50,000	50,000 to 100,000	100,000 to 250,000	250,000 to 500,000	500,000 to 2,500,000	2,500,000 and over
Number of Enterprises 1	591	234	129	6	100	3	52	14	11	14	11	12	6

Revenues ($ in Thousands)													
Net Sales 2	68864574	353170	283164	5978	525550	58608	1307467	894288	1417753	3371482	5311221	15625446	39710447
Interest 3	457805	226	0	2	0	0	104	59	461	2520	6720	50172	397541
Rents 4	29937	0	0	0	0	0	177	110	36	5	1036	12792	15781
Royalties 5	584941	5	0	0	5	0	0	378	0	3735	15247	34365	531207
Other Portfolio Income 6	259947	73	0	51	0	0	362	20	1428	5164	51289	29257	172303
Other Receipts 7	1599658	4564	3135	3681	663	0	9943	5686	9324	22345	34924	126442	1378949
Total Receipts 8	71796862	358038	286299	9712	526218	58608	1318053	900541	1429002	3405251	5420437	15878474	42206228
Average Total Receipts 9	121484	1530	2219	1619	5262	19536	25347	64324	129909	243232	492767	1323206	7034371

Operating Costs/Operating Income (%)													
Cost of Operations 10	71.1	64.4	50.4	59.6	63.0	54.7	75.7	79.3	83.5	75.1	81.2	83.2	64.2
Salaries and Wages 11	3.0	19.5	6.7	73.0	4.4	7.4	4.3	2.2	3.2	4.9	4.3	1.9	2.9
Taxes Paid 12	0.6	1.3	1.8	0.6	1.6	1.0	1.5	1.6	1.2	1.0	0.9	0.5	0.4
Interest Paid 13	2.6	0.7	•	24.2	5.7	0.5	0.8	0.9	0.3	0.8	1.5	2.1	3.2
Depreciation 14	4.7	1.9	0.5	3.9	1.8	0.2	2.7	4.1	1.9	2.7	2.6	3.4	5.8
Amortization and Depletion 15	0.7	0.9	0.1	•	0.0	•	0.1	0.4	0.0	0.3	0.2	0.3	1.1
Pensions and Other Deferred Comp. 16	1.3	0.4	1.0	•	2.8	•	0.2	0.2	0.6	0.8	0.4	0.5	1.8
Employee Benefits 17	1.5	1.0	2.0	5.4	1.2	0.5	1.6	0.9	0.8	0.8	1.3	0.9	1.9
Advertising 18	0.3	0.3	0.1	1.3	0.0	0.6	0.6	0.3	0.1	0.2	0.1	0.1	0.4
Other Expenses 19	13.6	11.0	7.7	135.0	8.1	20.7	6.2	6.4	4.0	6.3	5.8	4.7	19.5
Officers' Compensation 20	0.5	17.2	6.2	31.1	4.6	•	2.9	0.7	0.6	1.2	0.4	0.5	0.2
Operating Margin 21	0.2	•	23.6	•	6.9	14.5	3.5	2.9	3.7	5.7	1.2	1.8	•
Operating Margin Before Officers' Comp. 22	0.7	•	29.8	•	11.5	14.5	6.4	3.6	4.3	6.9	1.6	2.3	•

Selected Average Balance Sheet ($ in Thousands)

Net Receivables 23	20925	0	107	102	514	3607	4417	6481	17851	26804	68932	202414	1368466
Inventories 24	15478	0	39	388	783	4041	2876	8546	17481	29406	57662	134099	989025
Net Property, Plant and Equipment 25	40172	0	134	283	654	253	4676	14368	16098	46301	102697	364639	2813628
Total Assets 26	187540	0	378	918	3464	7672	15831	39126	74279	169986	389725	1154932	14616418
Notes and Loans Payable 27	98642	0	113	1131	1477	4652	3188	8310	14610	43965	136410	427164	8404927
All Other Liabilities 28	44676	0	88	835	862	1636	4943	11699	21996	39176	111492	317925	3340543
Net Worth 29	44222	0	177	-1048	1124	1384	7701	19116	37673	86846	141823	409844	2870948

Selected Financial Ratios (Times to 1)

Current Ratio 30	1.4	•	1.9	0.6	1.8	5.0	2.7	1.8	2.1	1.7	1.7	1.7	1.3
Quick Ratio 31	0.8	•	1.5	0.2	0.7	3.5	1.8	0.8	1.1	0.8	0.9	1.0	0.7
Net Sales to Working Capital 32	7.7	•	20.0	•	7.2	3.0	3.8	7.3	4.9	7.0	7.0	7.0	8.6
Coverage Ratio 33	2.9	•	•	•	2.2	32.4	6.3	4.9	16.8	9.1	3.6	2.7	2.8
Total Asset Turnover 34	0.6	•	5.8	1.1	1.5	2.5	1.6	1.6	1.7	1.4	1.2	1.1	0.5
Inventory Turnover 35	5.4	•	28.4	1.5	4.2	2.6	6.6	5.9	6.2	6.2	6.8	8.1	4.3
Receivables Turnover 36	5.8	•	20.3	19.6	10.4	2.2	5.8	7.9	7.4	8.6	5.9	7.5	5.0
Total Liabilities to Net Worth 37	3.2	•	1.1	•	2.1	4.5	1.1	1.0	1.0	1.0	1.7	1.8	4.1
Current Assets to Working Capital 38	3.3	•	2.1	•	2.3	1.2	1.6	2.3	1.9	2.4	2.3	2.4	4.2
Current Liabilities to Working Capital 39	2.3	•	1.1	•	1.3	0.2	0.6	1.3	0.9	1.4	1.3	1.4	3.2
Working Capital to Net Sales 40	0.1	•	0.1	•	0.1	0.3	0.3	0.1	0.2	0.1	0.1	0.1	0.1
Inventory to Working Capital 41	1.0	•	0.4	•	1.2	0.4	0.4	1.1	0.6	0.9	0.9	0.8	1.3
Total Receipts to Cash Flow 42	6.5	•	3.5	•	6.7	3.1	11.6	11.1	13.5	8.3	12.4	15.1	4.8
Cost of Goods to Cash Flow 43	4.6	•	1.7	•	4.3	1.7	8.7	8.8	11.3	6.2	10.1	12.6	3.1
Cash Flow to Total Debt 44	0.1	•	3.2	•	0.3	1.0	0.3	0.3	0.3	0.3	0.2	0.1	0.1

Selected Financial Factors (in Percentages)

Debt Ratio 45	76.4	•	53.1	214.2	67.5	82.0	51.4	51.1	49.3	48.9	63.6	64.5	80.4
Return on Total Assets 46	4.7	•	143.3	•	19.3	38.0	8.1	7.4	8.3	11.0	6.5	6.4	4.1
Return on Equity Before Income Taxes 47	13.3	•	305.8	163.2	32.9	204.3	13.9	12.0	15.5	19.1	12.8	11.3	13.3
Return on Equity After Income Taxes 48	8.4	•	305.8	163.2	32.7	134.9	11.3	6.7	12.0	15.4	9.1	6.9	8.0
Profit Margin (Before Income Tax) 49	5.0	•	24.7	•	7.0	14.5	4.3	3.6	4.5	6.9	3.8	3.5	5.8
Profit Margin (After Income Tax) 50	3.2	•	24.7	•	7.0	9.6	3.4	2.0	3.5	5.6	2.7	2.2	3.5

Table II
Corporations with Net Income

RESIN, SYNTHETIC RUBBER AND FIBERS AND FILAMENTS

MONEY AMOUNTS AND SIZE OF ASSETS IN THOUSANDS OF DOLLARS

Item Description for Accounting Period 7/12 Through 6/13	Total	Zero Assets	Under 500	500 to 1,000	1,000 to 5,000	5,000 to 10,000	10,000 to 25,000	25,000 to 50,000	50,000 to 100,000	100,000 to 250,000	250,000 to 500,000	500,000 to 2,500,000	2,500,000 and over
Number of Enterprises 1	244	3	41	3	•	3	43	•	•	11	8	•	3

Revenues ($ in Thousands)

	Total	Zero Assets	Under 500	500 to 1,000	1,000 to 5,000	5,000 to 10,000	10,000 to 25,000	25,000 to 50,000	50,000 to 100,000	100,000 to 250,000	250,000 to 500,000	500,000 to 2,500,000	2,500,000 and over
Net Sales 2	54759082	327585	202388	4497	•	58608	1193813	•	•	2827165	3821988	•	29870887
Interest 3	451176	203	0	0	•	0	37	•	•	2123	6265	•	394105
Rents 4	23237	0	0	0	•	0	0	•	•	0	956	•	15103
Royalties 5	547173	5	0	0	•	0	0	•	•	2535	10856	•	502415
Other Portfolio Income 6	258924	69	0	0	•	0	362	•	•	5164	50430	•	172195
Other Receipts 7	1189045	4565	3135	24	•	0	8108	•	•	3742	30097	•	1037559
Total Receipts 8	57228637	332427	205523	4521	•	58608	1202320	•	•	2840729	3920592	•	31992264
Average Total Receipts 9	234544	110809	5013	1507	•	19536	27961	•	•	258248	490074	•	10664088

Operating Costs/Operating Income (%)

	Total	Zero Assets	Under 500	500 to 1,000	1,000 to 5,000	5,000 to 10,000	10,000 to 25,000	25,000 to 50,000	50,000 to 100,000	100,000 to 250,000	250,000 to 500,000	500,000 to 2,500,000	2,500,000 and over
Cost of Operations 10	69.3	65.6	42.6	68.0	•	54.7	73.6	•	•	77.9	77.9	•	60.4
Salaries and Wages 11	2.2	9.5	9.4	1.2	•	7.4	4.3	•	•	3.4	5.3	•	1.5
Taxes Paid 12	0.6	1.4	1.3	0.7	•	1.0	1.5	•	•	1.0	1.1	•	0.4
Interest Paid 13	2.1	0.3	•	2.5	•	0.5	0.6	•	•	1.0	1.0	•	2.7
Depreciation 14	4.6	1.9	0.1	2.6	•	0.2	2.3	•	•	1.4	2.4	•	6.6
Amortization and Depletion 15	0.5	0.9	•	•	•	•	0.0	•	•	0.4	0.2	•	0.6
Pensions and Other Deferred Comp. 16	1.3	0.4	1.4	•	•	•	0.2	•	•	0.6	0.3	•	1.8
Employee Benefits 17	1.7	1.1	1.1	•	•	0.5	1.7	•	•	0.5	1.5	•	2.3
Advertising 18	0.3	0.2	0.2	0.0	•	0.6	0.6	•	•	0.2	0.1	•	0.4
Other Expenses 19	14.7	7.2	4.2	11.6	•	20.7	6.0	•	•	3.8	6.6	•	22.6
Officers' Compensation 20	0.4	4.7	5.1	13.1	•	•	2.9	•	•	1.1	0.4	•	0.1
Operating Margin 21	2.5	6.7	34.7	0.3	•	14.5	6.4	•	•	8.6	3.3	•	0.5
Operating Margin Before Officers' Comp. 22	2.9	11.5	39.8	13.4	•	14.5	9.2	•	•	9.8	3.7	•	0.6

Selected Average Balance Sheet ($ in Thousands)

Net Receivables 23	43431	0	0	168	•	3607	4235	•	•	26644	75490	•	2350101
Inventories 24	29377	0	40	225	•	3967	2803	•	•	27912	57444	•	1518317
Net Property, Plant and Equipment 25	78247	0	210	417	•	253	4890	•	•	39437	111063	•	4737798
Total Assets 26	392257	0	380	928	•	7672	16205	•	•	169495	405526	•	25587356
Notes and Loans Payable 27	202743	0	99	226	•	4652	3072	•	•	39229	106466	•	14652218
All Other Liabilities 28	91305	0	115	669	•	1636	4973	•	•	38143	110308	•	5644237
Net Worth 29	98209	0	167	34	•	1384	8160	•	•	92123	188753	•	5290901

Selected Financial Ratios (Times to 1)

Current Ratio 30	1.4	•	0.8	0.5	•	5.0	3.0	•	•	2.2	1.8	•	1.3
Quick Ratio 31	0.8	•	0.8	0.2	•	3.5	2.0	•	•	1.1	1.0	•	0.7
Net Sales to Working Capital 32	7.4	•	•	•	•	3.0	3.9	•	•	5.5	5.8	•	8.5
Coverage Ratio 33	4.8	25.7	•	1.3	•	32.4	12.6	•	•	10.6	7.3	•	4.3
Total Asset Turnover 34	0.6	•	13.0	1.6	•	2.5	1.7	•	•	1.5	1.2	•	0.4
Inventory Turnover 35	5.3	•	53.3	4.5	•	2.7	7.3	•	•	7.2	6.5	•	4.0
Receivables Turnover 36	5.5	•	29.0	17.9	•	2.5	6.3	•	•	10.1	6.0	•	4.5
Total Liabilities to Net Worth 37	3.0	•	1.3	26.6	•	4.5	1.0	•	•	0.8	1.1	•	3.8
Current Assets to Working Capital 38	3.3	•	•	•	•	1.2	1.5	•	•	1.9	2.2	•	4.7
Current Liabilities to Working Capital 39	2.3	•	•	•	•	0.2	0.5	•	•	0.9	1.2	•	3.7
Working Capital to Net Sales 40	0.1	•	•	•	•	0.3	0.3	•	•	0.2	0.2	•	0.1
Inventory to Working Capital 41	1.0	•	•	•	•	0.4	0.4	•	•	0.7	0.8	•	1.3
Total Receipts to Cash Flow 42	5.3	7.0	2.6	13.0	•	3.1	8.9	•	•	8.3	8.8	•	3.8
Cost of Goods to Cash Flow 43	3.7	4.6	1.1	8.8	•	1.7	6.6	•	•	6.5	6.8	•	2.3
Cash Flow to Total Debt 44	0.1	•	8.9	0.1	•	1.0	0.4	•	•	0.4	0.3	•	0.1

Selected Financial Factors (in Percentages)

Debt Ratio 45	75.0	•	56.2	96.4	•	82.0	49.6	•	•	45.6	53.5	•	79.3
Return on Total Assets 46	5.6	•	469.9	5.4	•	38.0	13.2	•	•	15.5	8.3	•	4.5
Return on Equity Before Income Taxes 47	17.6	•	1071.9	35.6	•	204.3	24.1	•	•	25.8	15.5	•	16.6
Return on Equity After Income Taxes 48	12.3	•	1071.9	30.7	•	134.9	21.0	•	•	21.4	11.6	•	10.9
Profit Margin (Before Income Tax) 49	7.7	8.2	36.2	0.8	•	14.5	7.1	•	•	9.3	6.1	•	8.8
Profit Margin (After Income Tax) 50	5.4	6.6	36.2	0.7	•	9.6	6.2	•	•	7.7	4.6	•	5.8

Table I

Corporations with and without Net Income

PHARMACEUTICAL AND MEDICINE

MONEY AMOUNTS AND SIZE OF ASSETS IN THOUSANDS OF DOLLARS

Item Description for Accounting Period 7/12 Through 6/13	Total	Zero Assets	Under 500	500 to 1,000	1,000 to 5,000	5,000 to 10,000	10,000 to 25,000	25,000 to 50,000	50,000 to 100,000	100,000 to 250,000	250,000 to 500,000	500,000 to 2,500,000	2,500,000 and over
Number of Enterprises 1	1640	356	607	3	228	73	121	73	48	50	22	28	32

Revenues ($ in Thousands)

	Total	Zero Assets	Under 500	500 to 1,000	1,000 to 5,000	5,000 to 10,000	10,000 to 25,000	25,000 to 50,000	50,000 to 100,000	100,000 to 250,000	250,000 to 500,000	500,000 to 2,500,000	2,500,000 and over
Net Sales 2	356863413	3918447	144825	0	1311150	786047	2400831	2533129	2929090	4824282	5011508	15317193	317686912
Interest 3	4556930	9645	19	3	249	1263	2271	3425	5755	17844	16235	56674	4443546
Rents 4	159962	0	0	0	0	0	738	1070	2296	997	2383	1853	150625
Royalties 5	29785321	383464	2304	0	0	0	69480	18613	89064	109021	89551	681123	28342700
Other Portfolio Income 6	13810626	49182	924	0	7977	872	8437	1281	38000	72375	19000	332799	13279779
Other Receipts 7	23292365	587089	8252	0	9206	4734	14393	57841	118184	220577	28921	1842161	20401006
Total Receipts 8	428468617	4947827	156324	3	1328582	792916	2496150	2615359	3182389	5245096	5167598	18231803	384304568
Average Total Receipts 9	261261	13898	258	1	5827	10862	20629	35827	66300	104902	234891	651136	12009518

Operating Costs/Operating Income (%)

	Total	Zero Assets	Under 500	500 to 1,000	1,000 to 5,000	5,000 to 10,000	10,000 to 25,000	25,000 to 50,000	50,000 to 100,000	100,000 to 250,000	250,000 to 500,000	500,000 to 2,500,000	2,500,000 and over
Cost of Operations 10	53.3	40.4	90.4	•	70.0	57.4	61.5	61.6	59.9	50.9	42.8	40.3	54.0
Salaries and Wages 11	13.9	17.6	10.0	•	5.8	15.0	9.3	10.3	13.2	16.1	12.9	22.3	13.5
Taxes Paid 12	1.5	1.3	2.9	•	1.3	3.0	2.3	2.4	1.9	2.3	2.1	2.1	1.5
Interest Paid 13	5.3	2.5	9.4	•	0.6	2.1	2.8	2.1	1.2	2.0	2.2	2.7	5.7
Depreciation 14	2.4	4.1	0.7	•	1.8	3.0	2.6	3.3	2.2	3.5	2.7	3.1	2.3
Amortization and Depletion 15	2.2	2.5	4.4	•	0.9	1.5	1.2	2.2	2.1	2.1	2.7	1.8	2.3
Pensions and Other Deferred Comp. 16	1.5	0.3	0.1	•	0.1	0.6	0.3	0.5	0.2	1.4	0.3	0.7	1.6
Employee Benefits 17	2.3	3.5	0.4	•	0.4	2.5	1.8	2.0	1.9	2.4	2.0	2.4	2.3
Advertising 18	3.3	2.6	3.1	•	0.2	0.6	1.7	0.6	2.1	2.1	1.6	2.2	3.5
Other Expenses 19	23.8	38.2	52.4	•	11.8	24.2	22.4	19.1	18.3	24.8	20.9	28.5	23.5
Officers' Compensation 20	0.5	1.9	21.4	•	6.6	8.6	3.4	3.1	1.8	2.2	1.8	2.1	0.3
Operating Margin 21	•	•	•	•	0.6	•	•	•	•	•	8.1	•	•
Operating Margin Before Officers' Comp. 22	•	•	•	•	7.1	•	•	•	•	•	9.9	•	•

Selected Average Balance Sheet ($ in Thousands)													
Net Receivables **23**	54592	0	51	0	428	1422	3141	5642	11403	23015	30160	155450	2556010
Inventories **24**	29602	0	25	215	513	2081	2656	6288	9238	15645	39649	87264	1341917
Net Property, Plant and Equipment **25**	43912	0	2	42	239	1672	3510	9040	10560	27929	55926	110447	2016476
Total Assets **26**	714951	0	125	876	1890	8226	14795	34679	70602	162086	307067	1078520	34957526
Notes and Loans Payable **27**	269433	0	578	141	1775	3514	7935	11378	17207	44101	88155	254111	13343162
All Other Liabilities **28**	208766	0	318	504	742	2231	4364	13100	18961	43099	60508	314912	10223465
Net Worth **29**	236752	0	-772	231	-627	2481	2496	10202	34434	74886	158404	509497	11390900

Selected Financial Ratios (Times to 1)													
Current Ratio **30**	0.8	•	0.3	1.7	2.3	1.6	1.8	1.4	2.3	2.5	2.3	1.9	0.8
Quick Ratio **31**	0.4	•	0.2	1.7	1.2	0.9	1.1	0.8	1.5	1.6	1.2	1.1	0.3
Net Sales to Working Capital **32**	•	•	•	•	5.8	5.5	4.9	5.9	2.6	1.9	3.1	2.2	•
Coverage Ratio **33**	3.4	5.6	•	•	4.3	•	•	•	4.3	0.6	6.3	5.1	3.4
Total Asset Turnover **34**	0.3	•	1.9	•	3.0	1.3	1.3	1.0	0.9	0.6	0.7	0.5	0.3
Inventory Turnover **35**	3.9	•	8.8	•	7.9	3.0	4.6	3.4	4.0	3.1	2.5	2.5	4.0
Receivables Turnover **36**	3.8	•	4.6	•	14.3	8.2	6.2	6.0	4.9	4.5	6.4	3.9	3.7
Total Liabilities to Net Worth **37**	2.0	•	•	2.8	•	2.3	4.9	2.4	1.1	1.2	0.9	1.1	2.1
Current Assets to Working Capital **38**	•	•	•	2.4	1.8	2.8	2.3	3.4	1.7	1.7	1.7	2.1	•
Current Liabilities to Working Capital **39**	•	•	•	1.4	0.8	1.8	1.3	2.4	0.7	0.7	0.7	1.1	•
Working Capital to Net Sales **40**	•	•	•	•	0.2	0.2	0.2	0.2	0.4	0.5	0.3	0.4	•
Inventory to Working Capital **41**	•	•	•	•	0.8	1.1	0.7	1.1	0.4	0.3	0.5	0.3	•
Total Receipts to Cash Flow **42**	3.5	2.2	•	•	8.8	579.3	7.1	9.1	5.0	5.0	3.4	2.9	3.5
Cost of Goods to Cash Flow **43**	1.9	0.9	•	•	6.2	332.7	4.4	5.6	3.0	2.6	1.5	1.2	1.9
Cash Flow to Total Debt **44**	0.1	•	•	•	0.3	0.0	0.2	0.2	0.3	0.2	0.4	0.3	0.1

Selected Financial Factors (in Percentages)													
Debt Ratio **45**	66.9	•	717.9	73.7	133.2	69.8	83.1	70.6	51.2	53.8	48.4	52.8	67.4
Return on Total Assets **46**	5.6	•	•	•	7.5	•	•	•	4.3	0.8	10.1	6.9	5.6
Return on Equity Before Income Taxes **47**	12.0	•	27.0	•	•	•	•	•	6.8	•	16.5	11.8	12.2
Return on Equity After Income Taxes **48**	8.0	•	27.5	•	•	•	•	•	3.4	•	10.3	7.8	8.3
Profit Margin (Before Income Tax) **49**	13.1	11.5	•	•	1.9	•	•	•	3.8	•	11.5	11.0	14.0
Profit Margin (After Income Tax) **50**	8.8	6.6	•	•	1.8	•	•	•	1.9	•	7.1	7.2	9.5

Table II		MANUFACTURING
Corporations with Net Income		325410

PHARMACEUTICAL AND MEDICINE

MONEY AMOUNTS AND SIZE OF ASSETS IN THOUSANDS OF DOLLARS

Item Description for Accounting Period 7/12 Through 6/13		Total	Zero Assets	Under 500	500 to 1,000	1,000 to 5,000	5,000 to 10,000	10,000 to 25,000	25,000 to 50,000	50,000 to 100,000	100,000 to 250,000	250,000 to 500,000	500,000 to 2,500,000	2,500,000 and over
Number of Enterprises	1	492	44	3	0	165	42	68	45	•	25	18	21	•

Revenues ($ in Thousands)

Net Sales	2	346522572	3531587	0	0	1237496	612055	1584286	1989156	•	3355031	4794819	12728121	•
Interest	3	4486453	9245	1	0	0	838	682	2898	•	4145	12661	20612	•
Rents	4	158248	0	0	0	0	0	0	1040	•	667	2383	1693	•
Royalties	5	29623233	378286	0	0	0	0	25900	5655	•	87386	89512	677874	•
Other Portfolio Income	6	13741030	39553	123	0	32	777	428	126	•	38046	19000	327116	•
Other Receipts	7	22469533	585468	7708	0	4582	317	11386	31954	•	79155	28887	1288296	•
Total Receipts	8	417001069	4544139	7832	0	1242110	613987	1622682	2030829	•	3564430	4947262	15043712	•
Average Total Receipts	9	847563	103276	2611	•	7528	14619	23863	45130	•	142577	274848	716367	•

Operating Costs/Operating Income (%)

Cost of Operations	10	53.1	41.5	•	•	70.2	53.9	57.2	57.1	•	48.2	43.2	41.2	•
Salaries and Wages	11	13.5	15.9	•	•	4.3	8.6	6.9	8.4	•	10.8	11.5	18.3	•
Taxes Paid	12	1.5	1.1	•	•	0.8	2.1	1.9	2.2	•	1.8	2.0	2.0	•
Interest Paid	13	5.3	2.7	•	•	0.2	0.7	0.4	1.1	•	1.4	1.8	0.9	•
Depreciation	14	2.3	4.3	•	•	0.3	2.0	1.8	2.7	•	3.0	2.7	2.4	•
Amortization and Depletion	15	2.2	2.5	•	•	0.0	0.7	0.3	0.8	•	1.7	2.3	1.5	•
Pensions and Other Deferred Comp.	16	1.5	0.2	•	•	0.1	0.6	0.4	0.6	•	1.0	0.3	0.8	•
Employee Benefits	17	2.3	3.4	•	•	0.2	1.3	1.6	1.5	•	1.7	1.9	2.4	•
Advertising	18	3.4	0.8	•	•	0.2	0.3	0.7	0.7	•	2.2	1.1	2.0	•
Other Expenses	19	23.6	35.9	•	•	6.2	13.7	12.6	16.7	•	16.3	19.6	27.8	•
Officers' Compensation	20	0.4	1.8	•	•	6.1	8.0	3.2	2.3	•	1.6	1.7	2.2	•
Operating Margin	21	•	•	•	•	11.3	8.1	13.1	5.9	•	10.2	11.8	•	•
Operating Margin Before Officers' Comp.	22	•	•	•	•	17.4	16.1	16.2	8.2	•	11.8	13.5	0.7	•

Selected Average Balance Sheet ($ in Thousands)

Net Receivables 23	176155	0	0	•	496	1757	3533	6869	•	26499	35596	136151	•
Inventories 24	94336	0	0	•	471	2600	3198	7773	•	19631	44961	104306	•
Net Property, Plant and Equipment 25	139802	0	46	•	139	1223	3833	9136	•	29391	58192	106676	•
Total Assets 26	2333683	0	386	•	1585	8387	15483	33495	•	166689	316514	1019594	•
Notes and Loans Payable 27	875861	0	0	•	217	2281	2346	10889	•	39326	84636	158826	•
All Other Liabilities 28	681950	0	1665	•	490	1092	3487	12173	•	41059	64689	302851	•
Net Worth 29	775873	0	-1279	•	878	5014	9650	10433	•	86304	167189	557917	•

Selected Financial Ratios (Times to 1)

Current Ratio 30	0.8	•	1.4	•	3.3	3.0	3.3	1.3	•	2.7	2.1	1.9	•
Quick Ratio 31	0.3	•	1.2	•	2.0	1.2	2.1	0.7	•	1.4	1.1	1.1	•
Net Sales to Working Capital 32	•	•	•	•	6.4	3.8	3.4	9.0	•	2.7	3.8	2.6	•
Coverage Ratio 33	3.7	8.1	•	•	54.3	12.9	41.3	8.5	•	13.0	9.6	20.1	•
Total Asset Turnover 34	0.3	•	•	•	4.7	1.7	1.5	1.3	•	0.8	0.8	0.6	•
Inventory Turnover 35	4.0	•	•	•	11.2	3.0	4.2	3.2	•	3.3	2.6	2.4	•
Receivables Turnover 36	3.8	•	•	•	16.1	10.9	6.2	6.5	•	5.1	6.5	4.8	•
Total Liabilities to Net Worth 37	2.0	•	•	•	0.8	0.7	0.6	2.2	•	0.9	0.9	0.8	•
Current Assets to Working Capital 38	•	•	3.3	•	1.4	1.5	1.4	3.9	•	1.6	1.9	2.1	•
Current Liabilities to Working Capital 39	•	•	2.3	•	0.4	0.5	0.4	2.9	•	0.6	0.9	1.1	•
Working Capital to Net Sales 40	•	•	•	•	0.2	0.3	0.3	0.1	•	0.4	0.3	0.4	•
Inventory to Working Capital 41	•	•	•	•	0.6	0.9	0.4	1.6	•	0.4	0.6	0.4	•
Total Receipts to Cash Flow 42	3.4	2.0	•	•	6.1	6.2	3.9	4.8	•	3.3	3.1	2.5	•
Cost of Goods to Cash Flow 43	1.8	0.8	•	•	4.3	3.3	2.2	2.8	•	1.6	1.4	1.0	•
Cash Flow to Total Debt 44	0.1	•	1.4	•	1.7	0.7	1.0	0.4	•	0.5	0.6	0.5	•

Selected Financial Factors (in Percentages)

Debt Ratio 45	66.8	•	431.7	•	44.6	40.2	37.7	68.9	•	48.2	47.2	45.3	•
Return on Total Assets 46	5.9	•	626.4	•	56.4	15.9	23.9	12.0	•	14.8	14.4	10.5	•
Return on Equity Before Income Taxes 47	13.0	•	•	•	100.0	24.5	37.5	34.0	•	26.4	24.4	18.2	•
Return on Equity After Income Taxes 48	8.9	•	•	•	99.4	20.4	34.1	28.3	•	20.4	17.1	13.3	•
Profit Margin (Before Income Tax) 49	14.3	18.8	•	•	11.7	8.4	15.5	8.0	•	17.0	15.3	16.8	•
Profit Margin (After Income Tax) 50	9.8	13.3	•	•	11.6	7.0	14.1	6.7	•	13.1	10.8	12.3	•

Table I

Corporations with and without Net Income

PAINT, COATING, AND ADHESIVE

MONEY AMOUNTS AND SIZE OF ASSETS IN THOUSANDS OF DOLLARS

Item Description for Accounting Period 7/12 Through 6/13	Total	Zero Assets	Under 500	500 to 1,000	1,000 to 5,000	5,000 to 10,000	10,000 to 25,000	25,000 to 50,000	50,000 to 100,000	100,000 to 250,000	250,000 to 500,000	500,000 to 2,500,000	2,500,000 and over
Number of Enterprises 1	1880	9	764	244	599	106	83	31	13	18	3	5	7

Revenues ($ in Thousands)

	Total	Zero Assets	Under 500	500 to 1,000	1,000 to 5,000	5,000 to 10,000	10,000 to 25,000	25,000 to 50,000	50,000 to 100,000	100,000 to 250,000	250,000 to 500,000	500,000 to 2,500,000	2,500,000 and over
Net Sales 2	52767533	186806	394481	633644	3971860	1694115	2096889	1762959	1329832	3088360	1384137	3311160	32913289
Interest 3	115168	305	0	16	26	216	668	1447	756	4141	5954	21336	80302
Rents 4	21465	426	0	0	0	1681	786	442	104	4019	24	1600	12383
Royalties 5	435628	2490	0	0	0	0	0	941	2461	648	3378	52685	373025
Other Portfolio Income 6	463485	2538	0	0	862	6911	10148	994	113	73329	15904	102267	250418
Other Receipts 7	426728	1206	0	1	3348	985	12678	19435	8916	20637	64888	40857	253779
Total Receipts 8	54230007	193771	394481	633661	3976096	1703908	2121169	1786218	1342182	3191134	1474285	3529905	33883196
Average Total Receipts 9	28846	21530	516	2597	6638	16075	25556	57620	103245	177285	491428	705981	4840457

Operating Costs/Operating Income (%)

	Total	Zero Assets	Under 500	500 to 1,000	1,000 to 5,000	5,000 to 10,000	10,000 to 25,000	25,000 to 50,000	50,000 to 100,000	100,000 to 250,000	250,000 to 500,000	500,000 to 2,500,000	2,500,000 and over
Cost of Operations 10	64.1	67.6	57.3	57.9	64.1	69.7	65.6	67.0	64.4	64.8	57.7	69.6	63.3
Salaries and Wages 11	10.1	1.3	13.4	7.0	6.1	7.6	9.6	10.7	8.8	10.5	14.6	8.7	10.7
Taxes Paid 12	1.6	3.3	2.4	4.5	1.6	3.1	1.5	1.6	4.0	1.9	2.0	1.5	1.3
Interest Paid 13	2.5	0.1	•	1.1	0.2	0.6	1.4	0.6	0.6	2.7	1.7	2.6	3.2
Depreciation 14	1.9	1.3	2.7	1.0	0.5	1.0	1.3	2.2	2.0	1.8	2.2	2.4	2.1
Amortization and Depletion 15	1.3	1.5	•	0.0	0.2	0.2	0.4	0.1	0.2	1.3	2.0	1.6	1.6
Pensions and Other Deferred Comp. 16	1.0	0.4	•	0.0	1.4	0.3	0.7	0.6	0.6	1.1	0.6	1.9	1.0
Employee Benefits 17	1.6	1.6	1.6	3.4	0.6	1.2	1.5	1.0	1.5	1.9	2.1	2.2	1.6
Advertising 18	1.6	0.8	2.0	0.1	1.2	0.2	0.9	0.6	0.8	1.0	1.0	0.3	2.1
Other Expenses 19	12.0	16.6	29.8	9.1	10.2	11.6	9.8	10.1	9.8	10.2	21.7	10.2	12.3
Officers' Compensation 20	1.7	3.9	1.8	3.8	8.6	3.3	3.3	1.3	1.8	1.1	0.4	0.8	0.9
Operating Margin 21	0.8	1.5	•	12.2	5.5	1.2	4.1	4.3	5.5	1.8	•	•	•
Operating Margin Before Officers' Comp. 22	2.5	5.4	•	15.9	14.1	4.5	7.4	5.6	7.2	2.9	•	•	0.9

Selected Average Balance Sheet ($ in Thousands)

Net Receivables 23	3535	0	42	331	553	1459	3610	7297	14501	27275	76296	70242	608838
Inventories 24	2602	0	2	272	587	1341	3803	7231	11624	18817	78976	57856	396335
Net Property, Plant and Equipment 25	3739	0	55	215	171	1523	2213	8035	17885	35134	55394	112929	663349
Total Assets 26	26475	0	126	827	2226	6777	15230	35507	73580	176854	380949	923230	5022970
Notes and Loans Payable 27	11334	0	382	385	253	2629	5183	7318	7264	63364	92594	312454	2394220
All Other Liabilities 28	11574	0	23	169	761	1420	3406	9014	25562	36635	130623	187363	2601679
Net Worth 29	3567	0	-279	272	1212	2728	6641	19176	40754	76855	157732	423413	27071

Selected Financial Ratios (Times to 1)

Current Ratio 30	1.0	•	0.7	1.8	2.2	1.7	2.2	1.9	1.8	1.8	1.5	2.0	0.8
Quick Ratio 31	0.5	•	0.7	1.3	1.3	0.8	1.2	1.1	0.9	1.0	0.9	0.9	0.3
Net Sales to Working Capital 32	•	•	•	9.8	6.9	10.1	4.7	6.1	6.0	5.6	10.6	6.1	•
Coverage Ratio 33	2.6	38.9	•	12.6	30.2	4.0	4.8	11.3	11.6	2.9	1.6	3.5	2.1
Total Asset Turnover 34	1.1	•	4.1	3.1	3.0	2.4	1.7	1.6	1.4	1.0	1.2	0.7	0.9
Inventory Turnover 35	6.9	•	127.6	5.5	7.2	8.3	4.4	5.3	5.7	5.9	3.4	8.0	7.5
Receivables Turnover 36	7.8	•	13.2	5.2	13.0	11.2	7.0	7.8	6.8	7.1	4.6	9.1	7.6
Total Liabilities to Net Worth 37	6.4	•	•	2.0	0.8	1.5	1.3	0.9	0.8	1.3	1.4	1.2	184.5
Current Assets to Working Capital 38	•	•	•	2.3	1.8	2.5	1.8	2.1	2.2	2.3	3.2	2.0	•
Current Liabilities to Working Capital 39	•	•	•	1.3	0.8	1.5	0.8	1.1	1.2	1.3	2.2	1.0	•
Working Capital to Net Sales 40	•	•	•	0.1	0.1	0.1	0.2	0.2	0.2	0.2	0.1	0.2	•
Inventory to Working Capital 41	•	•	•	0.6	0.7	1.0	0.7	0.8	0.7	0.7	1.2	0.6	•
Total Receipts to Cash Flow 42	8.0	5.4	7.4	6.5	7.4	11.4	7.5	7.4	6.8	8.2	5.4	8.2	8.3
Cost of Goods to Cash Flow 43	5.1	3.7	4.3	3.8	4.7	8.0	4.9	5.0	4.4	5.3	3.1	5.7	5.3
Cash Flow to Total Debt 44	0.2	•	0.2	0.7	0.9	0.3	0.4	0.5	0.5	0.2	0.4	0.2	0.1

Selected Financial Factors (in Percentages)

Debt Ratio 45	86.5	•	322.1	67.1	45.6	59.7	56.4	46.0	44.6	56.5	58.6	54.1	99.5
Return on Total Assets 46	6.9	•	•	41.6	17.1	5.6	10.9	10.9	9.9	7.6	3.3	6.5	6.3
Return on Equity Before Income Taxes 47	31.7	•	20.3	116.1	30.4	10.5	19.8	18.4	16.3	11.5	2.9	10.1	600.9
Return on Equity After Income Taxes 48	20.4	•	20.3	115.6	30.3	5.7	16.2	14.7	14.1	8.8	•	6.0	314.9
Profit Margin (Before Income Tax) 49	4.0	5.2	•	12.2	5.6	1.8	5.2	6.2	6.5	5.2	1.0	6.4	3.5
Profit Margin (After Income Tax) 50	2.6	3.5	•	12.1	5.5	1.0	4.3	5.0	5.6	4.0	•	3.8	1.8

Table II

Corporations with Net Income

PAINT, COATING, AND ADHESIVE

MONEY AMOUNTS AND SIZE OF ASSETS IN THOUSANDS OF DOLLARS

Item Description for Accounting Period 7/12 Through 6/13	Total	Zero Assets	Under 500	500 to 1,000	1,000 to 5,000	5,000 to 10,000	10,000 to 25,000	25,000 to 50,000	50,000 to 100,000	100,000 to 250,000	250,000 to 500,000	500,000 to 2,500,000	2,500,000 and over
Number of Enterprises 1	1048	9	0	244	599	62	67	•	13	18	0	•	4

Revenues ($ in Thousands)

	Total	Zero Assets	Under 500	500 to 1,000	1,000 to 5,000	5,000 to 10,000	10,000 to 25,000	25,000 to 50,000	50,000 to 100,000	100,000 to 250,000	250,000 to 500,000	500,000 to 2,500,000	2,500,000 and over
Net Sales 2	37315732	186806	0	633644	3971860	1084430	1615111	•	1329832	3757887	0	•	20520601
Interest 3	67287	305	0	16	26	214	668	•	756	3855	0	•	48039
Rents 4	9176	426	0	0	0	1681	786	•	104	714	0	•	3423
Royalties 5	363795	2490	0	0	0	0	0	•	2461	539	0	•	329193
Other Portfolio Income 6	437142	2538	0	0	862	6911	9931	•	113	83713	0	•	230767
Other Receipts 7	211544	1206	0	1	3348	981	12592	•	8916	32524	0	•	105354
Total Receipts 8	38404676	193771	0	633661	3976096	1094217	1639088	•	1342182	3879232	0	•	21237377
Average Total Receipts 9	36646	21530	•	2597	6638	17649	24464	•	103245	215513	•	•	5309344

Operating Costs/Operating Income (%)

	Total	Zero Assets	Under 500	500 to 1,000	1,000 to 5,000	5,000 to 10,000	10,000 to 25,000	25,000 to 50,000	50,000 to 100,000	100,000 to 250,000	250,000 to 500,000	500,000 to 2,500,000	2,500,000 and over
Cost of Operations 10	62.2	67.6	•	57.9	64.1	67.5	63.8	•	64.4	62.9	•	•	60.4
Salaries and Wages 11	10.6	1.3	•	7.0	6.1	9.4	9.5	•	8.8	10.0	•	•	12.1
Taxes Paid 12	1.8	3.3	•	4.5	1.6	1.2	1.6	•	4.0	1.7	•	•	1.6
Interest Paid 13	1.6	0.1	•	1.1	0.2	0.4	0.7	•	0.6	2.5	•	•	1.9
Depreciation 14	1.7	1.3	•	1.0	0.5	1.2	1.3	•	2.0	1.7	•	•	1.9
Amortization and Depletion 15	0.6	1.5	•	0.0	0.2	0.2	0.5	•	0.2	1.3	•	•	0.6
Pensions and Other Deferred Comp. 16	0.7	0.4	•	0.0	1.4	0.5	0.6	•	0.6	0.7	•	•	0.6
Employee Benefits 17	1.7	1.6	•	3.4	0.6	0.6	1.2	•	1.5	1.9	•	•	2.0
Advertising 18	1.3	0.8	•	0.1	1.2	0.2	1.0	•	0.8	0.9	•	•	1.6
Other Expenses 19	11.6	16.6	•	9.1	10.2	10.1	9.6	•	9.8	11.1	•	•	12.5
Officers' Compensation 20	2.2	3.9	•	3.8	8.6	1.4	3.9	•	1.8	1.0	•	•	1.3
Operating Margin 21	4.0	1.5	•	12.2	5.5	7.1	6.2	•	5.5	4.1	•	•	3.3
Operating Margin Before Officers' Comp. 22	6.2	5.4	•	15.9	14.1	8.5	10.1	•	7.2	5.1	•	•	4.6

Selected Average Balance Sheet ($ in Thousands)

Net Receivables **23**	4371	0	•	331	553	1364	3696	•	14501	32403	•	•	641132
Inventories **24**	3259	0	•	185	587	1791	3163	•	12172	25504	•	•	422430
Net Property, Plant and Equipment **25**	4312	0	•	215	171	1377	1861	•	17885	37322	•	•	641496
Total Assets **26**	33015	0	•	827	2226	7583	14458	•	73580	201908	•	•	5578114
Notes and Loans Payable **27**	11027	0	•	385	253	1215	4237	•	7264	73597	•	•	2018078
All Other Liabilities **28**	16026	0	•	169	761	1822	3360	•	25562	48000	•	•	3452040
Net Worth **29**	5962	0	•	272	1212	4546	6860	•	40754	80310	•	•	107997

Selected Financial Ratios (Times to 1)

Current Ratio **30**	0.9	•	•	1.8	2.2	2.8	2.2	•	1.8	1.5	•	•	0.7
Quick Ratio **31**	0.4	•	•	1.3	1.3	1.2	1.3	•	0.9	0.9	•	•	0.2
Net Sales to Working Capital **32**	•	•	•	9.8	6.9	5.5	4.5	•	6.0	8.3	•	•	•
Coverage Ratio **33**	5.8	38.9	•	12.6	30.2	20.1	11.3	•	11.6	4.0	•	•	5.1
Total Asset Turnover **34**	1.1	•	•	3.1	3.0	2.3	1.7	•	1.4	1.0	•	•	0.9
Inventory Turnover **35**	6.8	•	•	8.1	7.2	6.6	4.9	•	5.4	5.1	•	•	7.3
Receivables Turnover **36**	7.9	•	•	5.8	13.0	17.3	7.0	•	•	•	•	•	•
Total Liabilities to Net Worth **37**	4.5	•	•	2.0	0.8	0.7	1.1	•	0.8	1.5	•	•	50.7
Current Assets to Working Capital **38**	•	•	•	2.3	1.8	1.5	1.8	•	2.2	2.9	•	•	•
Current Liabilities to Working Capital **39**	•	•	•	1.3	0.8	0.5	0.8	•	1.2	1.9	•	•	•
Working Capital to Net Sales **40**	•	•	•	0.1	0.1	0.2	0.2	•	0.2	0.1	•	•	•
Inventory to Working Capital **41**	•	•	•	0.6	0.7	0.7	0.6	•	0.7	1.0	•	•	•
Total Receipts to Cash Flow **42**	6.4	5.4	•	6.5	7.4	6.3	6.4	•	6.8	6.2	•	•	6.3
Cost of Goods to Cash Flow **43**	4.0	3.7	•	3.8	4.7	4.3	4.1	•	4.4	3.9	•	•	3.8
Cash Flow to Total Debt **44**	0.2	•	•	0.7	0.9	0.9	0.5	•	0.5	0.3	•	•	0.1

Selected Financial Factors (in Percentages)

Debt Ratio **45**	81.9	•	•	67.1	45.6	40.1	52.5	•	44.6	60.2	•	•	98.1
Return on Total Assets **46**	9.9	•	•	41.6	17.1	19.4	14.1	•	9.9	10.4	•	•	8.8
Return on Equity Before Income Taxes **47**	45.3	•	•	116.1	30.4	30.8	27.1	•	16.3	19.6	•	•	366.3
Return on Equity After Income Taxes **48**	33.2	•	•	115.6	30.3	25.9	22.7	•	14.1	15.6	•	•	240.8
Profit Margin (Before Income Tax) **49**	7.6	5.2	•	12.2	5.6	8.0	7.7	•	6.5	7.5	•	•	7.7
Profit Margin (After Income Tax) **50**	5.6	3.5	•	12.1	5.5	6.7	6.5	•	5.6	6.0	•	•	5.1

Table I

Corporations with and without Net Income

SOAP, CLEANING COMPOUND, AND TOILET PREPARATION

MONEY AMOUNTS AND SIZE OF ASSETS IN THOUSANDS OF DOLLARS

Item Description for Accounting Period 7/12 Through 6/13	Total	Zero Assets	Under 500	500 to 1,000	1,000 to 5,000	5,000 to 10,000	10,000 to 25,000	25,000 to 50,000	50,000 to 100,000	100,000 to 250,000	250,000 to 500,000	500,000 to 2,500,000	2,500,000 and over
Number of Enterprises 1	2282	748	808	260	267	61	71	15	18	12	7	6	10

Revenues ($ in Thousands)													
Net Sales 2	93722542	350422	407712	379896	2348632	986582	2396277	1052015	2069125	2356023	3626116	7112484	70637259
Interest 3	389875	1823	51	55	4	17	169	893	626	2262	1247	6367	376362
Rents 4	25247	0	0	0	2456	0	326	74	1	1322	127	988	19953
Royalties 5	4029965	0	0	0	8535	0	73	229	719	0	12705	103036	3904667
Other Portfolio Income 6	3381326	20977	0	0	5548	193	306	962	1390	9800	62331	231849	3047970
Other Receipts 7	1962503	4181	86	-77075	8557	140	10796	1984	32294	65405	1959	102226	1811949
Total Receipts 8	103511458	377403	407849	302876	2373732	986932	2407947	1056157	2104155	2434812	3704485	7556950	79798160
Average Total Receipts 9	45360	505	505	1165	8890	16179	33915	70410	116898	202901	529212	1259492	7979816

Operating Costs/Operating Income (%)													
Cost of Operations 10	45.5	50.7	69.1	61.9	63.8	76.6	65.5	66.9	70.6	71.6	55.7	49.8	40.6
Salaries and Wages 11	9.9	9.1	5.0	12.4	13.5	3.9	10.6	12.8	7.5	7.0	9.0	9.1	10.1
Taxes Paid 12	1.8	1.9	3.6	3.1	2.0	1.1	1.4	1.5	1.2	1.3	1.5	1.8	1.9
Interest Paid 13	3.3	2.1	•	1.1	0.3	1.5	0.6	0.8	0.8	1.4	1.2	1.0	4.1
Depreciation 14	2.5	1.2	0.2	0.7	0.8	0.6	1.4	1.9	1.8	3.1	1.9	2.3	2.7
Amortization and Depletion 15	1.5	0.9	•	0.1	0.0	0.2	0.2	0.2	1.3	1.3	1.2	0.4	1.8
Pensions and Other Deferred Comp. 16	1.6	0.1	•	1.1	0.8	0.1	0.2	0.3	0.1	0.5	0.7	0.8	1.9
Employee Benefits 17	1.7	1.0	•	3.1	1.3	1.5	1.2	1.0	1.3	0.7	1.6	1.6	1.8
Advertising 18	8.1	6.2	0.1	0.6	0.2	0.7	1.3	0.7	1.0	1.4	6.4	4.0	9.8
Other Expenses 19	19.3	26.3	11.6	9.4	12.1	7.1	9.6	8.7	11.2	11.9	15.3	21.9	20.7
Officers' Compensation 20	1.1	6.8	10.5	6.7	5.0	0.9	1.8	2.6	2.6	0.5	0.9	1.9	0.7
Operating Margin 21	3.7	•	•	•	0.2	5.9	6.1	2.6	0.4	•	4.7	5.6	3.8
Operating Margin Before Officers' Comp. 22	4.7	0.6	10.5	6.5	5.2	6.8	7.8	5.3	3.1	•	5.6	7.5	4.5

Selected Average Balance Sheet ($ in Thousands)

Net Receivables 23	18058	0	56	177	823	1365	4683	9257	16518	29082	64384	134877	3843681
Inventories 24	3112	0	36	126	836	1670	4273	9314	11695	27406	55185	103602	472404
Net Property, Plant and Equipment 25	7623	0	13	77	343	1091	3285	11056	12324	35003	73248	179316	1457740
Total Assets 26	128575	0	166	812	2532	6453	16002	35114	72947	179693	364964	1294318	27654019
Notes and Loans Payable 27	33987	0	0	398	841	3090	3520	9051	28634	61343	105809	281360	7297484
All Other Liabilities 28	34033	0	11	111	460	2028	5264	11419	20693	47665	104226	369612	7294345
Net Worth 29	60555	0	155	304	1231	1336	7219	14644	23620	70685	154929	643345	13062190

Selected Financial Ratios (Times to 1)

Current Ratio 30	0.9	•	13.9	1.6	3.2	0.8	2.1	1.9	1.3	1.8	1.5	1.8	0.8
Quick Ratio 31	0.6	•	9.9	1.0	1.4	0.5	1.2	1.0	0.7	1.0	0.8	1.0	0.6
Net Sales to Working Capital 32	•	•	3.6	7.4	6.0	•	5.7	7.4	13.7	5.7	10.3	6.1	•
Coverage Ratio 33	6.3	1.7	•	•	4.7	5.0	12.2	4.7	3.7	2.9	7.3	14.7	6.2
Total Asset Turnover 34	0.3	•	3.0	1.8	3.5	2.5	2.1	2.0	1.6	1.1	1.4	0.9	0.3
Inventory Turnover 35	6.0	•	9.6	7.2	6.7	7.4	5.2	5.0	6.9	5.1	5.2	5.7	6.1
Receivables Turnover 36	2.3	•	9.4	8.5	10.9	9.9	8.0	6.3	7.2	6.8	8.5	9.9	1.9
Total Liabilities to Net Worth 37	1.1	•	0.1	1.7	1.1	3.8	1.2	1.4	2.1	1.5	1.4	1.0	1.1
Current Assets to Working Capital 38	•	•	1.1	2.6	1.4	•	1.9	2.1	4.2	2.2	3.1	2.3	•
Current Liabilities to Working Capital 39	•	•	0.1	1.6	0.4	•	0.9	1.1	3.2	1.2	2.1	1.3	•
Working Capital to Net Sales 40	•	•	0.3	0.1	0.2	•	0.2	0.1	0.1	0.2	0.1	0.2	•
Inventory to Working Capital 41	•	•	0.2	0.8	0.5	•	0.8	0.9	1.6	0.8	1.2	0.7	•
Total Receipts to Cash Flow 42	3.3	4.7	10.0	•	9.9	8.2	7.0	10.4	9.8	8.1	5.0	3.3	2.9
Cost of Goods to Cash Flow 43	1.5	2.4	6.9	•	6.3	6.3	4.6	6.9	6.9	5.8	2.8	1.6	1.2
Cash Flow to Total Debt 44	0.2	•	4.6	•	0.7	0.4	0.5	0.3	0.2	0.2	0.5	0.6	0.2

Selected Financial Factors (in Percentages)

Debt Ratio 45	52.9	•	6.6	62.6	51.4	79.3	54.9	58.3	67.6	60.7	57.5	50.3	52.8
Return on Total Assets 46	6.6	•	•	•	5.2	18.6	15.1	7.8	4.6	4.3	12.5	13.0	6.4
Return on Equity Before Income Taxes 47	11.8	•	•	•	8.4	72.2	30.8	14.8	10.3	7.2	25.5	24.4	11.3
Return on Equity After Income Taxes 48	7.7	•	•	•	6.5	71.5	29.7	13.5	7.3	4.2	19.8	15.9	7.4
Profit Margin (Before Income Tax) 49	17.4	1.5	•	•	1.2	6.0	6.6	3.1	2.1	2.6	7.6	13.2	21.0
Profit Margin (After Income Tax) 50	11.4	1.0	•	•	0.9	5.9	6.4	2.8	1.5	1.5	5.9	8.7	13.6

91

Table II
Corporations with Net Income

SOAP, CLEANING COMPOUND, AND TOILET PREPARATION

MONEY AMOUNTS AND SIZE OF ASSETS IN THOUSANDS OF DOLLARS

Item Description for Accounting Period 7/12 Through 6/13	Total	Zero Assets	Under 500	500 to 1,000	1,000 to 5,000	5,000 to 10,000	10,000 to 25,000	25,000 to 50,000	50,000 to 100,000	100,000 to 250,000	250,000 to 500,000	500,000 to 2,500,000	2,500,000 and over
Number of Enterprises 1	574	•	94	112	173	48	60	•	14	7	7	•	•

Revenues ($ in Thousands)

	Total	Zero Assets	Under 500	500 to 1,000	1,000 to 5,000	5,000 to 10,000	10,000 to 25,000	25,000 to 50,000	50,000 to 100,000	100,000 to 250,000	250,000 to 500,000	500,000 to 2,500,000	2,500,000 and over
Net Sales 2	85709615	•	79948	205521	1467775	683224	1954713	•	1824571	1227604	3626116	•	•
Interest 3	387182	•	51	55	4	0	168	•	414	1972	1247	•	•
Rents 4	21092	•	0	0	1248	0	326	•	1	0	127	•	•
Royalties 5	3871400	•	0	0	8535	0	73	•	479	0	12705	•	•
Other Portfolio Income 6	3378148	•	0	0	3993	193	76	•	1390	9590	62331	•	•
Other Receipts 7	2011115	•	0	257	5097	141	10706	•	29995	56881	1959	•	•
Total Receipts 8	95378552	•	79999	205833	1486652	683558	1966062	•	1856850	1296047	3704485	•	•
Average Total Receipts 9	166165	•	851	1838	8593	14241	32768	•	132632	185150	529212	•	•

Operating Costs/Operating Income (%)

	Total	Zero Assets	Under 500	500 to 1,000	1,000 to 5,000	5,000 to 10,000	10,000 to 25,000	25,000 to 50,000	50,000 to 100,000	100,000 to 250,000	250,000 to 500,000	500,000 to 2,500,000	2,500,000 and over
Cost of Operations 10	44.0	•	80.1	61.5	68.9	79.3	62.8	•	73.1	70.8	55.7	•	•
Salaries and Wages 11	9.8	•	5.8	7.5	6.8	2.9	10.5	•	5.8	5.9	9.0	•	•
Taxes Paid 12	1.7	•	1.1	2.8	1.9	1.0	1.4	•	1.0	1.2	1.5	•	•
Interest Paid 13	3.3	•	•	0.4	0.3	0.9	0.6	•	0.7	1.0	1.2	•	•
Depreciation 14	2.4	•	0.3	0.5	0.6	0.2	1.3	•	1.8	1.5	1.9	•	•
Amortization and Depletion 15	1.4	•	•	0.2	0.0	•	0.1	•	0.6	1.4	1.2	•	•
Pensions and Other Deferred Comp. 16	1.7	•	•	1.8	0.9	0.1	0.3	•	0.1	0.7	0.7	•	•
Employee Benefits 17	1.7	•	•	3.9	1.9	1.4	1.3	•	1.1	0.9	1.6	•	•
Advertising 18	8.5	•	0.0	0.6	0.2	0.7	1.6	•	1.2	1.4	6.4	•	•
Other Expenses 19	19.7	•	9.9	9.1	9.6	2.6	10.0	•	9.1	12.0	15.3	•	•
Officers' Compensation 20	1.0	•	2.6	8.6	5.3	0.7	2.1	•	2.8	0.6	0.9	•	•
Operating Margin 21	4.7	•	0.0	3.1	3.7	10.3	7.9	•	2.7	2.5	4.7	•	•
Operating Margin Before Officers' Comp. 22	5.7	•	2.6	11.7	9.0	11.0	10.0	•	5.5	3.1	5.6	•	•

Selected Average Balance Sheet ($ in Thousands)

Net Receivables 23	70274	•	45	243	762	1137	4713	•	17349	27872	64384	•	•
Inventories 24	10342	•	79	142	1035	1117	4258	•	12381	37243	59187	•	•
Net Property, Plant and Equipment 25	28305	•	10	63	282	1097	2916	•	14311	25130	73248	•	•
Total Assets 26	491611	•	479	907	2635	5912	15936	•	73855	172255	364964	•	•
Notes and Loans Payable 27	125506	•	0	139	637	2235	3039	•	25437	37908	105809	•	•
All Other Liabilities 28	129029	•	17	117	455	972	5158	•	21165	50176	104226	•	•
Net Worth 29	237075	•	462	651	1543	2705	7739	•	27253	84170	154929	•	•

Selected Financial Ratios (Times to 1)

Current Ratio 30	0.9	•	27.6	5.1	4.1	1.0	2.3	•	1.4	2.4	1.5	•	•
Quick Ratio 31	0.6	•	22.3	3.3	1.8	0.6	1.3	•	0.8	1.2	0.8	•	•
Net Sales to Working Capital 32	•	•	1.9	3.0	5.4	141.4	5.0	•	11.6	3.4	10.3	•	•
Coverage Ratio 33	7.0	•	•	9.0	20.6	12.3	14.6	•	7.6	9.0	7.3	•	•
Total Asset Turnover 34	0.3	•	1.8	2.0	3.2	2.4	2.0	•	1.8	1.0	1.4	•	•
Inventory Turnover 35	6.4	•	8.6	8.0	5.6	10.1	4.8	•	7.7	3.3	4.9	•	•
Receivables Turnover 36	2.2	•	18.7	7.6	•	11.1	7.8	•	8.2	4.3	16.1	•	•
Total Liabilities to Net Worth 37	1.1	•	0.0	0.4	0.7	1.2	1.1	•	1.7	1.0	1.4	•	•
Current Assets to Working Capital 38	•	•	1.0	1.2	1.3	22.5	1.8	•	3.3	1.7	3.1	•	•
Current Liabilities to Working Capital 39	•	•	0.0	0.2	0.3	21.5	0.8	•	2.3	0.7	2.1	•	•
Working Capital to Net Sales 40	•	•	0.5	0.3	0.2	0.0	0.2	•	0.1	0.3	0.1	•	•
Inventory to Working Capital 41	•	•	0.2	0.2	0.7	8.4	0.7	•	1.3	0.6	1.2	•	•
Total Receipts to Cash Flow 42	3.0	•	18.0	10.3	9.4	8.0	6.1	•	8.4	5.4	5.0	•	•
Cost of Goods to Cash Flow 43	1.3	•	14.5	6.3	6.5	6.4	3.8	•	6.2	3.9	2.8	•	•
Cash Flow to Total Debt 44	0.2	•	2.8	0.7	0.8	0.6	0.7	•	0.3	0.4	0.5	•	•

Selected Financial Factors (in Percentages)

Debt Ratio 45	51.8	•	3.5	28.2	41.5	54.2	51.4	•	63.1	51.1	57.5	•	•
Return on Total Assets 46	6.9	•	0.2	7.4	17.0	27.2	18.7	•	9.1	9.4	12.5	•	•
Return on Equity Before Income Taxes 47	12.3	•	0.2	9.2	27.6	54.6	35.8	•	21.4	17.0	25.5	•	•
Return on Equity After Income Taxes 48	8.2	•	0.2	7.5	25.3	54.2	34.7	•	18.1	12.7	19.8	•	•
Profit Margin (Before Income Tax) 49	19.6	•	0.1	3.2	5.0	10.4	8.5	•	4.5	8.2	7.6	•	•
Profit Margin (After Income Tax) 50	13.0	•	0.1	2.7	4.6	10.3	8.2	•	3.8	6.1	5.9	•	•

Table I

Corporations with and without Net Income

CHEMICAL PRODUCT AND PREPARATION

MONEY AMOUNTS AND SIZE OF ASSETS IN THOUSANDS OF DOLLARS

Item Description for Accounting Period 7/12 Through 6/13	Total	Zero Assets	Under 500	500 to 1,000	1,000 to 5,000	5,000 to 10,000	10,000 to 25,000	25,000 to 50,000	50,000 to 100,000	100,000 to 250,000	250,000 to 500,000	500,000 to 2,500,000	2,500,000 and over
Number of Enterprises 1	2022	46	999	221	385	87	107	68	43	28	14	18	6
Revenues ($ in Thousands)													
Net Sales 2	76798411	1056992	1023120	174961	1600885	1301615	2943949	4078564	4255671	6222689	4219685	18257919	31662361
Interest 3	219803	377	6	25	383	477	217	866	2461	6821	5799	42537	159834
Rents 4	19832	0	691	1280	1842	0	1112	2712	666	403	3665	1708	5753
Royalties 5	631602	1254	0	0	0	0	866	295	2166	19415	5068	83968	518570
Other Portfolio Income 6	590966	2262	6846	3627	8806	2324	973	9871	3110	11620	18709	170708	352110
Other Receipts 7	1574441	6162	16459	3	14604	20619	35874	64171	78364	149492	29069	325159	834466
Total Receipts 8	79835055	1067047	1047122	179896	1626520	1325035	2982991	4156479	4342438	6410440	4281995	18881999	33533094
Average Total Receipts 9	39483	23197	1048	814	4225	15230	27878	61125	100987	228944	305857	1049000	5588849
Operating Costs/Operating Income (%)													
Cost of Operations 10	68.1	83.0	54.5	66.9	57.9	63.3	71.6	67.0	77.7	77.2	68.7	72.0	63.1
Salaries and Wages 11	6.2	3.3	10.1	8.0	6.3	6.4	7.7	6.7	5.0	6.8	5.2	5.7	6.5
Taxes Paid 12	1.2	0.7	3.1	1.9	2.1	1.7	1.5	1.5	1.0	1.2	1.1	1.3	1.1
Interest Paid 13	1.9	1.3	0.2	1.2	0.4	2.0	0.6	0.7	0.5	0.7	1.8	3.1	2.0
Depreciation 14	2.4	2.4	0.1	1.3	2.2	1.8	2.3	2.2	2.2	1.4	2.8	2.7	2.6
Amortization and Depletion 15	0.9	0.1	0.0	0.0	0.1	0.3	1.6	0.2	0.4	0.4	1.7	0.6	1.2
Pensions and Other Deferred Comp. 16	0.6	0.1	0.3	1.6	3.0	0.6	0.2	0.3	0.4	0.6	0.3	0.7	0.5
Employee Benefits 17	1.0	1.0	2.1	1.7	1.6	1.6	1.3	0.4	0.9	0.9	1.1	1.2	0.8
Advertising 18	0.5	0.1	0.1	0.6	0.4	1.9	0.4	0.5	0.6	0.5	0.5	1.1	0.2
Other Expenses 19	10.3	10.1	16.8	25.8	14.7	13.4	8.1	14.0	6.6	7.2	9.0	7.4	12.4
Officers' Compensation 20	1.1	0.7	10.8	9.8	4.5	2.2	2.2	1.9	1.9	1.0	1.3	0.6	0.4
Operating Margin 21	5.9	•	1.8	•	6.7	4.9	2.4	4.5	2.8	2.0	6.5	3.7	9.2
Operating Margin Before Officers' Comp. 22	6.9	•	12.6	•	11.3	7.1	4.6	6.5	4.7	3.0	7.9	4.3	9.7

Selected Average Balance Sheet ($ in Thousands)

Net Receivables 23	5206	0	44	154	562	1809	3702	6362	14603	23012	57390	141957	769302
Inventories 24	5043	0	49	144	306	1235	3687	6253	17021	27470	53780	111863	800547
Net Property, Plant and Equipment 25	7588	0	1	82	525	1781	4393	8142	14337	29013	52228	201766	1358574
Total Assets 26	45458	0	131	797	2603	7523	16451	35206	68382	144228	361272	1189946	8723824
Notes and Loans Payable 27	12071	0	451	179	551	4978	4645	7091	14397	37521	124944	422214	1878954
All Other Liabilities 28	12305	0	389	88	633	2497	3348	9412	16223	29640	82460	396248	2199694
Net Worth 29	21083	0	-709	530	1419	48	8458	18702	37763	77067	153869	371484	4645177

Selected Financial Ratios (Times to 1)

Current Ratio 30	1.6	•	0.3	2.4	2.3	2.2	2.2	1.9	2.2	2.4	1.6	1.4	1.5
Quick Ratio 31	0.8	•	0.2	1.3	1.7	1.2	1.2	1.0	1.2	1.3	0.9	0.6	0.9
Net Sales to Working Capital 32	6.4	•	•	3.2	5.4	5.2	5.1	6.4	4.5	4.8	5.2	8.7	5.9
Coverage Ratio 33	6.5	•	20.5	•	20.0	4.4	6.9	9.8	10.4	9.0	5.4	3.4	9.1
Total Asset Turnover 34	0.8	•	7.8	1.0	1.6	2.0	1.7	1.7	1.4	1.5	0.8	0.9	0.6
Inventory Turnover 35	5.1	•	11.4	3.7	7.9	7.7	5.3	6.4	4.5	6.2	3.8	6.5	4.2
Receivables Turnover 36	6.7	•	28.6	6.9	7.7	7.9	7.3	9.2	6.7	9.6	5.2	7.8	5.5
Total Liabilities to Net Worth 37	1.2	•	•	0.5	0.8	155.7	0.9	0.9	0.8	0.9	1.3	2.2	0.9
Current Assets to Working Capital 38	2.8	•	•	1.7	1.8	1.9	1.8	2.2	1.8	1.7	2.7	3.8	3.0
Current Liabilities to Working Capital 39	1.8	•	•	0.7	0.8	0.9	0.8	1.2	0.8	0.7	1.7	2.8	2.0
Working Capital to Net Sales 40	0.2	•	•	0.3	0.2	0.2	0.2	0.2	0.2	0.2	0.2	0.1	0.2
Inventory to Working Capital 41	0.9	•	•	0.8	0.4	0.5	0.7	0.7	0.7	0.6	0.9	1.1	0.9
Total Receipts to Cash Flow 42	5.7	13.8	5.5	163.7	4.9	6.2	9.8	5.4	10.0	9.2	6.6	8.5	4.1
Cost of Goods to Cash Flow 43	3.9	11.5	3.0	109.4	2.9	3.9	7.0	3.6	7.8	7.1	4.5	6.1	2.6
Cash Flow to Total Debt 44	0.3	•	0.2	0.0	0.7	0.3	0.4	0.7	0.3	0.4	0.2	0.1	0.3

Selected Financial Factors (in Percentages)

Debt Ratio 45	53.6	•	642.2	33.5	45.5	99.4	48.6	46.9	44.8	46.6	57.4	68.8	46.8
Return on Total Assets 46	10.1	•	34.0	•	14.0	17.0	7.4	12.2	7.9	9.0	8.3	9.0	10.8
Return on Equity Before Income Taxes 47	18.5	•	•	•	24.4	2058.8	12.4	20.7	13.0	15.0	15.8	20.4	18.1
Return on Equity After Income Taxes 48	12.7	•	•	•	23.3	1618.0	10.4	18.6	9.5	11.5	12.5	14.1	11.9
Profit Margin (Before Income Tax) 49	10.2	•	4.1	•	8.3	6.6	3.8	6.4	4.9	5.2	8.1	7.5	15.9
Profit Margin (After Income Tax) 50	7.1	•	4.1	•	8.0	5.2	3.2	5.8	3.6	4.0	6.4	5.1	10.4

Table II

Corporations with Net Income

CHEMICAL PRODUCT AND PREPARATION

MONEY AMOUNTS AND SIZE OF ASSETS IN THOUSANDS OF DOLLARS

Item Description for Accounting Period 7/12 Through 6/13	Total	Zero Assets	Under 500	500 to 1,000	1,000 to 5,000	5,000 to 10,000	10,000 to 25,000	25,000 to 50,000	50,000 to 100,000	100,000 to 250,000	250,000 to 500,000	500,000 to 2,500,000	2,500,000 and over
Number of Enterprises **1**	1527	•	807	53	336	71	75	55	•	23	9	15	•

Revenues ($ in Thousands)

Net Sales **2**	69942001	•	972447	42298	1392586	1239907	2392361	3495048	•	5417083	3182286	17923144	•
Interest **3**	210228	•	0	0	346	385	47	679	•	6342	1807	42462	•
Rents **4**	14091	•	691	910	1159	0	1112	0	•	403	1691	1708	•
Royalties **5**	622244	•	0	0	0	0	0	130	•	17948	1045	83188	•
Other Portfolio Income **6**	531368	•	637	0	7351	2324	148	8824	•	9685	9012	148796	•
Other Receipts **7**	1508597	•	16459	0	2456	15066	29942	59082	•	143574	24693	304743	•
Total Receipts **8**	72828529	•	990234	43208	1403898	1257682	2423610	3563763	•	5595035	3220534	18504041	•
Average Total Receipts **9**	47694	•	1227	815	4178	17714	32315	64796	•	243262	357837	1233603	•

Operating Costs/Operating Income (%)

Cost of Operations **10**	67.7	•	53.5	38.3	56.1	62.9	71.1	67.7	•	75.5	66.7	72.4	•
Salaries and Wages **11**	5.9	•	8.7	15.7	4.4	5.0	7.6	6.0	•	7.2	4.3	5.5	•
Taxes Paid **12**	1.2	•	3.2	3.6	2.0	1.5	1.3	1.4	•	1.2	1.1	1.3	•
Interest Paid **13**	1.7	•	0.2	2.4	0.4	0.5	0.4	0.6	•	0.6	1.2	3.0	•
Depreciation **14**	2.2	•	0.2	0.9	1.6	1.3	1.5	1.8	•	1.3	3.2	2.4	•
Amortization and Depletion **15**	0.8	•	•	•	0.1	0.2	0.1	0.1	•	0.4	1.5	0.6	•
Pensions and Other Deferred Comp. **16**	0.5	•	0.3	5.2	3.5	0.6	0.2	0.4	•	0.7	0.3	0.7	•
Employee Benefits **17**	0.9	•	2.2	5.7	1.3	1.6	0.9	0.3	•	0.9	1.2	1.2	•
Advertising **18**	0.5	•	0.1	0.5	0.4	1.9	0.4	0.4	•	0.5	0.4	1.1	•
Other Expenses **19**	9.8	•	12.4	14.1	13.7	11.4	6.4	13.7	•	7.5	7.6	7.2	•
Officers' Compensation **20**	1.0	•	11.4	14.9	4.5	2.1	2.1	1.6	•	1.1	1.3	0.5	•
Operating Margin **21**	7.6	•	7.8	•	12.1	11.1	8.0	6.1	•	3.0	11.4	4.2	•
Operating Margin Before Officers' Comp. **22**	8.6	•	19.2	13.6	16.6	13.2	10.1	7.7	•	4.1	12.7	4.7	•

Selected Average Balance Sheet ($ in Thousands)

Net Receivables 23	6147	•	54	18	568	2080	3758	6808	•	25349	51161	158003	•
Inventories 24	5815	•	51	254	217	1142	4089	4628	•	29812	67340	111192	•
Net Property, Plant and Equipment 25	9097	•	1	101	380	1330	3941	8215	•	26790	68511	227977	•
Total Assets 26	53076	•	139	636	2495	7521	16265	34931	•	146366	363290	1213071	•
Notes and Loans Payable 27	12186	•	32	236	362	1671	3517	5800	•	38561	77441	402851	•
All Other Liabilities 28	14238	•	20	72	409	2062	3074	9902	•	26149	80369	435609	•
Net Worth 29	26652	•	87	329	1724	3787	9675	19230	•	81656	205480	374611	•

Selected Financial Ratios (Times to 1)

Current Ratio 30	1.6	•	2.6	1.4	2.4	2.9	2.4	1.8	•	2.4	1.8	1.4	•
Quick Ratio 31	0.9	•	1.6	0.5	1.8	1.7	1.4	1.0	•	1.4	1.0	0.6	•
Net Sales to Working Capital 32	6.3	•	14.2	16.3	5.3	4.7	5.5	7.3	•	4.7	4.7	9.0	•
Coverage Ratio 33	8.0	•	54.7	1.4	36.6	28.1	25.7	14.7	•	11.3	11.9	3.6	•
Total Asset Turnover 34	0.9	•	8.7	1.3	1.7	2.3	2.0	1.8	•	1.6	1.0	1.0	•
Inventory Turnover 35	5.3	•	12.6	1.2	10.7	9.6	5.5	9.3	•	6.0	3.5	7.8	•
Receivables Turnover 36	6.9	•	28.8	4.8	7.8	11.5	7.6	11.1	•	•	5.8	9.0	•
Total Liabilities to Net Worth 37	1.0	•	0.6	0.9	0.4	1.0	0.7	0.8	•	0.8	0.8	2.2	•
Current Assets to Working Capital 38	2.7	•	1.6	3.4	1.7	1.5	1.7	2.3	•	1.7	2.2	3.8	•
Current Liabilities to Working Capital 39	1.7	•	0.6	2.4	0.7	0.5	0.7	1.3	•	0.7	1.2	2.8	•
Working Capital to Net Sales 40	0.2	•	0.1	0.1	0.2	0.2	0.2	0.1	•	0.2	0.2	0.1	•
Inventory to Working Capital 41	0.8	•	0.6	2.0	0.3	0.4	0.7	0.7	•	0.6	0.8	1.1	•
Total Receipts to Cash Flow 42	5.2	•	5.2	10.1	4.1	5.0	7.1	5.0	•	8.1	5.5	8.4	•
Cost of Goods to Cash Flow 43	3.6	•	2.8	3.9	2.3	3.1	5.0	3.4	•	6.1	3.7	6.0	•
Cash Flow to Total Debt 44	0.3	•	4.5	0.3	1.3	0.9	0.7	0.8	•	0.5	0.4	0.2	•

Selected Financial Factors (in Percentages)

Debt Ratio 45	49.8	•	37.4	48.3	30.9	49.6	40.5	45.0	•	44.2	43.4	69.1	•
Return on Total Assets 46	11.9	•	84.8	4.1	22.1	30.0	19.0	15.7	•	11.4	13.4	10.6	•
Return on Equity Before Income Taxes 47	20.8	•	133.0	2.1	31.0	57.5	30.7	26.5	•	18.6	21.7	24.9	•
Return on Equity After Income Taxes 48	14.8	•	132.7	1.8	30.0	50.7	28.3	24.0	•	14.5	17.9	17.3	•
Profit Margin (Before Income Tax) 49	12.1	•	9.6	0.9	12.9	12.5	9.3	8.0	•	6.4	12.6	7.8	•
Profit Margin (After Income Tax) 50	8.6	•	9.6	0.7	12.5	11.0	8.6	7.3	•	5.0	10.4	5.4	•

Table I

Corporations with and without Net Income

PLASTICS PRODUCT

MONEY AMOUNTS AND SIZE OF ASSETS IN THOUSANDS OF DOLLARS

Item Description for Accounting Period 7/12 Through 6/13		Total	Zero Assets	Under 500	500 to 1,000	1,000 to 5,000	5,000 to 10,000	10,000 to 25,000	25,000 to 50,000	50,000 to 100,000	100,000 to 250,000	250,000 to 500,000	500,000 to 2,500,000	2,500,000 and over
Number of Enterprises	1	9733	2231	2173	1429	2409	586	455	170	110	104	38	25	3

Revenues ($ in Thousands)														
Net Sales	2	128968536	2546550	1308398	2554810	13191419	8425290	13447669	9417565	10922717	22095381	13711085	19713460	11634192
Interest	3	178528	894	263	9	1820	1740	1891	1236	8650	30664	41981	44991	44392
Rents	4	25323	138	2552	0	1017	296	2724	2190	2233	2989	8938	2246	0
Royalties	5	286795	2841	0	0	1610	942	226	2577	6625	19071	33407	61254	158243
Other Portfolio Income	6	785591	54694	942	160	23420	31978	9983	11629	24420	77843	39210	152746	358566
Other Receipts	7	805255	10023	253	6896	43008	13495	86231	59365	6587	142109	147302	262492	27490
Total Receipts	8	131050028	2615140	1312408	2561875	13262294	8473741	13548724	9494562	10971232	22368057	13981923	20237189	12222883
Average Total Receipts	9	13465	1172	604	1793	5505	14460	29777	55850	99738	215077	367945	809488	4074294

Operating Costs/Operating Income (%)														
Cost of Operations	10	72.4	72.6	55.2	53.7	67.4	71.7	73.2	71.7	73.0	73.6	74.7	75.8	72.7
Salaries and Wages	11	5.4	7.0	8.0	11.1	6.6	5.5	6.2	6.4	5.6	5.0	4.8	4.1	4.0
Taxes Paid	12	1.5	1.3	2.8	2.0	2.3	2.0	1.6	1.9	1.4	1.4	1.1	1.0	0.9
Interest Paid	13	2.0	2.8	0.3	0.3	0.5	0.8	1.0	0.8	1.1	1.3	2.8	3.0	7.1
Depreciation	14	2.8	1.9	4.2	1.1	2.1	1.9	2.6	2.8	2.9	3.2	2.5	3.5	3.7
Amortization and Depletion	15	0.5	1.0	•	0.2	0.1	0.1	0.3	0.4	0.3	0.5	1.0	0.9	1.0
Pensions and Other Deferred Comp.	16	0.4	0.6	0.3	0.1	0.3	0.4	0.3	0.4	0.4	0.5	0.4	0.5	0.6
Employee Benefits	17	1.6	1.3	0.5	2.9	1.5	1.5	1.4	1.6	1.8	1.4	1.6	1.5	2.4
Advertising	18	0.3	0.2	0.5	0.4	0.3	0.4	0.4	0.5	0.6	0.3	0.2	0.3	0.2
Other Expenses	19	8.1	9.3	18.0	12.0	10.5	8.2	7.9	7.7	6.8	7.9	7.9	6.9	8.0
Officers' Compensation	20	1.7	0.9	6.5	6.7	5.8	3.2	2.0	1.4	1.0	0.9	0.8	0.4	0.3
Operating Margin	21	3.0	1.0	3.7	9.6	2.5	4.5	3.2	4.3	5.0	4.0	2.3	2.3	•
Operating Margin Before Officers' Comp.	22	4.8	1.9	10.2	16.3	8.3	7.7	5.1	5.7	6.0	4.8	3.1	2.7	•

Selected Average Balance Sheet ($ in Thousands)

Net Receivables 23	1741	0	22	179	584	1891	3857	7525	14111	26493	49943	114821	671037
Inventories 24	1453	0	26	113	506	1429	3411	8065	13982	26470	34615	87985	381417
Net Property, Plant and Equipment 25	2416	0	49	106	473	1756	4544	10173	20883	46046	77189	192411	819907
Total Assets 26	10705	0	193	663	2183	7141	15739	33947	71091	156974	352052	978952	6150563
Notes and Loans Payable 27	4350	0	70	78	730	2191	5593	10071	23496	45035	158480	386943	3937844
All Other Liabilities 28	2869	0	46	271	518	1712	4878	8266	18922	41899	94189	216156	2045373
Net Worth 29	3486	0	77	314	935	3238	5269	15610	28673	70040	99384	375853	167347

Selected Financial Ratios (Times to 1)

Current Ratio 30	1.7	•	1.9	1.7	2.3	1.9	1.6	1.8	1.9	2.0	1.5	1.8	1.1
Quick Ratio 31	0.9	•	1.2	1.2	1.4	1.2	0.9	1.0	1.0	1.1	0.7	1.0	0.6
Net Sales to Working Capital 32	7.3	•	13.9	9.0	6.4	6.8	8.5	6.4	5.8	5.9	8.6	6.4	19.9
Coverage Ratio 33	3.3	2.4	13.1	35.2	6.9	7.3	5.0	7.1	6.1	4.9	2.5	2.7	1.6
Total Asset Turnover 34	1.2	•	3.1	2.7	2.5	2.0	1.9	1.6	1.4	1.4	1.0	0.8	0.6
Inventory Turnover 35	6.6	•	12.7	8.5	7.3	7.2	6.3	4.9	5.2	5.9	7.8	6.8	7.4
Receivables Turnover 36	7.7	•	16.9	8.9	9.8	8.2	7.8	7.0	6.4	8.0	8.9	6.5	6.4
Total Liabilities to Net Worth 37	2.1	•	1.5	1.1	1.3	1.2	2.0	1.2	1.5	1.2	2.5	1.6	35.8
Current Assets to Working Capital 38	2.4	•	2.1	2.5	1.8	2.1	2.7	2.2	2.2	2.0	3.0	2.3	8.2
Current Liabilities to Working Capital 39	1.4	•	1.1	1.5	0.8	1.1	1.7	1.2	1.2	1.0	2.0	1.3	7.2
Working Capital to Net Sales 40	0.1	•	0.1	0.1	0.2	0.1	0.1	0.2	0.2	0.2	0.1	0.2	0.1
Inventory to Working Capital 41	0.8	•	0.6	0.5	0.6	0.7	1.0	0.8	0.8	0.7	1.0	0.8	1.9
Total Receipts to Cash Flow 42	9.4	8.8	5.9	5.7	10.0	9.5	10.5	9.4	9.3	8.6	9.6	10.3	10.0
Cost of Goods to Cash Flow 43	6.8	6.4	3.2	3.1	6.7	6.8	7.7	6.7	6.8	6.3	7.1	7.8	7.3
Cash Flow to Total Debt 44	0.2	•	0.9	0.9	0.4	0.4	0.3	0.3	0.3	0.3	0.1	0.1	0.1

Selected Financial Factors (in Percentages)

Debt Ratio 45	67.4	•	60.3	52.7	57.2	54.7	66.5	54.0	59.7	55.4	71.8	61.6	97.3
Return on Total Assets 46	8.4	•	13.6	27.5	9.0	11.8	9.2	9.7	9.2	9.0	7.2	6.6	7.2
Return on Equity Before Income Taxes 47	18.1	•	31.5	56.4	18.1	22.4	22.0	18.1	19.0	16.2	15.6	10.9	100.8
Return on Equity After Income Taxes 48	15.7	•	31.1	56.3	17.4	21.0	20.3	16.4	16.9	14.0	12.5	9.0	73.9
Profit Margin (Before Income Tax) 49	4.8	3.7	4.0	9.9	3.1	5.0	3.9	5.1	5.5	5.3	4.3	5.2	4.4
Profit Margin (After Income Tax) 50	4.1	2.8	4.0	9.9	3.0	4.7	3.6	4.6	4.9	4.6	3.5	4.3	3.2

Table II

Corporations with Net Income

PLASTICS PRODUCT

MONEY AMOUNTS AND SIZE OF ASSETS IN THOUSANDS OF DOLLARS

Item Description for Accounting Period 7/12 Through 6/13	Total	Zero Assets	Under 500	500 to 1,000	1,000 to 5,000	5,000 to 10,000	10,000 to 25,000	25,000 to 50,000	50,000 to 100,000	100,000 to 250,000	250,000 to 500,000	500,000 to 2,500,000	2,500,000 and over
Number of Enterprises 1	7151	•	•	1128	1802	429	353	134	88	84	29	•	3

Revenues ($ in Thousands)

Net Sales 2	108888605	•	•	2020451	10623154	6776763	10780349	7767338	9444315	18833217	11879442	•	11634192
Interest 3	128493	•	•	8	1162	1452	631	630	5968	12421	29047	•	44392
Rents 4	20558	•	•	0	419	0	2700	1922	938	918	8938	•	0
Royalties 5	272366	•	•	0	1610	942	226	2516	6438	18556	25979	•	158243
Other Portfolio Income 6	752528	•	•	149	23240	30129	9269	9580	19091	75598	37708	•	358566
Other Receipts 7	675015	•	•	5364	49603	12059	59750	30642	2127	109438	135377	•	27490
Total Receipts 8	110737565	•	•	2025972	10699188	6821345	10852925	7812628	9478877	19050148	12116491	•	12222883
Average Total Receipts 9	15486	•	•	1796	5937	15901	30745	58303	107715	226787	417810	•	4074294

Operating Costs/Operating Income (%)

Cost of Operations 10	72.2	•	•	60.1	67.6	72.8	72.4	69.8	72.4	72.7	74.8	•	72.7
Salaries and Wages 11	5.2	•	•	7.6	5.9	4.5	6.1	6.8	5.6	5.1	4.6	•	4.0
Taxes Paid 12	1.4	•	•	1.3	2.2	1.7	1.5	2.0	1.4	1.5	1.1	•	0.9
Interest Paid 13	1.8	•	•	0.3	0.4	0.6	0.7	0.6	0.8	0.9	2.1	•	7.1
Depreciation 14	2.6	•	•	0.9	1.6	1.5	2.2	2.6	2.6	3.0	2.5	•	3.7
Amortization and Depletion 15	0.4	•	•	0.2	0.1	0.1	0.2	0.3	0.2	0.4	0.8	•	1.0
Pensions and Other Deferred Comp. 16	0.5	•	•	0.1	0.4	0.4	0.4	0.4	0.3	0.6	0.4	•	0.6
Employee Benefits 17	1.6	•	•	2.3	1.7	1.2	1.4	1.6	1.8	1.4	1.6	•	2.4
Advertising 18	0.3	•	•	0.4	0.3	0.2	0.3	0.5	0.7	0.4	0.2	•	0.2
Other Expenses 19	7.4	•	•	8.7	8.8	6.9	6.7	7.1	6.2	7.3	7.9	•	8.0
Officers' Compensation 20	1.6	•	•	4.2	5.9	2.8	2.0	1.5	1.0	0.9	0.8	•	0.3
Operating Margin 21	4.9	•	•	13.9	5.3	7.3	5.9	6.8	6.9	5.8	3.2	•	•
Operating Margin Before Officers' Comp. 22	6.5	•	•	18.1	11.1	10.1	8.0	8.3	7.9	6.7	3.9	•	•

Selected Average Balance Sheet ($ in Thousands)

Net Receivables 23	2040	•	•	176	623	2121	4072	8183	14660	27797	52866	•	671037
Inventories 24	1492	•	•	105	495	1379	3364	7429	13007	25784	35425	•	368204
Net Property, Plant and Equipment 25	2673	•	•	87	402	1774	4320	10133	20252	47052	87610	•	819907
Total Assets 26	11885	•	•	669	2173	7099	15489	33836	71162	158069	347109	•	6150563
Notes and Loans Payable 27	4530	•	•	75	492	2261	4034	8851	20470	37468	142826	•	3937844
All Other Liabilities 28	3134	•	•	128	495	1639	4175	7483	17675	42927	99198	•	2045373
Net Worth 29	4222	•	•	465	1185	3199	7279	17501	33017	77673	105085	•	167347

Selected Financial Ratios (Times to 1)

Current Ratio 30	1.8	•	•	3.1	2.8	2.0	1.9	2.2	2.0	2.2	1.5	•	1.1
Quick Ratio 31	1.0	•	•	2.4	1.7	1.3	1.1	1.2	1.1	1.2	0.7	•	0.6
Net Sales to Working Capital 32	6.7	•	•	5.0	5.8	6.7	6.6	5.3	5.7	5.4	9.0	•	19.9
Coverage Ratio 33	4.8	•	•	52.5	17.5	14.1	10.2	12.9	9.6	8.6	3.5	•	1.6
Total Asset Turnover 34	1.3	•	•	2.7	2.7	2.2	2.0	1.7	1.5	1.4	1.2	•	0.6
Inventory Turnover 35	7.4	•	•	10.2	8.1	8.3	6.6	5.4	6.0	6.3	8.6	•	7.7
Receivables Turnover 36	8.6	•	•	9.5	10.2	8.8	8.0	•	7.8	8.3	9.7	•	11.6
Total Liabilities to Net Worth 37	1.8	•	•	0.4	0.8	1.2	1.1	0.9	1.2	1.0	2.3	•	35.8
Current Assets to Working Capital 38	2.2	•	•	1.5	1.6	2.0	2.1	1.9	2.0	1.8	3.0	•	8.2
Current Liabilities to Working Capital 39	1.2	•	•	0.5	0.6	1.0	1.1	0.9	1.0	0.8	2.0	•	7.2
Working Capital to Net Sales 40	0.2	•	•	0.2	0.2	0.1	0.2	0.2	0.2	0.2	0.1	•	0.1
Inventory to Working Capital 41	0.7	•	•	0.3	0.5	0.6	0.8	0.7	0.7	0.7	1.0	•	1.9
Total Receipts to Cash Flow 42	8.3	•	•	5.2	8.6	8.0	8.9	8.0	8.3	7.8	8.7	•	10.0
Cost of Goods to Cash Flow 43	6.0	•	•	3.2	5.8	5.8	6.4	5.6	6.0	5.7	6.5	•	7.3
Cash Flow to Total Debt 44	0.2	•	•	1.7	0.7	0.5	0.4	0.4	0.3	0.4	0.2	•	0.1

Selected Financial Factors (in Percentages)

Debt Ratio 45	64.5	•	•	30.4	45.4	54.9	53.0	48.3	53.6	50.9	69.7	•	97.3
Return on Total Assets 46	10.9	•	•	38.8	17.2	19.2	14.4	13.8	12.3	11.4	8.6	•	7.2
Return on Equity Before Income Taxes 47	24.2	•	•	54.7	29.7	39.5	27.7	24.6	23.7	20.5	20.3	•	100.8
Return on Equity After Income Taxes 48	21.5	•	•	54.6	29.0	37.5	26.1	22.8	21.4	18.1	16.6	•	73.9
Profit Margin (Before Income Tax) 49	6.7	•	•	14.2	6.0	8.0	6.6	7.4	7.3	7.1	5.2	•	4.4
Profit Margin (After Income Tax) 50	6.0	•	•	14.2	5.8	7.6	6.2	6.9	6.6	6.3	4.2	•	3.2

Table I

Corporations with and without Net Income

RUBBER PRODUCT

MONEY AMOUNTS AND SIZE OF ASSETS IN THOUSANDS OF DOLLARS

Item Description for Accounting Period 7/12 Through 6/13		Total	Zero Assets	Under 500	500 to 1,000	1,000 to 5,000	5,000 to 10,000	10,000 to 25,000	25,000 to 50,000	50,000 to 100,000	100,000 to 250,000	250,000 to 500,000	500,000 to 2,500,000	2,500,000 and over
Number of Enterprises	1	1168	18	590	89	302	30	67	15	25	12	5	10	5

Revenues ($ in Thousands)														
Net Sales	2	65290497	722464	114290	266953	1549132	566045	1947226	953762	2345293	2180139	1870406	12750446	40024342
Interest	3	409685	358	0	170	599	805	2746	107	297	534	8089	157772	238208
Rents	4	12931	0	2	0	0	0	0	0	1763	58	0	4176	6931
Royalties	5	682210	719	0	0	0	0	310	0	3577	14	14294	100933	562362
Other Portfolio Income	6	391836	20323	0	2883	859	969	730	143	6122	10007	103789	157310	88697
Other Receipts	7	525709	7723	823	377	18059	370	26963	1704	9852	16889	21577	87466	333912
Total Receipts	8	67312868	751587	115115	270383	1568649	568189	1977975	955716	2366904	2207641	2018155	13258103	41254452
Average Total Receipts	9	57631	41755	195	3038	5194	18940	29522	63714	94676	183970	403631	1325810	8250890

Operating Costs/Operating Income (%)														
Cost of Operations	10	71.6	71.1	48.4	65.7	69.8	68.4	71.1	62.7	74.5	73.6	73.3	76.5	70.2
Salaries and Wages	11	6.2	5.8	6.2	7.2	7.5	7.1	6.4	4.9	6.2	4.3	4.6	4.3	6.9
Taxes Paid	12	1.3	1.4	1.6	2.3	1.9	2.1	1.6	1.8	1.5	1.2	1.4	0.7	1.4
Interest Paid	13	2.0	0.7	0.5	0.9	0.4	0.2	0.6	0.4	0.9	1.2	2.1	4.7	1.5
Depreciation	14	2.8	2.5	1.0	0.9	1.2	0.7	2.5	1.9	1.8	2.3	2.3	2.5	3.2
Amortization and Depletion	15	0.4	0.9	•	0.0	0.0	0.0	0.1	0.2	0.8	0.5	0.5	0.8	0.3
Pensions and Other Deferred Comp.	16	2.1	0.3	•	0.0	0.5	0.7	0.3	0.3	0.8	0.4	1.4	1.1	2.8
Employee Benefits	17	2.4	2.4	1.2	1.0	1.1	0.8	1.4	2.2	2.0	1.6	1.7	2.4	2.6
Advertising	18	1.2	0.2	0.5	0.4	0.2	0.3	0.3	3.1	0.5	0.2	0.7	1.0	1.4
Other Expenses	19	8.3	10.6	25.7	14.2	10.4	6.9	6.1	10.5	7.4	10.3	9.9	6.0	8.8
Officers' Compensation	20	0.5	0.7	4.6	4.8	4.0	4.7	1.6	1.8	1.4	0.7	0.8	0.6	0.1
Operating Margin	21	1.2	3.5	10.4	2.5	3.0	8.2	8.0	10.4	2.3	3.7	1.4	•	0.7
Operating Margin Before Officers' Comp.	22	1.7	4.2	15.0	7.2	7.0	12.9	9.6	12.2	3.7	4.4	2.2	0.0	0.8

Selected Average Balance Sheet ($ in Thousands)

	C1	C2	C3	C4	C5	C6	C7	C8	C9	C10	C11	C12	C13
Net Receivables 23	8118	0	57	77	573	2260	3650	8303	12478	28074	72215	215682	1132876
Inventories 24	7722	0	8	51	658	3424	3020	11475	14843	26161	68003	145852	1170136
Net Property, Plant and Equipment 25	9932	0	1	159	387	1345	4221	10692	13159	23511	59174	259334	1497154
Total Assets 26	46151	0	117	682	1857	7553	15638	37080	70417	153949	367384	1421160	6345466
Notes and Loans Payable 27	13991	0	20	334	490	630	2651	13082	20979	39425	109267	600068	1642895
All Other Liabilities 28	22626	0	120	213	687	1406	3579	8219	18808	63499	256622	477488	3686837
Net Worth 29	9534	0	-24	135	679	5517	9408	15779	30631	51024	1495	343603	1015734

Selected Financial Ratios (Times to 1)

	C1	C2	C3	C4	C5	C6	C7	C8	C9	C10	C11	C12	C13
Current Ratio 30	1.5	•	1.6	0.8	1.8	2.8	2.8	1.4	1.7	1.1	0.9	1.5	1.6
Quick Ratio 31	0.8	•	1.3	0.4	1.0	1.8	1.8	0.5	0.8	0.6	0.5	0.9	0.8
Net Sales to Working Capital 32	8.7	•	5.4	•	7.8	7.0	4.5	9.8	6.3	36.6	•	8.1	8.3
Coverage Ratio 33	3.4	11.5	25.6	5.1	10.6	61.2	17.6	28.7	4.8	5.3	5.4	1.9	3.9
Total Asset Turnover 34	1.2	•	1.7	4.4	2.8	2.5	1.9	1.7	1.3	1.2	1.0	0.9	1.3
Inventory Turnover 35	5.2	•	11.9	38.8	5.4	3.8	6.8	3.5	4.7	5.1	4.0	6.7	4.8
Receivables Turnover 36	6.4	•	3.9	57.8	8.9	3.9	8.5	8.7	7.1	7.4	3.7	7.2	6.1
Total Liabilities to Net Worth 37	3.8	•	•	4.1	1.7	0.4	0.7	1.3	1.3	2.0	244.7	3.1	5.2
Current Assets to Working Capital 38	2.9	•	2.8	•	2.2	1.6	1.6	3.5	2.3	13.9	•	3.0	2.7
Current Liabilities to Working Capital 39	1.9	•	1.8	•	1.2	0.6	0.6	2.5	1.3	12.9	•	2.0	1.7
Working Capital to Net Sales 40	0.1	•	0.2	•	0.1	0.1	0.2	0.1	0.2	0.0	•	0.1	0.1
Inventory to Working Capital 41	1.2	•	0.4	•	1.0	0.5	0.5	2.1	1.1	5.4	•	1.0	1.2
Total Receipts to Cash Flow 42	9.8	7.2	3.3	7.1	8.3	7.1	7.2	5.1	11.1	7.4	5.6	12.4	10.3
Cost of Goods to Cash Flow 43	7.0	5.1	1.6	4.7	5.8	4.8	5.1	3.2	8.3	5.5	4.1	9.5	7.2
Cash Flow to Total Debt 44	0.2	•	0.4	0.8	0.5	1.3	0.7	0.6	0.2	0.2	0.2	0.1	0.1

Selected Financial Factors (in Percentages)

	C1	C2	C3	C4	C5	C6	C7	C8	C9	C10	C11	C12	C13
Debt Ratio 45	79.3	•	120.4	80.2	63.4	27.0	39.8	57.4	56.5	66.9	99.6	75.8	84.0
Return on Total Assets 46	8.3	•	19.2	20.5	13.0	23.8	18.9	18.9	5.5	7.3	11.6	8.1	7.5
Return on Equity Before Income Taxes 47	28.3	•	•	83.3	32.2	32.0	29.6	42.8	10.0	17.9	2327.7	16.0	34.5
Return on Equity After Income Taxes 48	21.3	•	•	61.4	27.5	29.6	28.2	40.3	8.1	12.1	1947.5	10.6	25.2
Profit Margin (Before Income Tax) 49	4.8	7.5	11.1	3.7	4.3	9.4	9.6	10.6	3.3	5.0	9.3	4.3	4.4
Profit Margin (After Income Tax) 50	3.6	6.2	11.1	2.8	3.6	8.7	9.1	10.0	2.6	3.4	7.8	2.9	3.2

Table II

Corporations with Net Income

RUBBER PRODUCT

MONEY AMOUNTS AND SIZE OF ASSETS IN THOUSANDS OF DOLLARS

Item Description for Accounting Period 7/12 Through 6/13	Total	Zero Assets	Under 500	500 to 1,000	1,000 to 5,000	5,000 to 10,000	10,000 to 25,000	25,000 to 50,000	50,000 to 100,000	100,000 to 250,000	250,000 to 500,000	500,000 to 2,500,000	2,500,000 and over
Number of Enterprises 1	571	•	•	89	225	30	59	15	16	9	•	•	•

Revenues ($ in Thousands)

Net Sales 2	50982559	•	•	266953	1159964	566045	1782065	953762	1681242	1860964	•	•	•
Interest 3	339084	•	•	170	33	805	225	107	269	250	•	•	•
Rents 4	12333	•	•	0	0	0	0	0	1754	41	•	•	•
Royalties 5	187244	•	•	0	0	0	0	0	3394	14	•	•	•
Other Portfolio Income 6	299093	•	•	2883	729	969	653	143	6069	3976	•	•	•
Other Receipts 7	318936	•	•	377	17207	370	23791	1704	6664	10994	•	•	•
Total Receipts 8	52139249	•	•	270383	1177933	568189	1806734	955716	1699392	1876239	•	•	•
Average Total Receipts 9	91312	•	•	3038	5235	18940	30623	63714	106212	208471	•	•	•

Operating Costs/Operating Income (%)

Cost of Operations 10	71.3	•	•	65.7	68.8	68.4	70.1	62.7	75.1	71.3	•	•	•
Salaries and Wages 11	5.2	•	•	7.2	6.9	7.1	6.5	4.9	5.9	4.3	•	•	•
Taxes Paid 12	1.2	•	•	2.3	1.9	2.1	1.6	1.8	1.5	1.2	•	•	•
Interest Paid 13	1.8	•	•	0.9	0.4	0.2	0.2	0.4	0.8	1.4	•	•	•
Depreciation 14	2.8	•	•	0.9	1.1	0.7	2.3	1.9	1.5	2.4	•	•	•
Amortization and Depletion 15	0.3	•	•	0.0	0.0	0.0	0.0	0.2	0.6	1.0	•	•	•
Pensions and Other Deferred Comp. 16	1.4	•	•	0.0	0.6	0.7	0.4	0.3	0.9	0.4	•	•	•
Employee Benefits 17	2.5	•	•	1.0	0.8	0.8	1.4	2.2	2.1	1.5	•	•	•
Advertising 18	1.3	•	•	0.4	0.2	0.3	0.3	3.1	0.3	0.2	•	•	•
Other Expenses 19	7.8	•	•	14.2	9.9	6.9	5.8	10.5	5.1	10.6	•	•	•
Officers' Compensation 20	0.6	•	•	4.8	5.0	4.7	1.4	1.8	1.1	0.7	•	•	•
Operating Margin 21	3.8	•	•	2.5	4.5	8.2	10.1	10.4	5.0	5.1	•	•	•
Operating Margin Before Officers' Comp. 22	4.4	•	•	7.2	9.5	12.9	11.4	12.2	6.2	5.8	•	•	•

Net Receivables 23	13552	•	•	77	576	2260	3887	8303	13292	30555	•	•	•
Inventories 24	13075	•	•	51	622	3424	3222	13395	15719	25767	•	•	•
Net Property, Plant and Equipment 25	15483	•	•	159	411	1345	4130	10692	11564	26502	•	•	•
Total Assets 26	71190	•	•	682	1914	7553	15329	37080	67702	154305	•	•	•
Notes and Loans Payable 27	18669	•	•	334	458	630	1819	13082	16372	36934	•	•	•
All Other Liabilities 28	33852	•	•	213	749	1406	3483	8219	20691	64404	•	•	•
Net Worth 29	18669	•	•	135	707	5517	10027	15779	30639	52967	•	•	•

Selected Financial Ratios (Times to 1)

Current Ratio 30	1.5	•	•	0.8	2.0	2.8	3.3	1.4	1.7	1.1	•	•	•
Quick Ratio 31	0.8	•	•	0.4	1.0	1.8	2.2	0.5	0.8	0.6	•	•	•
Net Sales to Working Capital 32	8.4	•	•	•	7.0	7.0	4.1	9.8	6.9	46.7	•	•	•
Coverage Ratio 33	4.4	•	•	5.1	16.7	61.2	49.6	28.7	8.6	5.4	•	•	•
Total Asset Turnover 34	1.3	•	•	4.4	2.7	2.5	2.0	1.7	1.6	1.3	•	•	•
Inventory Turnover 35	4.9	•	•	38.8	5.7	3.8	6.6	3.0	5.0	5.7	•	•	•
Receivables Turnover 36	6.6	•	•	57.8	9.2	3.9	8.1	•	6.9	8.1	•	•	•
Total Liabilities to Net Worth 37	2.8	•	•	4.1	1.7	0.4	0.5	1.3	1.2	1.9	•	•	•
Current Assets to Working Capital 38	2.8	•	•	•	2.0	1.6	1.4	3.5	2.4	15.6	•	•	•
Current Liabilities to Working Capital 39	1.8	•	•	•	1.0	0.6	0.4	2.5	1.4	14.6	•	•	•
Working Capital to Net Sales 40	0.1	•	•	•	0.1	0.1	0.2	0.1	0.1	0.0	•	•	•
Inventory to Working Capital 41	1.2	•	•	•	0.9	0.5	0.4	2.1	1.0	5.9	•	•	•
Total Receipts to Cash Flow 42	8.5	•	•	7.1	7.3	7.1	6.3	5.1	10.4	6.8	•	•	•
Cost of Goods to Cash Flow 43	6.1	•	•	4.7	5.0	4.8	4.4	3.2	7.8	4.9	•	•	•
Cash Flow to Total Debt 44	0.2	•	•	0.8	0.6	1.3	0.9	0.6	0.3	0.3	•	•	•

Selected Financial Factors (in Percentages)

Debt Ratio 45	73.8	•	•	80.2	63.1	27.0	34.6	57.4	54.7	65.7	•	•	•
Return on Total Assets 46	10.3	•	•	20.5	17.2	23.8	23.0	18.9	10.8	9.8	•	•	•
Return on Equity Before Income Taxes 47	30.4	•	•	83.3	43.8	32.0	34.5	42.8	21.1	23.3	•	•	•
Return on Equity After Income Taxes 48	23.1	•	•	61.4	37.7	29.6	33.0	40.3	18.0	15.9	•	•	•
Profit Margin (Before Income Tax) 49	6.3	•	•	3.7	6.0	9.4	11.4	10.6	6.2	6.0	•	•	•
Profit Margin (After Income Tax) 50	4.8	•	•	2.8	5.2	8.7	11.0	10.0	5.3	4.1	•	•	•

Table I

Corporations with and without Net Income

CLAY, REFRACTORY AND OTHER NONMETALLIC MINERAL PRODUCT

MONEY AMOUNTS AND SIZE OF ASSETS IN THOUSANDS OF DOLLARS

Item Description for Accounting Period 7/12 Through 6/13	Total	Zero Assets	Under 500	500 to 1,000	1,000 to 5,000	5,000 to 10,000	10,000 to 25,000	25,000 to 50,000	50,000 to 100,000	100,000 to 250,000	250,000 to 500,000	500,000 to 2,500,000	2,500,000 and over
Number of Enterprises 1	2257	34	1404	366	265	35	75	37	11	11	8	10	0

Revenues ($ in Thousands)

Net Sales 2	20897201	835587	825311	462738	1382713	632730	2104717	1403354	871434	1427314	2300567	8650736	0
Interest 3	55576	2844	0	0	82	67	404	175	3	3053	2682	46265	0
Rents 4	1868	86	0	0	0	0	73	5	328	40	382	954	0
Royalties 5	84903	1328	0	0	0	0	619	1	0	0	803	82153	0
Other Portfolio Income 6	42438	12539	0	8013	44	260	5138	1616	1425	383	7658	5362	0
Other Receipts 7	209123	987	63	206	8369	12424	22573	6407	14771	14631	-67	128759	0
Total Receipts 8	21291109	853371	825374	470957	1391208	645481	2133524	1411558	887961	1445421	2312025	8914229	0
Average Total Receipts 9	9433	25099	588	1287	5250	18442	28447	38150	80724	131402	289003	891423	•

Operating Costs/Operating Income (%)

Cost of Operations 10	67.6	61.8	48.6	51.4	68.1	66.0	72.9	67.8	66.5	65.3	74.5	68.3	•
Salaries and Wages 11	6.3	6.4	5.6	5.0	8.0	8.9	3.7	7.7	10.4	6.0	4.9	6.5	•
Taxes Paid 12	1.7	1.1	2.7	5.1	2.3	3.2	1.8	1.9	1.8	1.9	0.8	1.4	•
Interest Paid 13	2.2	1.4	1.0	0.1	0.8	0.3	0.5	1.5	0.9	0.4	3.7	3.5	•
Depreciation 14	3.4	5.6	2.3	0.7	1.2	2.2	2.0	4.6	4.1	3.9	3.1	3.9	•
Amortization and Depletion 15	0.7	0.6	•	•	0.0	0.0	0.6	0.6	0.4	0.6	0.7	1.1	•
Pensions and Other Deferred Comp. 16	1.2	0.3	0.0	1.4	0.2	0.4	0.6	0.2	0.7	0.9	0.6	2.1	•
Employee Benefits 17	2.0	5.6	1.4	•	2.1	2.7	1.4	1.6	2.3	1.6	2.0	2.0	•
Advertising 18	0.6	0.4	0.2	0.3	0.8	0.1	0.4	0.4	1.1	0.4	1.0	0.7	•
Other Expenses 19	10.6	18.2	24.1	14.5	11.0	7.7	6.3	10.5	7.7	10.0	7.6	10.8	•
Officers' Compensation 20	2.1	3.8	6.1	11.6	4.3	1.5	2.8	1.8	1.8	0.9	0.4	1.2	•
Operating Margin 21	1.6	•	8.0	9.9	1.3	7.1	6.9	1.4	2.2	8.2	0.8	•	•
Operating Margin Before Officers' Comp. 22	3.7	•	14.2	21.5	5.6	8.6	9.8	3.2	4.0	9.1	1.1	•	•

Selected Average Balance Sheet ($ in Thousands)

Net Receivables 23	1187	0	22	72	430	2235	3200	5548	10637	21333	46054	126479	•
Inventories 24	1369	0	48	30	310	1629	3576	6795	21023	39616	45583	131951	•
Net Property, Plant and Equipment 25	2683	0	21	159	474	2007	3828	12864	23551	46972	90053	351168	•
Total Assets 26	10958	0	160	592	2249	7541	15585	36131	71075	174225	305480	1578247	•
Notes and Loans Payable 27	3896	0	110	111	1264	1339	2992	16922	19084	12352	118115	607636	•
All Other Liabilities 28	2658	0	6	97	479	1947	3738	8244	25158	29671	95536	380630	•
Net Worth 29	4404	0	44	384	506	4255	8855	10966	26833	132202	91829	589980	•

Selected Financial Ratios (Times to 1)

Current Ratio 30	1.6	•	18.6	5.9	1.7	2.3	2.1	1.6	2.7	4.3	2.2	1.2	•
Quick Ratio 31	0.8	•	11.8	5.0	0.9	1.4	1.1	0.7	1.1	1.9	1.2	0.6	•
Net Sales to Working Capital 32	6.3	•	5.3	4.1	12.9	5.9	5.9	6.7	3.7	1.9	4.6	11.0	•
Coverage Ratio 33	2.6	•	9.1	115.8	3.5	31.7	18.6	2.3	5.6	23.4	1.4	1.5	•
Total Asset Turnover 34	0.8	•	3.7	2.1	2.3	2.4	1.8	1.0	1.1	0.7	0.9	0.5	•
Inventory Turnover 35	4.6	•	5.9	21.9	11.5	7.3	5.7	3.8	2.5	2.1	4.7	4.5	•
Receivables Turnover 36	8.2	•	30.3	10.5	11.3	12.0	9.0	7.1	5.6	5.8	6.1	8.0	•
Total Liabilities to Net Worth 37	1.5	•	2.6	0.5	3.4	0.8	0.8	2.3	1.6	0.3	2.3	1.7	•
Current Assets to Working Capital 38	2.7	•	1.1	1.2	2.5	1.8	1.9	2.8	1.6	1.3	1.8	5.8	•
Current Liabilities to Working Capital 39	1.7	•	0.1	0.2	1.5	0.8	0.9	1.8	0.6	0.3	0.8	4.8	•
Working Capital to Net Sales 40	0.2	•	0.2	0.2	0.1	0.2	0.2	0.2	0.3	0.5	0.2	0.1	•
Inventory to Working Capital 41	0.9	•	0.4	0.1	1.0	0.6	0.8	1.4	0.9	0.6	0.7	1.7	•
Total Receipts to Cash Flow 42	9.1	8.2	4.5	4.2	11.1	7.4	7.8	9.5	10.8	5.5	14.9	11.0	•
Cost of Goods to Cash Flow 43	6.1	5.1	2.2	2.1	7.6	4.9	5.7	6.4	7.2	3.6	11.1	7.5	•
Cash Flow to Total Debt 44	0.2	•	1.1	1.5	0.3	0.7	0.5	0.2	0.2	0.6	0.1	0.1	•

Selected Financial Factors (in Percentages)

Debt Ratio 45	59.8	•	72.6	35.1	77.5	43.6	43.2	69.7	62.2	24.1	69.9	62.6	•
Return on Total Assets 46	4.9	•	33.2	25.2	6.2	22.6	15.8	3.6	5.7	7.4	4.7	3.0	•
Return on Equity Before Income Taxes 47	7.5	•	107.7	38.5	19.5	38.8	26.3	6.8	12.3	9.3	4.3	2.7	•
Return on Equity After Income Taxes 48	6.1	•	107.7	38.5	18.9	37.0	24.8	5.3	9.7	8.3	0.7	1.7	•
Profit Margin (Before Income Tax) 49	3.6	•	8.0	11.7	1.9	9.1	8.3	2.0	4.2	9.5	1.4	1.9	•
Profit Margin (After Income Tax) 50	2.9	•	8.0	11.7	1.8	8.7	7.8	1.5	3.3	8.4	0.2	1.1	•

Table II

Corporations with Net Income

CLAY, REFRACTORY AND OTHER NONMETALLIC MINERAL PRODUCT

MONEY AMOUNTS AND SIZE OF ASSETS IN THOUSANDS OF DOLLARS

Item Description for Accounting Period 7/12 Through 6/13		Total	Zero Assets	Under 500	500 to 1,000	1,000 to 5,000	5,000 to 10,000	10,000 to 25,000	25,000 to 50,000	50,000 to 100,000	100,000 to 250,000	250,000 to 500,000	500,000 to 2,500,000	2,500,000 and over
Number of Enterprises	1	1604	15	889	366	196	32	57	19	8	•	•	6	0

Revenues ($ in Thousands)

Net Sales	2	12569858	55244	747285	462738	993420	602328	1902911	869097	711803	•	•	3871035	0
Interest	3	31239	30	0	0	82	67	360	157	3	•	•	26199	0
Rents	4	906	0	0	0	0	0	73	0	328	•	•	84	0
Royalties	5	66357	0	0	0	0	0	44	1	0	•	•	66083	0
Other Portfolio Income	6	33454	12539	0	8013	44	0	329	359	1332	•	•	3117	0
Other Receipts	7	92393	196	63	206	7734	11402	27079	3296	13823	•	•	6430	0
Total Receipts	8	12794207	68009	747348	470957	1001280	613797	1930796	872910	727289	•	•	3972948	0
Average Total Receipts	9	7976	4534	841	1287	5109	19181	33874	45943	90911	•	•	662158	•

Operating Costs/Operating Income (%)

Cost of Operations	10	64.3	63.9	49.7	51.4	63.3	66.4	72.8	67.2	65.4	•	•	62.9	•
Salaries and Wages	11	6.2	1.0	4.4	5.0	7.9	8.8	3.2	7.7	11.0	•	•	6.7	•
Taxes Paid	12	1.9	3.0	2.4	5.1	2.7	3.1	1.7	2.0	1.8	•	•	1.4	•
Interest Paid	13	1.4	0.4	0.9	0.1	0.2	0.3	0.3	0.7	0.5	•	•	3.1	•
Depreciation	14	2.6	1.4	1.9	0.7	0.4	2.0	1.7	2.8	3.4	•	•	3.5	•
Amortization and Depletion	15	0.7	•	•	•	0.0	0.0	0.6	0.5	0.1	•	•	1.5	•
Pensions and Other Deferred Comp.	16	0.8	0.0	0.0	1.4	0.3	0.3	0.6	0.2	0.9	•	•	1.4	•
Employee Benefits	17	1.9	0.2	1.5	•	2.5	2.3	1.5	1.8	2.4	•	•	2.2	•
Advertising	18	0.4	0.0	0.1	0.3	0.5	0.1	0.5	0.4	1.3	•	•	0.1	•
Other Expenses	19	10.1	15.1	22.8	14.5	12.1	7.7	5.8	8.7	7.9	•	•	9.9	•
Officers' Compensation	20	2.5	0.5	5.1	11.6	5.1	1.2	2.8	1.9	2.0	•	•	1.7	•
Operating Margin	21	7.1	14.3	11.1	9.9	5.1	7.8	8.6	6.1	3.3	•	•	5.5	•
Operating Margin Before Officers' Comp.	22	9.6	14.9	16.2	21.5	10.2	9.0	11.4	8.0	5.3	•	•	7.3	•

Selected Average Balance Sheet ($ in Thousands)

Net Receivables 23	1196	0	33	72	468	2325	3599	6068	10342	•	•	156362	•
Inventories 24	1304	0	51	30	351	1645	4096	7839	14781	•	•	132806	•
Net Property, Plant and Equipment 25	1635	0	28	159	193	1812	3468	9557	16682	•	•	180214	•
Total Assets 26	8240	0	218	592	1447	7411	15759	33578	66417	•	•	1221935	•
Notes and Loans Payable 27	2541	0	143	111	288	981	2297	7448	11893	•	•	504644	•
All Other Liabilities 28	1552	0	6	97	437	1942	3500	8677	24942	•	•	173648	•
Net Worth 29	4146	0	70	384	722	4489	9963	17453	29582	•	•	543643	•

Selected Financial Ratios (Times to 1)

Current Ratio 30	2.3	•	28.1	5.9	1.9	2.2	2.5	1.4	2.4	•	•	2.0	•
Quick Ratio 31	1.2	•	20.5	5.0	1.1	1.4	1.4	0.7	1.0	•	•	1.0	•
Net Sales to Working Capital 32	4.1	•	5.5	4.1	9.2	6.3	5.4	9.1	4.2	•	•	3.5	•
Coverage Ratio 33	7.5	101.8	12.9	115.8	25.1	38.3	32.2	10.2	11.4	•	•	3.7	•
Total Asset Turnover 34	1.0	•	3.9	2.1	3.5	2.5	2.1	1.4	1.3	•	•	0.5	•
Inventory Turnover 35	3.9	•	8.1	21.9	9.1	7.6	5.9	3.9	3.9	•	•	3.1	•
Receivables Turnover 36	6.5	•	28.8	10.5	9.3	11.9	9.1	6.1	7.0	•	•	4.8	•
Total Liabilities to Net Worth 37	1.0	•	2.1	0.5	1.0	0.7	0.6	0.9	1.2	•	•	1.2	•
Current Assets to Working Capital 38	1.8	•	1.0	1.2	2.1	1.8	1.7	3.3	1.7	•	•	2.0	•
Current Liabilities to Working Capital 39	0.8	•	0.0	0.2	1.1	0.8	0.7	2.3	0.7	•	•	1.0	•
Working Capital to Net Sales 40	0.2	•	0.2	0.2	0.1	0.2	0.2	0.1	0.2	•	•	0.3	•
Inventory to Working Capital 41	0.6	•	0.3	0.1	0.8	0.6	0.6	1.5	0.9	•	•	0.5	•
Total Receipts to Cash Flow 42	6.2	2.8	4.2	4.2	7.7	7.2	7.1	7.5	9.1	•	•	6.2	•
Cost of Goods to Cash Flow 43	4.0	1.8	2.1	2.1	4.9	4.8	5.1	5.1	6.0	•	•	3.9	•
Cash Flow to Total Debt 44	0.3	•	1.4	1.5	0.9	0.9	0.8	0.4	0.3	•	•	0.2	•

Selected Financial Factors (in Percentages)

Debt Ratio 45	49.7	•	67.9	35.1	50.1	39.4	36.8	48.0	55.5	•	•	55.5	•
Return on Total Assets 46	9.8	•	46.5	25.2	21.5	25.2	22.0	9.9	8.2	•	•	6.0	•
Return on Equity Before Income Taxes 47	16.9	•	133.5	38.5	41.4	40.5	33.8	17.2	16.8	•	•	9.9	•
Return on Equity After Income Taxes 48	14.8	•	133.5	38.5	40.8	38.6	32.0	15.3	13.6	•	•	7.9	•
Profit Margin (Before Income Tax) 49	9.0	37.4	11.1	11.7	5.9	9.7	10.1	6.6	5.6	•	•	8.3	•
Profit Margin (After Income Tax) 50	7.9	26.5	11.1	11.7	5.8	9.2	9.6	5.8	4.5	•	•	6.7	•

Table I

Corporations with and without Net Income

GLASS AND GLASS PRODUCT

MONEY AMOUNTS AND SIZE OF ASSETS IN THOUSANDS OF DOLLARS

Item Description for Accounting Period 7/12 Through 6/13	Total	Zero Assets	Under 500	500 to 1,000	1,000 to 5,000	5,000 to 10,000	10,000 to 25,000	25,000 to 50,000	50,000 to 100,000	100,000 to 250,000	250,000 to 500,000	500,000 to 2,500,000	2,500,000 and over
Number of Enterprises 1	1988	9	1429	108	270	112	22	12	7	5	4	7	3

Revenues ($ in Thousands)

	Total	Zero Assets	Under 500	500 to 1,000	1,000 to 5,000	5,000 to 10,000	10,000 to 25,000	25,000 to 50,000	50,000 to 100,000	100,000 to 250,000	250,000 to 500,000	500,000 to 2,500,000	2,500,000 and over
Net Sales 2	27897974	509407	594855	228083	1214898	1888486	852902	562350	435903	778185	1429335	7809097	11594474
Interest 3	35318	11	0	17	2156	67	778	75	98	214	5876	5546	20479
Rents 4	10761	381	0	0	291	702	656	322	670	77	319	2561	4782
Royalties 5	1078027	0	0	0	0	2	0	0	250	0	5413	14080	1058282
Other Portfolio Income 6	323096	144	0	0	22703	1210	109	2634	311	140	22703	46234	226906
Other Receipts 7	379972	184	3073	11732	760	4106	14141	10011	7051	8066	22359	66291	232201
Total Receipts 8	29725148	510127	597928	239832	1240808	1894573	868586	575392	444283	786682	1486005	7943809	13137124
Average Total Receipts 9	14952	56681	418	2221	4596	16916	39481	47949	63469	157336	371501	1134830	4379041

Operating Costs/Operating Income (%)

	Total	Zero Assets	Under 500	500 to 1,000	1,000 to 5,000	5,000 to 10,000	10,000 to 25,000	25,000 to 50,000	50,000 to 100,000	100,000 to 250,000	250,000 to 500,000	500,000 to 2,500,000	2,500,000 and over
Cost of Operations 10	67.8	71.6	42.6	57.6	59.4	67.1	79.1	69.8	74.1	69.4	74.0	72.1	65.3
Salaries and Wages 11	6.0	1.3	22.7	18.5	9.7	4.9	4.0	8.5	10.0	3.9	6.5	7.4	4.0
Taxes Paid 12	1.8	0.5	3.2	2.3	2.4	2.6	1.8	1.2	2.3	2.7	1.5	2.2	1.4
Interest Paid 13	1.8	4.7	0.0	0.6	1.4	0.3	1.3	1.4	2.3	2.8	4.3	1.1	2.3
Depreciation 14	3.8	4.6	0.1	2.1	4.0	1.9	2.8	3.0	8.3	13.1	3.4	5.8	2.3
Amortization and Depletion 15	0.5	0.2	•	•	0.0	0.1	0.2	1.0	0.5	0.1	0.8	0.3	0.8
Pensions and Other Deferred Comp. 16	1.3	1.4	•	0.1	0.0	0.1	0.1	0.3	0.4	0.9	0.6	1.2	2.1
Employee Benefits 17	2.2	4.2	0.0	2.3	1.0	2.1	1.4	1.0	4.1	2.7	1.8	2.8	2.0
Advertising 18	0.3	0.0	1.5	0.3	0.2	0.1	0.2	0.2	0.3	0.3	0.4	0.1	0.3
Other Expenses 19	15.9	3.7	25.5	15.6	13.8	10.2	8.7	8.7	15.6	9.8	9.9	9.6	23.4
Officers' Compensation 20	1.4	0.6	5.3	4.2	6.1	2.6	1.4	2.1	1.2	1.3	1.3	0.9	0.9
Operating Margin 21	•	7.2	•	•	1.9	7.9	•	2.8	•	•	•	•	•
Operating Margin Before Officers' Comp. 22	•	7.8	4.4	0.6	8.0	10.5	0.3	4.9	•	•	•	•	•

Selected Average Balance Sheet ($ in Thousands)

Net Receivables 23	2212	0	28	206	561	1412	3847	4586	9942	10718	44197	114452	927931
Inventories 24	1892	0	108	81	456	2289	2875	5410	17220	33903	65653	153117	488310
Net Property, Plant and Equipment 25	5358	0	8	120	636	2044	4901	8767	27576	76985	77296	405552	2095402
Total Assets 26	31146	0	210	645	2164	7397	15839	33055	71524	174845	362848	1207440	16037407
Notes and Loans Payable 27	7474	0	300	151	1228	1215	6189	5953	22520	73508	182999	303399	3452779
All Other Liabilities 28	7477	0	89	333	207	1937	5383	9132	26708	43115	190470	491735	3197974
Net Worth 29	16194	0	-179	162	729	4244	4267	17970	22296	58222	-10622	412306	9386655

Selected Financial Ratios (Times to 1)

Current Ratio 30	1.4	•	2.1	1.6	2.7	2.1	1.6	2.4	1.4	1.7	0.9	1.5	1.4
Quick Ratio 31	0.8	•	0.6	1.0	1.8	1.0	1.0	1.2	0.7	1.0	0.4	0.7	0.9
Net Sales to Working Capital 32	7.6	•	4.4	10.8	4.9	7.3	10.9	4.3	7.5	4.7	•	10.0	6.3
Coverage Ratio 33	3.4	2.6	•	3.5	3.9	24.7	1.6	4.6	•	•	0.9	0.2	5.2
Total Asset Turnover 34	0.5	•	2.0	3.3	2.1	2.3	2.4	1.4	0.9	0.9	1.0	0.9	0.2
Inventory Turnover 35	5.0	•	1.6	15.1	5.9	4.9	10.7	6.0	2.7	3.2	4.0	5.3	5.2
Receivables Turnover 36	6.9	•	17.6	15.7	7.9	11.1	11.4	11.6	5.7	11.5	7.6	9.9	4.8
Total Liabilities to Net Worth 37	0.9	•	•	3.0	2.0	0.7	2.7	0.8	2.2	2.0	•	1.9	0.7
Current Assets to Working Capital 38	3.3	•	1.9	2.7	1.6	1.9	2.6	1.7	3.6	2.4	•	3.0	3.8
Current Liabilities to Working Capital 39	2.3	•	0.9	1.7	0.6	0.9	1.6	0.7	2.6	1.4	•	2.0	2.8
Working Capital to Net Sales 40	0.1	•	0.2	0.1	0.2	0.1	0.1	0.2	0.1	0.2	•	0.1	0.2
Inventory to Working Capital 41	1.1	•	1.3	0.7	0.5	1.0	0.9	0.8	1.4	0.9	•	1.5	0.9
Total Receipts to Cash Flow 42	6.0	9.8	6.2	6.8	9.4	6.9	13.6	8.7	•	38.2	14.0	19.2	3.4
Cost of Goods to Cash Flow 43	4.1	7.0	2.7	3.9	5.6	4.6	10.8	6.1	•	26.5	10.3	13.9	2.2
Cash Flow to Total Debt 44	0.2	•	0.2	0.6	0.3	0.8	0.2	0.4	•	0.0	0.1	0.1	0.2

Selected Financial Factors (in Percentages)

Debt Ratio 45	48.0	•	185.4	74.9	66.3	42.6	73.1	45.6	68.8	66.7	102.9	65.9	41.5
Return on Total Assets 46	2.8	•	•	7.4	11.3	19.6	5.2	9.3	•	•	3.8	0.2	2.9
Return on Equity Before Income Taxes 47	3.8	•	1.1	21.2	25.0	32.8	7.1	13.4	•	•	12.9	•	4.0
Return on Equity After Income Taxes 48	3.1	•	1.1	18.0	24.2	31.7	•	8.8	•	•	30.4	•	3.6
Profit Margin (Before Income Tax) 49	4.4	7.4	•	1.6	4.0	8.3	0.8	5.2	•	•	•	•	9.8
Profit Margin (After Income Tax) 50	3.6	7.2	•	1.4	3.9	8.0	•	3.4	•	•	•	•	8.8

Table II

Corporations with Net Income

GLASS AND GLASS PRODUCT

MONEY AMOUNTS AND SIZE OF ASSETS IN THOUSANDS OF DOLLARS

Item Description for Accounting Period 7/12 Through 6/13	Total	Zero Assets	Under 500	500 to 1000	1,000 to 5,000	5,000 to 10,000	10,000 to 25,000	25,000 to 50,000	50,000 to 100,000	100,000 to 250,000	250,000 to 500,000	500,000 to 2,500,000	2,500,000 and over
Number of Enterprises 1	1223	9	•	108	242	109	11	8	3	0	•	0	3

Revenues ($ in Thousands)

	Total	Zero Assets	Under 500	500 to 1000	1,000 to 5,000	5,000 to 10,000	10,000 to 25,000	25,000 to 50,000	50,000 to 100,000	100,000 to 250,000	250,000 to 500,000	500,000 to 2,500,000	2,500,000 and over
Net Sales 2	19600080	509407	•	228083	1114997	1868976	537598	513266	365599	0	•	0	11594474
Interest 3	25784	11	•	17	2154	59	246	60	251	0	•	0	20479
Rents 4	7168	381	•	0	291	702	656	322	5	0	•	0	4782
Royalties 5	1064812	0	•	0	0	0	0	0	0	0	•	0	1058282
Other Portfolio Income 6	254921	144	•	0	22114	827	26	1725	126	0	•	0	226906
Other Receipts 7	284245	184	•	11732	760	3637	12886	9177	3938	0	•	0	232201
Total Receipts 8	21237010	510127	•	239832	1140316	1874201	551412	524550	369919	0	•	0	13137124
Average Total Receipts 9	17365	56681	•	2221	4712	17195	50128	65569	123306	•	•	•	4379041

Operating Costs/Operating Income (%)

	Total	Zero Assets	Under 500	500 to 1000	1,000 to 5,000	5,000 to 10,000	10,000 to 25,000	25,000 to 50,000	50,000 to 100,000	100,000 to 250,000	250,000 to 500,000	500,000 to 2,500,000	2,500,000 and over
Cost of Operations 10	66.2	71.6	•	57.6	61.9	67.1	82.4	70.5	61.4	•	•	•	65.3
Salaries and Wages 11	4.8	1.3	•	18.5	8.0	4.8	2.6	7.8	6.4	•	•	•	4.0
Taxes Paid 12	1.6	0.5	•	2.3	2.4	2.6	1.2	1.1	2.5	•	•	•	1.4
Interest Paid 13	1.7	4.7	•	0.6	1.5	0.3	0.1	0.1	0.4	•	•	•	2.3
Depreciation 14	2.8	4.6	•	2.1	3.9	1.9	1.5	1.9	7.0	•	•	•	2.3
Amortization and Depletion 15	0.5	0.2	•	•	0.0	0.0	0.0	•	0.5	•	•	•	0.8
Pensions and Other Deferred Comp. 16	1.5	1.4	•	0.1	0.0	0.1	0.0	0.4	1.7	•	•	•	2.1
Employee Benefits 17	2.1	4.2	•	2.3	1.0	2.1	1.2	1.0	4.3	•	•	•	2.0
Advertising 18	0.3	0.0	•	0.3	0.2	0.1	0.1	0.1	0.6	•	•	•	0.3
Other Expenses 19	17.6	3.7	•	15.6	12.5	10.2	4.7	8.1	8.7	•	•	•	23.4
Officers' Compensation 20	1.6	0.6	•	4.2	6.4	2.6	1.1	2.3	1.8	•	•	•	0.9
Operating Margin 21	•	7.2	•	•	2.1	8.2	5.1	6.8	4.8	•	•	•	•
Operating Margin Before Officers' Comp. 22	0.9	7.8	•	0.6	8.5	10.7	6.2	9.1	6.6	•	•	•	•

Selected Average Balance Sheet ($ in Thousands)

Net Receivables 23	2912	0	•	206	596	1435	5076	6358	13465	•	•	•	927931
Inventories 24	2200	0	•	81	294	2338	4040	5933	12917	•	•	•	488310
Net Property, Plant and Equipment 25	6316	0	•	120	661	2028	3266	5554	31325	•	•	•	2095402
Total Assets 26	43128	0	•	645	2279	7346	17142	32180	142879	•	•	•	16037407
Notes and Loans Payable 27	9379	0	•	151	1321	1248	1884	2787	26551	•	•	•	3452779
All Other Liabilities 28	9223	0	•	333	206	1982	5135	8391	36338	•	•	•	3197974
Net Worth 29	24526	0	•	162	753	4116	10123	21002	79990	•	•	•	9386655

Selected Financial Ratios (Times to 1)

Current Ratio 30	1.4	•	•	1.6	2.7	2.0	2.0	2.3	2.8	•	•	•	1.4
Quick Ratio 31	0.8	•	•	1.0	1.8	1.0	1.2	1.2	2.0	•	•	•	0.9
Net Sales to Working Capital 32	7.7	•	•	10.8	4.7	7.4	8.1	5.1	2.1	•	•	•	6.3
Coverage Ratio 33	6.0	2.6	•	3.5	4.0	25.9	139.4	119.8	15.3	•	•	•	5.2
Total Asset Turnover 34	0.4	•	•	3.3	2.0	2.3	2.9	2.0	0.9	•	•	•	0.2
Inventory Turnover 35	4.8	•	•	15.1	9.7	4.9	10.0	7.6	5.8	•	•	•	5.2
Receivables Turnover 36	5.7	•	•	15.7	12.2	11.1	10.1	11.5	9.9	•	•	•	4.8
Total Liabilities to Net Worth 37	0.8	•	•	3.0	2.0	0.8	0.7	0.5	0.8	•	•	•	0.7
Current Assets to Working Capital 38	3.6	•	•	2.7	1.6	2.0	2.0	1.8	1.6	•	•	•	3.8
Current Liabilities to Working Capital 39	2.6	•	•	1.7	0.6	1.0	1.0	0.8	0.6	•	•	•	2.8
Working Capital to Net Sales 40	0.1	•	•	0.1	0.2	0.1	0.1	0.2	0.5	•	•	•	0.2
Inventory to Working Capital 41	1.0	•	•	0.7	0.5	1.0	0.7	0.7	0.3	•	•	•	0.9
Total Receipts to Cash Flow 42	4.5	9.8	•	6.8	9.7	6.8	9.2	6.6	7.7	•	•	•	3.4
Cost of Goods to Cash Flow 43	2.9	7.0	•	3.9	6.0	4.6	7.6	4.7	4.7	•	•	•	2.2
Cash Flow to Total Debt 44	0.2	•	•	0.6	0.3	0.8	0.8	0.9	0.3	•	•	•	0.2

Selected Financial Factors (in Percentages)

Debt Ratio 45	43.1	•	•	74.9	67.0	44.0	40.9	34.7	44.0	•	•	•	41.5
Return on Total Assets 46	3.8	•	•	7.4	11.9	20.5	22.1	18.0	5.4	•	•	•	2.9
Return on Equity Before Income Taxes 47	5.5	•	•	21.2	27.0	35.2	37.2	27.4	9.1	•	•	•	4.0
Return on Equity After Income Taxes 48	4.8	•	•	18.0	26.2	34.0	26.8	21.5	6.4	•	•	•	3.6
Profit Margin (Before Income Tax) 49	8.5	7.4	•	1.6	4.4	8.4	7.7	9.0	5.9	•	•	•	9.8
Profit Margin (After Income Tax) 50	7.4	7.2	•	1.4	4.3	8.2	5.6	7.0	4.2	•	•	•	8.8

Table I

Corporations with and without Net Income

CEMENT, CONCRETE, LIME AND GYPSUM PRODUCT

MONEY AMOUNTS AND SIZE OF ASSETS IN THOUSANDS OF DOLLARS

Item Description for Accounting Period 7/12 Through 6/13		Total	Zero Assets	Under 500	500 to 1,000	1,000 to 5,000	5,000 to 10,000	10,000 to 25,000	25,000 to 50,000	50,000 to 100,000	100,000 to 250,000	250,000 to 500,000	500,000 to 2,500,000	2,500,000 and over
Number of Enterprises	1	3878	9	1523	629	1177	271	139	46	29	17	11	20	7

Revenues ($ in Thousands)

Net Sales	2	59847153	508414	909928	992555	5448077	3510426	3123897	1721833	2074490	2905505	3059056	11444203	24148769
Interest	3	185056	127	62	1325	3160	4353	1299	358	896	3595	3914	58674	107292
Rents	4	69168	678	0	0	71	2409	3931	1551	1359	140	10092	6675	42262
Royalties	5	36115	441	0	0	0	0	1	1604	0	137	8712	12997	12224
Other Portfolio Income	6	662859	16643	1416	6186	15754	7740	35520	17832	15581	13008	11433	200241	321503
Other Receipts	7	749188	5300	7861	203	102768	105793	16927	23493	13280	-10268	22084	203780	257970
Total Receipts	8	61549539	531603	919267	1000269	5569830	3630721	3181575	1766671	2105606	2912117	3115291	11926570	24890020
Average Total Receipts	9	15871	59067	604	1590	4732	13397	22889	38406	72607	171301	283208	596328	3555717

Operating Costs/Operating Income (%)

Cost of Operations	10	71.1	83.1	47.3	58.1	70.0	71.3	71.9	70.1	74.9	72.1	76.1	71.0	71.5
Salaries and Wages	11	5.9	1.5	16.1	6.0	7.0	5.8	5.3	7.0	4.9	5.1	4.3	5.2	6.0
Taxes Paid	12	2.0	2.4	4.5	3.4	2.5	2.4	2.7	1.9	2.2	2.2	1.5	2.0	1.6
Interest Paid	13	3.4	1.1	1.4	0.5	0.9	1.1	0.9	0.8	1.4	1.3	1.2	3.9	5.5
Depreciation	14	5.7	8.3	3.8	1.5	1.8	3.1	3.7	5.1	4.5	4.4	4.2	10.0	5.9
Amortization and Depletion	15	1.4	3.8	0.1	0.0	0.0	0.2	0.2	0.3	0.5	0.7	1.4	2.6	1.9
Pensions and Other Deferred Comp.	16	0.8	0.1	0.2	0.6	0.3	0.3	0.6	0.3	0.6	0.7	0.8	0.9	1.2
Employee Benefits	17	2.4	4.4	0.4	2.1	1.3	1.1	1.5	1.3	2.0	2.8	1.5	2.5	3.0
Advertising	18	0.4	0.1	0.2	0.8	1.2	0.1	0.4	0.8	0.5	0.5	0.2	0.2	0.3
Other Expenses	19	9.8	10.4	19.9	15.9	10.0	10.0	9.0	8.5	6.4	8.3	5.3	8.5	10.8
Officers' Compensation	20	1.2	0.5	7.2	5.4	3.3	3.0	1.6	2.0	1.2	1.0	0.7	0.8	0.2
Operating Margin	21	•	•	•	5.6	1.7	1.7	2.1	2.0	1.0	1.0	2.7	•	•
Operating Margin Before Officers' Comp.	22	•	•	6.1	11.0	4.9	4.7	3.7	4.0	2.1	2.0	3.4	•	•

Selected Average Balance Sheet ($ in Thousands)

Net Receivables 23	2132	0	31	150	525	2051	3138	5894	13264	27791	39592	77669	485462
Inventories 24	1609	0	19	93	244	1047	2256	3997	7356	17154	28614	66529	419292
Net Property, Plant and Equipment 25	10858	0	52	250	711	3442	5607	14313	29798	56537	103855	591916	3408172
Total Assets 26	27960	0	140	602	2236	7131	15296	35131	68837	147167	328200	1311650	9312622
Notes and Loans Payable 27	8973	0	108	97	961	4167	4868	8332	23797	42188	38243	380293	3116848
All Other Liabilities 28	5566	0	89	128	496	1933	3130	5790	11789	26114	56658	359318	1566389
Net Worth 29	13420	0	-57	377	779	1031	7298	21009	33251	78864	233299	572039	4629384

Selected Financial Ratios (Times to 1)

Current Ratio 30	1.7	•	0.7	2.1	1.7	2.0	2.1	2.2	1.9	2.3	3.4	0.9	2.0
Quick Ratio 31	0.9	•	0.4	1.4	1.2	1.2	1.4	1.3	1.3	1.5	2.2	0.5	0.9
Net Sales to Working Capital 32	6.1	•	•	9.9	9.3	6.0	5.3	4.2	5.3	4.8	3.1	•	4.0
Coverage Ratio 33	0.7	•	1.0	15.0	5.3	5.8	5.1	6.8	2.7	2.0	4.7	0.2	0.1
Total Asset Turnover 34	0.6	•	4.3	2.6	2.1	1.8	1.5	1.1	1.0	1.2	0.8	0.4	0.4
Inventory Turnover 35	6.8	•	14.6	9.9	13.3	8.8	7.2	6.6	7.3	7.2	7.4	6.1	5.9
Receivables Turnover 36	7.3	•	15.9	9.3	9.1	5.6	7.0	8.0	5.7	5.9	7.5	7.4	7.3
Total Liabilities to Net Worth 37	1.1	•	•	0.6	1.9	5.9	1.1	0.7	1.1	0.9	0.4	1.3	1.0
Current Assets to Working Capital 38	2.5	•	•	1.9	2.4	2.0	1.9	1.8	2.1	1.8	1.4	•	2.0
Current Liabilities to Working Capital 39	1.5	•	•	0.9	1.4	1.0	0.9	0.8	1.1	0.8	0.4	•	1.0
Working Capital to Net Sales 40	0.2	•	•	0.1	0.1	0.2	0.2	0.2	0.2	0.2	0.3	•	0.2
Inventory to Working Capital 41	0.7	•	•	0.6	0.5	0.5	0.5	0.5	0.6	0.4	0.4	•	0.5
Total Receipts to Cash Flow 42	18.3	•	6.3	6.0	8.8	8.7	9.7	9.9	14.4	14.2	12.3	64.5	34.8
Cost of Goods to Cash Flow 43	13.0	•	3.0	3.5	6.2	6.2	7.0	6.9	10.8	10.2	9.4	45.8	24.9
Cash Flow to Total Debt 44	0.1	•	0.5	1.2	0.4	0.2	0.3	0.3	0.1	0.2	0.2	0.0	0.0

Selected Financial Factors (in Percentages)

Debt Ratio 45	52.0	•	141.0	37.3	65.2	85.5	52.3	40.2	51.7	46.4	28.9	56.4	50.3
Return on Total Assets 46	1.2	•	5.9	18.0	9.9	11.2	7.1	5.8	4.0	2.9	4.8	0.4	0.2
Return on Equity Before Income Taxes 47	•	•	0.2	26.7	23.1	64.0	11.9	8.2	5.3	2.7	5.4	•	•
Return on Equity After Income Taxes 48	•	•	0.7	26.2	22.9	63.6	11.3	7.2	4.4	2.0	4.6	•	•
Profit Margin (Before Income Tax) 49	•	•	•	6.4	3.9	5.1	3.9	4.6	2.5	1.2	4.5	•	•
Profit Margin (After Income Tax) 50	•	•	•	6.3	3.9	5.1	3.7	4.1	2.0	0.9	3.8	•	•

Table II
Corporations with Net Income

CEMENT, CONCRETE, LIME AND GYPSUM PRODUCT

MONEY AMOUNTS AND SIZE OF ASSETS IN THOUSANDS OF DOLLARS

Item Description for Accounting Period 7/12 Through 6/13	Total	Zero Assets	Under 500	500 to 1,000	1,000 to 5,000	5,000 to 10,000	10,000 to 25,000	25,000 to 50,000	50,000 to 100,000	100,000 to 250,000	250,000 to 500,000	500,000 to 2,500,000	2,500,000 and over
Number of Enterprises 1	2582	3	•	519	746	231	89	40	17	•	8	13	0

Revenues ($ in Thousands)

Net Sales 2	36280018	15732	•	863449	3260906	3124148	2245181	1489334	1450211	•	2392696	19214646	0
Interest 3	72996	6	•	725	1615	2687	624	294	746	•	2247	60567	0
Rents 4	28413	0	•	0	0	802	2720	1551	1274	•	9464	12461	0
Royalties 5	8133	0	•	0	0	0	1	1604	0	•	45	6346	0
Other Portfolio Income 6	268899	0	•	672	1807	7054	33875	15159	7122	•	11012	187010	0
Other Receipts 7	606748	211	•	171	90146	103783	9501	22678	7789	•	21546	337815	0
Total Receipts 8	37265207	15949	•	865017	3354474	3238474	2291902	1530620	1467142	•	2437010	19818845	0
Average Total Receipts 9	14433	5316	•	1667	4497	14019	25752	38266	86302	•	304626	1524527	•

Operating Costs/Operating Income (%)

Cost of Operations 10	70.2	76.8	•	55.1	64.9	70.9	72.4	68.7	73.4	•	76.7	71.6	•
Salaries and Wages 11	5.3	0.4	•	6.5	7.0	5.9	4.4	7.5	3.6	•	3.3	4.7	•
Taxes Paid 12	2.0	2.1	•	3.5	2.7	2.3	2.4	1.9	2.3	•	1.8	1.7	•
Interest Paid 13	2.3	0.7	•	0.3	1.2	1.1	0.5	0.8	1.1	•	0.4	3.6	•
Depreciation 14	4.0	3.4	•	1.3	1.8	3.1	2.9	5.3	3.9	•	4.1	4.6	•
Amortization and Depletion 15	1.3	•	•	0.0	0.1	0.1	0.2	0.2	0.5	•	1.4	2.1	•
Pensions and Other Deferred Comp. 16	0.8	0.0	•	0.7	0.4	0.2	0.6	0.3	0.7	•	1.1	1.1	•
Employee Benefits 17	1.8	5.3	•	2.1	1.6	0.9	1.3	1.2	1.8	•	1.0	2.1	•
Advertising 18	0.4	0.0	•	0.5	0.4	0.1	0.3	0.9	0.5	•	0.1	0.3	•
Other Expenses 19	8.4	4.5	•	16.6	9.8	9.8	7.9	8.1	5.6	•	4.0	7.9	•
Officers' Compensation 20	1.3	0.3	•	6.2	3.1	3.1	1.7	2.0	0.9	•	0.7	0.4	•
Operating Margin 21	2.2	6.3	•	7.3	7.1	2.6	5.2	3.0	5.6	•	5.5	•	•
Operating Margin Before Officers' Comp. 22	3.5	6.6	•	13.5	10.1	5.7	6.9	5.0	6.5	•	6.2	0.3	•

Selected Average Balance Sheet ($ in Thousands)

Net Receivables 23	1743	0	•	162	572	1981	3397	6190	12619	•	38818	166764	•
Inventories 24	1053	0	•	98	216	933	2027	3660	6803	•	30411	182492	•
Net Property, Plant and Equipment 25	6954	0	•	207	673	3583	4708	14690	30636	•	124187	1023175	•
Total Assets 26	16630	0	•	576	2179	7096	15107	35158	72046	•	317916	2398133	•
Notes and Loans Payable 27	6360	0	•	58	1056	4323	2515	8420	18386	•	24318	1005152	•
All Other Liabilities 28	3857	0	•	80	476	1907	2979	5437	13255	•	50329	585289	•
Net Worth 29	6412	0	•	439	647	865	9612	21301	40405	•	243268	807692	•

Selected Financial Ratios (Times to 1)

Current Ratio 30	1.8	•	•	3.6	1.9	2.1	2.5	2.3	2.6	•	3.9	1.5	•
Quick Ratio 31	1.2	•	•	2.5	1.3	1.2	1.8	1.5	1.8	•	2.7	0.9	•
Net Sales to Working Capital 32	6.2	•	•	7.3	6.9	6.0	4.9	4.0	4.5	•	2.9	8.5	•
Coverage Ratio 33	3.1	11.6	•	26.6	9.4	6.9	14.9	8.6	7.1	•	21.8	1.9	•
Total Asset Turnover 34	0.8	•	•	2.9	2.0	1.9	1.7	1.1	1.2	•	0.9	0.6	•
Inventory Turnover 35	9.4	•	•	9.3	13.1	10.3	9.0	7.0	9.2	•	7.5	5.8	•
Receivables Turnover 36	10.3	•	•	9.0	8.0	6.5	8.0	8.2	8.4	•	•	•	•
Total Liabilities to Net Worth 37	1.6	•	•	0.3	2.4	7.2	0.6	0.7	0.8	•	0.3	2.0	•
Current Assets to Working Capital 38	2.2	•	•	1.4	2.2	1.9	1.7	1.8	1.6	•	1.3	3.1	•
Current Liabilities to Working Capital 39	1.2	•	•	0.4	1.2	0.9	0.7	0.8	0.6	•	0.3	2.1	•
Working Capital to Net Sales 40	0.2	•	•	0.1	0.1	0.2	0.2	0.3	0.2	•	0.3	0.1	•
Inventory to Working Capital 41	0.6	•	•	0.4	0.4	0.5	0.4	0.5	0.4	•	0.3	1.0	•
Total Receipts to Cash Flow 42	9.6	9.2	•	5.6	6.2	8.1	7.8	8.8	9.2	•	10.4	12.0	•
Cost of Goods to Cash Flow 43	6.7	7.0	•	3.1	4.0	5.7	5.7	6.1	6.8	•	8.0	8.6	•
Cash Flow to Total Debt 44	0.1	•	•	2.2	0.5	0.3	0.6	0.3	0.3	•	0.4	0.1	•

Selected Financial Factors (in Percentages)

Debt Ratio 45	61.4	•	•	23.9	70.3	87.8	36.4	39.4	43.9	•	23.5	66.3	•
Return on Total Assets 46	6.1	•	•	22.5	22.3	13.9	13.0	7.0	9.3	•	7.2	4.2	•
Return on Equity Before Income Taxes 47	10.9	•	•	28.5	67.2	97.8	19.1	10.2	14.2	•	9.0	5.8	•
Return on Equity After Income Taxes 48	9.8	•	•	27.9	66.8	97.1	18.3	9.0	13.0	•	8.0	4.7	•
Profit Margin (Before Income Tax) 49	5.0	7.7	•	7.5	9.9	6.3	7.3	5.8	6.7	•	7.3	3.2	•
Profit Margin (After Income Tax) 50	4.5	7.7	•	7.4	9.9	6.2	7.0	5.2	6.1	•	6.5	2.6	•

Table I

Corporations with and without Net Income

IRON, STEEL MILLS AND STEEL PRODUCT

MONEY AMOUNTS AND SIZE OF ASSETS IN THOUSANDS OF DOLLARS

Item Description for Accounting Period 7/12 Through 6/13		Total	Zero Assets	Under 500	500 to 1,000	1,000 to 5,000	5,000 to 10,000	10,000 to 25,000	25,000 to 50,000	50,000 to 100,000	100,000 to 250,000	250,000 to 500,000	500,000 to 2,500,000	2,500,000 and over
Number of Enterprises	1	2703	454	•	•	593	138	135	82	37	38	18	13	15

Revenues ($ in Thousands)

Net Sales	2	154816426	2052284	•	•	2726718	2837728	3604213	5392796	4729072	9815506	8506512	19386923	94344589
Interest	3	579934	112	•	•	46	535	990	1074	4897	5033	70069	85926	410958
Rents	4	78349	0	•	•	0	78	1480	176	689	6870	9546	3216	56295
Royalties	5	96003	0	•	•	0	0	0	0	0	57	6981	13428	75537
Other Portfolio Income	6	744595	0	•	•	292	440	11710	82792	8155	12538	5608	22915	600123
Other Receipts	7	1681972	818	•	•	10420	34002	50423	17232	16290	6457	57091	153626	1202311
Total Receipts	8	157997279	2053214	•	•	2737476	2872783	3668816	5494070	4759103	9846461	8655807	19666034	96689813
Average Total Receipts	9	58453	4522	•	•	4616	20817	27176	67001	128624	259117	480878	1512772	6445988

Operating Costs/Operating Income (%)

Cost of Operations	10	83.7	99.1	•	•	69.4	83.2	77.1	80.4	84.4	85.7	85.8	87.9	83.2
Salaries and Wages	11	2.5	0.6	•	•	7.2	3.5	4.7	4.6	2.6	2.6	3.2	2.5	2.0
Taxes Paid	12	0.9	0.3	•	•	1.3	0.8	1.6	1.4	0.9	0.8	0.9	0.8	0.8
Interest Paid	13	1.8	0.7	•	•	0.4	0.5	0.5	0.8	0.5	0.8	2.8	1.4	2.2
Depreciation	14	2.8	1.5	•	•	1.3	0.9	2.4	2.4	2.0	2.6	3.0	2.1	3.1
Amortization and Depletion	15	0.6	1.0	•	•	0.0	0.0	0.1	0.1	0.1	0.2	0.3	0.7	0.7
Pensions and Other Deferred Comp.	16	0.5	0.0	•	•	0.0	0.2	0.6	0.6	0.3	0.3	0.6	0.2	0.6
Employee Benefits	17	1.3	0.1	•	•	0.8	0.9	1.3	1.3	1.0	1.0	2.1	0.9	1.4
Advertising	18	0.1	0.0	•	•	0.1	0.1	0.2	0.1	0.0	0.1	0.1	0.1	0.0
Other Expenses	19	5.7	1.5	•	•	4.6	2.5	6.2	5.2	2.9	3.9	5.0	3.1	6.7
Officers' Compensation	20	0.5	0.5	•	•	6.3	1.3	2.5	1.2	1.0	0.5	0.4	0.3	0.2
Operating Margin	21	•	•	•	•	8.7	6.1	2.7	1.8	4.3	1.5	•	0.0	•
Operating Margin Before Officers' Comp.	22	0.3	•	•	•	14.9	7.4	5.2	2.9	5.3	2.0	•	0.3	•

Selected Average Balance Sheet ($ in Thousands)

Net Receivables 23	6176	0	•	•	502	1867	4019	7499	13197	28496	41828	127348	723690
Inventories 24	7928	0	•	•	477	2920	3470	9194	24684	43091	87251	191496	855336
Net Property, Plant and Equipment 25	14468	0	•	•	431	1347	4429	10080	16303	46233	86987	338697	1922159
Total Assets 26	45888	0	•	•	1952	7816	16066	35433	67587	157960	356212	1113762	5793428
Notes and Loans Payable 27	15146	0	•	•	435	2107	3310	13611	19233	46664	110830	347134	1973438
All Other Liabilities 28	15798	0	•	•	293	1831	4822	11313	15626	52140	149481	271303	2119450
Net Worth 29	14944	0	•	•	1224	3878	7933	10509	32728	59157	95901	495326	1700540

Selected Financial Ratios (Times to 1)

Current Ratio 30	1.9	•	•	•	3.3	2.3	1.9	1.5	2.2	1.9	1.8	1.4	2.0
Quick Ratio 31	0.8	•	•	•	2.0	1.0	1.2	0.7	0.9	0.8	0.7	0.6	0.9
Net Sales to Working Capital 32	6.9	•	•	•	4.7	6.4	5.9	10.0	5.1	6.2	6.1	12.3	6.5
Coverage Ratio 33	2.0	•	•	•	26.2	16.5	9.5	5.3	11.7	3.3	0.1	2.0	1.7
Total Asset Turnover 34	1.2	•	•	•	2.4	2.6	1.7	1.9	1.9	1.6	1.3	1.3	1.1
Inventory Turnover 35	6.0	•	•	•	6.7	5.9	5.9	5.8	4.4	5.1	4.6	6.8	6.1
Receivables Turnover 36	9.1	•	•	•	9.9	10.6	5.9	8.7	8.6	9.2	9.9	12.3	8.5
Total Liabilities to Net Worth 37	2.1	•	•	•	0.6	1.0	1.0	2.4	1.1	1.7	2.7	1.2	2.4
Current Assets to Working Capital 38	2.2	•	•	•	1.4	1.7	2.1	3.1	1.8	2.2	2.2	3.5	2.0
Current Liabilities to Working Capital 39	1.2	•	•	•	0.4	0.7	1.1	2.1	0.8	1.2	1.2	2.5	1.0
Working Capital to Net Sales 40	0.1	•	•	•	0.2	0.2	0.2	0.1	0.2	0.2	0.2	0.1	0.2
Inventory to Working Capital 41	1.0	•	•	•	0.5	0.9	0.7	1.4	1.0	1.1	0.9	1.8	0.9
Total Receipts to Cash Flow 42	19.9	•	•	•	8.7	11.3	11.0	16.3	14.2	21.0	67.8	26.5	19.7
Cost of Goods to Cash Flow 43	16.6	•	•	•	6.0	9.4	8.5	13.1	11.9	18.0	58.2	23.3	16.4
Cash Flow to Total Debt 44	0.1	•	•	•	0.7	0.5	0.3	0.2	0.3	0.1	0.0	0.1	0.1

Selected Financial Factors (in Percentages)

Debt Ratio 45	67.4	•	•	•	37.3	50.4	50.6	70.3	51.6	62.5	73.1	55.5	70.6
Return on Total Assets 46	4.5	•	•	•	22.2	20.5	8.4	8.3	10.2	4.3	0.5	3.9	4.1
Return on Equity Before Income Taxes 47	7.0	•	•	•	34.0	38.8	15.2	22.7	19.2	8.1	•	4.4	5.9
Return on Equity After Income Taxes 48	4.3	•	•	•	33.8	37.2	12.9	20.6	16.4	5.5	•	1.3	3.2
Profit Margin (Before Income Tax) 49	1.8	•	•	•	9.1	7.3	4.5	3.6	4.9	1.9	•	1.5	1.6
Profit Margin (After Income Tax) 50	1.1	•	•	•	9.0	7.0	3.8	3.3	4.2	1.3	•	0.4	0.9

Table II

Corporations with Net Income

IRON, STEEL MILLS AND STEEL PRODUCT

MONEY AMOUNTS AND SIZE OF ASSETS IN THOUSANDS OF DOLLARS

Item Description for Accounting Period 7/12 Through 6/13	Total	Zero Assets	Under 500	500 to 1,000	1,000 to 5,000	5,000 to 10,000	10,000 to 25,000	25,000 to 50,000	50,000 to 100,000	100,000 to 250,000	250,000 to 500,000	500,000 to 2,500,000	2,500,000 and over
Number of Enterprises **1**	2034	•	829	293	530	130	110	55	•	•	13	•	11

Revenues ($ in Thousands)													
Net Sales **2**	120792325	•	467274	938633	2188052	2737807	3044618	3594025	•	•	5602763	•	75879428
Interest **3**	514903	•	89	204	9	534	985	660	•	•	42435	•	385331
Rents **4**	76763	•	0	0	0	78	1480	176	•	•	9158	•	55218
Royalties **5**	46058	•	0	0	0	0	0	0	•	•	6759	•	25814
Other Portfolio Income **6**	712173	•	24	0	292	440	11612	81249	•	•	2666	•	575252
Other Receipts **7**	1383678	•	127545	5755	10176	32953	48795	12166	•	•	29203	•	964253
Total Receipts **8**	123525900	•	594932	944592	2198529	2771812	3107490	3688276	•	•	5692984	•	77885296
Average Total Receipts **9**	60731	•	718	3224	4148	21322	28250	67060	•	•	437922	•	7080481

Operating Costs/Operating Income (%)													
Cost of Operations **10**	81.5	•	43.2	72.0	66.4	82.8	75.7	75.4	•	•	79.2	•	81.6
Salaries and Wages **11**	2.4	•	26.3	5.4	8.3	3.4	4.6	4.8	•	•	3.7	•	1.7
Taxes Paid **12**	1.0	•	5.2	1.9	1.3	0.8	1.5	1.5	•	•	1.0	•	0.9
Interest Paid **13**	1.8	•	0.0	0.1	0.4	0.4	0.4	0.5	•	•	2.4	•	2.3
Depreciation **14**	2.7	•	5.5	0.8	1.5	0.9	2.0	2.8	•	•	2.6	•	3.2
Amortization and Depletion **15**	0.6	•	0.1	0.0	0.0	0.0	0.1	0.2	•	•	0.2	•	0.8
Pensions and Other Deferred Comp. **16**	0.5	•	1.7	0.1	0.0	0.2	0.6	0.7	•	•	0.8	•	0.6
Employee Benefits **17**	1.2	•	0.4	1.6	0.9	0.9	1.1	1.4	•	•	1.3	•	1.3
Advertising **18**	0.1	•	•	0.1	0.2	0.1	0.2	0.2	•	•	0.1	•	0.0
Other Expenses **19**	6.1	•	10.7	7.3	3.6	2.2	6.1	5.6	•	•	4.2	•	7.4
Officers' Compensation **20**	0.6	•	24.7	2.3	5.6	1.3	2.7	1.4	•	•	0.4	•	0.2
Operating Margin **21**	1.6	•	•	8.5	11.8	7.0	4.9	5.6	•	•	4.1	•	0.1
Operating Margin Before Officers' Comp. **22**	2.2	•	6.8	10.8	17.5	8.3	7.6	6.9	•	•	4.5	•	0.2

Selected Average Balance Sheet ($ in Thousands)

Net Receivables 23	6526	•	38	391	534	1899	3976	7196	•	•	42590	•	797101
Inventories 24	7877	•	26	111	371	2553	3270	10336	•	•	92453	•	868979
Net Property, Plant and Equipment 25	14303	•	69	73	454	1330	4308	10085	•	•	79587	•	2076742
Total Assets 26	48981	•	198	817	2044	7923	15683	36273	•	•	353644	•	6684533
Notes and Loans Payable 27	15071	•	81	366	426	1969	2495	12790	•	•	78571	•	2239260
All Other Liabilities 28	15987	•	16	389	303	1808	4063	7899	•	•	111127	•	2355659
Net Worth 29	17923	•	102	62	1314	4146	9126	15585	•	•	163946	•	2089613

Selected Financial Ratios (Times to 1)

Current Ratio 30	2.3	•	4.6	1.8	3.6	2.6	2.0	1.9	•	•	3.6	•	2.1
Quick Ratio 31	1.0	•	3.4	1.6	2.2	1.1	1.2	0.9	•	•	1.4	•	0.9
Net Sales to Working Capital 32	5.8	•	6.7	10.1	3.9	6.0	5.8	6.8	•	•	3.5	•	6.0
Coverage Ratio 33	3.1	•	342.9	98.8	36.1	19.5	17.0	15.9	•	•	3.4	•	2.2
Total Asset Turnover 34	1.2	•	2.8	3.9	2.0	2.7	1.8	1.8	•	•	1.2	•	1.0
Inventory Turnover 35	6.1	•	9.5	20.9	7.4	6.8	6.4	4.8	•	•	3.7	•	6.5
Receivables Turnover 36	9.0	•	•	13.6	8.9	13.0	7.1	8.9	•	•	8.6	•	8.7
Total Liabilities to Net Worth 37	1.7	•	1.0	12.1	0.6	0.9	0.7	1.3	•	•	1.2	•	2.2
Current Assets to Working Capital 38	1.8	•	1.3	2.3	1.4	1.6	2.0	2.1	•	•	1.4	•	1.9
Current Liabilities to Working Capital 39	0.8	•	0.3	1.3	0.4	0.6	1.0	1.1	•	•	0.4	•	0.9
Working Capital to Net Sales 40	0.2	•	0.1	0.1	0.3	0.2	0.2	0.1	•	•	0.3	•	0.2
Inventory to Working Capital 41	0.8	•	0.3	0.2	0.4	0.9	0.6	1.0	•	•	0.6	•	0.9
Total Receipts to Cash Flow 42	13.7	•	6.5	7.2	7.2	10.4	8.7	9.8	•	•	10.9	•	15.0
Cost of Goods to Cash Flow 43	11.2	•	2.8	5.2	4.8	8.6	6.6	7.4	•	•	8.7	•	12.3
Cash Flow to Total Debt 44	0.1	•	0.9	0.6	0.8	0.5	0.5	0.3	•	•	0.2	•	0.1

Selected Financial Factors (in Percentages)

Debt Ratio 45	63.4	•	48.8	92.4	35.7	47.7	41.8	57.0	•	•	53.6	•	68.7
Return on Total Assets 46	6.9	•	26.9	36.2	25.6	23.1	13.0	15.7	•	•	9.9	•	5.2
Return on Equity Before Income Taxes 47	12.8	•	52.3	470.1	38.6	41.8	21.0	34.3	•	•	15.1	•	9.0
Return on Equity After Income Taxes 48	9.8	•	52.3	466.2	38.4	40.2	18.6	32.2	•	•	12.5	•	6.0
Profit Margin (Before Income Tax) 49	3.9	•	9.4	9.1	12.3	8.2	6.9	8.2	•	•	5.8	•	2.7
Profit Margin (After Income Tax) 50	3.0	•	9.4	9.1	12.2	7.9	6.1	7.7	•	•	4.8	•	1.8

Table I

Corporations with and without Net Income

NONFERROUS METAL PRODUCTION AND PROCESSING

MONEY AMOUNTS AND SIZE OF ASSETS IN THOUSANDS OF DOLLARS

Item Description for Accounting Period 7/12 Through 6/13	Total	Zero Assets	Under 500	500 to 1,000	1,000 to 5,000	5,000 to 10,000	10,000 to 25,000	25,000 to 50,000	50,000 to 100,000	100,000 to 250,000	250,000 to 500,000	500,000 to 2,500,000	2,500,000 and over
Number of Enterprises 1	921	4	•	•	457	29	156	59	36	27	16	23	4

Revenues ($ in Thousands)

	Total	Zero Assets	Under 500	500 to 1,000	1,000 to 5,000	5,000 to 10,000	10,000 to 25,000	25,000 to 50,000	50,000 to 100,000	100,000 to 250,000	250,000 to 500,000	500,000 to 2,500,000	2,500,000 and over
Net Sales 2	112332497	1813953	•	•	2159008	602439	11448963	5436532	6514163	7717689	12028565	34921713	29098009
Interest 3	1519442	1207	•	•	63	333	205	884	591	3873	15646	119127	1377513
Rents 4	64874	0	•	•	3235	0	1292	303	64	853	3819	4554	50755
Royalties 5	121449	0	•	•	0	0	1715	180	0	4227	572	25157	89597
Other Portfolio Income 6	859360	8766	•	•	0	7672	24572	6952	17098	9090	4040	170183	610987
Other Receipts 7	1872650	2917	•	•	1546	1751	38587	20252	2938	49456	65411	587631	1102161
Total Receipts 8	116770272	1826843	•	•	2163852	612195	11515334	5465103	6534854	7785188	12118053	35828365	32329022
Average Total Receipts 9	126786	456711	•	•	4735	21110	73816	92629	181524	288340	757378	1557755	8082256

Operating Costs/Operating Income (%)

	Total	Zero Assets	Under 500	500 to 1,000	1,000 to 5,000	5,000 to 10,000	10,000 to 25,000	25,000 to 50,000	50,000 to 100,000	100,000 to 250,000	250,000 to 500,000	500,000 to 2,500,000	2,500,000 and over
Cost of Operations 10	85.8	78.5	•	•	67.4	88.9	91.4	89.1	88.1	87.3	86.3	85.8	83.7
Salaries and Wages 11	2.6	2.0	•	•	7.1	3.8	1.8	2.1	1.9	1.9	2.7	2.7	2.8
Taxes Paid 12	0.5	1.3	•	•	1.4	0.6	0.6	0.6	0.6	0.7	0.4	0.5	0.3
Interest Paid 13	3.6	1.6	•	•	0.9	0.8	0.2	0.4	0.4	1.9	1.4	1.9	10.0
Depreciation 14	2.0	3.1	•	•	1.0	2.0	0.7	1.7	1.4	2.0	1.3	2.0	3.0
Amortization and Depletion 15	0.5	0.2	•	•	•	0.1	0.0	0.1	0.1	0.5	0.1	0.4	1.0
Pensions and Other Deferred Comp. 16	0.9	0.5	•	•	0.5	0.5	0.2	0.1	0.4	0.3	0.2	0.5	2.5
Employee Benefits 17	0.7	0.4	•	•	0.3	0.5	0.5	0.7	0.6	1.3	0.8	0.9	0.3
Advertising 18	0.1	0.1	•	•	0.1	0.1	0.1	0.1	0.0	0.1	0.0	0.1	0.2
Other Expenses 19	5.7	6.2	•	•	13.4	4.4	2.4	3.3	2.4	4.4	7.0	4.6	9.0
Officers' Compensation 20	0.5	0.2	•	•	2.3	0.4	0.8	1.1	1.1	0.6	0.2	0.4	0.0
Operating Margin 21	•	5.8	•	•	5.6	•	1.3	0.8	3.0	•	•	0.3	•
Operating Margin Before Officers' Comp. 22	•	6.0	•	•	7.9	•	2.1	1.9	4.1	•	•	0.7	•

Selected Average Balance Sheet ($ in Thousands)

Net Receivables	23	55660	0	•	•	414	1178	3687	8206	16243	31249	94040	158313	10850443
Inventories	24	10681	0	•	•	413	1192	4069	8781	17315	35398	77928	203275	465352
Net Property, Plant and Equipment	25	19481	0	•	•	461	2613	3460	8819	14734	49025	86833	240757	1948754
Total Assets	26	195255	0	•	•	2267	6140	15677	35090	67546	165380	382711	1122498	33795756
Notes and Loans Payable	27	73609	0	•	•	2762	2731	4343	13560	16605	54528	107361	447126	12723160
All Other Liabilities	28	58497	0	•	•	1628	1234	4165	9434	15427	56026	180193	271073	10173712
Net Worth	29	63148	0	•	•	-2123	2175	7168	12095	35515	54827	95158	404300	10898884

Selected Financial Ratios (Times to 1)

Current Ratio	30	1.3	•	•	•	0.9	1.9	2.0	1.6	2.1	1.6	1.7	2.1	1.1
Quick Ratio	31	1.0	•	•	•	0.4	1.1	1.1	0.8	1.2	0.7	0.9	1.1	1.1
Net Sales to Working Capital	32	6.9	•	•	•	•	14.5	14.5	11.4	8.1	9.3	8.3	6.3	4.7
Coverage Ratio	33	1.4	5.1	•	•	7.6	1.0	8.8	4.2	9.3	0.9	1.2	2.7	0.9
Total Asset Turnover	34	0.6	•	•	•	2.1	3.4	4.7	2.6	2.7	1.7	2.0	1.4	0.2
Inventory Turnover	35	9.8	•	•	•	7.7	15.5	16.5	9.3	9.2	7.1	8.3	6.4	13.1
Receivables Turnover	36	2.4	•	•	•	9.0	•	19.0	11.2	10.5	10.0	8.6	1.6	•
Total Liabilities to Net Worth	37	2.1	•	•	•	•	1.8	1.2	1.9	0.9	2.0	3.0	1.8	2.1
Current Assets to Working Capital	38	4.3	•	•	•	•	2.1	2.0	2.7	1.9	2.8	2.4	1.9	7.7
Current Liabilities to Working Capital	39	3.3	•	•	•	•	1.1	1.0	1.7	0.9	1.8	1.4	0.9	6.7
Working Capital to Net Sales	40	0.1	•	•	•	•	0.1	0.1	0.1	0.1	0.1	0.1	0.2	0.2
Inventory to Working Capital	41	0.6	•	•	•	•	0.8	0.9	1.1	0.7	1.3	1.0	0.7	0.3
Total Receipts to Cash Flow	42	17.6	8.4	•	•	5.8	56.5	27.3	27.0	20.5	28.6	17.3	15.1	18.9
Cost of Goods to Cash Flow	43	15.1	6.6	•	•	3.9	50.3	24.9	24.0	18.0	25.0	14.9	12.9	15.8
Cash Flow to Total Debt	44	0.1	•	•	•	0.2	0.1	0.3	0.1	0.3	0.1	0.2	0.1	0.0

Selected Financial Factors (in Percentages)

Debt Ratio	45	67.7	•	•	•	193.7	64.6	54.3	65.5	47.4	66.8	75.1	64.0	67.8
Return on Total Assets	46	3.1	•	•	•	14.0	2.9	9.9	4.6	10.0	3.2	3.3	6.7	1.9
Return on Equity Before Income Taxes	47	2.7	•	•	•	•	0.3	19.1	10.1	17.0	•	2.2	11.5	•
Return on Equity After Income Taxes	48	1.9	•	•	•	•	•	18.0	8.1	14.8	•	•	9.7	•
Profit Margin (Before Income Tax)	49	1.4	6.7	•	•	5.8	0.0	1.9	1.3	3.3	•	0.3	3.1	•
Profit Margin (After Income Tax)	50	1.0	4.4	•	•	5.7	•	1.8	1.1	2.9	•	•	2.6	•

Table II

Corporations with Net Income

NONFERROUS METAL PRODUCTION AND PROCESSING

MONEY AMOUNTS AND SIZE OF ASSETS IN THOUSANDS OF DOLLARS

Item Description for Accounting Period 7/12 Through 6/13	Total	Zero Assets	Under 500	500 to 1,000	1,000 to 5,000	5,000 to 10,000	10,000 to 25,000	25,000 to 50,000	50,000 to 100,000	100,000 to 250,000	250,000 to 500,000	500,000 to 2,500,000	2,500,000 and over
Number of Enterprises 1	734	4	0	109	371	0	139	37	28	17	9	20	•

Revenues ($ in Thousands)

	Total	Zero Assets	Under 500	500 to 1,000	1,000 to 5,000	5,000 to 10,000	10,000 to 25,000	25,000 to 50,000	50,000 to 100,000	100,000 to 250,000	250,000 to 500,000	500,000 to 2,500,000	2,500,000 and over
Net Sales 2	85340677	1813953	0	591464	2257469	0	11130997	4116747	5463110	5020923	6988525	47957489	•
Interest 3	1230293	1207	0	0	65	0	205	634	584	2247	11145	1214207	•
Rents 4	56027	0	0	0	3235	0	1292	303	55	0	3793	47349	•
Royalties 5	73154	0	0	0	0	0	1715	180	0	3616	572	67070	•
Other Portfolio Income 6	734514	8766	0	0	7672	0	24572	5991	16903	229	3972	666408	•
Other Receipts 7	1663100	2917	0	0	1685	0	33970	6455	6013	37972	25490	1548599	•
Total Receipts 8	89097765	1826843	0	591464	2270126	0	11192751	4130310	5486665	5064987	7033497	51501122	•
Average Total Receipts 9	121387	456711	•	5426	6119	•	80523	111630	195952	297940	781500	2575056	•

Operating Costs/Operating Income (%)

	Total	Zero Assets	Under 500	500 to 1,000	1,000 to 5,000	5,000 to 10,000	10,000 to 25,000	25,000 to 50,000	50,000 to 100,000	100,000 to 250,000	250,000 to 500,000	500,000 to 2,500,000	2,500,000 and over
Cost of Operations 10	85.8	78.5	•	84.9	67.2	•	91.4	90.2	88.0	86.0	81.8	85.6	•
Salaries and Wages 11	2.5	2.0	•	0.7	7.2	•	1.8	1.8	1.9	2.0	2.5	2.7	•
Taxes Paid 12	0.5	1.3	•	0.8	1.4	•	0.6	0.5	0.6	0.6	0.5	0.4	•
Interest Paid 13	2.8	1.6	•	0.1	0.9	•	0.2	0.4	0.4	0.8	2.0	4.5	•
Depreciation 14	1.7	3.1	•	0.1	1.0	•	0.6	1.1	1.1	1.4	1.1	2.2	•
Amortization and Depletion 15	0.4	0.2	•	•	0.0	•	0.0	0.1	0.1	0.2	0.1	0.6	•
Pensions and Other Deferred Comp. 16	1.0	0.5	•	0.2	0.6	•	0.2	0.1	0.4	0.3	0.2	1.5	•
Employee Benefits 17	0.5	0.4	•	0.7	0.3	•	0.5	0.4	0.6	0.5	0.8	0.5	•
Advertising 18	0.1	0.1	•	0.3	0.1	•	0.1	0.1	0.0	0.1	0.0	0.1	•
Other Expenses 19	5.7	6.2	•	1.5	13.1	•	2.3	2.4	1.8	4.6	8.2	6.6	•
Officers' Compensation 20	0.5	0.2	•	4.4	2.3	•	0.8	1.0	1.0	0.6	0.2	0.3	•
Operating Margin 21	•	5.8	•	6.3	6.0	•	1.6	2.0	4.1	2.9	2.6	•	•
Operating Margin Before Officers' Comp. 22	•	6.0	•	10.7	8.3	•	2.4	3.0	5.1	3.5	2.8	•	•

Selected Average Balance Sheet ($ in Thousands)

Net Receivables 23	60265	0	•	38	518	•	3996	9383	16179	34127	129546	2046814	•
Inventories 24	9918	0	•	249	406	•	4181	10932	16739	37330	80657	200288	•
Net Property, Plant and Equipment 25	17206	0	•	178	569	•	3252	8036	15414	40352	67353	496261	•
Total Assets 26	197176	0	•	723	2126	•	15764	35753	68212	150523	381190	6622302	•
Notes and Loans Payable 27	65998	0	•	78	1051	•	3470	12180	15838	36066	57521	2276856	•
All Other Liabilities 28	61323	0	•	77	411	•	4196	10119	14914	50442	222090	2030937	•
Net Worth 29	69855	0	•	568	664	•	8098	13453	37461	64015	101578	2314509	•

Selected Financial Ratios (Times to 1)

Current Ratio 30	1.2	•	•	7.1	2.3	•	2.3	1.8	2.3	1.8	2.8	1.1	•
Quick Ratio 31	1.0	•	•	3.5	1.5	•	1.2	1.0	1.3	0.8	1.7	1.0	•
Net Sales to Working Capital 32	7.9	•	•	11.6	7.3	•	13.1	10.9	8.0	8.0	4.6	7.6	•
Coverage Ratio 33	2.1	5.1	•	47.6	8.8	•	12.2	7.5	12.3	5.6	2.6	1.6	•
Total Asset Turnover 34	0.6	•	•	7.5	2.9	•	5.1	3.1	2.9	2.0	2.0	0.4	•
Inventory Turnover 35	10.1	•	•	18.5	10.1	•	17.5	9.2	10.3	6.8	7.9	10.3	•
Receivables Turnover 36	2.0	•	•	287.7	10.7	•	20.3	11.3	11.1	•	6.4	•	•
Total Liabilities to Net Worth 37	1.8	•	•	0.3	2.2	•	0.9	1.7	0.8	1.4	2.8	1.9	•
Current Assets to Working Capital 38	5.4	•	•	1.2	1.8	•	1.8	2.3	1.8	2.3	1.5	7.8	•
Current Liabilities to Working Capital 39	4.4	•	•	0.2	0.8	•	0.8	1.3	0.8	1.3	0.5	6.8	•
Working Capital to Net Sales 40	0.1	•	•	0.1	0.1	•	0.1	0.1	0.1	0.1	0.2	0.1	•
Inventory to Working Capital 41	0.7	•	•	0.5	0.5	•	0.8	0.9	0.7	1.0	0.5	0.6	•
Total Receipts to Cash Flow 42	13.6	8.4	•	13.4	5.8	•	25.4	25.4	18.1	13.3	10.3	13.1	•
Cost of Goods to Cash Flow 43	11.7	6.6	•	11.4	3.9	•	23.3	22.9	16.0	11.4	8.4	11.2	•
Cash Flow to Total Debt 44	0.1	•	•	2.6	0.7	•	0.4	0.2	0.4	0.3	0.3	0.0	•

Selected Financial Factors (in Percentages)

Debt Ratio 45	64.6	•	•	21.4	68.7	•	48.6	62.4	45.1	57.5	73.4	65.0	•
Return on Total Assets 46	3.5	•	•	48.3	21.6	•	11.8	8.4	13.8	9.1	10.6	2.6	•
Return on Equity Before Income Taxes 47	5.2	•	•	60.2	61.4	•	21.1	19.2	23.1	17.5	24.6	2.9	•
Return on Equity After Income Taxes 48	4.3	•	•	60.2	59.1	•	20.0	16.4	20.5	12.6	17.3	2.5	•
Profit Margin (Before Income Tax) 49	3.1	6.7	•	6.3	6.7	•	2.1	2.3	4.4	3.8	3.2	2.8	•
Profit Margin (After Income Tax) 50	2.6	4.4	•	6.3	6.5	•	2.0	2.0	3.9	2.7	2.3	2.4	•

Table I

Corporations with and without Net Income

FOUNDRIES

MONEY AMOUNTS AND SIZE OF ASSETS IN THOUSANDS OF DOLLARS

Item Description for Accounting Period 7/12 Through 6/13		Total	Zero Assets	Under 500	500 to 1,000	1,000 to 5,000	5,000 to 10,000	10,000 to 25,000	25,000 to 50,000	50,000 to 100,000	100,000 to 250,000	250,000 to 500,000	500,000 to 2,500,000	2,500,000 and over
Number of Enterprises	1	1602	4	1182	0	193	131	46	13	11	9	3	10	0
Revenues ($ in Thousands)														
Net Sales	2	27712201	132730	1156722	0	1298993	1903943	1307085	766587	1003026	2009106	1560988	16573019	0
Interest	3	47399	0	0	0	87	62	312	22	207	3059	840	42811	0
Rents	4	4279	0	0	0	833	23	645	305	264	0	1347	862	0
Royalties	5	10504	0	0	0	0	0	0	4	0	415	0	10085	0
Other Portfolio Income	6	242904	7	0	0	194	2929	263	384	1284	11493	957	225395	0
Other Receipts	7	201905	119	129	0	26778	2694	7694	-180	8255	15346	15174	125896	0
Total Receipts	8	28219192	132856	1156851	0	1326885	1909651	1315999	767122	1013036	2039419	1579306	16978068	0
Average Total Receipts	9	17615	33214	979	•	6875	14577	28609	59009	92094	226602	526435	1697807	•
Operating Costs/Operating Income (%)														
Cost of Operations	10	72.6	83.0	65.6	•	68.1	73.3	75.9	76.7	73.4	74.6	79.4	71.9	•
Salaries and Wages	11	4.4	1.2	4.3	•	12.2	4.2	4.6	2.9	5.6	4.0	3.6	3.9	•
Taxes Paid	12	1.6	1.1	2.6	•	2.8	2.0	1.8	1.5	2.2	1.2	1.6	1.3	•
Interest Paid	13	1.2	0.7	0.2	•	0.7	0.8	0.7	4.1	0.8	0.9	2.3	1.3	•
Depreciation	14	2.6	2.3	2.2	•	2.1	1.6	3.4	3.8	4.4	2.6	3.5	2.5	•
Amortization and Depletion	15	0.9	0.2	0.2	•	0.0	0.0	0.2	0.4	0.0	0.2	0.3	1.3	•
Pensions and Other Deferred Comp.	16	0.8	0.0	0.0	•	0.6	0.5	0.3	0.2	0.7	1.1	0.9	1.0	•
Employee Benefits	17	1.6	1.5	0.1	•	2.1	2.6	2.7	2.3	0.9	2.4	1.9	1.3	•
Advertising	18	0.1	0.0	0.6	•	0.2	0.2	0.1	0.0	0.3	0.1	0.2	0.1	•
Other Expenses	19	4.8	3.0	9.8	•	6.5	6.6	5.0	5.3	6.2	4.3	5.9	4.0	•
Officers' Compensation	20	1.4	0.4	7.3	•	2.6	1.7	1.9	0.8	1.3	0.8	0.8	1.0	•
Operating Margin	21	8.1	6.6	7.2	•	2.0	6.5	3.5	1.8	4.0	7.9	•	10.5	•
Operating Margin Before Officers' Comp.	22	9.4	7.0	14.5	•	4.7	8.3	5.3	2.7	5.3	8.7	0.5	11.4	•

Net Receivables 23	2459	0	94	•	1123	2137	3154	8709	11042	28394	72268	247955	•
Inventories 24	2672	0	8	•	762	1340	3190	7988	10182	26265	81567	309315	•
Net Property, Plant and Equipment 25	3483	0	20	•	438	2121	5047	10002	27667	45736	104624	380168	•
Total Assets 26	20148	0	147	•	2808	7144	15084	37848	69833	166489	370707	2606133	•
Notes and Loans Payable 27	4981	0	73	•	748	1982	3464	13130	19849	36838	82687	636205	•
All Other Liabilities 28	4298	0	41	•	711	1668	4056	9590	15684	45416	187351	502629	•
Net Worth 29	10869	0	33	•	1348	3494	7564	15128	34300	84236	100669	1467299	•

Selected Financial Ratios (Times to 1)

Current Ratio 30	2.2	•	2.9	•	3.0	2.4	1.7	2.0	1.7	1.9	1.4	2.3	•
Quick Ratio 31	1.0	•	2.6	•	1.8	1.6	1.0	1.1	0.9	1.0	0.7	1.0	•
Net Sales to Working Capital 32	5.0	•	12.3	•	4.9	5.4	8.1	5.5	7.4	6.1	9.9	4.2	•
Coverage Ratio 33	9.1	10.5	41.2	•	6.9	9.4	7.3	1.5	6.9	10.8	1.4	11.3	•
Total Asset Turnover 34	0.9	•	6.7	•	2.4	2.0	1.9	1.6	1.3	1.3	1.4	0.6	•
Inventory Turnover 35	4.7	•	85.4	•	6.0	7.9	6.8	5.7	6.6	6.3	5.1	3.9	•
Receivables Turnover 36	7.3	•	•	•	5.7	•	8.0	6.6	8.8	9.5	6.1	7.0	•
Total Liabilities to Net Worth 37	0.9	•	3.5	•	1.1	1.0	1.0	1.5	1.0	1.0	2.7	0.8	•
Current Assets to Working Capital 38	1.9	•	1.5	•	1.5	1.7	2.4	2.0	2.5	2.1	3.2	1.8	•
Current Liabilities to Working Capital 39	0.9	•	0.5	•	0.5	0.7	1.4	1.0	1.5	1.1	2.2	0.8	•
Working Capital to Net Sales 40	0.2	•	0.1	•	0.2	0.2	0.1	0.2	0.1	0.2	0.1	0.2	•
Inventory to Working Capital 41	0.9	•	0.1	•	0.5	0.5	0.9	0.8	0.8	0.9	1.4	0.9	•
Total Receipts to Cash Flow 42	8.1	10.4	7.5	•	12.4	9.1	12.6	16.2	10.1	7.9	16.6	7.1	•
Cost of Goods to Cash Flow 43	5.9	8.6	4.9	•	8.4	6.7	9.5	12.5	7.4	5.9	13.2	5.1	•
Cash Flow to Total Debt 44	0.2	•	1.1	•	0.4	0.4	0.3	0.2	0.3	0.3	0.1	0.2	•

Selected Financial Factors (in Percentages)

Debt Ratio 45	46.1	•	77.6	•	52.0	51.1	49.9	60.0	50.9	49.4	72.8	43.7	•
Return on Total Assets 46	9.6	•	49.3	•	11.8	15.4	9.1	9.3	7.6	13.7	4.5	9.1	•
Return on Equity Before Income Taxes 47	15.8	•	214.4	•	20.9	28.1	15.6	7.5	13.3	24.5	4.9	14.7	•
Return on Equity After Income Taxes 48	12.2	•	214.4	•	20.1	27.8	13.1	5.9	12.5	20.4	2.4	10.8	•
Profit Margin (Before Income Tax) 49	9.9	6.7	7.2	•	4.2	6.8	4.1	1.9	5.0	9.3	1.0	13.0	•
Profit Margin (After Income Tax) 50	7.6	6.7	7.2	•	4.0	6.7	3.5	1.5	4.7	7.7	0.5	9.5	•

Table II
Corporations with Net Income

FOUNDRIES

MONEY AMOUNTS AND SIZE OF ASSETS IN THOUSANDS OF DOLLARS

Item Description for Accounting Period 7/12 Through 6/13	Total	Zero Assets	Under 500	500 to 1,000	1,000 to 5,000	5,000 to 10,000	10,000 to 25,000	25,000 to 50,000	50,000 to 100,000	100,000 to 250,000	250,000 to 500,000	500,000 to 2,500,000	2,500,000 and over
Number of Enterprises 1	1117	•	760	0	175	112	33	8	•	•	0	•	0

Revenues ($ in Thousands)

	Total	Zero Assets	Under 500	500 to 1,000	1,000 to 5,000	5,000 to 10,000	10,000 to 25,000	25,000 to 50,000	50,000 to 100,000	100,000 to 250,000	250,000 to 500,000	500,000 to 2,500,000	2,500,000 and over
Net Sales 2	25739316	•	1152050	0	1234046	1705396	801200	567911	•	•	0	•	0
Interest 3	12097	•	0	0	38	41	312	22	•	•	0	•	0
Rents 4	3714	•	0	0	833	23	645	23	•	•	0	•	0
Royalties 5	10500	•	0	0	0	0	0	0	•	•	0	•	0
Other Portfolio Income 6	242671	•	0	0	194	2830	263	264	•	•	0	•	0
Other Receipts 7	192108	•	128	0	25369	1351	7539	231	•	•	0	•	0
Total Receipts 8	26200406	•	1152178	0	1260480	1709641	809959	568451	•	•	0	•	0
Average Total Receipts 9	23456	•	1516	•	7203	15265	24544	71056	•	•	•	•	•

Operating Costs/Operating Income (%)

	Total	Zero Assets	Under 500	500 to 1,000	1,000 to 5,000	5,000 to 10,000	10,000 to 25,000	25,000 to 50,000	50,000 to 100,000	100,000 to 250,000	250,000 to 500,000	500,000 to 2,500,000	2,500,000 and over
Cost of Operations 10	72.0	•	65.5	•	68.1	72.7	70.5	76.7	•	•	•	•	•
Salaries and Wages 11	4.4	•	4.3	•	12.4	4.0	5.3	2.6	•	•	•	•	•
Taxes Paid 12	1.5	•	2.6	•	2.6	1.8	2.1	1.6	•	•	•	•	•
Interest Paid 13	1.0	•	0.2	•	0.6	0.8	0.6	2.4	•	•	•	•	•
Depreciation 14	2.5	•	2.1	•	2.0	1.0	3.7	3.6	•	•	•	•	•
Amortization and Depletion 15	0.9	•	•	•	0.0	0.0	0.2	0.3	•	•	•	•	•
Pensions and Other Deferred Comp. 16	0.9	•	•	•	0.6	0.5	0.4	0.2	•	•	•	•	•
Employee Benefits 17	1.5	•	0.1	•	2.2	2.6	2.6	2.4	•	•	•	•	•
Advertising 18	0.1	•	0.6	•	0.2	0.1	0.1	0.1	•	•	•	•	•
Other Expenses 19	4.6	•	9.7	•	6.3	6.7	5.3	5.1	•	•	•	•	•
Officers' Compensation 20	1.4	•	7.3	•	2.4	1.7	2.5	0.9	•	•	•	•	•
Operating Margin 21	9.2	•	7.6	•	2.7	8.0	6.8	4.3	•	•	•	•	•
Operating Margin Before Officers' Comp. 22	10.6	•	14.9	•	5.1	9.7	9.3	5.2	•	•	•	•	•

Selected Average Balance Sheet ($ in Thousands)

Net Receivables 23	3304	•	145	•	1180	2261	2540	10364	•	•	•	•	•
Inventories 24	3299	•	11	•	451	1471	2786	8921	•	•	•	•	•
Net Property, Plant and Equipment 25	4573	•	30	•	397	1848	4488	9540	•	•	•	•	•
Total Assets 26	27098	•	216	•	2595	6928	14425	37570	•	•	•	•	•
Notes and Loans Payable 27	6190	•	113	•	547	1747	2028	7443	•	•	•	•	•
All Other Liabilities 28	5605	•	64	•	717	1767	2799	8332	•	•	•	•	•
Net Worth 29	15303	•	39	•	1332	3414	9598	21795	•	•	•	•	•

Selected Financial Ratios (Times to 1)

Current Ratio 30	2.4	•	2.9	•	2.7	2.4	3.8	2.8	•	•	•	•	•
Quick Ratio 31	1.1	•	2.6	•	1.9	1.7	2.3	1.5	•	•	•	•	•
Net Sales to Working Capital 32	4.6	•	12.3	•	5.9	5.2	4.2	4.2	•	•	•	•	•
Coverage Ratio 33	12.3	•	43.5	•	9.6	11.5	15.3	2.9	•	•	•	•	•
Total Asset Turnover 34	0.9	•	7.0	•	2.7	2.2	1.7	1.9	•	•	•	•	•
Inventory Turnover 35	5.0	•	87.2	•	10.6	7.5	6.1	6.1	•	•	•	•	•
Receivables Turnover 36	8.2	•	•	•	7.4	8.2	8.7	7.6	•	•	•	•	•
Total Liabilities to Net Worth 37	0.8	•	4.5	•	0.9	1.0	0.5	0.7	•	•	•	•	•
Current Assets to Working Capital 38	1.7	•	1.5	•	1.6	1.7	1.4	1.5	•	•	•	•	•
Current Liabilities to Working Capital 39	0.7	•	0.5	•	0.6	0.7	0.4	0.5	•	•	•	•	•
Working Capital to Net Sales 40	0.2	•	0.1	•	0.2	0.2	0.2	0.2	•	•	•	•	•
Inventory to Working Capital 41	0.8	•	0.1	•	0.4	0.5	0.5	0.6	•	•	•	•	•
Total Receipts to Cash Flow 42	7.6	•	7.3	•	11.7	8.1	8.6	12.1	•	•	•	•	•
Cost of Goods to Cash Flow 43	5.5	•	4.8	•	8.0	5.9	6.1	9.3	•	•	•	•	•
Cash Flow to Total Debt 44	0.3	•	1.2	•	0.5	0.5	0.6	0.4	•	•	•	•	•

Selected Financial Factors (in Percentages)

Debt Ratio 45	43.5	•	81.9	•	48.7	50.7	33.5	42.0	•	•	•	•	•
Return on Total Assets 46	10.2	•	54.9	•	14.7	19.7	14.2	12.8	•	•	•	•	•
Return on Equity Before Income Taxes 47	16.6	•	297.0	•	25.6	36.5	20.0	14.4	•	•	•	•	•
Return on Equity After Income Taxes 48	12.9	•	297.0	•	24.8	36.1	17.3	12.7	•	•	•	•	•
Profit Margin (Before Income Tax) 49	11.0	•	7.6	•	4.8	8.2	7.9	4.4	•	•	•	•	•
Profit Margin (After Income Tax) 50	8.5	•	7.6	•	4.7	8.1	6.8	3.9	•	•	•	•	•

Table I

Corporations with and without Net Income

FORGING AND STAMPING

MONEY AMOUNTS AND SIZE OF ASSETS IN THOUSANDS OF DOLLARS

Item Description for Accounting Period 7/12 Through 6/13	Total	Zero Assets	Under 500	500 to 1,000	1,000 to 5,000	5,000 to 10,000	10,000 to 25,000	25,000 to 50,000	50,000 to 100,000	100,000 to 250,000	250,000 to 500,000	500,000 to 2,500,000	2,500,000 and over
Number of Enterprises **1**	2072	4	1045	345	384	71	142	32	27	16	3	3	0

Revenues ($ in Thousands)													
Net Sales **2**	19097801	605617	186333	424615	2059300	840894	4623543	2108175	2986690	3484242	638493	1139898	0
Interest **3**	45299	1681	9	46	956	330	1174	121	1199	924	1477	37383	0
Rents **4**	6049	0	0	446	0	891	1470	0	747	2440	0	56	0
Royalties **5**	1244	807	0	0	9	191	231	1	0	0	0	6	0
Other Portfolio Income **6**	41145	57	0	0	9052	9029	2337	12180	6234	1681	34	544	0
Other Receipts **7**	226403	496	18481	291	6451	27085	19549	11687	39642	22459	59165	21091	0
Total Receipts **8**	19417941	608658	204823	425398	2075768	878420	4648304	2132164	3034512	3511746	699169	1198978	0
Average Total Receipts **9**	9372	152164	196	1233	5406	12372	32735	66630	112389	219484	233056	399659	•

Operating Costs/Operating Income (%)													
Cost of Operations **10**	73.3	76.1	70.9	65.5	65.8	59.7	75.4	75.7	79.2	75.4	70.8	64.7	•
Salaries and Wages **11**	4.8	6.6	8.8	1.3	7.2	5.0	4.6	4.6	4.6	3.5	5.6	4.7	•
Taxes Paid **12**	1.7	2.5	2.0	2.4	2.1	2.6	1.7	1.5	1.5	1.6	1.9	1.0	•
Interest Paid **13**	1.0	2.9	0.3	0.2	0.5	0.6	0.4	0.6	0.8	0.8	1.7	5.8	•
Depreciation **14**	2.9	3.2	0.6	0.3	2.4	4.7	2.1	2.3	3.0	3.9	4.6	3.5	•
Amortization and Depletion **15**	0.2	0.4	•	0.1	0.0	0.3	0.0	0.4	0.4	0.2	1.0	0.6	•
Pensions and Other Deferred Comp. **16**	0.8	0.0	1.0	0.2	1.8	0.4	0.5	0.4	0.7	0.4	0.9	2.8	•
Employee Benefits **17**	2.0	•	1.8	2.5	3.2	2.0	2.1	1.1	1.7	2.6	1.7	0.5	•
Advertising **18**	0.1	0.1	•	0.3	0.2	0.2	0.2	0.1	0.0	0.0	0.1	0.0	•
Other Expenses **19**	5.4	4.6	32.9	13.9	4.8	9.4	4.7	6.1	3.4	4.9	5.4	4.7	•
Officers' Compensation **20**	2.3	9.0	11.0	8.5	4.3	2.7	2.5	0.9	1.1	1.0	0.2	0.5	•
Operating Margin **21**	5.6	•	•	4.8	7.6	12.5	5.7	6.4	3.5	5.6	6.1	11.2	•
Operating Margin Before Officers' Comp. **22**	7.8	3.6	•	13.2	11.9	15.1	8.2	7.3	4.6	6.6	6.3	11.7	•

	Selected Average Balance Sheet ($ in Thousands)												
Net Receivables 23	1294	0	20	133	717	1369	4142	7905	19605	34146	22292	86185	•
Inventories 24	1096	0	10	144	507	1429	3025	8246	13956	27135	40204	104225	•
Net Property, Plant and Equipment 25	1667	0	8	17	538	2089	4222	10354	21781	50220	83775	170256	•
Total Assets 26	7176	0	60	682	2267	7706	15351	36200	74362	161328	354901	1386889	•
Notes and Loans Payable 27	2096	0	169	95	517	1710	3396	10917	21920	35313	100136	508450	•
All Other Liabilities 28	1784	0	247	123	523	1002	3512	8271	19674	42870	57792	323605	•
Net Worth 29	3295	0	-356	464	1227	4993	8443	17012	32768	83146	196972	554834	•

	Selected Financial Ratios (Times to 1)												
Current Ratio 30	2.2	•	0.2	4.3	3.3	4.1	2.2	1.9	2.2	2.0	3.2	2.5	•
Quick Ratio 31	1.3	•	0.1	3.2	2.3	2.7	1.4	1.0	1.3	1.1	2.0	1.2	•
Net Sales to Working Capital 32	5.1	•	•	2.5	4.7	3.5	6.1	6.8	4.8	5.2	2.7	2.4	•
Coverage Ratio 33	8.2	•	•	22.6	17.0	28.3	16.4	14.8	7.6	8.7	10.4	3.8	•
Total Asset Turnover 34	1.3	•	3.0	1.8	2.4	1.5	2.1	1.8	1.5	1.3	0.6	0.3	•
Inventory Turnover 35	6.2	•	12.3	5.6	7.0	4.9	8.1	6.0	6.3	6.1	3.7	2.4	•
Receivables Turnover 36	6.9	•	8.9	7.2	6.5	7.0	8.4	•	6.0	6.3	•	8.8	•
Total Liabilities to Net Worth 37	1.2	•	•	0.5	0.8	0.5	0.8	1.1	1.3	0.9	0.8	1.5	•
Current Assets to Working Capital 38	1.8	•	•	1.3	1.4	1.3	1.8	2.2	1.8	2.0	1.5	1.7	•
Current Liabilities to Working Capital 39	0.8	•	•	0.3	0.4	0.3	0.8	1.2	0.8	1.0	0.5	0.7	•
Working Capital to Net Sales 40	0.2	•	•	0.4	0.2	0.3	0.2	0.1	0.2	0.2	0.4	0.4	•
Inventory to Working Capital 41	0.6	•	•	0.3	0.4	0.3	0.6	0.9	0.6	0.7	0.5	0.6	•
Total Receipts to Cash Flow 42	9.5	•	•	6.5	10.1	4.3	11.1	9.4	13.9	10.2	5.2	4.9	•
Cost of Goods to Cash Flow 43	7.0	•	•	4.3	6.6	2.6	8.4	7.1	11.0	7.7	3.7	3.2	•
Cash Flow to Total Debt 44	0.2	•	•	0.9	0.5	1.0	0.4	0.4	0.2	0.3	0.3	0.1	•

	Selected Financial Factors (in Percentages)												
Debt Ratio 45	54.1	•	697.2	32.0	45.9	35.2	45.0	53.0	55.9	48.5	44.5	60.0	•
Return on Total Assets 46	10.7	•	•	9.3	21.1	27.0	14.1	15.6	8.7	9.7	10.5	6.1	•
Return on Equity Before Income Taxes 47	20.4	•	9.7	13.1	36.7	40.1	24.1	30.9	17.1	16.7	17.1	11.3	•
Return on Equity After Income Taxes 48	18.6	•	11.1	12.9	35.3	36.6	22.7	26.9	15.2	14.9	14.5	11.3	•
Profit Margin (Before Income Tax) 49	7.3	•	•	5.0	8.4	16.9	6.3	8.0	5.1	6.4	15.8	16.4	•
Profit Margin (After Income Tax) 50	6.7	•	•	4.9	8.1	15.4	5.9	7.0	4.5	5.7	13.4	16.4	•

111

Table II

Corporations with Net Income

FORGING AND STAMPING

MONEY AMOUNTS AND SIZE OF ASSETS IN THOUSANDS OF DOLLARS

Item Description for Accounting Period 7/12 Through 6/13	Total	Zero Assets	Under 500	500 to 1,000	1,000 to 5,000	5,000 to 10,000	10,000 to 25,000	25,000 to 50,000	50,000 to 100,000	100,000 to 250,000	250,000 to 500,000	500,000 to 2,500,000	2,500,000 and over
Number of Enterprises 1	1375	•	458	291	368	71	117	•	23	12	•	0	0
Revenues ($ in Thousands)													
Net Sales 2	15883009	•	5414	328544	1992770	840894	3962533	•	2691386	3100575	•	0	0
Interest 3	4754	•	0	13	819	330	752	•	1131	140	•	0	0
Rents 4	3541	•	0	446	0	891	1470	•	663	71	•	0	0
Royalties 5	437	•	0	0	9	191	231	•	0	0	•	0	0
Other Portfolio Income 6	39980	•	0	0	9052	9029	1966	•	6178	1525	•	0	0
Other Receipts 7	193226	•	18011	221	4581	27085	7654	•	33697	15557	•	0	0
Total Receipts 8	16124947	•	23425	329224	2007231	878420	3974606	•	2733055	3117868	•	0	0
Average Total Receipts 9	11727	•	51	1131	5454	12372	33971	•	118828	259822	•	•	•
Operating Costs/Operating Income (%)													
Cost of Operations 10	72.3	•	60.2	66.7	65.5	59.7	74.2	•	79.2	75.4	•	•	•
Salaries and Wages 11	4.7	•	•	1.1	7.0	5.0	4.7	•	4.5	3.5	•	•	•
Taxes Paid 12	1.7	•	5.3	1.7	2.2	2.6	1.8	•	1.4	1.6	•	•	•
Interest Paid 13	0.6	•	6.8	0.3	0.4	0.6	0.3	•	0.7	0.6	•	•	•
Depreciation 14	2.8	•	0.1	0.3	2.4	4.7	2.0	•	2.9	3.5	•	•	•
Amortization and Depletion 15	0.2	•	•	0.1	0.0	0.3	0.0	•	0.2	0.2	•	•	•
Pensions and Other Deferred Comp. 16	0.9	•	•	0.3	1.9	0.4	0.5	•	0.8	0.4	•	•	•
Employee Benefits 17	1.9	•	•	1.7	3.1	2.0	1.5	•	1.8	2.6	•	•	•
Advertising 18	0.1	•	•	0.4	0.2	0.2	0.2	•	0.0	0.0	•	•	•
Other Expenses 19	4.8	•	52.2	14.2	4.8	9.4	4.6	•	3.1	4.4	•	•	•
Officers' Compensation 20	1.9	•	•	5.9	4.3	2.7	2.4	•	1.1	0.8	•	•	•
Operating Margin 21	8.1	•	•	7.2	8.2	12.5	7.6	•	4.3	7.1	•	•	•
Operating Margin Before Officers' Comp. 22	10.0	•	•	13.1	12.5	15.1	10.1	•	5.3	7.9	•	•	•

Net Receivables	23	1578	•	6	132	723	1369	4388	•	18500	32590	•	•	•
Inventories	24	1226	•	1	151	411	1372	2733	•	12311	26906	•	•	•
Net Property, Plant and Equipment	25	2010	•	4	16	525	2089	4008	•	22293	53226	•	•	•
Total Assets	26	8097	•	10	640	2231	7706	15000	•	73721	165858	•	•	•
Notes and Loans Payable	27	1798	•	33	45	444	1710	2765	•	17898	32183	•	•	•
All Other Liabilities	28	1862	•	481	125	521	1002	3545	•	20680	39036	•	•	•
Net Worth	29	4437	•	-504	470	1266	4993	8690	•	35143	94639	•	•	•

Selected Financial Ratios (Times to 1)

Current Ratio	30	2.3	•	0.0	3.8	3.2	4.1	2.3	•	2.1	2.2	•	•	•
Quick Ratio	31	1.4	•	0.0	2.8	2.3	2.7	1.4	•	1.2	1.3	•	•	•
Net Sales to Working Capital	32	5.0	•	•	2.6	4.9	3.5	6.1	•	5.6	5.4	•	•	•
Coverage Ratio	33	18.4	•	46.6	25.9	21.5	28.3	24.1	•	9.1	14.5	•	•	•
Total Asset Turnover	34	1.4	•	1.1	1.8	2.4	1.5	2.3	•	1.6	1.6	•	•	•
Inventory Turnover	35	6.8	•	9.9	5.0	8.6	5.2	9.2	•	7.5	7.2	•	•	•
Receivables Turnover	36	7.5	•	0.6	•	7.2	7.4	8.4	•	7.3	7.6	•	•	•
Total Liabilities to Net Worth	37	0.8	•	•	0.4	0.8	0.5	0.7	•	1.1	0.8	•	•	•
Current Assets to Working Capital	38	1.8	•	•	1.4	1.5	1.3	1.8	•	1.9	1.9	•	•	•
Current Liabilities to Working Capital	39	0.8	•	•	0.4	0.5	0.3	0.8	•	0.9	0.9	•	•	•
Working Capital to Net Sales	40	0.2	•	•	0.4	0.2	0.3	0.2	•	0.2	0.2	•	•	•
Inventory to Working Capital	41	0.6	•	•	0.4	0.4	0.3	0.6	•	0.6	0.6	•	•	•
Total Receipts to Cash Flow	42	8.1	•	0.3	5.4	9.7	4.3	9.3	•	13.2	9.3	•	•	•
Cost of Goods to Cash Flow	43	5.8	•	0.2	3.6	6.4	2.6	6.9	•	10.4	7.0	•	•	•
Cash Flow to Total Debt	44	0.4	•	0.1	1.2	0.6	1.0	0.6	•	0.2	0.4	•	•	•

Selected Financial Factors (in Percentages)

Debt Ratio	45	45.2	•	4905.2	26.6	43.3	35.2	42.1	•	52.3	42.9	•	•	•
Return on Total Assets	46	14.6	•	355.2	13.6	22.6	27.0	18.7	•	10.4	12.7	•	•	•
Return on Equity Before Income Taxes	47	25.1	•	•	17.8	38.0	40.1	31.0	•	19.3	20.7	•	•	•
Return on Equity After Income Taxes	48	23.2	•	•	17.5	36.7	36.6	29.3	•	17.2	18.6	•	•	•
Profit Margin (Before Income Tax)	49	9.7	•	308.2	7.4	8.9	16.9	8.0	•	5.8	7.6	•	•	•
Profit Margin (After Income Tax)	50	8.9	•	208.7	7.3	8.6	15.4	7.5	•	5.2	6.8	•	•	•

Table I

Corporations with and without Net Income

CUTLERY, HARDWARE, SPRING AND WIRE MACHINE SHOPS, NUT, BOLT

MONEY AMOUNTS AND SIZE OF ASSETS IN THOUSANDS OF DOLLARS

Item Description for Accounting Period 7/12 Through 6/13	Total	Zero Assets	Under 500	500 to 1,000	1,000 to 5,000	5,000 to 10,000	10,000 to 25,000	25,000 to 50,000	50,000 to 100,000	100,000 to 250,000	250,000 to 500,000	500,000 to 2,500,000	2,500,000 and over
Number of Enterprises **1**	20729	3344	11673	1492	3203	473	355	105	44	22	6	9	3

Revenues ($ in Thousands)													
Net Sales **2**	70922821	1347100	5540211	3537382	12587300	6305087	9543842	5646923	4741920	3832792	2916453	4828736	10095076
Interest **3**	202911	59	608	1477	5483	1664	1633	724	10052	3384	1465	27296	149067
Rents **4**	13213	167	657	0	683	203	1341	627	1221	5682	1	2432	198
Royalties **5**	381715	0	0	0	29	32	2251	0	2946	5253	6879	13170	351155
Other Portfolio Income **6**	275775	92841	26443	16469	54188	2697	7858	2526	12912	16848	2964	14529	25497
Other Receipts **7**	742371	22192	4712	6805	157751	17502	54325	35512	31368	16413	173919	44344	177530
Total Receipts **8**	72538806	1462359	5572631	3562133	12805434	6327185	9611250	5686312	4800419	3880372	3101681	4930507	10798523
Average Total Receipts **9**	3499	437	477	2387	3998	13377	27074	54155	109100	176381	516947	547834	3599508

Operating Costs/Operating Income (%)													
Cost of Operations **10**	65.7	64.4	60.5	58.4	60.3	66.6	68.0	71.0	73.7	72.7	78.1	67.2	61.9
Salaries and Wages **11**	7.1	3.8	7.2	8.3	8.4	6.0	5.7	5.5	5.5	5.5	9.2	6.2	9.4
Taxes Paid **12**	2.2	4.7	2.1	3.9	3.1	2.6	2.1	1.8	1.4	1.7	0.9	1.5	1.4
Interest Paid **13**	1.6	1.2	0.6	0.5	1.0	0.4	1.2	0.6	0.8	1.6	2.6	2.5	4.7
Depreciation **14**	2.5	2.8	1.7	2.9	2.6	3.4	3.1	2.7	3.1	2.5	2.2	2.1	1.6
Amortization and Depletion **15**	0.5	1.1	0.0	0.0	0.1	0.0	0.2	0.3	0.5	0.9	0.6	1.2	1.6
Pensions and Other Deferred Comp. **16**	0.7	1.5	0.0	1.0	0.3	0.4	0.5	0.4	0.6	0.6	0.5	1.0	1.7
Employee Benefits **17**	1.8	0.8	1.3	2.5	2.0	1.6	1.7	1.6	1.1	1.5	0.9	1.8	2.5
Advertising **18**	0.6	0.1	0.7	0.1	0.3	0.4	0.6	0.6	0.6	0.5	0.7	1.9	1.0
Other Expenses **19**	10.5	32.1	14.7	10.1	10.7	6.5	7.9	7.0	6.8	8.2	7.3	9.5	16.2
Officers' Compensation **20**	3.4	3.9	6.9	6.3	6.3	4.8	2.5	2.5	1.2	0.9	0.6	1.2	0.8
Operating Margin **21**	3.4	•	4.3	6.1	4.8	7.2	6.6	5.9	4.7	3.5	•	3.8	•
Operating Margin Before Officers' Comp. **22**	6.8	•	11.2	12.4	11.2	12.1	9.1	8.4	5.9	4.4	•	5.0	•

Selected Average Balance Sheet ($ in Thousands)													
Net Receivables 23	447	0	24	273	481	1683	3255	7445	13976	23798	109045	65285	641457
Inventories 24	400	0	21	104	300	1743	4510	9324	15572	30233	61808	149018	310594
Net Property, Plant and Equipment 25	432	0	26	130	577	1660	4124	8388	17861	29068	53338	86242	320374
Total Assets 26	3651	0	131	671	2112	7054	15695	33389	72309	150264	409520	689576	12936628
Notes and Loans Payable 27	892	0	76	254	807	1485	5274	8116	20863	49952	224385	254065	1852000
All Other Liabilities 28	697	0	27	230	418	1237	2968	8535	17602	48225	84760	139280	2105220
Net Worth 29	2062	0	29	187	887	4332	7452	16738	33845	52087	100376	296230	8979408

Selected Financial Ratios (Times to 1)													
Current Ratio 30	1.9	•	2.8	1.8	2.6	3.1	2.3	2.4	2.2	1.8	2.2	2.5	1.0
Quick Ratio 31	1.1	•	1.7	1.5	1.8	1.7	1.2	1.2	1.0	0.8	1.3	1.2	0.6
Net Sales to Working Capital 32	6.0	•	7.5	10.4	5.3	4.0	4.9	4.4	5.1	6.0	4.4	3.5	•
Coverage Ratio 33	4.6	•	9.4	13.7	7.5	18.1	7.0	11.3	8.3	4.1	2.0	3.4	2.1
Total Asset Turnover 34	0.9	•	3.6	3.5	1.9	1.9	1.7	1.6	1.5	1.2	1.2	0.8	0.3
Inventory Turnover 35	5.6	•	13.6	13.4	7.9	5.1	4.1	4.1	5.1	4.2	6.1	2.4	6.7
Receivables Turnover 36	7.7	•	19.0	9.0	8.2	8.4	7.9	7.4	8.3	7.4	4.3	3.1	10.5
Total Liabilities to Net Worth 37	0.8	•	3.6	2.6	1.4	0.6	1.1	1.0	1.1	1.9	3.1	1.3	0.4
Current Assets to Working Capital 38	2.1	•	1.5	2.2	1.6	1.5	1.8	1.7	1.9	2.3	1.9	1.7	•
Current Liabilities to Working Capital 39	1.1	•	0.5	1.2	0.6	0.5	0.8	0.7	0.9	1.3	0.9	0.7	•
Working Capital to Net Sales 40	0.2	•	0.1	0.1	0.2	0.3	0.2	0.2	0.2	0.2	0.2	0.3	•
Inventory to Working Capital 41	0.7	•	0.4	0.4	0.4	0.6	0.8	0.7	0.8	1.0	0.5	0.6	•
Total Receipts to Cash Flow 42	7.5	25.8	6.6	7.4	7.5	8.7	7.7	8.4	8.9	8.8	11.7	7.3	5.3
Cost of Goods to Cash Flow 43	4.9	16.6	4.0	4.3	4.5	5.8	5.2	5.9	6.5	6.4	9.1	4.9	3.3
Cash Flow to Total Debt 44	0.3	•	0.7	0.7	0.4	0.6	0.4	0.4	0.3	0.2	0.1	0.2	0.2

Selected Financial Factors (in Percentages)													
Debt Ratio 45	43.5	•	78.1	72.1	58.0	38.6	52.5	49.9	53.2	65.3	75.5	57.0	30.6
Return on Total Assets 46	7.0	•	19.8	25.7	14.1	15.2	14.7	11.7	10.1	7.5	6.4	6.6	2.6
Return on Equity Before Income Taxes 47	9.7	•	80.7	85.4	29.1	23.3	26.5	21.2	19.0	16.3	13.4	10.9	1.9
Return on Equity After Income Taxes 48	8.4	•	78.7	78.0	27.6	21.7	24.7	19.5	15.8	12.6	8.0	8.8	1.3
Profit Margin (Before Income Tax) 49	5.8	•	4.9	6.8	6.6	7.6	7.3	6.6	6.0	4.9	2.8	6.0	5.1
Profit Margin (After Income Tax) 50	5.1	•	4.8	6.2	6.2	7.1	6.9	6.1	4.9	3.8	1.6	4.8	3.4

Table II

Corporations with Net Income

CUTLERY, HARDWARE, SPRING AND WIRE MACHINE SHOPS, NUT, BOLT

MONEY AMOUNTS AND SIZE OF ASSETS IN THOUSANDS OF DOLLARS

Item Description for Accounting Period 7/12 Through 6/13	Total	Zero Assets	Under 500	500 to 1,000	1,000 to 5,000	5,000 to 10,000	10,000 to 25,000	25,000 to 50,000	50,000 to 100,000	100,000 to 250,000	250,000 to 500,000	500,000 to 2,500,000	2,500,000 and over
Number of Enterprises **1**	14245	2652	6630	1327	2720	455	306	81	41	15	•	•	3

Revenues ($ in Thousands)

	Total	Zero Assets	Under 500	500 to 1,000	1,000 to 5,000	5,000 to 10,000	10,000 to 25,000	25,000 to 50,000	50,000 to 100,000	100,000 to 250,000	250,000 to 500,000	500,000 to 2,500,000	2,500,000 and over
Net Sales **2**	62920922	982843	3935336	3180668	11292859	6157661	8285582	4402313	4585728	2769961	•	•	10095076
Interest **3**	198986	5	283	1476	3515	1654	1632	683	9989	2080	•	•	149067
Rents **4**	11733	0	23	0	583	203	946	627	1221	5499	•	•	198
Royalties **5**	381278	0	0	0	0	32	2251	0	2946	4911	•	•	351155
Other Portfolio Income **6**	254189	92838	22574	16301	50960	2391	6871	2228	12912	11304	•	•	25497
Other Receipts **7**	552097	10077	906	6799	154738	16867	50378	29773	30616	12938	•	•	177530
Total Receipts **8**	64319205	1085763	3959122	3205244	11502655	6178808	8347660	4435624	4643412	2806693	•	•	10798523
Average Total Receipts **9**	4515	409	597	2415	4229	13580	27280	54761	113254	187113	•	•	3599508

Operating Costs/Operating Income (%)

	Total	Zero Assets	Under 500	500 to 1,000	1,000 to 5,000	5,000 to 10,000	10,000 to 25,000	25,000 to 50,000	50,000 to 100,000	100,000 to 250,000	250,000 to 500,000	500,000 to 2,500,000	2,500,000 and over
Cost of Operations **10**	65.3	62.6	62.5	60.8	59.5	66.4	67.4	66.3	73.5	70.0	•	•	61.9
Salaries and Wages **11**	6.8	2.5	6.3	5.3	8.7	6.0	5.5	6.2	5.6	5.6	•	•	9.4
Taxes Paid **12**	2.1	1.8	1.5	3.9	3.1	2.5	2.1	2.0	1.4	1.8	•	•	1.4
Interest Paid **13**	1.6	1.5	0.3	0.5	1.0	0.4	0.7	0.5	0.7	1.2	•	•	4.7
Depreciation **14**	2.4	2.5	1.2	3.1	2.2	3.4	2.9	2.8	2.8	2.1	•	•	1.6
Amortization and Depletion **15**	0.4	0.2	0.0	0.0	0.1	0.0	0.1	0.1	0.3	0.7	•	•	1.6
Pensions and Other Deferred Comp. **16**	0.7	1.8	0.0	1.1	0.3	0.4	0.5	0.4	0.6	0.7	•	•	1.7
Employee Benefits **17**	1.7	0.5	0.5	2.5	1.9	1.6	1.8	1.9	1.1	1.6	•	•	2.5
Advertising **18**	0.6	0.1	0.8	0.1	0.3	0.4	0.5	0.5	0.6	0.6	•	•	1.0
Other Expenses **19**	9.9	14.7	12.5	10.1	10.7	6.1	7.4	7.2	6.9	8.3	•	•	16.2
Officers' Compensation **20**	3.1	3.3	5.1	5.5	6.0	4.9	2.5	2.9	1.2	0.9	•	•	0.8
Operating Margin **21**	5.4	8.5	9.3	7.0	6.2	7.8	8.6	9.1	5.2	6.5	•	•	•
Operating Margin Before Officers' Comp. **22**	8.5	11.8	14.4	12.5	12.2	12.6	11.0	12.0	6.4	7.4	•	•	•

Selected Average Balance Sheet ($ in Thousands)

	C1	C2	C3	C4	C5	C6	C7	C8	C9	C10	C11	C12	C13
Net Receivables 23	584	0	20	269	516	1687	3327	7933	14553	22965	•	•	641457
Inventories 24	490	0	18	106	286	1731	4292	9320	18717	31166	•	•	310594
Net Property, Plant and Equipment 25	531	0	24	130	564	1674	4116	7430	17495	28215	•	•	320374
Total Assets 26	4905	0	118	674	2138	7093	15633	33745	73111	148017	•	•	12936628
Notes and Loans Payable 27	1092	0	53	264	824	1471	4219	6658	20499	31622	•	•	1852000
All Other Liabilities 28	899	0	23	241	396	1235	2888	6814	18161	45009	•	•	2105220
Net Worth 29	2914	0	43	169	918	4386	8527	20273	34451	71385	•	•	8979408

Selected Financial Ratios (Times to 1)

	C1	C2	C3	C4	C5	C6	C7	C8	C9	C10	C11	C12	C13
Current Ratio 30	2.0	•	2.6	1.9	2.6	3.2	2.6	3.1	2.2	2.5	•	•	1.0
Quick Ratio 31	1.2	•	1.7	1.5	1.9	1.8	1.3	1.7	1.0	1.2	•	•	0.6
Net Sales to Working Capital 32	5.8	•	10.1	10.3	5.3	3.9	4.5	3.6	4.9	4.5	•	•	•
Coverage Ratio 33	5.9	13.3	38.8	15.2	9.0	19.7	13.7	21.2	9.9	7.5	•	•	2.1
Total Asset Turnover 34	0.9	•	5.0	3.6	1.9	1.9	1.7	1.6	1.5	1.2	•	•	0.3
Inventory Turnover 35	5.9	•	20.2	13.7	8.7	5.2	4.3	3.9	4.4	4.1	•	•	6.7
Receivables Turnover 36	7.8	•	21.5	8.7	8.8	8.8	8.2	7.0	•	7.9	•	•	10.5
Total Liabilities to Net Worth 37	0.7	•	1.8	3.0	1.3	0.6	0.8	0.7	1.1	1.1	•	•	0.4
Current Assets to Working Capital 38	2.0	•	1.6	2.1	1.6	1.5	1.6	1.5	1.8	1.7	•	•	•
Current Liabilities to Working Capital 39	1.0	•	0.6	1.1	0.6	0.5	0.6	0.5	0.8	0.7	•	•	•
Working Capital to Net Sales 40	0.2	•	0.1	0.1	0.2	0.3	0.2	0.3	0.2	0.2	•	•	•
Inventory to Working Capital 41	0.7	•	0.3	0.4	0.4	0.6	0.7	0.6	0.8	0.7	•	•	•
Total Receipts to Cash Flow 42	6.6	3.3	5.3	6.9	6.7	8.5	6.9	6.6	8.5	6.9	•	•	5.3
Cost of Goods to Cash Flow 43	4.3	2.1	3.3	4.2	4.0	5.6	4.6	4.4	6.2	4.8	•	•	3.3
Cash Flow to Total Debt 44	0.3	•	1.5	0.7	0.5	0.6	0.6	0.6	0.3	0.3	•	•	0.2

Selected Financial Factors (in Percentages)

	C1	C2	C3	C4	C5	C6	C7	C8	C9	C10	C11	C12	C13
Debt Ratio 45	40.6	•	63.7	74.9	57.1	38.2	45.5	39.9	52.9	51.8	•	•	30.6
Return on Total Assets 46	8.4	•	51.0	29.5	17.7	16.3	17.4	16.6	11.0	11.5	•	•	2.6
Return on Equity Before Income Taxes 47	11.7	•	136.7	109.6	36.6	25.0	29.6	26.4	21.0	20.7	•	•	1.9
Return on Equity After Income Taxes 48	10.5	•	134.3	100.3	34.9	23.3	27.8	24.5	17.5	16.8	•	•	1.3
Profit Margin (Before Income Tax) 49	7.7	19.0	9.9	7.7	8.1	8.1	9.3	9.8	6.5	8.0	•	•	5.1
Profit Margin (After Income Tax) 50	6.9	18.8	9.7	7.1	7.7	7.6	8.8	9.2	5.4	6.5	•	•	3.4

114

Table I

Corporations with and without Net Income

ARCHITECTURAL AND STRUCTURAL METALS

MONEY AMOUNTS AND SIZE OF ASSETS IN THOUSANDS OF DOLLARS

Item Description for Accounting Period 7/12 Through 6/13	Total	Zero Assets	Under 500	500 to 1,000	1,000 to 5,000	5,000 to 10,000	10,000 to 25,000	25,000 to 50,000	50,000 to 100,000	100,000 to 250,000	250,000 to 500,000	500,000 to 2,500,000	2,500,000 and over
Number of Enterprises 1	8032	544	4308	1087	1466	270	217	86	25	15	8	7	0

Revenues ($ in Thousands)													
Net Sales 2	42994221	373011	2982231	1731277	7518126	3219848	6854689	4188634	2645193	3595861	2608881	7276469	0
Interest 3	80674	0	603	78	2535	1669	2809	4032	308	11197	1953	55490	0
Rents 4	9864	0	0	0	996	747	1202	305	0	1836	280	4498	0
Royalties 5	39986	0	0	0	0	0	0	0	0	406	111	39468	0
Other Portfolio Income 6	208385	31998	13260	123	59796	1615	32130	2759	6238	18919	1551	39997	0
Other Receipts 7	305295	2143	15897	2079	42757	17360	20800	18902	35921	15119	3240	131077	0
Total Receipts 8	43638425	407152	3011991	1733557	7624210	3241239	6911630	4214632	2687660	3643338	2616016	7546999	0
Average Total Receipts 9	5433	748	699	1595	5201	12005	31851	49007	107506	242889	327002	1078143	•

Operating Costs/Operating Income (%)													
Cost of Operations 10	72.3	76.2	66.4	65.8	69.8	71.0	71.8	76.3	76.5	72.7	81.2	72.2	•
Salaries and Wages 11	6.4	12.7	5.0	5.4	6.0	4.8	7.4	5.8	5.6	7.8	5.2	7.2	•
Taxes Paid 12	2.0	2.0	2.7	2.7	2.3	2.7	2.0	1.5	1.9	1.8	1.7	1.7	•
Interest Paid 13	1.2	0.4	0.3	0.5	0.4	0.9	0.6	0.6	0.4	2.0	1.7	3.2	•
Depreciation 14	2.2	1.5	0.9	4.5	1.6	2.6	1.4	1.7	1.6	1.9	3.3	3.6	•
Amortization and Depletion 15	0.2	0.1	0.0	0.0	0.0	0.0	0.2	0.3	0.1	0.7	0.6	0.4	•
Pensions and Other Deferred Comp. 16	0.6	•	0.3	0.1	0.6	0.4	0.6	0.3	0.7	0.4	0.4	1.0	•
Employee Benefits 17	1.9	0.5	0.7	2.5	1.8	1.2	2.3	0.9	1.2	2.1	1.4	3.1	•
Advertising 18	0.4	0.1	0.3	1.0	0.1	0.5	0.2	0.5	0.4	0.6	0.1	0.7	•
Other Expenses 19	8.7	12.1	12.5	12.5	8.2	10.1	8.7	6.4	7.6	9.2	4.9	9.0	•
Officers' Compensation 20	2.3	0.1	6.1	6.4	4.3	2.1	1.7	1.2	1.3	0.7	1.1	0.6	•
Operating Margin 21	1.9	•	4.8	•	4.8	3.7	3.1	4.5	2.7	0.1	•	•	•
Operating Margin Before Officers' Comp. 22	4.2	•	10.9	5.0	9.1	5.9	4.8	5.7	4.0	0.8	•	•	•

Selected Average Balance Sheet ($ in Thousands)

Net Receivables	23	807	0	69	129	726	2452	4389	6743	18596	30224	57680	200960	•
Inventories	24	513	0	7	159	318	1334	3763	5641	15374	24262	32937	110283	•
Net Property, Plant and Equipment	25	779	0	30	217	466	1633	3515	7062	15025	34017	97311	247803	•
Total Assets	26	3806	0	162	686	2244	6995	15411	33966	71070	169182	314679	1550320	•
Notes and Loans Payable	27	1181	0	67	424	429	1495	3778	5630	15676	63071	100804	607928	•
All Other Liabilities	28	981	0	41	94	684	1690	4587	8339	17680	45613	76193	384430	•
Net Worth	29	1644	0	54	168	1130	3810	7046	19997	37714	60498	137682	557962	•

Selected Financial Ratios (Times to 1)

Current Ratio	30	1.9	•	1.4	4.1	2.1	2.6	1.8	2.2	2.6	1.5	2.1	1.4	•
Quick Ratio	31	1.2	•	1.2	2.5	1.6	1.8	1.1	1.3	1.4	0.8	1.3	0.9	•
Net Sales to Working Capital	32	6.0	•	19.4	4.6	6.1	4.2	7.0	4.3	3.7	8.7	4.3	8.1	•
Coverage Ratio	33	3.9	10.5	22.8	•	15.2	6.0	7.9	9.0	11.5	1.7	0.2	1.3	•
Total Asset Turnover	34	1.4	•	4.3	2.3	2.3	1.7	2.0	1.4	1.5	1.4	1.0	0.7	•
Inventory Turnover	35	7.5	•	61.5	6.6	11.2	6.3	6.0	6.6	5.3	7.2	8.0	6.8	•
Receivables Turnover	36	6.8	•	11.2	10.7	6.8	5.2	7.0	7.9	5.8	9.0	5.1	5.4	•
Total Liabilities to Net Worth	37	1.3	•	2.0	3.1	1.0	0.8	1.2	0.7	0.9	1.8	1.3	1.8	•
Current Assets to Working Capital	38	2.1	•	3.5	1.3	1.9	1.6	2.3	1.8	1.6	2.9	1.9	3.3	•
Current Liabilities to Working Capital	39	1.1	•	2.5	0.3	0.9	0.6	1.3	0.8	0.6	1.9	0.9	2.3	•
Working Capital to Net Sales	40	0.2	•	0.1	0.2	0.2	0.2	0.1	0.2	0.3	0.1	0.2	0.1	•
Inventory to Working Capital	41	0.6	•	0.2	0.5	0.4	0.4	0.8	0.6	0.6	1.0	0.4	1.0	•
Total Receipts to Cash Flow	42	10.6	7.5	8.2	12.4	8.5	9.2	9.8	9.9	9.6	12.4	78.8	13.3	•
Cost of Goods to Cash Flow	43	7.7	5.7	5.5	8.2	5.9	6.5	7.1	7.6	7.3	9.0	64.0	9.6	•
Cash Flow to Total Debt	44	0.2	•	0.8	0.2	0.5	0.4	0.4	0.4	0.3	0.2	0.0	0.1	•

Selected Financial Factors (in Percentages)

Debt Ratio	45	56.8	•	66.9	75.5	49.6	45.5	54.3	41.1	46.9	64.2	56.2	64.0	•
Return on Total Assets	46	6.4	•	25.8	•	15.1	9.0	9.2	8.2	7.1	4.9	0.4	2.9	•
Return on Equity Before Income Taxes	47	11.0	•	74.7	•	28.0	13.8	17.5	12.4	12.1	5.7	•	1.9	•
Return on Equity After Income Taxes	48	9.7	•	74.6	•	27.5	12.5	16.4	10.9	11.5	3.5	•	•	•
Profit Margin (Before Income Tax)	49	3.4	3.5	5.8	•	6.2	4.4	3.9	5.1	4.3	1.4	•	1.0	•
Profit Margin (After Income Tax)	50	3.0	2.4	5.8	•	6.1	4.0	3.7	4.5	4.1	0.9	•	•	•

Table II

Corporations with Net Income

ARCHITECTURAL AND STRUCTURAL METALS

MONEY AMOUNTS AND SIZE OF ASSETS IN THOUSANDS OF DOLLARS

Item Description for Accounting Period 7/12 Through 6/13	Total	Zero Assets	Under 500	500 to 1,000	1,000 to 5,000	5,000 to 10,000	10,000 to 25,000	25,000 to 50,000	50,000 to 100,000	100,000 to 250,000	250,000 to 500,000	500,000 to 2,500,000	2,500,000 and over
Number of Enterprises **1**	5383	58	2697	966	1183	189	180	71	21	•	0	•	0
Revenues ($ in Thousands)													
Net Sales **2**	33422795	122546	2223459	1483672	5998208	2455082	5984114	3688876	2478568	•	0	•	0
Interest **3**	32650	0	603	73	2514	1628	1140	2684	149	•	0	•	0
Rents **4**	5888	0	0	0	996	747	415	305	0	•	0	•	0
Royalties **5**	25749	0	0	0	0	0	0	0	0	•	0	•	0
Other Portfolio Income **6**	186020	31975	1721	105	58746	215	31599	1500	1578	•	0	•	0
Other Receipts **7**	242256	0	15897	1549	14452	15510	19630	25997	37512	•	0	•	0
Total Receipts **8**	33915358	154521	2241680	1485399	6074916	2473182	6036898	3719362	2517807	•	0	•	0
Average Total Receipts **9**	6300	2664	831	1538	5135	13086	33538	52385	119896	•	•	•	•
Operating Costs/Operating Income (%)													
Cost of Operations **10**	70.7	71.2	62.2	64.7	66.8	71.7	70.6	76.2	76.6	•	•	•	•
Salaries and Wages **11**	6.1	17.4	6.3	3.1	6.2	4.0	7.3	5.1	5.3	•	•	•	•
Taxes Paid **12**	1.9	1.9	2.5	2.8	2.1	2.6	1.9	1.4	1.9	•	•	•	•
Interest Paid **13**	0.8	0.2	0.3	0.5	0.4	0.4	0.6	0.5	0.4	•	•	•	•
Depreciation **14**	2.0	1.6	1.2	5.2	1.7	2.2	1.3	1.6	1.6	•	•	•	•
Amortization and Depletion **15**	0.1	0.2	0.0	0.0	0.0	0.0	0.1	0.1	0.1	•	•	•	•
Pensions and Other Deferred Comp. **16**	0.6	•	0.4	0.1	0.7	0.4	0.7	0.3	0.7	•	•	•	•
Employee Benefits **17**	1.8	0.2	0.9	2.3	1.8	1.0	2.2	0.8	1.0	•	•	•	•
Advertising **18**	0.4	0.3	0.4	1.1	0.2	0.5	0.2	0.4	0.4	•	•	•	•
Other Expenses **19**	8.1	17.0	12.5	9.0	8.2	9.2	8.5	5.5	7.1	•	•	•	•
Officers' Compensation **20**	2.3	0.1	4.8	6.6	4.5	2.2	1.8	1.3	1.1	•	•	•	•
Operating Margin **21**	5.0	•	8.5	4.5	7.4	5.9	4.7	6.8	3.8	•	•	•	•
Operating Margin Before Officers' Comp. **22**	7.3	•	13.3	11.1	11.9	8.1	6.6	8.1	4.9	•	•	•	•

Net Receivables 23	861	0	54	110	683	2613	4534	7322	21051	•	•	•	•
Inventories 24	541	0	8	147	257	1646	3549	5378	16367	•	•	•	•
Net Property, Plant and Equipment 25	824	0	43	242	410	1624	3672	7122	15696	•	•	•	•
Total Assets 26	3928	0	177	693	2003	7088	15264	33632	72251	•	•	•	•
Notes and Loans Payable 27	1158	0	87	227	443	1175	3689	5900	16264	•	•	•	•
All Other Liabilities 28	1000	0	29	97	567	1463	4731	8692	18279	•	•	•	•
Net Worth 29	1769	0	60	369	992	4449	6844	19040	37709	•	•	•	•

Selected Financial Ratios (Times to 1)

Current Ratio 30	2.0	•	1.3	3.7	2.4	3.2	1.9	2.2	2.6	•	•	•	•
Quick Ratio 31	1.2	•	1.1	2.3	1.9	2.2	1.2	1.3	1.4	•	•	•	•
Net Sales to Working Capital 32	6.2	•	27.5	4.8	5.6	3.6	6.9	4.6	3.9	•	•	•	•
Coverage Ratio 33	8.9	73.9	27.8	10.8	23.9	17.5	11.1	15.4	14.1	•	•	•	•
Total Asset Turnover 34	1.6	•	4.7	2.2	2.5	1.8	2.2	1.5	1.6	•	•	•	•
Inventory Turnover 35	8.1	•	64.3	6.8	13.2	5.7	6.6	7.4	5.5	•	•	•	•
Receivables Turnover 36	7.7	•	15.8	•	7.1	4.9	8.1	8.5	6.0	•	•	•	•
Total Liabilities to Net Worth 37	1.2	•	1.9	0.9	1.0	0.6	1.2	0.8	0.9	•	•	•	•
Current Assets to Working Capital 38	2.0	•	4.1	1.4	1.7	1.4	2.1	1.8	1.6	•	•	•	•
Current Liabilities to Working Capital 39	1.0	•	3.1	0.4	0.7	0.4	1.1	0.8	0.6	•	•	•	•
Working Capital to Net Sales 40	0.2	•	0.0	0.2	0.2	0.3	0.1	0.2	0.3	•	•	•	•
Inventory to Working Capital 41	0.6	•	0.2	0.5	0.3	0.4	0.7	0.6	0.6	•	•	•	•
Total Receipts to Cash Flow 42	8.2	3.4	6.4	9.3	7.1	7.6	8.5	8.6	9.0	•	•	•	•
Cost of Goods to Cash Flow 43	5.8	2.4	4.0	6.0	4.7	5.4	6.0	6.6	6.9	•	•	•	•
Cash Flow to Total Debt 44	0.3	•	1.1	0.5	0.7	0.7	0.5	0.4	0.4	•	•	•	•

Selected Financial Factors (in Percentages)

Debt Ratio 45	55.0	•	65.9	46.8	50.5	37.2	55.2	43.4	47.8	•	•	•	•
Return on Total Assets 46	11.6	•	44.8	11.2	22.9	12.8	13.4	12.6	9.6	•	•	•	•
Return on Equity Before Income Taxes 47	22.8	•	126.6	19.0	44.3	19.2	27.3	20.8	17.1	•	•	•	•
Return on Equity After Income Taxes 48	21.0	•	126.5	18.2	43.6	17.7	25.9	18.9	16.3	•	•	•	•
Profit Margin (Before Income Tax) 49	6.5	16.0	9.3	4.6	8.7	6.6	5.6	7.6	5.4	•	•	•	•
Profit Margin (After Income Tax) 50	6.0	12.5	9.3	4.4	8.5	6.0	5.3	6.9	5.2	•	•	•	•

Table I

Corporations with and without Net Income

BOILER, TANK, AND SHIPPING CONTAINER

MONEY AMOUNTS AND SIZE OF ASSETS IN THOUSANDS OF DOLLARS

Item Description for Accounting Period 7/12 Through 6/13	Total	Zero Assets	Under 500	500 to 1,000	1,000 to 5,000	5,000 to 10,000	10,000 to 25,000	25,000 to 50,000	50,000 to 100,000	100,000 to 250,000	250,000 to 500,000	500,000 to 2,500,000	2,500,000 and over
Number of Enterprises **1**	886	8	317	208	223	22	54	16	17	6	5	6	5

Revenues ($ in Thousands)

	Total	Zero Assets	Under 500	500 to 1,000	1,000 to 5,000	5,000 to 10,000	10,000 to 25,000	25,000 to 50,000	50,000 to 100,000	100,000 to 250,000	250,000 to 500,000	500,000 to 2,500,000	2,500,000 and over
Net Sales **2**	29525872	316324	39570	361985	1146171	452528	1680823	871946	1646681	1085357	1571560	3619299	16733629
Interest **3**	25749	13	0	0	277	14	539	14	220	251	873	8279	15269
Rents **4**	8801	0	0	0	2199	0	533	0	0	0	91	3740	2238
Royalties **5**	152643	128	0	0	213	0	0	0	2912	23	80	13646	135640
Other Portfolio Income **6**	170922	0	0	0	0	957	1855	222	3551	214	2199	32005	129921
Other Receipts **7**	390319	-55	0	1242	189	1751	6125	739	17465	16264	7190	13232	326174
Total Receipts **8**	30274306	316410	39570	363227	1149049	455250	1689875	872921	1670829	1102109	1581993	3690201	17342871
Average Total Receipts **9**	34170	39551	125	1746	5153	20693	31294	54558	98284	183685	316399	615034	3468574

Operating Costs/Operating Income (%)

	Total	Zero Assets	Under 500	500 to 1,000	1,000 to 5,000	5,000 to 10,000	10,000 to 25,000	25,000 to 50,000	50,000 to 100,000	100,000 to 250,000	250,000 to 500,000	500,000 to 2,500,000	2,500,000 and over
Cost of Operations **10**	76.7	63.2	4.3	65.6	66.4	79.9	76.5	73.5	72.9	65.8	77.3	71.9	80.2
Salaries and Wages **11**	4.4	11.1	91.5	6.5	9.0	5.3	5.3	5.4	5.8	3.9	4.3	3.8	3.6
Taxes Paid **12**	1.2	1.7	3.4	2.8	3.5	0.6	1.8	1.6	1.6	1.0	2.9	1.7	0.7
Interest Paid **13**	2.6	14.1	•	0.3	0.1	0.8	0.3	0.6	0.9	2.6	4.1	3.2	2.9
Depreciation **14**	2.5	2.0	35.8	0.3	2.4	3.2	2.0	1.0	3.2	2.4	1.5	3.3	2.5
Amortization and Depletion **15**	0.7	0.7	0.9	•	•	•	0.1	0.1	0.3	0.3	1.0	0.4	0.9
Pensions and Other Deferred Comp. **16**	1.2	0.9	•	0.5	0.7	0.2	0.4	0.5	0.8	0.2	0.2	0.3	1.8
Employee Benefits **17**	1.4	1.9	•	1.7	3.4	0.0	1.2	1.3	2.5	1.1	1.6	1.2	1.3
Advertising **18**	0.1	0.3	•	0.4	0.4	0.2	0.1	1.1	0.4	0.1	0.2	0.3	0.0
Other Expenses **19**	6.0	39.7	61.1	7.4	11.9	6.6	5.3	6.5	6.1	7.6	4.0	7.9	4.5
Officers' Compensation **20**	1.0	1.4	•	5.3	2.3	1.2	1.5	2.0	1.3	0.8	2.2	1.3	0.5
Operating Margin **21**	2.1	•	•	9.3	0.0	2.1	5.5	6.3	4.1	14.3	0.7	4.6	1.1
Operating Margin Before Officers' Comp. **22**	3.1	•	•	14.6	2.3	3.2	7.0	8.4	5.4	15.0	2.9	5.8	1.6

Selected Average Balance Sheet ($ in Thousands)

Net Receivables 23	3886	0	0	173	464	2713	4223	8598	15280	26007	47741	92998	333235
Inventories 24	3624	0	0	114	709	1613	3332	6711	15248	16478	56380	107315	301134
Net Property, Plant and Equipment 25	5087	0	0	242	231	2243	2714	4713	15430	37024	44064	112832	550386
Total Assets 26	35495	0	0	765	2319	7851	16794	32551	70134	175738	319208	1163768	3669303
Notes and Loans Payable 27	16038	0	0	69	3612	3175	1887	6481	12804	65149	128560	492691	1781395
All Other Liabilities 28	11363	0	0	81	882	2771	4268	8552	23408	41167	125081	335448	1228542
Net Worth 29	8094	0	0	615	-2174	1905	10639	17518	33922	69422	65568	335629	659365

Selected Financial Ratios (Times to 1)

Current Ratio 30	1.6	•	•	4.4	2.1	1.8	3.6	2.2	1.6	2.3	1.3	2.0	1.4
Quick Ratio 31	0.9	•	•	3.2	1.0	1.2	2.5	1.3	0.8	1.2	0.7	0.9	0.8
Net Sales to Working Capital 32	7.7	•	•	4.3	5.3	8.8	3.6	4.8	6.3	3.8	11.1	4.8	11.8
Coverage Ratio 33	3.4	•	•	38.8	3.8	4.2	19.7	12.0	7.5	7.2	1.4	3.2	3.6
Total Asset Turnover 34	0.9	•	•	2.3	2.2	2.6	1.9	1.7	1.4	1.0	1.0	0.5	0.9
Inventory Turnover 35	7.1	•	•	10.0	4.8	10.2	7.1	6.0	4.6	7.2	4.3	4.0	8.9
Receivables Turnover 36	9.6	•	•	13.9	10.1	10.3	7.3	•	6.5	6.8	6.4	•	•
Total Liabilities to Net Worth 37	3.4	•	•	0.2	•	3.1	0.6	0.9	1.1	1.5	3.9	2.5	4.6
Current Assets to Working Capital 38	2.6	•	•	1.3	1.9	2.3	1.4	1.8	2.6	1.7	4.2	2.0	3.6
Current Liabilities to Working Capital 39	1.6	•	•	0.3	0.9	1.3	0.4	0.8	1.6	0.7	3.2	1.0	2.6
Working Capital to Net Sales 40	0.1	•	•	0.2	0.2	0.1	0.3	0.2	0.2	0.3	0.1	0.2	0.1
Inventory to Working Capital 41	0.8	•	•	0.3	0.9	0.6	0.3	0.6	1.1	0.3	1.6	0.9	1.1
Total Receipts to Cash Flow 42	11.2	63.4	•	8.6	12.4	12.7	10.6	8.8	9.9	4.5	30.0	8.3	12.6
Cost of Goods to Cash Flow 43	8.6	40.1	•	5.6	8.3	10.1	8.1	6.5	7.2	3.0	23.2	6.0	10.1
Cash Flow to Total Debt 44	0.1	•	•	1.4	0.1	0.3	0.5	0.4	0.3	0.4	0.0	0.1	0.1

Selected Financial Factors (in Percentages)

Debt Ratio 45	77.2	•	•	19.6	193.8	75.7	36.7	46.2	51.6	60.5	79.5	71.2	82.0
Return on Total Assets 46	8.3	•	•	22.4	0.9	9.1	11.7	11.7	8.8	18.9	5.4	5.3	9.4
Return on Equity Before Income Taxes 47	25.7	•	•	27.2	•	28.7	17.6	20.0	15.8	41.2	6.8	12.6	37.9
Return on Equity After Income Taxes 48	17.9	•	•	27.2	0.2	12.1	16.1	16.5	14.4	37.1	5.5	7.6	25.9
Profit Margin (Before Income Tax) 49	6.2	•	•	9.6	0.3	2.7	6.0	6.4	5.5	15.8	1.4	7.0	7.5
Profit Margin (After Income Tax) 50	4.3	•	•	9.6	•	1.1	5.5	5.3	5.0	14.2	1.2	4.2	5.1

Table II

Corporations with Net Income

BOILER, TANK, AND SHIPPING CONTAINER

MONEY AMOUNTS AND SIZE OF ASSETS IN THOUSANDS OF DOLLARS

Item Description for Accounting Period 7/12 Through 6/13	Total	Zero Assets	Under 500	500 to 1,000	1,000 to 5,000	5,000 to 10,000	10,000 to 25,000	25,000 to 50,000	50,000 to 100,000	100,000 to 250,000	250,000 to 500,000	500,000 to 2,500,000	2,500,000 and over
Number of Enterprises **1**	417	0	0	179	129	15	46	13	•	•	5	•	5
Revenues ($ in Thousands)													
Net Sales **2**	27910823	0	0	217183	879012	270420	1612965	736845	•	•	1571560	•	16733629
Interest **3**	24296	0	0	0	277	14	301	14	•	•	873	•	15269
Rents **4**	6602	0	0	0	0	0	533	0	•	•	91	•	2238
Royalties **5**	151291	0	0	0	213	0	0	0	•	•	80	•	135640
Other Portfolio Income **6**	170474	0	0	0	0	957	1821	17	•	•	2199	•	129921
Other Receipts **7**	400013	0	0	1242	124	1595	4770	346	•	•	7190	•	326174
Total Receipts **8**	28663499	0	0	218425	879626	272986	1620390	737222	•	•	1581993	•	17342871
Average Total Receipts **9**	68737	•	•	1220	6819	18199	35226	56709	•	•	316399	•	3468574
Operating Costs/Operating Income (%)													
Cost of Operations **10**	76.9	•	•	50.5	65.7	70.2	75.8	72.7	•	•	77.3	•	80.2
Salaries and Wages **11**	4.0	•	•	10.5	4.3	7.0	5.3	4.5	•	•	4.3	•	3.6
Taxes Paid **12**	1.1	•	•	3.0	1.7	0.9	1.8	1.8	•	•	2.9	•	0.7
Interest Paid **13**	2.5	•	•	0.4	0.1	1.2	0.3	0.5	•	•	4.1	•	2.9
Depreciation **14**	2.6	•	•	0.4	3.0	4.6	2.0	0.8	•	•	1.5	•	2.5
Amortization and Depletion **15**	0.7	•	•	•	•	•	0.1	0.1	•	•	1.0	•	0.9
Pensions and Other Deferred Comp. **16**	1.2	•	•	0.8	0.6	0.3	0.4	0.5	•	•	0.2	•	1.8
Employee Benefits **17**	1.3	•	•	2.3	1.7	0.1	1.2	1.1	•	•	1.6	•	1.3
Advertising **18**	0.1	•	•	0.6	0.4	0.3	0.1	1.3	•	•	0.2	•	0.0
Other Expenses **19**	5.3	•	•	8.3	10.7	7.1	5.4	5.9	•	•	4.0	•	4.5
Officers' Compensation **20**	0.9	•	•	6.6	2.2	1.5	1.5	2.0	•	•	2.2	•	0.5
Operating Margin **21**	3.3	•	•	16.5	9.6	6.7	6.1	8.9	•	•	0.7	•	1.1
Operating Margin Before Officers' Comp. **22**	4.3	•	•	23.1	11.8	8.2	7.6	10.9	•	•	2.9	•	1.6

Selected Average Balance Sheet ($ in Thousands)

Net Receivables 23	7574	•	•	133	542	3017	4893	8891	•	•	47741	•	333235
Inventories 24	6790	•	•	121	1019	1178	3527	9190	•	•	45172	•	301134
Net Property, Plant and Equipment 25	10111	•	•	258	357	2337	3040	3699	•	•	44064	•	550386
Total Assets 26	68194	•	•	748	2756	8569	17846	32412	•	•	319208	•	3669303
Notes and Loans Payable 27	28956	•	•	75	325	3719	2020	5358	•	•	128560	•	1781395
All Other Liabilities 28	21792	•	•	55	922	2927	4879	8810	•	•	125081	•	1228542
Net Worth 29	17446	•	•	618	1509	1923	10947	18244	•	•	65568	•	659365

Selected Financial Ratios (Times to 1)

Current Ratio 30	1.6	•	•	5.2	2.4	1.7	3.3	2.3	•	•	1.3	•	1.4
Quick Ratio 31	0.9	•	•	3.8	1.2	1.2	2.4	1.3	•	•	0.7	•	0.8
Net Sales to Working Capital 32	7.9	•	•	3.1	5.3	7.3	4.0	4.8	•	•	11.1	•	11.8
Coverage Ratio 33	4.1	•	•	42.6	77.5	7.2	22.7	19.3	•	•	1.4	•	3.6
Total Asset Turnover 34	1.0	•	•	1.6	2.5	2.1	2.0	1.7	•	•	1.0	•	0.9
Inventory Turnover 35	7.6	•	•	5.1	4.4	10.7	7.5	4.5	•	•	5.4	•	8.9
Receivables Turnover 36	10.6	•	•	11.0	10.0	8.9	7.2	5.9	•	•	•	•	•
Total Liabilities to Net Worth 37	2.9	•	•	0.2	0.8	3.5	0.6	0.8	•	•	3.9	•	4.6
Current Assets to Working Capital 38	2.6	•	•	1.2	1.7	2.4	1.4	1.8	•	•	4.2	•	3.6
Current Liabilities to Working Capital 39	1.6	•	•	0.2	0.7	1.4	0.4	0.8	•	•	3.2	•	2.6
Working Capital to Net Sales 40	0.1	•	•	0.3	0.2	0.1	0.3	0.2	•	•	0.1	•	0.1
Inventory to Working Capital 41	0.8	•	•	0.3	0.8	0.6	0.3	0.6	•	•	1.6	•	1.1
Total Receipts to Cash Flow 42	10.3	•	•	5.8	6.1	7.4	9.9	7.5	•	•	30.0	•	12.6
Cost of Goods to Cash Flow 43	8.0	•	•	2.9	4.0	5.2	7.5	5.4	•	•	23.2	•	10.1
Cash Flow to Total Debt 44	0.1	•	•	1.6	0.9	0.4	0.5	0.5	•	•	0.0	•	0.1

Selected Financial Factors (in Percentages)

Debt Ratio 45	74.4	•	•	17.4	45.2	77.6	38.7	43.7	•	•	79.5	•	82.0
Return on Total Assets 46	10.1	•	•	28.4	24.3	18.7	13.5	16.6	•	•	5.4	•	9.4
Return on Equity Before Income Taxes 47	29.8	•	•	33.5	43.8	71.7	21.0	27.9	•	•	6.8	•	37.9
Return on Equity After Income Taxes 48	22.1	•	•	33.5	41.5	47.5	19.3	23.8	•	•	5.5	•	25.9
Profit Margin (Before Income Tax) 49	7.8	•	•	17.1	9.7	7.6	6.6	9.0	•	•	1.4	•	7.5
Profit Margin (After Income Tax) 50	5.8	•	•	17.1	9.2	5.1	6.0	7.7	•	•	1.2	•	5.1

Table I

Corporations with and without Net Income

COATING, ENGRAVING, HEAT TREATING, AND ALLIED ACTIVITIES

MONEY AMOUNTS AND SIZE OF ASSETS IN THOUSANDS OF DOLLARS

Item Description for Accounting Period 7/12 Through 6/13	Total	Zero Assets	Under 500	500 to 1,000	1,000 to 5,000	5,000 to 10,000	10,000 to 25,000	25,000 to 50,000	50,000 to 100,000	100,000 to 250,000	250,000 to 500,000	500,000 to 2,500,000	2,500,000 and over
Number of Enterprises 1	2450	266	487	869	651	57	91	10	8	8	0	4	0
Revenues ($ in Thousands)													
Net Sales 2	12546809	156643	210472	1455791	2751949	572001	1862198	599354	788544	1163877	0	2985981	0
Interest 3	6377	13	0	100	245	1022	598	49	229	2112	0	2007	0
Rents 4	9268	109	0	838	41	999	718	579	928	4332	0	724	0
Royalties 5	17348	0	0	0	0	0	65	0	0	9261	0	8022	0
Other Portfolio Income 6	265104	12675	74	6944	2386	7191	12178	19	334	9157	0	214147	0
Other Receipts 7	144193	22933	3672	2119	14805	3937	10584	-1150	1212	4498	0	81584	0
Total Receipts 8	12989099	192373	214218	1465792	2769426	585150	1886341	598851	791247	1193237	0	3292465	0
Average Total Receipts 9	5302	723	440	1687	4254	10266	20729	59885	98906	149155	•	823116	•
Operating Costs/Operating Income (%)													
Cost of Operations 10	59.1	73.3	74.8	37.9	52.2	59.3	58.3	71.9	73.3	66.6	•	65.0	•
Salaries and Wages 11	7.8	3.2	5.7	8.9	9.4	10.4	8.4	3.3	7.9	7.1	•	6.5	•
Taxes Paid 12	2.7	2.8	2.1	2.8	4.0	2.6	2.9	2.3	1.9	1.8	•	2.0	•
Interest Paid 13	2.2	0.9	0.2	0.1	0.6	0.4	1.4	1.3	0.5	1.4	•	6.5	•
Depreciation 14	3.5	1.8	1.2	1.2	3.4	5.5	4.8	5.3	2.0	3.0	•	3.9	•
Amortization and Depletion 15	0.4	0.0	•	•	0.0	0.3	0.1	0.1	0.2	1.6	•	0.9	•
Pensions and Other Deferred Comp. 16	0.8	0.9	•	0.7	1.0	0.6	1.0	0.3	0.4	0.4	•	0.9	•
Employee Benefits 17	2.6	4.5	2.0	2.1	3.5	0.9	2.5	2.1	1.4	3.3	•	2.7	•
Advertising 18	0.2	0.1	0.1	0.1	0.2	0.1	0.3	0.1	0.3	0.2	•	0.2	•
Other Expenses 19	12.0	16.1	19.0	20.9	13.0	14.0	11.3	4.6	4.0	10.5	•	10.2	•
Officers' Compensation 20	4.4	3.4	•	9.3	9.5	4.2	3.3	1.3	1.1	1.5	•	1.1	•
Operating Margin 21	4.4	•	•	15.9	3.3	1.6	5.7	7.4	7.0	2.6	•	0.0	•
Operating Margin Before Officers' Comp. 22	8.8	•	•	25.2	12.8	5.8	9.0	8.8	8.1	4.2	•	1.1	•

Selected Average Balance Sheet ($ in Thousands)

Net Receivables 23	623	0	28	136	537	1242	3345	7299	12448	19596	•	85050	•
Inventories 24	390	0	1	64	148	537	1154	4134	9511	21690	•	96309	•
Net Property, Plant and Equipment 25	1140	0	73	121	788	2748	5496	18151	21449	36952	•	208329	•
Total Assets 26	4158	0	109	636	2033	7407	15641	38639	61985	140221	•	1101788	•
Notes and Loans Payable 27	1800	0	151	97	848	696	5915	19051	14895	37386	•	628241	•
All Other Liabilities 28	893	0	19	181	376	1220	2617	9147	15900	39528	•	233588	•
Net Worth 29	1465	0	-60	358	809	5491	7109	10441	31191	63306	•	239960	•

Selected Financial Ratios (Times to 1)

Current Ratio 30	1.9	•	0.2	3.3	2.3	2.6	2.0	1.3	2.0	1.7	•	1.7	•
Quick Ratio 31	1.3	•	0.2	2.6	1.8	2.2	1.5	0.8	1.2	0.9	•	0.9	•
Net Sales to Working Capital 32	7.2	•	•	5.5	7.6	4.9	5.7	17.4	7.1	6.0	•	7.5	•
Coverage Ratio 33	4.6	17.9	•	135.1	7.1	9.6	6.1	6.6	15.8	4.7	•	2.6	•
Total Asset Turnover 34	1.2	•	4.0	2.6	2.1	1.4	1.3	1.6	1.6	1.0	•	0.7	•
Inventory Turnover 35	7.8	•	245.9	10.0	14.9	11.1	10.3	10.4	7.6	4.5	•	5.0	•
Receivables Turnover 36	8.0	•	4.8	16.3	7.5	8.7	6.8	•	9.0	6.1	•	•	•
Total Liabilities to Net Worth 37	1.8	•	•	0.8	1.5	0.3	1.2	2.7	1.0	1.2	•	3.6	•
Current Assets to Working Capital 38	2.1	•	•	1.4	1.8	1.6	2.0	4.5	2.0	2.4	•	2.5	•
Current Liabilities to Working Capital 39	1.1	•	•	0.4	0.8	0.6	1.0	3.5	1.0	1.4	•	1.5	•
Working Capital to Net Sales 40	0.1	•	•	0.2	0.1	0.2	0.2	0.1	0.1	0.2	•	0.1	•
Inventory to Working Capital 41	0.5	•	•	0.2	0.2	0.2	0.4	1.2	0.6	0.8	•	1.0	•
Total Receipts to Cash Flow 42	6.4	3.2	10.4	3.0	7.9	6.6	6.6	9.5	9.8	8.4	•	7.5	•
Cost of Goods to Cash Flow 43	3.8	2.4	7.8	1.1	4.1	3.9	3.9	6.8	7.2	5.6	•	4.8	•
Cash Flow to Total Debt 44	0.3	•	0.2	2.0	0.4	0.8	0.4	0.2	0.3	0.2	•	0.1	•

Selected Financial Factors (in Percentages)

Debt Ratio 45	64.8	•	155.3	43.7	60.2	25.9	54.5	73.0	49.7	54.9	•	78.2	•
Return on Total Assets 46	12.4	•	•	44.0	9.5	5.9	10.9	13.4	12.5	6.9	•	11.5	•
Return on Equity Before Income Taxes 47	27.7	•	24.2	77.7	20.4	7.1	20.1	42.1	23.2	12.0	•	32.6	•
Return on Equity After Income Taxes 48	25.2	•	24.6	75.9	19.4	7.0	19.0	34.9	21.2	8.5	•	28.2	•
Profit Margin (Before Income Tax) 49	7.9	15.7	•	16.6	3.9	3.9	7.0	7.3	7.3	5.2	•	10.5	•
Profit Margin (After Income Tax) 50	7.2	15.7	•	16.2	3.7	3.8	6.6	6.1	6.7	3.7	•	9.1	•

Table II
Corporations with Net Income

COATING, ENGRAVING, HEAT TREATING, AND ALLIED ACTIVITIES

MONEY AMOUNTS AND SIZE OF ASSETS IN THOUSANDS OF DOLLARS

Item Description for Accounting Period 7/12 Through 6/13	Total	Zero Assets	Under 500	500 to 1,000	1,000 to 5,000	5,000 to 10,000	10,000 to 25,000	25,000 to 50,000	50,000 to 100,000	100,000 to 250,000	250,000 to 500,000	500,000 to 2,500,000	2,500,000 and over
Number of Enterprises 1	1784	•	238	686	452	37	77	•	•	8	0	4	0

Revenues ($ in Thousands)

Net Sales 2	11124309	•	144446	1056971	2352067	466961	1558505	•	•	1163877	0	2985981	0
Interest 3	5749	•	0	60	183	521	575	•	•	2112	0	2007	0
Rents 4	7851	•	0	0	41	999	718	•	•	4332	0	724	0
Royalties 5	17348	•	0	0	0	0	65	•	•	9261	0	8022	0
Other Portfolio Income 6	264937	•	74	6869	2386	7191	12090	•	•	9157	0	214147	0
Other Receipts 7	150932	•	3672	1712	14571	3933	17989	•	•	4498	0	81584	0
Total Receipts 8	11571126	•	148192	1065612	2369248	479605	1589942	•	•	1193237	0	3292465	0
Average Total Receipts 9	6486	•	623	1553	5242	12962	20649	•	•	149155	•	823116	•

Operating Costs/Operating Income (%)

Cost of Operations 10	59.2	•	71.5	36.6	51.1	59.7	57.8	•	•	66.6	•	65.0	•
Salaries and Wages 11	7.8	•	0.0	10.1	9.5	9.7	8.1	•	•	7.1	•	6.5	•
Taxes Paid 12	2.6	•	1.1	2.8	4.0	2.4	2.9	•	•	1.8	•	2.0	•
Interest Paid 13	2.3	•	0.2	0.1	0.4	0.4	1.3	•	•	1.4	•	6.5	•
Depreciation 14	3.1	•	0.5	1.6	2.1	5.4	3.6	•	•	3.0	•	3.9	•
Amortization and Depletion 15	0.4	•	•	•	0.0	0.0	0.1	•	•	1.6	•	0.9	•
Pensions and Other Deferred Comp. 16	0.8	•	•	1.0	1.0	0.7	1.1	•	•	0.4	•	0.9	•
Employee Benefits 17	2.6	•	0.0	2.0	3.5	0.8	2.5	•	•	3.3	•	2.7	•
Advertising 18	0.2	•	0.1	0.0	0.3	0.1	0.2	•	•	0.2	•	0.2	•
Other Expenses 19	9.9	•	25.4	10.5	12.2	5.9	8.8	•	•	10.5	•	10.2	•
Officers' Compensation 20	4.4	•	•	11.3	9.1	4.9	3.6	•	•	1.5	•	1.1	•
Operating Margin 21	6.7	•	1.2	24.2	6.9	10.0	10.1	•	•	2.6	•	0.0	•
Operating Margin Before Officers' Comp. 22	11.1	•	1.2	35.4	16.0	14.9	13.7	•	•	4.2	•	1.1	•

Selected Average Balance Sheet ($ in Thousands)

Net Receivables 23	774	•	57	122	718	1664	3266	•	•	19596	•	85050	•
Inventories 24	413	•	3	61	190	685	1010	•	•	20370	•	96309	•
Net Property, Plant and Equipment 25	1294	•	9	138	718	2562	4750	•	•	36952	•	208329	•
Total Assets 26	5169	•	79	618	2283	7706	15334	•	•	140221	•	1101788	•
Notes and Loans Payable 27	2052	•	46	58	393	489	4619	•	•	37386	•	628241	•
All Other Liabilities 28	1046	•	34	80	366	1095	1912	•	•	39528	•	233588	•
Net Worth 29	2071	•	-1	480	1524	6122	8803	•	•	63306	•	239960	•

Selected Financial Ratios (Times to 1)

Current Ratio 30	2.2	•	0.9	5.7	3.0	3.9	2.9	•	•	1.7	•	1.7	•
Quick Ratio 31	1.5	•	0.9	4.9	2.4	3.2	2.2	•	•	0.9	•	0.9	•
Net Sales to Working Capital 32	6.1	•	•	4.2	6.5	3.8	4.2	•	•	6.0	•	7.5	•
Coverage Ratio 33	5.7	•	16.6	461.9	19.6	29.8	10.3	•	•	4.7	•	2.6	•
Total Asset Turnover 34	1.2	•	7.7	2.5	2.3	1.6	1.3	•	•	1.0	•	0.7	•
Inventory Turnover 35	8.9	•	161.2	9.3	14.0	11.0	11.6	•	•	4.8	•	5.0	•
Receivables Turnover 36	8.4	•	4.9	15.8	6.6	7.8	6.8	•	•	•	•	17.6	•
Total Liabilities to Net Worth 37	1.5	•	•	0.3	0.5	0.3	0.7	•	•	1.2	•	3.6	•
Current Assets to Working Capital 38	1.8	•	•	1.2	1.5	1.3	1.5	•	•	2.4	•	2.5	•
Current Liabilities to Working Capital 39	0.8	•	•	0.2	0.5	0.3	0.5	•	•	1.4	•	1.5	•
Working Capital to Net Sales 40	0.2	•	•	0.2	0.2	0.3	0.2	•	•	0.2	•	0.1	•
Inventory to Working Capital 41	0.5	•	•	0.1	0.2	0.2	0.3	•	•	0.8	•	1.0	•
Total Receipts to Cash Flow 42	6.0	•	4.9	3.1	6.4	5.9	5.4	•	•	8.4	•	7.5	•
Cost of Goods to Cash Flow 43	3.6	•	3.5	1.1	3.3	3.5	3.1	•	•	5.6	•	4.8	•
Cash Flow to Total Debt 44	0.3	•	1.5	3.6	1.1	1.3	0.6	•	•	0.2	•	0.1	•

Selected Financial Factors (in Percentages)

Debt Ratio 45	59.9	•	101.8	22.4	33.2	20.6	42.6	•	•	54.9	•	78.2	•
Return on Total Assets 46	15.8	•	30.6	62.4	18.2	21.5	17.7	•	•	6.9	•	11.5	•
Return on Equity Before Income Taxes 47	32.4	•	•	80.2	25.9	26.2	27.8	•	•	12.0	•	32.6	•
Return on Equity After Income Taxes 48	30.0	•	•	78.5	25.1	26.0	26.7	•	•	8.5	•	28.2	•
Profit Margin (Before Income Tax) 49	10.8	•	3.8	25.0	7.6	12.7	12.1	•	•	5.2	•	10.5	•
Profit Margin (After Income Tax) 50	9.9	•	3.7	24.5	7.4	12.6	11.6	•	•	3.7	•	9.1	•

Table I

Corporations with and without Net Income

OTHER FABRICATED METAL PRODUCT

MONEY AMOUNTS AND SIZE OF ASSETS IN THOUSANDS OF DOLLARS

Item Description for Accounting Period 7/12 Through 6/13	Total	Zero Assets	Under 500	500 to 1,000	1,000 to 5,000	5,000 to 10,000	10,000 to 25,000	25,000 to 50,000	50,000 to 100,000	100,000 to 250,000	250,000 to 500,000	500,000 to 2,500,000	2,500,000 and over
Number of Enterprises 1	14981	1829	7444	1237	2940	840	345	153	93	51	21	23	5

Revenues ($ in Thousands)

Net Sales 2	127460472	1237147	4668149	2315269	15361281	11015607	9794946	8592316	8935724	10391607	7986341	21421688	25740396
Interest 3	600574	4845	623	1086	2854	1953	1947	4100	7536	13322	5675	81090	475542
Rents 4	16617	114	0	7	531	2249	1729	786	3848	531	534	4293	1995
Royalties 5	404047	5	0	0	140	0	592	6469	7995	4554	13235	44045	327013
Other Portfolio Income 6	1366700	63742	123	1458	31148	11551	36852	16586	11091	33008	37144	35033	1088966
Other Receipts 7	905530	13366	21479	1356	113376	69483	56540	43234	52327	81455	65637	296540	90736
Total Receipts 8	130753940	1319219	4690374	2319176	15509330	11100843	9892606	8663491	9018521	10524477	8108566	21882689	27724648
Average Total Receipts 9	8728	721	630	1875	5275	13215	28674	56624	96973	206362	386122	951421	5544930

Operating Costs/Operating Income (%)

Cost of Operations 10	67.5	67.4	57.9	60.6	65.0	63.0	70.8	69.7	69.0	67.7	66.0	71.6	67.9
Salaries and Wages 11	6.8	12.8	9.0	7.5	6.8	8.3	6.5	6.5	5.9	7.1	6.5	5.5	6.9
Taxes Paid 12	1.9	1.0	3.0	2.6	2.5	2.1	2.0	1.8	1.9	1.6	1.6	1.6	1.9
Interest Paid 13	2.0	1.7	0.5	0.9	0.6	0.6	0.5	1.0	1.2	0.8	0.7	3.6	4.4
Depreciation 14	2.2	2.3	1.4	2.7	1.5	2.0	2.5	2.5	2.5	2.4	2.6	2.5	1.8
Amortization and Depletion 15	1.0	1.2	0.1	0.3	0.0	0.1	0.2	0.2	0.5	0.4	0.5	1.0	3.4
Pensions and Other Deferred Comp. 16	1.1	15.5	0.3	0.3	0.5	0.2	0.6	0.5	0.8	0.7	1.3	0.9	2.3
Employee Benefits 17	1.9	3.1	1.7	2.2	1.5	1.7	1.7	1.9	1.8	1.4	1.7	1.6	2.7
Advertising 18	0.5	0.6	0.3	0.3	0.4	0.3	0.3	0.7	0.6	0.6	0.7	0.5	0.8
Other Expenses 19	8.2	16.1	13.0	11.8	8.6	8.8	6.6	8.3	8.3	7.3	8.4	8.1	7.3
Officers' Compensation 20	2.2	4.8	7.3	7.2	5.3	3.6	2.4	1.9	1.8	1.3	1.5	0.5	0.3
Operating Margin 21	4.7	•	5.5	3.5	7.3	9.3	6.2	4.9	5.8	8.8	8.5	2.7	0.3
Operating Margin Before Officers' Comp. 22	6.9	•	12.9	10.7	12.6	13.0	8.6	6.8	7.6	10.1	10.0	3.2	0.6

Selected Average Balance Sheet ($ in Thousands)													
Net Receivables 23	1054	0	45	213	548	1786	3927	6915	12987	26782	67317	123957	565649
Inventories 24	1139	0	26	116	538	1760	4559	10193	14276	34108	58245	153650	541110
Net Property, Plant and Equipment 25	1156	0	42	126	509	1578	3668	7845	15776	31243	69876	158464	677939
Total Assets 26	19835	0	178	672	2281	7045	16457	35433	68848	151031	344032	1219310	44380299
Notes and Loans Payable 27	6848	0	94	299	659	1518	3217	9872	17405	30813	54343	477981	16071318
All Other Liabilities 28	2053	0	43	163	516	1598	3458	9201	15999	41081	90967	298172	2484667
Net Worth 29	10935	0	41	210	1106	3928	9781	16360	35443	79137	198722	443158	25824313
Selected Financial Ratios (Times to 1)													
Current Ratio 30	1.9	•	2.4	1.5	2.6	2.8	2.7	2.2	2.1	2.3	2.6	1.8	1.1
Quick Ratio 31	1.0	•	1.6	1.1	1.6	1.8	1.4	1.0	1.2	1.1	1.4	0.9	0.5
Net Sales to Working Capital 32	5.8	•	8.9	13.3	5.4	4.2	4.0	4.6	5.0	4.4	3.0	5.0	74.0
Coverage Ratio 33	4.8	•	12.3	4.9	15.8	19.3	15.1	6.5	6.6	13.6	16.0	2.4	3.1
Total Asset Turnover 34	0.4	•	3.5	2.8	2.3	1.9	1.7	1.6	1.4	1.3	1.1	0.8	0.1
Inventory Turnover 35	5.0	•	13.9	9.8	6.3	4.7	4.4	3.8	4.6	4.0	4.3	4.3	6.5
Receivables Turnover 36	6.6	•	14.7	8.9	9.7	7.0	7.4	8.1	7.3	7.2	6.7	6.9	4.0
Total Liabilities to Net Worth 37	0.8	•	3.3	2.2	1.1	0.8	0.7	1.2	0.9	0.9	0.7	1.8	0.7
Current Assets to Working Capital 38	2.1	•	1.7	3.0	1.6	1.6	1.6	1.8	1.9	1.8	1.6	2.2	20.2
Current Liabilities to Working Capital 39	1.1	•	0.7	2.0	0.6	0.6	0.6	0.8	0.9	0.8	0.6	1.2	19.2
Working Capital to Net Sales 40	0.2	•	0.1	0.1	0.2	0.2	0.3	0.2	0.2	0.2	0.3	0.2	0.0
Inventory to Working Capital 41	0.8	•	0.5	0.7	0.6	0.5	0.7	0.9	0.7	0.8	0.5	0.8	7.5
Total Receipts to Cash Flow 42	7.7	•	7.2	9.8	7.2	6.2	8.4	8.3	7.5	6.5	6.1	8.8	8.2
Cost of Goods to Cash Flow 43	5.2	•	4.2	5.9	4.7	3.9	6.0	5.8	5.2	4.4	4.0	6.3	5.6
Cash Flow to Total Debt 44	0.1	•	0.6	0.4	0.6	0.7	0.5	0.4	0.4	0.4	0.4	0.1	0.0
Selected Financial Factors (in Percentages)													
Debt Ratio 45	44.9	•	77.0	68.7	51.5	44.2	40.6	53.8	48.5	47.6	42.2	63.7	41.8
Return on Total Assets 46	4.1	•	23.0	12.8	20.2	19.9	13.3	10.8	11.1	14.7	12.1	6.5	1.6
Return on Equity Before Income Taxes 47	5.9	•	92.0	32.6	39.0	33.8	20.9	19.8	18.3	26.0	19.6	10.2	1.9
Return on Equity After Income Taxes 48	4.8	•	87.3	30.7	37.7	32.5	19.6	17.4	16.6	22.1	14.6	6.6	1.2
Profit Margin (Before Income Tax) 49	7.6	•	6.0	3.7	8.3	10.1	7.2	5.8	6.8	10.1	10.2	4.9	9.4
Profit Margin (After Income Tax) 50	6.1	•	5.7	3.4	8.0	9.7	6.8	5.1	6.1	8.6	7.6	3.1	6.1

Table II
Corporations with Net Income

OTHER FABRICATED METAL PRODUCT

MONEY AMOUNTS AND SIZE OF ASSETS IN THOUSANDS OF DOLLARS

Item Description for Accounting Period 7/12 Through 6/13	Total	Zero Assets	Under 500	500 to 1,000	1,000 to 5,000	5,000 to 10,000	10,000 to 25,000	25,000 to 50,000	50,000 to 100,000	100,000 to 250,000	250,000 to 500,000	500,000 to 2,500,000	2,500,000 and over
Number of Enterprises 1	10666	288	5985	580	2513	720	290	125	79	45	18	19	5

Revenues ($ in Thousands)

	Total	Zero Assets	Under 500	500 to 1,000	1,000 to 5,000	5,000 to 10,000	10,000 to 25,000	25,000 to 50,000	50,000 to 100,000	100,000 to 250,000	250,000 to 500,000	500,000 to 2,500,000	2,500,000 and over
Net Sales 2	111331544	298631	3563103	1251760	14084861	9594880	8406812	6985250	7936595	9301794	7128756	17038706	25740396
Interest 3	573902	4092	611	926	2689	1663	1782	3750	7389	13213	4905	57342	475542
Rents 4	15446	114	0	0	470	2081	1729	426	3645	224	533	4229	1995
Royalties 5	396134	5	0	0	140	0	592	6469	525	4554	13235	43601	327013
Other Portfolio Income 6	1275785	14236	123	1432	21090	11536	15296	12227	7834	32779	35236	35031	1088966
Other Receipts 7	809147	5855	18605	647	99474	65132	55055	30236	45439	77912	61636	258416	90736
Total Receipts 8	114401958	322933	3582442	1254765	14208724	9675292	8481266	7038358	8001427	9430476	7244301	17437325	27724648
Average Total Receipts 9	10726	1121	599	2163	5654	13438	29246	56307	101284	209566	402461	917754	5544930

Operating Costs/Operating Income (%)

	Total	Zero Assets	Under 500	500 to 1,000	1,000 to 5,000	5,000 to 10,000	10,000 to 25,000	25,000 to 50,000	50,000 to 100,000	100,000 to 250,000	250,000 to 500,000	500,000 to 2,500,000	2,500,000 and over
Cost of Operations 10	66.5	71.4	52.9	54.7	64.6	60.1	68.4	69.5	67.7	65.8	65.4	71.5	67.9
Salaries and Wages 11	6.7	6.8	9.4	6.8	6.3	8.8	6.7	5.8	5.9	7.7	6.5	5.5	6.9
Taxes Paid 12	1.9	1.4	2.7	2.6	2.4	2.1	2.0	1.7	1.9	1.6	1.7	1.7	1.9
Interest Paid 13	1.8	3.0	0.5	0.6	0.5	0.4	0.5	0.8	0.9	0.8	0.7	2.6	4.4
Depreciation 14	2.1	2.0	1.2	1.4	1.4	2.0	2.4	2.3	2.2	2.5	2.4	2.4	1.8
Amortization and Depletion 15	1.0	0.4	0.2	0.0	0.0	0.0	0.1	0.2	0.5	0.4	0.5	0.9	3.4
Pensions and Other Deferred Comp. 16	1.1	0.2	0.4	0.3	0.5	0.3	0.6	0.5	0.9	0.7	1.3	0.9	2.3
Employee Benefits 17	1.8	1.7	1.6	3.3	1.3	1.7	1.7	1.8	1.8	1.4	1.8	1.5	2.7
Advertising 18	0.5	0.1	0.3	0.5	0.4	0.3	0.3	0.4	0.6	0.7	0.7	0.4	0.8
Other Expenses 19	7.8	9.8	13.5	11.7	8.0	8.8	6.6	7.2	8.5	6.6	7.7	7.8	7.3
Officers' Compensation 20	2.2	2.5	7.8	8.1	5.4	3.8	2.5	2.1	1.9	1.3	1.6	0.6	0.3
Operating Margin 21	6.4	0.7	9.5	10.1	9.1	11.6	8.1	7.7	7.3	10.4	9.7	4.3	0.3
Operating Margin Before Officers' Comp. 22	8.6	3.2	17.3	18.2	14.5	15.4	10.6	9.8	9.2	11.8	11.3	4.8	0.6

Selected Average Balance Sheet ($ in Thousands)

Net Receivables 23	1282	0	39	199	579	1809	3813	7173	13612	26611	67666	118210	565649
Inventories 24	1370	0	24	125	522	1660	4736	10011	14118	34728	63568	150619	519899
Net Property, Plant and Equipment 25	1408	0	43	131	529	1567	3757	7440	15309	32680	69688	151620	677939
Total Assets 26	26642	0	174	678	2363	7032	16148	34867	69178	153369	350984	1163031	44380299
Notes and Loans Payable 27	8966	0	46	244	557	1006	2877	7983	14071	31690	52653	390301	16071318
All Other Liabilities 28	2559	0	22	77	503	1563	3277	7792	16376	39084	96504	294405	2484667
Net Worth 29	15117	0	106	357	1303	4464	9994	19092	38732	82595	201828	478325	25824313

Selected Financial Ratios (Times to 1)

Current Ratio 30	2.0	•	3.9	3.8	2.9	3.1	2.9	2.9	2.3	2.4	2.7	1.8	1.1
Quick Ratio 31	1.0	•	2.6	2.8	1.8	2.1	1.5	1.4	1.3	1.2	1.4	0.8	0.5
Net Sales to Working Capital 32	5.6	•	6.9	6.0	5.1	3.9	3.9	3.8	4.6	4.2	2.9	5.0	74.0
Coverage Ratio 33	6.2	3.9	21.1	18.5	20.6	31.1	19.4	11.1	10.5	16.5	17.3	3.5	3.1
Total Asset Turnover 34	0.4	•	3.4	3.2	2.4	1.9	1.8	1.6	1.5	1.3	1.1	0.8	0.1
Inventory Turnover 35	5.1	•	13.0	9.4	6.9	4.8	4.2	3.9	4.8	3.9	4.1	4.3	6.7
Receivables Turnover 36	6.7	•	14.4	•	10.3	7.4	7.6	8.3	7.7	7.4	7.1	7.2	•
Total Liabilities to Net Worth 37	0.8	•	0.6	0.9	0.8	0.6	0.6	0.8	0.8	0.9	0.7	1.4	0.7
Current Assets to Working Capital 38	2.0	•	1.3	1.4	1.5	1.5	1.5	1.5	1.8	1.7	1.6	2.3	20.2
Current Liabilities to Working Capital 39	1.0	•	0.3	0.4	0.5	0.5	0.5	0.5	0.8	0.7	0.6	1.3	19.2
Working Capital to Net Sales 40	0.2	•	0.1	0.2	0.2	0.3	0.3	0.3	0.2	0.2	0.3	0.2	0.0
Inventory to Working Capital 41	0.8	•	0.4	0.3	0.5	0.4	0.7	0.7	0.7	0.7	0.5	0.9	7.5
Total Receipts to Cash Flow 42	6.8	9.1	5.4	5.3	6.6	5.5	7.3	7.1	6.7	6.0	5.8	7.7	8.2
Cost of Goods to Cash Flow 43	4.6	6.5	2.9	2.9	4.3	3.3	5.0	5.0	4.5	4.0	3.8	5.5	5.6
Cash Flow to Total Debt 44	0.1	•	1.6	1.3	0.8	1.0	0.6	0.5	0.5	0.5	0.5	0.2	0.0

Selected Financial Factors (in Percentages)

Debt Ratio 45	43.3	•	38.8	47.3	44.9	36.5	38.1	45.2	44.0	46.1	42.5	58.9	41.8
Return on Total Assets 46	4.4	•	36.1	34.7	24.8	24.4	17.1	14.9	13.0	17.0	13.9	7.1	1.6
Return on Equity Before Income Taxes 47	6.6	•	56.2	62.4	42.8	37.3	26.2	24.8	21.1	29.7	22.8	12.5	1.9
Return on Equity After Income Taxes 48	5.4	•	54.0	60.0	41.5	36.0	24.7	22.3	19.2	25.4	17.0	8.4	1.2
Profit Margin (Before Income Tax) 49	9.5	8.8	10.0	10.3	10.0	12.5	9.0	8.5	8.1	11.8	11.6	6.6	9.4
Profit Margin (After Income Tax) 50	7.9	6.1	9.6	9.9	9.7	12.1	8.5	7.6	7.4	10.2	8.7	4.5	6.1

Table I

Corporations with and without Net Income

AGRICULTURE, CONSTRUCTION, AND MINING MACHINERY

MONEY AMOUNTS AND SIZE OF ASSETS IN THOUSANDS OF DOLLARS

Item Description for Accounting Period 7/12 Through 6/13	Total	Zero Assets	Under 500	500 to 1,000	1,000 to 5,000	5,000 to 10,000	10,000 to 25,000	25,000 to 50,000	50,000 to 100,000	100,000 to 250,000	250,000 to 500,000	500,000 to 2,500,000	2,500,000 and over
Number of Enterprises 1	3590	15	1845	507	705	231	139	42	43	22	14	13	13

Revenues ($ in Thousands)													
Net Sales 2	179642534	402259	940995	981214	4349141	2618095	3601268	2737421	3700020	4086173	5117808	13607376	137500766
Interest 3	2667668	204	0	238	427	677	2959	1015	1925	4999	13353	35278	2606593
Rents 4	1620264	615	0	179	0	0	8354	203	659	2788	5175	3939	1598351
Royalties 5	1389350	0	0	0	0	0	228	253	285	868	12051	43310	1332355
Other Portfolio Income 6	1600401	4894	1036	62	153815	31224	19114	55648	2369	1972	19676	42750	1267841
Other Receipts 7	2468467	1367	7044	7136	22092	10316	73568	8440	28716	71214	12524	73917	2152132
Total Receipts 8	189388684	409339	949075	988829	4525475	2660312	3705491	2802980	3733974	4168014	5180587	13806570	146458038
Average Total Receipts 9	52755	27289	514	1950	6419	11517	26658	66738	86837	189455	370042	1062044	11266003

Operating Costs/Operating Income (%)													
Cost of Operations 10	71.8	61.1	51.2	50.3	74.9	64.2	71.5	73.6	70.3	70.3	68.0	77.0	71.8
Salaries and Wages 11	5.5	11.8	9.0	11.7	6.5	9.4	6.9	5.1	7.9	5.9	8.1	5.4	5.1
Taxes Paid 12	0.8	1.3	1.6	1.6	1.3	1.9	1.8	1.8	1.5	1.4	1.5	1.2	0.7
Interest Paid 13	2.4	1.9	0.5	2.2	0.3	0.5	0.8	0.6	1.1	0.9	1.7	1.5	2.7
Depreciation 14	3.0	2.1	0.4	3.7	2.4	2.3	2.0	1.7	1.7	2.4	1.8	2.3	3.3
Amortization and Depletion 15	0.3	0.6	0.0	•	0.1	0.1	0.2	0.1	0.4	0.5	0.8	0.6	0.3
Pensions and Other Deferred Comp. 16	0.9	0.1	0.4	0.1	0.7	0.2	0.5	0.6	0.5	0.5	0.8	0.8	1.0
Employee Benefits 17	2.2	0.7	1.2	0.2	0.9	0.7	1.7	1.5	1.4	1.2	1.7	1.2	2.5
Advertising 18	0.3	0.3	0.2	0.7	0.8	1.3	0.5	0.6	0.7	0.5	0.8	0.7	0.2
Other Expenses 19	9.3	10.5	12.4	18.5	6.7	11.3	8.2	6.9	7.6	8.3	9.6	5.7	9.8
Officers' Compensation 20	0.6	2.4	5.5	3.5	4.5	3.4	2.7	2.0	1.1	1.0	0.9	0.4	0.2
Operating Margin 21	2.9	7.2	17.6	7.4	1.0	4.6	3.0	5.4	5.7	7.1	4.3	3.3	2.5
Operating Margin Before Officers' Comp. 22	3.5	9.5	23.1	11.0	5.4	8.1	5.7	7.4	6.8	8.1	5.2	3.6	2.7

Selected Average Balance Sheet ($ in Thousands)

Net Receivables 23	24472	0	21	53	353	1108	3521	7136	13367	33645	94453	155339	6295406
Inventories 24	7849	0	57	97	642	2086	4618	15294	18126	40118	71045	193943	1586642
Net Property, Plant and Equipment 25	7996	0	12	213	472	1239	2444	8666	10347	25329	41934	164271	1809696
Total Assets 26	81950	0	132	808	2267	6950	15248	39425	72768	166849	367026	1046400	20078998
Notes and Loans Payable 27	30317	0	90	761	491	1076	3471	8040	20280	33653	98772	289328	7701100
All Other Liabilities 28	29525	0	41	65	789	1832	4914	10002	22130	41035	125706	305589	7401371
Net Worth 29	22109	0	2	-17	987	4042	6863	21383	30358	92161	142549	451483	4976526

Selected Financial Ratios (Times to 1)

Current Ratio 30	1.4	•	2.5	4.2	2.2	2.7	2.0	2.6	1.8	2.1	1.9	1.8	1.4
Quick Ratio 31	1.0	•	0.7	2.7	1.3	1.3	0.9	1.0	0.9	1.1	1.0	0.8	1.0
Net Sales to Working Capital 32	4.3	•	7.1	6.4	6.7	3.6	4.6	4.1	4.3	3.6	3.6	5.4	4.2
Coverage Ratio 33	5.1	5.7	35.9	4.7	20.5	13.5	8.2	13.0	6.9	10.7	4.3	4.2	4.9
Total Asset Turnover 34	0.6	•	3.9	2.4	2.7	1.6	1.7	1.7	1.2	1.1	1.0	1.0	0.5
Inventory Turnover 35	4.6	•	4.6	10.0	7.2	3.5	4.0	3.1	3.3	3.3	3.5	4.2	4.8
Receivables Turnover 36	2.1	•	21.3	32.2	18.5	9.3	7.5	7.9	7.5	5.0	4.8	5.6	1.7
Total Liabilities to Net Worth 37	2.7	•	60.9	•	1.3	0.7	1.2	0.8	1.4	0.8	1.6	1.3	3.0
Current Assets to Working Capital 38	3.4	•	1.6	1.3	1.9	1.6	2.0	1.6	2.2	1.9	2.1	2.3	3.8
Current Liabilities to Working Capital 39	2.4	•	0.6	0.3	0.9	0.6	1.0	0.6	1.2	0.9	1.1	1.3	2.8
Working Capital to Net Sales 40	0.2	•	0.1	0.2	0.1	0.3	0.2	0.2	0.2	0.3	0.3	0.2	0.2
Inventory to Working Capital 41	0.7	•	0.7	0.4	0.7	0.7	0.9	0.9	1.0	0.7	0.8	1.1	0.7
Total Receipts to Cash Flow 42	6.3	6.0	4.0	4.2	10.1	6.8	8.0	8.7	7.7	6.2	7.7	11.2	5.9
Cost of Goods to Cash Flow 43	4.5	3.7	2.0	2.1	7.6	4.4	5.7	6.4	5.4	4.4	5.3	8.6	4.2
Cash Flow to Total Debt 44	0.1	•	1.0	0.6	0.5	0.6	0.4	0.4	0.3	0.4	0.2	0.2	0.1

Selected Financial Factors (in Percentages)

Debt Ratio 45	73.0	•	98.4	102.1	56.5	41.8	55.0	45.8	58.3	44.8	61.2	56.9	75.2
Return on Total Assets 46	7.4	•	73.0	25.0	14.4	11.0	11.4	13.9	9.3	11.2	7.3	6.4	7.1
Return on Equity Before Income Taxes 47	21.9	•	4393.0	•	31.4	17.4	22.2	23.7	19.1	18.4	14.3	11.3	22.8
Return on Equity After Income Taxes 48	14.9	•	4393.0	•	29.0	15.6	18.0	18.7	16.8	15.1	9.9	8.0	14.9
Profit Margin (Before Income Tax) 49	9.7	8.9	18.4	8.2	5.0	6.2	5.9	7.8	6.7	9.1	5.6	4.9	10.7
Profit Margin (After Income Tax) 50	6.6	7.2	18.4	8.2	4.6	5.5	4.8	6.1	5.9	7.5	3.9	3.4	7.0

Table II

Corporations with Net Income

AGRICULTURE, CONSTRUCTION, AND MINING MACHINERY

MONEY AMOUNTS AND SIZE OF ASSETS IN THOUSANDS OF DOLLARS

Item Description for Accounting Period 7/12 Through 6/13		Total	Zero Assets	Under 500	500 to 1,000	1,000 to 5,000	5,000 to 10,000	10,000 to 25,000	25,000 to 50,000	50,000 to 100,000	100,000 to 250,000	250,000 to 500,000	500,000 to 2,500,000	2,500,000 and over
Number of Enterprises	1	2816	11	1409	389	584	196	111	34	30	17	•	•	13
Revenues ($ in Thousands)														
Net Sales	2	174879148	184968	759412	943385	4179613	2313354	3019245	2424941	2746274	3206251	•	•	137500766
Interest	3	2662475	166	0	0	426	407	2514	1004	1338	1426	•	•	2606593
Rents	4	1617607	615	0	179	0	0	8319	203	263	562	•	•	1598351
Royalties	5	1377147	0	0	0	0	0	228	253	44	417	•	•	1332355
Other Portfolio Income	6	1538407	2578	0	62	153575	14877	7792	55639	1152	1916	•	•	1267841
Other Receipts	7	2449195	2166	7045	7136	21939	10286	80822	7747	13066	67864	•	•	2152132
Total Receipts	8	184523979	190493	766457	950762	4355553	2338924	3118920	2489787	2762137	3278436	•	•	146458038
Average Total Receipts	9	65527	17318	544	2444	7458	11933	28098	73229	92071	192849	•	•	11266003
Operating Costs/Operating Income (%)														
Cost of Operations	10	71.7	60.8	45.5	49.4	75.2	63.5	70.8	73.0	67.2	69.1	•	•	71.8
Salaries and Wages	11	5.4	8.3	8.6	11.8	6.2	9.1	6.2	5.0	6.7	6.0	•	•	5.1
Taxes Paid	12	0.8	1.8	1.4	1.5	1.2	2.0	1.7	1.7	1.6	1.3	•	•	0.7
Interest Paid	13	2.3	0.3	0.2	2.3	0.2	0.5	0.4	0.5	0.6	0.6	•	•	2.7
Depreciation	14	3.0	0.5	0.1	3.5	2.4	1.6	1.7	1.6	1.7	2.4	•	•	3.3
Amortization and Depletion	15	0.3	0.2	0.0	•	0.1	0.1	0.1	0.1	0.2	0.3	•	•	0.3
Pensions and Other Deferred Comp.	16	0.9	0.3	0.5	0.1	0.7	0.3	0.4	0.6	0.6	0.5	•	•	1.0
Employee Benefits	17	2.2	1.0	1.2	0.3	0.9	0.7	1.5	1.3	1.5	1.1	•	•	2.5
Advertising	18	0.3	0.1	0.2	0.7	0.7	1.4	0.5	0.6	0.7	0.4	•	•	0.2
Other Expenses	19	9.2	2.2	10.9	18.7	6.1	10.1	8.2	5.8	6.3	6.8	•	•	9.8
Officers' Compensation	20	0.5	4.8	5.7	3.4	4.4	3.7	2.8	2.1	1.2	1.0	•	•	0.2
Operating Margin	21	3.3	19.9	25.5	8.4	1.9	6.9	5.6	7.7	11.7	10.4	•	•	2.5
Operating Margin Before Officers' Comp.	22	3.8	24.7	31.2	11.7	6.3	10.7	8.4	9.7	12.9	11.4	•	•	2.7

Selected Average Balance Sheet ($ in Thousands)

	C1	C2	C3	C4	C5	C6	C7	C8	C9	C10	C11	C12	C13
Net Receivables 23	30913	0	18	66	392	1107	3498	8244	13234	30711	•	•	6295406
Inventories 24	9587	0	33	86	631	2230	4925	16391	16871	44604	•	•	1711817
Net Property, Plant and Equipment 25	9742	0	8	254	548	1019	2159	7077	10421	24989	•	•	1809696
Total Assets 26	102501	0	67	837	2431	6815	15203	39794	71688	170140	•	•	20078998
Notes and Loans Payable 27	37742	0	21	892	319	824	2402	5317	16269	33768	•	•	7701100
All Other Liabilities 28	36807	0	20	67	599	1728	4785	10674	16892	34278	•	•	7401371
Net Worth 29	27952	0	27	-122	1514	4264	8015	23803	38527	102095	•	•	4976526

Selected Financial Ratios (Times to 1)

	C1	C2	C3	C4	C5	C6	C7	C8	C9	C10	C11	C12	C13
Current Ratio 30	1.4	•	3.0	4.4	2.7	2.9	2.1	2.9	2.4	2.3	•	•	1.4
Quick Ratio 31	1.0	•	1.6	2.9	1.7	1.4	1.0	1.2	1.3	1.2	•	•	1.0
Net Sales to Working Capital 32	4.3	•	13.6	6.8	6.4	3.5	4.5	3.9	3.4	3.3	•	•	4.2
Coverage Ratio 33	5.4	85.4	112.0	5.0	28.9	18.4	22.1	20.8	21.3	22.9	•	•	4.9
Total Asset Turnover 34	0.6	•	8.0	2.9	2.9	1.7	1.8	1.8	1.3	1.1	•	•	0.5
Inventory Turnover 35	4.6	•	7.5	13.9	8.5	3.4	3.9	3.2	3.6	2.9	•	•	4.4
Receivables Turnover 36	2.0	•	28.3	60.8	19.3	8.8	7.7	7.3	8.4	5.1	•	•	•
Total Liabilities to Net Worth 37	2.7	•	1.5	•	0.6	0.6	0.9	0.7	0.9	0.7	•	•	3.0
Current Assets to Working Capital 38	3.4	•	1.5	1.3	1.6	1.5	1.9	1.5	1.7	1.8	•	•	3.8
Current Liabilities to Working Capital 39	2.4	•	0.5	0.3	0.6	0.5	0.9	0.5	0.7	0.8	•	•	2.8
Working Capital to Net Sales 40	0.2	•	0.1	0.1	0.2	0.3	0.2	0.3	0.3	0.3	•	•	0.2
Inventory to Working Capital 41	0.7	•	0.7	0.4	0.6	0.7	0.9	0.8	0.7	0.7	•	•	0.7
Total Receipts to Cash Flow 42	6.2	4.7	3.0	4.0	9.4	6.3	6.4	7.9	5.7	5.5	•	•	5.9
Cost of Goods to Cash Flow 43	4.4	2.9	1.4	2.0	7.1	4.0	4.6	5.8	3.9	3.8	•	•	4.2
Cash Flow to Total Debt 44	0.1	•	4.4	0.6	0.8	0.7	0.6	0.6	0.5	0.5	•	•	0.1

Selected Financial Factors (in Percentages)

	C1	C2	C3	C4	C5	C6	C7	C8	C9	C10	C11	C12	C13
Debt Ratio 45	72.7	•	60.3	114.6	37.7	37.4	47.3	40.2	46.3	40.0	•	•	75.2
Return on Total Assets 46	7.5	•	213.2	33.2	18.7	14.7	16.7	19.4	16.5	14.7	•	•	7.1
Return on Equity Before Income Taxes 47	22.5	•	532.7	•	29.0	22.2	30.2	30.8	29.3	23.4	•	•	22.8
Return on Equity After Income Taxes 48	15.5	•	532.7	•	27.1	20.1	25.7	25.3	26.7	19.5	•	•	14.9
Profit Margin (Before Income Tax) 49	10.1	22.9	26.4	9.2	6.1	8.0	8.9	10.3	12.3	12.6	•	•	10.7
Profit Margin (After Income Tax) 50	7.0	19.1	26.4	9.1	5.7	7.3	7.6	8.5	11.2	10.6	•	•	7.0

Table I

Corporations with and without Net Income

INDUSTRIAL MACHINERY

MONEY AMOUNTS AND SIZE OF ASSETS IN THOUSANDS OF DOLLARS

Item Description for Accounting Period 7/12 Through 6/13	Total	Zero Assets	Under 500	500 to 1,000	1,000 to 5,000	5,000 to 10,000	10,000 to 25,000	25,000 to 50,000	50,000 to 100,000	100,000 to 250,000	250,000 to 500,000	500,000 to 2,500,000	2,500,000 and over
Number of Enterprises **1**	3264	37	1706	290	523	388	165	65	30	35	9	16	0

Revenues ($ in Thousands)

Net Sales **2**	49747269	956711	761318	472890	2671800	4274109	3574711	2902909	2584086	5165139	3331779	23051817	0
Interest **3**	97242	1020	910	0	449	1128	2273	2420	4338	19517	4754	60432	0
Rents **4**	81524	8	0	0	1582	1859	37	2656	2550	2674	16717	53441	0
Royalties **5**	299936	2811	0	0	1138	809	146	557	505	4770	10273	278926	0
Other Portfolio Income **6**	507902	4719	98	0	4186	2283	19931	6254	14177	33587	6328	416336	0
Other Receipts **7**	404009	24695	2277	726	62816	7320	8569	22108	27313	17667	23268	207256	0
Total Receipts **8**	51137882	989964	764603	473616	2741971	4287508	3605667	2936904	2632969	5243354	3393119	24068208	0
Average Total Receipts **9**	15667	26756	448	1633	5243	11050	21853	45183	87766	149810	377013	1504263	•

Operating Costs/Operating Income (%)

Cost of Operations **10**	64.8	69.9	53.6	62.2	65.2	63.0	71.3	65.8	68.8	67.7	74.0	61.7	•
Salaries and Wages **11**	9.8	10.2	9.2	3.7	8.8	10.5	7.9	10.1	8.1	7.7	7.5	11.2	•
Taxes Paid **12**	1.7	1.6	3.1	1.8	2.5	2.4	2.2	2.2	1.9	1.4	1.3	1.4	•
Interest Paid **13**	1.3	1.2	0.6	0.9	1.2	0.5	0.5	1.0	0.8	1.2	0.8	1.8	•
Depreciation **14**	2.0	1.5	2.1	0.1	1.3	1.1	1.3	1.5	1.8	1.7	2.0	2.5	•
Amortization and Depletion **15**	0.7	1.2	0.1	0.0	0.1	0.1	0.1	0.3	0.7	1.0	0.5	1.0	•
Pensions and Other Deferred Comp. **16**	0.9	1.3	0.0	•	0.2	1.3	0.5	0.9	0.6	0.8	0.9	1.0	•
Employee Benefits **17**	2.1	2.1	2.7	2.4	2.2	2.2	1.8	1.8	2.1	1.7	1.9	2.2	•
Advertising **18**	0.4	0.6	1.6	1.7	0.5	0.4	0.4	0.7	0.3	0.3	0.3	0.4	•
Other Expenses **19**	9.1	12.2	18.0	9.3	7.4	8.2	6.0	10.3	8.2	9.6	6.2	9.7	•
Officers' Compensation **20**	1.7	7.4	7.1	7.4	3.6	3.5	2.8	1.5	2.0	1.3	0.7	0.7	•
Operating Margin **21**	5.6	•	1.8	10.5	6.9	6.8	5.3	4.0	4.8	5.7	3.9	6.5	•
Operating Margin Before Officers' Comp. **22**	7.4	•	8.9	17.9	10.5	10.3	8.1	5.5	6.7	7.0	4.7	7.2	•

Selected Average Balance Sheet ($ in Thousands)

Net Receivables 23	4085	0	39	224	843	1518	3119	8037	14420	26225	75228	569120	•
Inventories 24	2153	0	23	268	912	1673	3866	8188	12613	21858	58180	134503	•
Net Property, Plant and Equipment 25	1799	0	31	21	365	1046	1749	5212	10116	17374	37405	208821	•
Total Assets 26	22244	0	150	754	2636	6195	14797	33103	69514	153336	367371	3312371	•
Notes and Loans Payable 27	4422	0	61	172	993	2119	2375	8346	11462	33639	51705	626163	•
All Other Liabilities 28	6185	0	81	205	497	1507	5716	9618	22484	52871	145265	859040	•
Net Worth 29	11637	0	8	376	1146	2568	6706	15139	35568	66827	170401	1827168	•

Selected Financial Ratios (Times to 1)

Current Ratio 30	1.5	•	1.1	3.5	3.0	2.4	1.8	2.0	1.8	2.0	1.7	1.3	•
Quick Ratio 31	1.0	•	0.7	1.7	1.8	1.2	1.0	1.1	1.1	1.1	0.9	0.9	•
Net Sales to Working Capital 32	4.9	•	74.3	3.2	3.9	4.0	4.6	4.2	4.7	3.4	4.4	5.7	•
Coverage Ratio 33	8.5	•	4.8	12.4	8.7	16.5	14.2	6.2	9.5	7.4	8.1	8.4	•
Total Asset Turnover 34	0.7	•	3.0	2.2	1.9	1.8	1.5	1.3	1.2	1.0	1.0	0.4	•
Inventory Turnover 35	4.6	•	10.3	3.8	3.7	4.2	4.0	3.6	4.7	4.6	4.7	6.6	•
Receivables Turnover 36	3.8	•	13.6	6.2	5.2	7.9	6.9	5.6	5.5	5.2	4.7	4.2	•
Total Liabilities to Net Worth 37	0.9	•	17.8	1.0	1.3	1.4	1.2	1.2	1.0	1.3	1.2	0.8	•
Current Assets to Working Capital 38	2.9	•	15.6	1.4	1.5	1.7	2.2	2.0	2.3	2.0	2.5	4.2	•
Current Liabilities to Working Capital 39	1.9	•	14.6	0.4	0.5	0.7	1.2	1.0	1.3	1.0	1.5	3.2	•
Working Capital to Net Sales 40	0.2	•	0.0	0.3	0.3	0.2	0.2	0.2	0.2	0.3	0.2	0.2	•
Inventory to Working Capital 41	0.7	•	5.4	0.6	0.6	0.6	0.8	0.8	0.6	0.5	0.6	0.8	•
Total Receipts to Cash Flow 42	6.6	18.9	6.4	6.3	7.0	7.7	9.4	7.5	7.9	6.8	9.2	5.6	•
Cost of Goods to Cash Flow 43	4.3	13.2	3.4	3.9	4.5	4.9	6.7	4.9	5.4	4.6	6.8	3.4	•
Cash Flow to Total Debt 44	0.2	•	0.5	0.7	0.5	0.4	0.3	0.3	0.3	0.3	0.2	0.2	•

Selected Financial Factors (in Percentages)

Debt Ratio 45	47.7	•	94.7	50.0	56.5	58.5	54.7	54.3	48.8	56.4	53.6	44.8	•
Return on Total Assets 46	7.4	•	8.3	25.1	20.9	13.4	9.6	8.3	9.2	8.3	6.8	6.5	•
Return on Equity Before Income Taxes 47	12.4	•	124.0	46.2	42.5	30.4	19.7	15.2	16.1	16.5	12.9	10.3	•
Return on Equity After Income Taxes 48	9.1	•	109.3	46.2	40.6	29.0	17.9	12.3	12.4	13.0	9.1	7.0	•
Profit Margin (Before Income Tax) 49	9.5	•	2.2	10.7	9.5	7.1	6.1	5.2	6.7	7.5	5.9	13.1	•
Profit Margin (After Income Tax) 50	7.0	•	1.9	10.7	9.1	6.8	5.6	4.2	5.1	5.9	4.2	8.9	•

Table II
Corporations with Net Income

INDUSTRIAL MACHINERY

MONEY AMOUNTS AND SIZE OF ASSETS IN THOUSANDS OF DOLLARS

Item Description for Accounting Period 7/12 Through 6/13	Total	Zero Assets	Under 500	500 to 1,000	1,000 to 5,000	5,000 to 10,000	10,000 to 25,000	25,000 to 50,000	50,000 to 100,000	100,000 to 250,000	250,000 to 500,000	500,000 to 2,500,000	2,500,000 and over
Number of Enterprises 1	2313	13	1019	290	454	266	137	53	•	32	•	16	0

Revenues ($ in Thousands)													
Net Sales 2	45146462	308798	288172	472890	2330665	2980839	3021765	2481880	•	4744730	•	23051817	0
Interest 3	91963	31	897	0	302	620	1816	1673	•	17793	•	60432	0
Rents 4	80024	0	0	0	1006	1859	37	2581	•	2187	•	53441	0
Royalties 5	293634	1172	0	0	1138	0	0	557	•	2667	•	278926	0
Other Portfolio Income 6	493875	2447	52	0	2124	353	18477	6254	•	28426	•	416336	0
Other Receipts 7	389108	22578	1718	726	56656	4638	8467	20502	•	18273	•	207256	0
Total Receipts 8	46495066	335026	290839	473616	2391891	2988309	3050562	2513447	•	4814076	•	24068208	0
Average Total Receipts 9	20102	25771	285	1633	5268	11234	22267	47424	•	150440	•	1504263	•

Operating Costs/Operating Income (%)													
Cost of Operations 10	63.8	62.0	34.2	62.2	64.6	57.4	68.7	64.0	•	68.0	•	61.7	•
Salaries and Wages 11	10.0	10.0	14.2	3.7	8.9	12.6	7.9	10.0	•	7.6	•	11.2	•
Taxes Paid 12	1.6	1.7	2.3	1.8	2.5	2.4	2.3	2.2	•	1.3	•	1.4	•
Interest Paid 13	1.3	0.3	0.6	0.9	1.1	0.4	0.4	0.8	•	1.2	•	1.8	•
Depreciation 14	2.0	2.0	0.3	0.1	1.1	1.1	1.2	1.6	•	1.7	•	2.5	•
Amortization and Depletion 15	0.7	1.0	•	0.0	0.1	0.0	0.1	0.2	•	0.9	•	1.0	•
Pensions and Other Deferred Comp. 16	0.9	0.6	•	•	0.2	1.0	0.6	1.0	•	0.7	•	1.0	•
Employee Benefits 17	2.0	2.2	0.2	2.4	1.9	2.1	1.9	1.9	•	1.5	•	2.2	•
Advertising 18	0.4	0.3	2.6	1.7	0.3	0.4	0.3	0.7	•	0.3	•	0.4	•
Other Expenses 19	8.8	9.6	19.6	9.3	6.1	9.1	5.7	9.8	•	8.5	•	9.7	•
Officers' Compensation 20	1.5	8.7	9.1	7.4	3.4	2.9	3.0	1.6	•	1.3	•	0.7	•
Operating Margin 21	7.0	1.7	17.0	10.5	9.6	10.5	8.0	6.1	•	7.1	•	6.5	•
Operating Margin Before Officers' Comp. 22	8.5	10.4	26.1	17.9	13.0	13.4	11.0	7.8	•	8.4	•	7.2	•

Selected Average Balance Sheet ($ in Thousands)

Net Receivables 23	5496	0	0	224	923	1567	3419	8135	•	26042	•	569120	•
Inventories 24	2671	0	30	268	867	1478	3769	8163	•	19956	•	190319	•
Net Property, Plant and Equipment 25	2381	0	4	21	318	1199	1711	5930	•	17917	•	208821	•
Total Assets 26	30002	0	97	754	2524	6217	14885	33755	•	154589	•	3312371	•
Notes and Loans Payable 27	5693	0	73	172	912	1356	1699	8130	•	31363	•	626163	•
All Other Liabilities 28	8169	0	30	205	479	1371	5192	8532	•	50030	•	859040	•
Net Worth 29	16140	0	-6	376	1133	3489	7994	17092	•	73195	•	1827168	•

Selected Financial Ratios (Times to 1)

Current Ratio 30	1.5	•	1.8	3.5	3.2	2.4	2.0	2.2	•	2.0	•	1.3	•
Quick Ratio 31	1.0	•	0.9	1.7	2.0	1.3	1.1	1.2	•	1.1	•	0.9	•
Net Sales to Working Capital 32	4.8	•	11.1	3.2	3.9	4.2	4.0	3.9	•	3.5	•	5.7	•
Coverage Ratio 33	9.8	33.4	31.5	12.4	11.9	25.4	23.9	10.4	•	8.4	•	8.4	•
Total Asset Turnover 34	0.7	•	2.9	2.2	2.0	1.8	1.5	1.4	•	1.0	•	0.4	•
Inventory Turnover 35	4.7	•	3.2	3.8	3.8	4.3	4.0	3.7	•	5.1	•	4.7	•
Receivables Turnover 36	3.7	•	5287.6	6.4	5.2	7.3	7.1	5.9	•	5.9	•	•	•
Total Liabilities to Net Worth 37	0.9	•	•	1.0	1.2	0.8	0.9	1.0	•	1.1	•	0.8	•
Current Assets to Working Capital 38	2.9	•	2.3	1.4	1.4	1.7	2.0	1.9	•	2.0	•	4.2	•
Current Liabilities to Working Capital 39	1.9	•	1.3	0.4	0.4	0.7	1.0	0.9	•	1.0	•	3.2	•
Working Capital to Net Sales 40	0.2	•	0.1	0.3	0.3	0.2	0.3	0.3	•	0.3	•	0.2	•
Inventory to Working Capital 41	0.7	•	1.2	0.6	0.5	0.5	0.7	0.7	•	0.5	•	0.8	•
Total Receipts to Cash Flow 42	6.1	5.5	2.9	6.3	6.2	5.8	7.5	6.6	•	6.6	•	5.6	•
Cost of Goods to Cash Flow 43	3.9	3.4	1.0	3.9	4.0	3.3	5.2	4.2	•	4.5	•	3.4	•
Cash Flow to Total Debt 44	0.2	•	1.0	0.7	0.6	0.7	0.4	0.4	•	0.3	•	0.2	•

Selected Financial Factors (in Percentages)

Debt Ratio 45	46.2	•	105.9	50.0	55.1	43.9	46.3	49.4	•	52.7	•	44.8	•
Return on Total Assets 46	8.1	•	53.7	25.1	27.1	20.1	13.9	11.4	•	9.5	•	6.5	•
Return on Equity Before Income Taxes 47	13.5	•	•	46.2	55.3	34.4	24.8	20.3	•	17.7	•	10.3	•
Return on Equity After Income Taxes 48	10.1	•	•	46.2	53.1	33.0	23.0	17.1	•	14.1	•	7.0	•
Profit Margin (Before Income Tax) 49	11.1	10.2	17.9	10.7	12.2	10.7	9.0	7.4	•	8.7	•	13.1	•
Profit Margin (After Income Tax) 50	8.4	7.0	17.2	10.7	11.7	10.3	8.3	6.2	•	7.0	•	8.9	•

126

Table I

Corporations with and without Net Income

COMMERCIAL AND SERVICE INDUSTRY MACHINERY

MONEY AMOUNTS AND SIZE OF ASSETS IN THOUSANDS OF DOLLARS

Item Description for Accounting Period 7/12 Through 6/13	Total	Zero Assets	Under 500	500 to 1,000	1,000 to 5,000	5,000 to 10,000	10,000 to 25,000	25,000 to 50,000	50,000 to 100,000	100,000 to 250,000	250,000 to 500,000	500,000 to 2,500,000	2,500,000 and over
Number of Enterprises **1**	2005	405	525	357	440	119	79	25	19	16	5	10	4

Revenues ($ in Thousands)

Net Sales **2**	44884616	328432	374752	754700	2167661	1386914	1700361	946650	1497535	2467061	1304355	7144959	24811237
Interest **3**	472387	592	0	14	520	142	2927	1008	2433	5620	2137	57378	399615
Rents **4**	1471216	0	0	0	0	0	1496	271	2940	4777	733	59108	1401892
Royalties **5**	581481	2969	0	0	0	0	33	269	19	38	29	56663	521461
Other Portfolio Income **6**	303998	0	0	7721	5125	570	3457	5511	1999	8039	3258	38200	230116
Other Receipts **7**	1076943	272	13232	1461	50360	15957	10757	4236	9927	34138	2384	6178	928042
Total Receipts **8**	48790641	332265	387984	763896	2223666	1403583	1719031	957945	1514853	2519673	1312896	7362486	28292363
Average Total Receipts **9**	24334	820	739	2140	5054	11795	21760	38318	79729	157480	262579	736249	7073091

Operating Costs/Operating Income (%)

Cost of Operations **10**	50.3	45.8	73.0	53.9	59.6	56.7	69.5	57.6	69.2	62.5	62.3	51.2	43.8
Salaries and Wages **11**	18.3	30.5	2.7	4.3	8.8	16.1	8.2	13.5	9.2	12.9	10.4	15.4	22.9
Taxes Paid **12**	2.7	10.6	0.9	1.1	2.8	2.6	1.9	2.4	1.5	2.4	2.3	1.9	3.2
Interest Paid **13**	2.3	0.3	0.0	0.3	0.9	0.2	0.9	0.8	2.7	0.5	1.1	2.0	3.2
Depreciation **14**	4.1	1.8	0.6	0.2	1.5	1.6	1.0	2.1	1.6	2.2	3.3	2.7	5.7
Amortization and Depletion **15**	3.1	0.1	•	0.1	0.2	0.1	0.5	0.5	0.7	0.6	0.6	1.3	5.1
Pensions and Other Deferred Comp. **16**	1.8	0.5	1.9	1.6	0.4	0.3	0.4	0.6	0.8	0.8	1.0	0.6	2.8
Employee Benefits **17**	2.5	0.5	4.1	1.2	2.2	3.1	1.3	2.2	1.9	2.8	2.0	1.5	2.9
Advertising **18**	0.8	0.3	0.2	0.7	0.4	2.4	0.5	0.8	1.4	0.5	1.1	0.5	0.9
Other Expenses **19**	18.8	34.6	5.0	6.7	12.1	6.8	8.1	15.7	7.6	11.8	12.0	17.7	23.4
Officers' Compensation **20**	1.5	11.7	5.6	11.6	5.6	2.5	1.8	2.7	1.6	1.7	1.3	1.7	0.5
Operating Margin **21**	•	•	6.1	18.1	5.4	7.5	6.0	1.0	1.8	1.3	2.6	3.5	•
Operating Margin Before Officers' Comp. **22**	•	•	11.7	29.7	11.0	10.1	7.7	3.7	3.3	3.0	3.9	5.2	•

	Selected Average Balance Sheet ($ in Thousands)												
Net Receivables 23	4516	0	18	359	427	1357	4170	6106	12533	23223	89821	99988	1506842
Inventories 24	2129	0	22	68	581	1298	4043	9431	14722	26013	58922	81028	366827
Net Property, Plant and Equipment 25	2627	0	6	53	297	957	1954	4035	7320	18612	45183	101998	765445
Total Assets 26	30813	0	163	719	1922	6282	16033	33454	63767	133761	342180	913844	10885009
Notes and Loans Payable 27	11921	0	0	303	530	1024	4138	4182	9938	16328	50520	315042	4788584
All Other Liabilities 28	9995	0	8	403	695	1284	5076	11185	22739	48754	121503	258222	3587875
Net Worth 29	8896	0	155	13	698	3975	6820	18087	31090	68678	170157	340580	2508550

	Selected Financial Ratios (Times to 1)												
Current Ratio 30	1.4	•	12.2	1.2	1.7	2.8	2.0	1.8	1.8	1.7	1.2	1.5	1.3
Quick Ratio 31	0.7	•	11.0	0.9	1.0	1.7	1.1	1.1	0.9	0.9	0.8	0.8	0.6
Net Sales to Working Capital 32	7.0	•	8.0	19.8	8.9	3.8	3.7	4.0	4.3	4.5	9.3	7.7	8.1
Coverage Ratio 33	2.7	•	17960.5	65.7	9.4	49.8	9.2	3.8	2.1	9.1	3.9	4.7	1.7
Total Asset Turnover 34	0.7	•	4.4	2.9	2.6	1.9	1.3	1.1	1.2	1.2	0.8	0.8	0.6
Inventory Turnover 35	5.3	•	23.7	16.7	5.1	5.1	3.7	2.3	3.7	3.7	2.8	4.5	7.4
Receivables Turnover 36	4.5	•	5.6	11.5	10.3	9.0	5.8	4.7	6.1	5.0	2.2	8.4	3.6
Total Liabilities to Net Worth 37	2.5	•	0.1	53.5	1.8	0.6	1.4	0.8	1.1	0.9	1.0	1.7	3.3
Current Assets to Working Capital 38	3.5	•	1.1	6.2	2.5	1.5	2.0	2.3	2.2	2.4	5.5	3.1	4.5
Current Liabilities to Working Capital 39	2.5	•	0.1	5.2	1.5	0.5	1.0	1.3	1.2	1.4	4.5	2.1	3.5
Working Capital to Net Sales 40	0.1	•	0.1	0.1	0.1	0.3	0.3	0.3	0.2	0.2	0.1	0.1	0.1
Inventory to Working Capital 41	0.7	•	0.1	1.2	0.9	0.5	0.7	0.6	0.9	0.9	1.3	1.0	0.5
Total Receipts to Cash Flow 42	5.6	•	7.1	4.0	5.7	7.6	7.4	7.4	10.7	7.5	7.4	4.7	5.3
Cost of Goods to Cash Flow 43	2.8	•	5.2	2.1	3.4	4.3	5.2	4.3	7.4	4.7	4.6	2.4	2.3
Cash Flow to Total Debt 44	0.2	•	12.6	0.8	0.7	0.7	0.3	0.3	0.2	0.3	0.2	0.3	0.1

	Selected Financial Factors (in Percentages)												
Debt Ratio 45	71.1	•	4.9	98.2	63.7	36.7	57.5	45.9	51.2	48.7	50.3	62.7	77.0
Return on Total Assets 46	4.5	•	41.9	57.8	23.0	16.5	10.6	3.3	6.9	4.9	3.4	7.2	3.0
Return on Equity Before Income Taxes 47	9.7	•	44.0	3101.6	56.7	25.6	22.3	4.5	7.4	8.5	5.1	15.3	5.3
Return on Equity After Income Taxes 48	6.0	•	44.0	3101.4	56.1	25.3	19.1	3.2	5.8	6.0	3.6	10.4	1.2
Profit Margin (Before Income Tax) 49	3.9	•	9.6	19.3	8.0	8.7	7.1	2.2	2.9	3.8	3.3	7.3	2.1
Profit Margin (After Income Tax) 50	2.4	•	9.6	19.3	7.9	8.6	6.1	1.5	2.3	2.7	2.4	5.0	0.5

Table II

Corporations with Net Income

COMMERCIAL AND SERVICE INDUSTRY MACHINERY

MONEY AMOUNTS AND SIZE OF ASSETS IN THOUSANDS OF DOLLARS

Item Description for Accounting Period 7/12 Through 6/13	Total	Zero Assets	Under 500	500 to 1,000	1,000 to 5,000	5,000 to 10,000	10,000 to 25,000	25,000 to 50,000	50,000 to 100,000	100,000 to 250,000	250,000 to 500,000	500,000 to 2,500,000	2,500,000 and over
Number of Enterprises **1**	1510	281	425	309	305	69	63	•	12	10	•	10	•

Revenues ($ in Thousands)													
Net Sales **2**	39210410	138009	316683	732979	1332178	934267	1415422	•	1034275	1751464	•	7144959	•
Interest **3**	465531	141	0	0	0	142	2888	•	1126	4925	•	57378	•
Rents **4**	1408660	0	0	0	0	0	1496	•	2875	2627	•	59108	•
Royalties **5**	533323	0	0	0	0	0	0	•	19	0	•	56663	•
Other Portfolio Income **6**	191715	0	0	7721	662	570	3457	•	767	4613	•	38200	•
Other Receipts **7**	986185	-18	13233	0	2051	10520	10523	•	9776	11887	•	6178	•
Total Receipts **8**	42795824	138132	329916	740700	1334891	945499	1433786	•	1048838	1775516	•	7362486	•
Average Total Receipts **9**	28342	492	776	2397	4377	13703	22759	•	87403	177552	•	736249	•

Operating Costs/Operating Income (%)													
Cost of Operations **10**	46.1	54.2	75.9	52.2	53.0	57.8	66.5	•	68.6	58.1	•	51.2	•
Salaries and Wages **11**	19.3	5.1	3.2	2.9	7.5	12.5	8.0	•	9.6	13.7	•	15.4	•
Taxes Paid **12**	2.8	21.2	0.9	1.1	3.4	2.1	2.0	•	1.4	2.9	•	1.9	•
Interest Paid **13**	2.2	0.6	0.0	0.1	0.3	0.2	0.7	•	1.2	0.3	•	2.0	•
Depreciation **14**	4.3	0.9	0.6	0.2	1.5	1.7	1.0	•	1.6	1.5	•	2.7	•
Amortization and Depletion **15**	3.2	•	•	0.1	0.2	0.1	0.6	•	0.3	0.5	•	1.3	•
Pensions and Other Deferred Comp. **16**	1.7	0.4	1.3	1.7	0.6	0.0	0.5	•	0.9	0.9	•	0.6	•
Employee Benefits **17**	2.0	1.2	•	1.2	1.8	2.6	1.4	•	2.3	2.7	•	1.5	•
Advertising **18**	0.5	0.5	0.3	0.7	0.3	0.4	0.4	•	1.7	0.6	•	0.5	•
Other Expenses **19**	19.3	7.2	3.9	4.6	10.5	5.5	8.5	•	5.4	10.9	•	17.7	•
Officers' Compensation **20**	1.3	0.6	6.6	11.7	4.4	3.1	1.7	•	1.7	2.0	•	1.7	•
Operating Margin **21**	•	8.2	7.2	23.4	16.5	13.9	8.7	•	5.4	5.9	•	3.5	•
Operating Margin Before Officers' Comp. **22**	•	8.7	13.8	35.1	20.8	17.0	10.4	•	7.1	7.9	•	5.2	•

Selected Average Balance Sheet ($ in Thousands)

Net Receivables 23	5531	0	0	409	385	1424	4481	•	11185	24579	•	99988	•
Inventories 24	2061	0	0	60	553	1277	3872	•	18175	25118	•	89682	•
Net Property, Plant and Equipment 25	3007	0	6	58	154	1033	1967	•	8574	23553	•	101998	•
Total Assets 26	35074	0	135	693	1624	7142	16117	•	61786	138018	•	913844	•
Notes and Loans Payable 27	12704	0	0	30	352	641	3967	•	8826	12536	•	315042	•
All Other Liabilities 28	9685	0	6	241	313	1002	5278	•	22509	40165	•	258222	•
Net Worth 29	12685	0	128	421	960	5500	6873	•	30451	85316	•	340580	•

Selected Financial Ratios (Times to 1)

Current Ratio 30	1.7	•	13.5	2.7	3.4	5.0	2.0	•	1.9	2.2	•	1.5	•
Quick Ratio 31	1.0	•	13.5	2.4	2.2	3.5	1.2	•	0.9	1.2	•	0.8	•
Net Sales to Working Capital 32	5.5	•	9.7	6.0	4.5	3.1	3.9	•	4.3	3.8	•	7.7	•
Coverage Ratio 33	4.4	14.9	18026.0	357.9	61.8	73.4	15.4	•	6.8	26.9	•	4.7	•
Total Asset Turnover 34	0.7	•	5.5	3.4	2.7	1.9	1.4	•	1.4	1.3	•	0.8	•
Inventory Turnover 35	5.8	•	•	20.7	4.2	6.1	3.9	•	3.3	4.1	•	4.1	•
Receivables Turnover 36	4.4	•	•	11.6	9.9	9.6	5.8	•	6.4	5.5	•	•	•
Total Liabilities to Net Worth 37	1.8	•	0.0	0.6	0.7	0.3	1.3	•	1.0	0.6	•	1.7	•
Current Assets to Working Capital 38	2.4	•	1.1	1.6	1.4	1.3	2.0	•	2.1	1.9	•	3.1	•
Current Liabilities to Working Capital 39	1.4	•	0.1	0.6	0.4	0.3	1.0	•	1.1	0.9	•	2.1	•
Working Capital to Net Sales 40	0.2	•	0.1	0.2	0.2	0.3	0.3	•	0.2	0.3	•	0.1	•
Inventory to Working Capital 41	0.5	•	•	0.2	0.5	0.3	0.6	•	0.9	0.6	•	1.0	•
Total Receipts to Cash Flow 42	4.6	7.9	6.6	3.5	4.2	5.5	6.0	•	9.1	6.1	•	4.7	•
Cost of Goods to Cash Flow 43	2.1	4.3	5.0	1.8	2.2	3.2	4.0	•	6.3	3.5	•	2.4	•
Cash Flow to Total Debt 44	0.3	•	18.5	2.5	1.6	1.5	0.4	•	0.3	0.5	•	0.3	•

Selected Financial Factors (in Percentages)

Debt Ratio 45	63.8	•	4.6	39.2	40.9	23.0	57.4	•	50.7	38.2	•	62.7	•
Return on Total Assets 46	7.3	•	63.1	84.1	45.5	29.0	14.9	•	11.1	10.3	•	7.2	•
Return on Equity Before Income Taxes 47	15.6	•	66.1	137.9	75.8	37.2	32.7	•	19.3	16.0	•	15.3	•
Return on Equity After Income Taxes 48	12.2	•	66.1	137.9	75.2	36.7	28.9	•	16.7	12.8	•	10.4	•
Profit Margin (Before Income Tax) 49	7.6	8.2	11.4	24.5	16.7	15.1	10.0	•	6.8	7.8	•	7.3	•
Profit Margin (After Income Tax) 50	6.0	5.8	11.4	24.5	16.5	14.9	8.8	•	5.9	6.2	•	5.0	•

Table I

Corporations with and without Net Income

VENTILATION, HEATING, A.C. & COMMERCIAL REFRIGERATION EQUIP.

MONEY AMOUNTS AND SIZE OF ASSETS IN THOUSANDS OF DOLLARS

Item Description for Accounting Period 7/12 Through 6/13	Total	Zero Assets	Under 500	500 to 1,000	1,000 to 5,000	5,000 to 10,000	10,000 to 25,000	25,000 to 50,000	50,000 to 100,000	100,000 to 250,000	250,000 to 500,000	500,000 to 2,500,000	2,500,000 and over
Number of Enterprises 1	942	9	271	170	210	106	76	35	29	20	5	7	3

Revenues ($ in Thousands)

	Total	Zero Assets	Under 500	500 to 1,000	1,000 to 5,000	5,000 to 10,000	10,000 to 25,000	25,000 to 50,000	50,000 to 100,000	100,000 to 250,000	250,000 to 500,000	500,000 to 2,500,000	2,500,000 and over
Net Sales 2	35502958	2110570	11047	381893	1452652	1042696	1967116	1920835	3204962	4503429	1261902	8056959	9588898
Interest 3	79632	3710	0	38	214	115	788	1227	1134	2052	8645	10110	51599
Rents 4	9914	82	0	0	36	215	440	5565	444	1800	306	985	41
Royalties 5	182811	2649	0	0	0	0	0	5629	3677	3836	2046	71128	93846
Other Portfolio Income 6	80019	10188	0	3	442	439	3295	4188	1037	11366	625	22965	25471
Other Receipts 7	542294	41053	0	1282	67419	3897	14672	24254	17111	26525	35090	46202	264788
Total Receipts 8	36397628	2168252	11047	383216	1520763	1047362	1986311	1961698	3228365	4549008	1308614	8208349	10024643
Average Total Receipts 9	38639	240917	41	2254	7242	9881	26136	56049	111323	227450	261723	1172621	3341548

Operating Costs/Operating Income (%)

	Total	Zero Assets	Under 500	500 to 1,000	1,000 to 5,000	5,000 to 10,000	10,000 to 25,000	25,000 to 50,000	50,000 to 100,000	100,000 to 250,000	250,000 to 500,000	500,000 to 2,500,000	2,500,000 and over
Cost of Operations 10	70.5	72.9	88.2	69.9	77.4	68.6	66.4	66.2	73.9	68.6	75.1	68.9	71.5
Salaries and Wages 11	8.7	5.9	0.9	13.6	7.1	8.8	10.0	9.6	7.4	7.0	6.1	11.3	8.2
Taxes Paid 12	1.3	1.6	2.5	2.9	2.3	1.5	1.6	1.6	1.5	1.7	1.0	1.6	0.6
Interest Paid 13	3.1	7.3	0.1	0.6	0.8	0.9	0.3	0.6	0.6	1.6	5.6	2.1	6.1
Depreciation 14	1.5	1.3	13.9	0.7	1.0	1.4	0.8	1.5	1.7	1.7	1.4	1.9	1.4
Amortization and Depletion 15	1.1	3.9	0.5	0.1	0.1	0.1	0.3	0.4	0.3	0.3	1.4	1.0	1.6
Pensions and Other Deferred Comp. 16	0.8	0.1	•	0.0	0.2	0.6	0.5	0.6	0.5	1.0	0.0	0.8	1.4
Employee Benefits 17	2.6	0.8	0.2	0.5	0.8	1.0	1.3	2.4	1.8	2.2	1.8	2.5	4.3
Advertising 18	0.8	0.5	2.9	1.2	0.4	0.5	1.0	1.2	0.5	0.5	0.7	1.3	0.8
Other Expenses 19	8.5	11.3	14.9	14.6	11.5	12.4	9.3	10.5	7.5	7.8	12.0	8.5	6.5
Officers' Compensation 20	1.0	1.4	2.3	5.9	3.4	2.5	2.6	1.3	0.9	0.7	0.3	0.7	0.3
Operating Margin 21	0.1	•	•	•	•	1.7	5.8	4.4	3.1	7.0	•	•	•
Operating Margin Before Officers' Comp. 22	1.1	•	•	•	•	4.2	8.4	5.6	4.1	7.6	•	0.3	•

Selected Average Balance Sheet ($ in Thousands)

Net Receivables 23	5094	0	0	149	595	1521	4497	8081	15543	28341	91469	151473	442321
Inventories 24	4027	0	4	119	509	1621	4060	6423	10366	29875	34647	196895	340355
Net Property, Plant and Equipment 25	4177	0	38	120	314	1366	2320	7270	14827	27380	41852	163963	309247
Total Assets 26	42120	0	43	758	2293	7034	16567	38152	66141	150294	399415	1108008	7012564
Notes and Loans Payable 27	17347	0	94	150	1170	2005	2213	6261	13695	55341	127281	486010	3300681
All Other Liabilities 28	11876	0	4	444	2723	1444	5138	9823	21219	54606	107844	402906	1528191
Net Worth 29	12897	0	-56	165	-1600	3585	9217	22068	31227	40347	164290	219091	2183692

Selected Financial Ratios (Times to 1)

Current Ratio 30	1.7	•	0.8	1.1	1.6	2.8	2.4	2.9	1.5	1.9	2.1	1.1	1.9
Quick Ratio 31	1.0	•	0.8	0.7	0.9	1.4	1.4	1.9	0.9	1.0	1.5	0.6	1.2
Net Sales to Working Capital 32	7.0	•	•	39.5	10.3	3.5	3.6	3.9	8.9	5.5	3.2	30.5	5.5
Coverage Ratio 33	1.9	0.4	•	•	0.6	3.3	26.3	12.5	7.1	6.1	0.7	2.3	1.4
Total Asset Turnover 34	0.9	•	0.9	3.0	3.0	1.4	1.6	1.4	1.7	1.5	0.6	1.0	0.5
Inventory Turnover 35	6.6	•	8.6	13.2	10.5	4.2	4.2	5.7	7.9	5.2	5.5	4.0	6.7
Receivables Turnover 36	7.4	•	76.7	13.2	10.9	6.1	6.3	5.9	7.5	7.6	2.9	4.7	14.5
Total Liabilities to Net Worth 37	2.3	•	•	3.6	•	1.0	0.8	0.7	1.1	2.7	1.4	4.1	2.2
Current Assets to Working Capital 38	2.4	•	•	9.0	2.8	1.6	1.7	1.5	2.9	2.2	1.9	9.4	2.1
Current Liabilities to Working Capital 39	1.4	•	•	8.0	1.8	0.6	0.7	0.5	1.9	1.2	0.9	8.4	1.1
Working Capital to Net Sales 40	0.1	•	•	0.0	0.1	0.3	0.3	0.3	0.1	0.2	0.3	0.0	0.2
Inventory to Working Capital 41	0.8	•	•	1.9	0.9	0.6	0.6	0.4	0.9	0.7	0.5	3.3	0.6
Total Receipts to Cash Flow 42	10.6	21.6	•	33.5	11.8	7.7	6.9	6.4	9.9	7.1	11.8	12.5	14.1
Cost of Goods to Cash Flow 43	7.5	15.8	•	23.4	9.2	5.3	4.6	4.2	7.3	4.9	8.9	8.6	10.1
Cash Flow to Total Debt 44	0.1	•	•	0.1	0.2	0.4	0.5	0.5	0.3	0.3	0.1	0.1	0.0

Selected Financial Factors (in Percentages)

Debt Ratio 45	69.4	•	229.5	78.3	169.8	49.0	44.4	42.2	52.8	73.2	58.9	80.2	68.9
Return on Total Assets 46	5.4	•	•	•	1.4	4.3	10.9	10.2	7.5	14.3	2.4	4.9	3.8
Return on Equity Before Income Taxes 47	8.5	•	19.4	•	1.4	5.9	18.8	16.2	13.6	44.6	•	13.8	3.2
Return on Equity After Income Taxes 48	6.1	•	19.4	•	4.4	4.5	17.2	12.4	11.0	35.1	•	9.5	2.3
Profit Margin (Before Income Tax) 49	2.9	•	•	•	•	2.2	6.7	6.5	3.9	8.0	•	2.6	2.2
Profit Margin (After Income Tax) 50	2.1	•	•	•	•	1.6	6.1	5.0	3.1	6.3	•	1.8	1.6

Table II
Corporations with Net Income

VENTILATION, HEATING, A.C. & COMMERCIAL REFRIGERATION EQUIP.

MONEY AMOUNTS AND SIZE OF ASSETS IN THOUSANDS OF DOLLARS

Item Description for Accounting Period 7/12 Through 6/13	Total	Zero Assets	Under 500	500 to 1,000	1,000 to 5,000	5,000 to 10,000	10,000 to 25,000	25,000 to 50,000	50,000 to 100,000	100,000 to 250,000	250,000 to 500,000	500,000 to 2,500,000	2,500,000 and over
Number of Enterprises **1**	331	3	0	28	85	72	62	28	24	•	0	•	3
Revenues ($ in Thousands)													
Net Sales **2**	29335036	8259	0	97414	709622	834405	1731210	1706712	2737921	•	0	•	9588898
Interest **3**	62409	152	0	1	106	87	655	969	907	•	0	•	51599
Rents **4**	9757	0	0	0	0	215	440	5565	405	•	0	•	41
Royalties **5**	172182	0	0	0	0	0	0	5629	91	•	0	•	93846
Other Portfolio Income **6**	78621	10188	0	0	85	439	2912	4173	1027	•	0	•	25471
Other Receipts **7**	459506	18	0	162	66018	1253	14417	20608	14375	•	0	•	264788
Total Receipts **8**	30117511	18617	0	97577	775831	836399	1749634	1743656	2754726	•	0	•	10024643
Average Total Receipts **9**	90989	6206	•	3485	9127	11617	28220	62273	114780	•	•	•	3341548
Operating Costs/Operating Income (%)													
Cost of Operations **10**	69.2	67.8	•	67.5	66.7	67.4	66.6	64.1	70.9	•	•	•	71.5
Salaries and Wages **11**	8.7	6.4	•	8.1	9.4	7.8	9.3	10.3	7.0	•	•	•	8.2
Taxes Paid **12**	1.3	3.7	•	1.9	3.2	1.1	1.5	1.5	1.5	•	•	•	0.6
Interest Paid **13**	2.9	3.2	•	0.7	1.4	0.5	0.2	0.3	0.6	•	•	•	6.1
Depreciation **14**	1.5	2.5	•	0.0	1.6	1.3	0.6	1.3	1.9	•	•	•	1.4
Amortization and Depletion **15**	0.9	•	•	•	0.1	0.0	0.1	0.2	0.4	•	•	•	1.6
Pensions and Other Deferred Comp. **16**	1.0	•	•	0.0	0.3	0.8	0.6	0.6	0.6	•	•	•	1.4
Employee Benefits **17**	2.7	1.0	•	0.1	0.9	0.7	1.3	2.4	2.0	•	•	•	4.3
Advertising **18**	0.8	0.1	•	0.0	0.2	0.4	0.8	1.3	0.5	•	•	•	0.8
Other Expenses **19**	8.4	30.2	•	12.6	11.4	10.7	8.9	11.2	8.3	•	•	•	6.5
Officers' Compensation **20**	0.9	1.2	•	1.9	5.5	1.5	2.8	1.2	1.0	•	•	•	0.3
Operating Margin **21**	1.7	•	•	7.3	•	8.0	7.3	5.4	5.3	•	•	•	•
Operating Margin Before Officers' Comp. **22**	2.6	•	•	9.2	4.8	9.4	10.1	6.6	6.3	•	•	•	•

Selected Average Balance Sheet ($ in Thousands)

Net Receivables 23	12475	0	•	117	938	1829	4624	9332	16446	•	•	•	442321
Inventories 24	9417	0	•	364	660	1873	3976	6707	10484	•	•	•	340355
Net Property, Plant and Equipment 25	10335	0	•	198	490	1544	1730	7760	16241	•	•	•	309247
Total Assets 26	108256	0	•	940	3051	6692	16164	39564	65590	•	•	•	7012564
Notes and Loans Payable 27	44497	0	•	263	508	1449	1332	5515	14498	•	•	•	3300681
All Other Liabilities 28	29233	0	•	279	2101	1398	5426	9354	19490	•	•	•	1528191
Net Worth 29	34526	0	•	398	443	3845	9406	24695	31602	•	•	•	2183692

Selected Financial Ratios (Times to 1)

Current Ratio 30	1.7	•	•	1.4	2.6	3.1	2.4	3.1	1.6	•	•	•	1.9
Quick Ratio 31	1.0	•	•	1.3	1.9	1.6	1.4	2.0	1.0	•	•	•	1.2
Net Sales to Working Capital 32	6.6	•	•	19.0	5.5	3.5	3.7	3.7	8.0	•	•	•	5.5
Coverage Ratio 33	2.7	35.5	•	11.3	7.2	19.0	39.7	24.7	10.8	•	•	•	1.4
Total Asset Turnover 34	0.8	•	•	3.7	2.7	1.7	1.7	1.5	1.7	•	•	•	0.5
Inventory Turnover 35	6.5	•	•	6.4	8.4	4.2	4.7	5.8	7.7	•	•	•	6.7
Receivables Turnover 36	7.6	•	•	5.8	8.4	5.5	7.2	5.9	8.5	•	•	•	14.5
Total Liabilities to Net Worth 37	2.1	•	•	1.4	5.9	0.7	0.7	0.6	1.1	•	•	•	2.2
Current Assets to Working Capital 38	2.4	•	•	3.7	1.6	1.5	1.7	1.5	2.6	•	•	•	2.1
Current Liabilities to Working Capital 39	1.4	•	•	2.7	0.6	0.5	0.7	0.5	1.6	•	•	•	1.1
Working Capital to Net Sales 40	0.2	•	•	0.1	0.2	0.3	0.3	0.3	0.1	•	•	•	0.2
Inventory to Working Capital 41	0.8	•	•	0.1	0.4	0.6	0.6	0.4	0.8	•	•	•	0.6
Total Receipts to Cash Flow 42	9.0	2.7	•	6.8	6.0	5.5	6.4	5.8	7.8	•	•	•	14.1
Cost of Goods to Cash Flow 43	6.2	1.8	•	4.6	4.0	3.7	4.2	3.7	5.5	•	•	•	10.1
Cash Flow to Total Debt 44	0.1	•	•	0.9	0.5	0.7	0.6	0.7	0.4	•	•	•	0.0

Selected Financial Factors (in Percentages)

Debt Ratio 45	68.1	•	•	57.7	85.5	42.5	41.8	37.6	51.8	•	•	•	68.9
Return on Total Assets 46	6.2	•	•	30.2	27.4	15.0	14.7	12.3	11.3	•	•	•	3.8
Return on Equity Before Income Taxes 47	12.2	•	•	65.1	162.8	24.7	24.7	18.8	21.2	•	•	•	3.2
Return on Equity After Income Taxes 48	9.7	•	•	62.7	135.3	22.8	22.7	14.6	18.0	•	•	•	2.3
Profit Margin (Before Income Tax) 49	4.7	109.4	•	7.4	8.6	8.2	8.3	7.6	5.9	•	•	•	2.2
Profit Margin (After Income Tax) 50	3.8	107.5	•	7.2	7.2	7.6	7.7	5.9	5.0	•	•	•	1.6

Table I

Corporations with and without Net Income

METALWORKING MACHINERY

MONEY AMOUNTS AND SIZE OF ASSETS IN THOUSANDS OF DOLLARS

Item Description for Accounting Period 7/12 Through 6/13	Total	Zero Assets	Under 500	500 to 1,000	1,000 to 5,000	5,000 to 10,000	10,000 to 25,000	25,000 to 50,000	50,000 to 100,000	100,000 to 250,000	250,000 to 500,000	500,000 to 2,500,000	2,500,000 and over
Number of Enterprises **1**	6185	344	3981	734	751	170	112	42	27	10	7	6	0

Revenues ($ in Thousands)

Net Sales **2**	28335950	713056	1826947	1150963	4009261	2428913	2510398	1780836	2546087	1866166	1823657	7679666	0
Interest **3**	86883	70	74	89	3047	560	325	431	1462	3156	1637	76034	0
Rents **4**	9117	333	884	0	1469	2376	122	433	464	1019	1241	776	0
Royalties **5**	11283	158	0	0	0	2257	571	0	232	2202	285	5578	0
Other Portfolio Income **6**	648626	48315	618	331	18574	10258	2461	1641	10542	8583	10002	537303	0
Other Receipts **7**	211099	6196	3051	7861	36268	7130	21727	8384	15135	24915	11435	68994	0
Total Receipts **8**	29302958	768128	1831574	1159244	4068619	2451494	2535604	1791725	2573922	1906041	1848257	8368351	0
Average Total Receipts **9**	4738	2233	460	1579	5418	14421	22639	42660	95330	190604	264037	1394725	•

Operating Costs/Operating Income (%)

Cost of Operations **10**	66.8	70.9	45.4	50.2	69.9	67.4	69.0	70.0	71.5	68.2	61.1	70.3	•
Salaries and Wages **11**	7.0	6.8	6.7	10.6	6.6	5.0	5.0	5.7	5.3	9.4	11.3	7.3	•
Taxes Paid **12**	2.0	2.4	3.5	3.6	2.9	2.1	2.2	2.3	1.6	1.5	2.2	0.9	•
Interest Paid **13**	1.6	1.8	1.3	1.2	0.4	0.6	0.6	1.3	0.6	1.3	2.3	3.4	•
Depreciation **14**	3.0	1.3	2.0	2.6	2.9	3.4	2.8	4.5	2.6	2.1	4.2	3.0	•
Amortization and Depletion **15**	0.4	0.5	0.0	0.0	0.0	0.0	0.0	0.3	0.2	0.3	0.7	1.1	•
Pensions and Other Deferred Comp. **16**	1.6	0.2	0.1	0.2	0.3	0.7	0.4	0.8	0.6	0.9	0.7	4.4	•
Employee Benefits **17**	2.5	2.0	1.5	3.2	1.2	0.8	3.1	2.4	1.9	3.2	1.8	4.1	•
Advertising **18**	0.4	0.2	0.2	0.1	0.3	0.1	0.4	0.2	0.4	0.5	0.5	0.5	•
Other Expenses **19**	8.9	11.9	28.2	8.4	6.6	6.0	6.9	7.0	6.5	7.6	12.1	7.5	•
Officers' Compensation **20**	2.5	1.3	6.6	6.4	4.9	5.0	2.2	1.8	1.3	1.1	0.5	0.3	•
Operating Margin **21**	3.4	0.6	4.5	13.7	4.0	8.8	7.2	3.8	7.3	3.8	2.6	•	•
Operating Margin Before Officers' Comp. **22**	5.8	1.9	11.1	20.1	8.9	13.8	9.5	5.6	8.6	5.0	3.1	•	•

	Selected Average Balance Sheet ($ in Thousands)												
Net Receivables 23	665	0	46	223	614	1884	3309	9193	15627	32692	40952	198112	•
Inventories 24	657	0	14	100	710	1551	4099	7199	18125	39048	38706	204032	•
Net Property, Plant and Equipment 25	660	0	21	282	540	2040	4016	9894	14233	16987	47736	213658	•
Total Assets 26	4365	0	130	758	2533	7413	15040	34954	68112	156064	315949	2332583	•
Notes and Loans Payable 27	1545	0	87	328	597	1773	3238	9394	14085	33697	81753	1028686	•
All Other Liabilities 28	1258	0	47	162	814	2006	3671	10508	19928	46700	121522	635475	•
Net Worth 29	1562	0	-4	268	1122	3634	8130	15051	34098	75666	112673	668422	•

	Selected Financial Ratios (Times to 1)												
Current Ratio 30	1.6	•	1.9	2.1	1.9	2.2	2.0	1.6	2.1	1.9	1.1	1.3	•
Quick Ratio 31	0.9	•	1.5	1.5	1.1	1.4	1.1	0.9	1.1	1.0	0.6	0.6	•
Net Sales to Working Capital 32	6.9	•	9.7	6.9	6.5	5.2	4.6	6.1	3.9	4.9	21.6	11.0	•
Coverage Ratio 33	5.4	5.6	4.6	13.5	14.4	17.3	14.4	4.4	14.1	6.3	3.3	3.1	•
Total Asset Turnover 34	1.0	•	3.5	2.1	2.1	1.9	1.5	1.2	1.4	1.2	0.8	0.5	•
Inventory Turnover 35	4.7	•	14.7	7.9	5.3	6.2	3.8	4.1	3.7	3.3	4.1	4.4	•
Receivables Turnover 36	7.0	•	12.3	6.9	8.2	9.7	5.8	5.5	6.4	5.5	7.6	6.2	•
Total Liabilities to Net Worth 37	1.8	•	•	1.8	1.3	1.0	0.8	1.3	1.0	1.1	1.8	2.5	•
Current Assets to Working Capital 38	2.7	•	2.1	1.9	2.2	1.8	2.0	2.8	1.9	2.1	9.4	4.7	•
Current Liabilities to Working Capital 39	1.7	•	1.1	0.9	1.2	0.8	1.0	1.8	0.9	1.1	8.4	3.7	•
Working Capital to Net Sales 40	0.1	•	0.1	0.1	0.2	0.2	0.2	0.2	0.3	0.2	0.0	0.1	•
Inventory to Working Capital 41	1.0	•	0.3	0.4	0.8	0.6	0.8	1.0	0.8	0.8	3.9	1.8	•
Total Receipts to Cash Flow 42	8.1	6.0	3.7	4.9	10.6	7.4	7.8	10.1	7.6	8.3	7.1	12.7	•
Cost of Goods to Cash Flow 43	5.4	4.3	1.7	2.5	7.4	5.0	5.4	7.1	5.4	5.7	4.3	8.9	•
Cash Flow to Total Debt 44	0.2	•	0.9	0.6	0.4	0.5	0.4	0.2	0.4	0.3	0.2	0.1	•

	Selected Financial Factors (in Percentages)												
Debt Ratio 45	64.2	•	103.0	64.7	55.7	51.0	45.9	56.9	49.9	51.5	64.3	71.3	•
Return on Total Assets 46	9.2	•	21.5	32.2	12.1	19.9	13.2	6.9	12.7	9.4	6.2	5.8	•
Return on Equity Before Income Taxes 47	21.0	•	•	84.4	25.3	38.2	22.8	12.3	23.5	16.4	12.1	13.7	•
Return on Equity After Income Taxes 48	17.4	•	•	83.7	23.9	36.3	21.1	10.4	20.1	11.8	8.0	9.0	•
Profit Margin (Before Income Tax) 49	7.2	8.4	4.8	14.4	5.3	9.7	8.3	4.4	8.5	6.6	5.2	7.1	•
Profit Margin (After Income Tax) 50	5.9	7.7	4.6	14.3	5.0	9.2	7.7	3.7	7.3	4.8	3.5	4.7	•

Table II

Corporations with Net Income

METALWORKING MACHINERY

MONEY AMOUNTS AND SIZE OF ASSETS IN THOUSANDS OF DOLLARS

Item Description for Accounting Period 7/12 Through 6/13	Total	Zero Assets	Under 500	500 to 1,000	1,000 to 5,000	5,000 to 10,000	10,000 to 25,000	25,000 to 50,000	50,000 to 100,000	100,000 to 250,000	250,000 to 500,000	500,000 to 2,500,000	2,500,000 and over
Number of Enterprises 1	5112	83	3451	562	664	170	106	32	24	•	•	•	0

Revenues ($ in Thousands)

	Total	Zero Assets	Under 500	500 to 1,000	1,000 to 5,000	5,000 to 10,000	10,000 to 25,000	25,000 to 50,000	50,000 to 100,000	100,000 to 250,000	250,000 to 500,000	500,000 to 2,500,000	2,500,000 and over
Net Sales 2	26258969	536582	1679557	957744	3793627	2428913	2436121	1322908	2387990	•	•	•	0
Interest 3	84773	31	62	89	1887	560	286	234	1316	•	•	•	0
Rents 4	7580	333	0	0	1469	2376	55	0	337	•	•	•	0
Royalties 5	10670	158	0	0	0	2257	571	0	232	•	•	•	0
Other Portfolio Income 6	639212	48315	23	331	11963	10258	2445	1539	9952	•	•	•	0
Other Receipts 7	201318	1413	2435	7860	36115	7130	21512	6382	14110	•	•	•	0
Total Receipts 8	27202522	586832	1682077	966024	3845061	2451494	2460990	1331063	2413937	•	•	•	0
Average Total Receipts 9	5321	7070	487	1719	5791	14421	23217	41596	100581	•	•	•	•

Operating Costs/Operating Income (%)

	Total	Zero Assets	Under 500	500 to 1,000	1,000 to 5,000	5,000 to 10,000	10,000 to 25,000	25,000 to 50,000	50,000 to 100,000	100,000 to 250,000	250,000 to 500,000	500,000 to 2,500,000	2,500,000 and over
Cost of Operations 10	66.5	66.0	44.0	46.7	69.8	67.4	68.8	67.8	71.1	•	•	•	•
Salaries and Wages 11	7.1	8.6	6.8	11.6	6.9	5.0	5.0	5.9	5.3	•	•	•	•
Taxes Paid 12	2.0	3.1	3.5	3.4	2.8	2.1	2.2	2.3	1.6	•	•	•	•
Interest Paid 13	1.5	2.4	1.4	1.2	0.4	0.6	0.6	0.7	0.6	•	•	•	•
Depreciation 14	2.9	1.8	2.1	2.4	2.7	3.4	2.6	5.2	2.5	•	•	•	•
Amortization and Depletion 15	0.4	0.6	0.0	0.0	0.0	0.0	0.0	0.1	0.2	•	•	•	•
Pensions and Other Deferred Comp. 16	1.7	0.3	0.1	0.2	0.3	0.7	0.4	1.0	0.6	•	•	•	•
Employee Benefits 17	2.5	2.7	1.2	3.3	1.0	0.8	3.1	2.1	1.8	•	•	•	•
Advertising 18	0.4	0.3	0.0	0.1	0.3	0.1	0.4	0.3	0.4	•	•	•	•
Other Expenses 19	8.7	10.5	29.1	8.4	6.6	6.0	6.8	6.7	6.3	•	•	•	•
Officers' Compensation 20	2.4	1.7	5.9	6.1	4.8	5.0	2.2	1.9	1.3	•	•	•	•
Operating Margin 21	4.0	2.0	5.8	16.6	4.3	8.8	7.7	6.2	8.3	•	•	•	•
Operating Margin Before Officers' Comp. 22	6.4	3.7	11.7	22.7	9.1	13.8	10.0	8.1	9.7	•	•	•	•

Selected Average Balance Sheet ($ in Thousands)

Net Receivables 23	729	0	39	239	637	1884	3272	9467	16089	•	•	•	•
Inventories 24	707	0	13	76	697	1501	3896	7323	16712	•	•	•	•
Net Property, Plant and Equipment 25	740	0	22	333	550	2040	4002	10571	14859	•	•	•	•
Total Assets 26	4801	0	119	808	2616	7413	14956	33855	69110	•	•	•	•
Notes and Loans Payable 27	1693	0	85	327	619	1773	2944	8269	14390	•	•	•	•
All Other Liabilities 28	1368	0	53	170	853	2006	3573	9185	20127	•	•	•	•
Net Worth 29	1740	0	-19	311	1144	3634	8440	16400	34593	•	•	•	•

Selected Financial Ratios (Times to 1)

Current Ratio 30	1.7	•	1.5	1.9	1.9	2.2	2.2	2.0	2.1	•	•	•	•
Quick Ratio 31	0.9	•	1.2	1.5	1.1	1.4	1.2	1.2	1.1	•	•	•	•
Net Sales to Working Capital 32	6.7	•	16.5	8.0	6.5	5.2	4.5	4.2	4.1	•	•	•	•
Coverage Ratio 33	6.3	5.7	5.2	15.8	16.1	17.3	15.5	10.3	16.0	•	•	•	•
Total Asset Turnover 34	1.1	•	4.1	2.1	2.2	1.9	1.5	1.2	1.4	•	•	•	•
Inventory Turnover 35	4.8	•	16.3	10.5	5.7	6.4	4.1	3.8	4.2	•	•	•	•
Receivables Turnover 36	7.3	•	13.6	7.9	9.2	9.9	6.2	5.3	7.0	•	•	•	•
Total Liabilities to Net Worth 37	1.8	•	•	1.6	1.3	1.0	0.8	1.1	1.0	•	•	•	•
Current Assets to Working Capital 38	2.5	•	3.1	2.1	2.1	1.8	1.9	2.0	1.9	•	•	•	•
Current Liabilities to Working Capital 39	1.5	•	2.1	1.1	1.1	0.8	0.9	1.0	0.9	•	•	•	•
Working Capital to Net Sales 40	0.1	•	0.1	0.1	0.2	0.2	0.2	0.2	0.2	•	•	•	•
Inventory to Working Capital 41	0.9	•	0.4	0.3	0.8	0.6	0.8	0.7	0.7	•	•	•	•
Total Receipts to Cash Flow 42	7.8	5.8	3.4	4.3	10.4	7.4	7.6	8.1	7.1	•	•	•	•
Cost of Goods to Cash Flow 43	5.2	3.8	1.5	2.0	7.3	5.0	5.2	5.5	5.1	•	•	•	•
Cash Flow to Total Debt 44	0.2	•	1.0	0.8	0.4	0.5	0.5	0.3	0.4	•	•	•	•

Selected Financial Factors (in Percentages)

Debt Ratio 45	63.8	•	116.0	61.5	56.3	51.0	43.6	51.6	49.9	•	•	•	•
Return on Total Assets 46	10.2	•	30.1	39.3	13.3	19.9	14.4	9.2	14.6	•	•	•	•
Return on Equity Before Income Taxes 47	23.6	•	•	95.8	28.5	38.2	23.9	17.1	27.3	•	•	•	•
Return on Equity After Income Taxes 48	19.7	•	•	95.0	26.9	36.3	22.2	14.8	23.5	•	•	•	•
Profit Margin (Before Income Tax) 49	8.0	11.4	5.9	17.5	5.7	9.7	8.8	6.8	9.5	•	•	•	•
Profit Margin (After Income Tax) 50	6.7	10.5	5.7	17.3	5.4	9.2	8.2	5.9	8.2	•	•	•	•

Table I

Corporations with and without Net Income

ENGINE, TURBINE AND POWER TRANSMISSION EQUIPMENT

MONEY AMOUNTS AND SIZE OF ASSETS IN THOUSANDS OF DOLLARS

Item Description for Accounting Period 7/12 Through 6/13		Total	Zero Assets	Under 500	500 to 1,000	1,000 to 5,000	5,000 to 10,000	10,000 to 25,000	25,000 to 50,000	50,000 to 100,000	100,000 to 250,000	250,000 to 500,000	500,000 to 2,500,000	2,500,000 and over
Number of Enterprises	1	268	8	0	7	137	24	32	19	10	11	8	5	8

Revenues ($ in Thousands)														
Net Sales	2	61846670	0	0	378	875077	139570	653375	875547	1193104	1765080	2647102	7787312	45910126
Interest	3	533832	0	0	0	1	15	99	501	747	6737	12999	8798	503934
Rents	4	337635	0	0	0	0	0	0	0	139	29	7	553	336906
Royalties	5	768444	0	0	0	0	0	0	0	0	278	3060	22234	742872
Other Portfolio Income	6	506400	0	0	0	13513	0	1311	145	433	4560	5102	65745	415590
Other Receipts	7	648468	0	0	0	-34286	10407	6735	42094	15869	5867	14760	38652	548372
Total Receipts	8	64641449	0	0	378	854305	149992	661520	918287	1210292	1782551	2683030	7923294	48457800
Average Total Receipts	9	241199	0	•	54	6236	6250	20672	48331	121029	162050	335379	1584659	6057225

Operating Costs/Operating Income (%)														
Cost of Operations	10	71.8	•	•	56.6	77.2	60.7	65.9	72.0	74.4	82.6	72.7	72.7	71.2
Salaries and Wages	11	14.2	•	•	875.9	4.9	10.6	10.1	8.0	5.8	4.2	8.6	6.4	16.8
Taxes Paid	12	1.5	•	•	172.2	2.4	4.3	2.1	2.1	1.4	0.8	1.9	1.4	1.5
Interest Paid	13	1.5	•	•	1.9	0.6	1.1	1.3	1.0	1.3	1.3	1.3	2.1	1.5
Depreciation	14	2.5	•	•	124.1	0.6	5.2	4.1	2.8	1.5	4.4	1.8	1.9	2.5
Amortization and Depletion	15	0.4	•	•	•	0.0	0.0	0.5	0.1	0.3	0.7	0.3	1.0	0.3
Pensions and Other Deferred Comp.	16	1.8	•	•	•	0.0	0.9	0.3	0.1	0.4	0.8	0.6	1.0	2.2
Employee Benefits	17	3.1	•	•	•	1.4	1.3	0.8	2.3	0.9	0.9	1.9	3.4	3.3
Advertising	18	0.4	•	•	0.5	0.5	1.3	0.2	0.2	0.3	0.3	0.2	0.9	0.3
Other Expenses	19	1.1	•	•	2598.7	21.0	16.7	14.1	10.5	8.5	5.7	7.1	4.7	•
Officers' Compensation	20	0.6	•	•	351.6	3.2	5.3	2.1	1.7	1.3	1.0	0.7	0.5	0.5
Operating Margin	21	1.1	•	•	•	•	•	•	•	•	3.8	•	2.9	4.0	1.0
Operating Margin Before Officers' Comp.	22	1.8	•	•	•	•	•	0.6	0.9	5.1	•	3.6	4.5	1.5

Selected Average Balance Sheet ($ in Thousands)

Net Receivables 23	40530	0	•	0	418	978	3286	7797	22260	31138	73871	187714	1054169
Inventories 24	33352	0	•	0	1189	1193	3696	9943	17074	32642	35703	247290	797688
Net Property, Plant and Equipment 25	34101	0	•	10	497	2587	3288	10421	11053	46683	38038	219506	834964
Total Assets 26	316617	0	•	859	2771	7600	13808	37021	76468	172141	346231	1158135	8990158
Notes and Loans Payable 27	42098	0	•	7336	1115	4188	4627	7382	25298	46187	119724	246983	966937
All Other Liabilities 28	153316	0	•	7064	1085	1491	3919	13355	24062	67609	206000	574930	4371084
Net Worth 29	121203	0	•	-13541	571	1921	5262	16283	27108	58345	20508	336222	3652137

Selected Financial Ratios (Times to 1)

Current Ratio 30	0.9	•	•	0.0	1.7	4.2	2.2	1.3	2.2	1.6	1.1	1.9	0.8
Quick Ratio 31	0.4	•	•	0.0	0.4	2.2	1.1	0.6	1.3	0.8	0.6	1.0	0.4
Net Sales to Working Capital 32	•	•	•	•	6.8	1.7	4.1	8.6	4.0	5.4	13.3	5.5	•
Coverage Ratio 33	5.2	•	•	•	•	1.0	0.8	5.2	5.1	0.1	4.4	3.9	6.1
Total Asset Turnover 34	0.7	•	•	0.1	2.3	0.8	1.5	1.2	1.6	0.9	1.0	1.3	0.6
Inventory Turnover 35	5.0	•	•	•	4.1	3.0	3.6	3.3	5.2	4.1	6.7	4.6	5.1
Receivables Turnover 36	6.1	•	•	•	15.4	5.7	7.2	5.9	6.4	5.6	4.4	8.3	5.9
Total Liabilities to Net Worth 37	1.6	•	•	•	3.9	3.0	1.6	1.3	1.8	2.0	15.9	2.4	1.5
Current Assets to Working Capital 38	•	•	•	•	2.4	1.3	1.8	3.9	1.8	2.8	8.9	2.1	•
Current Liabilities to Working Capital 39	•	•	•	•	1.4	0.3	0.8	2.9	0.8	1.8	7.9	1.1	•
Working Capital to Net Sales 40	•	•	•	•	0.1	0.6	0.2	0.1	0.2	0.2	0.1	0.2	•
Inventory to Working Capital 41	•	•	•	•	1.3	0.4	0.8	1.8	0.7	1.2	1.6	0.9	•
Total Receipts to Cash Flow 42	20.6	•	•	•	104.1	8.4	8.6	7.9	8.6	33.8	10.2	11.4	27.6
Cost of Goods to Cash Flow 43	14.8	•	•	•	80.4	5.1	5.6	5.7	6.4	27.9	7.4	8.3	19.7
Cash Flow to Total Debt 44	0.1	•	•	•	0.0	0.1	0.3	0.3	0.3	0.0	0.1	0.2	0.0

Selected Financial Factors (in Percentages)

Debt Ratio 45	61.7	•	•	1677.2	79.4	74.7	61.9	56.0	64.5	66.1	94.1	71.0	59.4
Return on Total Assets 46	5.7	•	•	•	•	0.8	1.7	6.2	10.2	0.1	5.3	11.0	5.6
Return on Equity Before Income Taxes 47	12.0	•	•	16.3	•	•	•	11.3	23.1	•	69.5	28.2	11.6
Return on Equity After Income Taxes 48	7.7	•	•	16.3	•	•	•	9.4	16.0	•	43.5	20.7	7.5
Profit Margin (Before Income Tax) 49	6.3	•	•	•	•	•	•	4.0	5.2	•	4.3	6.1	7.4
Profit Margin (After Income Tax) 50	4.0	•	•	•	•	•	•	3.3	3.6	•	2.7	4.5	4.8

Table II

Corporations with Net Income

ENGINE, TURBINE AND POWER TRANSMISSION EQUIPMENT

MONEY AMOUNTS AND SIZE OF ASSETS IN THOUSANDS OF DOLLARS

Item Description for Accounting Period 7/12 Through 6/13	Total	Zero Assets	Under 500	500 to 1,000	1,000 to 5,000	5,000 to 10,000	10,000 to 25,000	25,000 to 50,000	50,000 to 100,000	100,000 to 250,000	250,000 to 500,000	500,000 to 2,500,000	2,500,000 and over
Number of Enterprises **1**	142	0	0	0	66	12	19	•	•	4	5	5	•
Revenues ($ in Thousands)													
Net Sales **2**	54892408	0	0	0	524852	125918	434335	•	•	1183005	2066828	7787312	•
Interest **3**	519773	0	0	0	0	15	89	•	•	1663	12732	8798	•
Rents **4**	337202	0	0	0	0	0	0	•	•	0	7	553	•
Royalties **5**	761267	0	0	0	0	0	0	•	•	278	2633	22234	•
Other Portfolio Income **6**	489670	0	0	0	0	0	84	•	•	4560	3187	65745	•
Other Receipts **7**	540890	0	0	0	0	9950	16	•	•	1858	11792	38652	•
Total Receipts **8**	57541210	0	0	0	524852	135883	434524	•	•	1191364	2097179	7923294	•
Average Total Receipts **9**	405220	•	•	•	7952	11324	22870	•	•	297841	419436	1584659	•
Operating Costs/Operating Income (%)													
Cost of Operations **10**	73.6	•	•	•	79.1	55.5	69.1	•	•	81.4	73.4	72.7	•
Salaries and Wages **11**	13.9	•	•	•	3.0	3.7	6.7	•	•	4.4	9.3	6.4	•
Taxes Paid **12**	1.2	•	•	•	1.5	4.3	1.4	•	•	0.6	1.8	1.4	•
Interest Paid **13**	1.3	•	•	•	0.3	0.6	0.6	•	•	0.2	0.3	2.1	•
Depreciation **14**	2.3	•	•	•	0.1	0.8	1.4	•	•	2.6	1.5	1.9	•
Amortization and Depletion **15**	0.3	•	•	•	0.0	0.0	0.0	•	•	0.1	0.3	1.0	•
Pensions and Other Deferred Comp. **16**	1.8	•	•	•	•	0.7	0.2	•	•	0.7	0.5	1.0	•
Employee Benefits **17**	3.0	•	•	•	1.7	0.8	0.6	•	•	1.0	1.5	3.4	•
Advertising **18**	0.4	•	•	•	0.7	1.3	0.3	•	•	0.4	0.2	0.9	•
Other Expenses **19**	•	•	•	•	4.0	6.4	7.9	•	•	4.9	5.8	4.7	•
Officers' Compensation **20**	0.6	•	•	•	4.1	3.2	1.4	•	•	1.3	0.6	0.5	•
Operating Margin **21**	2.5	•	•	•	5.4	22.7	10.5	•	•	2.4	4.7	4.0	•
Operating Margin Before Officers' Comp. **22**	3.0	•	•	•	9.5	25.9	11.9	•	•	3.8	5.4	4.5	•

Selected Average Balance Sheet ($ in Thousands)

Net Receivables 23	67836	•	•	•	850	715	3640	•	•	59902	48849	187714	•
Inventories 24	53826	•	•	•	2025	1688	4501	•	•	66270	41418	245275	•
Net Property, Plant and Equipment 25	54163	•	•	•	396	1416	2927	•	•	44193	36187	219506	•
Total Assets 26	511544	•	•	•	3246	6662	13251	•	•	212467	333456	1158135	•
Notes and Loans Payable 27	59687	•	•	•	539	1906	1795	•	•	17116	70027	246983	•
All Other Liabilities 28	258728	•	•	•	520	372	2853	•	•	107084	133430	574930	•
Net Worth 29	193128	•	•	•	2186	4383	8603	•	•	88267	129999	336222	•

Selected Financial Ratios (Times to 1)

Current Ratio 30	0.9	•	•	•	3.6	4.8	2.9	•	•	1.7	1.6	1.9	•
Quick Ratio 31	0.5	•	•	•	1.1	2.2	1.5	•	•	0.9	0.7	1.0	•
Net Sales to Working Capital 32	•	•	•	•	3.9	3.0	3.5	•	•	4.9	4.5	5.5	•
Coverage Ratio 33	6.9	•	•	•	21.3	49.5	19.7	•	•	24.5	21.5	3.9	•
Total Asset Turnover 34	0.8	•	•	•	2.4	1.6	1.7	•	•	1.4	1.2	1.3	•
Inventory Turnover 35	5.3	•	•	•	3.1	3.5	3.5	•	•	3.6	7.3	4.6	•
Receivables Turnover 36	6.2	•	•	•	9.6	10.1	6.7	•	•	5.0	7.7	•	•
Total Liabilities to Net Worth 37	1.6	•	•	•	0.5	0.5	0.5	•	•	1.4	1.6	2.4	•
Current Assets to Working Capital 38	•	•	•	•	1.4	1.3	1.5	•	•	2.5	2.6	2.1	•
Current Liabilities to Working Capital 39	•	•	•	•	0.4	0.3	0.5	•	•	1.5	1.6	1.1	•
Working Capital to Net Sales 40	•	•	•	•	0.3	0.3	0.3	•	•	0.2	0.2	0.2	•
Inventory to Working Capital 41	•	•	•	•	0.9	0.6	0.7	•	•	1.0	0.5	0.9	•
Total Receipts to Cash Flow 42	22.0	•	•	•	13.1	2.9	5.8	•	•	14.4	9.6	11.4	•
Cost of Goods to Cash Flow 43	16.2	•	•	•	10.4	1.6	4.0	•	•	11.7	7.0	8.3	•
Cash Flow to Total Debt 44	0.1	•	•	•	0.6	1.6	0.8	•	•	0.2	0.2	0.2	•

Selected Financial Factors (in Percentages)

Debt Ratio 45	62.2	•	•	•	32.6	34.2	35.1	•	•	58.5	61.0	71.0	•
Return on Total Assets 46	7.1	•	•	•	13.9	49.2	19.2	•	•	5.7	8.1	11.0	•
Return on Equity Before Income Taxes 47	16.0	•	•	•	19.7	73.3	28.1	•	•	13.1	19.8	28.2	•
Return on Equity After Income Taxes 48	10.9	•	•	•	19.7	65.0	24.3	•	•	8.6	13.3	20.7	•
Profit Margin (Before Income Tax) 49	8.0	•	•	•	5.4	30.6	10.6	•	•	3.9	6.2	6.1	•
Profit Margin (After Income Tax) 50	5.4	•	•	•	5.4	27.2	9.1	•	•	2.6	4.2	4.5	•

Table I
Corporations with and without Net Income

OTHER GENERAL PURPOSE MACHINERY

MONEY AMOUNTS AND SIZE OF ASSETS IN THOUSANDS OF DOLLARS

Item Description for Accounting Period 7/12 Through 6/13	Total	Zero Assets	Under 500	500 to 1,000	1,000 to 5,000	5,000 to 10,000	10,000 to 25,000	25,000 to 50,000	50,000 to 100,000	100,000 to 250,000	250,000 to 500,000	500,000 to 2,500,000	2,500,000 and over
Number of Enterprises 1	4971	478	2510	743	522	305	229	70	44	29	14	18	9

Revenues ($ in Thousands)													
Net Sales 2	82770450	3594971	955410	2629276	2491687	3678530	6162836	3818088	3969654	5221796	6295439	16946853	27005910
Interest 3	352411	136504	2488	157	347	677	2140	3790	701	6642	5862	21069	172036
Rents 4	206065	2552	0	0	45	290	2007	473	10365	639	827	187644	1224
Royalties 5	355471	1319	0	0	0	0	40	243	3956	8500	6894	193108	141410
Other Portfolio Income 6	1215275	84139	885	260	776	7379	129617	35977	19319	25368	26703	61212	823640
Other Receipts 7	919775	25747	207	1718	8638	14271	79918	24961	18188	32183	18233	72160	623550
Total Receipts 8	85819447	3845232	958990	2631411	2501493	3701147	6376558	3883532	4022183	5295128	6353958	17482046	28767770
Average Total Receipts 9	17264	8044	382	3542	4792	12135	27845	55479	91413	182591	453854	971225	3196419

Operating Costs/Operating Income (%)													
Cost of Operations 10	68.8	62.6	42.2	55.1	64.2	62.3	67.7	74.2	70.0	72.5	69.0	66.8	72.9
Salaries and Wages 11	9.2	12.3	15.1	11.0	8.4	9.0	10.0	6.9	8.1	9.2	7.1	9.8	8.9
Taxes Paid 12	1.5	1.2	3.0	3.0	2.2	2.5	2.0	1.4	1.7	1.2	1.3	1.9	0.9
Interest Paid 13	1.9	6.8	0.5	0.3	0.4	0.4	0.9	1.3	1.0	1.4	0.3	1.3	3.0
Depreciation 14	2.1	1.4	1.0	0.8	1.3	1.2	1.9	1.4	2.3	1.2	1.8	1.9	3.0
Amortization and Depletion 15	0.7	1.9	0.0	0.0	0.1	0.0	0.3	0.3	0.3	0.9	0.4	1.0	1.0
Pensions and Other Deferred Comp. 16	1.3	1.2	0.6	1.4	1.1	0.4	0.5	0.2	0.8	0.8	1.2	1.0	2.1
Employee Benefits 17	2.0	4.1	1.4	1.4	1.5	1.8	1.6	0.9	1.6	2.3	1.8	2.6	1.8
Advertising 18	0.6	0.4	0.4	0.9	0.6	0.6	1.0	0.3	0.4	0.4	0.5	0.5	0.7
Other Expenses 19	9.6	8.7	20.3	11.6	9.8	10.5	7.6	7.0	6.3	8.8	7.2	8.7	11.5
Officers' Compensation 20	1.5	1.1	10.6	8.2	6.9	2.6	2.0	2.2	1.2	0.9	1.2	0.9	0.4
Operating Margin 21	0.9	•	4.9	6.3	3.7	8.6	4.5	3.9	6.2	0.6	8.1	3.7	•
Operating Margin Before Officers' Comp. 22	2.4	•	15.5	14.6	10.5	11.2	6.5	6.1	7.5	1.5	9.4	4.5	•

Selected Average Balance Sheet ($ in Thousands)

Net Receivables 23	3926	0	35	153	625	1548	3798	9618	15438	34702	69973	150392	1288925
Inventories 24	2372	0	14	138	729	2315	3983	9339	17412	21683	62503	138372	471207
Net Property, Plant and Equipment 25	2285	0	21	47	324	979	2656	5148	12472	16176	48939	113926	675693
Total Assets 26	22683	0	109	750	2214	7144	15608	33891	67778	145583	361075	926119	8190619
Notes and Loans Payable 27	4800	0	40	354	427	1190	3627	10012	16069	38692	33916	343106	1433583
All Other Liabilities 28	7341	0	25	223	762	2044	4963	9841	23112	51428	116815	332422	2587874
Net Worth 29	10542	0	44	173	1026	3910	7018	14038	28597	55464	210344	250591	4169162

Selected Financial Ratios (Times to 1)

Current Ratio 30	1.4	•	2.1	2.2	2.2	2.7	1.9	1.7	1.9	1.5	2.0	1.3	1.2
Quick Ratio 31	0.8	•	1.7	1.5	1.4	1.5	1.0	1.0	1.0	0.8	1.1	0.6	0.8
Net Sales to Working Capital 32	7.1	•	11.0	11.5	4.9	3.5	5.2	5.4	4.6	6.5	4.7	11.3	8.2
Coverage Ratio 33	3.9	1.9	12.2	22.9	11.8	22.3	10.3	5.5	9.0	2.6	33.6	7.0	1.6
Total Asset Turnover 34	0.7	•	3.5	4.7	2.2	1.7	1.7	1.6	1.3	1.2	1.2	1.0	0.4
Inventory Turnover 35	4.8	•	11.6	14.1	4.2	3.2	4.6	4.3	3.6	6.0	5.0	4.5	4.6
Receivables Turnover 36	5.0	•	11.3	26.7	7.7	7.9	7.3	5.9	5.4	5.9	6.1	6.1	3.1
Total Liabilities to Net Worth 37	1.2	•	1.5	3.3	1.2	0.8	1.2	1.4	1.4	1.6	0.7	2.7	1.0
Current Assets to Working Capital 38	3.7	•	1.9	1.9	1.9	1.6	2.1	2.4	2.1	2.9	2.0	4.6	6.4
Current Liabilities to Working Capital 39	2.7	•	0.9	0.9	0.9	0.6	1.1	1.4	1.1	1.9	1.0	3.6	5.4
Working Capital to Net Sales 40	0.1	•	0.1	0.1	0.2	0.3	0.2	0.2	0.2	0.2	0.2	0.1	0.1
Inventory to Working Capital 41	1.1	•	0.4	0.5	0.7	0.7	0.8	0.8	0.9	1.0	0.6	1.7	1.5
Total Receipts to Cash Flow 42	8.3	8.1	5.4	6.1	8.9	5.7	7.5	10.0	7.9	10.7	7.0	7.5	10.3
Cost of Goods to Cash Flow 43	5.7	5.1	2.3	3.4	5.7	3.6	5.1	7.4	5.5	7.8	4.8	5.0	7.5
Cash Flow to Total Debt 44	0.2	•	1.1	1.0	0.5	0.7	0.4	0.3	0.3	0.2	0.4	0.2	0.1

Selected Financial Factors (in Percentages)

Debt Ratio 45	53.5	•	59.5	76.9	53.7	45.3	55.0	58.6	57.8	61.9	41.7	72.9	49.1
Return on Total Assets 46	5.3	•	20.0	31.6	9.6	16.3	15.2	11.0	11.7	4.5	11.9	9.4	1.8
Return on Equity Before Income Taxes 47	8.5	•	45.4	131.0	18.9	28.5	30.4	21.8	24.6	7.3	19.8	29.7	1.3
Return on Equity After Income Taxes 48	5.8	•	44.9	128.5	16.6	26.0	27.6	18.4	20.6	3.6	13.6	19.7	0.2
Profit Margin (Before Income Tax) 49	5.4	6.3	5.3	6.4	4.1	9.2	7.9	5.6	7.8	2.2	9.3	7.9	1.8
Profit Margin (After Income Tax) 50	3.7	4.1	5.2	6.3	3.6	8.4	7.2	4.7	6.5	1.1	6.4	5.2	0.2

Table II

Corporations with Net Income

OTHER GENERAL PURPOSE MACHINERY

MONEY AMOUNTS AND SIZE OF ASSETS IN THOUSANDS OF DOLLARS

Item Description for Accounting Period 7/12 Through 6/13	Total	Zero Assets	Under 500	500 to 1,000	1,000 to 5,000	5,000 to 10,000	10,000 to 25,000	25,000 to 50,000	50,000 to 100,000	100,000 to 250,000	250,000 to 500,000	500,000 to 2,500,000	2,500,000 and over
Number of Enterprises 1	3242	260	1230	725	419	277	176	59	41	20	•	•	6

Revenues ($ in Thousands)

Net Sales 2	66856074	3287498	827056	2629276	2159280	3324794	4954249	3505242	3737077	3966245	•	•	15410624
Interest 3	273115	136139	771	16	136	676	1421	814	693	5379	•	•	100139
Rents 4	205308	2552	0	0	0	290	1994	350	10365	639	•	•	648
Royalties 5	345977	788	0	0	0	0	30	243	3956	124	•	•	140835
Other Portfolio Income 6	698964	77181	7	124	530	1292	127710	30074	19299	24976	•	•	329856
Other Receipts 7	812086	23545	207	1353	7371	13573	69858	19388	18136	18062	•	•	550884
Total Receipts 8	69191524	3527703	828041	2630769	2167317	3340625	5155262	3556111	3789526	4015425	•	•	16532986
Average Total Receipts 9	21342	13568	673	3629	5173	12060	29291	60273	92427	200771	•	•	2755498

Operating Costs/Operating Income (%)

Cost of Operations 10	66.3	64.6	45.4	55.1	65.2	60.7	65.7	74.4	69.0	72.3	•	•	65.2
Salaries and Wages 11	9.2	9.9	17.2	11.0	7.9	9.4	9.0	6.5	8.4	8.5	•	•	10.0
Taxes Paid 12	1.6	1.2	2.8	3.0	1.8	2.6	1.9	1.3	1.7	1.3	•	•	0.8
Interest Paid 13	1.7	7.2	0.5	0.3	0.3	0.4	0.8	1.0	0.8	0.8	•	•	3.2
Depreciation 14	1.7	1.4	0.9	0.8	0.9	1.2	1.4	1.2	2.4	1.1	•	•	1.9
Amortization and Depletion 15	0.7	1.8	•	0.0	0.1	0.0	0.3	0.3	0.2	0.9	•	•	1.0
Pensions and Other Deferred Comp. 16	1.0	1.3	0.6	1.4	1.1	0.5	0.6	0.2	0.8	0.9	•	•	1.1
Employee Benefits 17	2.1	4.0	1.4	1.4	1.0	1.8	1.6	0.8	1.6	2.3	•	•	2.2
Advertising 18	0.7	0.4	0.2	0.9	0.5	0.5	1.1	0.3	0.5	0.4	•	•	1.2
Other Expenses 19	9.5	7.4	14.0	11.4	8.8	9.7	8.0	5.3	6.5	6.5	•	•	14.3
Officers' Compensation 20	1.6	0.2	7.5	8.2	6.4	2.6	1.8	2.2	1.3	0.9	•	•	0.5
Operating Margin 21	4.1	0.6	9.4	6.5	6.0	10.6	7.8	6.3	6.8	4.2	•	•	•
Operating Margin Before Officers' Comp. 22	5.6	0.8	16.9	14.8	12.4	13.2	9.6	8.5	8.1	5.1	•	•	•

Selected Average Balance Sheet ($ in Thousands)												
Net Receivables 23	4552	0	61	154	663	1516	4030	10255	15011	38720	•	•	1266763
Inventories 24	2992	0	27	119	790	2387	4075	8458	15883	26461	•	•	649629
Net Property, Plant and Equipment 25	2311	0	42	49	307	967	2172	4940	12227	17419	•	•	485289
Total Assets 26	26433	0	160	756	2311	7060	15628	34184	66737	151641	•	•	8607926
Notes and Loans Payable 27	5345	0	74	363	386	1075	3291	8806	14449	30165	•	•	1408875
All Other Liabilities 28	7759	0	43	224	772	1993	5097	10464	22992	51468	•	•	2239226
Net Worth 29	13329	0	43	169	1153	3992	7240	14913	29295	70008	•	•	4959825

Selected Financial Ratios (Times to 1)												
Current Ratio 30	1.5	•	1.9	2.1	2.3	2.8	2.1	1.8	1.9	1.9	•	•	1.3
Quick Ratio 31	0.9	•	1.5	1.5	1.5	1.6	1.2	1.1	1.0	1.0	•	•	0.8
Net Sales to Working Capital 32	5.5	•	13.0	11.9	4.6	3.5	4.7	5.4	4.4	4.5	•	•	4.0
Coverage Ratio 33	6.0	2.2	19.2	23.5	20.4	26.5	15.4	8.7	11.4	8.5	•	•	3.6
Total Asset Turnover 34	0.8	•	4.2	4.8	2.2	1.7	1.8	1.7	1.4	1.3	•	•	0.3
Inventory Turnover 35	4.6	•	11.4	16.7	4.3	3.1	4.5	5.2	4.0	5.4	•	•	2.6
Receivables Turnover 36	5.6	•	10.6	28.0	8.0	7.6	7.3	6.2	6.4	5.4	•	•	•
Total Liabilities to Net Worth 37	1.0	•	2.7	3.5	1.0	0.8	1.2	1.3	1.3	1.2	•	•	0.7
Current Assets to Working Capital 38	2.8	•	2.1	1.9	1.7	1.6	1.9	2.2	2.1	2.2	•	•	4.0
Current Liabilities to Working Capital 39	1.8	•	1.1	0.9	0.7	0.6	0.9	1.2	1.1	1.2	•	•	3.0
Working Capital to Net Sales 40	0.2	•	0.1	0.1	0.2	0.3	0.2	0.2	0.2	0.2	•	•	0.2
Inventory to Working Capital 41	0.9	•	0.5	0.5	0.6	0.6	0.7	0.7	0.9	0.7	•	•	1.0
Total Receipts to Cash Flow 42	6.6	7.3	5.4	6.1	7.9	5.4	5.7	9.2	7.4	9.6	•	•	5.4
Cost of Goods to Cash Flow 43	4.4	4.7	2.5	3.4	5.2	3.3	3.7	6.8	5.1	6.9	•	•	3.5
Cash Flow to Total Debt 44	0.2	•	1.1	1.0	0.6	0.7	0.6	0.3	0.3	0.3	•	•	0.1

Selected Financial Factors (in Percentages)												
Debt Ratio 45	49.6	•	72.9	77.7	50.1	43.5	53.7	56.4	56.1	53.8	•	•	42.4
Return on Total Assets 46	8.0	•	42.2	33.0	15.0	19.6	22.9	15.2	12.8	8.5	•	•	3.5
Return on Equity Before Income Taxes 47	13.1	•	147.7	141.4	28.5	33.4	46.2	30.9	26.5	16.2	•	•	4.4
Return on Equity After Income Taxes 48	10.0	•	146.7	138.7	26.0	30.7	42.6	27.1	22.3	11.9	•	•	2.9
Profit Margin (Before Income Tax) 49	8.5	8.9	9.5	6.6	6.4	11.1	11.9	7.8	8.5	5.7	•	•	8.4
Profit Margin (After Income Tax) 50	6.4	6.5	9.5	6.5	5.8	10.2	11.0	6.8	7.2	4.2	•	•	5.6

Table I

Corporations with and without Net Income

COMPUTER AND PERIPHERAL EQUIPMENT

MONEY AMOUNTS AND SIZE OF ASSETS IN THOUSANDS OF DOLLARS

Item Description for Accounting Period 7/12 Through 6/13	Total	Zero Assets	Under 500	500 to 1,000	1,000 to 5,000	5,000 to 10,000	10,000 to 25,000	25,000 to 50,000	50,000 to 100,000	100,000 to 250,000	250,000 to 500,000	500,000 to 2,500,000	2,500,000 and over
Number of Enterprises 1	2240	1151	147	205	421	103	100	33	30	12	10	16	12

Revenues ($ in Thousands)

	Total	Zero Assets	Under 500	500 to 1,000	1,000 to 5,000	5,000 to 10,000	10,000 to 25,000	25,000 to 50,000	50,000 to 100,000	100,000 to 250,000	250,000 to 500,000	500,000 to 2,500,000	2,500,000 and over
Net Sales 2	244903166	763611	94421	353314	2584278	867202	2459967	1514140	2963930	2815813	3269282	11492937	215724272
Interest 3	1432163	1055	17	120	316	726	2010	530	1615	9550	5857	23864	1386502
Rents 4	2631577	0	0	0	0	0	0	0	215	0	0	17980	2613382
Royalties 5	23683314	6252	0	1439	0	0	21765	2774	26586	8151	52653	234543	23329153
Other Portfolio Income 6	1913391	5966	11109	0	1	1951	2817	4689	443	89	33022	32434	1820870
Other Receipts 7	5535462	5680	4572	0	801	2152	8546	23098	25963	21126	63125	673347	4707050
Total Receipts 8	280099073	782564	110119	354873	2585396	872031	2495105	1545231	3018752	2854729	3423939	12475105	249581229
Average Total Receipts 9	125044	680	749	1731	6141	8466	24951	46825	100625	237894	342394	779694	20798436

Operating Costs/Operating Income (%)

	Total	Zero Assets	Under 500	500 to 1,000	1,000 to 5,000	5,000 to 10,000	10,000 to 25,000	25,000 to 50,000	50,000 to 100,000	100,000 to 250,000	250,000 to 500,000	500,000 to 2,500,000	2,500,000 and over
Cost of Operations 10	58.5	51.1	35.0	50.1	64.7	55.2	58.6	51.5	66.1	70.1	65.3	66.5	57.8
Salaries and Wages 11	15.3	26.0	33.1	10.3	12.2	16.2	18.6	16.7	15.2	13.1	13.1	18.0	15.1
Taxes Paid 12	1.8	1.5	4.4	3.1	1.9	2.4	2.1	2.1	1.8	1.1	1.3	1.5	1.8
Interest Paid 13	1.4	2.0	1.6	2.5	0.4	0.5	0.4	1.3	1.2	0.9	1.0	0.6	1.5
Depreciation 14	2.9	2.0	2.0	3.0	1.2	1.3	1.5	1.3	1.6	1.1	2.2	2.7	3.0
Amortization and Depletion 15	•	1.1	1.8	1.8	0.0	1.7	1.0	1.4	1.0	0.3	1.2	1.1	•
Pensions and Other Deferred Comp. 16	0.8	0.1	•	0.2	0.0	0.7	0.2	0.1	0.2	0.2	0.2	0.1	0.9
Employee Benefits 17	1.4	1.6	1.5	1.5	1.0	2.2	1.7	1.5	1.5	1.0	1.1	1.7	1.3
Advertising 18	1.3	0.8	0.1	3.8	0.2	0.8	1.5	1.0	0.8	2.3	1.8	0.8	1.3
Other Expenses 19	21.5	26.3	38.4	31.6	16.2	11.5	17.4	16.9	14.0	6.9	15.2	13.5	22.5
Officers' Compensation 20	0.8	1.7	11.5	10.2	3.9	5.2	2.9	3.2	1.3	1.5	0.9	1.7	0.6
Operating Margin 21	•	•	•	•	•	2.1	•	3.2	•	1.5	•	•	•
Operating Margin Before Officers' Comp. 22	•	•	•	•	2.2	7.4	•	6.3	•	3.0	•	•	•

Selected Average Balance Sheet ($ in Thousands)

Net Receivables 23	23233	0	0	252	244	1398	4472	8694	15277	46835	76946	156505	3893000
Inventories 24	4222	0	0	102	401	1133	3110	9046	9540	20612	29038	72744	546087
Net Property, Plant and Equipment 25	13175	0	11	23	143	1056	1327	2019	5467	10814	20669	69286	2294084
Total Assets 26	185257	0	209	741	1808	6709	15980	35046	69460	171678	371966	964876	32273756
Notes and Loans Payable 27	48762	0	236	466	304	1123	2659	7691	11513	33041	75639	217741	8612629
All Other Liabilities 28	65240	0	373	275	920	1427	5453	15759	31650	83772	147171	276050	11382000
Net Worth 29	71255	0	-401	-1	584	4159	7868	11595	26297	54866	149156	471085	12279128

Selected Financial Ratios (Times to 1)

Current Ratio 30	1.0	•	3.3	0.9	1.9	3.5	2.4	1.8	1.6	1.4	1.6	2.0	1.0
Quick Ratio 31	0.6	•	2.9	0.7	1.1	2.1	1.6	1.2	0.9	1.0	1.2	1.1	0.5
Net Sales to Working Capital 32	54.5	•	5.0	•	9.0	2.8	3.3	4.1	6.0	7.8	4.8	2.8	•
Coverage Ratio 33	8.9	•	•	•	•	6.1	•	5.3	•	4.2	3.6	2.3	9.5
Total Asset Turnover 34	0.6	•	3.1	2.3	3.4	1.3	1.5	1.3	1.4	1.4	0.9	0.7	0.6
Inventory Turnover 35	15.2	•	•	8.5	9.9	4.1	4.6	2.6	6.8	8.0	7.3	6.6	19.0
Receivables Turnover 36	4.6	•	37.1	8.7	18.6	6.9	5.7	3.3	7.4	5.6	5.0	5.1	4.5
Total Liabilities to Net Worth 37	1.6	•	•	•	2.1	0.6	1.0	2.0	1.6	2.1	1.5	1.0	1.6
Current Assets to Working Capital 38	29.0	•	1.4	•	2.1	1.4	1.7	2.2	2.7	3.3	2.7	2.0	•
Current Liabilities to Working Capital 39	28.0	•	0.4	•	1.1	0.4	0.7	1.2	1.7	2.3	1.7	1.0	•
Working Capital to Net Sales 40	0.0	•	0.2	•	0.1	0.4	0.3	0.2	0.2	0.1	0.2	0.4	•
Inventory to Working Capital 41	2.1	•	•	•	0.8	0.4	0.4	0.6	0.6	0.8	0.4	0.3	•
Total Receipts to Cash Flow 42	3.5	8.7	29.0	10.8	9.9	9.5	9.4	5.0	10.3	11.7	6.8	8.2	3.3
Cost of Goods to Cash Flow 43	2.1	4.4	10.2	5.4	6.4	5.2	5.5	2.6	6.8	8.2	4.5	5.4	1.9
Cash Flow to Total Debt 44	0.3	•	0.0	0.2	0.5	0.3	0.3	0.4	0.2	0.2	0.2	0.2	0.3

Selected Financial Factors (in Percentages)

Debt Ratio 45	61.5	•	291.4	100.2	67.7	38.0	50.8	66.9	62.1	68.0	59.9	51.2	62.0
Return on Total Assets 46	7.3	•	•	•	•	4.1	•	9.1	•	5.3	3.1	1.0	7.7
Return on Equity Before Income Taxes 47	16.8	•	20.6	26510.2	•	5.5	•	22.3	•	12.5	5.6	1.2	18.2
Return on Equity After Income Taxes 48	10.6	•	21.1	26891.5	•	5.4	•	12.0	•	5.4	3.4	•	11.7
Profit Margin (Before Income Tax) 49	10.9	•	•	•	•	2.7	•	5.6	•	2.9	2.6	0.8	12.4
Profit Margin (After Income Tax) 50	6.9	•	•	•	•	2.7	•	3.0	•	1.3	1.6	•	8.0

Table II
Corporations with Net Income

COMPUTER AND PERIPHERAL EQUIPMENT

MONEY AMOUNTS AND SIZE OF ASSETS IN THOUSANDS OF DOLLARS

Item Description for Accounting Period 7/12 Through 6/13	Total	Zero Assets	Under 500	500 to 1,000	1,000 to 5,000	5,000 to 10,000	10,000 to 25,000	25,000 to 50,000	50,000 to 100,000	100,000 to 250,000	250,000 to 500,000	500,000 to 2,500,000	2,500,000 and over
Number of Enterprises 1	973	420	•	60	193	49	71	28	15	8	7	9	•

Revenues ($ in Thousands)

Net Sales 2	197822510	636906	•	183676	1282003	484418	2086058	1392756	2229130	2192853	2341390	7641243	•
Interest 3	1289290	871	•	0	221	69	1669	438	1055	868	5614	11106	•
Rents 4	1086060	0	•	0	0	0	0	0	160	0	0	17980	•
Royalties 5	20231814	6252	•	0	0	0	21744	2694	0	7880	5928	221953	•
Other Portfolio Income 6	1762367	3078	•	0	0	1937	2160	4689	55	41	10312	10637	•
Other Receipts 7	2766040	5100	•	0	0	840	7980	14679	24208	21079	66497	481077	•
Total Receipts 8	224958081	652207	•	183676	1282224	487264	2119611	1415256	2254608	2222721	2429741	8383996	•
Average Total Receipts 9	231200	1553	•	3061	6644	9944	29854	50545	150307	277840	347106	931555	•

Operating Costs/Operating Income (%)

Cost of Operations 10	52.3	52.2	•	59.0	66.5	54.5	58.7	50.9	68.5	70.6	63.4	58.6	•
Salaries and Wages 11	14.7	14.5	•	6.6	11.4	12.3	14.7	15.5	12.5	11.0	12.8	19.1	•
Taxes Paid 12	1.9	1.4	•	3.9	0.9	1.7	1.8	2.0	1.4	0.9	1.0	1.9	•
Interest Paid 13	1.2	2.3	•	0.4	0.4	0.3	0.3	1.4	0.5	0.5	0.6	0.6	•
Depreciation 14	2.4	2.0	•	5.2	1.4	0.4	1.0	1.2	1.1	0.8	2.0	3.2	•
Amortization and Depletion 15	0.5	1.2	•	0.0	0.0	0.2	0.2	1.4	0.8	0.2	0.7	1.0	•
Pensions and Other Deferred Comp. 16	0.6	0.1	•	0.4	0.1	1.1	0.2	0.1	0.2	0.2	0.1	0.0	•
Employee Benefits 17	1.4	1.0	•	1.4	0.3	1.6	1.5	1.4	0.9	0.9	1.5	2.0	•
Advertising 18	1.1	0.7	•	0.0	0.2	0.8	1.3	1.0	0.6	2.7	2.4	0.9	•
Other Expenses 19	23.3	13.6	•	12.7	7.8	8.7	10.4	13.9	10.1	5.7	13.3	15.5	•
Officers' Compensation 20	0.8	1.2	•	7.9	1.5	4.8	2.6	2.9	0.9	1.6	0.9	1.2	•
Operating Margin 21	•	9.9	•	2.6	9.4	13.7	7.2	8.3	2.9	4.9	1.3	•	•
Operating Margin Before Officers' Comp. 22	0.6	11.1	•	10.4	11.0	18.5	9.9	11.2	3.7	6.6	2.2	•	•

	Selected Average Balance Sheet ($ in Thousands)											
Net Receivables 23	40131	0	•	456	392	1711	4275	9507	17188	47206	74238	190839	•
Inventories 24	6264	0	•	279	388	1045	3527	6864	11580	24265	18127	75583	•
Net Property, Plant and Equipment 25	24289	0	•	50	255	297	1390	2196	5780	12514	23497	98904	•
Total Assets 26	358421	0	•	888	2000	6756	15737	36058	74982	172680	366473	1085997	•
Notes and Loans Payable 27	66943	0	•	339	196	952	2403	8529	11010	30430	31006	169879	•
All Other Liabilities 28	124942	0	•	279	850	974	4381	16003	36102	97548	155500	347680	•
Net Worth 29	166536	0	•	270	955	4830	8953	11525	27870	44701	179967	568438	•

	Selected Financial Ratios (Times to 1)											
Current Ratio 30	1.2	•	•	1.9	4.4	5.0	3.0	1.8	1.6	1.2	1.6	1.6	•
Quick Ratio 31	0.6	•	•	1.2	3.3	3.4	1.9	1.1	0.9	0.8	1.2	1.0	•
Net Sales to Working Capital 32	11.3	•	•	7.7	5.3	2.7	3.5	4.6	9.0	13.7	4.7	4.6	•
Coverage Ratio 33	14.0	6.4	•	7.4	22.6	55.5	31.4	8.6	9.7	13.7	11.8	10.7	•
Total Asset Turnover 34	0.6	•	•	3.4	3.3	1.5	1.9	1.4	2.0	1.6	0.9	0.8	•
Inventory Turnover 35	17.0	•	•	6.5	11.4	5.2	4.9	3.7	8.8	8.0	11.7	6.6	•
Receivables Turnover 36	4.9	•	•	7.0	17.9	6.6	6.5	5.1	•	6.2	5.6	4.7	•
Total Liabilities to Net Worth 37	1.2	•	•	2.3	1.1	0.4	0.8	2.1	1.7	2.9	1.0	0.9	•
Current Assets to Working Capital 38	6.1	•	•	2.1	1.3	1.3	1.5	2.3	2.8	5.0	2.7	2.7	•
Current Liabilities to Working Capital 39	5.1	•	•	1.1	0.3	0.3	0.5	1.3	1.8	4.0	1.7	1.7	•
Working Capital to Net Sales 40	0.1	•	•	0.1	0.2	0.4	0.3	0.2	0.1	0.1	0.2	0.2	•
Inventory to Working Capital 41	0.4	•	•	0.8	0.3	0.3	0.4	0.6	0.7	1.5	0.3	0.4	•
Total Receipts to Cash Flow 42	2.9	4.1	•	9.9	7.0	5.0	5.7	4.6	8.0	9.1	6.2	5.1	•
Cost of Goods to Cash Flow 43	1.5	2.1	•	5.9	4.7	2.8	3.4	2.3	5.5	6.4	3.9	3.0	•
Cash Flow to Total Debt 44	0.4	•	•	0.5	0.9	1.0	0.8	0.4	0.4	0.2	0.3	0.3	•

	Selected Financial Factors (in Percentages)											
Debt Ratio 45	53.5	•	•	69.6	52.3	28.5	43.1	68.0	62.8	74.1	50.9	47.7	•
Return on Total Assets 46	9.3	•	•	10.2	32.8	21.3	17.1	16.1	9.1	10.8	6.5	5.4	•
Return on Equity Before Income Taxes 47	18.5	•	•	29.0	65.8	29.2	29.0	44.4	21.9	38.8	12.0	9.4	•
Return on Equity After Income Taxes 48	12.4	•	•	23.5	64.2	29.0	26.6	32.2	17.3	25.6	9.5	6.7	•
Profit Margin (Before Income Tax) 49	15.1	12.3	•	2.6	9.5	14.3	8.8	10.3	4.1	6.3	6.5	6.3	•
Profit Margin (After Income Tax) 50	10.1	10.3	•	2.1	9.2	14.1	8.1	7.5	3.2	4.2	5.1	4.5	•

Table I

Corporations with and without Net Income

COMMUNICATIONS EQUIPMENT

MONEY AMOUNTS AND SIZE OF ASSETS IN THOUSANDS OF DOLLARS

Item Description for Accounting Period 7/12 Through 6/13		Total	Zero Assets	Under 500	500 to 1,000	1,000 to 5,000	5,000 to 10,000	10,000 to 25,000	25,000 to 50,000	50,000 to 100,000	100,000 to 250,000	250,000 to 500,000	500,000 to 2,500,000	2,500,000 and over
Number of Enterprises	1	1658	30	1076	53	292	42	72	33	17	15	6	14	8

Revenues ($ in Thousands)

		Total	Zero Assets	Under 500	500 to 1,000	1,000 to 5,000	5,000 to 10,000	10,000 to 25,000	25,000 to 50,000	50,000 to 100,000	100,000 to 250,000	250,000 to 500,000	500,000 to 2,500,000	2,500,000 and over
Net Sales	2	69247595	5713752	317942	127772	1340561	579361	2037604	1147561	1515626	2030879	2916690	9532984	41986863
Interest	3	221717	3081	65	0	285	90	165	827	1511	4439	39355	46992	124907
Rents	4	43694	0	0	0	0	347	147	228	249	459	8918	7114	26232
Royalties	5	651068	178833	0	0	0	5	0	955	250	3598	4736	32667	430024
Other Portfolio Income	6	4744149	2098695	0	0	338	10	583	34	3702	12403	474141	26178	2128068
Other Receipts	7	794369	332770	3564	514	5677	472	8752	14537	55927	23399	59599	79170	209984
Total Receipts	8	75702592	8327131	321571	128286	1346861	580285	2047251	1164142	1577265	2075177	3503439	9725105	44906078
Average Total Receipts	9	45659	277571	299	2420	4613	13816	28434	35277	92780	138345	583906	694650	5613260

Operating Costs/Operating Income (%)

		Total	Zero Assets	Under 500	500 to 1,000	1,000 to 5,000	5,000 to 10,000	10,000 to 25,000	25,000 to 50,000	50,000 to 100,000	100,000 to 250,000	250,000 to 500,000	500,000 to 2,500,000	2,500,000 and over
Cost of Operations	10	60.2	76.1	35.1	57.2	27.8	52.6	62.2	54.3	63.2	63.0	77.4	67.1	56.4
Salaries and Wages	11	12.7	15.5	32.1	9.9	32.4	14.6	15.3	15.7	14.3	12.0	11.6	11.5	11.6
Taxes Paid	12	2.1	2.3	1.4	2.1	4.2	1.4	2.4	2.5	1.6	1.2	1.7	1.4	2.2
Interest Paid	13	2.9	0.1	2.8	0.1	0.1	1.8	1.3	0.8	2.0	2.5	0.8	3.3	3.6
Depreciation	14	2.1	1.3	0.2	0.2	0.6	2.9	1.1	1.9	1.3	1.5	2.6	4.2	1.8
Amortization and Depletion	15	2.6	3.8	0.6	0.3	0.8	0.0	0.7	3.0	2.5	1.4	0.6	3.3	2.7
Pensions and Other Deferred Comp.	16	1.9	0.0	•	1.0	0.1	0.5	0.3	0.3	0.3	0.2	1.8	0.6	2.8
Employee Benefits	17	2.1	1.1	1.2	2.0	1.3	1.1	1.9	2.9	2.1	2.0	3.9	2.6	2.0
Advertising	18	0.8	2.7	0.2	0.0	1.3	0.6	0.6	0.9	0.9	0.5	0.2	0.6	0.6
Other Expenses	19	12.5	8.7	28.9	7.2	21.7	14.7	9.7	12.1	10.6	13.1	11.3	10.9	13.2
Officers' Compensation	20	1.0	2.5	•	19.0	8.2	5.5	2.5	2.1	1.8	1.8	1.5	0.5	0.4
Operating Margin	21	•	•	•	1.0	1.5	4.2	2.0	3.5	•	0.8	•	•	2.8
Operating Margin Before Officers' Comp.	22	0.3	•	•	19.9	9.7	9.7	4.4	5.6	1.2	2.6	•	•	3.2

Selected Average Balance Sheet ($ in Thousands)

Net Receivables 23	10905	0	30	98	913	2289	3738	4374	15340	24358	101134	163964	1717230
Inventories 24	4168	0	20	260	571	1438	2379	5671	11104	21132	42989	85279	541488
Net Property, Plant and Equipment 25	4490	0	1	13	379	1413	1083	3854	6173	9890	28830	148896	569675
Total Assets 26	58203	0	128	512	2640	7154	15482	31138	69266	156419	398608	1277092	8665814
Notes and Loans Payable 27	21382	0	67	129	1083	5453	3585	3570	26676	27014	60975	324460	3585437
All Other Liabilities 28	25776	0	30	72	1647	2325	6680	7460	19358	29917	146599	718620	3709664
Net Worth 29	11045	0	31	311	-89	-625	5217	20107	23232	99487	191034	234012	1370713

Selected Financial Ratios (Times to 1)

Current Ratio 30	1.5	•	3.4	5.7	1.2	2.6	2.0	2.8	2.8	2.7	2.2	0.8	1.8
Quick Ratio 31	1.0	•	2.7	2.1	0.9	1.7	1.3	1.8	1.9	1.7	1.6	0.6	1.1
Net Sales to Working Capital 32	5.1	•	3.9	7.1	11.1	4.1	5.4	2.8	3.3	2.8	3.3	•	3.6
Coverage Ratio 33	4.5	450.3	0.5	19.9	15.7	3.5	2.8	7.0	2.7	2.3	9.5	0.1	4.1
Total Asset Turnover 34	0.7	•	2.3	4.7	1.7	1.9	1.8	1.1	1.3	0.9	1.2	0.5	0.6
Inventory Turnover 35	6.0	•	5.1	5.3	2.2	5.0	7.4	3.3	5.1	4.0	8.8	5.4	5.5
Receivables Turnover 36	3.6	•	14.9	7.2	5.2	5.7	7.6	6.1	5.7	5.1	4.2	4.1	2.9
Total Liabilities to Net Worth 37	4.3	•	3.2	0.6	•	•	2.0	0.5	2.0	0.6	1.1	4.5	5.3
Current Assets to Working Capital 38	2.9	•	1.4	1.2	5.0	1.6	2.1	1.6	1.6	1.6	1.8	•	2.2
Current Liabilities to Working Capital 39	1.9	•	0.4	0.2	4.0	0.6	1.1	0.6	0.6	0.6	0.8	•	1.2
Working Capital to Net Sales 40	0.2	•	0.3	0.1	0.1	0.2	0.2	0.4	0.3	0.4	0.3	•	0.3
Inventory to Working Capital 41	0.5	•	0.3	0.8	1.1	0.5	0.4	0.4	0.4	0.5	0.4	•	0.4
Total Receipts to Cash Flow 42	5.9	2.5	4.8	17.5	5.6	5.8	10.1	6.6	8.2	7.1	125.3	22.6	5.4
Cost of Goods to Cash Flow 43	3.5	1.9	1.7	10.0	1.6	3.1	6.3	3.6	5.2	4.5	97.0	15.2	3.0
Cash Flow to Total Debt 44	0.2	•	0.6	0.7	0.3	0.3	0.3	0.5	0.2	0.3	0.0	0.0	0.1

Selected Financial Factors (in Percentages)

Debt Ratio 45	81.0	•	76.0	39.2	103.4	108.7	66.3	35.4	66.5	36.4	52.1	81.7	84.2
Return on Total Assets 46	9.3	•	3.2	6.9	3.7	11.8	6.9	6.4	7.2	4.9	9.0	0.2	9.0
Return on Equity Before Income Taxes 47	38.0	•	•	10.7	•	•	13.1	8.5	13.5	4.3	16.8	•	43.0
Return on Equity After Income Taxes 48	28.0	•	•	10.6	•	•	9.7	7.3	6.8	3.5	13.1	•	31.3
Profit Margin (Before Income Tax) 49	10.1	36.0	•	1.4	2.0	4.4	2.4	4.9	3.5	3.2	6.6	•	11.2
Profit Margin (After Income Tax) 50	7.4	30.0	•	1.4	1.9	3.0	1.8	4.2	1.8	2.5	5.2	•	8.2

Table II

Corporations with Net Income

COMMUNICATIONS EQUIPMENT

MONEY AMOUNTS AND SIZE OF ASSETS IN THOUSANDS OF DOLLARS

Item Description for Accounting Period 7/12 Through 6/13	Total	Zero Assets	Under 500	500 to 1,000	1,000 to 5,000	5,000 to 10,000	10,000 to 25,000	25,000 to 50,000	50,000 to 100,000	100,000 to 250,000	250,000 to 500,000	500,000 to 2,500,000	2,500,000 and over
Number of Enterprises **1**	1068	18	692	53	167	23	54	21	12	12	0	7	8

Revenues ($ in Thousands)

	Total	Zero Assets	Under 500	500 to 1,000	1,000 to 5,000	5,000 to 10,000	10,000 to 25,000	25,000 to 50,000	50,000 to 100,000	100,000 to 250,000	250,000 to 500,000	500,000 to 2,500,000	2,500,000 and over
Net Sales **2**	61321296	5293710	250820	127772	931152	378594	1751659	886625	1271976	3168176	0	5273948	41986863
Interest **3**	182336	3051	0	0	0	89	141	138	689	26124	0	27196	124907
Rents **4**	29378	0	0	0	0	49	0	228	248	459	0	2161	26232
Royalties **5**	612498	149100	0	0	0	0	0	955	250	8300	0	23870	430024
Other Portfolio Income **6**	4735216	2095804	0	0	338	10	436	34	3614	482230	0	24684	2128068
Other Receipts **7**	710822	331665	0	514	4949	312	5227	12004	55599	30547	0	60020	209984
Total Receipts **8**	67591546	7873330	250820	128286	936439	379054	1757463	899984	1332376	3715836	0	5411879	44906078
Average Total Receipts **9**	63288	437407	362	2420	5607	16481	32546	42856	111031	309653	•	773126	5613260

Operating Costs/Operating Income (%)

	Total	Zero Assets	Under 500	500 to 1,000	1,000 to 5,000	5,000 to 10,000	10,000 to 25,000	25,000 to 50,000	50,000 to 100,000	100,000 to 250,000	250,000 to 500,000	500,000 to 2,500,000	2,500,000 and over
Cost of Operations **10**	59.9	78.4	26.8	57.2	23.8	51.1	64.5	53.8	64.2	74.8	•	67.2	56.4
Salaries and Wages **11**	11.8	15.1	29.5	9.9	30.0	11.4	11.2	12.4	12.1	8.9	•	8.4	11.6
Taxes Paid **12**	2.1	2.3	1.6	2.1	4.3	1.4	2.2	2.4	1.4	1.5	•	1.2	2.2
Interest Paid **13**	3.0	0.1	3.3	0.1	0.1	0.6	0.7	0.9	2.4	1.1	•	4.3	3.6
Depreciation **14**	1.7	1.4	•	0.2	0.4	0.8	1.0	1.7	1.3	1.4	•	1.7	1.8
Amortization and Depletion **15**	2.5	4.0	•	0.3	1.1	0.0	0.2	0.2	1.2	0.6	•	2.7	2.7
Pensions and Other Deferred Comp. **16**	2.1	0.0	•	1.0	0.1	0.4	0.3	0.3	0.3	1.7	•	0.6	2.8
Employee Benefits **17**	2.0	1.0	1.5	2.0	0.4	1.4	1.3	2.9	1.7	3.5	•	2.3	2.0
Advertising **18**	0.8	2.8	0.2	0.0	1.4	0.9	0.5	1.0	0.8	0.1	•	0.5	0.6
Other Expenses **19**	12.1	7.0	27.5	7.2	23.7	8.4	7.3	11.0	10.4	10.7	•	9.4	13.2
Officers' Compensation **20**	0.9	1.5	•	19.0	7.5	6.0	2.2	2.0	1.8	2.0	•	0.5	0.4
Operating Margin **21**	1.2	•	9.7	1.0	7.2	17.5	8.5	11.4	2.3	•	•	1.1	2.8
Operating Margin Before Officers' Comp. **22**	2.1	•	9.7	19.9	14.7	23.6	10.7	13.5	4.1	•	•	1.6	3.2

Selected Average Balance Sheet ($ in Thousands)

Net Receivables 23	14928	0	37	98	1230	1862	4487	4569	16950	35895	•	136261	1717230
Inventories 24	5344	0	13	260	525	2019	2033	5514	11922	24864	•	101838	499882
Net Property, Plant and Equipment 25	5161	0	0	13	609	246	910	4062	8113	11879	•	67480	569675
Total Assets 26	76601	0	144	512	3290	6567	14689	29921	72000	183911	•	1023299	8665814
Notes and Loans Payable 27	30865	0	0	129	1591	2077	3831	4382	36331	23247	•	420777	3585437
All Other Liabilities 28	30911	0	2	72	2267	1263	5190	6767	19193	55460	•	229294	3709664
Net Worth 29	14825	0	142	311	-569	3227	5668	18772	16476	105204	•	373228	1370713

Selected Financial Ratios (Times to 1)

Current Ratio 30	1.9	•	48.3	5.7	1.1	4.1	2.1	3.0	2.5	2.1	•	2.1	1.8
Quick Ratio 31	1.2	•	42.6	2.1	0.9	2.4	1.4	1.8	1.7	1.4	•	1.4	1.1
Net Sales to Working Capital 32	4.1	•	3.3	7.1	25.6	3.5	5.5	3.2	4.0	5.2	•	3.7	3.6
Coverage Ratio 33	5.3	506.7	4.0	19.9	75.5	29.4	13.2	15.9	4.0	11.0	•	2.2	4.1
Total Asset Turnover 34	0.7	•	2.5	4.7	1.7	2.5	2.2	1.4	1.5	1.4	•	0.7	0.6
Inventory Turnover 35	6.4	•	7.3	5.3	2.5	4.2	10.3	4.1	5.7	7.9	•	5.0	5.9
Receivables Turnover 36	3.9	•	19.6	49.0	5.8	5.6	8.3	8.7	•	9.5	•	•	3.1
Total Liabilities to Net Worth 37	4.2	•	0.0	0.6	•	1.0	1.6	0.6	3.4	0.7	•	1.7	5.3
Current Assets to Working Capital 38	2.1	•	1.0	1.2	11.4	1.3	1.9	1.5	1.7	1.9	•	1.9	2.2
Current Liabilities to Working Capital 39	1.1	•	0.0	0.2	10.4	0.3	0.9	0.5	0.7	0.9	•	0.9	1.2
Working Capital to Net Sales 40	0.2	•	0.3	0.1	0.0	0.3	0.2	0.3	0.2	0.2	•	0.3	0.3
Inventory to Working Capital 41	0.4	•	0.1	0.8	1.6	0.5	0.3	0.4	0.5	0.5	•	0.5	0.4
Total Receipts to Cash Flow 42	5.2	2.4	3.3	17.5	3.9	4.1	6.9	4.5	6.2	15.4	•	8.9	5.4
Cost of Goods to Cash Flow 43	3.1	1.9	0.9	10.0	0.9	2.1	4.5	2.4	4.0	11.5	•	6.0	3.0
Cash Flow to Total Debt 44	0.2	•	46.8	0.7	0.4	1.2	0.5	0.8	0.3	0.2	•	0.1	0.1

Selected Financial Factors (in Percentages)

Debt Ratio 45	80.6	•	1.6	39.2	117.3	50.9	61.4	37.3	77.1	42.8	•	63.5	84.2
Return on Total Assets 46	12.0	•	32.5	6.9	13.4	45.8	21.0	19.5	14.0	17.6	•	7.1	9.0
Return on Equity Before Income Taxes 47	50.4	•	24.7	10.7	•	89.9	50.3	29.1	45.8	28.0	•	10.7	43.0
Return on Equity After Income Taxes 48	38.8	•	24.5	10.6	•	79.5	46.1	27.1	32.4	23.7	•	7.1	31.3
Profit Margin (Before Income Tax) 49	13.0	39.8	9.7	1.4	7.8	17.6	8.8	13.0	7.1	11.1	•	5.3	11.2
Profit Margin (After Income Tax) 50	10.0	33.3	9.6	1.4	7.7	15.6	8.1	12.1	5.0	9.4	•	3.5	8.2

Table I

Corporations with and without Net Income

AUDIO AND VIDEO EQUIP., REPRODUCING MAGNETIC & OPTICAL MEDIA

MONEY AMOUNTS AND SIZE OF ASSETS IN THOUSANDS OF DOLLARS

Item Description for Accounting Period 7/12 Through 6/13	Total	Zero Assets	Under 500	500 to 1,000	1,000 to 5,000	5,000 to 10,000	10,000 to 25,000	25,000 to 50,000	50,000 to 100,000	100,000 to 250,000	250,000 to 500,000	500,000 to 2,500,000	2,500,000 and over
Number of Enterprises 1	1270	286	401	268	202	30	30	20	15	9	3	6	0

Revenues ($ in Thousands)

	Total	Zero Assets	Under 500	500 to 1,000	1,000 to 5,000	5,000 to 10,000	10,000 to 25,000	25,000 to 50,000	50,000 to 100,000	100,000 to 250,000	250,000 to 500,000	500,000 to 2,500,000	2,500,000 and over
Net Sales 2	28424627	0	546605	472566	963611	312405	592608	939581	1343178	1822769	958024	20473280	0
Interest 3	24984	68	0	3	434	500	189	326	3508	309	2734	16914	0
Rents 4	10161	0	0	0	0	0	0	2	0	328	224	9607	0
Royalties 5	91079	0	0	0	17775	0	1	0	0	0	6224	67079	0
Other Portfolio Income 6	102334	0	0	0	209	0	0	430	604	2047	37249	61795	0
Other Receipts 7	210353	3715	19817	31263	4033	170	2940	18590	48429	8036	5459	67901	0
Total Receipts 8	28863538	3783	566422	503832	986062	313075	595738	958929	1395719	1833489	1009914	20696576	0
Average Total Receipts 9	22727	13	1413	1880	4881	10436	19858	47946	93048	203721	336638	3449429	•

Operating Costs/Operating Income (%)

	Total	Zero Assets	Under 500	500 to 1,000	1,000 to 5,000	5,000 to 10,000	10,000 to 25,000	25,000 to 50,000	50,000 to 100,000	100,000 to 250,000	250,000 to 500,000	500,000 to 2,500,000	2,500,000 and over
Cost of Operations 10	64.1	•	47.0	72.3	61.0	52.4	51.6	61.8	72.1	69.1	57.4	64.5	•
Salaries and Wages 11	10.7	•	15.0	19.3	12.8	11.5	16.7	14.5	10.5	12.6	15.3	9.5	•
Taxes Paid 12	1.1	•	2.7	2.9	2.1	1.8	2.0	2.2	1.7	1.9	2.0	0.7	•
Interest Paid 13	2.0	•	0.1	0.3	0.8	0.3	1.2	1.5	2.7	0.5	0.1	2.5	•
Depreciation 14	1.6	•	0.1	1.0	0.5	0.7	1.2	1.1	0.9	1.9	1.8	1.8	•
Amortization and Depletion 15	0.7	•	•	0.2	0.0	0.4	1.1	0.8	0.5	0.8	0.1	0.8	•
Pensions and Other Deferred Comp. 16	0.7	•	0.5	0.0	0.7	0.1	0.2	0.2	0.0	0.2	1.6	0.8	•
Employee Benefits 17	1.7	•	1.5	0.8	0.9	1.1	1.8	1.3	1.1	1.2	1.6	1.9	•
Advertising 18	1.8	•	0.1	2.3	0.4	0.2	1.3	0.5	1.9	1.4	2.3	2.1	•
Other Expenses 19	13.4	•	10.9	27.2	15.9	19.1	21.5	15.7	15.8	12.6	11.3	12.6	•
Officers' Compensation 20	1.2	•	8.4	5.5	11.4	8.4	2.3	1.4	1.1	1.0	1.6	0.3	•
Operating Margin 21	0.9	•	13.6	•	•	3.9	•	•	•	•	4.9	2.5	•
Operating Margin Before Officers' Comp. 22	2.1	•	22.0	•	4.7	12.3	1.4	0.4	•	•	6.5	2.8	•

Selected Average Balance Sheet ($ in Thousands)

Net Receivables 23	11369	0	38	208	360	1338	4933	9094	14972	34843	95793	2183261	•
Inventories 24	3074	0	39	351	276	1058	3563	5256	17455	23380	61489	473083	•
Net Property, Plant and Equipment 25	1790	0	1	70	102	1228	1312	2465	5868	18314	43826	287354	•
Total Assets 26	43940	0	396	931	2395	6498	17020	33620	67513	156835	354567	8340857	•
Notes and Loans Payable 27	12200	0	88	171	220	1034	51061	16074	20360	91001	36647	2041589	•
All Other Liabilities 28	13732	0	117	473	996	2720	12739	14455	25645	74492	143213	2471244	•
Net Worth 29	18007	0	191	287	1178	2745	-46780	3091	21508	-8659	174708	3828024	•

Selected Financial Ratios (Times to 1)

Current Ratio 30	1.1	•	2.8	1.8	1.5	1.3	1.1	1.4	2.0	1.5	1.4	1.1	•
Quick Ratio 31	0.7	•	2.4	0.7	1.3	0.9	0.8	0.9	0.9	0.9	0.9	0.7	•
Net Sales to Working Capital 32	9.0	•	5.4	4.8	7.8	12.3	21.1	10.7	3.6	6.9	5.0	10.9	•
Coverage Ratio 33	2.2	•	217.2	•	•	15.1	0.6	1.7	•	•	117.3	2.5	•
Total Asset Turnover 34	0.5	•	3.4	1.9	2.0	1.6	1.2	1.4	1.3	1.3	0.9	0.4	•
Inventory Turnover 35	4.7	•	16.4	3.6	10.6	5.2	2.9	5.5	3.7	6.0	3.0	4.7	•
Receivables Turnover 36	2.8	•	52.6	13.3	13.3	6.4	2.9	4.9	6.5	6.7	3.0	2.3	•
Total Liabilities to Net Worth 37	1.4	•	1.1	2.2	1.0	1.4	•	9.9	2.1	•	1.0	1.2	•
Current Assets to Working Capital 38	8.0	•	1.6	2.3	2.9	4.8	14.7	3.7	2.0	3.0	3.2	11.5	•
Current Liabilities to Working Capital 39	7.0	•	0.6	1.3	1.9	3.8	13.7	2.7	1.0	2.0	2.2	10.5	•
Working Capital to Net Sales 40	0.1	•	0.2	0.2	0.1	0.1	0.0	0.1	0.3	0.1	0.2	0.1	•
Inventory to Working Capital 41	1.2	•	0.2	1.4	0.5	1.1	3.6	1.1	0.8	0.8	0.7	1.5	•
Total Receipts to Cash Flow 42	7.2	•	4.0	•	14.9	4.9	5.3	8.3	10.0	13.3	6.1	6.8	•
Cost of Goods to Cash Flow 43	4.6	•	1.9	•	9.1	2.6	2.7	5.2	7.2	9.2	3.5	4.4	•
Cash Flow to Total Debt 44	0.1	•	1.6	•	0.3	0.6	0.1	0.2	0.2	0.1	0.3	0.1	•

Selected Financial Factors (in Percentages)

Debt Ratio 45	59.0	•	51.8	69.2	50.8	57.8	374.8	90.8	68.1	105.5	50.7	54.1	•
Return on Total Assets 46	2.3	•	59.4	•	•	7.0	0.9	3.6	•	•	10.0	2.5	•
Return on Equity Before Income Taxes 47	3.1	•	122.8	•	•	15.5	0.2	16.1	•	63.0	20.1	3.3	•
Return on Equity After Income Taxes 48	2.2	•	122.8	•	•	6.5	0.8	8.3	•	63.1	15.5	2.6	•
Profit Margin (Before Income Tax) 49	2.5	•	17.2	•	•	4.1	•	1.1	•	•	11.0	3.7	•
Profit Margin (After Income Tax) 50	1.7	•	17.2	•	•	1.7	•	0.5	•	•	8.5	2.9	•

Table II

Corporations with Net Income

AUDIO AND VIDEO EQUIP., REPRODUCING MAGNETIC & OPTICAL MEDIA

MONEY AMOUNTS AND SIZE OF ASSETS IN THOUSANDS OF DOLLARS

Item Description for Accounting Period 7/12 Through 6/13	Total	Zero Assets	Under 500	500 to 1,000	1,000 to 5,000	5,000 to 10,000	10,000 to 25,000	25,000 to 50,000	50,000 to 100,000	100,000 to 250,000	250,000 to 500,000	500,000 to 2,500,000	2,500,000 and over
Number of Enterprises 1	582	15	401	0	102	11	20	12	7	4	3	6	0

Revenues ($ in Thousands)

	Total	Zero Assets	Under 500	500 to 1,000	1,000 to 5,000	5,000 to 10,000	10,000 to 25,000	25,000 to 50,000	50,000 to 100,000	100,000 to 250,000	250,000 to 500,000	500,000 to 2,500,000	2,500,000 and over
Net Sales 2	25539802	0	546605	0	727299	147642	492079	547852	554026	1092994	958024	20473280	0
Interest 3	20952	68	0	0	328	219	189	289	64	147	2734	16914	0
Rents 4	9833	0	0	0	0	0	0	2	0	0	224	9607	0
Royalties 5	91078	0	0	0	17775	0	0	0	0	0	6224	67079	0
Other Portfolio Income 6	99413	0	0	0	209	0	0	16	28	117	37249	61795	0
Other Receipts 7	171318	3715	19817	0	2126	30	2280	16564	47306	6120	5459	67901	0
Total Receipts 8	25932396	3783	566422	0	747737	147891	494548	564723	601424	1099378	1009914	20696576	0
Average Total Receipts 9	44557	252	1413	•	7331	13445	24727	47060	85918	274844	336638	3449429	•

Operating Costs/Operating Income (%)

	Total	Zero Assets	Under 500	500 to 1,000	1,000 to 5,000	5,000 to 10,000	10,000 to 25,000	25,000 to 50,000	50,000 to 100,000	100,000 to 250,000	250,000 to 500,000	500,000 to 2,500,000	2,500,000 and over
Cost of Operations 10	64.1	•	47.0	•	61.2	45.2	56.1	56.3	68.4	80.1	57.4	64.5	•
Salaries and Wages 11	9.8	•	15.0	•	8.3	12.5	11.8	14.5	8.3	5.6	15.3	9.5	•
Taxes Paid 12	0.9	•	2.7	•	1.5	1.2	1.3	2.4	2.2	0.9	2.0	0.7	•
Interest Paid 13	2.1	•	0.1	•	0.7	0.4	1.0	0.8	1.5	0.1	0.1	2.5	•
Depreciation 14	1.6	•	0.1	•	0.3	0.5	1.2	1.5	0.8	1.0	1.8	1.8	•
Amortization and Depletion 15	0.7	•	•	•	0.0	•	0.2	0.6	0.9	0.0	0.1	0.8	•
Pensions and Other Deferred Comp. 16	0.7	•	0.5	•	0.9	0.0	0.2	0.3	0.1	0.3	1.6	0.8	•
Employee Benefits 17	1.8	•	1.5	•	0.1	0.7	1.3	1.1	0.7	1.1	1.6	1.9	•
Advertising 18	1.8	•	0.1	•	0.4	0.2	1.1	0.6	0.7	1.0	2.3	2.1	•
Other Expenses 19	12.2	•	10.9	•	8.9	10.3	17.3	13.1	10.5	5.7	11.3	12.6	•
Officers' Compensation 20	1.0	•	8.4	•	13.3	1.5	2.0	2.0	1.2	0.3	1.6	0.3	•
Operating Margin 21	3.3	•	13.6	•	4.3	27.5	6.4	6.9	5.0	4.0	4.9	2.5	•
Operating Margin Before Officers' Comp. 22	4.3	•	22.0	•	17.6	29.0	8.3	8.9	6.1	4.3	6.5	2.8	•

Selected Average Balance Sheet ($ in Thousands)

Net Receivables 23	23870	0	38	•	434	2348	3755	8972	12626	37249	95793	2183261	•
Inventories 24	5329	0	48	•	275	1453	3628	5040	16917	20542	37627	474948	•
Net Property, Plant and Equipment 25	3528	0	1	•	66	119	1624	2863	8397	15866	43826	287354	•
Total Assets 26	91841	0	396	•	2719	6751	16134	33373	66081	161637	354567	8340857	•
Notes and Loans Payable 27	21761	0	88	•	93	653	2787	3914	14126	12893	36647	2041589	•
All Other Liabilities 28	27364	0	117	•	859	1823	4399	6771	17597	55383	143213	2471244	•
Net Worth 29	42717	0	191	•	1768	4275	8947	22688	34358	93360	174708	3828024	•

Selected Financial Ratios (Times to 1)

Current Ratio 30	1.1	•	2.8	•	2.0	2.9	2.9	2.4	2.6	1.6	1.4	1.1	•
Quick Ratio 31	0.7	•	2.4	•	1.7	2.4	1.8	1.6	1.2	1.0	0.9	0.7	•
Net Sales to Working Capital 32	8.7	•	5.4	•	8.1	3.4	2.7	4.5	3.3	6.5	5.0	10.9	•
Coverage Ratio 33	3.4	•	217.2	•	11.7	66.1	7.7	13.9	10.0	52.1	117.3	2.5	•
Total Asset Turnover 34	0.5	•	3.4	•	2.6	2.0	1.5	1.4	1.2	1.7	0.9	0.4	•
Inventory Turnover 35	5.3	•	13.2	•	15.8	4.2	3.8	5.1	3.2	10.7	4.9	4.6	•
Receivables Turnover 36	2.8	•	•	•	18.1	6.9	3.4	6.2	5.3	8.8	4.4	•	•
Total Liabilities to Net Worth 37	1.1	•	1.1	•	0.5	0.6	0.8	0.5	0.9 ·	0.7	1.0	1.2	•
Current Assets to Working Capital 38	8.1	•	1.6	•	2.0	1.5	1.5	1.7	1.6	2.6	3.2	11.5	•
Current Liabilities to Working Capital 39	7.1	•	0.6	•	1.0	0.5	0.5	0.7	0.6	1.6	2.2	10.5	•
Working Capital to Net Sales 40	0.1	•	0.2	•	0.1	0.3	0.4	0.2	0.3	0.2	0.2	0.1	•
Inventory to Working Capital 41	1.1	•	0.2	•	0.2	0.3	0.5	0.5	0.5	0.6	0.7	1.5	•
Total Receipts to Cash Flow 42	6.5	•	4.0	•	6.9	2.7	4.5	4.8	4.3	10.9	6.1	6.8	•
Cost of Goods to Cash Flow 43	4.2	•	1.9	•	4.2	1.2	2.5	2.7	2.9	8.7	3.5	4.4	•
Cash Flow to Total Debt 44	0.1	•	1.6	•	1.1	2.0	0.8	0.9	0.6	0.4	0.3	0.1	•

Selected Financial Factors (in Percentages)

Debt Ratio 45	53.5	•	51.8	•	35.0	36.7	44.5	32.0	48.0	42.2	50.7	54.1	•
Return on Total Assets 46	3.4	•	59.4	•	20.4	55.8	12.0	14.7	18.0	7.9	10.0	2.5	•
Return on Equity Before Income Taxes 47	5.1	•	122.8	•	28.6	86.8	18.9	20.1	31.1	13.5	20.1	3.3	•
Return on Equity After Income Taxes 48	4.2	•	122.8	•	27.6	73.5	14.4	18.3	29.4	13.5	15.5	2.6	•
Profit Margin (Before Income Tax) 49	4.9	•	17.2	•	7.1	27.6	6.9	10.0	13.5	4.6	11.0	3.7	•
Profit Margin (After Income Tax) 50	4.1	•	17.2	•	6.8	23.4	5.2	9.1	12.7	4.6	8.5	2.9	•

Table I

Corporations with and without Net Income

SEMICONDUCTOR AND OTHER ELECTRONIC COMPONENT

MONEY AMOUNTS AND SIZE OF ASSETS IN THOUSANDS OF DOLLARS

Item Description for Accounting Period 7/12 Through 6/13	Total	Zero Assets	Under 500	500 to 1,000	1,000 to 5,000	5,000 to 10,000	10,000 to 25,000	25,000 to 50,000	50,000 to 100,000	100,000 to 250,000	250,000 to 500,000	500,000 to 2,500,000	2,500,000 and over
Number of Enterprises 1	4291	557	1214	550	1064	386	235	74	41	64	30	53	23

Revenues ($ in Thousands)

	Total	Zero Assets	Under 500	500 to 1,000	1,000 to 5,000	5,000 to 10,000	10,000 to 25,000	25,000 to 50,000	50,000 to 100,000	100,000 to 250,000	250,000 to 500,000	500,000 to 2,500,000	2,500,000 and over
Net Sales 2	205807607	966490	764382	1308649	5982550	4563104	5744793	3008708	3372685	11007242	8326302	33421586	127341116
Interest 3	617664	52559	268	1630	777	6400	2931	2818	7992	14467	17459	112519	397846
Rents 4	78302	0	0	0	0	2138	149	3347	1810	2138	3158	25593	39968
Royalties 5	9057951	12507	0	0	0	404	11030	42923	37235	34113	44911	961537	7913291
Other Portfolio Income 6	5464577	71782	0	0	13113	12648	56648	381730	17205	128012	71501	955581	3756358
Other Receipts 7	4459432	12402	84	1047	28321	49442	70537	40457	29513	408234	244132	1264231	2311029
Total Receipts 8	225485533	1115740	764734	1311326	6024761	4634136	5886088	3479983	3466440	11594206	8707463	36741047	141759608
Average Total Receipts 9	52548	2003	630	2384	5662	12006	25047	47027	84547	181159	290249	693227	6163461

Operating Costs/Operating Income (%)

	Total	Zero Assets	Under 500	500 to 1,000	1,000 to 5,000	5,000 to 10,000	10,000 to 25,000	25,000 to 50,000	50,000 to 100,000	100,000 to 250,000	250,000 to 500,000	500,000 to 2,500,000	2,500,000 and over
Cost of Operations 10	64.6	65.8	44.0	51.7	59.6	62.1	69.9	65.9	69.7	75.6	68.3	66.1	63.2
Salaries and Wages 11	13.6	14.2	8.5	16.0	10.1	12.6	11.4	11.9	10.4	10.9	13.0	15.0	13.9
Taxes Paid 12	1.3	2.6	2.8	2.3	2.9	2.1	1.8	2.2	2.1	1.3	1.4	1.4	1.1
Interest Paid 13	1.7	6.4	0.5	1.1	0.8	1.0	0.9	1.3	1.6	0.9	1.6	2.7	1.6
Depreciation 14	4.8	2.9	1.6	1.1	1.9	2.2	2.1	2.9	2.6	2.6	3.3	4.2	5.8
Amortization and Depletion 15	1.2	1.3	•	0.7	0.2	0.3	0.5	0.7	0.5	1.0	3.0	1.5	1.2
Pensions and Other Deferred Comp. 16	0.5	0.8	•	0.0	0.6	1.2	0.3	0.6	0.8	0.2	0.3	0.6	0.5
Employee Benefits 17	2.0	2.7	1.1	1.5	1.9	2.4	1.3	2.3	1.7	1.5	1.9	2.4	1.9
Advertising 18	1.3	0.6	0.0	1.2	0.6	0.6	0.3	0.3	0.3	0.3	0.6	0.3	1.9
Other Expenses 19	10.5	27.0	18.8	18.2	11.9	11.6	8.0	16.0	16.2	11.1	10.4	11.4	9.7
Officers' Compensation 20	1.0	2.1	6.9	4.6	7.2	3.4	3.3	2.0	1.9	1.4	1.1	1.2	0.2
Operating Margin 21	•	•	15.9	1.4	2.3	0.5	0.2	•	•	•	•	•	•
Operating Margin Before Officers' Comp. 22	•	•	22.8	6.0	9.5	4.0	3.5	•	•	•	•	•	•

Selected Average Balance Sheet ($ in Thousands)

Net Receivables 23	8736	0	40	217	649	1922	3182	7209	17988	31349	56709	153481	957616
Inventories 24	4241	0	47	127	713	1927	3570	7541	11727	24120	38363	62050	378590
Net Property, Plant and Equipment 25	12250	0	15	83	659	1015	2011	6083	10496	26881	42612	125190	1757541
Total Assets 26	78080	0	203	748	2844	7404	14955	35330	74140	157365	340979	1119521	10421594
Notes and Loans Payable 27	16708	0	43	228	1123	1983	3683	11973	18398	28199	56221	249506	2188468
All Other Liabilities 28	20592	0	64	299	734	1826	4642	11090	26940	56086	63340	261414	2794371
Net Worth 29	40781	0	96	221	986	3596	6630	12268	28802	73080	221418	608600	5438755

Selected Financial Ratios (Times to 1)

Current Ratio 30	1.9	•	2.1	1.7	2.2	2.4	2.2	2.0	1.6	1.7	3.1	2.2	1.8
Quick Ratio 31	1.0	•	1.7	1.1	1.2	1.5	1.2	1.2	1.1	1.0	2.1	1.4	0.9
Net Sales to Working Capital 32	3.8	•	7.3	12.0	5.1	3.7	4.3	3.9	5.4	4.8	2.5	2.6	4.2
Coverage Ratio 33	5.8	•	35.1	2.4	4.6	3.0	4.1	8.8	•	•	1.1	2.7	8.3
Total Asset Turnover 34	0.6	•	3.1	3.2	2.0	1.6	1.6	1.2	1.1	1.1	0.8	0.6	0.5
Inventory Turnover 35	7.3	•	5.9	9.7	4.7	3.8	4.8	3.6	4.9	5.4	4.9	6.7	9.2
Receivables Turnover 36	5.3	•	14.8	14.1	9.5	6.0	8.4	5.4	3.9	5.3	4.7	4.2	5.5
Total Liabilities to Net Worth 37	0.9	•	1.1	2.4	1.9	1.1	1.3	1.9	1.6	1.2	0.5	0.8	0.9
Current Assets to Working Capital 38	2.1	•	1.9	2.5	1.8	1.7	1.8	2.0	2.8	2.4	1.5	1.8	2.3
Current Liabilities to Working Capital 39	1.1	•	0.9	1.5	0.8	0.7	0.8	1.0	1.8	1.4	0.5	0.8	1.3
Working Capital to Net Sales 40	0.3	•	0.1	0.1	0.2	0.3	0.2	0.3	0.2	0.2	0.4	0.4	0.2
Inventory to Working Capital 41	0.3	•	0.4	0.8	0.7	0.6	0.6	0.7	0.7	0.7	0.3	0.3	0.3
Total Receipts to Cash Flow 42	7.0	•	3.5	8.2	8.9	10.0	12.9	9.5	12.5	13.6	12.1	8.0	6.0
Cost of Goods to Cash Flow 43	4.5	•	1.6	4.2	5.3	6.2	9.0	6.3	8.7	10.3	8.2	5.3	3.8
Cash Flow to Total Debt 44	0.2	•	1.7	0.6	0.3	0.3	0.2	0.2	0.1	0.1	0.2	0.2	0.2

Selected Financial Factors (in Percentages)

Debt Ratio 45	47.8	•	52.4	70.5	65.3	51.4	55.7	65.3	61.2	53.6	35.1	45.6	47.8
Return on Total Assets 46	6.1	•	51.1	8.8	7.6	5.0	5.9	12.8	•	•	1.5	4.1	7.1
Return on Equity Before Income Taxes 47	9.6	•	104.4	17.5	17.1	6.9	10.1	32.6	•	•	0.3	4.8	11.9
Return on Equity After Income Taxes 48	5.9	•	104.3	16.9	16.0	4.8	7.3	19.6	•	•	•	2.8	7.5
Profit Margin (Before Income Tax) 49	8.2	•	16.0	1.6	3.0	2.1	2.7	9.8	•	•	0.2	4.6	11.7
Profit Margin (After Income Tax) 50	5.0	•	16.0	1.6	2.8	1.5	2.0	5.9	•	•	•	2.7	7.3

143

Table II

Corporations with Net Income

SEMICONDUCTOR AND OTHER ELECTRONIC COMPONENT

MONEY AMOUNTS AND SIZE OF ASSETS IN THOUSANDS OF DOLLARS

Item Description for Accounting Period 7/12 Through 6/13		Total	Zero Assets	Under 500	500 to 1,000	1,000 to 5,000	5,000 to 10,000	10,000 to 25,000	25,000 to 50,000	50,000 to 100,000	100,000 to 250,000	250,000 to 500,000	500,000 to 2,500,000	2,500,000 and over
Number of Enterprises	1	2342	3	826	337	608	233	173	39	23	32	19	32	16

Revenues ($ in Thousands)

Net Sales	2	150247158	187908	573923	815202	4557066	3133694	4603902	1800944	2177558	7051407	6628092	21968162	96749300
Interest	3	409523	835	0	1619	217	6001	2256	2471	3651	6376	11259	50060	324778
Rents	4	71757	0	0	0	0	1508	142	63	766	1810	2768	24733	39968
Royalties	5	8629791	12507	0	0	0	3	10391	41567	25534	15789	43300	584602	7896098
Other Portfolio Income	6	4904086	71737	0	0	2096	1448	51321	381682	10701	78520	57925	773558	3475098
Other Receipts	7	3439653	10320	84	4	21431	12921	54567	23634	11335	416439	194172	1029029	1665714
Total Receipts	8	167701968	283307	574007	816825	4580810	3155575	4722579	2250361	2229545	7570341	6937516	24430144	110150956
Average Total Receipts	9	71606	94436	695	2424	7534	13543	27298	57702	96937	236573	365132	763442	6884435

Operating Costs/Operating Income (%)

Cost of Operations	10	58.9	69.2	45.8	45.8	57.6	58.3	70.3	65.3	67.6	75.6	68.6	64.3	55.3
Salaries and Wages	11	14.1	19.6	1.0	14.7	8.0	8.9	9.3	11.6	8.2	9.1	11.1	14.0	15.6
Taxes Paid	12	1.4	2.7	2.4	2.5	2.5	1.8	1.6	2.2	2.1	1.2	1.1	1.5	1.3
Interest Paid	13	1.5	0.8	0.6	1.5	0.4	0.9	0.6	0.9	0.9	0.7	0.3	2.4	1.5
Depreciation	14	5.1	4.6	2.0	1.1	1.7	1.5	1.6	1.5	1.7	2.0	1.8	3.2	6.6
Amortization and Depletion	15	1.1	0.4	•	1.2	0.1	0.3	0.2	0.6	0.4	0.6	0.8	1.1	1.2
Pensions and Other Deferred Comp.	16	0.5	0.5	•	0.0	0.3	1.1	0.3	0.3	0.3	0.3	0.2	0.7	0.5
Employee Benefits	17	2.1	2.5	1.1	1.6	2.1	2.0	1.2	1.6	1.9	1.2	1.7	2.5	2.2
Advertising	18	1.5	0.4	0.0	0.3	0.5	0.8	0.4	0.3	0.3	0.3	0.7	0.3	2.1
Other Expenses	19	10.0	16.3	13.8	17.2	9.3	9.1	5.5	10.7	7.0	8.6	8.3	10.9	10.3
Officers' Compensation	20	0.9	0.8	6.6	7.0	7.8	3.7	2.8	2.2	1.3	1.4	1.0	1.0	0.3
Operating Margin	21	2.9	•	26.7	7.1	9.7	11.7	6.2	2.9	8.4	•	4.3	•	3.1
Operating Margin Before Officers' Comp.	22	3.8	•	33.3	14.1	17.5	15.3	9.0	5.1	9.7	0.6	5.3	•	3.3

Selected Average Balance Sheet ($ in Thousands)

Net Receivables 23	9541	0	14	247	760	2168	3354	8375	21239	35121	60738	154770	791046
Inventories 24	5268	0	25	138	829	2242	3605	8421	12572	27687	42525	66585	386154
Net Property, Plant and Equipment 25	16700	0	18	72	690	786	1960	3396	11321	20810	37692	111394	2049407
Total Assets 26	103645	0	169	885	3282	7554	15031	33501	76593	161972	347158	1122056	11574303
Notes and Loans Payable 27	23067	0	35	267	626	1858	2861	6579	15565	22752	19433	255603	2669037
All Other Liabilities 28	24505	0	82	273	765	1629	4448	7598	21998	54329	67282	258697	2720025
Net Worth 29	56072	0	53	345	1892	4067	7722	19323	39029	84890	260443	607756	6185241

Selected Financial Ratios (Times to 1)

Current Ratio 30	2.1	•	1.5	2.1	2.9	2.8	2.5	2.6	2.0	1.9	3.0	2.3	2.0
Quick Ratio 31	1.0	•	1.2	1.5	1.6	1.8	1.4	1.5	1.5	1.1	2.0	1.5	0.8
Net Sales to Working Capital 32	3.5	•	13.5	8.7	4.6	3.5	4.0	3.4	4.1	4.9	2.8	2.5	3.7
Coverage Ratio 33	11.9	40.6	43.8	5.9	26.9	14.3	16.1	33.1	13.3	10.2	33.2	5.7	13.3
Total Asset Turnover 34	0.6	•	4.1	2.7	2.3	1.8	1.8	1.4	1.2	1.4	1.0	0.6	0.5
Inventory Turnover 35	7.2	•	12.7	8.0	5.2	3.5	5.2	3.6	5.1	6.0	5.6	6.6	8.7
Receivables Turnover 36	6.8	•	21.5	11.7	10.5	6.0	8.7	5.0	4.3	6.6	6.3	4.9	7.4
Total Liabilities to Net Worth 37	0.8	•	2.2	1.6	0.7	0.9	0.9	0.7	1.0	0.9	0.3	0.8	0.9
Current Assets to Working Capital 38	1.9	•	2.9	1.9	1.5	1.6	1.7	1.6	2.0	2.1	1.5	1.8	2.0
Current Liabilities to Working Capital 39	0.9	•	1.9	0.9	0.5	0.6	0.7	0.6	1.0	1.1	0.5	0.8	1.0
Working Capital to Net Sales 40	0.3	•	0.1	0.1	0.2	0.3	0.2	0.3	0.2	0.2	0.4	0.4	0.3
Inventory to Working Capital 41	0.3	•	0.7	0.5	0.6	0.5	0.5	0.6	0.5	0.6	0.4	0.3	0.3
Total Receipts to Cash Flow 42	4.7	3.2	2.9	5.1	6.3	5.4	8.6	6.1	6.1	7.3	6.2	5.4	4.2
Cost of Goods to Cash Flow 43	2.8	2.2	1.3	2.3	3.6	3.2	6.1	4.0	4.1	5.5	4.2	3.5	2.3
Cash Flow to Total Debt 44	0.3	•	2.1	0.9	0.9	0.7	0.4	0.5	0.4	0.4	0.6	0.2	0.3

Selected Financial Factors (in Percentages)

Debt Ratio 45	45.9	•	69.0	61.0	42.4	46.2	48.6	42.3	49.0	47.6	25.0	45.8	46.6
Return on Total Assets 46	10.8	•	112.0	24.1	24.2	23.7	16.9	39.6	14.5	10.2	10.0	8.3	10.6
Return on Equity Before Income Taxes 47	18.3	•	352.8	51.5	40.4	40.9	30.8	66.6	26.3	17.5	12.9	12.6	18.4
Return on Equity After Income Taxes 48	13.3	•	352.7	50.9	39.4	37.9	27.5	50.9	22.5	13.5	11.3	9.4	12.8
Profit Margin (Before Income Tax) 49	16.0	33.0	26.7	7.3	10.2	12.4	8.9	27.9	10.8	6.8	9.7	11.2	18.8
Profit Margin (After Income Tax) 50	11.6	31.7	26.7	7.3	9.9	11.4	8.0	21.3	9.3	5.2	8.5	8.3	13.1

Table I

Corporations with and without Net Income

NAVIGATIONAL, MEASURING, ELECTROMEDICAL, AND CONTROL

MONEY AMOUNTS AND SIZE OF ASSETS IN THOUSANDS OF DOLLARS

Item Description for Accounting Period 7/12 Through 6/13	Total	Zero Assets	Under 500	500 to 1,000	1,000 to 5,000	5,000 to 10,000	10,000 to 25,000	25,000 to 50,000	50,000 to 100,000	100,000 to 250,000	250,000 to 500,000	500,000 to 2,500,000	2,500,000 and over
Number of Enterprises **1**	3997	559	1754	609	370	302	185	74	41	36	22	26	21

Revenues ($ in Thousands)													
Net Sales **2**	109513591	750975	603701	815046	1917227	3355850	4287344	3051620	2901771	5422114	4956018	16842563	64609361
Interest **3**	2899836	5538	0	30	94	675	2015	925	3930	15498	33057	69562	2768512
Rents **4**	102233	103	0	1141	47	2491	949	1645	1497	4107	53	58839	31362
Royalties **5**	843236	7483	0	0	164	4	0	686	6703	8656	23917	198298	597326
Other Portfolio Income **6**	1382841	8456	29036	0	362	424	24993	24024	62446	130841	74245	143231	884781
Other Receipts **7**	3299179	30470	0	-13653	19986	22120	57128	47635	73239	148207	91508	248029	2574512
Total Receipts **8**	118040916	803025	632737	802564	1937880	3381564	4372429	3126535	3049586	5729423	5178798	17560522	71465854
Average Total Receipts **9**	29532	1437	361	1318	5238	11197	23635	42250	74380	159151	235400	675405	3403136

Operating Costs/Operating Income (%)													
Cost of Operations **10**	57.2	43.6	36.2	37.2	63.8	58.9	53.6	59.8	57.5	63.8	52.6	59.4	56.8
Salaries and Wages **11**	13.7	30.0	10.9	22.1	13.3	13.3	15.4	13.3	14.3	12.2	15.3	13.0	13.6
Taxes Paid **12**	1.9	2.5	2.3	3.2	2.6	2.8	2.4	2.1	1.9	1.8	2.0	1.8	1.8
Interest Paid **13**	4.6	0.6	0.1	0.3	1.0	0.6	0.5	1.4	0.6	1.0	3.0	2.2	6.7
Depreciation **14**	1.7	4.4	0.7	0.4	1.6	0.7	1.6	1.8	1.9	2.1	2.6	2.1	1.6
Amortization and Depletion **15**	1.5	1.5	0.0	0.1	0.8	0.2	0.3	0.8	1.0	0.9	2.2	1.5	1.7
Pensions and Other Deferred Comp. **16**	1.3	0.4	1.3	0.6	0.3	0.5	0.8	0.5	0.8	0.8	0.4	0.9	1.7
Employee Benefits **17**	2.3	2.3	2.4	2.6	1.9	2.2	2.3	2.3	2.2	2.1	3.1	2.3	2.3
Advertising **18**	0.7	1.8	1.6	1.1	0.7	0.7	0.9	0.4	1.6	0.7	1.6	0.7	0.5
Other Expenses **19**	14.8	27.8	18.6	21.0	11.7	11.4	12.6	11.5	13.6	11.7	14.7	12.8	16.0
Officers' Compensation **20**	1.5	12.8	15.6	8.8	4.2	4.2	4.3	3.0	2.1	2.0	1.5	1.2	0.7
Operating Margin **21**	•	•	10.2	2.7	•	4.5	5.3	3.1	2.4	1.0	0.8	2.1	•
Operating Margin Before Officers' Comp. **22**	0.3	•	25.8	11.4	2.5	8.6	9.6	6.1	4.5	3.0	2.3	3.3	•

Selected Average Balance Sheet ($ in Thousands)

Net Receivables 23	5560	0	15	199	806	2115	3543	8092	11767	31859	67502	143287	621211
Inventories 24	3010	0	40	90	785	1535	3564	7116	10490	24588	34841	91726	261957
Net Property, Plant and Equipment 25	3022	0	3	32	229	706	2067	4413	7344	18408	37203	71667	352417
Total Assets 26	79589	0	103	662	2364	7162	15227	34499	68465	161584	347209	1236008	12415575
Notes and Loans Payable 27	16124	0	33	260	936	1091	2888	8263	8536	28624	71416	323386	2430900
All Other Liabilities 28	33924	0	17	108	1019	1977	4355	11242	17298	38905	115685	342150	5682655
Net Worth 29	29541	0	52	294	409	4095	7985	14994	42631	94055	160108	570472	4302020

Selected Financial Ratios (Times to 1)

Current Ratio 30	1.1	•	3.1	5.2	1.7	2.6	2.0	2.2	2.4	2.3	1.5	1.1	0.9
Quick Ratio 31	0.7	•	2.0	4.1	1.0	1.7	1.2	1.3	1.3	1.2	0.9	0.7	0.6
Net Sales to Working Capital 32	16.3	•	6.6	2.7	6.5	3.2	4.3	3.5	3.1	2.9	4.3	16.1	•
Coverage Ratio 33	2.7	•	134.5	4.4	0.3	9.3	15.3	5.1	14.3	8.1	3.1	4.5	2.3
Total Asset Turnover 34	0.3	•	3.4	2.0	2.2	1.6	1.5	1.2	1.0	0.9	0.6	0.5	0.2
Inventory Turnover 35	5.2	•	3.2	5.6	4.2	4.3	3.5	3.5	3.9	3.9	3.4	4.2	6.7
Receivables Turnover 36	5.0	•	12.2	7.6	6.1	4.6	7.0	5.4	5.7	5.2	2.9	4.4	5.2
Total Liabilities to Net Worth 37	1.7	•	1.0	1.3	4.8	0.7	0.9	1.3	0.6	0.7	1.2	1.2	1.9
Current Assets to Working Capital 38	8.4	•	1.5	1.2	2.5	1.6	2.0	1.9	1.7	1.8	2.8	9.3	•
Current Liabilities to Working Capital 39	7.4	•	0.5	0.2	1.5	0.6	1.0	0.9	0.7	0.8	1.8	8.3	•
Working Capital to Net Sales 40	0.1	•	0.2	0.4	0.2	0.3	0.2	0.3	0.3	0.3	0.2	0.1	•
Inventory to Working Capital 41	1.8	•	0.4	0.3	0.9	0.4	0.7	0.6	0.5	0.5	0.6	2.2	•
Total Receipts to Cash Flow 42	5.4	128.1	4.0	5.4	11.4	6.9	5.7	6.8	5.7	6.7	5.5	5.9	4.9
Cost of Goods to Cash Flow 43	3.1	55.9	1.5	2.0	7.3	4.1	3.0	4.0	3.3	4.3	2.9	3.5	2.8
Cash Flow to Total Debt 44	0.1	•	1.7	0.7	0.2	0.5	0.6	0.3	0.5	0.3	0.2	0.2	0.1

Selected Financial Factors (in Percentages)

Debt Ratio 45	62.9	•	49.0	55.6	82.7	42.8	47.6	56.5	37.7	41.8	53.9	53.8	65.3
Return on Total Assets 46	4.2	•	50.7	3.0	0.7	9.1	11.9	8.4	8.9	7.2	6.0	5.1	3.8
Return on Equity Before Income Taxes 47	7.1	•	98.7	5.2	•	14.2	21.2	15.4	13.3	10.9	8.9	8.6	6.2
Return on Equity After Income Taxes 48	4.9	•	96.0	4.4	•	13.0	18.4	12.5	10.8	7.8	5.8	6.0	4.2
Profit Margin (Before Income Tax) 49	7.6	•	15.0	1.1	•	5.2	7.3	5.6	8.0	6.8	6.3	7.6	8.6
Profit Margin (After Income Tax) 50	5.3	•	14.6	1.0	•	4.8	6.3	4.6	6.5	4.9	4.1	5.2	5.9

Table II
Corporations with Net Income

NAVIGATIONAL, MEASURING, ELECTROMEDICAL, AND CONTROL

MONEY AMOUNTS AND SIZE OF ASSETS IN THOUSANDS OF DOLLARS

Item Description for Accounting Period 7/12 Through 6/13	Total	Zero Assets	Under 500	500 to 1,000	1,000 to 5,000	5,000 to 10,000	10,000 to 25,000	25,000 to 50,000	50,000 to 100,000	100,000 to 250,000	250,000 to 500,000	500,000 to 2,500,000	2,500,000 and over
Number of Enterprises 1	2407	16	•	551	239	262	152	58	32	30	15	22	•
Revenues ($ in Thousands)													
Net Sales 2	101431472	195100	•	721611	1490885	3143596	3852717	2648571	2491483	4975256	3165248	14950945	•
Interest 3	2875396	5227	•	0	71	443	1835	549	3757	8555	28949	61204	•
Rents 4	97011	103	•	1141	47	9	949	1645	762	2140	14	58839	•
Royalties 5	788475	0	•	0	0	0	0	659	6703	8239	18094	170102	•
Other Portfolio Income 6	1340482	3852	•	0	0	334	24576	23785	61356	116147	56979	140230	•
Other Receipts 7	3073933	17099	•	6410	1879	11241	54764	46674	73549	137009	52320	183284	•
Total Receipts 8	109606769	221381	•	729162	1492882	3155623	3934841	2721883	2637610	5247346	3321604	15564604	•
Average Total Receipts 9	45537	13836	•	1323	6246	12044	25887	46929	82425	174912	221440	707482	•
Operating Costs/Operating Income (%)													
Cost of Operations 10	56.8	47.1	•	32.4	63.4	58.2	52.8	60.3	58.3	63.8	47.5	58.5	•
Salaries and Wages 11	13.3	7.7	•	23.0	9.3	11.7	14.0	12.6	12.6	11.8	14.6	13.2	•
Taxes Paid 12	1.9	1.9	•	3.4	2.4	2.7	2.4	2.1	1.9	1.8	2.3	1.9	•
Interest Paid 13	4.7	0.3	•	0.3	0.4	0.4	0.5	1.2	0.5	0.7	1.9	1.7	•
Depreciation 14	1.7	2.2	•	0.4	1.6	0.5	1.2	1.7	1.6	2.1	2.0	2.2	•
Amortization and Depletion 15	1.3	0.3	•	0.0	0.0	0.1	0.2	0.3	0.8	0.5	1.1	0.9	•
Pensions and Other Deferred Comp. 16	1.3	0.1	•	0.7	0.3	0.5	0.9	0.6	0.9	0.8	0.5	1.0	•
Employee Benefits 17	2.3	1.6	•	2.8	1.8	2.1	2.2	2.4	2.0	2.1	2.6	2.5	•
Advertising 18	0.7	3.5	•	1.2	0.2	0.7	0.8	0.4	1.8	0.7	2.2	0.6	•
Other Expenses 19	14.6	25.9	•	13.8	7.1	10.3	12.9	9.5	12.5	10.7	16.5	12.8	•
Officers' Compensation 20	1.4	1.4	•	9.4	3.4	4.0	4.3	3.2	2.0	1.6	1.8	1.2	•
Operating Margin 21	0.1	8.0	•	12.5	10.2	8.8	7.9	5.6	5.2	3.4	7.0	3.5	•
Operating Margin Before Officers' Comp. 22	1.4	9.4	•	22.0	13.5	12.8	12.2	8.8	7.2	5.0	8.9	4.7	•

Selected Average Balance Sheet ($ in Thousands)

Net Receivables 23	8461	0	•	203	988	2310	3724	7974	12554	34290	70958	137240	•
Inventories 24	4541	0	•	96	982	1461	3619	8058	11363	25036	38529	104005	•
Net Property, Plant and Equipment 25	4614	0	•	34	269	726	1921	4706	7295	19326	30759	77663	•
Total Assets 26	126487	0	•	669	2555	7210	15368	33788	67975	163121	331970	1281718	•
Notes and Loans Payable 27	24881	0	•	101	415	840	2378	8807	8570	24958	57326	258508	•
All Other Liabilities 28	53563	0	•	102	900	1609	4384	10305	18945	40292	89367	367944	•
Net Worth 29	48043	0	•	467	1240	4761	8607	14676	40460	97871	185277	655266	•

Selected Financial Ratios (Times to 1)

Current Ratio 30	1.2	•	•	5.8	2.1	2.9	2.3	2.2	2.3	2.4	2.1	1.2	•
Quick Ratio 31	0.7	•	•	4.5	1.2	1.9	1.3	1.2	1.3	1.3	1.4	0.7	•
Net Sales to Working Capital 32	14.4	•	•	2.5	5.5	3.3	4.1	3.7	3.4	3.0	2.9	11.1	•
Coverage Ratio 33	3.0	76.9	•	43.6	26.6	26.6	22.8	7.9	22.9	13.0	8.1	6.3	•
Total Asset Turnover 34	0.3	•	•	2.0	2.4	1.7	1.6	1.4	1.1	1.0	0.6	0.5	•
Inventory Turnover 35	5.3	•	•	4.4	4.0	4.8	3.7	3.4	4.0	4.2	2.6	3.8	•
Receivables Turnover 36	5.2	•	•	8.4	5.6	4.6	7.5	5.8	6.1	5.4	2.6	4.6	•
Total Liabilities to Net Worth 37	1.6	•	•	0.4	1.1	0.5	0.8	1.3	0.7	0.7	0.8	1.0	•
Current Assets to Working Capital 38	7.3	•	•	1.2	1.9	1.5	1.8	1.8	1.8	1.7	1.9	6.6	•
Current Liabilities to Working Capital 39	6.3	•	•	0.2	0.9	0.5	0.8	0.8	0.8	0.7	0.9	5.6	•
Working Capital to Net Sales 40	0.1	•	•	0.4	0.2	0.3	0.2	0.3	0.3	0.3	0.3	0.1	•
Inventory to Working Capital 41	1.6	•	•	0.3	0.7	0.4	0.6	0.7	0.6	0.5	0.4	1.7	•
Total Receipts to Cash Flow 42	5.0	2.2	•	4.3	6.4	5.7	4.8	6.4	5.1	6.2	3.7	5.5	•
Cost of Goods to Cash Flow 43	2.9	1.0	•	1.4	4.0	3.3	2.6	3.8	2.9	4.0	1.8	3.2	•
Cash Flow to Total Debt 44	0.1	•	•	1.5	0.7	0.9	0.8	0.4	0.6	0.4	0.4	0.2	•

Selected Financial Factors (in Percentages)

Debt Ratio 45	62.0	•	•	30.3	51.5	34.0	44.0	56.6	40.5	40.0	44.2	48.9	•
Return on Total Assets 46	4.7	•	•	27.2	26.2	15.8	17.2	13.1	14.0	9.8	9.6	5.7	•
Return on Equity Before Income Taxes 47	8.1	•	•	38.1	51.9	23.1	29.4	26.2	22.5	15.1	15.1	9.4	•
Return on Equity After Income Taxes 48	5.9	•	•	37.5	47.1	21.9	26.2	22.4	19.0	11.6	11.2	6.6	•
Profit Margin (Before Income Tax) 49	9.3	24.8	•	13.6	10.3	9.2	10.0	8.4	11.7	8.9	13.3	9.0	•
Profit Margin (After Income Tax) 50	6.8	17.1	•	13.4	9.4	8.7	8.9	7.2	9.9	6.9	9.8	6.4	•

146

Table I

Corporations with and without Net Income

ELECTRICAL LIGHTING EQUIPMENT AND HOUSEHOLD APPLIANCE

MONEY AMOUNTS AND SIZE OF ASSETS IN THOUSANDS OF DOLLARS

Item Description for Accounting Period 7/12 Through 6/13	Total	Zero Assets	Under 500	500 to 1,000	1,000 to 5,000	5,000 to 10,000	10,000 to 25,000	25,000 to 50,000	50,000 to 100,000	100,000 to 250,000	250,000 to 500,000	500,000 to 2,500,000	2,500,000 and over
Number of Enterprises 1	1289	183	688	58	135	54	90	24	17	21	7	8	5

Revenues ($ in Thousands)

Net Sales 2	139187165	5635806	82482	162083	876305	847546	2183480	1186555	1795721	3699845	2470290	14796168	105450881
Interest 3	35836384	16696	0	0	603	117	182	8	284	7653	6478	27443	35776918
Rents 4	8358891	2820	0	0	0	620	2174	471	1229	2036	0	838	8348703
Royalties 5	2606540	1622	0	0	0	0	866	0	171	1393	289	25714	2576485
Other Portfolio Income 6	7202413	30541	356	0	0	1704	1062	114	1114	15037	16687	60111	7075687
Other Receipts 7	31071244	78276	5288	0	5389	8794	12167	8666	6358	7900	10255	70740	30857416
Total Receipts 8	224262637	5765761	88126	162083	882297	858781	2199931	1195814	1804877	3733864	2503999	14981014	190086090
Average Total Receipts 9	173982	31507	128	2795	6536	15903	24444	49826	106169	177803	357714	1872627	38017218

Operating Costs/Operating Income (%)

Cost of Operations 10	68.5	64.6	63.0	74.5	60.4	65.0	63.6	68.9	66.8	62.9	63.2	71.2	68.9
Salaries and Wages 11	11.8	12.9	31.5	7.0	12.2	7.0	12.3	8.0	8.4	10.6	6.8	6.2	12.9
Taxes Paid 12	1.2	1.6	1.2	0.9	1.7	1.8	1.9	2.1	1.2	1.6	1.3	1.4	1.1
Interest Paid 13	23.5	6.4	0.7	•	0.3	0.8	0.7	0.8	1.4	3.5	0.9	0.9	30.3
Depreciation 14	7.6	1.5	1.8	0.1	0.3	1.7	1.9	1.6	1.3	3.1	1.7	3.7	9.2
Amortization and Depletion 15	0.9	1.6	16.2	•	0.5	0.2	0.3	0.2	1.1	1.1	0.4	0.5	1.0
Pensions and Other Deferred Comp. 16	0.5	1.7	0.0	•	1.2	0.7	0.7	0.3	0.6	0.6	0.6	0.5	0.4
Employee Benefits 17	2.0	1.5	1.6	0.4	1.6	1.7	2.3	1.2	1.4	2.0	1.6	1.7	2.1
Advertising 18	1.3	0.7	0.5	0.3	0.3	0.9	0.8	1.2	1.0	1.1	3.9	3.0	1.0
Other Expenses 19	39.2	14.9	43.4	11.8	12.0	17.8	11.2	10.6	9.4	13.6	10.0	7.9	48.3
Officers' Compensation 20	0.6	0.5	4.4	3.4	5.5	2.1	3.4	1.4	2.4	1.2	2.0	0.7	0.3
Operating Margin 21	•	•	•	1.6	3.8	0.1	0.8	3.8	5.2	•	7.5	2.2	•
Operating Margin Before Officers' Comp. 22	•	•	•	5.0	9.3	2.2	4.3	5.2	7.5	•	9.6	2.9	•

Selected Average Balance Sheet ($ in Thousands)

	23–29												
Net Receivables 23	119823	0	0	253	948	1729	3121	7439	15746	30644	70566	264172	30047545
Inventories 24	10887	0	7	163	1196	2533	4496	9404	15364	29833	52042	176928	2084495
Net Property, Plant and Equipment 25	27969	0	5	4	191	1493	2676	6976	7928	27698	50556	268813	6462467
Total Assets 26	684515	0	18	504	3268	7654	15531	34066	72648	157683	321270	1559818	171990873
Notes and Loans Payable 27	357395	0	89	19	319	2255	4310	11221	22551	72232	70672	198544	91162920
All Other Liabilities 28	109951	0	17	230	1902	2810	4054	9031	20575	31751	111987	492512	26994238
Net Worth 29	217169	0	-88	256	1046	2589	7168	13815	29522	53700	138611	868762	53833715

Selected Financial Ratios (Times to 1)

Current Ratio 30	0.9	•	0.7	2.2	2.5	1.8	2.0	1.8	2.2	2.7	1.4	1.7	0.8
Quick Ratio 31	0.8	•	0.1	1.5	1.3	0.8	1.0	0.8	1.2	1.3	0.7	1.0	0.7
Net Sales to Working Capital 32	•	•	•	10.3	3.7	6.3	4.9	5.2	4.7	3.4	8.4	7.2	•
Coverage Ratio 33	1.3	0.3	•	•	14.2	2.7	3.3	6.6	5.1	1.0	11.9	5.1	1.3
Total Asset Turnover 34	0.2	•	6.6	5.5	2.0	2.1	1.6	1.5	1.5	1.1	1.1	1.2	0.1
Inventory Turnover 35	6.8	•	10.6	12.8	3.3	4.0	3.4	3.6	4.6	3.7	4.3	7.4	7.0
Receivables Turnover 36	0.9	•	•	22.1	4.7	•	7.3	7.1	8.1	5.7	5.7	7.6	0.7
Total Liabilities to Net Worth 37	2.2	•	•	1.0	2.1	2.0	1.2	1.5	1.5	1.9	1.3	0.8	2.2
Current Assets to Working Capital 38	•	•	•	1.8	1.7	2.3	2.0	2.2	1.8	1.6	3.6	2.4	•
Current Liabilities to Working Capital 39	•	•	•	0.8	0.7	1.3	1.0	1.2	0.8	0.6	2.6	1.4	•
Working Capital to Net Sales 40	•	•	•	0.1	0.3	0.2	0.2	0.2	0.2	0.3	0.1	0.1	•
Inventory to Working Capital 41	•	•	•	0.6	0.6	1.0	0.9	1.1	0.7	0.6	1.4	0.9	•
Total Receipts to Cash Flow 42	2.5	12.9	•	9.8	6.9	6.5	9.3	7.7	7.2	9.2	5.7	10.2	2.0
Cost of Goods to Cash Flow 43	1.7	8.3	•	7.3	4.2	4.2	5.9	5.3	4.8	5.8	3.6	7.3	1.4
Cash Flow to Total Debt 44	0.1	•	•	1.1	0.4	0.5	0.3	0.3	0.3	0.2	0.3	0.3	0.1

Selected Financial Factors (in Percentages)

Debt Ratio 45	68.3	•	585.1	49.3	68.0	66.2	53.9	59.4	59.4	65.9	56.9	44.3	68.7
Return on Total Assets 46	4.8	•	•	9.0	9.6	4.6	3.6	7.8	10.3	4.1	11.4	5.2	4.8
Return on Equity Before Income Taxes 47	3.6	•	78.0	17.8	27.9	8.5	5.4	16.2	20.3	0.5	24.2	7.5	3.4
Return on Equity After Income Taxes 48	2.4	•	78.0	15.1	27.9	6.2	3.6	11.4	17.5	•	21.0	4.9	2.3
Profit Margin (Before Income Tax) 49	7.2	•	•	1.6	4.5	1.4	1.6	4.5	5.7	0.1	9.5	3.5	8.8
Profit Margin (After Income Tax) 50	4.8	•	•	1.4	4.5	1.0	1.1	3.2	4.9	•	8.3	2.3	5.9

Table II

Corporations with Net Income

ELECTRICAL LIGHTING EQUIPMENT AND HOUSEHOLD APPLIANCE

MONEY AMOUNTS AND SIZE OF ASSETS IN THOUSANDS OF DOLLARS

Item Description for Accounting Period 7/12 Through 6/13	Total	Zero Assets	Under 500	500 to 1,000	1,000 to 5,000	5,000 to 10,000	10,000 to 25,000	25,000 to 50,000	50,000 to 100,000	100,000 to 250,000	250,000 to 500,000	500,000 to 2,500,000	2,500,000 and over
Number of Enterprises 1	965	20	•	58	79	40	59	17	14	11	•	•	5
Revenues ($ in Thousands)													
Net Sales 2	132458081	4170627	•	162083	753140	788210	1478774	1034398	1579385	2190763	•	•	105450881
Interest 3	35821980	16696	•	0	520	93	91	7	281	2163	•	•	35776918
Rents 4	8355452	204	•	0	0	620	2102	0	1229	1755	•	•	8348703
Royalties 5	2601064	1622	•	0	0	0	866	0	171	161	•	•	2576485
Other Portfolio Income 6	7179066	9478	•	0	0	1704	866	38	1109	13416	•	•	7075687
Other Receipts 7	31030417	75767	•	0	3941	8708	11791	998	-728	2681	•	•	30857416
Total Receipts 8	217446060	4274394	•	162083	757601	799335	1494490	1035441	1581447	2210939	•	•	190086090
Average Total Receipts 9	225333	213720	•	2795	9590	19983	25330	60908	112960	200994	•	•	38017218
Operating Costs/Operating Income (%)													
Cost of Operations 10	68.5	61.3	•	74.5	57.5	62.7	65.9	67.3	66.3	56.2	•	•	68.9
Salaries and Wages 11	11.9	15.1	•	7.0	11.1	6.3	9.7	8.2	8.0	11.7	•	•	12.9
Taxes Paid 12	1.2	1.8	•	0.9	1.5	1.7	1.6	1.5	1.1	1.5	•	•	1.1
Interest Paid 13	24.5	7.6	•	•	0.2	0.7	0.4	0.5	1.1	1.2	•	•	30.3
Depreciation 14	7.9	1.1	•	0.1	0.2	1.5	1.5	1.4	1.2	2.7	•	•	9.2
Amortization and Depletion 15	0.9	1.1	•	•	•	0.0	0.1	0.1	1.1	0.4	•	•	1.0
Pensions and Other Deferred Comp. 16	0.5	2.0	•	•	1.4	0.7	0.6	0.3	0.3	0.7	•	•	0.4
Employee Benefits 17	2.0	1.6	•	0.4	1.5	1.7	1.8	0.9	1.3	2.6	•	•	2.1
Advertising 18	1.2	0.3	•	0.3	0.1	0.9	0.9	1.2	1.0	0.8	•	•	1.0
Other Expenses 19	40.3	10.5	•	11.8	9.3	17.1	7.3	8.2	9.3	13.6	•	•	48.3
Officers' Compensation 20	0.5	0.0	•	3.4	6.1	2.0	2.3	1.3	2.5	1.4	•	•	0.3
Operating Margin 21	•	•	•	1.6	11.0	4.6	7.8	9.2	6.8	7.1	•	•	•
Operating Margin Before Officers' Comp. 22	•	•	•	5.0	17.1	6.5	10.1	10.5	9.3	8.5	•	•	•

	Selected Average Balance Sheet ($ in Thousands)												
Net Receivables 23	158691	0	•	253	1474	1878	2965	7814	15140	35721	•	•	30047545
Inventories 24	13032	0	•	163	1134	2483	4885	9243	16457	31414	•	•	2133171
Net Property, Plant and Equipment 25	36516	0	•	4	285	1720	2663	7630	6659	26538	•	•	6462467
Total Assets 26	908574	0	•	504	3504	8279	15390	32641	70677	160840	•	•	171990873
Notes and Loans Payable 27	474879	0	•	19	450	1898	2633	7949	20415	41095	•	•	91162920
All Other Liabilities 28	144791	0	•	230	2230	3367	2941	8061	13749	37809	•	•	26994238
Net Worth 29	288904	0	•	256	825	3015	9817	16632	36514	81935	•	•	53833715

	Selected Financial Ratios (Times to 1)												
Current Ratio 30	0.9	•	•	2.2	2.0	1.6	2.7	2.7	2.5	2.6	•	•	0.8
Quick Ratio 31	0.8	•	•	1.5	1.2	0.7	1.3	1.2	1.3	1.4	•	•	0.7
Net Sales to Working Capital 32	•	•	•	10.3	5.8	8.0	4.0	4.2	4.5	3.6	•	•	•
Coverage Ratio 33	1.3	1.2	•	•	63.2	9.1	23.4	21.6	7.4	8.0	•	•	1.3
Total Asset Turnover 34	0.2	•	•	5.5	2.7	2.4	1.6	1.9	1.6	1.2	•	•	0.1
Inventory Turnover 35	7.2	•	•	12.8	4.8	5.0	3.4	4.4	4.5	3.6	•	•	6.8
Receivables Turnover 36	0.9	•	•	22.1	7.0	13.7	7.7	9.3	8.5	•	•	•	•
Total Liabilities to Net Worth 37	2.1	•	•	1.0	3.2	1.7	0.6	1.0	0.9	1.0	•	•	2.2
Current Assets to Working Capital 38	•	•	•	1.8	2.0	2.5	1.6	1.6	1.7	1.6	•	•	•
Current Liabilities to Working Capital 39	•	•	•	0.8	1.0	1.5	0.6	0.6	0.7	0.6	•	•	•
Working Capital to Net Sales 40	•	•	•	0.1	0.2	0.1	0.2	0.2	0.2	0.3	•	•	•
Inventory to Working Capital 41	•	•	•	0.6	0.8	1.2	0.7	0.8	0.7	0.6	•	•	•
Total Receipts to Cash Flow 42	2.4	10.5	•	9.8	5.3	5.2	6.9	6.5	6.7	5.2	•	•	2.0
Cost of Goods to Cash Flow 43	1.6	6.5	•	7.3	3.0	3.3	4.6	4.4	4.4	2.9	•	•	1.4
Cash Flow to Total Debt 44	0.1	•	•	1.1	0.7	0.7	0.6	0.6	0.5	0.5	•	•	0.1

	Selected Financial Factors (in Percentages)												
Debt Ratio 45	68.2	•	•	49.3	76.5	63.6	36.2	49.0	48.3	49.1	•	•	68.7
Return on Total Assets 46	4.9	•	•	9.0	32.1	16.0	15.1	18.2	12.8	11.8	•	•	4.8
Return on Equity Before Income Taxes 47	3.9	•	•	17.8	134.3	39.0	22.7	34.0	21.4	20.3	•	•	3.4
Return on Equity After Income Taxes 48	2.7	•	•	15.1	134.2	36.4	20.6	28.3	18.7	15.7	•	•	2.3
Profit Margin (Before Income Tax) 49	8.2	1.3	•	1.6	11.6	6.0	8.9	9.3	6.9	8.4	•	•	8.8
Profit Margin (After Income Tax) 50	5.6	0.9	•	1.4	11.6	5.6	8.1	7.7	6.0	6.5	•	•	5.9

Table I

Corporations with and without Net Income

ELECTRICAL EQUIPMENT

MONEY AMOUNTS AND SIZE OF ASSETS IN THOUSANDS OF DOLLARS

Item Description for Accounting Period 7/12 Through 6/13	Total	Zero Assets	Under 500	500 to 1,000	1,000 to 5,000	5,000 to 10,000	10,000 to 25,000	25,000 to 50,000	50,000 to 100,000	100,000 to 250,000	250,000 to 500,000	500,000 to 2,500,000	2,500,000 and over
Number of Enterprises 1	940	10	•	•	325	135	59	23	14	7	12	0	3

Revenues ($ in Thousands)

Net Sales 2	39803774	413892	•	•	1336842	2344116	1790126	955966	1266597	1058830	5931414	0	23930012
Interest 3	184656	312	•	•	121	524	214	611	1277	592	2420	0	178585
Rents 4	34438	0	•	•	2523	0	0	27	452	0	0	0	30049
Royalties 5	208479	0	•	•	0	0	0	0	0	3307	18209	0	186964
Other Portfolio Income 6	741710	36305	•	•	5	4017	939	5626	2741	13337	42254	0	636488
Other Receipts 7	463030	9396	•	•	3059	8248	5016	10112	8769	6748	42566	0	366390
Total Receipts 8	41436087	459905	•	•	1342550	2356905	1796295	972342	1279836	1082814	6036863	0	25328488
Average Total Receipts 9	44081	45990	•	•	4131	17459	30446	42276	91417	154688	503072	•	8442829

Operating Costs/Operating Income (%)

Cost of Operations 10	63.5	58.9	•	•	64.2	62.1	66.1	71.5	68.3	70.6	65.3	•	61.8
Salaries and Wages 11	9.0	20.5	•	•	9.0	7.1	7.0	9.2	8.6	9.9	9.4	•	9.1
Taxes Paid 12	1.7	1.3	•	•	3.5	2.2	1.2	1.6	1.4	1.8	1.5	•	1.6
Interest Paid 13	2.1	13.5	•	•	1.1	0.3	0.4	0.9	0.8	3.1	1.2	•	2.6
Depreciation 14	1.6	1.1	•	•	1.1	1.0	1.4	2.1	1.4	1.7	1.9	•	1.6
Amortization and Depletion 15	1.3	6.9	•	•	0.1	0.2	0.1	1.2	0.5	0.8	2.6	•	1.3
Pensions and Other Deferred Comp. 16	1.1	0.1	•	•	0.4	0.3	0.8	0.3	0.2	1.1	1.4	•	1.3
Employee Benefits 17	2.1	1.7	•	•	2.3	3.0	2.3	2.6	1.2	2.0	1.9	•	2.1
Advertising 18	0.5	0.0	•	•	0.3	0.2	0.5	0.3	0.6	0.4	0.5	•	0.5
Other Expenses 19	10.5	13.3	•	•	13.5	8.3	10.4	10.0	7.9	6.4	9.8	•	10.9
Officers' Compensation 20	1.5	•	•	•	5.2	7.3	2.0	1.7	1.4	1.2	1.3	•	0.6
Operating Margin 21	5.3	•	•	•	•	7.9	7.8	•	7.9	1.1	3.2	•	6.6
Operating Margin Before Officers' Comp. 22	6.7	•	•	•	4.5	15.2	9.8	0.3	9.3	2.3	4.6	•	7.2

Selected Average Balance Sheet ($ in Thousands)

Net Receivables	23	11506	0	•	•	320	2092	3529	6356	17547	23396	78562	•	2881389
Inventories	24	4657	0	•	•	776	1765	4600	6265	17703	20433	56313	•	737402
Net Property, Plant and Equipment	25	5205	0	•	•	481	1070	2870	6465	9194	34068	78842	•	979847
Total Assets	26	75973	0	•	•	2064	8995	15232	36470	73996	166115	475995	•	19881897
Notes and Loans Payable	27	21198	0	•	•	976	1695	2729	9864	13620	28913	142782	•	5616428
All Other Liabilities	28	17387	0	•	•	389	1609	4133	10899	17454	52174	106025	•	4493225
Net Worth	29	37389	0	•	•	699	5692	8370	15707	42922	85028	227189	•	9772243

Selected Financial Ratios (Times to 1)

Current Ratio	30	1.2	•	•	•	3.1	2.7	2.3	1.5	2.0	1.6	1.8	•	1.0
Quick Ratio	31	0.8	•	•	•	1.5	1.8	1.2	0.7	1.1	1.0	1.0	•	0.7
Net Sales to Working Capital	32	11.9	•	•	•	4.0	4.0	4.8	8.1	4.1	5.1	5.2	•	106.3
Coverage Ratio	33	6.1	0.5	•	•	0.7	33.7	20.9	1.5	13.3	2.1	5.5	•	6.5
Total Asset Turnover	34	0.6	•	•	•	2.0	1.9	2.0	1.1	1.2	0.9	1.0	•	0.4
Inventory Turnover	35	5.8	•	•	•	3.4	6.1	4.4	4.7	3.5	5.2	5.7	•	6.7
Receivables Turnover	36	3.5	•	•	•	10.3	•	7.5	6.1	4.5	7.0	7.2	•	2.7
Total Liabilities to Net Worth	37	1.0	•	•	•	2.0	0.6	0.8	1.3	0.7	1.0	1.1	•	1.0
Current Assets to Working Capital	38	5.6	•	•	•	1.5	1.6	1.8	3.2	2.0	2.8	2.3	•	54.4
Current Liabilities to Working Capital	39	4.6	•	•	•	0.5	0.6	0.8	2.2	1.0	1.8	1.3	•	53.4
Working Capital to Net Sales	40	0.1	•	•	•	0.3	0.2	0.2	0.1	0.2	0.2	0.2	•	0.0
Inventory to Working Capital	41	1.3	•	•	•	0.7	0.4	0.7	1.3	0.7	0.8	0.7	•	8.9
Total Receipts to Cash Flow	42	5.7	132.2	•	•	9.5	6.7	6.1	11.3	6.3	11.8	7.7	•	4.8
Cost of Goods to Cash Flow	43	3.6	77.9	•	•	6.1	4.2	4.0	8.1	4.3	8.4	5.0	•	3.0
Cash Flow to Total Debt	44	0.2	•	•	•	0.3	0.8	0.7	0.2	0.5	0.2	0.3	•	0.2

Selected Financial Factors (in Percentages)

Debt Ratio	45	50.8	•	•	•	66.1	36.7	45.1	56.9	42.0	48.8	52.3	•	50.8
Return on Total Assets	46	7.0	•	•	•	1.6	16.7	17.1	1.5	12.3	5.9	6.8	•	6.7
Return on Equity Before Income Taxes	47	11.9	•	•	•	•	25.7	29.6	1.1	19.7	6.1	11.7	•	11.6
Return on Equity After Income Taxes	48	8.6	•	•	•	•	25.3	26.7	•	17.5	3.4	9.0	•	8.0
Profit Margin (Before Income Tax)	49	10.5	•	•	•	•	8.4	8.2	0.4	9.3	3.4	5.4	•	14.2
Profit Margin (After Income Tax)	50	7.6	•	•	•	•	8.3	7.4	•	8.3	1.9	4.1	•	9.8

Table II

Corporations with Net Income

ELECTRICAL EQUIPMENT

MONEY AMOUNTS AND SIZE OF ASSETS IN THOUSANDS OF DOLLARS

Item Description for Accounting Period 7/12 Through 6/13	Total	Zero Assets	Under 500	500 to 1,000	1,000 to 5,000	5,000 to 10,000	10,000 to 25,000	25,000 to 50,000	50,000 to 100,000	100,000 to 250,000	250,000 to 500,000	500,000 to 2,500,000	2,500,000 and over
Number of Enterprises 1	595	•	•	•	199	129	50	13	11	•	•	0	3

Revenues ($ in Thousands)

Net Sales 2	37581259	•	•	•	982802	2243743	1642042	637176	1157404	•	•	0	23930012
Interest 3	182754	•	•	•	102	336	198	563	1277	•	•	0	178585
Rents 4	34411	•	•	•	2523	0	0	0	452	•	•	0	30049
Royalties 5	208479	•	•	•	0	0	0	0	0	•	•	0	186964
Other Portfolio Income 6	688692	•	•	•	4	3931	611	5222	2678	•	•	0	636488
Other Receipts 7	447901	•	•	•	734	8248	4843	5687	9676	•	•	0	366390
Total Receipts 8	39143496	•	•	•	986165	2256258	1647694	648648	1171487	•	•	0	25328488
Average Total Receipts 9	65787	•	•	•	4956	17490	32954	49896	106499	•	•	•	8442829

Operating Costs/Operating Income (%)

Cost of Operations 10	63.2	•	•	•	63.5	61.1	66.7	65.9	67.8	•	•	•	61.8
Salaries and Wages 11	8.8	•	•	•	7.7	7.4	6.0	10.9	8.4	•	•	•	9.1
Taxes Paid 12	1.6	•	•	•	3.0	2.1	1.1	1.7	1.3	•	•	•	1.6
Interest Paid 13	1.9	•	•	•	1.0	0.3	0.4	1.1	0.7	•	•	•	2.6
Depreciation 14	1.5	•	•	•	0.6	1.0	1.3	1.9	1.3	•	•	•	1.6
Amortization and Depletion 15	1.3	•	•	•	0.1	0.2	0.0	1.3	0.4	•	•	•	1.3
Pensions and Other Deferred Comp. 16	1.1	•	•	•	0.4	0.3	0.8	0.4	0.2	•	•	•	1.3
Employee Benefits 17	2.0	•	•	•	1.5	2.9	2.2	2.7	1.2	•	•	•	2.1
Advertising 18	0.5	•	•	•	0.3	0.2	0.5	0.2	0.7	•	•	•	0.5
Other Expenses 19	10.2	•	•	•	11.9	8.6	10.2	10.3	7.5	•	•	•	10.9
Officers' Compensation 20	1.4	•	•	•	5.0	7.4	1.9	1.5	1.5	•	•	•	0.6
Operating Margin 21	6.4	•	•	•	5.1	8.4	9.0	2.0	9.2	•	•	•	6.6
Operating Margin Before Officers' Comp. 22	7.9	•	•	•	10.0	15.8	10.9	3.5	10.7	•	•	•	7.2

Net Receivables 23	17612	•	•	•	286	2064	3745	7294	20759	•	•	•	2881389
Inventories 24	6744	•	•	•	1089	1273	4938	7294	18632	•	•	•	665962
Net Property, Plant and Equipment 25	7683	•	•	•	576	1054	2765	6140	9593	•	•	•	979847
Total Assets 26	116866	•	•	•	2435	8964	15160	37991	74660	•	•	•	19881897
Notes and Loans Payable 27	32706	•	•	•	1036	1773	2703	9686	13373	•	•	•	5616428
All Other Liabilities 28	26305	•	•	•	407	1632	3861	12806	18745	•	•	•	4493225
Net Worth 29	57855	•	•	•	992	5559	8596	15499	42541	•	•	•	9772243

Selected Financial Ratios (Times to 1)

Current Ratio 30	1.2	•	•	•	4.0	2.6	2.3	1.4	2.3	•	•	•	1.0
Quick Ratio 31	0.8	•	•	•	1.8	1.8	1.2	0.7	1.4	•	•	•	0.7
Net Sales to Working Capital 32	11.9	•	•	•	3.6	4.0	4.8	8.6	3.9	•	•	•	106.3
Coverage Ratio 33	7.1	•	•	•	6.3	34.3	27.1	4.5	17.0	•	•	•	6.5
Total Asset Turnover 34	0.5	•	•	•	2.0	1.9	2.2	1.3	1.4	•	•	•	0.4
Inventory Turnover 35	5.9	•	•	•	2.9	8.4	4.4	4.4	3.8	•	•	•	7.4
Receivables Turnover 36	3.5	•	•	•	10.0	12.2	7.7	6.6	4.7	•	•	•	•
Total Liabilities to Net Worth 37	1.0	•	•	•	1.5	0.6	0.8	1.5	0.8	•	•	•	1.0
Current Assets to Working Capital 38	5.6	•	•	•	1.3	1.6	1.8	3.4	1.8	•	•	•	54.4
Current Liabilities to Working Capital 39	4.6	•	•	•	0.3	0.6	0.8	2.4	0.8	•	•	•	53.4
Working Capital to Net Sales 40	0.1	•	•	•	0.3	0.2	0.2	0.1	0.3	•	•	•	0.0
Inventory to Working Capital 41	1.2	•	•	•	0.7	0.4	0.7	1.4	0.6	•	•	•	8.9
Total Receipts to Cash Flow 42	5.4	•	•	•	6.6	6.4	5.7	7.9	5.9	•	•	•	4.8
Cost of Goods to Cash Flow 43	3.4	•	•	•	4.2	3.9	3.8	5.2	4.0	•	•	•	3.0
Cash Flow to Total Debt 44	0.2	•	•	•	0.5	0.8	0.9	0.3	0.6	•	•	•	0.2

Selected Financial Factors (in Percentages)

Debt Ratio 45	50.5	•	•	•	59.3	38.0	43.3	59.2	43.0	•	•	•	50.8
Return on Total Assets 46	7.4	•	•	•	13.0	17.9	21.1	6.5	16.2	•	•	•	6.7
Return on Equity Before Income Taxes 47	12.9	•	•	•	26.9	28.0	35.8	12.4	26.8	•	•	•	11.6
Return on Equity After Income Taxes 48	9.5	•	•	•	25.0	27.6	32.5	9.0	24.1	•	•	•	8.0
Profit Margin (Before Income Tax) 49	11.8	•	•	•	5.4	8.9	9.4	3.9	10.8	•	•	•	14.2
Profit Margin (After Income Tax) 50	8.7	•	•	•	5.0	8.8	8.5	2.8	9.7	•	•	•	9.8

Table I

Corporations with and without Net Income

OTHER ELECTRICAL EQUIPMENT AND COMPONENT

MONEY AMOUNTS AND SIZE OF ASSETS IN THOUSANDS OF DOLLARS

Item Description for Accounting Period 7/12 Through 6/13	Total	Zero Assets	Under 500	500 to 1,000	1,000 to 5,000	5,000 to 10,000	10,000 to 25,000	25,000 to 50,000	50,000 to 100,000	100,000 to 250,000	250,000 to 500,000	500,000 to 2,500,000	2,500,000 and over
Number of Enterprises 1	3678	781	•	•	813	327	177	93	57	34	16	18	5

Revenues ($ in Thousands)

Net Sales 2	62208008	536457	•	•	3096816	3967498	4539261	4541014	5009895	5172655	4493227	11107541	17972532
Interest 3	256523	697	•	•	236	300	1214	3187	6044	6472	11924	53582	172864
Rents 4	10005	7	•	•	371	910	2656	1469	1617	892	284	1750	0
Royalties 5	132197	924	•	•	0	640	787	2376	6616	5224	48012	41419	26118
Other Portfolio Income 6	460494	22124	•	•	1672	9489	12180	6442	43796	9044	35908	6206	313636
Other Receipts 7	423856	6619	•	•	47322	22739	28350	30656	51290	47588	13893	90804	82088
Total Receipts 8	63491083	566828	•	•	3146417	4001576	4584448	4585144	5119258	5241875	4603248	11301302	18567238
Average Total Receipts 9	17262	726	•	•	3870	12237	25901	49303	89812	154173	287703	627850	3713448

Operating Costs/Operating Income (%)

Cost of Operations 10	67.7	61.8	•	•	56.4	69.6	69.4	68.1	69.3	71.0	63.4	68.0	70.7
Salaries and Wages 11	8.9	13.1	•	•	13.2	7.9	7.3	9.2	9.0	8.8	11.4	8.8	7.9
Taxes Paid 12	1.8	2.4	•	•	2.5	2.1	2.1	1.9	2.2	1.7	1.3	1.9	1.5
Interest Paid 13	2.4	2.7	•	•	0.5	1.1	0.5	0.7	1.0	1.8	1.6	2.8	4.6
Depreciation 14	2.0	2.4	•	•	1.8	1.3	1.4	2.4	2.0	2.8	2.3	3.4	1.2
Amortization and Depletion 15	1.4	7.9	•	•	0.2	0.4	0.2	0.6	0.8	0.9	2.7	1.4	2.2
Pensions and Other Deferred Comp. 16	0.6	0.1	•	•	0.5	0.2	0.4	0.4	0.3	0.7	0.5	0.8	0.8
Employee Benefits 17	1.6	2.1	•	•	1.9	1.2	1.8	2.0	1.9	1.9	2.2	1.6	1.3
Advertising 18	1.1	0.3	•	•	0.5	0.6	0.4	0.8	0.5	0.5	1.2	0.9	2.1
Other Expenses 19	9.6	15.8	•	•	14.7	6.8	9.0	10.3	9.3	9.2	11.6	10.9	7.0
Officers' Compensation 20	2.0	1.0	•	•	8.9	3.6	3.8	1.6	1.5	1.3	1.4	1.1	0.3
Operating Margin 21	0.7	•	•	•	•	5.1	3.5	2.0	2.2	•	0.4	•	0.5
Operating Margin Before Officers' Comp. 22	2.7	•	•	•	7.6	8.8	7.3	3.6	3.6	0.8	1.8	•	0.7

		Selected Average Balance Sheet ($ in Thousands)											
Net Receivables	23	3299	0	•	•	354	1472	4106	8409	14884	28308	66855	102135	989605
Inventories	24	2278	0	•	•	494	2021	4692	8085	13226	25760	45224	100139	297902
Net Property, Plant and Equipment	25	2509	0	•	•	523	1033	2214	6340	9571	39877	59944	175404	289220
Total Assets	26	27775	0	•	•	2017	6837	15863	33916	70398	167566	326571	956626	11902183
Notes and Loans Payable	27	5777	0	•	•	526	2349	2816	7290	17306	56929	93139	267897	1867646
All Other Liabilities	28	9666	0	•	•	641	1513	4740	9558	24191	58479	74726	268645	4625461
Net Worth	29	12332	0	•	•	849	2976	8307	17068	28902	52158	158706	420084	5409077

		Selected Financial Ratios (Times to 1)											
Current Ratio	30	1.5	•	•	•	1.8	2.1	2.3	2.2	1.8	1.9	1.7	2.1	1.0
Quick Ratio	31	0.9	•	•	•	1.2	1.0	1.3	1.3	1.0	1.0	1.0	1.2	0.7
Net Sales to Working Capital	32	6.7	•	•	•	7.4	4.8	3.8	4.1	4.9	4.3	4.9	4.4	263.0
Coverage Ratio	33	2.3	•	•	•	1.7	6.3	9.5	5.6	5.3	1.6	3.9	1.2	2.0
Total Asset Turnover	34	0.6	•	•	•	1.9	1.8	1.6	1.4	1.2	0.9	0.9	0.6	0.3
Inventory Turnover	35	5.0	•	•	•	4.3	4.2	3.8	4.1	4.6	4.2	3.9	4.2	8.5
Receivables Turnover	36	4.8	•	•	•	7.4	8.6	5.8	5.9	6.0	5.6	4.0	5.8	3.1
Total Liabilities to Net Worth	37	1.3	•	•	•	1.4	1.3	0.9	1.0	1.4	2.2	1.1	1.3	1.2
Current Assets to Working Capital	38	2.9	•	•	•	2.2	1.9	1.8	1.9	2.3	2.1	2.4	1.9	117.9
Current Liabilities to Working Capital	39	1.9	•	•	•	1.2	0.9	0.8	0.9	1.3	1.1	1.4	0.9	116.9
Working Capital to Net Sales	40	0.1	•	•	•	0.1	0.2	0.3	0.2	0.2	0.2	0.2	0.2	0.0
Inventory to Working Capital	41	0.9	•	•	•	0.7	0.9	0.7	0.7	0.7	0.7	0.7	0.7	22.7
Total Receipts to Cash Flow	42	10.1	17.9	•	•	8.2	9.2	8.6	8.6	8.5	12.4	8.0	11.2	12.7
Cost of Goods to Cash Flow	43	6.8	11.1	•	•	4.6	6.4	6.0	5.9	5.9	8.8	5.1	7.6	9.0
Cash Flow to Total Debt	44	0.1	•	•	•	0.4	0.3	0.4	0.3	0.3	0.1	0.2	0.1	0.0

		Selected Financial Factors (in Percentages)											
Debt Ratio	45	55.6	•	•	•	57.9	56.5	47.6	49.7	58.9	68.9	51.4	56.1	54.6
Return on Total Assets	46	3.4	•	•	•	1.6	12.7	8.1	5.4	6.8	2.6	5.2	2.1	2.8
Return on Equity Before Income Taxes	47	4.4	•	•	•	1.5	24.4	13.8	8.8	13.5	3.0	8.0	0.7	3.0
Return on Equity After Income Taxes	48	2.6	•	•	•	•	23.3	11.7	5.5	10.5	•	4.5	•	1.8
Profit Margin (Before Income Tax)	49	3.2	•	•	•	0.3	6.0	4.5	3.1	4.4	1.0	4.5	0.5	4.5
Profit Margin (After Income Tax)	50	1.9	•	•	•	•	5.7	3.8	1.9	3.5	•	2.6	•	2.7

Table II
Corporations with Net Income

OTHER ELECTRICAL EQUIPMENT AND COMPONENT

MONEY AMOUNTS AND SIZE OF ASSETS IN THOUSANDS OF DOLLARS

Item Description for Accounting Period 7/12 Through 6/13		Total	Zero Assets	Under 500	500 to 1000	1,000 to 5,000	5,000 to 10,000	10,000 to 25,000	25,000 to 50,000	50,000 to 100,000	100,000 to 250,000	250,000 to 500,000	500,000 to 2,500,000	2,500,000 and over
Number of Enterprises	1	2178	•	341	•	502	262	132	69	41	20	12	•	•

Revenues ($ in Thousands)

Net Sales	2	48995407	•	331529	•	2426732	3548036	3891432	3413406	3947646	3917787	3646735	•	•
Interest	3	221479	•	0	•	200	258	570	1728	5667	3553	11918	•	•
Rents	4	9473	•	0	•	371	830	2656	1253	1617	796	270	•	•
Royalties	5	114089	•	0	•	0	0	787	2376	6532	2717	42173	•	•
Other Portfolio Income	6	418915	•	0	•	1299	816	3611	6006	38134	5114	35792	•	•
Other Receipts	7	324320	•	170	•	16775	7306	23770	18709	47232	4632	12121	•	•
Total Receipts	8	50083683	•	331699	•	2445377	3557246	3922826	3443478	4046828	3934599	3749009	•	•
Average Total Receipts	9	22995	•	973	•	4871	13577	29718	49905	98703	196730	312417	•	•

Operating Costs/Operating Income (%)

Cost of Operations	10	66.4	•	0.3	•	56.1	68.7	69.3	63.8	66.7	67.4	62.2	•	•
Salaries and Wages	11	8.4	•	12.1	•	11.0	7.0	6.4	9.4	9.0	8.6	11.1	•	•
Taxes Paid	12	1.8	•	2.3	•	2.8	2.1	1.9	2.0	2.3	1.8	1.5	•	•
Interest Paid	13	1.9	•	0.1	•	0.4	0.9	0.5	0.7	0.8	1.4	1.5	•	•
Depreciation	14	1.7	•	1.1	•	2.0	0.9	1.2	1.5	1.7	2.2	2.2	•	•
Amortization and Depletion	15	1.0	•	•	•	0.1	0.3	0.2	0.2	0.5	0.5	0.6	•	•
Pensions and Other Deferred Comp.	16	0.7	•	5.1	•	0.6	0.2	0.4	0.4	0.4	0.6	0.5	•	•
Employee Benefits	17	1.5	•	0.7	•	1.6	1.0	1.6	1.7	1.7	1.4	2.0	•	•
Advertising	18	1.2	•	0.0	•	0.6	0.5	0.3	0.9	0.6	0.6	1.4	•	•
Other Expenses	19	8.2	•	15.5	•	10.5	5.1	7.9	10.6	9.1	6.1	11.3	•	•
Officers' Compensation	20	1.9	•	43.4	•	9.9	3.6	2.1	1.5	1.4	1.0	1.6	•	•
Operating Margin	21	5.1	•	19.4	•	4.4	9.6	8.1	7.4	5.9	8.4	4.0	•	•
Operating Margin Before Officers' Comp.	22	7.1	•	62.8	•	14.3	13.3	10.2	8.9	7.3	9.4	5.6	•	•

Selected Average Balance Sheet ($ in Thousands)

Net Receivables 23	4498	•	0	•	474	1634	4758	7665	15233	27820	72868	•	•
Inventories 24	2793	•	3	•	710	1738	4962	8670	14050	27718	47350	•	•
Net Property, Plant and Equipment 25	2745	•	11	•	342	936	2167	5113	9257	30958	43921	•	•
Total Assets 26	35611	•	342	•	1989	6722	16095	33079	70468	157814	333875	•	•
Notes and Loans Payable 27	6888	•	66	•	348	2116	3021	6177	16139	64640	105080	•	•
All Other Liabilities 28	13486	•	52	•	445	1371	4812	8092	23680	37646	67700	•	•
Net Worth 29	15236	•	225	•	1196	3235	8262	18810	30650	55528	161096	•	•

Selected Financial Ratios (Times to 1)

Current Ratio 30	1.6	•	2.1	•	2.9	2.3	2.3	2.4	1.9	2.5	1.9	•	•
Quick Ratio 31	1.0	•	2.1	•	1.9	1.2	1.3	1.5	1.1	1.2	1.1	•	•
Net Sales to Working Capital 32	5.8	•	7.5	•	4.8	4.8	4.2	3.9	4.7	3.9	4.3	•	•
Coverage Ratio 33	5.1	•	150.7	•	13.5	11.8	18.0	13.4	11.2	7.3	6.7	•	•
Total Asset Turnover 34	0.6	•	2.8	•	2.4	2.0	1.8	1.5	1.4	1.2	0.9	•	•
Inventory Turnover 35	5.3	•	0.9	•	3.8	5.4	4.1	3.6	4.6	4.8	4.0	•	•
Receivables Turnover 36	4.7	•	21.2	•	7.4	9.9	6.0	5.9	6.8	7.5	4.2	•	•
Total Liabilities to Net Worth 37	1.3	•	0.5	•	0.7	1.1	0.9	0.8	1.3	1.8	1.1	•	•
Current Assets to Working Capital 38	2.6	•	1.9	•	1.5	1.8	1.8	1.7	2.1	1.6	2.2	•	•
Current Liabilities to Working Capital 39	1.6	•	0.9	•	0.5	0.8	0.8	0.7	1.1	0.6	1.2	•	•
Working Capital to Net Sales 40	0.2	•	0.1	•	0.2	0.2	0.2	0.3	0.2	0.3	0.2	•	•
Inventory to Working Capital 41	0.8	•	0.0	•	0.5	0.8	0.7	0.6	0.7	0.6	0.7	•	•
Total Receipts to Cash Flow 42	7.6	•	3.3	•	7.8	7.4	6.6	5.8	6.3	7.7	6.2	•	•
Cost of Goods to Cash Flow 43	5.0	•	0.0	•	4.4	5.1	4.6	3.7	4.2	5.2	3.9	•	•
Cash Flow to Total Debt 44	0.1	•	2.5	•	0.8	0.5	0.6	0.6	0.4	0.2	0.3	•	•

Selected Financial Factors (in Percentages)

Debt Ratio 45	57.2	•	34.3	•	39.9	51.9	48.7	43.1	56.5	64.8	51.7	•	•
Return on Total Assets 46	6.2	•	55.5	•	13.6	21.8	17.2	13.6	12.8	12.9	9.4	•	•
Return on Equity Before Income Taxes 47	11.6	•	84.0	•	20.9	41.4	31.7	22.2	26.8	31.6	16.6	•	•
Return on Equity After Income Taxes 48	9.1	•	84.0	•	16.8	40.1	29.0	18.1	22.9	25.9	12.1	•	•
Profit Margin (Before Income Tax) 49	7.8	•	19.4	•	5.2	9.9	8.9	8.4	8.5	8.9	8.8	•	•
Profit Margin (After Income Tax) 50	6.2	•	19.4	•	4.2	9.6	8.1	6.9	7.3	7.3	6.4	•	•

Table I

Corporations with and without Net Income

MOTOR VEHICLES AND PARTS

MONEY AMOUNTS AND SIZE OF ASSETS IN THOUSANDS OF DOLLARS

Item Description for Accounting Period 7/12 Through 6/13	Total	Zero Assets	Under 500	500 to 1,000	1,000 to 5,000	5,000 to 10,000	10,000 to 25,000	25,000 to 50,000	50,000 to 100,000	100,000 to 250,000	250,000 to 500,000	500,000 to 2,500,000	2,500,000 and over
Number of Enterprises **1**	6352	646	3373	490	823	277	205	174	106	110	63	60	26

Revenues ($ in Thousands)

Net Sales **2**	672387951	4778204	2003964	1338824	5562854	4113005	6054681	12412654	13573396	29382839	36502170	81660809	475004552
Interest **3**	8873931	1591	32	27	1089	737	1232	2143	6347	17444	52577	340399	8450312
Rents **4**	10211420	384	0	0	433	3597	1534	1898	1159	4517	10959	76098	10110841
Royalties **5**	6666161	8871	0	0	0	3740	25858	693	5417	9097	24967	418866	6168653
Other Portfolio Income **6**	6894061	172153	25897	0	12060	13212	7419	10537	55228	19996	80713	248035	6248810
Other Receipts **7**	9439762	24646	9025	1937	37361	46303	40126	76363	106910	402472	280866	885128	7528625
Total Receipts **8**	714473286	4985849	2038918	1340788	5613797	4180594	6130850	12504288	13748457	29836365	36952252	83629335	513511793
Average Total Receipts **9**	112480	7718	604	2736	6821	15092	29907	71864	129702	271240	586544	1393822	19750454

Operating Costs/Operating Income (%)

Cost of Operations **10**	81.2	81.9	70.7	40.4	74.6	86.3	80.4	80.9	82.3	83.1	85.4	82.8	80.6
Salaries and Wages **11**	3.1	6.1	8.8	27.1	6.0	3.5	4.5	4.2	3.5	3.0	3.4	4.2	2.6
Taxes Paid **12**	0.8	1.6	4.8	4.2	1.8	1.7	1.5	1.6	1.1	1.0	1.0	1.1	0.6
Interest Paid **13**	1.6	1.6	0.5	0.3	0.8	1.1	0.8	0.6	0.7	0.9	1.0	1.5	1.7
Depreciation **14**	4.9	3.0	0.5	0.5	1.4	2.0	2.8	2.6	2.6	3.2	2.9	2.7	5.8
Amortization and Depletion **15**	0.9	0.3	0.3	0.0	0.0	0.0	0.1	0.1	0.3	0.3	0.5	0.4	1.1
Pensions and Other Deferred Comp. **16**	1.1	0.2	0.2	0.1	0.1	0.2	0.1	0.2	0.3	0.4	0.5	0.7	1.4
Employee Benefits **17**	1.4	1.9	0.7	0.7	0.6	1.1	1.3	1.5	1.5	1.4	1.2	1.6	1.4
Advertising **18**	1.7	0.1	0.9	0.8	1.0	0.2	0.3	0.3	0.2	0.3	0.2	0.3	2.3
Other Expenses **19**	6.1	6.0	12.5	10.9	8.4	4.6	6.7	5.4	5.2	4.8	4.5	5.5	6.4
Officers' Compensation **20**	0.3	1.0	2.3	6.8	4.0	1.3	1.4	1.1	0.6	0.4	0.3	0.3	0.1
Operating Margin **21**	•	•	•	8.0	1.3	•	0.2	1.7	1.9	1.2	•	•	•
Operating Margin Before Officers' Comp. **22**	•	•	0.2	14.8	5.3	•	1.6	2.7	2.4	1.6	•	•	•

Selected Average Balance Sheet ($ in Thousands)

Net Receivables **23**	36348	0	28	137	433	1314	3610	8706	17053	30673	66645	198970	7939403
Inventories **24**	7111	0	51	246	1124	3216	5025	8359	13776	26910	59986	125935	954561
Net Property, Plant and Equipment **25**	23452	0	4	225	362	2379	4590	9744	21317	43095	95136	224573	4568455
Total Assets **26**	137064	0	121	759	2542	7532	16830	35366	70786	156753	342012	1019653	28792293
Notes and Loans Payable **27**	42246	0	82	136	1038	5778	5276	11180	22899	48465	115601	344330	8723743
All Other Liabilities **28**	53078	0	53	130	1026	1883	4532	13624	24774	52719	120033	370116	11309502
Net Worth **29**	41741	0	-14	493	478	-129	7022	10561	23114	55569	106378	305206	8759048

Selected Financial Ratios (Times to 1)

Current Ratio **30**	1.5	•	1.4	3.6	2.1	1.9	1.7	1.5	1.3	1.3	1.3	1.4	1.5
Quick Ratio **31**	1.0	•	0.6	2.0	0.7	0.8	0.8	0.8	0.7	0.7	0.6	0.8	1.0
Net Sales to Working Capital **32**	5.4	•	19.5	7.1	6.5	6.4	6.7	10.2	12.7	14.1	17.1	11.0	4.4
Coverage Ratio **33**	3.4	1.6	0.2	24.3	3.8	0.7	2.9	5.1	5.7	4.1	1.5	2.0	3.7
Total Asset Turnover **34**	0.8	•	4.9	3.6	2.7	2.0	1.8	2.0	1.8	1.7	1.7	1.3	0.6
Inventory Turnover **35**	12.1	•	8.3	4.5	4.5	4.0	4.7	6.9	7.6	8.2	8.2	8.9	15.4
Receivables Turnover **36**	2.9	•	31.6	7.9	17.4	12.1	7.9	8.1	7.5	8.6	8.9	7.0	2.3
Total Liabilities to Net Worth **37**	2.3	•	•	0.5	4.3	•	1.4	2.3	2.1	1.8	2.2	2.3	2.3
Current Assets to Working Capital **38**	3.1	•	3.3	1.4	1.9	2.1	2.4	3.0	4.0	4.0	5.0	3.7	3.1
Current Liabilities to Working Capital **39**	2.1	•	2.3	0.4	0.9	1.1	1.4	2.0	3.0	3.0	4.0	2.7	2.1
Working Capital to Net Sales **40**	0.2	•	0.1	0.1	0.2	0.2	0.1	0.1	0.1	0.1	0.1	0.1	0.2
Inventory to Working Capital **41**	0.4	•	1.9	0.6	1.2	1.2	1.1	1.2	1.4	1.4	1.9	1.1	0.2
Total Receipts to Cash Flow **42**	11.6	20.5	12.2	6.2	12.0	39.3	15.3	15.4	14.1	15.0	26.1	17.3	10.2
Cost of Goods to Cash Flow **43**	9.4	16.8	8.7	2.5	8.9	33.9	12.3	12.5	11.6	12.5	22.3	14.3	8.2
Cash Flow to Total Debt **44**	0.1	•	0.4	1.6	0.3	0.0	0.2	0.2	0.2	0.2	0.1	0.1	0.1

Selected Financial Factors (in Percentages)

Debt Ratio **45**	69.5	•	111.8	35.1	81.2	101.7	58.3	70.1	67.3	64.5	68.9	70.1	69.6
Return on Total Assets **46**	4.1	•	0.3	30.4	7.9	1.5	4.0	6.0	7.0	6.2	2.6	4.1	4.1
Return on Equity Before Income Taxes **47**	9.6	•	16.0	44.9	31.0	41.6	6.2	16.3	17.8	13.2	2.7	6.7	9.8
Return on Equity After Income Taxes **48**	8.3	•	18.0	44.2	30.0	54.2	3.5	14.0	14.3	9.1	0.4	3.5	8.8
Profit Margin (Before Income Tax) **49**	3.8	1.0	•	8.1	2.2	•	1.5	2.4	3.2	2.7	0.5	1.5	4.7
Profit Margin (After Income Tax) **50**	3.3	•	•	8.0	2.1	•	0.8	2.1	2.6	1.9	0.1	0.8	4.2

Table II

Corporations with Net Income

MOTOR VEHICLES AND PARTS

MONEY AMOUNTS AND SIZE OF ASSETS IN THOUSANDS OF DOLLARS

Item Description for Accounting Period 7/12 Through 6/13	Total	Zero Assets	Under 500	500 to 1,000	1,000 to 5,000	5,000 to 10,000	10,000 to 25,000	25,000 to 50,000	50,000 to 100,000	100,000 to 250,000	250,000 to 500,000	500,000 to 2,500,000	2,500,000 and over
Number of Enterprises **1**	2555	21	•	432	604	114	131	135	74	80	40	39	•
Revenues ($ in Thousands)													
Net Sales **2**	574267174	3096042	•	1230778	4636866	1182543	4128945	10400712	10940163	23947031	24380780	59308423	•
Interest **3**	8242692	1379	•	27	701	728	714	1445	3990	8866	30679	241917	•
Rents **4**	9587757	384	•	0	216	3597	974	298	673	4508	7394	7715	•
Royalties **5**	6046346	8463	•	0	0	0	15501	693	3753	7031	12263	146303	•
Other Portfolio Income **6**	6371588	140473	•	0	9913	36	6755	10181	54693	16225	48903	197372	•
Other Receipts **7**	8238696	12586	•	1801	12439	13615	26093	58949	93560	267218	210795	716925	•
Total Receipts **8**	612754253	3259327	•	1232606	4660135	1200519	4178982	10472278	11096832	24250879	24690814	60618655	•
Average Total Receipts **9**	239826	155206	•	2853	7715	10531	31901	77572	149957	303136	617270	1554324	•
Operating Costs/Operating Income (%)													
Cost of Operations **10**	80.5	82.2	•	36.4	73.4	74.1	77.1	79.2	81.4	82.3	83.9	81.7	•
Salaries and Wages **11**	2.9	3.3	•	29.1	5.3	4.7	4.2	4.2	3.3	3.2	3.5	4.2	•
Taxes Paid **12**	0.7	1.3	•	4.5	1.8	2.1	1.6	1.4	1.1	1.1	1.0	1.1	•
Interest Paid **13**	1.5	1.1	•	0.2	0.4	0.7	0.5	0.6	0.5	0.9	0.7	1.3	•
Depreciation **14**	5.1	2.9	•	0.5	1.3	2.8	2.5	2.1	2.3	2.2	2.5	1.9	•
Amortization and Depletion **15**	0.9	0.3	•	0.0	0.0	0.0	0.0	0.1	0.2	0.4	0.3	0.4	•
Pensions and Other Deferred Comp. **16**	1.1	0.1	•	0.1	0.1	0.3	0.2	0.2	0.3	0.2	0.4	0.8	•
Employee Benefits **17**	1.4	1.8	•	0.8	0.5	1.6	1.5	1.4	1.5	1.2	1.3	1.7	•
Advertising **18**	1.9	0.0	•	0.8	0.9	0.3	0.2	0.3	0.2	0.3	0.1	0.2	•
Other Expenses **19**	5.8	4.0	•	11.7	8.0	6.4	5.2	5.4	4.8	4.4	3.8	4.5	•
Officers' Compensation **20**	0.2	0.6	•	7.1	4.1	2.4	1.6	1.2	0.6	0.4	0.3	0.3	•
Operating Margin **21**	•	2.3	•	8.8	4.2	4.7	5.5	3.9	4.0	3.5	2.1	2.0	•
Operating Margin Before Officers' Comp. **22**	•	2.9	•	15.9	8.3	7.1	7.0	5.2	4.5	3.9	2.4	2.3	•

Selected Average Balance Sheet ($ in Thousands)

Net Receivables 23	80985	0	•	123	459	1183	3670	9339	17762	32592	66933	192251	•
Inventories 24	12560	0	•	210	1305	1337	5977	7834	12934	27126	53463	122399	•
Net Property, Plant and Equipment 25	51277	0	•	249	343	1760	4599	8476	21645	39064	85998	205859	•
Total Assets 26	296562	0	•	749	2773	6079	16622	35176	71758	156500	332446	1026683	•
Notes and Loans Payable 27	90087	0	•	117	555	1641	3998	10035	17990	40778	82149	283261	•
All Other Liabilities 28	109639	0	•	144	586	1084	4024	11010	25032	55226	107720	343124	•
Net Worth 29	96836	0	•	488	1632	3354	8600	14132	28735	60496	142577	400298	•

Selected Financial Ratios (Times to 1)

Current Ratio 30	1.5	•	•	3.1	3.3	2.5	2.2	1.6	1.4	1.5	1.4	1.7	•
Quick Ratio 31	1.0	•	•	1.9	1.1	1.2	1.0	0.9	0.8	0.8	0.7	1.0	•
Net Sales to Working Capital 32	4.7	•	•	8.5	5.1	4.4	5.3	8.9	11.1	11.6	12.0	7.8	•
Coverage Ratio 33	4.5	8.2	•	39.4	13.5	10.5	15.1	9.4	12.1	6.5	5.6	4.3	•
Total Asset Turnover 34	0.8	•	•	3.8	2.8	1.7	1.9	2.2	2.1	1.9	1.8	1.5	•
Inventory Turnover 35	14.4	•	•	4.9	4.3	5.7	4.1	7.8	9.3	9.1	9.6	10.1	•
Receivables Turnover 36	3.1	•	•	10.8	18.7	11.8	7.6	9.0	9.2	9.8	10.7	8.5	•
Total Liabilities to Net Worth 37	2.1	•	•	0.5	0.7	0.8	0.9	1.5	1.5	1.6	1.3	1.6	•
Current Assets to Working Capital 38	2.9	•	•	1.5	1.4	1.7	1.9	2.6	3.3	3.2	3.5	2.5	•
Current Liabilities to Working Capital 39	1.9	•	•	0.5	0.4	0.7	0.9	1.6	2.3	2.2	2.5	1.5	•
Working Capital to Net Sales 40	0.2	•	•	0.1	0.2	0.2	0.2	0.1	0.1	0.1	0.1	0.1	•
Inventory to Working Capital 41	0.3	•	•	0.5	0.9	0.7	0.8	1.0	1.1	1.1	1.3	0.7	•
Total Receipts to Cash Flow 42	10.1	9.3	•	5.7	9.8	9.6	9.7	11.5	11.1	12.2	16.7	12.8	•
Cost of Goods to Cash Flow 43	8.1	7.6	•	2.1	7.2	7.1	7.4	9.1	9.1	10.0	14.0	10.4	•
Cash Flow to Total Debt 44	0.1	•	•	1.9	0.7	0.4	0.4	0.3	0.3	0.3	0.2	0.2	•

Selected Financial Factors (in Percentages)

Debt Ratio 45	67.3	•	•	34.8	41.2	44.8	48.3	59.8	60.0	61.3	57.1	61.0	•
Return on Total Assets 46	5.1	•	•	34.8	14.0	11.8	13.5	11.4	12.2	10.7	7.6	8.4	•
Return on Equity Before Income Taxes 47	12.2	•	•	52.1	22.1	19.3	24.4	25.4	27.9	23.5	14.6	16.6	•
Return on Equity After Income Taxes 48	10.7	•	•	51.2	21.7	18.2	21.0	23.2	23.9	18.4	11.9	12.8	•
Profit Margin (Before Income Tax) 49	5.2	8.0	•	8.9	4.7	6.2	6.7	4.7	5.4	4.8	3.4	4.4	•
Profit Margin (After Income Tax) 50	4.6	6.0	•	8.8	4.6	5.9	5.7	4.3	4.6	3.7	2.8	3.4	•

Table I

Corporations with and without Net Income

AEROSPACE PRODUCT AND PARTS

MONEY AMOUNTS AND SIZE OF ASSETS IN THOUSANDS OF DOLLARS

Item Description for Accounting Period 7/12 Through 6/13		Total	Zero Assets	Under 500	500 to 1,000	1,000 to 5,000	5,000 to 10,000	10,000 to 25,000	25,000 to 50,000	50,000 to 100,000	100,000 to 250,000	250,000 to 500,000	500,000 to 2,500,000	2,500,000 and over
Number of Enterprises	1	1625	292	630	58	308	98	114	47	18	22	5	15	19

Revenues ($ in Thousands)

Net Sales	2	318365181	4806394	650489	101247	1202701	1122805	2400327	1879084	1271164	3088622	1383665	17692307	282766376
Interest	3	654649	2612	12	0	568	706	908	762	1301	5653	416	23044	618667
Rents	4	583670	2746	0	0	878	0	279	580	74	135	140	11626	567211
Royalties	5	1968155	27560	0	0	0	0	0	0	312	2977	0	6760	1930547
Other Portfolio Income	6	4000644	6702	337	0	139	82	4725	2740	5187	140610	1654	48663	3789805
Other Receipts	7	3853802	12584	12595	0	3778	661	9288	5258	14982	27611	14057	179441	3573546
Total Receipts	8	329426101	4858598	663433	101247	1208064	1124254	2415527	1888424	1293020	3265608	1399932	17961841	293246152
Average Total Receipts	9	202724	16639	1053	1746	3922	11472	21189	40179	71834	148437	279986	1197456	15434008

Operating Costs/Operating Income (%)

Cost of Operations	10	71.9	68.7	58.2	29.1	54.6	61.5	64.8	66.1	66.7	67.8	68.8	73.4	72.2
Salaries and Wages	11	5.1	17.5	1.7	30.2	14.5	9.8	6.6	7.4	8.3	9.2	5.7	7.5	4.5
Taxes Paid	12	1.4	0.6	1.1	2.8	2.7	2.8	2.6	2.4	2.5	1.6	2.0	1.5	1.4
Interest Paid	13	1.6	2.2	0.6	0.0	0.8	1.1	1.1	1.2	1.8	1.8	1.7	1.9	1.6
Depreciation	14	2.0	2.5	1.1	15.6	3.2	1.1	3.0	2.4	2.6	3.1	2.9	2.9	1.9
Amortization and Depletion	15	0.7	1.4	•	•	0.9	0.1	0.3	0.3	0.4	0.9	0.8	1.8	0.6
Pensions and Other Deferred Comp.	16	3.3	1.5	•	0.0	0.3	0.2	0.6	1.1	0.8	0.3	0.4	1.0	3.6
Employee Benefits	17	2.1	0.8	0.3	•	0.8	2.6	3.3	2.7	2.4	2.1	1.2	3.2	2.1
Advertising	18	0.2	0.2	0.0	•	0.1	0.0	0.3	0.2	0.3	0.2	0.1	0.3	0.3
Other Expenses	19	9.8	14.8	17.5	22.3	14.7	7.7	9.0	9.5	7.1	9.5	13.7	5.8	9.9
Officers' Compensation	20	0.3	1.5	7.0	•	4.2	2.0	3.8	2.5	3.3	0.9	1.0	0.6	0.2
Operating Margin	21	1.6	•	12.4	•	3.2	11.2	4.6	4.1	3.8	2.6	1.7	0.1	1.8
Operating Margin Before Officers' Comp.	22	1.9	•	19.4	•	7.4	13.2	8.5	6.6	7.1	3.5	2.7	0.7	2.0

Selected Average Balance Sheet ($ in Thousands)

Net Receivables 23	26007	0	12	28	331	2173	3186	6234	14668	20254	38501	209804	1959539
Inventories 24	42255	0	3	70	407	3235	4830	10320	18505	32947	112735	188427	3301713
Net Property, Plant and Equipment 25	26749	0	8	505	361	953	3148	6839	13093	30079	46778	209362	2014496
Total Assets 26	261236	0	157	661	1840	7702	16436	35133	71899	156092	315847	1341057	20689513
Notes and Loans Payable 27	51875	0	134	0	666	2352	4085	9009	19438	54854	163814	404237	3918295
All Other Liabilities 28	146997	0	4	358	292	3950	5671	9390	16980	39679	90414	649262	11890109
Net Worth 29	62364	0	18	303	882	1399	6680	16734	35481	61559	61619	287557	4881109

Selected Financial Ratios (Times to 1)

Current Ratio 30	1.3	•	1.0	0.4	3.2	3.3	2.4	2.3	2.7	1.9	2.8	1.7	1.2
Quick Ratio 31	0.6	•	0.9	0.4	2.4	1.5	1.2	0.9	1.4	0.8	1.0	0.8	0.6
Net Sales to Working Capital 32	10.3	•	•	•	4.5	2.7	3.4	3.2	2.4	4.1	2.3	4.4	12.3
Coverage Ratio 33	4.5	•	26.8	1.0	5.4	11.7	6.0	4.8	4.0	5.5	2.6	1.9	4.9
Total Asset Turnover 34	0.7	•	6.6	2.6	2.1	1.5	1.3	1.1	1.0	0.9	0.9	0.9	0.7
Inventory Turnover 35	3.3	•	183.3	7.2	5.2	2.2	2.8	2.6	2.5	2.9	1.7	4.6	3.3
Receivables Turnover 36	7.8	•	170.4	13.9	7.6	6.4	6.1	6.4	5.2	6.2	6.4	6.5	7.9
Total Liabilities to Net Worth 37	3.2	•	7.6	1.2	1.1	4.5	1.5	1.1	1.0	1.5	4.1	3.7	3.2
Current Assets to Working Capital 38	5.0	•	•	•	1.4	1.4	1.7	1.8	1.6	2.2	1.6	2.4	6.0
Current Liabilities to Working Capital 39	4.0	•	•	•	0.4	0.4	0.7	0.8	0.6	1.2	0.6	1.4	5.0
Working Capital to Net Sales 40	0.1	•	•	•	0.2	0.4	0.3	0.3	0.4	0.2	0.4	0.2	0.1
Inventory to Working Capital 41	2.3	•	•	•	0.3	0.7	0.8	0.9	0.6	0.9	0.8	0.9	2.8
Total Receipts to Cash Flow 42	8.1	27.9	4.0	6.5	7.4	6.3	8.5	8.3	9.8	7.1	6.5	19.8	7.8
Cost of Goods to Cash Flow 43	5.8	19.1	2.3	1.9	4.1	3.9	5.5	5.5	6.5	4.8	4.5	14.5	5.6
Cash Flow to Total Debt 44	0.1	•	1.9	0.8	0.5	0.3	0.3	0.3	0.2	0.2	0.2	0.1	0.1

Selected Financial Factors (in Percentages)

Debt Ratio 45	76.1	•	88.3	54.2	52.1	81.8	59.4	52.4	50.7	60.6	80.5	78.6	76.4
Return on Total Assets 46	5.4	•	98.6	0.0	9.4	18.5	8.1	6.6	7.2	9.1	4.0	3.1	5.5
Return on Equity Before Income Taxes 47	17.6	•	813.7	•	16.0	93.1	16.6	11.0	10.9	19.0	12.8	6.7	18.5
Return on Equity After Income Taxes 48	11.4	•	813.0	•	12.7	88.0	14.4	9.5	7.7	13.4	12.8	0.3	12.2
Profit Margin (Before Income Tax) 49	5.6	•	14.4	•	3.6	11.4	5.3	4.6	5.5	8.3	2.9	1.6	6.1
Profit Margin (After Income Tax) 50	3.6	•	14.4	•	2.9	10.8	4.6	4.0	3.9	5.9	2.9	0.1	4.0

Table II
Corporations with Net Income

AEROSPACE PRODUCT AND PARTS

MONEY AMOUNTS AND SIZE OF ASSETS IN THOUSANDS OF DOLLARS

Item Description for Accounting Period 7/12 Through 6/13	Total	Zero Assets	Under 500	500 to 1,000	1,000 to 5,000	5,000 to 10,000	10,000 to 25,000	25,000 to 50,000	50,000 to 100,000	100,000 to 250,000	250,000 to 500,000	500,000 to 2,500,000	2,500,000 and over
Number of Enterprises **1**	1083	4	630	0	207	68	74	38	•	17	•	11	•

Revenues ($ in Thousands)													
Net Sales **2**	301689233	100658	650489	0	469621	971706	2004297	1660373	•	2349869	•	13182746	•
Interest **3**	599592	429	12	0	554	673	678	166	•	5351	•	17778	•
Rents **4**	568202	1	0	0	878	0	279	392	•	135	•	9765	•
Royalties **5**	1940205	0	0	0	0	0	0	0	•	2806	•	6568	•
Other Portfolio Income **6**	3981571	0	337	0	139	82	4429	2695	•	140082	•	48638	•
Other Receipts **7**	3588548	6513	12595	0	166	152	46	3432	•	21207	•	58487	•
Total Receipts **8**	312367351	107601	663433	0	471358	972613	2009729	1667058	•	2519450	•	13323982	•
Average Total Receipts **9**	288428	26900	1053	•	2277	14303	27158	43870	•	148203	•	1211271	•

Operating Costs/Operating Income (%)													
Cost of Operations **10**	71.6	63.8	58.2	•	47.5	60.7	62.7	66.0	•	64.9	•	72.5	•
Salaries and Wages **11**	4.8	4.3	1.7	•	8.3	7.8	5.5	7.1	•	10.5	•	7.6	•
Taxes Paid **12**	1.4	2.4	1.1	•	2.7	2.5	2.4	2.4	•	1.6	•	1.4	•
Interest Paid **13**	1.5	4.3	0.6	•	0.4	0.5	0.8	1.1	•	1.3	•	1.1	•
Depreciation **14**	1.9	2.2	1.1	•	1.1	0.6	2.3	1.9	•	2.9	•	2.0	•
Amortization and Depletion **15**	0.6	1.2	•	•	2.2	0.1	0.3	0.3	•	0.7	•	0.7	•
Pensions and Other Deferred Comp. **16**	3.4	0.4	•	•	0.7	0.2	0.7	1.1	•	0.4	•	0.7	•
Employee Benefits **17**	2.2	1.3	0.3	•	1.8	2.4	3.6	2.7	•	2.1	•	3.6	•
Advertising **18**	0.2	0.2	0.0	•	0.2	0.0	0.1	0.2	•	0.3	•	0.2	•
Other Expenses **19**	9.7	14.3	17.5	•	9.5	6.4	7.6	7.9	•	9.9	•	3.4	•
Officers' Compensation **20**	0.3	2.7	7.0	•	6.8	1.3	3.9	2.3	•	1.0	•	0.7	•
Operating Margin **21**	2.4	2.9	12.4	•	18.8	17.5	10.0	6.9	•	4.6	•	5.9	•
Operating Margin Before Officers' Comp. **22**	2.7	5.6	19.4	•	25.6	18.8	14.0	9.2	•	5.6	•	6.7	•

Selected Average Balance Sheet ($ in Thousands)

Net Receivables **23**	37110	0	12	•	280	2327	3826	5890	•	20124	•	247025	•
Inventories **24**	44191	0	3	•	487	2690	5895	10276	•	24494	•	194266	•
Net Property, Plant and Equipment **25**	37111	0	8	•	61	1098	3358	6161	•	28758	•	186614	•
Total Assets **26**	378846	0	157	•	1736	7705	17101	34281	•	153534	•	1362341	•
Notes and Loans Payable **27**	72775	0	134	•	439	1550	4236	8512	•	37029	•	228460	•
All Other Liabilities **28**	213353	0	4	•	191	4028	2866	7311	•	35122	•	639429	•
Net Worth **29**	92718	0	18	•	1106	2127	9999	18457	•	81384	•	494451	•

Selected Financial Ratios (Times to 1)

Current Ratio **30**	1.2	•	1.0	•	7.1	4.6	3.0	2.7	•	1.9	•	2.1	•
Quick Ratio **31**	0.6	•	0.9	•	5.9	2.5	1.4	1.1	•	0.9	•	1.1	•
Net Sales to Working Capital **32**	10.4	•	•	•	1.9	3.1	3.4	3.2	•	3.9	•	3.6	•
Coverage Ratio **33**	5.2	3.3	26.8	•	45.6	35.8	14.5	7.5	•	10.0	•	7.3	•
Total Asset Turnover **34**	0.7	•	6.6	•	1.3	1.9	1.6	1.3	•	0.9	•	0.9	•
Inventory Turnover **35**	4.5	•	183.3	•	2.2	3.2	2.9	2.8	•	3.7	•	4.5	•
Receivables Turnover **36**	8.8	•	170.4	•	3.4	7.0	6.6	7.6	•	•	•	•	•
Total Liabilities to Net Worth **37**	3.1	•	7.6	•	0.6	2.6	0.7	0.9	•	0.9	•	1.8	•
Current Assets to Working Capital **38**	5.0	•	•	•	1.2	1.3	1.5	1.6	•	2.1	•	1.9	•
Current Liabilities to Working Capital **39**	4.0	•	•	•	0.2	0.3	0.5	0.6	•	1.1	•	0.9	•
Working Capital to Net Sales **40**	0.1	•	•	•	0.5	0.3	0.3	0.3	•	0.3	•	0.3	•
Inventory to Working Capital **41**	2.3	•	•	•	0.1	0.5	0.7	0.9	•	0.7	•	0.6	•
Total Receipts to Cash Flow **42**	7.7	4.5	4.0	•	3.9	4.8	6.4	7.5	•	5.7	•	12.1	•
Cost of Goods to Cash Flow **43**	5.5	2.9	2.3	•	1.8	2.9	4.0	5.0	•	3.7	•	8.8	•
Cash Flow to Total Debt **44**	0.1	•	1.9	•	0.9	0.5	0.6	0.4	•	0.3	•	0.1	•

Selected Financial Factors (in Percentages)

Debt Ratio **45**	75.5	•	88.3	•	36.3	72.4	41.5	46.2	•	47.0	•	63.7	•
Return on Total Assets **46**	5.9	•	98.6	•	25.7	33.5	17.5	10.7	•	11.8	•	7.2	•
Return on Equity Before Income Taxes **47**	19.5	•	813.7	•	39.4	118.0	27.9	17.3	•	20.0	•	17.1	•
Return on Equity After Income Taxes **48**	13.3	•	813.0	•	35.5	113.1	25.5	15.7	•	14.5	•	12.1	•
Profit Margin (Before Income Tax) **49**	6.5	9.8	14.4	•	19.2	17.6	10.3	7.3	•	11.8	•	7.1	•
Profit Margin (After Income Tax) **50**	4.4	6.6	14.4	•	17.3	16.8	9.4	6.6	•	8.5	•	5.0	•

Table I
Corporations with and without Net Income

SHIP AND BOAT BUILDING

MONEY AMOUNTS AND SIZE OF ASSETS IN THOUSANDS OF DOLLARS

Item Description for Accounting Period 7/12 Through 6/13		Total	Zero Assets	Under 500	500 to 1,000	1,000 to 5,000	5,000 to 10,000	10,000 to 25,000	25,000 to 50,000	50,000 to 100,000	100,000 to 250,000	250,000 to 500,000	500,000 to 2,500,000	2,500,000 and over
Number of Enterprises	1	743	26	398	0	146	53	60	29	13	9	4	4	0
Revenues ($ in Thousands)														
Net Sales	2	45462696	59608	237779	0	671077	845345	1842995	1002580	1310778	1520954	1551401	36420180	0
Interest	3	16282	35	0	0	750	0	596	617	381	362	1763	11778	0
Rents	4	6481	0	205	0	0	0	0	620	556	376	3699	1025	0
Royalties	5	510	0	0	0	0	0	0	0	0	0	0	510	0
Other Portfolio Income	6	203334	0	7416	0	159	17	107	5265	8837	44257	132549	4728	0
Other Receipts	7	567202	206	1313	0	59002	6127	21508	21297	13434	16084	16240	411988	0
Total Receipts	8	46256505	59849	246713	0	730988	851489	1865206	1030379	1333986	1582033	1705652	36850209	0
Average Total Receipts	9	62256	2302	620	•	5007	16066	31087	35530	102614	175781	426413	9212552	•
Operating Costs/Operating Income (%)														
Cost of Operations	10	75.7	100.5	33.9	•	65.7	67.8	80.5	68.8	82.3	83.8	73.8	75.7	•
Salaries and Wages	11	5.1	4.7	37.3	•	3.6	11.6	2.4	4.5	3.3	2.8	9.6	4.9	•
Taxes Paid	12	1.5	2.2	5.4	•	4.1	2.4	1.2	1.8	1.5	1.9	1.6	1.4	•
Interest Paid	13	1.0	2.0	0.5	•	2.5	0.5	0.6	0.7	1.8	0.6	0.9	1.1	•
Depreciation	14	1.5	2.0	2.2	•	2.2	0.9	2.4	2.3	2.3	2.3	2.2	1.4	•
Amortization and Depletion	15	0.7	0.2	•	•	0.0	0.0	0.0	0.1	0.6	0.0	0.1	0.9	•
Pensions and Other Deferred Comp.	16	1.0	•	0.7	•	0.1	0.3	0.2	0.1	0.3	0.3	0.9	1.1	•
Employee Benefits	17	1.7	0.0	9.8	•	1.0	3.5	0.9	2.0	0.7	1.7	4.1	1.6	•
Advertising	18	0.6	1.5	0.5	•	0.1	0.4	0.6	0.4	0.9	0.2	0.1	0.6	•
Other Expenses	19	4.7	37.9	20.1	•	17.5	5.3	4.6	12.6	6.5	2.3	6.2	4.1	•
Officers' Compensation	20	0.8	2.4	14.3	•	3.5	1.9	2.4	1.3	1.6	0.9	0.3	0.5	•
Operating Margin	21	5.6	•	•	•	•	5.4	4.3	5.4	•	3.3	0.2	6.7	•
Operating Margin Before Officers' Comp.	22	6.4	•	•	•	3.1	7.3	6.7	6.6	•	4.2	0.5	7.2	•

Selected Average Balance Sheet ($ in Thousands)

Net Receivables 23	5156	0	175	•	303	1922	2717	2651	8548	24022	37580	724372	•
Inventories 24	6611	0	7	•	586	4155	2875	3185	7974	22718	2324	1005265	•
Net Property, Plant and Equipment 25	9856	0	96	•	1047	1604	4929	11643	23131	34791	104377	1345522	•
Total Assets 26	60621	0	297	•	2785	9524	14647	37483	71203	159978	387746	9532473	•
Notes and Loans Payable 27	11251	0	100	•	1377	1342	2958	8103	41201	32849	52022	1648932	•
All Other Liabilities 28	29065	0	280	•	1295	3225	5866	14755	18829	54132	141146	4761973	•
Net Worth 29	20305	0	-83	•	113	4956	5824	14625	11172	72997	194578	3121569	•

Selected Financial Ratios (Times to 1)

Current Ratio 30	1.4	•	0.6	•	1.1	2.2	1.6	1.4	1.1	1.5	1.3	1.5	•
Quick Ratio 31	0.7	•	0.6	•	0.4	0.9	0.9	0.6	0.5	0.9	0.5	0.7	•
Net Sales to Working Capital 32	8.5	•	•	•	38.1	4.0	9.7	6.8	68.8	5.6	11.7	8.3	•
Coverage Ratio 33	8.1	•	•	•	4.5	12.7	10.5	12.5	1.0	13.1	11.9	8.5	•
Total Asset Turnover 34	1.0	•	2.0	•	1.7	1.7	2.1	0.9	1.4	1.1	1.0	1.0	•
Inventory Turnover 35	7.0	•	29.0	•	5.2	2.6	8.6	7.5	10.4	6.2	123.2	6.9	•
Receivables Turnover 36	13.4	•	3.4	•	18.5	7.3	9.0	10.8	14.1	7.3	13.6	14.8	•
Total Liabilities to Net Worth 37	2.0	•	•	•	23.7	0.9	1.5	1.6	5.4	1.2	1.0	2.1	•
Current Assets to Working Capital 38	3.3	•	•	•	12.8	1.8	2.8	3.4	19.5	3.0	4.6	3.2	•
Current Liabilities to Working Capital 39	2.3	•	•	•	11.8	0.8	1.8	2.4	18.5	2.0	3.6	2.2	•
Working Capital to Net Sales 40	0.1	•	•	•	0.0	0.3	0.1	0.1	0.0	0.2	0.1	0.1	•
Inventory to Working Capital 41	0.9	•	•	•	5.2	1.1	0.6	0.7	7.3	0.7	0.1	0.9	•
Total Receipts to Cash Flow 42	10.1	•	•	•	4.4	11.6	11.5	5.4	19.7	18.2	6.8	10.1	•
Cost of Goods to Cash Flow 43	7.6	•	•	•	2.9	7.9	9.2	3.7	16.2	15.3	5.0	7.7	•
Cash Flow to Total Debt 44	0.2	•	•	•	0.4	0.3	0.3	0.3	0.1	0.1	0.3	0.1	•

Selected Financial Factors (in Percentages)

Debt Ratio 45	66.5	•	127.8	•	96.0	48.0	60.2	61.0	84.3	54.4	49.8	67.3	•
Return on Total Assets 46	8.5	•	•	•	18.2	11.2	12.8	8.2	2.6	8.3	11.1	8.6	•
Return on Equity Before Income Taxes 47	22.4	•	150.9	•	348.4	19.8	29.0	19.2	0.4	16.9	20.3	23.2	•
Return on Equity After Income Taxes 48	15.4	•	151.3	•	337.6	19.8	27.3	18.8	•	13.8	18.4	15.2	•
Profit Margin (Before Income Tax) 49	7.4	•	•	•	8.5	6.2	5.5	8.1	0.0	7.3	10.2	8.0	•
Profit Margin (After Income Tax) 50	5.1	•	•	•	8.3	6.2	5.2	7.9	•	5.9	9.2	5.2	•

Table II

Corporations with Net Income

SHIP AND BOAT BUILDING

MONEY AMOUNTS AND SIZE OF ASSETS IN THOUSANDS OF DOLLARS

Item Description for Accounting Period 7/12 Through 6/13	Total	Zero Assets	Under 500	500 to 1,000	1,000 to 5,000	5,000 to 10,000	10,000 to 25,000	25,000 to 50,000	50,000 to 100,000	100,000 to 250,000	250,000 to 500,000	500,000 to 2,500,000	2,500,000 and over
Number of Enterprises **1**	262	8	•	0	106	47	54	23	9	•	•	•	0

Revenues ($ in Thousands)													
Net Sales **2**	43253787	0	•	0	607170	794830	1622492	643829	915704	•	•	•	0
Interest **3**	15397	0	•	0	749	0	297	153	381	•	•	•	0
Rents **4**	5861	0	•	0	0	0	0	0	556	•	•	•	0
Royalties **5**	510	0	•	0	0	0	0	0	0	•	•	•	0
Other Portfolio Income **6**	202350	0	•	0	10	17	107	5224	8652	•	•	•	0
Other Receipts **7**	484440	25	•	0	7339	6078	20012	15093	2751	•	•	•	0
Total Receipts **8**	43962345	25	•	0	615268	800925	1642908	664299	928044	•	•	•	0
Average Total Receipts **9**	167795	3	•	•	5804	17041	30424	28883	103116	•	•	•	•

Operating Costs/Operating Income (%)													
Cost of Operations **10**	75.5	•	•	•	65.6	65.5	79.7	64.0	77.7	•	•	•	•
Salaries and Wages **11**	5.0	•	•	•	2.4	12.0	2.3	4.3	3.8	•	•	•	•
Taxes Paid **12**	1.5	•	•	•	4.2	2.3	1.1	1.8	1.5	•	•	•	•
Interest Paid **13**	1.1	•	•	•	2.5	0.2	0.6	0.8	2.1	•	•	•	•
Depreciation **14**	1.5	•	•	•	2.3	0.9	2.1	2.8	2.5	•	•	•	•
Amortization and Depletion **15**	0.7	•	•	•	0.0	•	0.1	0.1	0.5	•	•	•	•
Pensions and Other Deferred Comp. **16**	1.0	•	•	•	0.1	0.3	0.2	0.2	0.3	•	•	•	•
Employee Benefits **17**	1.7	•	•	•	1.0	3.6	0.6	1.5	0.5	•	•	•	•
Advertising **18**	0.6	•	•	•	0.1	0.5	0.7	0.3	0.9	•	•	•	•
Other Expenses **19**	4.3	•	•	•	9.7	5.0	3.8	11.5	5.6	•	•	•	•
Officers' Compensation **20**	0.7	•	•	•	3.0	1.9	2.5	1.3	1.7	•	•	•	•
Operating Margin **21**	6.6	•	•	•	9.0	7.7	6.5	11.5	3.1	•	•	•	•
Operating Margin Before Officers' Comp. **22**	7.2	•	•	•	12.0	9.6	9.0	12.8	4.8	•	•	•	•

Selected Average Balance Sheet ($ in Thousands)

Net Receivables 23	13677	0	•	•	358	2161	2755	1975	8862	•	•	•	•
Inventories 24	17196	0	•	•	69	4528	1807	3148	9360	•	•	•	•
Net Property, Plant and Equipment 25	26238	0	•	•	1381	1221	4617	12619	20645	•	•	•	•
Total Assets 26	165643	0	•	•	2639	9626	14771	37033	69905	•	•	•	•
Notes and Loans Payable 27	29187	0	•	•	1332	629	2645	5904	26098	•	•	•	•
All Other Liabilities 28	78463	0	•	•	595	3054	5304	13700	15056	•	•	•	•
Net Worth 29	57993	0	•	•	711	5942	6822	17429	28751	•	•	•	•

Selected Financial Ratios (Times to 1)

Current Ratio 30	1.5	•	•	•	1.8	2.6	1.8	1.5	1.2	•	•	•	•
Quick Ratio 31	0.7	•	•	•	1.1	1.0	1.1	0.7	0.6	•	•	•	•
Net Sales to Working Capital 32	7.6	•	•	•	10.4	3.4	7.1	5.6	19.9	•	•	•	•
Coverage Ratio 33	8.8	•	•	•	5.1	38.2	14.9	20.5	3.1	•	•	•	•
Total Asset Turnover 34	1.0	•	•	•	2.2	1.8	2.0	0.8	1.5	•	•	•	•
Inventory Turnover 35	7.2	•	•	•	54.6	2.4	13.2	5.7	8.4	•	•	•	•
Receivables Turnover 36	14.0	•	•	•	23.2	9.0	9.6	8.5	23.0	•	•	•	•
Total Liabilities to Net Worth 37	1.9	•	•	•	2.7	0.6	1.2	1.1	1.4	•	•	•	•
Current Assets to Working Capital 38	2.9	•	•	•	2.2	1.6	2.2	2.9	5.1	•	•	•	•
Current Liabilities to Working Capital 39	1.9	•	•	•	1.2	0.6	1.2	1.9	4.1	•	•	•	•
Working Capital to Net Sales 40	0.1	•	•	•	0.1	0.3	0.1	0.2	0.1	•	•	•	•
Inventory to Working Capital 41	0.8	•	•	•	0.2	1.0	0.5	0.6	1.8	•	•	•	•
Total Receipts to Cash Flow 42	9.7	•	•	•	5.8	9.5	9.5	4.2	12.1	•	•	•	•
Cost of Goods to Cash Flow 43	7.3	•	•	•	3.8	6.2	7.6	2.7	9.4	•	•	•	•
Cash Flow to Total Debt 44	0.2	•	•	•	0.5	0.5	0.4	0.3	0.2	•	•	•	•

Selected Financial Factors (in Percentages)

Debt Ratio 45	65.0	•	•	•	73.0	38.3	53.8	52.9	58.9	•	•	•	•
Return on Total Assets 46	9.3	•	•	•	27.9	15.3	16.9	11.7	9.3	•	•	•	•
Return on Equity Before Income Taxes 47	23.5	•	•	•	83.1	24.1	34.2	23.6	15.2	•	•	•	•
Return on Equity After Income Taxes 48	16.6	•	•	•	80.7	24.1	32.6	23.1	12.1	•	•	•	•
Profit Margin (Before Income Tax) 49	8.3	•	•	•	10.3	8.5	7.8	14.7	4.3	•	•	•	•
Profit Margin (After Income Tax) 50	5.8	•	•	•	10.0	8.5	7.4	14.4	3.4	•	•	•	•

Table I

Corporations with and without Net Income

OTHER TRANSPORTATION EQUIPMENT AND RAILROAD ROLLING STOCK

MONEY AMOUNTS AND SIZE OF ASSETS IN THOUSANDS OF DOLLARS

Item Description for Accounting Period 7/12 Through 6/13		Total	Zero Assets	Under 500	500 to 1,000	1,000 to 5,000	5,000 to 10,000	10,000 to 25,000	25,000 to 50,000	50,000 to 100,000	100,000 to 250,000	250,000 to 500,000	500,000 to 2,500,000	2,500,000 and over
Number of Enterprises	1	2136	231	1280	248	172	96	49	22	11	11	6	9	0

Revenues ($ in Thousands)

Net Sales	2	29744998	0	228189	78568	578473	1601382	1232006	1458326	1210792	2048278	3949999	17358985	0
Interest	3	583046	0	0	226	39	10	636	5352	559	1689	895	573641	0
Rents	4	78045	0	0	0	0	0	845	1279	119	688	1758	73355	0
Royalties	5	101441	0	0	0	0	0	0	733	63	99	1	100545	0
Other Portfolio Income	6	235457	0	0	0	311	1467	583	1572	164	5027	10776	215556	0
Other Receipts	7	258537	0	301	418	891	1007	8066	39719	5781	63610	31075	107671	0
Total Receipts	8	31001524	0	228490	79212	579714	1603866	1242136	1506981	1217478	2119391	3994504	18429753	0
Average Total Receipts	9	14514	0	179	319	3370	16707	25350	68499	110680	192672	665751	2047750	•

Operating Costs/Operating Income (%)

Cost of Operations	10	69.5	•	65.3	45.6	69.0	74.1	75.0	75.0	74.6	73.8	82.4	64.5	•
Salaries and Wages	11	6.2	•	6.0	0.5	5.8	10.4	5.7	4.6	6.1	3.7	4.2	6.9	•
Taxes Paid	12	1.3	•	5.7	1.3	1.9	1.7	1.4	1.7	1.7	0.9	0.9	1.3	•
Interest Paid	13	2.2	•	1.9	1.4	0.9	0.4	0.5	0.5	0.5	2.0	0.2	3.2	•
Depreciation	14	3.6	•	2.0	1.9	4.2	1.3	1.4	1.0	2.2	2.3	1.9	4.8	•
Amortization and Depletion	15	0.6	•	0.8	•	0.4	•	0.3	0.7	0.3	1.0	0.3	0.7	•
Pensions and Other Deferred Comp.	16	1.3	•	•	•	0.2	0.1	0.2	0.1	0.9	0.2	0.3	2.1	•
Employee Benefits	17	1.6	•	•	0.3	0.9	1.5	0.8	1.0	1.4	2.3	1.4	1.8	•
Advertising	18	1.0	•	0.7	0.4	0.3	0.1	0.4	0.8	0.2	0.2	2.0	1.2	•
Other Expenses	19	8.6	•	21.5	43.9	9.9	8.0	7.6	8.9	2.6	5.4	5.8	9.7	•
Officers' Compensation	20	0.9	•	3.6	3.2	3.4	2.9	1.8	0.7	1.8	0.5	0.2	0.7	•
Operating Margin	21	3.1	•	•	1.5	3.0	•	4.9	5.0	7.8	7.6	0.5	3.1	•
Operating Margin Before Officers' Comp.	22	4.1	•	•	4.8	6.4	2.4	6.7	5.8	9.6	8.2	0.7	3.9	•

Selected Average Balance Sheet ($ in Thousands)

Net Receivables 23	4033	0	8	378	582	2260	3446	7428	18087	27622	64454	774588	•
Inventories 24	1768	0	56	97	782	2867	3611	7664	15960	27420	54468	235714	•
Net Property, Plant and Equipment 25	3027	0	15	17	276	955	2732	4648	15746	23254	71469	578939	•
Total Assets 26	13836	0	95	593	2089	7593	15890	36928	74737	165705	361190	2421400	•
Notes and Loans Payable 27	5386	0	116	197	925	2348	4985	6551	17548	61970	64020	1030662	•
All Other Liabilities 28	3808	0	28	345	409	2285	4187	9053	28879	51014	181451	594565	•
Net Worth 29	4641	0	-49	52	755	2960	6717	21324	28309	52721	115719	796173	•

Selected Financial Ratios (Times to 1)

Current Ratio 30	1.6	•	0.9	1.4	2.3	2.2	1.8	2.5	1.8	2.0	1.3	1.6	•
Quick Ratio 31	1.0	•	0.1	1.1	1.1	0.8	0.9	1.3	1.1	1.1	0.6	1.1	•
Net Sales to Working Capital 32	4.5	•	•	2.1	3.5	4.6	5.7	4.8	5.0	3.9	13.1	3.9	•
Coverage Ratio 33	4.4	•	•	2.7	4.5	0.1	13.3	17.6	17.2	6.5	9.2	3.9	•
Total Asset Turnover 34	1.0	•	1.9	0.5	1.6	2.2	1.6	1.8	1.5	1.1	1.8	0.8	•
Inventory Turnover 35	5.5	•	2.1	1.5	3.0	4.3	5.2	6.5	5.1	5.0	10.0	5.3	•
Receivables Turnover 36	3.5	•	13.7	1.7	7.1	7.8	7.8	8.3	5.1	8.2	10.4	2.5	•
Total Liabilities to Net Worth 37	2.0	•	•	10.5	1.8	1.6	1.4	0.7	1.6	2.1	2.1	2.0	•
Current Assets to Working Capital 38	2.7	•	•	3.3	1.8	1.8	2.3	1.7	2.3	2.0	4.7	2.8	•
Current Liabilities to Working Capital 39	1.7	•	•	2.3	0.8	0.8	1.3	0.7	1.3	1.0	3.7	1.8	•
Working Capital to Net Sales 40	0.2	•	•	0.5	0.3	0.2	0.2	0.2	0.2	0.3	0.1	0.3	•
Inventory to Working Capital 41	0.6	•	•	0.7	0.9	1.1	1.0	0.6	0.8	0.6	1.1	0.5	•
Total Receipts to Cash Flow 42	7.2	•	11.6	2.4	10.7	17.4	8.3	6.3	11.4	6.4	15.0	6.1	•
Cost of Goods to Cash Flow 43	5.0	•	7.6	1.1	7.4	12.9	6.3	4.8	8.5	4.7	12.4	3.9	•
Cash Flow to Total Debt 44	0.2	•	0.1	0.2	0.2	0.2	0.3	0.7	0.2	0.3	0.2	0.2	•

Selected Financial Factors (in Percentages)

Debt Ratio 45	66.5	•	151.2	91.3	63.8	61.0	57.7	42.3	62.1	68.2	68.0	67.1	•
Return on Total Assets 46	9.7	•	•	2.0	6.7	0.1	9.7	15.9	13.0	14.8	3.4	10.1	•
Return on Equity Before Income Taxes 47	22.3	•	26.8	14.4	14.3	•	21.2	26.0	32.4	39.3	9.4	22.8	•
Return on Equity After Income Taxes 48	17.0	•	26.8	13.3	11.4	•	21.2	24.9	26.0	33.7	8.1	16.6	•
Profit Margin (Before Income Tax) 49	7.4	•	•	2.4	3.2	•	5.7	8.4	8.3	11.1	1.7	9.4	•
Profit Margin (After Income Tax) 50	5.7	•	•	2.2	2.6	•	5.7	8.0	6.7	9.5	1.4	6.9	•

Table II

Corporations with Net Income

OTHER TRANSPORTATION EQUIPMENT AND RAILROAD ROLLING STOCK

MONEY AMOUNTS AND SIZE OF ASSETS IN THOUSANDS OF DOLLARS

Item Description for Accounting Period 7/12 Through 6/13	Total	Zero Assets	Under 500	500 to 1,000	1,000 to 5,000	5,000 to 10,000	10,000 to 25,000	25,000 to 50,000	50,000 to 100,000	100,000 to 250,000	250,000 to 500,000	500,000 to 2,500,000	2,500,000 and over
Number of Enterprises 1	871	0	418	248	72	49	35	17	•	•	•	•	0

Revenues ($ in Thousands)

Net Sales 2	25490173	0	69558	78568	376709	835491	1026322	1296805	•	•	•	•	0
Interest 3	580594	0	0	226	39	10	6	4612	•	•	•	•	0
Rents 4	75921	0	0	0	0	0	0	0	•	•	•	•	0
Royalties 5	100707	0	0	0	0	0	0	0	•	•	•	•	0
Other Portfolio Income 6	230043	0	0	0	0	118	4	229	•	•	•	•	0
Other Receipts 7	230105	0	207	418	272	838	3974	30889	•	•	•	•	0
Total Receipts 8	26707543	0	69765	79212	377020	836457	1030306	1332535	•	•	•	•	0
Average Total Receipts 9	30663	•	167	319	5236	17071	29437	78384	•	•	•	•	•

Operating Costs/Operating Income (%)

Cost of Operations 10	68.1	•	77.3	45.6	70.5	77.8	76.5	76.2	•	•	•	•	•
Salaries and Wages 11	6.0	•	•	0.5	3.1	4.3	5.3	3.8	•	•	•	•	•
Taxes Paid 12	1.3	•	1.2	1.3	1.5	1.4	1.4	1.6	•	•	•	•	•
Interest Paid 13	2.2	•	•	1.4	0.6	0.3	0.4	0.2	•	•	•	•	•
Depreciation 14	3.8	•	•	1.9	2.0	0.5	1.2	0.5	•	•	•	•	•
Amortization and Depletion 15	0.6	•	•	•	0.5	•	0.0	0.5	•	•	•	•	•
Pensions and Other Deferred Comp. 16	1.6	•	•	•	0.3	0.1	0.2	0.1	•	•	•	•	•
Employee Benefits 17	1.7	•	•	0.3	1.4	0.1	0.4	0.7	•	•	•	•	•
Advertising 18	0.9	•	1.1	0.4	0.3	0.0	0.4	0.6	•	•	•	•	•
Other Expenses 19	8.4	•	12.7	43.9	7.0	2.3	5.5	8.2	•	•	•	•	•
Officers' Compensation 20	1.0	•	5.0	3.2	4.8	4.9	1.8	0.6	•	•	•	•	•
Operating Margin 21	4.5	•	2.8	1.5	8.1	8.1	7.0	7.0	•	•	•	•	•
Operating Margin Before Officers' Comp. 22	5.5	•	7.7	4.8	12.9	13.0	8.8	7.5	•	•	•	•	•

Selected Average Balance Sheet ($ in Thousands)

Net Receivables 23	8937	•	0	378	482	2419	2956	7458	•	•	•	•	•
Inventories 24	3274	•	23	50	1111	2621	4640	8889	•	•	•	•	•
Net Property, Plant and Equipment 25	6919	•	0	17	169	955	2660	3233	•	•	•	•	•
Total Assets 26	30163	•	0	593	1962	6177	16187	36456	•	•	•	•	•
Notes and Loans Payable 27	11648	•	0	197	444	1651	4888	3091	•	•	•	•	•
All Other Liabilities 28	7656	•	0	345	725	1077	2730	6822	•	•	•	•	•
Net Worth 29	10858	•	0	52	793	3448	8569	26543	•	•	•	•	•

Selected Financial Ratios (Times to 1)

Current Ratio 30	1.6	•	•	1.4	2.5	2.0	2.1	3.5	•	•	•	•	•
Quick Ratio 31	1.1	•	•	1.1	1.4	1.1	1.0	1.9	•	•	•	•	•
Net Sales to Working Capital 32	4.1	•	•	2.1	5.8	6.5	5.0	4.2	•	•	•	•	•
Coverage Ratio 33	5.2	•	•	2.7	14.7	24.7	20.7	49.5	•	•	•	•	•
Total Asset Turnover 34	1.0	•	•	0.5	2.7	2.8	1.8	2.1	•	•	•	•	•
Inventory Turnover 35	6.1	•	5.7	2.9	3.3	5.1	4.8	6.5	•	•	•	•	•
Receivables Turnover 36	3.3	•	19.5	1.7	8.0	5.5	9.5	8.9	•	•	•	•	•
Total Liabilities to Net Worth 37	1.8	•	•	10.5	1.5	0.8	0.9	0.4	•	•	•	•	•
Current Assets to Working Capital 38	2.6	•	•	3.3	1.7	2.0	1.9	1.4	•	•	•	•	•
Current Liabilities to Working Capital 39	1.6	•	•	2.3	0.7	1.0	0.9	0.4	•	•	•	•	•
Working Capital to Net Sales 40	0.2	•	•	0.5	0.2	0.2	0.2	0.2	•	•	•	•	•
Inventory to Working Capital 41	0.5	•	•	0.7	0.6	0.8	0.9	0.5	•	•	•	•	•
Total Receipts to Cash Flow 42	6.5	•	7.7	2.4	7.7	11.0	8.6	6.0	•	•	•	•	•
Cost of Goods to Cash Flow 43	4.4	•	5.9	1.1	5.4	8.6	6.6	4.6	•	•	•	•	•
Cash Flow to Total Debt 44	0.2	•	•	0.2	0.6	0.6	0.4	1.3	•	•	•	•	•

Selected Financial Factors (in Percentages)

Debt Ratio 45	64.0	•	•	91.3	59.6	44.2	47.1	27.2	•	•	•	•	•
Return on Total Assets 46	11.2	•	•	2.0	23.5	23.6	14.1	20.8	•	•	•	•	•
Return on Equity Before Income Taxes 47	25.1	•	•	14.4	54.1	40.6	25.4	28.0	•	•	•	•	•
Return on Equity After Income Taxes 48	19.6	•	•	13.3	47.5	36.4	25.3	26.8	•	•	•	•	•
Profit Margin (Before Income Tax) 49	9.3	•	3.1	2.4	8.2	8.2	7.4	9.7	•	•	•	•	•
Profit Margin (After Income Tax) 50	7.3	•	3.1	2.2	7.2	7.4	7.4	9.3	•	•	•	•	•

Table I

Corporations with and without Net Income

FURNITURE AND RELATED PRODUCT MANUFACTURING

MONEY AMOUNTS AND SIZE OF ASSETS IN THOUSANDS OF DOLLARS

Item Description for Accounting Period 7/12 Through 6/13	Total	Zero Assets	Under 500	500 to 1,000	1,000 to 5,000	5,000 to 10,000	10,000 to 25,000	25,000 to 50,000	50,000 to 100,000	100,000 to 250,000	250,000 to 500,000	500,000 to 2,500,000	2,500,000 and over
Number of Enterprises 1	12471	2705	•	787	965	106	164	68	18	24	6	•	•

Revenues ($ in Thousands)

Net Sales 2	60019734	2268592	•	2059097	6066424	1924240	4930051	5023964	2315746	5035260	4050591	•	•
Interest 3	48225	425	•	30	1303	195	1576	1561	515	4124	3406	•	•
Rents 4	35332	35	•	0	626	194	916	1938	78	7776	2396	•	•
Royalties 5	102836	37022	•	0	0	0	0	968	1596	223	0	•	•
Other Portfolio Income 6	129014	0	•	0	2727	546	4391	6053	633	7357	2526	•	•
Other Receipts 7	746803	11537	•	6705	10588	37926	14459	43734	14415	103250	2159	•	•
Total Receipts 8	61081944	2317611	•	2065832	6081668	1963101	4951393	5078218	2332983	5157990	4061078	•	•
Average Total Receipts 9	4898	857	•	2625	6302	18520	30191	74680	129610	214916	676846	•	•

Operating Costs/Operating Income (%)

Cost of Operations 10	66.1	57.4	•	67.2	69.3	69.7	70.7	75.4	69.5	70.9	62.5	•	•
Salaries and Wages 11	8.3	9.1	•	6.3	9.3	5.9	7.6	6.9	7.5	7.2	10.1	•	•
Taxes Paid 12	2.1	1.6	•	2.5	2.8	2.8	2.0	1.7	1.5	1.8	1.9	•	•
Interest Paid 13	1.1	3.4	•	0.4	0.6	0.5	0.6	0.7	0.8	0.9	0.2	•	•
Depreciation 14	1.5	0.7	•	0.9	1.1	1.0	1.4	1.4	1.2	2.0	2.1	•	•
Amortization and Depletion 15	0.4	2.1	•	0.1	0.0	0.1	0.1	0.5	0.2	0.4	0.2	•	•
Pensions and Other Deferred Comp. 16	0.5	0.2	•	0.3	0.1	0.3	0.3	0.3	0.5	0.3	0.5	•	•
Employee Benefits 17	1.9	0.4	•	2.5	1.2	2.5	1.8	1.6	2.2	2.1	1.4	•	•
Advertising 18	2.7	11.9	•	0.9	0.7	1.9	2.1	1.6	0.5	1.3	4.5	•	•
Other Expenses 19	12.5	18.1	•	9.8	10.7	8.9	9.2	9.3	10.5	9.0	11.9	•	•
Officers' Compensation 20	1.9	5.4	•	7.0	1.8	3.0	2.1	1.4	0.9	1.0	0.8	•	•
Operating Margin 21	1.1	•	•	2.1	2.4	3.4	1.9	•	4.9	3.2	3.9	•	•
Operating Margin Before Officers' Comp. 22	3.0	•	•	9.1	4.2	6.4	4.1	0.7	5.8	4.1	4.6	•	•

	Selected Average Balance Sheet ($ in Thousands)												
Net Receivables 23	495	0	•	274	594	2207	3368	8096	16085	23308	64356	•	•
Inventories 24	441	0	•	49	639	1787	4001	7279	21868	29330	51486	•	•
Net Property, Plant and Equipment 25	528	0	•	101	556	1993	3180	7747	14698	31817	84115	•	•
Total Assets 26	3137	0	•	601	2313	7482	14554	35452	66633	140480	331141	•	•
Notes and Loans Payable 27	949	0	•	186	928	2126	3997	11638	13394	28283	37396	•	•
All Other Liabilities 28	1053	0	•	264	692	1988	4028	9124	19628	51056	112256	•	•
Net Worth 29	1134	0	•	151	693	3368	6529	14690	33611	61142	181489	•	•

	Selected Financial Ratios (Times to 1)												
Current Ratio 30	1.6	•	•	1.3	2.1	2.2	1.9	1.7	2.0	2.6	2.5	•	•
Quick Ratio 31	0.8	•	•	1.1	1.1	1.4	0.9	0.9	1.1	1.2	1.7	•	•
Net Sales to Working Capital 32	9.5	•	•	22.3	7.3	6.5	6.2	8.5	5.9	4.6	5.9	•	•
Coverage Ratio 33	3.9	•	•	7.2	5.0	12.9	4.9	1.5	8.3	7.1	22.0	•	•
Total Asset Turnover 34	1.5	•	•	4.4	2.7	2.4	2.1	2.1	1.9	1.5	2.0	•	•
Inventory Turnover 35	7.2	•	•	35.6	6.8	7.1	5.3	7.7	4.1	5.1	8.2	•	•
Receivables Turnover 36	10.2	•	•	12.5	11.6	8.1	9.4	9.5	6.1	9.3	10.4	•	•
Total Liabilities to Net Worth 37	1.8	•	•	3.0	2.3	1.2	1.2	1.4	1.0	1.3	0.8	•	•
Current Assets to Working Capital 38	2.7	•	•	3.9	1.9	1.8	2.1	2.4	2.0	1.6	1.7	•	•
Current Liabilities to Working Capital 39	1.7	•	•	2.9	0.9	0.8	1.1	1.4	1.0	0.6	0.7	•	•
Working Capital to Net Sales 40	0.1	•	•	0.0	0.1	0.2	0.2	0.1	0.2	0.2	0.2	•	•
Inventory to Working Capital 41	0.9	•	•	0.5	0.8	0.6	0.9	0.9	0.8	0.7	0.5	•	•
Total Receipts to Cash Flow 42	8.0	13.5	•	13.0	9.9	8.9	11.1	12.8	7.0	8.2	7.3	•	•
Cost of Goods to Cash Flow 43	5.3	7.7	•	8.8	6.9	6.2	7.8	9.6	4.9	5.8	4.6	•	•
Cash Flow to Total Debt 44	0.3	•	•	0.4	0.4	0.5	0.3	0.3	0.6	0.3	0.6	•	•

	Selected Financial Factors (in Percentages)												
Debt Ratio 45	63.8	•	•	74.9	70.0	55.0	55.1	58.6	49.6	56.5	45.2	•	•
Return on Total Assets 46	6.4	•	•	12.4	8.8	14.3	6.2	2.3	12.4	9.7	8.8	•	•
Return on Equity Before Income Taxes 47	13.2	•	•	42.4	23.7	29.3	10.9	1.7	21.5	19.2	15.3	•	•
Return on Equity After Income Taxes 48	10.2	•	•	41.3	22.8	28.6	10.2	1.0	21.0	15.1	12.1	•	•
Profit Margin (Before Income Tax) 49	3.1	•	•	2.4	2.6	5.4	2.4	0.3	5.6	5.6	4.1	•	•
Profit Margin (After Income Tax) 50	2.4	•	•	2.4	2.5	5.3	2.2	0.2	5.5	4.4	3.2	•	•

Table II

Corporations with Net Income

FURNITURE AND RELATED PRODUCT MANUFACTURING

MONEY AMOUNTS AND SIZE OF ASSETS IN THOUSANDS OF DOLLARS

Item Description for Accounting Period 7/12 Through 6/13		Total	Zero Assets	Under 500	500 to 1,000	1,000 to 5,000	5,000 to 10,000	10,000 to 25,000	25,000 to 50,000	50,000 to 100,000	100,000 to 250,000	250,000 to 500,000	500,000 to 2,500,000	2,500,000 and over
Number of Enterprises	1	8119	1745	4757	676	673	82	102	39	13	16	6	11	0

Revenues ($ in Thousands)

Net Sales	2	46534483	233826	2096958	1894164	4745239	1537064	3193858	2784110	1704047	4086072	4050591	20208553	0
Interest	3	36740	113	75	24	755	168	405	1121	29	809	3406	29836	0
Rents	4	32770	0	0	0	13	0	601	1701	38	7511	2396	20511	0
Royalties	5	47481	0	0	0	0	0	0	908	0	71	0	46503	0
Other Portfolio Income	6	111594	0	0	0	263	357	2814	4460	252	2863	2526	98057	0
Other Receipts	7	614254	35	2685	35	4442	37218	12216	21403	6387	91937	2159	435737	0
Total Receipts	8	47377322	233974	2099718	1894223	4750712	1574807	3209894	2813703	1710753	4189263	4061078	20839197	0
Average Total Receipts	9	5835	134	441	2802	7059	19205	31470	72146	131596	261829	676846	1894472	•

Operating Costs/Operating Income (%)

Cost of Operations	10	64.9	59.5	43.1	67.4	67.8	68.3	70.1	72.2	68.4	70.7	62.5	63.1	•
Salaries and Wages	11	8.3	6.1	12.1	5.9	9.2	4.7	6.0	6.4	7.6	7.1	10.1	8.7	•
Taxes Paid	12	2.1	1.8	2.8	2.6	2.6	2.9	1.7	1.9	1.4	1.7	1.9	2.0	•
Interest Paid	13	0.9	1.1	1.0	0.2	0.5	0.2	0.3	0.6	0.3	0.6	0.2	1.4	•
Depreciation	14	1.5	0.8	2.2	0.9	1.1	0.7	1.2	1.2	1.0	1.9	2.1	1.5	•
Amortization and Depletion	15	0.3	1.4	0.2	0.1	0.0	0.1	0.1	0.3	0.2	0.3	0.2	0.5	•
Pensions and Other Deferred Comp.	16	0.5	0.0	0.8	0.3	0.2	0.4	0.4	0.1	0.3	0.3	0.5	0.8	•
Employee Benefits	17	1.9	0.0	1.7	2.6	1.2	3.0	1.4	1.6	2.2	2.1	1.4	2.2	•
Advertising	18	2.5	0.6	0.4	0.9	0.7	2.0	2.5	2.1	0.5	1.1	4.5	3.4	•
Other Expenses	19	11.7	13.8	21.5	9.3	10.5	8.3	8.9	8.1	8.9	7.2	11.9	13.6	•
Officers' Compensation	20	1.8	1.8	9.2	6.9	1.8	2.9	2.2	1.3	0.8	1.1	0.8	0.9	•
Operating Margin	21	3.7	13.2	4.9	2.8	4.6	6.5	5.3	4.2	8.4	5.9	3.9	1.9	•
Operating Margin Before Officers' Comp.	22	5.5	14.9	14.1	9.7	6.4	9.4	7.6	5.5	9.2	6.9	4.6	2.8	•

Selected Average Balance Sheet ($ in Thousands)

Net Receivables 23	569	0	14	301	658	2478	3572	6587	16357	27508	64356	185679	•
Inventories 24	449	0	26	52	644	1357	3637	6363	17354	36866	52106	123220	•
Net Property, Plant and Equipment 25	610	0	20	70	512	1676	2618	8167	12374	35584	84115	227822	•
Total Assets 26	3472	0	96	581	2419	7069	14117	34005	65403	142060	331141	1568356	•
Notes and Loans Payable 27	934	0	57	116	648	1452	2510	7836	11646	26817	37396	482578	•
All Other Liabilities 28	1112	0	26	265	737	1434	3173	7260	14442	39425	112256	546248	•
Net Worth 29	1426	0	13	200	1033	4184	8434	18909	39316	75817	181489	539531	•

Selected Financial Ratios (Times to 1)

Current Ratio 30	1.6	•	2.3	1.4	2.3	2.5	2.5	1.8	2.5	2.7	2.5	1.2	•
Quick Ratio 31	0.8	•	1.3	1.1	1.2	1.7	1.3	0.9	1.5	1.3	1.7	0.5	•
Net Sales to Working Capital 32	9.3	•	12.3	21.2	6.7	6.1	4.8	9.2	4.8	4.8	5.9	22.1	•
Coverage Ratio 33	7.8	13.4	6.1	15.9	11.0	38.6	22.5	9.7	33.2	14.2	22.0	5.1	•
Total Asset Turnover 34	1.7	•	4.6	4.8	2.9	2.7	2.2	2.1	2.0	1.8	2.0	1.2	•
Inventory Turnover 35	8.3	•	7.4	36.6	7.4	9.4	6.0	8.1	5.2	4.9	8.1	9.4	•
Receivables Turnover 36	11.6	•	24.9	12.0	13.0	8.3	10.2	10.8	7.8	8.4	21.0	11.5	•
Total Liabilities to Net Worth 37	1.4	•	6.5	1.9	1.3	0.7	0.7	0.8	0.7	0.9	0.8	1.9	•
Current Assets to Working Capital 38	2.7	•	1.8	3.6	1.8	1.7	1.7	2.3	1.7	1.6	1.7	7.0	•
Current Liabilities to Working Capital 39	1.7	•	0.8	2.6	0.8	0.7	0.7	1.3	0.7	0.6	0.7	6.0	•
Working Capital to Net Sales 40	0.1	•	0.1	0.0	0.1	0.2	0.2	0.1	0.2	0.2	0.2	0.0	•
Inventory to Working Capital 41	0.9	•	0.4	0.4	0.7	0.5	0.7	0.9	0.6	0.7	0.5	2.0	•
Total Receipts to Cash Flow 42	6.8	4.0	4.6	13.6	8.2	7.0	7.8	9.0	6.1	7.5	7.3	6.1	•
Cost of Goods to Cash Flow 43	4.4	2.4	2.0	9.2	5.6	4.8	5.4	6.5	4.2	5.3	4.6	3.9	•
Cash Flow to Total Debt 44	0.4	•	1.2	0.5	0.6	0.9	0.7	0.5	0.8	0.5	0.6	0.3	•

Selected Financial Factors (in Percentages)

Debt Ratio 45	58.9	•	86.7	65.6	57.3	40.8	40.3	44.4	39.9	46.6	45.2	65.6	•
Return on Total Assets 46	11.0	•	27.7	14.5	15.1	24.3	13.6	12.2	18.1	16.2	8.8	8.3	•
Return on Equity Before Income Taxes 47	23.3	•	173.6	39.6	32.2	39.9	21.7	19.7	29.2	28.2	15.3	19.5	•
Return on Equity After Income Taxes 48	19.7	•	172.7	38.7	31.3	39.2	20.7	18.7	28.5	23.2	12.1	14.6	•
Profit Margin (Before Income Tax) 49	5.8	13.2	5.1	2.8	4.7	8.9	5.8	5.2	8.7	8.4	4.1	5.7	•
Profit Margin (After Income Tax) 50	4.9	12.0	5.0	2.8	4.6	8.7	5.6	5.0	8.5	6.9	3.2	4.3	•

Table I

Corporations with and without Net Income

MEDICAL EQUIPMENT AND SUPPLIES

MONEY AMOUNTS AND SIZE OF ASSETS IN THOUSANDS OF DOLLARS

Item Description for Accounting Period 7/12 Through 6/13	Total	Zero Assets	Under 500	500 to 1,000	1,000 to 5,000	5,000 to 10,000	10,000 to 25,000	25,000 to 50,000	50,000 to 100,000	100,000 to 250,000	250,000 to 500,000	500,000 to 2,500,000	2,500,000 and over
Number of Enterprises **1**	9300	2035	5466	348	755	210	202	86	63	51	24	37	22

Revenues ($ in Thousands)													
Net Sales **2**	132141895	1830424	2205535	556969	4021014	2296374	3850432	3671578	4746659	6562305	4977355	27379054	70044196
Interest **3**	640972	8065	57	767	314	1050	4173	2909	5008	9604	169974	73329	365721
Rents **4**	71710	3153	0	0	0	763	398	147	64	3960	3464	50903	8860
Royalties **5**	3021634	3702	0	0	0	359	15569	1877	19482	14205	76461	166352	2723628
Other Portfolio Income **6**	1557404	45674	2182	0	13120	796	21799	5846	48014	20757	16317	437204	945695
Other Receipts **7**	3044539	35313	397	457	32605	18475	46707	51546	43097	53520	211598	135692	2415130
Total Receipts **8**	140478154	1926331	2208171	558193	4067053	2317817	3939078	3733903	4862324	6664351	5455169	28242534	76503230
Average Total Receipts **9**	15105	947	404	1604	5387	11037	19500	43417	77180	130674	227299	763312	3477420

Operating Costs/Operating Income (%)													
Cost of Operations **10**	51.8	54.0	23.9	57.8	56.7	55.2	48.7	58.0	55.3	53.0	45.0	51.3	52.3
Salaries and Wages **11**	16.3	20.2	23.4	15.9	12.0	12.1	18.5	16.6	18.7	15.4	18.3	15.9	16.1
Taxes Paid **12**	1.8	2.0	4.0	1.8	3.3	2.5	2.8	2.3	2.2	1.7	1.8	1.7	1.6
Interest Paid **13**	3.8	2.6	0.4	1.1	1.0	1.0	1.2	1.1	1.7	2.3	8.3	2.7	4.9
Depreciation **14**	2.8	1.8	2.1	0.4	1.6	1.7	2.2	2.0	2.4	2.5	3.5	2.8	3.0
Amortization and Depletion **15**	1.5	1.8	0.2	0.0	0.3	0.3	0.8	0.9	1.6	1.9	1.8	1.9	1.5
Pensions and Other Deferred Comp. **16**	0.8	2.8	0.2	•	0.3	0.1	0.4	0.4	0.3	0.4	0.5	0.6	1.0
Employee Benefits **17**	2.7	0.9	1.2	1.7	1.7	1.7	2.4	1.9	1.9	2.3	2.5	2.2	3.2
Advertising **18**	0.8	0.4	0.3	3.0	1.1	0.8	1.7	1.2	1.8	1.1	1.0	0.7	0.7
Other Expenses **19**	16.0	27.5	25.9	22.6	16.9	15.1	25.2	17.2	17.2	16.1	21.5	14.7	14.8
Officers' Compensation **20**	1.8	8.6	14.0	5.5	6.5	10.2	5.9	3.0	2.5	1.7	2.2	1.4	0.5
Operating Margin **21**	•	•	4.4	•	•	•	•	•	•	1.6	•	4.1	0.4
Operating Margin Before Officers' Comp. **22**	1.8	•	18.4	•	5.1	9.5	•	•	•	3.4	•	5.6	0.9

Selected Average Balance Sheet ($ in Thousands)

Net Receivables 23	2925	0	21	251	644	1463	3283	7455	12671	24699	35590	154558	739829
Inventories 24	2015	0	13	220	524	1346	2927	6594	10105	16786	33611	109166	473440
Net Property, Plant and Equipment 25	2255	0	25	14	299	1058	2064	4587	9938	18918	37509	140232	540398
Total Assets 26	24800	0	100	773	1963	6891	15956	35117	70384	162361	362675	1092608	7218614
Notes and Loans Payable 27	8954	0	47	38	861	2368	4337	6897	19423	42732	134366	332282	2793874
All Other Liabilities 28	7242	0	30	629	672	1750	3567	10912	19389	32529	76839	282032	2239983
Net Worth 29	8604	0	24	106	430	2773	8052	17308	31572	87100	151470	478293	2184757

Selected Financial Ratios (Times to 1)

Current Ratio 30	1.9	•	1.2	1.1	1.7	2.6	2.8	2.3	2.0	2.3	2.2	1.8	1.9
Quick Ratio 31	1.0	•	0.8	0.5	1.0	1.8	1.8	1.4	1.2	1.4	1.2	1.0	1.0
Net Sales to Working Capital 32	3.7	•	44.7	24.0	8.7	3.4	2.5	3.3	4.3	3.3	2.8	4.1	3.4
Coverage Ratio 33	3.1	•	11.6	•	0.8	1.2	•	•	•	2.5	1.4	4.2	3.4
Total Asset Turnover 34	0.6	•	4.0	2.1	2.7	1.6	1.2	1.2	1.1	0.8	0.6	0.7	0.4
Inventory Turnover 35	3.7	•	7.4	4.2	5.8	4.5	3.2	3.8	4.1	4.1	2.8	3.5	3.5
Receivables Turnover 36	5.0	•	19.7	4.8	7.1	8.4	6.4	6.0	6.3	5.5	4.5	4.8	4.5
Total Liabilities to Net Worth 37	1.9	•	3.2	6.3	3.6	1.5	1.0	1.0	1.2	0.9	1.4	1.3	2.3
Current Assets to Working Capital 38	2.1	•	5.4	10.2	2.5	1.6	1.5	1.8	2.0	1.8	1.8	2.2	2.2
Current Liabilities to Working Capital 39	1.1	•	4.4	9.2	1.5	0.6	0.5	0.8	1.0	0.8	0.8	1.2	1.2
Working Capital to Net Sales 40	0.3	•	0.0	0.0	0.1	0.3	0.4	0.3	0.2	0.3	0.4	0.2	0.3
Inventory to Working Capital 41	0.5	•	1.2	5.3	0.8	0.4	0.4	0.5	0.6	0.5	0.4	0.6	0.5
Total Receipts to Cash Flow 42	5.0	18.0	4.0	10.0	7.8	7.8	6.9	8.3	8.4	5.8	4.4	5.1	4.4
Cost of Goods to Cash Flow 43	2.6	9.7	1.0	5.8	4.4	4.3	3.4	4.8	4.6	3.1	2.0	2.6	2.3
Cash Flow to Total Debt 44	0.2	•	1.3	0.2	0.4	0.3	0.3	0.3	0.2	0.3	0.2	0.2	0.1

Selected Financial Factors (in Percentages)

Debt Ratio 45	65.3	•	76.3	86.3	78.1	59.8	49.5	50.7	55.1	46.4	58.2	56.2	69.7
Return on Total Assets 46	6.7	•	20.1	•	2.1	1.9	•	•	•	4.4	6.8	7.6	7.5
Return on Equity Before Income Taxes 47	13.0	•	77.5	•	•	0.9	•	•	•	4.9	4.8	13.2	17.6
Return on Equity After Income Taxes 48	8.4	•	75.1	•	•	•	•	•	•	2.6	1.5	9.2	12.2
Profit Margin (Before Income Tax) 49	7.9	•	4.5	•	•	0.2	•	•	•	3.3	3.5	8.5	12.1
Profit Margin (After Income Tax) 50	5.1	•	4.4	•	•	•	•	•	•	1.7	1.1	6.0	8.4

Table II

Corporations with Net Income

MEDICAL EQUIPMENT AND SUPPLIES

MONEY AMOUNTS AND SIZE OF ASSETS IN THOUSANDS OF DOLLARS

Item Description for Accounting Period 7/12 Through 6/13	Total	Zero Assets	Under 500	500 to 1,000	1,000 to 5,000	5,000 to 10,000	10,000 to 25,000	25,000 to 50,000	50,000 to 100,000	100,000 to 250,000	250,000 to 500,000	500,000 to 2,500,000	2,500,000 and over
Number of Enterprises 1	6219	943	4164	•	572	160	103	42	33	33	12	29	•

Revenues ($ in Thousands)

	Total	Zero Assets	Under 500	500 to 1,000	1,000 to 5,000	5,000 to 10,000	10,000 to 25,000	25,000 to 50,000	50,000 to 100,000	100,000 to 250,000	250,000 to 500,000	500,000 to 2,500,000	2,500,000 and over
Net Sales 2	115796574	604776	1715234	•	3502870	2111275	2752706	2172682	2931106	4930755	2824850	22848662	•
Interest 3	451516	788	52	•	163	485	1705	868	3484	7733	3726	67094	•
Rents 4	65489	0	0	•	0	763	398	98	0	3960	616	50794	•
Royalties 5	2871389	702	0	•	0	343	3969	371	4227	11142	64270	62737	•
Other Portfolio Income 6	1428832	35329	277	•	11161	305	19625	3055	1218	19096	604	392471	•
Other Receipts 7	2726314	23683	237	•	24018	16754	33801	20889	16482	51357	25601	99784	•
Total Receipts 8	123340114	665278	1715800	•	3538212	2129925	2812204	2197963	2956517	5024043	2919667	23521542	•
Average Total Receipts 9	19833	705	412	•	6186	13312	27303	52332	89591	152244	243306	811088	•

Operating Costs/Operating Income (%)

	Total	Zero Assets	Under 500	500 to 1,000	1,000 to 5,000	5,000 to 10,000	10,000 to 25,000	25,000 to 50,000	50,000 to 100,000	100,000 to 250,000	250,000 to 500,000	500,000 to 2,500,000	2,500,000 and over
Cost of Operations 10	51.9	39.7	18.1	•	56.3	56.3	47.0	55.8	58.5	54.7	37.3	52.6	•
Salaries and Wages 11	15.1	5.3	25.0	•	9.4	8.0	14.1	12.5	12.2	12.9	19.3	13.8	•
Taxes Paid 12	1.7	1.7	4.2	•	3.1	2.2	2.5	2.1	1.7	1.6	2.0	1.7	•
Interest Paid 13	3.4	1.4	0.4	•	0.6	0.7	0.4	0.7	0.8	1.4	0.9	2.0	•
Depreciation 14	2.8	1.6	1.5	•	1.5	1.5	1.7	1.5	2.3	2.1	3.2	2.9	•
Amortization and Depletion 15	1.3	1.2	0.0	•	0.0	0.1	0.3	0.7	1.0	1.4	1.2	1.2	•
Pensions and Other Deferred Comp. 16	0.8	0.8	0.2	•	0.3	0.1	0.5	0.6	0.3	0.5	0.6	0.7	•
Employee Benefits 17	2.7	0.7	1.3	•	1.4	1.5	2.0	1.6	1.7	2.2	2.8	2.1	•
Advertising 18	0.7	0.4	0.2	•	1.2	0.7	1.3	0.5	1.2	1.1	0.8	0.6	•
Other Expenses 19	14.8	26.0	23.4	•	13.6	10.0	16.5	12.5	12.8	14.5	19.4	14.5	•
Officers' Compensation 20	1.5	12.3	14.1	•	5.6	10.2	5.2	2.3	1.7	1.4	2.8	1.2	•
Operating Margin 21	3.3	9.0	11.5	•	6.9	8.9	8.7	9.1	5.9	6.3	9.8	6.5	•
Operating Margin Before Officers' Comp. 22	4.8	21.3	25.6	•	12.6	19.1	13.9	11.4	7.7	7.7	12.6	7.8	•

Selected Average Balance Sheet ($ in Thousands)

Net Receivables 23	3851	0	9	•	751	1459	4067	8098	15419	23512	36056	159418	•
Inventories 24	2643	0	12	•	575	1504	3317	7609	12673	20467	35870	119629	•
Net Property, Plant and Equipment 25	2999	0	21	•	288	1234	2395	3411	10916	19114	46453	153686	•
Total Assets 26	33057	0	79	•	1875	6911	16023	36091	71931	163497	367754	1092296	•
Notes and Loans Payable 27	11534	0	32	•	788	2411	2509	4871	14760	33974	59450	301556	•
All Other Liabilities 28	9818	0	10	•	583	1095	3143	11394	19901	34374	70005	281493	•
Net Worth 29	11705	0	37	•	504	3405	10372	19827	37270	95150	238298	509246	•

Selected Financial Ratios (Times to 1)

Current Ratio 30	1.9	•	1.3	•	2.0	3.8	2.6	2.4	2.5	2.8	2.3	1.8	•
Quick Ratio 31	1.0	•	0.8	•	1.2	2.4	1.6	1.3	1.4	1.7	1.2	1.0	•
Net Sales to Working Capital 32	3.6	•	55.5	•	7.8	3.5	3.7	3.6	3.7	3.4	2.6	4.2	•
Coverage Ratio 33	4.4	15.1	33.1	•	14.0	15.3	30.2	15.9	10.7	7.1	15.3	6.4	•
Total Asset Turnover 34	0.6	•	5.2	•	3.3	1.9	1.7	1.4	1.2	0.9	0.6	0.7	•
Inventory Turnover 35	3.7	•	6.3	•	6.0	4.9	3.8	3.8	4.1	4.0	2.4	3.5	•
Receivables Turnover 36	5.0	•	25.2	•	7.5	10.0	6.8	6.0	6.0	6.2	4.3	4.7	•
Total Liabilities to Net Worth 37	1.8	•	1.2	•	2.7	1.0	0.5	0.8	0.9	0.7	0.5	1.1	•
Current Assets to Working Capital 38	2.1	•	4.5	•	2.0	1.4	1.6	1.7	1.7	1.6	1.8	2.2	•
Current Liabilities to Working Capital 39	1.1	•	3.5	•	1.0	0.4	0.6	0.7	0.7	0.6	0.8	1.2	•
Working Capital to Net Sales 40	0.3	•	0.0	•	0.1	0.3	0.3	0.3	0.3	0.3	0.4	0.2	•
Inventory to Working Capital 41	0.5	•	1.2	•	0.7	0.4	0.5	0.5	0.5	0.5	0.3	0.6	•
Total Receipts to Cash Flow 42	4.5	2.3	3.3	•	5.6	5.7	4.1	4.8	5.7	4.8	3.3	4.6	•
Cost of Goods to Cash Flow 43	2.3	0.9	0.6	•	3.2	3.2	1.9	2.7	3.3	2.6	1.2	2.4	•
Cash Flow to Total Debt 44	0.2	•	2.9	•	0.8	0.7	1.2	0.7	0.5	0.5	0.6	0.3	•

Selected Financial Factors (in Percentages)

Debt Ratio 45	64.6	•	53.6	•	73.1	50.7	35.3	45.1	48.2	41.8	35.2	53.4	•
Return on Total Assets 46	8.4	•	62.3	•	28.0	20.0	18.8	15.7	10.1	8.8	9.2	9.2	•
Return on Equity Before Income Taxes 47	18.3	•	130.3	•	96.8	37.9	28.1	26.8	17.7	13.0	13.3	16.7	•
Return on Equity After Income Taxes 48	13.3	•	128.3	•	90.1	35.8	25.3	23.8	13.7	9.7	9.2	11.9	•
Profit Margin (Before Income Tax) 49	11.5	19.0	11.6	•	8.0	9.8	10.9	10.3	7.4	8.3	13.4	10.8	•
Profit Margin (After Income Tax) 50	8.4	18.4	11.4	•	7.4	9.2	9.8	9.1	5.8	6.2	9.3	7.7	•

Table I

Corporations with and without Net Income

OTHER MISCELLANEOUS MANUFACTURING

MONEY AMOUNTS AND SIZE OF ASSETS IN THOUSANDS OF DOLLARS

Item Description for Accounting Period 7/12 Through 6/13	Total	Zero Assets	Under 500	500 to 1,000	1,000 to 5,000	5,000 to 10,000	10,000 to 25,000	25,000 to 50,000	50,000 to 100,000	100,000 to 250,000	250,000 to 500,000	500,000 to 2,500,000	2,500,000 and over
Number of Enterprises 1	20526	1227	15971	581	1700	525	281	93	60	40	25	19	4

Revenues ($ in Thousands)

Net Sales 2	77242796	550557	6487550	705674	7321951	7503549	6909444	4756840	5846777	6182689	7204328	12993604	10779833
Interest 3	474119	223	148	404	972	3552	1284	2574	11568	11027	28904	28156	385305
Rents 4	21953	5160	0	0	1400	1562	2186	159	273	5484	2457	2242	1031
Royalties 5	1124087	27	10232	0	1440	93	298	5696	8611	27246	13856	73720	982868
Other Portfolio Income 6	417956	219	46707	351	23656	3564	7089	13393	21207	156708	34292	47556	63213
Other Receipts 7	885400	6681	146433	1486	16929	51724	52565	14174	43229	141512	187129	38665	184874
Total Receipts 8	80166311	562867	6691070	707915	7366348	7564044	6972866	4792836	5931665	6524666	7470966	13183943	12397124
Average Total Receipts 9	3906	459	419	1218	4333	14408	24814	51536	98861	163117	298839	693892	3099281

Operating Costs/Operating Income (%)

Cost of Operations 10	59.7	63.7	47.2	53.3	61.2	67.4	68.1	63.3	65.8	63.7	60.3	55.9	52.9
Salaries and Wages 11	10.3	9.7	10.5	13.9	9.6	8.8	8.1	11.1	8.8	9.0	12.0	11.1	12.2
Taxes Paid 12	2.0	1.6	2.9	2.6	2.3	1.7	2.0	1.8	1.8	2.2	1.7	2.0	2.0
Interest Paid 13	2.3	1.4	0.9	1.0	0.6	0.7	1.1	0.8	1.4	1.5	2.9	3.0	6.3
Depreciation 14	2.3	2.3	0.8	1.6	1.7	1.1	1.7	1.9	1.8	2.6	2.5	3.3	3.5
Amortization and Depletion 15	0.8	0.8	0.3	0.6	0.5	0.2	0.5	0.6	0.5	0.7	0.7	1.4	1.6
Pensions and Other Deferred Comp. 16	0.6	0.1	0.0	0.7	0.4	0.3	0.2	0.8	0.4	1.1	0.5	0.9	1.2
Employee Benefits 17	1.7	0.8	1.3	1.4	0.9	1.7	1.4	1.7	1.6	1.8	2.0	2.3	1.7
Advertising 18	1.9	0.8	1.9	1.3	1.0	0.7	1.0	1.6	2.3	2.3	2.1	1.6	3.7
Other Expenses 19	13.3	12.9	22.1	18.5	13.8	9.7	8.7	11.3	10.4	10.9	12.8	13.5	17.1
Officers' Compensation 20	2.5	2.5	7.2	3.3	5.1	3.5	2.4	2.0	2.1	1.0	1.0	1.1	1.1
Operating Margin 21	2.5	3.3	4.7	1.8	2.8	4.1	4.7	3.1	3.0	3.3	1.5	3.7	•
Operating Margin Before Officers' Comp. 22	5.0	5.8	11.9	5.1	8.0	7.7	7.1	5.1	5.1	4.3	2.5	4.8	•

Selected Average Balance Sheet ($ in Thousands)													
Net Receivables 23	545	0	21	99	593	1525	3748	5683	13739	23340	51758	120255	518401
Inventories 24	586	0	21	320	500	2161	4359	10067	14437	26951	55069	88378	590718
Net Property, Plant and Equipment 25	471	0	21	40	306	1159	2866	5561	11339	27959	55570	100922	438544
Total Assets 26	3473	0	104	599	2183	6719	16026	33983	68421	162660	336890	1024413	3970686
Notes and Loans Payable 27	1227	0	82	145	796	2251	5144	7253	21878	49312	118250	324561	1681470
All Other Liabilities 28	1045	0	64	227	676	1503	4043	10449	19437	37730	87559	352415	1172341
Net Worth 29	1202	0	-41	227	710	2965	6839	16281	27106	75618	131081	347437	1116874

Selected Financial Ratios (Times to 1)													
Current Ratio 30	1.9	•	1.1	2.1	1.9	2.1	1.8	2.3	1.9	2.0	2.0	2.0	1.9
Quick Ratio 31	1.0	•	0.6	0.8	1.2	1.1	1.0	1.0	1.0	1.0	1.0	1.1	0.8
Net Sales to Working Capital 32	4.8	•	57.2	5.2	5.8	5.8	5.2	4.2	4.8	4.0	4.1	4.0	3.6
Coverage Ratio 33	3.9	5.8	9.3	3.1	6.9	8.0	6.2	6.3	4.3	7.0	3.1	2.8	3.0
Total Asset Turnover 34	1.1	•	3.9	2.0	2.0	2.1	1.5	1.5	1.4	1.0	0.9	0.7	0.7
Inventory Turnover 35	3.8	•	9.2	2.0	5.3	4.5	3.8	3.2	4.4	3.7	3.2	4.3	2.4
Receivables Turnover 36	6.9	•	22.0	9.3	7.6	9.8	6.2	7.5	7.8	5.9	6.1	6.0	4.7
Total Liabilities to Net Worth 37	1.9	•	•	1.6	2.1	1.3	1.3	1.1	1.5	1.2	1.6	1.9	2.6
Current Assets to Working Capital 38	2.1	•	9.9	1.9	2.2	1.9	2.2	1.8	2.1	2.0	2.0	2.0	2.1
Current Liabilities to Working Capital 39	1.1	•	8.9	0.9	1.2	0.9	1.2	0.8	1.1	1.0	1.0	1.0	1.1
Working Capital to Net Sales 40	0.2	•	0.0	0.2	0.2	0.2	0.2	0.2	0.2	0.3	0.2	0.3	0.3
Inventory to Working Capital 41	0.8	•	3.5	0.9	0.7	0.9	0.9	0.8	0.8	0.7	0.8	0.5	0.8
Total Receipts to Cash Flow 42	6.1	6.3	4.1	6.5	7.4	8.4	8.3	7.9	7.9	6.2	6.6	6.1	4.2
Cost of Goods to Cash Flow 43	3.6	4.0	1.9	3.5	4.5	5.7	5.6	5.0	5.2	4.0	4.0	3.4	2.2
Cash Flow to Total Debt 44	0.3	•	0.7	0.5	0.4	0.5	0.3	0.4	0.3	0.3	0.2	0.2	0.2

Selected Financial Factors (in Percentages)													
Debt Ratio 45	65.4	•	139.8	62.1	67.5	55.9	57.3	52.1	60.4	53.5	61.1	66.1	71.9
Return on Total Assets 46	9.6	•	34.4	6.2	8.0	12.1	10.4	7.3	8.4	10.1	7.8	5.6	12.9
Return on Equity Before Income Taxes 47	20.7	•	•	11.2	20.9	23.9	20.3	12.9	16.2	18.6	13.6	10.7	30.5
Return on Equity After Income Taxes 48	16.7	•	•	9.4	20.0	22.4	19.1	10.5	12.4	16.4	11.6	7.3	19.9
Profit Margin (Before Income Tax) 49	6.6	6.6	7.9	2.1	3.4	5.0	5.7	4.1	4.5	9.1	6.2	5.4	12.6
Profit Margin (After Income Tax) 50	5.3	5.7	7.8	1.8	3.3	4.7	5.3	3.3	3.4	8.0	5.3	3.7	8.2

Table II

Corporations with Net Income

OTHER MISCELLANEOUS MANUFACTURING

MONEY AMOUNTS AND SIZE OF ASSETS IN THOUSANDS OF DOLLARS

Item Description for Accounting Period 7/12 Through 6/13	Total	Zero Assets	Under 500	500 to 1,000	1,000 to 5,000	5,000 to 10,000	10,000 to 25,000	25,000 to 50,000	50,000 to 100,000	100,000 to 250,000	250,000 to 500,000	500,000 to 2,500,000	2,500,000 and over
Number of Enterprises 1	12182	445	9488	•	1114	378	207	73	42	32	20	•	4

Revenues ($ in Thousands)

	Total	Zero Assets	Under 500	500 to 1,000	1,000 to 5,000	5,000 to 10,000	10,000 to 25,000	25,000 to 50,000	50,000 to 100,000	100,000 to 250,000	250,000 to 500,000	500,000 to 2,500,000	2,500,000 and over
Net Sales 2	66526968	444939	4885324	•	6309752	6091026	5341722	3690981	4588413	5500905	5996178	•	10779833
Interest 3	463781	219	34	•	281	1155	1036	1655	10758	10236	25436	•	385305
Rents 4	21218	5160	0	•	1335	1562	2186	91	177	5484	2074	•	1031
Royalties 5	1095480	27	0	•	1393	0	0	4805	7990	27246	4021	•	982868
Other Portfolio Income 6	360496	192	46707	•	727	2071	4040	4992	19931	153171	33386	•	63213
Other Receipts 7	844383	6516	126332	•	40048	46910	46575	11122	38979	141474	162877	•	184874
Total Receipts 8	69312326	457053	5058397	•	6353536	6142724	5395559	3713646	4666248	5838516	6223972	•	12397124
Average Total Receipts 9	5690	1027	533	•	5703	16251	26066	50872	111101	182454	311199	•	3099281

Operating Costs/Operating Income (%)

	Total	Zero Assets	Under 500	500 to 1,000	1,000 to 5,000	5,000 to 10,000	10,000 to 25,000	25,000 to 50,000	50,000 to 100,000	100,000 to 250,000	250,000 to 500,000	500,000 to 2,500,000	2,500,000 and over
Cost of Operations 10	58.8	67.2	45.5	•	60.4	65.7	67.9	63.3	64.8	61.6	61.1	•	52.9
Salaries and Wages 11	10.2	8.7	11.2	•	8.8	8.6	7.1	10.2	7.9	9.3	11.9	•	12.2
Taxes Paid 12	2.0	1.7	2.9	•	2.3	1.6	1.8	1.8	1.7	2.3	1.7	•	2.0
Interest Paid 13	2.2	1.0	0.5	•	0.4	0.7	0.7	0.7	1.1	1.4	2.3	•	6.3
Depreciation 14	2.2	1.5	0.5	•	1.3	1.0	1.3	2.0	1.7	2.4	2.4	•	3.5
Amortization and Depletion 15	0.7	0.5	0.2	•	0.1	0.1	0.2	0.3	0.4	0.6	0.6	•	1.6
Pensions and Other Deferred Comp. 16	0.7	0.1	0.0	•	0.4	0.3	0.3	0.7	0.4	1.2	0.6	•	1.2
Employee Benefits 17	1.7	0.9	1.3	•	0.8	1.9	1.3	2.0	1.3	1.8	1.7	•	1.7
Advertising 18	1.8	0.7	1.3	•	0.9	0.7	0.6	1.4	2.4	2.6	2.0	•	3.7
Other Expenses 19	12.6	10.1	19.1	•	12.2	8.8	8.0	10.5	9.7	10.7	11.6	•	17.1
Officers' Compensation 20	2.3	1.9	7.1	•	4.7	3.5	2.3	1.4	2.0	0.9	1.0	•	1.1
Operating Margin 21	4.9	5.6	10.3	•	7.9	7.2	8.5	5.8	6.6	5.3	3.1	•	•
Operating Margin Before Officers' Comp. 22	7.1	7.5	17.4	•	12.6	10.7	10.8	7.2	8.6	6.2	4.0	•	•

Selected Average Balance Sheet ($ in Thousands)

Net Receivables 23	793	0	27	•	719	1624	3479	5573	15145	24661	55460	•	518401
Inventories 24	797	0	16	•	590	2198	4517	10087	16225	25462	48997	•	590718
Net Property, Plant and Equipment 25	660	0	7	•	290	1217	2628	5470	11169	30818	58648	•	438544
Total Assets 26	4936	0	95	•	2366	6684	15455	33509	69660	167846	334379	•	3970686
Notes and Loans Payable 27	1643	0	53	•	475	2020	4649	7253	19490	43190	98021	•	1681470
All Other Liabilities 28	1397	0	49	•	643	1459	3271	11120	20550	38019	87342	•	1172341
Net Worth 29	1896	0	-7	•	1248	3205	7535	15136	29620	86636	149017	•	1116874

Selected Financial Ratios (Times to 1)

Current Ratio 30	2.1	•	1.7	•	2.8	2.1	2.1	2.1	2.0	2.3	2.0	•	1.9
Quick Ratio 31	1.1	•	1.2	•	1.8	1.0	1.1	0.9	1.0	1.1	1.0	•	0.8
Net Sales to Working Capital 32	4.6	•	16.8	•	4.7	6.1	4.6	4.3	4.8	4.0	4.4	•	3.6
Coverage Ratio 33	5.2	10.3	27.7	•	25.3	13.4	14.3	10.8	8.7	9.4	4.5	•	3.0
Total Asset Turnover 34	1.1	•	5.4	•	2.4	2.4	1.7	1.5	1.6	1.0	0.9	•	0.7
Inventory Turnover 35	4.0	•	14.5	•	5.8	4.8	3.9	3.2	4.4	4.2	3.7	•	2.4
Receivables Turnover 36	7.2	•	25.5	•	7.6	11.2	6.9	7.8	8.0	7.9	6.2	•	4.7
Total Liabilities to Net Worth 37	1.6	•	•	•	0.9	1.1	1.1	1.2	1.4	0.9	1.2	•	2.6
Current Assets to Working Capital 38	1.9	•	2.4	•	1.6	1.9	1.9	1.9	2.0	1.8	2.0	•	2.1
Current Liabilities to Working Capital 39	0.9	•	1.4	•	0.6	0.9	0.9	0.9	1.0	0.8	1.0	•	1.1
Working Capital to Net Sales 40	0.2	•	0.1	•	0.2	0.2	0.2	0.2	0.2	0.3	0.2	•	0.3
Inventory to Working Capital 41	0.7	•	0.6	•	0.5	0.9	0.8	0.9	0.8	0.7	0.8	•	0.8
Total Receipts to Cash Flow 42	5.4	6.0	3.5	•	5.7	7.0	6.5	6.8	6.3	5.5	6.1	•	4.2
Cost of Goods to Cash Flow 43	3.2	4.0	1.6	•	3.4	4.6	4.4	4.3	4.1	3.4	3.8	•	2.2
Cash Flow to Total Debt 44	0.3	•	1.4	•	0.9	0.7	0.5	0.4	0.4	0.4	0.3	•	0.2

Selected Financial Factors (in Percentages)

Debt Ratio 45	61.6	•	107.3	•	47.3	52.0	51.2	54.8	57.5	48.4	55.4	•	71.9
Return on Total Assets 46	12.9	•	77.9	•	21.3	21.0	17.0	11.3	14.8	13.4	9.3	•	12.9
Return on Equity Before Income Taxes 47	27.0	•	•	•	38.9	40.5	32.5	22.7	30.7	23.2	16.2	•	30.5
Return on Equity After Income Taxes 48	22.7	•	•	•	38.1	38.6	31.0	19.4	25.8	20.9	14.0	•	19.9
Profit Margin (Before Income Tax) 49	9.4	9.5	13.8	•	8.6	8.1	9.5	6.8	8.3	11.7	8.1	•	12.6
Profit Margin (After Income Tax) 50	7.9	8.4	13.7	•	8.4	7.7	9.1	5.8	7.0	10.5	6.9	•	8.2

Table I

Corporations with and without Net Income

MOTOR VEHICLE AND MOTOR VEHICLE PARTS AND SUPPLIES

MONEY AMOUNTS AND SIZE OF ASSETS IN THOUSANDS OF DOLLARS

Item Description for Accounting Period 7/12 Through 6/13	Total	Zero Assets	Under 500	500 to 1,000	1,000 to 5,000	5,000 to 10,000	10,000 to 25,000	25,000 to 50,000	50,000 to 100,000	100,000 to 250,000	250,000 to 500,000	500,000 to 2,500,000	2,500,000 and over
Number of Enterprises **1**	20243	1352	12554	2339	2979	438	297	150	48	40	19	18	8

Revenues ($ in Thousands)

Net Sales **2**	264105179	899644	10474114	5195160	21776563	7151504	10959128	14193861	6993337	11331749	17454714	46664565	111010839
Interest **3**	2504517	38	2091	566	7471	12593	6901	3891	1567	7104	11395	126400	2324500
Rents **4**	5701087	0	977	385	436	2130	2582	4790	6864	9158	465	56592	5616707
Royalties **5**	58196	0	0	2746	2777	2868	271	0	0	321	240	10006	38968
Other Portfolio Income **6**	981431	6372	2600	48	20812	42470	10712	25101	53871	25259	12740	49023	732424
Other Receipts **7**	1650217	2360	33329	17946	94168	29584	74887	127985	63354	131470	73197	415752	586184
Total Receipts **8**	275000627	908414	10513111	5216851	21902227	7241149	11054481	14355628	7118993	11505061	17552751	47322338	120309622
Average Total Receipts **9**	13585	672	837	2230	7352	16532	37220	95704	148312	287627	923829	2629019	15038703

Operating Costs/Operating Income (%)

Cost of Operations **10**	83.6	79.5	86.0	79.4	80.2	77.7	80.1	81.5	78.7	81.7	86.6	86.8	84.1
Salaries and Wages **11**	3.9	6.0	4.5	6.7	5.0	7.5	6.1	6.0	6.5	5.5	3.2	3.5	2.8
Taxes Paid **12**	0.8	0.8	0.9	1.2	1.2	1.4	1.1	1.2	1.5	1.1	0.5	0.8	0.5
Interest Paid **13**	0.9	0.7	0.3	0.5	0.3	0.6	0.5	0.4	0.6	1.0	0.7	0.6	1.3
Depreciation **14**	3.6	0.4	0.3	0.4	0.4	0.7	1.0	1.0	1.0	1.3	0.6	0.8	7.5
Amortization and Depletion **15**	0.1	0.0	0.0	0.1	0.0	0.1	0.1	0.1	0.2	0.3	0.1	0.1	0.1
Pensions and Other Deferred Comp. **16**	0.2	0.1	0.0	0.1	0.2	0.3	0.2	0.1	0.1	0.2	0.1	0.1	0.3
Employee Benefits **17**	0.5	1.3	0.2	0.5	0.5	0.7	0.6	0.8	0.7	0.7	0.5	0.5	0.4
Advertising **18**	1.5	0.1	0.2	0.5	0.5	0.6	0.4	0.6	0.6	0.6	1.1	1.9	2.2
Other Expenses **19**	5.4	7.9	6.0	7.3	7.3	7.3	6.1	5.4	7.9	5.0	4.1	4.5	5.1
Officers' Compensation **20**	0.7	0.8	2.0	2.4	2.3	1.9	1.3	1.1	1.1	0.6	0.3	0.3	0.1
Operating Margin **21**	•	2.4	•	0.8	2.2	1.3	2.4	1.8	1.1	2.1	2.2	0.1	•
Operating Margin Before Officers' Comp. **22**	•	3.2	1.6	3.2	4.4	3.1	3.7	2.9	2.2	2.7	2.5	0.4	•

Selected Average Balance Sheet ($ in Thousands)

Net Receivables 23	3210	0	27	106	616	1557	4250	7903	12803	24801	67862	349009	6283279
Inventories 24	1512	0	36	350	846	2946	7361	14197	26350	53192	115787	417744	1011910
Net Property, Plant and Equipment 25	2262	0	10	92	174	1077	1981	4264	9490	19923	44874	121916	4866603
Total Assets 26	9284	0	104	710	2158	6875	15938	35513	69127	156248	357064	1250706	15825228
Notes and Loans Payable 27	3213	0	49	201	476	1974	4556	11226	21713	64547	86531	474924	5604181
All Other Liabilities 28	4200	0	43	266	802	2370	5683	11521	21214	44953	161131	501452	7764764
Net Worth 29	1870	0	13	243	879	2531	5698	12766	26199	46747	109402	274330	2456282

Selected Financial Ratios (Times to 1)

Current Ratio 30	1.4	•	1.7	1.9	1.9	1.9	1.8	1.7	1.5	1.4	1.6	1.4	1.3
Quick Ratio 31	0.9	•	0.9	0.8	0.9	0.8	0.8	0.6	0.5	0.5	0.6	0.7	1.0
Net Sales to Working Capital 32	8.2	•	24.1	7.8	8.1	6.4	6.4	8.2	8.5	10.5	11.4	9.7	7.1
Coverage Ratio 33	4.3	5.9	0.9	3.6	10.0	5.0	7.2	8.6	6.0	4.6	4.9	3.5	3.8
Total Asset Turnover 34	1.4	•	8.0	3.1	3.4	2.4	2.3	2.7	2.1	1.8	2.6	2.1	0.9
Inventory Turnover 35	7.2	•	20.1	5.0	6.9	4.3	4.0	5.4	4.3	4.3	6.9	5.4	11.5
Receivables Turnover 36	4.3	•	32.7	18.0	13.8	9.4	8.4	12.3	11.0	11.1	14.8	8.1	2.3
Total Liabilities to Net Worth 37	4.0	•	7.0	1.9	1.5	1.7	1.8	1.8	1.6	2.3	2.3	3.6	5.4
Current Assets to Working Capital 38	3.5	•	2.4	2.1	2.1	2.2	2.3	2.4	2.9	3.7	2.8	3.2	4.4
Current Liabilities to Working Capital 39	2.5	•	1.4	1.1	1.1	1.2	1.3	1.4	1.9	2.7	1.8	2.2	3.4
Working Capital to Net Sales 40	0.1	•	0.0	0.1	0.1	0.2	0.2	0.1	0.1	0.1	0.1	0.1	0.1
Inventory to Working Capital 41	1.0	•	0.9	1.2	1.0	1.2	1.2	1.3	1.7	2.0	1.6	1.4	0.6
Total Receipts to Cash Flow 42	14.0	11.2	24.0	14.7	12.7	13.8	12.9	14.8	10.8	13.9	16.6	19.9	12.1
Cost of Goods to Cash Flow 43	11.7	8.9	20.7	11.7	10.2	10.7	10.4	12.1	8.5	11.4	14.3	17.3	10.2
Cash Flow to Total Debt 44	0.1	•	0.4	0.3	0.4	0.3	0.3	0.3	0.3	0.2	0.2	0.1	0.1

Selected Financial Factors (in Percentages)

Debt Ratio 45	79.9	•	87.5	65.7	59.3	63.2	64.2	64.1	62.1	70.1	69.4	78.1	84.5
Return on Total Assets 46	5.4	•	2.0	5.3	10.5	7.5	8.8	8.9	7.4	8.3	9.0	4.5	4.5
Return on Equity Before Income Taxes 47	20.4	•	•	11.2	23.1	16.2	21.1	21.9	16.2	21.8	23.4	14.7	21.6
Return on Equity After Income Taxes 48	17.1	•	•	10.3	21.1	14.4	18.7	20.4	14.4	16.4	20.2	10.6	18.0
Profit Margin (Before Income Tax) 49	2.9	3.4	•	1.2	2.8	2.5	3.3	3.0	2.9	3.6	2.8	1.6	3.8
Profit Margin (After Income Tax) 50	2.4	3.3	•	1.1	2.5	2.2	2.9	2.7	2.6	2.7	2.4	1.1	3.2

167

Table II
Corporations with Net Income

MOTOR VEHICLE AND MOTOR VEHICLE PARTS AND SUPPLIES

MONEY AMOUNTS AND SIZE OF ASSETS IN THOUSANDS OF DOLLARS

Item Description for Accounting Period 7/12 Through 6/13		Total	Zero Assets	Under 500	500 to 1,000	1,000 to 5,000	5,000 to 10,000	10,000 to 25,000	25,000 to 50,000	50,000 to 100,000	100,000 to 250,000	250,000 to 500,000	500,000 to 2,500,000	2,500,000 and over
Number of Enterprises	1	13124	770	7347	1548	2578	369	270	133	38	34	14	15	8

Revenues ($ in Thousands)

		Total	Zero Assets	Under 500	500 to 1,000	1,000 to 5,000	5,000 to 10,000	10,000 to 25,000	25,000 to 50,000	50,000 to 100,000	100,000 to 250,000	250,000 to 500,000	500,000 to 2,500,000	2,500,000 and over
Net Sales	2	239128701	806654	4789521	4201362	19658722	6069456	9987326	13153139	5709351	10273643	16202284	37266404	111010839
Interest	3	2492384	11	2001	103	6836	10176	6265	3754	1479	3269	7654	126338	2324500
Rents	4	5694332	0	977	385	350	1541	2582	4686	6689	3427	430	56558	5616707
Royalties	5	57896	0	0	2746	2777	2808	271	0	0	321	0	10006	38968
Other Portfolio Income	6	967392	6372	2038	0	20284	42219	8331	24878	53032	16195	12598	49023	732424
Other Receipts	7	1528813	1666	31542	6767	75367	22543	65831	120545	57768	120870	52199	387526	586184
Total Receipts	8	249869518	814703	4826079	4211363	19764336	6148743	10070606	13307002	5828319	10417725	16275165	37895855	120309622
Average Total Receipts	9	19039	1058	657	2721	7667	16663	37299	100053	153377	306404	1162512	2526390	15038703

Operating Costs/Operating Income (%)

		Total	Zero Assets	Under 500	500 to 1,000	1,000 to 5,000	5,000 to 10,000	10,000 to 25,000	25,000 to 50,000	50,000 to 100,000	100,000 to 250,000	250,000 to 500,000	500,000 to 2,500,000	2,500,000 and over
Cost of Operations	10	83.3	79.3	79.8	79.5	79.4	76.9	79.4	81.4	79.8	82.6	87.0	86.2	84.1
Salaries and Wages	11	3.9	6.0	6.1	6.2	5.1	7.3	6.0	5.9	6.0	5.3	2.9	4.0	2.8
Taxes Paid	12	0.8	0.8	1.0	1.1	1.2	1.4	1.1	1.3	1.6	1.1	0.5	0.9	0.5
Interest Paid	13	0.9	0.7	0.4	0.3	0.3	0.6	0.5	0.4	0.5	0.8	0.4	0.7	1.3
Depreciation	14	3.9	0.4	0.4	0.3	0.4	0.7	1.0	1.0	0.8	1.0	0.4	0.9	7.5
Amortization and Depletion	15	0.1	0.0	0.0	0.1	0.0	0.0	0.0	0.1	0.1	0.3	0.1	0.1	0.1
Pensions and Other Deferred Comp.	16	0.2	0.1	0.0	0.1	0.2	0.3	0.2	0.2	0.1	0.2	0.1	0.1	0.3
Employee Benefits	17	0.5	1.4	0.2	0.4	0.5	0.7	0.6	0.8	0.6	0.7	0.5	0.5	0.4
Advertising	18	1.4	0.1	0.3	0.5	0.5	0.5	0.4	0.6	0.4	0.6	1.2	1.3	2.2
Other Expenses	19	5.3	6.4	8.0	7.1	7.3	6.9	6.2	5.1	7.1	4.2	3.7	4.2	5.1
Officers' Compensation	20	0.6	0.7	2.0	2.0	2.3	2.0	1.3	0.9	1.0	0.6	0.3	0.3	0.1
Operating Margin	21	•	4.0	1.7	2.4	2.9	2.6	3.2	2.3	2.0	2.7	2.9	0.7	•
Operating Margin Before Officers' Comp.	22	•	4.7	3.7	4.4	5.2	4.6	4.5	3.2	3.0	3.3	3.3	1.1	•

		Selected Average Balance Sheet ($ in Thousands)										
Net Receivables 23	4776	0	24	108	643	1632	4184	8024	13056	24846	72935	350193	6283279
Inventories 24	1817	0	28	315	798	2817	7216	13819	27067	54593	128117	384330	728497
Net Property, Plant and Equipment 25	3407	0	6	124	182	1197	1941	4330	8745	16817	40769	137406	4866603
Total Assets 26	13520	0	114	760	2195	6972	15714	35295	68688	154706	359439	1250352	15825228
Notes and Loans Payable 27	4603	0	40	168	420	1776	4209	10442	21450	60195	83040	449218	5604181
All Other Liabilities 28	6077	0	34	289	795	2373	5401	11490	19973	42693	147526	450086	7764764
Net Worth 29	2840	0	40	304	980	2823	6105	13363	27265	51818	128873	351048	2456282

		Selected Financial Ratios (Times to 1)										
Current Ratio 30	1.4	•	2.6	1.8	2.0	2.0	1.8	1.6	1.6	1.5	1.7	1.5	1.3
Quick Ratio 31	0.9	•	1.2	0.9	1.0	0.9	0.8	0.6	0.5	0.6	0.6	0.8	1.0
Net Sales to Working Capital 32	7.8	•	11.7	9.8	8.0	6.0	6.3	9.2	8.0	8.7	11.1	8.6	7.1
Coverage Ratio 33	4.9	7.9	7.7	9.0	13.3	7.5	9.5	10.2	9.1	6.4	10.0	4.3	3.8
Total Asset Turnover 34	1.3	•	5.7	3.6	3.5	2.4	2.4	2.8	2.2	2.0	3.2	2.0	0.9
Inventory Turnover 35	8.4	•	18.5	6.9	7.6	4.5	4.1	5.8	4.4	4.6	7.9	5.6	16.0
Receivables Turnover 36	6.0	•	31.3	21.6	14.1	10.1	8.6	12.7	11.2	11.3	17.4	8.2	3.9
Total Liabilities to Net Worth 37	3.8	•	1.8	1.5	1.2	1.5	1.6	1.6	1.5	2.0	1.8	2.6	5.4
Current Assets to Working Capital 38	3.5	•	1.6	2.2	2.0	2.0	2.2	2.6	2.7	2.9	2.5	3.0	4.4
Current Liabilities to Working Capital 39	2.5	•	0.6	1.2	1.0	1.0	1.2	1.6	1.7	1.9	1.5	2.0	3.4
Working Capital to Net Sales 40	0.1	•	0.1	0.1	0.1	0.2	0.2	0.1	0.1	0.1	0.1	0.1	0.1
Inventory to Working Capital 41	0.9	•	0.7	1.1	0.9	1.1	1.2	1.4	1.5	1.5	1.5	1.3	0.6
Total Receipts to Cash Flow 42	13.1	11.1	12.1	12.5	11.7	12.2	11.7	14.2	10.1	14.1	16.0	18.3	12.1
Cost of Goods to Cash Flow 43	10.9	8.8	9.6	10.0	9.3	9.4	9.3	11.5	8.1	11.6	13.9	15.8	10.2
Cash Flow to Total Debt 44	0.1	•	0.7	0.5	0.5	0.3	0.3	0.3	0.4	0.2	0.3	0.2	0.1

		Selected Financial Factors (in Percentages)										
Debt Ratio 45	79.0	•	64.7	60.0	55.3	59.5	61.2	62.1	60.3	66.5	64.1	71.9	84.5
Return on Total Assets 46	6.0	•	16.1	10.4	13.1	10.6	10.6	10.9	10.0	9.6	12.2	6.3	4.5
Return on Equity Before Income Taxes 47	22.6	•	39.6	23.2	27.0	22.7	24.4	25.9	22.5	24.1	30.5	17.2	21.6
Return on Equity After Income Taxes 48	19.2	•	38.4	22.1	24.9	20.7	21.9	24.2	20.4	18.3	26.8	13.4	18.0
Profit Margin (Before Income Tax) 49	3.5	5.0	2.4	2.6	3.5	3.9	4.0	3.5	4.1	4.1	3.4	2.4	3.8
Profit Margin (After Income Tax) 50	3.0	4.9	2.4	2.5	3.2	3.6	3.6	3.3	3.7	3.1	3.0	1.9	3.2

Table I

Corporations with and without Net Income

LUMBER AND OTHER CONSTRUCTION MATERIALS

MONEY AMOUNTS AND SIZE OF ASSETS IN THOUSANDS OF DOLLARS

Item Description for Accounting Period 7/12 Through 6/13	Total	Zero Assets	Under 500	500 to 1,000	1,000 to 5,000	5,000 to 10,000	10,000 to 25,000	25,000 to 50,000	50,000 to 100,000	100,000 to 250,000	250,000 to 500,000	500,000 to 2,500,000	2,500,000 and over
Number of Enterprises **1**	14306	1609	5992	1394	3978	769	397	87	49	17	6	7	0

Revenues ($ in Thousands)													
Net Sales **2**	104320490	635238	4018984	3708764	23390990	19817029	14940205	7899022	7876165	6264239	3058621	12711233	0
Interest **3**	46551	468	153	605	9400	4718	4645	4223	1142	5514	6160	9522	0
Rents **4**	42254	0	0	12	16214	1417	6953	1956	290	1274	439	13698	0
Royalties **5**	14	0	0	0	0	14	1	0	0	0	0	0	0
Other Portfolio Income **6**	175180	455	55013	1692	30783	27693	13791	7777	2677	9253	12911	13137	0
Other Receipts **7**	491927	405	70168	288	164424	29476	104179	32752	37915	23825	5342	23152	0
Total Receipts **8**	105076416	636566	4144318	3711361	23611811	19880347	15069774	7945730	7918189	6304105	3083473	12770742	0
Average Total Receipts **9**	7345	396	692	2662	5936	25852	37959	91330	161596	370830	513912	1824392	•

Operating Costs/Operating Income (%)													
Cost of Operations **10**	79.0	74.5	56.3	72.8	75.5	84.2	80.5	82.8	81.3	84.3	72.5	79.7	•
Salaries and Wages **11**	7.0	3.8	9.8	9.5	7.7	5.5	7.3	6.1	7.1	5.3	11.0	6.8	•
Taxes Paid **12**	1.2	1.0	1.7	2.1	1.7	0.8	1.2	0.9	1.0	0.9	1.8	1.0	•
Interest Paid **13**	0.6	0.6	0.4	0.4	0.6	0.4	0.4	0.6	0.4	0.5	0.8	1.5	•
Depreciation **14**	0.8	0.2	0.5	0.8	0.9	0.4	0.7	0.7	0.8	1.2	1.2	0.9	•
Amortization and Depletion **15**	0.1	0.6	0.2	0.0	0.0	0.1	0.0	0.1	0.1	0.2	0.2	0.6	•
Pensions and Other Deferred Comp. **16**	0.2	0.1	0.3	0.2	0.3	0.1	0.2	0.1	0.2	0.2	0.0	0.2	•
Employee Benefits **17**	0.6	0.3	0.5	0.2	0.7	0.5	0.8	0.6	0.7	0.7	0.6	0.5	•
Advertising **18**	0.3	0.1	1.9	0.9	0.2	0.1	0.2	0.2	0.2	0.2	0.2	0.1	•
Other Expenses **19**	7.2	23.5	19.5	8.0	8.4	5.5	5.5	5.9	6.4	5.5	8.6	6.3	•
Officers' Compensation **20**	1.6	12.7	3.8	2.8	2.5	1.3	1.4	0.9	0.7	0.5	1.3	0.4	•
Operating Margin **21**	1.5	•	5.0	2.5	1.7	1.0	1.8	1.1	1.2	0.5	1.7	1.9	•
Operating Margin Before Officers' Comp. **22**	3.1	•	8.8	5.2	4.2	2.3	3.2	2.0	1.9	1.0	3.0	2.3	•

	Selected Average Balance Sheet ($ in Thousands)												
Net Receivables 23	759	0	26	183	700	2650	4171	9597	17690	39735	64018	172278	•
Inventories 24	799	0	47	218	714	2442	4457	12326	20181	40219	72722	166954	•
Net Property, Plant and Equipment 25	450	0	14	97	408	921	2224	4355	9193	30175	69290	178843	•
Total Assets 26	2777	0	148	708	2308	7579	14851	35469	63418	159242	311110	883082	•
Notes and Loans Payable 27	899	0	75	270	744	2682	3734	15586	15187	55872	69302	293713	•
All Other Liabilities 28	793	0	54	225	621	2184	3253	9680	17446	50582	85933	313599	•
Net Worth 29	1086	0	20	213	943	2713	7864	10203	30785	52788	155875	275770	•

	Selected Financial Ratios (Times to 1)												
Current Ratio 30	2.0	•	1.9	2.3	2.1	1.7	2.4	1.7	2.0	1.6	1.6	2.1	•
Quick Ratio 31	1.0	•	1.0	1.5	1.1	0.9	1.2	0.7	0.9	0.8	0.8	0.9	•
Net Sales to Working Capital 32	7.7	•	13.8	8.0	6.3	9.8	5.7	8.9	7.1	9.8	8.9	8.3	•
Coverage Ratio 33	4.7	•	20.1	8.2	5.8	4.3	7.5	3.9	5.5	3.5	4.4	2.7	•
Total Asset Turnover 34	2.6	•	4.5	3.8	2.5	3.4	2.5	2.6	2.5	2.3	1.6	2.1	•
Inventory Turnover 35	7.2	•	8.0	8.9	6.2	8.9	6.8	6.1	6.5	7.7	5.1	8.7	•
Receivables Turnover 36	9.9	•	21.1	16.3	8.3	10.5	8.9	9.9	9.6	10.0	7.1	12.1	•
Total Liabilities to Net Worth 37	1.6	•	6.6	2.3	1.4	1.8	0.9	2.5	1.1	2.0	1.0	2.2	•
Current Assets to Working Capital 38	2.0	•	2.1	1.8	1.9	2.3	1.7	2.5	2.0	2.6	2.6	1.9	•
Current Liabilities to Working Capital 39	1.0	•	1.1	0.8	0.9	1.3	0.7	1.5	1.0	1.6	1.6	0.9	•
Working Capital to Net Sales 40	0.1	•	0.1	0.1	0.2	0.1	0.2	0.1	0.1	0.1	0.1	0.1	•
Inventory to Working Capital 41	0.9	•	1.0	0.6	0.8	0.9	0.7	1.3	0.9	1.2	1.1	0.9	•
Total Receipts to Cash Flow 42	14.0	38.6	4.7	12.8	11.6	19.8	16.2	17.9	16.4	20.8	12.7	14.5	•
Cost of Goods to Cash Flow 43	11.1	28.7	2.6	9.3	8.8	16.7	13.0	14.8	13.3	17.6	9.2	11.6	•
Cash Flow to Total Debt 44	0.3	•	1.1	0.4	0.4	0.3	0.3	0.2	0.3	0.2	0.3	0.2	•

	Selected Financial Factors (in Percentages)												
Debt Ratio 45	60.9	•	86.8	70.0	59.2	64.2	47.0	71.2	51.5	66.9	49.9	68.8	•
Return on Total Assets 46	7.4	•	38.7	10.9	8.1	5.9	7.7	5.8	5.4	3.6	5.4	8.1	•
Return on Equity Before Income Taxes 47	14.9	•	279.5	31.9	16.4	12.7	12.6	14.9	9.1	7.8	8.2	16.1	•
Return on Equity After Income Taxes 48	13.2	•	275.2	30.7	15.9	11.9	11.6	13.9	8.7	7.1	5.6	9.0	•
Profit Margin (Before Income Tax) 49	2.2	•	8.1	2.5	2.6	1.3	2.6	1.7	1.7	1.1	2.5	2.4	•
Profit Margin (After Income Tax) 50	2.0	•	8.0	2.5	2.5	1.2	2.4	1.6	1.7	1.0	1.7	1.4	•

Table II

Corporations with Net Income

LUMBER AND OTHER CONSTRUCTION MATERIALS

MONEY AMOUNTS AND SIZE OF ASSETS IN THOUSANDS OF DOLLARS

Item Description for Accounting Period 7/12 Through 6/13	Total	Zero Assets	Under 500	500 to 1,000	1,000 to 5,000	5,000 to 10,000	10,000 to 25,000	25,000 to 50,000	50,000 to 100,000	100,000 to 250,000	250,000 to 500,000	500,000 to 2,500,000	2,500,000 and over
Number of Enterprises **1**	10782	650	5110	780	3224	541	•	76	36	11	•	4	0
Revenues ($ in Thousands)													
Net Sales **2**	83792143	351854	3846620	2906437	19813098	14365825	•	7442703	6603375	5053558	•	8262333	0
Interest **3**	31537	282	134	275	6889	3166	•	1892	299	640	•	8024	0
Rents **4**	38566	0	0	12	15958	1263	•	1043	232	733	•	11962	0
Royalties **5**	1	0	0	0	0	0	•	0	0	0	•	0	0
Other Portfolio Income **6**	143956	0	53682	1691	26040	25718	•	3877	2211	3971	•	1113	0
Other Receipts **7**	411492	7	69535	68	146205	18213	•	31467	33419	13596	•	12551	0
Total Receipts **8**	84417695	352143	3969971	2908483	20008190	14414185	•	7480982	6639536	5072498	•	8295983	0
Average Total Receipts **9**	7830	542	777	3729	6206	26644	•	98434	184432	461136	•	2073996	•
Operating Costs/Operating Income (%)													
Cost of Operations **10**	78.5	74.0	55.9	78.8	75.1	85.0	•	82.7	81.5	83.7	•	76.8	•
Salaries and Wages **11**	6.8	0.3	9.9	8.6	7.6	4.6	•	6.0	6.7	5.4	•	7.0	•
Taxes Paid **12**	1.2	0.8	1.7	1.4	1.6	0.8	•	0.9	0.9	0.9	•	1.2	•
Interest Paid **13**	0.5	0.2	0.3	0.0	0.6	0.3	•	0.5	0.3	0.3	•	1.1	•
Depreciation **14**	0.7	0.0	0.5	0.2	0.9	0.2	•	0.5	0.7	1.2	•	1.0	•
Amortization and Depletion **15**	0.1	0.2	0.0	•	0.0	0.1	•	0.1	0.1	0.2	•	0.6	•
Pensions and Other Deferred Comp. **16**	0.2	0.2	0.3	0.2	0.3	0.2	•	0.1	0.2	0.2	•	0.3	•
Employee Benefits **17**	0.6	0.0	0.3	0.3	0.6	0.4	•	0.6	0.8	0.8	•	0.6	•
Advertising **18**	0.3	0.2	2.0	0.8	0.2	0.1	•	0.2	0.2	0.2	•	0.1	•
Other Expenses **19**	6.8	16.5	19.3	4.1	7.9	4.5	•	5.7	6.0	5.0	•	6.3	•
Officers' Compensation **20**	1.6	2.2	3.5	1.6	2.4	1.5	•	0.9	0.7	0.6	•	0.6	•
Operating Margin **21**	2.9	5.4	6.3	4.0	2.9	2.4	•	1.8	2.0	1.5	•	4.5	•
Operating Margin Before Officers' Comp. **22**	4.4	7.6	9.8	5.7	5.3	3.9	•	2.7	2.7	2.1	•	5.0	•

Selected Average Balance Sheet ($ in Thousands)

Net Receivables **23**	801	0	29	192	747	2911	•	10110	19289	42303	•	198192	•
Inventories **24**	773	0	48	164	650	2547	•	11637	19989	37002	•	238906	•
Net Property, Plant and Equipment **25**	422	0	15	17	443	523	•	3712	7905	27720	•	197700	•
Total Assets **26**	2821	0	151	713	2408	7470	•	35366	63160	149620	•	1012440	•
Notes and Loans Payable **27**	841	0	70	64	797	2141	•	15617	15285	51243	•	283306	•
All Other Liabilities **28**	717	0	56	299	603	1771	•	9269	16784	38358	•	284201	•
Net Worth **29**	1264	0	25	350	1008	3558	•	10481	31091	60018	•	444933	•

Selected Financial Ratios (Times to 1)

Current Ratio **30**	2.1	•	2.4	2.2	2.2	2.0	•	1.6	2.0	2.0	•	2.0	•
Quick Ratio **31**	1.1	•	1.3	1.6	1.2	1.0	•	0.7	1.0	0.9	•	0.9	•
Net Sales to Working Capital **32**	7.3	•	11.3	10.0	6.1	8.0	•	9.5	7.4	8.7	•	8.5	•
Coverage Ratio **33**	8.3	27.7	29.6	1297.7	7.8	8.8	•	5.4	8.9	6.6	•	5.6	•
Total Asset Turnover **34**	2.8	•	5.0	5.2	2.6	3.6	•	2.8	2.9	3.1	•	2.0	•
Inventory Turnover **35**	7.9	•	8.8	17.9	7.1	8.9	•	7.0	7.5	10.4	•	6.6	•
Receivables Turnover **36**	10.7	•	24.0	•	9.0	10.0	•	11.3	11.0	13.9	•	20.8	•
Total Liabilities to Net Worth **37**	1.2	•	5.1	1.0	1.4	1.1	•	2.4	1.0	1.5	•	1.3	•
Current Assets to Working Capital **38**	1.9	•	1.7	1.8	1.9	2.0	•	2.6	2.0	2.0	•	2.0	•
Current Liabilities to Working Capital **39**	0.9	•	0.7	0.8	0.9	1.0	•	1.6	1.0	1.0	•	1.0	•
Working Capital to Net Sales **40**	0.1	•	0.1	0.1	0.2	0.1	•	0.1	0.1	0.1	•	0.1	•
Inventory to Working Capital **41**	0.8	•	0.8	0.4	0.7	0.8	•	1.3	0.9	0.9	•	1.0	•
Total Receipts to Cash Flow **42**	12.1	5.5	4.4	14.1	10.3	17.7	•	16.7	15.3	19.2	•	10.6	•
Cost of Goods to Cash Flow **43**	9.5	4.1	2.5	11.1	7.8	15.1	•	13.8	12.4	16.1	•	8.1	•
Cash Flow to Total Debt **44**	0.4	•	1.4	0.7	0.4	0.4	•	0.2	0.4	0.3	•	0.3	•

Selected Financial Factors (in Percentages)

Debt Ratio **45**	55.2	•	83.6	50.9	58.1	52.4	•	70.4	50.8	59.9	•	56.1	•
Return on Total Assets **46**	11.3	•	49.4	21.5	11.4	10.9	•	7.7	8.3	6.9	•	12.4	•
Return on Equity Before Income Taxes **47**	22.2	•	290.6	43.7	23.8	20.2	•	21.1	15.0	14.5	•	23.1	•
Return on Equity After Income Taxes **48**	20.3	•	286.6	42.4	23.1	19.3	•	20.0	14.6	13.6	•	15.4	•
Profit Margin (Before Income Tax) **49**	3.6	5.5	9.5	4.1	3.9	2.7	•	2.3	2.5	1.9	•	5.0	•
Profit Margin (After Income Tax) **50**	3.3	4.8	9.4	4.0	3.8	2.6	•	2.1	2.5	1.8	•	3.3	•

Table I

Corporations with and without Net Income

PROFESSIONAL AND COMMERCIAL EQUIPMENT AND SUPPLIES

MONEY AMOUNTS AND SIZE OF ASSETS IN THOUSANDS OF DOLLARS

Item Description for Accounting Period 7/12 Through 6/13	Total	Zero Assets	Under 500	500 to 1,000	1,000 to 5,000	5,000 to 10,000	10,000 to 25,000	25,000 to 50,000	50,000 to 100,000	100,000 to 250,000	250,000 to 500,000	500,000 to 2,500,000	2,500,000 and over
Number of Enterprises 1	35977	3366	23994	3171	4084	546	417	162	105	62	29	30	10

Revenues ($ in Thousands)

	Total	Zero Assets	Under 500	500 to 1,000	1,000 to 5,000	5,000 to 10,000	10,000 to 25,000	25,000 to 50,000	50,000 to 100,000	100,000 to 250,000	250,000 to 500,000	500,000 to 2,500,000	2,500,000 and over
Net Sales 2	274126468	17170080	12442441	7218839	27533065	9419136	16226713	11880003	13141413	18543675	14364738	48999419	77186948
Interest 3	532930	727	927	1371	2711	3069	3007	9429	11078	16608	11406	93069	379526
Rents 4	379853	929	0	382	8521	991	1450	1097	16889	2471	35686	44197	267241
Royalties 5	249460	8	187	0	0	8220	3720	23	339	21558	120015	42166	53225
Other Portfolio Income 6	1278428	21866	8773	7799	28888	22068	11841	3886	169814	45665	23916	198567	735349
Other Receipts 7	2405849	21388	279760	61786	145815	129059	59859	44456	108736	86244	227376	826100	415263
Total Receipts 8	278972988	17214998	12732088	7290177	27719000	9582543	16306590	11938894	13448269	18716221	14783137	50203518	79037552
Average Total Receipts 9	7754	5114	531	2299	6787	17550	39105	73697	128079	301875	509763	1673451	7903755

Operating Costs/Operating Income (%)

	Total	Zero Assets	Under 500	500 to 1,000	1,000 to 5,000	5,000 to 10,000	10,000 to 25,000	25,000 to 50,000	50,000 to 100,000	100,000 to 250,000	250,000 to 500,000	500,000 to 2,500,000	2,500,000 and over
Cost of Operations 10	73.1	91.0	57.3	56.3	69.4	70.8	72.8	70.7	73.9	75.3	72.4	79.5	70.8
Salaries and Wages 11	10.8	3.8	9.0	12.7	10.6	10.9	9.7	10.6	9.8	8.0	10.8	7.9	15.4
Taxes Paid 12	1.1	0.4	2.0	2.3	1.4	1.4	1.4	1.2	1.3	1.1	1.4	0.8	0.7
Interest Paid 13	1.1	0.1	0.2	0.5	0.5	0.4	0.4	0.9	0.8	1.0	1.1	1.0	2.0
Depreciation 14	1.3	0.4	0.5	0.7	0.7	0.6	0.6	0.9	1.0	1.1	1.3	0.9	2.4
Amortization and Depletion 15	0.4	0.1	0.1	0.1	0.1	0.2	0.1	0.4	0.4	0.5	0.6	0.9	0.3
Pensions and Other Deferred Comp. 16	0.2	0.3	0.2	0.5	0.3	0.1	0.3	0.3	0.2	0.3	0.3	0.2	0.1
Employee Benefits 17	0.8	0.4	0.8	0.9	1.0	1.0	0.8	0.8	1.0	1.0	1.0	0.9	0.5
Advertising 18	0.9	0.1	1.2	1.2	0.8	0.6	0.8	1.2	1.0	1.3	0.9	1.1	0.8
Other Expenses 19	6.8	2.1	18.2	16.9	8.9	11.2	8.9	9.4	8.9	7.6	10.4	6.3	2.0
Officers' Compensation 20	1.5	1.1	7.8	5.0	3.8	2.1	2.1	1.2	1.1	0.8	0.5	0.3	0.3
Operating Margin 21	2.2	0.2	2.8	2.9	2.7	0.7	2.1	2.3	0.7	2.2	•	0.2	4.7
Operating Margin Before Officers' Comp. 22	3.7	1.3	10.6	7.9	6.5	2.8	4.2	3.6	1.7	3.0	•	0.6	5.0

Selected Average Balance Sheet ($ in Thousands)

Net Receivables 23	1032	0	17	190	621	1969	5453	11383	19002	51919	85964	227647	1385290
Inventories 24	603	0	29	197	588	1800	4057	7683	12300	30287	52654	148127	493029
Net Property, Plant and Equipment 25	343	0	10	85	235	705	1245	2996	5787	13334	25960	63462	537307
Total Assets 26	4751	0	108	754	2124	6579	15531	34876	71166	156157	337934	1049941	8309361
Notes and Loans Payable 27	1566	0	62	289	973	1807	3505	8034	17185	47003	75495	305405	3015374
All Other Liabilities 28	1771	0	44	286	907	2487	7604	12829	26706	66127	111337	372172	3014696
Net Worth 29	1413	0	2	178	243	2284	4422	14014	27274	43027	151102	372364	2279291

Selected Financial Ratios (Times to 1)

Current Ratio 30	1.4	•	1.6	1.6	1.7	1.8	1.5	1.8	1.4	1.6	1.6	1.6	1.1
Quick Ratio 31	0.8	•	1.0	1.0	1.0	1.0	0.9	1.1	0.9	0.9	1.0	0.8	0.8
Net Sales to Working Capital 32	10.8	•	16.5	10.4	9.7	7.5	9.2	6.8	8.7	8.1	6.6	7.7	19.4
Coverage Ratio 33	5.5	7.4	25.0	9.1	7.9	6.8	7.7	4.0	4.8	4.3	3.0	3.6	5.9
Total Asset Turnover 34	1.6	•	4.8	3.0	3.2	2.6	2.5	2.1	1.8	1.9	1.5	1.6	0.9
Inventory Turnover 35	9.2	•	10.3	6.5	8.0	6.8	7.0	6.7	7.5	7.4	6.8	8.8	11.1
Receivables Turnover 36	7.4	•	27.4	10.0	10.6	7.5	7.2	6.5	7.5	6.0	5.4	7.3	5.6
Total Liabilities to Net Worth 37	2.4	•	48.1	3.2	7.7	1.9	2.5	1.5	1.6	2.6	1.2	1.8	2.6
Current Assets to Working Capital 38	3.5	•	2.7	2.6	2.5	2.3	2.9	2.3	3.3	2.8	2.6	2.8	7.7
Current Liabilities to Working Capital 39	2.5	•	1.7	1.6	1.5	1.3	1.9	1.3	2.3	1.8	1.6	1.8	6.7
Working Capital to Net Sales 40	0.1	•	0.1	0.1	0.1	0.1	0.1	0.1	0.1	0.1	0.2	0.1	0.1
Inventory to Working Capital 41	0.9	•	0.9	0.9	0.8	0.8	0.9	0.8	1.0	0.8	0.7	0.7	1.2
Total Receipts to Cash Flow 42	11.1	60.4	5.0	5.7	9.8	8.6	10.0	9.5	10.7	10.5	9.2	13.0	13.8
Cost of Goods to Cash Flow 43	8.1	55.0	2.9	3.2	6.8	6.1	7.3	6.7	7.9	7.9	6.7	10.3	9.8
Cash Flow to Total Debt 44	0.2	•	1.0	0.7	0.4	0.5	0.3	0.4	0.3	0.3	0.3	0.2	0.1

Selected Financial Factors (in Percentages)

Debt Ratio 45	70.3	•	98.0	76.3	88.5	65.3	71.5	59.8	61.7	72.4	55.3	64.5	72.6
Return on Total Assets 46	9.3	•	25.7	13.2	12.3	7.8	7.5	7.9	6.7	8.0	4.7	5.9	10.7
Return on Equity Before Income Taxes 47	25.5	•	1208.4	49.8	93.7	19.2	23.0	14.8	13.9	22.4	7.0	12.1	32.4
Return on Equity After Income Taxes 48	18.5	•	1200.7	48.3	89.6	14.6	19.2	12.3	9.6	16.9	3.8	8.4	22.1
Profit Margin (Before Income Tax) 49	4.7	0.5	5.2	3.9	3.4	2.5	2.6	2.8	3.0	3.2	2.1	2.8	9.6
Profit Margin (After Income Tax) 50	3.4	•	5.1	3.8	3.2	1.9	2.2	2.3	2.1	2.4	1.2	1.9	6.5

Table II

Corporations with Net Income

PROFESSIONAL AND COMMERCIAL EQUIPMENT AND SUPPLIES

MONEY AMOUNTS AND SIZE OF ASSETS IN THOUSANDS OF DOLLARS

Item Description for Accounting Period 7/12 Through 6/13	Total	Zero Assets	Under 500	500 to 1,000	1,000 to 5,000	5,000 to 10,000	10,000 to 25,000	25,000 to 50,000	50,000 to 100,000	100,000 to 250,000	250,000 to 500,000	500,000 to 2,500,000	2,500,000 and over
Number of Enterprises 1	24195	2548	15572	2039	2971	409	351	120	81	48	23	25	10

Revenues ($ in Thousands)

	Total	Zero Assets	Under 500	500 to 1,000	1,000 to 5,000	5,000 to 10,000	10,000 to 25,000	25,000 to 50,000	50,000 to 100,000	100,000 to 250,000	250,000 to 500,000	500,000 to 2,500,000	2,500,000 and over
Net Sales 2	247380380	15902563	9348458	5143823	23182395	8098595	14422847	10176714	11225981	14957902	12541332	45192821	77186948
Interest 3	515298	723	897	1233	2507	2879	2657	4685	8709	14573	8362	88548	379526
Rents 4	377968	929	0	0	8424	407	1171	1097	16584	2232	35686	44197	267241
Royalties 5	161983	8	187	0	0	8220	3632	0	339	20525	41688	34159	53225
Other Portfolio Income 6	1228317	15942	0	7799	24465	21537	5432	3816	163796	41233	23173	185779	735349
Other Receipts 7	2233583	20649	276481	30725	111931	119001	51282	32336	95046	69118	210923	800826	415263
Total Receipts 8	251897529	15940814	9626023	5183580	23329722	8250639	14487021	10218648	11510455	15105583	12861164	46346330	79037552
Average Total Receipts 9	10411	6256	618	2542	7852	20173	41274	85155	142104	314700	559181	1853853	7903755

Operating Costs/Operating Income (%)

	Total	Zero Assets	Under 500	500 to 1,000	1,000 to 5,000	5,000 to 10,000	10,000 to 25,000	25,000 to 50,000	50,000 to 100,000	100,000 to 250,000	250,000 to 500,000	500,000 to 2,500,000	2,500,000 and over
Cost of Operations 10	74.0	92.5	60.0	54.4	70.8	71.0	74.0	72.8	72.2	74.6	74.9	80.2	70.8
Salaries and Wages 11	10.4	2.6	7.1	12.4	9.4	9.7	9.0	9.5	9.7	7.7	9.9	7.8	15.4
Taxes Paid 12	1.0	0.4	1.7	2.5	1.3	1.2	1.4	1.1	1.3	1.1	1.2	0.8	0.7
Interest Paid 13	1.0	0.1	0.2	0.3	0.3	0.3	0.4	0.6	0.7	0.8	0.6	0.8	2.0
Depreciation 14	1.3	0.3	0.4	0.7	0.6	0.6	0.6	0.8	1.0	1.2	1.3	0.8	2.4
Amortization and Depletion 15	0.3	0.1	0.0	0.2	0.0	0.1	0.1	0.3	0.2	0.4	0.4	0.5	0.3
Pensions and Other Deferred Comp. 16	0.2	0.0	0.2	0.2	0.3	0.1	0.3	0.3	0.2	0.3	0.3	0.3	0.1
Employee Benefits 17	0.7	0.2	0.5	0.8	0.9	0.9	0.8	0.7	1.0	0.9	1.0	0.8	0.5
Advertising 18	0.8	0.0	0.6	1.1	0.5	0.6	0.6	0.9	1.0	1.3	0.9	1.1	0.8
Other Expenses 19	5.8	1.6	16.9	15.0	7.5	10.2	7.5	7.9	8.3	7.5	8.2	6.1	2.0
Officers' Compensation 20	1.1	0.1	5.4	4.8	3.2	2.0	1.8	1.2	1.0	0.8	0.4	0.3	0.3
Operating Margin 21	3.5	2.2	7.2	7.6	5.1	3.1	3.6	4.0	3.3	3.5	0.9	0.5	4.7
Operating Margin Before Officers' Comp. 22	4.6	2.2	12.6	12.4	8.3	5.1	5.4	5.2	4.3	4.2	1.3	0.8	5.0

Net Receivables **23**	1369	0	14	191	699	1933	5459	11751	21447	51743	91111	245878	1385290
Inventories **24**	718	0	33	231	562	1763	4162	7682	13187	30695	50905	155238	402460
Net Property, Plant and Equipment **25**	457	0	10	73	236	741	1246	3100	6295	14338	27340	69733	537307
Total Assets **26**	6354	0	115	773	2209	6649	15289	35191	71891	155700	337415	1093820	8309361
Notes and Loans Payable **27**	1946	0	37	184	585	1098	3554	7302	15552	46963	59038	271448	3015374
All Other Liabilities **28**	2340	0	43	286	799	2458	6435	12961	28865	64079	118171	395562	3014696
Net Worth **29**	2068	0	35	303	825	3093	5300	14928	27475	44657	160205	426810	2279291

Selected Financial Ratios (Times to 1)

Current Ratio **30**	1.4	•	1.8	1.9	2.1	1.9	1.7	1.8	1.5	1.7	1.6	1.5	1.1
Quick Ratio **31**	0.9	•	1.2	1.0	1.3	1.0	1.0	1.1	0.9	1.0	1.0	0.8	0.8
Net Sales to Working Capital **32**	10.8	•	15.6	8.8	8.3	7.6	8.0	7.3	7.7	7.5	7.2	8.1	19.4
Coverage Ratio **33**	7.3	49.4	56.5	28.9	18.5	17.6	12.2	8.7	9.0	6.9	7.1	5.0	5.9
Total Asset Turnover **34**	1.6	•	5.2	3.3	3.5	3.0	2.7	2.4	1.9	2.0	1.6	1.7	0.9
Inventory Turnover **35**	10.5	•	10.9	5.9	9.8	8.0	7.3	8.0	7.6	7.6	8.0	9.3	13.6
Receivables Turnover **36**	8.1	•	30.5	12.1	10.8	8.1	7.7	7.8	7.4	6.6	5.7	8.0	6.5
Total Liabilities to Net Worth **37**	2.1	•	2.3	1.5	1.7	1.1	1.9	1.4	1.6	2.5	1.1	1.6	2.6
Current Assets to Working Capital **38**	3.4	•	2.2	2.1	1.9	2.1	2.4	2.3	2.9	2.5	2.6	2.8	7.7
Current Liabilities to Working Capital **39**	2.4	•	1.2	1.1	0.9	1.1	1.4	1.3	1.9	1.5	1.6	1.8	6.7
Working Capital to Net Sales **40**	0.1	•	0.1	0.1	0.1	0.1	0.1	0.1	0.1	0.1	0.1	0.1	0.1
Inventory to Working Capital **41**	0.8	•	0.8	0.9	0.6	0.7	0.8	0.7	0.8	0.8	0.7	0.8	1.2
Total Receipts to Cash Flow **42**	10.5	28.2	4.1	5.0	8.9	7.5	9.9	9.0	8.7	9.2	9.8	12.5	13.8
Cost of Goods to Cash Flow **43**	7.8	26.1	2.5	2.7	6.3	5.3	7.3	6.6	6.3	6.8	7.3	10.0	9.8
Cash Flow to Total Debt **44**	0.2	•	1.8	1.1	0.6	0.7	0.4	0.5	0.4	0.3	0.3	0.2	0.1

Selected Financial Factors (in Percentages)

Debt Ratio **45**	67.4	•	69.9	60.8	62.6	53.5	65.3	57.6	61.8	71.3	52.5	61.0	72.6
Return on Total Assets **46**	11.4	•	53.7	28.5	21.4	16.0	11.8	12.0	12.6	10.6	6.7	6.4	10.7
Return on Equity Before Income Taxes **47**	30.2	•	175.5	70.1	54.1	32.4	31.4	25.1	29.3	31.7	12.1	13.2	32.4
Return on Equity After Income Taxes **48**	23.1	•	174.7	68.7	52.4	27.9	27.6	21.9	23.7	24.8	8.3	9.4	22.1
Profit Margin (Before Income Tax) **49**	6.1	2.4	10.1	8.4	5.7	5.1	4.0	4.4	5.8	4.5	3.6	3.1	9.6
Profit Margin (After Income Tax) **50**	4.7	1.7	10.1	8.3	5.5	4.4	3.6	3.9	4.7	3.6	2.4	2.2	6.5

Table I

Corporations with and without Net Income

METAL AND MINERAL (EXCEPT PETROLEUM)

MONEY AMOUNTS AND SIZE OF ASSETS IN THOUSANDS OF DOLLARS

Item Description for Accounting Period 7/12 Through 6/13	Total	Zero Assets	Under 500	500 to 1,000	1,000 to 5,000	5,000 to 10,000	10,000 to 25,000	25,000 to 50,000	50,000 to 100,000	100,000 to 250,000	250,000 to 500,000	500,000 to 2,500,000	2,500,000 and over
Number of Enterprises 1	5808	401	2785	586	1022	430	305	117	66	54	20	19	3

Revenues ($ in Thousands)													
Net Sales 2	140767344	1625420	2833473	1798941	6286979	12170392	11839710	11091615	11116752	20827562	11517954	31321644	18336900
Interest 3	128739	3091	85	8	1946	2170	3638	4004	7929	7554	13895	30412	54008
Rents 4	68187	0	1895	0	10	1900	1045	2393	196	1218	10395	7639	41495
Royalties 5	180	0	0	0	0	0	105	0	0	0	0	0	75
Other Portfolio Income 6	260794	0	0	95	371	2510	7781	8871	2967	92144	14682	27931	103442
Other Receipts 7	905255	1450	40	2753	13077	25646	74095	23595	49424	446375	87288	106368	75148
Total Receipts 8	142130499	1629961	2835493	1801797	6302383	12202618	11926374	11130478	11177268	21374853	11644214	31493994	18611068
Average Total Receipts 9	24472	4065	1018	3075	6167	28378	39103	95132	169353	395831	582211	1657579	6203689

Operating Costs/Operating Income (%)													
Cost of Operations 10	87.9	80.1	66.8	76.5	80.5	91.1	87.0	88.5	88.3	92.6	88.8	88.2	87.1
Salaries and Wages 11	3.3	9.7	6.0	4.0	6.0	1.7	3.7	2.7	2.9	2.2	2.3	3.7	3.6
Taxes Paid 12	0.6	1.1	1.4	1.0	0.9	0.4	0.7	0.6	0.5	0.4	0.6	0.6	0.7
Interest Paid 13	0.7	6.2	0.2	0.1	0.3	0.2	0.4	0.4	0.4	0.4	0.4	1.4	0.8
Depreciation 14	0.7	1.4	0.2	0.7	0.3	0.2	0.6	0.8	0.5	0.3	0.6	0.8	1.4
Amortization and Depletion 15	0.2	0.8	0.0	0.0	0.0	0.0	0.0	0.0	0.0	0.1	0.2	0.3	0.3
Pensions and Other Deferred Comp. 16	0.2	0.0	•	0.3	0.2	0.1	0.1	0.1	0.2	0.1	0.2	0.2	0.2
Employee Benefits 17	0.5	0.3	0.4	0.3	0.8	0.2	0.5	0.4	0.4	0.4	0.3	0.9	0.2
Advertising 18	0.1	0.1	0.1	0.1	0.1	0.0	0.1	0.0	0.1	0.0	0.0	0.0	0.0
Other Expenses 19	4.1	35.3	5.7	7.0	6.0	3.1	4.0	3.7	3.3	3.3	4.0	2.9	5.0
Officers' Compensation 20	1.0	0.8	13.2	5.1	2.9	1.2	1.0	0.9	0.9	0.3	0.6	0.3	0.4
Operating Margin 21	0.8	•	5.9	4.8	1.9	1.6	2.0	1.8	2.7	•	2.0	0.6	0.3
Operating Margin Before Officers' Comp. 22	1.8	•	19.1	9.9	4.8	2.8	3.0	2.7	3.5	0.2	2.5	0.9	0.7

Selected Average Balance Sheet ($ in Thousands)

Net Receivables 23	2552	0	39	198	703	2425	4598	10597	19425	35738	76746	177922	688956
Inventories 24	3597	0	16	164	667	3112	5875	14512	29662	68475	123244	318772	708914
Net Property, Plant and Equipment 25	1615	0	30	111	92	369	1420	4340	4991	11137	31421	175530	1047024
Total Assets 26	11558	0	145	693	2448	7242	15944	36399	69999	153814	344352	950808	4568715
Notes and Loans Payable 27	3649	0	36	141	268	1742	4237	11209	23239	48969	98342	337400	1608567
All Other Liabilities 28	3809	0	5	177	910	3302	4814	11469	20831	49633	107403	414560	921660
Net Worth 29	4101	0	104	375	1270	2197	6893	13720	25929	55212	138607	198849	2038488

Selected Financial Ratios (Times to 1)

Current Ratio 30	1.8	•	4.1	2.3	2.2	1.7	1.9	1.6	2.0	1.8	1.8	1.5	2.2
Quick Ratio 31	0.8	•	3.2	1.6	1.3	0.9	0.9	0.7	0.8	0.7	0.7	0.5	1.1
Net Sales to Working Capital 32	7.3	•	12.7	10.1	5.6	10.4	6.5	8.7	5.8	6.9	5.4	8.2	6.9
Coverage Ratio 33	3.6	•	28.4	37.0	7.3	8.8	8.0	6.4	8.9	7.6	8.3	1.9	3.3
Total Asset Turnover 34	2.1	•	7.0	4.4	2.5	3.9	2.4	2.6	2.4	2.5	1.7	1.7	1.3
Inventory Turnover 35	5.9	•	41.8	14.3	7.4	8.3	5.7	5.8	5.0	5.2	4.1	4.6	7.5
Receivables Turnover 36	9.8	•	26.6	12.8	10.4	13.1	8.3	9.5	8.1	10.3	7.0	8.1	17.7
Total Liabilities to Net Worth 37	1.8	•	0.4	0.8	0.9	2.3	1.3	1.7	1.7	1.8	1.5	3.8	1.2
Current Assets to Working Capital 38	2.3	•	1.3	1.8	1.9	2.4	2.2	2.6	2.0	2.2	2.2	3.0	1.8
Current Liabilities to Working Capital 39	1.3	•	0.3	0.8	0.9	1.4	1.2	1.6	1.0	1.2	1.2	2.0	0.8
Working Capital to Net Sales 40	0.1	•	0.1	0.1	0.2	0.1	0.2	0.1	0.2	0.1	0.2	0.1	0.1
Inventory to Working Capital 41	1.2	•	0.2	0.6	0.7	1.1	1.0	1.4	1.1	1.2	1.2	1.6	0.8
Total Receipts to Cash Flow 42	20.2	•	9.4	9.7	15.7	23.2	17.7	19.7	17.9	19.2	16.5	32.3	18.3
Cost of Goods to Cash Flow 43	17.7	•	6.3	7.5	12.6	21.2	15.4	17.4	15.8	17.8	14.6	28.5	15.9
Cash Flow to Total Debt 44	0.2	•	2.6	1.0	0.3	0.2	0.2	0.2	0.2	0.2	0.2	0.1	0.1

Selected Financial Factors (in Percentages)

Debt Ratio 45	64.5	•	28.5	45.8	48.1	69.7	56.8	62.3	63.0	64.1	59.7	79.1	55.4
Return on Total Assets 46	5.3	•	43.7	22.5	6.3	8.1	7.6	6.8	8.7	7.3	5.9	4.6	3.5
Return on Equity Before Income Taxes 47	10.8	•	59.0	40.4	10.4	23.6	15.3	15.2	20.8	17.7	12.8	10.5	5.5
Return on Equity After Income Taxes 48	7.9	•	57.2	39.3	9.7	22.4	13.8	13.4	18.0	13.6	8.6	6.8	2.8
Profit Margin (Before Income Tax) 49	1.8	•	6.0	4.9	2.1	1.8	2.7	2.2	3.2	2.5	3.1	1.3	1.8
Profit Margin (After Income Tax) 50	1.3	•	5.8	4.8	2.0	1.7	2.4	1.9	2.8	1.9	2.1	0.8	0.9

Table II

Corporations with Net Income

METAL AND MINERAL (EXCEPT PETROLEUM)

MONEY AMOUNTS AND SIZE OF ASSETS IN THOUSANDS OF DOLLARS

Item Description for Accounting Period 7/12 Through 6/13	Total	Zero Assets	Under 500	500 to 1,000	1,000 to 5,000	5,000 to 10,000	10,000 to 25,000	25,000 to 50,000	50,000 to 100,000	100,000 to 250,000	250,000 to 500,000	500,000 to 2,500,000	2,500,000 and over
Number of Enterprises 1	4833	388	2425	578	631	344	252	91	54	38	16	16	0

Revenues ($ in Thousands)													
Net Sales 2	111956190	801806	2688092	1489581	5111261	9910417	10034146	8692872	10105893	17899682	10085881	35136559	0
Interest 3	56468	2065	85	8	1837	1903	3144	3834	7184	5297	11731	19381	0
Rents 4	27556	0	1895	0	10	1255	977	2393	196	900	10365	9564	0
Royalties 5	0	0	0	0	0	0	0	0	0	0	0	0	0
Other Portfolio Income 6	147518	0	0	37	371	2473	6936	8309	2860	81707	14682	30143	0
Other Receipts 7	733659	1259	39	2752	11889	15703	40917	17352	39687	431451	87052	85557	0
Total Receipts 8	112921391	805130	2690111	1492378	5125368	9931751	10086120	8724760	10155820	18419037	10209711	35281204	0
Average Total Receipts 9	23365	2075	1109	2582	8123	28871	40024	95876	188071	484712	638107	2205075	•

Operating Costs/Operating Income (%)													
Cost of Operations 10	86.5	88.8	65.7	71.5	81.3	90.1	85.9	87.8	88.1	92.5	88.8	84.0	•
Salaries and Wages 11	3.4	2.9	6.3	4.8	4.2	1.7	3.8	2.9	2.8	2.2	2.1	4.7	•
Taxes Paid 12	0.7	0.7	1.5	1.2	1.0	0.4	0.7	0.6	0.5	0.4	0.6	0.7	•
Interest Paid 13	0.6	0.3	0.2	0.2	0.4	0.3	0.3	0.4	0.4	0.3	0.4	1.2	•
Depreciation 14	0.6	0.1	0.2	0.8	0.2	0.2	0.5	0.9	0.4	0.3	0.6	1.0	•
Amortization and Depletion 15	0.1	0.0	0.0	0.0	0.0	0.0	0.0	0.0	0.0	0.0	0.1	0.3	•
Pensions and Other Deferred Comp. 16	0.2	0.0	•	0.4	0.3	0.1	0.2	0.2	0.2	0.1	0.2	0.3	•
Employee Benefits 17	0.5	0.2	0.4	0.4	0.7	0.2	0.5	0.4	0.3	0.4	0.3	0.9	•
Advertising 18	0.1	0.0	0.1	0.2	0.1	0.0	0.1	0.0	0.1	0.0	0.0	0.1	•
Other Expenses 19	3.7	4.3	5.8	7.7	5.8	3.0	3.7	3.2	3.1	3.2	3.5	3.9	•
Officers' Compensation 20	1.1	0.1	13.4	6.1	2.7	1.2	1.1	0.9	0.8	0.3	0.6	0.4	•
Operating Margin 21	2.5	2.5	6.3	6.8	3.4	2.8	3.3	2.6	3.3	0.3	2.7	2.5	•
Operating Margin Before Officers' Comp. 22	3.6	2.6	19.7	12.9	6.1	4.1	4.4	3.5	4.1	0.5	3.3	2.9	•

Selected Average Balance Sheet ($ in Thousands)

Net Receivables 23	2435	0	44	197	946	2409	4449	10424	20810	41937	80376	252989	•
Inventories 24	3427	0	17	171	847	3389	5859	15550	31575	79000	108957	383970	•
Net Property, Plant and Equipment 25	1137	0	34	109	51	351	1268	4530	5184	13468	37499	192020	•
Total Assets 26	9786	0	152	693	2982	7297	15443	36649	71222	161038	338748	1220231	•
Notes and Loans Payable 27	2623	0	42	131	381	1333	3436	10768	19699	43715	80795	371142	•
All Other Liabilities 28	3196	0	6	161	923	3296	4588	10387	21859	54861	98302	417794	•
Net Worth 29	3967	0	105	401	1678	2667	7420	15494	29663	62462	159651	431295	•

Selected Financial Ratios (Times to 1)

Current Ratio 30	2.0	•	3.8	2.4	2.6	1.8	2.0	1.8	2.0	1.7	1.9	2.1	•
Quick Ratio 31	0.9	•	3.2	1.7	1.6	0.9	1.0	0.7	0.8	0.7	0.8	0.8	•
Net Sales to Working Capital 32	6.7	•	13.6	8.0	4.8	10.1	6.4	7.4	6.1	8.6	6.0	5.7	•
Coverage Ratio 33	6.6	11.9	28.5	43.7	11.2	13.1	11.9	8.3	11.1	13.1	10.4	3.4	•
Total Asset Turnover 34	2.4	•	7.3	3.7	2.7	3.9	2.6	2.6	2.6	2.9	1.9	1.8	•
Inventory Turnover 35	5.8	•	43.8	10.8	7.8	7.7	5.8	5.4	5.2	5.5	5.1	4.8	•
Receivables Turnover 36	9.5	•	26.0	•	10.2	12.1	8.5	9.1	8.6	10.3	7.8	•	•
Total Liabilities to Net Worth 37	1.5	•	0.5	0.7	0.8	1.7	1.1	1.4	1.4	1.6	1.1	1.8	•
Current Assets to Working Capital 38	2.0	•	1.4	1.7	1.6	2.3	2.0	2.3	2.0	2.4	2.1	1.9	•
Current Liabilities to Working Capital 39	1.0	•	0.4	0.7	0.6	1.3	1.0	1.3	1.0	1.4	1.1	0.9	•
Working Capital to Net Sales 40	0.2	•	0.1	0.1	0.2	0.1	0.2	0.1	0.2	0.1	0.2	0.2	•
Inventory to Working Capital 41	1.0	•	0.2	0.5	0.6	1.0	1.0	1.2	1.0	1.3	1.0	1.0	•
Total Receipts to Cash Flow 42	16.3	17.2	9.0	7.7	12.5	18.8	15.4	18.4	16.4	17.2	15.5	18.0	•
Cost of Goods to Cash Flow 43	14.1	15.3	5.9	5.5	10.2	16.9	13.2	16.2	14.5	15.9	13.7	15.2	•
Cash Flow to Total Debt 44	0.2	•	2.6	1.1	0.5	0.3	0.3	0.2	0.3	0.3	0.2	0.2	•

Selected Financial Factors (in Percentages)

Debt Ratio 45	59.5	•	31.2	42.1	43.7	63.4	52.0	57.7	58.4	61.2	52.9	64.7	•
Return on Total Assets 46	9.5	•	47.9	26.6	10.9	13.1	10.7	9.0	10.9	10.1	8.0	7.5	•
Return on Equity Before Income Taxes 47	19.9	•	67.2	44.8	17.6	33.1	20.4	18.8	23.8	24.0	15.4	15.0	•
Return on Equity After Income Taxes 48	16.3	•	65.2	43.8	16.7	31.8	18.6	16.7	20.8	18.8	10.8	10.6	•
Profit Margin (Before Income Tax) 49	3.4	2.9	6.4	7.0	3.6	3.1	3.8	3.0	3.8	3.2	3.9	3.0	•
Profit Margin (After Income Tax) 50	2.8	2.6	6.2	6.8	3.5	2.9	3.5	2.7	3.3	2.5	2.7	2.1	•

Table I

Corporations with and without Net Income

ELECTRICAL GOODS

MONEY AMOUNTS AND SIZE OF ASSETS IN THOUSANDS OF DOLLARS

Item Description for Accounting Period 7/12 Through 6/13	Total	Zero Assets	Under 500	500 to 1,000	1,000 to 5,000	5,000 to 10,000	10,000 to 25,000	25,000 to 50,000	50,000 to 100,000	100,000 to 250,000	250,000 to 500,000	500,000 to 2,500,000	2,500,000 and over
Number of Enterprises 1	31885	4768	17478	3719	4251	665	500	206	125	94	27	34	16

Revenues ($ in Thousands)													
Net Sales 2	399775758	7593806	12206733	8386731	24157598	13625512	18881205	17543181	19988674	34571870	14978686	84791268	143050492
Interest 3	280479	512	1769	686	2222	2601	6977	9872	8988	20076	21587	43003	162186
Rents 4	109363	0	0	713	1067	3532	3401	2959	3170	3131	4904	16548	69940
Royalties 5	2229077	124	0	1	0	0	765	4299	4153	105305	28630	84902	2000897
Other Portfolio Income 6	2137752	27100	19914	14724	24555	3773	17960	4921	8651	17617	22945	184981	1790610
Other Receipts 7	3613398	41060	51705	66567	319402	104867	104552	94584	125705	204219	111313	953168	1436259
Total Receipts 8	408145827	7662602	12280121	8469422	24504844	13740285	19014860	17659816	20139341	34922218	15168065	86073870	148510384
Average Total Receipts 9	12801	1607	703	2277	5764	20662	38030	85727	161115	371513	561780	2531584	9281899

Operating Costs/Operating Income (%)													
Cost of Operations 10	82.5	88.8	63.8	70.3	73.3	79.8	81.0	80.9	82.1	83.7	79.4	89.5	82.5
Salaries and Wages 11	6.1	4.2	8.7	8.3	8.9	7.2	6.8	6.7	6.6	5.9	8.0	4.3	5.8
Taxes Paid 12	0.8	0.5	2.0	1.6	1.5	1.0	0.9	0.9	0.9	0.7	0.9	0.5	0.6
Interest Paid 13	0.4	0.2	0.9	0.5	0.3	0.2	0.3	0.4	0.4	0.2	0.7	0.2	0.7
Depreciation 14	1.1	0.2	0.4	0.5	0.5	0.4	0.4	0.3	0.5	0.5	0.7	0.4	2.3
Amortization and Depletion 15	0.9	0.1	0.1	0.0	0.1	0.0	0.1	0.2	0.2	0.1	0.3	0.2	2.2
Pensions and Other Deferred Comp. 16	0.3	0.1	0.2	0.3	0.4	0.2	0.1	0.3	0.2	0.3	0.3	0.4	0.3
Employee Benefits 17	0.7	0.3	0.8	0.7	0.8	0.7	0.5	0.6	0.6	0.8	0.8	0.5	0.8
Advertising 18	0.7	0.2	0.6	0.8	0.4	0.5	0.6	0.4	0.7	0.7	0.3	0.4	1.1
Other Expenses 19	5.4	5.2	11.7	9.6	10.1	6.8	6.1	6.1	5.2	4.7	8.2	2.9	4.9
Officers' Compensation 20	0.9	1.1	6.8	5.7	3.4	1.9	1.2	1.2	0.6	0.5	0.6	0.2	0.1
Operating Margin 21	0.3	•	4.0	1.6	0.5	1.2	1.9	2.1	2.1	1.9	•	0.4	•
Operating Margin Before Officers' Comp. 22	1.2	0.3	10.8	7.2	3.9	3.1	3.2	3.3	2.7	2.4	0.4	0.7	•

Net Receivables 23	1920	0	21	165	615	2786	5031	12808	23509	56154	110411	393998	1625245
Inventories 24	1067	0	22	169	746	2327	4234	10635	19670	36634	54654	192879	627626
Net Property, Plant and Equipment 25	575	0	9	114	134	526	962	1790	4993	11254	21743	62645	723840
Total Assets 26	6761	0	108	709	2194	7020	15004	35303	70081	157456	356760	1051204	7084830
Notes and Loans Payable 27	1670	0	91	316	492	2245	2984	6337	13384	24595	61079	92122	2208751
All Other Liabilities 28	2818	0	53	268	845	3411	6410	16247	31412	63109	141174	558167	2678720
Net Worth 29	2273	0	-36	125	858	1364	5609	12720	25285	69752	154508	400915	2197359

Current Ratio 30	1.4	•	1.3	1.5	1.9	1.6	1.6	1.6	1.7	1.8	1.7	1.4	1.2
Quick Ratio 31	0.8	•	0.9	0.8	1.0	1.0	0.9	0.9	0.9	1.1	1.2	0.9	0.7
Net Sales to Working Capital 32	11.3	•	34.9	13.5	6.3	9.3	8.0	7.6	7.2	7.0	6.0	11.6	20.2
Coverage Ratio 33	6.8	1.4	6.2	5.9	8.1	9.4	8.9	8.4	8.3	13.6	2.7	11.9	5.3
Total Asset Turnover 34	1.9	•	6.5	3.2	2.6	2.9	2.5	2.4	2.3	2.3	1.6	2.4	1.3
Inventory Turnover 35	9.7	•	20.6	9.4	5.6	7.0	7.2	6.5	6.7	8.4	8.1	11.6	11.8
Receivables Turnover 36	6.9	•	29.8	13.8	8.2	6.9	8.1	6.7	6.8	6.6	5.3	6.3	6.2
Total Liabilities to Net Worth 37	2.0	•	•	4.7	1.6	4.1	1.7	1.8	1.8	1.3	1.3	1.6	2.2
Current Assets to Working Capital 38	3.7	•	4.1	3.1	2.1	2.8	2.6	2.7	2.5	2.3	2.3	3.5	7.6
Current Liabilities to Working Capital 39	2.7	•	3.1	2.1	1.1	1.8	1.6	1.7	1.5	1.3	1.3	2.5	6.6
Working Capital to Net Sales 40	0.1	•	0.0	0.1	0.2	0.1	0.1	0.1	0.1	0.1	0.2	0.1	0.0
Inventory to Working Capital 41	1.0	•	1.0	1.1	0.9	0.9	0.9	1.0	0.9	0.7	0.6	0.8	1.6
Total Receipts to Cash Flow 42	15.2	26.4	7.6	10.3	10.5	13.0	13.4	12.9	14.2	14.7	12.1	23.6	16.1
Cost of Goods to Cash Flow 43	12.5	23.4	4.9	7.2	7.7	10.4	10.8	10.5	11.6	12.3	9.6	21.1	13.2
Cash Flow to Total Debt 44	0.2	•	0.6	0.4	0.4	0.3	0.3	0.3	0.3	0.3	0.2	0.2	0.1

Debt Ratio 45	66.4	•	133.6	82.4	60.9	80.6	62.6	64.0	63.9	55.7	56.7	61.9	69.0
Return on Total Assets 46	5.5	•	35.5	9.8	5.8	6.7	7.5	7.6	7.5	7.4	2.7	5.2	4.4
Return on Equity Before Income Taxes 47	13.9	•	•	46.0	13.0	30.7	17.8	18.5	18.2	15.5	4.0	12.6	11.6
Return on Equity After Income Taxes 48	10.9	•	•	42.6	11.7	25.2	15.3	16.1	15.3	12.4	2.4	9.0	8.6
Profit Margin (Before Income Tax) 49	2.5	0.1	4.6	2.5	2.0	2.0	2.6	2.8	2.9	2.9	1.1	2.0	2.9
Profit Margin (After Income Tax) 50	2.0	0.0	4.5	2.4	1.8	1.7	2.3	2.4	2.4	2.3	0.7	1.4	2.1

Table II

Corporations with Net Income

ELECTRICAL GOODS

MONEY AMOUNTS AND SIZE OF ASSETS IN THOUSANDS OF DOLLARS

Item Description for Accounting Period 7/12 Through 6/13	Total	Zero Assets	Under 500	500 to 1,000	1,000 to 5,000	5,000 to 10,000	10,000 to 25,000	25,000 to 50,000	50,000 to 100,000	100,000 to 250,000	250,000 to 500,000	500,000 to 2,500,000	2,500,000 and over
Number of Enterprises 1	19798	2042	11035	2520	2844	•	406	167	107	81	18	25	•

Revenues ($ in Thousands)

Net Sales 2	358318469	6419967	10426811	6058896	19448517	•	16335838	15540384	18054387	32469208	11962092	69801401	•
Interest 3	236567	121	39	500	1154	•	4687	8431	6067	12101	10259	38491	•
Rents 4	92395	0	0	713	301	•	1838	2721	2317	1468	4904	4837	•
Royalties 5	2105995	124	0	0	0	•	330	0	4153	19194	7660	73638	•
Other Portfolio Income 6	1990476	26900	17232	14724	20739	•	17772	3964	8480	14884	19495	169325	•
Other Receipts 7	3431895	41777	51553	56379	313441	•	88273	83456	112376	179809	75915	934248	•
Total Receipts 8	366175797	6488889	10495635	6131212	19784152	•	16448738	15638956	18187780	32696664	12080325	71021940	•
Average Total Receipts 9	18496	3178	951	2433	6956	•	40514	93646	169979	403663	671129	2840878	•

Operating Costs/Operating Income (%)

Cost of Operations 10	82.4	88.4	63.0	66.5	73.9	•	80.4	80.7	82.0	83.7	82.1	88.2	•
Salaries and Wages 11	5.9	3.9	8.4	8.1	8.1	•	6.5	6.8	6.3	5.7	5.7	4.8	•
Taxes Paid 12	0.7	0.4	1.9	1.5	1.4	•	0.8	0.9	0.9	0.7	0.6	0.5	•
Interest Paid 13	0.4	0.2	0.1	0.5	0.2	•	0.3	0.3	0.3	0.2	0.5	0.2	•
Depreciation 14	1.0	0.2	0.4	0.5	0.4	•	0.4	0.3	0.5	0.5	0.5	0.4	•
Amortization and Depletion 15	0.9	0.0	0.1	0.0	0.0	•	0.1	0.2	0.1	0.1	0.3	0.1	•
Pensions and Other Deferred Comp. 16	0.3	0.1	0.2	0.4	0.4	•	0.1	0.3	0.2	0.3	0.3	0.4	•
Employee Benefits 17	0.7	0.2	0.8	0.7	0.6	•	0.5	0.6	0.5	0.7	0.6	0.5	•
Advertising 18	0.7	0.1	0.3	0.9	0.3	•	0.6	0.4	0.6	0.6	0.2	0.5	•
Other Expenses 19	5.1	4.6	10.7	9.0	8.6	•	5.7	5.5	5.0	4.2	6.8	3.1	•
Officers' Compensation 20	0.8	0.7	6.3	6.6	3.2	•	1.2	1.1	0.7	0.5	0.6	0.2	•
Operating Margin 21	1.1	1.2	7.7	5.2	2.9	•	3.3	3.0	3.0	2.7	1.8	1.1	•
Operating Margin Before Officers' Comp. 22	1.9	1.9	14.0	11.8	6.1	•	4.5	4.1	3.6	3.2	2.4	1.3	•

Selected Average Balance Sheet ($ in Thousands)

Net Receivables 23	2758	0	20	173	686	•	5218	13700	24482	59351	130546	427216	•
Inventories 24	1536	0	24	177	809	•	4368	11707	20451	38586	60843	239396	•
Net Property, Plant and Equipment 25	724	0	10	111	144	•	994	1903	5060	11693	16807	69548	•
Total Assets 26	9423	0	123	725	2218	•	14869	35911	70069	157989	353426	1101911	•
Notes and Loans Payable 27	2299	0	67	172	375	•	2680	6161	13449	26375	66373	109295	•
All Other Liabilities 28	3888	0	43	275	797	•	6036	16410	27868	63733	154848	542963	•
Net Worth 29	3237	0	13	279	1046	•	6153	13340	28751	67882	132205	449652	•

Selected Financial Ratios (Times to 1)

Current Ratio 30	1.4	•	1.7	1.7	2.2	•	1.8	1.7	1.9	1.8	1.8	1.5	•
Quick Ratio 31	0.8	•	1.1	1.0	1.1	•	1.0	0.9	1.0	1.1	1.1	1.0	•
Net Sales to Working Capital 32	11.4	•	26.2	11.0	6.5	•	7.4	7.5	6.4	7.1	6.4	11.1	•
Coverage Ratio 33	9.8	13.6	61.3	12.9	22.5	•	15.2	12.4	13.0	16.6	6.3	15.8	•
Total Asset Turnover 34	1.9	•	7.7	3.3	3.1	•	2.7	2.6	2.4	2.5	1.9	2.5	•
Inventory Turnover 35	9.7	•	24.5	9.1	6.3	•	7.4	6.4	6.8	8.7	9.0	10.3	•
Receivables Turnover 36	6.9	•	36.2	•	8.1	•	8.4	6.7	7.0	7.2	5.8	6.0	•
Total Liabilities to Net Worth 37	1.9	•	8.8	1.6	1.1	•	1.4	1.7	1.4	1.3	1.7	1.5	•
Current Assets to Working Capital 38	3.7	•	2.5	2.4	1.9	•	2.3	2.5	2.2	2.2	2.3	3.2	•
Current Liabilities to Working Capital 39	2.7	•	1.5	1.4	0.9	•	1.3	1.5	1.2	1.2	1.3	2.2	•
Working Capital to Net Sales 40	0.1	•	0.0	0.1	0.2	•	0.1	0.1	0.2	0.1	0.2	0.1	•
Inventory to Working Capital 41	1.0	•	0.6	0.8	0.8	•	0.8	1.0	0.8	0.7	0.6	0.8	•
Total Receipts to Cash Flow 42	13.8	17.6	6.3	7.5	8.9	•	11.8	12.6	12.9	14.5	11.3	19.3	•
Cost of Goods to Cash Flow 43	11.3	15.5	3.9	5.0	6.5	•	9.5	10.2	10.5	12.1	9.3	17.0	•
Cash Flow to Total Debt 44	0.2	•	1.4	0.7	0.7	•	0.4	0.3	0.3	0.3	0.3	0.2	•

Selected Financial Factors (in Percentages)

Debt Ratio 45	65.6	•	89.8	61.6	52.8	•	58.6	62.9	59.0	57.0	62.6	59.2	•
Return on Total Assets 46	7.3	•	65.3	22.9	14.9	•	11.5	10.1	9.7	9.4	6.4	7.7	•
Return on Equity Before Income Taxes 47	19.1	•	632.3	55.1	30.2	•	25.9	25.1	21.9	20.5	14.3	17.7	•
Return on Equity After Income Taxes 48	15.7	•	623.9	52.9	28.6	•	23.1	22.3	19.0	16.8	11.5	13.4	•
Profit Margin (Before Income Tax) 49	3.4	2.2	8.4	6.4	4.6	•	4.0	3.6	3.7	3.5	2.8	2.9	•
Profit Margin (After Income Tax) 50	2.8	2.2	8.3	6.1	4.4	•	3.5	3.2	3.2	2.8	2.3	2.2	•

Table I

Corporations with and without Net Income

HARDWARE, PLUMBING, HEATING EQUIPMENT, AND SUPPLIES

MONEY AMOUNTS AND SIZE OF ASSETS IN THOUSANDS OF DOLLARS

Item Description for Accounting Period 7/12 Through 6/13	Total	Zero Assets	Under 500	500 to 1,000	1,000 to 5,000	5,000 to 10,000	10,000 to 25,000	25,000 to 50,000	50,000 to 100,000	100,000 to 250,000	250,000 to 500,000	500,000 to 2,500,000	2,500,000 and over
Number of Enterprises 1	13624	1551	6603	1564	2876	455	369	110	52	29	5	10	0

Revenues ($ in Thousands)

Net Sales 2	91705269	396280	3015276	3084287	16764811	7122674	13238874	8405262	7602251	6676673	3301755	22097126	0
Interest 3	40268	1	4	259	4442	3671	3673	3633	3711	3833	328	16714	0
Rents 4	32921	0	0	620	2996	319	1557	4146	490	119	0	22674	0
Royalties 5	5573	0	0	0	0	0	0	0	0	0	0	5573	0
Other Portfolio Income 6	169944	1812	1853	0	54942	848	12295	13584	2128	8238	707	73533	0
Other Receipts 7	837073	11684	-411	22261	258970	99917	102589	71002	51208	24067	47632	148157	0
Total Receipts 8	92791048	409777	3016722	3107427	17086161	7227429	13358988	8497627	7659788	6712930	3350422	22363777	0
Average Total Receipts 9	6811	264	457	1987	5941	15884	36203	77251	147304	231480	670084	2236378	•

Operating Costs/Operating Income (%)

Cost of Operations 10	72.0	61.4	61.7	67.8	73.3	68.3	74.6	75.1	74.5	75.1	77.8	68.8	•
Salaries and Wages 11	10.1	11.4	12.0	9.4	9.7	12.1	9.3	9.9	8.9	9.0	8.7	11.0	•
Taxes Paid 12	1.5	3.1	2.3	1.8	1.5	1.5	1.2	1.3	1.2	1.3	1.3	1.6	•
Interest Paid 13	0.7	1.0	0.6	0.3	0.3	0.6	0.4	0.5	0.4	0.7	1.1	1.5	•
Depreciation 14	0.7	0.7	0.5	0.4	0.4	0.4	0.3	0.6	0.6	1.1	0.5	1.2	•
Amortization and Depletion 15	0.2	0.0	0.2	0.2	0.0	0.0	0.1	0.0	0.1	0.3	0.5	0.4	•
Pensions and Other Deferred Comp. 16	0.4	0.5	0.3	0.4	0.4	0.4	0.4	0.3	0.4	0.3	0.1	0.5	•
Employee Benefits 17	1.0	0.5	0.5	0.4	1.0	1.2	0.8	1.0	1.0	1.1	1.0	1.2	•
Advertising 18	0.5	0.6	0.9	0.3	0.4	0.6	0.5	0.5	0.9	0.6	0.1	0.3	•
Other Expenses 19	8.5	16.8	15.7	11.3	8.9	9.7	6.7	6.8	7.7	8.4	5.9	8.9	•
Officers' Compensation 20	2.1	1.7	6.1	6.6	3.9	2.7	2.3	1.3	0.9	0.7	0.8	0.5	•
Operating Margin 21	2.5	2.2	•	1.1	0.4	2.5	3.3	2.6	3.2	1.5	2.3	4.2	•
Operating Margin Before Officers' Comp. 22	4.5	3.9	5.3	7.7	4.2	5.2	5.6	3.9	4.2	2.2	3.1	4.6	•

Selected Average Balance Sheet ($ in Thousands)

Net Receivables 23	824	0	30	210	669	2072	4250	8814	18777	40257	66154	281942	•
Inventories 24	1065	0	22	190	811	3970	6256	13637	24209	48017	114295	290212	•
Net Property, Plant and Equipment 25	381	0	6	38	151	599	978	3948	8056	19693	20133	249437	•
Total Assets 26	3370	0	95	659	2382	7138	15457	33308	68917	147144	367483	1509884	•
Notes and Loans Payable 27	986	0	105	227	453	2173	3458	8960	14779	37639	113025	540726	•
All Other Liabilities 28	982	0	41	187	729	1822	4293	8839	20705	53701	112189	413854	•
Net Worth 29	1401	0	-52	245	1200	3142	7705	15509	33433	55805	142269	555305	•

Selected Financial Ratios (Times to 1)

Current Ratio 30	2.2	•	1.4	2.6	2.3	2.3	2.1	2.0	2.3	1.7	2.4	2.6	•
Quick Ratio 31	1.1	•	1.0	1.5	1.2	0.9	0.9	0.9	1.1	0.8	1.2	1.4	•
Net Sales to Working Capital 32	5.2	•	21.2	6.0	5.2	4.4	5.4	6.0	4.8	5.1	5.7	4.6	•
Coverage Ratio 33	6.1	6.4	•	7.7	8.0	7.6	12.6	8.1	10.3	3.7	4.5	4.7	•
Total Asset Turnover 34	2.0	•	4.8	3.0	2.4	2.2	2.3	2.3	2.1	1.6	1.8	1.5	•
Inventory Turnover 35	4.5	•	12.7	7.0	5.3	2.7	4.3	4.2	4.5	3.6	4.5	5.2	•
Receivables Turnover 36	7.9	•	11.4	10.9	8.3	6.1	8.7	8.2	8.2	5.9	7.8	8.0	•
Total Liabilities to Net Worth 37	1.4	•	•	1.7	1.0	1.3	1.0	1.1	1.1	1.6	1.6	1.7	•
Current Assets to Working Capital 38	1.8	•	3.4	1.6	1.8	1.8	1.9	2.0	1.8	2.4	1.7	1.6	•
Current Liabilities to Working Capital 39	0.8	•	2.4	0.6	0.8	0.8	0.9	1.0	0.8	1.4	0.7	0.6	•
Working Capital to Net Sales 40	0.2	•	0.0	0.2	0.2	0.2	0.2	0.2	0.2	0.2	0.2	0.2	•
Inventory to Working Capital 41	0.8	•	1.0	0.6	0.8	1.0	1.0	1.1	0.9	1.1	0.8	0.7	•
Total Receipts to Cash Flow 42	10.2	5.3	7.9	9.6	11.3	8.6	11.7	12.2	10.5	12.0	13.4	8.5	•
Cost of Goods to Cash Flow 43	7.3	3.3	4.9	6.5	8.3	5.9	8.7	9.2	7.8	9.0	10.4	5.8	•
Cash Flow to Total Debt 44	0.3	•	0.4	0.5	0.4	0.5	0.4	0.4	0.4	0.2	0.2	0.3	•

Selected Financial Factors (in Percentages)

Debt Ratio 45	58.4	•	154.5	62.8	49.6	56.0	50.1	53.4	51.5	62.1	61.3	63.2	•
Return on Total Assets 46	8.7	•	•	6.4	6.3	9.9	10.6	9.7	9.3	4.3	8.6	10.2	•
Return on Equity Before Income Taxes 47	17.5	•	6.6	15.0	11.0	19.6	19.5	18.2	17.4	8.2	17.4	21.7	•
Return on Equity After Income Taxes 48	14.4	•	7.4	14.3	8.9	17.9	17.9	15.5	15.9	6.6	13.2	16.0	•
Profit Margin (Before Income Tax) 49	3.7	5.6	•	1.9	2.3	3.9	4.2	3.7	4.0	2.0	3.7	5.5	•
Profit Margin (After Income Tax) 50	3.0	5.6	•	1.8	1.8	3.6	3.8	3.1	3.6	1.6	2.8	4.0	•

Table II

Corporations with Net Income

HARDWARE, PLUMBING, HEATING EQUIPMENT, AND SUPPLIES

MONEY AMOUNTS AND SIZE OF ASSETS IN THOUSANDS OF DOLLARS

Item Description for Accounting Period 7/12 Through 6/13		Total	Zero Assets	Under 500	500 to 1,000	1,000 to 5,000	5,000 to 10,000	10,000 to 25,000	25,000 to 50,000	50,000 to 100,000	100,000 to 250,000	250,000 to 500,000	500,000 to 2,500,000	2,500,000 and over
Number of Enterprises	1	9247	831	4264	1203	2022	408	•	•	•	23	•	7	0
Revenues ($ in Thousands)														
Net Sales	2	78971245	381631	2104698	2439571	12175654	6495514	•	•	•	5386470	•	19878211	0
Interest	3	35414	1	0	184	3508	3507	•	•	•	3437	•	15463	0
Rents	4	29848	0	0	0	674	319	•	•	•	71	•	22670	0
Royalties	5	5573	0	0	0	0	0	•	•	•	0	•	5573	0
Other Portfolio Income	6	124696	1812	1853	0	38314	848	•	•	•	8000	•	46688	0
Other Receipts	7	720026	11637	-10684	21310	194585	96987	•	•	•	22980	•	131079	0
Total Receipts	8	79886802	395081	2095867	2461065	12412735	6597175	•	•	•	5420958	•	20099684	0
Average Total Receipts	9	8639	475	492	2046	6139	16170	•	•	•	235694	•	2871383	•
Operating Costs/Operating Income (%)														
Cost of Operations	10	72.1	57.7	57.1	68.6	73.0	67.1	•	•	•	75.6	•	70.3	•
Salaries and Wages	11	9.7	11.8	9.2	9.1	8.5	12.4	•	•	•	8.4	•	10.5	•
Taxes Paid	12	1.4	2.9	2.3	1.5	1.5	1.6	•	•	•	1.2	•	1.5	•
Interest Paid	13	0.6	0.5	0.4	0.1	0.4	0.6	•	•	•	0.5	•	1.0	•
Depreciation	14	0.6	0.5	0.4	0.2	0.4	0.4	•	•	•	1.0	•	0.9	•
Amortization and Depletion	15	0.1	0.0	0.1	0.0	0.0	0.0	•	•	•	0.2	•	0.3	•
Pensions and Other Deferred Comp.	16	0.4	0.5	0.4	0.5	0.4	0.4	•	•	•	0.3	•	0.6	•
Employee Benefits	17	1.0	0.5	0.5	0.2	0.8	1.1	•	•	•	1.1	•	1.2	•
Advertising	18	0.5	0.6	1.2	0.3	0.3	0.6	•	•	•	0.6	•	0.3	•
Other Expenses	19	7.7	12.2	15.1	10.3	7.8	9.7	•	•	•	7.1	•	7.6	•
Officers' Compensation	20	2.1	1.7	8.0	5.9	4.7	2.8	•	•	•	0.7	•	0.3	•
Operating Margin	21	3.9	11.1	5.3	3.3	2.2	3.3	•	•	•	3.3	•	5.4	•
Operating Margin Before Officers' Comp.	22	6.0	12.8	13.3	9.2	6.9	6.1	•	•	•	4.0	•	5.8	•

Selected Average Balance Sheet ($ in Thousands)

Net Receivables **23**	1075	0	29	214	762	2128	•	•	•	43347	•	375500	•
Inventories **24**	1345	0	13	187	926	4130	•	•	•	44721	•	390118	•
Net Property, Plant and Equipment **25**	372	0	3	26	143	558	•	•	•	18040	•	192000	•
Total Assets **26**	3926	0	73	632	2367	7082	•	•	•	149234	•	1556259	•
Notes and Loans Payable **27**	1041	0	24	111	486	1970	•	•	•	31851	•	536568	•
All Other Liabilities **28**	1094	0	41	159	768	1698	•	•	•	53186	•	382361	•
Net Worth **29**	1791	0	7	362	1113	3413	•	•	•	64197	•	637330	•

Selected Financial Ratios (Times to 1)

Current Ratio **30**	2.3	•	1.6	2.9	2.2	2.4	•	•	•	2.0	•	2.6	•
Quick Ratio **31**	1.1	•	1.3	1.8	1.1	1.0	•	•	•	1.0	•	1.5	•
Net Sales to Working Capital **32**	5.1	•	19.7	5.9	5.3	4.3	•	•	•	4.3	•	4.7	•
Coverage Ratio **33**	9.6	32.1	14.9	31.5	12.5	9.2	•	•	•	8.7	•	7.4	•
Total Asset Turnover **34**	2.2	•	6.8	3.2	2.5	2.2	•	•	•	1.6	•	1.8	•
Inventory Turnover **35**	4.6	•	21.5	7.4	4.7	2.6	•	•	•	4.0	•	5.1	•
Receivables Turnover **36**	7.8	•	11.9	10.3	7.4	6.1	•	•	•	5.8	•	•	•
Total Liabilities to Net Worth **37**	1.2	•	9.1	0.7	1.1	1.1	•	•	•	1.3	•	1.4	•
Current Assets to Working Capital **38**	1.8	•	2.7	1.5	1.8	1.7	•	•	•	2.0	•	1.6	•
Current Liabilities to Working Capital **39**	0.8	•	1.7	0.5	0.8	0.7	•	•	•	1.0	•	0.6	•
Working Capital to Net Sales **40**	0.2	•	0.1	0.2	0.2	0.2	•	•	•	0.2	•	0.2	•
Inventory to Working Capital **41**	0.8	•	0.5	0.5	0.8	1.0	•	•	•	0.9	•	0.6	•
Total Receipts to Cash Flow **42**	9.5	4.2	5.7	8.3	10.3	8.0	•	•	•	11.1	•	8.5	•
Cost of Goods to Cash Flow **43**	6.9	2.4	3.3	5.7	7.5	5.4	•	•	•	8.4	•	6.0	•
Cash Flow to Total Debt **44**	0.4	•	1.3	0.9	0.5	0.5	•	•	•	0.2	•	0.4	•

Selected Financial Factors (in Percentages)

Debt Ratio **45**	54.4	•	90.1	42.7	53.0	51.8	•	•	•	57.0	•	59.0	•
Return on Total Assets **46**	12.2	•	35.4	13.8	11.5	12.2	•	•	•	7.0	•	14.0	•
Return on Equity Before Income Taxes **47**	24.0	•	333.9	23.4	22.5	22.6	•	•	•	14.4	•	29.5	•
Return on Equity After Income Taxes **48**	20.4	•	325.4	22.7	19.3	20.9	•	•	•	12.6	•	22.3	•
Profit Margin (Before Income Tax) **49**	5.0	14.6	4.9	4.2	4.2	4.8	•	•	•	4.0	•	6.6	•
Profit Margin (After Income Tax) **50**	4.3	14.6	4.8	4.1	3.6	4.5	•	•	•	3.5	•	5.0	•

Table I

Corporations with and without Net Income

MACHINERY, EQUIPMENT, AND SUPPLIES

MONEY AMOUNTS AND SIZE OF ASSETS IN THOUSANDS OF DOLLARS

Item Description for Accounting Period 7/12 Through 6/13	Total	Zero Assets	Under 500	500 to 1,000	1,000 to 5,000	5,000 to 10,000	10,000 to 25,000	25,000 to 50,000	50,000 to 100,000	100,000 to 250,000	250,000 to 500,000	500,000 to 2,500,000	2,500,000 and over
Number of Enterprises 1	48730	4909	25212	6084	8769	1722	1230	421	191	110	42	34	6
Revenues ($ in Thousands)													
Net Sales 2	322268785	9198810	15553792	10610137	50557507	28043912	40325443	28845913	23437170	25000426	16061649	37065334	37568692
Interest 3	337398	7274	502	3034	13975	7392	12623	14621	20564	20069	22066	39550	175728
Rents 4	197593	1100	1089	14021	14958	13159	18740	13505	12889	39500	29145	34874	4613
Royalties 5	35811	479	0	0	10144	8008	982	158	7313	3050	302	3050	2326
Other Portfolio Income 6	1609862	77802	30950	24964	140953	58716	141789	166730	154435	234724	173711	298611	106474
Other Receipts 7	2882011	51695	136505	103823	563616	228965	410872	214989	307637	342092	171036	214253	136530
Total Receipts 8	327331460	9337160	15722838	10755979	51301153	28360152	40910449	29255916	23940008	25639861	16457909	37655672	37994363
Average Total Receipts 9	6717	1902	624	1768	5850	16469	33261	69491	125340	233090	391855	1107520	6332394
Operating Costs/Operating Income (%)													
Cost of Operations 10	75.9	87.3	62.1	70.6	71.3	75.9	76.9	78.8	79.0	77.1	73.2	72.1	85.1
Salaries and Wages 11	6.8	3.1	6.4	7.3	8.3	7.2	7.5	6.4	6.5	6.9	8.1	7.5	3.9
Taxes Paid 12	1.1	0.5	1.6	1.5	1.6	1.3	1.1	1.0	1.0	1.0	1.2	1.2	0.6
Interest Paid 13	0.7	0.5	0.2	0.4	0.5	0.5	0.4	0.5	0.6	0.9	0.8	1.1	1.3
Depreciation 14	1.6	0.5	0.5	1.4	0.8	0.8	1.2	1.6	2.0	2.5	4.5	3.4	0.7
Amortization and Depletion 15	0.2	0.2	0.0	0.0	0.1	0.1	0.1	0.1	0.2	0.2	0.1	0.7	0.5
Pensions and Other Deferred Comp. 16	0.4	1.5	0.5	0.4	0.4	0.2	0.2	0.3	0.3	0.2	0.5	0.6	0.5
Employee Benefits 17	0.9	0.5	0.5	0.8	0.9	0.7	0.8	0.8	0.8	0.9	1.6	1.5	0.8
Advertising 18	0.4	0.1	0.4	0.3	0.4	0.4	0.4	0.3	0.4	0.3	0.3	0.3	0.5
Other Expenses 19	7.0	4.5	16.7	10.5	8.9	7.3	6.4	5.7	5.1	6.7	6.9	6.0	3.9
Officers' Compensation 20	2.0	2.2	7.6	4.6	4.0	2.5	1.7	1.5	0.9	0.8	0.6	0.7	0.3
Operating Margin 21	3.0	•	3.5	2.3	2.9	3.2	3.3	2.9	3.2	2.5	2.1	4.9	2.1
Operating Margin Before Officers' Comp. 22	5.0	1.5	11.1	6.9	6.9	5.7	5.1	4.4	4.2	3.3	2.7	5.5	2.4

Selected Average Balance Sheet ($ in Thousands)													
Net Receivables 23	836	0	35	160	590	1905	3765	7448	12558	33083	69354	172431	1310210
Inventories 24	1086	0	41	178	765	3053	5599	14662	25079	51694	99217	245130	468985
Net Property, Plant and Equipment 25	480	0	15	81	232	739	1806	4557	9755	25245	65275	179670	263142
Total Assets 26	3519	0	141	660	2245	7232	15198	34969	69091	153302	341929	906370	3853288
Notes and Loans Payable 27	1042	0	54	245	639	2108	3890	8876	17898	47675	103610	301914	1145147
All Other Liabilities 28	1150	0	42	184	764	2316	5201	12870	24595	49738	106684	265113	1281337
Net Worth 29	1328	0	45	230	843	2808	6108	13224	26598	55888	131636	339343	1426804
Selected Financial Ratios (Times to 1)													
Current Ratio 30	1.8	•	2.4	2.5	1.9	1.9	1.7	1.6	1.7	1.6	1.6	1.9	2.2
Quick Ratio 31	0.8	•	1.4	1.4	1.0	0.8	0.8	0.6	0.6	0.6	0.7	0.7	1.2
Net Sales to Working Capital 32	5.9	•	9.2	5.7	6.9	5.7	6.5	6.6	6.0	5.9	5.0	4.4	4.7
Coverage Ratio 33	7.6	2.8	20.4	9.5	10.1	9.3	11.9	9.0	9.8	6.7	6.6	6.8	3.6
Total Asset Turnover 34	1.9	•	4.4	2.6	2.6	2.3	2.2	2.0	1.8	1.5	1.1	1.2	1.6
Inventory Turnover 35	4.6	•	9.4	6.9	5.4	4.0	4.5	3.7	3.9	3.4	2.8	3.2	11.4
Receivables Turnover 36	8.3	•	17.5	11.9	9.8	9.3	9.1	9.4	9.7	6.7	5.2	7.1	5.3
Total Liabilities to Net Worth 37	1.7	•	2.2	1.9	1.7	1.6	1.5	1.6	1.6	1.7	1.6	1.7	1.7
Current Assets to Working Capital 38	2.3	•	1.7	1.7	2.2	2.1	2.4	2.6	2.5	2.8	2.7	2.2	1.8
Current Liabilities to Working Capital 39	1.3	•	0.7	0.7	1.2	1.1	1.4	1.6	1.5	1.8	1.7	1.2	0.8
Working Capital to Net Sales 40	0.2	•	0.1	0.2	0.1	0.2	0.2	0.2	0.2	0.2	0.2	0.2	0.2
Inventory to Working Capital 41	1.1	•	0.6	0.6	0.9	1.1	1.2	1.5	1.4	1.5	1.3	1.2	0.4
Total Receipts to Cash Flow 42	10.0	21.2	5.3	8.5	8.9	9.8	10.4	11.6	10.8	9.8	10.0	9.3	15.6
Cost of Goods to Cash Flow 43	7.6	18.5	3.3	6.0	6.4	7.4	8.0	9.1	8.5	7.6	7.3	6.7	13.2
Cash Flow to Total Debt 44	0.3	•	1.2	0.5	0.5	0.4	0.3	0.3	0.3	0.2	0.2	0.2	0.2
Selected Financial Factors (in Percentages)													
Debt Ratio 45	62.3	•	68.3	65.1	62.5	61.2	59.8	62.2	61.5	63.5	61.5	62.6	63.0
Return on Total Assets 46	9.9	•	21.2	10.9	12.5	10.9	11.3	9.6	10.7	8.8	6.2	9.2	7.4
Return on Equity Before Income Taxes 47	22.7	•	63.6	27.9	30.0	25.0	25.7	22.5	24.9	20.5	13.6	20.9	14.4
Return on Equity After Income Taxes 48	18.9	•	61.6	26.2	27.7	22.9	22.3	19.3	22.5	17.1	10.5	14.8	9.0
Profit Margin (Before Income Tax) 49	4.6	0.8	4.6	3.7	4.4	4.3	4.8	4.3	5.4	5.0	4.7	6.5	3.3
Profit Margin (After Income Tax) 50	3.8	0.5	4.5	3.5	4.1	3.9	4.2	3.7	4.9	4.2	3.6	4.6	2.0

Table II

Corporations with Net Income

MACHINERY, EQUIPMENT, AND SUPPLIES

MONEY AMOUNTS AND SIZE OF ASSETS IN THOUSANDS OF DOLLARS

Item Description for Accounting Period 7/12 Through 6/13	Total	Zero Assets	Under 500	500 to 1,000	1,000 to 5,000	5,000 to 10,000	10,000 to 25,000	25,000 to 50,000	50,000 to 100,000	100,000 to 250,000	250,000 to 500,000	500,000 to 2,500,000	2,500,000 and over
Number of Enterprises 1	35137	2300	18158	4153	7231	•	1103	377	169	97	38	31	•

Revenues ($ in Thousands)

	Total	Zero Assets	Under 500	500 to 1,000	1,000 to 5,000	5,000 to 10,000	10,000 to 25,000	25,000 to 50,000	50,000 to 100,000	100,000 to 250,000	250,000 to 500,000	500,000 to 2,500,000	2,500,000 and over
Net Sales 2	285638442	7674933	13607800	8821622	43812484	•	37307504	27522880	21902397	23232411	14443901	34045286	•
Interest 3	281292	6462	281	1645	11930	•	11836	12477	19421	16753	20322	30513	•
Rents 4	185483	1100	1089	12733	13638	•	17425	11792	12534	38645	27202	34550	•
Royalties 5	30883	0	0	0	9324	•	982	60	7313	441	302	2875	•
Other Portfolio Income 6	1362682	76699	30510	20136	104526	•	113785	132966	145158	171739	125325	295989	•
Other Receipts 7	2627772	48758	119929	83177	518627	•	374873	198803	306529	315598	156379	203309	•
Total Receipts 8	290126554	7807952	13759609	8939313	44470529	•	37826405	27878978	22393352	23775587	14773431	34612522	•
Average Total Receipts 9	8257	3395	758	2152	6150	•	34294	73950	132505	245109	388774	1116533	•

Operating Costs/Operating Income (%)

	Total	Zero Assets	Under 500	500 to 1,000	1,000 to 5,000	5,000 to 10,000	10,000 to 25,000	25,000 to 50,000	50,000 to 100,000	100,000 to 250,000	250,000 to 500,000	500,000 to 2,500,000	2,500,000 and over
Cost of Operations 10	75.4	88.7	61.0	70.8	70.2	•	76.6	79.3	79.2	77.2	73.0	71.1	•
Salaries and Wages 11	6.8	2.0	5.6	6.5	8.2	•	7.4	6.2	6.5	6.8	8.3	7.6	•
Taxes Paid 12	1.1	0.4	1.5	1.2	1.6	•	1.1	1.0	1.0	1.0	1.2	1.2	•
Interest Paid 13	0.6	0.2	0.2	0.3	0.5	•	0.4	0.5	0.5	0.8	0.8	1.1	•
Depreciation 14	1.4	0.5	0.4	1.1	0.8	•	1.1	1.2	1.6	2.0	3.8	3.2	•
Amortization and Depletion 15	0.2	0.0	0.0	0.0	0.1	•	0.1	0.1	0.1	0.2	0.1	0.7	•
Pensions and Other Deferred Comp. 16	0.4	1.8	0.5	0.4	0.4	•	0.2	0.3	0.3	0.2	0.6	0.6	•
Employee Benefits 17	0.9	0.2	0.5	0.6	0.9	•	0.7	0.8	0.8	0.9	1.6	1.6	•
Advertising 18	0.3	0.0	0.3	0.2	0.4	•	0.4	0.3	0.4	0.3	0.3	0.3	•
Other Expenses 19	6.7	2.9	16.4	9.4	8.6	•	6.2	5.3	4.9	6.5	6.6	6.2	•
Officers' Compensation 20	2.0	2.2	7.7	4.6	3.9	•	1.7	1.5	1.0	0.8	0.6	0.6	•
Operating Margin 21	4.1	1.2	5.8	4.9	4.5	•	4.1	3.6	3.9	3.3	3.2	5.7	•
Operating Margin Before Officers' Comp. 22	6.2	3.3	13.6	9.6	8.4	•	5.8	5.1	4.8	4.1	3.7	6.3	•

Selected Average Balance Sheet ($ in Thousands)

Net Receivables **23**	1000	0	38	193	621	•	3867	7626	12549	34149	71580	166210	•
Inventories **24**	1285	0	42	143	784	•	5647	14927	24670	48591	92852	225701	•
Net Property, Plant and Equipment **25**	554	0	16	80	249	•	1607	4104	9647	24482	59815	164501	•
Total Assets **26**	4153	0	156	647	2284	•	15312	35077	68972	152828	344713	893956	•
Notes and Loans Payable **27**	1162	0	52	190	611	•	3589	8727	16109	45375	98010	302602	•
All Other Liabilities **28**	1345	0	40	175	691	•	5270	13027	25659	49558	108769	255002	•
Net Worth **29**	1646	0	64	283	982	•	6453	13323	27205	57895	137934	336352	•

Selected Financial Ratios (Times to 1)

Current Ratio **30**	1.9	•	2.8	2.7	2.1	•	1.8	1.6	1.7	1.6	1.6	2.0	•
Quick Ratio **31**	0.9	•	1.7	1.9	1.1	•	0.8	0.6	0.6	0.6	0.7	0.8	•
Net Sales to Working Capital **32**	5.7	•	8.7	6.6	6.3	•	6.1	6.7	6.2	6.0	4.6	4.2	•
Coverage Ratio **33**	10.4	17.5	34.7	23.2	13.6	•	14.6	11.4	14.2	8.5	8.2	7.5	•
Total Asset Turnover **34**	2.0	•	4.8	3.3	2.7	•	2.2	2.1	1.9	1.6	1.1	1.2	•
Inventory Turnover **35**	4.8	•	10.8	10.5	5.4	•	4.6	3.9	4.2	3.8	3.0	3.5	•
Receivables Turnover **36**	8.6	•	19.4	12.3	10.3	•	9.5	10.0	11.0	7.4	5.4	8.1	•
Total Liabilities to Net Worth **37**	1.5	•	1.5	1.3	1.3	•	1.4	1.6	1.5	1.6	1.5	1.7	•
Current Assets to Working Capital **38**	2.1	•	1.5	1.6	2.0	•	2.3	2.6	2.5	2.7	2.6	2.0	•
Current Liabilities to Working Capital **39**	1.1	•	0.5	0.6	1.0	•	1.3	1.6	1.5	1.7	1.6	1.0	•
Working Capital to Net Sales **40**	0.2	•	0.1	0.2	0.2	•	0.2	0.1	0.2	0.2	0.2	0.2	•
Inventory to Working Capital **41**	1.0	•	0.6	0.4	0.9	•	1.1	1.5	1.4	1.4	1.2	1.1	•
Total Receipts to Cash Flow **42**	9.2	19.2	4.7	7.4	8.0	•	9.8	11.0	10.2	9.3	9.3	8.5	•
Cost of Goods to Cash Flow **43**	6.9	17.0	2.9	5.3	5.6	•	7.5	8.7	8.1	7.2	6.8	6.0	•
Cash Flow to Total Debt **44**	0.4	•	1.7	0.8	0.6	•	0.4	0.3	0.3	0.3	0.2	0.2	•

Selected Financial Factors (in Percentages)

Debt Ratio **45**	60.4	•	59.2	56.3	57.0	•	57.9	62.0	60.6	62.1	60.0	62.4	•
Return on Total Assets **46**	12.4	•	34.4	21.5	17.2	•	13.0	11.3	12.4	10.0	7.1	10.5	•
Return on Equity Before Income Taxes **47**	28.3	•	81.8	47.2	37.0	•	28.8	27.2	29.2	23.3	15.5	24.2	•
Return on Equity After Income Taxes **48**	24.1	•	79.8	45.1	34.6	•	25.2	23.7	26.6	19.6	12.2	17.4	•
Profit Margin (Before Income Tax) **49**	5.7	2.9	6.9	6.3	6.0	•	5.5	5.0	6.1	5.6	5.6	7.4	•
Profit Margin (After Income Tax) **50**	4.9	2.5	6.8	6.0	5.6	•	4.8	4.3	5.6	4.7	4.4	5.3	•

Table I

Corporations with and without Net Income

FURNITURE, SPORTS, TOYS, JEWELRY, OTHER DURABLE GOODS

MONEY AMOUNTS AND SIZE OF ASSETS IN THOUSANDS OF DOLLARS

Item Description for Accounting Period 7/12 Through 6/13		Total	Zero Assets	Under 500	500 to 1,000	1,000 to 5,000	5,000 to 10,000	10,000 to 25,000	25,000 to 50,000	50,000 to 100,000	100,000 to 250,000	250,000 to 500,000	500,000 to 2,500,000	2,500,000 and over
Number of Enterprises	1	76106	13853	46024	5736	7543	1564	837	286	153	75	20	9	5
Revenues ($ in Thousands)														
Net Sales	2	277997963	3272266	17548951	12719127	47193618	27630109	31887492	20475327	25663936	23718048	17867839	12051173	37970077
Interest	3	270474	6922	4175	1294	11057	8486	6282	17190	15154	13472	16670	5401	164373
Rents	4	82982	283	9997	20	9647	1278	2493	4390	7202	7518	2401	18194	19560
Royalties	5	408577	2466	0	0	85	1627	0	1272	9472	161514	57696	61327	113117
Other Portfolio Income	6	555558	40489	8302	1127	39101	30736	68522	7518	12979	16992	1079	56164	272550
Other Receipts	7	2210723	112077	96020	19093	435538	143777	201192	156580	96842	207131	63120	128816	550532
Total Receipts	8	281526277	3434503	17667445	12740661	47689046	27816013	32165981	20662277	25805585	24124675	18008805	12321075	39090209
Average Total Receipts	9	3699	248	384	2221	6322	17785	38430	72246	168664	321662	900440	1369008	7818042
Operating Costs/Operating Income (%)														
Cost of Operations	10	80.8	82.0	65.7	73.4	75.4	82.3	78.7	79.9	83.6	84.4	85.3	79.7	92.1
Salaries and Wages	11	5.3	4.3	6.7	5.8	7.6	5.3	6.1	5.6	4.3	4.2	3.6	6.0	3.0
Taxes Paid	12	0.9	1.3	1.7	1.3	1.2	0.9	1.1	1.0	0.8	0.7	0.5	1.0	0.3
Interest Paid	13	0.6	0.5	0.4	0.4	0.5	0.3	0.5	0.7	0.5	0.7	0.7	1.4	0.7
Depreciation	14	0.7	1.4	0.6	1.1	0.4	0.6	0.6	0.7	0.7	0.7	0.6	0.8	1.0
Amortization and Depletion	15	0.2	0.4	0.2	0.2	0.0	0.1	0.2	0.1	0.2	0.4	0.3	0.6	0.4
Pensions and Other Deferred Comp.	16	0.2	0.0	0.3	0.0	0.3	0.1	0.2	0.1	0.2	0.2	0.0	0.3	0.3
Employee Benefits	17	0.5	0.5	0.5	0.5	0.4	0.4	0.5	0.4	0.5	0.5	0.8	0.8	0.1
Advertising	18	1.1	0.8	1.0	1.3	0.7	0.6	1.2	1.3	1.1	1.6	1.9	0.8	1.5
Other Expenses	19	6.8	13.8	14.5	10.6	9.1	6.1	7.1	6.8	5.6	5.3	4.4	6.4	1.9
Officers' Compensation	20	1.7	0.9	6.2	2.7	2.9	2.1	1.8	1.2	0.8	0.6	0.4	0.4	0.3
Operating Margin	21	1.2	•	2.3	2.6	1.6	1.2	2.1	2.1	1.8	0.6	1.6	1.9	•
Operating Margin Before Officers' Comp.	22	2.9	•	8.5	5.3	4.5	3.4	3.9	3.3	2.6	1.2	2.0	2.3	•

Selected Average Balance Sheet ($ in Thousands)

Net Receivables 23	363	0	10	148	554	2082	4317	9937	18247	37550	97947	161046	678042
Inventories 24	463	0	38	277	784	2807	5907	10585	22695	36494	91775	193685	757846
Net Property, Plant and Equipment 25	140	0	13	87	161	392	1332	3756	6932	13059	37974	87354	397991
Total Assets 26	1607	0	104	710	2127	6902	15202	34099	68659	148814	340006	956348	5417396
Notes and Loans Payable 27	500	0	59	360	639	1566	4024	11043	20901	40765	116365	278515	1674324
All Other Liabilities 28	732	0	31	218	2434	3268	5896	12368	22321	48910	131364	306323	1722511
Net Worth 29	375	0	13	131	-945	2068	5282	10687	25437	59139	92277	371511	2020561

Selected Financial Ratios (Times to 1)

Current Ratio 30	1.6	•	2.0	2.2	1.7	1.5	1.6	1.6	1.6	1.7	1.5	1.4	1.5
Quick Ratio 31	0.8	•	0.9	1.0	0.8	0.7	0.8	0.8	0.7	0.9	0.8	0.7	0.6
Net Sales to Working Capital 32	8.7	•	10.1	7.3	8.5	9.1	7.9	7.3	9.0	7.6	12.7	11.3	8.6
Coverage Ratio 33	5.4	•	8.8	7.3	6.9	7.1	7.4	5.0	5.9	4.3	4.7	4.7	2.8
Total Asset Turnover 34	2.3	•	3.7	3.1	2.9	2.6	2.5	2.1	2.4	2.1	2.6	1.4	1.4
Inventory Turnover 35	6.4	•	6.6	5.9	6.0	5.2	5.1	5.4	6.2	7.3	8.3	5.5	9.2
Receivables Turnover 36	10.3	•	35.3	13.0	11.1	9.6	8.5	7.8	9.0	9.1	7.6	8.9	12.7
Total Liabilities to Net Worth 37	3.3	•	7.0	4.4	•	2.3	1.9	2.2	1.7	1.5	2.7	1.6	1.7
Current Assets to Working Capital 38	2.6	•	2.0	1.9	2.4	3.0	2.6	2.7	2.7	2.4	3.2	3.4	3.0
Current Liabilities to Working Capital 39	1.6	•	1.0	0.9	1.4	2.0	1.6	1.7	1.7	1.4	2.2	2.4	2.0
Working Capital to Net Sales 40	0.1	•	0.1	0.1	0.1	0.1	0.1	0.1	0.1	0.1	0.1	0.1	0.1
Inventory to Working Capital 41	1.1	•	1.0	0.9	1.0	1.5	1.2	1.2	1.3	0.9	1.2	1.6	1.0
Total Receipts to Cash Flow 42	13.6	14.2	7.7	9.2	10.5	15.6	12.6	12.0	14.6	15.0	17.4	11.8	53.6
Cost of Goods to Cash Flow 43	11.0	11.6	5.1	6.8	7.9	12.8	9.9	9.6	12.2	12.7	14.9	9.4	49.4
Cash Flow to Total Debt 44	0.2	•	0.5	0.4	0.2	0.2	0.3	0.3	0.3	0.2	0.2	0.2	0.0

Selected Financial Factors (in Percentages)

Debt Ratio 45	76.7	•	87.5	81.5	144.4	70.0	65.3	68.7	63.0	60.3	72.9	61.2	62.7
Return on Total Assets 46	7.0	•	12.5	10.1	9.2	5.8	8.8	7.8	7.0	6.8	8.3	9.0	2.7
Return on Equity Before Income Taxes 47	24.3	•	88.5	47.3	•	16.5	21.8	19.9	15.7	13.1	24.2	18.2	4.6
Return on Equity After Income Taxes 48	20.3	•	85.2	44.6	•	14.5	20.5	17.5	13.7	9.6	19.0	11.3	2.1
Profit Margin (Before Income Tax) 49	2.5	•	3.0	2.8	2.7	1.9	3.0	3.0	2.4	2.4	2.5	5.0	1.2
Profit Margin (After Income Tax) 50	2.1	•	2.9	2.6	2.5	1.7	2.8	2.6	2.1	1.8	2.0	3.1	0.6

Table II
Corporations with Net Income

FURNITURE, SPORTS, TOYS, JEWELRY, OTHER DURABLE GOODS

MONEY AMOUNTS AND SIZE OF ASSETS IN THOUSANDS OF DOLLARS

Item Description for Accounting Period 7/12 Through 6/13		Total	Zero Assets	Under 500	500 to 1,000	1,000 to 5,000	5,000 to 10,000	10,000 to 25,000	25,000 to 50,000	50,000 to 100,000	100,000 to 250,000	250,000 to 500,000	500,000 to 2,500,000	2,500,000 and over
Number of Enterprises	1	38878	3540	23438	3931	5697	1169	•	246	120	59	16	•	•

Revenues ($ in Thousands)														
Net Sales	2	211882512	819982	12507534	10024150	41505249	19117934	•	18253403	21289164	19919159	9949022	•	•
Interest	3	199599	6488	3392	1143	7726	7305	•	13514	7528	7999	5477	•	•
Rents	4	66638	275	5213	20	3716	1094	•	3577	6562	5603	2401	•	•
Royalties	5	359203	2418	0	0	85	680	•	262	7727	140810	55543	•	•
Other Portfolio Income	6	346335	38505	5168	987	23768	29586	•	3661	11079	11561	670	•	•
Other Receipts	7	1785472	85508	87095	18754	395266	127111	•	122868	91653	55675	44284	•	•
Total Receipts	8	214639759	953176	12608402	10045054	41935810	19283710	•	18397285	21413713	20140807	10057397	•	•
Average Total Receipts	9	5521	269	538	2555	7361	16496	•	74786	178448	341370	628587	•	•

Operating Costs/Operating Income (%)														
Cost of Operations	10	79.2	74.3	63.2	73.7	76.5	80.4	•	80.0	83.4	84.2	75.5	•	•
Salaries and Wages	11	5.5	3.5	6.8	5.9	6.8	5.4	•	5.4	4.2	3.9	5.8	•	•
Taxes Paid	12	0.9	1.4	1.7	1.2	1.0	1.0	•	1.1	0.7	0.6	0.8	•	•
Interest Paid	13	0.5	0.2	0.3	0.2	0.3	0.3	•	0.6	0.4	0.7	1.1	•	•
Depreciation	14	0.5	0.5	0.5	0.4	0.3	0.2	•	0.6	0.5	0.6	1.1	•	•
Amortization and Depletion	15	0.2	0.0	0.1	0.2	0.0	0.1	•	0.1	0.1	0.3	0.4	•	•
Pensions and Other Deferred Comp.	16	0.2	0.1	0.2	0.1	0.3	0.1	•	0.1	0.1	0.2	0.1	•	•
Employee Benefits	17	0.4	0.4	0.6	0.5	0.3	0.3	•	0.4	0.4	0.5	1.2	•	•
Advertising	18	1.1	1.3	1.1	1.4	0.6	0.5	•	1.3	1.1	1.3	3.2	•	•
Other Expenses	19	6.5	12.0	12.9	8.8	7.7	6.4	•	6.2	5.1	4.8	6.8	•	•
Officers' Compensation	20	1.8	2.3	5.8	3.1	2.9	2.3	•	1.2	0.8	0.6	0.4	•	•
Operating Margin	21	3.0	4.0	6.6	4.4	3.1	2.9	•	3.0	3.0	2.5	3.6	•	•
Operating Margin Before Officers' Comp.	22	4.8	6.4	12.4	7.4	6.0	5.2	•	4.2	3.8	3.1	4.0	•	•

Selected Average Balance Sheet ($ in Thousands)

Net Receivables 23	561	0	12	177	617	2055	•	10134	19203	40721	102911	•	•
Inventories 24	695	0	48	263	774	3021	•	10985	23964	37643	95143	•	•
Net Property, Plant and Equipment 25	194	0	15	56	155	258	•	3611	6257	12081	40502	•	•
Total Assets 26	2292	0	130	720	2156	6854	•	34148	68420	144410	341967	•	•
Notes and Loans Payable 27	600	0	41	170	487	1195	•	9798	18969	38494	123977	•	•
All Other Liabilities 28	829	0	28	234	861	3016	•	12171	23120	42273	131115	•	•
Net Worth 29	863	0	61	316	808	2643	•	12179	26332	63643	86875	•	•

Selected Financial Ratios (Times to 1)

Current Ratio 30	1.7	•	2.8	2.1	1.8	1.7	•	1.6	1.7	1.9	1.4	•	•
Quick Ratio 31	0.8	•	1.3	1.1	0.9	0.7	•	0.8	0.8	1.1	0.8	•	•
Net Sales to Working Capital 32	8.3	•	8.7	8.2	8.7	6.9	•	7.3	8.4	7.1	9.4	•	•
Coverage Ratio 33	9.4	117.3	22.7	21.4	13.0	14.3	•	7.2	9.3	6.4	5.3	•	•
Total Asset Turnover 34	2.4	•	4.1	3.5	3.4	2.4	•	2.2	2.6	2.3	1.8	•	•
Inventory Turnover 35	6.2	•	7.1	7.2	7.2	4.4	•	5.4	6.2	7.5	4.9	•	•
Receivables Turnover 36	9.6	•	41.5	•	12.0	8.5	•	7.8	8.9	9.1	4.8	•	•
Total Liabilities to Net Worth 37	1.7	•	1.1	1.3	1.7	1.6	•	1.8	1.6	1.3	2.9	•	•
Current Assets to Working Capital 38	2.4	•	1.5	1.9	2.2	2.5	•	2.7	2.5	2.1	3.4	•	•
Current Liabilities to Working Capital 39	1.4	•	0.5	0.9	1.2	1.5	•	1.7	1.5	1.1	2.4	•	•
Working Capital to Net Sales 40	0.1	•	0.1	0.1	0.1	0.1	•	0.1	0.1	0.1	0.1	•	•
Inventory to Working Capital 41	1.0	•	0.7	0.8	0.9	1.3	•	1.2	1.2	0.8	1.3	•	•
Total Receipts to Cash Flow 42	11.0	3.9	5.9	8.8	10.0	11.7	•	11.5	13.1	13.3	10.3	•	•
Cost of Goods to Cash Flow 43	8.7	2.9	3.7	6.5	7.7	9.4	•	9.2	10.9	11.2	7.8	•	•
Cash Flow to Total Debt 44	0.3	•	1.3	0.7	0.5	0.3	•	0.3	0.3	0.3	0.2	•	•

Selected Financial Factors (in Percentages)

Debt Ratio 45	62.4	•	52.9	56.1	62.5	61.4	•	64.3	61.5	55.9	74.6	•	•
Return on Total Assets 46	11.6	•	31.8	17.0	15.2	9.9	•	9.4	10.3	10.0	10.8	•	•
Return on Equity Before Income Taxes 47	27.5	•	64.5	36.8	37.6	23.8	•	22.8	23.9	19.1	34.4	•	•
Return on Equity After Income Taxes 48	24.2	•	63.2	35.2	35.9	21.7	•	20.3	21.4	15.1	27.5	•	•
Profit Margin (Before Income Tax) 49	4.4	20.3	7.4	4.6	4.2	3.8	•	3.7	3.5	3.6	4.8	•	•
Profit Margin (After Income Tax) 50	3.8	19.1	7.3	4.4	4.0	3.5	•	3.3	3.2	2.8	3.8	•	•

Table I

Corporations with and without Net Income

PAPER AND PAPER PRODUCT

MONEY AMOUNTS AND SIZE OF ASSETS IN THOUSANDS OF DOLLARS

Item Description for Accounting Period 7/12 Through 6/13	Total	Zero Assets	Under 500	500 to 1,000	1,000 to 5,000	5,000 to 10,000	10,000 to 25,000	25,000 to 50,000	50,000 to 100,000	100,000 to 250,000	250,000 to 500,000	500,000 to 2,500,000	2,500,000 and over
Number of Enterprises 1	9777	1925	5790	744	850	220	152	52	20	16	3	5	0

Revenues ($ in Thousands)

Net Sales 2	54933440	394989	2394522	2382113	5197084	3992632	7301035	5707307	4239811	6849316	4204195	12270435	0
Interest 3	17185	188	0	6	2653	380	1750	1239	300	1825	2310	6534	0
Rents 4	8352	0	0	0	267	2355	79	1003	1161	201	166	3120	0
Royalties 5	18709	0	5360	0	0	0	0	0	0	0	0	13349	0
Other Portfolio Income 6	130837	9986	41	2	14541	4714	8931	60309	2171	77	122	29943	0
Other Receipts 7	347515	51540	377	1784	35346	25480	46935	41046	14641	44543	60243	25580	0
Total Receipts 8	55456038	456703	2400300	2383905	5249891	4025561	7358730	5810904	4258084	6895962	4267036	12348961	0
Average Total Receipts 9	5672	237	415	3204	6176	18298	48413	111748	212904	430998	1422345	2469792	•

Operating Costs/Operating Income (%)

Cost of Operations 10	82.6	80.1	68.0	72.8	72.7	76.8	82.2	83.4	87.7	88.0	91.7	85.7	•
Salaries and Wages 11	6.0	7.9	7.4	8.5	8.7	9.4	6.7	6.5	4.3	3.8	3.2	5.3	•
Taxes Paid 12	0.8	1.4	1.2	1.0	1.4	1.3	0.9	0.9	0.6	0.5	0.4	0.6	•
Interest Paid 13	0.6	3.4	0.4	0.0	0.3	0.5	0.3	0.6	0.3	0.2	0.9	1.0	•
Depreciation 14	0.5	0.6	0.6	0.4	0.5	0.7	0.4	0.7	0.7	0.7	0.3	0.5	•
Amortization and Depletion 15	0.1	0.2	0.1	0.0	0.1	0.0	0.1	0.2	0.0	0.1	0.1	0.2	•
Pensions and Other Deferred Comp. 16	0.2	0.8	0.0	0.3	0.5	0.1	0.2	0.3	0.1	0.1	0.0	0.4	•
Employee Benefits 17	0.5	1.3	0.4	0.6	0.7	0.4	0.4	0.6	0.4	0.2	0.5	0.5	•
Advertising 18	0.2	0.1	0.6	0.2	0.3	0.1	0.4	0.2	0.1	0.0	0.1	0.1	•
Other Expenses 19	5.9	12.5	13.2	9.8	9.0	7.0	5.5	4.9	4.1	5.3	3.8	4.1	•
Officers' Compensation 20	1.2	4.0	5.7	2.6	2.5	1.6	1.2	1.1	0.6	0.5	0.2	0.2	•
Operating Margin 21	1.3	•	2.4	4.0	3.4	2.2	1.8	0.6	1.0	0.5	•	1.3	•
Operating Margin Before Officers' Comp. 22	2.5	•	8.1	6.6	5.9	3.8	3.0	1.7	1.7	1.0	•	1.5	•

Selected Average Balance Sheet ($ in Thousands)													
Net Receivables **23**	660	0	21	270	660	2034	5681	12272	23049	62391	221228	298824	•
Inventories **24**	438	0	28	181	447	1872	3818	10614	24073	32094	78168	166909	•
Net Property, Plant and Equipment **25**	189	0	4	136	190	1040	1574	3734	5777	20016	27067	75554	•
Total Assets **26**	1887	0	101	857	2087	6199	16017	34721	68225	150725	325010	1019196	•
Notes and Loans Payable **27**	555	0	87	188	552	2059	3174	11621	27286	45137	116282	232392	•
All Other Liabilities **28**	819	0	28	233	457	1609	5850	11800	22828	65927	195555	666572	•
Net Worth **29**	512	0	-13	436	1078	2530	6993	11299	18110	39660	13172	120232	•

Selected Financial Ratios (Times to 1)													
Current Ratio **30**	1.4	•	2.2	1.8	2.2	1.7	1.7	1.7	1.7	1.5	1.6	0.8	•
Quick Ratio **31**	0.8	•	1.2	1.2	1.5	0.9	1.1	0.9	0.8	0.9	1.2	0.5	•
Net Sales to Working Capital **32**	14.7	•	9.5	10.1	7.4	9.5	8.8	10.1	9.2	10.9	11.6	•	•
Coverage Ratio **33**	5.1	2.0	8.2	85.6	17.3	7.4	9.4	5.5	6.2	5.9	1.5	2.9	•
Total Asset Turnover **34**	3.0	•	4.1	3.7	2.9	2.9	3.0	3.2	3.1	2.8	4.3	2.4	•
Inventory Turnover **35**	10.6	•	9.9	12.9	9.9	7.4	10.3	8.6	7.7	11.7	16.4	12.6	•
Receivables Turnover **36**	8.4	•	19.0	13.1	9.0	8.9	9.9	8.1	8.8	6.8	5.5	8.3	•
Total Liabilities to Net Worth **37**	2.7	•	•	1.0	0.9	1.4	1.3	2.1	2.8	2.8	23.7	7.5	•
Current Assets to Working Capital **38**	3.5	•	1.8	2.2	1.8	2.4	2.3	2.5	2.5	2.9	2.6	•	•
Current Liabilities to Working Capital **39**	2.5	•	0.8	1.2	0.8	1.4	1.3	1.5	1.5	1.9	1.6	•	•
Working Capital to Net Sales **40**	0.1	•	0.1	0.1	0.1	0.1	0.1	0.1	0.1	0.1	0.1	•	•
Inventory to Working Capital **41**	1.2	•	0.8	0.7	0.5	1.0	0.8	1.0	1.0	0.8	0.6	•	•
Total Receipts to Cash Flow **42**	15.5	8.0	8.9	8.6	9.4	13.1	15.2	17.7	23.6	18.6	31.0	20.7	•
Cost of Goods to Cash Flow **43**	12.8	6.4	6.1	6.2	6.8	10.0	12.5	14.8	20.7	16.4	28.4	17.7	•
Cash Flow to Total Debt **44**	0.3	•	0.4	0.9	0.6	0.4	0.4	0.3	0.2	0.2	0.1	0.1	•

Selected Financial Factors (in Percentages)													
Debt Ratio **45**	72.9	•	113.3	49.1	48.3	59.2	56.3	67.5	73.5	73.7	95.9	88.2	•
Return on Total Assets **46**	8.5	•	12.4	15.5	13.9	10.3	8.6	9.6	5.4	4.1	5.9	7.3	•
Return on Equity Before Income Taxes **47**	25.2	•	•	30.0	25.3	21.7	17.6	24.0	16.9	12.9	46.4	40.9	•
Return on Equity After Income Taxes **48**	22.1	•	•	29.9	24.2	20.3	16.0	19.4	14.4	11.3	43.0	29.6	•
Profit Margin (Before Income Tax) **49**	2.3	3.3	2.7	4.1	4.5	3.0	2.6	2.5	1.4	1.2	0.4	2.0	•
Profit Margin (After Income Tax) **50**	2.0	2.8	2.6	4.1	4.3	2.8	2.3	2.0	1.2	1.0	0.4	1.4	•

Table II
Corporations with Net Income

PAPER AND PAPER PRODUCT

MONEY AMOUNTS AND SIZE OF ASSETS IN THOUSANDS OF DOLLARS

Item Description for Accounting Period 7/12 Through 6/13	Total	Zero Assets	Under 500	500 to 1,000	1,000 to 5,000	5,000 to 10,000	10,000 to 25,000	25,000 to 50,000	50,000 to 100,000	100,000 to 250,000	250,000 to 500,000	500,000 to 2,500,000	2,500,000 and over
Number of Enterprises 1	6565	1502	3331	577	729	207	138	43	17	12	3	5	0

Revenues ($ in Thousands)

Net Sales 2	49187379	93510	1350784	2065854	4287026	3717098	6863631	5200183	3139205	5995458	4204195	12270435	0
Interest 3	15202	0	0	6	2100	249	1750	400	146	1708	2310	6534	0
Rents 4	7814	0	0	0	267	2355	79	465	1161	201	166	3120	0
Royalties 5	18709	0	5360	0	0	0	0	0	0	0	0	13349	0
Other Portfolio Income 6	109413	0	0	0	14447	0	5511	58108	1206	77	122	29943	0
Other Receipts 7	288378	18909	0	1264	34388	23994	44567	21752	13796	43883	60243	25580	0
Total Receipts 8	49626895	112419	1356144	2067124	4338228	3743696	6915538	5280908	3155514	6041327	4267036	12348961	0
Average Total Receipts 9	7559	75	407	3583	5951	18085	50113	122812	185618	503444	1422345	2469792	•

Operating Costs/Operating Income (%)

Cost of Operations 10	82.7	45.9	67.7	70.7	72.9	76.8	82.0	83.3	86.1	87.3	91.7	85.7	•
Salaries and Wages 11	5.8	•	4.6	9.2	7.5	8.9	6.7	6.1	4.8	4.2	3.2	5.3	•
Taxes Paid 12	0.8	1.3	0.9	1.0	1.3	1.2	0.9	0.9	0.6	0.5	0.4	0.6	•
Interest Paid 13	0.5	11.6	0.6	0.0	0.2	0.5	0.3	0.3	0.3	0.2	0.9	1.0	•
Depreciation 14	0.4	•	0.7	0.4	0.4	0.7	0.3	0.4	0.4	0.4	0.3	0.5	•
Amortization and Depletion 15	0.1	•	•	•	0.1	0.0	0.1	0.1	0.0	0.1	0.1	0.2	•
Pensions and Other Deferred Comp. 16	0.2	•	•	0.3	0.5	0.1	0.2	0.3	0.1	0.1	0.0	0.4	•
Employee Benefits 17	0.5	5.3	0.5	0.6	0.7	0.3	0.4	0.5	0.4	0.2	0.5	0.5	•
Advertising 18	0.2	0.2	0.9	0.2	0.2	0.1	0.4	0.2	0.2	0.0	0.1	0.1	•
Other Expenses 19	5.6	21.1	11.9	9.6	8.8	7.1	5.5	4.8	4.3	5.4	3.8	4.1	•
Officers' Compensation 20	1.1	10.6	4.6	2.7	2.5	1.6	1.2	1.1	0.8	0.5	0.2	0.2	•
Operating Margin 21	2.1	3.9	7.6	5.3	4.9	2.6	2.1	2.1	2.1	1.1	•	1.3	•
Operating Margin Before Officers' Comp. 22	3.1	14.5	12.2	8.0	7.4	4.2	3.3	3.2	2.9	1.6	•	1.5	•

Selected Average Balance Sheet ($ in Thousands)

Net Receivables 23	897	0	26	320	612	1994	5960	13217	24382	66204	221228	298824	•
Inventories 24	523	0	12	120	434	1469	3786	10716	23316	33972	78168	175723	•
Net Property, Plant and Equipment 25	233	0	7	125	168	1080	1460	2509	4707	20017	27067	75554	•
Total Assets 26	2467	0	82	864	2000	6041	16216	34414	65955	150148	325010	1019196	•
Notes and Loans Payable 27	637	0	106	101	416	2079	2919	9880	19182	31024	116282	232392	•
All Other Liabilities 28	1106	0	28	247	431	1612	6104	10292	22061	66621	195555	666572	•
Net Worth 29	723	0	-51	516	1152	2351	7194	14242	24712	52503	13172	120232	•

Selected Financial Ratios (Times to 1)

Current Ratio 30	1.4	•	2.1	2.1	2.3	1.6	1.8	1.8	1.8	1.7	1.6	0.8	•
Quick Ratio 31	0.9	•	1.5	1.6	1.6	0.9	1.1	1.0	0.9	1.1	1.2	0.5	•
Net Sales to Working Capital 32	15.2	•	11.4	9.5	7.2	11.1	8.5	9.5	7.5	11.1	11.6	•	•
Coverage Ratio 33	6.4	3.1	15.2	109.3	28.5	8.0	11.3	12.6	10.9	8.9	1.5	2.9	•
Total Asset Turnover 34	3.0	•	4.9	4.1	2.9	3.0	3.1	3.5	2.8	3.3	4.3	2.4	•
Inventory Turnover 35	11.8	•	22.4	21.1	9.9	9.4	10.8	9.4	6.8	12.8	16.4	12.0	•
Receivables Turnover 36	9.0	•	17.7	12.4	9.1	9.4	10.5	8.6	7.2	•	5.5	•	•
Total Liabilities to Net Worth 37	2.4	•	•	0.7	0.7	1.6	1.3	1.4	1.7	1.9	23.7	7.5	•
Current Assets to Working Capital 38	3.5	•	1.9	1.9	1.8	2.7	2.3	2.2	2.2	2.5	2.6	•	•
Current Liabilities to Working Capital 39	2.5	•	0.9	0.9	0.8	1.7	1.3	1.2	1.2	1.5	1.6	•	•
Working Capital to Net Sales 40	0.1	•	0.1	0.1	0.1	0.1	0.1	0.1	0.1	0.1	0.1	•	•
Inventory to Working Capital 41	1.1	•	0.5	0.4	0.4	1.1	0.7	0.8	0.9	0.8	0.6	•	•
Total Receipts to Cash Flow 42	14.4	2.3	6.0	8.0	8.3	12.6	14.4	14.7	18.4	16.9	31.0	20.7	•
Cost of Goods to Cash Flow 43	11.9	1.1	4.0	5.7	6.1	9.7	11.8	12.2	15.8	14.7	28.4	17.7	•
Cash Flow to Total Debt 44	0.3	•	0.5	1.3	0.8	0.4	0.4	0.4	0.2	0.3	0.1	0.1	•

Selected Financial Factors (in Percentages)

Debt Ratio 45	70.7	•	162.4	40.3	42.4	61.1	55.6	58.6	62.5	65.0	95.9	88.2	•
Return on Total Assets 46	10.7	•	41.9	22.3	18.6	11.3	9.7	13.9	8.0	6.9	5.9	7.3	•
Return on Equity Before Income Taxes 47	30.9	•	•	37.0	31.2	25.3	19.9	30.9	19.3	17.4	46.4	40.9	•
Return on Equity After Income Taxes 48	27.6	•	•	36.8	30.0	23.7	18.2	26.5	17.1	15.8	43.0	29.6	•
Profit Margin (Before Income Tax) 49	3.0	24.2	8.0	5.3	6.1	3.3	2.9	3.6	2.6	1.8	0.4	2.0	•
Profit Margin (After Income Tax) 50	2.7	22.2	7.8	5.3	5.9	3.1	2.6	3.1	2.3	1.7	0.4	1.4	•

Table I

Corporations with and without Net Income

DRUGS AND DRUGGISTS' SUNDRIES

MONEY AMOUNTS AND SIZE OF ASSETS IN THOUSANDS OF DOLLARS

Item Description for Accounting Period 7/12 Through 6/13	Total	Zero Assets	Under 500	500 to 1,000	1,000 to 5,000	5,000 to 10,000	10,000 to 25,000	25,000 to 50,000	50,000 to 100,000	100,000 to 250,000	250,000 to 500,000	500,000 to 2,500,000	2,500,000 and over
Number of Enterprises 1	5483	443	3268	459	698	236	170	78	44	30	18	20	18

Revenues ($ in Thousands)													
Net Sales 2	489465218	8013930	829326	635953	5559505	3183667	6350579	5927886	5293903	6862007	8102527	27145329	411560606
Interest 3	363767	4270	85	64	654	1304	1278	5008	5008	2691	5008	128122	210273
Rents 4	47748	459	0	882	10605	0	562	334	541	567	2663	1326	29808
Royalties 5	2853349	510	0	0	138	37205	18828	20955	22560	17848	49722	82186	2603397
Other Portfolio Income 6	3821078	2245819	10908	0	5380	16333	11413	18054	23155	34065	15919	44395	1395638
Other Receipts 7	6031138	3900	855	-4638	30064	44945	124477	33049	51097	106423	118125	1435146	4087697
Total Receipts 8	502582298	10268888	841174	632261	5606346	3283454	6507137	6005286	5396264	7023601	8293964	28836504	419887419
Average Total Receipts 9	91662	23180	257	1377	8032	13913	38277	76991	122642	234120	460776	1441825	23327079

Operating Costs/Operating Income (%)													
Cost of Operations 10	85.1	73.6	57.3	69.1	58.9	76.5	71.7	74.9	66.0	59.0	69.0	67.4	88.3
Salaries and Wages 11	3.6	8.3	8.0	10.0	10.1	6.6	9.0	7.8	8.5	11.2	6.8	8.0	2.7
Taxes Paid 12	0.5	0.8	1.9	1.5	1.5	1.0	1.0	1.0	0.9	1.0	0.9	1.3	0.3
Interest Paid 13	0.7	2.0	0.9	0.5	0.4	0.7	0.3	0.5	0.9	1.8	1.3	1.3	0.7
Depreciation 14	0.4	1.0	2.6	1.1	0.2	0.5	0.4	0.5	0.8	1.4	0.5	0.7	0.3
Amortization and Depletion 15	0.5	1.5	0.2	0.0	0.1	0.5	0.2	0.2	0.9	1.2	0.8	1.2	0.4
Pensions and Other Deferred Comp. 16	0.1	0.3	•	0.5	0.1	0.1	0.3	0.1	0.1	0.2	0.3	0.3	0.1
Employee Benefits 17	0.5	0.8	0.2	0.6	0.6	0.4	0.6	0.7	0.7	0.9	1.0	1.4	0.4
Advertising 18	0.8	1.4	0.3	0.5	1.8	1.7	1.4	1.5	3.4	4.1	2.1	1.3	0.6
Other Expenses 19	5.8	11.6	25.5	9.5	17.8	13.7	10.6	8.6	14.0	14.9	9.7	15.6	4.3
Officers' Compensation 20	0.5	2.5	11.1	4.0	5.4	2.4	2.6	1.4	1.0	1.1	0.8	0.5	0.3
Operating Margin 21	1.6	•	•	2.7	3.2	•	2.0	2.8	2.7	3.3	6.8	1.0	1.6
Operating Margin Before Officers' Comp. 22	2.0	•	3.2	6.7	8.6	•	4.5	4.2	3.7	4.4	7.6	1.6	1.8

Selected Average Balance Sheet ($ in Thousands)

Net Receivables 23	8444	0	3	111	652	1984	3965	10097	15303	32235	72540	195795	2055056
Inventories 24	6735	0	23	221	861	1759	5092	7388	13591	34126	75723	139192	1584708
Net Property, Plant and Equipment 25	2568	0	11	111	459	311	995	2083	6062	20178	20463	58398	603264
Total Assets 26	50786	0	67	845	2887	6828	15732	33891	72123	163824	347551	1104712	12914844
Notes and Loans Payable 27	12258	0	44	81	875	1667	3161	8582	19505	59614	120234	247079	3059136
All Other Liabilities 28	21522	0	64	84	1269	2959	5616	14060	27049	61078	129329	431757	5563250
Net Worth 29	17006	0	-40	681	743	2201	6955	11249	25569	43132	97988	425875	4292458

Selected Financial Ratios (Times to 1)

Current Ratio 30	1.1	•	2.4	3.3	1.5	1.5	1.8	1.5	1.7	1.3	1.6	1.6	1.0
Quick Ratio 31	0.6	•	1.0	2.0	0.9	0.8	0.9	0.9	0.9	0.7	0.8	0.9	0.6
Net Sales to Working Capital 32	47.0	•	11.4	6.2	11.6	7.2	6.7	9.7	6.9	12.3	5.5	7.2	336.6
Coverage Ratio 33	7.0	13.4	•	5.3	11.5	•	14.4	9.8	6.4	4.2	8.2	7.1	6.7
Total Asset Turnover 34	1.8	•	3.8	1.6	2.8	2.0	2.4	2.2	1.7	1.4	1.3	1.2	1.8
Inventory Turnover 35	11.3	•	6.4	4.3	5.4	5.9	5.3	7.7	5.8	4.0	4.1	6.6	12.7
Receivables Turnover 36	11.1	•	74.4	10.3	12.2	7.3	9.6	7.2	8.6	8.3	6.2	6.9	11.8
Total Liabilities to Net Worth 37	2.0	•	•	0.2	2.9	2.1	1.3	2.0	1.8	2.8	2.5	1.6	2.0
Current Assets to Working Capital 38	10.9	•	1.7	1.4	2.9	3.0	2.3	3.1	2.4	5.0	2.7	2.8	71.0
Current Liabilities to Working Capital 39	9.9	•	0.7	0.4	1.9	2.0	1.3	2.1	1.4	4.0	1.7	1.8	70.0
Working Capital to Net Sales 40	0.0	•	0.1	0.2	0.1	0.1	0.1	0.1	0.1	0.1	0.2	0.1	0.0
Inventory to Working Capital 41	3.6	•	0.8	0.5	1.1	1.0	1.0	1.0	0.8	1.7	1.0	0.6	23.7
Total Receipts to Cash Flow 42	11.5	12.1	8.5	11.4	5.3	13.2	7.3	8.9	6.0	5.2	5.8	4.6	14.0
Cost of Goods to Cash Flow 43	9.8	8.9	4.8	7.9	3.1	10.1	5.3	6.6	3.9	3.1	4.0	3.1	12.4
Cash Flow to Total Debt 44	0.2	•	0.3	0.7	0.7	0.2	0.6	0.4	0.4	0.4	0.3	0.4	0.2

Selected Financial Factors (in Percentages)

Debt Ratio 45	66.5	•	160.1	19.5	74.3	67.8	55.8	66.8	64.5	73.7	71.8	61.4	66.8
Return on Total Assets 46	9.1	•	•	4.3	12.2	•	11.3	10.2	9.4	10.8	13.5	10.9	7.9
Return on Equity Before Income Taxes 47	23.3	•	40.8	4.4	43.1	•	23.7	27.6	22.4	31.1	42.1	24.3	20.3
Return on Equity After Income Taxes 48	16.0	•	40.9	4.0	39.0	•	21.7	22.9	15.2	23.3	27.5	15.5	13.3
Profit Margin (Before Income Tax) 49	4.4	24.4	•	2.2	4.0	•	4.4	4.1	4.8	5.9	9.2	7.6	3.8
Profit Margin (After Income Tax) 50	3.0	22.0	•	2.0	3.6	•	4.0	3.4	3.2	4.4	6.0	4.9	2.5

Table II

Corporations with Net Income

DRUGS AND DRUGGISTS' SUNDRIES

MONEY AMOUNTS AND SIZE OF ASSETS IN THOUSANDS OF DOLLARS

Item Description for Accounting Period 7/12 Through 6/13		Total	Zero Assets	Under 500	500 to 1,000	1,000 to 5,000	5,000 to 10,000	10,000 to 25,000	25,000 to 50,000	50,000 to 100,000	100,000 to 250,000	250,000 to 500,000	500,000 to 2,500,000	2,500,000 and over
Number of Enterprises	1	3211	264	•	346	482	194	128	62	31	25	14	15	•

Revenues ($ in Thousands)

Net Sales	2	474365211	7292163	•	429269	5323517	2917014	5289309	5668010	4474532	5638419	5799397	21120887	•
Interest	3	322947	1584	•	64	541	506	831	2087	3427	2681	3438	105595	•
Rents	4	36416	459	•	882	338	0	562	334	0	87	2663	1282	•
Royalties	5	2666005	389	•	0	138	37205	18828	18938	5278	16708	49658	27474	•
Other Portfolio Income	6	3719987	2243231	•	0	4805	494	10544	17387	23155	24817	15919	43765	•
Other Receipts	7	5800160	2673	•	578	30014	36748	125116	27447	30868	67475	117633	1276772	•
Total Receipts	8	486910726	9540499	•	430793	5359353	2991967	5445190	5734203	4537260	5750187	5988708	22575775	•
Average Total Receipts	9	151638	36138	•	1245	11119	15423	42541	92487	146363	230007	427765	1505052	•

Operating Costs/Operating Income (%)

Cost of Operations	10	85.5	79.3	•	75.0	59.7	77.7	70.4	75.9	71.4	52.3	64.2	63.5	•
Salaries and Wages	11	3.4	6.2	•	6.4	9.6	5.4	9.2	7.3	6.7	13.0	7.5	8.6	•
Taxes Paid	12	0.4	0.6	•	1.0	1.4	1.0	1.0	1.0	0.8	1.1	1.0	1.4	•
Interest Paid	13	0.6	1.5	•	0.2	0.3	0.4	0.3	0.2	0.6	1.2	1.1	1.1	•
Depreciation	14	0.4	0.9	•	0.2	0.2	0.4	0.3	0.4	0.7	1.6	0.5	0.7	•
Amortization and Depletion	15	0.4	0.5	•	0.0	0.1	0.0	0.1	0.2	0.4	0.8	0.8	1.1	•
Pensions and Other Deferred Comp.	16	0.1	0.3	•	0.7	0.1	0.1	0.2	0.1	0.1	0.2	0.4	0.4	•
Employee Benefits	17	0.5	0.6	•	0.5	0.5	0.2	0.4	0.7	0.6	1.0	1.1	1.6	•
Advertising	18	0.7	1.1	•	0.6	1.6	1.1	1.4	1.4	2.5	4.6	2.0	0.8	•
Other Expenses	19	5.4	9.3	•	7.4	14.9	8.0	9.8	7.1	9.0	16.5	10.4	16.6	•
Officers' Compensation	20	0.4	2.3	•	3.5	5.3	1.8	2.4	1.4	0.8	1.3	0.9	0.5	•
Operating Margin	21	2.1	•	•	4.4	6.4	3.8	4.6	4.3	6.4	6.4	10.1	3.6	•
Operating Margin Before Officers' Comp.	22	2.5	•	•	7.9	11.7	5.7	7.0	5.7	7.3	7.7	11.0	4.1	•

Selected Average Balance Sheet ($ in Thousands)

Net Receivables 23	13736	0	•	75	897	2208	4308	11993	17796	37645	81497	205185	•
Inventories 24	10875	0	•	120	1102	1993	5648	8397	15937	30565	61511	152499	•
Net Property, Plant and Equipment 25	4114	0	•	50	193	341	983	1965	4989	22000	23611	63350	•
Total Assets 26	79568	0	•	832	3332	6807	15837	35327	70420	165966	336449	1179978	•
Notes and Loans Payable 27	17282	0	•	14	672	1685	2945	7091	18783	36309	88925	224128	•
All Other Liabilities 28	34355	0	•	72	1620	3413	5787	15783	23372	69568	152602	449885	•
Net Worth 29	27931	0	•	747	1040	1708	7104	12453	28265	60089	94922	505965	•

Selected Financial Ratios (Times to 1)

Current Ratio 30	1.1	•	•	4.2	1.5	1.4	1.9	1.6	1.9	1.4	1.3	1.7	•
Quick Ratio 31	0.6	•	•	2.5	0.9	0.8	0.9	0.9	1.0	0.8	0.7	1.0	•
Net Sales to Working Capital 32	55.5	•	•	5.5	12.8	8.7	6.1	9.0	6.3	8.4	7.9	6.3	•
Coverage Ratio 33	9.0	19.3	•	23.9	23.8	15.8	26.9	23.8	13.8	8.3	13.6	10.6	•
Total Asset Turnover 34	1.9	•	•	1.5	3.3	2.2	2.6	2.6	2.0	1.4	1.2	1.2	•
Inventory Turnover 35	11.6	•	•	7.8	6.0	5.9	5.1	8.3	6.5	3.9	4.3	5.9	•
Receivables Turnover 36	11.2	•	•	18.7	12.6	7.5	9.7	7.2	9.2	7.3	4.9	6.7	•
Total Liabilities to Net Worth 37	1.8	•	•	0.1	2.2	3.0	1.2	1.8	1.5	1.8	2.5	1.3	•
Current Assets to Working Capital 38	12.4	•	•	1.3	3.0	3.4	2.1	2.7	2.1	3.7	4.0	2.5	•
Current Liabilities to Working Capital 39	11.4	•	•	0.3	2.0	2.4	1.1	1.7	1.1	2.7	3.0	1.5	•
Working Capital to Net Sales 40	0.0	•	•	0.2	0.1	0.1	0.2	0.1	0.2	0.1	0.1	0.2	•
Inventory to Working Capital 41	4.1	•	•	0.5	1.1	1.2	0.9	0.9	0.7	1.1	1.1	0.5	•
Total Receipts to Cash Flow 42	11.3	13.7	•	10.6	5.1	7.8	6.3	9.0	6.5	4.3	4.5	3.9	•
Cost of Goods to Cash Flow 43	9.7	10.9	•	7.9	3.0	6.0	4.4	6.8	4.6	2.2	2.9	2.5	•
Cash Flow to Total Debt 44	0.3	•	•	1.4	0.9	0.4	0.8	0.4	0.5	0.5	0.4	0.5	•

Selected Financial Factors (in Percentages)

Debt Ratio 45	64.9	•	•	10.3	68.8	74.9	55.1	64.7	59.9	63.8	71.8	57.1	•
Return on Total Assets 46	10.2	•	•	7.3	24.5	15.0	20.4	14.8	17.6	13.4	17.7	14.0	•
Return on Equity Before Income Taxes 47	25.9	•	•	7.8	75.1	56.1	43.7	40.1	40.7	32.5	58.1	29.6	•
Return on Equity After Income Taxes 48	18.2	•	•	7.4	70.8	48.3	41.2	34.8	31.5	25.8	38.7	19.7	•
Profit Margin (Before Income Tax) 49	4.9	28.2	•	4.7	7.1	6.4	7.5	5.5	8.0	8.7	13.3	10.6	•
Profit Margin (After Income Tax) 50	3.4	25.6	•	4.4	6.7	5.5	7.1	4.7	6.2	6.9	8.9	7.1	•

Table I

Corporations with and without Net Income

APPAREL, PIECE GOODS, AND NOTIONS

MONEY AMOUNTS AND SIZE OF ASSETS IN THOUSANDS OF DOLLARS

Item Description for Accounting Period 7/12 Through 6/13	Total	Zero Assets	Under 500	500 to 1,000	1,000 to 5,000	5,000 to 10,000	10,000 to 25,000	25,000 to 50,000	50,000 to 100,000	100,000 to 250,000	250,000 to 500,000	500,000 to 2,500,000	2,500,000 and over
Number of Enterprises 1	22110	2039	15282	1422	2478	387	288	95	53	28	16	19	4

Revenues ($ in Thousands)													
Net Sales 2	117693712	1721181	8362519	3391248	15887495	6704227	11244580	6939541	6955022	6231957	7168601	18598176	24489165
Interest 3	61785	47	457	87	1800	676	6002	1211	1834	4882	3824	27620	13346
Rents 4	47559	0	0	4	438	2030	1453	527	6980	935	24393	7461	3338
Royalties 5	1254991	596	0	0	2937	684	7233	4968	20368	57535	43536	177969	939164
Other Portfolio Income 6	577694	5	0	0	3302	2507	10795	299	506	9163	17208	40313	493596
Other Receipts 7	1110196	177	28783	5131	77998	24755	103022	41389	79623	29964	148838	117537	452978
Total Receipts 8	120745937	1722006	8391759	3396470	15973970	6734879	11373085	6987935	7064333	6334436	7406400	18969076	26391587
Average Total Receipts 9	5461	845	549	2389	6446	17403	39490	73557	133289	226230	462900	998372	6597897

Operating Costs/Operating Income (%)													
Cost of Operations 10	66.9	82.5	66.8	76.8	74.2	77.3	74.3	73.0	71.9	69.4	61.7	56.9	59.0
Salaries and Wages 11	8.9	4.0	4.5	5.0	5.9	5.8	7.3	7.1	7.5	8.7	10.1	12.2	12.8
Taxes Paid 12	2.1	0.3	1.2	1.4	1.9	2.8	3.0	1.6	1.7	2.2	2.9	2.5	1.9
Interest Paid 13	0.6	0.3	0.4	0.3	0.5	0.6	0.6	0.5	0.7	1.0	1.7	0.8	0.2
Depreciation 14	0.9	0.1	0.5	0.1	0.1	0.3	0.3	0.6	0.7	0.9	1.7	1.9	1.4
Amortization and Depletion 15	0.3	0.0	0.1	0.1	0.0	0.1	0.2	0.1	0.2	0.4	0.9	0.4	0.5
Pensions and Other Deferred Comp. 16	0.2	0.0	0.3	0.1	0.3	0.6	0.1	0.2	0.2	0.2	0.1	0.3	0.2
Employee Benefits 17	0.6	0.0	0.2	0.3	0.5	0.4	0.4	0.5	0.7	0.7	1.1	0.8	0.6
Advertising 18	2.1	0.2	0.3	1.3	0.5	0.7	0.8	1.0	1.5	2.3	2.1	2.8	4.6
Other Expenses 19	13.2	12.1	17.8	12.4	10.2	7.6	8.0	9.4	10.7	11.9	14.5	15.4	18.0
Officers' Compensation 20	1.9	0.0	5.8	1.9	2.7	2.5	2.6	1.9	1.6	2.4	0.9	0.8	0.9
Operating Margin 21	2.2	0.4	2.2	0.2	3.1	1.4	2.4	4.0	2.8	•	2.2	5.1	•
Operating Margin Before Officers' Comp. 22	4.1	0.4	7.9	2.1	5.8	3.9	5.0	5.9	4.4	2.2	3.1	5.9	0.9

Selected Average Balance Sheet ($ in Thousands)

Net Receivables 23	603	0	14	196	674	2221	4420	9813	17062	32773	55833	132037	723972
Inventories 24	757	0	29	149	728	2292	5429	15090	21149	54911	93599	177397	807984
Net Property, Plant and Equipment 25	323	0	11	18	94	716	842	2966	4799	12137	41880	114444	618620
Total Assets 26	5214	0	97	664	2213	6967	15772	34649	69898	149185	358456	899496	16531058
Notes and Loans Payable 27	802	0	91	292	538	2266	5043	6748	17876	44408	140547	116981	1238266
All Other Liabilities 28	1061	0	38	441	1121	3562	6339	11707	23365	42658	90533	225030	1747456
Net Worth 29	3351	0	-33	-69	554	1140	4390	16194	28656	62119	127377	557485	13545336

Selected Financial Ratios (Times to 1)

Current Ratio 30	1.7	•	1.5	1.3	1.5	1.4	1.7	2.0	1.6	2.0	2.5	2.4	1.4
Quick Ratio 31	0.8	•	0.8	0.6	0.8	0.8	0.7	0.9	0.7	0.9	1.0	1.2	0.7
Net Sales to Working Capital 32	6.6	•	19.8	18.1	9.8	9.5	7.0	5.1	7.1	4.8	3.7	3.9	8.1
Coverage Ratio 33	10.3	2.3	7.4	2.1	9.1	4.0	6.8	9.9	7.6	2.6	4.2	9.7	52.9
Total Asset Turnover 34	1.0	•	5.7	3.6	2.9	2.5	2.5	2.1	1.9	1.5	1.2	1.1	0.4
Inventory Turnover 35	4.7	•	12.8	12.3	6.5	5.8	5.3	3.5	4.5	2.8	3.0	3.1	4.5
Receivables Turnover 36	8.1	•	37.3	14.1	10.6	7.2	9.1	7.0	8.4	6.0	8.6	•	5.8
Total Liabilities to Net Worth 37	0.6	•	•	•	3.0	5.1	2.6	1.1	1.4	1.4	1.8	0.6	0.2
Current Assets to Working Capital 38	2.4	•	2.8	4.7	2.9	3.2	2.4	2.0	2.8	2.0	1.7	1.7	3.7
Current Liabilities to Working Capital 39	1.4	•	1.8	3.7	1.9	2.2	1.4	1.0	1.8	1.0	0.7	0.7	2.7
Working Capital to Net Sales 40	0.2	•	0.1	0.1	0.1	0.1	0.1	0.2	0.1	0.2	0.3	0.3	0.1
Inventory to Working Capital 41	0.9	•	1.0	1.8	1.1	1.3	1.1	1.0	1.2	1.0	0.8	0.7	1.0
Total Receipts to Cash Flow 42	6.8	9.1	6.4	11.5	8.8	12.8	10.2	8.5	8.0	9.6	6.6	5.7	4.5
Cost of Goods to Cash Flow 43	4.5	7.5	4.2	8.8	6.5	9.9	7.6	6.2	5.8	6.7	4.1	3.3	2.6
Cash Flow to Total Debt 44	0.4	•	0.7	0.3	0.4	0.2	0.3	0.5	0.4	0.3	0.3	0.5	0.5

Selected Financial Factors (in Percentages)

Debt Ratio 45	35.7	•	133.7	110.4	75.0	83.6	72.2	53.3	59.0	58.4	64.5	38.0	18.1
Return on Total Assets 46	6.3	•	16.6	2.4	11.9	6.2	10.3	10.9	9.4	3.9	9.2	8.8	4.3
Return on Equity Before Income Taxes 47	8.9	•	•	•	42.3	28.3	31.6	21.0	19.8	5.8	19.7	12.7	5.1
Return on Equity After Income Taxes 48	6.5	•	•	•	41.5	24.5	29.9	18.9	18.8	4.1	11.8	8.7	3.2
Profit Margin (Before Income Tax) 49	5.6	0.4	2.5	0.3	3.7	1.9	3.6	4.7	4.3	1.6	5.6	7.2	11.4
Profit Margin (After Income Tax) 50	4.1	0.2	2.5	0.3	3.6	1.6	3.4	4.2	4.1	1.1	3.4	5.0	7.1

Table II
Corporations with Net Income

APPAREL, PIECE GOODS, AND NOTIONS

MONEY AMOUNTS AND SIZE OF ASSETS IN THOUSANDS OF DOLLARS

Item Description for Accounting Period 7/12 Through 6/13	Total	Zero Assets	Under 500	500 to 1,000	1,000 to 5,000	5,000 to 10,000	10,000 to 25,000	25,000 to 50,000	50,000 to 100,000	100,000 to 250,000	250,000 to 500,000	500,000 to 2,500,000	2,500,000 and over
Number of Enterprises 1	12544	706	7799	1178	2152	318	223	81	43	17	11	16	0

Revenues ($ in Thousands)

	Total	Zero Assets	Under 500	500 to 1,000	1,000 to 5,000	5,000 to 10,000	10,000 to 25,000	25,000 to 50,000	50,000 to 100,000	100,000 to 250,000	250,000 to 500,000	500,000 to 2,500,000	2,500,000 and over
Net Sales 2	91341188	759001	5320002	3072217	14701848	5968630	9821295	6051386	5945603	3972816	4768941	30959449	0
Interest 3	49915	40	431	52	913	152	3893	940	837	1054	1900	39701	0
Rents 4	36651	0	0	4	371	2030	52	527	2269	783	21751	8863	0
Royalties 5	1016167	596	0	0	2937	0	2859	4697	2086	12829	14527	975636	0
Other Portfolio Income 6	547783	0	0	0	3302	2507	7086	296	491	3163	6601	524337	0
Other Receipts 7	1113779	1	20554	5099	43307	20798	73766	24001	68073	7489	119900	730795	0
Total Receipts 8	94105483	759638	5340987	3077372	14752678	5994117	9908951	6081847	6019359	3998134	4933620	33238781	0
Average Total Receipts 9	7502	1076	685	2612	6855	18849	44435	75085	139985	235184	448511	2077424	•

Operating Costs/Operating Income (%)

	Total	Zero Assets	Under 500	500 to 1,000	1,000 to 5,000	5,000 to 10,000	10,000 to 25,000	25,000 to 50,000	50,000 to 100,000	100,000 to 250,000	250,000 to 500,000	500,000 to 2,500,000	2,500,000 and over
Cost of Operations 10	66.0	79.3	67.8	75.9	73.3	77.5	74.3	72.1	72.0	67.6	56.5	55.1	•
Salaries and Wages 11	8.7	5.4	3.3	4.4	5.7	5.4	6.8	6.8	6.7	7.6	9.9	13.6	•
Taxes Paid 12	2.2	0.5	1.2	0.9	2.0	2.8	3.3	1.6	1.6	2.3	3.5	2.3	•
Interest Paid 13	0.4	0.8	0.2	0.2	0.4	0.4	0.5	0.5	0.7	0.7	0.7	0.4	•
Depreciation 14	0.9	0.1	0.6	0.1	0.1	0.3	0.2	0.5	0.6	0.7	2.0	1.8	•
Amortization and Depletion 15	0.2	0.0	0.0	0.0	0.0	0.0	0.1	0.1	0.2	0.2	0.2	0.3	•
Pensions and Other Deferred Comp. 16	0.2	0.0	0.5	0.1	0.3	0.6	0.1	0.2	0.2	0.2	0.2	0.2	•
Employee Benefits 17	0.5	0.1	0.1	0.1	0.5	0.4	0.4	0.4	0.5	0.7	1.1	0.6	•
Advertising 18	2.0	0.3	0.3	1.3	0.5	0.5	0.7	1.0	1.3	2.2	2.6	4.2	•
Other Expenses 19	11.8	10.1	11.8	10.1	9.1	6.7	6.9	8.6	9.6	12.4	15.8	16.3	•
Officers' Compensation 20	2.1	0.0	6.2	2.0	2.7	2.6	2.7	2.1	1.6	2.0	1.1	1.1	•
Operating Margin 21	4.8	3.4	8.0	4.8	5.3	2.9	4.0	6.1	5.1	3.5	6.4	4.2	•
Operating Margin Before Officers' Comp. 22	6.8	3.4	14.1	6.7	8.0	5.4	6.7	8.2	6.6	5.6	7.5	5.3	•

Selected Average Balance Sheet ($ in Thousands)													
Net Receivables 23	804	0	17	205	680	2326	4652	10198	18512	31193	50471	235589	•
Inventories 24	1046	0	20	142	602	2445	5697	15752	21427	61272	94699	211128	•
Net Property, Plant and Equipment 25	443	0	19	20	75	773	548	2851	3950	10720	51242	231552	•
Total Assets 26	7620	0	105	671	2147	6955	15731	34659	68530	147619	344470	4473605	•
Notes and Loans Payable 27	763	0	34	236	495	1879	4092	5829	17560	32999	78502	237363	•
All Other Liabilities 28	1345	0	38	297	982	3184	6375	11199	24544	37071	80709	512615	•
Net Worth 29	5512	0	33	138	671	1893	5264	17631	26426	77549	185258	3723627	•
Selected Financial Ratios (Times to 1)													
Current Ratio 30	2.0	•	1.9	2.0	1.6	1.6	1.9	2.1	1.6	2.5	2.5	2.2	•
Quick Ratio 31	1.0	•	1.5	1.0	0.9	0.8	0.8	0.9	0.7	1.0	1.0	1.2	•
Net Sales to Working Capital 32	5.4	•	19.6	8.1	10.0	8.2	6.5	4.8	7.1	4.0	3.6	3.8	•
Coverage Ratio 33	20.8	5.5	43.0	21.1	14.3	9.5	10.8	14.4	10.6	7.2	16.1	38.7	•
Total Asset Turnover 34	1.0	•	6.5	3.9	3.2	2.7	2.8	2.2	2.0	1.6	1.3	0.4	•
Inventory Turnover 35	4.6	•	23.5	13.9	8.3	5.9	5.7	3.4	4.6	2.6	2.6	5.0	•
Receivables Turnover 36	8.0	•	39.7	14.8	12.4	7.0	9.9	7.0	8.6	5.8	8.8	12.2	•
Total Liabilities to Net Worth 37	0.4	•	2.2	3.9	2.2	2.7	2.0	1.0	1.6	0.9	0.9	0.2	•
Current Assets to Working Capital 38	2.0	•	2.1	2.0	2.7	2.6	2.1	1.9	2.7	1.7	1.6	1.8	•
Current Liabilities to Working Capital 39	1.0	•	1.1	1.0	1.7	1.6	1.1	0.9	1.7	0.7	0.6	0.8	•
Working Capital to Net Sales 40	0.2	•	0.1	0.1	0.1	0.1	0.2	0.2	0.1	0.3	0.3	0.3	•
Inventory to Working Capital 41	0.7	•	0.4	0.7	0.9	1.1	1.0	0.9	1.2	0.9	0.8	0.6	•
Total Receipts to Cash Flow 42	6.0	7.9	5.8	8.4	7.8	11.8	9.9	7.6	7.3	7.0	5.0	4.3	•
Cost of Goods to Cash Flow 43	4.0	6.2	3.9	6.3	5.7	9.1	7.4	5.5	5.2	4.7	2.8	2.4	•
Cash Flow to Total Debt 44	0.6	•	1.7	0.6	0.6	0.3	0.4	0.6	0.5	0.5	0.5	0.6	•
Selected Financial Factors (in Percentages)													
Debt Ratio 45	27.7	•	68.4	79.4	68.8	72.8	66.5	49.1	61.4	47.5	46.2	16.8	•
Return on Total Assets 46	8.8	•	55.7	20.2	19.3	9.9	15.1	15.3	14.1	7.7	13.3	6.4	•
Return on Equity Before Income Taxes 47	11.6	•	172.2	93.4	57.3	32.6	41.0	27.9	33.0	12.6	23.2	7.5	•
Return on Equity After Income Taxes 48	9.0	•	170.9	92.8	56.6	29.8	39.2	25.7	31.6	10.3	15.3	5.0	•
Profit Margin (Before Income Tax) 49	8.8	3.5	8.4	4.9	5.6	3.3	4.9	6.6	6.3	4.2	9.9	14.5	•
Profit Margin (After Income Tax) 50	6.8	3.1	8.3	4.9	5.6	3.0	4.7	6.1	6.0	3.4	6.5	9.7	•

Table I

Corporations with and without Net Income

GROCERY AND RELATED PRODUCT

MONEY AMOUNTS AND SIZE OF ASSETS IN THOUSANDS OF DOLLARS

Item Description for Accounting Period 7/12 Through 6/13		Total	Zero Assets	Under 500	500 to 1,000	1,000 to 5,000	5,000 to 10,000	10,000 to 25,000	25,000 to 50,000	50,000 to 100,000	100,000 to 250,000	250,000 to 500,000	500,000 to 2,500,000	2,500,000 and over
Number of Enterprises	1	36786	4896	21340	3322	5165	900	687	228	135	73	14	21	6
Revenues ($ in Thousands)														
Net Sales	2	595281033	6923888	16524590	11055493	63174961	26435509	48850409	29214659	35409230	36018759	18255844	75091215	228326477
Interest	3	5122827	724	4532	478	8242	9295	6775	8070	18083	7361	19339	59583	4980345
Rents	4	1786226	670	1251	3852	17195	6697	6591	5181	7142	7757	9786	31043	1689063
Royalties	5	641024	0	18387	0	61	0	10816	1210	524	0	270	22306	587450
Other Portfolio Income	6	6341698	95330	7083	901	24112	18563	28171	21106	8545	42390	4296	207416	5883785
Other Receipts	7	4536962	101838	80101	97538	189502	195670	224513	345867	182802	410441	131084	1049684	1527918
Total Receipts	8	613709770	7122450	16635944	11158262	63414073	26665734	49127275	29596093	35626326	36486708	18420619	76461247	242995038
Average Total Receipts	9	16683	1455	780	3359	12278	29629	71510	129807	263899	499818	1315758	3641012	40499173
Operating Costs/Operating Income (%)														
Cost of Operations	10	79.8	91.8	75.2	80.2	85.0	86.2	87.9	87.5	86.2	87.2	90.3	85.3	69.9
Salaries and Wages	11	5.9	2.9	4.7	4.2	4.3	3.8	4.1	4.1	4.2	4.5	3.4	4.4	8.6
Taxes Paid	12	1.1	0.5	1.0	1.1	1.0	0.7	0.6	0.6	1.2	0.7	0.5	0.7	1.7
Interest Paid	13	1.2	0.1	0.2	0.4	0.2	0.2	0.3	0.3	0.4	0.5	0.3	0.5	2.5
Depreciation	14	1.7	0.1	0.4	0.6	0.4	0.3	0.3	0.6	0.5	0.6	0.5	0.8	3.6
Amortization and Depletion	15	0.2	0.0	0.1	0.1	0.0	0.1	0.0	0.0	0.1	0.2	0.1	0.2	0.5
Pensions and Other Deferred Comp.	16	0.4	0.1	0.2	0.1	0.2	0.2	0.2	0.1	0.1	0.2	0.2	0.2	0.7
Employee Benefits	17	0.8	0.2	0.5	0.6	0.4	0.4	0.4	0.5	0.5	0.6	0.5	0.5	1.2
Advertising	18	0.7	0.1	0.5	0.3	0.2	0.2	0.4	0.3	0.7	0.6	0.1	0.7	1.0
Other Expenses	19	6.6	5.1	10.5	8.3	5.1	5.7	3.6	4.3	4.3	4.0	3.8	5.5	9.1
Officers' Compensation	20	0.8	0.5	4.4	2.3	1.7	1.2	1.2	0.7	0.8	0.5	0.2	0.3	0.2
Operating Margin	21	0.9	•	2.4	2.0	1.5	1.0	1.0	0.9	0.9	0.5	0.1	0.8	0.9
Operating Margin Before Officers' Comp.	22	1.7	•	6.8	4.4	3.3	2.3	2.2	1.7	1.7	1.0	0.3	1.1	1.1

Selected Average Balance Sheet ($ in Thousands)

Net Receivables 23	1403	0	22	210	752	2364	5674	10137	19299	35044	79548	210951	4586021
Inventories 24	993	0	14	137	480	1539	4057	10427	20982	44194	112964	195117	2502386
Net Property, Plant and Equipment 25	3263	0	16	165	250	500	1726	4917	10710	22226	58112	240843	17694158
Total Assets 26	17160	0	107	701	2074	7110	15755	35480	68998	152541	357074	1122701	90261598
Notes and Loans Payable 27	2900	0	46	235	572	1599	4268	8551	19351	52102	103820	287181	13622453
All Other Liabilities 28	6158	0	35	308	749	2400	5862	13109	24733	52036	122318	419801	32340216
Net Worth 29	8102	0	26	158	753	3111	5626	13819	24914	48403	130937	415718	44298929

Selected Financial Ratios (Times to 1)

Current Ratio 30	1.1	•	2.0	1.3	1.9	1.9	1.6	1.7	1.6	1.6	1.5	1.6	0.9
Quick Ratio 31	0.7	•	1.3	0.8	1.2	1.1	0.9	0.9	0.8	0.7	0.7	0.7	0.6
Net Sales to Working Capital 32	56.8	•	24.4	35.9	15.8	10.7	16.6	11.7	14.9	13.2	17.7	16.3	•
Coverage Ratio 33	4.5	13.4	14.6	8.6	10.6	9.1	6.9	9.4	4.9	5.0	4.3	6.9	4.0
Total Asset Turnover 34	0.9	•	7.2	4.7	5.9	4.1	4.5	3.6	3.8	3.2	3.7	3.2	0.4
Inventory Turnover 35	13.0	•	41.6	19.4	21.7	16.4	15.4	10.7	10.8	9.7	10.4	15.6	10.6
Receivables Turnover 36	12.7	•	37.0	14.4	15.8	14.1	13.2	11.9	13.6	14.3	15.9	19.9	9.6
Total Liabilities to Net Worth 37	1.1	•	3.1	3.4	1.8	1.3	1.8	1.6	1.8	2.2	1.7	1.7	1.0
Current Assets to Working Capital 38	15.5	•	2.0	4.5	2.2	2.1	2.8	2.5	2.8	2.7	2.9	2.7	•
Current Liabilities to Working Capital 39	14.5	•	1.0	3.5	1.2	1.1	1.8	1.5	1.8	1.7	1.9	1.7	•
Working Capital to Net Sales 40	0.0	•	0.0	0.0	0.1	0.1	0.1	0.1	0.1	0.1	0.1	0.1	•
Inventory to Working Capital 41	3.5	•	0.4	1.3	0.6	0.6	1.0	0.9	1.2	1.2	1.5	1.0	•
Total Receipts to Cash Flow 42	11.3	20.2	9.1	10.6	17.7	15.2	23.2	19.4	20.2	19.8	25.7	15.2	7.3
Cost of Goods to Cash Flow 43	9.0	18.6	6.8	8.5	15.1	13.1	20.4	16.9	17.4	17.3	23.2	12.9	5.1
Cash Flow to Total Debt 44	0.2	•	1.0	0.6	0.5	0.5	0.3	0.3	0.3	0.2	0.2	0.3	0.1

Selected Financial Factors (in Percentages)

Debt Ratio 45	52.8	•	75.9	77.5	63.7	56.2	64.3	61.1	63.9	68.3	63.3	63.0	50.9
Return on Total Assets 46	5.0	•	23.7	15.8	12.4	8.9	8.3	9.1	7.3	7.5	5.0	9.9	4.2
Return on Equity Before Income Taxes 47	8.2	•	91.5	62.2	31.0	18.1	20.0	20.8	16.1	19.0	10.4	23.0	6.4
Return on Equity After Income Taxes 48	6.1	•	90.7	62.0	29.6	16.9	18.5	19.2	14.4	16.1	8.0	15.8	4.4
Profit Margin (Before Income Tax) 49	4.1	1.4	3.1	2.9	1.9	1.9	1.6	2.2	1.5	1.9	1.0	2.7	7.5
Profit Margin (After Income Tax) 50	3.0	1.2	3.0	2.9	1.8	1.8	1.5	2.1	1.4	1.6	0.8	1.8	5.1

Table II

Corporations with Net Income

GROCERY AND RELATED PRODUCT

MONEY AMOUNTS AND SIZE OF ASSETS IN THOUSANDS OF DOLLARS

Item Description for Accounting Period 7/12 Through 6/13		Total	Zero Assets	Under 500	500 to 1,000	1,000 to 5,000	5,000 to 10,000	10,000 to 25,000	25,000 to 50,000	50,000 to 100,000	100,000 to 250,000	250,000 to 500,000	500,000 to 2,500,000	2,500,000 and over
Number of Enterprises	1	24481	1891	14019	2638	4162	798	580	188	111	61	•	17	•
Revenues ($ in Thousands)														
Net Sales	2	514517896	5990075	13133429	9262631	55670238	24342392	44727798	25838755	29311291	32597888	•	50349321	•
Interest	3	5079015	679	2408	88	6582	5343	5446	7230	13229	7068	•	47303	•
Rents	4	1755588	626	0	1730	11424	4632	5937	5181	5944	4466	•	26088	•
Royalties	5	638569	0	18387	0	0	0	10816	43	413	0	•	21460	•
Other Portfolio Income	6	6284358	95330	5269	901	21995	17972	16332	17906	8308	27795	•	187200	•
Other Receipts	7	3690470	98379	2119	97393	164984	190243	209900	339796	126822	395093	•	591671	•
Total Receipts	8	531965896	6185089	13161612	9362743	55875223	24560582	44976229	26208911	29466007	33032310	•	51223043	•
Average Total Receipts	9	21730	3271	939	3549	13425	30778	77545	139409	265460	541513	•	3013120	•
Operating Costs/Operating Income (%)														
Cost of Operations	10	78.7	92.4	75.2	79.0	85.6	86.1	87.9	87.8	85.2	87.5	•	81.7	•
Salaries and Wages	11	6.0	2.6	3.5	4.3	3.9	3.7	4.0	4.0	4.5	4.4	•	5.5	•
Taxes Paid	12	1.2	0.5	0.8	1.0	0.9	0.7	0.6	0.6	1.4	0.6	•	0.9	•
Interest Paid	13	1.2	0.1	0.2	0.4	0.2	0.2	0.3	0.3	0.4	0.3	•	0.4	•
Depreciation	14	1.9	0.1	0.3	0.6	0.4	0.3	0.3	0.4	0.6	0.6	•	1.0	•
Amortization and Depletion	15	0.2	0.0	0.1	0.1	0.0	0.0	0.0	0.0	0.1	0.1	•	0.2	•
Pensions and Other Deferred Comp.	16	0.4	0.1	0.2	0.1	0.1	0.2	0.1	0.1	0.1	0.2	•	0.3	•
Employee Benefits	17	0.8	0.2	0.2	0.5	0.3	0.4	0.3	0.5	0.5	0.5	•	0.6	•
Advertising	18	0.7	0.1	0.5	0.3	0.1	0.2	0.4	0.3	0.8	0.6	•	1.1	•
Other Expenses	19	6.7	4.0	10.4	8.5	4.6	5.5	3.3	3.9	4.2	3.8	•	5.6	•
Officers' Compensation	20	0.7	0.3	3.8	2.0	1.6	1.2	1.2	0.7	0.8	0.5	•	0.4	•
Operating Margin	21	1.5	•	4.8	3.2	2.2	1.5	1.5	1.5	1.6	0.9	•	2.4	•
Operating Margin Before Officers' Comp.	22	2.3	•	8.6	5.2	3.8	2.7	2.8	2.2	2.3	1.3	•	2.8	•

Selected Average Balance Sheet ($ in Thousands)

Net Receivables 23	1894	0	24	170	791	2438	5834	10498	19334	35796	•	208333	•
Inventories 24	1303	0	8	142	485	1648	4195	10939	21403	46653	•	216343	•
Net Property, Plant and Equipment 25	4706	0	18	161	226	480	1741	4451	11470	22332	•	215520	•
Total Assets 26	24679	0	111	681	2130	7211	15640	35285	69131	149296	•	1035938	•
Notes and Loans Payable 27	3928	0	43	253	514	1671	4059	8350	19044	47550	•	252936	•
All Other Liabilities 28	8830	0	26	307	759	2396	5614	13290	23510	49944	•	340463	•
Net Worth 29	11920	0	41	121	857	3144	5967	13645	26577	51802	•	442539	•

Selected Financial Ratios (Times to 1)

Current Ratio 30	1.1	•	3.1	1.2	1.9	2.0	1.6	1.7	1.7	1.6	•	1.9	•
Quick Ratio 31	0.7	•	2.2	0.7	1.3	1.1	1.0	0.9	0.8	0.7	•	0.9	•
Net Sales to Working Capital 32	69.1	•	20.7	62.7	15.7	10.1	16.3	11.7	13.6	14.3	•	11.1	•
Coverage Ratio 33	5.1	29.7	30.4	11.0	16.0	11.8	9.2	12.4	6.6	7.7	•	10.7	•
Total Asset Turnover 34	0.9	•	8.5	5.2	6.3	4.2	4.9	3.9	3.8	3.6	•	2.9	•
Inventory Turnover 35	12.7	•	89.7	19.5	23.6	15.9	16.2	11.0	10.5	10.0	•	11.2	•
Receivables Turnover 36	12.3	•	43.0	18.3	16.6	14.2	13.6	12.7	13.7	14.9	•	•	•
Total Liabilities to Net Worth 37	1.1	•	1.7	4.6	1.5	1.3	1.6	1.6	1.6	1.9	•	1.3	•
Current Assets to Working Capital 38	20.1	•	1.5	6.8	2.1	2.0	2.6	2.4	2.5	2.7	•	2.2	•
Current Liabilities to Working Capital 39	19.1	•	0.5	5.8	1.1	1.0	1.6	1.4	1.5	1.7	•	1.2	•
Working Capital to Net Sales 40	0.0	•	0.0	0.0	0.1	0.1	0.1	0.1	0.1	0.1	•	0.1	•
Inventory to Working Capital 41	4.3	•	0.2	2.5	0.6	0.6	0.9	0.9	1.1	1.3	•	0.8	•
Total Receipts to Cash Flow 42	10.4	19.6	7.8	9.2	17.3	14.5	21.9	17.5	18.5	18.8	•	12.6	•
Cost of Goods to Cash Flow 43	8.1	18.1	5.8	7.3	14.8	12.5	19.2	15.4	15.8	16.5	•	10.3	•
Cash Flow to Total Debt 44	0.2	•	1.7	0.7	0.6	0.5	0.4	0.4	0.3	0.3	•	0.4	•

Selected Financial Factors (in Percentages)

Debt Ratio 45	51.7	•	62.6	82.3	59.8	56.4	61.8	61.3	61.6	65.3	•	57.3	•
Return on Total Assets 46	5.3	•	44.1	24.1	17.2	11.2	11.6	12.4	9.5	9.3	•	13.2	•
Return on Equity Before Income Taxes 47	8.8	•	113.8	123.6	40.0	23.5	27.2	29.5	20.9	23.3	•	28.0	•
Return on Equity After Income Taxes 48	6.6	•	113.1	123.4	38.5	22.2	25.5	27.6	19.0	20.0	•	19.7	•
Profit Margin (Before Income Tax) 49	5.0	2.8	5.0	4.2	2.6	2.4	2.1	2.9	2.1	2.3	•	4.2	•
Profit Margin (After Income Tax) 50	3.7	2.5	5.0	4.2	2.5	2.3	2.0	2.7	1.9	1.9	•	2.9	•

Table I

Corporations with and without Net Income

FARM PRODUCT RAW MATERIAL

MONEY AMOUNTS AND SIZE OF ASSETS IN THOUSANDS OF DOLLARS

Item Description for Accounting Period 7/12 Through 6/13	Total	Zero Assets	Under 500	500 to 1,000	1,000 to 5,000	5,000 to 10,000	10,000 to 25,000	25,000 to 50,000	50,000 to 100,000	100,000 to 250,000	250,000 to 500,000	500,000 to 2,500,000	2,500,000 and over
Number of Enterprises **1**	4278	436	1450	617	1185	299	180	49	25	21	4	9	3

Revenues ($ in Thousands)

	Total	Zero Assets	Under 500	500 to 1,000	1,000 to 5,000	5,000 to 10,000	10,000 to 25,000	25,000 to 50,000	50,000 to 100,000	100,000 to 250,000	250,000 to 500,000	500,000 to 2,500,000	2,500,000 and over
Net Sales **2**	188144048	378253	967204	3449188	11277888	8638198	10866882	8074225	5120673	11488615	1779134	32460772	93643018
Interest **3**	428281	86	0	137	5562	5840	4686	1938	1412	2991	2096	46459	357075
Rents **4**	143128	0	11	171	5432	2721	839	226	785	4275	3157	105976	19536
Royalties **5**	151557	0	0	0	0	293	0	0	0	3495	621	3409	143738
Other Portfolio Income **6**	456562	2235	3461	2376	8711	11646	17740	1081	2632	8118	13212	139570	245780
Other Receipts **7**	2742106	4651	62411	85450	130340	39125	96500	66157	55987	74844	56021	176046	1894571
Total Receipts **8**	192065682	385225	1033087	3537322	11427933	8697823	10986647	8143627	5181489	11582338	1854241	32932232	96303718
Average Total Receipts **9**	44896	884	712	5733	9644	29090	61037	166196	207260	551540	463560	3659137	32101239

Operating Costs/Operating Income (%)

	Total	Zero Assets	Under 500	500 to 1,000	1,000 to 5,000	5,000 to 10,000	10,000 to 25,000	25,000 to 50,000	50,000 to 100,000	100,000 to 250,000	250,000 to 500,000	500,000 to 2,500,000	2,500,000 and over
Cost of Operations **10**	93.9	89.3	78.2	92.1	88.3	92.7	92.6	95.1	93.1	94.5	93.1	95.9	94.4
Salaries and Wages **11**	1.6	0.6	3.0	2.3	2.3	1.7	2.5	1.5	1.7	1.4	2.6	1.1	1.6
Taxes Paid **12**	0.3	0.3	1.0	0.5	0.6	0.4	0.3	0.2	0.3	0.4	0.5	0.2	0.3
Interest Paid **13**	0.8	0.3	2.0	0.2	0.2	0.2	0.4	0.2	0.3	0.4	1.8	0.5	1.2
Depreciation **14**	0.8	0.2	2.5	0.9	0.4	0.7	0.4	0.4	0.9	0.8	0.5	0.6	0.9
Amortization and Depletion **15**	0.1	•	0.0	•	0.0	0.0	0.0	0.0	0.0	0.0	0.1	0.1	0.1
Pensions and Other Deferred Comp. **16**	0.2	0.0	•	0.1	0.2	0.0	0.1	0.0	0.1	0.1	0.4	0.1	0.2
Employee Benefits **17**	0.4	0.0	0.3	0.0	0.2	0.2	0.2	0.2	0.1	0.1	0.2	0.2	0.6
Advertising **18**	0.1	0.0	0.4	0.1	0.1	0.0	0.0	0.0	0.0	0.1	0.0	0.1	0.1
Other Expenses **19**	2.3	4.6	14.7	3.6	5.4	2.4	2.2	1.6	3.0	1.8	2.7	1.6	2.1
Officers' Compensation **20**	0.4	0.2	3.9	1.4	1.6	0.7	0.6	0.4	0.2	0.3	0.9	0.2	0.3
Operating Margin **21**	•	4.5	•	•	0.6	0.9	0.6	0.4	0.3	0.2	•	•	•
Operating Margin Before Officers' Comp. **22**	•	4.7	•	0.1	2.2	1.6	1.2	0.8	0.5	0.5	•	•	•

Selected Average Balance Sheet ($ in Thousands)

Net Receivables 23	4939	0	34	302	539	2000	3309	10352	19846	34851	53747	303010	4794181
Inventories 24	3946	0	6	53	403	1179	4476	12295	25197	57024	171105	421087	2879918
Net Property, Plant and Equipment 25	2528	0	35	50	257	1960	1996	5073	10612	28673	24855	193946	2173671
Total Assets 26	21657	0	185	719	2161	6419	14977	35712	71169	151967	298855	1303377	21705073
Notes and Loans Payable 27	7783	0	303	597	559	1793	4114	9466	20699	37700	160256	502983	7869949
All Other Liabilities 28	5362	0	10	80	739	2682	6320	15948	27636	55155	48633	424089	4472940
Net Worth 29	8511	0	-128	42	862	1944	4544	10298	22833	59112	89966	376304	9362184

Selected Financial Ratios (Times to 1)

Current Ratio 30	1.7	•	4.5	1.0	1.9	1.2	1.5	1.4	1.4	1.3	1.5	1.4	1.9
Quick Ratio 31	0.9	•	3.7	0.9	1.1	0.8	0.8	0.6	0.6	0.6	0.4	0.6	1.2
Net Sales to Working Capital 32	10.3	•	7.9	•	12.4	45.1	15.1	20.2	12.5	22.8	5.4	16.0	7.4
Coverage Ratio 33	3.0	22.8	1.4	8.7	11.5	7.5	5.4	6.2	5.5	3.9	1.8	2.8	2.6
Total Asset Turnover 34	2.0	•	3.6	7.8	4.4	4.5	4.0	4.6	2.9	3.6	1.5	2.8	1.4
Inventory Turnover 35	10.5	•	80.3	96.4	20.9	22.7	12.5	12.7	7.6	9.1	2.4	8.2	10.2
Receivables Turnover 36	9.5	•	17.1	•	17.1	16.3	16.4	15.1	•	11.4	16.6	14.0	7.0
Total Liabilities to Net Worth 37	1.5	•	•	16.0	1.5	2.3	2.3	2.5	2.1	1.6	2.3	2.5	1.3
Current Assets to Working Capital 38	2.5	•	1.3	•	2.2	6.1	2.9	3.5	3.5	4.0	3.0	3.8	2.1
Current Liabilities to Working Capital 39	1.5	•	0.3	•	1.2	5.1	1.9	2.5	2.5	3.0	2.0	2.8	1.1
Working Capital to Net Sales 40	0.1	•	0.1	•	0.1	0.0	0.1	0.0	0.1	0.0	0.2	0.1	0.1
Inventory to Working Capital 41	0.9	•	0.1	•	0.5	1.6	1.2	1.4	1.5	1.9	2.1	1.8	0.7
Total Receipts to Cash Flow 42	37.0	9.8	8.4	27.6	16.5	31.2	29.4	42.1	25.4	42.6	34.2	58.3	42.5
Cost of Goods to Cash Flow 43	34.8	8.7	6.6	25.4	14.6	28.9	27.2	40.0	23.6	40.3	31.8	56.0	40.1
Cash Flow to Total Debt 44	0.1	•	0.3	0.3	0.4	0.2	0.2	0.2	0.2	0.1	0.1	0.1	0.1

Selected Financial Factors (in Percentages)

Debt Ratio 45	60.7	•	168.7	94.1	60.1	69.7	69.7	71.2	67.9	61.1	69.9	71.1	56.9
Return on Total Assets 46	5.1	•	10.0	10.6	9.5	8.5	8.4	6.9	5.1	4.9	4.8	4.1	4.7
Return on Equity Before Income Taxes 47	8.6	•	•	160.1	21.8	24.3	22.5	20.1	13.0	9.4	7.3	9.1	6.7
Return on Equity After Income Taxes 48	6.2	•	•	158.2	20.8	22.4	20.5	18.6	11.8	6.4	3.8	4.9	4.5
Profit Margin (Before Income Tax) 49	1.7	6.3	0.8	1.2	2.0	1.6	1.7	1.3	1.4	1.0	1.5	1.0	2.0
Profit Margin (After Income Tax) 50	1.2	4.9	0.5	1.2	1.9	1.5	1.5	1.2	1.3	0.7	0.8	0.5	1.3

Table II

Corporations with Net Income

FARM PRODUCT RAW MATERIAL

MONEY AMOUNTS AND SIZE OF ASSETS IN THOUSANDS OF DOLLARS

Item Description for Accounting Period 7/12 Through 6/13		Total	Zero Assets	Under 500	500 to 1,000	1,000 to 5,000	5,000 to 10,000	10,000 to 25,000	25,000 to 50,000	50,000 to 100,000	100,000 to 250,000	250,000 to 500,000	500,000 to 2,500,000	2,500,000 and over
Number of Enterprises	1	3010	425	•	421	852	240	147	43	22	18	0	•	3
Revenues ($ in Thousands)														
Net Sales	2	173790096	313254	•	2170266	9602506	7962272	9202721	7424583	4603734	9354890	0	•	93643018
Interest	3	421841	3	•	137	5140	5836	3966	1373	1274	3420	0	•	357075
Rents	4	141699	0	•	171	5431	2721	839	164	785	6067	0	•	19536
Royalties	5	148348	0	•	0	0	293	0	0	0	4116	0	•	143738
Other Portfolio Income	6	430314	1985	•	324	2742	11646	16921	943	1664	9911	0	•	245780
Other Receipts	7	2605069	2554	•	85305	61534	38595	103054	60119	37413	121441	0	•	1894571
Total Receipts	8	177537367	317796	•	2256203	9677353	8021363	9327501	7487182	4644870	9499845	0	•	96303718
Average Total Receipts	9	58983	748	•	5359	11358	33422	63452	174121	211130	527769	•	•	32101239
Operating Costs/Operating Income (%)														
Cost of Operations	10	93.8	88.4	•	88.4	88.0	92.8	92.2	95.1	93.4	93.4	•	•	94.4
Salaries and Wages	11	1.6	0.2	•	3.0	2.4	1.6	2.8	1.5	1.5	1.7	•	•	1.6
Taxes Paid	12	0.3	0.2	•	0.7	0.5	0.4	0.3	0.2	0.3	0.5	•	•	0.3
Interest Paid	13	0.8	0.1	•	0.2	0.1	0.2	0.3	0.2	0.3	0.4	•	•	1.2
Depreciation	14	0.7	0.1	•	1.5	0.4	0.4	0.4	0.3	0.7	0.9	•	•	0.9
Amortization and Depletion	15	0.0	•	•	•	•	0.0	0.0	0.0	0.0	0.0	•	•	0.1
Pensions and Other Deferred Comp.	16	0.2	0.0	•	0.2	0.1	0.0	0.2	0.0	0.1	0.1	•	•	0.2
Employee Benefits	17	0.4	0.0	•	•	0.1	0.2	0.2	0.2	0.1	0.1	•	•	0.6
Advertising	18	0.1	0.0	•	0.1	0.1	0.0	0.0	0.0	0.1	0.1	•	•	0.1
Other Expenses	19	2.2	3.4	•	4.6	4.8	2.4	2.0	1.5	2.4	2.1	•	•	2.1
Officers' Compensation	20	0.4	•	•	1.9	1.4	0.7	0.7	0.4	0.2	0.3	•	•	0.3
Operating Margin	21	•	7.6	•	•	2.0	1.4	1.0	0.6	1.0	0.3	•	•	•
Operating Margin Before Officers' Comp.	22	•	7.6	•	1.1	3.3	2.1	1.6	1.0	1.3	0.7	•	•	•

Selected Average Balance Sheet ($ in Thousands)

Net Receivables	23	6735	0	•	202	635	2305	3453	10881	20719	34268	•	•	4794181
Inventories	24	3992	0	•	165	442	1164	4227	11786	20157	53530	•	•	2735827
Net Property, Plant and Equipment	25	3315	0	•	67	268	1450	1883	4835	9053	28339	•	•	2173671
Total Assets	26	28738	0	•	671	2161	6262	15108	35404	69133	161579	•	•	21705073
Notes and Loans Payable	27	9872	0	•	260	537	916	3760	8341	17219	44341	•	•	7869949
All Other Liabilities	28	7103	0	•	115	650	3161	6330	16682	29661	52645	•	•	4472940
Net Worth	29	11763	0	•	296	974	2185	5018	10381	22252	64593	•	•	9362184

Selected Financial Ratios (Times to 1)

Current Ratio	30	1.7	•	•	2.0	2.3	1.3	1.6	1.4	1.4	1.3	•	•	1.9
Quick Ratio	31	1.0	•	•	1.6	1.3	0.9	0.7	0.6	0.7	0.5	•	•	1.2
Net Sales to Working Capital	32	9.7	•	•	22.5	11.0	31.8	14.9	20.6	13.4	19.6	•	•	7.4
Coverage Ratio	33	3.5	162.0	•	13.9	19.4	12.2	9.4	8.1	7.5	5.5	•	•	2.6
Total Asset Turnover	34	2.0	•	•	7.7	5.2	5.3	4.1	4.9	3.0	3.2	•	•	1.4
Inventory Turnover	35	13.6	•	•	27.7	22.4	26.4	13.6	13.9	9.7	9.1	•	•	10.8
Receivables Turnover	36	12.4	•	•	28.2	19.0	16.6	17.4	16.8	9.7	10.5	•	•	•
Total Liabilities to Net Worth	37	1.4	•	•	1.3	1.2	1.9	2.0	2.4	2.1	1.5	•	•	1.3
Current Assets to Working Capital	38	2.3	•	•	2.0	1.8	4.2	2.8	3.5	3.6	3.9	•	•	2.1
Current Liabilities to Working Capital	39	1.3	•	•	1.0	0.8	3.2	1.8	2.5	2.6	2.9	•	•	1.1
Working Capital to Net Sales	40	0.1	•	•	0.0	0.1	0.0	0.1	0.0	0.1	0.1	•	•	0.1
Inventory to Working Capital	41	0.8	•	•	0.3	0.4	1.0	1.1	1.4	1.5	2.1	•	•	0.7
Total Receipts to Cash Flow	42	34.5	8.5	•	15.8	15.5	27.8	25.7	40.3	25.4	29.8	•	•	42.5
Cost of Goods to Cash Flow	43	32.3	7.5	•	14.0	13.7	25.8	23.6	38.3	23.8	27.9	•	•	40.1
Cash Flow to Total Debt	44	0.1	•	•	0.9	0.6	0.3	0.2	0.2	0.2	0.2	•	•	0.1

Selected Financial Factors (in Percentages)

Debt Ratio	45	59.1	•	•	55.8	54.9	65.1	66.8	70.7	67.8	60.0	•	•	56.9
Return on Total Assets	46	5.7	•	•	26.4	15.1	12.2	10.9	7.9	6.8	7.4	•	•	4.7
Return on Equity Before Income Taxes	47	10.0	•	•	55.5	31.7	32.2	29.4	23.7	18.2	15.0	•	•	6.7
Return on Equity After Income Taxes	48	7.4	•	•	55.1	30.5	30.1	27.1	22.1	16.8	10.7	•	•	4.5
Profit Margin (Before Income Tax)	49	2.0	9.1	•	3.2	2.7	2.1	2.4	1.4	1.9	1.9	•	•	2.0
Profit Margin (After Income Tax)	50	1.5	7.4	•	3.2	2.6	2.0	2.2	1.3	1.8	1.3	•	•	1.3

Table I

Corporations with and without Net Income

CHEMICAL AND ALLIED PRODUCTS

MONEY AMOUNTS AND SIZE OF ASSETS IN THOUSANDS OF DOLLARS

Item Description for Accounting Period 7/12 Through 6/13	Total	Zero Assets	Under 500	500 to 1,000	1,000 to 5,000	5,000 to 10,000	10,000 to 25,000	25,000 to 50,000	50,000 to 100,000	100,000 to 250,000	250,000 to 500,000	500,000 to 2,500,000	2,500,000 and over
Number of Enterprises 1	9699	2536	4828	532	1175	235	233	78	36	24	9	8	3

Revenues ($ in Thousands)

Net Sales 2	92790457	2374507	2835457	1877174	9635055	5266923	10362514	7224072	5562093	9606460	5276880	15669908	17099415
Interest 3	82794	326	58	604	2836	1421	4562	1400	1753	7070	598	22403	39763
Rents 4	18284	264	0	0	710	800	817	942	3184	298	6790	1818	2662
Royalties 5	5210	0	4240	0	0	0	0	0	0	518	0	452	0
Other Portfolio Income 6	211388	44743	0	34	19559	1755	2466	1098	2351	13980	7747	77590	40066
Other Receipts 7	1192175	37675	6420	29287	102263	21277	25547	19386	20993	35360	9751	241775	642437
Total Receipts 8	94300308	2457515	2846175	1907099	9760423	5292176	10395906	7246898	5590374	9663686	5301766	16013946	17824343
Average Total Receipts 9	9723	969	590	3585	8307	22520	44618	92909	155288	402654	589085	2001743	5941448

Operating Costs/Operating Income (%)

Cost of Operations 10	81.1	74.3	65.8	76.2	76.5	76.6	81.7	83.2	83.9	89.3	91.5	84.7	75.8
Salaries and Wages 11	5.4	5.2	7.4	5.8	6.1	7.6	5.3	4.7	5.0	2.4	1.8	4.0	8.3
Taxes Paid 12	0.8	0.9	1.2	1.3	1.1	1.1	0.9	1.1	0.8	0.4	0.4	0.7	0.8
Interest Paid 13	0.7	0.6	0.1	0.1	0.5	0.3	0.2	0.3	0.4	0.3	0.3	1.1	1.9
Depreciation 14	1.2	0.5	0.1	0.3	0.7	0.5	0.7	0.9	1.1	0.7	2.4	0.8	2.8
Amortization and Depletion 15	0.5	0.1	0.3	•	0.2	0.0	0.1	0.1	0.1	0.2	0.3	0.7	1.7
Pensions and Other Deferred Comp. 16	0.3	0.6	0.1	0.5	0.2	0.6	0.3	0.4	0.4	0.2	0.1	0.2	0.4
Employee Benefits 17	0.8	0.7	0.2	0.3	0.6	0.4	0.5	0.5	0.6	0.4	0.4	0.6	2.0
Advertising 18	0.1	0.1	0.7	0.3	0.1	0.2	0.2	0.2	0.1	0.0	0.1	0.1	0.0
Other Expenses 19	5.7	10.9	20.1	8.9	8.2	6.7	4.7	4.3	3.7	3.1	2.0	4.1	6.5
Officers' Compensation 20	1.2	1.3	3.1	6.4	2.7	3.0	1.3	1.3	0.8	0.4	0.2	0.6	0.3
Operating Margin 21	2.1	4.7	0.9	•	3.0	3.0	4.2	3.3	2.9	2.4	0.5	2.5	•
Operating Margin Before Officers' Comp. 22	3.4	6.1	4.0	6.3	5.7	6.0	5.5	4.5	3.7	2.9	0.7	3.1	•

Selected Average Balance Sheet ($ in Thousands)

Net Receivables 23	1202	0	43	389	759	2487	5363	11236	20834	46288	40584	228247	1195575
Inventories 24	857	0	36	110	568	2428	4993	10433	19078	37689	48489	205945	493951
Net Property, Plant and Equipment 25	921	0	3	51	217	565	2485	4551	10157	18951	44775	166588	1671846
Total Assets 26	5906	0	161	773	2326	7128	16499	33469	70693	150203	308588	1444720	8249580
Notes and Loans Payable 27	2107	0	58	189	585	1447	3021	8961	17455	29510	48175	565719	3777581
All Other Liabilities 28	1561	0	28	314	1148	2819	5683	12100	21730	53965	86666	342101	1655697
Net Worth 29	2238	0	75	270	593	2862	7794	12408	31508	66728	173747	536900	2816301

Selected Financial Ratios (Times to 1)

Current Ratio 30	1.6	•	2.4	1.8	1.5	1.9	1.9	1.6	1.6	1.5	1.4	2.0	1.5
Quick Ratio 31	0.8	•	1.7	1.4	0.9	1.1	1.1	0.8	0.9	0.9	0.5	1.1	0.5
Net Sales to Working Capital 32	8.1	•	7.3	11.6	16.4	7.8	7.6	9.4	8.1	12.0	12.5	7.3	5.0
Coverage Ratio 33	6.1	15.6	14.6	13.8	9.2	14.1	23.8	13.0	8.7	11.2	4.6	5.5	2.9
Total Asset Turnover 34	1.6	•	3.6	4.6	3.5	3.1	2.7	2.8	2.2	2.7	1.9	1.4	0.7
Inventory Turnover 35	9.1	•	10.7	24.4	11.1	7.1	7.3	7.4	6.8	9.5	11.1	8.1	8.7
Receivables Turnover 36	7.9	•	14.3	12.0	8.9	8.8	7.7	8.3	6.9	8.0	•	•	4.9
Total Liabilities to Net Worth 37	1.6	•	1.1	1.9	2.9	1.5	1.1	1.7	1.2	1.3	0.8	1.7	1.9
Current Assets to Working Capital 38	2.6	•	1.7	2.2	3.2	2.1	2.1	2.6	2.5	2.9	3.4	2.0	3.2
Current Liabilities to Working Capital 39	1.6	•	0.7	1.2	2.2	1.1	1.1	1.6	1.5	1.9	2.4	1.0	2.2
Working Capital to Net Sales 40	0.1	•	0.1	0.1	0.1	0.1	0.1	0.1	0.1	0.1	0.1	0.1	0.2
Inventory to Working Capital 41	0.7	•	0.5	0.5	1.1	0.9	0.8	1.1	1.0	0.9	1.0	0.8	0.5
Total Receipts to Cash Flow 42	12.6	5.9	5.2	11.7	9.3	11.5	12.1	14.6	16.4	18.3	38.6	12.9	14.2
Cost of Goods to Cash Flow 43	10.2	4.4	3.4	8.9	7.1	8.8	9.9	12.1	13.8	16.4	35.3	10.9	10.7
Cash Flow to Total Debt 44	0.2	•	1.3	0.6	0.5	0.5	0.4	0.3	0.2	0.3	0.1	0.2	0.1

Selected Financial Factors (in Percentages)

Debt Ratio 45	62.1	•	53.4	65.1	74.5	59.9	52.8	62.9	55.4	55.6	43.7	62.8	65.9
Return on Total Assets 46	7.3	•	5.0	7.1	17.3	11.8	12.8	10.7	8.4	9.1	2.5	7.8	3.9
Return on Equity Before Income Taxes 47	16.2	•	9.9	18.8	60.3	27.3	25.9	26.6	16.6	18.6	3.5	17.2	7.6
Return on Equity After Income Taxes 48	13.1	•	8.7	17.0	58.1	24.4	24.0	22.6	14.5	13.3	2.9	12.9	4.9
Profit Margin (Before Income Tax) 49	3.8	8.2	1.3	1.4	4.4	3.5	4.5	3.6	3.4	3.1	1.0	4.7	3.8
Profit Margin (After Income Tax) 50	3.1	7.1	1.1	1.3	4.2	3.1	4.2	3.0	3.0	2.2	0.9	3.5	2.4

Table II

Corporations with Net Income

CHEMICAL AND ALLIED PRODUCTS

MONEY AMOUNTS AND SIZE OF ASSETS IN THOUSANDS OF DOLLARS

Item Description for Accounting Period 7/12 Through 6/13	Total	Zero Assets	Under 500	500 to 1,000	1,000 to 5,000	5,000 to 10,000	10,000 to 25,000	25,000 to 50,000	50,000 to 100,000	100,000 to 250,000	250,000 to 500,000	500,000 to 2,500,000	2,500,000 and over
Number of Enterprises 1	6029	1437	2503	528	997	214	215	67	32	•	5	•	0

Revenues ($ in Thousands)													
Net Sales 2	77512689	2095947	2399827	1874515	8446691	4829915	10011776	6199292	5123825	•	1931862	•	0
Interest 3	63207	326	13	604	2312	1418	2132	1379	1689	•	307	•	0
Rents 4	7891	264	0	0	710	729	187	942	3184	•	0	•	0
Royalties 5	4974	0	4240	0	0	0	0	0	0	•	0	•	0
Other Portfolio Income 6	205152	44743	0	29	17534	1692	2466	1098	2328	•	3759	•	0
Other Receipts 7	1114368	25253	6143	29288	94513	20803	24153	18780	18026	•	2905	•	0
Total Receipts 8	78908281	2166533	2410223	1904436	8561760	4854557	10040714	6221491	5149052	•	1938833	•	0
Average Total Receipts 9	13088	1508	963	3607	8588	22685	46701	92858	160908	•	387767	•	•

Operating Costs/Operating Income (%)													
Cost of Operations 10	80.3	72.1	64.2	76.2	77.4	75.5	81.9	81.4	83.5	•	79.0	•	•
Salaries and Wages 11	5.6	5.8	7.1	5.8	6.1	7.9	5.2	5.0	5.2	•	3.9	•	•
Taxes Paid 12	0.8	1.0	1.2	1.3	1.0	1.1	0.8	1.2	0.8	•	0.8	•	•
Interest Paid 13	0.5	0.6	0.1	0.1	0.5	0.3	0.2	0.3	0.4	•	0.2	•	•
Depreciation 14	1.1	0.6	0.1	0.3	0.6	0.5	0.6	0.8	1.1	•	1.0	•	•
Amortization and Depletion 15	0.5	0.2	0.4	•	0.1	0.0	0.1	0.1	0.1	•	0.6	•	•
Pensions and Other Deferred Comp. 16	0.3	0.4	0.0	0.5	0.2	0.6	0.3	0.4	0.4	•	0.3	•	•
Employee Benefits 17	0.8	0.8	0.2	0.3	0.5	0.4	0.5	0.5	0.6	•	0.9	•	•
Advertising 18	0.1	0.1	0.7	0.3	0.1	0.2	0.2	0.2	0.1	•	0.1	•	•
Other Expenses 19	5.4	10.9	19.3	8.5	6.8	6.6	4.4	4.4	3.6	•	4.2	•	•
Officers' Compensation 20	1.3	1.5	3.0	6.4	2.7	3.2	1.3	1.4	0.9	•	0.2	•	•
Operating Margin 21	3.2	6.1	3.6	0.3	3.9	3.7	4.6	4.4	3.3	•	8.9	•	•
Operating Margin Before Officers' Comp. 22	4.5	7.6	6.7	6.7	6.5	6.9	5.9	5.8	4.2	•	9.1	•	•

Selected Average Balance Sheet ($ in Thousands)

Net Receivables 23	1692	0	44	391	795	2489	5566	12050	21189	•	40451	•	•
Inventories 24	1187	0	57	105	511	2443	5170	10470	19615	•	45453	•	•
Net Property, Plant and Equipment 25	1228	0	4	51	231	573	2383	3834	10315	•	23918	•	•
Total Assets 26	7599	0	181	774	2274	7196	16152	33706	71631	•	290769	•	•
Notes and Loans Payable 27	2461	0	23	165	618	1389	2813	9371	16402	•	41035	•	•
All Other Liabilities 28	1959	0	28	317	1117	2619	5587	11032	22061	•	53024	•	•
Net Worth 29	3179	0	130	293	539	3188	7751	13303	33169	•	196711	•	•

Selected Financial Ratios (Times to 1)

Current Ratio 30	1.6	•	4.8	1.8	1.5	2.1	1.9	1.7	1.7	•	2.4	•	•
Quick Ratio 31	0.8	•	2.6	1.4	0.9	1.1	1.1	0.9	1.0	•	0.7	•	•
Net Sales to Working Capital 32	7.5	•	7.8	11.7	16.5	7.0	7.9	8.1	7.8	•	3.8	•	•
Coverage Ratio 33	11.8	16.8	54.1	17.8	11.0	17.2	29.6	18.6	11.0	•	54.8	•	•
Total Asset Turnover 34	1.7	•	5.3	4.6	3.7	3.1	2.9	2.7	2.2	•	1.3	•	•
Inventory Turnover 35	8.7	•	10.7	25.9	12.8	7.0	7.4	7.2	6.8	•	6.7	•	•
Receivables Turnover 36	7.6	•	19.3	12.8	9.4	9.1	7.8	7.8	7.0	•	•	•	•
Total Liabilities to Net Worth 37	1.4	•	0.4	1.6	3.2	1.3	1.1	1.5	1.2	•	0.5	•	•
Current Assets to Working Capital 38	2.5	•	1.3	2.2	3.1	2.0	2.1	2.4	2.4	•	1.7	•	•
Current Liabilities to Working Capital 39	1.5	•	0.3	1.2	2.1	1.0	1.1	1.4	1.4	•	0.7	•	•
Working Capital to Net Sales 40	0.1	•	0.1	0.1	0.1	0.1	0.1	0.1	0.1	•	0.3	•	•
Inventory to Working Capital 41	0.7	•	0.6	0.5	1.0	0.8	0.8	1.0	0.9	•	0.4	•	•
Total Receipts to Cash Flow 42	11.3	5.6	4.6	11.7	9.5	10.7	12.0	12.3	15.8	•	7.9	•	•
Cost of Goods to Cash Flow 43	9.1	4.0	3.0	8.9	7.4	8.1	9.8	10.0	13.2	•	6.2	•	•
Cash Flow to Total Debt 44	0.3	•	4.1	0.6	0.5	0.5	0.5	0.4	0.3	•	0.5	•	•

Selected Financial Factors (in Percentages)

Debt Ratio 45	58.2	•	28.1	62.1	76.3	55.7	52.0	60.5	53.7	•	32.3	•	•
Return on Total Assets 46	9.2	•	21.9	9.0	21.6	14.1	14.5	13.9	9.4	•	12.7	•	•
Return on Equity Before Income Taxes 47	20.2	•	29.9	22.5	83.0	30.0	29.2	33.3	18.5	•	18.4	•	•
Return on Equity After Income Taxes 48	16.7	•	28.6	20.8	80.2	27.2	27.1	28.9	16.2	•	17.5	•	•
Profit Margin (Before Income Tax) 49	5.0	9.5	4.1	1.9	5.3	4.2	4.9	4.8	3.8	•	9.3	•	•
Profit Margin (After Income Tax) 50	4.1	8.2	3.9	1.7	5.1	3.8	4.5	4.2	3.4	•	8.9	•	•

Table I

Corporations with and without Net Income

PETROLEUM AND PETROLEUM PRODUCTS

MONEY AMOUNTS AND SIZE OF ASSETS IN THOUSANDS OF DOLLARS

Item Description for Accounting Period 7/12 Through 6/13	Total	Zero Assets	Under 500	500 to 1,000	1,000 to 5,000	5,000 to 10,000	10,000 to 25,000	25,000 to 50,000	50,000 to 100,000	100,000 to 250,000	250,000 to 500,000	500,000 to 2,500,000	2,500,000 and over
Number of Enterprises 1	6566	699	1968	652	2014	571	342	162	74	37	15	25	7

Revenues ($ in Thousands)													
Net Sales 2	677522172	52920033	1995498	3889901	59496692	45280917	57503388	43689352	40984380	48771511	42951657	152541978	127496865
Interest 3	395596	3091	1347	2278	6300	3992	8016	6551	2216	3543	12079	29673	316510
Rents 4	200327	13	8175	390	12594	14171	33486	19020	8037	23378	22764	45575	12722
Royalties 5	71778	0	96	0	0	3065	599	0	137	298	2	5980	61602
Other Portfolio Income 6	2008940	13953	21487	0	95937	45466	20154	31107	25880	77072	92943	412994	1171946
Other Receipts 7	3295760	303633	1964	2855	220366	125789	119920	153543	92410	177188	350557	290639	1456899
Total Receipts 8	683494573	53240723	2028567	3895424	59831889	45473400	57685563	43899573	41113060	49052990	43430002	153326839	130516544
Average Total Receipts 9	104096	76167	1031	5975	29708	79638	168671	270985	555582	1325756	2895333	6133074	18645221

Operating Costs/Operating Income (%)													
Cost of Operations 10	94.9	98.2	90.0	93.3	92.0	95.5	95.6	94.7	95.4	96.4	98.2	97.9	89.3
Salaries and Wages 11	1.0	0.9	3.9	1.0	1.6	1.5	1.2	1.7	1.3	0.7	0.6	0.5	1.1
Taxes Paid 12	0.6	0.1	1.2	0.9	3.1	0.3	0.4	0.3	0.2	0.4	0.1	0.1	0.7
Interest Paid 13	0.4	0.2	0.4	0.3	0.1	0.2	0.1	0.2	0.1	0.1	0.1	0.2	1.7
Depreciation 14	0.6	0.1	0.3	0.1	0.2	0.3	0.3	0.6	0.4	0.2	0.2	0.2	1.8
Amortization and Depletion 15	0.3	0.0	0.3	0.0	0.0	0.1	0.0	0.0	0.0	0.0	0.1	0.1	1.5
Pensions and Other Deferred Comp. 16	0.1	0.0	0.0	0.0	0.0	0.1	0.0	0.0	0.0	0.0	0.0	0.1	0.1
Employee Benefits 17	0.1	0.0	0.1	0.2	0.1	0.1	0.1	0.1	0.1	0.1	0.1	0.1	0.1
Advertising 18	0.0	0.0	0.1	0.0	0.1	0.0	0.0	0.1	0.0	0.0	0.0	0.0	0.0
Other Expenses 19	2.2	1.3	4.3	2.8	2.5	1.6	1.7	2.0	1.7	1.6	1.2	0.9	5.2
Officers' Compensation 20	0.2	0.0	2.4	1.9	0.4	0.3	0.3	0.3	0.2	0.2	0.2	0.1	0.2
Operating Margin 21	•	•	•	•	•	0.1	0.2	0.1	0.3	0.3	•	•	•
Operating Margin Before Officers' Comp. 22	•	•	•	1.4	0.2	0.4	0.5	0.5	0.6	0.5	•	•	•

Net Receivables 23	4516	0	27	451	935	2743	5013	10893	25279	58183	121318	274010	1383410
Inventories 24	2530	0	21	96	403	1015	2352	4735	8773	27647	83032	205847	783054
Net Property, Plant and Equipment 25	9902	0	22	56	449	1869	4075	11217	15773	26151	52898	93659	7783582
Total Assets 26	25236	0	178	772	2547	7486	15955	34869	68628	159148	349046	957660	14884565
Notes and Loans Payable 27	9701	0	72	166	840	2162	3820	10704	19204	48775	89738	235948	6715454
All Other Liabilities 28	8158	0	50	214	990	2646	6034	12177	28736	75920	168517	416087	3988480
Net Worth 29	7378	0	57	391	717	2678	6101	11988	20689	34452	90791	305626	4180630

Current Ratio 30	1.4	•	2.2	2.3	1.6	1.5	1.4	1.3	1.3	1.3	1.4	1.2	1.6
Quick Ratio 31	0.9	•	1.5	2.0	1.2	1.1	1.0	0.9	0.9	0.8	0.8	0.7	1.0
Net Sales to Working Capital 32	38.5	•	13.9	15.4	42.1	50.2	63.4	59.2	51.4	52.8	43.1	65.4	15.6
Coverage Ratio 33	2.1	•	•	•	4.2	4.2	5.5	4.7	6.2	7.5	2.8	2.9	1.5
Total Asset Turnover 34	4.1	•	5.7	7.7	11.6	10.6	10.5	7.7	8.1	8.3	8.2	6.4	1.2
Inventory Turnover 35	38.7	•	43.9	57.7	67.5	74.6	68.3	53.9	60.2	46.0	33.9	29.0	20.8
Receivables Turnover 36	22.7	•	37.1	14.9	35.7	25.0	31.2	26.3	21.3	27.9	21.6	22.3	12.6
Total Liabilities to Net Worth 37	2.4	•	2.1	1.0	2.6	1.8	1.6	1.9	2.3	3.6	2.8	2.1	2.6
Current Assets to Working Capital 38	3.4	•	1.8	1.7	2.6	3.1	3.7	4.3	4.0	4.5	3.8	5.9	2.6
Current Liabilities to Working Capital 39	2.4	•	0.8	0.7	1.6	2.1	2.7	3.3	3.0	3.5	2.8	4.9	1.6
Working Capital to Net Sales 40	0.0	•	0.1	0.1	0.0	0.0	0.0	0.0	0.0	0.0	0.0	0.0	0.1
Inventory to Working Capital 41	0.9	•	0.4	0.3	0.6	0.6	0.8	1.1	0.8	1.5	1.1	2.1	0.7
Total Receipts to Cash Flow 42	46.6	125.1	60.0	53.8	44.0	62.2	57.0	47.6	51.8	52.5	92.2	137.6	19.0
Cost of Goods to Cash Flow 43	44.3	122.8	54.0	50.2	40.5	59.5	54.4	45.1	49.4	50.6	90.6	134.7	17.0
Cash Flow to Total Debt 44	0.1	•	0.1	0.3	0.4	0.3	0.3	0.2	0.2	0.2	0.1	0.1	0.1

Debt Ratio 45	70.8	•	68.0	49.3	71.9	64.2	61.8	65.6	69.9	78.4	74.0	68.1	71.9
Return on Total Assets 46	3.7	•	•	•	4.8	6.8	6.2	6.0	6.2	8.6	3.1	3.4	3.0
Return on Equity Before Income Taxes 47	6.5	•	•	•	13.0	14.6	13.2	13.7	17.2	34.5	7.6	6.9	3.6
Return on Equity After Income Taxes 48	5.7	•	•	•	12.0	14.0	12.0	12.8	15.5	31.6	4.8	5.6	3.3
Profit Margin (Before Income Tax) 49	0.5	•	•	•	0.3	0.5	0.5	0.6	0.6	0.9	0.2	0.3	0.8
Profit Margin (After Income Tax) 50	0.4	•	•	•	0.3	0.5	0.4	0.6	0.6	0.8	0.2	0.3	0.8

Table II

Corporations with Net Income

PETROLEUM AND PETROLEUM PRODUCTS

MONEY AMOUNTS AND SIZE OF ASSETS IN THOUSANDS OF DOLLARS

Item Description for Accounting Period 7/12 Through 6/13		Total	Zero Assets	Under 500	500 to 1,000	1,000 to 5,000	5,000 to 10,000	10,000 to 25,000	25,000 to 50,000	50,000 to 100,000	100,000 to 250,000	250,000 to 500,000	500,000 to 2,500,000	2,500,000 and over
Number of Enterprises	1	3849	394	•	333	1366	440	275	125	64	28	12	15	•

Revenues ($ in Thousands)

Net Sales	2	510512921	8183152	•	1228114	43140897	41434349	47587990	36650091	35957892	41012992	33575547	110839215	•
Interest	3	183677	3	•	1037	5204	2938	6989	5279	1860	2836	12056	24984	•
Rents	4	146719	13	•	0	10960	12233	31673	17864	4043	2192	22764	24659	•
Royalties	5	71435	0	•	0	0	3012	565	0	137	277	2	5745	•
Other Portfolio Income	6	1959600	13872	•	0	77985	36013	15816	26045	23563	75576	92565	404730	•
Other Receipts	7	2774263	32271	•	554	170112	113537	103021	117987	83160	162314	336067	248041	•
Total Receipts	8	515648615	8229311	•	1229705	43405158	41602082	47746054	36817266	36070655	41256187	34039001	111547374	•
Average Total Receipts	9	133970	20887	•	3693	31775	94550	173622	294538	563604	1473435	2836583	7436492	•

Operating Costs/Operating Income (%)

Cost of Operations	10	94.4	98.9	•	87.1	90.9	95.9	95.5	94.5	95.4	96.3	98.0	97.8	•
Salaries and Wages	11	1.0	0.1	•	1.4	1.4	1.4	1.2	1.7	1.2	0.7	0.6	0.5	•
Taxes Paid	12	0.7	0.0	•	1.2	4.1	0.3	0.5	0.3	0.2	0.4	0.1	0.1	•
Interest Paid	13	0.5	0.0	•	0.3	0.1	0.1	0.1	0.1	0.1	0.1	0.1	0.2	•
Depreciation	14	0.6	0.0	•	0.1	0.2	0.2	0.3	0.5	0.4	0.2	0.3	0.2	•
Amortization and Depletion	15	0.2	•	•	•	0.0	0.0	0.0	0.0	0.0	0.0	0.0	0.1	•
Pensions and Other Deferred Comp.	16	0.1	0.0	•	0.2	0.0	0.1	0.0	0.0	0.0	0.0	0.0	0.1	•
Employee Benefits	17	0.1	•	•	0.0	0.1	0.1	0.1	0.1	0.1	0.0	0.1	0.1	•
Advertising	18	0.0	0.0	•	0.1	0.1	0.0	0.0	0.1	0.0	0.0	0.0	0.0	•
Other Expenses	19	2.4	0.8	•	4.6	2.6	1.4	1.6	2.0	1.7	1.4	1.4	0.7	•
Officers' Compensation	20	0.2	0.0	•	2.8	0.4	0.3	0.3	0.3	0.2	0.2	0.1	0.1	•
Operating Margin	21	•	0.2	•	2.3	0.2	0.3	0.4	0.4	0.5	0.6	•	0.0	•
Operating Margin Before Officers' Comp.	22	0.1	0.2	•	5.1	0.5	0.6	0.7	0.7	0.7	0.7	•	0.2	•

Selected Average Balance Sheet ($ in Thousands)

Net Receivables 23	5366	0	•	505	937	3219	5288	12411	25629	64658	128338	288604	•
Inventories 24	2975	0	•	143	423	1031	2477	5205	7481	27751	71186	218078	•
Net Property, Plant and Equipment 25	13518	0	•	40	389	1211	4058	9540	14875	23904	58425	88550	•
Total Assets 26	31439	0	•	755	2489	7510	15970	34830	68406	164788	348858	923751	•
Notes and Loans Payable 27	10954	0	•	137	640	1615	3578	9402	17737	51097	96046	241257	•
All Other Liabilities 28	11071	0	•	167	991	2775	6123	13394	28798	78441	162609	379298	•
Net Worth 29	9415	0	•	451	857	3120	6269	12034	21871	35251	90203	303195	•

Selected Financial Ratios (Times to 1)

Current Ratio 30	1.4	•	•	3.9	1.6	1.6	1.4	1.4	1.4	1.3	1.3	1.3	•
Quick Ratio 31	0.9	•	•	3.2	1.2	1.3	1.0	0.9	1.0	0.8	0.8	0.8	•
Net Sales to Working Capital 32	43.0	•	•	7.0	47.0	44.2	60.3	48.3	49.2	49.6	46.3	54.3	•
Coverage Ratio 33	2.9	70.5	•	10.4	14.1	7.2	8.1	8.0	8.1	10.1	5.1	5.3	•
Total Asset Turnover 34	4.2	•	•	4.9	12.7	12.5	10.8	8.4	8.2	8.9	8.0	8.0	•
Inventory Turnover 35	42.1	•	•	22.5	67.9	87.6	66.7	53.2	71.7	50.8	38.5	33.1	•
Receivables Turnover 36	25.6	•	•	7.1	34.6	28.2	30.2	26.2	22.8	30.3	•	24.5	•
Total Liabilities to Net Worth 37	2.3	•	•	0.7	1.9	1.4	1.5	1.9	2.1	3.7	2.9	2.0	•
Current Assets to Working Capital 38	3.5	•	•	1.3	2.7	2.6	3.5	3.6	3.8	4.1	4.4	3.9	•
Current Liabilities to Working Capital 39	2.5	•	•	0.3	1.7	1.6	2.5	2.6	2.8	3.1	3.4	2.9	•
Working Capital to Net Sales 40	0.0	•	•	0.1	0.0	0.0	0.0	0.0	0.0	0.0	0.0	0.0	•
Inventory to Working Capital 41	0.9	•	•	0.2	0.6	0.5	0.8	0.9	0.7	1.4	1.2	1.3	•
Total Receipts to Cash Flow 42	37.1	76.8	•	16.0	35.3	60.6	52.0	42.4	49.8	49.7	70.2	110.9	•
Cost of Goods to Cash Flow 43	35.0	76.0	•	14.0	32.1	58.1	49.7	40.1	47.5	47.8	68.8	108.5	•
Cash Flow to Total Debt 44	0.2	•	•	0.8	0.5	0.4	0.3	0.3	0.2	0.2	0.2	0.1	•

Selected Financial Factors (in Percentages)

Debt Ratio 45	70.1	•	•	40.3	65.6	58.5	60.7	65.5	68.0	78.6	74.1	67.2	•
Return on Total Assets 46	5.7	•	•	12.9	10.5	9.6	8.7	8.2	7.3	11.4	5.2	6.9	•
Return on Equity Before Income Taxes 47	12.5	•	•	19.6	28.4	19.8	19.5	20.8	19.9	47.9	16.3	17.1	•
Return on Equity After Income Taxes 48	11.5	•	•	18.6	27.1	19.2	18.0	19.6	18.1	44.1	12.8	14.9	•
Profit Margin (Before Income Tax) 49	0.9	0.7	•	2.4	0.8	0.7	0.7	0.9	0.8	1.2	0.5	0.7	•
Profit Margin (After Income Tax) 50	0.8	0.6	•	2.3	0.7	0.6	0.7	0.8	0.7	1.1	0.4	0.6	•

Table I

Corporations with and without Net Income

424800

BEER, WINE, AND DISTILLED ALCOHOLIC BEVERAGE

MONEY AMOUNTS AND SIZE OF ASSETS IN THOUSANDS OF DOLLARS

Item Description for Accounting Period 7/12 Through 6/13	Total	Zero Assets	Under 500	500 to 1,000	1,000 to 5,000	5,000 to 10,000	10,000 to 25,000	25,000 to 50,000	50,000 to 100,000	100,000 to 250,000	250,000 to 500,000	500,000 to 2,500,000	2,500,000 and over
Number of Enterprises 1	3755	901	1237	142	688	364	243	57	61	39	10	10	3

Revenues ($ in Thousands)

Net Sales 2	83694376	498043	373562	221743	5777909	9586092	11245087	4694465	8736229	10885655	6477128	11769707	13428756
Interest 3	39998	7	0	1	1874	890	396	474	6700	743	5728	6028	17157
Rents 4	44371	118	0	0	0	101	339	100	116	29	14544	28341	683
Royalties 5	80599	0	0	0	0	0	0	3470	0	34789	585	5931	35825
Other Portfolio Income 6	183057	36881	0	162	44936	13331	9098	6124	19075	12939	497	28712	11302
Other Receipts 7	834017	370	1732	10	7404	36273	96909	20574	150063	202560	77070	175294	65758
Total Receipts 8	84876418	535419	375294	221916	5832123	9636687	11351829	4725207	8912183	11136715	6575552	12014013	13559481
Average Total Receipts 9	22604	594	303	1563	8477	26474	46715	82898	146101	285557	657555	1201401	4519827

Operating Costs/Operating Income (%)

Cost of Operations 10	75.8	72.8	39.1	63.7	77.0	75.3	74.5	74.3	76.8	74.6	78.0	78.0	75.8
Salaries and Wages 11	8.1	8.8	0.6	7.8	7.5	8.7	8.3	9.4	7.5	7.9	7.5	7.2	9.1
Taxes Paid 12	2.0	1.9	2.2	5.3	2.0	2.5	3.2	1.8	1.9	1.7	2.1	1.6	1.1
Interest Paid 13	0.8	0.0	•	0.8	0.3	0.3	0.5	0.5	0.6	0.5	0.7	0.8	2.1
Depreciation 14	0.6	0.2	1.0	1.0	0.5	0.4	0.7	0.6	0.8	0.6	0.5	0.9	0.3
Amortization and Depletion 15	1.4	0.5	0.9	1.1	0.2	0.3	0.6	1.0	1.0	0.7	1.1	1.6	4.6
Pensions and Other Deferred Comp. 16	0.4	0.7	•	•	0.7	0.5	0.3	0.3	0.2	0.3	0.2	0.3	0.5
Employee Benefits 17	0.8	1.3	•	1.0	0.6	0.8	1.0	1.0	1.0	0.9	0.5	0.5	1.1
Advertising 18	1.9	1.1	0.4	1.3	0.6	0.7	0.7	1.0	1.4	3.3	1.5	2.3	3.7
Other Expenses 19	5.4	7.5	26.6	20.4	7.5	4.9	5.9	6.0	6.1	5.9	4.8	5.5	3.0
Officers' Compensation 20	1.0	1.3	15.0	0.5	2.5	1.6	1.2	1.1	0.8	1.2	0.5	0.3	0.2
Operating Margin 21	1.8	3.8	14.2	•	0.6	3.9	3.1	3.0	1.9	2.4	2.5	1.0	•
Operating Margin Before Officers' Comp. 22	2.8	5.1	29.2	•	3.1	5.5	4.4	4.1	2.7	3.6	3.0	1.3	•

Selected Average Balance Sheet ($ in Thousands)

Net Receivables 23	1926	0	12	169	483	1120	1755	3920	8866	31722	44612	148190	698627
Inventories 24	2542	0	39	215	843	2265	3092	8805	9401	32371	61105	174542	872606
Net Property, Plant and Equipment 25	1096	0	12	42	238	1161	1751	4391	7836	11515	37735	89495	211438
Total Assets 26	13877	0	109	698	2195	7713	16363	35896	70206	155562	336753	1029419	5841348
Notes and Loans Payable 27	4370	0	48	149	510	1047	5501	10554	25107	43524	108863	231286	2342948
All Other Liabilities 28	3631	0	40	304	743	2580	2804	7299	12127	43854	90214	311548	1508579
Net Worth 29	5876	0	22	246	942	4086	8058	18043	32972	68183	137676	486584	1989821

Selected Financial Ratios (Times to 1)

Current Ratio 30	1.4	•	1.4	1.3	2.2	2.3	2.1	1.9	1.7	1.7	1.5	2.0	0.7
Quick Ratio 31	0.6	•	0.4	0.6	1.0	1.1	1.2	0.9	1.0	0.9	0.7	0.8	0.3
Net Sales to Working Capital 32	14.6	•	15.5	16.2	9.2	9.7	10.5	10.5	12.7	8.1	15.8	5.4	•
Coverage Ratio 33	5.1	404.1	•	•	6.1	14.9	8.9	8.8	7.8	10.2	6.5	4.7	0.8
Total Asset Turnover 34	1.6	•	2.8	2.2	3.8	3.4	2.8	2.3	2.0	1.8	1.9	1.1	0.8
Inventory Turnover 35	6.6	•	3.0	4.6	7.7	8.8	11.2	6.9	11.7	6.4	8.3	5.3	3.9
Receivables Turnover 36	11.4	•	26.3	8.0	17.6	24.4	24.9	16.1	14.9	9.1	13.2	8.3	6.3
Total Liabilities to Net Worth 37	1.4	•	4.1	1.8	1.3	0.9	1.0	1.0	1.1	1.3	1.4	1.1	1.9
Current Assets to Working Capital 38	3.8	•	3.3	4.9	1.9	1.8	1.9	2.1	2.4	2.3	3.2	2.0	•
Current Liabilities to Working Capital 39	2.8	•	2.3	3.9	0.9	0.8	0.9	1.1	1.4	1.3	2.2	1.0	•
Working Capital to Net Sales 40	0.1	•	0.1	0.1	0.1	0.1	0.1	0.1	0.1	0.1	0.1	0.2	•
Inventory to Working Capital 41	1.7	•	2.4	2.6	0.9	0.8	0.7	0.9	0.8	0.9	1.5	0.9	•
Total Receipts to Cash Flow 42	13.7	7.3	3.2	7.3	13.5	12.2	11.8	12.4	11.7	10.5	12.5	13.7	69.8
Cost of Goods to Cash Flow 43	10.4	5.3	1.2	4.6	10.4	9.2	8.8	9.2	9.0	7.8	9.8	10.6	52.9
Cash Flow to Total Debt 44	0.2	•	1.1	0.5	0.5	0.6	0.5	0.4	0.3	0.3	0.3	0.2	0.0

Selected Financial Factors (in Percentages)

Debt Ratio 45	57.7	•	80.3	64.8	57.1	47.0	50.8	49.7	53.0	56.2	59.1	52.7	65.9
Return on Total Assets 46	6.4	•	40.5	•	6.8	16.3	13.0	9.4	9.2	9.4	9.2	4.5	1.3
Return on Equity Before Income Taxes 47	12.1	•	205.4	•	13.3	28.8	23.4	16.6	17.1	19.3	19.1	7.4	•
Return on Equity After Income Taxes 48	11.2	•	202.8	•	10.7	27.8	22.8	15.3	16.8	17.8	16.0	6.0	•
Profit Margin (Before Income Tax) 49	3.2	11.3	14.7	•	1.5	4.5	4.1	3.6	3.9	4.7	4.1	3.1	•
Profit Margin (After Income Tax) 50	2.9	11.2	14.5	•	1.2	4.3	4.0	3.4	3.9	4.3	3.4	2.5	•

Table II
Corporations with Net Income

BEER, WINE, AND DISTILLED ALCOHOLIC BEVERAGE

MONEY AMOUNTS AND SIZE OF ASSETS IN THOUSANDS OF DOLLARS

Item Description for Accounting Period 7/12 Through 6/13		Total	Zero Assets	Under 500	500 to 1,000	1,000 to 5,000	5,000 to 10,000	10,000 to 25,000	25,000 to 50,000	50,000 to 100,000	100,000 to 250,000	250,000 to 500,000	500,000 to 2,500,000	2,500,000 and over
Number of Enterprises	1	1803	14	511	57	519	339	198	53	53	•	•	•	0

Revenues ($ in Thousands)

Net Sales	2	76035979	466284	283043	32031	4729626	9210393	9787540	4506654	7811298	•	•	•	0
Interest	3	21512	7	0	0	703	889	343	474	6600	•	•	•	0
Rents	4	43584	118	0	0	0	101	264	100	116	•	•	•	0
Royalties	5	44775	0	0	0	0	0	0	3470	0	•	•	•	0
Other Portfolio Income	6	163338	36872	0	0	43174	13331	7203	6124	14575	•	•	•	0
Other Receipts	7	837897	363	1732	0	17881	36660	96348	17191	134063	•	•	•	0
Total Receipts	8	77147085	503644	284775	32031	4791384	9261374	9891698	4534013	7966652	•	•	•	0
Average Total Receipts	9	42788	35975	557	562	9232	27320	49958	85547	150314	•	•	•	•

Operating Costs/Operating Income (%)

Cost of Operations	10	76.6	73.7	29.9	3.3	74.7	75.4	74.3	74.1	77.6	•	•	•	•
Salaries and Wages	11	8.0	8.9	0.8	•	7.6	8.6	8.1	9.5	7.2	•	•	•	•
Taxes Paid	12	2.0	2.1	2.3	0.8	2.2	2.5	3.4	1.9	1.8	•	•	•	•
Interest Paid	13	0.5	0.0	•	•	0.2	0.3	0.4	0.5	0.6	•	•	•	•
Depreciation	14	0.5	0.1	1.1	•	0.5	0.4	0.7	0.6	0.6	•	•	•	•
Amortization and Depletion	15	0.7	0.5	0.1	•	0.0	0.3	0.6	0.8	1.1	•	•	•	•
Pensions and Other Deferred Comp.	16	0.3	0.8	•	•	0.2	0.5	0.3	0.3	0.2	•	•	•	•
Employee Benefits	17	0.8	1.4	•	•	0.5	0.8	1.0	1.0	0.9	•	•	•	•
Advertising	18	1.3	1.2	0.0	•	0.5	0.7	0.7	0.9	1.3	•	•	•	•
Other Expenses	19	5.1	4.6	22.5	86.4	7.8	4.6	5.5	6.0	5.2	•	•	•	•
Officers' Compensation	20	1.0	1.4	16.3	•	2.6	1.6	1.2	1.1	0.8	•	•	•	•
Operating Margin	21	2.9	5.4	26.9	9.5	3.1	4.3	4.0	3.3	2.7	•	•	•	•
Operating Margin Before Officers' Comp.	22	3.9	6.8	43.2	9.5	5.7	5.8	5.1	4.4	3.5	•	•	•	•

Selected Average Balance Sheet ($ in Thousands)													
Net Receivables 23	3453	0	29	323	407	1132	1745	3715	8894	•	•	•	•
Inventories 24	4670	0	45	399	930	2212	3230	8194	8208	•	•	•	•
Net Property, Plant and Equipment 25	2005	0	28	1	198	1195	1955	4670	7043	•	•	•	•
Total Assets 26	21250	0	119	696	2079	7753	16352	35527	70755	•	•	•	•
Notes and Loans Payable 27	5866	0	0	5	294	906	5009	10750	24019	•	•	•	•
All Other Liabilities 28	5886	0	71	654	699	2537	2892	6132	12572	•	•	•	•
Net Worth 29	9498	0	47	37	1086	4310	8450	18645	34164	•	•	•	•

Selected Financial Ratios (Times to 1)													
Current Ratio 30	2.0	•	1.1	1.1	2.5	2.6	2.3	2.0	1.7	•	•	•	•
Quick Ratio 31	0.9	•	0.5	0.5	1.1	1.3	1.3	0.9	0.9	•	•	•	•
Net Sales to Working Capital 32	8.0	•	60.6	13.6	9.2	9.5	10.2	10.4	14.0	•	•	•	•
Coverage Ratio 33	9.4	446.4	•	•	23.7	16.0	12.8	9.0	9.2	•	•	•	•
Total Asset Turnover 34	2.0	•	4.7	0.8	4.4	3.5	3.0	2.4	2.1	•	•	•	•
Inventory Turnover 35	6.9	•	3.7	0.0	7.3	9.3	11.4	7.7	13.9	•	•	•	•
Receivables Turnover 36	12.6	•	•	1.3	20.6	24.3	25.1	18.1	•	•	•	•	•
Total Liabilities to Net Worth 37	1.2	•	1.5	18.0	0.9	0.8	0.9	0.9	1.1	•	•	•	•
Current Assets to Working Capital 38	2.0	•	8.8	16.8	1.7	1.6	1.7	2.0	2.5	•	•	•	•
Current Liabilities to Working Capital 39	1.0	•	7.8	15.8	0.7	0.6	0.7	1.0	1.5	•	•	•	•
Working Capital to Net Sales 40	0.1	•	0.0	0.1	0.1	0.1	0.1	0.1	0.1	•	•	•	•
Inventory to Working Capital 41	0.9	•	5.0	8.7	0.8	0.7	0.7	0.9	0.8	•	•	•	•
Total Receipts to Cash Flow 42	12.3	6.8	2.4	1.0	9.7	12.1	11.0	12.1	11.7	•	•	•	•
Cost of Goods to Cash Flow 43	9.4	5.0	0.7	0.0	7.2	9.2	8.2	9.0	9.1	•	•	•	•
Cash Flow to Total Debt 44	0.3	•	3.3	0.8	0.9	0.7	0.6	0.4	0.3	•	•	•	•

Selected Financial Factors (in Percentages)													
Debt Ratio 45	55.3	•	60.2	94.7	47.7	44.4	48.3	47.5	51.7	•	•	•	•
Return on Total Assets 46	9.6	•	128.3	7.7	20.1	18.1	16.5	10.4	11.0	•	•	•	•
Return on Equity Before Income Taxes 47	19.3	•	322.6	146.1	36.9	30.5	29.4	17.6	20.2	•	•	•	•
Return on Equity After Income Taxes 48	18.0	•	319.7	123.2	33.8	29.4	28.6	16.4	19.9	•	•	•	•
Profit Margin (Before Income Tax) 49	4.3	13.4	27.5	9.5	4.4	4.8	5.0	3.9	4.7	•	•	•	•
Profit Margin (After Income Tax) 50	4.0	13.3	27.2	8.0	4.0	4.7	4.9	3.6	4.6	•	•	•	•

Table I

Corporations with and without Net Income

MISCELLANEOUS NONDURABLE GOODS

MONEY AMOUNTS AND SIZE OF ASSETS IN THOUSANDS OF DOLLARS

Item Description for Accounting Period 7/12 Through 6/13	Total	Zero Assets	Under 500	500 to 1,000	1,000 to 5,000	5,000 to 10,000	10,000 to 25,000	25,000 to 50,000	50,000 to 100,000	100,000 to 250,000	250,000 to 500,000	500,000 to 2,500,000	2,500,000 and over
Number of Enterprises 1	28664	3639	17821	2357	3649	477	424	132	83	42	15	18	5

Revenues ($ in Thousands)

Net Sales 2	192696926	1988030	10016012	6617947	28069753	9213258	20936569	14623549	16269126	14722858	5736517	34512215	29991093
Interest 3	185542	460	2102	193	5594	5330	11434	1848	4787	9214	15456	31467	97659
Rents 4	31654	1054	218	202	6433	1440	1906	896	1494	405	117	6513	10976
Royalties 5	574214	61	0	0	10	73	113	3119	1878	3926	12666	5317	547051
Other Portfolio Income 6	1304381	58504	8994	14212	28971	21786	6731	4224	13189	5965	3472	25995	1112340
Other Receipts 7	2903105	22778	25999	14711	247016	80708	237864	164044	124038	192211	208628	145538	1439566
Total Receipts 8	197695822	2070887	10053325	6647265	28357777	9322595	21194617	14797680	16414512	14934579	5976856	34727045	33198685
Average Total Receipts 9	6897	569	564	2820	7771	19544	49987	112104	197765	355585	398457	1929280	6639737

Operating Costs/Operating Income (%)

Cost of Operations 10	79.2	76.9	71.8	78.6	82.4	81.0	80.1	83.8	87.2	77.5	83.1	80.3	70.4
Salaries and Wages 11	5.3	4.0	5.0	6.2	4.7	5.1	5.7	5.2	3.8	6.8	5.2	5.5	5.7
Taxes Paid 12	1.5	0.9	1.8	1.1	0.9	0.7	2.7	0.7	0.9	1.5	0.8	2.2	1.3
Interest Paid 13	0.7	0.7	0.4	0.2	0.3	0.2	0.3	0.3	0.4	1.1	0.8	1.2	1.4
Depreciation 14	0.8	1.0	0.6	0.3	0.4	0.5	0.5	0.5	0.6	0.9	1.0	1.1	1.6
Amortization and Depletion 15	0.3	0.3	0.1	0.0	0.0	0.0	0.1	0.1	0.2	0.4	0.7	0.4	1.1
Pensions and Other Deferred Comp. 16	0.3	0.1	0.3	0.0	0.3	0.2	0.1	0.2	0.1	0.2	0.2	0.3	0.5
Employee Benefits 17	0.5	0.4	0.2	0.4	0.3	0.3	0.5	0.5	0.4	0.6	0.5	0.7	0.9
Advertising 18	1.1	0.2	0.7	0.6	0.4	0.6	0.8	0.9	0.6	2.2	0.2	1.2	2.0
Other Expenses 19	7.5	10.4	13.2	9.1	6.6	5.8	6.7	5.6	4.3	5.6	6.6	5.5	13.1
Officers' Compensation 20	1.1	2.6	3.1	2.9	2.0	2.2	1.2	1.0	0.6	0.5	0.5	0.3	0.3
Operating Margin 21	1.7	2.6	2.7	0.7	1.8	3.3	1.3	1.2	0.8	2.6	0.4	1.4	1.9
Operating Margin Before Officers' Comp. 22	2.8	5.2	5.8	3.5	3.8	5.5	2.6	2.2	1.4	3.1	0.9	1.7	2.2

	Selected Average Balance Sheet ($ in Thousands)												
Net Receivables 23	574	0	12	205	682	1609	4331	9808	18751	30038	64450	149012	581804
Inventories 24	695	0	34	238	622	1832	4800	11400	20025	46859	65391	170879	877894
Net Property, Plant and Equipment 25	467	0	17	66	239	827	1813	4649	8822	20788	29225	164539	1050668
Total Assets 26	3689	0	124	702	2287	6504	15479	35827	68789	149821	334931	904673	9164695
Notes and Loans Payable 27	1031	0	58	220	550	1894	4581	9674	19578	71288	70208	326754	2067082
All Other Liabilities 28	1425	0	36	301	904	2812	4879	14037	28327	57562	113962	363266	3586220
Net Worth 29	1232	0	31	182	833	1797	6020	12116	20884	20971	150761	214653	3511393

	Selected Financial Ratios (Times to 1)												
Current Ratio 30	1.4	•	2.0	1.6	1.7	1.5	1.8	1.5	1.4	1.5	1.3	1.4	1.1
Quick Ratio 31	0.6	•	0.9	0.9	1.0	0.7	0.9	0.7	0.6	0.7	0.6	0.6	0.4
Net Sales to Working Capital 32	12.0	•	13.3	13.0	10.3	11.6	9.8	12.1	13.4	10.8	8.9	13.7	14.1
Coverage Ratio 33	6.8	10.5	8.6	7.8	10.6	19.7	8.4	8.5	4.8	4.6	6.9	2.7	10.0
Total Asset Turnover 34	1.8	•	4.5	4.0	3.4	3.0	3.2	3.1	2.8	2.3	1.1	2.1	0.7
Inventory Turnover 35	7.7	•	11.8	9.3	10.2	8.5	8.2	8.1	8.5	5.8	4.9	9.0	4.8
Receivables Turnover 36	12.3	•	42.0	14.2	11.7	14.8	10.8	11.4	11.1	10.4	5.9	14.0	12.3
Total Liabilities to Net Worth 37	2.0	•	3.1	2.9	1.7	2.6	1.6	2.0	2.3	6.1	1.2	3.2	1.6
Current Assets to Working Capital 38	3.7	•	2.0	2.7	2.5	3.1	2.3	2.9	3.5	2.8	3.9	3.4	9.5
Current Liabilities to Working Capital 39	2.7	•	1.0	1.7	1.5	2.1	1.3	1.9	2.5	1.8	2.9	2.4	8.5
Working Capital to Net Sales 40	0.1	•	0.1	0.1	0.1	0.1	0.1	0.1	0.1	0.1	0.1	0.1	0.1
Inventory to Working Capital 41	1.3	•	0.9	1.1	0.9	1.3	1.0	1.3	1.6	1.3	1.5	1.4	2.2
Total Receipts to Cash Flow 42	9.8	6.7	7.4	12.6	12.2	11.7	12.7	14.6	20.2	11.7	9.8	16.4	4.3
Cost of Goods to Cash Flow 43	7.8	5.2	5.3	9.9	10.1	9.5	10.2	12.3	17.6	9.0	8.1	13.2	3.0
Cash Flow to Total Debt 44	0.3	•	0.8	0.4	0.4	0.4	0.4	0.3	0.2	0.2	0.2	0.2	0.2

	Selected Financial Factors (in Percentages)												
Debt Ratio 45	66.6	•	75.4	74.1	63.6	72.4	61.1	66.2	69.6	86.0	55.0	76.3	61.7
Return on Total Assets 46	9.2	•	15.8	5.7	10.5	14.1	9.3	8.5	6.1	12.1	6.1	7.0	9.3
Return on Equity Before Income Taxes 47	23.5	•	56.8	19.2	26.0	48.3	21.0	22.2	15.9	67.4	11.7	18.4	21.8
Return on Equity After Income Taxes 48	19.1	•	55.5	17.0	25.2	44.8	18.6	19.7	14.0	58.6	9.1	15.1	15.6
Profit Margin (Before Income Tax) 49	4.3	6.8	3.1	1.2	2.8	4.5	2.6	2.4	1.7	4.0	4.6	2.1	12.7
Profit Margin (After Income Tax) 50	3.5	6.5	3.0	1.1	2.7	4.2	2.3	2.2	1.5	3.5	3.6	1.7	9.1

Table II

Corporations with Net Income

MISCELLANEOUS NONDURABLE GOODS

MONEY AMOUNTS AND SIZE OF ASSETS IN THOUSANDS OF DOLLARS

Item Description for Accounting Period 7/12 Through 6/13	Total	Zero Assets	Under 500	500 to 1,000	1,000 to 5,000	5,000 to 10,000	10,000 to 25,000	25,000 to 50,000	50,000 to 100,000	100,000 to 250,000	250,000 to 500,000	500,000 to 2,500,000	2,500,000 and over
Number of Enterprises 1	17329	1304	10638	1530	2889	370	348	120	68	34	•	11	•

Revenues ($ in Thousands)													
Net Sales 2	162987044	1783883	7608792	5081402	23733834	8246987	18690193	13315435	14129570	12640022	•	27689917	•
Interest 3	162753	332	2087	106	4152	2837	10840	1759	4274	8509	•	22026	•
Rents 4	24442	1054	218	200	5250	1318	1194	896	1452	403	•	1372	•
Royalties 5	406410	0	0	0	10	73	0	3119	1231	3240	•	3124	•
Other Portfolio Income 6	1274428	58432	3508	11006	26703	21733	4446	1045	6751	5959	•	20385	•
Other Receipts 7	2405387	22308	8061	11211	229797	65123	170031	117488	72671	189080	•	97319	•
Total Receipts 8	167260464	1866009	7622666	5103925	23999746	8338071	18876704	13439742	14215949	12847213	•	27834143	•
Average Total Receipts 9	9652	1431	717	3336	8307	22535	54243	111998	209058	377859	•	2530377	•

Operating Costs/Operating Income (%)													
Cost of Operations 10	79.4	76.7	70.2	77.0	81.5	79.9	79.9	83.5	87.2	76.2	•	81.1	•
Salaries and Wages 11	5.0	3.5	4.5	6.1	4.6	5.3	5.4	5.0	3.4	7.0	•	5.0	•
Taxes Paid 12	1.5	0.7	1.9	1.0	0.9	0.7	2.9	0.7	0.9	1.7	•	2.5	•
Interest Paid 13	0.5	0.5	0.3	0.2	0.3	0.3	0.3	0.3	0.4	1.1	•	0.6	•
Depreciation 14	0.7	1.0	0.3	0.3	0.4	0.5	0.4	0.5	0.5	0.8	•	0.9	•
Amortization and Depletion 15	0.3	0.1	0.1	0.0	0.0	0.0	0.1	0.1	0.1	0.2	•	0.2	•
Pensions and Other Deferred Comp. 16	0.3	0.1	0.3	0.1	0.3	0.2	0.1	0.2	0.1	0.2	•	0.3	•
Employee Benefits 17	0.5	0.4	0.2	0.3	0.2	0.4	0.4	0.5	0.3	0.6	•	0.5	•
Advertising 18	1.1	0.2	0.8	0.7	0.4	0.6	0.6	0.8	0.7	2.6	•	1.3	•
Other Expenses 19	6.5	7.8	11.4	7.8	6.4	5.3	6.1	5.5	3.8	5.5	•	4.7	•
Officers' Compensation 20	1.1	2.6	3.0	3.0	2.0	2.3	1.2	1.0	0.6	0.5	•	0.3	•
Operating Margin 21	3.2	6.4	6.9	3.6	3.0	4.6	2.6	2.1	2.0	3.6	•	2.6	•
Operating Margin Before Officers' Comp. 22	4.3	9.0	9.9	6.6	4.9	6.9	3.8	3.1	2.6	4.1	•	2.9	•

Selected Average Balance Sheet ($ in Thousands)

Net Receivables 23	762	0	13	198	773	1709	4588	9538	18406	30337	•	164002	•
Inventories 24	897	0	40	236	607	1965	4860	11643	19450	46842	•	160196	•
Net Property, Plant and Equipment 25	610	0	10	46	221	657	1743	4533	8575	19359	•	207215	•
Total Assets 26	4941	0	132	701	2331	6375	15586	35400	68255	146750	•	866885	•
Notes and Loans Payable 27	1305	0	53	201	507	1265	3710	8984	17600	76854	•	264473	•
All Other Liabilities 28	1711	0	38	271	860	2364	4944	12928	25523	52654	•	386142	•
Net Worth 29	1926	0	41	229	964	2746	6932	13488	25132	17241	•	216270	•

Selected Financial Ratios (Times to 1)

Current Ratio 30	1.4	•	2.1	1.7	1.9	1.9	1.9	1.6	1.6	1.6	•	1.3	•
Quick Ratio 31	0.6	•	1.0	0.9	1.1	0.9	1.0	0.7	0.7	0.7	•	0.6	•
Net Sales to Working Capital 32	12.5	•	14.1	13.5	8.9	8.7	9.1	11.6	11.6	10.2	•	24.8	•
Coverage Ratio 33	12.1	23.7	25.2	23.4	16.1	23.6	12.8	10.9	7.7	5.8	•	6.3	•
Total Asset Turnover 34	1.9	•	5.4	4.7	3.5	3.5	3.4	3.1	3.0	2.5	•	2.9	•
Inventory Turnover 35	8.3	•	12.6	10.9	11.0	9.1	8.8	8.0	9.3	6.0	•	12.8	•
Receivables Turnover 36	12.7	•	44.9	19.7	11.6	15.6	11.2	11.3	12.3	11.0	•	16.3	•
Total Liabilities to Net Worth 37	1.6	•	2.2	2.1	1.4	1.3	1.2	1.6	1.7	7.5	•	3.0	•
Current Assets to Working Capital 38	3.7	•	1.9	2.4	2.2	2.1	2.1	2.8	2.8	2.6	•	4.6	•
Current Liabilities to Working Capital 39	2.7	•	0.9	1.4	1.2	1.1	1.1	1.8	1.8	1.6	•	3.6	•
Working Capital to Net Sales 40	0.1	•	0.1	0.1	0.1	0.1	0.1	0.1	0.1	0.1	•	0.0	•
Inventory to Working Capital 41	1.2	•	0.9	1.0	0.7	0.9	0.9	1.3	1.3	1.2	•	1.6	•
Total Receipts to Cash Flow 42	9.2	6.0	6.2	9.8	10.7	10.6	11.8	13.6	18.1	10.4	•	15.5	•
Cost of Goods to Cash Flow 43	7.3	4.6	4.3	7.6	8.8	8.5	9.4	11.3	15.8	7.9	•	12.6	•
Cash Flow to Total Debt 44	0.3	•	1.3	0.7	0.6	0.6	0.5	0.4	0.3	0.3	•	0.2	•

Selected Financial Factors (in Percentages)

Debt Ratio 45	61.0	•	69.0	67.4	58.6	56.9	55.5	61.9	63.2	88.3	•	75.1	•
Return on Total Assets 46	12.3	•	40.1	20.8	15.4	20.7	13.3	10.4	9.3	15.9	•	10.9	•
Return on Equity Before Income Taxes 47	28.9	•	124.4	61.0	34.9	46.0	27.6	24.8	22.0	112.1	•	36.6	•
Return on Equity After Income Taxes 48	24.2	•	122.7	58.3	34.0	43.0	25.2	22.3	20.1	99.0	•	31.3	•
Profit Margin (Before Income Tax) 49	5.9	11.0	7.1	4.2	4.1	5.7	3.6	3.0	2.7	5.2	•	3.1	•
Profit Margin (After Income Tax) 50	5.0	10.7	7.0	4.0	4.0	5.3	3.2	2.7	2.4	4.6	•	2.7	•

Table I

Corporations with and without Net Income

WHOLESALE ELECTRONIC MARKETS AND AGENTS AND BROKERS

MONEY AMOUNTS AND SIZE OF ASSETS IN THOUSANDS OF DOLLARS

Item Description for Accounting Period 7/12 Through 6/13		Total	Zero Assets	Under 500	500 to 1,000	1,000 to 5,000	5,000 to 10,000	10,000 to 25,000	25,000 to 50,000	50,000 to 100,000	100,000 to 250,000	250,000 to 500,000	500,000 to 2,500,000	2,500,000 and over
Number of Enterprises	1	13831	3093	10548	3	133	25	20	5	3	0	0	0	0
Revenues ($ in Thousands)														
Net Sales	2	4500056	812416	2476331	4668	117232	107883	207703	7120	766704	0	0	0	0
Interest	3	1738	312	78	0	482	50	305	373	138	0	0	0	0
Rents	4	4558	2861	0	0	0	0	0	294	1403	0	0	0	0
Royalties	5	10126	484	0	0	0	0	0	0	9642	0	0	0	0
Other Portfolio Income	6	43915	15310	9652	0	7448	41	229	6243	4994	0	0	0	0
Other Receipts	7	157340	5469	67059	21	35180	2275	38666	5839	2827	0	0	0	0
Total Receipts	8	4717733	836852	2553120	4689	160342	110249	246903	19869	785708	0	0	0	0
Average Total Receipts	9	341	271	242	1563	1206	4410	12345	3974	261903	•	•	•	•
Operating Costs/Operating Income (%)														
Cost of Operations	10	1.7	4.5	•	•	•	•	0.2	•	5.0	•	•	•	•
Salaries and Wages	11	26.2	51.4	19.1	97.1	23.9	33.1	36.2	22.9	18.4	•	•	•	•
Taxes Paid	12	4.4	5.5	3.4	9.2	4.2	6.2	4.2	10.7	5.8	•	•	•	•
Interest Paid	13	0.9	1.4	0.3	•	0.5	1.9	0.5	18.6	2.1	•	•	•	•
Depreciation	14	1.5	0.6	0.4	0.0	0.3	2.4	1.1	1.5	6.0	•	•	•	•
Amortization and Depletion	15	0.5	0.7	0.3	•	•	0.6	0.2	12.5	0.8	•	•	•	•
Pensions and Other Deferred Comp.	16	1.3	1.4	1.1	•	2.2	•	1.0	•	1.5	•	•	•	•
Employee Benefits	17	2.3	3.6	2.3	5.7	1.6	0.6	0.9	1.2	1.8	•	•	•	•
Advertising	18	0.6	0.2	0.6	15.5	0.1	2.2	1.5	0.1	0.8	•	•	•	•
Other Expenses	19	30.8	24.6	32.0	194.3	24.9	49.8	41.6	34.2	27.6	•	•	•	•
Officers' Compensation	20	15.4	4.6	23.3	26.0	45.2	7.0	5.2	70.3	0.4	•	•	•	•
Operating Margin	21	14.5	1.5	17.0	•	•	•	7.5	•	29.7	•	•	•	•
Operating Margin Before Officers' Comp.	22	29.9	6.2	40.3	•	42.3	3.1	12.7	•	30.1	•	•	•	•

Selected Average Balance Sheet ($ in Thousands)

Net Receivables 23	29	0	2	5	689	0	2680	1715	77595	•	•	•	•
Inventories 24	5	0	1	0	190	1902	354	0	957	•	•	•	•
Net Property, Plant and Equipment 25	46	0	8	64	34	525	2157	130	165677	•	•	•	•
Total Assets 26	275	0	67	880	2096	5273	12633	43649	736244	•	•	•	•
Notes and Loans Payable 27	113	0	33	7027	785	1533	1320	15906	315455	•	•	•	•
All Other Liabilities 28	70	0	14	154	888	2360	4612	17104	154674	•	•	•	•
Net Worth 29	92	0	20	-6300	423	1380	6702	10639	266114	•	•	•	•

Selected Financial Ratios (Times to 1)

Current Ratio 30	1.4	•	2.7	6.6	2.3	1.8	1.2	0.6	1.0	•	•	•	•
Quick Ratio 31	1.0	•	2.0	2.1	1.8	0.3	1.1	0.2	0.6	•	•	•	•
Net Sales to Working Capital 32	10.3	•	8.7	2.9	0.8	2.6	12.2	•	•	•	•	•	•
Coverage Ratio 33	23.3	4.2	75.1	•	71.1	0.1	58.3	6.8	16.4	•	•	•	•
Total Asset Turnover 34	1.2	•	3.5	1.8	0.4	0.8	0.8	0.0	0.3	•	•	•	•
Inventory Turnover 35	1.1	•	•	•	•	•	0.1	•	13.4	•	•	•	•
Receivables Turnover 36	7.1	•	110.0	•	1.5	•	4.8	1.1	•	•	•	•	•
Total Liabilities to Net Worth 37	2.0	•	2.3	•	4.0	2.8	0.9	3.1	1.8	•	•	•	•
Current Assets to Working Capital 38	3.3	•	1.6	1.2	1.8	2.2	5.5	•	•	•	•	•	•
Current Liabilities to Working Capital 39	2.3	•	0.6	0.2	0.8	1.2	4.5	•	•	•	•	•	•
Working Capital to Net Sales 40	0.1	•	0.1	0.3	1.2	0.4	0.1	•	•	•	•	•	•
Inventory to Working Capital 41	0.1	•	•	•	0.1	1.2	0.0	•	•	•	•	•	•
Total Receipts to Cash Flow 42	2.2	3.8	2.1	•	1.8	2.7	1.7	0.7	1.8	•	•	•	•
Cost of Goods to Cash Flow 43	0.0	0.2	•	•	•	•	0.0	•	0.1	•	•	•	•
Cash Flow to Total Debt 44	0.8	•	2.4	•	0.3	0.4	1.1	0.1	0.3	•	•	•	•

Selected Financial Factors (in Percentages)

Debt Ratio 45	66.5	•	69.7	815.7	79.8	73.8	47.0	75.6	63.9	•	•	•	•
Return on Total Assets 46	23.9	•	71.7	•	14.4	0.2	22.1	4.1	11.9	•	•	•	•
Return on Equity Before Income Taxes 47	68.5	•	233.5	61.1	70.5	•	40.9	14.3	30.9	•	•	•	•
Return on Equity After Income Taxes 48	58.8	•	227.9	61.1	69.2	•	37.6	11.2	19.5	•	•	•	•
Profit Margin (Before Income Tax) 49	19.3	4.5	20.1	•	33.9	•	26.4	107.1	32.2	•	•	•	•
Profit Margin (After Income Tax) 50	16.6	3.0	19.6	•	33.2	•	24.3	83.3	20.4	•	•	•	•

Table II

Corporations with Net Income

WHOLESALE ELECTRONIC MARKETS AND AGENTS AND BROKERS

MONEY AMOUNTS AND SIZE OF ASSETS IN THOUSANDS OF DOLLARS

Item Description for Accounting Period 7/12 Through 6/13	Total	Zero Assets	Under 500	500 to 1000	1,000 to 5,000	5,000 to 10,000	10,000 to 25,000	25,000 to 50,000	50,000 to 100,000	100,000 to 250,000	250,000 to 500,000	500,000 to 2,500,000	2,500,000 and over
Number of Enterprises **1**	9035	1279	7609	0	111	•	20	•	•	0	0	•	0
Revenues ($ in Thousands)													
Net Sales **2**	4353836	761170	2416195	0	98104	•	207703	•	•	0	0	•	0
Interest **3**	1738	312	78	0	482	•	305	•	•	0	0	•	0
Rents **4**	4558	2861	0	0	0	•	0	•	•	0	0	•	0
Royalties **5**	10126	484	0	0	0	•	0	•	•	0	0	•	0
Other Portfolio Income **6**	43001	15310	9187	0	6998	•	229	•	•	0	0	•	0
Other Receipts **7**	138114	5433	66755	0	22305	•	38666	•	•	0	0	•	0
Total Receipts **8**	4551373	785570	2492215	0	127889	•	246903	•	•	0	0	•	0
Average Total Receipts **9**	504	614	328	•	1152	•	12345	•	•	•	•	•	•
Operating Costs/Operating Income (%)													
Cost of Operations **10**	0.9	•	•	•	•	•	0.2	•	•	•	•	•	•
Salaries and Wages **11**	25.5	54.8	17.9	•	18.1	•	36.2	•	•	•	•	•	•
Taxes Paid **12**	4.3	5.8	3.4	•	3.7	•	4.2	•	•	•	•	•	•
Interest Paid **13**	0.8	1.5	0.2	•	0.6	•	0.5	•	•	•	•	•	•
Depreciation **14**	1.5	0.5	0.4	•	0.3	•	1.1	•	•	•	•	•	•
Amortization and Depletion **15**	0.4	0.8	0.1	•	•	•	0.2	•	•	•	•	•	•
Pensions and Other Deferred Comp. **16**	1.0	1.5	1.2	•	2.6	•	1.0	•	•	•	•	•	•
Employee Benefits **17**	2.3	3.6	2.2	•	1.5	•	0.9	•	•	•	•	•	•
Advertising **18**	0.6	0.0	0.6	•	0.2	•	1.5	•	•	•	•	•	•
Other Expenses **19**	29.0	20.3	30.5	•	21.3	•	41.6	•	•	•	•	•	•
Officers' Compensation **20**	14.9	4.9	23.4	•	23.4	•	5.2	•	•	•	•	•	•
Operating Margin **21**	18.8	6.2	20.0	•	28.5	•	7.5	•	•	•	•	•	•
Operating Margin Before Officers' Comp. **22**	33.7	11.2	43.4	•	51.8	•	12.7	•	•	•	•	•	•

Net Receivables 23	31	0	0	•	688	•	2680	•	•	•	•	•
Inventories 24	4	0	1	•	215	•	3	•	•	•	•	•
Net Property, Plant and Equipment 25	63	0	6	•	40	•	2157	•	•	•	•	•
Total Assets 26	263	0	70	•	1830	•	12633	•	•	•	•	•
Notes and Loans Payable 27	88	0	20	•	928	•	1320	•	•	•	•	•
All Other Liabilities 28	57	0	10	•	588	•	4612	•	•	•	•	•
Net Worth 29	118	0	40	•	314	•	6702	•	•	•	•	•

Current Ratio 30	1.8	•	2.8	•	3.0	•	1.2	•	•	•	•	•
Quick Ratio 31	1.2	•	2.0	•	2.1	•	1.1	•	•	•	•	•
Net Sales to Working Capital 32	9.6	•	10.1	•	0.8	•	12.2	•	•	•	•	•
Coverage Ratio 33	29.2	7.3	98.3	•	104.5	•	58.3	•	•	•	•	•
Total Asset Turnover 34	1.8	•	4.6	•	0.5	•	0.8	•	•	•	•	•
Inventory Turnover 35	1.1	•	•	•	•	•	5.9	•	•	•	•	•
Receivables Turnover 36	7.9	•	295.0	•	1.5	•	6.1	•	•	•	•	•
Total Liabilities to Net Worth 37	1.2	•	0.7	•	4.8	•	0.9	•	•	•	•	•
Current Assets to Working Capital 38	2.3	•	1.6	•	1.5	•	5.5	•	•	•	•	•
Current Liabilities to Working Capital 39	1.3	•	0.6	•	0.5	•	4.5	•	•	•	•	•
Working Capital to Net Sales 40	0.1	•	0.1	•	1.3	•	0.1	•	•	•	•	•
Inventory to Working Capital 41	0.0	•	•	•	0.1	•	0.0	•	•	•	•	•
Total Receipts to Cash Flow 42	2.1	3.7	2.0	•	1.3	•	1.7	•	•	•	•	•
Cost of Goods to Cash Flow 43	0.0	•	•	•	•	•	0.0	•	•	•	•	•
Cash Flow to Total Debt 44	1.6	•	5.3	•	0.5	•	1.1	•	•	•	•	•

Debt Ratio 45	55.1	•	42.5	•	82.8	•	47.0	•	•	•	•	•
Return on Total Assets 46	44.2	•	106.5	•	28.7	•	22.1	•	•	•	•	•
Return on Equity Before Income Taxes 47	95.2	•	183.2	•	165.6	•	40.9	•	•	•	•	•
Return on Equity After Income Taxes 48	83.7	•	179.3	•	163.5	•	37.6	•	•	•	•	•
Profit Margin (Before Income Tax) 49	23.3	9.4	23.2	•	58.8	•	26.4	•	•	•	•	•
Profit Margin (After Income Tax) 50	20.5	7.8	22.7	•	58.1	•	24.3	•	•	•	•	•

Table I

Corporations with and without Net Income

NEW AND USED CAR DEALERS

MONEY AMOUNTS AND SIZE OF ASSETS IN THOUSANDS OF DOLLARS

Item Description for Accounting Period 7/12 Through 6/13	Total	Zero Assets	Under 500	500 to 1,000	1,000 to 5,000	5,000 to 10,000	10,000 to 25,000	25,000 to 50,000	50,000 to 100,000	100,000 to 250,000	250,000 to 500,000	500,000 to 2,500,000	2,500,000 and over
Number of Enterprises **1**	45963	6434	20021	3231	7806	3594	3745	829	209	70	14	5	5

Revenues ($ in Thousands)

Net Sales **2**	643349694	5705272	17166988	13546823	72812282	92844160	208587757	92831076	43390062	27697952	9737135	11347113	47683075
Interest **3**	824806	761	8496	4030	109204	64342	129498	64870	31688	61099	7852	14727	328238
Rents **4**	264517	1458	1189	1130	12618	7176	18198	25721	16810	27132	2351	15029	135705
Royalties **5**	9061	0	0	0	13	23	304	5	621	0	0	8095	0
Other Portfolio Income **6**	919135	51979	25058	24050	128562	55037	150445	167370	60863	59183	12406	132038	52146
Other Receipts **7**	14300314	130609	83898	77394	1321465	1965482	5271190	2257895	1021627	726946	218231	392108	833465
Total Receipts **8**	659667527	5890079	17285629	13653427	74384144	94936220	214157392	95346937	44521671	28572312	9977975	11909110	49032629
Average Total Receipts **9**	14352	915	863	4226	9529	26415	57185	115014	213022	408176	712712	2381822	9806526

Operating Costs/Operating Income (%)

Cost of Operations **10**	88.0	87.3	81.9	89.2	87.3	88.5	88.8	88.4	88.5	88.2	84.9	82.6	86.8
Salaries and Wages **11**	5.0	5.7	3.3	2.8	5.0	4.7	5.1	4.9	5.1	5.3	5.9	7.1	6.1
Taxes Paid **12**	0.9	1.2	2.0	1.1	0.9	0.8	0.8	0.8	0.8	0.8	0.9	0.8	1.2
Interest Paid **13**	0.4	0.4	0.5	0.4	0.5	0.4	0.3	0.4	0.4	0.4	0.6	1.2	0.8
Depreciation **14**	0.4	1.2	0.3	0.2	0.2	0.3	0.3	0.6	0.6	0.7	0.8	1.0	0.5
Amortization and Depletion **15**	0.1	0.0	0.0	0.0	0.0	0.1	0.1	0.1	0.1	0.1	0.1	0.7	0.5
Pensions and Other Deferred Comp. **16**	0.0	0.0	0.0	0.1	0.1	0.0	0.0	0.0	0.0	0.1	0.1	0.0	0.1
Employee Benefits **17**	0.4	0.4	0.1	0.2	0.4	0.4	0.4	0.4	0.4	0.4	0.5	0.7	0.4
Advertising **18**	1.0	1.0	0.6	0.6	1.1	1.1	1.1	1.0	1.0	1.0	0.8	1.0	0.6
Other Expenses **19**	4.1	6.7	8.5	4.0	4.9	4.0	3.7	3.7	3.5	3.7	5.9	7.8	3.2
Officers' Compensation **20**	0.7	0.5	2.0	1.8	1.0	0.8	0.7	0.6	0.5	0.5	0.5	0.1	0.1
Operating Margin **21**	•	•	0.8	•	•	•	•	•	•	•	•	•	•
Operating Margin Before Officers' Comp. **22**	•	•	2.8	1.4	•	•	•	•	•	•	•	•	•

Selected Average Balance Sheet ($ in Thousands)

Net Receivables 23	494	0	18	73	375	812	1719	3965	8089	18153	47653	244504	335376
Inventories 24	2061	0	94	323	1613	4906	8249	15125	26307	51222	86560	422720	1141263
Net Property, Plant and Equipment 25	527	0	29	49	161	472	1412	4478	10419	24397	76995	290865	1018062
Total Assets 26	4286	0	187	720	2661	7379	15449	33882	67470	145535	322555	1460158	4320997
Notes and Loans Payable 27	2745	0	116	267	1680	5157	10868	23031	43001	88461	183362	539369	2218358
All Other Liabilities 28	522	0	21	144	421	640	1547	3275	8777	17716	43628	529407	535878
Net Worth 29	1020	0	50	309	559	1582	3034	7576	15693	39358	95564	391381	1566761

Selected Financial Ratios (Times to 1)

Current Ratio 30	1.3	•	3.6	4.0	1.6	1.4	1.3	1.3	1.2	1.2	1.2	1.1	1.2
Quick Ratio 31	0.4	•	1.2	1.7	0.5	0.3	0.3	0.4	0.4	0.4	0.4	0.4	0.3
Net Sales to Working Capital 32	17.3	•	8.1	9.0	10.3	15.4	20.4	20.6	23.3	24.2	20.1	33.2	25.3
Coverage Ratio 33	4.4	•	4.0	2.2	2.2	3.8	5.4	6.1	6.1	6.7	3.3	2.6	4.1
Total Asset Turnover 34	3.3	•	4.6	5.8	3.5	3.5	3.6	3.3	3.1	2.7	2.2	1.6	2.2
Inventory Turnover 35	6.0	•	7.4	11.6	5.1	4.7	6.0	6.5	7.0	6.8	6.8	4.4	7.3
Receivables Turnover 36	29.4	•	49.5	40.5	24.6	29.6	34.1	31.1	29.1	24.0	15.7	8.8	33.4
Total Liabilities to Net Worth 37	3.2	•	2.7	1.3	3.8	3.7	4.1	3.5	3.3	2.7	2.4	2.7	1.8
Current Assets to Working Capital 38	4.0	•	1.4	1.3	2.6	3.8	4.7	4.8	5.6	6.0	5.1	10.2	5.1
Current Liabilities to Working Capital 39	3.0	•	0.4	0.3	1.6	2.8	3.7	3.8	4.6	5.0	4.1	9.2	4.1
Working Capital to Net Sales 40	0.1	•	0.1	0.1	0.1	0.1	0.0	0.0	0.0	0.0	0.0	0.0	0.0
Inventory to Working Capital 41	2.8	•	0.9	0.7	1.7	2.8	3.4	3.3	3.6	3.8	3.0	5.6	3.7
Total Receipts to Cash Flow 42	23.9	40.0	13.1	31.5	24.6	26.0	25.9	22.6	23.6	21.5	20.7	16.8	23.5
Cost of Goods to Cash Flow 43	21.1	34.9	10.7	28.1	21.5	23.0	23.0	20.0	20.8	18.9	17.5	13.9	20.4
Cash Flow to Total Debt 44	0.2	•	0.5	0.3	0.2	0.2	0.2	0.2	0.2	0.2	0.1	0.1	0.1

Selected Financial Factors (in Percentages)

Debt Ratio 45	76.2	•	73.2	57.1	79.0	78.6	80.4	77.6	76.7	73.0	70.4	73.2	63.7
Return on Total Assets 46	6.2	•	9.0	4.8	4.0	5.6	6.2	7.6	6.9	6.5	4.6	5.0	7.1
Return on Equity Before Income Taxes 47	20.1	•	25.1	6.2	10.4	19.2	25.6	28.5	24.7	20.4	10.7	11.5	14.9
Return on Equity After Income Taxes 48	18.4	•	24.7	5.8	9.5	18.8	25.0	27.7	23.3	19.2	9.2	8.2	9.5
Profit Margin (Before Income Tax) 49	1.5	•	1.5	0.5	0.6	1.2	1.4	1.9	1.9	2.0	1.5	2.0	2.4
Profit Margin (After Income Tax) 50	1.3	•	1.4	0.4	0.6	1.2	1.4	1.9	1.8	1.9	1.3	1.4	1.6

Table II

Corporations with Net Income

NEW AND USED CAR DEALERS

MONEY AMOUNTS AND SIZE OF ASSETS IN THOUSANDS OF DOLLARS

Item Description for Accounting Period 7/12 Through 6/13		Total	Zero Assets	Under 500	500 to 1,000	1,000 to 5,000	5,000 to 10,000	10,000 to 25,000	25,000 to 50,000	50,000 to 100,000	100,000 to 250,000	250,000 to 500,000	500,000 to 2,500,000	2,500,000 and over
Number of Enterprises	1	26980	1863	11269	2263	4679	•	3115	758	191	67	•	5	•
Revenues ($ in Thousands)														
Net Sales	2	534610115	3160861	10949874	10405453	46171040	•	178643725	85903506	40113858	26559764	•	11347113	•
Interest	3	746348	265	4550	270	85452	•	108510	57532	31391	57637	•	14727	•
Rents	4	251600	0	0	0	12373	•	14340	22349	16507	26566	•	15029	•
Royalties	5	9061	0	0	0	13	•	304	5	621	0	•	8095	•
Other Portfolio Income	6	798885	51799	6036	16357	98901	•	134274	159829	50278	57975	•	132038	•
Other Receipts	7	11982337	88814	27373	67412	689724	•	4657096	2118244	960041	701088	•	392108	•
Total Receipts	8	548398346	3301739	10987833	10489492	47057503	•	183558249	88261465	41172696	27403030	•	11909110	•
Average Total Receipts	9	20326	1772	975	4635	10057	•	58927	116440	215564	409000	•	2381822	•
Operating Costs/Operating Income (%)														
Cost of Operations	10	87.9	86.8	80.2	88.4	86.4	•	88.7	88.5	88.5	88.2	•	82.6	•
Salaries and Wages	11	5.0	4.1	3.1	2.4	5.0	•	5.1	4.9	5.1	5.3	•	7.1	•
Taxes Paid	12	0.9	1.1	2.0	1.2	0.9	•	0.8	0.7	0.8	0.8	•	0.8	•
Interest Paid	13	0.4	0.5	0.2	0.4	0.4	•	0.3	0.4	0.3	0.4	•	1.2	•
Depreciation	14	0.4	0.2	0.3	0.2	0.2	•	0.3	0.5	0.5	0.7	•	1.0	•
Amortization and Depletion	15	0.1	0.0	0.0	0.0	0.0	•	0.1	0.1	0.1	0.1	•	0.7	•
Pensions and Other Deferred Comp.	16	0.0	0.0	•	0.1	0.0	•	0.0	0.0	0.0	0.1	•	0.0	•
Employee Benefits	17	0.4	0.3	0.1	0.1	0.4	•	0.4	0.4	0.4	0.4	•	0.7	•
Advertising	18	1.0	1.0	0.5	0.6	1.0	•	1.1	1.0	1.0	0.9	•	1.0	•
Other Expenses	19	3.8	5.1	7.5	3.8	4.6	•	3.6	3.5	3.4	3.6	•	7.8	•
Officers' Compensation	20	0.7	0.7	1.9	1.5	0.9	•	0.7	0.6	0.5	0.5	•	0.1	•
Operating Margin	21	•	0.2	4.1	1.3	0.0	•	•	•	•	•	•	•	•
Operating Margin Before Officers' Comp.	22	0.1	0.9	6.0	2.8	0.9	•	•	•	•	•	•	•	•

Selected Average Balance Sheet ($ in Thousands)

Net Receivables 23	710	0	17	57	414	•	1763	4027	8201	18465	•	244504	•
Inventories 24	2892	0	100	392	1898	•	8310	14579	26213	47803	•	382689	•
Net Property, Plant and Equipment 25	755	0	23	21	150	•	1360	4564	9852	24806	•	290865	•
Total Assets 26	6029	0	188	725	2787	•	15562	33980	67905	144536	•	1460158	•
Notes and Loans Payable 27	3750	0	70	217	1521	•	10792	22952	42513	87309	•	539369	•
All Other Liabilities 28	724	0	17	192	387	•	1593	3125	8801	17891	•	529407	•
Net Worth 29	1556	0	102	317	878	•	3177	7903	16591	39337	•	391381	•

Selected Financial Ratios (Times to 1)

Current Ratio 30	1.3	•	3.9	3.9	1.8	•	1.3	1.3	1.2	1.2	•	1.1	•
Quick Ratio 31	0.4	•	1.4	1.3	0.6	•	0.3	0.4	0.4	0.4	•	0.4	•
Net Sales to Working Capital 32	16.8	•	8.1	9.6	8.9	•	19.6	20.3	21.5	22.9	•	33.2	•
Coverage Ratio 33	6.0	10.0	18.6	6.6	5.4	•	6.8	6.8	7.1	7.1	•	2.6	•
Total Asset Turnover 34	3.3	•	5.2	6.3	3.5	•	3.7	3.3	3.1	2.7	•	1.6	•
Inventory Turnover 35	6.0	•	7.8	10.4	4.5	•	6.1	6.9	7.1	7.3	•	4.9	•
Receivables Turnover 36	29.7	•	55.1	39.1	22.5	•	34.0	32.1	29.6	26.4	•	•	•
Total Liabilities to Net Worth 37	2.9	•	0.9	1.3	2.2	•	3.9	3.3	3.1	2.7	•	2.7	•
Current Assets to Working Capital 38	3.9	•	1.3	1.3	2.2	•	4.5	4.7	5.2	5.7	•	10.2	•
Current Liabilities to Working Capital 39	2.9	•	0.3	0.3	1.2	•	3.5	3.7	4.2	4.7	•	9.2	•
Working Capital to Net Sales 40	0.1	•	0.1	0.1	0.1	•	0.1	0.0	0.0	0.0	•	0.0	•
Inventory to Working Capital 41	2.7	•	0.8	0.8	1.5	•	3.2	3.2	3.3	3.5	•	5.6	•
Total Receipts to Cash Flow 42	21.9	13.7	10.1	20.5	19.1	•	24.1	22.3	22.7	21.0	•	16.8	•
Cost of Goods to Cash Flow 43	19.2	11.9	8.1	18.1	16.5	•	21.4	19.7	20.1	18.5	•	13.9	•
Cash Flow to Total Debt 44	0.2	•	1.1	0.6	0.3	•	0.2	0.2	0.2	0.2	•	0.1	•

Selected Financial Factors (in Percentages)

Debt Ratio 45	74.2	•	46.0	56.3	68.5	•	79.6	76.7	75.6	72.8	•	73.2	•
Return on Total Assets 46	8.1	•	24.0	15.6	8.4	•	7.6	8.3	7.5	6.9	•	5.0	•
Return on Equity Before Income Taxes 47	26.2	•	42.1	30.3	21.8	•	31.9	30.5	26.2	21.7	•	11.5	•
Return on Equity After Income Taxes 48	24.4	•	41.7	29.9	20.9	•	31.3	29.5	24.8	20.4	•	8.2	•
Profit Margin (Before Income Tax) 49	2.1	4.7	4.4	2.1	1.9	•	1.8	2.1	2.1	2.2	•	2.0	•
Profit Margin (After Income Tax) 50	1.9	4.7	4.4	2.1	1.9	•	1.7	2.1	2.0	2.0	•	1.4	•

Table I

Corporations with and without Net Income

OTHER MOTOR VEHICLE AND PARTS DEALERS

MONEY AMOUNTS AND SIZE OF ASSETS IN THOUSANDS OF DOLLARS

Item Description for Accounting Period 7/12 Through 6/13		Total	Zero Assets	Under 500	500 to 1,000	1,000 to 5,000	5,000 to 10,000	10,000 to 25,000	25,000 to 50,000	50,000 to 100,000	100,000 to 250,000	250,000 to 500,000	500,000 to 2,500,000	2,500,000 and over
Number of Enterprises	1	36265	4706	19975	3555	6724	837	300	88	38	26	8	4	4
Revenues ($ in Thousands)														
Net Sales	2	134436924	1251806	13998002	6237684	33487238	13797832	10533700	6812656	6156002	7494281	3805739	6669428	24192555
Interest	3	72506	998	2034	1706	10211	2740	12972	3939	9712	914	19381	185	7714
Rents	4	46399	0	121	1312	21879	2326	2511	599	8137	6488	0	1934	1093
Royalties	5	15912	0	0	0	296	0	287	0	0	0	887	97	14345
Other Portfolio Income	6	236401	13857	1659	66679	49849	5406	26217	3957	11740	19581	34873	865	1719
Other Receipts	7	1790482	14986	196251	98045	384751	203375	148762	48460	100182	63850	52263	367019	112536
Total Receipts	8	136598624	1281647	14198067	6405426	33954224	14011679	10724449	6869611	6285773	7585114	3913143	7039528	24329962
Average Total Receipts	9	3767	272	711	1802	5050	16740	35748	78064	165415	291735	489143	1759882	6082490
Operating Costs/Operating Income (%)														
Cost of Operations	10	68.8	74.2	65.8	67.0	73.7	78.1	79.5	80.0	75.7	73.0	69.6	60.9	49.6
Salaries and Wages	11	10.6	5.3	8.6	10.1	9.1	7.3	7.8	7.4	9.2	9.6	9.3	16.4	17.7
Taxes Paid	12	1.9	1.1	2.3	2.3	1.7	1.2	1.2	1.1	1.5	1.5	1.5	2.5	3.2
Interest Paid	13	0.9	0.8	0.6	0.6	0.9	1.0	0.6	0.8	0.8	0.5	0.9	1.9	1.0
Depreciation	14	1.2	0.4	0.6	0.9	0.9	0.6	0.6	0.8	1.7	1.8	5.3	1.3	1.8
Amortization and Depletion	15	0.1	0.1	0.1	0.1	0.1	0.0	0.1	0.1	0.1	0.1	0.3	0.4	0.2
Pensions and Other Deferred Comp.	16	0.2	0.1	0.1	0.0	0.1	0.1	0.1	0.2	0.2	0.3	0.3	0.3	0.2
Employee Benefits	17	0.8	0.3	0.4	0.8	0.6	0.5	0.7	0.6	0.9	1.0	1.4	1.0	1.4
Advertising	18	1.1	1.2	1.1	1.3	1.1	1.2	0.9	0.7	0.8	1.0	0.8	2.2	1.0
Other Expenses	19	10.5	17.3	14.2	13.6	8.7	9.4	6.6	5.8	7.7	8.8	8.9	17.4	13.2
Officers' Compensation	20	1.6	0.9	4.5	3.3	2.3	1.0	0.9	0.9	1.1	0.7	0.5	0.5	0.3
Operating Margin	21	2.3	•	1.8	•	0.8	•	1.0	1.8	0.3	1.6	1.2	•	10.4
Operating Margin Before Officers' Comp.	22	3.9	•	6.3	3.2	3.1	0.5	1.9	2.6	1.4	2.4	1.8	•	10.6

Selected Average Balance Sheet ($ in Thousands)

Net Receivables 23	166	0	13	87	162	610	1432	3902	10735	22673	31914	275398	177835
Inventories 24	837	0	71	407	1258	4086	7000	16065	34280	54103	110217	290799	1834820
Net Property, Plant and Equipment 25	339	0	22	93	284	751	2096	6052	12780	31028	91367	208628	1245072
Total Assets 26	1771	0	143	701	2098	6535	14546	32746	67930	137748	332039	1129150	4680066
Notes and Loans Payable 27	704	0	67	357	832	3200	7043	14749	30584	46848	141954	314113	1617118
All Other Liabilities 28	624	0	44	148	635	2243	3413	7563	17560	44941	49270	541652	2248263
Net Worth 29	443	0	31	196	630	1092	4090	10434	19787	45960	140814	273385	814685

Selected Financial Ratios (Times to 1)

Current Ratio 30	1.5	•	2.5	2.4	1.8	1.3	1.4	1.4	1.5	1.5	1.6	1.7	1.1
Quick Ratio 31	0.4	•	1.0	0.7	0.3	0.3	0.4	0.4	0.5	0.5	0.5	0.8	0.2
Net Sales to Working Capital 32	9.6	•	10.7	5.6	7.0	12.6	10.6	10.8	10.1	8.7	6.5	5.9	26.5
Coverage Ratio 33	5.4	1.8	6.8	5.0	3.4	2.1	5.4	4.2	4.1	6.3	5.4	1.4	12.5
Total Asset Turnover 34	2.1	•	4.9	2.5	2.4	2.5	2.4	2.4	2.4	2.1	1.4	1.5	1.3
Inventory Turnover 35	3.0	•	6.5	2.9	2.9	3.2	4.0	3.9	3.6	3.9	3.0	3.5	1.6
Receivables Turnover 36	21.0	•	47.3	19.8	29.8	27.3	23.4	20.0	13.4	11.9	15.9	6.2	25.6
Total Liabilities to Net Worth 37	3.0	•	3.5	2.6	2.3	5.0	2.6	2.1	2.4	2.0	1.4	3.1	4.7
Current Assets to Working Capital 38	3.1	•	1.7	1.7	2.3	4.1	3.3	3.3	3.0	2.9	2.7	2.4	10.4
Current Liabilities to Working Capital 39	2.1	•	0.7	0.7	1.3	3.1	2.3	2.3	2.0	1.9	1.7	1.4	9.4
Working Capital to Net Sales 40	0.1	•	0.1	0.2	0.1	0.1	0.1	0.1	0.1	0.1	0.2	0.2	0.0
Inventory to Working Capital 41	2.2	•	1.0	1.1	1.8	3.1	2.3	2.1	1.9	1.8	1.6	1.1	8.5
Total Receipts to Cash Flow 42	9.0	7.3	7.3	8.6	11.9	12.1	14.1	14.9	13.5	11.1	10.1	7.6	5.3
Cost of Goods to Cash Flow 43	6.2	5.4	4.8	5.8	8.8	9.5	11.2	11.9	10.2	8.1	7.0	4.6	2.6
Cash Flow to Total Debt 44	0.3	•	0.9	0.4	0.3	0.2	0.2	0.2	0.2	0.3	0.2	0.3	0.3

Selected Financial Factors (in Percentages)

Debt Ratio 45	75.0	•	78.0	72.1	69.9	83.3	71.9	68.1	70.9	66.6	57.6	75.8	82.6
Return on Total Assets 46	10.0	•	18.7	8.0	7.5	5.3	8.3	8.1	7.5	7.1	7.1	4.0	15.5
Return on Equity Before Income Taxes 47	32.6	•	72.5	22.8	17.5	16.6	24.0	19.5	19.3	17.9	13.7	5.1	82.1
Return on Equity After Income Taxes 48	26.0	•	71.4	22.0	16.9	15.3	22.2	17.8	18.3	16.5	13.1	5.0	53.4
Profit Margin (Before Income Tax) 49	3.9	0.7	3.3	2.5	2.2	1.1	2.8	2.6	2.4	2.8	4.1	0.8	11.1
Profit Margin (After Income Tax) 50	3.1	0.4	3.2	2.5	2.1	1.0	2.6	2.4	2.2	2.6	3.9	0.8	7.2

Table II

Corporations with Net Income

OTHER MOTOR VEHICLE AND PARTS DEALERS

MONEY AMOUNTS AND SIZE OF ASSETS IN THOUSANDS OF DOLLARS

Item Description for Accounting Period 7/12 Through 6/13	Total	Zero Assets	Under 500	500 to 1,000	1,000 to 5,000	5,000 to 10,000	10,000 to 25,000	25,000 to 50,000	50,000 to 100,000	100,000 to 250,000	250,000 to 500,000	500,000 to 2,500,000	2,500,000 and over
Number of Enterprises 1	22613	2375	12400	2183	4555	•	279	78	33	21	•	0	4

Revenues ($ in Thousands)

Net Sales 2	114878370	1063026	10570817	4602298	25579061	•	10199341	6667118	5584419	6059241	•	0	24192555
Interest 3	49605	925	1706	1187	8422	•	12721	3809	9640	653	•	0	7714
Rents 4	24505	0	118	0	9021	•	1946	599	7535	1320	•	0	1093
Royalties 5	15527	0	0	0	296	•	0	0	0	0	•	0	14345
Other Portfolio Income 6	221640	12211	1303	58524	47633	•	25283	3957	11616	18442	•	0	1719
Other Receipts 7	1511948	11554	165572	34411	302431	•	147086	48296	89543	59436	•	0	112536
Total Receipts 8	116701595	1087716	10739516	4696420	25946864	•	10386377	6723779	5702753	6139092	•	0	24329962
Average Total Receipts 9	5161	458	866	2151	5696	•	37227	86202	172811	292338	•	•	6082490

Operating Costs/Operating Income (%)

Cost of Operations 10	67.8	74.4	64.9	65.1	72.7	•	79.7	80.1	75.6	72.8	•	•	49.6
Salaries and Wages 11	10.7	5.0	8.1	9.7	8.9	•	7.6	7.4	9.1	9.4	•	•	17.7
Taxes Paid 12	1.9	0.9	2.3	2.3	1.6	•	1.2	1.0	1.5	1.5	•	•	3.2
Interest Paid 13	0.8	0.2	0.5	0.5	0.8	•	0.6	0.7	0.7	0.5	•	•	1.0
Depreciation 14	1.2	0.2	0.6	0.7	0.6	•	0.6	0.5	1.7	1.9	•	•	1.8
Amortization and Depletion 15	0.1	0.1	0.1	0.2	0.1	•	0.1	0.1	0.0	0.1	•	•	0.2
Pensions and Other Deferred Comp. 16	0.2	0.1	0.1	0.0	0.1	•	0.2	0.2	0.2	0.4	•	•	0.2
Employee Benefits 17	0.8	0.2	0.3	0.7	0.6	•	0.6	0.6	0.9	1.1	•	•	1.4
Advertising 18	1.1	0.7	1.2	1.4	1.2	•	0.9	0.7	0.9	0.9	•	•	1.0
Other Expenses 19	10.2	13.2	13.5	11.6	8.4	•	6.3	5.7	7.5	8.2	•	•	13.2
Officers' Compensation 20	1.5	0.9	4.5	3.5	2.3	•	1.0	0.9	1.1	0.8	•	•	0.3
Operating Margin 21	3.7	4.1	4.0	4.3	2.6	•	1.3	2.2	0.6	2.5	•	•	10.4
Operating Margin Before Officers' Comp. 22	5.2	5.0	8.5	7.8	5.0	•	2.3	3.1	1.8	3.3	•	•	10.6

Selected Average Balance Sheet ($ in Thousands)

Net Receivables	23	212	0	11	102	212	•	1417	4260	11107	23364	•	•	177835
Inventories	24	1090	0	72	464	1275	•	6499	15560	34849	56672	•	•	1834820
Net Property, Plant and Equipment	25	468	0	19	100	289	•	1904	4451	12209	29785	•	•	1245072
Total Assets	26	2352	0	141	743	2098	•	14340	33391	68097	138874	•	•	4680066
Notes and Loans Payable	27	886	0	47	276	839	•	6646	14261	29969	47605	•	•	1617118
All Other Liabilities	28	836	0	53	174	536	•	3316	7086	17206	43990	•	•	2248263
Net Worth	29	630	0	41	293	723	•	4378	12044	20922	47279	•	•	814685

Selected Financial Ratios (Times to 1)

Current Ratio	30	1.5	•	2.6	2.9	1.9	•	1.5	1.6	1.6	1.6	•	•	1.1
Quick Ratio	31	0.4	•	1.2	0.9	0.4	•	0.4	0.4	0.5	0.6	•	•	0.2
Net Sales to Working Capital	32	10.0	•	12.3	5.5	7.2	•	10.4	9.2	9.3	7.5	•	•	26.5
Coverage Ratio	33	7.9	31.6	11.3	14.7	6.1	•	5.9	5.5	4.9	9.2	•	•	12.5
Total Asset Turnover	34	2.2	•	6.0	2.8	2.7	•	2.5	2.6	2.5	2.1	•	•	1.3
Inventory Turnover	35	3.2	•	7.6	3.0	3.2	•	4.5	4.4	3.7	3.7	•	•	1.6
Receivables Turnover	36	22.3	•	57.4	19.3	26.3	•	27.7	22.3	13.3	12.3	•	•	25.6
Total Liabilities to Net Worth	37	2.7	•	2.5	1.5	1.9	•	2.3	1.8	2.3	1.9	•	•	4.7
Current Assets to Working Capital	38	3.1	•	1.6	1.5	2.2	•	3.2	2.8	2.7	2.5	•	•	10.4
Current Liabilities to Working Capital	39	2.1	•	0.6	0.5	1.2	•	2.2	1.8	1.7	1.5	•	•	9.4
Working Capital to Net Sales	40	0.1	•	0.1	0.2	0.1	•	0.1	0.1	0.1	0.1	•	•	0.0
Inventory to Working Capital	41	2.2	•	0.8	1.0	1.6	•	2.2	1.8	1.7	1.6	•	•	8.5
Total Receipts to Cash Flow	42	8.1	5.8	6.4	7.0	9.6	•	13.9	14.1	13.2	10.3	•	•	5.3
Cost of Goods to Cash Flow	43	5.5	4.3	4.1	4.6	7.0	•	11.0	11.3	10.0	7.5	•	•	2.6
Cash Flow to Total Debt	44	0.4	•	1.3	0.7	0.4	•	0.3	0.3	0.3	0.3	•	•	0.3

Selected Financial Factors (in Percentages)

Debt Ratio	45	73.2	•	71.1	60.6	65.5	•	69.5	63.9	69.3	66.0	•	•	82.6
Return on Total Assets	46	13.1	•	37.0	19.3	13.0	•	9.6	9.6	8.5	8.9	•	•	15.5
Return on Equity Before Income Taxes	47	42.8	•	116.7	45.6	31.6	•	26.2	21.8	22.1	23.2	•	•	82.1
Return on Equity After Income Taxes	48	35.4	•	115.4	44.7	30.8	•	24.3	20.2	21.1	21.6	•	•	53.4
Profit Margin (Before Income Tax)	49	5.3	6.4	5.6	6.3	4.1	•	3.1	3.1	2.7	3.8	•	•	11.1
Profit Margin (After Income Tax)	50	4.4	6.1	5.5	6.2	4.0	•	2.9	2.8	2.6	3.5	•	•	7.2

Table I

Corporations with and without Net Income

FURNITURE AND HOME FURNISHINGS STORES

MONEY AMOUNTS AND SIZE OF ASSETS IN THOUSANDS OF DOLLARS

Item Description for Accounting Period 7/12 Through 6/13	Total	Zero Assets	Under 500	500 to 1,000	1,000 to 5,000	5,000 to 10,000	10,000 to 25,000	25,000 to 50,000	50,000 to 100,000	100,000 to 250,000	250,000 to 500,000	500,000 to 2,500,000	2,500,000 and over
Number of Enterprises **1**	32358	5463	20831	2968	2626	224	145	49	21	12	9	9	0
Revenues ($ in Thousands)													
Net Sales **2**	80078026	1070339	9745391	5659956	13163561	3463565	5860226	4242315	3028143	3634346	5065221	25144964	0
Interest **3**	202212	21	4811	9235	23068	15411	5363	9	66	26009	107434	10787	0
Rents **4**	29152	67	3750	24	3666	2302	1146	53	2955	2009	2061	11119	0
Royalties **5**	10945	0	0	0	0	0	0	0	57	0	0	10888	0
Other Portfolio Income **6**	50062	4	22268	2938	14483	966	876	512	1129	473	5208	1204	0
Other Receipts **7**	877913	836	67150	26199	106021	53917	56524	38606	92455	52437	93167	290600	0
Total Receipts **8**	81248310	1071267	9843370	5698352	13310799	3536161	5924135	4281495	3124805	3715274	5273091	25469562	0
Average Total Receipts **9**	2511	196	473	1920	5069	15786	40856	87377	148800	309606	585899	2829951	•
Operating Costs/Operating Income (%)													
Cost of Operations **10**	57.9	61.7	59.2	65.2	59.9	63.4	61.4	59.9	54.6	54.0	54.7	54.3	•
Salaries and Wages **11**	12.0	7.3	9.5	8.9	12.7	10.7	13.6	13.2	14.4	14.3	16.5	11.5	•
Taxes Paid **12**	2.3	2.6	2.7	2.3	2.1	1.6	2.0	1.6	2.4	2.4	2.8	2.6	•
Interest Paid **13**	0.6	0.9	0.5	0.7	0.5	0.9	0.4	0.5	0.4	1.1	0.6	0.7	•
Depreciation **14**	1.4	1.7	0.6	0.8	0.7	1.2	0.8	0.9	1.3	1.7	2.1	2.4	•
Amortization and Depletion **15**	0.2	•	0.1	0.0	0.1	0.0	0.2	0.1	0.2	0.2	0.1	0.3	•
Pensions and Other Deferred Comp. **16**	0.1	0.0	0.2	0.1	0.1	0.0	0.1	0.2	0.2	0.1	0.7	0.1	•
Employee Benefits **17**	0.9	0.7	0.7	0.6	0.5	0.5	0.9	1.2	0.9	1.3	1.2	1.2	•
Advertising **18**	3.7	2.6	2.3	2.2	2.8	3.4	5.2	4.0	3.7	4.6	5.1	4.5	•
Other Expenses **19**	15.7	25.3	16.6	15.0	14.3	18.6	12.2	15.3	19.8	21.4	18.6	14.4	•
Officers' Compensation **20**	2.3	1.1	6.9	3.5	3.5	2.6	1.3	1.2	1.1	0.4	0.8	0.9	•
Operating Margin **21**	2.8	•	0.7	0.7	2.9	•	1.9	1.9	0.9	•	•	7.4	•
Operating Margin Before Officers' Comp. **22**	5.1	•	7.6	4.2	6.4	•	3.2	3.2	2.0	•	•	8.3	•

Selected Average Balance Sheet ($ in Thousands)

Net Receivables 23	208	0	17	83	307	1287	2924	7426	7756	23758	88781	333321	•
Inventories 24	372	0	48	249	840	2987	5941	9597	23584	40774	96832	469822	•
Net Property, Plant and Equipment 25	316	0	23	146	399	2292	2414	7151	19063	52922	80116	589029	•
Total Assets 26	1267	0	123	686	2104	7486	15656	33781	72798	153212	382514	2051067	•
Notes and Loans Payable 27	339	0	73	191	741	2408	3457	9509	17723	33771	93129	422424	•
All Other Liabilities 28	468	0	46	204	720	2332	6907	11284	26095	74010	109593	796603	•
Net Worth 29	460	0	3	292	643	2745	5292	12988	28979	45431	179792	832040	•

Selected Financial Ratios (Times to 1)

Current Ratio 30	1.5	•	1.8	1.8	1.9	1.8	1.4	1.7	1.8	1.2	1.9	1.3	•
Quick Ratio 31	0.6	•	0.8	0.8	0.8	0.7	0.6	0.6	0.7	0.5	0.9	0.5	•
Net Sales to Working Capital 32	9.3	•	12.0	9.5	7.1	7.3	11.2	9.3	7.2	26.7	5.2	10.6	•
Coverage Ratio 33	7.8	•	4.1	3.1	9.1	•	7.8	7.1	11.6	1.6	2.6	14.0	•
Total Asset Turnover 34	2.0	•	3.8	2.8	2.4	2.1	2.6	2.6	2.0	2.0	1.5	1.4	•
Inventory Turnover 35	3.9	•	5.8	5.0	3.6	3.3	4.2	5.4	3.3	4.0	3.2	3.2	•
Receivables Turnover 36	12.1	•	25.8	18.2	15.8	13.6	16.9	12.6	18.7	16.6	5.9	8.6	•
Total Liabilities to Net Worth 37	1.8	•	37.6	1.4	2.3	1.7	2.0	1.6	1.5	2.4	1.1	1.5	•
Current Assets to Working Capital 38	2.9	•	2.3	2.3	2.1	2.3	3.3	2.5	2.2	7.4	2.2	4.3	•
Current Liabilities to Working Capital 39	1.9	•	1.3	1.3	1.1	1.3	2.3	1.5	1.2	6.4	1.2	3.3	•
Working Capital to Net Sales 40	0.1	•	0.1	0.1	0.1	0.1	0.1	0.1	0.1	0.0	0.2	0.1	•
Inventory to Working Capital 41	1.4	•	1.2	1.1	1.1	1.4	1.5	1.3	1.3	3.9	1.0	1.9	•
Total Receipts to Cash Flow 42	7.4	10.4	8.1	8.6	7.8	9.5	10.5	8.1	5.7	6.9	8.9	6.1	•
Cost of Goods to Cash Flow 43	4.3	6.4	4.8	5.6	4.6	6.0	6.4	4.9	3.1	3.7	4.9	3.3	•
Cash Flow to Total Debt 44	0.4	•	0.5	0.6	0.4	0.3	0.4	0.5	0.6	0.4	0.3	0.4	•

Selected Financial Factors (in Percentages)

Debt Ratio 45	63.7	•	97.4	57.5	69.5	63.3	66.2	61.6	60.2	70.3	53.0	59.4	•
Return on Total Assets 46	9.4	•	8.6	5.6	10.7	•	8.8	8.5	8.8	3.5	2.4	12.8	•
Return on Equity Before Income Taxes 47	22.7	•	252.8	9.0	31.3	•	22.6	19.0	20.1	4.3	3.1	29.2	•
Return on Equity After Income Taxes 48	17.3	•	244.3	8.3	30.6	•	21.2	18.9	19.3	2.6	1.6	19.6	•
Profit Margin (Before Income Tax) 49	4.2	•	1.7	1.4	4.0	•	3.0	2.9	4.0	0.6	1.0	8.7	•
Profit Margin (After Income Tax) 50	3.2	•	1.7	1.3	3.9	•	2.8	2.8	3.9	0.4	0.5	5.8	•

Table II
Corporations with Net Income

FURNITURE AND HOME FURNISHINGS STORES

MONEY AMOUNTS AND SIZE OF ASSETS IN THOUSANDS OF DOLLARS

Item Description for Accounting Period 7/12 Through 6/13	Total	Zero Assets	Under 500	500 to 1,000	1,000 to 5,000	5,000 to 10,000	10,000 to 25,000	25,000 to 50,000	50,000 to 100,000	100,000 to 250,000	250,000 to 500,000	500,000 to 2,500,000	2,500,000 and over
Number of Enterprises 1	18674	2278	12012	1764	2307	112	119	42	15	•	6	•	0
Revenues ($ in Thousands)													
Net Sales 2	67961632	254182	6616075	4189563	11954397	2391442	4883601	4081485	2379332	•	3003122	•	0
Interest 3	159070	21	512	8982	18169	7709	5361	7	21	•	107425	•	0
Rents 4	24237	0	3175	1	3666	1310	1120	53	2357	•	1925	•	0
Royalties 5	10888	0	0	0	0	0	0	0	0	•	0	•	0
Other Portfolio Income 6	30939	0	14136	2735	9695	121	792	512	591	•	679	•	0
Other Receipts 7	828420	346	67246	24665	105567	40159	52203	38132	88537	•	79746	•	0
Total Receipts 8	69015186	254549	6701144	4225946	12091494	2440741	4943077	4120189	2470838	•	3192897	•	0
Average Total Receipts 9	3696	112	558	2396	5241	21792	41538	98100	164723	•	532150	•	•
Operating Costs/Operating Income (%)													
Cost of Operations 10	57.7	48.3	59.2	70.6	60.0	60.9	60.9	60.6	53.4	•	52.5	•	•
Salaries and Wages 11	11.8	2.4	7.9	8.3	12.4	11.5	13.4	13.0	13.9	•	16.7	•	•
Taxes Paid 12	2.3	2.2	2.4	2.0	2.0	1.5	1.8	1.5	2.4	•	2.9	•	•
Interest Paid 13	0.4	1.2	0.5	0.3	0.5	0.4	0.3	0.4	0.3	•	0.8	•	•
Depreciation 14	1.5	0.9	0.6	0.6	0.7	1.3	0.8	0.9	1.3	•	2.6	•	•
Amortization and Depletion 15	0.1	•	0.1	0.0	0.1	0.0	0.2	0.0	0.0	•	0.1	•	•
Pensions and Other Deferred Comp. 16	0.2	•	0.1	0.1	0.1	0.1	0.1	0.2	0.2	•	1.1	•	•
Employee Benefits 17	0.9	0.3	0.7	0.4	0.5	0.6	1.0	1.2	1.0	•	0.6	•	•
Advertising 18	3.7	1.0	1.6	1.6	2.8	3.7	5.5	3.9	3.8	•	4.5	•	•
Other Expenses 19	14.7	27.1	15.3	10.6	13.9	14.9	11.8	14.8	19.6	•	20.6	•	•
Officers' Compensation 20	2.1	1.1	6.6	3.6	3.3	3.0	1.3	1.2	1.1	•	0.7	•	•
Operating Margin 21	4.5	15.5	5.0	1.8	3.6	2.1	2.9	2.3	3.0	•	•	•	•
Operating Margin Before Officers' Comp. 22	6.6	16.6	11.6	5.5	6.9	5.1	4.2	3.6	4.1	•	•	•	•

Net Receivables 23	307	0	20	115	292	1370	2915	7791	9267	•	84504	•	•
Inventories 24	523	0	48	264	775	3428	6186	9593	25927	•	93011	•	•
Net Property, Plant and Equipment 25	472	0	24	93	401	1897	2623	6629	18907	•	87078	•	•
Total Assets 26	1838	0	126	719	2055	7860	15505	34454	72931	•	385448	•	•
Notes and Loans Payable 27	459	0	87	120	768	1740	2652	9792	18619	•	88012	•	•
All Other Liabilities 28	682	0	49	261	620	1992	6272	11867	28764	•	98226	•	•
Net Worth 29	697	0	-10	338	667	4128	6580	12795	25548	•	199210	•	•

Selected Financial Ratios (Times to 1)

Current Ratio 30	1.5	•	1.6	1.6	2.2	1.9	1.6	1.6	1.8	•	2.2	•	•
Quick Ratio 31	0.6	•	0.7	0.7	0.8	0.7	0.7	0.6	0.6	•	1.0	•	•
Net Sales to Working Capital 32	9.6	•	17.2	12.3	6.7	7.7	9.7	10.3	7.6	•	4.6	•	•
Coverage Ratio 33	14.6	13.8	13.7	10.2	11.0	10.3	13.6	9.0	21.3	•	4.9	•	•
Total Asset Turnover 34	2.0	•	4.4	3.3	2.5	2.7	2.6	2.8	2.2	•	1.3	•	•
Inventory Turnover 35	4.0	•	6.8	6.4	4.0	3.8	4.0	6.1	3.3	•	2.8	•	•
Receivables Turnover 36	12.2	•	34.1	19.2	17.8	•	17.1	13.7	18.4	•	5.0	•	•
Total Liabilities to Net Worth 37	1.6	•	•	1.1	2.1	0.9	1.4	1.7	1.9	•	0.9	•	•
Current Assets to Working Capital 38	3.0	•	2.8	2.7	1.9	2.1	2.7	2.6	2.3	•	1.8	•	•
Current Liabilities to Working Capital 39	2.0	•	1.8	1.7	0.9	1.1	1.7	1.6	1.3	•	0.8	•	•
Working Capital to Net Sales 40	0.1	•	0.1	0.1	0.1	0.1	0.1	0.1	0.1	•	0.2	•	•
Inventory to Working Capital 41	1.4	•	1.3	1.2	1.1	1.2	1.3	1.3	1.4	•	0.8	•	•
Total Receipts to Cash Flow 42	6.7	2.9	5.9	11.0	7.3	8.3	9.5	8.1	5.1	•	6.2	•	•
Cost of Goods to Cash Flow 43	3.9	1.4	3.5	7.8	4.4	5.1	5.8	4.9	2.7	•	3.3	•	•
Cash Flow to Total Debt 44	0.5	•	0.7	0.6	0.5	0.7	0.5	0.6	0.7	•	0.4	•	•

Selected Financial Factors (in Percentages)

Debt Ratio 45	62.1	•	108.0	53.0	67.6	47.5	57.6	62.9	65.0	•	48.3	•	•
Return on Total Assets 46	12.9	•	29.5	9.9	13.2	12.6	11.7	10.3	15.5	•	5.1	•	•
Return on Equity Before Income Taxes 47	31.6	•	•	19.1	36.9	21.6	25.6	24.8	42.3	•	7.9	•	•
Return on Equity After Income Taxes 48	25.5	•	•	18.1	36.0	20.2	24.2	24.6	41.0	•	5.9	•	•
Profit Margin (Before Income Tax) 49	6.1	15.6	6.3	2.7	4.7	4.2	4.1	3.3	6.8	•	3.1	•	•
Profit Margin (After Income Tax) 50	4.9	15.6	6.2	2.6	4.6	3.9	3.9	3.2	6.6	•	2.3	•	•

Table I

Corporations with and without Net Income

ELECTRONICS AND APPLIANCE STORES

MONEY AMOUNTS AND SIZE OF ASSETS IN THOUSANDS OF DOLLARS

Item Description for Accounting Period 7/12 Through 6/13	Total	Zero Assets	Under 500	500 to 1,000	1,000 to 5,000	5,000 to 10,000	10,000 to 25,000	25,000 to 50,000	50,000 to 100,000	100,000 to 250,000	250,000 to 500,000	500,000 to 2,500,000	2,500,000 and over
Number of Enterprises **1**	20935	3767	14501	1102	1375	45	81	30	9	13	3	9	0

Revenues ($ in Thousands)

	Total	Zero Assets	Under 500	500 to 1,000	1,000 to 5,000	5,000 to 10,000	10,000 to 25,000	25,000 to 50,000	50,000 to 100,000	100,000 to 250,000	250,000 to 500,000	500,000 to 2,500,000	2,500,000 and over
Net Sales **2**	93124352	1003170	7647473	2490147	6950670	664907	3383107	2674170	1885883	3446668	2801713	60176443	0
Interest **3**	176567	0	1022	406	94	17	208	186	425	2208	3030	168971	0
Rents **4**	27919	0	3227	1318	414	0	0	0	0	1561	0	21399	0
Royalties **5**	47921	0	0	0	0	0	0	0	0	7573	0	40348	0
Other Portfolio Income **6**	128707	49275	239	1103	25338	164	1806	643	6252	1495	14099	28293	0
Other Receipts **7**	1194165	41295	30374	69645	32829	5366	10367	10671	14189	65564	17992	895876	0
Total Receipts **8**	94699631	1093740	7682335	2562619	7009345	670454	3395488	2685670	1906749	3525069	2836834	61331330	0
Average Total Receipts **9**	4524	290	530	2325	5098	14899	41920	89522	211861	271159	945611	6814592	•

Operating Costs/Operating Income (%)

	Total	Zero Assets	Under 500	500 to 1,000	1,000 to 5,000	5,000 to 10,000	10,000 to 25,000	25,000 to 50,000	50,000 to 100,000	100,000 to 250,000	250,000 to 500,000	500,000 to 2,500,000	2,500,000 and over
Cost of Operations **10**	72.5	70.4	50.4	64.7	68.0	51.0	72.5	78.8	63.1	73.7	82.9	75.9	•
Salaries and Wages **11**	9.8	8.7	15.7	15.0	13.1	14.3	11.7	8.8	24.4	12.8	8.2	7.8	•
Taxes Paid **12**	1.5	1.5	2.7	2.3	1.9	1.7	1.2	1.5	1.5	1.1	1.1	1.3	•
Interest Paid **13**	0.4	0.5	0.5	0.7	0.6	0.7	0.4	0.4	0.4	0.4	0.6	0.4	•
Depreciation **14**	0.8	0.6	1.1	1.0	0.5	0.7	0.9	0.5	2.3	1.0	0.4	0.7	•
Amortization and Depletion **15**	0.2	0.2	0.1	0.0	0.2	0.2	0.1	0.3	0.1	0.2	0.4	0.2	•
Pensions and Other Deferred Comp. **16**	0.1	0.0	0.4	0.2	0.2	0.2	0.1	0.1	0.1	0.0	0.0	0.1	•
Employee Benefits **17**	0.8	0.2	0.9	1.2	1.3	0.9	0.5	0.6	0.8	0.5	0.5	0.7	•
Advertising **18**	2.0	0.5	1.5	1.2	1.3	3.9	1.0	1.1	1.1	1.4	0.0	2.4	•
Other Expenses **19**	10.3	21.0	17.8	11.9	7.9	18.7	8.5	5.7	5.9	9.7	4.7	10.0	•
Officers' Compensation **20**	1.1	0.8	6.5	3.1	2.7	2.9	1.1	1.0	0.6	0.6	0.4	0.1	•
Operating Margin **21**	0.6	•	2.3	•	2.3	4.6	2.1	1.2	•	•	0.8	0.3	•
Operating Margin Before Officers' Comp. **22**	1.6	•	8.8	1.9	5.0	7.5	3.2	2.2	0.3	•	1.2	0.5	•

Selected Average Balance Sheet ($ in Thousands)													
Net Receivables 23	291	0	13	80	438	1769	5379	16021	14060	18869	63690	406183	•
Inventories 24	489	0	35	232	651	3319	3295	4489	24321	23110	64666	812928	•
Net Property, Plant and Equipment 25	248	0	20	190	228	580	1346	1944	8728	22238	12638	418539	•
Total Assets 26	1869	0	123	767	1956	7765	14820	32372	73052	152705	332575	3072981	•
Notes and Loans Payable 27	319	0	81	149	556	2028	2535	8791	18032	26025	36354	378758	•
All Other Liabilities 28	919	0	60	369	760	2025	7499	19110	32063	48397	171263	1579074	•
Net Worth 29	631	0	-18	249	640	3712	4785	4471	22957	78284	124958	1115149	•

Selected Financial Ratios (Times to 1)													
Current Ratio 30	1.2	•	1.3	2.1	1.7	2.2	1.5	1.2	1.2	1.3	1.5	1.1	•
Quick Ratio 31	0.5	•	0.7	1.0	0.8	1.0	0.9	0.9	0.5	0.7	0.7	0.4	•
Net Sales to Working Capital 32	24.2	•	30.1	9.7	7.9	5.3	10.5	18.2	27.6	16.5	11.0	44.9	•
Coverage Ratio 33	6.7	10.3	6.4	3.6	6.6	8.7	8.1	4.9	3.4	2.8	4.2	7.4	•
Total Asset Turnover 34	2.4	•	4.3	2.9	2.6	1.9	2.8	2.8	2.9	1.7	2.8	2.2	•
Inventory Turnover 35	6.6	•	7.5	6.3	5.3	2.3	9.2	15.6	5.4	8.5	12.0	6.2	•
Receivables Turnover 36	14.4	•	32.5	20.9	10.8	5.5	6.5	8.1	8.7	9.3	15.2	16.1	•
Total Liabilities to Net Worth 37	2.0	•	•	2.1	2.1	1.1	2.1	6.2	2.2	1.0	1.7	1.8	•
Current Assets to Working Capital 38	5.9	•	4.8	1.9	2.4	1.8	3.0	5.6	5.8	4.0	3.1	11.3	•
Current Liabilities to Working Capital 39	4.9	•	3.8	0.9	1.4	0.8	2.0	4.6	4.8	3.0	2.1	10.3	•
Working Capital to Net Sales 40	0.0	•	0.0	0.1	0.1	0.2	0.1	0.1	0.0	0.1	0.1	0.0	•
Inventory to Working Capital 41	2.8	•	1.7	0.8	1.1	0.9	0.8	1.1	1.9	1.3	1.4	5.8	•
Total Receipts to Cash Flow 42	10.6	6.1	6.1	9.7	11.3	5.1	11.0	18.4	23.4	12.9	23.6	11.1	•
Cost of Goods to Cash Flow 43	7.7	4.3	3.1	6.3	7.7	2.6	8.0	14.5	14.8	9.5	19.5	8.4	•
Cash Flow to Total Debt 44	0.3	•	0.6	0.5	0.3	0.7	0.4	0.2	0.2	0.3	0.2	0.3	•

Selected Financial Factors (in Percentages)													
Debt Ratio 45	66.2	•	114.9	67.5	67.3	52.2	67.7	86.2	68.6	48.7	62.4	63.7	•
Return on Total Assets 46	7.0	•	14.1	6.9	9.5	11.6	8.0	5.5	3.6	2.0	7.5	6.4	•
Return on Equity Before Income Taxes 47	17.6	•	•	15.2	24.8	21.6	21.6	31.8	8.0	2.5	15.3	15.4	•
Return on Equity After Income Taxes 48	12.9	•	•	14.3	23.7	17.3	20.4	28.6	6.7	2.1	13.7	9.6	•
Profit Margin (Before Income Tax) 49	2.5	4.7	2.8	1.7	3.1	5.4	2.5	1.6	0.9	0.7	2.0	2.6	•
Profit Margin (After Income Tax) 50	1.8	4.6	2.8	1.6	3.0	4.3	2.3	1.4	0.7	0.6	1.8	1.6	•

Table II

Corporations with Net Income

ELECTRONICS AND APPLIANCE STORES

MONEY AMOUNTS AND SIZE OF ASSETS IN THOUSANDS OF DOLLARS

Item Description for Accounting Period 7/12 Through 6/13	Total	Zero Assets	Under 500	500 to 1,000	1,000 to 5,000	5,000 to 10,000	10,000 to 25,000	25,000 to 50,000	50,000 to 100,000	100,000 to 250,000	250,000 to 500,000	500,000 to 2,500,000	2,500,000 and over
Number of Enterprises 1	11440	1801	7745	753	1005	31	63	20	4	•	3	•	0
Revenues ($ in Thousands)													
Net Sales 2	78270680	757171	5575189	1182410	4904027	622653	2834922	1831566	667254	•	2801713	•	0
Interest 3	159368	0	1019	178	84	17	196	144	380	•	3030	•	0
Rents 4	25695	0	3227	1318	0	0	0	0	0	•	0	•	0
Royalties 5	46003	0	0	0	0	0	0	0	0	•	0	•	0
Other Portfolio Income 6	127511	49275	238	1102	24989	164	1806	643	6251	•	14099	•	0
Other Receipts 7	1075458	41660	28125	14506	11409	4995	8626	3928	12345	•	17992	•	0
Total Receipts 8	79704715	848106	5607798	1199514	4940509	627829	2845550	1836281	686230	•	2836834	•	0
Average Total Receipts 9	6967	471	724	1593	4916	20253	45167	91814	171558	•	945611	•	•
Operating Costs/Operating Income (%)													
Cost of Operations 10	73.3	72.2	46.8	66.1	65.9	50.5	72.9	82.6	27.9	•	82.9	•	•
Salaries and Wages 11	8.9	6.6	16.5	9.2	13.2	13.9	11.1	5.7	54.6	•	8.2	•	•
Taxes Paid 12	1.4	1.7	2.9	2.4	1.9	1.8	1.1	0.9	2.1	•	1.1	•	•
Interest Paid 13	0.4	0.7	0.2	1.2	0.5	0.8	0.3	0.3	0.5	•	0.6	•	•
Depreciation 14	0.7	0.6	1.0	1.6	0.4	0.7	1.0	0.2	5.4	•	0.4	•	•
Amortization and Depletion 15	0.2	0.2	0.1	0.0	0.2	0.2	0.1	0.3	0.0	•	0.4	•	•
Pensions and Other Deferred Comp. 16	0.1	0.0	0.5	0.2	0.2	0.1	0.1	0.1	0.2	•	0.0	•	•
Employee Benefits 17	0.8	0.3	1.1	0.7	1.4	0.8	0.4	0.5	1.1	•	0.5	•	•
Advertising 18	1.9	0.1	1.6	0.9	1.2	3.8	0.7	0.6	0.1	•	0.0	•	•
Other Expenses 19	9.8	22.0	15.9	9.5	7.9	16.7	8.1	3.1	6.0	•	4.7	•	•
Officers' Compensation 20	1.0	1.0	7.7	4.0	2.8	3.1	1.1	1.2	1.1	•	0.4	•	•
Operating Margin 21	1.5	•	5.7	4.3	4.3	7.5	3.1	4.6	1.0	•	0.8	•	•
Operating Margin Before Officers' Comp. 22	2.6	•	13.3	8.3	7.1	10.6	4.2	5.8	2.1	•	1.2	•	•

	Selected Average Balance Sheet ($ in Thousands)												
Net Receivables 23	437	0	17	77	518	1571	5791	16518	9161	•	63690	•	•
Inventories 24	721	0	36	159	569	3529	3374	3268	24127	•	114626	•	•
Net Property, Plant and Equipment 25	371	0	12	255	146	698	1195	1458	5795	•	12638	•	•
Total Assets 26	2861	0	144	792	1995	7825	15356	30988	69247	•	332575	•	•
Notes and Loans Payable 27	357	0	29	176	447	2452	2725	5218	23511	•	36354	•	•
All Other Liabilities 28	1423	0	53	343	824	2181	7400	16855	12420	•	171263	•	•
Net Worth 29	1081	0	62	273	723	3192	5231	8915	33316	•	124958	•	•

	Selected Financial Ratios (Times to 1)												
Current Ratio 30	1.2	•	1.9	1.8	1.8	2.2	1.5	1.4	1.5	•	1.5	•	•
Quick Ratio 31	0.5	•	1.3	0.8	1.0	0.8	1.0	1.1	1.1	•	0.7	•	•
Net Sales to Working Capital 32	32.3	•	13.9	7.5	7.1	6.3	10.4	11.3	17.5	•	11.0	•	•
Coverage Ratio 33	10.9	11.3	26.4	6.0	10.5	12.0	11.4	19.9	8.1	•	4.2	•	•
Total Asset Turnover 34	2.4	•	5.0	2.0	2.4	2.6	2.9	3.0	2.4	•	2.8	•	•
Inventory Turnover 35	7.0	•	9.2	6.5	5.6	2.9	9.7	23.1	1.9	•	6.8	•	•
Receivables Turnover 36	15.6	•	38.3	17.8	9.1	•	6.9	7.5	4.3	•	29.3	•	•
Total Liabilities to Net Worth 37	1.6	•	1.3	1.9	1.8	1.5	1.9	2.5	1.1	•	1.7	•	•
Current Assets to Working Capital 38	7.6	•	2.2	2.2	2.3	1.8	2.9	3.4	2.9	•	3.1	•	•
Current Liabilities to Working Capital 39	6.6	•	1.2	1.2	1.3	0.8	1.9	2.4	1.9	•	2.1	•	•
Working Capital to Net Sales 40	0.0	•	0.1	0.1	0.1	0.2	0.1	0.1	0.1	•	0.1	•	•
Inventory to Working Capital 41	3.6	•	0.7	1.0	0.9	1.1	0.8	0.6	0.7	•	1.4	•	•
Total Receipts to Cash Flow 42	9.8	4.9	5.4	7.5	9.4	4.7	10.5	14.2	16.0	•	23.6	•	•
Cost of Goods to Cash Flow 43	7.2	3.6	2.5	5.0	6.2	2.4	7.6	11.8	4.5	•	19.5	•	•
Cash Flow to Total Debt 44	0.4	•	1.6	0.4	0.4	0.9	0.4	0.3	0.3	•	0.2	•	•

	Selected Financial Factors (in Percentages)												
Debt Ratio 45	62.2	•	56.7	65.6	63.7	59.2	65.9	71.2	51.9	•	62.4	•	•
Return on Total Assets 46	9.5	•	32.5	13.6	13.5	23.3	11.2	15.1	10.7	•	7.5	•	•
Return on Equity Before Income Taxes 47	22.9	•	72.0	33.0	33.8	52.4	29.9	50.0	19.4	•	15.3	•	•
Return on Equity After Income Taxes 48	17.9	•	71.7	31.7	32.5	45.1	29.8	47.6	17.4	•	13.7	•	•
Profit Margin (Before Income Tax) 49	3.6	6.7	6.2	5.7	5.0	8.3	3.5	4.9	3.9	•	2.0	•	•
Profit Margin (After Income Tax) 50	2.8	6.6	6.2	5.5	4.8	7.2	3.5	4.6	3.5	•	1.8	•	•

Table I

Corporations with and without Net Income

HOMES CENTERS; PAINT AND WALLPAPER STORES

MONEY AMOUNTS AND SIZE OF ASSETS IN THOUSANDS OF DOLLARS

Item Description for Accounting Period 7/12 Through 6/13	Total	Zero Assets	Under 500	500 to 1,000	1,000 to 5,000	5,000 to 10,000	10,000 to 25,000	25,000 to 50,000	50,000 to 100,000	100,000 to 250,000	250,000 to 500,000	500,000 to 2,500,000	2,500,000 and over
Number of Enterprises 1	2899	•	1726	575	527	•	41	6	•	0	0	0	3

Revenues ($ in Thousands)

Net Sales 2	137059263	•	1063784	1117205	3385877	•	1482818	592559	•	0	0	0	128237943
Interest 3	33133	•	317	729	3665	•	835	282	•	0	0	0	26835
Rents 4	410691	•	0	305	308	•	1555	0	•	0	0	0	405219
Royalties 5	262545	•	0	0	0	•	0	0	•	0	0	0	262545
Other Portfolio Income 6	227045	•	0	1443	1382	•	298	10	•	0	0	0	222864
Other Receipts 7	2735272	•	281	575	12315	•	14190	3095	•	0	0	0	2699257
Total Receipts 8	140727949	•	1064382	1120257	3403547	•	1499696	595946	•	0	0	0	131854663
Average Total Receipts 9	48544	•	617	1948	6458	•	36578	99324	•	•	•	•	43951554

Operating Costs/Operating Income (%)

Cost of Operations 10	66.5	•	61.4	64.9	70.8	•	72.7	72.0	•	•	•	•	66.3
Salaries and Wages 11	12.9	•	6.1	12.1	11.9	•	11.5	11.5	•	•	•	•	13.0
Taxes Paid 12	2.3	•	2.0	7.6	2.1	•	1.7	1.7	•	•	•	•	2.3
Interest Paid 13	0.8	•	0.2	1.0	0.2	•	0.4	0.3	•	•	•	•	0.8
Depreciation 14	1.8	•	0.5	0.6	0.6	•	0.9	2.0	•	•	•	•	1.9
Amortization and Depletion 15	0.0	•	0.0	•	0.0	•	0.0	0.1	•	•	•	•	0.0
Pensions and Other Deferred Comp. 16	0.2	•	0.0	0.0	0.4	•	0.3	0.1	•	•	•	•	0.2
Employee Benefits 17	1.6	•	1.1	0.3	0.8	•	0.7	1.4	•	•	•	•	1.6
Advertising 18	1.4	•	0.8	0.5	0.7	•	0.8	0.6	•	•	•	•	1.4
Other Expenses 19	6.8	•	18.0	9.8	7.9	•	9.2	7.8	•	•	•	•	6.7
Officers' Compensation 20	0.3	•	8.1	2.9	2.5	•	1.2	1.6	•	•	•	•	0.1
Operating Margin 21	5.4	•	1.9	0.3	2.2	•	0.5	0.9	•	•	•	•	5.6
Operating Margin Before Officers' Comp. 22	5.7	•	10.0	3.1	4.7	•	1.7	2.5	•	•	•	•	5.8

Selected Average Balance Sheet ($ in Thousands)

Net Receivables 23	1697	•	39	116	589	•	3492	8533	•	•	•	•	1407715
Inventories 24	7000	•	58	163	804	•	5021	11058	•	•	•	•	6373884
Net Property, Plant and Equipment 25	13388	•	13	217	204	•	3630	10804	•	•	•	•	12727620
Total Assets 26	47359	•	128	755	2390	•	16406	35454	•	•	•	•	44641206
Notes and Loans Payable 27	16200	•	27	329	254	•	5839	9034	•	•	•	•	15393083
All Other Liabilities 28	18447	•	46	269	462	•	3231	9244	•	•	•	•	17554141
Net Worth 29	12713	•	55	157	1673	•	7337	17177	•	•	•	•	11693982

Selected Financial Ratios (Times to 1)

Current Ratio 30	1.2	•	2.2	1.2	3.7	•	1.7	2.6	•	•	•	•	1.2
Quick Ratio 31	0.1	•	1.1	0.7	2.0	•	0.8	1.1	•	•	•	•	0.1
Net Sales to Working Capital 32	14.9	•	9.7	21.7	4.4	•	8.0	7.6	•	•	•	•	16.5
Coverage Ratio 33	11.2	•	10.5	1.5	14.4	•	5.2	5.9	•	•	•	•	11.4
Total Asset Turnover 34	1.0	•	4.8	2.6	2.7	•	2.2	2.8	•	•	•	•	1.0
Inventory Turnover 35	4.5	•	6.6	7.7	5.7	•	5.2	6.4	•	•	•	•	4.4
Receivables Turnover 36	29.9	•	18.1	17.2	12.1	•	11.3	12.5	•	•	•	•	32.6
Total Liabilities to Net Worth 37	2.7	•	1.3	3.8	0.4	•	1.2	1.1	•	•	•	•	2.8
Current Assets to Working Capital 38	6.6	•	1.8	5.4	1.4	•	2.4	1.6	•	•	•	•	7.4
Current Liabilities to Working Capital 39	5.6	•	0.8	4.4	0.4	•	1.4	0.6	•	•	•	•	6.4
Working Capital to Net Sales 40	0.1	•	0.1	0.0	0.2	•	0.1	0.1	•	•	•	•	0.1
Inventory to Working Capital 41	2.2	•	0.9	2.0	0.6	•	1.3	0.9	•	•	•	•	2.5
Total Receipts to Cash Flow 42	8.3	•	6.4	15.0	12.0	•	12.8	15.6	•	•	•	•	8.1
Cost of Goods to Cash Flow 43	5.5	•	3.9	9.7	8.5	•	9.3	11.2	•	•	•	•	5.4
Cash Flow to Total Debt 44	0.2	•	1.3	0.2	0.7	•	0.3	0.3	•	•	•	•	0.2

Selected Financial Factors (in Percentages)

Debt Ratio 45	73.2	•	57.0	79.2	30.0	•	55.3	51.6	•	•	•	•	73.8
Return on Total Assets 46	8.9	•	10.2	4.0	7.9	•	4.5	4.8	•	•	•	•	8.9
Return on Equity Before Income Taxes 47	30.2	•	21.5	6.5	10.5	•	8.2	8.3	•	•	•	•	31.2
Return on Equity After Income Taxes 48	20.8	•	21.5	6.3	10.2	•	7.1	7.0	•	•	•	•	21.4
Profit Margin (Before Income Tax) 49	8.1	•	1.9	0.5	2.7	•	1.7	1.4	•	•	•	•	8.5
Profit Margin (After Income Tax) 50	5.6	•	1.9	0.5	2.6	•	1.4	1.2	•	•	•	•	5.8

Table II

Corporations with Net Income

HOMES CENTERS; PAINT AND WALLPAPER STORES

MONEY AMOUNTS AND SIZE OF ASSETS IN THOUSANDS OF DOLLARS

Item Description for Accounting Period 7/12 Through 6/13	Total	Zero Assets	Under 500	500 to 1,000	1,000 to 5,000	5,000 to 10,000	10,000 to 25,000	25,000 to 50,000	50,000 to 100,000	100,000 to 250,000	250,000 to 500,000	500,000 to 2,500,000	2,500,000 and over
Number of Enterprises 1	1732	0	862	356	457	•	30	6	•	•	0	0	3

Revenues ($ in Thousands)

Net Sales 2	135417977	0	862401	947461	2885755	•	982492	592559	•	•	0	0	128237943
Interest 3	29601	0	0	729	531	•	835	282	•	•	0	0	26835
Rents 4	410077	0	0	0	0	•	1555	0	•	•	0	0	405219
Royalties 5	262545	0	0	0	0	•	0	0	•	•	0	0	262545
Other Portfolio Income 6	224748	0	0	0	1312	•	240	10	•	•	0	0	222864
Other Receipts 7	2727839	0	281	313	11789	•	7976	3095	•	•	0	0	2699257
Total Receipts 8	139072787	0	862682	948503	2899387	•	993098	595946	•	•	0	0	131854663
Average Total Receipts 9	80296	•	1001	2664	6344	•	33103	99324	•	•	•	•	43951554

Operating Costs/Operating Income (%)

Cost of Operations 10	66.5	•	62.6	64.2	71.3	•	69.1	72.0	•	•	•	•	66.3
Salaries and Wages 11	12.9	•	5.0	11.3	11.1	•	13.0	11.5	•	•	•	•	13.0
Taxes Paid 12	2.3	•	1.5	8.1	2.0	•	1.9	1.7	•	•	•	•	2.3
Interest Paid 13	0.8	•	0.0	0.3	0.2	•	0.4	0.3	•	•	•	•	0.8
Depreciation 14	1.8	•	0.4	0.3	0.5	•	0.9	2.0	•	•	•	•	1.9
Amortization and Depletion 15	0.0	•	•	•	0.0	•	0.0	0.1	•	•	•	•	0.0
Pensions and Other Deferred Comp. 16	0.2	•	•	0.0	0.3	•	0.4	0.1	•	•	•	•	0.2
Employee Benefits 17	1.6	•	1.1	0.2	0.7	•	0.7	1.4	•	•	•	•	1.6
Advertising 18	1.4	•	0.9	0.5	0.6	•	0.9	0.6	•	•	•	•	1.4
Other Expenses 19	6.8	•	17.3	8.5	7.4	•	7.9	7.8	•	•	•	•	6.7
Officers' Compensation 20	0.3	•	8.3	2.8	2.5	•	1.1	1.6	•	•	•	•	0.1
Operating Margin 21	5.5	•	3.0	3.7	3.3	•	3.6	0.9	•	•	•	•	5.6
Operating Margin Before Officers' Comp. 22	5.8	•	11.3	6.4	5.9	•	4.7	2.5	•	•	•	•	5.8

Selected Average Balance Sheet ($ in Thousands)													
Net Receivables 23	2766	•	71	179	586	•	2440	8533	•	•	•	•	1407715
Inventories 24	11470	•	35	158	667	•	5592	11080	•	•	•	•	6373884
Net Property, Plant and Equipment 25	22295	•	21	80	152	•	4200	10804	•	•	•	•	12727620
Total Assets 26	78840	•	173	762	2348	•	16127	35454	•	•	•	•	44641206
Notes and Loans Payable 27	26885	•	6	161	234	•	2591	9034	•	•	•	•	15393083
All Other Liabilities 28	30772	•	67	311	449	•	2528	9244	•	•	•	•	17554141
Net Worth 29	21183	•	100	290	1665	•	11008	17177	•	•	•	•	11693982
Selected Financial Ratios (Times to 1)													
Current Ratio 30	1.2	•	2.2	1.9	3.9	•	2.7	2.6	•	•	•	•	1.2
Quick Ratio 31	0.1	•	1.5	1.2	2.1	•	1.2	1.1	•	•	•	•	0.1
Net Sales to Working Capital 32	14.9	•	12.1	8.8	4.2	•	5.0	7.6	•	•	•	•	16.5
Coverage Ratio 33	11.5	•	323.3	12.7	25.3	•	14.0	5.9	•	•	•	•	11.4
Total Asset Turnover 34	1.0	•	5.8	3.5	2.7	•	2.0	2.8	•	•	•	•	1.0
Inventory Turnover 35	4.5	•	18.1	10.8	6.8	•	4.0	6.4	•	•	•	•	4.4
Receivables Turnover 36	30.8	•	16.6	24.2	13.3	•	•	23.1	•	•	•	•	32.6
Total Liabilities to Net Worth 37	2.7	•	0.7	1.6	0.4	•	0.5	1.1	•	•	•	•	2.8
Current Assets to Working Capital 38	6.6	•	1.9	2.1	1.3	•	1.6	1.6	•	•	•	•	7.4
Current Liabilities to Working Capital 39	5.6	•	0.9	1.1	0.3	•	0.6	0.6	•	•	•	•	6.4
Working Capital to Net Sales 40	0.1	•	0.1	0.1	0.2	•	0.2	0.1	•	•	•	•	0.1
Inventory to Working Capital 41	2.2	•	0.5	0.8	0.6	•	0.9	0.9	•	•	•	•	2.5
Total Receipts to Cash Flow 42	8.2	•	6.0	12.2	11.2	•	10.3	15.6	•	•	•	•	8.1
Cost of Goods to Cash Flow 43	5.5	•	3.8	7.9	8.0	•	7.1	11.2	•	•	•	•	5.4
Cash Flow to Total Debt 44	0.2	•	2.3	0.5	0.8	•	0.6	0.3	•	•	•	•	0.2
Selected Financial Factors (in Percentages)													
Debt Ratio 45	73.1	•	42.3	62.0	29.1	•	31.7	51.6	•	•	•	•	73.8
Return on Total Assets 46	9.0	•	17.3	14.3	10.7	•	10.2	4.8	•	•	•	•	8.9
Return on Equity Before Income Taxes 47	30.5	•	29.9	34.8	14.5	•	13.9	8.3	•	•	•	•	31.2
Return on Equity After Income Taxes 48	21.1	•	29.9	34.6	14.0	•	12.9	7.0	•	•	•	•	21.4
Profit Margin (Before Income Tax) 49	8.3	•	3.0	3.8	3.8	•	4.7	1.4	•	•	•	•	8.5
Profit Margin (After Income Tax) 50	5.7	•	3.0	3.8	3.7	•	4.3	1.2	•	•	•	•	5.8

Table I

Corporations with and without Net Income

HARDWARE STORES

MONEY AMOUNTS AND SIZE OF ASSETS IN THOUSANDS OF DOLLARS

Item Description for Accounting Period 7/12 Through 6/13	Total	Zero Assets	Under 500	500 to 1,000	1,000 to 5,000	5,000 to 10,000	10,000 to 25,000	25,000 to 50,000	50,000 to 100,000	100,000 to 250,000	250,000 to 500,000	500,000 to 2,500,000	2,500,000 and over
Number of Enterprises 1	7933	519	2243	2981	2069	•	41	14	•	•	0	•	0

Revenues ($ in Thousands)

Net Sales 2	20559271	402382	1472062	5199358	8282619	•	938741	1196943	•	•	0	•	0
Interest 3	11473	5	4384	196	5899	•	17	121	•	•	0	•	0
Rents 4	12283	568	591	528	9172	•	61	1328	•	•	0	•	0
Royalties 5	22	0	0	22	0	•	0	0	•	•	0	•	0
Other Portfolio Income 6	14651	0	1682	1101	7746	•	2219	116	•	•	0	•	0
Other Receipts 7	185166	12248	22569	78311	53972	•	8659	4220	•	•	0	•	0
Total Receipts 8	20782866	415203	1501288	5279516	8359408	•	949697	1202728	•	•	0	•	0
Average Total Receipts 9	2620	800	669	1771	4040	•	23163	85909	•	•	•	•	•

Operating Costs/Operating Income (%)

Cost of Operations 10	64.3	70.8	63.4	63.6	64.0	•	65.7	64.8	•	•	•	•	•
Salaries and Wages 11	12.3	11.1	10.4	11.9	13.0	•	12.8	14.9	•	•	•	•	•
Taxes Paid 12	2.3	1.9	2.6	2.3	2.5	•	2.4	2.7	•	•	•	•	•
Interest Paid 13	0.9	1.1	0.7	0.7	0.7	•	0.5	0.6	•	•	•	•	•
Depreciation 14	1.1	0.8	1.2	0.8	1.3	•	1.2	1.1	•	•	•	•	•
Amortization and Depletion 15	0.0	0.4	0.0	0.0	0.0	•	0.0	0.3	•	•	•	•	•
Pensions and Other Deferred Comp. 16	0.2	0.0	0.1	0.2	0.2	•	0.4	0.3	•	•	•	•	•
Employee Benefits 17	0.9	1.6	1.3	0.6	0.9	•	0.7	1.5	•	•	•	•	•
Advertising 18	1.9	1.3	0.7	2.1	1.5	•	1.6	1.1	•	•	•	•	•
Other Expenses 19	10.6	13.6	13.1	13.3	11.6	•	8.9	10.1	•	•	•	•	•
Officers' Compensation 20	3.3	2.0	7.5	4.3	3.0	•	1.7	1.3	•	•	•	•	•
Operating Margin 21	2.1	•	•	0.2	1.3	•	3.9	1.2	•	•	•	•	•
Operating Margin Before Officers' Comp. 22	5.4	•	6.5	4.4	4.3	•	5.6	2.5	•	•	•	•	•

	Selected Average Balance Sheet ($ in Thousands)												
Net Receivables 23	100	0	45	47	195	•	1150	3561	•	•	•	•	•
Inventories 24	544	0	140	386	822	•	5573	15001	•	•	•	•	•
Net Property, Plant and Equipment 25	185	0	25	60	269	•	4139	9555	•	•	•	•	•
Total Assets 26	1110	0	275	709	1820	•	13418	32372	•	•	•	•	•
Notes and Loans Payable 27	505	0	168	371	566	•	2684	10285	•	•	•	•	•
All Other Liabilities 28	203	0	42	144	272	•	2015	8729	•	•	•	•	•
Net Worth 29	402	0	65	194	981	•	8719	13359	•	•	•	•	•

	Selected Financial Ratios (Times to 1)												
Current Ratio 30	3.2	•	4.3	3.0	3.9	•	2.9	1.8	•	•	•	•	•
Quick Ratio 31	0.8	•	1.3	0.5	1.3	•	0.7	0.4	•	•	•	•	•
Net Sales to Working Capital 32	4.7	•	4.4	4.9	3.9	•	4.4	10.1	•	•	•	•	•
Coverage Ratio 33	4.6	•	2.4	3.4	4.3	•	10.7	3.6	•	•	•	•	•
Total Asset Turnover 34	2.3	•	2.4	2.5	2.2	•	1.7	2.6	•	•	•	•	•
Inventory Turnover 35	3.1	•	3.0	2.9	3.1	•	2.7	3.7	•	•	•	•	•
Receivables Turnover 36	28.0	•	18.9	38.4	22.6	•	•	28.3	•	•	•	•	•
Total Liabilities to Net Worth 37	1.8	•	3.2	2.7	0.9	•	0.5	1.4	•	•	•	•	•
Current Assets to Working Capital 38	1.5	•	1.3	1.5	1.3	•	1.5	2.3	•	•	•	•	•
Current Liabilities to Working Capital 39	0.5	•	0.3	0.5	0.3	•	0.5	1.3	•	•	•	•	•
Working Capital to Net Sales 40	0.2	•	0.2	0.2	0.3	•	0.2	0.1	•	•	•	•	•
Inventory to Working Capital 41	1.0	•	0.9	1.2	0.9	•	1.1	1.7	•	•	•	•	•
Total Receipts to Cash Flow 42	11.2	14.2	10.6	11.4	11.3	•	8.2	13.3	•	•	•	•	•
Cost of Goods to Cash Flow 43	7.2	10.1	6.7	7.3	7.2	•	5.4	8.6	•	•	•	•	•
Cash Flow to Total Debt 44	0.3	•	0.3	0.3	0.4	•	0.6	0.3	•	•	•	•	•

	Selected Financial Factors (in Percentages)												
Debt Ratio 45	63.8	•	76.3	72.7	46.1	•	35.0	58.7	•	•	•	•	•
Return on Total Assets 46	9.5	•	4.1	6.0	6.3	•	9.5	6.2	•	•	•	•	•
Return on Equity Before Income Taxes 47	20.5	•	9.9	15.4	9.0	•	13.3	10.8	•	•	•	•	•
Return on Equity After Income Taxes 48	19.5	•	7.9	15.2	8.5	•	12.3	9.5	•	•	•	•	•
Profit Margin (Before Income Tax) 49	3.2	•	1.0	1.7	2.2	•	5.1	1.7	•	•	•	•	•
Profit Margin (After Income Tax) 50	3.0	•	0.8	1.7	2.1	•	4.7	1.5	•	•	•	•	•

Table II

Corporations with Net Income

HARDWARE STORES

MONEY AMOUNTS AND SIZE OF ASSETS IN THOUSANDS OF DOLLARS

Item Description for Accounting Period 7/12 Through 6/13	Total	Zero Assets	Under 500	500 to 1,000	1,000 to 5,000	5,000 to 10,000	10,000 to 25,000	25,000 to 50,000	50,000 to 100,000	100,000 to 250,000	250,000 to 500,000	500,000 to 2,500,000	2,500,000 and over
Number of Enterprises 1	5705	107	1545	2303	1649	•	33	9	•	•	0	0	0
Revenues ($ in Thousands)													
Net Sales 2	16813821	29875	951802	4439079	6706967	•	760909	915736	•	•	0	0	0
Interest 3	6098	1	575	193	4536	•	15	22	•	•	0	0	0
Rents 4	6207	0	0	259	4913	•	61	974	•	•	0	0	0
Royalties 5	22	0	0	22	0	•	0	0	•	•	0	0	0
Other Portfolio Income 6	10435	0	36	239	6386	•	2174	99	•	•	0	0	0
Other Receipts 7	147686	0	18990	72218	40015	•	7664	3822	•	•	0	0	0
Total Receipts 8	16984269	29876	971403	4512010	6762817	•	770823	920653	•	•	0	0	0
Average Total Receipts 9	2977	279	629	1959	4101	•	23358	102295	•	•	•	•	•
Operating Costs/Operating Income (%)													
Cost of Operations 10	63.1	67.5	61.0	63.0	62.1	•	62.7	66.5	•	•	•	•	•
Salaries and Wages 11	12.7	8.6	10.4	12.3	13.7	•	13.4	14.5	•	•	•	•	•
Taxes Paid 12	2.2	1.2	2.1	2.2	2.5	•	2.6	2.5	•	•	•	•	•
Interest Paid 13	0.8	0.0	0.5	0.6	0.6	•	0.6	0.4	•	•	•	•	•
Depreciation 14	1.0	0.2	1.7	0.4	1.2	•	1.4	0.6	•	•	•	•	•
Amortization and Depletion 15	0.0	0.0	0.0	0.0	0.0	•	0.0	0.0	•	•	•	•	•
Pensions and Other Deferred Comp. 16	0.2	0.0	0.1	0.2	0.2	•	0.5	0.2	•	•	•	•	•
Employee Benefits 17	0.9	0.1	1.0	0.7	0.9	•	0.8	1.4	•	•	•	•	•
Advertising 18	2.0	0.7	0.6	1.7	1.7	•	1.8	0.9	•	•	•	•	•
Other Expenses 19	10.4	4.2	14.1	13.3	11.9	•	9.2	9.7	•	•	•	•	•
Officers' Compensation 20	3.0	7.4	6.7	3.4	2.9	•	1.8	1.4	•	•	•	•	•
Operating Margin 21	3.7	10.0	1.9	2.2	2.1	•	5.2	1.9	•	•	•	•	•
Operating Margin Before Officers' Comp. 22	6.6	17.4	8.6	5.7	5.1	•	7.0	3.2	•	•	•	•	•

Selected Average Balance Sheet ($ in Thousands)

	C1	C2	C3	C4	C5	C6	C7	C8	C9	C10	C11	C12	C13
Net Receivables 23	98	0	38	50	164	•	813	4150	•	•	•	•	•
Inventories 24	587	0	126	317	848	•	4155	18006	•	•	•	•	•
Net Property, Plant and Equipment 25	203	0	16	39	285	•	4435	7193	•	•	•	•	•
Total Assets 26	1239	0	246	708	1883	•	12812	28894	•	•	•	•	•
Notes and Loans Payable 27	532	0	143	281	569	•	2997	7929	•	•	•	•	•
All Other Liabilities 28	212	0	32	119	275	•	1414	7802	•	•	•	•	•
Net Worth 29	495	0	71	308	1039	•	8400	13163	•	•	•	•	•

Selected Financial Ratios (Times to 1)

	C1	C2	C3	C4	C5	C6	C7	C8	C9	C10	C11	C12	C13
Current Ratio 30	3.6	•	5.1	4.0	4.1	•	3.3	1.8	•	•	•	•	•
Quick Ratio 31	0.9	•	1.4	0.8	1.3	•	0.9	0.5	•	•	•	•	•
Net Sales to Working Capital 32	4.5	•	4.3	4.5	3.9	•	4.7	11.4	•	•	•	•	•
Coverage Ratio 33	6.6	299.8	8.4	7.4	5.7	•	11.7	7.2	•	•	•	•	•
Total Asset Turnover 34	2.4	•	2.5	2.7	2.2	•	1.8	3.5	•	•	•	•	•
Inventory Turnover 35	3.2	•	3.0	3.8	3.0	•	3.5	3.8	•	•	•	•	•
Receivables Turnover 36	31.7	•	21.8	47.5	25.0	•	20.8	29.1	•	•	•	•	•
Total Liabilities to Net Worth 37	1.5	•	2.5	1.3	0.8	•	0.5	1.2	•	•	•	•	•
Current Assets to Working Capital 38	1.4	•	1.2	1.3	1.3	•	1.4	2.2	•	•	•	•	•
Current Liabilities to Working Capital 39	0.4	•	0.2	0.3	0.3	•	0.4	1.2	•	•	•	•	•
Working Capital to Net Sales 40	0.2	•	0.2	0.2	0.3	•	0.2	0.1	•	•	•	•	•
Inventory to Working Capital 41	1.0	•	0.9	1.0	0.9	•	1.0	1.6	•	•	•	•	•
Total Receipts to Cash Flow 42	9.9	7.4	8.2	9.2	10.2	•	7.3	12.8	•	•	•	•	•
Cost of Goods to Cash Flow 43	6.2	5.0	5.0	5.8	6.3	•	4.6	8.5	•	•	•	•	•
Cash Flow to Total Debt 44	0.4	•	0.4	0.5	0.5	•	0.7	0.5	•	•	•	•	•

Selected Financial Factors (in Percentages)

	C1	C2	C3	C4	C5	C6	C7	C8	C9	C10	C11	C12	C13
Debt Ratio 45	60.0	•	71.1	56.5	44.8	•	34.4	54.4	•	•	•	•	•
Return on Total Assets 46	13.1	•	11.2	12.2	7.8	•	12.7	9.8	•	•	•	•	•
Return on Equity Before Income Taxes 47	27.9	•	34.1	24.2	11.6	•	17.7	18.5	•	•	•	•	•
Return on Equity After Income Taxes 48	26.8	•	31.3	24.0	11.0	•	16.5	16.4	•	•	•	•	•
Profit Margin (Before Income Tax) 49	4.7	10.0	3.9	3.9	3.0	•	6.5	2.4	•	•	•	•	•
Profit Margin (After Income Tax) 50	4.5	10.0	3.6	3.8	2.8	•	6.0	2.1	•	•	•	•	•

Table I

Corporations with and without Net Income

OTHER BUILDING MATERIAL DEALERS

MONEY AMOUNTS AND SIZE OF ASSETS IN THOUSANDS OF DOLLARS

Item Description for Accounting Period 7/12 Through 6/13		Total	Zero Assets	Under 500	500 to 1,000	1,000 to 5,000	5,000 to 10,000	10,000 to 25,000	25,000 to 50,000	50,000 to 100,000	100,000 to 250,000	250,000 to 500,000	500,000 to 2,500,000	2,500,000 and over
Number of Enterprises	1	17897	•	11536	1761	2720	471	160	32	17	•	5	•	0
Revenues ($ in Thousands)														
Net Sales	2	49933455	•	6917584	3789239	14636458	7919593	4707698	2318733	2299377	•	2749911	•	0
Interest	3	386157	•	848	5250	8937	2038	2403	859	2297	•	1520	•	0
Rents	4	21738	•	0	505	3950	868	3135	799	129	•	2407	•	0
Royalties	5	617	•	0	0	0	0	0	87	0	•	0	•	0
Other Portfolio Income	6	126309	•	21694	9469	4163	37500	6859	783	3680	•	5241	•	0
Other Receipts	7	521237	•	28981	19015	62798	18642	42386	20350	24832	•	4262	•	0
Total Receipts	8	50989513	•	6969107	3823478	14716306	7978641	4762481	2341611	2330315	•	2763341	•	0
Average Total Receipts	9	2849	•	604	2171	5410	16940	29766	73175	137077	•	552668	•	•
Operating Costs/Operating Income (%)														
Cost of Operations	10	71.7	•	59.7	69.8	71.9	76.6	74.8	74.6	75.3	•	74.6	•	•
Salaries and Wages	11	9.4	•	9.6	7.2	8.6	9.8	10.4	10.4	11.1	•	8.6	•	•
Taxes Paid	12	1.8	•	1.9	2.6	1.8	1.7	1.9	1.6	1.6	•	0.9	•	•
Interest Paid	13	2.6	•	0.9	0.3	0.5	0.5	0.5	0.5	0.6	•	0.6	•	•
Depreciation	14	0.9	•	1.4	0.6	0.5	0.4	0.9	0.8	1.3	•	1.5	•	•
Amortization and Depletion	15	0.2	•	0.0	0.0	0.0	0.0	0.1	0.1	0.2	•	0.3	•	•
Pensions and Other Deferred Comp.	16	0.2	•	0.0	0.5	0.2	0.2	0.6	0.3	0.6	•	0.2	•	•
Employee Benefits	17	0.9	•	1.1	1.2	0.8	0.5	0.9	1.3	1.3	•	1.0	•	•
Advertising	18	0.8	•	1.2	2.1	0.5	0.4	0.6	0.5	0.5	•	2.2	•	•
Other Expenses	19	11.3	•	19.1	9.0	9.3	8.0	8.5	7.0	5.4	•	5.9	•	•
Officers' Compensation	20	2.4	•	4.7	4.4	2.9	1.3	1.1	0.9	0.7	•	1.2	•	•
Operating Margin	21	•	•	0.5	2.3	3.0	0.6	•	1.9	1.5	•	3.0	•	•
Operating Margin Before Officers' Comp.	22	0.0	•	5.2	6.7	5.9	1.9	0.7	2.8	2.2	•	4.2	•	•

Selected Average Balance Sheet ($ in Thousands)

Net Receivables 23	305	•	27	146	446	1626	3307	10335	14565	•	55103	•	•
Inventories 24	398	•	53	297	870	2331	4205	10228	19385	•	84666	•	•
Net Property, Plant and Equipment 25	239	•	29	107	244	873	2808	7506	19951	•	59048	•	•
Total Assets 26	1717	•	153	769	2106	6940	14530	36917	73487	•	346960	•	•
Notes and Loans Payable 27	852	•	111	204	598	2126	4862	9780	18814	•	62656	•	•
All Other Liabilities 28	463	•	60	101	509	1295	3916	5685	14238	•	137709	•	•
Net Worth 29	403	•	-19	464	1000	3520	5751	21452	40435	•	146595	•	•

Selected Financial Ratios (Times to 1)

Current Ratio 30	2.0	•	1.3	5.4	2.7	2.5	2.0	2.5	2.4	•	2.8	•	•
Quick Ratio 31	0.9	•	0.5	3.0	1.2	1.3	0.9	1.2	1.1	•	1.6	•	•
Net Sales to Working Capital 32	5.5	•	22.7	4.2	5.0	4.8	5.6	4.9	5.9	•	3.9	•	•
Coverage Ratio 33	0.9	•	2.4	11.3	8.3	3.6	2.5	6.3	5.8	•	6.7	•	•
Total Asset Turnover 34	1.6	•	3.9	2.8	2.6	2.4	2.0	2.0	1.8	•	1.6	•	•
Inventory Turnover 35	5.0	•	6.8	5.1	4.4	5.5	5.2	5.3	5.3	•	4.8	•	•
Receivables Turnover 36	9.8	•	26.1	12.4	12.3	11.4	9.7	6.6	•	•	•	•	•
Total Liabilities to Net Worth 37	3.3	•	•	0.7	1.1	1.0	1.5	0.7	0.8	•	1.4	•	•
Current Assets to Working Capital 38	2.0	•	4.3	1.2	1.6	1.7	2.0	1.7	1.7	•	1.5	•	•
Current Liabilities to Working Capital 39	1.0	•	3.3	0.2	0.6	0.7	1.0	0.7	0.7	•	0.5	•	•
Working Capital to Net Sales 40	0.2	•	0.0	0.2	0.2	0.2	0.2	0.2	0.2	•	0.3	•	•
Inventory to Working Capital 41	0.8	•	2.1	0.5	0.8	0.7	0.9	0.7	0.9	•	0.6	•	•
Total Receipts to Cash Flow 42	12.5	•	6.5	10.7	9.8	14.9	16.1	12.8	16.6	•	13.3	•	•
Cost of Goods to Cash Flow 43	9.0	•	3.9	7.5	7.1	11.4	12.0	9.5	12.5	•	9.9	•	•
Cash Flow to Total Debt 44	0.2	•	0.5	0.7	0.5	0.3	0.2	0.4	0.2	•	0.2	•	•

Selected Financial Factors (in Percentages)

Debt Ratio 45	76.6	•	112.1	39.7	52.5	49.3	60.4	41.9	45.0	•	57.7	•	•
Return on Total Assets 46	4.0	•	8.4	9.8	10.3	4.4	2.6	6.7	6.3	•	6.5	•	•
Return on Equity Before Income Taxes 47	•	•	•	14.8	19.1	6.2	3.9	9.7	9.5	•	13.1	•	•
Return on Equity After Income Taxes 48	•	•	•	14.3	18.7	6.1	3.0	9.5	8.9	•	10.1	•	•
Profit Margin (Before Income Tax) 49	•	•	1.2	3.2	3.5	1.3	0.8	2.9	2.8	•	3.5	•	•
Profit Margin (After Income Tax) 50	•	•	1.1	3.1	3.5	1.3	0.6	2.8	2.6	•	2.7	•	•

215

Table II

Corporations with Net Income

OTHER BUILDING MATERIAL DEALERS

MONEY AMOUNTS AND SIZE OF ASSETS IN THOUSANDS OF DOLLARS

Item Description for Accounting Period 7/12 Through 6/13	Total	Zero Assets	Under 500	500 to 1,000	1,000 to 5,000	5,000 to 10,000	10,000 to 25,000	25,000 to 50,000	50,000 to 100,000	100,000 to 250,000	250,000 to 500,000	500,000 to 2,500,000	2,500,000 and over
Number of Enterprises 1	10580	512	6172	1275	2183	269	121	23	•	•	5	0	0

Revenues ($ in Thousands)

Net Sales 2	35616747	57460	3293741	3308788	12249987	5507229	3667704	1901376	•	•	2353338	0	0
Interest 3	20363	0	6	4472	7323	1499	1326	318	•	•	2966	0	0
Rents 4	6774	0	0	331	3754	848	766	62	•	•	885	0	0
Royalties 5	617	0	0	0	0	0	0	87	•	•	530	0	0
Other Portfolio Income 6	76985	0	21099	4109	3679	33476	6596	708	•	•	3534	0	0
Other Receipts 7	221829	20951	6550	16856	45469	14618	33185	19544	•	•	35155	0	0
Total Receipts 8	35943315	78411	3321396	3334556	12310212	5557670	3709577	1922095	•	•	2396408	0	0
Average Total Receipts 9	3397	153	538	2615	5639	20660	30658	83569	•	•	479282	•	•

Operating Costs/Operating Income (%)

Cost of Operations 10	71.6	53.3	55.5	70.7	70.7	76.3	76.9	74.4	•	•	73.4	•	•
Salaries and Wages 11	8.5	•	5.7	6.4	8.4	9.4	9.6	10.1	•	•	8.1	•	•
Taxes Paid 12	1.7	•	1.2	2.5	1.8	1.4	1.7	1.5	•	•	1.3	•	•
Interest Paid 13	0.5	0.0	0.8	0.2	0.5	0.6	0.4	0.3	•	•	0.8	•	•
Depreciation 14	0.8	1.3	1.3	0.5	0.5	0.5	0.8	0.7	•	•	1.6	•	•
Amortization and Depletion 15	0.1	•	•	0.0	0.0	0.0	0.0	0.1	•	•	0.2	•	•
Pensions and Other Deferred Comp. 16	0.2	•	0.0	0.5	0.2	0.1	0.2	0.3	•	•	0.2	•	•
Employee Benefits 17	0.8	•	0.7	1.1	0.9	0.5	0.9	1.0	•	•	1.1	•	•
Advertising 18	0.8	4.2	1.3	2.2	0.4	0.3	0.3	0.6	•	•	2.5	•	•
Other Expenses 19	9.3	34.5	21.8	8.7	9.4	7.8	6.5	7.0	•	•	6.1	•	•
Officers' Compensation 20	2.3	•	4.1	3.7	3.0	1.3	1.2	0.8	•	•	1.2	•	•
Operating Margin 21	3.5	6.6	7.6	3.5	4.1	1.8	1.6	3.2	•	•	3.5	•	•
Operating Margin Before Officers' Comp. 22	5.7	6.6	11.7	7.1	7.1	3.0	2.7	4.0	•	•	4.7	•	•

Selected Average Balance Sheet ($ in Thousands)

Net Receivables 23	330	0	16	176	424	1904	3535	11428	•	•	116425	•	•
Inventories 24	491	0	47	284	880	2827	3883	10362	•	•	144550	•	•
Net Property, Plant and Equipment 25	260	0	33	100	247	655	2403	5345	•	•	151586	•	•
Total Assets 26	1613	0	148	750	2108	7301	14209	36703	•	•	834769	•	•
Notes and Loans Payable 27	500	0	71	195	638	2966	3200	7172	•	•	270971	•	•
All Other Liabilities 28	390	0	33	120	478	1438	3058	6040	•	•	297854	•	•
Net Worth 29	723	0	44	435	993	2897	7951	23492	•	•	265944	•	•

Selected Financial Ratios (Times to 1)

Current Ratio 30	2.4	•	1.7	4.7	2.8	2.4	2.3	3.3	•	•	1.9	•	•
Quick Ratio 31	1.1	•	0.7	2.3	1.2	1.2	1.1	1.5	•	•	0.8	•	•
Net Sales to Working Capital 32	5.1	•	12.9	5.3	5.1	5.5	5.0	4.3	•	•	2.4	•	•
Coverage Ratio 33	9.7	1906.2	11.4	20.0	10.9	5.3	8.5	13.7	•	•	7.9	•	•
Total Asset Turnover 34	2.1	•	3.6	3.5	2.7	2.8	2.1	2.3	•	•	0.6	•	•
Inventory Turnover 35	4.9	•	6.3	6.5	4.5	5.5	6.0	5.9	•	•	2.4	•	•
Receivables Turnover 36	11.4	•	36.0	14.6	14.0	11.6	10.7	8.9	•	•	•	•	•
Total Liabilities to Net Worth 37	1.2	•	2.4	0.7	1.1	1.5	0.8	0.6	•	•	2.1	•	•
Current Assets to Working Capital 38	1.7	•	2.4	1.3	1.6	1.7	1.7	1.4	•	•	2.2	•	•
Current Liabilities to Working Capital 39	0.7	•	1.4	0.3	0.6	0.7	0.7	0.4	•	•	1.2	•	•
Working Capital to Net Sales 40	0.2	•	0.1	0.2	0.2	0.2	0.2	0.2	•	•	0.4	•	•
Inventory to Working Capital 41	0.8	•	1.2	0.6	0.8	0.8	0.8	0.6	•	•	0.7	•	•
Total Receipts to Cash Flow 42	9.0	1.3	3.9	10.0	8.8	12.9	14.7	10.8	•	•	10.1	•	•
Cost of Goods to Cash Flow 43	6.5	0.7	2.2	7.1	6.2	9.9	11.3	8.0	•	•	7.4	•	•
Cash Flow to Total Debt 44	0.4	•	1.3	0.8	0.6	0.4	0.3	0.6	•	•	0.1	•	•

Selected Financial Factors (in Percentages)

Debt Ratio 45	55.2	•	70.3	42.0	52.9	60.3	44.0	36.0	•	•	68.1	•	•
Return on Total Assets 46	10.2	•	33.3	15.5	13.5	9.2	6.6	10.3	•	•	3.5	•	•
Return on Equity Before Income Taxes 47	20.4	•	102.4	25.5	26.0	18.9	10.3	14.9	•	•	9.5	•	•
Return on Equity After Income Taxes 48	19.6	•	99.8	24.8	25.6	18.6	9.5	14.7	•	•	7.7	•	•
Profit Margin (Before Income Tax) 49	4.4	43.1	8.4	4.3	4.6	2.7	2.7	4.2	•	•	5.4	•	•
Profit Margin (After Income Tax) 50	4.2	43.1	8.2	4.2	4.5	2.6	2.5	4.2	•	•	4.4	•	•

Table I

Corporations with and without Net Income

LAWN AND GARDEN EQUIPMENT AND SUPPLIES STORES

MONEY AMOUNTS AND SIZE OF ASSETS IN THOUSANDS OF DOLLARS

Item Description for Accounting Period 7/12 Through 6/13	Total	Zero Assets	Under 500	500 to 1,000	1,000 to 5,000	5,000 to 10,000	10,000 to 25,000	25,000 to 50,000	50,000 to 100,000	100,000 to 250,000	250,000 to 500,000	500,000 to 2,500,000	2,500,000 and over
Number of Enterprises 1	7770	1079	4124	1410	1013	•	39	22	•	0	0	0	0

Revenues ($ in Thousands)

Net Sales 2	16572080	339683	2396232	2981715	5146656	•	1249152	2620593	•	0	0	0	0
Interest 3	12294	0	230	307	9593	•	336	334	•	0	0	0	0
Rents 4	3497	0	0	1090	2219	•	0	26	•	0	0	0	0
Royalties 5	0	0	0	0	0	•	0	0	•	0	0	0	0
Other Portfolio Income 6	24689	212	0	210	7335	•	778	169	•	0	0	0	0
Other Receipts 7	80297	2438	4011	2542	31781	•	21225	5708	•	0	0	0	0
Total Receipts 8	16692857	342333	2400473	2985864	5197584	•	1271491	2626830	•	0	0	0	0
Average Total Receipts 9	2148	317	582	2118	5131	•	32602	119401	•	•	•	•	•

Operating Costs/Operating Income (%)

Cost of Operations 10	71.1	93.4	60.2	62.7	73.7	•	70.4	74.9	•	•	•	•	•
Salaries and Wages 11	9.2	0.7	9.6	14.5	7.6	•	7.5	10.0	•	•	•	•	•
Taxes Paid 12	2.1	1.0	2.6	3.7	1.8	•	2.6	1.5	•	•	•	•	•
Interest Paid 13	0.6	•	0.8	0.7	0.6	•	0.4	0.7	•	•	•	•	•
Depreciation 14	1.1	1.3	1.4	0.8	1.6	•	0.8	0.7	•	•	•	•	•
Amortization and Depletion 15	0.0	•	0.0	0.0	0.0	•	0.0	0.1	•	•	•	•	•
Pensions and Other Deferred Comp. 16	0.1	•	•	0.1	0.2	•	0.4	0.1	•	•	•	•	•
Employee Benefits 17	0.8	0.0	1.1	0.9	0.8	•	0.7	0.7	•	•	•	•	•
Advertising 18	1.0	1.6	1.5	0.9	0.9	•	1.3	0.7	•	•	•	•	•
Other Expenses 19	9.8	5.0	16.5	9.8	9.1	•	12.4	6.9	•	•	•	•	•
Officers' Compensation 20	2.5	4.3	4.4	3.3	2.9	•	0.8	1.0	•	•	•	•	•
Operating Margin 21	1.6	•	2.0	2.5	1.0	•	2.6	2.8	•	•	•	•	•
Operating Margin Before Officers' Comp. 22	4.2	•	6.4	5.8	3.8	•	3.4	3.8	•	•	•	•	•

Selected Average Balance Sheet ($ in Thousands)

Net Receivables 23	83	0	9	36	224	•	1004	6971	•	•	•	•	•
Inventories 24	366	0	102	360	949	•	7745	15278	•	•	•	•	•
Net Property, Plant and Equipment 25	176	0	72	143	635	•	1982	4305	•	•	•	•	•
Total Assets 26	845	0	206	761	2217	•	13812	39376	•	•	•	•	•
Notes and Loans Payable 27	373	0	102	332	814	•	4243	15753	•	•	•	•	•
All Other Liabilities 28	238	0	99	164	507	•	4392	11463	•	•	•	•	•
Net Worth 29	234	0	5	265	897	•	5177	12160	•	•	•	•	•

Selected Financial Ratios (Times to 1)

Current Ratio 30	1.6	•	1.2	3.1	1.9	•	1.8	1.9	•	•	•	•	•
Quick Ratio 31	0.5	•	0.3	1.2	0.7	•	0.3	0.6	•	•	•	•	•
Net Sales to Working Capital 32	9.5	•	33.7	5.3	7.5	•	7.2	7.8	•	•	•	•	•
Coverage Ratio 33	4.7	•	3.7	4.6	4.4	•	10.8	5.3	•	•	•	•	•
Total Asset Turnover 34	2.5	•	2.8	2.8	2.3	•	2.3	3.0	•	•	•	•	•
Inventory Turnover 35	4.1	•	3.4	3.7	3.9	•	2.9	5.8	•	•	•	•	•
Receivables Turnover 36	27.6	•	54.8	31.3	23.5	•	•	24.9	•	•	•	•	•
Total Liabilities to Net Worth 37	2.6	•	39.4	1.9	1.5	•	1.7	2.2	•	•	•	•	•
Current Assets to Working Capital 38	2.6	•	7.3	1.5	2.2	•	2.2	2.1	•	•	•	•	•
Current Liabilities to Working Capital 39	1.6	•	6.3	0.5	1.2	•	1.2	1.1	•	•	•	•	•
Working Capital to Net Sales 40	0.1	•	0.0	0.2	0.1	•	0.1	0.1	•	•	•	•	•
Inventory to Working Capital 41	1.7	•	5.6	0.9	1.2	•	1.7	1.4	•	•	•	•	•
Total Receipts to Cash Flow 42	10.9	•	6.8	10.8	11.9	•	7.1	15.3	•	•	•	•	•
Cost of Goods to Cash Flow 43	7.7	•	4.1	6.8	8.7	•	5.0	11.5	•	•	•	•	•
Cash Flow to Total Debt 44	0.3	•	0.4	0.4	0.3	•	0.5	0.3	•	•	•	•	•

Selected Financial Factors (in Percentages)

Debt Ratio 45	72.3	•	97.5	65.2	59.6	•	62.5	69.1	•	•	•	•	•
Return on Total Assets 46	7.5	•	8.3	9.2	5.8	•	11.2	11.2	•	•	•	•	•
Return on Equity Before Income Taxes 47	21.3	•	243.5	20.7	11.1	•	27.2	29.4	•	•	•	•	•
Return on Equity After Income Taxes 48	19.9	•	243.3	20.2	9.5	•	27.1	28.8	•	•	•	•	•
Profit Margin (Before Income Tax) 49	2.3	•	2.1	2.6	2.0	•	4.4	3.0	•	•	•	•	•
Profit Margin (After Income Tax) 50	2.2	•	2.1	2.5	1.7	•	4.4	2.9	•	•	•	•	•

217

Table II

Corporations with Net Income

LAWN AND GARDEN EQUIPMENT AND SUPPLIES STORES

MONEY AMOUNTS AND SIZE OF ASSETS IN THOUSANDS OF DOLLARS

Item Description for Accounting Period 7/12 Through 6/13	Total	Zero Assets	Under 500	500 to 1,000	1,000 to 5,000	5,000 to 10,000	10,000 to 25,000	25,000 to 50,000	50,000 to 100,000	100,000 to 250,000	250,000 to 500,000	500,000 to 2,500,000	2,500,000 and over
Number of Enterprises 1	4657	410	2296	889	924	•	39	17	•	0	0	0	0
Revenues ($ in Thousands)													
Net Sales 2	13535695	0	1504197	2297740	4837851	•	1249152	1808706	•	0	0	0	0
Interest 3	11340	0	230	296	8652	•	336	334	•	0	0	0	0
Rents 4	3497	0	0	1090	2219	•	0	26	•	0	0	0	0
Royalties 5	0	0	0	0	0	•	0	0	•	0	0	0	0
Other Portfolio Income 6	24180	0	0	3	7335	•	778	80	•	0	0	0	0
Other Receipts 7	74039	2434	1571	2167	31730	•	21225	2333	•	0	0	0	0
Total Receipts 8	13648751	2434	1505998	2301296	4887787	•	1271491	1811479	•	0	0	0	0
Average Total Receipts 9	2931	6	656	2589	5290	•	32602	106558	•	•	•	•	•
Operating Costs/Operating Income (%)													
Cost of Operations 10	71.1	•	62.9	61.7	74.0	•	70.4	70.7	•	•	•	•	•
Salaries and Wages 11	9.2	•	9.0	15.3	7.8	•	7.5	9.6	•	•	•	•	•
Taxes Paid 12	2.1	•	2.3	3.5	1.7	•	2.6	1.6	•	•	•	•	•
Interest Paid 13	0.6	•	0.8	0.4	0.5	•	0.4	0.7	•	•	•	•	•
Depreciation 14	1.0	•	0.9	0.7	1.5	•	0.8	0.8	•	•	•	•	•
Amortization and Depletion 15	0.0	•	0.0	•	0.0	•	0.0	0.1	•	•	•	•	•
Pensions and Other Deferred Comp. 16	0.1	•	•	0.1	0.1	•	0.4	0.1	•	•	•	•	•
Employee Benefits 17	0.7	•	1.3	0.8	0.7	•	0.7	0.6	•	•	•	•	•
Advertising 18	1.0	•	1.5	0.6	0.9	•	1.3	1.0	•	•	•	•	•
Other Expenses 19	9.3	•	12.6	9.1	8.9	•	12.4	9.1	•	•	•	•	•
Officers' Compensation 20	2.2	•	3.8	2.6	2.6	•	0.8	1.1	•	•	•	•	•
Operating Margin 21	2.8	•	4.8	5.0	1.3	•	2.6	4.5	•	•	•	•	•
Operating Margin Before Officers' Comp. 22	5.0	•	8.7	7.7	3.9	•	3.4	5.6	•	•	•	•	•

Selected Average Balance Sheet ($ in Thousands)

Net Receivables 23	114	0	13	52	238	•	1004	4650	•	•	•	•	•
Inventories 24	425	0	101	312	677	•	7745	16886	•	•	•	•	•
Net Property, Plant and Equipment 25	200	0	42	80	600	•	1982	4742	•	•	•	•	•
Total Assets 26	1106	0	205	808	2190	•	13812	39121	•	•	•	•	•
Notes and Loans Payable 27	408	0	84	226	779	•	4243	14615	•	•	•	•	•
All Other Liabilities 28	271	0	74	182	477	•	4392	8281	•	•	•	•	•
Net Worth 29	427	0	47	399	934	•	5177	16225	•	•	•	•	•

Selected Financial Ratios (Times to 1)

Current Ratio 30	2.0	•	1.9	3.5	1.9	•	1.8	2.6	•	•	•	•	•
Quick Ratio 31	0.6	•	0.4	1.6	0.7	•	0.3	0.6	•	•	•	•	•
Net Sales to Working Capital 32	7.1	•	8.7	5.1	7.6	•	7.2	5.7	•	•	•	•	•
Coverage Ratio 33	7.6	•	7.3	13.3	5.6	•	10.8	8.1	•	•	•	•	•
Total Asset Turnover 34	2.6	•	3.2	3.2	2.4	•	2.3	2.7	•	•	•	•	•
Inventory Turnover 35	4.9	•	4.1	5.1	5.7	•	2.9	4.5	•	•	•	•	•
Receivables Turnover 36	30.3	•	72.9	29.7	27.7	•	•	26.6	•	•	•	•	•
Total Liabilities to Net Worth 37	1.6	•	3.4	1.0	1.3	•	1.7	1.4	•	•	•	•	•
Current Assets to Working Capital 38	2.0	•	2.1	1.4	2.1	•	2.2	1.6	•	•	•	•	•
Current Liabilities to Working Capital 39	1.0	•	1.1	0.4	1.1	•	1.2	0.6	•	•	•	•	•
Working Capital to Net Sales 40	0.1	•	0.1	0.2	0.1	•	0.1	0.2	•	•	•	•	•
Inventory to Working Capital 41	1.3	•	1.6	0.7	1.2	•	1.7	1.2	•	•	•	•	•
Total Receipts to Cash Flow 42	10.0	•	8.0	8.8	11.5	•	7.1	9.8	•	•	•	•	•
Cost of Goods to Cash Flow 43	7.1	•	5.0	5.4	8.5	•	5.0	6.9	•	•	•	•	•
Cash Flow to Total Debt 44	0.4	•	0.5	0.7	0.4	•	0.5	0.5	•	•	•	•	•

Selected Financial Factors (in Percentages)

Debt Ratio 45	61.4	•	77.2	50.6	57.3	•	62.5	58.5	•	•	•	•	•
Return on Total Assets 46	11.0	•	18.3	17.9	6.8	•	11.2	14.5	•	•	•	•	•
Return on Equity Before Income Taxes 47	24.7	•	69.2	33.4	13.1	•	27.2	30.5	•	•	•	•	•
Return on Equity After Income Taxes 48	23.5	•	69.2	32.9	11.4	•	27.1	29.9	•	•	•	•	•
Profit Margin (Before Income Tax) 49	3.6	•	4.9	5.2	2.3	•	4.4	4.7	•	•	•	•	•
Profit Margin (After Income Tax) 50	3.5	•	4.9	5.1	2.0	•	4.4	4.6	•	•	•	•	•

Table I

Corporations with and without Net Income

FOOD AND BEVERAGE STORES

MONEY AMOUNTS AND SIZE OF ASSETS IN THOUSANDS OF DOLLARS

Item Description for Accounting Period 7/12 Through 6/13		Total	Zero Assets	Under 500	500 to 1,000	1,000 to 5,000	5,000 to 10,000	10,000 to 25,000	25,000 to 50,000	50,000 to 100,000	100,000 to 250,000	250,000 to 500,000	500,000 to 2,500,000	2,500,000 and over
Number of Enterprises	1	76531	8664	58159	3995	4832	479	208	49	50	40	14	28	13
Revenues ($ in Thousands)														
Net Sales	2	579980086	3322871	44105652	12298818	38792557	15170742	14352534	7475871	13125687	23266370	17031911	89035088	302001986
Interest	3	485148	1548	2849	543	6376	2852	1431	109	2748	1056	2215	39987	423435
Rents	4	596651	21	3689	432	7859	9336	15831	5415	5762	20791	19019	121813	386682
Royalties	5	1881370	3318	0	0	0	0	2767	9083	12143	9393	0	73675	1770990
Other Portfolio Income	6	587793	14951	46664	1576	10900	12857	9268	8586	3999	22634	3554	99209	353595
Other Receipts	7	6153041	27298	506533	80961	462514	148736	142416	70113	182118	181708	124340	1610616	2615689
Total Receipts	8	589684089	3370007	44665387	12382330	39280206	15344523	14524247	7569177	13332457	23501952	17181039	90980388	307552377
Average Total Receipts	9	7705	389	768	3099	8129	32034	69828	154473	266649	587549	1227217	3249300	23657875
Operating Costs/Operating Income (%)														
Cost of Operations	10	74.5	66.0	73.2	74.6	74.4	74.2	75.0	78.4	74.6	72.6	74.3	75.3	74.7
Salaries and Wages	11	9.9	10.2	7.1	9.0	9.4	10.4	9.3	8.7	10.0	11.1	10.7	10.0	10.2
Taxes Paid	12	1.5	2.4	2.2	1.4	1.5	1.5	1.4	1.6	1.6	1.7	1.6	1.6	1.4
Interest Paid	13	0.6	0.2	0.2	0.3	0.3	0.3	0.3	0.2	0.3	0.3	0.4	0.7	0.7
Depreciation	14	1.6	1.3	0.7	0.7	0.9	0.7	0.9	1.0	1.2	1.7	2.0	2.0	1.8
Amortization and Depletion	15	0.2	0.2	0.3	0.3	0.1	0.2	0.1	0.1	0.1	0.1	0.2	0.3	0.1
Pensions and Other Deferred Comp.	16	0.5	0.1	0.0	0.0	0.2	0.2	0.1	0.2	0.4	0.2	0.3	0.6	0.7
Employee Benefits	17	1.3	0.6	0.1	0.4	0.7	0.7	1.0	1.2	1.6	1.5	1.3	1.8	1.4
Advertising	18	0.7	0.6	0.4	0.5	1.1	0.8	0.9	0.6	0.8	0.9	0.7	0.7	0.6
Other Expenses	19	8.4	21.3	12.8	9.2	10.2	8.0	10.1	7.4	8.3	9.0	7.7	7.8	7.4
Officers' Compensation	20	0.5	2.4	2.4	1.6	1.0	1.1	0.7	0.5	0.5	0.3	0.3	0.2	0.1
Operating Margin	21	0.5	•	0.6	2.1	0.4	1.9	0.2	0.2	0.6	0.5	0.6	•	0.8
Operating Margin Before Officers' Comp.	22	0.9	•	3.0	3.7	1.4	3.0	0.9	0.7	1.1	0.8	0.8	•	0.9

Selected Average Balance Sheet ($ in Thousands)

Net Receivables 23	208	0	3	66	180	519	861	2073	5184	7308	19396	50699	913043
Inventories 24	366	0	38	160	407	1703	3511	7635	11287	29290	54629	168656	1081201
Net Property, Plant and Equipment 25	1109	0	30	235	662	2131	4897	13729	23110	67496	193550	549165	4175768
Total Assets 26	2722	0	124	738	1853	7156	15791	35575	68966	152183	349270	1269860	10060416
Notes and Loans Payable 27	750	0	63	295	687	2750	4901	10512	17999	39307	115212	292271	2622510
All Other Liabilities 28	1157	0	17	113	412	1519	4618	13445	20979	53813	107171	465169	5003762
Net Worth 29	815	0	44	330	755	2886	6272	11617	29988	59063	126887	512420	2434144

Selected Financial Ratios (Times to 1)

Current Ratio 30	1.0	•	3.2	2.5	2.1	1.9	1.6	1.2	1.5	1.2	1.0	1.1	0.9
Quick Ratio 31	0.5	•	1.3	1.4	0.9	0.7	0.7	0.5	0.9	0.4	0.3	0.4	0.4
Net Sales to Working Capital 32	450.7	•	16.6	13.5	17.9	20.8	24.6	66.9	24.7	65.5	•	129.7	•
Coverage Ratio 33	4.9	•	12.2	11.1	5.9	12.1	5.5	8.3	7.6	5.4	4.6	2.6	5.0
Total Asset Turnover 34	2.8	•	6.1	4.2	4.3	4.4	4.4	4.3	3.8	3.8	3.5	2.5	2.3
Inventory Turnover 35	15.4	•	14.7	14.4	14.7	13.8	14.7	15.7	17.4	14.4	16.5	14.2	16.1
Receivables Turnover 36	38.9	•	305.8	45.9	38.3	72.2	84.0	55.1	51.6	79.0	63.5	68.4	27.8
Total Liabilities to Net Worth 37	2.3	•	1.8	1.2	1.5	1.5	1.5	2.1	1.3	1.6	1.8	1.5	3.1
Current Assets to Working Capital 38	55.3	•	1.5	1.7	1.9	2.2	2.7	6.3	2.8	6.0	•	13.9	•
Current Liabilities to Working Capital 39	54.3	•	0.5	0.7	0.9	1.2	1.7	5.3	1.8	5.0	•	12.9	•
Working Capital to Net Sales 40	0.0	•	0.1	0.1	0.1	0.0	0.0	0.0	0.0	0.0	•	0.0	•
Inventory to Working Capital 41	22.9	•	0.8	0.7	1.0	1.1	1.2	3.2	1.0	3.4	•	7.0	•
Total Receipts to Cash Flow 42	13.4	12.1	11.1	11.6	11.8	12.0	12.5	16.5	13.5	14.4	15.5	15.9	13.5
Cost of Goods to Cash Flow 43	10.0	8.0	8.1	8.7	8.8	8.9	9.3	13.0	10.0	10.4	11.5	11.9	10.1
Cash Flow to Total Debt 44	0.3	•	0.9	0.6	0.6	0.6	0.6	0.4	0.5	0.4	0.4	0.3	0.2

Selected Financial Factors (in Percentages)

Debt Ratio 45	70.0	•	64.5	55.3	59.3	59.7	60.3	67.3	56.5	61.2	63.7	59.6	75.8
Return on Total Assets 46	7.5	•	12.7	12.6	8.4	14.8	7.4	7.1	9.7	7.1	6.3	4.9	7.7
Return on Equity Before Income Taxes 47	20.0	•	32.9	25.6	17.2	33.6	15.1	19.2	19.3	14.8	13.7	7.4	25.6
Return on Equity After Income Taxes 48	14.5	•	32.0	24.7	16.2	32.1	14.0	17.6	17.6	13.3	9.2	5.0	16.7
Profit Margin (Before Income Tax) 49	2.2	•	1.9	2.7	1.6	3.1	1.4	1.5	2.2	1.5	1.4	1.2	2.7
Profit Margin (After Income Tax) 50	1.6	•	1.9	2.6	1.5	2.9	1.3	1.3	2.0	1.3	1.0	0.8	1.8

Table II

Corporations with Net Income

FOOD AND BEVERAGE STORES

MONEY AMOUNTS AND SIZE OF ASSETS IN THOUSANDS OF DOLLARS

Item Description for Accounting Period 7/12 Through 6/13	Total	Zero Assets	Under 500	500 to 1,000	1,000 to 5,000	5,000 to 10,000	10,000 to 25,000	25,000 to 50,000	50,000 to 100,000	100,000 to 250,000	250,000 to 500,000	500,000 to 2,500,000	2,500,000 and over
Number of Enterprises 1	44959	2178	35984	2806	3232	449	•	34	41	•	9	21	13

Revenues ($ in Thousands)													
Net Sales 2	524454684	1113811	33713753	10920683	30127920	14526061	•	5464587	11253214	•	11835350	71174865	302001986
Interest 3	482468	1380	2150	150	6210	2699	•	85	2630	•	2150	39550	423435
Rents 4	545684	0	3661	50	5681	8709	•	3372	4838	•	14725	86905	386682
Royalties 5	1864493	0	0	0	0	0	•	9083	0	•	0	73290	1770990
Other Portfolio Income 6	536308	10754	46664	1084	10070	12848	•	7795	3547	•	2677	64723	353595
Other Receipts 7	5442720	16690	294134	71518	357999	136269	•	59940	165364	•	69577	1402438	2615689
Total Receipts 8	533326357	1142635	34060362	10993485	30507880	14686586	•	5544862	11429593	•	11924479	72841771	307552377
Average Total Receipts 9	11863	525	947	3918	9439	32710	•	163084	278771	•	1324942	3468656	23657875

Operating Costs/Operating Income (%)													
Cost of Operations 10	74.9	71.1	73.9	75.5	76.3	74.3	•	78.4	75.3	•	73.8	75.9	74.7
Salaries and Wages 11	9.7	5.3	6.4	8.4	8.1	10.3	•	8.5	9.6	•	10.9	9.8	10.2
Taxes Paid 12	1.5	1.9	2.1	1.3	1.3	1.5	•	1.4	1.6	•	1.7	1.5	1.4
Interest Paid 13	0.5	0.3	0.1	0.2	0.3	0.3	•	0.2	0.2	•	0.2	0.5	0.7
Depreciation 14	1.6	1.1	0.5	0.6	0.6	0.7	•	0.9	1.1	•	1.8	2.0	1.8
Amortization and Depletion 15	0.2	0.1	0.2	0.3	0.1	0.2	•	0.0	0.1	•	0.1	0.2	0.1
Pensions and Other Deferred Comp. 16	0.5	0.1	0.0	0.0	0.2	0.2	•	0.2	0.4	•	0.2	0.6	0.7
Employee Benefits 17	1.2	0.7	0.1	0.3	0.6	0.7	•	0.9	1.5	•	1.5	1.5	1.4
Advertising 18	0.6	0.1	0.3	0.4	1.0	0.8	•	0.6	0.7	•	0.7	0.6	0.6
Other Expenses 19	7.9	15.0	11.5	8.8	8.8	7.8	•	7.3	7.8	•	7.1	7.3	7.4
Officers' Compensation 20	0.4	2.1	2.2	1.4	1.1	1.1	•	0.6	0.5	•	0.3	0.2	0.1
Operating Margin 21	1.0	2.2	2.5	2.8	1.6	2.2	•	1.0	1.2	•	1.9	•	0.8
Operating Margin Before Officers' Comp. 22	1.4	4.3	4.7	4.2	2.7	3.3	•	1.6	1.7	•	2.1	0.1	0.9

Selected Average Balance Sheet ($ in Thousands)

Net Receivables 23	330	0	3	86	141	484	•	1726	4780	•	16747	53511	913043
Inventories 24	547	0	44	175	404	1601	•	7285	10811	•	63687	174319	1081201
Net Property, Plant and Equipment 25	1709	0	34	157	600	2175	•	12993	21937	•	215428	561631	4175768
Total Assets 26	4192	0	140	749	1816	7125	•	36109	69187	•	358900	1267419	10060416
Notes and Loans Payable 27	1080	0	53	236	546	2523	•	6987	15380	•	77123	270830	2622510
All Other Liabilities 28	1810	0	17	119	374	1451	•	11561	19980	•	114034	415457	5003762
Net Worth 29	1302	0	71	394	896	3151	•	17561	33827	•	167743	581133	2434144

Selected Financial Ratios (Times to 1)

Current Ratio 30	1.0	•	3.9	3.0	2.1	1.9	•	1.3	1.7	•	1.1	1.2	0.9
Quick Ratio 31	0.5	•	1.7	1.8	0.9	0.7	•	0.5	0.9	•	0.3	0.5	0.4
Net Sales to Working Capital 32	1129.1	•	15.9	12.6	19.9	20.5	•	53.9	22.0	•	147.5	60.3	•
Coverage Ratio 33	6.2	15.5	25.6	15.2	11.4	13.3	•	13.1	15.9	•	15.2	5.3	5.0
Total Asset Turnover 34	2.8	•	6.7	5.2	5.1	4.5	•	4.5	4.0	•	3.7	2.7	2.3
Inventory Turnover 35	16.0	•	15.7	16.7	17.6	15.0	•	17.3	19.1	•	15.2	14.8	16.1
Receivables Turnover 36	38.2	•	306.7	44.2	53.0	84.0	•	57.6	69.2	•	86.4	68.9	27.8
Total Liabilities to Net Worth 37	2.2	•	1.0	0.9	1.0	1.3	•	1.1	1.0	•	1.1	1.2	3.1
Current Assets to Working Capital 38	140.3	•	1.3	1.5	1.9	2.1	•	4.9	2.5	•	11.6	6.5	•
Current Liabilities to Working Capital 39	139.3	•	0.3	0.5	0.9	1.1	•	3.9	1.5	•	10.6	5.5	•
Working Capital to Net Sales 40	0.0	•	0.1	0.1	0.1	0.0	•	0.0	0.0	•	0.0	0.0	•
Inventory to Working Capital 41	56.5	•	0.7	0.6	1.0	1.1	•	2.5	0.9	•	6.8	3.1	•
Total Receipts to Cash Flow 42	13.0	7.4	10.2	11.1	11.1	11.7	•	14.3	13.1	•	14.2	14.1	13.5
Cost of Goods to Cash Flow 43	9.7	5.3	7.5	8.4	8.5	8.7	•	11.2	9.9	•	10.5	10.7	10.1
Cash Flow to Total Debt 44	0.3	•	1.3	1.0	0.9	0.7	•	0.6	0.6	•	0.5	0.3	0.2

Selected Financial Factors (in Percentages)

Debt Ratio 45	68.9	•	49.6	47.4	50.7	55.8	•	51.4	51.1	•	53.3	54.1	75.8
Return on Total Assets 46	8.9	•	24.4	19.2	16.3	16.3	•	11.9	11.8	•	10.2	7.5	7.7
Return on Equity Before Income Taxes 47	24.1	•	46.6	34.0	30.1	34.0	•	22.6	22.6	•	20.4	13.2	25.6
Return on Equity After Income Taxes 48	18.2	•	45.8	33.0	28.8	32.5	•	21.2	20.8	•	15.1	10.3	16.7
Profit Margin (Before Income Tax) 49	2.7	4.8	3.5	3.4	2.9	3.3	•	2.5	2.8	•	2.6	2.3	2.7
Profit Margin (After Income Tax) 50	2.0	4.6	3.5	3.3	2.8	3.2	•	2.3	2.6	•	1.9	1.8	1.8

Table I

Corporations with and without Net Income

BEER, WINE, AND LIQUOR STORES

MONEY AMOUNTS AND SIZE OF ASSETS IN THOUSANDS OF DOLLARS

Item Description for Accounting Period 7/12 Through 6/13	Total	Zero Assets	Under 500	500 to 1,000	1,000 to 5,000	5,000 to 10,000	10,000 to 25,000	25,000 to 50,000	50,000 to 100,000	100,000 to 250,000	250,000 to 500,000	500,000 to 2,500,000	2,500,000 and over
Number of Enterprises **1**	20565	653	16136	2778	878	88	19	8	0	5	0	0	0

Revenues ($ in Thousands)													
Net Sales **2**	28145557	41352	12432664	6240095	4130194	1033750	1107300	566038	0	2594165	0	0	0
Interest **3**	2241	0	657	322	556	0	388	0	0	318	0	0	0
Rents **4**	2872	0	1195	43	533	90	0	0	0	1011	0	0	0
Royalties **5**	0	0	0	0	0	0	0	0	0	0	0	0	0
Other Portfolio Income **6**	14398	972	3273	0	2535	6351	4	61	0	1202	0	0	0
Other Receipts **7**	416256	1171	279000	89178	14832	9266	10067	3544	0	9198	0	0	0
Total Receipts **8**	28581324	43495	12716789	6329638	4148650	1049457	1117759	569643	0	2605894	0	0	0
Average Total Receipts **9**	1390	67	788	2278	4725	11926	58829	71205	•	521179	•	•	•

Operating Costs/Operating Income (%)													
Cost of Operations **10**	78.1	34.5	77.8	80.9	76.3	73.2	82.3	78.8	•	76.1	•	•	•
Salaries and Wages **11**	5.4	3.5	5.0	4.8	5.6	6.6	5.4	5.9	•	8.0	•	•	•
Taxes Paid **12**	2.2	3.9	2.9	1.6	2.0	0.8	0.9	1.1	•	1.3	•	•	•
Interest Paid **13**	0.5	0.8	0.4	0.3	0.7	0.1	0.1	1.5	•	1.0	•	•	•
Depreciation **14**	0.6	0.1	0.5	0.7	0.8	0.3	0.1	0.6	•	1.4	•	•	•
Amortization and Depletion **15**	0.4	4.7	0.5	0.4	0.2	0.2	0.1	0.5	•	0.1	•	•	•
Pensions and Other Deferred Comp. **16**	0.1	•	0.1	0.0	0.1	0.1	0.1	0.0	•	0.1	•	•	•
Employee Benefits **17**	0.3	•	0.2	0.1	0.3	0.1	0.3	0.3	•	0.7	•	•	•
Advertising **18**	0.4	•	0.2	0.5	0.5	0.6	0.7	0.6	•	1.3	•	•	•
Other Expenses **19**	9.3	51.8	9.9	8.2	9.2	11.4	8.7	10.4	•	7.9	•	•	•
Officers' Compensation **20**	2.6	•	4.0	1.2	2.1	1.7	1.4	1.5	•	0.6	•	•	•
Operating Margin **21**	0.2	0.5	•	1.3	2.3	4.9	•	•	•	1.4	•	•	•
Operating Margin Before Officers' Comp. **22**	2.8	0.5	2.5	2.5	4.4	6.6	1.4	0.3	•	2.0	•	•	•

Selected Average Balance Sheet ($ in Thousands)

Net Receivables 23	16	0	5	5	121	393	486	5500	•	6512	•	•	•
Inventories 24	225	0	100	400	1135	3271	5992	17191	•	75119	•	•	•
Net Property, Plant and Equipment 25	81	0	38	87	456	269	1967	7191	•	57855	•	•	•
Total Assets 26	473	0	221	763	2073	6626	11403	44353	•	212215	•	•	•
Notes and Loans Payable 27	224	0	124	343	1034	967	2347	17513	•	96694	•	•	•
All Other Liabilities 28	99	0	38	187	309	1047	6354	15322	•	61327	•	•	•
Net Worth 29	149	0	60	233	730	4612	2702	11518	•	54194	•	•	•

Selected Financial Ratios (Times to 1)

Current Ratio 30	2.8	•	3.1	3.3	3.3	3.3	1.1	2.1	•	1.7	•	•	•
Quick Ratio 31	0.7	•	0.8	0.9	0.6	1.4	0.3	0.4	•	0.2	•	•	•
Net Sales to Working Capital 32	6.5	•	7.8	5.6	4.8	2.7	158.0	4.3	•	11.3	•	•	•
Coverage Ratio 33	4.8	8.1	3.0	9.2	4.9	65.7	7.5	0.6	•	2.8	•	•	•
Total Asset Turnover 34	2.9	•	3.5	2.9	2.3	1.8	5.1	1.6	•	2.4	•	•	•
Inventory Turnover 35	4.7	•	6.0	4.5	3.2	2.6	8.0	3.2	•	5.3	•	•	•
Receivables Turnover 36	97.7	•	245.1	257.2	47.7	21.8	174.4	13.6	•	83.7	•	•	•
Total Liabilities to Net Worth 37	2.2	•	2.7	2.3	1.8	0.4	3.2	2.9	•	2.9	•	•	•
Current Assets to Working Capital 38	1.6	•	1.5	1.4	1.4	1.4	20.2	1.9	•	2.5	•	•	•
Current Liabilities to Working Capital 39	0.6	•	0.5	0.4	0.4	0.4	19.2	0.9	•	1.5	•	•	•
Working Capital to Net Sales 40	0.2	•	0.1	0.2	0.2	0.4	0.0	0.2	•	0.1	•	•	•
Inventory to Working Capital 41	1.1	•	1.1	1.0	1.1	0.8	13.2	1.1	•	1.7	•	•	•
Total Receipts to Cash Flow 42	14.2	2.7	16.2	13.3	12.8	7.4	12.4	15.1	•	18.5	•	•	•
Cost of Goods to Cash Flow 43	11.1	0.9	12.6	10.7	9.8	5.4	10.2	11.9	•	14.1	•	•	•
Cash Flow to Total Debt 44	0.3	•	0.3	0.3	0.3	0.8	0.5	0.1	•	0.2	•	•	•

Selected Financial Factors (in Percentages)

Debt Ratio 45	68.4	•	73.0	69.5	64.8	30.4	76.3	74.0	•	74.5	•	•	•
Return on Total Assets 46	6.6	•	3.9	9.1	7.8	11.6	5.5	1.6	•	7.1	•	•	•
Return on Equity Before Income Taxes 47	16.4	•	9.8	26.6	17.6	16.4	20.1	•	•	18.1	•	•	•
Return on Equity After Income Taxes 48	15.6	•	9.1	26.4	16.0	16.3	19.4	•	•	16.2	•	•	•
Profit Margin (Before Income Tax) 49	1.8	5.7	0.8	2.8	2.7	6.5	0.9	•	•	1.9	•	•	•
Profit Margin (After Income Tax) 50	1.7	5.1	0.7	2.7	2.5	6.4	0.9	•	•	1.7	•	•	•

Table II
Corporations with Net Income

BEER, WINE, AND LIQUOR STORES

MONEY AMOUNTS AND SIZE OF ASSETS IN THOUSANDS OF DOLLARS

Item Description for Accounting Period 7/12 Through 6/13	Total	Zero Assets	Under 500	500 to 1,000	1,000 to 5,000	5,000 to 10,000	10,000 to 25,000	25,000 to 50,000	50,000 to 100,000	100,000 to 250,000	250,000 to 500,000	500,000 to 2,500,000	2,500,000 and over
Number of Enterprises **1**	14247	283	10792	2401	661	85	•	4	0	•	0	0	0

Revenues ($ in Thousands)

Net Sales **2**	23246866	41352	9478183	5961594	3504922	1017606	•	349516	0	•	0	0	0
Interest **3**	1589	0	626	26	378	0	•	0	0	•	0	0	0
Rents **4**	2829	0	1195	0	533	90	•	0	0	•	0	0	0
Royalties **5**	0	0	0	0	0	0	•	0	0	•	0	0	0
Other Portfolio Income **6**	11011	972	2292	0	190	6351	•	0	0	•	0	0	0
Other Receipts **7**	361346	1171	243425	82739	10801	9263	•	3437	0	•	0	0	0
Total Receipts **8**	23623641	43495	9725721	6044359	3516824	1033310	•	352953	0	•	0	0	0
Average Total Receipts **9**	1658	154	901	2517	5320	12157	•	88238	•	•	•	•	•

Operating Costs/Operating Income (%)

Cost of Operations **10**	78.5	34.5	78.1	80.8	76.9	73.5	•	80.4	•	•	•	•	•
Salaries and Wages **11**	5.0	3.5	4.4	4.8	4.9	6.2	•	5.0	•	•	•	•	•
Taxes Paid **12**	1.9	3.9	2.4	1.6	2.1	0.7	•	1.0	•	•	•	•	•
Interest Paid **13**	0.3	0.8	0.2	0.3	0.5	0.1	•	1.1	•	•	•	•	•
Depreciation **14**	0.4	0.1	0.3	0.6	0.4	0.3	•	0.2	•	•	•	•	•
Amortization and Depletion **15**	0.3	4.7	0.4	0.3	0.1	0.1	•	0.1	•	•	•	•	•
Pensions and Other Deferred Comp. **16**	0.1	•	0.1	0.0	0.1	0.1	•	0.0	•	•	•	•	•
Employee Benefits **17**	0.2	•	0.2	0.1	0.3	0.1	•	0.2	•	•	•	•	•
Advertising **18**	0.4	•	0.2	0.5	0.5	0.6	•	0.5	•	•	•	•	•
Other Expenses **19**	8.9	51.8	9.5	7.9	9.1	10.7	•	8.8	•	•	•	•	•
Officers' Compensation **20**	2.4	•	3.9	1.2	1.6	1.6	•	2.4	•	•	•	•	•
Operating Margin **21**	1.6	0.5	0.3	1.7	3.5	6.0	•	0.2	•	•	•	•	•
Operating Margin Before Officers' Comp. **22**	3.9	0.5	4.2	2.9	5.1	7.6	•	2.6	•	•	•	•	•

Selected Average Balance Sheet ($ in Thousands)

	1	2	3	4	5	6	7	8	9	10	11	12	13
Net Receivables 23	17	0	7	4	119	407	•	2794	•	•	•	•	•
Inventories 24	263	0	115	353	1293	3349	•	24103	•	•	•	•	•
Net Property, Plant and Equipment 25	72	0	17	74	543	269	•	2662	•	•	•	•	•
Total Assets 26	531	0	237	769	2196	6672	•	48077	•	•	•	•	•
Notes and Loans Payable 27	188	0	72	308	1038	1001	•	14117	•	•	•	•	•
All Other Liabilities 28	114	0	42	200	327	993	•	23686	•	•	•	•	•
Net Worth 29	229	0	122	261	832	4678	•	10274	•	•	•	•	•

Selected Financial Ratios (Times to 1)

	1	2	3	4	5	6	7	8	9	10	11	12	13
Current Ratio 30	3.1	•	4.9	3.1	3.3	3.4	•	1.8	•	•	•	•	•
Quick Ratio 31	0.8	•	1.4	0.9	0.6	1.4	•	0.2	•	•	•	•	•
Net Sales to Working Capital 32	6.0	•	6.1	5.9	4.9	2.7	•	4.5	•	•	•	•	•
Coverage Ratio 33	11.9	8.1	17.1	11.5	8.0	75.3	•	2.1	•	•	•	•	•
Total Asset Turnover 34	3.1	•	3.7	3.2	2.4	1.8	•	1.8	•	•	•	•	•
Inventory Turnover 35	4.9	•	6.0	5.7	3.2	2.6	•	2.9	•	•	•	•	•
Receivables Turnover 36	114.8	•	216.3	402.4	59.1	21.5	•	34.7	•	•	•	•	•
Total Liabilities to Net Worth 37	1.3	•	0.9	1.9	1.6	0.4	•	3.7	•	•	•	•	•
Current Assets to Working Capital 38	1.5	•	1.3	1.5	1.4	1.4	•	2.3	•	•	•	•	•
Current Liabilities to Working Capital 39	0.5	•	0.3	0.5	0.4	0.4	•	1.3	•	•	•	•	•
Working Capital to Net Sales 40	0.2	•	0.2	0.2	0.2	0.4	•	0.2	•	•	•	•	•
Inventory to Working Capital 41	1.0	•	0.9	1.0	1.1	0.8	•	1.3	•	•	•	•	•
Total Receipts to Cash Flow 42	12.3	2.7	12.7	12.9	11.1	7.1	•	13.7	•	•	•	•	•
Cost of Goods to Cash Flow 43	9.7	0.9	9.9	10.4	8.5	5.3	•	11.0	•	•	•	•	•
Cash Flow to Total Debt 44	0.4	•	0.6	0.4	0.4	0.8	•	0.2	•	•	•	•	•

Selected Financial Factors (in Percentages)

	1	2	3	4	5	6	7	8	9	10	11	12	13
Debt Ratio 45	56.8	•	48.3	66.0	62.1	29.9	•	78.6	•	•	•	•	•
Return on Total Assets 46	10.6	•	11.4	11.0	10.5	13.7	•	4.2	•	•	•	•	•
Return on Equity Before Income Taxes 47	22.6	•	20.8	29.5	24.2	19.2	•	10.5	•	•	•	•	•
Return on Equity After Income Taxes 48	21.8	•	20.3	29.3	22.4	19.1	•	10.5	•	•	•	•	•
Profit Margin (Before Income Tax) 49	3.2	5.7	2.9	3.1	3.8	7.5	•	1.2	•	•	•	•	•
Profit Margin (After Income Tax) 50	3.1	5.1	2.8	3.1	3.5	7.5	•	1.2	•	•	•	•	•

Table I

Corporations with and without Net Income

HEALTH AND PERSONAL CARE STORES

MONEY AMOUNTS AND SIZE OF ASSETS IN THOUSANDS OF DOLLARS

Item Description for Accounting Period 7/12 Through 6/13	Total	Zero Assets	Under 500	500 to 1,000	1,000 to 5,000	5,000 to 10,000	10,000 to 25,000	25,000 to 50,000	50,000 to 100,000	100,000 to 250,000	250,000 to 500,000	500,000 to 2,500,000	2,500,000 and over
Number of Enterprises **1**	44725	6176	29731	4525	4026	93	106	24	13	19	0	5	7

Revenues ($ in Thousands)

Net Sales **2**	324145864	2439836	24680302	15854587	23545451	1223763	3890049	2635890	2155254	7980003	0	9063310	230677418
Interest **3**	98946	124	1307	1224	2248	873	3218	26	186	2500	0	1760	85481
Rents **4**	169070	176	3697	1957	1931	1167	691	0	0	7978	0	1322	150150
Royalties **5**	114024	0	0	0	0	0	7	0	0	3773	0	3729	106514
Other Portfolio Income **6**	241294	29317	55014	13463	31745	1932	9786	3	38	8777	0	77185	14033
Other Receipts **7**	4591315	40832	128781	21354	132354	27756	54361	35577	29326	67681	0	26652	4026644
Total Receipts **8**	329360513	2510285	24869101	15892585	23713729	1255491	3958112	2671496	2184804	8070712	0	9173958	235060240
Average Total Receipts **9**	7364	406	836	3512	5890	13500	37341	111312	168062	424774	•	1834792	33580034

Operating Costs/Operating Income (%)

Cost of Operations **10**	70.1	64.7	67.7	75.8	67.8	59.3	63.2	71.0	67.8	71.1	•	58.8	70.9
Salaries and Wages **11**	9.2	10.5	7.9	7.7	11.7	17.1	16.0	10.9	14.1	12.8	•	14.2	8.6
Taxes Paid **12**	1.2	1.8	1.9	1.4	1.6	1.6	1.5	1.5	1.4	1.4	•	2.2	1.1
Interest Paid **13**	0.8	1.0	0.1	0.2	0.4	0.1	0.6	0.9	3.5	1.1	•	2.0	0.9
Depreciation **14**	1.0	0.6	0.4	0.4	0.5	2.0	1.4	1.0	0.9	1.1	•	1.8	1.1
Amortization and Depletion **15**	0.3	0.5	0.1	0.2	0.3	0.1	0.4	0.2	0.7	0.4	•	0.7	0.4
Pensions and Other Deferred Comp. **16**	0.3	0.3	0.3	0.3	0.4	0.5	0.3	0.1	0.2	0.2	•	0.2	0.3
Employee Benefits **17**	0.8	0.9	0.3	0.4	0.5	1.5	0.9	0.7	1.2	1.3	•	0.6	0.9
Advertising **18**	0.9	1.7	1.0	0.5	0.7	0.6	2.1	1.0	0.8	1.3	•	1.0	0.9
Other Expenses **19**	11.8	15.2	10.6	7.5	8.7	13.6	10.1	11.9	10.0	9.7	•	12.6	12.6
Officers' Compensation **20**	1.1	4.3	6.9	4.1	3.0	1.1	1.4	0.5	0.6	0.7	•	1.3	0.1
Operating Margin **21**	2.4	•	2.7	1.7	4.4	2.5	2.0	0.5	•	•	•	4.6	2.4
Operating Margin Before Officers' Comp. **22**	3.5	2.8	9.6	5.8	7.4	3.6	3.4	1.0	•	•	•	5.9	2.4

Selected Average Balance Sheet ($ in Thousands)

Net Receivables 23	705	0	15	82	243	1590	3826	7525	18870	31726	•	81567	3966637
Inventories 24	665	0	60	269	468	1551	2362	8418	10441	26027	•	263452	3170060
Net Property, Plant and Equipment 25	537	0	18	63	221	1622	2491	4946	7909	23021	•	158639	2922900
Total Assets 26	3842	0	146	707	1646	7166	14658	31875	75565	168021	•	1049566	20751120
Notes and Loans Payable 27	1006	0	56	143	629	2169	5026	10456	33904	72972	•	429552	5030263
All Other Liabilities 28	1062	0	36	179	388	1336	4299	16031	23810	61031	•	279984	5745673
Net Worth 29	1774	0	54	385	629	3662	5333	5388	17851	34018	•	340030	9975184

Selected Financial Ratios (Times to 1)

Current Ratio 30	1.5	•	3.1	2.8	2.4	1.7	1.7	1.4	1.5	1.3	•	2.7	1.3
Quick Ratio 31	0.8	•	1.4	1.2	1.2	1.0	1.1	0.7	0.9	0.8	•	1.1	0.7
Net Sales to Working Capital 32	13.7	•	10.6	10.6	8.7	6.2	9.2	19.0	15.2	23.3	•	5.5	16.2
Coverage Ratio 33	6.1	2.4	28.2	12.0	13.5	45.1	7.0	3.0	1.1	1.1	•	3.9	6.0
Total Asset Turnover 34	1.9	•	5.7	5.0	3.6	1.8	2.5	3.4	2.2	2.5	•	1.7	1.6
Inventory Turnover 35	7.6	•	9.4	9.9	8.5	5.0	9.8	9.3	10.8	11.5	•	4.0	7.4
Receivables Turnover 36	10.7	•	57.4	45.5	22.8	5.0	9.1	12.8	9.2	14.2	•	17.6	8.8
Total Liabilities to Net Worth 37	1.2	•	1.7	0.8	1.6	1.0	1.7	4.9	3.2	3.9	•	2.1	1.1
Current Assets to Working Capital 38	3.2	•	1.5	1.6	1.7	2.4	2.4	3.7	3.2	4.3	•	1.6	4.1
Current Liabilities to Working Capital 39	2.2	•	0.5	0.6	0.7	1.4	1.4	2.7	2.2	3.3	•	0.6	3.1
Working Capital to Net Sales 40	0.1	•	0.1	0.1	0.1	0.2	0.1	0.1	0.1	0.0	•	0.2	0.1
Inventory to Working Capital 41	1.3	•	0.8	0.9	0.7	0.6	0.6	1.5	1.0	1.5	•	0.7	1.6
Total Receipts to Cash Flow 42	8.0	10.5	10.5	14.3	8.6	6.2	8.8	9.3	12.8	16.2	•	7.7	7.4
Cost of Goods to Cash Flow 43	5.6	6.8	7.1	10.8	5.8	3.6	5.5	6.6	8.7	11.5	•	4.5	5.3
Cash Flow to Total Debt 44	0.4	•	0.9	0.8	0.7	0.6	0.4	0.4	0.2	0.2	•	0.3	0.4

Selected Financial Factors (in Percentages)

Debt Ratio 45	53.8	•	62.9	45.5	61.8	48.9	63.6	83.1	76.4	79.8	•	67.6	51.9
Return on Total Assets 46	9.1	•	20.6	10.2	19.5	9.5	10.9	9.3	8.1	3.2	•	13.4	8.1
Return on Equity Before Income Taxes 47	16.5	•	53.5	17.2	47.3	18.2	25.6	37.1	1.8	1.8	•	30.9	14.1
Return on Equity After Income Taxes 48	11.8	•	51.6	16.8	45.4	16.0	22.4	34.5	1.0	•	•	21.0	9.3
Profit Margin (Before Income Tax) 49	4.0	1.4	3.5	1.9	5.1	5.1	3.7	1.8	0.2	0.1	•	5.8	4.3
Profit Margin (After Income Tax) 50	2.9	1.2	3.4	1.8	4.9	4.5	3.3	1.7	0.1	•	•	3.9	2.8

Table II

Corporations with Net Income

HEALTH AND PERSONAL CARE STORES

MONEY AMOUNTS AND SIZE OF ASSETS IN THOUSANDS OF DOLLARS

Item Description for Accounting Period 7/12 Through 6/13	Total	Zero Assets	Under 500	500 to 1,000	1,000 to 5,000	5,000 to 10,000	10,000 to 25,000	25,000 to 50,000	50,000 to 100,000	100,000 to 250,000	250,000 to 500,000	500,000 to 2,500,000	2,500,000 and over
Number of Enterprises **1**	31690	4028	20421	3869	3188	62	71	18	9	12	0	5	7

Revenues ($ in Thousands)

	Total	Zero Assets	Under 500	500 to 1,000	1,000 to 5,000	5,000 to 10,000	10,000 to 25,000	25,000 to 50,000	50,000 to 100,000	100,000 to 250,000	250,000 to 500,000	500,000 to 2,500,000	2,500,000 and over
Net Sales **2**	309736273	1970322	19847004	13729558	20397153	1066265	2873870	1989465	1502679	6619229	0	9063310	230677418
Interest **3**	92633	1	836	972	1751	181	366	1	65	1219	0	1760	85481
Rents **4**	168020	176	3697	1803	1698	1167	550	0	0	7456	0	1322	150150
Royalties **5**	110250	0	0	0	0	0	7	0	0	0	0	3729	106514
Other Portfolio Income **6**	229461	29317	55012	12336	29401	430	2929	3	38	8777	0	77185	14033
Other Receipts **7**	4467034	11762	122000	7098	104670	9970	34841	34915	27431	61053	0	26652	4026644
Total Receipts **8**	314803671	2011578	20028549	13751767	20534673	1078013	2912563	2024384	1530213	6697734	0	9173958	235060240
Average Total Receipts **9**	9934	499	981	3554	6441	17387	41022	112466	170024	558144	•	1834792	33580034

Operating Costs/Operating Income (%)

	Total	Zero Assets	Under 500	500 to 1,000	1,000 to 5,000	5,000 to 10,000	10,000 to 25,000	25,000 to 50,000	50,000 to 100,000	100,000 to 250,000	250,000 to 500,000	500,000 to 2,500,000	2,500,000 and over
Cost of Operations **10**	70.2	62.4	67.2	75.5	68.0	58.5	61.1	69.9	66.7	74.2	•	58.8	70.9
Salaries and Wages **11**	9.0	10.6	7.6	7.1	11.1	17.4	15.2	10.9	13.8	11.6	•	14.2	8.6
Taxes Paid **12**	1.2	2.0	1.9	1.4	1.5	1.5	1.4	1.5	1.3	1.2	•	2.2	1.1
Interest Paid **13**	0.8	1.0	0.1	0.2	0.4	0.1	0.5	0.8	0.7	0.7	•	2.0	0.9
Depreciation **14**	1.0	0.4	0.4	0.3	0.3	1.4	1.3	0.9	1.0	0.9	•	1.8	1.1
Amortization and Depletion **15**	0.3	0.4	0.1	0.2	0.2	0.1	0.2	0.1	0.9	0.2	•	0.7	0.4
Pensions and Other Deferred Comp. **16**	0.3	0.3	0.2	0.3	0.4	0.6	0.3	0.1	0.3	0.2	•	0.2	0.3
Employee Benefits **17**	0.8	0.8	0.3	0.4	0.5	1.4	0.9	0.7	1.4	1.2	•	0.6	0.9
Advertising **18**	0.9	1.8	0.8	0.4	0.7	0.6	2.6	1.2	1.1	0.9	•	1.0	0.9
Other Expenses **19**	11.7	12.3	10.0	7.5	8.3	11.3	9.4	10.9	9.7	8.0	•	12.6	12.6
Officers' Compensation **20**	0.9	3.6	6.3	3.8	2.7	0.9	1.8	0.5	0.6	0.5	•	1.3	0.1
Operating Margin **21**	2.9	4.4	5.1	2.9	5.8	6.2	5.2	2.5	2.5	0.5	•	4.6	2.4
Operating Margin Before Officers' Comp. **22**	3.8	7.9	11.5	6.7	8.4	7.1	7.0	3.0	3.1	1.0	•	5.9	2.4

Selected Average Balance Sheet ($ in Thousands)

Net Receivables 23	970	0	16	79	248	1768	4212	7181	20926	33464	•	81567	3966637
Inventories 24	847	0	70	241	472	1816	2660	7621	9047	42770	•	263452	3184921
Net Property, Plant and Equipment 25	733	0	19	52	192	1905	2561	5347	9453	25706	•	158639	2922900
Total Assets 26	5265	0	166	693	1692	7376	14635	31588	78895	176184	•	1049566	20751120
Notes and Loans Payable 27	1328	0	44	123	546	2261	4643	8126	25526	64368	•	429552	5030263
All Other Liabilities 28	1454	0	32	176	405	1823	4489	16021	24181	73361	•	279984	5745673
Net Worth 29	2483	0	89	393	741	3292	5502	7441	29189	38455	•	340030	9975184

Selected Financial Ratios (Times to 1)

Current Ratio 30	1.5	•	3.9	2.7	2.6	1.3	1.9	1.3	1.5	1.2	•	2.7	1.3
Quick Ratio 31	0.8	•	1.7	1.1	1.4	0.8	1.2	0.7	1.0	0.7	•	1.1	0.7
Net Sales to Working Capital 32	13.9	•	10.1	11.0	8.3	14.9	8.5	21.1	14.0	31.2	•	5.5	16.2
Coverage Ratio 33	6.9	7.2	44.9	20.9	17.0	59.7	13.6	6.2	7.5	3.7	•	3.9	6.0
Total Asset Turnover 34	1.9	•	5.9	5.1	3.8	2.3	2.8	3.5	2.1	3.1	•	1.7	1.6
Inventory Turnover 35	8.1	•	9.4	11.1	9.2	5.5	9.3	10.1	12.3	9.6	•	4.0	7.3
Receivables Turnover 36	10.8	•	65.3	49.0	23.7	5.3	8.7	11.6	•	17.9	•	17.6	•
Total Liabilities to Net Worth 37	1.1	•	0.9	0.8	1.3	1.2	1.7	3.2	1.7	3.6	•	2.1	1.1
Current Assets to Working Capital 38	3.2	•	1.3	1.6	1.6	4.2	2.1	3.9	3.0	5.2	•	1.6	4.1
Current Liabilities to Working Capital 39	2.2	•	0.3	0.6	0.6	3.2	1.1	2.9	2.0	4.2	•	0.6	3.1
Working Capital to Net Sales 40	0.1	•	0.1	0.1	0.1	0.1	0.1	0.0	0.1	0.0	•	0.2	0.1
Inventory to Working Capital 41	1.3	•	0.7	0.9	0.6	1.2	0.6	1.6	0.8	2.2	•	0.7	1.6
Total Receipts to Cash Flow 42	7.7	7.8	8.5	12.4	7.8	6.1	7.3	8.3	8.2	15.5	•	7.7	7.4
Cost of Goods to Cash Flow 43	5.4	4.9	5.7	9.4	5.3	3.5	4.5	5.8	5.5	11.5	•	4.5	5.3
Cash Flow to Total Debt 44	0.5	•	1.5	1.0	0.9	0.7	0.6	0.6	0.4	0.3	•	0.3	0.4

Selected Financial Factors (in Percentages)

Debt Ratio 45	52.8	•	46.1	43.2	56.2	55.4	62.4	76.4	63.0	78.2	•	67.6	51.9
Return on Total Assets 46	9.8	•	36.2	16.7	26.0	17.2	19.6	17.8	10.6	7.5	•	13.4	8.1
Return on Equity Before Income Taxes 47	17.8	•	65.6	27.9	55.8	38.0	48.3	63.3	24.8	25.0	•	30.9	14.1
Return on Equity After Income Taxes 48	13.1	•	63.9	27.5	53.7	34.4	43.7	60.8	24.2	21.2	•	21.0	9.3
Profit Margin (Before Income Tax) 49	4.5	6.5	6.0	3.1	6.5	7.3	6.6	4.3	4.3	1.7	•	5.8	4.3
Profit Margin (After Income Tax) 50	3.3	6.2	5.9	3.1	6.2	6.6	5.9	4.1	4.2	1.5	•	3.9	2.8

Table I

Corporations with and without Net Income

GASOLINE STATIONS

MONEY AMOUNTS AND SIZE OF ASSETS IN THOUSANDS OF DOLLARS

Item Description for Accounting Period 7/12 Through 6/13	Total	Zero Assets	Under 500	500 to 1,000	1,000 to 5,000	5,000 to 10,000	10,000 to 25,000	25,000 to 50,000	50,000 to 100,000	100,000 to 250,000	250,000 to 500,000	500,000 to 2,500,000	2,500,000 and over
Number of Enterprises 1	45514	4214	30029	6199	4379	362	191	60	42	20	3	16	0

Revenues ($ in Thousands)

Net Sales 2	360729541	3114833	69160721	33795702	47928686	10414563	24335644	19004999	15803906	16622851	6564497	113983140	0
Interest 3	89825	58	1474	2148	2006	560	1118	2292	715	266	787	78400	0
Rents 4	112214	0	10887	30	14842	9454	9545	7825	9325	8422	177	41708	0
Royalties 5	44602	0	0	0	390	0	0	1	0	607	0	43604	0
Other Portfolio Income 6	314750	54039	93025	9317	27791	24314	63486	7867	4877	5130	814	24092	0
Other Receipts 7	2326555	29089	390432	136157	244948	63372	164437	121649	107468	100994	-1221	969226	0
Total Receipts 8	363617487	3198019	69656539	33943354	48218663	10512263	24574230	19144633	15926291	16738270	6565054	115140170	0
Average Total Receipts 9	7989	759	2320	5476	11011	29039	128661	319077	379197	836914	2188351	7196261	•

Operating Costs/Operating Income (%)

Cost of Operations 10	90.5	86.2	90.0	91.4	90.8	91.1	91.0	92.8	92.1	90.6	91.3	89.8	•
Salaries and Wages 11	2.8	4.4	2.4	2.0	2.8	2.4	3.6	2.5	2.3	3.4	2.1	3.0	•
Taxes Paid 12	0.9	1.4	0.8	0.9	0.9	0.7	0.6	0.5	0.7	0.5	0.5	1.0	•
Interest Paid 13	0.3	0.2	0.1	0.3	0.5	0.6	0.2	0.2	0.2	0.3	0.3	0.4	•
Depreciation 14	0.8	0.4	0.3	0.5	0.7	0.7	0.6	0.6	0.9	0.9	1.6	1.3	•
Amortization and Depletion 15	0.1	0.0	0.1	0.1	0.1	0.2	0.0	0.0	0.0	0.1	0.1	0.1	•
Pensions and Other Deferred Comp. 16	0.0	0.0	0.0	0.0	0.0	0.0	0.0	0.0	0.0	0.0	0.0	0.1	•
Employee Benefits 17	0.1	0.2	0.0	0.0	0.1	0.2	0.2	0.1	0.1	0.1	0.1	0.3	•
Advertising 18	0.1	0.3	0.1	0.0	0.1	0.1	0.1	0.1	0.1	0.1	0.1	0.1	•
Other Expenses 19	4.0	8.2	5.9	3.7	3.9	3.5	3.7	3.3	3.2	3.6	2.8	3.5	•
Officers' Compensation 20	0.4	1.7	0.8	0.8	0.4	0.3	0.2	0.2	0.2	0.1	0.6	0.1	•
Operating Margin 21	0.0	•	•	0.2	•	0.3	•	•	0.2	0.3	0.5	0.5	•
Operating Margin Before Officers' Comp. 22	0.4	•	0.3	0.9	0.1	0.6	•	•	0.4	0.4	1.1	0.5	•

Selected Average Balance Sheet ($ in Thousands)												
Net Receivables **23**	94	0	8	35	87	479	2233	4843	5436	17086	14718	121182	•
Inventories **24**	140	0	47	101	190	546	1936	4766	5768	23545	18051	119237	•
Net Property, Plant and Equipment **25**	640	0	54	351	1160	3322	6523	16367	33196	85045	258441	808888	•
Total Assets **26**	1269	0	179	719	1912	6218	15993	35361	64389	177551	337997	1554943	•
Notes and Loans Payable **27**	466	0	112	406	1465	3707	4918	12470	19602	44905	100415	242069	•
All Other Liabilities **28**	385	0	42	96	228	1107	4565	12702	16400	53780	130501	655521	•
Net Worth **29**	418	0	25	218	219	1404	6509	10188	28387	78866	107081	657353	•

Selected Financial Ratios (Times to 1)												
Current Ratio **30**	1.4	•	2.2	2.4	1.9	1.7	1.4	1.1	1.4	1.3	0.6	1.1	•
Quick Ratio **31**	0.7	•	0.9	1.3	1.0	0.9	0.9	0.6	0.8	0.7	0.4	0.6	•
Net Sales to Working Capital **32**	70.2	•	44.2	37.6	47.3	38.8	67.4	169.4	61.7	64.3	•	212.4	•
Coverage Ratio **33**	3.8	•	3.2	2.8	1.6	3.1	4.5	3.1	6.2	4.8	3.0	5.4	•
Total Asset Turnover **34**	6.2	•	12.9	7.6	5.7	4.6	8.0	9.0	5.8	4.7	6.5	4.6	•
Inventory Turnover **35**	51.2	•	43.8	49.3	52.2	48.0	59.9	61.7	60.1	32.0	110.7	53.6	•
Receivables Turnover **36**	87.3	•	343.6	181.0	99.1	90.9	59.0	64.7	66.7	49.9	297.3	61.8	•
Total Liabilities to Net Worth **37**	2.0	•	6.3	2.3	7.7	3.4	1.5	2.5	1.3	1.3	2.2	1.4	•
Current Assets to Working Capital **38**	3.6	•	1.8	1.7	2.2	2.5	3.5	8.2	3.8	4.4	•	12.6	•
Current Liabilities to Working Capital **39**	2.6	•	0.8	0.7	1.2	1.5	2.5	7.2	2.8	3.4	•	11.6	•
Working Capital to Net Sales **40**	0.0	•	0.0	0.0	0.0	0.0	0.0	0.0	0.0	0.0	•	0.0	•
Inventory to Working Capital **41**	1.3	•	1.0	0.6	0.8	0.8	1.0	2.5	1.0	1.7	•	4.0	•
Total Receipts to Cash Flow **42**	29.3	32.4	25.7	33.5	33.6	25.8	33.0	35.0	30.1	29.6	38.9	27.4	•
Cost of Goods to Cash Flow **43**	26.5	27.9	23.1	30.6	30.5	23.5	30.0	32.5	27.7	26.8	35.6	24.6	•
Cash Flow to Total Debt **44**	0.3	•	0.6	0.3	0.2	0.2	0.4	0.4	0.3	0.3	0.2	0.3	•

Selected Financial Factors (in Percentages)												
Debt Ratio **45**	67.1	•	86.3	69.7	88.6	77.4	59.3	71.2	55.9	55.6	68.3	57.7	•
Return on Total Assets **46**	7.2	•	5.4	7.3	4.7	8.5	7.1	5.6	6.5	5.9	5.3	8.7	•
Return on Equity Before Income Taxes **47**	16.0	•	27.1	15.5	15.3	25.2	13.5	13.1	12.3	10.6	11.1	16.8	•
Return on Equity After Income Taxes **48**	13.9	•	25.2	15.4	14.3	23.3	12.8	12.0	11.4	9.8	8.0	13.8	•
Profit Margin (Before Income Tax) **49**	0.8	•	0.3	0.6	0.3	1.2	0.7	0.4	0.9	1.0	0.5	1.5	•
Profit Margin (After Income Tax) **50**	0.7	•	0.3	0.6	0.3	1.1	0.7	0.4	0.9	0.9	0.4	1.3	•

Table II

Corporations with Net Income

GASOLINE STATIONS

MONEY AMOUNTS AND SIZE OF ASSETS IN THOUSANDS OF DOLLARS

Item Description for Accounting Period 7/12 Through 6/13	Total	Zero Assets	Under 500	500 to 1,000	1,000 to 5,000	5,000 to 10,000	10,000 to 25,000	25,000 to 50,000	50,000 to 100,000	100,000 to 250,000	250,000 to 500,000	500,000 to 2,500,000	2,500,000 and over
Number of Enterprises 1	30175	1656	20771	3993	3201	306	134	48	34	16	3	13	0

Revenues ($ in Thousands)

Net Sales 2	285046689	2016639	53942265	22347604	35302475	8091217	18413093	14748518	13631699	14423016	6564497	95565667	0
Interest 3	85724	0	1399	627	1693	366	872	1009	595	56	787	78320	0
Rents 4	94247	0	7935	0	13703	9203	7063	5496	7404	7405	177	35861	0
Royalties 5	43995	0	0	0	390	0	0	1	0	0	0	43604	0
Other Portfolio Income 6	292508	50641	92813	3853	26958	18879	59876	6200	3909	5130	814	23436	0
Other Receipts 7	2083387	16582	324398	95988	231986	50950	118320	96966	89531	100238	-1221	959647	0
Total Receipts 8	287646550	2083862	54368810	22448072	35577205	8170615	18599224	14858190	13733138	14535845	6565054	96706535	0
Average Total Receipts 9	9533	1258	2618	5622	11114	26701	138800	309546	403916	908490	2188351	7438964	•

Operating Costs/Operating Income (%)

Cost of Operations 10	90.3	87.9	90.2	91.0	90.9	90.4	90.5	92.4	92.4	90.6	91.3	89.4	•
Salaries and Wages 11	2.7	3.2	2.1	1.5	2.8	2.5	3.8	2.6	2.1	3.3	2.1	3.1	•
Taxes Paid 12	0.9	0.7	0.7	1.0	0.8	0.7	0.7	0.5	0.7	0.5	0.5	1.1	•
Interest Paid 13	0.3	0.2	0.1	0.4	0.4	0.6	0.2	0.2	0.2	0.3	0.3	0.3	•
Depreciation 14	0.8	0.3	0.2	0.4	0.6	0.7	0.6	0.6	0.8	0.9	1.6	1.4	•
Amortization and Depletion 15	0.1	•	0.1	0.2	0.1	0.1	0.0	0.0	0.0	0.1	0.1	0.0	•
Pensions and Other Deferred Comp. 16	0.0	•	0.0	•	0.0	0.0	0.0	0.0	0.0	0.1	0.0	0.1	•
Employee Benefits 17	0.1	•	0.0	0.0	0.1	0.2	0.2	0.1	0.1	0.1	0.1	0.3	•
Advertising 18	0.1	0.0	0.1	0.0	0.1	0.1	0.1	0.1	0.1	0.1	0.1	0.2	•
Other Expenses 19	3.8	7.2	5.2	3.6	3.5	3.7	3.6	3.4	3.0	3.4	2.8	3.6	•
Officers' Compensation 20	0.3	2.1	0.7	0.8	0.4	0.4	0.2	0.2	0.2	0.1	0.6	0.1	•
Operating Margin 21	0.5	•	0.6	1.0	0.2	0.7	0.1	•	0.5	0.5	0.5	0.6	•
Operating Margin Before Officers' Comp. 22	0.8	0.4	1.3	1.8	0.6	1.1	0.3	0.1	0.7	0.6	1.1	0.6	•

Selected Average Balance Sheet ($ in Thousands)

Net Receivables 23	117	0	9	27	80	540	2402	5683	5181	14537	14718	136566	•
Inventories 24	160	0	50	107	184	593	1885	3887	5248	25413	18051	117546	•
Net Property, Plant and Equipment 25	738	0	47	346	1045	3227	6251	15625	32425	91380	258441	818672	•
Total Assets 26	1504	0	190	725	1760	6197	16064	36000	65145	182630	337997	1613572	•
Notes and Loans Payable 27	400	0	93	344	932	3470	3949	11314	17498	49247	100415	152178	•
All Other Liabilities 28	491	0	40	91	219	1009	4909	13138	16297	52654	130501	732731	•
Net Worth 29	613	0	57	290	609	1718	7206	11548	31350	80729	107081	728662	•

Selected Financial Ratios (Times to 1)

Current Ratio 30	1.4	•	2.5	2.5	2.2	2.0	1.5	1.1	1.4	1.2	0.6	1.1	•
Quick Ratio 31	0.7	•	1.0	1.3	1.2	1.0	1.0	0.6	0.9	0.6	0.4	0.6	•
Net Sales to Working Capital 32	66.3	•	41.1	38.2	39.0	28.0	60.1	146.5	57.5	93.9	•	178.4	•
Coverage Ratio 33	6.0	7.8	14.0	4.7	3.4	3.8	7.3	4.5	8.9	5.7	3.0	6.5	•
Total Asset Turnover 34	6.3	•	13.7	7.7	6.3	4.3	8.6	8.5	6.2	4.9	6.5	4.6	•
Inventory Turnover 35	53.4	•	46.4	47.6	54.4	40.3	65.9	73.0	70.6	32.2	110.7	55.9	•
Receivables Turnover 36	86.9	•	351.6	199.5	124.4	74.4	58.7	59.3	78.0	56.1	297.3	59.6	•
Total Liabilities to Net Worth 37	1.5	•	2.3	1.5	1.9	2.6	1.2	2.1	1.1	1.3	2.2	1.2	•
Current Assets to Working Capital 38	3.5	•	1.7	1.7	1.9	2.0	3.1	7.7	3.5	5.4	•	11.0	•
Current Liabilities to Working Capital 39	2.5	•	0.7	0.7	0.9	1.0	2.1	6.7	2.5	4.4	•	10.0	•
Working Capital to Net Sales 40	0.0	•	0.0	0.0	0.0	0.0	0.0	0.0	0.0	0.0	•	0.0	•
Inventory to Working Capital 41	1.2	•	0.9	0.6	0.6	0.7	0.9	2.1	0.8	2.4	•	3.4	•
Total Receipts to Cash Flow 42	26.0	26.1	23.1	27.0	29.1	22.5	30.6	31.0	29.2	28.0	38.9	24.4	•
Cost of Goods to Cash Flow 43	23.5	22.9	20.9	24.5	26.4	20.3	27.7	28.7	27.0	25.4	35.6	21.8	•
Cash Flow to Total Debt 44	0.4	•	0.8	0.5	0.3	0.3	0.5	0.4	0.4	0.3	0.2	0.3	•

Selected Financial Factors (in Percentages)

Debt Ratio 45	59.2	•	69.9	60.0	65.4	72.3	55.1	67.9	51.9	55.8	68.3	54.8	•
Return on Total Assets 46	10.7	•	20.0	14.4	8.9	9.7	10.8	7.3	8.3	7.4	5.3	10.1	•
Return on Equity Before Income Taxes 47	21.9	•	61.6	28.3	18.1	25.9	20.8	17.6	15.3	13.8	11.1	19.0	•
Return on Equity After Income Taxes 48	19.8	•	60.4	28.1	17.7	24.1	19.9	16.4	14.3	12.8	8.0	15.6	•
Profit Margin (Before Income Tax) 49	1.4	1.7	1.4	1.5	1.0	1.7	1.1	0.7	1.2	1.2	0.5	1.9	•
Profit Margin (After Income Tax) 50	1.3	1.7	1.3	1.5	1.0	1.6	1.0	0.6	1.1	1.1	0.4	1.5	•

226

Table I

Corporations with and without Net Income

CLOTHING AND CLOTHING ACCESSORIES STORES

MONEY AMOUNTS AND SIZE OF ASSETS IN THOUSANDS OF DOLLARS

Item Description for Accounting Period 7/12 Through 6/13	Total	Zero Assets	Under 500	500 to 1,000	1,000 to 5,000	5,000 to 10,000	10,000 to 25,000	25,000 to 50,000	50,000 to 100,000	100,000 to 250,000	250,000 to 500,000	500,000 to 2,500,000	2,500,000 and over
Number of Enterprises **1**	49646	10965	32144	3326	2615	288	140	49	32	20	23	32	12

Revenues ($ in Thousands)													
Net Sales **2**	212655648	5412364	13608956	4926292	10704034	3555451	3823203	3560509	3870451	6573795	15968617	55365121	85286856
Interest **3**	881133	52775	711	1132	3473	1372	734	1088	910	326	3176	381937	433500
Rents **4**	139655	8	15027	180	2716	13128	36	939	107	3158	1496	41012	61848
Royalties **5**	1019420	19767	0	0	37	0	115	0	1570	0	52431	225990	719508
Other Portfolio Income **6**	329936	212357	22	4592	6627	565	983	494	9910	16136	3151	24023	51077
Other Receipts **7**	3244175	67600	90965	31572	100416	38768	71190	65845	38610	53831	194405	982998	1507975
Total Receipts **8**	218269967	5764871	13715681	4963768	10817303	3609284	3896261	3628875	3921558	6647246	16223276	57021081	88060764
Average Total Receipts **9**	4397	526	427	1492	4137	12532	27830	74059	122549	332362	705360	1781909	7338397

Operating Costs/Operating Income (%)													
Cost of Operations **10**	52.7	52.1	54.1	55.8	60.1	60.8	56.9	56.0	55.2	51.9	53.3	50.8	51.9
Salaries and Wages **11**	14.0	12.0	10.4	10.9	11.2	11.5	14.3	14.5	14.9	16.3	14.7	14.9	14.4
Taxes Paid **12**	2.4	2.7	3.4	3.1	2.1	2.1	2.5	3.8	2.5	2.3	2.1	2.5	2.1
Interest Paid **13**	1.0	1.5	0.4	0.5	0.6	0.6	0.7	0.6	0.8	0.6	0.8	0.9	1.5
Depreciation **14**	2.3	1.3	0.6	0.7	0.8	1.5	1.7	1.7	2.3	2.2	3.0	2.9	2.5
Amortization and Depletion **15**	0.2	0.2	0.1	0.0	0.1	0.1	0.2	0.1	0.3	0.2	0.2	0.3	0.3
Pensions and Other Deferred Comp. **16**	0.3	0.2	0.2	0.2	0.3	0.3	0.2	0.1	0.1	0.1	0.1	0.2	0.5
Employee Benefits **17**	1.1	0.7	0.3	0.7	0.6	0.5	0.9	0.9	1.0	0.9	1.5	1.0	1.3
Advertising **18**	2.3	2.9	1.9	3.4	2.0	2.9	3.2	3.0	2.5	1.7	2.3	2.6	2.2
Other Expenses **19**	18.4	28.0	20.2	16.1	16.2	18.2	19.7	18.8	20.5	22.4	19.6	21.0	15.5
Officers' Compensation **20**	1.5	1.2	6.1	5.3	3.8	2.0	1.5	1.3	0.9	0.5	0.8	0.6	1.0
Operating Margin **21**	3.7	•	2.2	3.3	2.3	•	•	•	•	0.9	1.6	2.2	7.0
Operating Margin Before Officers' Comp. **22**	5.2	•	8.4	8.6	6.2	1.7	•	0.5	•	1.4	2.4	2.8	8.0

Selected Average Balance Sheet ($ in Thousands)

Net Receivables 23	170	0	5	32	85	194	1399	3140	3850	5214	15858	47672	452981
Inventories 24	674	0	81	478	1074	3486	7360	14412	28900	54656	106097	296807	810415
Net Property, Plant and Equipment 25	591	0	11	43	277	1025	3171	5752	15857	45674	97184	326816	1082260
Total Assets 26	2559	0	143	710	1912	7189	16592	35085	71914	165346	349604	1116510	4968845
Notes and Loans Payable 27	715	0	61	225	507	1979	4419	9302	15597	32575	55179	264769	1577652
All Other Liabilities 28	947	0	40	137	663	2375	6541	15804	34886	79873	134986	370467	1958608
Net Worth 29	897	0	41	348	742	2835	5632	9979	21431	52898	159440	481274	1432585

Selected Financial Ratios (Times to 1)

Current Ratio 30	1.6	•	2.5	3.2	2.2	2.2	1.4	1.5	1.6	1.3	2.0	1.6	1.3
Quick Ratio 31	0.5	•	0.7	0.7	0.5	0.3	0.3	0.4	0.4	0.4	0.6	0.4	0.6
Net Sales to Working Capital 32	9.4	•	5.9	3.4	5.1	3.9	7.9	9.2	7.2	19.3	7.2	9.5	13.9
Coverage Ratio 33	7.2	3.8	9.0	9.7	6.9	2.9	1.2	2.7	1.6	4.2	5.2	6.8	8.1
Total Asset Turnover 34	1.7	•	3.0	2.1	2.1	1.7	1.6	2.1	1.7	2.0	2.0	1.5	1.4
Inventory Turnover 35	3.4	•	2.8	1.7	2.3	2.2	2.1	2.8	2.3	3.1	3.5	3.0	4.6
Receivables Turnover 36	27.0	•	95.0	37.7	49.8	60.7	18.9	25.4	27.8	35.1	54.5	35.0	17.8
Total Liabilities to Net Worth 37	1.9	•	2.4	1.0	1.6	1.5	1.9	2.5	2.4	2.1	1.2	1.3	2.5
Current Assets to Working Capital 38	2.8	•	1.7	1.5	1.8	1.9	3.4	3.2	2.8	4.8	2.1	2.8	4.0
Current Liabilities to Working Capital 39	1.8	•	0.7	0.5	0.8	0.9	2.4	2.2	1.8	3.8	1.1	1.8	3.0
Working Capital to Net Sales 40	0.1	•	0.2	0.3	0.2	0.3	0.1	0.1	0.1	0.1	0.1	0.1	0.1
Inventory to Working Capital 41	1.5	•	1.2	1.1	1.3	1.3	2.1	2.2	1.6	2.9	1.2	1.6	1.7
Total Receipts to Cash Flow 42	6.3	5.4	7.2	7.7	8.8	8.5	9.5	9.7	10.5	8.4	8.3	6.4	5.3
Cost of Goods to Cash Flow 43	3.3	2.8	3.9	4.3	5.3	5.2	5.4	5.4	5.8	4.3	4.4	3.2	2.8
Cash Flow to Total Debt 44	0.4	•	0.6	0.5	0.4	0.3	0.3	0.3	0.2	0.3	0.4	0.4	0.4

Selected Financial Factors (in Percentages)

Debt Ratio 45	65.0	•	71.0	51.0	61.2	60.6	66.1	71.6	70.2	68.0	54.4	56.9	71.2
Return on Total Assets 46	12.5	•	10.1	9.5	8.4	3.1	1.4	3.6	2.2	5.3	8.0	9.6	16.9
Return on Equity Before Income Taxes 47	30.8	•	30.9	17.4	18.6	5.2	0.7	8.0	2.7	12.5	14.2	19.0	51.5
Return on Equity After Income Taxes 48	20.4	•	30.4	16.3	17.5	3.0	•	3.1	0.0	6.7	6.4	12.5	33.3
Profit Margin (Before Income Tax) 49	6.5	4.0	3.0	4.1	3.4	1.2	0.1	1.1	0.5	2.0	3.3	5.3	10.4
Profit Margin (After Income Tax) 50	4.3	2.9	3.0	3.8	3.2	0.7	•	0.4	0.0	1.1	1.5	3.5	6.7

Table II

Corporations with Net Income

CLOTHING AND CLOTHING ACCESSORIES STORES

MONEY AMOUNTS AND SIZE OF ASSETS IN THOUSANDS OF DOLLARS

Item Description for Accounting Period 7/12 Through 6/13	Total	Zero Assets	Under 500	500 to 1,000	1,000 to 5,000	5,000 to 10,000	10,000 to 25,000	25,000 to 50,000	50,000 to 100,000	100,000 to 250,000	250,000 to 500,000	500,000 to 2,500,000	2,500,000 and over
Number of Enterprises 1	30909	4879	20880	2579	2103	261	95	33	•	11	14	25	•

Revenues ($ in Thousands)

	Total	Zero Assets	Under 500	500 to 1,000	1,000 to 5,000	5,000 to 10,000	10,000 to 25,000	25,000 to 50,000	50,000 to 100,000	100,000 to 250,000	250,000 to 500,000	500,000 to 2,500,000	2,500,000 and over
Net Sales 2	182327134	4529798	9818156	4337069	8683249	3084384	2602534	2258590	•	3975469	10718640	49171792	•
Interest 3	541469	49514	426	1054	2152	864	544	919	•	236	2100	51805	•
Rents 4	107172	8	0	180	2678	74	36	0	•	1248	451	40542	•
Royalties 5	473946	19767	0	0	37	0	102	0	•	0	14639	164188	•
Other Portfolio Income 6	282990	211544	20	3513	2535	428	249	351	•	1644	2939	11353	•
Other Receipts 7	2847103	62289	74871	18066	79635	29342	51683	30163	•	35363	57310	923832	•
Total Receipts 8	186579814	4872920	9893473	4359882	8770286	3115092	2655148	2290023	•	4013960	10796079	50363512	•
Average Total Receipts 9	6036	999	474	1691	4170	11935	27949	69395	•	364905	771148	2014540	•

Operating Costs/Operating Income (%)

	Total	Zero Assets	Under 500	500 to 1,000	1,000 to 5,000	5,000 to 10,000	10,000 to 25,000	25,000 to 50,000	50,000 to 100,000	100,000 to 250,000	250,000 to 500,000	500,000 to 2,500,000	2,500,000 and over
Cost of Operations 10	52.6	51.3	53.9	55.1	60.6	62.8	57.3	54.4	•	48.8	53.3	50.8	•
Salaries and Wages 11	13.6	11.0	8.1	10.8	10.3	10.0	13.1	14.1	•	16.4	13.3	14.8	•
Taxes Paid 12	2.3	2.6	3.2	3.1	2.0	1.6	2.4	4.4	•	2.4	2.3	2.5	•
Interest Paid 13	0.8	1.5	0.3	0.4	0.4	0.4	0.5	0.5	•	0.6	0.2	0.6	•
Depreciation 14	2.2	1.2	0.6	0.6	0.7	1.0	1.0	1.6	•	2.4	2.3	2.8	•
Amortization and Depletion 15	0.2	0.2	0.0	0.0	0.1	0.0	0.2	0.0	•	0.2	0.1	0.3	•
Pensions and Other Deferred Comp. 16	0.2	0.3	0.2	0.2	0.3	0.4	0.2	0.1	•	0.1	0.0	0.2	•
Employee Benefits 17	1.0	0.7	0.1	0.6	0.5	0.3	0.7	0.8	•	0.7	1.0	0.9	•
Advertising 18	2.2	3.2	1.4	3.4	1.8	2.9	3.2	2.8	•	1.1	2.0	2.5	•
Other Expenses 19	17.3	26.3	19.4	15.3	15.1	15.0	16.0	14.0	•	20.6	17.6	19.9	•
Officers' Compensation 20	1.4	0.8	6.0	4.9	4.1	2.0	1.4	1.2	•	0.4	0.9	0.6	•
Operating Margin 21	6.2	1.1	6.8	5.5	4.1	3.6	4.0	6.2	•	6.3	7.0	4.1	•
Operating Margin Before Officers' Comp. 22	7.6	1.8	12.7	10.5	8.1	5.6	5.4	7.4	•	6.7	7.9	4.7	•

Selected Average Balance Sheet ($ in Thousands)

	C1	C2	C3	C4	C5	C6	C7	C8		C9	C10	C11	
Net Receivables 23	234	0	4	34	80	177	1600	4161	•	7528	14530	44973	•
Inventories 24	852	0	84	455	1091	3277	7017	14381	•	55613	100930	280156	•
Net Property, Plant and Equipment 25	816	0	10	43	265	963	2234	4634	•	47074	96632	363724	•
Total Assets 26	3287	0	145	717	1896	7214	15746	35256	•	182649	360862	1156027	•
Notes and Loans Payable 27	739	0	51	192	309	1867	2690	7268	•	24568	18813	189139	•
All Other Liabilities 28	1205	0	38	140	709	1793	4860	13608	•	83076	124426	384228	•
Net Worth 29	1343	0	56	385	878	3553	8195	14381	•	75006	217623	582660	•

Selected Financial Ratios (Times to 1)

	C1	C2	C3	C4	C5	C6	C7	C8		C9	C10	C11	
Current Ratio 30	1.6	•	2.9	3.1	2.1	2.7	2.0	1.7	•	1.4	2.1	1.6	•
Quick Ratio 31	0.5	•	0.8	0.7	0.5	0.3	0.6	0.5	•	0.4	0.6	0.5	•
Net Sales to Working Capital 32	9.6	•	6.0	3.8	5.2	3.2	4.7	5.9	•	15.3	7.0	9.2	•
Coverage Ratio 33	11.6	6.8	25.7	16.6	12.9	12.5	12.6	17.8	•	13.2	36.0	11.6	•
Total Asset Turnover 34	1.8	•	3.3	2.3	2.2	1.6	1.7	1.9	•	2.0	2.1	1.7	•
Inventory Turnover 35	3.6	•	3.0	2.0	2.3	2.3	2.2	2.6	•	3.2	4.0	3.6	•
Receivables Turnover 36	27.4	•	132.1	37.2	57.2	87.4	15.1	21.0	•	•	64.9	49.0	•
Total Liabilities to Net Worth 37	1.4	•	1.6	0.9	1.2	1.0	0.9	1.5	•	1.4	0.7	1.0	•
Current Assets to Working Capital 38	2.8	•	1.5	1.5	1.9	1.6	2.0	2.4	•	3.6	1.9	2.6	•
Current Liabilities to Working Capital 39	1.8	•	0.5	0.5	0.9	0.6	1.0	1.4	•	2.6	0.9	1.6	•
Working Capital to Net Sales 40	0.1	•	0.2	0.3	0.2	0.3	0.2	0.2	•	0.1	0.1	0.1	•
Inventory to Working Capital 41	1.5	•	1.1	1.1	1.3	1.1	1.2	1.5	•	2.4	1.1	1.5	•
Total Receipts to Cash Flow 42	5.7	4.5	5.9	6.9	8.2	7.1	6.6	7.1	•	6.0	6.2	6.2	•
Cost of Goods to Cash Flow 43	3.0	2.3	3.2	3.8	5.0	4.4	3.8	3.9	•	2.9	3.3	3.1	•
Cash Flow to Total Debt 44	0.5	•	0.9	0.7	0.5	0.5	0.6	0.5	•	0.6	0.9	0.6	•

Selected Financial Factors (in Percentages)

	C1	C2	C3	C4	C5	C6	C7	C8		C9	C10	C11	
Debt Ratio 45	59.1	•	61.5	46.3	53.7	50.7	48.0	59.2	•	58.9	39.7	49.6	•
Return on Total Assets 46	16.9	•	25.5	15.1	12.0	8.2	11.3	15.6	•	15.6	16.8	12.2	•
Return on Equity Before Income Taxes 47	37.9	•	63.7	26.5	23.9	15.4	20.1	36.2	•	35.1	27.1	22.1	•
Return on Equity After Income Taxes 48	26.8	•	63.2	25.2	22.7	13.5	19.3	31.1	•	27.6	17.8	15.3	•
Profit Margin (Before Income Tax) 49	8.6	8.9	7.5	6.1	5.1	4.6	6.0	7.6	•	7.3	7.7	6.6	•
Profit Margin (After Income Tax) 50	6.1	7.5	7.5	5.8	4.8	4.1	5.8	6.5	•	5.7	5.1	4.5	•

Table I

Corporations with and without Net Income

SPORTING GOODS, HOBBY, BOOK, AND MUSIC STORES

MONEY AMOUNTS AND SIZE OF ASSETS IN THOUSANDS OF DOLLARS

Item Description for Accounting Period 7/12 Through 6/13		Total	Zero Assets	Under 500	500 to 1,000	1,000 to 5,000	5,000 to 10,000	10,000 to 25,000	25,000 to 50,000	50,000 to 100,000	100,000 to 250,000	250,000 to 500,000	500,000 to 2,500,000	2,500,000 and over
Number of Enterprises	1	23732	2871	17226	1392	1893	226	63	21	6	13	10	7	4
Revenues ($ in Thousands)														
Net Sales	2	79387545	3309887	6081783	2170228	8015570	2984632	1621691	1122009	1069046	4655112	5629085	18673214	24055289
Interest	3	630735	57	872	528	3377	825	2232	148	6	286	1425	1015	619964
Rents	4	48903	2185	4020	0	3782	40	0	6299	0	223	9899	1737	20718
Royalties	5	122635	0	0	33	0	0	0	0	0	13786	0	6500	102316
Other Portfolio Income	6	126640	26337	31622	325	9990	411	216	3628	234	15519	3878	2099	32381
Other Receipts	7	1105057	39497	13736	159156	76378	26449	10650	6611	16362	50348	93949	113147	498774
Total Receipts	8	81421515	3377963	6132033	2330270	8109097	3012357	1634789	1138695	1085648	4735274	5738236	18797712	25329442
Average Total Receipts	9	3431	1177	356	1674	4284	13329	25949	54224	180941	364252	573824	2685387	6332360
Operating Costs/Operating Income (%)														
Cost of Operations	10	59.8	61.2	58.7	67.5	60.5	72.4	61.0	66.1	59.3	59.7	61.7	51.9	62.6
Salaries and Wages	11	12.6	12.4	10.4	10.8	12.6	9.3	12.7	9.2	13.8	13.8	13.0	14.1	12.2
Taxes Paid	12	2.4	1.3	3.0	4.6	2.8	1.3	1.9	1.7	1.7	2.2	1.8	2.8	2.2
Interest Paid	13	1.8	1.0	0.9	0.6	0.5	0.8	0.6	0.5	0.5	0.8	1.8	3.1	2.2
Depreciation	14	1.8	1.8	0.6	0.7	1.5	0.4	0.9	3.3	0.9	1.9	1.7	2.3	2.0
Amortization and Depletion	15	0.2	0.1	0.1	0.0	0.1	0.1	0.2	0.1	0.6	0.2	1.2	0.1	0.2
Pensions and Other Deferred Comp.	16	0.2	0.1	0.1	0.1	0.4	0.0	0.1	0.1	0.4	0.2	0.1	0.1	0.2
Employee Benefits	17	0.7	1.6	0.7	0.7	0.7	0.3	0.9	0.8	1.4	0.8	0.7	0.3	0.8
Advertising	18	2.5	4.7	1.0	1.2	1.6	1.6	2.5	3.7	2.4	2.7	2.3	2.7	3.0
Other Expenses	19	15.5	11.7	19.1	15.6	13.0	9.2	13.8	14.2	20.2	16.6	14.0	16.3	16.3
Officers' Compensation	20	1.5	1.5	4.2	4.5	4.0	0.8	1.9	0.9	0.3	0.7	0.6	0.4	1.1
Operating Margin	21	1.0	2.5	1.1	•	2.2	3.7	3.4	•	•	0.4	1.1	5.6	•
Operating Margin Before Officers' Comp.	22	2.5	3.9	5.3	•	6.2	4.5	5.3	0.3	•	1.1	1.7	6.0	•

Selected Average Balance Sheet ($ in Thousands)

Net Receivables 23	216	0	3	31	118	597	1610	2238	6028	9974	23479	51128	944102
Inventories 24	696	0	82	488	885	3332	5424	12597	41114	91620	121645	579242	1170050
Net Property, Plant and Equipment 25	422	0	10	78	359	429	2009	5971	6304	27364	69423	365055	1268607
Total Assets 26	1994	0	126	736	1998	6947	15207	35616	66391	163342	341631	1610412	4964301
Notes and Loans Payable 27	835	0	84	580	517	1808	2453	9750	25885	55665	138303	847244	1906713
All Other Liabilities 28	778	0	37	153	509	1400	6235	11728	22960	71067	107134	769869	2040123
Net Worth 29	382	0	6	3	972	3738	6518	14138	17547	36610	96194	-6701	1017466

Selected Financial Ratios (Times to 1)

Current Ratio 30	1.7	•	2.8	3.7	2.9	1.7	1.5	1.8	1.6	1.7	1.7	1.5	1.5
Quick Ratio 31	0.6	•	0.6	0.8	1.0	0.4	0.4	0.4	0.3	0.3	0.4	0.2	0.8
Net Sales to Working Capital 32	6.9	•	5.1	3.4	4.2	7.9	8.1	4.4	9.6	7.0	7.6	10.5	6.6
Coverage Ratio 33	2.9	5.5	3.2	2.6	7.2	7.1	7.7	3.0	1.3	3.6	2.7	3.0	2.1
Total Asset Turnover 34	1.7	•	2.8	2.1	2.1	1.9	1.7	1.5	2.7	2.2	1.6	1.7	1.2
Inventory Turnover 35	2.9	•	2.5	2.2	2.9	2.9	2.9	2.8	2.6	2.3	2.9	2.4	3.2
Receivables Turnover 36	15.8	•	87.9	43.3	37.1	20.9	19.1	28.2	14.9	49.8	26.8	52.4	6.5
Total Liabilities to Net Worth 37	4.2	•	21.5	220.8	1.1	0.9	1.3	1.5	2.8	3.5	2.6	•	3.9
Current Assets to Working Capital 38	2.4	•	1.6	1.4	1.5	2.5	2.9	2.2	2.7	2.4	2.5	2.9	2.9
Current Liabilities to Working Capital 39	1.4	•	0.6	0.4	0.5	1.5	1.9	1.2	1.7	1.4	1.5	1.9	1.9
Working Capital to Net Sales 40	0.1	•	0.2	0.3	0.2	0.1	0.1	0.2	0.1	0.1	0.1	0.1	0.2
Inventory to Working Capital 41	1.4	•	1.2	1.1	1.0	1.7	2.0	1.2	2.0	1.8	1.8	2.2	1.2
Total Receipts to Cash Flow 42	8.2	8.5	7.6	10.7	8.9	10.3	7.8	8.6	8.3	11.3	9.7	6.9	8.3
Cost of Goods to Cash Flow 43	4.9	5.2	4.5	7.2	5.4	7.4	4.8	5.7	4.9	6.7	6.0	3.6	5.2
Cash Flow to Total Debt 44	0.3	•	0.4	0.2	0.5	0.4	0.4	0.3	0.4	0.3	0.2	0.2	0.2

Selected Financial Factors (in Percentages)

Debt Ratio 45	80.9	•	95.5	99.5	51.4	46.2	57.1	60.3	73.6	77.6	71.8	100.4	79.5
Return on Total Assets 46	9.0	•	7.9	3.4	8.3	10.3	8.2	2.1	1.6	6.6	8.1	15.7	5.6
Return on Equity Before Income Taxes 47	31.1	•	122.9	452.8	14.7	16.4	16.7	3.5	1.4	21.2	18.1	•	14.2
Return on Equity After Income Taxes 48	24.7	•	121.6	368.9	13.8	15.5	16.4	2.5	0.3	16.8	8.7	•	9.7
Profit Margin (Before Income Tax) 49	3.6	4.7	2.0	1.0	3.4	4.7	4.2	0.9	0.1	2.2	3.1	6.3	2.4
Profit Margin (After Income Tax) 50	2.8	2.5	1.9	0.8	3.2	4.4	4.1	0.7	0.0	1.7	1.5	5.3	1.6

Table II

Corporations with Net Income

SPORTING GOODS, HOBBY, BOOK, AND MUSIC STORES

MONEY AMOUNTS AND SIZE OF ASSETS IN THOUSANDS OF DOLLARS

Item Description for Accounting Period 7/12 Through 6/13	Total	Zero Assets	Under 500	500 to 1,000	1,000 to 5,000	5,000 to 10,000	10,000 to 25,000	25,000 to 50,000	50,000 to 100,000	100,000 to 250,000	250,000 to 500,000	500,000 to 2,500,000	2,500,000 and over
Number of Enterprises 1	10854	745	7450	957	1447	166	47	15	•	7	5	•	4

Revenues ($ in Thousands)

	Total	Zero Assets	Under 500	500 to 1,000	1,000 to 5,000	5,000 to 10,000	10,000 to 25,000	25,000 to 50,000	50,000 to 100,000	100,000 to 250,000	250,000 to 500,000	500,000 to 2,500,000	2,500,000 and over
Net Sales 2	67217997	2579173	3635111	1602978	6886119	2823560	1260309	855235	•	2825913	3421815	•	24055289
Interest 3	628077	20	749	435	2911	408	2229	144	•	138	93	•	619964
Rents 4	32955	0	0	0	3782	40	0	6299	•	0	379	•	20718
Royalties 5	108817	0	0	0	0	0	0	0	•	0	0	•	102316
Other Portfolio Income 6	113084	22485	31441	0	7153	402	216	1165	•	15508	0	•	32381
Other Receipts 7	990146	31620	5154	158529	70767	26253	10475	5782	•	28962	39531	•	498774
Total Receipts 8	69091076	2633298	3672455	1761942	6970732	2850663	1273229	868625	•	2870521	3461818	•	25329442
Average Total Receipts 9	6365	3535	493	1841	4817	17173	27090	57908	•	410074	692364	•	6332360

Operating Costs/Operating Income (%)

	Total	Zero Assets	Under 500	500 to 1,000	1,000 to 5,000	5,000 to 10,000	10,000 to 25,000	25,000 to 50,000	50,000 to 100,000	100,000 to 250,000	250,000 to 500,000	500,000 to 2,500,000	2,500,000 and over
Cost of Operations 10	59.4	60.3	57.0	70.3	60.9	74.7	58.7	67.1	•	60.4	59.7	•	62.6
Salaries and Wages 11	12.5	11.6	9.0	9.8	12.4	8.6	13.2	7.6	•	12.7	14.2	•	12.2
Taxes Paid 12	2.4	1.0	3.1	5.6	2.6	1.1	2.0	1.4	•	2.2	2.2	•	2.2
Interest Paid 13	1.6	0.9	0.7	0.4	0.4	0.6	0.5	0.6	•	0.5	0.3	•	2.2
Depreciation 14	1.7	1.8	0.6	0.7	0.8	0.2	0.8	1.6	•	1.6	1.6	•	2.0
Amortization and Depletion 15	0.1	0.0	0.1	0.0	0.1	0.0	0.1	0.1	•	0.1	0.1	•	0.2
Pensions and Other Deferred Comp. 16	0.2	0.1	0.0	0.2	0.4	0.0	0.2	0.1	•	0.0	0.1	•	0.2
Employee Benefits 17	0.7	2.0	0.4	0.6	0.8	0.3	1.0	0.5	•	0.7	0.5	•	0.8
Advertising 18	2.5	5.2	0.8	1.1	1.5	1.6	1.4	2.0	•	2.3	2.4	•	3.0
Other Expenses 19	15.1	9.5	18.1	9.5	12.4	8.0	14.4	15.1	•	15.5	12.1	•	16.3
Officers' Compensation 20	1.4	0.4	3.8	5.2	3.9	0.8	2.1	0.6	•	0.8	0.5	•	1.1
Operating Margin 21	2.3	7.3	6.4	•	3.7	4.1	5.7	3.4	•	3.2	6.4	•	•
Operating Margin Before Officers' Comp. 22	3.7	7.7	10.2	1.9	7.7	4.9	7.8	4.1	•	4.0	6.9	•	•

Selected Average Balance Sheet ($ in Thousands)

	1	2	3	4	5	6	7	8		9	10		11
Net Receivables 23	439	0	2	37	129	752	1579	2095	•	15423	14396	•	944102
Inventories 24	1111	0	96	440	844	4387	5394	13706	•	80080	144938	•	1086183
Net Property, Plant and Equipment 25	823	0	7	83	328	226	2402	5715	•	25577	91798	•	1268607
Total Assets 26	3665	0	134	726	2127	7370	13838	38508	•	165576	348126	•	4964301
Notes and Loans Payable 27	1491	0	63	224	480	1882	1743	12119	•	51917	35120	•	1906713
All Other Liabilities 28	1356	0	27	110	510	1637	6137	12831	•	74497	141676	•	2040123
Net Worth 29	818	0	44	392	1137	3851	5958	13558	•	39162	171329	•	1017466

Selected Financial Ratios (Times to 1)

Current Ratio 30	1.7	•	4.0	4.7	3.2	1.7	1.8	1.9	•	2.0	1.8	•	1.5
Quick Ratio 31	0.6	•	1.2	1.3	1.2	0.4	0.6	0.3	•	0.5	0.3	•	0.8
Net Sales to Working Capital 32	7.0	•	5.5	3.4	4.1	7.8	6.5	4.0	•	6.0	7.0	•	6.6
Coverage Ratio 33	4.1	11.4	12.4	19.8	13.2	9.1	14.0	9.5	•	10.4	22.7	•	2.1
Total Asset Turnover 34	1.7	•	3.6	2.3	2.2	2.3	1.9	1.5	•	2.4	2.0	•	1.2
Inventory Turnover 35	3.3	•	2.9	2.7	3.4	2.9	2.9	2.8	•	3.0	2.8	•	3.5
Receivables Turnover 36	14.9	•	90.3	36.9	38.4	23.3	22.3	28.7	•	45.0	49.6	•	•
Total Liabilities to Net Worth 37	3.5	•	2.1	0.9	0.9	0.9	1.3	1.8	•	3.2	1.0	•	3.9
Current Assets to Working Capital 38	2.4	•	1.3	1.3	1.5	2.4	2.2	2.1	•	2.0	2.3	•	2.9
Current Liabilities to Working Capital 39	1.4	•	0.3	0.3	0.5	1.4	1.2	1.1	•	1.0	1.3	•	1.9
Working Capital to Net Sales 40	0.1	•	0.2	0.3	0.2	0.1	0.2	0.2	•	0.2	0.1	•	0.2
Inventory to Working Capital 41	1.4	•	0.9	0.9	0.9	1.8	1.5	1.1	•	1.4	1.7	•	1.2
Total Receipts to Cash Flow 42	7.4	6.3	5.8	7.5	8.0	10.8	6.7	6.1	•	8.8	7.5	•	8.3
Cost of Goods to Cash Flow 43	4.4	3.8	3.3	5.2	4.9	8.0	3.9	4.1	•	5.3	4.5	•	5.2
Cash Flow to Total Debt 44	0.3	•	0.9	0.7	0.6	0.4	0.5	0.4	•	0.4	0.5	•	0.2

Selected Financial Factors (in Percentages)

Debt Ratio 45	77.7	•	67.3	46.1	46.5	47.7	56.9	64.8	•	76.3	50.8	•	79.5
Return on Total Assets 46	11.4	•	29.3	16.0	12.0	13.1	14.0	8.2	•	12.9	15.5	•	5.6
Return on Equity Before Income Taxes 47	38.8	•	82.4	28.2	20.8	22.3	30.2	20.9	•	49.3	30.2	•	14.2
Return on Equity After Income Taxes 48	32.2	•	82.0	27.2	19.8	21.1	29.7	19.4	•	41.6	19.6	•	9.7
Profit Margin (Before Income Tax) 49	5.1	9.7	7.4	6.6	5.0	5.1	6.7	5.0	•	4.8	7.6	•	2.4
Profit Margin (After Income Tax) 50	4.3	6.9	7.4	6.4	4.7	4.8	6.6	4.6	•	4.0	4.9	•	1.6

Table I

Corporations with and without Net Income

GENERAL MERCHANDISE STORES

MONEY AMOUNTS AND SIZE OF ASSETS IN THOUSANDS OF DOLLARS

Item Description for Accounting Period 7/12 Through 6/13	Total	Zero Assets	Under 500	500 to 1,000	1,000 to 5,000	5,000 to 10,000	10,000 to 25,000	25,000 to 50,000	50,000 to 100,000	100,000 to 250,000	250,000 to 500,000	500,000 to 2,500,000	2,500,000 and over
Number of Enterprises 1	8712	1591	5673	1090	241	32	25	15	6	10	6	9	15
Revenues ($ in Thousands)													
Net Sales 2	679015751	1123376	3783399	1940919	1782084	666043	587652	1326251	381227	3533708	3782305	23211377	636897411
Interest 3	519374	467	1183	479	2541	573	140	18	12	1122	7071	3837	501930
Rents 4	895661	4918	0	0	217	0	0	8	5449	2859	2903	17428	861878
Royalties 5	1571902	0	0	0	58	0	0	0	0	0	2535	112535	1456773
Other Portfolio Income 6	2432702	3040	1025	162	1923	64	1389	192	22	1316	68	1973	2421527
Other Receipts 7	13034815	8997	113896	9667	2238	28464	3863	4818	21585	36582	26243	207605	12570861
Total Receipts 8	697470205	1140798	3899503	1951227	1789061	695144	593044	1331287	408295	3575587	3821125	23554755	654710380
Average Total Receipts 9	80059	717	687	1790	7423	21723	23722	88752	68049	357559	636854	2617195	43647359
Operating Costs/Operating Income (%)													
Cost of Operations 10	73.6	67.2	75.9	65.0	61.0	73.8	61.5	71.7	67.1	68.8	59.6	65.4	74.1
Salaries and Wages 11	10.8	5.4	6.5	10.2	12.0	8.3	10.3	9.6	13.4	11.7	13.9	12.5	10.8
Taxes Paid 12	1.8	1.4	1.7	1.4	1.9	1.8	1.2	1.5	2.3	1.9	1.6	2.6	1.8
Interest Paid 13	0.8	0.4	0.3	0.4	0.6	0.1	0.2	0.2	0.5	0.3	0.2	0.9	0.8
Depreciation 14	1.8	0.9	0.4	0.4	0.5	0.2	0.8	0.5	1.7	1.3	3.0	1.8	1.8
Amortization and Depletion 15	0.1	0.4	0.0	0.1	0.0	0.0	0.0	0.1	0.1	0.0	0.2	0.1	0.1
Pensions and Other Deferred Comp. 16	0.4	0.0	•	0.8	0.2	0.1	0.2	0.2	0.4	0.3	0.1	0.2	0.4
Employee Benefits 17	0.9	0.2	0.1	0.5	0.6	1.2	1.9	0.9	1.1	1.3	1.9	1.1	0.9
Advertising 18	1.2	2.9	0.4	5.5	1.3	1.1	1.3	1.0	1.8	3.0	1.7	1.5	1.2
Other Expenses 19	6.6	23.8	12.4	8.9	18.1	8.0	18.0	11.1	17.7	12.1	14.7	11.3	6.2
Officers' Compensation 20	0.2	0.4	2.3	4.1	2.4	0.8	1.6	0.5	0.3	0.1	1.9	0.6	0.1
Operating Margin 21	1.8	•	•	2.5	1.5	4.6	3.2	2.7	•	•	1.2	2.1	1.8
Operating Margin Before Officers' Comp. 22	2.0	•	2.1	6.6	3.9	5.4	4.7	3.2	•	•	3.1	2.7	1.9

Selected Average Balance Sheet ($ in Thousands)

Net Receivables 23	745	0	1	34	295	1279	1691	801	12657	15230	20481	28994	377782
Inventories 24	8796	0	60	199	1283	2579	4269	19187	23831	67526	125647	517641	4603652
Net Property, Plant and Equipment 25	17611	0	15	100	284	680	1179	6223	5593	36029	106078	381594	9903824
Total Assets 26	43989	0	116	672	2423	7430	12627	35291	59060	163305	366337	1334618	24265265
Notes and Loans Payable 27	12201	0	66	293	564	422	658	16370	5498	23693	67981	328719	6770558
All Other Liabilities 28	15611	0	42	114	986	1868	86965	6392	26702	55595	114262	440003	8514007
Net Worth 29	16177	0	8	264	873	5141	-74996	12529	26860	84017	184095	565896	8980699

Selected Financial Ratios (Times to 1)

Current Ratio 30	0.9	•	2.1	2.5	2.0	2.8	0.1	3.5	2.4	2.0	1.4	1.8	0.8
Quick Ratio 31	0.1	•	0.4	1.1	0.8	1.1	0.1	0.4	1.1	0.6	0.3	0.2	0.1
Net Sales to Working Capital 32	•	•	13.7	7.3	7.6	6.4	•	5.5	2.6	6.9	13.2	9.0	•
Coverage Ratio 33	7.3	•	9.1	7.9	4.4	69.4	19.6	14.3	2.8	2.0	10.2	5.1	7.4
Total Asset Turnover 34	1.8	•	5.8	2.7	3.1	2.8	1.9	2.5	1.1	2.2	1.7	1.9	1.7
Inventory Turnover 35	6.5	•	8.4	5.8	3.5	6.0	3.4	3.3	1.8	3.6	3.0	3.3	6.8
Receivables Turnover 36	111.0	•	247.7	80.5	21.9	23.8	11.9	145.5	4.1	27.7	24.4	103.7	119.9
Total Liabilities to Net Worth 37	1.7	•	12.9	1.5	1.8	0.4	•	1.8	1.2	0.9	1.0	1.4	1.7
Current Assets to Working Capital 38	•	•	1.9	1.7	2.0	1.6	•	1.4	1.7	2.0	3.6	2.2	•
Current Liabilities to Working Capital 39	•	•	0.9	0.7	1.0	0.6	•	0.4	0.7	1.0	2.6	1.2	•
Working Capital to Net Sales 40	•	•	0.1	0.1	0.1	0.2	•	0.2	0.4	0.1	0.1	0.1	•
Inventory to Working Capital 41	•	•	1.3	0.9	1.1	0.9	•	1.2	0.6	1.3	2.6	1.8	•
Total Receipts to Cash Flow 42	11.2	6.1	10.8	11.3	7.2	6.7	5.4	9.6	7.8	12.8	10.1	10.5	11.2
Cost of Goods to Cash Flow 43	8.2	4.1	8.2	7.4	4.4	5.0	3.3	6.9	5.3	8.8	6.0	6.9	8.3
Cash Flow to Total Debt 44	0.3	•	0.6	0.4	0.7	1.4	0.0	0.4	0.3	0.3	0.3	0.3	0.2

Selected Financial Factors (in Percentages)

Debt Ratio 45	63.2	•	92.8	60.7	64.0	30.8	693.9	64.5	54.5	48.6	49.7	57.6	63.0
Return on Total Assets 46	10.3	•	18.3	9.2	7.5	25.5	7.5	8.3	1.5	1.3	4.2	8.7	10.4
Return on Equity Before Income Taxes 47	24.2	•	226.2	20.4	16.0	36.3	•	21.6	2.1	1.3	7.6	16.5	24.4
Return on Equity After Income Taxes 48	15.5	•	226.1	19.9	14.1	33.9	•	21.6	1.2	•	6.1	10.9	15.5
Profit Margin (Before Income Tax) 49	5.0	•	2.8	3.0	1.9	9.0	3.8	3.1	0.9	0.3	2.2	3.6	5.2
Profit Margin (After Income Tax) 50	3.2	•	2.8	3.0	1.7	8.4	3.7	3.1	0.5	•	1.8	2.4	3.3

Table II
Corporations with Net Income

GENERAL MERCHANDISE STORES

MONEY AMOUNTS AND SIZE OF ASSETS IN THOUSANDS OF DOLLARS

Item Description for Accounting Period 7/12 Through 6/13	Total	Zero Assets	Under 500	500 to 1,000	1,000 to 5,000	5,000 to 10,000	10,000 to 25,000	25,000 to 50,000	50,000 to 100,000	100,000 to 250,000	250,000 to 500,000	500,000 to 2,500,000	2,500,000 and over
Number of Enterprises **1**	5795	630	3946	939	187	32	16	8	•	7	•	•	•
Revenues ($ in Thousands)													
Net Sales **2**	659289034	355271	3053430	1876065	1424152	666043	571784	884822	•	2980970	•	•	•
Interest **3**	507077	4	1183	454	2128	573	29	0	•	200	•	•	•
Rents **4**	783315	0	0	0	54	0	0	0	•	2820	•	•	•
Royalties **5**	1569654	0	0	0	58	0	0	0	•	0	•	•	•
Other Portfolio Income **6**	2052457	3040	0	7	168	64	0	11	•	385	•	•	•
Other Receipts **7**	11470426	8318	78471	7808	1624	28464	3270	3657	•	32493	•	•	•
Total Receipts **8**	675671963	366633	3133084	1884334	1428184	695144	575083	888490	•	3016868	•	•	•
Average Total Receipts **9**	116596	582	794	2007	7637	21723	35943	111061	•	430981	•	•	•
Operating Costs/Operating Income (%)													
Cost of Operations **10**	73.8	63.1	78.1	65.2	62.3	73.8	62.0	72.5	•	68.2	•	•	•
Salaries and Wages **11**	10.6	8.8	3.9	9.7	10.6	8.3	9.6	9.0	•	11.8	•	•	•
Taxes Paid **12**	1.8	2.3	1.4	1.3	1.6	1.8	1.0	1.5	•	1.8	•	•	•
Interest Paid **13**	0.8	1.1	0.3	0.4	0.5	0.1	0.2	0.3	•	0.2	•	•	•
Depreciation **14**	1.7	1.3	0.3	0.4	0.3	0.2	0.2	0.3	•	1.2	•	•	•
Amortization and Depletion **15**	0.0	0.0	0.0	0.1	0.0	0.0	0.0	0.1	•	0.0	•	•	•
Pensions and Other Deferred Comp. **16**	0.4	0.1	•	0.9	0.3	0.1	0.2	0.1	•	0.3	•	•	•
Employee Benefits **17**	0.9	0.2	0.1	0.5	0.3	1.2	0.8	0.9	•	1.5	•	•	•
Advertising **18**	1.1	3.2	0.3	5.6	1.4	1.1	1.1	0.5	•	2.0	•	•	•
Other Expenses **19**	6.2	14.0	10.4	8.4	15.5	8.0	15.3	7.6	•	11.0	•	•	•
Officers' Compensation **20**	0.1	0.7	2.6	4.0	2.2	0.8	1.5	0.5	•	0.1	•	•	•
Operating Margin **21**	2.4	5.2	2.6	3.4	5.0	4.6	8.0	6.5	•	1.7	•	•	•
Operating Margin Before Officers' Comp. **22**	2.6	5.9	5.2	7.5	7.1	5.4	9.5	7.0	•	1.8	•	•	•

Selected Average Balance Sheet ($ in Thousands)

Net Receivables 23	1073	0	0	29	329	1279	2590	804	•	19491	•	•	•
Inventories 24	12106	0	67	175	1064	2956	6143	30301	•	68106	•	•	•
Net Property, Plant and Equipment 25	25819	0	12	106	210	680	527	5098	•	39028	•	•	•
Total Assets 26	63450	0	106	671	2312	7430	12699	33526	•	151313	•	•	•
Notes and Loans Payable 27	17614	0	62	303	510	422	841	12859	•	10433	•	•	•
All Other Liabilities 28	21818	0	10	121	433	1868	3616	7092	•	52179	•	•	•
Net Worth 29	24018	0	33	247	1369	5141	8242	13574	•	88700	•	•	•

Selected Financial Ratios (Times to 1)

Current Ratio 30	0.9	•	7.7	2.2	4.6	2.8	2.9	3.0	•	2.3	•	•	•
Quick Ratio 31	0.1	•	2.0	1.0	1.9	1.1	1.3	0.2	•	0.8	•	•	•
Net Sales to Working Capital 32	•	•	10.3	9.4	4.9	6.4	4.5	6.2	•	7.0	•	•	•
Coverage Ratio 33	8.0	8.7	17.8	9.8	11.3	69.4	42.5	24.0	•	18.5	•	•	•
Total Asset Turnover 34	1.8	•	7.3	3.0	3.3	2.8	2.8	3.3	•	2.8	•	•	•
Inventory Turnover 35	6.9	•	9.0	7.5	4.5	5.2	3.6	2.6	•	4.3	•	•	•
Receivables Turnover 36	117.1	•	323.4	123.6	24.2	•	11.9	142.0	•	•	•	•	•
Total Liabilities to Net Worth 37	1.6	•	2.2	1.7	0.7	0.4	0.5	1.5	•	0.7	•	•	•
Current Assets to Working Capital 38	•	•	1.1	1.8	1.3	1.6	1.5	1.5	•	1.8	•	•	•
Current Liabilities to Working Capital 39	•	•	0.1	0.8	0.3	0.6	0.5	0.5	•	0.8	•	•	•
Working Capital to Net Sales 40	•	•	0.1	0.1	0.2	0.2	0.2	0.2	•	0.1	•	•	•
Inventory to Working Capital 41	•	•	0.8	0.9	0.7	0.9	0.8	1.4	•	1.1	•	•	•
Total Receipts to Cash Flow 42	10.8	6.2	9.0	10.7	6.1	6.7	4.5	8.8	•	10.5	•	•	•
Cost of Goods to Cash Flow 43	8.0	3.9	7.1	7.0	3.8	5.0	2.8	6.4	•	7.1	•	•	•
Cash Flow to Total Debt 44	0.3	•	1.2	0.4	1.3	1.4	1.8	0.6	•	0.7	•	•	•

Selected Financial Factors (in Percentages)

Debt Ratio 45	62.1	•	68.6	63.2	40.8	30.8	35.1	59.5	•	41.4	•	•	•
Return on Total Assets 46	11.1	•	40.3	12.9	18.9	25.5	24.7	23.9	•	8.6	•	•	•
Return on Equity Before Income Taxes 47	25.7	•	121.0	31.4	29.2	36.3	37.2	56.6	•	13.8	•	•	•
Return on Equity After Income Taxes 48	16.9	•	121.0	30.7	27.6	33.9	36.6	56.6	•	11.0	•	•	•
Profit Margin (Before Income Tax) 49	5.4	8.4	5.2	3.9	5.2	9.0	8.6	6.9	•	2.9	•	•	•
Profit Margin (After Income Tax) 50	3.6	6.4	5.2	3.8	5.0	8.4	8.4	6.9	•	2.3	•	•	•

Table I

Corporations with and without Net Income

MISCELLANEOUS STORE RETAILERS

MONEY AMOUNTS AND SIZE OF ASSETS IN THOUSANDS OF DOLLARS

Item Description for Accounting Period 7/12 Through 6/13	Total	Zero Assets	Under 500	500 to 1,000	1,000 to 5,000	5,000 to 10,000	10,000 to 25,000	25,000 to 50,000	50,000 to 100,000	100,000 to 250,000	250,000 to 500,000	500,000 to 2,500,000	2,500,000 and over
Number of Enterprises 1	73442	11516	54405	3265	3618	316	218	51	19	13	9	8	4
Revenues ($ in Thousands)													
Net Sales 2	122004089	1903931	24300964	18254233	13131387	3441924	6161830	3046657	1876988	2157515	5312483	11570545	30845633
Interest 3	204941	391	1142	1311	9985	1210	8753	280	144	2149	2042	22389	155145
Rents 4	43135	0	5771	4317	3351	2315	10071	1556	0	1203	2718	1785	10048
Royalties 5	222985	9289	0	0	802	27339	7130	33774	0	0	4486	26645	113519
Other Portfolio Income 6	748038	4680	19308	10700	36015	452	4283	4216	657	92	1	15389	652247
Other Receipts 7	2038982	28585	169444	144109	441452	43518	90234	27024	16727	15955	96006	870504	95421
Total Receipts 8	125262170	1946876	24496629	18414670	13622992	3516758	6282301	3113507	1894516	2176914	5417736	12507257	31872013
Average Total Receipts 9	1706	169	450	5640	3765	11129	28818	61049	99711	167455	601971	1563407	7968003
Operating Costs/Operating Income (%)													
Cost of Operations 10	64.2	51.7	52.6	83.1	66.7	66.8	71.6	65.4	72.2	57.5	58.4	51.3	65.7
Salaries and Wages 11	11.5	15.3	11.9	6.1	10.5	12.4	9.5	11.0	8.0	13.3	13.6	18.8	12.0
Taxes Paid 12	2.0	4.0	2.7	0.9	2.5	1.4	1.5	1.8	1.4	2.1	2.0	3.1	1.5
Interest Paid 13	1.1	2.7	0.7	0.3	0.8	1.1	0.5	0.7	0.6	1.2	2.8	2.4	1.4
Depreciation 14	1.2	1.5	1.0	0.4	0.8	0.6	1.1	1.7	1.7	2.5	1.5	2.8	1.2
Amortization and Depletion 15	0.2	0.8	0.1	0.0	0.1	0.1	0.2	0.1	0.2	0.2	1.7	0.1	0.1
Pensions and Other Deferred Comp. 16	0.1	0.0	0.2	0.1	0.3	0.4	0.2	0.3	0.3	0.1	0.0	0.1	0.1
Employee Benefits 17	0.8	0.9	0.6	0.2	0.7	0.4	0.5	0.9	0.9	0.4	1.5	1.6	1.2
Advertising 18	1.7	2.6	1.4	0.4	0.8	1.2	1.9	0.8	1.1	1.9	2.7	2.1	2.7
Other Expenses 19	14.1	27.0	21.2	4.9	13.1	15.0	9.0	13.7	6.8	18.0	15.1	19.2	12.6
Officers' Compensation 20	2.5	8.0	5.2	3.1	4.0	1.6	2.5	1.6	1.3	1.0	0.5	1.7	0.1
Operating Margin 21	0.6	•	2.4	0.4	•	•	1.6	2.0	5.6	1.7	0.2	•	1.5
Operating Margin Before Officers' Comp. 22	3.1	•	7.6	3.5	3.8	0.6	4.1	3.7	6.9	2.7	0.7	•	1.5

Net Receivables **23**	124	0	9	94	297	1143	1826	5390	5795	13715	47112	111632	1141778
Inventories **24**	213	0	43	244	689	3933	5676	11220	20719	64487	77906	235516	785295
Net Property, Plant and Equipment **25**	126	0	24	126	275	380	2305	4884	10579	38666	40572	269139	604248
Total Assets **26**	838	0	112	696	2035	6808	14975	33235	67170	179468	342677	1199612	5602347
Notes and Loans Payable **27**	335	0	84	281	597	2456	4163	8589	12139	58001	239770	651616	1618715
All Other Liabilities **28**	269	0	27	228	372	2386	4871	13148	26872	65959	101891	315743	2231952
Net Worth **29**	234	0	1	187	1067	1966	5941	11498	28159	55507	1015	232252	1751680

	Selected Financial Ratios (Times to 1)												
Current Ratio **30**	2.0	•	2.2	1.9	3.0	1.8	2.2	1.8	1.5	1.7	1.6	1.4	2.0
Quick Ratio **31**	0.9	•	0.9	0.8	1.2	0.5	0.8	0.6	0.4	0.6	0.6	0.7	1.2
Net Sales to Working Capital **32**	7.1	•	11.1	21.8	4.0	4.4	4.7	5.6	7.3	3.8	8.6	9.7	5.4
Coverage Ratio **33**	4.0	•	5.9	5.9	5.7	2.1	8.3	7.4	11.8	3.2	1.8	3.1	4.6
Total Asset Turnover **34**	2.0	•	4.0	8.0	1.8	1.6	1.9	1.8	1.5	0.9	1.7	1.2	1.4
Inventory Turnover **35**	5.0	•	5.5	19.0	3.5	1.8	3.6	3.5	3.4	1.5	4.4	3.1	6.4
Receivables Turnover **36**	13.0	•	49.2	65.0	14.1	6.8	16.4	11.8	15.1	8.4	14.5	13.7	6.3
Total Liabilities to Net Worth **37**	2.6	•	90.5	2.7	0.9	2.5	1.5	1.9	1.4	2.2	336.5	4.2	2.2
Current Assets to Working Capital **38**	2.0	•	1.8	2.1	1.5	2.3	1.8	2.3	3.2	2.4	2.6	3.3	2.0
Current Liabilities to Working Capital **39**	1.0	•	0.8	1.1	0.5	1.3	0.8	1.3	2.2	1.4	1.6	2.3	1.0
Working Capital to Net Sales **40**	0.1	•	0.1	0.0	0.2	0.2	0.2	0.2	0.1	0.3	0.1	0.1	0.2
Inventory to Working Capital **41**	0.9	•	1.1	1.1	0.8	1.5	1.0	1.2	1.6	1.4	1.4	1.4	0.6
Total Receipts to Cash Flow **42**	8.8	33.8	6.2	23.2	8.2	8.6	11.7	8.6	9.3	7.5	9.6	6.6	9.1
Cost of Goods to Cash Flow **43**	5.7	17.5	3.3	19.3	5.5	5.7	8.4	5.6	6.7	4.3	5.6	3.4	6.0
Cash Flow to Total Debt **44**	0.3	•	0.7	0.5	0.5	0.3	0.3	0.3	0.3	0.2	0.2	0.2	0.2

	Selected Financial Factors (in Percentages)												
Debt Ratio **45**	72.1	•	98.9	73.1	47.6	71.1	60.3	65.4	58.1	69.1	99.7	80.6	68.7
Return on Total Assets **46**	8.7	•	15.3	12.2	7.6	3.6	7.6	8.8	10.4	3.5	8.6	9.1	8.7
Return on Equity Before Income Taxes **47**	23.5	•	1159.9	37.6	12.0	6.6	16.9	21.9	22.8	7.8	1289.4	32.1	21.7
Return on Equity After Income Taxes **48**	18.5	•	1145.7	35.8	11.4	5.9	15.6	20.2	18.8	5.1	704.1	18.2	15.7
Profit Margin (Before Income Tax) **49**	3.3	•	3.2	1.3	3.5	1.2	3.6	4.2	6.5	2.6	2.2	5.2	4.9
Profit Margin (After Income Tax) **50**	2.6	•	3.1	1.2	3.3	1.1	3.3	3.9	5.3	1.7	1.2	2.9	3.6

Table II

Corporations with Net Income

MISCELLANEOUS STORE RETAILERS

MONEY AMOUNTS AND SIZE OF ASSETS IN THOUSANDS OF DOLLARS

Item Description for Accounting Period 7/12 Through 6/13	Total	Zero Assets	Under 500	500 to 1,000	1,000 to 5,000	5,000 to 10,000	10,000 to 25,000	25,000 to 50,000	50,000 to 100,000	100,000 to 250,000	250,000 to 500,000	500,000 to 2,500,000	2,500,000 and over
Number of Enterprises 1	41730	5259	30843	2563	2586	225	174	40	15	9	•	•	•

Revenues ($ in Thousands)

Net Sales 2	99257049	569375	17956557	17165420	10591676	2935172	5749410	2510604	1446783	1964404	•	•	•
Interest 3	178586	296	898	609	8533	254	8719	157	144	2147	•	•	•
Rents 4	26720	0	0	272	3133	42	10060	1556	0	1203	•	•	•
Royalties 5	185674	0	0	0	802	0	7130	33774	0	0	•	•	•
Other Portfolio Income 6	735912	7	16106	10347	35613	452	4161	1687	176	14	•	•	•
Other Receipts 7	1879210	24778	138337	140511	391371	33666	84545	23704	16456	15726	•	•	•
Total Receipts 8	102263151	594456	18111898	17317159	11031128	2969586	5864025	2571482	1463559	1983494	•	•	•
Average Total Receipts 9	2451	113	587	6757	4266	13198	33701	64287	97571	220388	•	•	•

Operating Costs/Operating Income (%)

Cost of Operations 10	64.7	51.3	50.2	84.7	68.5	68.3	71.5	67.5	66.6	58.4	•	•	•
Salaries and Wages 11	11.0	4.1	11.9	5.6	9.2	11.2	9.4	9.7	9.0	14.1	•	•	•
Taxes Paid 12	1.9	4.1	2.6	0.8	2.3	1.1	1.5	1.6	1.6	2.0	•	•	•
Interest Paid 13	1.0	0.2	0.5	0.2	0.7	0.7	0.4	0.3	0.3	1.1	•	•	•
Depreciation 14	1.1	1.1	0.8	0.3	0.6	0.4	0.9	1.7	1.5	2.2	•	•	•
Amortization and Depletion 15	0.1	0.0	0.0	0.0	0.1	0.1	0.1	0.0	0.2	0.2	•	•	•
Pensions and Other Deferred Comp. 16	0.2	0.0	0.2	0.1	0.3	0.5	0.3	0.3	0.4	0.1	•	•	•
Employee Benefits 17	0.8	0.2	0.7	0.2	0.6	0.3	0.5	0.7	1.0	0.4	•	•	•
Advertising 18	1.5	1.3	1.3	0.4	0.8	1.1	1.3	0.6	1.3	2.1	•	•	•
Other Expenses 19	12.8	23.4	20.2	4.0	11.2	12.7	8.4	11.5	7.8	15.8	•	•	•
Officers' Compensation 20	2.4	5.6	5.4	3.1	3.5	1.3	2.5	1.7	1.4	1.0	•	•	•
Operating Margin 21	2.5	8.8	6.0	0.7	2.3	2.2	3.3	4.4	8.8	2.6	•	•	•
Operating Margin Before Officers' Comp. 22	4.8	14.4	11.4	3.7	5.7	3.5	5.8	6.1	10.2	3.6	•	•	•

Selected Average Balance Sheet ($ in Thousands)

Net Receivables 23	124	0	12	96	285	1279	2211	5615	6494	8425	•	•	•
Inventories 24	262	0	39	210	655	4551	4994	9612	15327	65298	•	•	•
Net Property, Plant and Equipment 25	160	0	27	92	226	200	2398	5146	9507	26042	•	•	•
Total Assets 26	1076	0	125	676	2011	7086	15288	31672	64922	181085	•	•	•
Notes and Loans Payable 27	426	0	65	247	642	1857	3336	7484	9016	70324	•	•	•
All Other Liabilities 28	294	0	28	263	367	2645	5487	9015	28832	38843	•	•	•
Net Worth 29	356	0	32	166	1002	2584	6466	15173	27074	71917	•	•	•

Selected Financial Ratios (Times to 1)

Current Ratio 30	2.0	•	2.3	1.9	3.1	2.0	2.0	2.1	1.5	3.4	•	•	•
Quick Ratio 31	0.8	•	1.0	0.9	1.3	0.6	0.8	0.8	0.4	1.2	•	•	•
Net Sales to Working Capital 32	8.3	•	12.6	25.5	4.4	4.1	5.9	5.2	6.8	2.9	•	•	•
Coverage Ratio 33	6.7	81.4	13.5	7.8	10.6	5.6	14.9	22.0	34.9	4.1	•	•	•
Total Asset Turnover 34	2.2	•	4.6	9.9	2.0	1.8	2.2	2.0	1.5	1.2	•	•	•
Inventory Turnover 35	5.9	•	7.5	27.0	4.3	2.0	4.7	4.4	4.2	2.0	•	•	•
Receivables Turnover 36	19.3	•	49.0	75.4	14.8	7.5	16.9	12.9	18.1	14.2	•	•	•
Total Liabilities to Net Worth 37	2.0	•	2.9	3.1	1.0	1.7	1.4	1.1	1.4	1.5	•	•	•
Current Assets to Working Capital 38	2.0	•	1.8	2.1	1.5	2.0	2.0	1.9	3.1	1.4	•	•	•
Current Liabilities to Working Capital 39	1.0	•	0.8	1.1	0.5	1.0	1.0	0.9	2.1	0.4	•	•	•
Working Capital to Net Sales 40	0.1	•	0.1	0.0	0.2	0.2	0.2	0.2	0.1	0.3	•	•	•
Inventory to Working Capital 41	1.0	•	0.9	1.1	0.8	1.3	1.0	1.0	1.4	0.8	•	•	•
Total Receipts to Cash Flow 42	7.9	3.7	5.3	24.6	7.3	7.9	10.3	7.3	6.8	8.2	•	•	•
Cost of Goods to Cash Flow 43	5.1	1.9	2.7	20.9	5.0	5.4	7.4	4.9	4.5	4.8	•	•	•
Cash Flow to Total Debt 44	0.4	•	1.2	0.5	0.6	0.4	0.4	0.5	0.4	0.2	•	•	•

Selected Financial Factors (in Percentages)

Debt Ratio 45	66.9	•	74.6	75.4	50.2	63.5	57.7	52.1	58.3	60.3	•	•	•
Return on Total Assets 46	14.4	•	34.3	17.5	14.5	7.6	12.3	14.2	15.3	5.7	•	•	•
Return on Equity Before Income Taxes 47	37.0	•	125.2	61.9	26.3	17.0	27.1	28.4	35.6	10.9	•	•	•
Return on Equity After Income Taxes 48	31.3	•	124.2	59.4	25.4	16.3	25.6	26.8	30.3	7.8	•	•	•
Profit Margin (Before Income Tax) 49	5.5	13.2	6.8	1.5	6.4	3.4	5.3	6.9	10.0	3.6	•	•	•
Profit Margin (After Income Tax) 50	4.7	13.0	6.8	1.5	6.2	3.2	5.0	6.5	8.5	2.6	•	•	•

Table I

Corporations with and without Net Income

NONSTORE RETAILERS

MONEY AMOUNTS AND SIZE OF ASSETS IN THOUSANDS OF DOLLARS

Item Description for Accounting Period 7/12 Through 6/13	Total	Zero Assets	Under 500	500 to 1,000	1,000 to 5,000	5,000 to 10,000	10,000 to 25,000	25,000 to 50,000	50,000 to 100,000	100,000 to 250,000	250,000 to 500,000	500,000 to 2,500,000	2,500,000 and over
Number of Enterprises 1	55577	12400	37949	2277	2137	431	167	92	46	39	14	14	10

Revenues ($ in Thousands)													
Net Sales 2	208132593	2487258	17183440	6422132	20013116	9475645	8890267	7906242	9130506	11887876	12147459	16906264	85682388
Interest 3	486503	408	2050	1917	1782	1178	2625	3379	7274	51792	23518	261429	129151
Rents 4	113874	8	1066	7011	1565	859	1316	2093	8175	5410	4165	39295	42911
Royalties 5	791872	411	0	245	264	0	0	0	4143	1889	162	92794	691964
Other Portfolio Income 6	1692267	36088	56910	369	28720	5945	11452	24020	33181	44231	46889	106172	1298287
Other Receipts 7	-1361838	132667	14868	18811	107054	43914	74718	75420	95746	97451	339231	454102	-2815816
Total Receipts 8	209855271	2656840	17258334	6450485	20152501	9527541	8980378	8011154	9279025	12088649	12561424	17860056	85028885
Average Total Receipts 9	3776	214	455	2833	9430	22106	53775	87078	201718	309965	897245	1275718	8502888

Operating Costs/Operating Income (%)													
Cost of Operations 10	65.9	44.8	64.8	73.9	73.2	79.0	71.4	62.1	77.2	62.4	79.7	71.6	58.9
Salaries and Wages 11	8.4	7.5	6.7	5.6	7.5	5.6	6.9	10.3	6.6	10.2	6.6	8.1	9.7
Taxes Paid 12	1.1	1.7	1.6	1.6	1.4	1.1	0.9	1.5	0.9	1.3	0.9	1.0	1.0
Interest Paid 13	1.1	1.2	0.3	0.3	0.4	0.4	0.3	0.4	0.5	0.9	0.5	1.6	1.8
Depreciation 14	1.5	1.7	0.6	0.6	0.5	0.7	0.6	1.3	0.9	1.6	0.5	1.2	2.4
Amortization and Depletion 15	0.3	0.7	0.0	0.0	0.2	0.2	0.3	0.3	0.1	0.3	0.3	0.4	0.4
Pensions and Other Deferred Comp. 16	0.2	0.2	0.2	0.4	0.1	0.1	0.2	0.3	0.1	0.2	0.1	0.2	0.3
Employee Benefits 17	0.8	1.8	0.5	0.6	0.6	0.6	0.4	1.0	1.0	0.9	0.8	1.0	0.9
Advertising 18	2.5	4.9	1.6	1.5	2.0	1.3	4.4	4.7	1.8	4.4	2.5	4.1	2.0
Other Expenses 19	14.0	35.6	16.3	7.8	9.3	6.7	13.0	17.6	10.8	15.7	8.0	12.5	16.2
Officers' Compensation 20	1.6	2.5	5.5	3.8	4.6	1.5	1.6	1.7	0.6	1.1	0.5	0.3	0.5
Operating Margin 21	2.6	•	2.0	4.0	0.3	2.9	•	•	•	1.0	•	•	5.8
Operating Margin Before Officers' Comp. 22	4.2	•	7.4	7.8	4.9	4.4	1.6	0.5	0.2	2.1	0.1	•	6.3

Selected Average Balance Sheet ($ in Thousands)

Net Receivables 23	441	0	12	136	680	1718	2251	5275	15802	31073	94271	274787	1359891
Inventories 24	252	0	17	124	555	902	3395	6430	13561	26725	87183	124602	572754
Net Property, Plant and Equipment 25	274	0	10	95	246	1201	1743	4678	10580	18334	24002	67663	1041296
Total Assets 26	2694	0	69	657	2255	6573	15147	35800	68845	163318	374410	1050105	10265131
Notes and Loans Payable 27	725	0	45	114	559	2692	3390	6474	17094	39242	63751	181335	2901959
All Other Liabilities 28	1078	0	23	239	1101	1989	6040	14143	25496	68743	128788	508680	4017499
Net Worth 29	892	0	1	304	596	1892	5717	15184	26255	55333	181871	360091	3345673

Selected Financial Ratios (Times to 1)

Current Ratio 30	1.5	•	2.3	2.0	1.4	1.7	1.7	1.5	1.5	1.3	1.9	1.4	1.5
Quick Ratio 31	1.0	•	1.4	1.3	0.9	1.2	0.9	0.8	0.9	0.8	1.0	1.0	1.0
Net Sales to Working Capital 32	8.6	•	15.7	13.5	18.3	12.9	13.8	11.7	13.6	13.2	7.6	9.1	5.9
Coverage Ratio 33	4.6	4.6	8.7	17.0	3.4	9.8	4.2	1.2	3.8	4.0	6.6	4.2	4.3
Total Asset Turnover 34	1.4	•	6.6	4.3	4.2	3.3	3.5	2.4	2.9	1.9	2.3	1.1	0.8
Inventory Turnover 35	9.8	•	17.1	16.7	12.4	19.3	11.2	8.3	11.3	7.1	7.9	6.9	8.8
Receivables Turnover 36	9.0	•	40.2	22.7	13.9	14.6	21.9	17.6	11.1	10.2	10.0	4.5	6.9
Total Liabilities to Net Worth 37	2.0	•	121.2	1.2	2.8	2.5	1.6	1.4	1.6	2.0	1.1	1.9	2.1
Current Assets to Working Capital 38	3.0	•	1.8	2.0	3.3	2.5	2.5	3.0	2.9	4.2	2.1	3.8	3.0
Current Liabilities to Working Capital 39	2.0	•	0.8	1.0	2.3	1.5	1.5	2.0	1.9	3.2	1.1	2.8	2.0
Working Capital to Net Sales 40	0.1	•	0.1	0.1	0.1	0.1	0.1	0.1	0.1	0.1	0.1	0.1	0.2
Inventory to Working Capital 41	0.6	•	0.5	0.7	1.0	0.6	0.9	1.1	0.8	1.1	0.8	0.9	0.4
Total Receipts to Cash Flow 42	6.3	2.7	6.7	9.4	11.3	10.8	7.8	6.4	9.2	6.0	10.0	6.9	5.1
Cost of Goods to Cash Flow 43	4.2	1.2	4.3	6.9	8.2	8.5	5.5	4.0	7.1	3.7	8.0	5.0	3.0
Cash Flow to Total Debt 44	0.3	•	1.0	0.9	0.5	0.4	0.7	0.7	0.5	0.5	0.4	0.3	0.2

Selected Financial Factors (in Percentages)

Debt Ratio 45	66.9	•	99.2	53.7	73.6	71.2	62.3	57.6	61.9	66.1	51.4	65.7	67.4
Return on Total Assets 46	7.1	•	17.9	20.2	5.7	12.9	4.7	1.0	5.1	6.8	8.1	7.9	6.6
Return on Equity Before Income Taxes 47	16.7	•	1930.8	41.0	15.3	40.3	9.4	0.4	9.9	15.0	14.2	17.6	15.5
Return on Equity After Income Taxes 48	13.6	•	1906.3	39.4	14.3	38.4	6.4	•	7.8	11.8	12.7	13.3	12.3
Profit Margin (Before Income Tax) 49	4.0	4.3	2.4	4.4	1.0	3.5	1.0	0.1	1.3	2.7	3.0	5.3	6.0
Profit Margin (After Income Tax) 50	3.2	3.0	2.4	4.2	0.9	3.3	0.7	•	1.0	2.1	2.7	4.0	4.8

Table II

Corporations with Net Income

NONSTORE RETAILERS

MONEY AMOUNTS AND SIZE OF ASSETS IN THOUSANDS OF DOLLARS

Item Description for Accounting Period 7/12 Through 6/13	Total	Zero Assets	Under 500	500 to 1,000	1,000 to 5,000	5,000 to 10,000	10,000 to 25,000	25,000 to 50,000	50,000 to 100,000	100,000 to 250,000	250,000 to 500,000	500,000 to 2,500,000	2,500,000 and over
Number of Enterprises 1	28649	4661	19645	2162	1570	332	120	69	30	30	•	10	•

Revenues ($ in Thousands)													
Net Sales 2	181295043	1271611	12646364	6193333	16508388	8026172	7671754	6400038	5841567	9349728	•	10586892	•
Interest 3	469965	22	474	195	391	937	1722	3299	6951	50610	•	259017	•
Rents 4	108743	0	0	7010	361	514	1253	1944	7681	5410	•	37494	•
Royalties 5	786234	0	0	245	4	0	0	0	4143	1889	•	88437	•
Other Portfolio Income 6	1491446	35863	41074	369	18019	5854	11399	23634	29508	16675	•	106161	•
Other Receipts 7	-1553923	134518	10253	18638	94129	42690	65191	64181	84758	39951	•	394456	•
Total Receipts 8	182597508	1442014	12698165	6219790	16621292	8076167	7751319	6493096	5974608	9464263	•	11472457	•
Average Total Receipts 9	6374	309	646	2877	10587	24326	64594	94103	199154	315475	•	1147246	•

Operating Costs/Operating Income (%)													
Cost of Operations 10	64.9	41.1	64.7	73.4	73.7	80.2	72.1	61.8	72.8	61.9	•	62.9	•
Salaries and Wages 11	8.4	4.5	6.1	5.7	6.7	6.0	5.5	8.9	7.3	10.3	•	10.1	•
Taxes Paid 12	1.1	1.3	1.4	1.6	1.3	0.9	0.7	1.5	1.1	1.4	•	1.1	•
Interest Paid 13	1.1	1.0	0.2	0.3	0.4	0.3	0.2	0.3	0.4	0.7	•	2.3	•
Depreciation 14	1.5	1.2	0.5	0.6	0.3	0.4	0.5	1.2	0.9	1.0	•	1.8	•
Amortization and Depletion 15	0.3	0.1	0.0	0.0	0.1	0.2	0.3	0.3	0.1	0.2	•	0.6	•
Pensions and Other Deferred Comp. 16	0.2	0.1	0.1	0.4	0.1	0.1	0.2	0.2	0.2	0.2	•	0.3	•
Employee Benefits 17	0.8	1.7	0.3	0.6	0.5	0.6	0.3	0.9	1.2	1.0	•	1.2	•
Advertising 18	2.3	1.9	1.3	1.5	1.7	1.2	3.2	4.5	1.1	4.1	•	5.1	•
Other Expenses 19	13.8	38.2	15.0	7.6	7.9	4.3	12.3	16.8	12.2	15.0	•	16.4	•
Officers' Compensation 20	1.5	4.5	4.9	3.7	5.0	1.3	1.6	1.1	0.7	0.9	•	0.4	•
Operating Margin 21	4.1	4.3	5.5	4.5	2.2	4.6	3.1	2.4	2.1	3.2	•	•	•
Operating Margin Before Officers' Comp. 22	5.6	8.8	10.4	8.3	7.2	5.9	4.8	3.6	2.7	4.1	•	•	•

Selected Average Balance Sheet ($ in Thousands)

Net Receivables 23	796	0	12	135	812	2075	2690	6281	19961	33148	•	328992	•
Inventories 24	364	0	23	121	615	1008	3764	5928	13879	26363	•	127143	•
Net Property, Plant and Equipment 25	483	0	12	96	229	910	1651	5074	10966	16171	•	83207	•
Total Assets 26	4642	0	86	662	2301	6489	14938	35931	69339	168290	•	993589	•
Notes and Loans Payable 27	1209	0	36	114	543	2155	2796	6246	16009	40600	•	219745	•
All Other Liabilities 28	1857	0	16	235	1094	1885	5962	13164	25160	67755	•	438100	•
Net Worth 29	1576	0	34	313	664	2449	6180	16521	28169	59936	•	335745	•

Selected Financial Ratios (Times to 1)

Current Ratio 30	1.5	•	3.3	2.0	1.5	1.8	1.6	1.5	1.7	1.3	•	1.3	•
Quick Ratio 31	1.0	•	2.2	1.3	0.9	1.4	0.8	0.8	1.1	0.8	•	1.0	•
Net Sales to Working Capital 32	8.0	•	13.8	13.6	18.6	11.3	16.7	12.3	10.4	14.4	•	8.5	•
Coverage Ratio 33	5.9	19.6	25.4	18.7	8.5	18.1	26.4	14.7	10.9	7.7	•	4.9	•
Total Asset Turnover 34	1.4	•	7.5	4.3	4.6	3.7	4.3	2.6	2.8	1.9	•	1.1	•
Inventory Turnover 35	11.3	•	18.1	17.4	12.6	19.2	12.2	9.7	10.2	7.3	•	5.2	•
Receivables Turnover 36	8.9	•	48.3	24.8	13.2	13.1	24.7	18.6	10.0	10.0	•	3.1	•
Total Liabilities to Net Worth 37	1.9	•	1.5	1.1	2.5	1.6	1.4	1.2	1.5	1.8	•	2.0	•
Current Assets to Working Capital 38	2.9	•	1.4	2.0	3.2	2.2	2.6	2.9	2.5	4.7	•	4.3	•
Current Liabilities to Working Capital 39	1.9	•	0.4	1.0	2.2	1.2	1.6	1.9	1.5	3.7	•	3.3	•
Working Capital to Net Sales 40	0.1	•	0.1	0.1	0.1	0.1	0.1	0.1	0.1	0.1	•	0.1	•
Inventory to Working Capital 41	0.5	•	0.4	0.7	0.9	0.5	0.9	1.1	0.7	1.2	•	0.8	•
Total Receipts to Cash Flow 42	5.9	1.9	6.0	9.0	10.4	11.3	6.4	5.3	6.5	5.6	•	4.7	•
Cost of Goods to Cash Flow 43	3.8	0.8	3.9	6.6	7.7	9.0	4.6	3.3	4.8	3.5	•	3.0	•
Cash Flow to Total Debt 44	0.4	•	2.1	0.9	0.6	0.5	1.1	0.9	0.7	0.5	•	0.3	•

Selected Financial Factors (in Percentages)

Debt Ratio 45	66.1	•	60.7	52.8	71.2	62.3	58.6	54.0	59.4	64.4	•	66.2	•
Return on Total Assets 46	9.0	•	46.5	22.7	15.0	20.7	18.6	10.7	13.8	9.5	•	11.9	•
Return on Equity Before Income Taxes 47	22.0	•	113.8	45.5	46.0	51.7	43.2	21.7	30.8	23.2	•	28.1	•
Return on Equity After Income Taxes 48	18.6	•	113.0	43.8	44.7	49.8	39.3	19.5	27.8	19.3	•	21.7	•
Profit Margin (Before Income Tax) 49	5.5	17.7	5.9	5.0	2.9	5.2	4.2	3.9	4.5	4.5	•	8.9	•
Profit Margin (After Income Tax) 50	4.6	15.1	5.9	4.8	2.8	5.0	3.8	3.5	4.0	3.7	•	6.9	•

Table I

Corporations with and without Net Income

AIR TRANSPORTATION

MONEY AMOUNTS AND SIZE OF ASSETS IN THOUSANDS OF DOLLARS

Item Description for Accounting Period 7/12 Through 6/13		Total	Zero Assets	Under 500	500 to 1,000	1,000 to 5,000	5,000 to 10,000	10,000 to 25,000	25,000 to 50,000	50,000 to 100,000	100,000 to 250,000	250,000 to 500,000	500,000 to 2,500,000	2,500,000 and over
Number of Enterprises	1	7336	1188	4602	500	733	118	100	32	24	8	6	14	10

Revenues ($ in Thousands)

		Total	Zero Assets	Under 500	500 to 1,000	1,000 to 5,000	5,000 to 10,000	10,000 to 25,000	25,000 to 50,000	50,000 to 100,000	100,000 to 250,000	250,000 to 500,000	500,000 to 2,500,000	2,500,000 and over
Net Sales	2	169149778	1339265	1103310	267818	886814	1633310	3234723	828010	3308073	791271	1575851	11504358	142676975
Interest	3	216967	29	1	17	293	254	821	405	595	180	1269	19647	193456
Rents	4	495517	0	0	1808	0	0	3666	2980	45	105	0	14325	472587
Royalties	5	195	0	0	0	0	0	192	0	0	0	0	0	2
Other Portfolio Income	6	900690	4379	81247	0	33001	2165	9408	8879	7822	1402	390	212867	539130
Other Receipts	7	4501829	4872	1307	84	230570	7883	34300	10834	8563	7326	16953	136254	4042884
Total Receipts	8	175264976	1348545	1185865	269727	1150678	1643612	3283110	851108	3325098	800284	1594463	11887451	147925034
Average Total Receipts	9	23891	1135	258	539	1570	13929	32831	26597	138546	100036	265744	849104	14792503

Operating Costs/Operating Income (%)

		Total	Zero Assets	Under 500	500 to 1,000	1,000 to 5,000	5,000 to 10,000	10,000 to 25,000	25,000 to 50,000	50,000 to 100,000	100,000 to 250,000	250,000 to 500,000	500,000 to 2,500,000	2,500,000 and over
Cost of Operations	10	28.6	2.7	82.4	19.9	26.3	76.9	67.3	61.5	46.9	30.2	50.1	29.7	26.1
Salaries and Wages	11	16.3	16.0	•	20.0	10.0	6.3	10.2	6.2	10.5	15.2	13.3	13.8	17.1
Taxes Paid	12	1.9	1.3	0.8	3.6	4.0	0.7	1.2	2.3	1.4	2.1	1.2	2.4	1.9
Interest Paid	13	2.2	0.9	0.4	1.3	1.9	0.5	1.1	2.0	1.5	2.0	3.9	3.6	2.1
Depreciation	14	5.6	7.5	5.0	17.0	40.4	3.6	3.0	7.8	3.4	6.6	2.9	8.8	5.2
Amortization and Depletion	15	0.5	•	0.0	0.6	0.0	0.0	0.1	0.1	0.8	0.1	0.8	0.3	0.6
Pensions and Other Deferred Comp.	16	1.8	0.0	•	•	0.3	0.0	0.1	0.0	0.1	0.3	0.3	0.7	2.1
Employee Benefits	17	2.8	0.9	0.2	4.2	0.4	0.3	0.6	1.1	1.2	2.0	3.0	1.9	3.0
Advertising	18	0.6	0.1	0.5	0.2	0.2	0.2	0.2	0.5	0.1	0.1	0.4	1.3	0.6
Other Expenses	19	43.4	97.3	26.3	59.0	55.1	15.4	15.0	19.4	37.5	32.9	29.9	42.0	44.4
Officers' Compensation	20	0.5	0.9	6.1	11.6	4.4	0.6	2.0	2.4	0.5	2.1	0.7	0.6	0.3
Operating Margin	21	•	•	•	•	•	•	•	•	•	6.3	•	•	•
Operating Margin Before Officers' Comp.	22	•	•	•	•	•	•	1.2	•	•	8.4	•	•	•

Selected Average Balance Sheet ($ in Thousands)

Net Receivables 23	1095	0	0	110	88	1099	4033	2861	12733	26341	116797	53746	531632
Inventories 24	347	0	19	7	43	40	243	841	2767	5940	28729	18349	182419
Net Property, Plant and Equipment 25	13031	0	40	419	1556	3087	6528	21666	33892	61946	57863	457282	8429242
Total Assets 26	24597	0	80	698	2175	5795	15320	34057	71818	138641	331660	910704	15725633
Notes and Loans Payable 27	9010	0	151	3318	1204	2071	6496	14164	39087	64452	85242	388070	5411550
All Other Liabilities 28	14658	0	18	2625	100	1492	4647	8108	32457	26712	226950	309296	9847901
Net Worth 29	929	0	-89	-5245	871	2233	4177	11785	274	47476	19468	213338	466182

Selected Financial Ratios (Times to 1)

Current Ratio 30	0.9	•	3.7	0.1	3.3	1.1	1.4	1.3	1.0	2.2	1.2	1.3	0.8
Quick Ratio 31	0.5	•	2.0	0.1	2.0	0.8	1.2	0.7	0.8	1.7	0.8	0.8	0.5
Net Sales to Working Capital 32	•	•	8.2	•	4.7	102.3	18.4	11.5	157.3	3.0	9.8	13.8	•
Coverage Ratio 33	0.8	•	•	•	•	•	1.6	0.7	•	4.7	•	0.7	1.1
Total Asset Turnover 34	0.9	•	3.0	0.8	0.6	2.4	2.1	0.8	1.9	0.7	0.8	0.9	0.9
Inventory Turnover 35	19.0	•	10.1	14.7	7.4	266.7	89.4	18.9	23.4	5.0	4.6	13.3	20.4
Receivables Turnover 36	21.4	•	121.2	5.2	12.0	10.1	8.5	9.3	11.1	2.8	2.7	14.1	27.7
Total Liabilities to Net Worth 37	25.5	•	•	•	1.5	1.6	2.7	1.9	261.2	1.9	16.0	3.3	32.7
Current Assets to Working Capital 38	•	•	1.4	•	1.4	13.8	3.6	4.6	34.9	1.8	7.3	4.2	•
Current Liabilities to Working Capital 39	•	•	0.4	•	0.4	12.8	2.6	3.6	33.9	0.8	6.3	3.2	•
Working Capital to Net Sales 40	•	•	0.1	•	0.2	0.0	0.1	0.1	0.0	0.3	0.1	0.1	•
Inventory to Working Capital 41	•	•	0.5	•	0.2	0.4	0.1	0.4	2.9	0.1	1.5	0.3	•
Total Receipts to Cash Flow 42	3.4	2.8	34.5	7.3	3.0	14.5	10.6	8.5	5.7	3.7	6.6	4.5	3.1
Cost of Goods to Cash Flow 43	1.0	0.1	28.4	1.5	0.8	11.1	7.1	5.2	2.7	1.1	3.3	1.3	0.8
Cash Flow to Total Debt 44	0.3	•	0.0	0.0	0.3	0.3	0.3	0.1	0.3	0.3	0.1	0.3	0.3

Selected Financial Factors (in Percentages)

Debt Ratio 45	96.2	•	212.1	851.1	59.9	61.5	72.7	65.4	99.6	65.8	94.1	76.6	97.0
Return on Total Assets 46	1.7	•	•	•	•	•	3.8	1.1	•	6.8	•	2.2	2.2
Return on Equity Before Income Taxes 47	•	•	38.2	3.8	•	•	5.2	•	•	15.5	•	•	8.3
Return on Equity After Income Taxes 48	•	•	38.2	3.8	•	•	4.6	•	•	13.1	•	•	5.9
Profit Margin (Before Income Tax) 49	•	•	•	•	•	•	0.7	•	•	7.4	•	•	0.3
Profit Margin (After Income Tax) 50	•	•	•	•	•	•	0.6	•	•	6.3	•	•	0.2

Table II

Corporations with Net Income

AIR TRANSPORTATION

MONEY AMOUNTS AND SIZE OF ASSETS IN THOUSANDS OF DOLLARS

Item Description for Accounting Period 7/12 Through 6/13	Total	Zero Assets	Under 500	500 to 1,000	1,000 to 5,000	5,000 to 10,000	10,000 to 25,000	25,000 to 50,000	50,000 to 100,000	100,000 to 250,000	250,000 to 500,000	500,000 to 2,500,000	2,500,000 and over
Number of Enterprises 1	1878	19	1545	0	•	42	38	20	•	4	3	7	5

Revenues ($ in Thousands)													
Net Sales 2	75454306	70852	36348	0	•	1448466	2192779	562573	•	672914	420194	5157236	63309069
Interest 3	115918	4	0	0	•	217	206	287	•	94	80	18677	95971
Rents 4	79689	0	0	0	•	0	0	2980	•	105	0	12958	63601
Royalties 5	2	0	0	0	•	0	0	0	•	0	0	0	2
Other Portfolio Income 6	702484	2386	39151	0	•	566	7869	8780	•	646	390	190695	415103
Other Receipts 7	384697	686	404	0	•	7841	17900	8353	•	7094	2045	41654	262553
Total Receipts 8	76737096	73928	75903	0	•	1457090	2218754	582973	•	680853	422709	5421220	64146299
Average Total Receipts 9	40861	3891	49	•	•	34693	58388	29149	•	170213	140903	774460	12829260

Operating Costs/Operating Income (%)													
Cost of Operations 10	30.5	50.7	13.7	•	•	82.4	62.8	65.3	•	33.4	43.1	14.4	28.7
Salaries and Wages 11	18.1	9.5	•	•	•	3.2	11.0	3.8	•	15.6	12.3	19.0	19.0
Taxes Paid 12	2.5	7.8	0.8	•	•	0.4	1.3	2.0	•	2.3	1.1	2.7	2.6
Interest Paid 13	1.6	0.9	1.1	•	•	0.2	0.5	1.9	•	0.5	1.9	2.7	1.6
Depreciation 14	5.7	1.2	5.0	•	•	0.4	1.0	5.9	•	3.6	5.6	8.3	5.8
Amortization and Depletion 15	0.2	0.2	•	•	•	0.0	0.0	0.1	•	0.1	0.5	0.1	0.3
Pensions and Other Deferred Comp. 16	1.6	•	•	•	•	0.0	0.1	0.0	•	0.3	1.2	0.8	1.8
Employee Benefits 17	3.3	•	•	•	•	0.2	0.7	1.1	•	2.3	3.1	2.5	3.6
Advertising 18	0.6	0.8	2.5	•	•	0.2	0.2	0.1	•	0.0	0.3	0.2	0.6
Other Expenses 19	34.1	23.1	42.6	•	•	11.1	17.1	12.1	•	28.8	20.2	48.3	34.6
Officers' Compensation 20	0.3	•	1.0	•	•	0.4	2.5	3.2	•	2.4	1.3	0.6	0.2
Operating Margin 21	1.5	5.8	33.5	•	•	1.5	2.9	4.5	•	10.8	9.3	0.3	1.2
Operating Margin Before Officers' Comp. 22	1.8	5.8	34.5	•	•	1.9	5.4	7.7	•	13.2	10.6	0.9	1.4

Selected Average Balance Sheet ($ in Thousands)

	C1	C2	C3	C4	C5	C6	C7	C8	C9	C10	C11	C12	C13
Net Receivables 23	1743	0	0	•	•	2407	5196	3960	•	29370	150748	36257	382677
Inventories 24	661	0	0	•	•	99	443	1099	•	14655	38005	12115	185740
Net Property, Plant and Equipment 25	21478	0	0	•	•	549	4355	16516	•	41234	64667	432411	7176338
Total Assets 26	38586	0	36	•	•	5959	14549	31308	•	125299	331767	986170	12246771
Notes and Loans Payable 27	12197	0	16	•	•	2022	5001	12965	•	23992	44666	326302	3856706
All Other Liabilities 28	22892	0	0	•	•	2050	5541	7164	•	25648	191856	318664	7873507
Net Worth 29	3497	0	20	•	•	1887	4006	11179	•	75658	95245	341204	516557

Selected Financial Ratios (Times to 1)

	C1	C2	C3	C4	C5	C6	C7	C8	C9	C10	C11	C12	C13
Current Ratio 30	1.1	•	105.9	•	•	1.4	1.4	2.1	•	2.8	3.5	1.9	1.0
Quick Ratio 31	0.7	•	105.9	•	•	1.0	1.2	0.9	•	2.2	2.8	1.0	0.6
Net Sales to Working Capital 32	56.5	•	0.7	•	•	35.6	21.5	4.2	•	3.6	0.9	5.6	•
Coverage Ratio 33	3.0	12.8	136.1	•	•	14.0	9.6	5.3	•	26.6	6.1	3.5	2.6
Total Asset Turnover 34	1.0	•	0.6	•	•	5.8	4.0	0.9	•	1.3	0.4	0.7	1.0
Inventory Turnover 35	18.6	•	•	•	•	286.6	81.9	16.7	•	3.8	1.6	8.8	19.5
Receivables Turnover 36	23.3	•	18.2	•	•	14.2	10.1	7.3	•	1.6	1.9	26.4	34.7
Total Liabilities to Net Worth 37	10.0	•	0.8	•	•	2.2	2.6	1.8	•	0.7	2.5	1.9	22.7
Current Assets to Working Capital 38	17.1	•	1.0	•	•	3.7	3.6	1.9	•	1.6	1.4	2.2	•
Current Liabilities to Working Capital 39	16.1	•	0.0	•	•	2.7	2.6	0.9	•	0.6	0.4	1.2	•
Working Capital to Net Sales 40	0.0	•	1.5	•	•	0.0	0.0	0.2	•	0.3	1.1	0.2	•
Inventory to Working Capital 41	1.3	•	•	•	•	0.1	0.2	0.2	•	0.1	0.2	0.1	•
Total Receipts to Cash Flow 42	4.2	5.5	0.5	•	•	9.8	7.2	7.4	•	3.7	3.4	3.3	4.3
Cost of Goods to Cash Flow 43	1.3	2.8	0.1	•	•	8.1	4.5	4.8	•	1.2	1.5	0.5	1.2
Cash Flow to Total Debt 44	0.3	•	2.7	•	•	0.9	0.8	0.2	•	0.9	0.2	0.3	0.3

Selected Financial Factors (in Percentages)

	C1	C2	C3	C4	C5	C6	C7	C8	C9	C10	C11	C12	C13
Debt Ratio 45	90.9	•	44.0	•	•	68.3	72.5	64.3	•	39.6	71.3	65.4	95.8
Return on Total Assets 46	5.1	•	92.9	•	•	13.0	18.1	9.0	•	16.8	5.0	7.1	4.3
Return on Equity Before Income Taxes 47	37.7	•	164.8	•	•	38.1	58.8	20.4	•	26.7	14.6	14.6	61.7
Return on Equity After Income Taxes 48	34.1	•	164.8	•	•	31.0	57.3	16.6	•	23.6	14.4	11.1	57.3
Profit Margin (Before Income Tax) 49	3.3	10.1	142.3	•	•	2.1	4.1	8.1	•	12.0	9.9	6.8	2.5
Profit Margin (After Income Tax) 50	3.0	7.4	142.3	•	•	1.7	4.0	6.6	•	10.6	9.8	5.1	2.3

Table I

Corporations with and without Net Income

RAIL TRANSPORTATION

MONEY AMOUNTS AND SIZE OF ASSETS IN THOUSANDS OF DOLLARS

Item Description for Accounting Period 7/12 Through 6/13		Total	Zero Assets	Under 500	500 to 1,000	1,000 to 5,000	5,000 to 10,000	10,000 to 25,000	25,000 to 50,000	50,000 to 100,000	100,000 to 250,000	250,000 to 500,000	500,000 to 2,500,000	2,500,000 and over
Number of Enterprises	1	231	20	101	0	23	8	26	18	10	10	3	3	8
Revenues ($ in Thousands)														
Net Sales	2	56423052	318468	31	0	34597	174630	295942	356555	269412	502959	504694	735740	53230024
Interest	3	147202	2541	247	0	9	312	557	642	490	1957	7	14657	125783
Rents	4	513203	14414	0	0	1991	0	2595	3147	3498	4803	3670	2985	476100
Royalties	5	44865	0	0	0	0	199	0	0	0	3593	2	0	41070
Other Portfolio Income	6	464573	20676	0	0	457	15314	338	11421	6662	3392	3929	4297	398089
Other Receipts	7	954312	119047	-1	0	14527	9817	6863	14831	6337	22218	3878	29913	726880
Total Receipts	8	58547207	475146	277	0	51581	200272	306295	386596	286399	538922	516180	787592	54997946
Average Total Receipts	9	253451	23757	3	•	2243	25034	11781	21478	28640	53892	172060	262531	6874743
Operating Costs/Operating Income (%)														
Cost of Operations	10	16.4	•	•	•	16.9	•	21.5	13.8	4.1	26.9	36.9	•	16.5
Salaries and Wages	11	17.8	28.1	•	•	21.7	2.2	17.6	10.7	15.8	18.7	9.2	15.7	17.9
Taxes Paid	12	5.1	6.2	248.4	•	9.8	0.3	4.1	7.0	4.4	3.7	2.2	3.3	5.1
Interest Paid	13	4.4	25.8	•	•	14.2	0.6	0.8	0.9	2.7	1.3	2.1	8.2	4.4
Depreciation	14	12.0	7.5	•	•	16.9	2.9	4.0	10.4	16.9	9.3	9.5	11.7	12.1
Amortization and Depletion	15	0.1	1.6	•	•	0.4	0.0	0.2	0.2	0.1	0.1	0.1	0.4	0.1
Pensions and Other Deferred Comp.	16	1.4	0.4	•	•	•	0.0	0.0	0.8	0.8	1.2	0.0	0.0	1.4
Employee Benefits	17	5.2	2.5	•	•	1.4	0.3	4.1	0.9	3.6	3.3	2.1	7.7	5.2
Advertising	18	0.1	0.1	•	•	0.4	0.0	0.1	0.2	0.1	0.3	0.0	•	0.2
Other Expenses	19	27.4	74.7	2738.7	•	85.3	95.9	31.7	37.9	34.0	31.0	19.6	40.7	26.6
Officers' Compensation	20	0.8	2.7	•	•	5.3	1.7	0.2	5.7	1.7	1.8	0.8	0.7	0.7
Operating Margin	21	9.3	•	•	•	•	•	15.8	11.4	15.5	2.2	17.5	11.6	9.7
Operating Margin Before Officers' Comp.	22	10.1	•	•	•	•	•	16.0	17.2	17.2	4.1	18.2	12.3	10.4

Selected Average Balance Sheet ($ in Thousands)

Net Receivables 23	21545	0	2	•	68	1532	1218	5990	4014	7080	31426	208448	499104
Inventories 24	5385	0	0	•	0	0	150	276	956	1123	7250	1613	148462
Net Property, Plant and Equipment 25	551250	0	101	•	1579	2234	7111	18909	43498	98668	271901	512240	15371885
Total Assets 26	682332	0	302	•	3077	8697	14633	37033	64323	137475	383485	1272933	18676695
Notes and Loans Payable 27	144962	0	0	•	293	4438	4690	3898	20467	29405	113359	247482	3958836
All Other Liabilities 28	286648	0	9	•	410	1932	2789	4481	10616	52429	106315	315336	8017663
Net Worth 29	250722	0	294	•	2374	2327	7154	28654	33240	55641	163811	710115	6700196

Selected Financial Ratios (Times to 1)

Current Ratio 30	0.8	•	23.5	•	1.4	1.3	1.1	2.3	1.6	1.3	1.0	1.7	0.7
Quick Ratio 31	0.6	•	23.5	•	1.2	0.8	0.7	1.8	1.3	0.8	0.6	1.6	0.5
Net Sales to Working Capital 32	•	•	0.0	•	8.9	31.6	28.9	3.7	4.8	11.5	•	2.2	•
Coverage Ratio 33	4.0	1.0	•	•	•	19.6	26.2	23.7	8.9	8.1	10.5	3.3	4.0
Total Asset Turnover 34	0.4	•	0.0	•	0.5	2.5	0.8	0.5	0.4	0.4	0.4	0.2	0.4
Inventory Turnover 35	7.4	•	•	•	1296.0	•	16.2	9.9	1.2	12.0	8.6	•	7.4
Receivables Turnover 36	10.5	•	0.2	•	19.3	11.1	5.6	4.9	7.4	6.6	5.4	1.1	12.2
Total Liabilities to Net Worth 37	1.7	•	0.0	•	0.3	2.7	1.0	0.3	0.9	1.5	1.3	0.8	1.8
Current Assets to Working Capital 38	•	•	1.0	•	3.4	4.5	9.1	1.8	2.7	4.8	•	2.4	•
Current Liabilities to Working Capital 39	•	•	0.0	•	2.4	3.5	8.1	0.8	1.7	3.8	•	1.4	•
Working Capital to Net Sales 40	•	•	628.9	•	0.1	0.0	0.0	0.3	0.2	0.1	•	0.5	•
Inventory to Working Capital 41	•	•	•	•	0.0	•	0.3	0.1	0.1	0.4	•	0.0	•
Total Receipts to Cash Flow 42	3.2	1.7	0.2	•	1.8	2.0	2.7	2.2	2.3	2.9	2.8	1.9	3.3
Cost of Goods to Cash Flow 43	0.5	•	•	•	0.3	•	0.6	0.3	0.1	0.8	1.0	•	0.5
Cash Flow to Total Debt 44	0.2	•	0.2	•	1.2	1.7	0.6	1.1	0.4	0.2	0.3	0.2	0.2

Selected Financial Factors (in Percentages)

Debt Ratio 45	63.3	•	2.8	•	22.8	73.2	51.1	22.6	48.3	59.5	57.3	44.2	64.1
Return on Total Assets 46	6.3	•	•	•	•	28.4	15.6	11.1	10.3	3.9	9.6	5.2	6.2
Return on Equity Before Income Taxes 47	12.8	•	•	•	•	100.9	30.7	13.7	17.7	8.5	20.3	6.4	12.9
Return on Equity After Income Taxes 48	8.3	•	•	•	•	100.9	25.9	11.5	12.6	6.9	20.3	3.8	8.3
Profit Margin (Before Income Tax) 49	13.1	•	•	•	•	10.8	19.3	19.8	21.8	9.4	19.7	18.6	13.0
Profit Margin (After Income Tax) 50	8.6	•	•	•	•	10.8	16.3	16.7	15.5	7.6	19.7	11.0	8.4

Table II

Corporations with Net Income

RAIL TRANSPORTATION

MONEY AMOUNTS AND SIZE OF ASSETS IN THOUSANDS OF DOLLARS

Item Description for Accounting Period 7/12 Through 6/13	Total	Zero Assets	Under 500	500 to 1,000	1,000 to 5,000	5,000 to 10,000	10,000 to 25,000	25,000 to 50,000	50,000 to 100,000	100,000 to 250,000	250,000 to 500,000	500,000 to 2,500,000	2,500,000 and over
Number of Enterprises 1	81	12	0	0	•	0	26	15	•	•	3	0	•

Revenues ($ in Thousands)

Net Sales 2	49995345	5658	0	0	•	0	295942	281844	•	•	804252	0	•
Interest 3	136563	46	0	0	•	0	557	642	•	•	14657	0	•
Rents 4	445216	1169	0	0	•	0	2595	3147	•	•	763	0	•
Royalties 5	44663	0	0	0	•	0	0	0	•	•	0	0	•
Other Portfolio Income 6	435709	17630	0	0	•	0	338	11418	•	•	4416	0	•
Other Receipts 7	224583	42492	0	0	•	0	6863	14832	•	•	29988	0	•
Total Receipts 8	51282079	66995	0	0	•	0	306295	311883	•	•	854076	0	•
Average Total Receipts 9	633112	5583	•	•	•	•	11781	20792	•	•	284692	•	•

Operating Costs/Operating Income (%)

Cost of Operations 10	16.5	•	•	•	•	•	21.5	17.5	•	•	18.6	•	•
Salaries and Wages 11	16.3	41.5	•	•	•	•	17.6	9.1	•	•	10.9	•	•
Taxes Paid 12	4.9	10.2	•	•	•	•	4.1	6.6	•	•	1.4	•	•
Interest Paid 13	4.4	462.4	•	•	•	•	0.8	0.9	•	•	0.7	•	•
Depreciation 14	12.6	6.0	•	•	•	•	4.0	8.2	•	•	7.6	•	•
Amortization and Depletion 15	0.1	9.2	•	•	•	•	0.2	0.0	•	•	•	•	•
Pensions and Other Deferred Comp. 16	0.8	•	•	•	•	•	0.0	1.0	•	•	0.0	•	•
Employee Benefits 17	5.6	2.7	•	•	•	•	4.1	0.6	•	•	6.0	•	•
Advertising 18	0.0	0.5	•	•	•	•	0.1	0.1	•	•	0.0	•	•
Other Expenses 19	24.9	169.0	•	•	•	•	31.7	36.8	•	•	26.7	•	•
Officers' Compensation 20	0.8	•	•	•	•	•	0.2	4.4	•	•	0.4	•	•
Operating Margin 21	13.1	•	•	•	•	•	15.8	14.5	•	•	27.7	•	•
Operating Margin Before Officers' Comp. 22	13.9	•	•	•	•	•	16.0	19.0	•	•	28.1	•	•

Selected Average Balance Sheet ($ in Thousands)

Net Receivables 23	54792	0	•	•	•	•	1218	6683	•	•	212116	•	•
Inventories 24	14667	0	•	•	•	•	147	330	•	•	9818	•	•
Net Property, Plant and Equipment 25	1374937	0	•	•	•	•	7111	14059	•	•	383443	•	•
Total Assets 26	1715550	0	•	•	•	•	14633	34413	•	•	1134588	•	•
Notes and Loans Payable 27	380279	0	•	•	•	•	4690	3999	•	•	80928	•	•
All Other Liabilities 28	729484	0	•	•	•	•	2789	4489	•	•	310131	•	•
Net Worth 29	605787	0	•	•	•	•	7154	25925	•	•	743529	•	•

Selected Financial Ratios (Times to 1)

Current Ratio 30	0.7	•	•	•	•	•	1.1	2.6	•	•	1.6	•	•
Quick Ratio 31	0.6	•	•	•	•	•	0.7	2.1	•	•	1.5	•	•
Net Sales to Working Capital 32	•	•	•	•	•	•	28.9	2.9	•	•	2.6	•	•
Coverage Ratio 33	4.6	2.0	•	•	•	•	26.2	27.6	•	•	52.7	•	•
Total Asset Turnover 34	0.4	•	•	•	•	•	0.8	0.5	•	•	0.2	•	•
Inventory Turnover 35	7.0	•	•	•	•	•	16.7	10.0	•	•	5.1	•	•
Receivables Turnover 36	10.3	•	•	•	•	•	6.6	•	•	•	2.5	•	•
Total Liabilities to Net Worth 37	1.8	•	•	•	•	•	1.0	0.3	•	•	0.5	•	•
Current Assets to Working Capital 38	•	•	•	•	•	•	9.1	1.6	•	•	2.6	•	•
Current Liabilities to Working Capital 39	•	•	•	•	•	•	8.1	0.6	•	•	1.6	•	•
Working Capital to Net Sales 40	•	•	•	•	•	•	0.0	0.3	•	•	0.4	•	•
Inventory to Working Capital 41	•	•	•	•	•	•	0.3	0.1	•	•	0.1	•	•
Total Receipts to Cash Flow 42	3.2	0.2	•	•	•	•	2.7	2.1	•	•	1.8	•	•
Cost of Goods to Cash Flow 43	0.5	•	•	•	•	•	0.6	0.4	•	•	0.3	•	•
Cash Flow to Total Debt 44	0.2	•	•	•	•	•	0.6	1.1	•	•	0.4	•	•

Selected Financial Factors (in Percentages)

Debt Ratio 45	64.7	•	•	•	•	•	51.1	24.7	•	•	34.5	•	•
Return on Total Assets 46	7.2	•	•	•	•	•	15.6	14.2	•	•	8.2	•	•
Return on Equity Before Income Taxes 47	16.0	•	•	•	•	•	30.7	18.2	•	•	12.2	•	•
Return on Equity After Income Taxes 48	10.8	•	•	•	•	•	25.9	15.4	•	•	9.7	•	•
Profit Margin (Before Income Tax) 49	15.7	482.5	•	•	•	•	19.3	25.2	•	•	33.9	•	•
Profit Margin (After Income Tax) 50	10.6	432.4	•	•	•	•	16.3	21.2	•	•	26.9	•	•

Table I

Corporations with and without Net Income

WATER TRANSPORTATION

MONEY AMOUNTS AND SIZE OF ASSETS IN THOUSANDS OF DOLLARS

Item Description for Accounting Period 7/12 Through 6/13	Total	Zero Assets	Under 500	500 to 1,000	1,000 to 5,000	5,000 to 10,000	10,000 to 25,000	25,000 to 50,000	50,000 to 100,000	100,000 to 250,000	250,000 to 500,000	500,000 to 2,500,000	2,500,000 and over
Number of Enterprises **1**	3486	954	1378	221	542	190	89	33	22	24	15	14	4

Revenues ($ in Thousands)

Net Sales **2**	29885779	1583955	296538	583217	1821631	890787	2157331	770981	1170719	1857540	1617180	10943149	6192751
Interest **3**	53617	335	10	631	101	17	368	207	1337	2139	1775	23967	22731
Rents **4**	71273	29	0	0	0	553	1980	355	21	645	2733	64957	0
Royalties **5**	531	524	0	0	0	0	0	0	0	0	7	0	0
Other Portfolio Income **6**	799586	6479	792	37832	16341	14	5312	52020	17024	25708	31937	405760	200366
Other Receipts **7**	1075018	366443	157637	1830	8977	302	35464	18210	-42560	15846	19163	309409	184296
Total Receipts **8**	31885804	1957765	454977	623510	1847050	891673	2200455	841773	1146541	1901878	1672795	11747242	6600144
Average Total Receipts **9**	9147	2052	330	2821	3408	4693	24724	25508	52116	79245	111520	839089	1650036

Operating Costs/Operating Income (%)

Cost of Operations **10**	37.5	29.9	3.3	42.7	43.9	46.3	38.6	34.7	33.8	34.5	38.1	44.6	26.3
Salaries and Wages **11**	10.4	5.4	25.4	17.0	18.7	18.0	8.0	14.5	7.2	10.9	11.9	8.3	11.1
Taxes Paid **12**	1.7	0.7	3.5	4.3	1.8	2.0	1.6	3.1	1.2	2.5	2.1	1.6	1.5
Interest Paid **13**	2.7	1.7	0.3	0.2	1.9	2.6	0.9	2.3	2.1	3.0	4.4	3.3	2.7
Depreciation **14**	9.6	4.1	0.3	4.3	6.3	26.1	5.0	6.5	5.3	17.3	21.2	6.1	14.3
Amortization and Depletion **15**	0.4	0.3	•	0.0	0.0	0.0	0.0	0.1	0.8	0.2	0.2	0.4	0.6
Pensions and Other Deferred Comp. **16**	0.7	0.1	4.1	0.0	0.3	0.1	0.5	0.5	0.4	0.7	0.4	1.0	0.7
Employee Benefits **17**	2.2	0.8	4.3	0.0	1.5	0.4	1.3	2.7	1.3	3.1	2.2	1.6	4.2
Advertising **18**	0.2	2.1	0.1	0.0	0.1	0.1	0.2	0.4	0.2	0.4	0.3	0.1	0.1
Other Expenses **19**	39.0	81.8	66.6	18.4	21.0	11.9	42.1	27.1	42.3	31.1	20.9	39.9	43.0
Officers' Compensation **20**	1.8	1.1	17.6	15.6	4.6	3.2	2.6	2.1	1.2	1.3	0.5	0.7	1.4
Operating Margin **21**	•	•	•	•	0.0	•	•	6.1	4.2	•	•	•	•
Operating Margin Before Officers' Comp. **22**	•	•	•	13.0	4.6	•	1.9	8.2	5.4	•	•	•	•

Selected Average Balance Sheet ($ in Thousands)

Net Receivables 23	1633	0	11	204	336	1713	4409	3331	8937	9824	19915	216741	213816
Inventories 24	147	0	0	0	2	45	137	169	366	693	2238	20891	67801
Net Property, Plant and Equipment 25	7124	0	67	280	1348	4953	6610	13538	36099	107148	202841	584091	1846658
Total Assets 26	13471	0	163	762	2572	7615	14621	33353	70540	156557	356446	1303839	3103495
Notes and Loans Payable 27	5098	0	77	135	1231	3107	6077	12846	21194	76415	92642	537331	1050187
All Other Liabilities 28	3297	0	66	305	449	595	6166	5330	17554	18976	109136	376075	627470
Net Worth 29	5076	0	20	322	892	3913	2379	15177	31792	61166	154667	390433	1425838

Selected Financial Ratios (Times to 1)

Current Ratio 30	1.3	•	0.3	1.6	1.4	7.1	1.3	2.1	1.4	1.3	0.6	1.2	2.2
Quick Ratio 31	1.0	•	0.2	1.6	1.1	6.5	1.1	1.6	0.9	1.0	0.5	0.9	1.5
Net Sales to Working Capital 32	11.1	•	•	18.6	17.5	2.3	15.8	5.0	7.1	12.7	•	14.3	4.9
Coverage Ratio 33	1.5	•	108.3	18.7	1.7	•	2.4	7.7	2.1	0.1	1.2	1.7	1.3
Total Asset Turnover 34	0.6	•	1.3	3.5	1.3	0.6	1.7	0.7	0.8	0.5	0.3	0.6	0.5
Inventory Turnover 35	21.8	•	136.1	•	604.5	48.4	68.5	47.9	49.2	38.5	18.4	16.7	6.0
Receivables Turnover 36	5.8	•	20.8	16.5	11.7	3.3	6.3	9.8	6.2	6.8	7.0	3.5	14.5
Total Liabilities to Net Worth 37	1.7	•	7.0	1.4	1.9	0.9	5.1	1.2	1.2	1.6	1.3	2.3	1.2
Current Assets to Working Capital 38	4.0	•	•	2.7	3.6	1.2	4.1	1.9	3.4	4.1	•	6.5	1.9
Current Liabilities to Working Capital 39	3.0	•	•	1.7	2.6	0.2	3.1	0.9	2.4	3.1	•	5.5	0.9
Working Capital to Net Sales 40	0.1	•	•	0.1	0.1	0.4	0.1	0.2	0.1	0.1	•	0.1	0.2
Inventory to Working Capital 41	0.2	•	•	•	•	0.0	0.1	0.0	0.0	0.1	•	0.3	0.2
Total Receipts to Cash Flow 42	3.3	1.4	1.1	5.2	6.6	84.6	6.2	3.2	2.6	4.4	5.7	3.2	3.1
Cost of Goods to Cash Flow 43	1.3	0.4	0.0	2.2	2.9	39.2	2.4	1.1	0.9	1.5	2.2	1.4	0.8
Cash Flow to Total Debt 44	0.3	•	1.4	1.1	0.3	0.0	0.3	0.4	0.5	0.2	0.1	0.3	0.3

Selected Financial Factors (in Percentages)

Debt Ratio 45	62.3	•	87.5	57.8	65.3	48.6	83.7	54.5	54.9	60.9	56.6	70.1	54.1
Return on Total Assets 46	2.6	•	37.2	15.7	4.3	•	3.7	12.3	3.3	0.2	1.6	3.3	1.7
Return on Equity Before Income Taxes 47	2.3	•	294.5	35.2	5.4	•	13.4	23.5	3.9	•	0.7	4.4	0.8
Return on Equity After Income Taxes 48	0.8	•	294.5	34.8	4.0	•	11.5	22.5	2.3	•	0.5	1.3	•
Profit Margin (Before Income Tax) 49	1.4	•	28.0	4.3	1.4	•	1.3	15.3	2.3	•	1.0	2.2	0.7
Profit Margin (After Income Tax) 50	0.5	•	28.0	4.2	1.1	•	1.1	14.6	1.4	•	0.8	0.7	•

Table II
Corporations with Net Income

WATER TRANSPORTATION

MONEY AMOUNTS AND SIZE OF ASSETS IN THOUSANDS OF DOLLARS

Item Description for Accounting Period 7/12 Through 6/13	Total	Zero Assets	Under 500	500 to 1,000	1,000 to 5,000	5,000 to 10,000	10,000 to 25,000	25,000 to 50,000	50,000 to 100,000	100,000 to 250,000	250,000 to 500,000	500,000 to 2,500,000	2,500,000 and over
Number of Enterprises **1**	1802	449	998	72	70	103	46	26	11	12	5	10	0

Revenues ($ in Thousands)

Net Sales **2**	21522076	1124141	223634	336349	831803	804913	1935986	725494	475961	1127552	953186	12983058	0
Interest **3**	43430	128	7	0	38	17	344	85	769	554	856	40631	0
Rents **4**	70897	29	0	0	0	553	1980	0	0	645	2733	64957	0
Royalties **5**	524	524	0	0	0	0	0	0	0	0	0	0	0
Other Portfolio Income **6**	697786	3875	0	37832	15636	14	4859	51877	13652	22329	18933	528776	0
Other Receipts **7**	561104	11142	157506	1466	537	243	32461	12180	-20620	11095	6366	348731	0
Total Receipts **8**	22895817	1139839	381147	375647	848014	805740	1975630	789636	469762	1162175	982074	13966153	0
Average Total Receipts **9**	12706	2539	382	5217	12114	7823	42948	30371	42706	96848	196415	1396615	•

Operating Costs/Operating Income (%)

Cost of Operations **10**	39.5	14.5	•	74.0	61.1	50.6	37.1	36.8	46.5	37.6	32.7	40.2	•
Salaries and Wages **11**	8.9	4.4	13.8	6.4	12.1	17.9	8.6	13.9	8.9	8.1	14.4	7.9	•
Taxes Paid **12**	1.8	0.5	3.2	4.7	1.7	1.9	1.6	3.1	1.7	2.7	2.1	1.7	•
Interest Paid **13**	1.7	0.4	0.3	0.4	0.3	2.1	0.4	1.4	1.5	2.0	2.2	2.0	•
Depreciation **14**	5.9	1.2	0.2	1.0	0.3	10.5	1.7	5.2	5.8	7.3	14.9	6.5	•
Amortization and Depletion **15**	0.2	0.0	•	0.0	0.0	0.0	0.0	0.1	0.1	0.1	0.0	0.3	•
Pensions and Other Deferred Comp. **16**	0.7	0.1	5.3	0.1	0.2	0.0	0.5	0.6	0.6	0.6	0.3	0.9	•
Employee Benefits **17**	1.8	0.5	5.6	0.0	1.4	0.2	1.4	2.6	1.2	3.4	2.3	1.8	•
Advertising **18**	0.3	2.8	0.0	•	0.1	0.1	0.1	0.4	0.1	0.1	0.4	0.1	•
Other Expenses **19**	38.7	73.2	79.9	8.9	12.2	12.5	42.9	24.5	15.8	31.4	23.5	41.9	•
Officers' Compensation **20**	1.4	0.1	23.3	6.5	1.4	1.5	2.8	2.2	2.3	1.3	0.3	0.8	•
Operating Margin **21**	•	2.2	•	•	9.3	2.6	2.7	9.1	15.5	5.5	6.9	•	•
Operating Margin Before Officers' Comp. **22**	0.6	2.3	•	4.6	10.7	4.1	5.5	11.4	17.7	6.7	7.2	•	•

Selected Average Balance Sheet ($ in Thousands)

Net Receivables 23	2357	0	13	628	1866	105	7146	2546	9627	11190	33525	324533	•
Inventories 24	176	0	0	0	11	54	263	192	480	1017	3372	28080	•
Net Property, Plant and Equipment 25	7299	0	3	30	115	7039	3469	15980	34036	85310	289835	899188	•
Total Assets 26	14277	0	130	875	3573	8275	15415	32131	66581	148640	370817	1851653	•
Notes and Loans Payable 27	4684	0	59	236	506	4144	5652	11213	13780	61045	69866	611781	•
All Other Liabilities 28	4386	0	22	500	1543	538	6993	4685	10024	21449	67352	653416	•
Net Worth 29	5207	0	50	139	1523	3593	2769	16232	42777	66147	233598	586456	•

Selected Financial Ratios (Times to 1)

Current Ratio 30	1.3	•	1.0	1.6	1.7	1.2	1.3	1.8	3.1	1.9	0.7	1.3	•
Quick Ratio 31	1.0	•	0.8	1.6	1.6	0.6	1.2	1.4	2.1	1.5	0.6	1.0	•
Net Sales to Working Capital 32	11.8	•	256.5	15.8	10.1	65.2	17.5	7.1	2.3	6.0	•	10.8	•
Coverage Ratio 33	5.0	12.6	113.0	27.4	41.8	2.3	11.6	13.6	10.1	5.2	5.5	3.6	•
Total Asset Turnover 34	0.8	•	1.7	5.3	3.3	0.9	2.7	0.9	0.6	0.6	0.5	0.7	•
Inventory Turnover 35	26.8	•	•	•	670.4	73.6	59.3	53.4	41.8	34.7	18.5	18.6	•
Receivables Turnover 36	5.7	•	17.6	9.5	7.7	85.0	7.2	•	•	8.2	9.1	•	•
Total Liabilities to Net Worth 37	1.7	•	1.6	5.3	1.3	1.3	4.6	1.0	0.6	1.2	0.6	2.2	•
Current Assets to Working Capital 38	4.0	•	29.3	2.7	2.4	6.0	4.2	2.2	1.5	2.1	•	4.4	•
Current Liabilities to Working Capital 39	3.0	•	28.3	1.7	1.4	5.0	3.2	1.2	0.5	1.1	•	3.4	•
Working Capital to Net Sales 40	0.1	•	0.0	0.1	0.1	0.0	0.1	0.1	0.4	0.2	•	0.1	•
Inventory to Working Capital 41	0.2	•	•	•	•	0.4	0.1	0.0	0.0	0.1	•	0.2	•
Total Receipts to Cash Flow 42	2.9	1.3	0.9	5.6	5.1	6.6	4.9	3.2	4.4	2.8	3.5	2.8	•
Cost of Goods to Cash Flow 43	1.1	0.2	•	4.2	3.1	3.4	1.8	1.2	2.0	1.1	1.1	1.1	•
Cash Flow to Total Debt 44	0.5	•	3.2	1.1	1.1	0.3	0.7	0.5	0.4	0.4	0.4	0.4	•

Selected Financial Factors (in Percentages)

Debt Ratio 45	63.5	•	61.8	84.1	57.4	56.6	82.0	49.5	35.8	55.5	37.0	68.3	•
Return on Total Assets 46	7.1	•	67.3	54.0	38.3	4.5	14.3	16.9	10.2	6.6	6.2	5.2	•
Return on Equity Before Income Taxes 47	15.5	•	174.6	327.3	87.8	5.8	72.6	30.9	14.3	12.1	8.1	11.8	•
Return on Equity After Income Taxes 48	12.6	•	174.6	324.5	81.7	5.4	69.3	29.7	12.0	10.2	7.8	8.1	•
Profit Margin (Before Income Tax) 49	6.8	4.7	38.8	9.7	11.2	2.7	4.8	18.0	14.1	8.5	9.9	5.3	•
Profit Margin (After Income Tax) 50	5.5	3.8	38.8	9.7	10.5	2.5	4.6	17.3	11.9	7.2	9.6	3.6	•

Table I

Corporations with and without Net Income

TRUCK TRANSPORTATION

MONEY AMOUNTS AND SIZE OF ASSETS IN THOUSANDS OF DOLLARS

Item Description for Accounting Period 7/12 Through 6/13		Total	Zero Assets	Under 500	500 to 1,000	1,000 to 5,000	5,000 to 10,000	10,000 to 25,000	25,000 to 50,000	50,000 to 100,000	100,000 to 250,000	250,000 to 500,000	500,000 to 2,500,000	2,500,000 and over
Number of Enterprises	1	120846	33592	74732	5404	5513	820	417	186	81	56	19	26	0
Revenues ($ in Thousands)														
Net Sales	2	256431484	5894740	55009090	18562462	42864295	17835796	15823025	14470589	10620810	15003080	10437157	49910440	0
Interest	3	869059	58	520	948	7160	3676	4371	2157	2711	16924	77561	752972	0
Rents	4	382068	112	562	2400	27364	6895	37890	35601	6576	18275	12482	233911	0
Royalties	5	14231	257	223	58	0	0	21	7	1	2062	3971	7631	0
Other Portfolio Income	6	1672428	122781	235664	71378	152024	109874	103299	121008	102769	113334	111849	428447	0
Other Receipts	7	2964063	328427	808150	174418	402925	92296	104147	192537	82494	145008	459885	173777	0
Total Receipts	8	262333333	6346375	56054209	18811664	43453768	18048537	16072753	14821899	10815361	15298683	11102905	51507178	0
Average Total Receipts	9	2171	189	750	3481	7882	22010	38544	79688	133523	273191	584363	1981045	•
Operating Costs/Operating Income (%)														
Cost of Operations	10	33.5	27.6	29.4	36.0	39.3	41.4	45.6	48.4	32.8	25.8	43.3	22.3	•
Salaries and Wages	11	14.7	7.3	10.1	12.4	11.3	14.1	14.5	11.4	19.0	20.9	14.8	23.0	•
Taxes Paid	12	3.2	2.5	2.7	2.6	2.9	2.5	3.3	2.5	4.1	3.5	3.2	4.2	•
Interest Paid	13	1.1	0.7	0.4	0.6	0.6	0.5	0.9	0.9	1.1	2.0	1.2	2.4	•
Depreciation	14	4.1	2.6	2.3	3.3	3.7	3.9	4.9	4.8	6.5	5.8	5.9	4.8	•
Amortization and Depletion	15	0.1	0.1	0.0	0.0	0.1	0.0	0.1	0.1	0.2	0.3	0.3	0.2	•
Pensions and Other Deferred Comp.	16	0.3	0.1	0.1	0.1	0.2	0.3	0.1	0.2	0.1	0.7	0.2	1.0	•
Employee Benefits	17	2.0	0.6	0.8	1.0	1.4	2.6	2.0	1.2	2.6	2.7	1.7	4.1	•
Advertising	18	0.2	0.1	0.4	0.1	0.3	0.2	0.2	0.2	0.2	0.2	0.2	0.2	•
Other Expenses	19	36.6	52.3	41.5	41.0	36.3	31.3	26.4	29.7	31.9	37.6	31.1	37.1	•
Officers' Compensation	20	3.3	5.5	10.8	2.0	1.7	1.5	1.7	1.1	1.0	0.7	0.4	0.3	•
Operating Margin	21	0.9	0.6	1.4	0.8	2.1	1.9	0.4	•	0.4	•	•	0.4	•
Operating Margin Before Officers' Comp.	22	4.2	6.1	12.2	2.9	3.9	3.4	2.0	0.5	1.5	0.5	•	0.7	•

Selected Average Balance Sheet ($ in Thousands)

Net Receivables 23	189	0	12	129	579	2137	4326	8560	14323	34536	81730	315698	•
Inventories 24	9	0	1	19	30	112	194	742	457	2227	4933	9882	•
Net Property, Plant and Equipment 25	349	0	33	281	799	2889	6510	14293	34107	76097	186049	594367	•
Total Assets 26	824	0	79	732	2148	7206	15225	34850	68234	160291	389413	1430871	•
Notes and Loans Payable 27	336	0	55	411	1135	2798	7036	13529	30935	81410	120045	418380	•
All Other Liabilities 28	232	0	17	126	491	1645	3929	6779	14639	40595	131915	505596	•
Net Worth 29	256	0	7	195	522	2763	4260	14541	22661	38286	137453	506895	•

Selected Financial Ratios (Times to 1)

Current Ratio 30	1.3	•	1.4	1.2	1.4	1.7	1.5	1.6	1.3	1.1	1.3	1.2	•
Quick Ratio 31	1.1	•	1.3	0.9	1.2	1.5	1.2	1.3	1.1	0.8	1.0	1.0	•
Net Sales to Working Capital 32	27.3	•	67.2	64.8	23.5	13.8	17.2	13.5	21.0	73.3	18.0	26.6	•
Coverage Ratio 33	4.0	12.3	8.7	4.9	6.7	7.4	3.2	3.1	3.0	1.9	4.4	2.5	•
Total Asset Turnover 34	2.6	•	9.3	4.7	3.6	3.0	2.5	2.2	1.9	1.7	1.4	1.3	•
Inventory Turnover 35	75.5	•	368.4	64.1	100.4	80.2	89.1	50.8	94.1	31.1	48.2	43.4	•
Receivables Turnover 36	11.7	•	64.4	31.0	12.7	9.6	9.1	9.5	9.8	8.3	7.2	6.5	•
Total Liabilities to Net Worth 37	2.2	•	10.0	2.7	3.1	1.6	2.6	1.4	2.0	3.2	1.8	1.8	•
Current Assets to Working Capital 38	4.1	•	3.3	5.5	3.3	2.5	3.2	2.6	4.0	16.2	4.6	6.2	•
Current Liabilities to Working Capital 39	3.1	•	2.3	4.5	2.3	1.5	2.2	1.6	3.0	15.2	3.6	5.2	•
Working Capital to Net Sales 40	0.0	•	0.0	0.0	0.0	0.1	0.1	0.1	0.0	0.0	0.1	0.0	•
Inventory to Working Capital 41	0.1	•	0.0	0.4	0.1	0.0	0.1	0.1	0.1	0.8	0.1	0.1	•
Total Receipts to Cash Flow 42	3.1	1.9	2.6	2.8	3.1	3.8	4.9	4.1	3.7	3.2	3.8	2.9	•
Cost of Goods to Cash Flow 43	1.0	0.5	0.8	1.0	1.2	1.6	2.3	2.0	1.2	0.8	1.6	0.6	•
Cash Flow to Total Debt 44	1.2	•	3.9	2.3	1.5	1.3	0.7	0.9	0.8	0.7	0.6	0.7	•

Selected Financial Factors (in Percentages)

Debt Ratio 45	68.9	•	90.9	73.3	75.7	61.7	72.0	58.3	66.8	76.1	64.7	64.6	•
Return on Total Assets 46	10.9	•	34.8	12.9	15.0	10.8	7.1	6.1	6.6	6.3	7.4	8.1	•
Return on Equity Before Income Taxes 47	26.1	•	338.1	38.5	52.4	24.3	17.4	9.8	13.2	12.7	16.3	13.8	•
Return on Equity After Income Taxes 48	23.5	•	333.7	37.1	50.6	23.2	15.8	8.7	12.6	11.9	10.6	10.3	•
Profit Margin (Before Income Tax) 49	3.2	8.2	3.3	2.2	3.5	3.1	1.9	1.8	2.3	1.8	4.1	3.6	•
Profit Margin (After Income Tax) 50	2.8	8.1	3.3	2.1	3.4	3.0	1.8	1.6	2.2	1.7	2.7	2.7	•

Table II
Corporations with Net Income

TRUCK TRANSPORTATION

MONEY AMOUNTS AND SIZE OF ASSETS IN THOUSANDS OF DOLLARS

Item Description for Accounting Period 7/12 Through 6/13		Total	Zero Assets	Under 500	500 to 1,000	1,000 to 5,000	5,000 to 10,000	10,000 to 25,000	25,000 to 50,000	50,000 to 100,000	100,000 to 250,000	250,000 to 500,000	500,000 to 2,500,000	2,500,000 and over
Number of Enterprises	1	82748	21028	52523	3917	4132	640	268	123	49	34	13	20	0
Revenues ($ in Thousands)														
Net Sales	2	193435955	4072630	44034576	14558068	31176471	14262922	11157103	10789157	6639213	9908722	7314800	39522293	0
Interest	3	108499	28	291	897	5722	1861	3934	1560	1990	4608	31440	56168	0
Rents	4	319770	112	562	454	17184	4903	36046	18651	4815	17415	12212	207417	0
Royalties	5	5476	0	223	0	0	0	21	0	0	0	2640	2593	0
Other Portfolio Income	6	1198743	102725	175591	42609	90133	74231	70058	93254	63163	70820	90551	325610	0
Other Receipts	7	2220993	327703	638718	152673	301651	63225	62660	95965	40104	82600	438769	16921	0
Total Receipts	8	197289436	4503198	44849961	14754701	31591161	14407142	11329822	10998587	6749285	10084165	7890412	40131002	0
Average Total Receipts	9	2384	214	854	3767	7645	22511	42275	89419	137741	296593	606955	2006550	•
Operating Costs/Operating Income (%)														
Cost of Operations	10	35.1	29.6	31.8	43.6	40.4	37.5	40.6	49.3	40.1	28.8	37.2	26.1	•
Salaries and Wages	11	13.4	5.8	8.7	8.7	10.5	15.1	15.5	10.7	14.6	19.7	15.7	20.7	•
Taxes Paid	12	2.9	2.3	2.3	2.1	2.8	2.5	3.5	2.1	3.5	3.2	3.3	4.0	•
Interest Paid	13	0.6	0.5	0.3	0.4	0.5	0.4	0.7	0.6	1.0	0.9	0.6	0.8	•
Depreciation	14	3.5	1.7	1.9	2.2	2.9	3.4	3.9	3.9	5.1	4.6	5.6	5.3	•
Amortization and Depletion	15	0.1	0.2	0.0	0.0	0.1	0.0	0.1	0.0	0.2	0.1	0.2	0.2	•
Pensions and Other Deferred Comp.	16	0.3	0.1	0.1	0.1	0.2	0.3	0.1	0.2	0.1	0.8	0.2	0.6	•
Employee Benefits	17	1.6	0.4	0.6	0.8	1.3	2.9	2.4	0.9	1.9	2.0	1.9	2.8	•
Advertising	18	0.2	0.1	0.4	0.1	0.2	0.2	0.2	0.2	0.2	0.2	0.1	0.1	•
Other Expenses	19	35.2	49.2	37.9	37.3	34.7	32.8	28.5	28.8	28.8	35.5	36.2	35.5	•
Officers' Compensation	20	3.9	5.0	12.6	2.0	1.9	1.6	1.9	1.3	1.2	0.7	0.4	0.3	•
Operating Margin	21	3.3	5.2	3.3	2.6	4.6	3.4	2.5	1.9	3.3	3.5	•	3.6	•
Operating Margin Before Officers' Comp.	22	7.2	10.1	15.9	4.6	6.5	5.1	4.4	3.2	4.5	4.2	•	3.9	•

Selected Average Balance Sheet ($ in Thousands)

Net Receivables 23	196	0	14	162	542	2097	4655	9205	16048	39945	95389	278440	•
Inventories 24	9	0	0	17	20	121	202	812	455	2825	3545	11045	•
Net Property, Plant and Equipment 25	359	0	31	232	750	2776	5826	13035	32479	77168	170266	636607	•
Total Assets 26	841	0	84	727	2112	7339	15278	35372	68895	163199	390378	1325813	•
Notes and Loans Payable 27	278	0	49	350	921	2362	6291	10813	29066	54261	101640	304732	•
All Other Liabilities 28	220	0	15	146	454	1602	3523	6292	14937	38809	128953	426837	•
Net Worth 29	344	0	20	231	737	3375	5464	18267	24892	70129	159785	594244	•

Selected Financial Ratios (Times to 1)

Current Ratio 30	1.5	•	2.0	1.2	1.8	2.0	1.6	2.0	1.5	1.3	1.5	1.3	•
Quick Ratio 31	1.3	•	1.8	1.0	1.5	1.8	1.4	1.6	1.3	1.0	1.2	1.1	•
Net Sales to Working Capital 32	19.3	•	42.5	69.4	15.4	10.9	14.6	10.8	15.1	17.8	10.7	20.0	•
Coverage Ratio 33	10.3	29.7	17.7	10.1	12.0	12.7	6.6	7.6	6.2	6.8	11.2	7.5	•
Total Asset Turnover 34	2.8	•	10.0	5.1	3.6	3.0	2.7	2.5	2.0	1.8	1.4	1.5	•
Inventory Turnover 35	86.8	•	884.2	96.8	149.7	69.3	83.7	53.3	119.5	29.7	59.0	46.6	•
Receivables Turnover 36	13.3	•	68.3	31.7	12.9	10.4	9.3	11.2	10.3	9.3	6.7	8.3	•
Total Liabilities to Net Worth 37	1.4	•	3.2	2.2	1.9	1.2	1.8	0.9	1.8	1.3	1.4	1.2	•
Current Assets to Working Capital 38	2.8	•	2.1	5.6	2.3	2.0	2.7	2.0	3.0	3.9	3.0	4.1	•
Current Liabilities to Working Capital 39	1.8	•	1.1	4.6	1.3	1.0	1.7	1.0	2.0	2.9	2.0	3.1	•
Working Capital to Net Sales 40	0.1	•	0.0	0.0	0.1	0.1	0.1	0.1	0.1	0.1	0.1	0.1	•
Inventory to Working Capital 41	0.1	•	0.0	0.3	0.1	0.0	0.1	0.1	0.1	0.2	0.0	0.1	•
Total Receipts to Cash Flow 42	3.0	1.8	2.7	2.8	3.0	3.5	4.2	3.8	3.5	3.1	3.1	2.8	•
Cost of Goods to Cash Flow 43	1.0	0.5	0.9	1.2	1.2	1.3	1.7	1.9	1.4	0.9	1.2	0.7	•
Cash Flow to Total Debt 44	1.6	•	4.9	2.7	1.8	1.6	1.0	1.4	0.9	1.0	0.8	0.9	•

Selected Financial Factors (in Percentages)

Debt Ratio 45	59.2	•	76.0	68.3	65.1	54.0	64.2	48.4	63.9	57.0	59.1	55.2	•
Return on Total Assets 46	16.3	•	54.9	22.1	23.1	14.6	13.1	11.0	11.7	11.0	10.3	8.9	•
Return on Equity Before Income Taxes 47	35.9	•	215.9	62.9	60.8	29.3	31.2	18.5	27.0	21.9	22.9	17.2	•
Return on Equity After Income Taxes 48	33.1	•	213.7	61.3	59.0	28.2	29.3	17.3	26.1	21.2	15.7	13.4	•
Profit Margin (Before Income Tax) 49	5.3	15.8	5.2	3.9	5.9	4.4	4.1	3.9	5.0	5.3	6.5	5.2	•
Profit Margin (After Income Tax) 50	4.9	15.6	5.1	3.8	5.8	4.3	3.8	3.6	4.8	5.1	4.5	4.0	•

Table I

Corporations with and without Net Income

TRANSIT AND GROUND PASSENGER TRANSPORTATION

MONEY AMOUNTS AND SIZE OF ASSETS IN THOUSANDS OF DOLLARS

Item Description for Accounting Period 7/12 Through 6/13	Total	Zero Assets	Under 500	500 to 1,000	1,000 to 5,000	5,000 to 10,000	10,000 to 25,000	25,000 to 50,000	50,000 to 100,000	100,000 to 250,000	250,000 to 500,000	500,000 to 2,500,000	2,500,000 and over
Number of Enterprises 1	29942	7108	17630	2901	2060	72	117	31	12	3	4	4	0

Revenues ($ in Thousands)

	Total	Zero Assets	Under 500	500 to 1,000	1,000 to 5,000	5,000 to 10,000	10,000 to 25,000	25,000 to 50,000	50,000 to 100,000	100,000 to 250,000	250,000 to 500,000	500,000 to 2,500,000	2,500,000 and over
Net Sales 2	26585026	446984	5022899	750109	5834239	1027556	2392575	1581986	876846	716291	1631709	6303830	0
Interest 3	105197	34	6	1406	915	75	3436	429	249	1262	818	96566	0
Rents 4	11019	0	0	0	1055	27	518	46	451	754	0	8169	0
Royalties 5	12054	0	0	0	0	0	0	0	0	0	0	12054	0
Other Portfolio Income 6	232273	21473	3461	35270	22302	11055	70950	17948	3279	24068	15012	7454	0
Other Receipts 7	472463	639	202814	15006	51399	16832	72219	11342	3883	2154	3221	92957	0
Total Receipts 8	27418032	469130	5229180	801791	5909910	1055545	2539698	1611751	884708	744529	1650760	6521030	0
Average Total Receipts 9	916	66	297	276	2869	14660	21707	51992	73726	248176	412690	1630258	•

Operating Costs/Operating Income (%)

	Total	Zero Assets	Under 500	500 to 1,000	1,000 to 5,000	5,000 to 10,000	10,000 to 25,000	25,000 to 50,000	50,000 to 100,000	100,000 to 250,000	250,000 to 500,000	500,000 to 2,500,000	2,500,000 and over
Cost of Operations 10	25.9	16.8	4.3	33.0	33.8	21.6	51.4	45.6	53.6	68.5	24.7	13.1	•
Salaries and Wages 11	27.5	5.5	34.6	17.4	18.5	26.9	13.8	18.2	12.8	4.9	34.4	43.4	•
Taxes Paid 12	4.5	2.9	4.6	2.2	3.7	5.8	3.4	3.8	5.0	3.9	5.0	5.8	•
Interest Paid 13	2.0	3.7	0.9	8.5	1.5	1.8	0.9	0.8	1.3	9.3	1.3	2.8	•
Depreciation 14	5.1	5.0	3.3	1.7	5.7	6.8	9.2	5.5	8.7	7.6	5.2	3.6	•
Amortization and Depletion 15	0.7	0.3	0.4	3.5	0.4	0.1	0.1	0.1	0.2	1.0	0.3	1.7	•
Pensions and Other Deferred Comp. 16	0.5	•	0.1	0.0	0.3	0.3	0.8	0.5	0.6	1.0	0.1	1.0	•
Employee Benefits 17	2.1	0.8	0.5	0.7	1.1	1.9	2.1	1.9	3.5	6.4	5.1	3.3	•
Advertising 18	0.5	0.3	0.7	0.2	0.6	1.0	0.4	0.5	0.4	0.3	0.7	0.3	•
Other Expenses 19	28.9	50.2	43.8	21.3	31.0	33.5	20.1	17.1	12.9	10.8	20.8	26.4	•
Officers' Compensation 20	2.8	13.4	5.6	7.0	4.2	1.1	1.2	1.1	1.6	0.2	0.7	0.3	•
Operating Margin 21	•	1.1	1.3	4.4	•	•	•	5.0	•	•	1.8	•	•
Operating Margin Before Officers' Comp. 22	2.2	14.4	6.9	11.4	3.2	0.4	•	6.0	1.1	•	2.4	•	•

Selected Average Balance Sheet ($ in Thousands)

	1	2	3	4	5	6	7	8	9	10	11	12	
Net Receivables 23	89	0	4	21	274	652	2228	6590	12690	47734	39428	253145	•
Inventories 24	4	0	0	0	6	11	76	162	1433	4450	1405	13996	•
Net Property, Plant and Equipment 25	228	0	25	70	587	3930	7078	11920	32910	80403	88830	621450	•
Total Assets 26	713	0	80	727	1781	7069	14338	30164	75217	146632	340380	2087302	•
Notes and Loans Payable 27	417	0	54	623	1245	3780	5558	10284	36378	131636	177724	1095005	•
All Other Liabilities 28	140	0	8	23	204	1442	3009	7183	12322	39518	108330	548368	•
Net Worth 29	156	0	18	81	331	1846	5771	12697	26516	-24521	54326	443929	•

Selected Financial Ratios (Times to 1)

Current Ratio 30	1.2	•	1.0	2.1	1.8	0.9	1.0	1.4	1.5	0.7	1.5	0.9	•
Quick Ratio 31	0.8	•	0.6	0.9	1.5	0.7	0.8	1.2	1.1	0.6	0.6	0.7	•
Net Sales to Working Capital 32	36.2	•	•	4.9	13.1	•	•	12.2	9.3	•	8.1	•	•
Coverage Ratio 33	2.3	2.6	7.3	2.3	1.2	2.1	4.0	9.3	1.3	•	3.3	1.6	•
Total Asset Turnover 34	1.2	•	3.6	0.4	1.6	2.0	1.4	1.7	1.0	1.6	1.2	0.8	•
Inventory Turnover 35	56.5	•	200.9	248.1	155.7	293.2	138.1	143.7	27.3	36.7	71.8	14.8	•
Receivables Turnover 36	10.7	•	60.4	24.1	10.0	19.7	9.3	12.2	6.6	2.1	13.0	8.4	•
Total Liabilities to Net Worth 37	3.6	•	3.4	8.0	4.4	2.8	1.5	1.4	1.8	•	5.3	3.7	•
Current Assets to Working Capital 38	7.3	•	•	1.9	2.3	•	•	3.4	3.2	•	2.9	•	•
Current Liabilities to Working Capital 39	6.3	•	•	0.9	1.3	•	•	2.4	2.2	•	1.9	•	•
Working Capital to Net Sales 40	0.0	•	•	0.2	0.1	•	•	0.1	0.1	•	0.1	•	•
Inventory to Working Capital 41	0.2	•	•	0.0	0.0	•	•	0.1	0.2	•	0.0	•	•
Total Receipts to Cash Flow 42	4.0	2.0	2.4	3.3	4.7	3.6	5.5	4.8	11.9	•	5.0	4.5	•
Cost of Goods to Cash Flow 43	1.0	0.3	0.1	1.1	1.6	0.8	2.9	2.2	6.4	•	1.2	0.6	•
Cash Flow to Total Debt 44	0.4	•	1.9	0.1	0.4	0.7	0.4	0.6	0.1	•	0.3	0.2	•

Selected Financial Factors (in Percentages)

Debt Ratio 45	78.1	•	77.3	88.9	81.4	73.9	59.8	57.9	64.7	116.7	84.0	78.7	•
Return on Total Assets 46	5.8	•	22.5	7.0	3.0	7.7	5.3	13.0	1.6	•	5.3	3.4	•
Return on Equity Before Income Taxes 47	14.9	•	85.6	36.2	2.9	15.6	9.9	27.6	1.0	94.3	23.0	6.3	•
Return on Equity After Income Taxes 48	14.1	•	83.8	33.7	2.8	12.4	9.2	27.3	0.7	94.3	18.5	6.1	•
Profit Margin (Before Income Tax) 49	2.6	6.0	5.5	11.3	0.3	2.0	2.8	6.9	0.4	•	3.1	1.8	•
Profit Margin (After Income Tax) 50	2.5	6.0	5.3	10.5	0.3	1.6	2.6	6.8	0.3	•	2.5	1.7	•

Table II

Corporations with Net Income

TRANSIT AND GROUND PASSENGER TRANSPORTATION

MONEY AMOUNTS AND SIZE OF ASSETS IN THOUSANDS OF DOLLARS

Item Description for Accounting Period 7/12 Through 6/13		Total	Zero Assets	Under 500	500 to 1,000	1,000 to 5,000	5,000 to 10,000	10,000 to 25,000	25,000 to 50,000	50,000 to 100,000	100,000 to 250,000	250,000 to 500,000	500,000 to 2,500,000	2,500,000 and over
Number of Enterprises	1	18741	2997	12073	1922	1570	44	90	•	8	0	4	•	0
Revenues ($ in Thousands)														
Net Sales	2	21498766	275674	4179180	715011	4281893	759653	1985355	•	521223	0	1631709	•	0
Interest	3	94409	0	0	533	256	63	106	•	1	0	818	•	0
Rents	4	8677	0	0	0	0	27	398	•	38	0	0	•	0
Royalties	5	12054	0	0	0	0	0	0	•	0	0	0	•	0
Other Portfolio Income	6	188403	21407	3461	35269	12055	9301	66036	•	575	0	15012	•	0
Other Receipts	7	225533	1	4438	14727	34150	16270	68258	•	2931	0	3221	•	0
Total Receipts	8	22027842	297082	4187079	765540	4328354	785314	2120153	•	524768	0	1650760	•	0
Average Total Receipts	9	1175	99	347	398	2757	17848	23557	•	65596	•	412690	•	•
Operating Costs/Operating Income (%)														
Cost of Operations	10	23.5	5.5	4.4	34.6	34.1	18.7	49.3	•	61.3	•	24.7	•	•
Salaries and Wages	11	28.7	3.8	36.2	18.2	14.1	26.5	14.2	•	4.2	•	34.4	•	•
Taxes Paid	12	4.6	3.2	4.7	2.2	3.5	6.3	3.1	•	4.3	•	5.0	•	•
Interest Paid	13	1.6	0.2	0.7	4.9	1.5	0.6	0.9	•	1.4	•	1.3	•	•
Depreciation	14	4.5	2.9	3.4	1.7	5.4	3.7	7.8	•	8.3	•	5.2	•	•
Amortization and Depletion	15	0.6	•	0.1	0.2	0.3	0.1	0.1	•	0.1	•	0.3	•	•
Pensions and Other Deferred Comp.	16	0.6	•	0.1	0.0	0.4	0.4	1.0	•	0.9	•	0.1	•	•
Employee Benefits	17	2.0	1.3	0.3	0.7	0.8	2.2	2.4	•	4.4	•	5.1	•	•
Advertising	18	0.5	0.5	0.8	0.2	0.8	0.5	0.3	•	0.3	•	0.7	•	•
Other Expenses	19	27.8	59.9	34.9	21.3	32.2	36.3	21.9	•	8.3	•	20.8	•	•
Officers' Compensation	20	3.1	17.3	6.1	7.1	5.1	0.7	1.1	•	1.9	•	0.7	•	•
Operating Margin	21	2.6	5.4	8.3	8.9	1.7	4.1	•	•	4.7	•	1.8	•	•
Operating Margin Before Officers' Comp.	22	5.7	22.7	14.4	16.0	6.8	4.8	•	•	6.6	•	2.4	•	•

Selected Average Balance Sheet ($ in Thousands)

Net Receivables 23	115	0	6	1	287	501	2334	•	13922	•	39428	•	•
Inventories 24	5	0	0	0	1	8	91	•	1027	•	1868	•	•
Net Property, Plant and Equipment 25	284	0	30	104	575	3048	6681	•	30889	•	88830	•	•
Total Assets 26	924	0	79	734	1819	6762	14688	•	73668	•	340380	•	•
Notes and Loans Payable 27	500	0	39	546	1168	2127	5410	•	37002	•	177724	•	•
All Other Liabilities 28	186	0	8	17	150	1881	3502	•	8616	•	108330	•	•
Net Worth 29	238	0	32	171	502	2754	5775	•	28050	•	54326	•	•

Selected Financial Ratios (Times to 1)

Current Ratio 30	1.3	•	1.8	2.2	2.1	1.2	1.0	•	1.8	•	1.5	•	•
Quick Ratio 31	0.9	•	1.0	1.3	1.8	0.8	0.8	•	1.4	•	0.6	•	•
Net Sales to Working Capital 32	23.2	•	28.8	13.4	10.4	48.0	2324.8	•	5.7	•	8.1	•	•
Coverage Ratio 33	4.2	54.7	13.5	4.3	2.9	13.5	6.4	•	4.7	•	3.3	•	•
Total Asset Turnover 34	1.2	•	4.4	0.5	1.5	2.6	1.5	•	0.9	•	1.2	•	•
Inventory Turnover 35	54.4	•	170.9	381.1	625.2	391.5	120.0	•	38.9	•	54.1	•	•
Receivables Turnover 36	11.1	•	56.6	495.5	8.6	28.7	9.0	•	7.7	•	20.7	•	•
Total Liabilities to Net Worth 37	2.9	•	1.5	3.3	2.6	1.5	1.5	•	1.6	•	5.3	•	•
Current Assets to Working Capital 38	4.7	•	2.3	1.8	1.9	6.8	487.8	•	2.3	•	2.9	•	•
Current Liabilities to Working Capital 39	3.7	•	1.3	0.8	0.9	5.8	486.8	•	1.3	•	1.9	•	•
Working Capital to Net Sales 40	0.0	•	0.0	0.1	0.1	0.0	0.0	•	0.2	•	0.1	•	•
Inventory to Working Capital 41	0.1	•	0.0	0.0	0.0	0.0	11.2	•	0.2	•	0.0	•	•
Total Receipts to Cash Flow 42	3.7	1.5	2.7	2.9	4.0	2.9	4.7	•	9.4	•	5.0	•	•
Cost of Goods to Cash Flow 43	0.9	0.1	0.1	1.0	1.4	0.5	2.3	•	5.8	•	1.2	•	•
Cash Flow to Total Debt 44	0.4	•	2.7	0.2	0.5	1.5	0.5	•	0.2	•	0.3	•	•

Selected Financial Factors (in Percentages)

Debt Ratio 45	74.2	•	60.0	76.7	72.4	59.3	60.7	•	61.9	•	84.0	•	•
Return on Total Assets 46	8.3	•	40.0	10.6	6.3	20.6	8.3	•	6.0	•	5.3	•	•
Return on Equity Before Income Taxes 47	24.5	•	92.6	34.7	14.9	46.9	17.9	•	12.4	•	23.0	•	•
Return on Equity After Income Taxes 48	23.7	•	91.1	32.9	14.8	43.4	17.0	•	11.9	•	18.5	•	•
Profit Margin (Before Income Tax) 49	5.1	13.2	8.5	16.0	2.7	7.5	4.7	•	5.3	•	3.1	•	•
Profit Margin (After Income Tax) 50	4.9	13.1	8.3	15.1	2.7	6.9	4.4	•	5.1	•	2.5	•	•

TRANSPORTATION AND WAREHOUSING
486000

Table I

Corporations with and without Net Income

PIPELINE TRANSPORTATION

MONEY AMOUNTS AND SIZE OF ASSETS IN THOUSANDS OF DOLLARS

Item Description for Accounting Period 7/12 Through 6/13	Total	Zero Assets	Under 500	500 to 1,000	1,000 to 5,000	5,000 to 10,000	10,000 to 25,000	25,000 to 50,000	50,000 to 100,000	100,000 to 250,000	250,000 to 500,000	500,000 to 2,500,000	2,500,000 and over
Number of Enterprises 1	600	19	313	0	169	57	14	4	9	5	0	5	4

Revenues ($ in Thousands)													
Net Sales 2	7599284	45623	240451	0	698718	162658	128837	141068	662158	555063	0	2192916	2771792
Interest 3	21186	1	0	0	69	226	138	30	275	106	0	700	19641
Rents 4	14540	51	0	0	0	0	438	2385	2053	0	0	4232	5381
Royalties 5	326	0	0	0	118	0	0	0	0	0	0	0	208
Other Portfolio Income 6	157261	26478	0	0	0	42290	78	9	1609	150	0	83295	3352
Other Receipts 7	926227	52605	0	0	7713	-8359	8696	1489	2248	55283	0	293687	512865
Total Receipts 8	8718824	124758	240451	0	706618	196815	138187	144981	668343	610602	0	2574830	3313239
Average Total Receipts 9	14531	6566	768	•	4181	3453	9870	36245	74260	122120	•	514966	828310

Operating Costs/Operating Income (%)													
Cost of Operations 10	24.3	16.2	66.0	•	69.0	16.8	30.6	•	63.3	26.7	•	15.4	8.3
Salaries and Wages 11	9.6	3.9	0.1	•	11.4	3.0	5.1	4.3	1.1	15.6	•	6.8	14.0
Taxes Paid 12	5.4	6.1	0.3	•	2.2	1.1	3.6	6.7	2.6	5.6	•	5.5	7.5
Interest Paid 13	14.3	17.8	3.7	•	0.6	0.2	•	0.4	0.3	3.6	•	8.4	31.1
Depreciation 14	15.9	13.3	30.6	•	0.3	7.8	5.1	5.8	8.3	8.3	•	11.5	26.9
Amortization and Depletion 15	0.5	•	•	•	0.2	0.9	0.0	•	0.1	0.3	•	1.2	0.3
Pensions and Other Deferred Comp. 16	0.4	0.0	•	•	0.4	0.0	•	•	0.2	0.9	•	0.9	0.1
Employee Benefits 17	2.2	•	•	•	1.8	2.5	1.0	1.2	0.1	4.6	•	0.9	3.7
Advertising 18	0.1	0.1	•	•	0.9	•	•	•	•	0.0	•	0.0	0.0
Other Expenses 19	25.6	90.6	29.5	•	10.5	37.6	20.8	34.3	9.8	16.6	•	35.1	25.2
Officers' Compensation 20	0.4	•	0.2	•	2.4	0.7	0.5	•	0.1	0.0	•	0.4	0.1
Operating Margin 21	1.1	•	•	•	0.5	29.2	33.3	47.4	14.2	17.8	•	13.8	•
Operating Margin Before Officers' Comp. 22	1.5	•	•	•	2.9	29.9	33.8	47.4	14.3	17.8	•	14.2	•

Selected Average Balance Sheet ($ in Thousands)

Net Receivables 23	2000	0	77	•	234	978	1047	3379	4647	19692	•	116921	81891
Inventories 24	468	0	0	•	185	70	765	684	1928	421	•	7918	43281
Net Property, Plant and Equipment 25	28745	0	177	•	210	635	7623	29299	42675	131362	•	716821	3067810
Total Assets 26	48452	0	261	•	1422	7327	14353	37487	66012	154043	•	1189953	5166653
Notes and Loans Payable 27	24157	0	1275	•	292	3785	0	4502	4709	86074	•	526172	2677038
All Other Liabilities 28	11755	0	85	•	123	227	1624	4879	23392	59355	•	414630	1092431
Net Worth 29	12541	0	-1100	•	1007	3315	12729	28106	37911	8614	•	249152	1397184

Selected Financial Ratios (Times to 1)

Current Ratio 30	0.9	•	0.7	•	2.9	9.4	4.6	1.0	2.2	1.1	•	0.9	0.6
Quick Ratio 31	0.6	•	0.7	•	1.7	8.6	4.0	1.0	1.5	0.8	•	0.8	0.3
Net Sales to Working Capital 32	•	•	•	•	8.7	1.3	3.8	312.1	8.0	36.6	•	•	•
Coverage Ratio 33	2.1	8.1	•	•	3.9	204.5	•	142.3	58.9	8.8	•	4.7	1.1
Total Asset Turnover 34	0.3	•	2.9	•	2.9	0.4	0.6	0.9	1.1	0.7	•	0.4	0.1
Inventory Turnover 35	6.6	•	•	•	15.4	6.9	3.7	•	24.2	70.3	•	8.5	1.3
Receivables Turnover 36	3.8	•	20.1	•	12.9	2.9	4.6	6.3	17.0	6.1	•	4.1	2.3
Total Liabilities to Net Worth 37	2.9	•	•	•	0.4	1.2	0.1	0.3	0.7	16.9	•	3.8	2.7
Current Assets to Working Capital 38	•	•	•	•	1.5	1.1	1.3	72.5	1.8	12.6	•	•	•
Current Liabilities to Working Capital 39	•	•	•	•	0.5	0.1	0.3	71.5	0.8	11.6	•	•	•
Working Capital to Net Sales 40	•	•	•	•	0.1	0.8	0.3	0.0	0.1	0.0	•	•	•
Inventory to Working Capital 41	•	•	•	•	0.5	0.1	0.1	1.0	0.4	0.1	•	•	•
Total Receipts to Cash Flow 42	2.9	0.7	•	•	13.4	1.2	1.7	1.2	4.1	2.6	•	1.7	5.0
Cost of Goods to Cash Flow 43	0.7	0.1	•	•	9.2	0.2	0.5	•	2.6	0.7	•	0.3	0.4
Cash Flow to Total Debt 44	0.1	•	•	•	0.7	0.6	3.2	3.1	0.6	0.3	•	0.3	0.0

Selected Financial Factors (in Percentages)

Debt Ratio 45	74.1	•	520.9	•	29.1	54.8	11.3	25.0	42.6	94.4	•	79.1	73.0
Return on Total Assets 46	7.9	•	•	•	6.3	19.6	26.0	47.6	17.2	22.6	•	14.6	4.5
Return on Equity Before Income Taxes 47	16.0	•	21.2	•	6.7	43.2	29.3	63.0	29.4	357.7	•	55.0	1.2
Return on Equity After Income Taxes 48	11.0	•	21.2	•	5.4	42.4	19.4	40.9	18.2	241.1	•	36.5	1.1
Profit Margin (Before Income Tax) 49	15.9	125.6	•	•	1.6	50.2	40.6	50.2	15.1	27.8	•	31.2	2.4
Profit Margin (After Income Tax) 50	10.9	104.2	•	•	1.3	49.2	26.8	32.6	9.4	18.7	•	20.7	2.3

Table II

Corporations with Net Income

PIPELINE TRANSPORTATION

MONEY AMOUNTS AND SIZE OF ASSETS IN THOUSANDS OF DOLLARS

Item Description for Accounting Period 7/12 Through 6/13	Total	Zero Assets	Under 500	500 to 1,000	1,000 to 5,000	5,000 to 10,000	10,000 to 25,000	25,000 to 50,000	50,000 to 100,000	100,000 to 250,000	250,000 to 500,000	500,000 to 2,500,000	2,500,000 and over
Number of Enterprises **1**	242	19	0	0	134	57	11	4	6	•	0	•	0
Revenues ($ in Thousands)													
Net Sales **2**	5136712	45623	0	0	622806	162658	125170	141068	254052	•	0	•	0
Interest **3**	1370	1	0	0	69	226	132	30	33	•	0	•	0
Rents **4**	8840	51	0	0	0	0	438	2385	2053	•	0	•	0
Royalties **5**	118	0	0	0	118	0	0	0	0	•	0	•	0
Other Portfolio Income **6**	148903	26478	0	0	0	42290	45	9	1551	•	0	•	0
Other Receipts **7**	433898	52605	0	0	7672	-8359	8696	1489	9	•	0	•	0
Total Receipts **8**	5729841	124758	0	0	630665	196815	134481	144981	257698	•	0	•	0
Average Total Receipts **9**	23677	6566	•	•	4706	3453	12226	36245	42950	•	•	•	•
Operating Costs/Operating Income (%)													
Cost of Operations **10**	16.5	16.2	•	•	69.0	16.8	30.5	•	15.2	•	•	•	•
Salaries and Wages **11**	7.4	3.9	•	•	11.9	3.0	4.9	4.3	2.3	•	•	•	•
Taxes Paid **12**	6.2	6.1	•	•	2.2	1.1	3.5	6.7	6.4	•	•	•	•
Interest Paid **13**	7.6	17.8	•	•	0.1	0.2	•	0.4	0.4	•	•	•	•
Depreciation **14**	13.1	13.3	•	•	0.1	7.8	5.1	5.8	11.8	•	•	•	•
Amortization and Depletion **15**	0.4	•	•	•	0.3	0.9	0.0	•	•	•	•	•	•
Pensions and Other Deferred Comp. **16**	0.6	0.0	•	•	0.4	0.0	•	•	0.6	•	•	•	•
Employee Benefits **17**	1.6	•	•	•	2.0	2.5	1.0	1.2	0.2	•	•	•	•
Advertising **18**	0.1	0.1	•	•	0.9	•	•	•	•	•	•	•	•
Other Expenses **19**	25.1	90.6	•	•	10.4	37.6	20.5	34.3	21.0	•	•	•	•
Officers' Compensation **20**	0.4	•	•	•	1.8	0.7	0.1	•	0.2	•	•	•	•
Operating Margin **21**	21.0	•	•	•	0.8	29.2	34.5	47.4	41.9	•	•	•	•
Operating Margin Before Officers' Comp. **22**	21.4	•	•	•	2.6	29.9	34.5	47.4	42.1	•	•	•	•

Selected Average Balance Sheet ($ in Thousands)

Net Receivables	23	2643	0	•	•	268	978	1196	3379	3385	•	•	•	•
Inventories	24	327	0	•	•	224	70	960	118	1039	•	•	•	•
Net Property, Plant and Equipment	25	50049	0	•	•	38	635	6104	29299	48526	•	•	•	•
Total Assets	26	65618	0	•	•	1481	7327	14117	37487	66636	•	•	•	•
Notes and Loans Payable	27	25040	0	•	•	159	3785	0	4502	4273	•	•	•	•
All Other Liabilities	28	21203	0	•	•	136	227	1556	4879	20658	•	•	•	•
Net Worth	29	19376	0	•	•	1186	3315	12561	28106	41704	•	•	•	•

Selected Financial Ratios (Times to 1)

Current Ratio	30	0.8	•	•	•	4.0	9.4	5.1	1.0	2.4	•	•	•	•
Quick Ratio	31	0.5	•	•	•	2.4	8.6	4.3	1.0	1.8	•	•	•	•
Net Sales to Working Capital	32	•	•	•	•	7.2	1.3	3.9	312.1	4.8	•	•	•	•
Coverage Ratio	33	5.3	8.1	•	•	19.2	204.5	•	142.3	108.4	•	•	•	•
Total Asset Turnover	34	0.3	•	•	•	3.1	0.4	0.8	0.9	0.6	•	•	•	•
Inventory Turnover	35	10.7	•	•	•	14.3	6.9	3.6	•	6.2	•	•	•	•
Receivables Turnover	36	9.4	•	•	•	11.9	5.3	4.6	•	9.0	•	•	•	•
Total Liabilities to Net Worth	37	2.4	•	•	•	0.2	1.2	0.1	0.3	0.6	•	•	•	•
Current Assets to Working Capital	38	•	•	•	•	1.3	1.1	1.2	72.5	1.7	•	•	•	•
Current Liabilities to Working Capital	39	•	•	•	•	0.3	0.1	0.2	71.5	0.7	•	•	•	•
Working Capital to Net Sales	40	•	•	•	•	0.1	0.8	0.3	0.0	0.2	•	•	•	•
Inventory to Working Capital	41	•	•	•	•	0.4	0.1	0.1	1.0	0.1	•	•	•	•
Total Receipts to Cash Flow	42	2.0	0.7	•	•	13.3	1.2	1.7	1.2	1.6	•	•	•	•
Cost of Goods to Cash Flow	43	0.3	0.1	•	•	9.1	0.2	0.5	•	0.2	•	•	•	•
Cash Flow to Total Debt	44	0.2	•	•	•	1.2	0.6	4.3	3.1	1.1	•	•	•	•

Selected Financial Factors (in Percentages)

Debt Ratio	45	70.5	•	•	•	19.9	54.8	11.0	25.0	37.4	•	•	•	•
Return on Total Assets	46	13.0	•	•	•	6.7	19.6	33.8	47.6	27.8	•	•	•	•
Return on Equity Before Income Taxes	47	35.7	•	•	•	7.9	43.2	38.0	63.0	44.0	•	•	•	•
Return on Equity After Income Taxes	48	27.6	•	•	•	6.5	42.4	25.1	40.9	28.7	•	•	•	•
Profit Margin (Before Income Tax)	49	32.5	125.6	•	•	2.0	50.2	41.9	50.2	43.3	•	•	•	•
Profit Margin (After Income Tax)	50	25.2	104.2	•	•	1.7	49.2	27.7	32.6	28.3	•	•	•	•

248

Table I

Corporations with and without Net Income

OTHER TRANSPORTATION AND SUPPORT ACTIVITIES

MONEY AMOUNTS AND SIZE OF ASSETS IN THOUSANDS OF DOLLARS

Item Description for Accounting Period 7/12 Through 6/13	Total	Zero Assets	Under 500	500 to 1,000	1,000 to 5,000	5,000 to 10,000	10,000 to 25,000	25,000 to 50,000	50,000 to 100,000	100,000 to 250,000	250,000 to 500,000	500,000 to 2,500,000	2,500,000 and over
Number of Enterprises 1	44864	10308	28265	2777	2582	370	291	98	64	55	24	23	6

Revenues ($ in Thousands)

	Total	Zero Assets	Under 500	500 to 1,000	1,000 to 5,000	5,000 to 10,000	10,000 to 25,000	25,000 to 50,000	50,000 to 100,000	100,000 to 250,000	250,000 to 500,000	500,000 to 2,500,000	2,500,000 and over
Net Sales 2	245419302	3078192	20789137	9491267	19471665	6510499	11462140	7874283	8693493	13885509	7809441	16521509	119832167
Interest 3	412180	368	230	323	3064	3401	2149	2755	11146	6610	24978	107967	249189
Rents 4	265190	538	2035	0	5475	2945	2926	4942	10629	32986	23768	76616	102331
Royalties 5	1860592	0	0	0	4	0	0	0	150	429	0	1507	1858502
Other Portfolio Income 6	1322784	205781	24361	49918	13954	4659	10560	14984	60675	38213	42685	282303	574693
Other Receipts 7	3708815	41991	44725	64132	116694	40622	60499	161784	191543	173978	147601	116869	2548376
Total Receipts 8	252988863	3326870	20860488	9605640	19610856	6562126	11538274	8058748	8967636	14137725	8048473	17106771	125165258
Average Total Receipts 9	5639	323	738	3459	7595	17735	39650	82232	140119	257050	335353	743773	20860876

Operating Costs/Operating Income (%)

	Total	Zero Assets	Under 500	500 to 1,000	1,000 to 5,000	5,000 to 10,000	10,000 to 25,000	25,000 to 50,000	50,000 to 100,000	100,000 to 250,000	250,000 to 500,000	500,000 to 2,500,000	2,500,000 and over
Cost of Operations 10	38.4	47.1	45.9	62.1	63.6	65.3	64.7	64.1	64.8	63.4	28.2	42.4	20.5
Salaries and Wages 11	15.9	17.4	6.0	10.0	12.8	11.3	11.2	10.4	10.5	9.1	19.6	12.1	21.0
Taxes Paid 12	2.6	2.5	1.8	1.8	2.9	4.6	1.7	1.2	3.1	2.1	2.3	1.9	2.9
Interest Paid 13	0.9	1.5	0.6	0.5	0.3	0.8	0.5	0.5	0.8	0.7	1.8	4.0	0.6
Depreciation 14	2.7	1.7	1.4	1.4	0.9	1.3	1.6	1.3	1.5	2.0	2.4	3.6	3.8
Amortization and Depletion 15	0.3	0.6	0.1	0.0	0.1	0.0	0.1	0.3	0.5	0.7	0.8	1.5	0.2
Pensions and Other Deferred Comp. 16	1.4	0.2	0.2	0.4	0.4	0.5	0.3	0.2	0.2	0.3	0.6	0.3	2.4
Employee Benefits 17	3.6	1.1	0.3	1.0	0.9	2.0	1.4	0.9	1.7	1.7	3.8	4.7	5.5
Advertising 18	0.3	0.1	0.2	0.4	0.2	0.1	0.2	0.2	0.2	0.2	0.2	0.1	0.5
Other Expenses 19	30.9	25.1	34.9	16.6	12.0	10.5	14.0	19.4	15.4	19.1	40.8	34.1	39.5
Officers' Compensation 20	1.4	4.0	4.4	4.4	3.3	2.4	1.8	1.6	0.9	0.6	1.4	0.2	0.4
Operating Margin 21	1.6	•	4.2	1.4	2.6	1.1	2.5	•	0.6	0.0	•	•	2.6
Operating Margin Before Officers' Comp. 22	3.0	2.7	8.6	5.8	5.9	3.5	4.3	1.5	1.5	0.7	•	•	3.0

Selected Average Balance Sheet ($ in Thousands)

Net Receivables 23	643	0	7	139	844	2401	5700	14677	20108	39576	74409	148372	2242682
Inventories 24	47	0	1	18	50	104	239	835	3337	5884	10831	14787	91375
Net Property, Plant and Equipment 25	1046	0	29	201	428	989	4848	6334	15920	38235	64610	178226	5547479
Total Assets 26	3608	0	88	665	2133	6723	16145	35450	72151	160213	362238	1108851	15626025
Notes and Loans Payable 27	1239	0	71	278	625	2189	4954	8587	23880	47079	168853	546053	4566784
All Other Liabilities 28	1379	0	33	188	840	3071	5299	18595	23049	57374	127222	253016	6703729
Net Worth 29	990	0	-16	198	669	1463	5893	8268	25222	55760	66163	309782	4355512

Selected Financial Ratios (Times to 1)

Current Ratio 30	0.9	•	1.6	1.5	1.5	1.4	1.5	1.1	1.5	1.3	1.2	1.0	0.7
Quick Ratio 31	0.8	•	1.4	1.3	1.3	1.1	1.3	0.9	1.1	0.9	1.0	0.7	0.6
Net Sales to Working Capital 32	•	•	43.9	30.8	15.9	16.0	14.0	32.3	10.8	16.9	13.8	•	•
Coverage Ratio 33	6.4	5.6	8.1	5.8	10.9	3.3	7.5	5.1	5.8	3.8	1.8	0.6	12.3
Total Asset Turnover 34	1.5	•	8.4	5.1	3.5	2.6	2.4	2.3	1.9	1.6	0.9	0.6	1.3
Inventory Turnover 35	45.1	•	298.0	117.5	95.9	110.9	106.7	61.6	26.4	27.2	8.5	20.6	44.7
Receivables Turnover 36	8.0	•	87.3	21.2	8.8	7.7	6.6	6.0	6.4	7.0	4.2	4.2	8.2
Total Liabilities to Net Worth 37	2.6	•	•	2.3	2.2	3.6	1.7	3.3	1.9	1.9	4.5	2.6	2.6
Current Assets to Working Capital 38	•	•	2.7	3.1	3.0	3.8	3.1	8.9	3.0	4.7	6.1	•	•
Current Liabilities to Working Capital 39	•	•	1.7	2.1	2.0	2.8	2.1	7.9	2.0	3.7	5.1	•	•
Working Capital to Net Sales 40	•	•	0.0	0.0	0.1	0.1	0.1	0.0	0.1	0.1	0.1	•	•
Inventory to Working Capital 41	•	•	0.1	0.1	0.1	0.1	0.1	0.5	0.3	0.5	0.1	•	•
Total Receipts to Cash Flow 42	3.4	4.1	2.9	6.1	7.9	12.1	7.2	5.2	6.8	6.0	2.8	3.5	2.6
Cost of Goods to Cash Flow 43	1.3	1.9	1.3	3.8	5.0	7.9	4.6	3.3	4.4	3.8	0.8	1.5	0.5
Cash Flow to Total Debt 44	0.6	•	2.4	1.2	0.6	0.3	0.5	0.6	0.4	0.4	0.4	0.3	0.7

Selected Financial Factors (in Percentages)

Debt Ratio 45	72.6	•	118.1	70.1	68.7	78.2	63.5	76.7	65.0	65.2	81.7	72.1	72.1
Return on Total Assets 46	8.6	•	43.3	16.0	12.9	6.9	8.9	6.3	8.6	4.1	2.9	1.7	9.9
Return on Equity Before Income Taxes 47	26.4	•	•	44.5	37.4	22.2	21.2	21.6	20.3	8.7	7.2	•	32.7
Return on Equity After Income Taxes 48	18.3	•	•	42.1	36.3	18.4	19.1	17.7	15.6	5.4	0.5	•	21.1
Profit Margin (Before Income Tax) 49	4.8	6.9	4.5	2.6	3.3	1.8	3.2	2.2	3.8	1.9	1.5	•	7.1
Profit Margin (After Income Tax) 50	3.3	6.1	4.5	2.4	3.2	1.5	2.9	1.8	2.9	1.2	0.1	•	4.6

Table II

Corporations with Net Income

OTHER TRANSPORTATION AND SUPPORT ACTIVITIES

MONEY AMOUNTS AND SIZE OF ASSETS IN THOUSANDS OF DOLLARS

Item Description for Accounting Period 7/12 Through 6/13	Total	Zero Assets	Under 500	500 to 1,000	1,000 to 5,000	5,000 to 10,000	10,000 to 25,000	25,000 to 50,000	50,000 to 100,000	100,000 to 250,000	250,000 to 500,000	500,000 to 2,500,000	2,500,000 and over
Number of Enterprises 1	27490	3978	18856	2075	1940	260	206	•	42	33	11	12	•
Revenues ($ in Thousands)													
Net Sales 2	204846400	1721952	16515863	7377773	17373660	4633033	9682654	•	6099821	8378926	3998223	12890169	•
Interest 3	254247	247	168	59	2652	2159	1664	•	7607	4974	2543	61370	•
Rents 4	226761	538	0	0	4736	2484	1450	•	7799	31545	17552	53594	•
Royalties 5	1843309	0	0	0	4	0	0	•	150	425	0	1507	•
Other Portfolio Income 6	1062022	185706	24361	49812	9115	3315	8502	•	53533	29971	41696	88719	•
Other Receipts 7	1268133	27648	45943	64247	81336	27912	42802	•	186049	111551	77418	96179	•
Total Receipts 8	209500872	1936091	16586335	7491891	17471503	4668903	9737072	•	6354959	8557392	4137432	13191538	•
Average Total Receipts 9	7621	487	880	3611	9006	17957	47267	•	151309	259315	376130	1099295	•
Operating Costs/Operating Income (%)													
Cost of Operations 10	36.9	50.4	43.9	64.0	64.0	63.1	64.9	•	60.9	60.4	39.8	39.9	•
Salaries and Wages 11	16.3	10.1	5.8	10.7	12.7	13.1	11.1	•	10.4	9.5	17.2	12.2	•
Taxes Paid 12	2.5	2.4	1.6	1.9	2.9	3.2	1.5	•	3.4	1.8	2.5	1.5	•
Interest Paid 13	0.6	2.4	0.5	0.6	0.2	0.4	0.3	•	0.4	0.8	1.1	2.3	•
Depreciation 14	2.9	1.9	1.4	1.6	0.5	1.1	1.2	•	1.4	1.9	3.4	2.7	•
Amortization and Depletion 15	0.2	0.9	0.1	0.1	0.1	0.0	0.1	•	0.3	0.5	0.8	0.6	•
Pensions and Other Deferred Comp. 16	1.5	0.4	0.3	0.4	0.2	0.4	0.3	•	0.3	0.4	0.8	0.2	•
Employee Benefits 17	3.8	1.2	0.3	1.1	0.9	2.2	1.3	•	1.7	2.0	3.8	3.1	•
Advertising 18	0.4	0.1	0.3	0.5	0.2	0.1	0.2	•	0.1	0.2	0.3	0.1	•
Other Expenses 19	29.2	20.9	35.5	12.4	11.3	9.4	13.1	•	17.9	19.3	24.7	36.2	•
Officers' Compensation 20	1.4	3.9	4.3	4.3	3.4	2.8	1.9	•	1.0	0.7	1.9	0.2	•
Operating Margin 21	4.3	5.4	6.0	2.4	3.8	4.1	4.1	•	2.3	2.5	3.8	1.2	•
Operating Margin Before Officers' Comp. 22	5.7	9.4	10.3	6.7	7.2	7.0	6.0	•	3.3	3.2	5.7	1.4	•

Selected Average Balance Sheet ($ in Thousands)

Net Receivables	23	823	0	7	94	944	2542	7185	•	24046	38072	78615	208569	•
Inventories	24	62	0	0	19	49	137	231	•	3259	7566	22530	19673	•
Net Property, Plant and Equipment	25	1511	0	32	217	385	1086	3415	•	14193	43539	94264	221184	•
Total Assets	26	4446	0	94	676	2221	6820	16215	•	73914	158011	354808	1074743	•
Notes and Loans Payable	27	1327	0	81	255	389	1453	3483	•	14949	41403	98711	384948	•
All Other Liabilities	28	1765	0	33	184	911	2860	6575	•	24657	52882	108005	299859	•
Net Worth	29	1354	0	-19	237	921	2507	6157	•	34307	63727	148093	389936	•

Selected Financial Ratios (Times to 1)

Current Ratio	30	1.0	•	1.6	1.4	1.6	1.6	1.5	•	1.8	1.5	1.9	1.7	•
Quick Ratio	31	0.8	•	1.4	1.3	1.4	1.4	1.3	•	1.4	1.1	1.4	1.3	•
Net Sales to Working Capital	32	•	•	51.5	35.5	16.0	10.4	13.2	•	7.5	10.2	4.8	7.0	•
Coverage Ratio	33	11.5	8.6	14.4	7.7	21.5	13.3	15.4	•	18.4	7.3	8.1	2.6	•
Total Asset Turnover	34	1.7	•	9.3	5.3	4.0	2.6	2.9	•	2.0	1.6	1.0	1.0	•
Inventory Turnover	35	44.7	•	1595.4	117.8	117.2	81.9	132.0	•	27.1	20.3	6.4	21.8	•
Receivables Turnover	36	8.1	•	96.9	26.8	9.9	7.1	6.4	•	5.9	7.8	4.4	4.1	•
Total Liabilities to Net Worth	37	2.3	•	•	1.9	1.4	1.7	1.6	•	1.2	1.5	1.4	1.8	•
Current Assets to Working Capital	38	•	•	2.6	3.2	2.8	2.6	3.0	•	2.3	3.0	2.2	2.5	•
Current Liabilities to Working Capital	39	•	•	1.6	2.2	1.8	1.6	2.0	•	1.3	2.0	1.2	1.5	•
Working Capital to Net Sales	40	•	•	0.0	0.0	0.1	0.1	0.1	•	0.1	0.1	0.2	0.1	•
Inventory to Working Capital	41	•	•	0.0	0.2	0.1	0.1	0.1	•	0.2	0.5	0.1	0.2	•
Total Receipts to Cash Flow	42	3.3	3.2	2.7	7.6	7.5	9.3	6.5	•	5.1	5.1	4.0	2.7	•
Cost of Goods to Cash Flow	43	1.2	1.6	1.2	4.9	4.8	5.9	4.2	•	3.1	3.1	1.6	1.1	•
Cash Flow to Total Debt	44	0.7	•	2.9	1.1	0.9	0.4	0.7	•	0.7	0.5	0.4	0.6	•

Selected Financial Factors (in Percentages)

Debt Ratio	45	69.6	•	120.5	64.9	58.5	63.2	62.0	•	53.6	59.7	58.3	63.7	•
Return on Total Assets	46	12.2	•	64.3	24.1	18.6	13.9	14.4	•	13.5	8.9	9.2	5.8	•
Return on Equity Before Income Taxes	47	36.5	•	•	59.9	42.8	34.9	35.4	•	27.5	19.0	19.4	9.8	•
Return on Equity After Income Taxes	48	26.9	•	•	57.2	41.7	31.8	32.6	•	22.3	14.5	12.9	6.9	•
Profit Margin (Before Income Tax)	49	6.6	18.1	6.5	4.0	4.4	4.9	4.6	•	6.5	4.8	7.9	3.5	•
Profit Margin (After Income Tax)	50	4.9	16.8	6.4	3.8	4.3	4.5	4.3	•	5.3	3.6	5.3	2.5	•

Table I

Corporations with and without Net Income

WAREHOUSING AND STORAGE

MONEY AMOUNTS AND SIZE OF ASSETS IN THOUSANDS OF DOLLARS

Item Description for Accounting Period 7/12 Through 6/13	Total	Zero Assets	Under 500	500 to 1,000	1,000 to 5,000	5,000 to 10,000	10,000 to 25,000	25,000 to 50,000	50,000 to 100,000	100,000 to 250,000	250,000 to 500,000	500,000 to 2,500,000	2,500,000 and over
Number of Enterprises 1	3971	304	1793	831	567	182	203	43	20	18	0	9	•

Revenues ($ in Thousands)

	Total	Zero Assets	Under 500	500 to 1,000	1,000 to 5,000	5,000 to 10,000	10,000 to 25,000	25,000 to 50,000	50,000 to 100,000	100,000 to 250,000	250,000 to 500,000	500,000 to 2,500,000	2,500,000 and over
Net Sales 2	26091400	915687	864504	2111105	3358542	1932165	4668601	1605910	1614518	1649022	0	7371345	•
Interest 3	87217	54	0	2413	813	346	5747	1255	1907	6718	0	67964	•
Rents 4	26574	60	2398	0	1746	7025	96	4124	4899	5052	0	1173	•
Royalties 5	25203	0	0	0	0	0	0	0	0	5	0	25198	•
Other Portfolio Income 6	269455	18555	26762	90724	33041	6930	9173	4008	32428	5192	0	42641	•
Other Receipts 7	771980	535	1533	3902	39572	135864	184106	36252	15265	178914	0	176040	•
Total Receipts 8	27271829	934891	895197	2208144	3433714	2082330	4867723	1651549	1669017	1844903	0	7684361	•
Average Total Receipts 9	6868	3075	499	2657	6056	11441	23979	38408	83451	102495	•	853818	•

Operating Costs/Operating Income (%)

	Total	Zero Assets	Under 500	500 to 1,000	1,000 to 5,000	5,000 to 10,000	10,000 to 25,000	25,000 to 50,000	50,000 to 100,000	100,000 to 250,000	250,000 to 500,000	500,000 to 2,500,000	2,500,000 and over
Cost of Operations 10	43.7	85.2	16.1	36.3	73.6	44.9	40.8	59.4	54.0	19.3	•	31.5	•
Salaries and Wages 11	18.4	4.6	33.7	19.0	7.8	22.1	19.9	9.7	14.2	21.3	•	23.1	•
Taxes Paid 12	3.1	0.2	2.7	3.6	1.8	4.3	3.5	3.0	1.9	4.7	•	3.4	•
Interest Paid 13	2.4	1.8	0.2	0.3	1.0	0.6	1.1	1.6	1.0	2.5	•	5.6	•
Depreciation 14	3.7	3.9	2.0	1.3	2.1	1.9	3.3	5.0	3.8	8.7	•	4.5	•
Amortization and Depletion 15	0.4	0.4	0.0	0.0	0.2	0.1	0.1	0.1	0.2	0.7	•	1.2	•
Pensions and Other Deferred Comp. 16	0.7	0.0	0.1	0.6	0.0	4.3	0.5	0.2	0.3	0.6	•	0.8	•
Employee Benefits 17	2.8	0.2	0.6	7.2	0.8	4.7	1.3	1.3	2.8	5.1	•	3.2	•
Advertising 18	0.2	0.0	0.5	0.7	0.1	0.2	0.1	0.1	0.1	0.1	•	0.3	•
Other Expenses 19	22.3	4.1	40.4	28.4	10.7	22.0	25.7	18.2	19.8	36.3	•	22.2	•
Officers' Compensation 20	1.6	0.9	1.2	3.8	1.5	1.9	3.2	1.0	1.3	1.3	•	0.3	•
Operating Margin 21	0.7	•	2.5	•	0.3	•	0.3	0.6	0.6	•	•	3.9	•
Operating Margin Before Officers' Comp. 22	2.2	•	3.8	2.6	1.8	•	3.5	1.6	1.9	0.8	•	4.2	•

Selected Average Balance Sheet ($ in Thousands)

Net Receivables 23	984	0	13	243	562	1539	2806	4291	10306	17924	•	199922	•
Inventories 24	228	0	0	19	449	475	557	2173	5800	7327	•	10252	•
Net Property, Plant and Equipment 25	2335	0	127	223	1329	1492	6277	15727	30959	94844	•	395357	•
Total Assets 26	7696	0	235	746	2795	6177	15583	36187	68735	182690	•	1936303	•
Notes and Loans Payable 27	2991	0	115	582	1191	868	6089	14586	22244	65091	•	763719	•
All Other Liabilities 28	1875	0	43	319	1094	2775	2650	6348	9804	52830	•	446540	•
Net Worth 29	2831	0	77	-154	510	2534	6845	15252	36688	64769	•	726044	•

Selected Financial Ratios (Times to 1)

Current Ratio 30	1.5	•	1.8	1.1	1.1	1.4	1.7	2.4	2.0	1.5	•	1.5	•
Quick Ratio 31	1.1	•	1.5	1.0	0.7	1.0	1.3	1.8	1.1	1.1	•	1.3	•
Net Sales to Working Capital 32	10.1	•	10.0	86.6	35.7	8.9	9.3	4.5	6.1	6.9	•	9.4	•
Coverage Ratio 33	3.2	1.4	27.6	11.1	3.5	2.4	5.0	3.2	5.1	5.6	•	2.5	•
Total Asset Turnover 34	0.9	•	2.0	3.4	2.1	1.7	1.5	1.0	1.2	0.5	•	0.4	•
Inventory Turnover 35	12.6	•	163.0	47.5	9.7	10.0	16.8	10.2	7.5	2.4	•	25.2	•
Receivables Turnover 36	5.6	•	15.4	15.2	9.7	7.3	9.3	7.2	7.6	5.8	•	2.8	•
Total Liabilities to Net Worth 37	1.7	•	2.0	•	4.5	1.4	1.3	1.4	0.9	1.8	•	1.7	•
Current Assets to Working Capital 38	2.9	•	2.2	14.1	8.3	3.4	2.4	1.7	2.0	3.0	•	3.1	•
Current Liabilities to Working Capital 39	1.9	•	1.2	13.1	7.3	2.4	1.4	0.7	1.0	2.0	•	2.1	•
Working Capital to Net Sales 40	0.1	•	0.1	0.0	0.0	0.1	0.1	0.2	0.2	0.1	•	0.1	•
Inventory to Working Capital 41	0.3	•	0.0	0.4	2.7	0.3	0.2	0.2	0.5	0.4	•	0.1	•
Total Receipts to Cash Flow 42	5.4	29.8	5.6	4.9	11.2	7.9	4.7	7.1	6.2	2.6	•	4.8	•
Cost of Goods to Cash Flow 43	2.4	25.4	0.9	1.8	8.2	3.6	1.9	4.2	3.4	0.5	•	1.5	•
Cash Flow to Total Debt 44	0.2	•	0.5	0.6	0.2	0.4	0.6	0.3	0.4	0.3	•	0.1	•

Selected Financial Factors (in Percentages)

Debt Ratio 45	63.2	•	67.1	120.7	81.8	59.0	56.1	57.9	46.6	64.5	•	62.5	•
Return on Total Assets 46	6.5	•	12.9	12.8	7.5	2.4	8.3	5.2	5.8	6.9	•	5.9	•
Return on Equity Before Income Taxes 47	12.1	•	37.8	•	29.3	3.4	15.1	8.4	8.8	16.1	•	9.3	•
Return on Equity After Income Taxes 48	9.4	•	31.7	•	25.7	1.5	14.0	6.9	5.7	13.5	•	6.5	•
Profit Margin (Before Income Tax) 49	5.2	0.7	6.1	3.4	2.5	0.8	4.5	3.4	4.0	11.4	•	8.2	•
Profit Margin (After Income Tax) 50	4.1	0.2	5.1	3.3	2.2	0.4	4.2	2.8	2.6	9.6	•	5.8	•

Table II
Corporations with Net Income

WAREHOUSING AND STORAGE

MONEY AMOUNTS AND SIZE OF ASSETS IN THOUSANDS OF DOLLARS

Item Description for Accounting Period 7/12 Through 6/13	Total	Zero Assets	Under 500	500 to 1000	1,000 to 5,000	5,000 to 10,000	10,000 to 25,000	25,000 to 50,000	50,000 to 100,000	100,000 to 250,000	250,000 to 500,000	500,000 to 2,500,000	2,500,000 and over
Number of Enterprises **1**	1851	295	479	352	403	100	156	32	14	14	0	6	•

Revenues ($ in Thousands)													
Net Sales **2**	18627294	871802	575401	1077359	1608654	1367710	3217195	1272249	1195969	1441681	0	5999274	•
Interest **3**	79359	54	0	2187	197	254	2223	1249	915	5450	0	66830	•
Rents **4**	18992	60	0	0	1746	7025	96	2943	2063	5052	0	6	•
Royalties **5**	25203	0	0	0	0	0	0	0	0	5	0	25198	•
Other Portfolio Income **6**	253804	18555	26762	90405	32178	3021	8104	3559	32183	4534	0	34504	•
Other Receipts **7**	545936	375	28	2651	39603	22233	79005	34609	13338	178266	0	175827	•
Total Receipts **8**	19550588	890846	602191	1172602	1682378	1400243	3306623	1314609	1244468	1634988	0	6301639	•
Average Total Receipts **9**	10562	3020	1257	3331	4175	14002	21196	41082	88891	116785	•	1050273	•

Operating Costs/Operating Income (%)													
Cost of Operations **10**	41.1	88.5	•	59.2	58.4	30.1	37.0	64.2	44.0	19.0	•	34.8	•
Salaries and Wages **11**	17.5	4.7	45.9	9.6	10.1	26.9	14.4	9.0	17.8	22.3	•	20.0	•
Taxes Paid **12**	3.0	0.1	2.7	2.2	2.4	4.0	2.7	1.9	2.2	4.8	•	3.7	•
Interest Paid **13**	2.7	0.1	0.1	0.3	1.6	0.5	1.2	1.5	0.8	1.9	•	6.2	•
Depreciation **14**	3.9	0.8	0.7	1.3	3.6	1.7	3.9	4.8	3.0	6.9	•	4.9	•
Amortization and Depletion **15**	0.4	0.0	•	0.0	0.0	0.2	0.1	0.0	0.2	0.3	•	1.1	•
Pensions and Other Deferred Comp. **16**	0.6	0.0	•	0.2	0.1	3.9	0.6	0.2	0.2	0.6	•	0.3	•
Employee Benefits **17**	2.3	0.2	0.6	0.9	1.2	5.8	1.5	0.5	3.5	4.9	•	2.4	•
Advertising **18**	0.2	0.0	0.0	0.6	0.0	0.2	0.1	0.1	0.1	0.1	•	0.3	•
Other Expenses **19**	22.4	3.9	40.4	16.5	17.1	19.6	30.3	13.8	23.5	36.9	•	20.4	•
Officers' Compensation **20**	1.1	0.2	0.0	2.5	2.1	1.4	1.9	0.9	0.8	1.1	•	0.3	•
Operating Margin **21**	4.9	1.4	9.6	6.8	3.4	5.7	6.2	3.1	3.9	1.3	•	5.5	•
Operating Margin Before Officers' Comp. **22**	5.9	1.6	9.7	9.3	5.4	7.2	8.1	4.0	4.7	2.4	•	5.8	•

Selected Average Balance Sheet ($ in Thousands)

Net Receivables 23	1318	0	47	213	376	1321	2579	4486	11950	18210	•	181904	•
Inventories 24	302	0	0	29	135	741	576	1701	3784	7664	•	12223	•
Net Property, Plant and Equipment 25	4020	0	92	231	1458	1169	7101	14481	28657	102334	•	534373	•
Total Assets 26	13025	0	364	795	2448	6069	15528	33013	69331	195168	•	2479886	•
Notes and Loans Payable 27	5205	0	65	319	1242	559	5678	12383	14331	71298	•	1075721	•
All Other Liabilities 28	2536	0	41	143	333	1903	2608	6313	12600	63404	•	437930	•
Net Worth 29	5283	0	258	334	873	3607	7242	14316	42400	60466	•	966236	•

Selected Financial Ratios (Times to 1)

Current Ratio 30	1.6	•	15.2	1.2	2.8	2.2	1.7	1.9	2.6	1.4	•	1.2	•
Quick Ratio 31	1.2	•	14.0	1.1	2.2	1.4	1.3	1.4	1.6	0.9	•	1.0	•
Net Sales to Working Capital 32	10.4	•	4.7	65.6	6.8	5.6	8.8	7.4	4.8	9.0	•	27.1	•
Coverage Ratio 33	4.6	30.3	125.8	60.2	5.9	15.9	8.3	5.4	11.5	8.9	•	2.7	•
Total Asset Turnover 34	0.8	•	3.3	3.9	1.6	2.3	1.3	1.2	1.2	0.5	•	0.4	•
Inventory Turnover 35	13.7	•	•	61.9	17.2	5.6	13.2	15.0	9.9	2.6	•	28.5	•
Receivables Turnover 36	5.5	•	17.6	19.2	10.9	10.4	9.0	•	6.9	•	•	2.9	•
Total Liabilities to Net Worth 37	1.5	•	0.4	1.4	1.8	0.7	1.1	1.3	0.6	2.2	•	1.6	•
Current Assets to Working Capital 38	2.7	•	1.1	7.4	1.6	1.8	2.3	2.1	1.6	3.7	•	7.0	•
Current Liabilities to Working Capital 39	1.7	•	0.1	6.4	0.6	0.8	1.3	1.1	0.6	2.7	•	6.0	•
Working Capital to Net Sales 40	0.1	•	0.2	0.0	0.1	0.2	0.1	0.1	0.2	0.1	•	0.0	•
Inventory to Working Capital 41	0.3	•	•	•	0.3	0.2	0.3	0.3	0.2	0.7	•	0.4	•
Total Receipts to Cash Flow 42	4.3	16.7	3.9	4.0	5.9	4.8	3.4	6.0	4.6	2.4	•	4.6	•
Cost of Goods to Cash Flow 43	1.8	14.8	•	2.3	3.4	1.4	1.3	3.9	2.0	0.4	•	1.6	•
Cash Flow to Total Debt 44	0.3	•	2.9	1.7	0.4	1.2	0.7	0.4	0.7	0.3	•	0.1	•

Selected Financial Factors (in Percentages)

Debt Ratio 45	59.4	•	29.2	58.0	64.4	40.6	53.4	56.6	38.8	69.0	•	61.0	•
Return on Total Assets 46	9.7	•	47.5	61.2	15.6	19.5	13.4	9.6	10.7	8.7	•	6.8	•
Return on Equity Before Income Taxes 47	18.8	•	66.6	143.4	36.3	30.8	25.3	18.0	16.0	25.0	•	11.1	•
Return on Equity After Income Taxes 48	15.8	•	59.7	141.5	33.3	28.3	23.9	15.9	12.1	21.5	•	7.9	•
Profit Margin (Before Income Tax) 49	9.9	3.6	14.3	15.6	7.9	8.1	8.9	6.5	7.9	14.7	•	10.7	•
Profit Margin (After Income Tax) 50	8.3	3.1	12.8	15.4	7.3	7.5	8.4	5.7	6.0	12.6	•	7.7	•

Table I

Corporations with and without Net Income

NEWSPAPER PUBLISHERS

MONEY AMOUNTS AND SIZE OF ASSETS IN THOUSANDS OF DOLLARS

Item Description for Accounting Period 7/12 Through 6/13	Total	Zero Assets	Under 500	500 to 1,000	1,000 to 5,000	5,000 to 10,000	10,000 to 25,000	25,000 to 50,000	50,000 to 100,000	100,000 to 250,000	250,000 to 500,000	500,000 to 2,500,000	2,500,000 and over
Number of Enterprises 1	4779	747	3281	118	384	81	84	32	20	13	7	6	6

Revenues ($ in Thousands)													
Net Sales 2	24638905	130606	1356695	117433	1376693	1624491	1290808	1095747	1083902	1809119	2233599	2464585	10055229
Interest 3	31114	15	200	0	17	832	6372	2867	725	4067	1095	2865	12059
Rents 4	65017	2	0	155	0	57	1641	3746	391	11897	5503	15609	26017
Royalties 5	24810	0	0	0	0	0	12	0	9	6	2	353	24427
Other Portfolio Income 6	720308	68	273	0	11	7860	8138	43800	4340	4565	404786	20798	225669
Other Receipts 7	1086634	8101	410	108	45082	1625	14819	17564	22551	22331	32849	54731	866461
Total Receipts 8	26566788	138792	1357578	117696	1421803	1634865	1321790	1163724	1111918	1851985	2677834	2558941	11209862
Average Total Receipts 9	5559	186	414	997	3703	20184	15736	36366	55596	142460	382548	426490	1868310

Operating Costs/Operating Income (%)													
Cost of Operations 10	32.8	31.5	37.3	33.0	37.6	75.9	33.5	25.2	33.2	22.5	14.7	28.9	32.0
Salaries and Wages 11	21.8	18.5	13.8	27.9	22.2	6.8	27.1	28.0	26.2	26.1	28.5	22.9	20.9
Taxes Paid 12	3.4	5.9	2.4	3.0	4.9	1.0	3.9	3.9	3.6	3.6	3.7	3.8	3.4
Interest Paid 13	6.2	0.7	0.8	1.6	3.1	0.3	0.9	1.2	3.1	1.8	5.5	9.3	10.1
Depreciation 14	2.9	1.4	1.6	4.5	1.6	0.2	2.6	3.2	4.2	3.8	3.1	3.5	3.1
Amortization and Depletion 15	4.6	3.8	0.1	3.6	0.6	0.4	0.4	1.7	2.8	2.7	7.6	9.9	5.8
Pensions and Other Deferred Comp. 16	2.4	0.2	0.0	•	0.0	1.5	1.1	2.6	1.3	0.8	3.5	1.5	3.9
Employee Benefits 17	3.3	1.0	1.2	1.8	3.6	0.8	3.6	4.3	4.5	3.7	4.3	3.1	3.6
Advertising 18	1.7	1.5	3.1	0.5	0.4	1.1	1.1	1.7	2.8	1.3	1.6	1.1	2.0
Other Expenses 19	23.5	74.6	30.6	15.4	23.1	5.5	25.4	30.8	23.0	30.6	38.0	24.2	19.2
Officers' Compensation 20	1.7	3.1	7.4	4.1	2.9	1.8	1.8	2.6	2.3	1.3	2.0	1.0	0.8
Operating Margin 21	•	•	1.7	4.7	0.0	4.9	•	•	•	1.7	•	•	•
Operating Margin Before Officers' Comp. 22	•	•	9.1	8.7	2.9	6.6	0.4	•	•	3.0	•	•	•

Selected Average Balance Sheet ($ in Thousands)

Net Receivables 23	899	0	28	150	453	3652	2020	5283	6132	21766	47562	46910	392574
Inventories 24	109	0	1	0	159	822	239	718	908	2411	5246	5945	37818
Net Property, Plant and Equipment 25	1815	0	29	176	803	447	3461	10104	21771	47805	103946	133122	836375
Total Assets 26	11972	0	86	671	2420	8099	14115	32746	65233	178915	355800	721350	7096972
Notes and Loans Payable 27	2389	0	53	379	1530	629	2289	8867	44034	45116	259497	459896	673814
All Other Liabilities 28	5878	0	34	44	631	5403	3684	6443	16709	65442	142122	225648	3873959
Net Worth 29	3705	0	-0	248	258	2067	8142	17436	4490	68357	-45820	35806	2549199

Selected Financial Ratios (Times to 1)

Current Ratio 30	1.7	•	1.5	3.5	0.9	1.6	2.2	1.3	1.0	1.3	0.9	0.8	2.3
Quick Ratio 31	1.4	•	1.5	3.5	0.8	1.0	1.7	1.1	0.7	0.9	0.7	0.6	1.8
Net Sales to Working Capital 32	4.4	•	23.6	5.3	•	8.7	5.2	14.1	73.6	8.1	•	•	2.0
Coverage Ratio 33	1.6	•	3.2	4.0	2.1	19.4	2.0	1.8	•	3.3	2.3	0.4	1.7
Total Asset Turnover 34	0.4	•	4.8	1.5	1.5	2.5	1.1	1.0	0.8	0.8	0.9	0.6	0.2
Inventory Turnover 35	15.5	•	274.2	704.3	8.5	18.5	21.5	12.0	19.8	13.0	9.0	20.0	14.2
Receivables Turnover 36	6.1	•	15.8	3.5	4.8	8.7	7.9	7.5	8.3	7.9	6.3	7.1	4.9
Total Liabilities to Net Worth 37	2.2	•	•	1.7	8.4	2.9	0.7	0.9	13.5	1.6	•	19.1	1.8
Current Assets to Working Capital 38	2.4	•	2.9	1.4	•	2.8	1.9	4.5	23.7	3.9	•	•	1.8
Current Liabilities to Working Capital 39	1.4	•	1.9	0.4	•	1.8	0.9	3.5	22.7	2.9	•	•	0.8
Working Capital to Net Sales 40	0.2	•	0.0	0.2	•	0.1	0.2	0.1	0.0	0.1	•	•	0.5
Inventory to Working Capital 41	0.1	•	0.0	0.0	•	0.6	0.1	0.4	1.2	0.2	•	•	0.1
Total Receipts to Cash Flow 42	4.6	3.1	3.7	6.1	4.1	10.3	4.5	4.0	6.3	3.3	3.9	7.6	4.5
Cost of Goods to Cash Flow 43	1.5	1.0	1.4	2.0	1.6	7.8	1.5	1.0	2.1	0.7	0.6	2.2	1.4
Cash Flow to Total Debt 44	0.1	•	1.3	0.4	0.4	0.3	0.6	0.6	0.1	0.4	0.2	0.1	0.1

Selected Financial Factors (in Percentages)

Debt Ratio 45	69.1	•	100.1	63.1	89.3	74.5	42.3	46.8	93.1	61.8	112.9	95.0	64.1
Return on Total Assets 46	4.2	•	12.0	9.7	9.4	14.4	2.0	2.3	•	4.5	11.6	2.1	4.0
Return on Equity Before Income Taxes 47	4.9	•	•	19.6	46.1	53.6	1.7	2.0	•	8.1	•	•	4.4
Return on Equity After Income Taxes 48	3.2	•	•	17.3	46.1	53.1	0.1	1.6	•	5.6	•	•	3.5
Profit Margin (Before Income Tax) 49	3.5	•	1.7	4.9	3.3	5.5	0.9	1.0	•	4.0	7.4	•	6.8
Profit Margin (After Income Tax) 50	2.3	•	1.6	4.3	3.3	5.5	0.1	0.8	•	2.7	3.4	•	5.3

Table II

Corporations with Net Income

NEWSPAPER PUBLISHERS

MONEY AMOUNTS AND SIZE OF ASSETS IN THOUSANDS OF DOLLARS

Item Description for Accounting Period 7/12 Through 6/13		Total	Zero Assets	Under 500	500 to 1,000	1,000 to 5,000	5,000 to 10,000	10,000 to 25,000	25,000 to 50,000	50,000 to 100,000	100,000 to 250,000	250,000 to 500,000	500,000 to 2,500,000	2,500,000 and over
Number of Enterprises	1	2725	33	2271	59	203	68	39	•	13	10	0	3	•
Revenues ($ in Thousands)														
Net Sales	2	15034544	72833	752763	77299	665306	1554556	634554	•	634384	1689544	0	979098	•
Interest	3	25227	15	199	0	1	584	3603	•	652	3123	0	2761	•
Rents	4	50642	0	0	155	0	30	157	•	336	7732	0	12615	•
Royalties	5	24635	0	0	0	0	0	0	•	9	5	0	193	•
Other Portfolio Income	6	692509	0	225	0	0	62	6093	•	2473	399887	0	14372	•
Other Receipts	7	666603	6556	241	90	37751	754	16752	•	17794	30428	0	18429	•
Total Receipts	8	16494160	79404	753428	77544	703058	1555986	661159	•	655648	2130719	0	1027468	•
Average Total Receipts	9	6053	2406	332	1314	3463	22882	16953	•	50434	213072	•	342489	•
Operating Costs/Operating Income (%)														
Cost of Operations	10	35.0	35.7	36.2	30.7	55.4	78.2	38.4	•	30.8	20.9	•	34.7	•
Salaries and Wages	11	20.5	31.5	12.3	19.9	4.4	5.3	22.3	•	24.4	26.1	•	15.7	•
Taxes Paid	12	3.2	2.1	2.3	2.8	3.7	0.7	4.2	•	3.2	3.9	•	3.9	•
Interest Paid	13	3.3	0.2	1.0	2.5	2.7	0.3	0.5	•	2.0	3.0	•	1.9	•
Depreciation	14	2.5	1.4	2.0	6.8	0.7	0.2	2.1	•	3.7	3.0	•	4.9	•
Amortization and Depletion	15	3.0	0.8	0.2	2.0	1.1	0.4	0.3	•	2.6	3.8	•	6.8	•
Pensions and Other Deferred Comp.	16	2.9	0.3	0.0	•	0.0	0.5	1.1	•	1.5	2.6	•	1.9	•
Employee Benefits	17	3.6	•	0.8	2.5	3.6	0.5	2.1	•	4.2	3.1	•	1.6	•
Advertising	18	1.7	0.5	3.3	0.6	0.8	0.9	0.7	•	1.1	1.3	•	1.8	•
Other Expenses	19	21.0	29.9	23.9	18.4	16.1	4.8	20.7	•	20.3	31.2	•	18.8	•
Officers' Compensation	20	2.3	2.5	12.7	6.0	3.9	1.2	2.2	•	2.7	2.5	•	1.7	•
Operating Margin	21	1.1	•	5.2	7.7	7.6	7.0	5.3	•	3.6	•	•	6.3	•
Operating Margin Before Officers' Comp.	22	3.4	•	17.9	13.7	11.5	8.2	7.5	•	6.3	1.2	•	8.0	•

Selected Average Balance Sheet ($ in Thousands)

Net Receivables	23	1069	0	32	161	436	4221	1476	•	5334	22716	•	38960 •
Inventories	24	145	0	0	1	284	972	216	•	701	2321	•	3952 •
Net Property, Plant and Equipment	25	2074	0	33	334	148	428	3415	•	19113	47215	•	135547 •
Total Assets	26	16015	0	96	805	1950	8524	14286	•	67713	220290	•	604822 •
Notes and Loans Payable	27	2091	0	52	527	1164	744	1084	•	21021	42013	•	115425 •
All Other Liabilities	28	4009	0	25	43	159	5145	3123	•	13287	72589	•	153807 •
Net Worth	29	9915	0	19	235	628	2635	10080	•	33405	105687	•	335590 •

Selected Financial Ratios (Times to 1)

Current Ratio	30	1.9	•	2.0	1.9	4.3	1.5	4.1	•	1.5	1.4	•	1.7 •
Quick Ratio	31	1.4	•	1.9	1.9	3.8	1.0	3.1	•	1.0	0.9	•	1.4 •
Net Sales to Working Capital	32	3.7	•	12.5	11.1	7.4	9.9	3.2	•	7.5	8.2	•	9.4 •
Coverage Ratio	33	4.2	20.7	6.1	4.2	5.9	24.0	19.5	•	4.4	9.2	•	7.0 •
Total Asset Turnover	34	0.3	•	3.5	1.6	1.7	2.7	1.1	•	0.7	0.8	•	0.5 •
Inventory Turnover	35	13.3	•	3922.5	559.0	6.4	18.4	28.9	•	21.4	15.2	•	28.7 •
Receivables Turnover	36	6.0	•	13.4	8.9	2.9	8.7	9.2	•	9.1	9.8	•	16.8 •
Total Liabilities to Net Worth	37	0.6	•	4.0	2.4	2.1	2.2	0.4	•	1.0	1.1	•	0.8 •
Current Assets to Working Capital	38	2.1	•	2.0	2.1	1.3	3.1	1.3	•	2.9	3.8	•	2.5 •
Current Liabilities to Working Capital	39	1.1	•	1.0	1.1	0.3	2.1	0.3	•	1.9	2.8	•	1.5 •
Working Capital to Net Sales	40	0.3	•	0.1	0.1	0.1	0.1	0.3	•	0.1	0.1	•	0.1 •
Inventory to Working Capital	41	0.1	•	0.0	0.0	0.0	0.8	0.0	•	0.1	0.1	•	0.1 •
Total Receipts to Cash Flow	42	3.9	3.3	4.4	4.5	3.8	9.3	3.7	•	4.0	3.2	•	3.7 •
Cost of Goods to Cash Flow	43	1.4	1.2	1.6	1.4	2.1	7.3	1.4	•	1.2	0.7	•	1.3 •
Cash Flow to Total Debt	44	0.2	•	1.0	0.5	0.6	0.4	1.0	•	0.4	0.5	•	0.3 •

Selected Financial Factors (in Percentages)

Debt Ratio	45	38.1	•	80.1	70.8	67.8	69.1	29.4	•	50.7	52.0	•	44.5 •
Return on Total Assets	46	4.9	•	21.9	17.1	26.9	20.0	11.3	•	6.5	21.3	•	7.1 •
Return on Equity Before Income Taxes	47	6.0	•	91.9	44.8	69.4	61.9	15.2	•	10.2	39.6	•	10.9 •
Return on Equity After Income Taxes	48	4.9	•	88.5	39.8	69.4	61.5	12.4	•	9.3	29.0	•	8.7 •
Profit Margin (Before Income Tax)	49	10.8	4.1	5.3	8.0	13.3	7.1	9.4	•	7.0	24.8	•	11.2 •
Profit Margin (After Income Tax)	50	8.8	2.9	5.1	7.1	13.3	7.1	7.7	•	6.3	18.1	•	8.9 •

Table I

Corporations with and without Net Income

PERIODICAL PUBLISHERS

MONEY AMOUNTS AND SIZE OF ASSETS IN THOUSANDS OF DOLLARS

Item Description for Accounting Period 7/12 Through 6/13	Total	Zero Assets	Under 500	500 to 1,000	1,000 to 5,000	5,000 to 10,000	10,000 to 25,000	25,000 to 50,000	50,000 to 100,000	100,000 to 250,000	250,000 to 500,000	500,000 to 2,500,000	2,500,000 and over
Number of Enterprises 1	5735	1385	3489	251	422	46	66	26	16	14	8	8	4
Revenues ($ in Thousands)													
Net Sales 2	27794550	65577	1282879	303996	2199624	377547	1595654	1026894	1005368	1743496	1684291	3697940	12811284
Interest 3	92312	32	187	0	3545	300	365	351	1378	2800	16891	5969	60494
Rents 4	106795	0	0	0	0	2665	1388	126	0	3113	6995	2021	90486
Royalties 5	379659	0	0	0	484	1	47	0	22880	55248	113008	18541	169449
Other Portfolio Income 6	928695	32169	21605	0	0	1478	20952	2412	2704	2685	133702	108507	602481
Other Receipts 7	1362877	6353	1797	164	50810	2561	16008	7999	18103	131965	103005	7366	1016748
Total Receipts 8	30664888	104131	1306468	304160	2254463	384552	1634414	1037782	1050433	1939307	2057892	3840344	14750942
Average Total Receipts 9	5347	75	374	1212	5342	8360	24764	39915	65652	138522	257236	480043	3687736
Operating Costs/Operating Income (%)													
Cost of Operations 10	30.7	9.2	16.3	31.6	59.9	55.3	55.8	39.1	30.5	36.5	34.3	27.2	22.4
Salaries and Wages 11	22.6	19.5	13.3	12.4	8.4	19.9	15.2	17.8	22.9	21.0	20.6	21.5	28.4
Taxes Paid 12	2.8	4.3	2.8	1.6	3.5	4.1	2.0	2.5	2.5	2.4	2.3	2.4	3.0
Interest Paid 13	7.1	0.1	0.2	0.1	1.7	1.1	2.7	0.4	3.3	3.4	10.1	5.8	11.0
Depreciation 14	1.8	3.3	1.5	0.0	0.7	1.7	2.0	1.5	1.8	2.3	1.4	1.4	2.1
Amortization and Depletion 15	3.6	3.0	1.5	3.6	0.6	1.9	1.1	1.0	4.1	4.3	5.0	5.8	3.9
Pensions and Other Deferred Comp. 16	1.7	•	0.2	1.0	1.3	0.6	0.4	1.0	1.0	1.1	0.2	1.2	2.6
Employee Benefits 17	3.1	2.2	2.0	•	1.2	3.0	2.5	2.5	3.8	2.8	2.8	2.0	4.2
Advertising 18	1.8	0.5	1.0	1.7	2.4	2.7	1.0	6.0	2.7	3.8	1.2	1.2	1.3
Other Expenses 19	28.6	70.6	37.4	32.8	16.2	15.4	16.5	28.7	21.9	28.4	40.4	25.6	31.3
Officers' Compensation 20	2.6	5.9	15.7	5.1	2.6	1.5	2.0	3.2	2.0	3.0	1.9	1.3	1.7
Operating Margin 21	•	•	8.1	9.9	1.4	•	•	•	3.5	•	•	4.6	•
Operating Margin Before Officers' Comp. 22	•	•	23.8	15.1	4.0	•	0.8	•	5.5	•	•	5.9	•

Selected Average Balance Sheet ($ in Thousands)

	1	2	3	4	5	6	7	8	9	10	11	12	13
Net Receivables 23	1785	0	30	183	725	1209	3273	5330	9525	22378	36525	66398	2020924
Inventories 24	89	0	7	0	22	206	1321	1171	1194	5447	3154	7435	42581
Net Property, Plant and Equipment 25	542	0	15	26	187	1312	3572	3646	6107	15226	17960	50255	431096
Total Assets 26	12736	0	92	730	2050	6724	16733	33289	75038	152803	384862	953767	13835183
Notes and Loans Payable 27	3353	0	73	0	528	3003	8502	6438	25046	50258	206395	389115	3003990
All Other Liabilities 28	6390	0	96	70	2089	3390	8425	17335	40172	66975	209388	290009	7168168
Net Worth 29	2993	0	-77	660	-567	330	-194	9517	9820	35570	-30921	274643	3663024

Selected Financial Ratios (Times to 1)

	1	2	3	4	5	6	7	8	9	10	11	12	13
Current Ratio 30	0.6	•	0.7	2.6	1.1	0.9	1.4	1.3	0.9	1.0	0.5	0.8	0.5
Quick Ratio 31	0.5	•	0.6	2.6	0.8	0.6	0.8	0.9	0.5	0.7	0.4	0.5	0.4
Net Sales to Working Capital 32	•	•	•	8.8	31.8	•	10.2	11.8	•	•	•	•	•
Coverage Ratio 33	1.6	356.3	56.5	73.0	3.2	•	1.5	•	3.5	1.7	1.3	2.5	1.3
Total Asset Turnover 34	0.4	•	4.0	1.7	2.5	1.2	1.4	1.2	0.8	0.8	0.5	0.5	0.2
Inventory Turnover 35	16.7	•	9.1	•	139.9	22.0	10.2	13.2	16.0	8.4	22.9	16.9	16.9
Receivables Turnover 36	3.9	•	13.8	6.9	7.5	6.5	7.8	8.0	6.4	5.7	6.1	6.5	2.6
Total Liabilities to Net Worth 37	3.3	•	•	0.1	•	19.3	•	2.5	6.6	3.3	•	2.5	2.8
Current Assets to Working Capital 38	•	•	•	1.6	9.4	•	3.3	4.8	•	•	•	•	•
Current Liabilities to Working Capital 39	•	•	•	0.6	8.4	•	2.3	3.8	•	•	•	•	•
Working Capital to Net Sales 40	•	•	•	0.1	0.0	•	0.1	0.1	•	•	•	•	•
Inventory to Working Capital 41	•	•	•	•	0.1	•	0.5	0.3	•	•	•	•	•
Total Receipts to Cash Flow 42	3.6	1.7	2.4	2.4	6.0	15.1	7.2	4.6	3.9	3.8	3.3	3.5	3.3
Cost of Goods to Cash Flow 43	1.1	0.2	0.4	0.8	3.6	8.4	4.0	1.8	1.2	1.4	1.1	0.9	0.7
Cash Flow to Total Debt 44	0.1	•	0.9	7.3	0.3	0.1	0.2	0.4	0.2	0.3	0.2	0.2	0.1

Selected Financial Factors (in Percentages)

	1	2	3	4	5	6	7	8	9	10	11	12	13
Debt Ratio 45	76.5	•	182.9	9.6	127.6	95.1	101.2	71.4	86.9	76.7	108.0	71.2	73.5
Return on Total Assets 46	4.3	•	40.1	16.8	14.2	•	5.8	•	9.8	4.8	7.0	7.0	3.4
Return on Equity Before Income Taxes 47	6.9	•	•	18.3	•	•	•	•	53.4	8.6	•	14.6	3.0
Return on Equity After Income Taxes 48	5.0	•	•	16.0	•	•	•	•	38.4	8.3	•	9.2	2.1
Profit Margin (Before Income Tax) 49	4.2	40.1	9.9	10.0	3.9	•	1.3	•	8.3	2.5	2.7	8.7	3.5
Profit Margin (After Income Tax) 50	3.1	37.6	9.7	8.7	3.8	•	1.2	•	6.0	2.4	1.3	5.5	2.4

Table II

Corporations with Net Income

PERIODICAL PUBLISHERS

MONEY AMOUNTS AND SIZE OF ASSETS IN THOUSANDS OF DOLLARS

Item Description for Accounting Period 7/12 Through 6/13	Total	Zero Assets	Under 500	500 to 1,000	1,000 to 5,000	5,000 to 10,000	10,000 to 25,000	25,000 to 50,000	50,000 to 100,000	100,000 to 250,000	250,000 to 500,000	500,000 to 2,500,000	2,500,000 and over
Number of Enterprises **1**	4240	277	3380	251	232	17	43	12	10	4	5	•	•

Revenues ($ in Thousands)													
Net Sales **2**	20086007	39494	1188526	303996	1912092	77267	977187	616755	680969	611247	1222869	•	•
Interest **3**	84666	32	187	0	392	202	79	22	884	91	16700	•	•
Rents **4**	92174	0	0	0	0	0	63	0	0	0	3918	•	•
Royalties **5**	211244	0	0	0	0	0	47	0	19420	0	4065	•	•
Other Portfolio Income **6**	915596	32169	21605	0	0	164	18715	0	2615	261	133702	•	•
Other Receipts **7**	1187603	6353	1797	164	34862	558	4762	6800	18073	6504	99795	•	•
Total Receipts **8**	22577290	78048	1212115	304160	1947346	78191	1000853	623577	721961	618103	1481049	•	•
Average Total Receipts **9**	5325	282	359	1212	8394	4599	23276	51965	72196	154526	296210	•	•

Operating Costs/Operating Income (%)													
Cost of Operations **10**	29.3	15.3	17.6	31.6	62.2	46.1	51.4	39.4	26.3	20.8	33.4	•	•
Salaries and Wages **11**	21.6	32.4	9.4	12.4	7.3	12.3	14.0	11.8	22.6	23.2	15.8	•	•
Taxes Paid **12**	2.8	6.7	2.6	1.6	3.4	4.9	1.8	2.3	2.5	1.9	1.8	•	•
Interest Paid **13**	5.2	0.2	0.1	0.1	1.8	0.1	0.9	0.1	1.6	0.6	9.9	•	•
Depreciation **14**	1.7	3.6	1.6	0.0	0.7	1.5	2.3	1.3	1.8	1.8	1.2	•	•
Amortization and Depletion **15**	3.2	5.1	1.6	3.6	0.6	0.0	1.0	1.0	2.0	2.1	4.5	•	•
Pensions and Other Deferred Comp. **16**	1.9	•	0.2	1.0	0.1	2.5	0.5	0.2	1.5	0.3	0.1	•	•
Employee Benefits **17**	3.1	3.7	1.7	•	0.9	2.1	2.9	2.2	4.2	4.0	2.0	•	•
Advertising **18**	1.7	0.4	0.2	1.7	2.5	2.4	0.8	9.4	2.6	6.5	0.7	•	•
Other Expenses **19**	28.2	46.1	33.4	32.8	14.3	21.1	14.3	17.8	22.1	19.1	41.8	•	•
Officers' Compensation **20**	3.1	9.8	17.0	5.1	2.2	0.2	2.0	4.4	1.9	3.4	2.1	•	•
Operating Margin **21**	•	•	14.6	9.9	4.0	6.7	8.0	9.9	10.9	16.2	•	•	•
Operating Margin Before Officers' Comp. **22**	1.4	•	31.6	15.1	6.3	7.0	10.0	14.3	12.8	19.6	•	•	•

Selected Average Balance Sheet ($ in Thousands)

Net Receivables 23	837	0	27	183	1073	450	3196	4338	11205	24441	40149	•	•
Inventories 24	70	0	6	0	14	360	1280	581	1828	8628	2314	•	•
Net Property, Plant and Equipment 25	567	0	15	26	324	586	4330	2671	7038	10631	15077	•	•
Total Assets 26	11899	0	88	730	2659	7812	16205	33600	77143	180658	382539	•	•
Notes and Loans Payable 27	3469	0	37	0	630	3278	4520	1500	15523	19042	98953	•	•
All Other Liabilities 28	4012	0	46	70	3024	1609	6487	14788	35907	99109	327314	•	•
Net Worth 29	4418	0	5	660	-995	2924	5199	17311	25713	62506	-43728	•	•

Selected Financial Ratios (Times to 1)

Current Ratio 30	1.1	•	1.3	2.6	1.0	2.1	2.0	1.2	1.1	0.8	0.5	•	•
Quick Ratio 31	0.7	•	1.2	2.6	0.8	1.8	1.3	1.0	0.5	0.6	0.4	•	•
Net Sales to Working Capital 32	25.0	•	22.9	8.8	97.9	2.3	6.2	20.1	26.6	•	•	•	•
Coverage Ratio 33	3.1	425.9	202.4	73.0	4.2	147.0	13.0	88.5	11.6	31.6	1.9	•	•
Total Asset Turnover 34	0.4	•	4.0	1.7	3.1	0.6	1.4	1.5	0.9	0.8	0.6	•	•
Inventory Turnover 35	19.7	•	9.8	•	366.9	5.8	9.1	34.9	9.8	3.7	35.3	•	•
Receivables Turnover 36	7.0	•	16.3	6.9	7.7	6.1	7.9	•	6.2	5.2	7.0	•	•
Total Liabilities to Net Worth 37	1.7	•	18.1	0.1	•	1.7	2.1	0.9	2.0	1.9	•	•	•
Current Assets to Working Capital 38	10.6	•	4.0	1.6	21.2	1.9	2.0	5.4	13.4	•	•	•	•
Current Liabilities to Working Capital 39	9.6	•	3.0	0.6	20.2	0.9	1.0	4.4	12.4	•	•	•	•
Working Capital to Net Sales 40	0.0	•	0.0	0.1	0.0	0.4	0.2	0.0	0.0	•	•	•	•
Inventory to Working Capital 41	0.4	•	0.4	•	0.2	0.3	0.4	0.2	0.7	•	•	•	•
Total Receipts to Cash Flow 42	3.0	3.1	2.2	2.4	6.0	3.8	5.0	3.9	2.8	2.9	2.8	•	•
Cost of Goods to Cash Flow 43	0.9	0.5	0.4	0.8	3.7	1.7	2.6	1.6	0.7	0.6	0.9	•	•
Cash Flow to Total Debt 44	0.2	•	1.9	7.3	0.4	0.2	0.4	0.8	0.5	0.4	0.2	•	•

Selected Financial Factors (in Percentages)

Debt Ratio 45	62.9	•	94.8	9.6	137.4	62.6	67.9	48.5	66.7	65.4	111.4	•	•
Return on Total Assets 46	6.5	•	66.3	16.8	23.9	4.6	15.9	17.0	16.8	15.8	11.9	•	•
Return on Equity Before Income Taxes 47	11.9	•	1260.8	18.3	•	12.3	45.7	32.7	46.1	44.3	•	•	•
Return on Equity After Income Taxes 48	10.2	•	1244.5	16.0	•	10.4	44.7	32.6	36.9	43.7	•	•	•
Profit Margin (Before Income Tax) 49	11.1	74.2	16.6	10.0	5.8	7.9	10.5	11.0	17.4	18.1	8.7	•	•
Profit Margin (After Income Tax) 50	9.5	70.1	16.4	8.7	5.8	6.7	10.2	11.0	13.9	17.9	6.8	•	•

256

Table I

Corporations with and without Net Income

BOOK PUBLISHERS

MONEY AMOUNTS AND SIZE OF ASSETS IN THOUSANDS OF DOLLARS

Item Description for Accounting Period 7/12 Through 6/13	Total	Zero Assets	Under 500	500 to 1,000	1,000 to 5,000	5,000 to 10,000	10,000 to 25,000	25,000 to 50,000	50,000 to 100,000	100,000 to 250,000	250,000 to 500,000	500,000 to 2,500,000	2,500,000 and over
Number of Enterprises **1**	5076	1717	2970	116	158	36	31	15	13	7	4	3	6
Revenues ($ in Thousands)													
Net Sales **2**	27649848	360956	1029996	191726	472230	324710	564217	546601	961688	965260	618366	2906409	18707687
Interest **3**	217796	1	20	1313	1695	0	51	470	1627	1740	6217	4997	199666
Rents **4**	28791	31	0	0	0	0	344	928	748	0	303	9658	16781
Royalties **5**	260056	0	1716	0	2433	179	314	271	19072	197	719	64074	171082
Other Portfolio Income **6**	118021	233	0	0	176	0	2917	5503	569	17335	1138	15674	74476
Other Receipts **7**	783551	6398	1647	8	252	2501	6556	18363	12367	47614	57184	149508	481152
Total Receipts **8**	29058063	367619	1033379	193047	476786	327390	574399	572136	996071	1032146	683927	3150320	19650844
Average Total Receipts **9**	5725	214	348	1664	3018	9094	18529	38142	76621	147449	170982	1050107	3275141
Operating Costs/Operating Income (%)													
Cost of Operations **10**	32.8	36.6	58.3	46.4	28.7	50.8	29.1	57.3	39.9	35.0	20.2	46.1	28.2
Salaries and Wages **11**	23.1	8.0	10.3	8.2	15.4	10.1	24.9	13.5	18.6	17.2	25.5	24.2	25.1
Taxes Paid **12**	2.6	1.0	1.8	1.1	2.6	1.4	3.0	2.0	2.3	2.0	1.6	3.4	2.7
Interest Paid **13**	6.3	0.8	0.2	0.8	0.0	0.8	0.8	0.9	1.6	6.4	12.2	1.2	8.3
Depreciation **14**	3.0	1.1	0.6	•	0.6	0.5	1.0	1.1	3.6	2.0	1.1	2.6	3.5
Amortization and Depletion **15**	4.9	0.2	0.1	•	0.0	0.0	1.2	2.1	2.7	4.9	5.5	3.5	6.0
Pensions and Other Deferred Comp. **16**	1.6	0.0	4.2	0.2	1.5	0.2	0.6	0.2	0.6	0.9	0.8	0.8	1.8
Employee Benefits **17**	2.7	1.4	1.2	1.6	0.9	1.5	3.4	2.3	1.7	1.7	2.9	3.6	2.8
Advertising **18**	1.4	2.9	0.7	0.3	1.7	1.3	2.3	4.1	3.8	1.8	1.5	2.9	1.0
Other Expenses **19**	19.9	40.7	16.0	28.2	30.4	23.6	23.5	13.7	20.4	35.7	38.7	18.1	18.1
Officers' Compensation **20**	1.5	1.1	7.3	12.1	10.1	4.8	4.2	2.8	2.3	2.9	2.1	0.8	0.6
Operating Margin **21**	0.2	6.4	•	1.0	8.1	5.0	6.0	•	2.5	•	•	•	1.7
Operating Margin Before Officers' Comp. **22**	1.7	7.4	6.6	13.1	18.2	9.8	10.2	2.7	4.8	•	•	•	2.3

Selected Average Balance Sheet ($ in Thousands)

Net Receivables 23	925	0	11	276	287	1719	2500	3960	15939	27121	79046	239028	492329
Inventories 24	498	0	22	418	774	1974	2709	7338	7544	19814	13426	108683	234804
Net Property, Plant and Equipment 25	417	0	41	0	89	437	3052	757	10336	9466	14543	130980	200870
Total Assets 26	9455	0	127	653	2977	6939	14554	38062	71950	170837	365267	1687479	6190284
Notes and Loans Payable 27	3632	0	230	425	3	1908	4208	1852	13728	110669	270158	315669	2415781
All Other Liabilities 28	3782	0	51	65	439	3536	3124	14011	33447	57517	151991	699317	2498430
Net Worth 29	2041	0	-154	163	2534	1496	7222	22199	24775	2651	-56882	672493	1276074

Selected Financial Ratios (Times to 1)

Current Ratio 30	0.7	•	1.0	3.9	6.0	1.4	1.7	2.7	1.4	0.8	0.8	1.5	0.6
Quick Ratio 31	0.3	•	0.4	3.9	3.9	0.7	1.1	1.0	0.8	0.5	0.6	0.8	0.2
Net Sales to Working Capital 32	•	•	•	6.7	1.4	6.8	5.9	3.0	6.5	•	•	5.5	•
Coverage Ratio 33	1.9	11.1	•	3.0	971.2	8.5	10.8	6.1	4.7	0.4	0.9	2.3	1.9
Total Asset Turnover 34	0.6	•	2.7	2.5	1.0	1.3	1.3	1.0	1.0	0.8	0.4	0.6	0.5
Inventory Turnover 35	3.6	•	9.3	1.8	1.1	2.3	2.0	2.8	3.9	2.4	2.3	4.1	3.8
Receivables Turnover 36	5.4	•	30.8	6.1	9.0	4.6	4.8	7.3	5.0	4.5	2.1	3.5	5.8
Total Liabilities to Net Worth 37	3.6	•	•	3.0	0.2	3.6	1.0	0.7	1.9	63.4	•	1.5	3.9
Current Assets to Working Capital 38	•	•	•	1.3	1.2	3.6	2.4	1.6	3.8	•	•	3.2	•
Current Liabilities to Working Capital 39	•	•	•	0.3	0.2	2.6	1.4	0.6	2.8	•	•	2.2	•
Working Capital to Net Sales 40	•	•	•	0.1	0.7	0.1	0.2	0.3	0.2	•	•	0.2	•
Inventory to Working Capital 41	•	•	•	0.0	0.3	1.3	0.6	0.5	0.7	•	•	0.6	•
Total Receipts to Cash Flow 42	4.7	2.3	11.3	3.5	2.8	3.6	3.5	6.9	4.4	3.6	3.0	7.0	4.7
Cost of Goods to Cash Flow 43	1.5	0.9	6.6	1.6	0.8	1.8	1.0	3.9	1.7	1.3	0.6	3.2	1.3
Cash Flow to Total Debt 44	0.2	•	0.1	1.0	2.4	0.5	0.7	0.3	0.4	0.2	0.1	0.1	0.1

Selected Financial Factors (in Percentages)

Debt Ratio 45	78.4	•	221.4	75.0	14.9	78.4	50.4	41.7	65.6	98.4	115.6	60.1	79.4
Return on Total Assets 46	6.9	•	•	6.3	9.1	8.5	10.7	5.5	7.9	2.3	4.5	1.5	7.7
Return on Equity Before Income Taxes 47	14.9	•	0.8	16.8	10.7	34.9	19.6	7.9	18.1	•	4.2	2.1	17.3
Return on Equity After Income Taxes 48	10.0	•	0.8	15.6	10.2	33.9	19.6	5.5	15.6	•	7.4	1.1	11.4
Profit Margin (Before Income Tax) 49	5.6	8.2	•	1.7	9.0	5.8	7.8	4.8	6.0	•	•	1.5	7.1
Profit Margin (After Income Tax) 50	3.7	6.5	•	1.5	8.6	5.6	7.8	3.4	5.2	•	•	0.8	4.7

Table II

Corporations with Net Income

BOOK PUBLISHERS

MONEY AMOUNTS AND SIZE OF ASSETS IN THOUSANDS OF DOLLARS

Item Description for Accounting Period 7/12 Through 6/13	Total	Zero Assets	Under 500	500 to 1,000	1,000 to 5,000	5,000 to 10,000	10,000 to 25,000	25,000 to 50,000	50,000 to 100,000	100,000 to 250,000	250,000 to 500,000	500,000 to 2,500,000	2,500,000 and over
Number of Enterprises **1**	1593	984	291	116	127	24	17	11	•	4	4	0	•
Revenues ($ in Thousands)													
Net Sales **2**	22992137	114588	800916	191726	472230	280869	396806	439195	•	638918	2631297	0	•
Interest **3**	183953	1	0	1313	1695	0	0	468	•	943	7165	0	•
Rents **4**	28417	0	0	0	0	0	0	928	•	0	9960	0	•
Royalties **5**	205687	0	1716	0	2433	0	0	271	•	0	37529	0	•
Other Portfolio Income **6**	115113	0	0	0	176	0	2913	5503	•	17335	14873	0	•
Other Receipts **7**	404692	112	1357	8	252	1493	3446	17789	•	42568	149847	0	•
Total Receipts **8**	23929999	114701	803989	193047	476786	282362	403165	464154	•	699764	2850671	0	•
Average Total Receipts **9**	15022	117	2763	1664	3754	11765	23716	42196	•	174941	712668	•	•
Operating Costs/Operating Income (%)													
Cost of Operations **10**	30.8	11.6	52.6	46.4	28.7	48.1	24.1	53.9	•	34.6	38.0	•	•
Salaries and Wages **11**	23.9	9.9	2.0	8.2	15.4	9.5	24.2	14.2	•	21.0	24.9	•	•
Taxes Paid **12**	2.7	1.2	1.0	1.1	2.6	1.3	3.3	2.0	•	2.5	3.6	•	•
Interest Paid **13**	4.3	•	•	0.8	0.0	0.4	0.6	0.3	•	1.5	2.9	•	•
Depreciation **14**	3.1	0.1	0.8	•	0.6	0.5	0.9	1.3	•	0.7	2.7	•	•
Amortization and Depletion **15**	2.9	0.1	0.0	•	0.0	0.0	0.0	2.4	•	0.9	3.4	•	•
Pensions and Other Deferred Comp. **16**	1.8	0.1	5.4	0.2	1.5	0.2	0.7	0.3	•	1.1	1.1	•	•
Employee Benefits **17**	2.8	2.2	•	1.6	0.9	1.0	3.2	2.2	•	1.7	3.4	•	•
Advertising **18**	1.3	0.5	0.7	0.3	1.7	1.5	2.1	4.3	•	2.6	1.9	•	•
Other Expenses **19**	19.7	28.1	16.0	28.2	30.4	15.6	22.5	15.2	•	35.4	22.2	•	•
Officers' Compensation **20**	1.5	•	7.2	12.1	10.1	5.3	3.0	3.5	•	4.1	0.8	•	•
Operating Margin **21**	5.2	46.1	14.3	1.0	8.1	16.4	15.3	0.5	•	•	•	•	•
Operating Margin Before Officers' Comp. **22**	6.7	46.1	21.5	13.1	18.2	21.8	18.4	4.0	•	•	•	•	•

Selected Average Balance Sheet ($ in Thousands)

	C1	C2	C3	C4	C5	C6	C7	C8	C9	C10	C11	C12	C13
Net Receivables 23	2437	0	82	276	356	2219	2877	4612	•	35521	184872	•	•
Inventories 24	1161	0	1	2	865	2455	2372	8454	•	15647	66126	•	•
Net Property, Plant and Equipment 25	980	0	316	0	111	411	4049	950	•	7364	94274	•	•
Total Assets 26	22379	0	421	653	3453	6292	13680	41111	•	140096	1090035	•	•
Notes and Loans Payable 27	6436	0	106	425	3	1599	2724	2117	•	41455	332708	•	•
All Other Liabilities 28	10027	0	156	65	527	2890	2913	12446	•	64966	445564	•	•
Net Worth 29	5916	0	160	163	2923	1804	8043	26547	•	33674	311763	•	•

Selected Financial Ratios (Times to 1)

	C1	C2	C3	C4	C5	C6	C7	C8	C9	C10	C11	C12	C13
Current Ratio 30	0.9	•	0.7	3.9	5.8	1.7	2.3	2.5	•	0.8	1.4	•	•
Quick Ratio 31	0.4	•	0.6	3.9	4.1	0.9	1.8	1.0	•	0.5	0.9	•	•
Net Sales to Working Capital 32	•	•	•	6.7	1.5	5.0	5.3	3.0	•	•	6.8	•	•
Coverage Ratio 33	3.2	•	•	3.0	973.0	39.9	31.4	20.3	•	3.4	2.3	•	•
Total Asset Turnover 34	0.6	•	6.5	2.5	1.1	1.9	1.7	1.0	•	1.1	0.6	•	•
Inventory Turnover 35	3.8	•	1537.7	366.1	1.2	2.3	2.4	2.5	•	3.5	3.8	•	•
Receivables Turnover 36	5.5	•	30.8	6.5	9.6	4.6	4.9	6.2	•	5.2	•	•	•
Total Liabilities to Net Worth 37	2.8	•	1.6	3.0	0.2	2.5	0.7	0.5	•	3.2	2.5	•	•
Current Assets to Working Capital 38	•	•	•	1.3	1.2	2.5	1.7	1.7	•	•	3.4	•	•
Current Liabilities to Working Capital 39	•	•	•	0.3	0.2	1.5	0.7	0.7	•	•	2.4	•	•
Working Capital to Net Sales 40	•	•	•	0.1	0.7	0.2	0.2	0.3	•	•	0.1	•	•
Inventory to Working Capital 41	•	•	•	0.0	0.3	1.0	0.3	0.5	•	•	0.7	•	•
Total Receipts to Cash Flow 42	4.0	1.4	4.4	3.5	2.8	3.2	2.7	5.7	•	3.0	4.8	•	•
Cost of Goods to Cash Flow 43	1.2	0.2	2.3	1.6	0.8	1.5	0.7	3.1	•	1.0	1.8	•	•
Cash Flow to Total Debt 44	0.2	•	2.4	1.0	2.5	0.8	1.5	0.5	•	0.5	0.2	•	•

Selected Financial Factors (in Percentages)

	C1	C2	C3	C4	C5	C6	C7	C8	C9	C10	C11	C12	C13
Debt Ratio 45	73.6	•	62.1	75.0	15.3	71.3	41.2	35.4	•	76.0	71.4	•	•
Return on Total Assets 46	8.9	•	96.0	6.3	9.8	32.4	29.9	6.7	•	5.7	3.9	•	•
Return on Equity Before Income Taxes 47	23.3	•	253.4	16.8	11.5	110.0	49.2	9.8	•	16.9	7.7	•	•
Return on Equity After Income Taxes 48	17.9	•	253.4	15.6	11.0	108.9	49.2	7.1	•	13.2	5.5	•	•
Profit Margin (Before Income Tax) 49	9.6	46.2	14.7	1.7	9.1	17.0	16.9	6.5	•	3.6	3.7	•	•
Profit Margin (After Income Tax) 50	7.3	40.8	14.7	1.5	8.6	16.8	16.9	4.7	•	2.8	2.6	•	•

Table I

Corporations with and without Net Income

DATABASE, DIRECTORY, AND OTHER PUBLISHERS

MONEY AMOUNTS AND SIZE OF ASSETS IN THOUSANDS OF DOLLARS

Item Description for Accounting Period 7/12 Through 6/13	Total	Zero Assets	Under 500	500 to 1,000	1,000 to 5,000	5,000 to 10,000	10,000 to 25,000	25,000 to 50,000	50,000 to 100,000	100,000 to 250,000	250,000 to 500,000	500,000 to 2,500,000	2,500,000 and over
Number of Enterprises **1**	3518	1118	2036	143	130	26	31	9	7	8	3	8	0

Revenues ($ in Thousands)

Net Sales **2**	15524785	191608	135212	131646	1431738	337379	445639	612819	740385	530968	354261	10613130	0
Interest **3**	28732	2186	0	316	268	109	75	708	3416	1342	3557	16755	0
Rents **4**	63646	0	0	0	0	62	0	60	280	0	0	63244	0
Royalties **5**	63055	0	0	1455	0	0	0	0	0	617	2646	58338	0
Other Portfolio Income **6**	371381	1302	0	0	192	9621	80	53	1296	2187	309584	47065	0
Other Receipts **7**	144322	-1506	1705	61	946	560	13586	4571	18195	9058	11794	85352	0
Total Receipts **8**	16195921	193590	136917	133478	1433144	347731	459380	618211	763572	544172	681842	10883884	0
Average Total Receipts **9**	4604	173	67	933	11024	13374	14819	68690	109082	68022	227281	1360486	•

Operating Costs/Operating Income (%)

Cost of Operations **10**	30.9	38.1	53.3	37.2	23.2	51.2	39.7	44.8	25.6	27.6	52.1	29.5	•
Salaries and Wages **11**	19.4	12.2	97.9	17.6	13.8	17.4	13.0	19.6	28.8	21.0	19.8	19.0	•
Taxes Paid **12**	3.3	0.9	4.5	4.5	2.5	1.7	2.3	1.8	2.7	2.3	3.9	3.6	•
Interest Paid **13**	5.1	11.8	6.8	0.2	0.1	1.1	1.8	0.2	2.7	18.0	0.7	5.9	•
Depreciation **14**	1.7	2.4	0.1	0.1	0.5	0.6	2.5	2.2	1.3	1.1	1.8	2.0	•
Amortization and Depletion **15**	4.3	47.7	0.3	0.0	0.1	1.3	1.8	0.1	1.1	19.8	4.0	4.1	•
Pensions and Other Deferred Comp. **16**	0.7	•	•	1.6	0.1	0.2	0.3	0.4	1.0	1.7	0.3	0.7	•
Employee Benefits **17**	2.1	0.9	2.8	3.7	0.3	1.8	1.2	1.2	3.3	4.0	4.5	2.1	•
Advertising **18**	3.2	1.1	6.6	•	1.0	0.6	6.1	1.4	12.6	2.1	0.5	3.1	•
Other Expenses **19**	24.5	24.2	42.0	12.4	9.1	19.9	15.3	16.6	30.4	25.7	20.9	27.1	•
Officers' Compensation **20**	5.3	0.5	8.3	18.4	42.5	3.4	2.4	1.3	1.6	1.5	13.9	0.8	•
Operating Margin **21**	•	•	•	4.1	6.9	0.7	13.6	10.2	•	•	•	2.2	•
Operating Margin Before Officers' Comp. **22**	4.9	•	•	22.5	49.4	4.2	16.0	11.6	•	•	•	3.0	•

Selected Average Balance Sheet ($ in Thousands)

Net Receivables 23	770	0	3	78	1651	962	3259	6731	22952	9762	15937	250570	•
Inventories 24	232	0	18	0	0	271	288	1443	15	600	22063	56906	•
Net Property, Plant and Equipment 25	432	0	0	2	228	251	2013	9235	12919	3134	9249	149075	•
Total Assets 26	4975	0	29	775	3124	6019	14666	30478	73485	172305	284689	1661612	•
Notes and Loans Payable 27	2291	0	137	0	292	1732	2855	6353	56392	184597	45323	693198	•
All Other Liabilities 28	2136	0	15	268	1405	3138	10087	7514	62624	36118	40080	744157	•
Net Worth 29	548	0	-123	506	1428	1150	1724	16611	-45530	-48410	199287	224257	•

Selected Financial Ratios (Times to 1)

Current Ratio 30	0.7	•	0.5	1.9	2.0	1.1	0.9	2.0	0.7	0.3	3.0	0.7	•
Quick Ratio 31	0.5	•	0.1	0.7	1.9	0.9	0.8	1.4	0.6	0.2	1.1	0.5	•
Net Sales to Working Capital 32	•	•	•	3.8	7.5	60.3	•	7.4	•	•	1.3	•	•
Coverage Ratio 33	2.1	•	•	31.5	72.9	4.6	10.2	45.9	8.5	•	109.7	1.8	•
Total Asset Turnover 34	0.9	•	2.3	1.2	3.5	2.2	1.0	2.2	1.4	0.4	0.4	0.8	•
Inventory Turnover 35	5.9	•	1.9	•	•	24.5	19.9	21.1	1762.4	30.6	2.8	6.9	•
Receivables Turnover 36	5.9	•	13.5	5.7	6.7	14.0	5.0	14.2	4.5	7.0	14.8	8.0	•
Total Liabilities to Net Worth 37	8.1	•	•	0.5	1.2	4.2	7.5	0.8	•	•	0.4	6.4	•
Current Assets to Working Capital 38	•	•	•	2.1	2.0	15.5	•	2.0	•	•	1.5	•	•
Current Liabilities to Working Capital 39	•	•	•	1.1	1.0	14.5	•	1.0	•	•	0.5	•	•
Working Capital to Net Sales 40	•	•	•	0.3	0.1	0.0	•	0.1	•	•	0.8	•	•
Inventory to Working Capital 41	•	•	•	•	•	2.0	•	0.2	•	•	0.2	•	•
Total Receipts to Cash Flow 42	5.1	•	•	7.7	6.9	5.2	3.5	4.0	5.1	57.6	•	4.3	•
Cost of Goods to Cash Flow 43	1.6	•	•	2.9	1.6	2.7	1.4	1.8	1.3	15.9	•	1.3	•
Cash Flow to Total Debt 44	0.2	•	•	0.4	0.9	0.5	0.3	1.2	0.2	0.0	•	0.2	•

Selected Financial Factors (in Percentages)

Debt Ratio 45	89.0	•	519.9	34.7	54.3	80.9	88.2	45.5	162.0	128.1	30.0	86.5	•
Return on Total Assets 46	9.3	•	•	6.8	24.9	10.5	18.1	25.4	32.5	•	31.4	8.6	•
Return on Equity Before Income Taxes 47	43.5	•	65.7	10.0	53.8	43.1	139.1	45.6	•	30.6	44.5	28.9	•
Return on Equity After Income Taxes 48	27.0	•	65.7	9.7	51.1	31.6	130.7	42.8	•	30.6	29.9	20.6	•
Profit Margin (Before Income Tax) 49	5.4	•	•	5.5	7.0	3.8	16.7	11.1	19.9	•	75.0	4.9	•
Profit Margin (After Income Tax) 50	3.3	•	•	5.4	6.6	2.8	15.7	10.5	11.3	•	50.5	3.5	•

Table II

Corporations with Net Income

DATABASE, DIRECTORY, AND OTHER PUBLISHERS

MONEY AMOUNTS AND SIZE OF ASSETS IN THOUSANDS OF DOLLARS

Item Description for Accounting Period 7/12 Through 6/13	Total	Zero Assets	Under 500	500 to 1,000	1,000 to 5,000	5,000 to 10,000	10,000 to 25,000	25,000 to 50,000	50,000 to 100,000	100,000 to 250,000	250,000 to 500,000	500,000 to 2,500,000	2,500,000 and over
Number of Enterprises 1	1823	676	812	143	124	16	28	•	•	5	0	•	0

Revenues ($ in Thousands)

	Total	Zero Assets	Under 500	500 to 1,000	1,000 to 5,000	5,000 to 10,000	10,000 to 25,000	25,000 to 50,000	50,000 to 100,000	100,000 to 250,000	250,000 to 500,000	500,000 to 2,500,000	2,500,000 and over
Net Sales 2	13152605	19870	11734	131646	1413451	167104	427692	•	•	434706	0	•	0
Interest 3	18736	172	0	316	255	64	75	•	•	3887	0	•	0
Rents 4	63646	0	0	0	0	62	0	•	•	0	0	•	0
Royalties 5	62823	0	0	1455	0	0	0	•	•	3030	0	•	0
Other Portfolio Income 6	369645	1283	0	0	192	9621	80	•	•	311355	0	•	0
Other Receipts 7	138262	500	0	61	824	715	13587	•	•	18192	0	•	0
Total Receipts 8	13805717	21825	11734	133478	1414722	177566	441434	•	•	771170	0	•	0
Average Total Receipts 9	7573	32	14	933	11409	11098	15766	•	•	154234	•	•	•

Operating Costs/Operating Income (%)

	Total	Zero Assets	Under 500	500 to 1,000	1,000 to 5,000	5,000 to 10,000	10,000 to 25,000	25,000 to 50,000	50,000 to 100,000	100,000 to 250,000	250,000 to 500,000	500,000 to 2,500,000	2,500,000 and over
Cost of Operations 10	29.6	10.4	81.7	37.2	22.7	25.6	41.1	•	•	52.1	•	•	•
Salaries and Wages 11	19.1	23.5	•	17.6	13.3	22.3	12.3	•	•	18.5	•	•	•
Taxes Paid 12	3.4	0.3	•	4.5	2.5	2.5	2.4	•	•	4.5	•	•	•
Interest Paid 13	4.4	1.9	•	0.2	0.0	0.9	1.4	•	•	0.9	•	•	•
Depreciation 14	1.9	0.8	•	0.1	0.4	0.6	2.5	•	•	1.5	•	•	•
Amortization and Depletion 15	2.4	5.3	•	0.0	0.0	1.9	1.8	•	•	3.9	•	•	•
Pensions and Other Deferred Comp. 16	0.7	•	•	1.6	0.1	0.4	0.3	•	•	0.3	•	•	•
Employee Benefits 17	1.9	4.5	•	3.7	0.3	2.4	1.1	•	•	4.1	•	•	•
Advertising 18	2.8	0.2	•	•	1.0	0.3	6.3	•	•	1.4	•	•	•
Other Expenses 19	24.4	19.7	11.5	12.4	8.5	30.1	13.1	•	•	17.7	•	•	•
Officers' Compensation 20	6.0	•	•	18.4	43.0	3.8	2.5	•	•	11.7	•	•	•
Operating Margin 21	3.5	33.4	6.7	4.1	8.1	9.2	15.2	•	•	•	•	•	•
Operating Margin Before Officers' Comp. 22	9.5	33.4	6.7	22.5	51.1	13.0	17.6	•	•	•	•	•	•

Selected Average Balance Sheet ($ in Thousands)

Net Receivables 23	932	0	0	78	1689	1163	3477	•	•	16846	•	•	•
Inventories 24	281	0	0	0	0	358	318	•	•	13451	•	•	•
Net Property, Plant and Equipment 25	784	0	0	2	233	300	2188	•	•	5677	•	•	•
Total Assets 26	7788	0	1	775	3113	6075	14754	•	•	199265	•	•	•
Notes and Loans Payable 27	3255	0	0	0	228	1308	2686	•	•	27218	•	•	•
All Other Liabilities 28	2581	0	0	268	1424	2204	10712	•	•	39973	•	•	•
Net Worth 29	1953	0	1	506	1462	2564	1356	•	•	132075	•	•	•

Selected Financial Ratios (Times to 1)

Current Ratio 30	0.8	•	•	1.9	2.0	1.3	1.0	•	•	3.4	•	•	•
Quick Ratio 31	0.5	•	•	0.7	1.8	0.9	0.8	•	•	1.4	•	•	•
Net Sales to Working Capital 32	•	•	23.5	3.8	7.9	15.5	•	•	•	1.1	•	•	•
Coverage Ratio 33	3.3	24.0	•	31.5	208.8	17.9	14.1	•	•	70.0	•	•	•
Total Asset Turnover 34	0.9	•	23.5	1.2	3.7	1.7	1.0	•	•	0.4	•	•	•
Inventory Turnover 35	7.6	•	•	•	•	7.5	19.7	•	•	3.4	•	•	•
Receivables Turnover 36	8.0	•	•	5.9	6.8	11.4	5.5	•	•	10.3	•	•	•
Total Liabilities to Net Worth 37	3.0	•	•	0.5	1.1	1.4	9.9	•	•	0.5	•	•	•
Current Assets to Working Capital 38	•	•	1.0	2.1	2.0	4.1	•	•	•	1.4	•	•	•
Current Liabilities to Working Capital 39	•	•	•	1.1	1.0	3.1	•	•	•	0.4	•	•	•
Working Capital to Net Sales 40	•	•	0.0	0.3	0.1	0.1	•	•	•	0.9	•	•	•
Inventory to Working Capital 41	•	•	•	•	•	1.0	•	•	•	0.2	•	•	•
Total Receipts to Cash Flow 42	4.4	1.8	5.5	7.7	6.6	2.7	3.5	•	•	27.9	•	•	•
Cost of Goods to Cash Flow 43	1.3	0.2	4.5	2.9	1.5	0.7	1.4	•	•	14.5	•	•	•
Cash Flow to Total Debt 44	0.3	•	•	0.4	1.1	1.1	0.3	•	•	0.0	•	•	•

Selected Financial Factors (in Percentages)

Debt Ratio 45	74.9	•	•	34.7	53.1	57.8	90.8	•	•	33.7	•	•	•
Return on Total Assets 46	13.6	•	158.1	6.8	30.2	28.1	20.5	•	•	28.6	•	•	•
Return on Equity Before Income Taxes 47	37.9	•	158.1	10.0	64.0	63.0	207.1	•	•	42.6	•	•	•
Return on Equity After Income Taxes 48	29.0	•	158.1	9.7	61.3	54.6	195.2	•	•	29.4	•	•	•
Profit Margin (Before Income Tax) 49	10.3	43.2	6.7	5.5	8.2	15.5	18.4	•	•	64.7	•	•	•
Profit Margin (After Income Tax) 50	7.8	42.5	6.7	5.4	7.9	13.4	17.3	•	•	44.7	•	•	•

Table I

Corporations with and without Net Income

SOFTWARE PUBLISHERS

MONEY AMOUNTS AND SIZE OF ASSETS IN THOUSANDS OF DOLLARS

Item Description for Accounting Period 7/12 Through 6/13	Total	Zero Assets	Under 500	500 to 1,000	1,000 to 5,000	5,000 to 10,000	10,000 to 25,000	25,000 to 50,000	50,000 to 100,000	100,000 to 250,000	250,000 to 500,000	500,000 to 2,500,000	2,500,000 and over
Number of Enterprises 1	9353	2093	5454	443	712	162	232	77	45	44	27	42	22
Revenues ($ in Thousands)													
Net Sales 2	127795813	4392527	3401978	769036	4549883	1305282	4291443	3011381	2526465	4757352	5603924	20730151	72456391
Interest 3	394202	5940	37	308	3233	1278	8276	5211	2912	14540	17929	96672	237867
Rents 4	176035	8	0	0	443	41	520	343	464	992	4745	60602	107878
Royalties 5	10686968	32525	17629	1	34	592	32383	453	34410	231239	22110	1421847	8893746
Other Portfolio Income 6	2736777	32446	211	195	26370	25155	54282	4399	783	55004	289329	315291	1933310
Other Receipts 7	45099158	43107	91970	3106	51012	137074	42510	37212	3089	233133	74796	278779	44103368
Total Receipts 8	186888953	4506553	3511825	772646	4630975	1469422	4429414	3058999	2568123	5292260	6012833	22903342	127732560
Average Total Receipts 9	19982	2153	644	1744	6504	9071	19092	39727	57069	120279	222698	545318	5806025
Operating Costs/Operating Income (%)													
Cost of Operations 10	33.4	27.7	7.6	8.5	63.6	17.7	19.6	26.3	21.2	28.0	21.4	19.0	40.6
Salaries and Wages 11	38.5	32.1	39.9	46.6	17.0	52.6	35.3	37.5	33.8	31.0	31.7	34.9	42.2
Taxes Paid 12	4.0	6.9	5.4	4.8	2.0	4.1	3.7	3.2	3.3	3.8	3.1	3.4	4.1
Interest Paid 13	3.1	1.9	0.6	0.4	0.5	3.3	1.1	1.3	1.3	1.5	2.7	4.1	3.5
Depreciation 14	3.6	1.0	0.5	0.3	0.4	1.8	1.9	1.7	2.5	1.4	3.1	2.6	4.8
Amortization and Depletion 15	2.1	1.2	0.1	0.4	0.9	3.7	1.8	0.7	1.7	2.4	2.7	2.7	2.2
Pensions and Other Deferred Comp. 16	0.4	0.1	0.1	0.1	0.2	0.8	0.6	0.4	0.4	0.3	0.4	0.8	0.3
Employee Benefits 17	3.7	1.8	2.3	1.9	1.4	4.0	3.1	3.3	3.4	2.6	3.0	4.0	4.1
Advertising 18	4.8	1.1	1.6	0.9	1.6	6.5	3.6	3.5	3.2	5.2	4.0	1.9	6.4
Other Expenses 19	35.5	37.7	31.4	38.7	13.3	34.6	31.7	23.2	28.1	26.3	26.1	24.1	42.6
Officers' Compensation 20	2.5	2.8	14.3	10.5	5.1	7.1	3.6	2.6	4.1	2.1	2.7	2.6	1.4
Operating Margin 21	•	•	•	•	•	•	•	•	•	•	•	•	•
Operating Margin Before Officers' Comp. 22	•	•	10.4	•	•	•	•	•	1.3	•	1.9	2.5	•

Selected Average Balance Sheet ($ in Thousands)

Net Receivables 23	4030	0	38	231	793	1372	3137	9568	12351	26533	44070	141911	1193619
Inventories 24	233	0	0	6	54	81	208	409	246	1177	3454	2645	80767
Net Property, Plant and Equipment 25	1962	0	16	17	97	798	984	2191	3486	5942	19833	64943	635546
Total Assets 26	37081	0	122	682	2370	7324	16064	35309	71711	160370	353657	1162657	12175662
Notes and Loans Payable 27	6219	0	391	312	632	3030	3971	8231	11273	28841	88783	282674	1697937
All Other Liabilities 28	18315	0	101	1132	1443	4789	9255	20791	35611	65925	121761	373509	6419160
Net Worth 29	12546	0	-370	-763	295	-495	2837	6288	24828	65604	143113	506474	4058565

Selected Financial Ratios (Times to 1)

Current Ratio 30	0.6	•	0.3	0.8	1.2	1.0	1.3	1.1	1.3	1.8	1.5	1.2	0.4
Quick Ratio 31	0.5	•	0.3	0.7	1.1	0.8	1.1	0.9	1.0	1.5	1.2	1.1	0.4
Net Sales to Working Capital 32	•	•	•	•	17.5	68.3	7.9	26.6	7.7	3.2	4.0	7.2	•
Coverage Ratio 33	6.4	•	•	•	•	•	•	•	0.2	5.8	3.5	3.6	8.6
Total Asset Turnover 34	0.4	•	5.1	2.5	2.7	1.1	1.2	1.1	0.8	0.7	0.6	0.4	0.3
Inventory Turnover 35	19.6	•	658.9	25.4	74.8	17.7	17.4	25.1	48.4	25.7	12.9	35.5	16.5
Receivables Turnover 36	3.6	•	28.9	7.3	10.4	4.3	6.3	4.1	5.0	4.4	4.2	3.4	3.0
Total Liabilities to Net Worth 37	2.0	•	•	•	7.0	•	4.7	4.6	1.9	1.4	1.5	1.3	2.0
Current Assets to Working Capital 38	•	•	•	•	5.0	38.5	4.3	16.2	4.7	2.3	3.0	5.1	•
Current Liabilities to Working Capital 39	•	•	•	•	4.0	37.5	3.3	15.2	3.7	1.3	2.0	4.1	•
Working Capital to Net Sales 40	•	•	•	•	0.1	0.0	0.1	0.0	0.1	0.3	0.2	0.1	•
Inventory to Working Capital 41	•	•	•	•	0.2	0.6	0.1	0.2	0.0	0.0	0.1	0.0	•
Total Receipts to Cash Flow 42	2.2	4.2	3.6	4.7	15.2	19.4	4.0	5.5	4.3	3.4	4.0	3.4	1.7
Cost of Goods to Cash Flow 43	0.7	1.2	0.3	0.4	9.7	3.4	0.8	1.4	0.9	0.9	0.9	0.6	0.7
Cash Flow to Total Debt 44	0.3	•	0.3	0.3	0.2	0.1	0.4	0.2	0.3	0.3	0.2	0.2	0.2

Selected Financial Factors (in Percentages)

Debt Ratio 45	66.2	•	403.0	211.9	87.6	106.8	82.3	82.2	65.4	59.1	59.5	56.4	66.7
Return on Total Assets 46	7.2	•	•	•	•	•	•	•	0.2	5.7	5.5	6.3	8.2
Return on Equity Before Income Taxes 47	18.0	•	1.2	28.5	•	384.4	•	•	•	11.6	9.7	10.5	21.7
Return on Equity After Income Taxes 48	11.2	•	1.2	32.1	•	398.9	•	•	•	8.4	5.6	8.0	13.9
Profit Margin (Before Income Tax) 49	16.5	•	•	•	•	•	•	•	•	7.0	6.7	10.8	26.7
Profit Margin (After Income Tax) 50	10.3	•	•	•	•	•	•	•	•	5.1	3.9	8.2	17.2

Table II

Corporations with Net Income

SOFTWARE PUBLISHERS

MONEY AMOUNTS AND SIZE OF ASSETS IN THOUSANDS OF DOLLARS

Item Description for Accounting Period 7/12 Through 6/13	Total	Zero Assets	Under 500	500 to 1,000	1,000 to 5,000	5,000 to 10,000	10,000 to 25,000	25,000 to 50,000	50,000 to 100,000	100,000 to 250,000	250,000 to 500,000	500,000 to 2,500,000	2,500,000 and over
Number of Enterprises 1	2666	15	1758	152	404	62	113	46	23	27	16	33	17

Revenues ($ in Thousands)

	Total	Zero Assets	Under 500	500 to 1,000	1,000 to 5,000	5,000 to 10,000	10,000 to 25,000	25,000 to 50,000	50,000 to 100,000	100,000 to 250,000	250,000 to 500,000	500,000 to 2,500,000	2,500,000 and over
Net Sales 2	105502833	1601427	1176515	429644	4043892	792079	2434188	2001815	1570764	3265855	3740437	17572318	66873899
Interest 3	305462	158	15	211	2171	765	1637	4269	1644	7560	14373	81239	191421
Rents 4	139925	0	0	0	443	41	440	331	86	78	4745	28597	105163
Royalties 5	10386121	0	17629	0	0	0	32259	0	32233	84887	21580	1346099	8851433
Other Portfolio Income 6	2705917	31306	171	195	26230	23079	51029	4399	30	54950	270781	310821	1932924
Other Receipts 7	44677022	4837	62134	303	48020	33070	22556	45392	1583	164541	50913	239411	44004266
Total Receipts 8	163717280	1637728	1256464	430353	4120756	849034	2542109	2056206	1606340	3577871	4102829	19578485	121959106
Average Total Receipts 9	61409	109182	715	2831	10200	13694	22497	44700	69841	132514	256427	593287	7174065

Operating Costs/Operating Income (%)

	Total	Zero Assets	Under 500	500 to 1,000	1,000 to 5,000	5,000 to 10,000	10,000 to 25,000	25,000 to 50,000	50,000 to 100,000	100,000 to 250,000	250,000 to 500,000	500,000 to 2,500,000	2,500,000 and over
Cost of Operations 10	36.4	63.3	4.5	0.9	68.3	15.8	22.2	23.5	20.3	27.2	16.8	16.6	42.8
Salaries and Wages 11	38.5	8.6	33.1	33.8	10.6	35.0	28.3	32.0	27.7	27.6	31.8	35.0	43.8
Taxes Paid 12	3.8	4.5	4.2	3.4	1.3	2.7	2.7	2.7	2.9	2.7	2.9	3.3	4.2
Interest Paid 13	2.8	0.4	0.2	0.0	0.1	2.8	0.6	0.7	1.7	1.4	2.3	4.3	3.0
Depreciation 14	3.8	0.7	0.4	0.4	0.2	1.6	1.2	0.9	1.7	1.3	2.5	2.6	5.0
Amortization and Depletion 15	2.1	0.5	0.3	0.0	0.2	0.4	0.9	0.8	1.4	2.1	2.5	2.3	2.3
Pensions and Other Deferred Comp. 16	0.4	0.0	0.2	0.1	0.2	1.1	0.8	0.5	0.5	0.3	0.5	0.8	0.2
Employee Benefits 17	3.8	0.4	0.2	1.2	0.9	2.7	2.8	2.8	2.2	2.6	2.8	4.1	4.3
Advertising 18	5.1	0.3	0.8	0.1	0.5	7.5	3.7	4.5	1.0	4.6	3.6	2.1	6.6
Other Expenses 19	33.7	14.5	30.0	37.0	6.8	18.5	25.4	19.9	27.3	18.8	25.0	24.8	40.5
Officers' Compensation 20	1.9	0.2	8.1	9.7	4.0	4.2	3.0	2.4	1.7	1.9	2.8	2.4	1.4
Operating Margin 21	•	6.5	18.0	13.4	7.0	7.7	8.4	9.2	11.6	9.5	6.4	1.8	•
Operating Margin Before Officers' Comp. 22	•	6.7	26.1	23.2	10.9	11.9	11.4	11.5	13.3	11.5	9.2	4.2	•

Selected Average Balance Sheet ($ in Thousands)

Net Receivables 23	12565	0	88	62	1148	2135	3286	10052	13794	21341	56742	160365	1459465
Inventories 24	741	0	0	5	73	162	152	394	246	287	965	2875	123231
Net Property, Plant and Equipment 25	6295	0	31	18	90	787	737	2154	4003	6571	17989	76904	785988
Total Assets 26	115560	0	119	698	2645	7477	16477	34952	77192	162530	368890	1218535	14734596
Notes and Loans Payable 27	16181	0	1006	10	230	1814	3577	3057	11471	33685	99218	291408	1661179
All Other Liabilities 28	59427	0	153	131	1552	4020	8919	18718	30404	53385	141102	402094	8101777
Net Worth 29	39952	0	-1041	558	864	1642	3981	13177	35317	75460	128569	525033	4971640

Selected Financial Ratios (Times to 1)

Current Ratio 30	0.5	•	0.1	4.1	1.5	2.3	1.4	1.4	1.2	1.7	1.4	1.3	0.4
Quick Ratio 31	0.4	•	0.1	4.0	1.4	1.9	1.2	1.1	1.0	1.3	1.1	1.1	0.3
Net Sales to Working Capital 32	•	•	•	7.0	12.9	4.6	6.7	6.6	9.6	4.3	4.6	6.3	•
Coverage Ratio 33	9.8	36.0	101.4	375.6	119.6	6.3	26.2	17.0	9.4	14.4	8.1	4.2	11.3
Total Asset Turnover 34	0.3	•	5.6	4.0	3.8	1.7	1.3	1.2	0.9	0.7	0.6	0.4	0.3
Inventory Turnover 35	19.4	•	416.4	5.8	93.1	12.5	31.4	26.0	56.1	114.3	40.8	30.7	13.7
Receivables Turnover 36	3.4	•	14.9	16.8	14.0	3.5	6.9	4.4	•	6.4	4.0	3.6	•
Total Liabilities to Net Worth 37	1.9	•	•	0.3	2.1	3.6	3.1	1.7	1.2	1.2	1.9	1.3	2.0
Current Assets to Working Capital 38	•	•	•	1.3	2.9	1.8	3.5	3.6	5.1	2.5	3.3	4.5	•
Current Liabilities to Working Capital 39	•	•	•	0.3	1.9	0.8	2.5	2.6	4.1	1.5	2.3	3.5	•
Working Capital to Net Sales 40	•	•	•	0.1	0.1	0.2	0.1	0.2	0.1	0.2	0.2	0.2	•
Inventory to Working Capital 41	•	•	•	0.0	0.1	0.0	0.0	0.1	0.0	0.0	0.0	0.0	•
Total Receipts to Cash Flow 42	2.0	4.8	1.9	2.3	7.2	3.5	2.9	3.4	2.6	2.9	3.2	3.0	1.6
Cost of Goods to Cash Flow 43	0.7	3.1	0.1	0.0	4.9	0.6	0.6	0.8	0.5	0.8	0.5	0.5	0.7
Cash Flow to Total Debt 44	0.3	•	0.3	8.9	0.8	0.6	0.6	0.6	0.6	0.5	0.3	0.3	0.3

Selected Financial Factors (in Percentages)

Debt Ratio 45	65.4	•	975.0	20.1	67.4	78.0	75.8	62.3	54.2	53.6	65.1	56.9	66.3
Return on Total Assets 46	9.5	•	141.0	55.2	33.8	30.2	19.9	15.8	13.8	15.5	11.8	7.8	9.1
Return on Equity Before Income Taxes 47	24.6	•	•	69.0	102.6	115.8	79.4	39.4	26.9	31.1	29.7	13.8	24.5
Return on Equity After Income Taxes 48	17.2	•	•	54.7	96.9	104.4	71.8	35.0	21.7	26.6	22.0	10.7	16.3
Profit Margin (Before Income Tax) 49	24.9	13.4	24.8	13.6	8.9	14.9	14.7	11.9	13.9	19.4	16.3	13.6	31.0
Profit Margin (After Income Tax) 50	17.4	11.3	24.8	10.8	8.4	13.4	13.3	10.6	11.2	16.6	12.1	10.5	20.6

Table I

Corporations with and without Net Income

MOTION PICTURE AND VIDEO INDUSTRIES (EXCEPT VIDEO RENTAL)

MONEY AMOUNTS AND SIZE OF ASSETS IN THOUSANDS OF DOLLARS

Item Description for Accounting Period 7/12 Through 6/13		Total	Zero Assets	Under 500	500 to 1,000	1,000 to 5,000	5,000 to 10,000	10,000 to 25,000	25,000 to 50,000	50,000 to 100,000	100,000 to 250,000	250,000 to 500,000	500,000 to 2,500,000	2,500,000 and over
Number of Enterprises	1	28577	5607	20206	1398	918	•	81	44	13	•	7	13	9
Revenues ($ in Thousands)														
Net Sales	2	94892244	1246496	5379151	1960475	2270787	•	1985425	1491385	627102	•	1462023	8147296	65495700
Interest	3	516743	10116	80	93	2356	•	84	1919	743	•	17878	55155	420296
Rents	4	355543	0	428	0	21	•	0	1435	235	•	5320	48923	297245
Royalties	5	10184964	317004	238	0	49	•	709	0	0	•	3509	78844	9782571
Other Portfolio Income	6	2308526	30269	16683	342	14645	•	17635	4018	628	•	14042	222556	1964508
Other Receipts	7	4189618	183514	67481	86973	43623	•	60428	38709	14956	•	21036	613099	2810934
Total Receipts	8	112447638	1787399	5464061	2047883	2331481	•	2064281	1537466	643664	•	1523808	9165873	80771254
Average Total Receipts	9	3935	319	270	1465	2540	•	25485	34942	49513	•	217687	705067	8974584
Operating Costs/Operating Income (%)														
Cost of Operations	10	23.2	19.0	19.0	43.6	38.4	•	64.7	55.2	42.4	•	59.9	32.9	17.6
Salaries and Wages	11	11.8	4.9	8.7	10.8	9.7	•	8.5	9.4	12.1	•	7.8	13.2	12.4
Taxes Paid	12	2.6	2.2	2.8	2.5	2.1	•	1.4	3.6	3.1	•	1.1	3.6	2.6
Interest Paid	13	4.8	12.6	0.4	1.1	1.3	•	0.6	2.1	2.1	•	10.4	4.1	5.7
Depreciation	14	7.1	5.1	0.9	3.7	6.0	•	1.4	5.1	3.7	•	6.0	4.3	8.1
Amortization and Depletion	15	15.6	1.2	0.0	0.8	2.6	•	2.1	5.2	6.5	•	2.6	3.8	21.5
Pensions and Other Deferred Comp.	16	0.5	0.9	2.5	0.7	0.6	•	0.1	0.1	0.0	•	0.1	0.5	0.3
Employee Benefits	17	1.6	0.6	1.4	1.3	0.5	•	0.8	1.4	1.1	•	3.7	1.7	1.7
Advertising	18	5.4	0.9	0.3	1.2	0.4	•	0.7	1.1	0.8	•	0.3	1.5	7.4
Other Expenses	19	30.3	73.9	31.0	21.7	33.7	•	12.7	29.2	25.0	•	15.8	37.0	29.1
Officers' Compensation	20	3.3	11.5	26.0	11.5	5.2	•	6.4	3.5	5.8	•	1.2	1.4	1.2
Operating Margin	21	•	•	7.2	1.1	•	•	0.7	•	•	•	•	•	•
Operating Margin Before Officers' Comp.	22	•	•	33.1	12.6	4.7	•	7.1	•	3.2	•	•	•	•

Selected Average Balance Sheet ($ in Thousands)

	1	2	3	4	5	6	7	8	9	10	11
Net Receivables 23	811	0	1	19	140	3057	3957	2754	106264	81123	2244490
Inventories 24	407	0	1	10	21	903	1405	1741	9773	5842	1235506
Net Property, Plant and Equipment 25	604	0	7	265	657	3143	8502	24684	51468	337855	1071662
Total Assets 26	7628	0	67	709	2098	16216	34123	69163	340352	1222158	20709209
Notes and Loans Payable 27	3004	0	183	541	1355	3942	24256	24743	193415	359776	7813087
All Other Liabilities 28	1162	0	35	418	574	7705	12768	22106	202170	561339	2110299
Net Worth 29	3463	0	-151	-251	170	4569	-2901	22313	-55233	301043	10785824

Selected Financial Ratios (Times to 1)

	1	2	3	4	5	6	7	8	9	10	11
Current Ratio 30	1.4	•	1.1	0.6	1.3	1.5	1.2	1.1	1.2	0.9	1.5
Quick Ratio 31	0.8	•	1.0	0.5	1.0	0.9	0.8	0.7	0.7	0.6	0.9
Net Sales to Working Capital 32	6.0	•	122.2	•	13.1	9.2	19.6	19.2	5.8	•	4.2
Coverage Ratio 33	3.7	1.8	25.7	6.0	2.7	8.5	•	1.0	0.6	3.1	4.0
Total Asset Turnover 34	0.4	•	4.0	2.0	1.2	1.5	1.0	0.7	0.6	0.5	0.4
Inventory Turnover 35	1.9	•	55.0	61.6	45.9	17.6	13.3	11.7	12.8	35.3	1.0
Receivables Turnover 36	3.5	•	228.6	79.6	22.2	6.9	7.9	8.3	1.7	8.9	2.7
Total Liabilities to Net Worth 37	1.2	•	•	•	11.3	2.5	•	2.1	•	3.1	0.9
Current Assets to Working Capital 38	3.7	•	15.9	•	4.2	3.1	7.5	8.2	6.5	•	3.1
Current Liabilities to Working Capital 39	2.7	•	14.9	•	3.2	2.1	6.5	7.2	5.5	•	2.1
Working Capital to Net Sales 40	0.2	•	0.0	•	0.1	0.1	0.1	0.1	0.2	•	0.2
Inventory to Working Capital 41	0.8	•	0.4	•	0.2	0.4	0.8	0.5	0.2	•	0.7
Total Receipts to Cash Flow 42	2.9	1.4	2.9	5.1	3.4	6.7	45.8	6.4	18.6	4.9	2.6
Cost of Goods to Cash Flow 43	0.7	0.3	0.6	2.2	1.3	4.3	25.3	2.7	11.1	1.6	0.5
Cash Flow to Total Debt 44	0.3	•	0.4	0.3	0.4	0.3	0.0	0.2	0.0	0.1	0.3

Selected Financial Factors (in Percentages)

	1	2	3	4	5	6	7	8	9	10	11
Debt Ratio 45	54.6	•	326.5	135.4	91.9	71.8	108.5	67.7	116.2	75.4	47.9
Return on Total Assets 46	7.8	•	36.3	13.3	4.1	8.0	•	1.5	3.6	6.5	7.9
Return on Equity Before Income Taxes 47	12.6	•	•	•	31.6	25.1	147.8	0.1	17.0	17.8	11.4
Return on Equity After Income Taxes 48	8.2	•	•	•	30.4	24.3	149.1	•	24.9	9.9	7.3
Profit Margin (Before Income Tax) 49	13.1	10.6	8.8	5.6	2.2	4.7	•	0.0	•	8.6	16.8
Profit Margin (After Income Tax) 50	8.6	9.6	8.6	5.2	2.1	4.5	•	•	•	4.7	10.9

Table II

Corporations with Net Income

MOTION PICTURE AND VIDEO INDUSTRIES (EXCEPT VIDEO RENTAL)

MONEY AMOUNTS AND SIZE OF ASSETS IN THOUSANDS OF DOLLARS

Item Description for Accounting Period 7/12 Through 6/13	Total	Zero Assets	Under 500	500 to 1,000	1,000 to 5,000	5,000 to 10,000	10,000 to 25,000	25,000 to 50,000	50,000 to 100,000	100,000 to 250,000	250,000 to 500,000	500,000 to 2,500,000	2,500,000 and over
Number of Enterprises 1	19154	4622	12846	914	533	131	51	16	7	•	3	•	•
Revenues ($ in Thousands)													
Net Sales 2	84473892	1209666	3834775	1578178	1526958	2112022	1902258	434024	355687	•	798693	•	•
Interest 3	418768	1255	78	19	881	59	72	102	740	•	10094	•	•
Rents 4	349432	0	428	0	0	660	0	141	235	•	1722	•	•
Royalties 5	10042266	246732	0	0	0	0	709	0	0	•	0	•	•
Other Portfolio Income 6	2259184	6059	16683	342	14194	11283	17635	8	571	•	0	•	•
Other Receipts 7	4106573	144428	65614	86791	28481	172519	46618	27042	6940	•	19075	•	•
Total Receipts 8	101650115	1608140	3917578	1665330	1570514	2296543	1967292	461317	364173	•	829584	•	•
Average Total Receipts 9	5307	348	305	1822	2947	17531	38574	28832	52025	•	276528	•	•
Operating Costs/Operating Income (%)													
Cost of Operations 10	20.5	18.6	13.4	46.1	27.7	27.3	65.5	25.0	20.4	•	69.9	•	•
Salaries and Wages 11	11.5	3.5	4.5	8.8	6.8	16.4	6.8	6.9	13.2	•	5.6	•	•
Taxes Paid 12	2.6	1.5	2.5	2.2	1.4	3.4	1.3	4.3	3.6	•	1.1	•	•
Interest Paid 13	4.6	0.2	0.3	0.8	0.4	0.9	0.5	1.4	2.4	•	0.8	•	•
Depreciation 14	7.4	5.0	0.7	3.4	5.8	15.5	0.9	4.2	4.1	•	0.4	•	•
Amortization and Depletion 15	17.0	0.0	0.0	0.6	3.0	1.6	1.1	0.7	0.4	•	0.3	•	•
Pensions and Other Deferred Comp. 16	0.5	0.9	3.3	0.8	0.9	0.1	0.1	0.1	0.0	•	0.2	•	•
Employee Benefits 17	1.6	0.2	1.5	0.9	0.1	0.5	0.7	0.9	1.3	•	2.1	•	•
Advertising 18	5.7	0.3	0.2	1.4	0.3	0.3	0.6	2.5	0.5	•	0.1	•	•
Other Expenses 19	29.1	64.4	26.6	20.4	35.1	28.6	10.2	37.8	32.9	•	11.7	•	•
Officers' Compensation 20	3.3	10.5	31.4	10.8	5.6	5.1	6.3	7.8	9.6	•	0.3	•	•
Operating Margin 21	•	•	15.6	3.8	12.8	0.1	6.1	8.5	11.6	•	7.5	•	•
Operating Margin Before Officers' Comp. 22	•	5.5	47.0	14.6	18.5	5.2	12.4	16.3	21.2	•	7.8	•	•

Selected Average Balance Sheet ($ in Thousands)

Net Receivables 23	1106	0	0	18	100	913	4150	2494	3157	•	140926	•	•
Inventories 24	585	0	0	11	8	50	97	116	1303	•	21032	•	•
Net Property, Plant and Equipment 25	657	0	9	192	492	3052	4390	8019	38950	•	13606	•	•
Total Assets 26	10282	0	72	641	1516	7042	16483	29853	67330	•	341592	•	•
Notes and Loans Payable 27	3910	0	50	364	659	3322	3716	8303	19817	•	42923	•	•
All Other Liabilities 28	1320	0	18	190	176	1641	7456	7511	19780	•	208273	•	•
Net Worth 29	5052	0	4	87	681	2079	5311	14040	27733	•	90395	•	•

Selected Financial Ratios (Times to 1)

Current Ratio 30	1.5	•	2.2	0.9	3.0	2.2	1.4	1.6	1.4	•	1.4	•	•
Quick Ratio 31	0.9	•	2.1	0.6	2.2	1.9	1.0	1.5	0.9	•	0.7	•	•
Net Sales to Working Capital 32	5.2	•	13.9	•	4.9	9.2	15.3	5.8	8.0	•	2.7	•	•
Coverage Ratio 33	4.8	160.1	59.7	13.3	39.4	10.3	18.9	11.9	7.0	•	15.2	•	•
Total Asset Turnover 34	0.4	•	4.1	2.7	1.9	2.3	2.3	0.9	0.8	•	0.8	•	•
Inventory Turnover 35	1.5	•	92.8	70.9	95.3	88.9	252.2	58.5	7.9	•	8.8	•	•
Receivables Turnover 36	3.4	•	434.9	125.6	46.5	•	8.1	•	7.3	•	2.0	•	•
Total Liabilities to Net Worth 37	1.0	•	15.6	6.4	1.2	2.4	2.1	1.1	1.4	•	2.8	•	•
Current Assets to Working Capital 38	3.2	•	1.8	•	1.5	1.8	3.7	2.6	3.7	•	3.2	•	•
Current Liabilities to Working Capital 39	2.2	•	0.8	•	0.5	0.8	2.7	1.6	2.7	•	2.2	•	•
Working Capital to Net Sales 40	0.2	•	0.1	•	0.2	0.1	0.1	0.2	0.1	•	0.4	•	•
Inventory to Working Capital 41	0.7	•	0.0	•	0.0	0.0	0.0	0.0	0.0	•	0.2	•	•
Total Receipts to Cash Flow 42	2.6	1.2	2.6	4.6	2.3	3.3	5.6	3.8	3.0	•	5.4	•	•
Cost of Goods to Cash Flow 43	0.5	0.2	0.3	2.1	0.6	0.9	3.7	0.9	0.6	•	3.7	•	•
Cash Flow to Total Debt 44	0.3	•	1.7	0.7	1.5	1.0	0.6	0.5	0.4	•	0.2	•	•

Selected Financial Factors (in Percentages)

Debt Ratio 45	50.9	•	94.0	86.4	55.1	70.5	67.8	53.0	58.8	•	73.5	•	•
Return on Total Assets 46	9.4	•	74.7	27.1	30.4	22.5	22.7	14.7	12.4	•	9.5	•	•
Return on Equity Before Income Taxes 47	15.2	•	1221.7	184.7	65.9	68.7	66.8	28.7	25.8	•	33.4	•	•
Return on Equity After Income Taxes 48	10.7	•	1208.2	175.4	65.4	67.2	65.6	27.9	24.7	•	22.3	•	•
Profit Margin (Before Income Tax) 49	17.4	28.0	17.7	9.3	15.7	8.9	9.5	14.8	14.1	•	11.4	•	•
Profit Margin (After Income Tax) 50	12.3	26.9	17.5	8.8	15.5	8.7	9.3	14.4	13.5	•	7.6	•	•

Table I

Corporations with and without Net Income

SOUND RECORDING INDUSTRIES

MONEY AMOUNTS AND SIZE OF ASSETS IN THOUSANDS OF DOLLARS

Item Description for Accounting Period 7/12 Through 6/13	Total	Zero Assets	Under 500	500 to 1,000	1,000 to 5,000	5,000 to 10,000	10,000 to 25,000	25,000 to 50,000	50,000 to 100,000	100,000 to 250,000	250,000 to 500,000	500,000 to 2,500,000	2,500,000 and over
Number of Enterprises 1	5857	1568	4162	0	45	•	0	13	7	•	0	3	3
Revenues ($ in Thousands)													
Net Sales 2	6592630	159021	804747	0	116706	•	0	327746	206214	•	0	377124	3484367
Interest 3	55692	57	0	0	95	•	0	667	949	•	0	13399	31643
Rents 4	6755	0	0	0	0	•	0	301	12	•	0	2463	3979
Royalties 5	2041862	5688	0	0	13496	•	0	37772	4273	•	0	177191	1715599
Other Portfolio Income 6	239068	0	0	0	100598	•	0	663	0	•	0	1206	136590
Other Receipts 7	743836	677	139	0	5648	•	0	3861	12487	•	0	59854	627627
Total Receipts 8	9679843	165443	804886	0	236543	•	0	371010	223935	•	0	631237	5999805
Average Total Receipts 9	1653	106	193	•	5257	•	•	28539	31991	•	•	210412	1999935
Operating Costs/Operating Income (%)													
Cost of Operations 10	38.5	29.9	37.6	•	20.5	•	•	70.4	52.8	•	•	46.4	41.1
Salaries and Wages 11	11.6	0.9	3.3	•	17.9	•	•	12.1	12.7	•	•	20.5	13.4
Taxes Paid 12	3.4	1.6	2.2	•	2.2	•	•	1.5	1.4	•	•	3.0	4.9
Interest Paid 13	8.7	0.5	0.1	•	5.3	•	•	0.2	1.1	•	•	25.5	13.3
Depreciation 14	4.5	0.2	1.0	•	1.2	•	•	0.8	2.7	•	•	6.7	6.0
Amortization and Depletion 15	6.5	0.0	•	•	5.5	•	•	1.9	6.0	•	•	18.2	9.3
Pensions and Other Deferred Comp. 16	0.8	0.0	1.1	•	0.1	•	•	0.1	0.2	•	•	0.1	1.2
Employee Benefits 17	1.2	0.1	2.8	•	1.0	•	•	0.9	1.5	•	•	2.8	1.0
Advertising 18	2.7	1.8	0.1	•	4.1	•	•	1.4	0.2	•	•	0.7	4.0
Other Expenses 19	67.0	44.1	30.7	•	50.3	•	•	21.4	34.3	•	•	58.3	82.8
Officers' Compensation 20	2.6	4.0	11.7	•	5.5	•	•	3.8	3.4	•	•	0.8	0.7
Operating Margin 21	•	17.0	9.5	•	•	•	•	•	•	•	•	•	•
Operating Margin Before Officers' Comp. 22	•	21.0	21.2	•	•	•	•	•	•	•	•	•	•

Selected Average Balance Sheet ($ in Thousands)

Net Receivables 23	155	0	2	•	0	•	•	2026	496	•	•	39112	214384
Inventories 24	48	0	0	•	0	•	•	84	3303	•	•	33554	62422
Net Property, Plant and Equipment 25	81	0	15	•	2	•	•	4105	1292	•	•	11777	62119
Total Assets 26	6084	0	70	•	1997	•	•	38081	67619	•	•	826955	10330448
Notes and Loans Payable 27	1721	0	311	•	602	•	•	7457	17828	•	•	400791	2385074
All Other Liabilities 28	2577	0	3	•	2429	•	•	19226	25768	•	•	167488	4622526
Net Worth 29	1786	0	-245	•	-1034	•	•	11398	24023	•	•	258676	3322848

Selected Financial Ratios (Times to 1)

Current Ratio 30	0.4	•	11.6	•	0.9	•	•	1.4	1.2	•	•	1.0	0.2
Quick Ratio 31	0.2	•	11.4	•	0.5	•	•	0.9	0.5	•	•	0.5	0.1
Net Sales to Working Capital 32	•	•	3.9	•	•	•	•	3.3	4.9	•	•	398.2	•
Coverage Ratio 33	1.0	45.2	184.6	•	17.8	•	•	•	•	•	•	0.5	0.6
Total Asset Turnover 34	0.2	•	2.8	•	1.3	•	•	0.7	0.4	•	•	0.2	0.1
Inventory Turnover 35	9.0	•	•	•	•	•	•	212.5	4.7	•	•	1.7	7.6
Receivables Turnover 36	8.3	•	84.9	•	19451.0	•	•	20.3	5.5	•	•	1.1	10.8
Total Liabilities to Net Worth 37	2.4	•	•	•	•	•	•	2.3	1.8	•	•	2.2	2.1
Current Assets to Working Capital 38	•	•	1.1	•	•	•	•	3.4	6.2	•	•	525.5	•
Current Liabilities to Working Capital 39	•	•	0.1	•	•	•	•	2.4	5.2	•	•	524.5	•
Working Capital to Net Sales 40	•	•	0.3	•	•	•	•	0.3	0.2	•	•	0.0	•
Inventory to Working Capital 41	•	•	•	•	•	•	•	0.0	•	•	•	21.4	•
Total Receipts to Cash Flow 42	1.6	2.0	3.3	•	0.7	•	•	5.2	4.2	•	•	2.5	1.3
Cost of Goods to Cash Flow 43	0.6	0.6	1.3	•	0.1	•	•	3.7	2.2	•	•	1.2	0.6
Cash Flow to Total Debt 44	0.2	•	0.2	•	1.2	•	•	0.2	0.2	•	•	0.1	0.1

Selected Financial Factors (in Percentages)

Debt Ratio 45	70.6	•	450.8	•	151.8	•	•	70.1	64.5	•	•	68.7	67.8
Return on Total Assets 46	1.5	•	26.6	•	122.6	•	•	•	•	•	•	1.8	0.9
Return on Equity Before Income Taxes 47	•	•	•	•	•	•	•	•	•	•	•	•	•
Return on Equity After Income Taxes 48	•	•	•	•	•	•	•	•	•	•	•	•	•
Profit Margin (Before Income Tax) 49	•	21.1	9.5	•	89.1	•	•	•	•	•	•	•	•
Profit Margin (After Income Tax) 50	•	16.8	9.0	•	89.1	•	•	•	•	•	•	•	•

Table II

Corporations with Net Income

SOUND RECORDING INDUSTRIES

MONEY AMOUNTS AND SIZE OF ASSETS IN THOUSANDS OF DOLLARS

Item Description for Accounting Period 7/12 Through 6/13	Total	Zero Assets	Under 500	500 to 1,000	1,000 to 5,000	5,000 to 10,000	10,000 to 25,000	25,000 to 50,000	50,000 to 100,000	100,000 to 250,000	250,000 to 500,000	500,000 to 2,500,000	2,500,000 and over
Number of Enterprises **1**	3395	1184	2107	0	42	53	0	6	0	•	0	•	•
Revenues ($ in Thousands)													
Net Sales **2**	3241327	159021	724261	0	116706	138990	0	58227	0	•	0	•	•
Interest **3**	2258	57	0	0	95	0	0	987	0	•	0	•	•
Rents **4**	3979	0	0	0	0	0	0	0	0	•	0	•	•
Royalties **5**	1473869	5688	0	0	13496	0	0	0	0	•	0	•	•
Other Portfolio Income **6**	224302	0	0	0	100598	0	0	647	0	•	0	•	•
Other Receipts **7**	313521	677	4	0	5648	0	0	12552	0	•	0	•	•
Total Receipts **8**	5259256	165443	724265	0	236543	138990	0	72413	0	•	0	•	•
Average Total Receipts **9**	1549	140	344	•	5632	2622	•	12069	•	•	•	•	•
Operating Costs/Operating Income (%)													
Cost of Operations **10**	33.6	29.9	40.4	•	20.5	32.3	•	10.7	•	•	•	•	•
Salaries and Wages **11**	10.2	0.9	1.6	•	17.9	9.2	•	27.6	•	•	•	•	•
Taxes Paid **12**	2.9	1.6	2.1	•	2.2	1.6	•	4.3	•	•	•	•	•
Interest Paid **13**	4.0	0.5	0.0	•	5.3	0.1	•	0.0	•	•	•	•	•
Depreciation **14**	0.7	0.2	0.9	•	1.2	0.4	•	2.5	•	•	•	•	•
Amortization and Depletion **15**	4.3	0.0	•	•	5.5	•	•	5.7	•	•	•	•	•
Pensions and Other Deferred Comp. **16**	1.7	0.0	1.2	•	0.1	0.1	•	0.5	•	•	•	•	•
Employee Benefits **17**	1.2	0.1	0.3	•	1.0	0.1	•	2.8	•	•	•	•	•
Advertising **18**	5.0	1.8	0.1	•	4.1	6.3	•	0.8	•	•	•	•	•
Other Expenses **19**	83.1	43.3	20.0	•	50.2	27.9	•	29.6	•	•	•	•	•
Officers' Compensation **20**	3.7	4.0	12.4	•	5.5	0.5	•	18.7	•	•	•	•	•
Operating Margin **21**	•	17.8	20.9	•	•	21.6	•	•	•	•	•	•	•
Operating Margin Before Officers' Comp. **22**	•	21.8	33.3	•	•	22.0	•	15.4	•	•	•	•	•

Selected Average Balance Sheet ($ in Thousands)

Net Receivables 23	78	0	4	•	0	683	•	163	•	•	•	•	•
Inventories 24	72	0	0	•	0	698	•	0	•	•	•	•	•
Net Property, Plant and Equipment 25	55	0	12	•	2	1645	•	834	•	•	•	•	•
Total Assets 26	6782	0	108	•	1953	5580	•	48631	•	•	•	•	•
Notes and Loans Payable 27	170	0	39	•	511	781	•	7125	•	•	•	•	•
All Other Liabilities 28	3824	0	3	•	2603	903	•	18889	•	•	•	•	•
Net Worth 29	2788	0	66	•	-1161	3896	•	22617	•	•	•	•	•

Selected Financial Ratios (Times to 1)

Current Ratio 30	0.2	•	22.7	•	0.7	2.3	•	1.7	•	•	•	•	•
Quick Ratio 31	0.1	•	22.5	•	0.5	0.9	•	1.2	•	•	•	•	•
Net Sales to Working Capital 32	•	•	3.7	•	•	1.2	•	0.9	•	•	•	•	•
Coverage Ratio 33	3.9	46.8	75750.5	•	17.8	297.8	•	455.7	•	•	•	•	•
Total Asset Turnover 34	0.1	•	3.2	•	1.4	0.5	•	0.2	•	•	•	•	•
Inventory Turnover 35	4.4	•	•	•	•	1.2	•	•	•	•	•	•	•
Receivables Turnover 36	9.1	•	76.4	•	19451.0	•	•	•	•	•	•	•	•
Total Liabilities to Net Worth 37	1.4	•	0.6	•	•	0.4	•	1.2	•	•	•	•	•
Current Assets to Working Capital 38	•	•	1.0	•	•	1.8	•	2.5	•	•	•	•	•
Current Liabilities to Working Capital 39	•	•	0.0	•	•	0.8	•	1.5	•	•	•	•	•
Working Capital to Net Sales 40	•	•	0.3	•	•	0.8	•	1.1	•	•	•	•	•
Inventory to Working Capital 41	•	•	•	•	•	0.3	•	•	•	•	•	•	•
Total Receipts to Cash Flow 42	1.1	2.0	2.9	•	0.7	2.2	•	2.3	•	•	•	•	•
Cost of Goods to Cash Flow 43	0.4	0.6	1.2	•	0.1	0.7	•	0.2	•	•	•	•	•
Cash Flow to Total Debt 44	0.2	•	2.9	•	1.2	0.7	•	0.2	•	•	•	•	•

Selected Financial Factors (in Percentages)

Debt Ratio 45	58.9	•	39.1	•	159.5	30.2	•	53.5	•	•	•	•	•
Return on Total Assets 46	2.2	•	66.7	•	134.5	10.2	•	4.2	•	•	•	•	•
Return on Equity Before Income Taxes 47	4.0	•	109.4	•	•	14.5	•	9.0	•	•	•	•	•
Return on Equity After Income Taxes 48	3.8	•	106.4	•	•	14.4	•	7.7	•	•	•	•	•
Profit Margin (Before Income Tax) 49	11.8	21.9	20.9	•	89.2	21.6	•	21.1	•	•	•	•	•
Profit Margin (After Income Tax) 50	11.1	17.6	20.3	•	89.2	21.4	•	18.0	•	•	•	•	•

Table I

Corporations with and without Net Income

BROADCASTING (EXCEPT INTERNET)

MONEY AMOUNTS AND SIZE OF ASSETS IN THOUSANDS OF DOLLARS

Item Description for Accounting Period 7/12 Through 6/13	Total	Zero Assets	Under 500	500 to 1,000	1,000 to 5,000	5,000 to 10,000	10,000 to 25,000	25,000 to 50,000	50,000 to 100,000	100,000 to 250,000	250,000 to 500,000	500,000 to 2,500,000	2,500,000 and over
Number of Enterprises 1	6377	556	4121	641	670	130	109	45	27	23	20	19	15

Revenues ($ in Thousands)													
Net Sales 2	101384319	484003	1170001	743461	1369652	857493	1675161	890105	850964	1905360	6360998	6536036	78541084
Interest 3	1983098	250	8	240	490	531	2743	1291	232	13392	26195	110840	1826885
Rents 4	267175	59	0	2972	3260	460	1520	3746	285	5201	16579	16089	217005
Royalties 5	4906172	0	0	0	0	0	11180	3	3406	0	47026	228	4844328
Other Portfolio Income 6	2485051	1042153	0	10846	40712	255	102811	55238	266	10301	114120	401646	706706
Other Receipts 7	7304328	43779	10664	53285	18115	25359	63451	25169	26798	21922	278248	139914	6597622
Total Receipts 8	118330143	1570244	1180673	810804	1432229	884098	1856866	975552	881951	1956176	6843166	7204753	92733630
Average Total Receipts 9	18556	2824	287	1265	2138	6801	17035	21679	32665	85051	342158	379198	6182242

Operating Costs/Operating Income (%)													
Cost of Operations 10	12.4	•	1.2	1.8	17.4	16.8	35.6	5.8	19.0	9.9	57.8	4.6	9.1
Salaries and Wages 11	16.3	18.4	11.0	41.6	28.5	33.6	16.3	22.8	24.6	22.6	9.6	24.1	15.3
Taxes Paid 12	2.4	2.8	14.9	8.2	4.4	3.5	3.0	2.9	3.1	3.7	1.6	3.6	2.0
Interest Paid 13	7.3	6.7	0.4	5.0	2.1	4.5	2.0	7.0	8.5	7.8	5.2	9.9	7.6
Depreciation 14	4.6	9.7	3.4	4.2	4.0	3.2	3.6	3.9	6.1	3.7	5.5	4.8	4.6
Amortization and Depletion 15	8.9	8.1	1.2	0.3	1.4	2.0	4.1	8.7	4.2	7.5	3.6	12.4	9.7
Pensions and Other Deferred Comp. 16	1.1	0.4	1.2	0.0	0.4	0.3	0.9	0.4	0.4	0.5	0.6	1.2	1.1
Employee Benefits 17	3.7	1.4	0.6	3.5	1.5	2.1	0.9	1.9	1.1	2.2	1.4	2.0	4.2
Advertising 18	3.1	0.5	0.1	0.6	2.2	0.8	1.1	3.6	1.6	1.8	1.3	1.5	3.5
Other Expenses 19	44.9	97.1	41.5	29.7	24.6	24.9	23.8	41.0	28.4	31.0	18.2	39.1	49.0
Officers' Compensation 20	2.9	1.4	26.3	11.5	7.9	12.3	2.2	3.7	3.4	2.7	1.3	1.9	2.5
Operating Margin 21	•	•	•	•	5.7	•	6.5	•	•	6.5	•	•	•
Operating Margin Before Officers' Comp. 22	•	•	24.6	5.0	13.7	8.4	8.7	2.0	3.0	9.2	•	•	•

Selected Average Balance Sheet ($ in Thousands)

Net Receivables 23	2848	0	6	130	362	715	1843	5129	7647	16399	46710	62622	971732
Inventories 24	198	0	0	11	16	5	4	147	482	2357	2270	863	73768
Net Property, Plant and Equipment 25	4934	0	31	186	469	829	2938	5283	12370	22880	67951	106348	1733066
Total Assets 26	43044	0	62	640	2158	6341	15428	36803	65157	148316	345175	1018792	15785800
Notes and Loans Payable 27	15638	0	104	889	1345	1921	3691	27000	30790	82641	165463	531516	5321095
All Other Liabilities 28	11562	0	9	-442	292	903	3885	5317	17564	28235	101838	294224	4283289
Net Worth 29	15845	0	-51	193	522	3517	7851	4485	16803	37440	77874	193053	6181416

Selected Financial Ratios (Times to 1)

Current Ratio 30	1.0	•	1.8	0.6	1.5	3.0	2.2	1.3	2.6	2.4	1.1	1.3	1.0
Quick Ratio 31	0.6	•	1.2	0.5	1.2	1.2	1.8	1.1	1.9	1.5	0.9	1.0	0.6
Net Sales to Working Capital 32	59.1	•	26.3	•	5.6	2.8	3.9	5.9	2.7	3.1	22.6	14.0	•
Coverage Ratio 33	2.3	27.6	•	1.5	6.0	0.8	9.7	2.1	1.4	2.2	1.3	1.6	2.3
Total Asset Turnover 34	0.4	•	4.6	1.8	0.9	1.0	1.0	0.5	0.5	0.6	0.9	0.3	0.3
Inventory Turnover 35	9.9	•	•	1.9	22.2	236.0	1287.5	7.8	12.4	3.5	81.0	18.2	6.5
Receivables Turnover 36	5.8	•	64.1	8.6	7.3	8.8	7.7	4.1	4.3	5.1	7.1	4.5	5.7
Total Liabilities to Net Worth 37	1.7	•	•	2.3	3.1	0.8	1.0	7.2	2.9	3.0	3.4	4.3	1.6
Current Assets to Working Capital 38	26.4	•	2.3	•	3.2	1.5	1.8	3.9	1.6	1.7	8.1	4.9	•
Current Liabilities to Working Capital 39	25.4	•	1.3	•	2.2	0.5	0.8	2.9	0.6	0.7	7.1	3.9	•
Working Capital to Net Sales 40	0.0	•	0.0	•	0.2	0.4	0.3	0.2	0.4	0.3	0.0	0.1	•
Inventory to Working Capital 41	0.9	•	•	•	0.1	0.0	0.0	0.0	0.1	0.2	0.2	0.0	•
Total Receipts to Cash Flow 42	2.0	0.6	2.8	4.7	3.2	4.9	2.7	2.3	3.6	2.8	6.0	2.7	1.9
Cost of Goods to Cash Flow 43	0.3	•	0.0	0.1	0.6	0.8	1.0	0.1	0.7	0.3	3.5	0.1	0.2
Cash Flow to Total Debt 44	0.3	•	0.9	0.6	0.4	0.5	0.7	0.3	0.2	0.3	0.2	0.2	0.3

Selected Financial Factors (in Percentages)

Debt Ratio 45	63.2	•	181.9	69.9	75.8	44.5	49.1	87.8	74.2	74.8	77.4	81.1	60.8
Return on Total Assets 46	6.2	•	•	13.7	11.7	3.9	19.2	8.0	5.7	9.4	6.0	5.3	5.7
Return on Equity Before Income Taxes 47	9.5	•	4.4	15.3	40.4	•	33.9	34.9	6.1	20.2	5.5	10.3	8.2
Return on Equity After Income Taxes 48	6.2	•	4.4	13.8	39.9	•	29.2	26.5	5.4	15.0	2.5	6.5	5.2
Profit Margin (Before Income Tax) 49	9.5	177.8	•	2.5	10.3	•	17.3	7.9	3.3	9.1	1.3	5.8	9.7
Profit Margin (After Income Tax) 50	6.2	122.3	•	2.3	10.2	•	14.9	6.0	2.9	6.8	0.6	3.7	6.2

Table II

Corporations with Net Income

BROADCASTING (EXCEPT INTERNET)

MONEY AMOUNTS AND SIZE OF ASSETS IN THOUSANDS OF DOLLARS

Item Description for Accounting Period 7/12 Through 6/13	Total	Zero Assets	Under 500	500 to 1,000	1,000 to 5,000	5,000 to 10,000	10,000 to 25,000	25,000 to 50,000	50,000 to 100,000	100,000 to 250,000	250,000 to 500,000	500,000 to 2,500,000	2,500,000 and over
Number of Enterprises 1	3370	259	1735	521	580	88	87	35	18	15	12	12	10

Revenues ($ in Thousands)

Net Sales 2	81954517	101443	1115350	633856	1233796	694662	1063271	722197	656209	1541388	4787594	4856013	64548738
Interest 3	1552899	52	8	125	460	470	2534	1173	61	11986	3268	11817	1520943
Rents 4	227258	59	0	0	2161	237	577	3746	279	4985	13642	12617	188954
Royalties 5	4905977	0	0	0	0	0	11180	3	3406	0	47026	228	4844133
Other Portfolio Income 6	1881725	1041302	0	10788	40712	31	101980	47139	229	4886	113964	132240	388457
Other Receipts 7	5980114	42826	-202	18831	18022	13515	59674	22981	25816	20024	111973	145309	5501348
Total Receipts 8	96502490	1185682	1115156	663600	1295151	708915	1239216	797239	686000	1583269	5077467	5158224	76992573
Average Total Receipts 9	28636	4578	643	1274	2233	8056	14244	22778	38111	105551	423122	429852	7699257

Operating Costs/Operating Income (%)

Cost of Operations 10	13.1	•	0.9	0.6	17.2	15.1	13.8	7.1	14.1	12.2	62.0	5.7	10.4
Salaries and Wages 11	14.9	12.1	10.4	41.3	29.1	34.5	21.1	22.7	24.9	23.6	9.0	21.0	13.7
Taxes Paid 12	2.2	5.0	15.4	8.8	4.4	3.5	4.3	2.7	3.2	3.6	1.7	3.7	1.6
Interest Paid 13	4.6	16.0	0.1	5.4	1.8	0.7	2.1	2.4	6.2	5.7	1.9	9.1	4.6
Depreciation 14	3.6	0.6	3.1	1.7	2.1	2.4	4.7	4.3	4.1	3.3	2.7	5.1	3.6
Amortization and Depletion 15	9.2	9.9	0.0	0.3	1.2	0.3	5.2	5.1	4.6	6.1	1.7	9.9	10.4
Pensions and Other Deferred Comp. 16	1.2	•	1.3	•	0.4	0.3	0.3	0.5	0.4	0.6	0.7	1.4	1.3
Employee Benefits 17	4.2	0.7	0.6	3.7	1.5	1.9	1.0	1.7	1.1	2.4	1.4	1.7	4.9
Advertising 18	3.4	1.2	0.1	0.4	2.3	0.5	1.6	3.2	1.5	2.1	1.4	1.3	3.9
Other Expenses 19	44.5	233.0	36.8	23.2	17.4	18.2	29.1	37.2	25.3	27.4	16.1	31.8	49.3
Officers' Compensation 20	3.3	2.0	27.5	8.5	8.5	14.8	3.1	2.6	3.9	2.9	1.0	1.7	2.9
Operating Margin 21	•	•	3.7	6.2	14.1	7.8	13.9	10.6	10.7	10.0	0.5	7.8	•
Operating Margin Before Officers' Comp. 22	•	•	31.2	14.7	22.6	22.6	17.0	13.1	14.5	12.9	1.4	9.5	•

Selected Average Balance Sheet ($ in Thousands)

Net Receivables 23	4622	0	14	130	265	780	1988	5586	7595	18679	55840	76437	1288910
Inventories 24	355	0	0	13	4	3	2	166	264	3612	2137	1218	108340
Net Property, Plant and Equipment 25	7043	0	65	121	418	652	2968	6007	9768	24082	70913	141931	1969962
Total Assets 26	65361	0	107	604	2046	6270	15116	35666	65469	156980	340004	1034387	19544001
Notes and Loans Payable 27	13912	0	12	823	1281	1793	2991	12415	24885	80738	96892	626324	3450048
All Other Liabilities 28	17151	0	20	969	149	647	2715	7072	18030	32520	108348	272091	5125291
Net Worth 29	34299	0	75	-1189	616	3830	9411	16180	22554	43722	134764	135972	10968661

Selected Financial Ratios (Times to 1)

Current Ratio 30	1.2	•	1.3	0.5	1.6	4.2	2.9	1.8	2.6	2.7	1.7	1.1	1.1
Quick Ratio 31	0.7	•	1.2	0.4	1.2	1.6	2.3	1.4	2.2	1.6	1.4	0.9	0.6
Net Sales to Working Capital 32	13.1	•	78.3	•	5.2	2.4	2.7	3.8	3.3	2.9	6.9	28.7	17.7
Coverage Ratio 33	4.0	56.5	37.9	3.0	11.4	15.9	15.6	9.8	3.5	3.2	4.4	2.6	3.8
Total Asset Turnover 34	0.4	•	6.0	2.0	1.0	1.3	0.8	0.6	0.6	0.7	1.2	0.4	0.3
Inventory Turnover 35	9.0	•	•	0.6	85.0	382.3	863.8	8.9	19.5	3.5	115.7	19.0	6.2
Receivables Turnover 36	5.6	•	89.2	8.6	9.8	9.4	5.5	4.3	5.8	5.2	9.4	5.0	5.3
Total Liabilities to Net Worth 37	0.9	•	0.4	•	2.3	0.6	0.6	1.2	1.9	2.6	1.5	6.6	0.8
Current Assets to Working Capital 38	6.3	•	4.9	•	2.7	1.3	1.5	2.2	1.6	1.6	2.5	10.2	8.9
Current Liabilities to Working Capital 39	5.3	•	3.9	•	1.7	0.3	0.5	1.2	0.6	0.6	1.5	9.2	7.9
Working Capital to Net Sales 40	0.1	•	0.0	•	0.2	0.4	0.4	0.3	0.3	0.4	0.1	0.0	0.1
Inventory to Working Capital 41	0.2	•	•	•	0.0	0.0	0.0	0.0	0.0	0.2	0.0	0.1	0.3
Total Receipts to Cash Flow 42	1.9	0.2	2.6	3.8	3.0	3.9	1.9	1.9	2.6	2.8	5.0	2.4	1.7
Cost of Goods to Cash Flow 43	0.2	•	0.0	0.0	0.5	0.6	0.3	0.1	0.4	0.3	3.1	0.1	0.2
Cash Flow to Total Debt 44	0.4	•	7.6	0.2	0.5	0.8	1.1	0.5	0.3	0.3	0.4	0.2	0.4

Selected Financial Factors (in Percentages)

Debt Ratio 45	47.5	•	30.2	297.0	69.9	38.9	37.7	54.6	65.6	72.1	60.4	86.9	43.9
Return on Total Assets 46	6.9	•	22.6	32.9	21.7	13.2	26.3	13.5	11.9	12.0	9.7	9.3	5.8
Return on Equity Before Income Taxes 47	9.8	•	31.5	•	65.6	20.3	39.5	26.7	24.6	29.7	18.9	43.7	7.5
Return on Equity After Income Taxes 48	7.0	•	31.5	•	65.2	19.2	34.6	23.7	23.7	22.8	16.0	35.2	5.0
Profit Margin (Before Income Tax) 49	13.9	888.3	3.7	10.9	19.0	9.8	30.4	21.0	15.2	12.6	6.4	14.7	12.8
Profit Margin (After Income Tax) 50	9.8	623.3	3.7	10.7	18.9	9.3	26.6	18.6	14.7	9.7	5.4	11.8	8.6

Table I

Corporations with and without Net Income

TELECOMMUNICATIONS (WIRED, WIRELESS, SATELLITE, INTERNET PROVIDERS)

MONEY AMOUNTS AND SIZE OF ASSETS IN THOUSANDS OF DOLLARS

Item Description for Accounting Period 7/12 Through 6/13		Total	Zero Assets	Under 500	500 to 1,000	1,000 to 5,000	5,000 to 10,000	10,000 to 25,000	25,000 to 50,000	50,000 to 100,000	100,000 to 250,000	250,000 to 500,000	500,000 to 2,500,000	2,500,000 and over
Number of Enterprises	1	16409	3134	10247	564	1206	402	348	188	127	86	37	38	30
Revenues ($ in Thousands)														
Net Sales	2	415537706	2318800	4779583	532571	8292041	4178269	3915550	4153928	4812275	6902116	10845862	26806866	337999845
Interest	3	8147931	69940	27	1969	10071	5113	7419	7671	21770	28406	41310	294693	7659542
Rents	4	7250160	1039	0	244	1153	18204	9230	7435	12434	21576	7145	63921	7107778
Royalties	5	5001940	0	11	0	0	0	1971	12	545	0	1154	197268	4800980
Other Portfolio Income	6	7630306	1153863	6511	4216	53600	25024	130525	69565	96278	89033	820912	73400	5107385
Other Receipts	7	28162200	340730	81051	2569	79841	69651	342547	204217	322168	325119	174275	1167865	25052159
Total Receipts	8	471730243	3884372	4867183	541569	8436706	4296261	4407242	4442828	5265470	7366250	11890658	28604013	387727689
Average Total Receipts	9	28748	1239	475	960	6996	10687	12664	23632	41460	85654	321369	752737	12924256
Operating Costs/Operating Income (%)														
Cost of Operations	10	23.3	35.1	46.5	40.6	56.9	57.8	36.1	32.8	36.6	42.0	49.1	36.6	18.9
Salaries and Wages	11	14.5	13.9	14.0	25.2	13.0	15.7	15.4	13.7	11.6	10.1	14.0	27.0	13.6
Taxes Paid	12	3.0	2.9	2.1	2.6	2.3	2.0	3.0	2.9	2.4	2.2	1.8	3.0	3.1
Interest Paid	13	7.5	19.9	1.5	3.5	0.7	1.0	2.5	2.2	2.7	3.1	4.7	4.5	8.4
Depreciation	14	9.7	6.5	1.1	1.5	1.6	4.8	9.9	10.2	11.5	11.5	6.6	7.6	10.3
Amortization and Depletion	15	1.7	1.2	0.2	0.2	0.2	0.3	0.8	1.7	1.0	1.4	1.5	1.6	1.8
Pensions and Other Deferred Comp.	16	3.0	0.6	0.4	0.4	0.2	0.2	0.4	0.3	0.2	0.2	0.2	3.7	3.3
Employee Benefits	17	2.5	1.9	0.4	1.0	2.9	1.1	1.7	1.7	1.3	1.5	1.6	3.5	2.6
Advertising	18	2.1	1.7	1.1	1.1	0.7	0.7	0.8	3.2	3.1	1.1	0.6	2.0	2.2
Other Expenses	19	40.7	61.6	22.2	26.8	16.8	17.0	36.7	33.2	34.0	28.3	46.7	17.1	43.9
Officers' Compensation	20	0.6	4.1	8.2	10.6	3.2	2.0	2.3	1.8	1.5	1.2	1.0	0.7	0.3
Operating Margin	21	•	•	2.2	•	1.4	•	•	•	•	•	•	•	•
Operating Margin Before Officers' Comp.	22	•	•	10.4	•	4.6	•	•	•	•	•	•	•	•

Selected Average Balance Sheet ($ in Thousands)

Net Receivables 23	10463	0	5	104	512	2108	1695	3076	6623	17315	49994	193540	5246922
Inventories 24	315	0	3	25	105	247	360	923	801	2997	7074	13015	116531
Net Property, Plant and Equipment 25	17589	0	16	34	500	2246	6459	13997	27220	55938	82317	278441	8672086
Total Assets 26	76869	0	81	635	2221	7560	16275	34602	69934	164306	340465	1107442	38819334
Notes and Loans Payable 27	28521	0	138	495	729	3245	4567	9579	17593	41200	99413	394080	14543476
All Other Liabilities 28	28130	0	154	47	1100	3101	4297	8496	15494	46196	178781	372947	14253040
Net Worth 29	20217	0	-212	92	392	1214	7411	16527	36847	76909	62271	340415	10022818

Selected Financial Ratios (Times to 1)

Current Ratio 30	1.0	•	0.3	4.2	1.1	1.2	1.4	1.8	1.7	1.4	1.0	1.5	0.9
Quick Ratio 31	0.8	•	0.2	2.3	0.9	1.0	1.1	1.1	1.3	0.9	0.7	1.3	0.8
Net Sales to Working Capital 32	•	•	•	2.5	42.3	14.0	6.5	4.5	4.9	5.7	•	6.2	•
Coverage Ratio 33	1.7	1.9	3.8	•	5.6	1.3	2.1	2.4	2.6	2.3	•	0.9	1.7
Total Asset Turnover 34	0.3	•	5.8	1.5	3.1	1.4	0.7	0.6	0.5	0.5	0.9	0.6	0.3
Inventory Turnover 35	18.7	•	84.8	15.4	37.4	24.3	11.3	7.9	17.3	11.3	20.4	19.9	18.3
Receivables Turnover 36	2.5	•	74.3	7.1	11.9	5.4	5.3	7.0	6.5	3.9	6.1	3.3	2.2
Total Liabilities to Net Worth 37	2.8	•	•	5.9	4.7	5.2	1.2	1.1	0.9	1.1	4.5	2.3	2.9
Current Assets to Working Capital 38	•	•	•	1.3	7.9	5.5	3.4	2.3	2.5	3.5	•	2.8	•
Current Liabilities to Working Capital 39	•	•	•	0.3	6.9	4.5	2.4	1.3	1.5	2.5	•	1.8	•
Working Capital to Net Sales 40	•	•	•	0.4	0.0	0.1	0.2	0.2	0.2	0.2	•	0.2	•
Inventory to Working Capital 41	•	•	•	0.0	0.6	0.3	0.2	0.2	0.1	0.2	•	0.1	•
Total Receipts to Cash Flow 42	2.6	4.1	5.0	9.7	5.9	7.6	3.1	3.3	3.2	3.7	•	7.4	2.3
Cost of Goods to Cash Flow 43	0.6	1.5	2.3	3.9	3.4	4.4	1.1	1.1	1.2	1.6	•	2.7	0.4
Cash Flow to Total Debt 44	0.2	•	0.3	0.2	0.6	0.2	0.4	0.4	0.4	0.2	•	0.1	0.2

Selected Financial Factors (in Percentages)

Debt Ratio 45	73.7	•	362.9	85.4	82.4	83.9	54.5	52.2	47.3	53.2	81.7	69.3	74.2
Return on Total Assets 46	4.1	•	32.0	•	11.8	1.7	3.7	3.5	3.8	3.5	•	2.7	4.3
Return on Equity Before Income Taxes 47	6.2	•	•	•	55.1	2.4	4.3	4.2	4.4	4.2	•	•	7.0
Return on Equity After Income Taxes 48	4.4	•	•	•	48.6	•	1.5	1.2	2.7	2.2	•	•	5.3
Profit Margin (Before Income Tax) 49	4.9	18.1	4.1	•	3.1	0.3	2.8	3.2	4.3	4.1	•	•	6.2
Profit Margin (After Income Tax) 50	3.5	17.3	3.9	•	2.8	•	1.0	0.9	2.7	2.1	•	•	4.7

Table II
Corporations with Net Income

TELECOMMUNICATIONS (WIRED, WIRELESS, SATELLITE, INTERNET PROVIDERS)

MONEY AMOUNTS AND SIZE OF ASSETS IN THOUSANDS OF DOLLARS

Item Description for Accounting Period 7/12 Through 6/13	Total	Zero Assets	Under 500	500 to 1,000	1,000 to 5,000	5,000 to 10,000	10,000 to 25,000	25,000 to 50,000	50,000 to 100,000	100,000 to 250,000	250,000 to 500,000	500,000 to 2,500,000	2,500,000 and over
Number of Enterprises 1	10729	1457	7524	311	669	225	229	112	75	60	23	26	18

Revenues ($ in Thousands)

Net Sales 2	253878647	1729116	3605850	377168	5042434	2512425	2747738	2712763	2913945	4686746	7052459	22812824	197685179
Interest 3	2648128	3178	9	20	1978	3726	6337	5721	10283	21237	11015	263171	2321453
Rents 4	3658034	0	0	0	804	17642	8834	5695	7445	21493	6643	59946	3529532
Royalties 5	301062	0	11	0	0	0	1	0	0	0	2	188543	112505
Other Portfolio Income 6	6010314	1152609	331	0	50740	23811	129673	64295	72185	85949	52464	29802	4348457
Other Receipts 7	23262082	331816	62136	190	62010	65065	213232	174574	263792	316156	159634	1070540	20542936
Total Receipts 8	289758267	3216719	3668337	377378	5157966	2622669	3105815	2963048	3267650	5131581	7282217	24424826	228540062
Average Total Receipts 9	27007	2208	488	1213	7710	11656	13563	26456	43569	85526	316618	939416	12696670

Operating Costs/Operating Income (%)

Cost of Operations 10	27.4	32.2	45.6	42.7	56.4	61.5	35.4	33.9	31.5	42.2	45.3	39.7	23.2
Salaries and Wages 11	14.7	12.1	9.7	25.2	11.3	8.9	9.8	10.0	7.8	8.3	13.3	28.9	13.7
Taxes Paid 12	3.0	2.9	1.9	2.3	2.1	1.7	2.6	2.8	2.2	2.2	1.7	3.1	3.1
Interest Paid 13	6.7	19.4	0.2	0.1	0.4	0.6	1.5	1.5	2.5	2.5	1.6	3.6	7.9
Depreciation 14	10.2	5.8	0.9	1.7	1.2	2.9	9.1	8.5	11.1	11.7	5.5	5.4	11.5
Amortization and Depletion 15	2.0	0.8	0.2	•	0.1	0.1	0.7	0.6	0.6	1.0	1.3	1.2	2.3
Pensions and Other Deferred Comp. 16	2.0	0.8	0.6	0.5	0.1	0.2	0.4	0.4	0.2	0.2	0.3	4.1	2.0
Employee Benefits 17	3.0	1.9	0.4	1.0	4.0	0.7	1.1	1.5	1.1	1.5	1.7	3.3	3.2
Advertising 18	2.1	1.1	1.4	1.3	1.0	0.3	0.5	4.1	4.5	1.1	0.3	2.2	2.2
Other Expenses 19	30.9	54.7	19.9	17.7	12.5	16.8	35.1	28.5	34.7	25.7	23.3	9.7	34.3
Officers' Compensation 20	0.7	2.2	8.5	1.9	2.0	1.7	1.4	1.7	1.3	1.0	1.0	0.7	0.4
Operating Margin 21	•	•	10.9	5.6	8.9	4.5	2.2	6.6	2.6	2.7	4.6	•	•
Operating Margin Before Officers' Comp. 22	•	•	19.4	7.5	10.9	6.2	3.6	8.3	3.8	3.6	5.7	•	•

Selected Average Balance Sheet ($ in Thousands)

Net Receivables 23	5302	0	1	96	486	2289	1602	3309	5902	18660	59262	263091	2527748
Inventories 24	274	0	1	33	112	215	342	643	566	3306	7850	12749	105707
Net Property, Plant and Equipment 25	16667	0	8	37	552	1803	6471	14003	29931	56751	73363	225340	8984730
Total Assets 26	65624	0	72	615	2406	7408	16441	34700	70110	164628	323965	1126112	35586492
Notes and Loans Payable 27	23232	0	25	80	371	2210	3298	6758	18603	38398	73243	389456	12848282
All Other Liabilities 28	25026	0	36	44	726	2041	3334	7773	13079	42843	137059	361794	13862584
Net Worth 29	17367	0	11	491	1309	3158	9810	20168	38428	83388	113663	374863	8875627

Selected Financial Ratios (Times to 1)

Current Ratio 30	1.0	•	1.3	5.7	2.1	1.8	2.3	2.2	1.9	1.6	1.2	1.8	0.9
Quick Ratio 31	0.8	•	1.1	2.0	1.6	1.4	1.7	1.6	1.4	1.1	1.0	1.5	0.7
Net Sales to Working Capital 32	170.0	•	51.3	3.3	11.1	5.9	3.5	4.1	4.3	4.3	11.3	4.8	•
Coverage Ratio 33	2.7	3.7	73.2	51.4	27.7	15.0	11.0	11.6	7.5	5.8	5.9	2.5	2.5
Total Asset Turnover 34	0.4	•	6.7	2.0	3.1	1.5	0.7	0.7	0.6	0.5	0.9	0.8	0.3
Inventory Turnover 35	23.7	•	415.1	15.7	38.1	31.9	12.4	12.8	21.6	10.0	17.7	27.3	24.1
Receivables Turnover 36	5.6	•	138.2	10.6	11.6	5.6	6.0	7.4	6.7	3.9	5.8	3.7	5.7
Total Liabilities to Net Worth 37	2.8	•	5.8	0.3	0.8	1.3	0.7	0.7	0.8	1.0	1.9	2.0	3.0
Current Assets to Working Capital 38	71.3	•	4.6	1.2	1.9	2.3	1.8	1.8	2.1	2.8	5.1	2.3	•
Current Liabilities to Working Capital 39	70.3	•	3.6	0.2	0.9	1.3	0.8	0.8	1.1	1.8	4.1	1.3	•
Working Capital to Net Sales 40	0.0	•	0.0	0.3	0.1	0.2	0.3	0.2	0.2	0.2	0.1	0.2	•
Inventory to Working Capital 41	2.1	•	0.0	0.0	0.1	0.2	0.1	0.1	0.1	0.1	0.3	0.1	•
Total Receipts to Cash Flow 42	2.8	2.8	3.5	4.8	5.0	4.9	2.4	2.7	2.3	3.0	3.6	7.9	2.5
Cost of Goods to Cash Flow 43	0.8	0.9	1.6	2.1	2.8	3.0	0.8	0.9	0.7	1.3	1.6	3.1	0.6
Cash Flow to Total Debt 44	0.2	•	2.3	2.0	1.4	0.5	0.8	0.6	0.5	0.3	0.4	0.1	0.2

Selected Financial Factors (in Percentages)

Debt Ratio 45	73.5	•	85.3	20.2	45.6	57.4	40.3	41.9	45.2	49.3	64.9	66.7	75.1
Return on Total Assets 46	6.6	•	85.1	11.4	36.4	14.3	12.2	12.0	10.2	6.9	9.0	6.9	6.1
Return on Equity Before Income Taxes 47	15.8	•	572.4	14.0	64.5	31.4	18.5	18.9	16.1	11.3	21.3	12.3	14.8
Return on Equity After Income Taxes 48	12.6	•	565.7	11.4	61.0	27.4	15.4	14.8	13.3	8.7	15.8	9.6	11.6
Profit Margin (Before Income Tax) 49	11.6	52.3	12.6	5.7	11.2	8.9	15.2	15.8	15.9	12.1	7.9	5.3	12.0
Profit Margin (After Income Tax) 50	9.2	51.2	12.4	4.6	10.6	7.7	12.6	12.3	13.2	9.3	5.9	4.1	9.3

Table I

Corporations with and without Net Income

DATA PROCESSING, HOSTING AND RELATED SERVICES

MONEY AMOUNTS AND SIZE OF ASSETS IN THOUSANDS OF DOLLARS

Item Description for Accounting Period 7/12 Through 6/13	Total	Zero Assets	Under 500	500 to 1,000	1,000 to 5,000	5,000 to 10,000	10,000 to 25,000	25,000 to 50,000	50,000 to 100,000	100,000 to 250,000	250,000 to 500,000	500,000 to 2,500,000	2,500,000 and over
Number of Enterprises **1**	9727	3014	5510	308	543	137	92	43	25	23	9	15	7

Revenues ($ in Thousands)

	Total	Zero Assets	Under 500	500 to 1,000	1,000 to 5,000	5,000 to 10,000	10,000 to 25,000	25,000 to 50,000	50,000 to 100,000	100,000 to 250,000	250,000 to 500,000	500,000 to 2,500,000	2,500,000 and over
Net Sales **2**	40456402	1059448	2724210	369429	2941442	1174135	1651075	1667902	1485786	2192434	1371320	6369570	17449653
Interest **3**	255426	8860	1	11	1661	443	1573	3220	369	6938	5538	18841	207971
Rents **4**	7289	174	0	0	13	217	106	0	1612	191	0	0	4976
Royalties **5**	1161803	25223	0	0	0	0	0	0	319	7074	1186	33432	1094569
Other Portfolio Income **6**	451710	22889	1023	57126	306	2051	1	643	15382	17536	10	41413	293327
Other Receipts **7**	1323621	13867	42401	8242	24837	16953	94388	26607	7708	11788	109293	67471	900067
Total Receipts **8**	43656251	1130461	2767635	434808	2968259	1193799	1747143	1698372	1511176	2235961	1487347	6530727	19950563
Average Total Receipts **9**	4488	375	502	1412	5466	8714	18991	39497	60447	97216	165261	435382	2850080

Operating Costs/Operating Income (%)

	Total	Zero Assets	Under 500	500 to 1,000	1,000 to 5,000	5,000 to 10,000	10,000 to 25,000	25,000 to 50,000	50,000 to 100,000	100,000 to 250,000	250,000 to 500,000	500,000 to 2,500,000	2,500,000 and over
Cost of Operations **10**	22.8	8.1	30.8	44.3	33.4	60.5	47.4	25.9	26.5	15.0	3.7	19.8	18.2
Salaries and Wages **11**	44.8	38.6	18.7	7.2	20.1	19.7	26.5	25.5	27.9	32.9	36.8	31.1	68.1
Taxes Paid **12**	3.1	2.9	2.7	1.8	2.3	1.8	3.1	3.5	3.1	3.5	4.2	4.1	3.0
Interest Paid **13**	4.5	4.4	0.5	1.7	0.7	1.1	1.1	2.2	1.7	2.3	6.6	3.5	7.3
Depreciation **14**	6.2	3.9	0.6	1.5	2.1	0.9	4.1	5.8	3.5	8.3	7.3	7.3	8.1
Amortization and Depletion **15**	2.2	2.0	0.1	4.5	0.5	1.0	1.1	0.8	1.1	2.4	7.1	4.5	2.0
Pensions and Other Deferred Comp. **16**	0.3	0.4	•	•	0.4	0.1	0.7	0.6	0.3	0.5	0.1	0.2	0.4
Employee Benefits **17**	2.8	2.4	1.7	0.9	1.3	1.1	2.6	2.3	2.4	2.2	2.3	2.5	3.8
Advertising **18**	2.0	8.5	2.1	1.1	1.4	1.8	2.0	7.7	1.2	2.6	3.2	1.4	1.3
Other Expenses **19**	28.2	40.9	32.6	67.4	28.3	20.0	21.2	32.9	29.1	33.9	36.9	28.0	25.2
Officers' Compensation **20**	11.6	10.2	7.0	7.4	10.8	2.2	3.0	3.3	2.4	1.5	2.1	5.9	19.8
Operating Margin **21**	•	•	3.3	•	•	•	•	•	•	0.7	•	•	•
Operating Margin Before Officers' Comp. **22**	•	•	10.3	•	9.4	•	•	•	•	3.1	•	•	•

Selected Average Balance Sheet ($ in Thousands)

Net Receivables	23	686	0	30	174	375	1705	2717	4472	10557	21689	32115	86352	460366
Inventories	24	8	0	0	0	52	23	104	63	400	456	442	500	100
Net Property, Plant and Equipment	25	1491	0	12	33	378	228	2444	8231	8953	29004	36340	110440	1534573
Total Assets	26	9106	0	118	684	2676	6469	14577	37463	65770	163219	391431	990235	8378296
Notes and Loans Payable	27	2926	0	129	193	897	1140	3064	9508	13456	38681	129263	251891	2883807
All Other Liabilities	28	2001	0	69	627	1333	2370	6710	14129	23537	51710	68211	309611	1367996
Net Worth	29	4180	0	-80	-136	446	2959	4802	13826	28778	72828	193958	428734	4126494

Selected Financial Ratios (Times to 1)

Current Ratio	30	1.5	•	1.2	0.6	1.6	2.1	1.6	1.5	1.4	1.7	1.7	1.4	1.4
Quick Ratio	31	1.0	•	0.9	0.5	1.4	2.0	1.3	1.2	1.2	1.3	1.4	0.8	1.0
Net Sales to Working Capital	32	6.2	•	31.8	•	7.3	3.6	6.1	6.7	7.0	3.6	5.2	5.2	5.9
Coverage Ratio	33	•	•	10.5	•	0.4	•	•	•	2.5	•	0.7	•	•
Total Asset Turnover	34	0.5	•	4.2	1.8	2.0	1.3	1.2	1.0	0.9	0.6	0.4	0.4	0.3
Inventory Turnover	35	117.5	•	322.9	40959.2	34.9	229.7	82.1	160.5	39.4	31.3	12.8	168.1	4536.3
Receivables Turnover	36	6.4	•	19.0	13.2	13.4	6.8	6.9	11.3	5.3	5.0	4.6	6.7	5.1
Total Liabilities to Net Worth	37	1.2	•	•	•	5.0	1.2	2.0	1.7	1.3	1.2	1.0	1.3	1.0
Current Assets to Working Capital	38	3.2	•	5.7	•	2.6	1.9	2.7	3.2	3.3	2.4	2.5	3.6	3.3
Current Liabilities to Working Capital	39	2.2	•	4.7	•	1.6	0.9	1.7	2.2	2.3	1.4	1.5	2.6	2.3
Working Capital to Net Sales	40	0.2	•	0.0	•	0.1	0.3	0.2	0.1	0.1	0.3	0.2	0.2	0.2
Inventory to Working Capital	41	0.0	•	0.0	•	0.1	•	0.0	0.0	0.0	0.0	0.0	0.0	0.0
Total Receipts to Cash Flow	42	109.4	4.6	3.1	2.8	4.1	10.2	8.9	4.6	3.8	4.0	3.2	5.5	•
Cost of Goods to Cash Flow	43	24.9	0.4	1.0	1.2	1.4	6.2	4.2	1.2	1.0	0.6	0.1	1.1	•
Cash Flow to Total Debt	44	0.0	•	0.8	0.5	0.6	0.2	0.2	0.4	0.4	0.3	0.2	0.1	•

Selected Financial Factors (in Percentages)

Debt Ratio	45	54.1	•	168.3	119.8	83.3	54.3	67.1	63.1	56.2	55.4	50.4	56.7	50.7
Return on Total Assets	46	•	•	22.6	•	0.6	•	•	•	4.0	•	1.8	•	•
Return on Equity Before Income Taxes	47	•	•	•	179.4	•	•	•	•	5.5	•	•	•	•
Return on Equity After Income Taxes	48	•	•	•	179.8	•	•	•	•	3.7	•	•	•	•
Profit Margin (Before Income Tax)	49	•	•	4.9	•	•	•	•	•	2.6	•	•	•	•
Profit Margin (After Income Tax)	50	•	•	4.9	•	•	•	•	•	1.8	•	•	•	•

Table II

Corporations with Net Income

DATA PROCESSING, HOSTING AND RELATED SERVICES

MONEY AMOUNTS AND SIZE OF ASSETS IN THOUSANDS OF DOLLARS

Item Description for Accounting Period 7/12 Through 6/13		Total	Zero Assets	Under 500	500 to 1,000	1,000 to 5,000	5,000 to 10,000	10,000 to 25,000	25,000 to 50,000	50,000 to 100,000	100,000 to 250,000	250,000 to 500,000	500,000 to 2,500,000	2,500,000 and over
Number of Enterprises	1	6137	1155	4426	•	336	72	34	14	15	10	4	8	•

Revenues ($ in Thousands)

		Total	Zero Assets	Under 500	500 to 1,000	1,000 to 5,000	5,000 to 10,000	10,000 to 25,000	25,000 to 50,000	50,000 to 100,000	100,000 to 250,000	250,000 to 500,000	500,000 to 2,500,000	2,500,000 and over
Net Sales	2	21039896	221335	2567007	•	2448513	928154	692063	613045	966390	1327118	985708	3586264	•
Interest	3	129330	8714	0	•	1218	81	1109	812	44	2997	885	14907	•
Rents	4	2642	0	0	•	0	0	106	0	686	16	0	0	•
Royalties	5	16463	6651	0	•	0	0	0	0	0	7074	0	2739	•
Other Portfolio Income	6	400680	22889	1023	•	18	423	1	12	14295	17335	0	6356	•
Other Receipts	7	498864	8550	41750	•	12322	1372	84134	37171	3437	9526	2161	11788	•
Total Receipts	8	22087875	268139	2609780	•	2462071	930030	777413	651040	984852	1364066	988754	3622054	•
Average Total Receipts	9	3599	232	590	•	7328	12917	22865	46503	65657	136407	247188	452757	•

Operating Costs/Operating Income (%)

		Total	Zero Assets	Under 500	500 to 1,000	1,000 to 5,000	5,000 to 10,000	10,000 to 25,000	25,000 to 50,000	50,000 to 100,000	100,000 to 250,000	250,000 to 500,000	500,000 to 2,500,000	2,500,000 and over
Cost of Operations	10	21.3	8.1	31.0	•	34.7	70.2	30.3	17.4	29.8	10.4	3.7	24.2	•
Salaries and Wages	11	23.8	19.4	18.2	•	15.5	3.3	26.9	16.3	21.3	33.4	35.1	23.6	•
Taxes Paid	12	2.4	2.2	2.7	•	1.7	0.7	4.2	4.5	3.5	3.7	4.6	3.5	•
Interest Paid	13	3.2	6.7	0.5	•	0.7	0.5	0.6	1.5	2.1	1.7	4.0	3.7	•
Depreciation	14	3.5	1.7	0.5	•	1.1	0.6	4.4	7.9	3.7	6.6	4.3	4.9	•
Amortization and Depletion	15	2.4	2.6	0.1	•	0.1	0.1	0.9	0.4	1.2	2.2	2.6	6.7	•
Pensions and Other Deferred Comp.	16	0.3	1.0	•	•	0.5	0.1	1.5	0.1	0.4	0.7	0.0	0.3	•
Employee Benefits	17	3.4	2.6	1.7	•	0.8	0.2	3.5	2.1	1.8	1.5	1.2	2.2	•
Advertising	18	1.5	0.6	0.9	•	0.6	0.4	2.7	16.3	0.6	3.6	3.8	1.4	•
Other Expenses	19	27.6	43.4	30.3	•	24.6	11.7	23.3	21.1	21.5	29.6	35.6	21.8	•
Officers' Compensation	20	2.8	10.1	7.1	•	9.6	0.7	3.0	2.4	2.0	1.3	2.1	0.9	•
Operating Margin	21	7.8	1.5	7.0	•	10.2	11.5	•	10.0	12.1	5.5	2.9	6.7	•
Operating Margin Before Officers' Comp.	22	10.6	11.7	14.1	•	19.8	12.2	1.8	12.4	14.0	6.7	5.0	7.7	•

Selected Average Balance Sheet ($ in Thousands)

	1	2	3	4	5	6	7	8	9	10	11	12	13
Net Receivables 23	497	0	35	•	395	2893	3189	1421	9434	21039	40964	111401	•
Inventories 24	7	0	0	•	68	0	88	76	225	275	838	836	•
Net Property, Plant and Equipment 25	729	0	11	•	341	247	2612	12929	8940	24130	25741	87067	•
Total Assets 26	6212	0	136	•	2481	6506	15186	36182	61542	178174	401428	1018474	•
Notes and Loans Payable 27	1906	0	142	•	1115	533	2386	11004	15850	39719	98896	263821	•
All Other Liabilities 28	1497	0	75	•	1339	2936	5393	9683	22002	47822	77078	364018	•
Net Worth 29	2809	0	-82	•	28	3037	7406	15496	23690	90633	225454	390635	•

Selected Financial Ratios (Times to 1)

	1	2	3	4	5	6	7	8	9	10	11	12	13
Current Ratio 30	1.1	•	1.3	•	1.5	1.5	2.2	1.3	1.0	1.8	1.8	1.0	•
Quick Ratio 31	0.9	•	1.0	•	1.2	1.5	1.8	0.7	0.9	1.5	1.5	0.8	•
Net Sales to Working Capital 32	25.3	•	23.3	•	12.3	8.2	4.9	16.3	73.2	4.6	5.2	•	•
Coverage Ratio 33	5.1	4.5	18.3	•	16.0	25.2	20.7	11.7	7.9	5.8	1.8	3.1	•
Total Asset Turnover 34	0.6	•	4.3	•	2.9	2.0	1.3	1.2	1.0	0.7	0.6	0.4	•
Inventory Turnover 35	102.5	•	1897.9	•	37.2	•	69.9	100.1	85.2	50.2	10.8	129.6	•
Receivables Turnover 36	6.2	•	23.4	•	21.6	6.6	5.2	25.1	6.7	6.8	7.0	5.5	•
Total Liabilities to Net Worth 37	1.2	•	•	•	87.6	1.1	1.1	1.3	1.6	1.0	0.8	1.6	•
Current Assets to Working Capital 38	8.1	•	4.1	•	3.1	2.9	1.8	4.0	22.4	2.2	2.3	•	•
Current Liabilities to Working Capital 39	7.1	•	3.1	•	2.1	1.9	0.8	3.0	21.4	1.2	1.3	•	•
Working Capital to Net Sales 40	0.0	•	0.0	•	0.1	0.1	0.2	0.1	0.0	0.2	0.2	•	•
Inventory to Working Capital 41	0.1	•	•	•	0.1	•	0.0	0.0	0.4	0.0	0.0	•	•
Total Receipts to Cash Flow 42	2.9	1.6	2.9	•	3.2	4.4	3.4	2.8	3.2	3.1	2.7	3.9	•
Cost of Goods to Cash Flow 43	0.6	0.1	0.9	•	1.1	3.1	1.0	0.5	1.0	0.3	0.1	0.9	•
Cash Flow to Total Debt 44	0.3	•	0.9	•	0.9	0.8	0.8	0.7	0.5	0.5	0.5	0.2	•

Selected Financial Factors (in Percentages)

	1	2	3	4	5	6	7	8	9	10	11	12	13
Debt Ratio 45	54.8	•	160.3	•	98.9	53.3	51.2	57.2	61.5	49.1	43.8	61.6	•
Return on Total Assets 46	8.9	•	39.2	•	33.7	24.2	15.7	21.4	17.0	7.5	4.5	5.0	•
Return on Equity Before Income Taxes 47	15.8	•	•	•	2799.1	49.8	30.6	45.7	38.6	12.1	3.6	8.9	•
Return on Equity After Income Taxes 48	13.3	•	•	•	2677.9	42.2	27.2	37.9	35.0	10.3	3.5	7.1	•
Profit Margin (Before Income Tax) 49	12.9	23.4	8.6	•	10.8	11.7	11.1	16.2	14.2	8.3	3.3	7.8	•
Profit Margin (After Income Tax) 50	10.9	23.3	8.6	•	10.3	10.0	9.9	13.4	12.9	7.1	3.2	6.2	•

Table I

Corporations with and without Net Income

OTHER INFORMATION SERVICES, INTERNET PUBLISHING, WEB PORTALS

MONEY AMOUNTS AND SIZE OF ASSETS IN THOUSANDS OF DOLLARS

Item Description for Accounting Period 7/12 Through 6/13		Total	Zero Assets	Under 500	500 to 1,000	1,000 to 5,000	5,000 to 10,000	10,000 to 25,000	25,000 to 50,000	50,000 to 100,000	100,000 to 250,000	250,000 to 500,000	500,000 to 2,500,000	2,500,000 and over
Number of Enterprises	1	23917	6967	14763	423	1156	327	129	45	43	28	12	15	9

Revenues ($ in Thousands)

		Total	Zero Assets	Under 500	500 to 1,000	1,000 to 5,000	5,000 to 10,000	10,000 to 25,000	25,000 to 50,000	50,000 to 100,000	100,000 to 250,000	250,000 to 500,000	500,000 to 2,500,000	2,500,000 and over
Net Sales	2	86842450	747368	2677373	1203526	6541713	5113040	2354720	1767767	2170776	3169452	2404686	10270038	48421990
Interest	3	903934	1935	78	74	3143	1189	1406	3955	2926	4765	3005	78756	802702
Rents	4	152422	0	862	0	1437	335	37	0	811	24	7693	8553	132669
Royalties	5	1573326	987	37330	0	0	0	1092	48	6471	924	603045	59780	863649
Other Portfolio Income	6	7458372	13257	20378	0	36343	37762	28276	17919	37743	7513	4960	44721	7209496
Other Receipts	7	5008290	-9711	146051	57	29030	156482	12340	28971	138906	21821	13582	151907	4318859
Total Receipts	8	101938794	753836	2882072	1203657	6611666	5308808	2397871	1818660	2357633	3204499	3036971	10613755	61749365
Average Total Receipts	9	4262	108	195	2846	5719	16235	18588	40415	54829	114446	253081	707584	6861041

Operating Costs/Operating Income (%)

		Total	Zero Assets	Under 500	500 to 1,000	1,000 to 5,000	5,000 to 10,000	10,000 to 25,000	25,000 to 50,000	50,000 to 100,000	100,000 to 250,000	250,000 to 500,000	500,000 to 2,500,000	2,500,000 and over
Cost of Operations	10	27.3	18.6	24.3	26.4	60.2	54.1	35.1	33.4	21.6	21.2	6.0	31.4	20.6
Salaries and Wages	11	25.3	36.2	14.0	23.2	15.2	21.4	28.1	23.8	30.8	29.4	33.4	25.2	26.7
Taxes Paid	12	2.5	4.9	2.6	2.5	1.5	3.5	3.0	2.5	3.1	3.0	4.0	2.1	2.4
Interest Paid	13	2.9	4.3	1.1	0.7	0.2	0.4	1.2	0.6	1.8	1.3	3.3	4.0	3.6
Depreciation	14	3.7	2.0	0.9	0.3	0.5	0.9	2.5	2.6	2.6	3.8	3.0	3.2	5.0
Amortization and Depletion	15	1.5	0.6	0.5	0.1	0.4	0.3	1.9	1.1	1.8	1.2	1.9	4.0	1.4
Pensions and Other Deferred Comp.	16	0.6	0.4	0.6	0.4	0.1	0.9	0.1	0.1	0.2	0.6	3.5	0.6	0.6
Employee Benefits	17	1.8	3.1	1.6	0.8	1.2	2.9	2.2	1.7	2.3	2.5	3.3	2.2	1.6
Advertising	18	3.5	1.6	8.7	0.9	1.8	2.3	9.9	19.2	3.2	6.0	12.1	3.4	2.2
Other Expenses	19	30.7	53.7	38.7	32.2	17.4	15.0	29.6	27.4	43.2	32.0	41.3	22.7	34.1
Officers' Compensation	20	2.4	9.8	12.0	16.0	5.8	3.0	4.6	2.0	2.3	2.3	2.5	1.9	0.9
Operating Margin	21	•	•	•	•	•	•	•	•	•	•	•	•	1.0
Operating Margin Before Officers' Comp.	22	0.1	•	7.0	12.3	1.5	•	•	•	•	•	•	1.3	1.8

Selected Average Balance Sheet ($ in Thousands)

Net Receivables 23	595	0	3	92	314	2283	3351	6399	11396	19820	33352	95992	1047967
Inventories 24	28	0	0	12	12	53	129	59	769	207	66	25651	20674
Net Property, Plant and Equipment 25	669	0	5	12	212	509	1470	3501	3991	13074	29688	99463	1421139
Total Assets 26	6498	0	55	770	1978	7071	15215	35420	67823	145370	362085	1255743	12884372
Notes and Loans Payable 27	1198	0	101	459	550	957	4397	5987	19287	18902	72043	537755	1655296
All Other Liabilities 28	1702	0	48	191	816	2871	7293	10812	27194	47276	116514	421111	2932377
Net Worth 29	3598	0	-95	120	612	3243	3524	18621	21342	79192	173528	296878	8296699

Selected Financial Ratios (Times to 1)

Current Ratio 30	1.9	•	0.9	2.6	1.4	2.1	1.4	2.1	1.2	1.3	1.3	1.2	2.3
Quick Ratio 31	1.1	•	0.6	2.5	1.3	1.7	1.3	1.8	0.9	1.2	1.2	0.7	1.1
Net Sales to Working Capital 32	3.4	•	•	8.9	14.3	5.4	5.8	3.8	9.5	7.7	6.0	12.4	2.2
Coverage Ratio 33	6.7	•	3.4	•	•	•	•	•	•	•	4.7	1.8	9.4
Total Asset Turnover 34	0.6	•	3.3	3.7	2.9	2.2	1.2	1.1	0.7	0.8	0.6	0.5	0.4
Inventory Turnover 35	35.5	•	255.2	60.5	293.3	159.5	49.8	224.3	14.2	116.0	182.7	8.4	53.7
Receivables Turnover 36	6.5	•	73.4	29.6	19.3	8.1	5.9	4.0	5.8	5.9	6.6	7.6	5.5
Total Liabilities to Net Worth 37	0.8	•	•	5.4	2.2	1.2	3.3	0.9	2.2	0.8	1.1	3.2	0.6
Current Assets to Working Capital 38	2.1	•	•	1.6	3.3	2.0	3.3	1.9	6.0	3.9	4.6	6.7	1.8
Current Liabilities to Working Capital 39	1.1	•	•	0.6	2.3	1.0	2.3	0.9	5.0	2.9	3.6	5.7	0.8
Working Capital to Net Sales 40	0.3	•	•	0.1	0.1	0.2	0.2	0.3	0.1	0.1	0.2	0.1	0.4
Inventory to Working Capital 41	0.0	•	•	0.0	0.0	0.0	0.1	0.0	0.1	0.0	0.0	0.5	0.0
Total Receipts to Cash Flow 42	2.8	27.9	2.7	3.8	8.3	8.6	9.8	7.9	2.9	3.8	2.1	4.4	2.1
Cost of Goods to Cash Flow 43	0.8	5.2	0.7	1.0	5.0	4.7	3.4	2.7	0.6	0.8	0.1	1.4	0.4
Cash Flow to Total Debt 44	0.4	•	0.4	1.2	0.5	0.5	0.2	0.3	0.4	0.4	0.5	0.2	0.6

Selected Financial Factors (in Percentages)

Debt Ratio 45	44.6	•	272.9	84.4	69.1	54.1	76.8	47.4	68.5	45.5	52.1	76.4	35.6
Return on Total Assets 46	10.7	•	12.2	•	•	•	•	•	•	•	8.6	3.9	14.3
Return on Equity Before Income Taxes 47	16.5	•	•	•	•	•	•	•	•	•	14.2	7.3	19.8
Return on Equity After Income Taxes 48	10.1	•	•	•	•	•	•	•	•	•	6.1	2.5	13.1
Profit Margin (Before Income Tax) 49	16.4	•	2.6	•	•	•	•	•	•	•	12.3	3.2	30.6
Profit Margin (After Income Tax) 50	10.0	•	2.4	•	•	•	•	•	•	•	5.3	1.1	20.2

Table II
Corporations with Net Income

OTHER INFORMATION SERVICES, INTERNET PUBLISHING, WEB PORTALS

MONEY AMOUNTS AND SIZE OF ASSETS IN THOUSANDS OF DOLLARS

Item Description for Accounting Period 7/12 Through 6/13		Total	Zero Assets	Under 500	500 to 1,000	1,000 to 5,000	5,000 to 10,000	10,000 to 25,000	25,000 to 50,000	50,000 to 100,000	100,000 to 250,000	250,000 to 500,000	500,000 to 2,500,000	2,500,000 and over
Number of Enterprises	1	13119	2894	8946	•	740	179	53	11	19	14	7	8	•
Revenues ($ in Thousands)														
Net Sales	2	73174906	288965	2160723	•	5591862	4277037	1167841	789665	1422547	1834760	1834668	7297227	•
Interest	3	423387	1776	25	•	2751	471	407	1241	656	2843	2831	75918	•
Rents	4	142080	0	862	•	827	289	37	0	633	0	3974	8159	•
Royalties	5	824649	0	0	•	0	0	1092	0	1249	199	7542	59626	•
Other Portfolio Income	6	7406000	13257	13205	•	24387	37752	27849	852	35950	5332	4930	36321	•
Other Receipts	7	4743573	6458	143197	•	214	145078	8203	23855	24854	17640	-3303	87886	•
Total Receipts	8	86714595	310456	2318012	•	5620041	4460627	1205429	815613	1485889	1860774	1850642	7565137	•
Average Total Receipts	9	6610	107	259	•	7595	24920	22744	74147	78205	132912	264377	945642	•
Operating Costs/Operating Income (%)														
Cost of Operations	10	28.3	4.1	27.5	•	64.1	60.3	35.8	49.2	17.6	15.5	0.8	31.9	•
Salaries and Wages	11	22.9	24.8	8.4	•	10.1	15.6	16.5	14.3	26.7	21.4	23.3	23.5	•
Taxes Paid	12	2.3	2.5	1.9	•	0.9	3.4	1.7	2.0	2.7	2.6	2.8	2.2	•
Interest Paid	13	2.1	0.2	0.2	•	0.1	0.1	1.0	0.5	1.5	1.3	0.2	1.9	•
Depreciation	14	3.7	0.8	0.4	•	0.3	0.4	1.3	3.4	2.2	4.8	2.1	2.2	•
Amortization and Depletion	15	1.2	0.0	0.1	•	0.1	0.0	0.7	0.3	0.5	0.9	1.9	2.0	•
Pensions and Other Deferred Comp.	16	0.6	0.1	0.2	•	0.1	1.1	0.1	0.2	0.2	0.3	2.1	0.8	•
Employee Benefits	17	1.7	0.9	1.2	•	1.0	2.8	1.7	1.3	1.9	2.5	2.4	2.3	•
Advertising	18	2.0	0.2	3.5	•	1.6	1.8	6.7	1.4	2.2	6.1	10.6	3.8	•
Other Expenses	19	28.9	37.9	26.9	•	10.4	9.5	23.8	22.3	35.2	36.1	26.6	22.4	•
Officers' Compensation	20	1.7	5.0	10.1	•	5.7	2.4	3.0	1.2	1.5	1.3	1.0	2.2	•
Operating Margin	21	4.6	23.4	19.7	•	5.8	2.6	7.7	3.9	7.9	7.2	26.3	4.8	•
Operating Margin Before Officers' Comp.	22	6.4	28.4	29.7	•	11.4	5.0	10.8	5.1	9.4	8.5	27.3	7.0	•

Selected Average Balance Sheet ($ in Thousands)

Net Receivables 23	927	0	2	•	261	3162	3806	6205	15062	20974	39267	129826	•
Inventories 24	34	0	0	•	6	1	31	6	649	296	0	30806	•
Net Property, Plant and Equipment 25	1064	0	4	•	213	439	1148	7840	4718	15765	24048	122384	•
Total Assets 26	9444	0	50	•	1869	6971	14947	40676	69459	147521	368694	1370289	•
Notes and Loans Payable 27	1528	0	30	•	329	468	5906	12054	6931	18031	44105	502492	•
All Other Liabilities 28	1713	0	10	•	622	2336	8622	13859	41508	41215	78465	556570	•
Net Worth 29	6203	0	9	•	918	4167	419	14763	21020	88275	246125	311227	•

Selected Financial Ratios (Times to 1)

Current Ratio 30	2.0	•	2.0	•	1.8	2.6	1.2	2.0	1.0	1.3	2.0	1.1	•
Quick Ratio 31	1.1	•	1.4	•	1.6	2.1	1.1	1.5	0.8	1.2	1.9	0.9	•
Net Sales to Working Capital 32	3.2	•	13.0	•	12.6	6.6	13.6	6.7	139.2	9.9	3.1	27.2	•
Coverage Ratio 33	12.9	127.3	124.4	•	87.4	47.6	13.4	16.4	9.3	7.5	130.1	5.7	•
Total Asset Turnover 34	0.6	•	4.9	•	4.0	3.4	1.5	1.8	1.1	0.9	0.7	0.7	•
Inventory Turnover 35	45.7	•	345.4	•	815.4	11883.0	256.8	6265.7	20.3	68.5	•	9.5	•
Receivables Turnover 36	7.3	•	103.6	•	26.5	9.7	5.9	9.9	6.6	6.5	6.9	7.8	•
Total Liabilities to Net Worth 37	0.5	•	4.3	•	1.0	0.7	34.7	1.8	2.3	0.7	0.5	3.4	•
Current Assets to Working Capital 38	2.0	•	2.0	•	2.2	1.6	5.7	2.0	67.2	4.1	2.0	11.8	•
Current Liabilities to Working Capital 39	1.0	•	1.0	•	1.2	0.6	4.7	1.0	66.2	3.1	1.0	10.8	•
Working Capital to Net Sales 40	0.3	•	0.1	•	0.1	0.2	0.1	0.1	0.0	0.1	0.3	0.0	•
Inventory to Working Capital 41	0.0	•	0.0	•	0.0	0.0	0.0	0.0	1.4	0.0	•	1.0	•
Total Receipts to Cash Flow 42	2.4	1.5	2.0	•	6.5	7.1	3.0	3.6	2.3	2.5	2.0	3.5	•
Cost of Goods to Cash Flow 43	0.7	0.1	0.5	•	4.2	4.3	1.1	1.8	0.4	0.4	0.0	1.1	•
Cash Flow to Total Debt 44	0.7	•	3.0	•	1.2	1.2	0.5	0.8	0.7	0.9	1.1	0.2	•

Selected Financial Factors (in Percentages)

Debt Ratio 45	34.3	•	81.3	•	50.9	40.2	97.2	63.7	69.7	40.2	33.2	77.3	•
Return on Total Assets 46	15.8	•	132.1	•	25.6	24.2	19.2	13.6	15.1	8.9	19.6	7.3	•
Return on Equity Before Income Taxes 47	22.1	•	699.0	•	51.5	39.7	634.4	35.3	44.4	12.8	29.1	26.4	•
Return on Equity After Income Taxes 48	15.3	•	692.9	•	49.4	38.2	526.1	27.6	39.9	10.1	19.3	17.8	•
Profit Margin (Before Income Tax) 49	24.6	30.8	27.0	•	6.3	6.9	12.1	7.3	12.5	8.6	27.4	9.0	•
Profit Margin (After Income Tax) 50	17.1	28.5	26.7	•	6.0	6.7	10.0	5.7	11.2	6.8	18.1	6.1	•

Table I

Corporations with and without Net Income

CREDIT INTERMEDIATION

MONEY AMOUNTS AND SIZE OF ASSETS IN THOUSANDS OF DOLLARS

Item Description for Accounting Period 7/12 Through 6/13	Total	Zero Assets	Under 500	500 to 1,000	1,000 to 5,000	5,000 to 10,000	10,000 to 25,000	25,000 to 50,000	50,000 to 100,000	100,000 to 250,000	250,000 to 500,000	500,000 to 2,500,000	2,500,000 and over
Number of Enterprises **1**	43122	10391	20215	3316	4187	926	919	666	694	870	407	397	133

Revenues ($ in Thousands)													
Net Sales **2**	473434938	44267605	4164875	1626213	4564513	2293091	4934277	5530284	8174230	14922472	13654593	34011856	335290930
Interest **3**	234894533	24319745	17346	6751	124577	58861	190488	388418	1078933	3971924	4646578	12584812	187506099
Rents **4**	1264037	103483	4347	2	2831	3871	4917	2120	10394	20972	40989	66028	1004084
Royalties **5**	1534735	21411	36	0	0	0	0	135	287	31979	18080	4776	1458031
Other Portfolio Income **6**	26667227	4307950	9555	315	53896	3006	23968	79706	128352	476936	1113623	1863034	18606888
Other Receipts **7**	209074406	15515016	4133591	1619145	4383209	2227353	4714904	5059905	6956264	10420661	7835323	19493206	126715828
Total Receipts **8**	473434938	44267605	4164875	1626213	4564513	2293091	4934277	5530284	8174230	14922472	13654593	34011856	335290930
Average Total Receipts **9**	10979	4260	206	490	1090	2476	5369	8304	11778	17152	33549	85672	2520984

Operating Costs/Operating Income (%)													
Cost of Operations **10**	0.3	•	•	•	•	0.1	0.0	0.1	•	0.2	0.1	0.3	0.4
Salaries and Wages **11**	10.3	9.3	18.4	14.1	23.7	24.4	24.3	22.1	22.3	21.9	22.4	20.1	7.3
Taxes Paid **12**	1.7	3.2	3.0	3.8	3.3	3.4	2.9	2.8	2.5	3.0	3.0	2.6	1.2
Interest Paid **13**	30.8	33.9	1.0	2.8	5.8	9.3	6.5	7.3	6.6	9.3	10.7	12.9	36.4
Depreciation **14**	2.8	1.3	0.7	1.5	0.9	2.0	1.2	0.9	1.2	2.5	1.9	2.1	3.2
Amortization and Depletion **15**	0.8	0.2	0.2	0.1	0.5	0.2	0.4	0.5	0.5	0.6	0.5	1.4	0.9
Pensions and Other Deferred Comp. **16**	0.6	0.5	0.5	0.7	1.1	0.3	0.4	0.6	0.5	0.7	0.8	1.0	0.6
Employee Benefits **17**	1.1	1.0	1.6	1.4	0.8	1.8	1.4	1.2	1.5	1.8	2.1	2.6	0.8
Advertising **18**	1.5	0.3	2.3	2.8	1.7	2.5	2.3	2.7	1.3	1.8	1.8	1.5	1.6
Other Expenses **19**	34.3	29.4	39.1	42.5	39.3	53.4	42.1	50.5	48.4	43.8	41.9	37.1	32.9
Officers' Compensation **20**	1.5	1.4	21.4	10.0	9.7	7.4	6.7	6.5	4.2	5.4	3.7	2.7	0.5
Operating Margin **21**	14.3	19.5	11.8	20.4	13.3	•	11.9	4.9	11.0	9.1	11.2	15.7	14.3
Operating Margin Before Officers' Comp. **22**	15.8	20.9	33.3	30.3	22.9	2.6	18.7	11.3	15.2	14.5	14.9	18.3	14.8

Selected Average Balance Sheet ($ in Thousands)

Net Receivables 23	23301	0	14	197	858	2070	7065	11245	24797	59278	101844	239621	5857154
Inventories 24	•	•	•	•	•	•	•	•	•	•	•	•	•
Net Property, Plant and Equipment 25	1668	0	8	95	148	273	376	658	1285	2866	5915	14380	438425
Total Assets 26	192976	0	84	708	2284	7085	15913	35899	72720	159099	347022	999603	56660646
Notes and Loans Payable 27	140278	0	48	436	1188	5432	6707	10786	13287	20199	46238	165138	44452233
All Other Liabilities 28	44453	0	18	62	419	2665	11152	30826	68303	129209	269817	738219	9914655
Net Worth 29	8245	0	18	211	677	-1013	-1947	-5713	-8870	9692	30968	96246	2293758

Selected Financial Ratios (Times to 1)

Current Ratio 30	0.8	•	4.3	3.7	2.4	1.3	1.5	1.0	0.8	0.8	0.6	0.6	0.9
Quick Ratio 31	0.7	•	3.4	2.9	2.0	1.0	1.3	0.8	0.7	0.7	0.6	0.5	0.8
Net Sales to Working Capital 32	•	•	4.7	1.2	1.1	2.4	1.5	•	•	•	•	•	•
Coverage Ratio 33	1.5	1.5	13.2	8.3	3.3	0.5	2.8	1.6	2.6	1.9	2.0	2.2	1.4
Total Asset Turnover 34	0.1	•	2.5	0.7	0.5	0.3	0.3	0.2	0.2	0.1	0.1	0.1	0.0
Inventory Turnover 35	•	•	•	•	•	•	•	•	•	•	•	•	•
Receivables Turnover 36	•	•	•	•	•	•	•	•	•	•	•	•	•
Total Liabilities to Net Worth 37	22.4	•	3.7	2.4	2.4	•	•	•	•	15.4	10.2	9.4	23.7
Current Assets to Working Capital 38	•	•	1.3	1.4	1.7	3.9	3.0	•	•	•	•	•	•
Current Liabilities to Working Capital 39	•	•	0.3	0.4	0.7	2.9	2.0	•	•	•	•	•	•
Working Capital to Net Sales 40	•	•	0.2	0.8	0.9	0.4	0.7	•	•	•	•	•	•
Inventory to Working Capital 41	•	•	•	•	0.0	0.0	0.0	•	•	•	•	•	•
Total Receipts to Cash Flow 42	2.2	2.4	2.2	1.9	2.2	2.3	2.3	2.2	2.0	2.3	2.4	2.1	2.2
Cost of Goods to Cash Flow 43	0.0	•	•	•	•	0.0	0.0	0.0	•	0.0	0.0	0.0	0.0
Cash Flow to Total Debt 44	0.0	•	1.4	0.5	0.3	0.1	0.1	0.1	0.1	0.1	0.0	0.0	0.0

Selected Financial Factors (in Percentages)

Debt Ratio 45	95.7	•	78.6	70.2	70.4	114.3	112.2	115.9	112.2	93.9	91.1	90.4	96.0
Return on Total Assets 46	2.6	•	31.4	16.0	9.1	1.6	6.2	2.8	2.8	1.9	2.0	2.4	2.3
Return on Equity Before Income Taxes 47	19.1	•	135.5	47.3	21.4	11.6	•	•	•	14.6	11.3	13.3	16.0
Return on Equity After Income Taxes 48	15.1	•	133.7	46.0	19.8	13.0	•	•	•	10.9	8.5	9.5	12.5
Profit Margin (Before Income Tax) 49	14.3	18.3	11.8	20.4	13.3	•	11.9	4.7	10.4	8.3	10.5	14.9	14.6
Profit Margin (After Income Tax) 50	11.3	15.6	11.7	19.8	12.3	•	11.2	3.7	9.2	6.1	7.9	10.7	11.4

Table II

Corporations with Net Income

CREDIT INTERMEDIATION

MONEY AMOUNTS AND SIZE OF ASSETS IN THOUSANDS OF DOLLARS

Item Description for Accounting Period 7/12 Through 6/13	Total	Zero Assets	Under 500	500 to 1,000	1,000 to 5,000	5,000 to 10,000	10,000 to 25,000	25,000 to 50,000	50,000 to 100,000	100,000 to 250,000	250,000 to 500,000	500,000 to 2,500,000	2,500,000 and over
Number of Enterprises 1	24986	4134	12084	2120	3019	579	652	446	510	667	326	337	112

Revenues ($ in Thousands)

Net Sales 2	434581642	34215358	3698021	1446834	4209157	1599968	3993797	3823699	5865576	11855748	11974676	28664257	323234551
Interest 3	222316803	18159234	8454	6102	99512	50380	86810	253925	773625	3017771	3864667	10996073	185000252
Rents 4	956377	59476	4347	2	2781	1554	3954	1254	7355	14716	27091	60500	773346
Royalties 5	1510915	116	0	0	0	0	0	19	8	31972	18080	3611	1457108
Other Portfolio Income 6	25273502	3609180	8420	106	48018	1352	17507	70634	108568	413346	1054828	1524326	18417220
Other Receipts 7	184524045	12387352	3676800	1440624	4058846	1546682	3885526	3497867	4976020	8377943	7010010	16079747	117586625
Total Receipts 8	434581642	34215358	3698021	1446834	4209157	1599968	3993797	3823699	5865576	11855748	11974676	28664257	323234551
Average Total Receipts 9	17393	8277	306	682	1394	2763	6125	8573	11501	17775	36732	85057	2886023

Operating Costs/Operating Income (%)

Cost of Operations 10	0.3	•	•	•	•	•	0.0	0.1	•	0.1	0.1	0.3	0.3
Salaries and Wages 11	9.8	7.8	18.3	11.6	22.3	23.0	26.0	25.4	27.9	24.0	22.4	20.6	7.1
Taxes Paid 12	1.7	3.4	2.9	3.3	3.0	3.2	3.1	3.1	3.1	3.2	3.0	2.8	1.2
Interest Paid 13	31.4	31.7	0.5	1.4	4.9	8.2	5.5	8.5	7.3	8.6	9.2	12.1	36.7
Depreciation 14	2.9	1.3	0.5	1.0	0.8	1.0	0.9	0.9	1.2	2.3	1.8	2.3	3.3
Amortization and Depletion 15	0.7	0.2	0.1	0.1	0.2	0.1	0.3	0.4	0.5	0.6	0.5	1.1	0.7
Pensions and Other Deferred Comp. 16	0.6	0.5	0.5	0.7	1.2	0.3	0.4	0.4	0.6	0.7	0.7	1.1	0.6
Employee Benefits 17	1.0	1.0	1.6	1.2	0.8	1.8	1.4	1.2	1.7	1.9	1.9	2.8	0.8
Advertising 18	1.5	0.2	2.4	2.8	1.5	3.0	2.5	3.5	1.6	2.0	1.8	1.5	1.5
Other Expenses 19	31.2	21.2	36.4	35.0	34.2	34.8	29.4	29.3	30.6	31.0	34.7	31.9	32.1
Officers' Compensation 20	1.4	1.0	19.1	9.7	9.9	9.9	7.2	7.3	5.0	5.7	3.6	2.9	0.5
Operating Margin 21	17.5	31.7	17.7	33.0	21.4	14.7	23.3	20.1	20.5	19.9	20.2	20.7	15.3
Operating Margin Before Officers' Comp. 22	18.9	32.7	36.8	42.8	31.2	24.6	30.5	27.3	25.5	25.6	23.8	23.6	15.8

Selected Average Balance Sheet ($ in Thousands)

Net Receivables 23	37521	0	15	206	782	2709	8215	13902	27219	63819	104635	239082	6698709
Inventories 24	•	•	•	•	•	•	•	•	•	•	•	•	•
Net Property, Plant and Equipment 25	2714	0	11	46	110	206	354	680	1201	2850	5968	14980	509800
Total Assets 26	319494	0	89	767	2162	6826	15922	36052	72905	160130	347410	998453	65620653
Notes and Loans Payable 27	236766	0	24	246	900	3921	6811	12696	11930	18957	45179	138563	51962375
All Other Liabilities 28	66380	0	11	76	381	1370	4486	18875	49151	119125	256501	712511	10863614
Net Worth 29	16348	0	53	445	881	1535	4625	4481	11824	22048	45731	147378	2794664

Selected Financial Ratios (Times to 1)

Current Ratio 30	0.9	•	6.3	3.7	2.4	1.7	1.6	1.0	0.9	0.8	0.6	0.6	0.9
Quick Ratio 31	0.8	•	5.6	2.8	2.0	1.4	1.5	0.9	0.8	0.8	0.6	0.5	0.8
Net Sales to Working Capital 32	•	•	6.4	1.4	1.5	1.4	1.4	10.4	•	•	•	•	•
Coverage Ratio 33	1.6	2.0	39.2	24.2	5.4	2.8	5.2	3.3	3.7	3.2	3.1	2.6	1.4
Total Asset Turnover 34	0.1	•	3.5	0.9	0.6	0.4	0.4	0.2	0.2	0.1	0.1	0.1	0.0
Inventory Turnover 35	•	•	•	•	•	•	•	•	•	•	•	•	•
Receivables Turnover 36	•	•	•	•	•	•	•	•	•	•	•	•	•
Total Liabilities to Net Worth 37	18.5	•	0.7	0.7	1.5	3.4	2.4	7.0	5.2	6.3	6.6	5.8	22.5
Current Assets to Working Capital 38	•	•	1.2	1.4	1.7	2.3	2.6	27.5	•	•	•	•	•
Current Liabilities to Working Capital 39	•	•	0.2	0.4	0.7	1.3	1.6	26.5	•	•	•	•	•
Working Capital to Net Sales 40	•	•	0.2	0.7	0.7	0.7	0.7	0.1	•	•	•	•	•
Inventory to Working Capital 41	•	•	•	•	•	•	0.0	0.0	•	•	•	•	•
Total Receipts to Cash Flow 42	2.1	2.1	2.0	1.7	2.0	2.2	2.0	2.2	2.1	2.1	2.2	2.1	2.2
Cost of Goods to Cash Flow 43	0.0	•	•	•	•	•	0.0	0.0	•	0.0	0.0	0.0	0.0
Cash Flow to Total Debt 44	0.0	•	4.2	1.3	0.5	0.2	0.3	0.1	0.1	0.1	0.1	0.0	0.0

Selected Financial Factors (in Percentages)

Debt Ratio 45	94.9	•	40.0	42.0	59.3	77.5	71.0	87.6	83.8	86.2	86.8	85.2	95.7
Return on Total Assets 46	2.7	•	62.7	30.6	16.9	9.3	11.1	6.7	4.3	3.1	3.0	2.7	2.3
Return on Equity Before Income Taxes 47	18.7	•	101.9	50.6	33.8	26.4	30.9	38.0	19.2	15.3	15.6	11.5	16.1
Return on Equity After Income Taxes 48	15.3	•	100.9	49.6	32.1	24.9	29.7	35.3	17.6	13.1	13.2	8.6	12.7
Profit Margin (Before Income Tax) 49	17.6	31.6	17.7	33.0	21.4	14.7	23.3	19.9	19.8	19.0	19.4	20.0	15.6
Profit Margin (After Income Tax) 50	14.3	28.1	17.5	32.4	20.3	13.8	22.4	18.4	18.1	16.3	16.5	14.9	12.3

Table I

Corporations with and without Net Income

COMMERCIAL BANKING

MONEY AMOUNTS AND SIZE OF ASSETS IN THOUSANDS OF DOLLARS

Item Description for Accounting Period 7/12 Through 6/13		Total	Zero Assets	Under 500	500 to 1,000	1,000 to 5,000	5,000 to 10,000	10,000 to 25,000	25,000 to 50,000	50,000 to 100,000	100,000 to 250,000	250,000 to 500,000	500,000 to 2,500,000	2,500,000 and over
Number of Enterprises	1	1674	217	0	•	•	18	150	205	351	449	154	85	20
Revenues ($ in Thousands)														
Net Sales	2	74537967	40200015	0	•	•	3960	613066	1139301	2677149	4730575	2717109	4879757	17542484
Interest	3	40062455	23740075	0	•	•	1124	57554	130476	558650	1949234	1447926	2295174	9874281
Rents	4	393433	98808	0	•	•	0	546	279	3030	6285	18821	8791	256831
Royalties	5	32221	21409	0	•	•	0	0	0	8	10710	0	0	93
Other Portfolio Income	6	3861981	2638331	0	•	•	0	2893	11449	66227	205385	159515	248211	529791
Other Receipts	7	30187877	13701392	0	•	•	2836	552073	997097	2049234	2558961	1090847	2327581	6881488
Total Receipts	8	74537967	40200015	0	•	•	3960	613066	1139301	2677149	4730575	2717109	4879757	17542484
Average Total Receipts	9	44527	185254	•	•	•	220	4087	5558	7627	10536	17644	57409	877124
Operating Costs/Operating Income (%)														
Cost of Operations	10	0.1	•	•	•	•	•	•	•	•	•	0.6	•	0.2
Salaries and Wages	11	12.2	8.7	•	•	•	0.9	2.7	4.6	7.3	13.4	18.1	16.6	19.4
Taxes Paid	12	3.0	3.3	•	•	•	0.2	0.7	0.8	1.4	2.5	3.4	2.4	3.0
Interest Paid	13	24.7	36.6	•	•	•	15.2	2.8	2.8	5.5	9.9	12.0	13.4	11.5
Depreciation	14	1.9	1.3	•	•	•	•	0.3	0.4	1.0	1.9	2.3	1.8	3.4
Amortization and Depletion	15	1.0	0.2	•	•	•	•	0.1	0.4	0.1	0.5	0.5	0.8	3.2
Pensions and Other Deferred Comp.	16	0.7	0.5	•	•	•	•	0.0	0.4	0.3	0.6	0.8	0.6	1.3
Employee Benefits	17	1.5	0.9	•	•	•	•	0.5	0.9	1.4	2.1	2.6	2.1	2.2
Advertising	18	0.4	0.1	•	•	•	•	0.1	0.4	0.4	0.6	0.9	0.7	0.8
Other Expenses	19	37.6	28.9	•	•	•	1645.2	99.3	94.3	75.3	57.9	51.4	46.4	35.3
Officers' Compensation	20	2.2	1.5	•	•	•	11.7	1.5	2.8	4.2	6.1	7.1	3.1	1.7
Operating Margin	21	14.8	17.9	•	•	•	•	•	•	3.1	4.5	0.5	12.0	18.0
Operating Margin Before Officers' Comp.	22	17.0	19.4	•	•	•	•	•	•	7.3	10.6	7.5	15.2	19.7

Selected Average Balance Sheet ($ in Thousands)

Net Receivables 23	184377	0	•	•	•	633	3672	12396	33270	86129	180298	462301	9406581
Inventories 24	•	•	•	•	•	•	•	•	•	•	•	•	•
Net Property, Plant and Equipment 25	3643	0	•	•	•	0	54	270	1044	2623	5144	10596	139960
Total Assets 26	368218	0	•	•	•	8270	18380	36400	72272	158980	338073	981339	18686444
Notes and Loans Payable 27	26573	0	•	•	•	667	0	973	1279	4358	8697	37953	1863690
All Other Liabilities 28	314167	0	•	•	•	44619	43615	60479	91965	152710	318689	951920	13749828
Net Worth 29	27477	0	•	•	•	-37016	-25235	-25052	-20972	1912	10687	-8534	3072926

Selected Financial Ratios (Times to 1)

Current Ratio 30	1.0	•	•	•	•	2.3	1.0	1.0	0.9	1.0	0.9	0.8	1.0
Quick Ratio 31	0.9	•	•	•	•	1.1	0.8	0.9	0.9	0.9	0.9	0.8	1.0
Net Sales to Working Capital 32	•	•	•	•	•	0.1	•	•	•	•	•	•	11.3
Coverage Ratio 33	1.5	1.5	•	•	•	•	•	•	1.3	1.3	0.8	1.8	2.3
Total Asset Turnover 34	0.1	•	•	•	•	0.0	0.2	0.2	0.1	0.1	0.1	0.1	0.0
Inventory Turnover 35	•	•	•	•	•	•	•	•	•	•	•	•	•
Receivables Turnover 36	•	•	•	•	•	•	•	•	•	•	•	•	•
Total Liabilities to Net Worth 37	12.4	•	•	•	•	•	•	•	•	82.1	30.6	•	5.1
Current Assets to Working Capital 38	•	•	•	•	•	1.8	•	•	•	•	•	•	170.1
Current Liabilities to Working Capital 39	•	•	•	•	•	0.8	•	•	•	•	•	•	169.1
Working Capital to Net Sales 40	•	•	•	•	•	12.4	•	•	•	•	•	•	0.1
Inventory to Working Capital 41	•	•	•	•	•	•	•	•	•	•	•	•	0.0
Total Receipts to Cash Flow 42	2.3	2.6	•	•	•	•	2.7	1.6	1.8	2.1	2.9	2.1	2.1
Cost of Goods to Cash Flow 43	0.0	•	•	•	•	•	•	•	•	•	0.0	•	0.0
Cash Flow to Total Debt 44	0.1	•	•	•	•	•	0.0	0.1	0.0	0.0	0.0	0.0	0.0

Selected Financial Factors (in Percentages)

Debt Ratio 45	92.5	•	•	•	•	547.6	237.3	168.8	129.0	98.8	96.8	100.9	83.6
Return on Total Assets 46	4.6	•	•	•	•	•	•	•	0.7	0.8	0.5	1.4	1.3
Return on Equity Before Income Taxes 47	22.0	•	•	•	•	9.4	1.3	1.9	•	14.4	•	•	4.4
Return on Equity After Income Taxes 48	16.6	•	•	•	•	9.4	1.4	2.0	•	3.8	•	•	2.9
Profit Margin (Before Income Tax) 49	13.6	17.5	•	•	•	•	•	•	1.6	2.6	•	10.3	15.5
Profit Margin (After Income Tax) 50	10.2	14.5	•	•	•	•	•	•	0.9	0.7	•	7.2	10.3

Table II

Corporations with Net Income

COMMERCIAL BANKING

MONEY AMOUNTS AND SIZE OF ASSETS IN THOUSANDS OF DOLLARS

Item Description for Accounting Period 7/12 Through 6/13	Total	Zero Assets	Under 500	500 to 1,000	1,000 to 5,000	5,000 to 10,000	10,000 to 25,000	25,000 to 50,000	50,000 to 100,000	100,000 to 250,000	250,000 to 500,000	500,000 to 2,500,000	2,500,000 and over
Number of Enterprises 1	1079	120	0	•	0	0	50	100	242	347	127	73	•

Revenues ($ in Thousands)

Net Sales 2	58471272	31082079	0	•	0	0	87094	309017	926910	2984760	2218683	3469459	•
Interest 3	32652887	17713878	0	•	0	0	28483	72532	388756	1543789	1202999	1946211	•
Rents 4	336185	55341	0	•	0	0	149	68	1047	4861	11375	6710	•
Royalties 5	10919	113	0	•	0	0	0	0	8	10703	0	0	•
Other Portfolio Income 6	3399552	2265122	0	•	0	0	1528	8336	56142	183377	126727	229612	•
Other Receipts 7	22071729	11047625	0	•	0	0	56934	228081	480957	1242030	877582	1286926	•
Total Receipts 8	58471272	31082079	0	•	0	0	87094	309017	926910	2984760	2218683	3469459	•
Average Total Receipts 9	54190	259017	•	•	•	•	1742	3090	3830	8602	17470	47527	•

Operating Costs/Operating Income (%)

Cost of Operations 10	0.1	•	•	•	•	•	•	•	•	•	0.7	•	•
Salaries and Wages 11	12.7	7.4	•	•	•	•	6.3	13.4	14.8	17.4	18.3	19.9	•
Taxes Paid 12	3.3	3.5	•	•	•	•	1.8	2.2	3.1	3.3	3.5	3.0	•
Interest Paid 13	23.9	34.3	•	•	•	•	5.4	6.7	12.0	12.3	12.0	15.2	•
Depreciation 14	2.1	1.3	•	•	•	•	1.0	1.0	2.1	2.3	2.2	2.1	•
Amortization and Depletion 15	1.2	0.2	•	•	•	•	0.1	0.5	0.2	0.8	0.5	1.1	•
Pensions and Other Deferred Comp. 16	0.8	0.5	•	•	•	•	0.3	0.4	0.7	0.8	0.8	0.7	•
Employee Benefits 17	1.6	0.9	•	•	•	•	2.1	2.2	3.2	2.8	2.7	2.5	•
Advertising 18	0.4	0.0	•	•	•	•	0.4	1.4	0.7	0.8	0.9	0.8	•
Other Expenses 19	26.5	20.5	•	•	•	•	24.8	53.3	32.1	31.5	24.5	29.8	•
Officers' Compensation 20	2.2	1.0	•	•	•	•	7.3	7.4	9.6	8.1	7.3	4.0	•
Operating Margin 21	25.3	30.3	•	•	•	•	50.4	11.6	21.4	19.9	26.5	20.7	•
Operating Margin Before Officers' Comp. 22	27.5	31.3	•	•	•	•	57.6	19.0	31.0	28.0	33.8	24.7	•

Selected Average Balance Sheet ($ in Thousands)

Net Receivables 23	265280	0	•	•	•	•	7679	18955	38614	93218	191450	440472	•
Inventories 24	•	•	•	•	•	•	•	•	•	•	•	•	•
Net Property, Plant and Equipment 25	4935	0	•	•	•	•	116	378	1051	2706	4841	10102	•
Total Assets 26	518627	0	•	•	•	•	19662	36889	73047	162002	340766	956831	•
Notes and Loans Payable 27	38929	0	•	•	•	•	0	997	1037	3566	8028	29075	•
All Other Liabilities 28	406113	0	•	•	•	•	20344	37699	64408	140217	296397	843733	•
Net Worth 29	73584	0	•	•	•	•	-683	-1807	7602	18218	36341	84023	•

Selected Financial Ratios (Times to 1)

Current Ratio 30	1.0	•	•	•	•	•	1.1	1.1	1.0	1.0	0.9	0.9	•
Quick Ratio 31	1.0	•	•	•	•	•	1.0	1.0	1.0	1.0	0.9	0.9	•
Net Sales to Working Capital 32	•	•	•	•	•	•	1.2	1.9	36.4	•	•	•	•
Coverage Ratio 33	2.0	1.9	•	•	•	•	10.0	2.4	2.5	2.4	3.0	2.2	•
Total Asset Turnover 34	0.1	•	•	•	•	•	0.1	0.1	0.1	0.1	0.1	0.0	•
Inventory Turnover 35	•	•	•	•	•	•	•	•	•	•	•	•	•
Receivables Turnover 36	•	•	•	•	•	•	•	•	•	•	•	•	•
Total Liabilities to Net Worth 37	6.0	•	•	•	•	•	•	•	8.6	7.9	8.4	10.4	•
Current Assets to Working Capital 38	•	•	•	•	•	•	12.2	20.0	599.8	•	•	•	•
Current Liabilities to Working Capital 39	•	•	•	•	•	•	11.2	19.0	598.8	•	•	•	•
Working Capital to Net Sales 40	•	•	•	•	•	•	0.8	0.5	0.0	•	•	•	•
Inventory to Working Capital 41	•	•	•	•	•	•	•	•	•	•	•	•	•
Total Receipts to Cash Flow 42	2.1	2.1	•	•	•	•	1.4	1.7	2.2	2.1	2.1	2.2	•
Cost of Goods to Cash Flow 43	0.0	•	•	•	•	•	•	•	•	•	0.0	•	•
Cash Flow to Total Debt 44	0.1	•	•	•	•	•	0.1	0.0	0.0	0.0	0.0	0.0	•

Selected Financial Factors (in Percentages)

Debt Ratio 45	85.8	•	•	•	•	•	103.5	104.9	89.6	88.8	89.3	91.2	•
Return on Total Assets 46	5.0	•	•	•	•	•	4.8	1.4	1.6	1.6	1.8	1.7	•
Return on Equity Before Income Taxes 47	17.7	•	•	•	•	•	•	•	8.9	8.1	11.5	10.4	•
Return on Equity After Income Taxes 48	14.6	•	•	•	•	•	•	•	7.9	6.7	9.0	7.9	•
Profit Margin (Before Income Tax) 49	24.0	30.2	•	•	•	•	49.0	9.7	17.7	17.1	23.8	18.3	•
Profit Margin (After Income Tax) 50	19.8	26.4	•	•	•	•	47.9	8.2	15.7	14.1	18.6	13.9	•

Table I

Corporations with and without Net Income

SAVINGS INSTITUTIONS AND OTHER DEPOSITORY CREDIT

MONEY AMOUNTS AND SIZE OF ASSETS IN THOUSANDS OF DOLLARS

Item Description for Accounting Period 7/12 Through 6/13		Total	Zero Assets	Under 500	500 to 1,000	1,000 to 5,000	5,000 to 10,000	10,000 to 25,000	25,000 to 50,000	50,000 to 100,000	100,000 to 250,000	250,000 to 500,000	500,000 to 2,500,000	2,500,000 and over
Number of Enterprises	1	1116	49	•	•	•	0	23	103	141	250	186	218	51

Revenues ($ in Thousands)

		Total	Zero Assets	Under 500	500 to 1,000	1,000 to 5,000	5,000 to 10,000	10,000 to 25,000	25,000 to 50,000	50,000 to 100,000	100,000 to 250,000	250,000 to 500,000	500,000 to 2,500,000	2,500,000 and over
Net Sales	2	52728871	1008464	•	•	•	0	13436	157436	521794	2292495	3654130	10932578	34050968
Interest	3	32686590	509136	•	•	•	0	10372	132909	360012	1456301	2382364	7199183	20632777
Rents	4	555503	697	•	•	•	0	47	720	5683	8033	12279	44182	483854
Royalties	5	5438	2	•	•	•	0	0	19	0	0	0	4776	640
Other Portfolio Income	6	5620164	419348	•	•	•	0	1373	8630	25554	216397	638197	978968	3326499
Other Receipts	7	13861176	79281	•	•	•	0	1644	15158	130545	611764	621290	2705469	9607198
Total Receipts	8	52728871	1008464	•	•	•	0	13436	157436	521794	2292495	3654130	10932578	34050968
Average Total Receipts	9	47248	20581	•	•	•	•	584	1529	3701	9170	19646	50149	667666

Operating Costs/Operating Income (%)

		Total	Zero Assets	Under 500	500 to 1,000	1,000 to 5,000	5,000 to 10,000	10,000 to 25,000	25,000 to 50,000	50,000 to 100,000	100,000 to 250,000	250,000 to 500,000	500,000 to 2,500,000	2,500,000 and over
Cost of Operations	10	0.0	•	•	•	•	•	•	•	•	0.5	•	•	•
Salaries and Wages	11	16.0	9.7	•	•	•	•	16.8	17.2	16.5	19.0	18.3	19.9	14.5
Taxes Paid	12	2.8	1.0	•	•	•	•	3.3	4.3	3.5	3.5	3.1	3.1	2.6
Interest Paid	13	18.6	13.3	•	•	•	•	17.3	17.0	17.9	15.4	15.7	15.8	20.2
Depreciation	14	2.8	1.1	•	•	•	•	2.2	2.6	2.3	3.6	2.3	2.2	3.1
Amortization and Depletion	15	1.5	0.1	•	•	•	•	0.3	0.3	0.1	0.4	0.2	0.6	2.1
Pensions and Other Deferred Comp.	16	1.6	1.3	•	•	•	•	0.6	5.5	2.5	1.8	2.1	2.1	1.4
Employee Benefits	17	2.5	3.8	•	•	•	•	3.1	4.3	3.2	3.2	3.4	3.1	2.1
Advertising	18	1.3	1.2	•	•	•	•	2.0	1.2	0.9	1.1	1.1	1.4	1.3
Other Expenses	19	35.5	24.9	•	•	•	•	57.7	104.5	46.7	45.4	35.6	35.6	34.5
Officers' Compensation	20	2.2	0.8	•	•	•	•	7.8	13.4	8.1	5.6	4.1	3.4	1.2
Operating Margin	21	15.3	42.9	•	•	•	•	•	•	•	0.4	14.1	12.9	17.1
Operating Margin Before Officers' Comp.	22	17.4	43.7	•	•	•	•	•	•	6.5	6.0	18.2	16.2	18.3

Selected Average Balance Sheet ($ in Thousands)

Net Receivables 23	87402	0	•	•	•	•	593	1548	5064	12708	24704	68088	1451490
Inventories 24	•	•	•	•	•	•	•	•	•	•	•	•	•
Net Property, Plant and Equipment 25	9739	0	•	•	•	•	200	557	1270	3207	6436	14900	105468
Total Assets 26	882591	0	•	•	•	•	13986	37780	76064	162619	352952	962194	12820359
Notes and Loans Payable 27	96516	0	•	•	•	•	266	836	3215	8422	21658	54325	1748816
All Other Liabilities 28	703035	0	•	•	•	•	57174	36722	66789	142214	292142	827381	9799177
Net Worth 29	83040	0	•	•	•	•	-43454	222	6059	11983	39152	80488	1272366

Selected Financial Ratios (Times to 1)

Current Ratio 30	0.3	•	•	•	•	•	0.5	0.3	0.4	0.3	0.3	0.3	0.3
Quick Ratio 31	0.3	•	•	•	•	•	0.5	0.3	0.3	0.3	0.3	0.3	0.3
Net Sales to Working Capital 32	•	•	•	•	•	•	•	•	•	•	•	•	•
Coverage Ratio 33	1.8	4.2	•	•	•	•	0.3	•	0.8	0.9	1.8	1.7	1.8
Total Asset Turnover 34	0.1	•	•	•	•	•	0.0	0.0	0.0	0.1	0.1	0.1	0.1
Inventory Turnover 35	•	•	•	•	•	•	•	•	•	•	•	•	•
Receivables Turnover 36	•	•	•	•	•	•	•	•	•	•	•	•	•
Total Liabilities to Net Worth 37	9.6	•	•	•	•	•	•	169.0	11.6	12.6	8.0	11.0	9.1
Current Assets to Working Capital 38	•	•	•	•	•	•	•	•	•	•	•	•	•
Current Liabilities to Working Capital 39	•	•	•	•	•	•	•	•	•	•	•	•	•
Working Capital to Net Sales 40	•	•	•	•	•	•	•	•	•	•	•	•	•
Inventory to Working Capital 41	•	•	•	•	•	•	•	•	•	•	•	•	•
Total Receipts to Cash Flow 42	2.2	1.7	•	•	•	•	2.4	•	2.6	2.6	3.5	2.3	2.1
Cost of Goods to Cash Flow 43	0.0	•	•	•	•	•	•	•	•	0.0	•	•	•
Cash Flow to Total Debt 44	0.0	•	•	•	•	•	0.0	•	0.0	0.0	0.0	0.0	0.0

Selected Financial Factors (in Percentages)

Debt Ratio 45	90.6	•	•	•	•	•	410.7	99.4	92.0	92.6	88.9	91.6	90.1
Return on Total Assets 46	1.8	•	•	•	•	•	0.2	•	0.7	0.8	1.6	1.4	1.9
Return on Equity Before Income Taxes 47	8.2	•	•	•	•	•	0.2	•	•	•	6.4	7.3	8.5
Return on Equity After Income Taxes 48	5.6	•	•	•	•	•	0.2	•	•	•	4.9	4.7	5.9
Profit Margin (Before Income Tax) 49	14.3	42.8	•	•	•	•	•	•	•	•	12.7	11.7	16.3
Profit Margin (After Income Tax) 50	9.8	42.1	•	•	•	•	•	•	•	•	9.7	7.6	11.2

Table II

Corporations with Net Income

SAVINGS INSTITUTIONS AND OTHER DEPOSITORY CREDIT

MONEY AMOUNTS AND SIZE OF ASSETS IN THOUSANDS OF DOLLARS

Item Description for Accounting Period 7/12 Through 6/13	Total	Zero Assets	Under 500	500 to 1,000	1,000 to 5,000	5,000 to 10,000	10,000 to 25,000	25,000 to 50,000	50,000 to 100,000	100,000 to 250,000	250,000 to 500,000	500,000 to 2,500,000	2,500,000 and over
Number of Enterprises 1	850	11	•	•	31	0	16	62	102	184	148	190	•
Revenues ($ in Thousands)													
Net Sales 2	45513874	862646	•	•	34637	0	10227	117747	355724	1579910	2974412	8992823	•
Interest 3	28666993	416001	•	•	51	0	8787	84851	268810	1055155	1924876	6371578	•
Rents 4	538909	185	•	•	0	0	47	164	4919	3885	8621	41215	•
Royalties 5	3632	2	•	•	0	0	0	19	0	0	0	3611	•
Other Portfolio Income 6	5378334	415752	•	•	0	0	1055	6485	18908	186766	612920	824252	•
Other Receipts 7	10926006	30706	•	•	34586	0	338	26228	63087	334104	427995	1752167	•
Total Receipts 8	45513874	862646	•	•	34637	0	10227	117747	355724	1579910	2974412	8992823	•
Average Total Receipts 9	53546	78422	•	•	1117	•	639	1899	3487	8586	20097	47331	•
Operating Costs/Operating Income (%)													
Cost of Operations 10	•	•	•	•	•	•	•	•	•	•	•	•	•
Salaries and Wages 11	16.3	7.6	•	•	33.4	•	18.5	13.3	15.9	19.6	17.6	20.8	•
Taxes Paid 12	2.9	0.7	•	•	2.9	•	3.4	3.9	3.8	3.7	3.1	3.3	•
Interest Paid 13	18.5	12.9	•	•	•	•	18.4	15.1	19.7	15.3	15.0	16.7	•
Depreciation 14	3.0	1.0	•	•	3.7	•	2.2	2.0	2.3	4.4	2.3	2.4	•
Amortization and Depletion 15	1.2	0.0	•	•	•	•	0.4	0.1	0.1	0.5	0.2	0.5	•
Pensions and Other Deferred Comp. 16	1.6	0.5	•	•	•	•	0.7	2.1	2.3	2.0	1.9	2.3	•
Employee Benefits 17	2.5	3.5	•	•	3.1	•	3.6	3.8	3.5	3.3	3.2	3.3	•
Advertising 18	1.1	1.3	•	•	0.4	•	2.6	1.0	1.0	1.2	1.1	1.5	•
Other Expenses 19	28.5	14.9	•	•	52.8	•	24.4	27.0	25.0	24.9	30.2	27.3	•
Officers' Compensation 20	2.2	0.3	•	•	•	•	10.3	12.9	8.7	6.2	3.9	3.6	•
Operating Margin 21	22.2	57.2	•	•	3.7	•	15.4	18.8	17.8	18.8	21.4	18.3	•
Operating Margin Before Officers' Comp. 22	24.4	57.5	•	•	3.7	•	25.7	31.8	26.5	25.0	25.3	22.0	•

Selected Average Balance Sheet ($ in Thousands)

Net Receivables 23	101564	0	•	•	104	•	223	1357	4197	12463	25374	65831	•
Inventories 24	•	•	•	•	•	•	•	•	•	•	•	•	•
Net Property, Plant and Equipment 25	11276	0	•	•	42	•	287	560	1111	2763	6391	15156	•
Total Assets 26	1010160	0	•	•	2076	•	14463	38205	75370	160807	351461	962365	•
Notes and Loans Payable 27	113460	0	•	•	0	•	383	1137	2905	6941	20165	53087	•
All Other Liabilities 28	771635	0	•	•	107	•	9986	31009	60766	132655	286261	798855	•
Net Worth 29	125065	0	•	•	1969	•	4094	6059	11699	21211	45035	110423	•

Selected Financial Ratios (Times to 1)

Current Ratio 30	0.3	•	•	•	19.1	•	0.3	0.3	0.3	0.3	0.3	0.3	•
Quick Ratio 31	0.3	•	•	•	18.6	•	0.3	0.3	0.3	0.3	0.3	0.3	•
Net Sales to Working Capital 32	•	•	•	•	0.6	•	•	•	•	•	•	•	•
Coverage Ratio 33	2.1	5.4	•	•	•	•	1.8	2.2	1.8	2.1	2.3	2.0	•
Total Asset Turnover 34	0.1	•	•	•	0.5	•	0.0	0.0	0.0	0.1	0.1	0.0	•
Inventory Turnover 35	•	•	•	•	•	•	•	•	•	•	•	•	•
Receivables Turnover 36	•	•	•	•	•	•	•	•	•	•	•	•	•
Total Liabilities to Net Worth 37	7.1	•	•	•	0.1	•	2.5	5.3	5.4	6.6	6.8	7.7	•
Current Assets to Working Capital 38	•	•	•	•	1.1	•	•	•	•	•	•	•	•
Current Liabilities to Working Capital 39	•	•	•	•	0.1	•	•	•	•	•	•	•	•
Working Capital to Net Sales 40	•	•	•	•	1.7	•	•	•	•	•	•	•	•
Inventory to Working Capital 41	•	•	•	•	•	•	•	•	•	•	•	•	•
Total Receipts to Cash Flow 42	2.2	1.5	•	•	2.7	•	2.8	2.4	2.5	2.5	3.5	2.4	•
Cost of Goods to Cash Flow 43	•	•	•	•	•	•	•	•	•	•	•	•	•
Cash Flow to Total Debt 44	0.0	•	•	•	3.9	•	0.0	0.0	0.0	0.0	0.0	0.0	•

Selected Financial Factors (in Percentages)

Debt Ratio 45	87.6	•	•	•	5.2	•	71.7	84.1	84.5	86.8	87.2	88.5	•
Return on Total Assets 46	2.1	•	•	•	2.0	•	1.5	1.6	1.6	1.7	2.0	1.7	•
Return on Equity Before Income Taxes 47	9.0	•	•	•	2.1	•	2.3	5.5	4.7	7.0	8.8	7.3	•
Return on Equity After Income Taxes 48	6.8	•	•	•	1.8	•	2.0	4.5	3.4	5.2	7.2	5.2	•
Profit Margin (Before Income Tax) 49	21.1	57.2	•	•	3.7	•	14.5	17.7	15.7	17.2	19.8	17.0	•
Profit Margin (After Income Tax) 50	15.9	56.4	•	•	3.1	•	13.1	14.3	11.5	12.8	16.1	12.0	•

Table I

Corporations with and without Net Income

CREDIT CARD ISSUING AND OTHER CONSUMER CREDIT

MONEY AMOUNTS AND SIZE OF ASSETS IN THOUSANDS OF DOLLARS

Item Description for Accounting Period 7/12 Through 6/13	Total	Zero Assets	Under 500	500 to 1,000	1,000 to 5,000	5,000 to 10,000	10,000 to 25,000	25,000 to 50,000	50,000 to 100,000	100,000 to 250,000	250,000 to 500,000	500,000 to 2,500,000	2,500,000 and over
Number of Enterprises 1	•	2620	3568	1157	1219	228	319	102	51	50	28	27	•

Revenues ($ in Thousands)

	Total	Zero Assets	Under 500	500 to 1,000	1,000 to 5,000	5,000 to 10,000	10,000 to 25,000	25,000 to 50,000	50,000 to 100,000	100,000 to 250,000	250,000 to 500,000	500,000 to 2,500,000	2,500,000 and over
Net Sales 2	•	638346	506741	266137	1028075	543119	1809745	1021478	1239194	1977664	3434300	6139002	•
Interest 3	•	46759	437	315	18826	41951	59862	40851	59770	327577	596496	1743412	•
Rents 4	•	310	0	0	533	30	233	0	0	1513	6395	3817	•
Royalties 5	•	0	0	0	0	0	0	0	0	21124	14811	0	•
Other Portfolio Income 6	•	20304	0	1	13497	785	3705	7	17622	35508	53528	361334	•
Other Receipts 7	•	570973	506304	265821	995219	500353	1745945	980620	1161802	1591942	2763070	4030439	•
Total Receipts 8	•	638346	506741	266137	1028075	543119	1809745	1021478	1239194	1977664	3434300	6139002	•
Average Total Receipts 9	•	244	142	230	843	2382	5673	10014	24298	39553	122654	227370	•

Operating Costs/Operating Income (%)

	Total	Zero Assets	Under 500	500 to 1,000	1,000 to 5,000	5,000 to 10,000	10,000 to 25,000	25,000 to 50,000	50,000 to 100,000	100,000 to 250,000	250,000 to 500,000	500,000 to 2,500,000	2,500,000 and over
Cost of Operations 10	•	•	•	•	•	•	0.0	•	•	0.1	0.0	0.6	•
Salaries and Wages 11	•	25.9	23.1	16.0	25.5	14.3	18.3	16.1	22.0	18.5	15.3	14.1	•
Taxes Paid 12	•	3.3	2.7	3.3	3.3	2.1	2.3	2.2	2.5	2.7	2.3	2.1	•
Interest Paid 13	•	4.8	2.0	3.6	9.6	8.7	8.8	11.4	6.9	10.6	7.6	13.2	•
Depreciation 14	•	2.2	0.8	0.9	0.8	5.0	1.2	0.6	1.7	6.1	2.1	1.5	•
Amortization and Depletion 15	•	0.8	0.1	0.0	0.6	0.1	0.1	0.1	0.3	0.9	0.9	0.4	•
Pensions and Other Deferred Comp. 16	•	0.1	1.2	•	0.3	0.3	0.4	0.3	0.7	0.3	0.3	0.2	•
Employee Benefits 17	•	1.3	0.0	0.6	1.4	2.1	1.5	1.0	1.6	1.0	1.0	1.6	•
Advertising 18	•	1.9	4.6	2.8	1.6	0.9	2.5	1.6	2.0	2.2	1.8	2.8	•
Other Expenses 19	•	59.4	42.8	67.7	42.4	53.3	41.8	37.4	38.3	29.7	53.4	43.0	•
Officers' Compensation 20	•	1.0	15.5	3.5	7.9	8.1	7.2	10.6	3.7	4.3	1.6	1.4	•
Operating Margin 21	•	•	7.3	1.5	6.7	5.1	15.8	18.7	20.3	23.7	13.7	19.1	•
Operating Margin Before Officers' Comp. 22	•	0.4	22.7	5.0	14.6	13.2	23.0	29.3	24.0	27.9	15.2	20.4	•

Selected Average Balance Sheet ($ in Thousands)

Net Receivables 23	•	0	58	355	1844	4043	11568	24834	42750	100713	185658	729995	•
Inventories 24	•	•	•	•	•	•	•	•	•	•	•	•	•
Net Property, Plant and Equipment 25	•	0	7	29	56	361	280	404	1631	1543	9396	12339	•
Total Assets 26	•	0	112	603	2557	7135	15608	36280	71657	161351	371778	1193073	•
Notes and Loans Payable 27	•	0	108	337	1338	4302	8906	24380	33377	98904	202336	732556	•
All Other Liabilities 28	•	0	24	74	295	739	3006	7998	12949	31305	102197	278842	•
Net Worth 29	•	0	-20	192	924	2094	3696	3902	25332	31143	67246	181675	•

Selected Financial Ratios (Times to 1)

Current Ratio 30	•	•	2.8	15.4	3.5	2.6	2.4	2.6	3.8	2.4	2.0	1.4	•
Quick Ratio 31	•	•	2.6	11.3	3.2	2.0	2.3	2.4	3.2	2.2	1.6	1.3	•
Net Sales to Working Capital 32	•	•	2.6	0.4	0.5	0.7	0.8	0.5	0.6	0.6	0.9	0.9	•
Coverage Ratio 33	•	0.9	4.7	1.4	1.7	1.6	2.8	2.6	3.9	3.2	2.8	2.4	•
Total Asset Turnover 34	•	•	1.3	0.4	0.3	0.3	0.4	0.3	0.3	0.2	0.3	0.2	•
Inventory Turnover 35	•	•	•	•	•	•	•	•	•	•	•	•	•
Receivables Turnover 36	•	•	•	•	•	•	•	•	•	•	•	•	•
Total Liabilities to Net Worth 37	•	•	•	2.1	1.8	2.4	3.2	8.3	1.8	4.2	4.5	5.6	•
Current Assets to Working Capital 38	•	•	1.6	1.1	1.4	1.6	1.7	1.6	1.4	1.7	2.0	3.5	•
Current Liabilities to Working Capital 39	•	•	0.6	0.1	0.4	0.6	0.7	0.6	0.4	0.7	1.0	2.5	•
Working Capital to Net Sales 40	•	•	0.4	2.3	1.8	1.5	1.3	1.9	1.7	1.7	1.1	1.1	•
Inventory to Working Capital 41	•	•	•	•	•	•	0.0	•	0.0	0.0	0.0	0.0	•
Total Receipts to Cash Flow 42	•	2.0	2.2	1.6	2.3	1.8	1.8	1.9	1.8	2.1	1.6	1.7	•
Cost of Goods to Cash Flow 43	•	•	•	•	•	•	0.0	•	•	0.0	0.0	0.0	•
Cash Flow to Total Debt 44	•	•	0.5	0.3	0.2	0.3	0.3	0.2	0.3	0.1	0.2	0.1	•

Selected Financial Factors (in Percentages)

Debt Ratio 45	•	•	117.9	68.1	63.9	70.6	76.3	89.2	64.6	80.7	81.9	84.8	•
Return on Total Assets 46	•	•	11.7	1.9	5.4	4.6	8.9	8.3	9.2	8.4	7.0	6.1	•
Return on Equity Before Income Taxes 47	•	•	•	1.8	6.1	5.8	24.2	48.0	19.4	30.0	24.8	23.6	•
Return on Equity After Income Taxes 48	•	•	•	1.8	5.2	5.1	23.3	45.6	17.4	26.8	21.2	16.8	•
Profit Margin (Before Income Tax) 49	•	•	7.3	1.5	6.7	5.1	15.8	18.7	20.2	23.6	13.6	18.8	•
Profit Margin (After Income Tax) 50	•	•	7.1	1.5	5.7	4.5	15.2	17.8	18.1	21.1	11.6	13.4	•

Table II

Corporations with Net Income

CREDIT CARD ISSUING AND OTHER CONSUMER CREDIT

MONEY AMOUNTS AND SIZE OF ASSETS IN THOUSANDS OF DOLLARS

Item Description for Accounting Period 7/12 Through 6/13	Total	Zero Assets	Under 500	500 to 1,000	1,000 to 5,000	5,000 to 10,000	10,000 to 25,000	25,000 to 50,000	50,000 to 100,000	100,000 to 250,000	250,000 to 500,000	500,000 to 2,500,000	2,500,000 and over
Number of Enterprises 1	•	1724	1424	•	873	183	252	80	41	39	22	22	•

Revenues ($ in Thousands)

Net Sales 2	•	435335	472558	•	918200	393849	1582630	852067	1158792	1777640	3345211	5906353	•
Interest 3	•	9911	206	•	12801	41951	19470	40363	44206	287018	551920	1652590	•
Rents 4	•	310	0	•	533	30	127	0	0	1513	6395	3817	•
Royalties 5	•	0	0	•	0	0	0	0	0	21124	14811	0	•
Other Portfolio Income 6	•	16535	0	•	11879	746	149	7	15194	33992	53528	359235	•
Other Receipts 7	•	408579	472352	•	892987	351122	1562884	811697	1099392	1433993	2718557	3890711	•
Total Receipts 8	•	435335	472558	•	918200	393849	1582630	852067	1158792	1777640	3345211	5906353	•
Average Total Receipts 9	•	253	332	•	1052	2152	6280	10651	28263	45581	152055	268471	•

Operating Costs/Operating Income (%)

Cost of Operations 10	•	•	•	•	•	•	0.0	•	•	•	0.0	0.7	•
Salaries and Wages 11	•	20.8	24.6	•	23.7	8.5	16.7	15.6	21.0	18.7	15.5	14.1	•
Taxes Paid 12	•	3.1	2.4	•	3.0	1.7	2.2	2.3	2.5	2.8	2.3	2.1	•
Interest Paid 13	•	3.6	0.5	•	7.1	9.3	7.8	12.3	6.2	7.4	6.4	10.6	•
Depreciation 14	•	0.7	0.7	•	0.5	0.7	0.4	0.5	1.3	3.9	2.1	1.6	•
Amortization and Depletion 15	•	0.3	•	•	0.1	0.0	0.1	0.1	0.2	0.5	0.7	0.4	•
Pensions and Other Deferred Comp. 16	•	0.0	1.3	•	0.3	0.2	0.4	0.3	0.8	0.3	0.3	0.2	•
Employee Benefits 17	•	1.1	0.0	•	1.1	0.9	1.4	0.9	1.4	0.9	1.0	1.6	•
Advertising 18	•	1.3	4.4	•	0.9	0.5	2.5	1.8	1.9	1.6	1.8	2.7	•
Other Expenses 19	•	45.4	32.9	•	39.4	55.6	38.3	30.3	36.0	28.0	52.9	42.6	•
Officers' Compensation 20	•	1.3	15.1	•	7.8	10.6	7.6	9.1	3.3	4.4	1.6	1.3	•
Operating Margin 21	•	22.4	18.3	•	16.1	12.1	22.7	26.9	25.5	31.6	15.4	22.2	•
Operating Margin Before Officers' Comp. 22	•	23.7	33.3	•	23.9	22.7	30.3	36.0	28.8	35.9	16.9	23.5	•

Selected Average Balance Sheet ($ in Thousands)

Net Receivables 23	•	0	83	•	1747	3622	12431	26647	46809	109391	149860	757724	•
Inventories 24	•	•	•	•	•	•	•	•	•	•	•	•	•
Net Property, Plant and Equipment 25	•	0	7	•	48	208	227	383	1678	1776	11921	14791	•
Total Assets 26	•	0	130	•	2319	6720	15664	36947	70959	165368	363807	1229357	•
Notes and Loans Payable 27	•	0	67	•	1003	4285	8561	21930	32787	98193	205846	659825	•
All Other Liabilities 28	•	0	20	•	310	806	2756	7803	11757	24117	75060	276592	•
Net Worth 29	•	0	43	•	1006	1629	4347	7214	26415	43058	82901	292939	•

Selected Financial Ratios (Times to 1)

Current Ratio 30	•	•	9.3	•	2.9	3.0	2.6	3.0	4.4	2.6	2.0	1.6	•
Quick Ratio 31	•	•	8.5	•	2.8	2.2	2.5	2.6	3.7	2.4	1.5	1.5	•
Net Sales to Working Capital 32	•	•	3.1	•	0.8	0.6	0.8	0.5	0.6	0.6	1.2	0.9	•
Coverage Ratio 33	•	7.2	38.6	•	3.3	2.3	3.9	3.2	5.1	5.2	3.4	3.1	•
Total Asset Turnover 34	•	•	2.6	•	0.5	0.3	0.4	0.3	0.4	0.3	0.4	0.2	•
Inventory Turnover 35	•	•	•	•	•	•	•	•	•	•	•	•	•
Receivables Turnover 36	•	•	•	•	•	•	•	•	•	•	•	•	•
Total Liabilities to Net Worth 37	•	•	2.0	•	1.3	3.1	2.6	4.1	1.7	2.8	3.4	3.2	•
Current Assets to Working Capital 38	•	•	1.1	•	1.5	1.5	1.6	1.5	1.3	1.6	2.0	2.8	•
Current Liabilities to Working Capital 39	•	•	0.1	•	0.5	0.5	0.6	0.5	0.3	0.6	1.0	1.8	•
Working Capital to Net Sales 40	•	•	0.3	•	1.3	1.7	1.3	2.0	1.6	1.7	0.8	1.2	•
Inventory to Working Capital 41	•	•	•	•	•	•	0.0	•	•	0.0	0.0	0.0	•
Total Receipts to Cash Flow 42	•	1.6	2.1	•	2.0	1.5	1.7	1.8	1.7	1.8	1.6	1.6	•
Cost of Goods to Cash Flow 43	•	•	•	•	•	•	0.0	•	•	•	0.0	0.0	•
Cash Flow to Total Debt 44	•	•	1.8	•	0.4	0.3	0.3	0.2	0.4	0.2	0.3	0.2	•

Selected Financial Factors (in Percentages)

Debt Ratio 45	•	•	67.1	•	56.6	75.8	72.2	80.5	62.8	74.0	77.2	76.2	•
Return on Total Assets 46	•	•	47.9	•	10.5	6.9	12.2	11.3	12.6	10.7	9.1	7.1	•
Return on Equity Before Income Taxes 47	•	•	141.7	•	16.8	16.0	32.7	39.7	27.2	33.4	28.1	20.2	•
Return on Equity After Income Taxes 48	•	•	140.3	•	15.6	14.9	31.8	38.0	24.8	30.4	24.3	15.0	•
Profit Margin (Before Income Tax) 49	•	22.4	18.3	•	16.1	12.1	22.7	26.9	25.5	31.5	15.3	22.0	•
Profit Margin (After Income Tax) 50	•	22.2	18.1	•	14.9	11.3	22.0	25.7	23.2	28.7	13.3	16.4	•

Table I

Corporations with and without Net Income

REAL ESTATE CREDIT INCL. MORTGAGE BANKERS AND ORIGINATORS

MONEY AMOUNTS AND SIZE OF ASSETS IN THOUSANDS OF DOLLARS

Item Description for Accounting Period 7/12 Through 6/13	Total	Zero Assets	Under 500	500 to 1,000	1,000 to 5,000	5,000 to 10,000	10,000 to 25,000	25,000 to 50,000	50,000 to 100,000	100,000 to 250,000	250,000 to 500,000	500,000 to 2,500,000	2,500,000 and over
Number of Enterprises 1	8569	2476	•	•	1063	310	213	132	74	58	16	22	7

Revenues ($ in Thousands)

Net Sales 2	26001378	1322140	•	•	996823	741389	1179239	1407175	2075293	2864415	2289388	3796080	8161755
Interest 3	1528116	5107	•	•	16959	10408	38477	42263	30624	91873	1510	355634	922442
Rents 4	22792	0	•	•	2248	2577	4090	746	112	4391	4	4866	0
Royalties 5	135	0	•	•	0	0	0	0	0	135	0	0	0
Other Portfolio Income 6	4779694	909822	•	•	21977	516	14134	55483	17539	5694	214606	169908	3365444
Other Receipts 7	19670641	407211	•	•	955639	727888	1122538	1308683	2027018	2762322	2073268	3265672	3873869
Total Receipts 8	26001378	1322140	•	•	996823	741389	1179239	1407175	2075293	2864415	2289388	3796080	8161755
Average Total Receipts 9	3034	534	•	•	938	2392	5536	10660	28044	49386	143087	172549	1165965

Operating Costs/Operating Income (%)

Cost of Operations 10	0.3	•	•	•	•	•	•	•	•	•	•	1.0	0.5
Salaries and Wages 11	26.8	11.9	•	•	14.2	37.6	35.3	39.2	38.8	35.6	43.9	30.2	15.8
Taxes Paid 12	2.9	2.3	•	•	2.7	4.6	4.1	3.9	3.4	3.3	3.3	2.7	2.1
Interest Paid 13	7.7	1.8	•	•	4.3	7.1	5.8	8.5	5.3	6.7	3.8	10.1	11.2
Depreciation 14	0.8	0.7	•	•	0.6	0.6	0.9	0.5	0.6	0.7	0.7	0.9	1.1
Amortization and Depletion 15	0.3	0.1	•	•	0.2	0.0	0.3	0.1	0.2	0.1	0.0	0.6	0.5
Pensions and Other Deferred Comp. 16	0.2	0.1	•	•	1.1	0.1	0.5	0.2	0.2	0.3	0.1	0.3	0.2
Employee Benefits 17	1.1	0.5	•	•	0.2	0.8	1.4	1.3	1.2	1.0	1.2	1.4	1.0
Advertising 18	2.6	3.6	•	•	0.4	3.2	3.1	4.2	1.9	3.0	3.2	2.0	2.6
Other Expenses 19	30.3	25.3	•	•	51.8	39.4	24.8	25.5	27.1	31.4	23.4	29.8	32.2
Officers' Compensation 20	4.0	0.6	•	•	7.6	9.0	6.2	6.6	4.4	6.1	2.6	2.9	0.4
Operating Margin 21	22.9	53.0	•	•	16.8	•	17.8	9.8	17.0	11.7	17.9	18.2	32.4
Operating Margin Before Officers' Comp. 22	26.9	53.6	•	•	24.5	6.6	24.0	16.4	21.4	17.8	20.6	21.1	32.8

Selected Average Balance Sheet ($ in Thousands)

Net Receivables 23	2157	0	•	•	386	622	4276	7334	11107	20014	15876	228593	1243484
Inventories 24	•	•	•	•	•	•	•	•	•	•	•	•	•
Net Property, Plant and Equipment 25	179	0	•	•	401	128	499	758	1327	3134	3763	4883	56905
Total Assets 26	12019	0	•	•	2261	7302	15326	34159	72135	158851	338876	1012571	6795319
Notes and Loans Payable 27	5445	0	•	•	1299	4860	7918	19281	59874	70939	215174	503139	2308132
All Other Liabilities 28	4160	0	•	•	261	3676	3484	10993	44878	75551	81707	378483	2083090
Net Worth 29	2414	0	•	•	701	-1234	3924	3884	-32617	12360	41995	130949	2404097

Selected Financial Ratios (Times to 1)

Current Ratio 30	0.6	•	•	•	1.5	0.4	1.1	0.8	0.3	0.4	0.3	0.5	0.9
Quick Ratio 31	0.6	•	•	•	1.2	0.3	0.9	0.6	0.3	0.3	0.1	0.5	0.9
Net Sales to Working Capital 32	•	•	•	•	3.5	•	13.8	•	•	•	•	•	•
Coverage Ratio 33	4.0	30.5	•	•	4.9	0.7	4.1	2.2	4.2	2.7	5.7	2.8	3.9
Total Asset Turnover 34	0.3	•	•	•	0.4	0.3	0.4	0.3	0.4	0.3	0.4	0.2	0.2
Inventory Turnover 35	•	•	•	•	•	•	•	•	•	•	•	•	•
Receivables Turnover 36	•	•	•	•	•	•	•	•	•	•	•	•	•
Total Liabilities to Net Worth 37	4.0	•	•	•	2.2	•	2.9	7.8	•	11.9	7.1	6.7	1.8
Current Assets to Working Capital 38	•	•	•	•	3.2	•	17.1	•	•	•	•	•	•
Current Liabilities to Working Capital 39	•	•	•	•	2.2	•	16.1	•	•	•	•	•	•
Working Capital to Net Sales 40	•	•	•	•	0.3	•	0.1	•	•	•	•	•	•
Inventory to Working Capital 41	•	•	•	•	•	•	•	•	•	•	•	•	•
Total Receipts to Cash Flow 42	2.0	1.3	•	•	1.6	3.2	2.5	4.0	2.4	2.5	2.6	2.2	1.6
Cost of Goods to Cash Flow 43	0.0	•	•	•	•	•	•	•	•	•	•	0.0	0.0
Cash Flow to Total Debt 44	0.2	•	•	•	0.4	0.1	0.2	0.1	0.1	0.1	0.2	0.1	0.2

Selected Financial Factors (in Percentages)

Debt Ratio 45	79.9	•	•	•	69.0	116.9	74.4	88.6	145.2	92.2	87.6	87.1	64.6
Return on Total Assets 46	7.7	•	•	•	8.8	1.5	8.5	5.7	8.7	5.7	9.2	4.7	7.5
Return on Equity Before Income Taxes 47	28.7	•	•	•	22.5	4.7	25.1	27.0	•	46.5	61.2	23.2	15.8
Return on Equity After Income Taxes 48	27.1	•	•	•	21.5	5.6	23.1	25.0	•	40.8	60.1	20.8	15.0
Profit Margin (Before Income Tax) 49	22.8	53.0	•	•	16.8	•	17.8	9.8	17.0	11.6	17.9	17.6	32.5
Profit Margin (After Income Tax) 50	21.6	51.8	•	•	16.1	•	16.3	9.1	15.9	10.2	17.6	15.8	31.0

Table II

Corporations with Net Income

REAL ESTATE CREDIT INCL. MORTGAGE BANKERS AND ORIGINATORS

MONEY AMOUNTS AND SIZE OF ASSETS IN THOUSANDS OF DOLLARS

Item Description for Accounting Period 7/12 Through 6/13		Total	Zero Assets	Under 500	500 to 1,000	1,000 to 5,000	5,000 to 10,000	10,000 to 25,000	25,000 to 50,000	50,000 to 100,000	100,000 to 250,000	250,000 to 500,000	500,000 to 2,500,000	2,500,000 and over
Number of Enterprises	1	4741	443	2511	414	784	158	168	115	64	47	•	16	•
Revenues ($ in Thousands)														
Net Sales	2	24382403	1307561	549629	355107	973423	604910	1107949	1324608	2040694	2804384	•	3312490	•
Interest	3	1187193	3879	3307	2404	12664	6744	19117	37388	18934	36267	•	245007	•
Rents	4	20550	0	3758	0	2248	1524	3630	691	112	3716	•	4866	•
Royalties	5	135	0	0	0	0	0	0	0	0	135	•	0	•
Other Portfolio Income	6	4492738	909822	3224	3	20769	81	14134	52796	17152	4582	•	6616	•
Other Receipts	7	18681787	393860	539340	352700	937742	596561	1071068	1233733	2004496	2759684	•	3056001	•
Total Receipts	8	24382403	1307561	549629	355107	973423	604910	1107949	1324608	2040694	2804384	•	3312490	•
Average Total Receipts	9	5143	2952	219	858	1242	3829	6595	11518	31886	59668	•	207031	•
Operating Costs/Operating Income (%)														
Cost of Operations	10	0.3	•	•	•	•	•	•	•	•	•	•	1.1	•
Salaries and Wages	11	26.6	11.9	26.0	5.7	14.3	33.9	36.4	38.4	39.3	35.1	•	28.7	•
Taxes Paid	12	2.8	2.2	3.5	5.6	2.4	3.9	4.0	3.7	3.4	3.2	•	2.6	•
Interest Paid	13	6.8	1.7	0.1	0.4	3.5	6.2	4.2	7.7	4.6	5.3	•	7.6	•
Depreciation	14	0.8	0.6	0.3	0.0	0.5	0.6	0.8	0.4	0.5	0.5	•	0.7	•
Amortization and Depletion	15	0.3	0.1	•	0.1	0.2	0.0	0.2	0.1	0.2	0.1	•	0.4	•
Pensions and Other Deferred Comp.	16	0.2	0.1	•	•	1.2	0.0	0.4	0.3	0.2	0.3	•	0.3	•
Employee Benefits	17	1.1	0.5	3.3	2.9	0.2	0.7	1.4	1.3	1.2	1.0	•	1.2	•
Advertising	18	2.8	3.6	0.6	5.5	0.4	3.8	3.1	4.3	1.9	3.1	•	2.3	•
Other Expenses	19	28.0	22.3	22.9	25.5	47.7	25.7	21.1	20.5	26.4	27.3	•	30.0	•
Officers' Compensation	20	3.3	0.6	7.8	8.3	7.8	10.4	4.9	6.7	4.3	6.1	•	3.1	•
Operating Margin	21	26.9	56.2	35.6	45.9	21.8	14.7	23.4	16.6	18.0	18.1	•	21.9	•
Operating Margin Before Officers' Comp.	22	30.2	56.8	43.5	54.3	29.6	25.0	28.3	23.3	22.3	24.2	•	25.1	•

Selected Average Balance Sheet ($ in Thousands)

Net Receivables 23	3319	0	0	47	212	694	4007	8216	9982	19868	•	212339	•
Inventories 24	•	•	•	•	•	•	•	•	•	•	•	•	•
Net Property, Plant and Equipment 25	244	0	5	7	227	185	559	834	850	3172	•	5883	•
Total Assets 26	18266	0	92	785	2055	7137	15232	34382	71356	155438	•	970854	•
Notes and Loans Payable 27	7432	0	33	387	1006	3880	6191	20196	37181	60216	•	348930	•
All Other Liabilities 28	5858	0	1	18	353	2380	3101	10337	21854	73193	•	413786	•
Net Worth 29	4976	0	58	379	696	878	5940	3849	12321	22029	•	208139	•

Selected Financial Ratios (Times to 1)

Current Ratio 30	0.6	•	6.0	2.1	1.5	0.4	1.0	0.7	0.4	0.4	•	0.6	•
Quick Ratio 31	0.6	•	5.9	1.2	1.2	0.3	0.8	0.6	0.3	0.3	•	0.6	•
Net Sales to Working Capital 32	•	•	12.0	2.3	4.4	•	31.7	•	•	•	•	•	•
Coverage Ratio 33	5.0	33.5	461.7	130.5	7.2	3.3	6.5	3.2	4.9	4.4	•	3.9	•
Total Asset Turnover 34	0.3	•	2.4	1.1	0.6	0.5	0.4	0.3	0.4	0.4	•	0.2	•
Inventory Turnover 35	•	•	•	•	•	•	•	•	•	•	•	•	•
Receivables Turnover 36	•	•	•	•	•	•	•	•	•	•	•	•	•
Total Liabilities to Net Worth 37	2.7	•	0.6	1.1	2.0	7.1	1.6	7.9	4.8	6.1	•	3.7	•
Current Assets to Working Capital 38	•	•	1.2	1.9	2.9	•	32.8	•	•	•	•	•	•
Current Liabilities to Working Capital 39	•	•	0.2	0.9	1.9	•	31.8	•	•	•	•	•	•
Working Capital to Net Sales 40	•	•	0.1	0.4	0.2	•	0.0	•	•	•	•	•	•
Inventory to Working Capital 41	•	•	•	•	•	•	•	•	•	•	•	•	•
Total Receipts to Cash Flow 42	1.9	1.3	1.9	1.6	1.6	2.8	2.4	3.3	2.4	2.3	•	2.0	•
Cost of Goods to Cash Flow 43	0.0	•	•	•	•	•	•	•	•	•	•	0.0	•
Cash Flow to Total Debt 44	0.2	•	3.5	1.3	0.6	0.2	0.3	0.1	0.2	0.2	•	0.1	•

Selected Financial Factors (in Percentages)

Debt Ratio 45	72.8	•	36.9	51.7	66.1	87.7	61.0	88.8	82.7	85.8	•	78.6	•
Return on Total Assets 46	9.5	•	85.0	50.6	15.3	11.2	11.9	8.2	10.1	9.0	•	6.3	•
Return on Equity Before Income Taxes 47	27.8	•	134.4	103.9	38.9	63.9	25.9	49.7	46.5	49.0	•	21.8	•
Return on Equity After Income Taxes 48	26.4	•	133.6	103.7	37.5	61.3	24.2	47.5	43.8	45.0	•	19.7	•
Profit Margin (Before Income Tax) 49	26.9	56.2	35.6	45.9	21.8	14.6	23.4	16.6	18.0	18.1	•	21.9	•
Profit Margin (After Income Tax) 50	25.6	54.9	35.4	45.8	21.0	14.1	21.8	15.9	16.9	16.6	•	19.8	•

Table I

Corporations with and without Net Income

INTL. TRADE, SECONDARY FINANCING, OTHER NONDEPOSITORY CREDIT

MONEY AMOUNTS AND SIZE OF ASSETS IN THOUSANDS OF DOLLARS

Item Description for Accounting Period 7/12 Through 6/13	Total	Zero Assets	Under 500	500 to 1,000	1,000 to 5,000	5,000 to 10,000	10,000 to 25,000	25,000 to 50,000	50,000 to 100,000	100,000 to 250,000	250,000 to 500,000	500,000 to 2,500,000	2,500,000 and over
Number of Enterprises **1**	5531	1046	2404	763	800	221	119	55	33	28	14	22	25

Revenues ($ in Thousands)

Net Sales **2**	156209957	619758	339180	430663	569744	371146	589385	555074	460845	440822	446678	2193764	149192900
Interest **3**	124280281	8287	707	2557	74989	2813	18716	25012	59600	107049	192288	713788	123074476
Rents **4**	32274	3640	0	2	0	860	0	56	413	24	3478	2655	21146
Royalties **5**	243	0	36	0	0	0	0	116	81	10	0	0	0
Other Portfolio Income **6**	8087650	318440	0	0	15414	1582	1363	1973	803	3937	11817	32884	7699436
Other Receipts **7**	23809509	289391	338437	428104	479341	365891	569306	527917	399948	329802	239095	1444437	18397842
Total Receipts **8**	156209957	619758	339180	430663	569744	371146	589385	555074	460845	440822	446678	2193764	149192900
Average Total Receipts **9**	28243	593	141	564	712	1679	4953	10092	13965	15744	31906	99717	5967716

Operating Costs/Operating Income (%)

Cost of Operations **10**	•	•	•	•	•	•	•	•	•	•	•	•	•
Salaries and Wages **11**	2.3	16.6	28.3	17.9	24.0	17.3	25.9	21.4	15.1	14.0	13.7	18.2	1.5
Taxes Paid **12**	0.3	1.2	5.6	4.9	4.5	4.0	3.6	3.0	1.9	2.8	2.7	3.2	0.1
Interest Paid **13**	59.8	2.0	0.0	5.2	2.7	24.6	9.3	11.2	12.0	20.8	30.9	15.9	62.0
Depreciation **14**	0.3	2.1	1.8	1.9	0.9	1.5	1.8	3.3	0.7	1.4	1.4	4.5	0.2
Amortization and Depletion **15**	0.2	0.0	0.4	0.0	1.9	0.4	0.5	0.5	1.6	0.6	2.6	2.0	0.1
Pensions and Other Deferred Comp. **16**	0.2	0.0	•	1.2	0.5	0.9	0.4	0.6	0.5	0.3	0.2	1.3	0.1
Employee Benefits **17**	0.3	0.1	•	0.8	3.0	3.3	1.7	1.2	1.1	1.3	1.6	1.4	0.2
Advertising **18**	0.2	0.7	5.2	2.7	2.1	5.8	3.0	2.9	1.1	0.7	2.0	0.5	0.1
Other Expenses **19**	25.4	25.7	43.7	31.8	40.1	32.4	30.6	33.1	54.5	28.7	41.2	25.0	25.0
Officers' Compensation **20**	0.4	3.2	16.0	13.0	8.4	3.4	6.7	8.1	4.5	3.4	3.4	2.3	0.2
Operating Margin **21**	10.7	48.4	•	20.7	11.8	6.4	16.7	14.7	7.1	26.0	0.2	25.7	10.3
Operating Margin Before Officers' Comp. **22**	11.2	51.6	15.0	33.7	20.2	9.8	23.4	22.8	11.6	29.4	3.6	27.9	10.5

Selected Average Balance Sheet ($ in Thousands)

Net Receivables 23	26952	0	21	257	480	3238	7965	15234	40986	84509	213384	583526	5055786
Inventories 24	•	•	•	•	•	•	•	•	•	•	•	•	•
Net Property, Plant and Equipment 25	621	0	3	135	90	281	753	2070	1295	1217	1518	15896	101487
Total Assets 26	1011145	0	89	772	1775	6694	15036	34589	72072	145024	336688	1217887	221892149
Notes and Loans Payable 27	979566	0	16	584	946	9181	8288	18070	33838	104157	221319	597185	215698320
All Other Liabilities 28	25157	0	4	30	210	922	2032	4570	17031	12027	106915	220104	5240390
Net Worth 29	6422	0	69	157	619	-3409	4716	11949	21203	28840	8454	400599	953439

Selected Financial Ratios (Times to 1)

Current Ratio 30	1.0	•	19.8	3.4	2.4	4.8	2.2	1.6	1.5	1.6	1.3	1.7	0.9
Quick Ratio 31	0.8	•	13.2	2.7	1.7	3.7	1.7	1.1	1.3	1.3	1.2	1.3	0.7
Net Sales to Working Capital 32	•	•	1.8	1.4	1.1	0.4	0.7	1.1	0.8	0.4	0.7	0.3	•
Coverage Ratio 33	1.2	•	•	5.0	5.4	1.3	2.8	2.3	1.6	2.3	1.0	2.6	1.2
Total Asset Turnover 34	0.0	•	1.6	0.7	0.4	0.3	0.3	0.3	0.2	0.1	0.1	0.1	0.0
Inventory Turnover 35	•	•	•	•	•	•	•	•	•	•	•	•	•
Receivables Turnover 36	•	•	•	•	•	•	•	•	•	•	•	•	•
Total Liabilities to Net Worth 37	156.4	•	0.3	3.9	1.9	•	2.2	1.9	2.4	4.0	38.8	2.0	231.7
Current Assets to Working Capital 38	•	•	1.1	1.4	1.7	1.3	1.8	2.8	2.9	2.7	5.0	2.3	•
Current Liabilities to Working Capital 39	•	•	0.1	0.4	0.7	0.3	0.8	1.8	1.9	1.7	4.0	1.3	•
Working Capital to Net Sales 40	•	•	0.6	0.7	0.9	2.4	1.3	0.9	1.3	2.6	1.5	3.7	•
Inventory to Working Capital 41	•	•	•	•	•	•	•	0.0	•	•	0.0	0.0	•
Total Receipts to Cash Flow 42	2.8	1.4	3.2	2.3	2.6	3.1	2.4	2.3	1.7	1.9	2.6	2.2	2.8
Cost of Goods to Cash Flow 43	•	•	•	•	•	•	•	•	•	•	•	•	•
Cash Flow to Total Debt 44	0.0	•	2.2	0.4	0.2	0.1	0.2	0.2	0.2	0.1	0.0	0.1	0.0

Selected Financial Factors (in Percentages)

Debt Ratio 45	99.4	•	22.8	79.6	65.1	150.9	68.6	65.5	70.6	80.1	97.5	67.1	99.6
Return on Total Assets 46	2.0	•	•	18.9	5.8	7.8	8.6	7.6	3.7	5.1	2.9	3.4	1.9
Return on Equity Before Income Taxes 47	44.4	•	•	74.2	13.6	•	17.6	12.4	4.7	14.2	0.6	6.4	61.7
Return on Equity After Income Taxes 48	40.8	•	•	72.2	9.8	•	17.0	10.8	3.1	11.0	•	4.3	57.6
Profit Margin (Before Income Tax) 49	10.1	•	•	20.7	11.8	6.4	16.7	14.7	7.1	26.0	0.2	25.8	9.9
Profit Margin (After Income Tax) 50	9.3	•	•	20.1	8.5	5.6	16.2	12.8	4.7	20.2	•	17.1	9.2

Table II
Corporations with Net Income

INTL. TRADE, SECONDARY FINANCING, OTHER NONDEPOSITORY CREDIT

MONEY AMOUNTS AND SIZE OF ASSETS IN THOUSANDS OF DOLLARS

Item Description for Accounting Period 7/12 Through 6/13	Total	Zero Assets	Under 500	500 to 1,000	1,000 to 5,000	5,000 to 10,000	10,000 to 25,000	25,000 to 50,000	50,000 to 100,000	100,000 to 250,000	250,000 to 500,000	500,000 to 2,500,000	2,500,000 and over
Number of Enterprises 1	3071	399	•	559	484	194	92	46	23	22	•	18	16

Revenues ($ in Thousands)

Net Sales 2	153124036	161835	•	328995	502675	360337	553456	438314	390683	394001	•	1923533	147374987
Interest 3	124043534	5251	•	2557	71536	2	5553	16904	43175	74812	•	626705	123018086
Rents 4	28434	3640	•	2	0	0	0	12	280	15	•	2655	21146
Royalties 5	10	0	•	0	0	0	0	0	0	10	•	0	0
Other Portfolio Income 6	7766589	549	•	0	15164	402	448	1934	585	3895	•	32884	7699436
Other Receipts 7	21285469	152395	•	326436	415975	359933	547455	419464	346643	315269	•	1261289	16636319
Total Receipts 8	153124036	161835	•	328995	502675	360337	553456	438314	390683	394001	•	1923533	147374987
Average Total Receipts 9	49861	406	•	589	1039	1857	6016	9529	16986	17909	•	106863	9210937

Operating Costs/Operating Income (%)

Cost of Operations 10	•	•	•	•	•	•	•	•	•	•	•	•	•
Salaries and Wages 11	2.0	11.5	•	12.6	25.9	17.7	24.1	16.8	13.4	13.2	•	17.2	1.4
Taxes Paid 12	0.2	2.2	•	4.1	4.8	3.3	3.5	2.6	1.9	2.8	•	3.3	0.1
Interest Paid 13	60.7	7.6	•	2.0	2.8	15.2	5.6	12.4	8.6	18.2	•	13.5	62.7
Depreciation 14	0.3	0.5	•	2.0	1.0	1.4	1.6	2.7	0.6	1.3	•	5.0	0.2
Amortization and Depletion 15	0.1	0.1	•	•	0.2	0.4	0.2	0.5	0.8	0.6	•	1.2	0.1
Pensions and Other Deferred Comp. 16	0.2	•	•	1.5	0.5	0.9	0.4	0.2	0.5	0.3	•	1.4	0.1
Employee Benefits 17	0.3	0.3	•	•	3.4	3.3	1.4	0.8	1.0	1.1	•	1.3	0.2
Advertising 18	0.2	2.5	•	2.9	1.9	6.0	2.8	1.1	0.9	0.8	•	0.5	0.1
Other Expenses 19	24.6	43.1	•	21.7	33.1	29.5	26.8	31.3	49.5	25.8	•	24.3	24.4
Officers' Compensation 20	0.4	0.1	•	12.4	9.2	3.5	6.2	8.4	4.4	3.6	•	2.4	0.2
Operating Margin 21	11.0	32.2	•	40.9	17.2	18.8	27.3	23.2	18.3	32.3	•	30.1	10.5
Operating Margin Before Officers' Comp. 22	11.4	32.3	•	53.2	26.4	22.2	33.5	31.6	22.8	35.9	•	32.4	10.7

Selected Average Balance Sheet ($ in Thousands)

Net Receivables 23	47080	0	•	278	488	3799	9476	16039	49973	78998	•	711392	7739374
Inventories 24	•	•	•	•	•	•	•	•	•	•	•	•	•
Net Property, Plant and Equipment 25	1012	0	•	134	148	130	427	1298	830	1342	•	18325	152326
Total Assets 26	1802391	0	•	743	1838	6674	15659	34837	75492	142092	•	1228412	343681916
Notes and Loans Payable 27	1747571	0	•	238	676	3962	7916	19574	35408	91541	•	515940	334342604
All Other Liabilities 28	42969	0	•	41	276	1007	1722	5028	17427	14428	•	247396	7838384
Net Worth 29	11852	0	•	464	886	1705	6021	10234	22657	36123	•	465076	1500928

Selected Financial Ratios (Times to 1)

Current Ratio 30	1.1	•	•	5.2	5.0	5.1	2.7	1.4	1.7	2.3	•	2.2	1.1
Quick Ratio 31	0.9	•	•	4.1	3.6	4.0	2.1	1.0	1.4	1.8	•	1.8	0.8
Net Sales to Working Capital 32	4.6	•	•	1.2	0.9	0.4	0.7	1.2	0.7	0.3	•	0.2	8.2
Coverage Ratio 33	1.2	5.2	•	21.3	7.0	2.2	5.9	2.9	3.1	2.8	•	3.2	1.2
Total Asset Turnover 34	0.0	•	•	0.8	0.6	0.3	0.4	0.3	0.2	0.1	•	0.1	0.0
Inventory Turnover 35	•	•	•	•	•	•	•	•	•	•	•	•	•
Receivables Turnover 36	•	•	•	•	•	•	•	•	•	•	•	•	•
Total Liabilities to Net Worth 37	151.1	•	•	0.6	1.1	2.9	1.6	2.4	2.3	2.9	•	1.6	228.0
Current Assets to Working Capital 38	12.1	•	•	1.2	1.2	1.2	1.6	3.3	2.5	1.8	•	1.8	20.7
Current Liabilities to Working Capital 39	11.1	•	•	0.2	0.2	0.2	0.6	2.3	1.5	0.8	•	0.8	19.7
Working Capital to Net Sales 40	0.2	•	•	0.8	1.1	2.6	1.4	0.8	1.5	3.3	•	4.9	0.1
Inventory to Working Capital 41	0.0	•	•	•	•	•	•	•	•	•	•	0.0	0.0
Total Receipts to Cash Flow 42	2.8	1.4	•	1.8	2.7	2.3	2.0	1.9	1.5	1.8	•	2.0	2.9
Cost of Goods to Cash Flow 43	•	•	•	•	•	•	•	•	•	•	•	•	•
Cash Flow to Total Debt 44	0.0	•	•	1.2	0.4	0.2	0.3	0.2	0.2	0.1	•	0.1	0.0

Selected Financial Factors (in Percentages)

Debt Ratio 45	99.3	•	•	37.6	51.8	74.5	61.5	70.6	70.0	74.6	•	62.1	99.6
Return on Total Assets 46	2.0	•	•	33.9	11.3	9.5	12.7	9.7	6.0	6.4	•	3.8	1.9
Return on Equity Before Income Taxes 47	44.6	•	•	51.8	20.1	20.4	27.3	21.6	13.7	16.0	•	6.9	61.4
Return on Equity After Income Taxes 48	41.1	•	•	50.9	15.7	19.6	26.7	19.3	11.6	12.8	•	4.7	57.4
Profit Margin (Before Income Tax) 49	10.6	32.2	•	40.9	17.2	18.7	27.3	23.2	18.3	32.3	•	30.2	10.0
Profit Margin (After Income Tax) 50	9.8	31.5	•	40.1	13.4	18.0	26.8	20.7	15.5	25.8	•	20.3	9.3

Table I

Corporations with and without Net Income

ACTIVITIES RELATED TO CREDIT INTERMEDIATION

MONEY AMOUNTS AND SIZE OF ASSETS IN THOUSANDS OF DOLLARS

Item Description for Accounting Period 7/12 Through 6/13	Total	Zero Assets	Under 500	500 to 1,000	1,000 to 5,000	5,000 to 10,000	10,000 to 25,000	25,000 to 50,000	50,000 to 100,000	100,000 to 250,000	250,000 to 500,000	500,000 to 2,500,000	2,500,000 and over
Number of Enterprises **1**	16848	3981	10637	744	1047	150	95	69	43	35	9	23	15

Revenues ($ in Thousands)

Net Sales **2**	56917868	478882	2520846	516094	1881494	633478	729407	1249820	1199955	2616501	1112989	6070676	37907727
Interest **3**	2459148	10381	3621	863	5086	2566	5507	16907	10278	39891	25993	277622	2060435
Rents **4**	239368	28	590	0	0	404	0	319	1155	726	12	1716	234417
Royalties **5**	840431	0	0	0	0	0	0	0	197	0	3269	0	836966
Other Portfolio Income **6**	983365	1705	0	0	2930	123	500	2163	606	10016	35960	71726	857637
Other Receipts **7**	52395556	466768	2516635	515231	1873478	630385	723400	1230431	1187719	2565868	1047755	5719612	33918272
Total Receipts **8**	56917868	478882	2520846	516094	1881494	633478	729407	1249820	1199955	2616501	1112989	6070676	37907727
Average Total Receipts **9**	3378	120	237	694	1797	4223	7678	18113	27906	74757	123665	263942	2527182

Operating Costs/Operating Income (%)

Cost of Operations **10**	0.4	•	•	•	•	0.2	•	0.3	•	0.5	•	0.4	0.5
Salaries and Wages **11**	18.9	18.5	16.1	16.2	27.8	22.1	38.1	24.7	32.9	28.5	27.4	23.7	15.9
Taxes Paid **12**	2.8	3.3	2.9	1.9	3.2	2.7	3.6	3.5	3.2	3.3	3.0	2.4	2.8
Interest Paid **13**	7.4	14.4	0.7	2.0	5.6	3.3	2.4	3.8	4.3	2.9	6.5	7.8	8.5
Depreciation **14**	1.9	0.9	0.7	2.1	1.1	1.4	1.9	0.9	1.9	2.2	1.6	2.8	1.9
Amortization and Depletion **15**	2.1	2.4	0.2	0.2	0.1	0.4	1.2	1.3	1.7	1.0	0.8	4.5	2.2
Pensions and Other Deferred Comp. **16**	0.7	0.0	0.5	1.1	1.8	0.2	0.4	0.6	0.3	0.5	0.2	0.5	0.7
Employee Benefits **17**	2.0	1.4	1.9	0.8	0.2	1.8	1.9	1.0	1.5	1.7	1.7	4.4	1.8
Advertising **18**	3.1	0.8	2.1	1.1	2.3	1.0	1.6	4.1	1.7	3.2	3.2	0.9	3.7
Other Expenses **19**	37.7	58.3	41.7	48.7	27.1	72.3	31.7	50.5	34.0	43.7	42.2	35.2	36.6
Officers' Compensation **20**	2.9	2.3	21.4	10.9	12.5	7.2	10.9	4.6	2.7	4.2	2.7	2.4	0.8
Operating Margin **21**	20.1	•	11.9	15.1	18.3	•	6.3	4.7	15.8	8.3	10.7	14.9	24.5
Operating Margin Before Officers' Comp. **22**	23.0	•	33.3	26.0	30.8	•	17.2	9.4	18.5	12.5	13.3	17.3	25.3

Selected Average Balance Sheet ($ in Thousands)

Net Receivables 23	1978	0	2	24	523	503	3993	6510	10763	33142	72191	148446	1743529
Inventories 24	•	•	•	•	•	•	•	•	•	•	•	•	•
Net Property, Plant and Equipment 25	289	0	11	233	49	460	501	1018	2844	6325	8174	33459	210072
Total Assets 26	11722	0	74	770	2357	6943	15922	35415	69864	143935	331148	973357	10350342
Notes and Loans Payable 27	4439	0	41	537	1124	3342	6781	12642	24864	43839	138280	282818	4027545
All Other Liabilities 28	4619	0	14	106	542	1021	4725	26538	27012	57357	81456	482301	3972396
Net Worth 29	2664	0	19	127	691	2580	4417	-3765	17988	42739	111412	208237	2350401

Selected Financial Ratios (Times to 1)

Current Ratio 30	1.1	•	4.3	2.0	2.2	1.7	1.2	0.9	0.9	1.1	1.0	0.7	1.2
Quick Ratio 31	0.8	•	3.1	2.0	1.6	1.2	1.0	0.7	0.6	0.9	1.0	0.6	0.9
Net Sales to Working Capital 32	5.6	•	6.0	2.8	1.6	3.7	5.7	•	•	14.1	26.6	•	3.6
Coverage Ratio 33	3.9	0.9	17.7	8.5	4.3	•	3.6	2.2	4.7	3.9	2.9	2.9	4.1
Total Asset Turnover 34	0.3	•	3.2	0.9	0.8	0.6	0.5	0.5	0.4	0.5	0.4	0.3	0.2
Inventory Turnover 35	•	•	•	•	•	•	•	•	•	•	•	•	•
Receivables Turnover 36	•	•	•	•	•	•	•	•	•	•	•	•	•
Total Liabilities to Net Worth 37	3.4	•	3.0	5.1	2.4	1.7	2.6	•	2.9	2.4	2.0	3.7	3.4
Current Assets to Working Capital 38	7.7	•	1.3	2.0	1.8	2.5	6.1	•	•	13.9	30.3	•	5.8
Current Liabilities to Working Capital 39	6.7	•	0.3	1.0	0.8	1.5	5.1	•	•	12.9	29.3	•	4.8
Working Capital to Net Sales 40	0.2	•	0.2	0.4	0.6	0.3	0.2	•	•	0.1	0.0	•	0.3
Inventory to Working Capital 41	0.0	•	•	•	0.0	0.0	0.0	•	•	0.0	0.0	•	0.0
Total Receipts to Cash Flow 42	1.8	2.0	2.1	1.9	2.4	1.9	2.9	1.9	2.1	2.2	2.1	2.2	1.7
Cost of Goods to Cash Flow 43	0.0	•	•	•	•	0.0	•	0.0	•	0.0	•	0.0	0.0
Cash Flow to Total Debt 44	0.2	•	2.1	0.6	0.4	0.5	0.2	0.2	0.3	0.3	0.3	0.2	0.2

Selected Financial Factors (in Percentages)

Debt Ratio 45	77.3	•	74.7	83.5	70.7	62.8	72.3	110.6	74.3	70.3	66.4	78.6	77.3
Return on Total Assets 46	8.2	•	40.7	15.4	18.2	•	4.2	4.3	8.0	5.8	7.1	6.2	8.4
Return on Equity Before Income Taxes 47	26.9	•	151.8	82.5	47.4	•	10.9	•	24.5	14.5	13.8	19.0	28.0
Return on Equity After Income Taxes 48	18.2	•	151.0	75.5	46.3	•	9.9	•	23.6	11.7	10.5	13.6	18.1
Profit Margin (Before Income Tax) 49	21.2	•	11.9	15.1	18.3	•	6.3	4.7	15.8	8.3	12.4	15.0	26.1
Profit Margin (After Income Tax) 50	14.4	•	11.8	13.8	17.8	•	5.7	3.4	15.2	6.7	9.4	10.8	16.8

Table II

Corporations with Net Income

ACTIVITIES RELATED TO CREDIT INTERMEDIATION

MONEY AMOUNTS AND SIZE OF ASSETS IN THOUSANDS OF DOLLARS

Item Description for Accounting Period 7/12 Through 6/13	Total	Zero Assets	Under 500	500 to 1,000	1,000 to 5,000	5,000 to 10,000	10,000 to 25,000	25,000 to 50,000	50,000 to 100,000	100,000 to 250,000	250,000 to 500,000	500,000 to 2,500,000	2,500,000 and over
Number of Enterprises 1	9979	1437	6940	493	847	43	74	44	37	28	5	18	12

Revenues ($ in Thousands)

Net Sales 2	47674086	365901	2382005	511080	1780222	240872	652440	781945	992773	2315053	918322	5059599	31673875
Interest 3	2241163	10313	2041	731	2459	1683	5400	1888	9743	20730	4653	153982	2027540
Rents 4	11737	0	590	0	0	0	0	319	997	726	12	1236	7857
Royalties 5	839952	0	0	0	0	0	0	0	0	0	3269	0	836683
Other Portfolio Income 6	916942	1402	0	0	205	123	194	1074	588	731	35960	71726	804941
Other Receipts 7	43664292	354186	2379374	510349	1777558	239066	646846	778664	981445	2292866	874428	4832655	27996854
Total Receipts 8	47674086	365901	2382005	511080	1780222	240872	652440	781945	992773	2315053	918322	5059599	31673875
Average Total Receipts 9	4777	255	343	1037	2102	5602	8817	17771	26832	82680	183664	281089	2639490

Operating Costs/Operating Income (%)

Cost of Operations 10	0.1	•	•	•	•	•	•	0.4	•	0.6	•	0.3	0.0
Salaries and Wages 11	18.4	13.4	14.8	15.3	24.7	27.1	35.4	25.5	34.8	27.9	23.4	24.3	15.6
Taxes Paid 12	3.0	3.0	2.5	1.9	2.8	3.6	3.4	3.4	3.4	3.2	3.1	2.3	3.1
Interest Paid 13	3.8	11.6	0.5	1.5	5.2	1.1	2.1	3.0	5.1	2.6	5.3	6.3	3.6
Depreciation 14	1.8	1.2	0.6	1.5	1.0	2.2	1.5	0.8	1.6	2.1	1.5	2.9	1.9
Amortization and Depletion 15	1.5	3.2	0.2	0.2	0.1	0.0	1.2	1.0	1.8	0.9	0.4	3.4	1.5
Pensions and Other Deferred Comp. 16	0.7	0.0	0.5	1.1	1.9	0.4	0.4	0.4	0.4	0.6	0.1	0.5	0.7
Employee Benefits 17	1.7	1.7	1.7	0.8	0.1	3.6	1.4	0.9	1.5	1.6	0.9	4.9	1.4
Advertising 18	3.5	0.7	2.0	1.0	2.3	0.4	1.2	6.5	1.8	3.4	2.2	0.5	4.4
Other Expenses 19	35.9	48.3	40.2	40.2	24.1	31.5	24.7	33.2	25.9	42.3	40.6	33.1	36.5
Officers' Compensation 20	3.1	1.6	22.6	10.8	12.4	17.3	10.6	4.6	2.9	3.0	3.1	2.6	0.8
Operating Margin 21	26.3	15.3	14.3	25.7	25.4	12.8	18.1	20.3	20.8	11.8	19.4	18.9	30.4
Operating Margin Before Officers' Comp. 22	29.4	16.9	36.9	36.4	37.8	30.1	28.7	24.9	23.7	14.9	22.5	21.5	31.2

Selected Average Balance Sheet ($ in Thousands)

	C1	C2	C3	C4	C5	C6	C7	C8	C9	C10	C11	C12	C13
Net Receivables 23	3127	0	3	30	508	1371	3930	9234	10857	35339	43819	168664	2111943
Inventories 24	•	•	•	•	•	•	•	•	•	•	•	•	•
Net Property, Plant and Equipment 25	370	0	15	38	47	627	400	1011	2764	7344	9831	37864	199262
Total Assets 26	14622	0	76	763	2288	6974	16485	34308	70372	147243	334444	1060530	9379128
Notes and Loans Payable 27	4524	0	15	302	857	2425	6879	11704	26990	52015	118554	283381	2907744
All Other Liabilities 28	5515	0	15	97	552	1736	5053	15490	27046	60504	64588	532363	3390896
Net Worth 29	4582	0	47	364	879	2813	4553	7114	16335	34724	151303	244786	3080488

Selected Financial Ratios (Times to 1)

	C1	C2	C3	C4	C5	C6	C7	C8	C9	C10	C11	C12	C13
Current Ratio 30	1.2	•	4.4	2.1	1.9	1.7	1.0	1.0	0.8	0.9	0.7	0.7	1.3
Quick Ratio 31	1.0	•	4.3	2.1	1.6	1.5	0.8	0.7	0.6	0.8	0.6	0.6	1.1
Net Sales to Working Capital 32	4.2	•	9.1	2.9	2.1	3.5	•	•	•	•	•	•	2.5
Coverage Ratio 33	8.1	2.3	27.1	17.6	5.9	12.7	9.8	7.8	5.1	5.5	5.1	4.0	9.7
Total Asset Turnover 34	0.3	•	4.5	1.4	0.9	0.8	0.5	0.5	0.4	0.6	0.5	0.3	0.3
Inventory Turnover 35	•	•	•	•	•	•	•	•	•	•	•	•	•
Receivables Turnover 36	•	•	•	•	•	•	•	•	•	•	•	•	•
Total Liabilities to Net Worth 37	2.2	•	0.6	1.1	1.6	1.5	2.6	3.8	3.3	3.2	1.2	3.3	2.0
Current Assets to Working Capital 38	5.7	•	1.3	1.9	2.1	2.5	•	•	•	•	•	•	4.0
Current Liabilities to Working Capital 39	4.7	•	0.3	0.9	1.1	1.5	•	•	•	•	•	•	3.0
Working Capital to Net Sales 40	0.2	•	0.1	0.3	0.5	0.3	•	•	•	•	•	•	0.4
Inventory to Working Capital 41	0.0	•	•	•	•	•	•	•	•	•	•	•	0.0
Total Receipts to Cash Flow 42	1.7	1.7	2.0	1.9	2.2	2.5	2.5	2.0	2.3	2.1	1.8	2.1	1.6
Cost of Goods to Cash Flow 43	0.0	•	•	•	•	•	•	0.0	•	0.0	•	0.0	0.0
Cash Flow to Total Debt 44	0.3	•	5.8	1.4	0.7	0.5	0.3	0.3	0.2	0.4	0.6	0.2	0.3

Selected Financial Factors (in Percentages)

	C1	C2	C3	C4	C5	C6	C7	C8	C9	C10	C11	C12	C13
Debt Ratio 45	68.7	•	38.6	52.3	61.6	59.7	72.4	79.3	76.8	76.4	54.8	76.9	67.2
Return on Total Assets 46	10.2	•	66.8	36.9	28.1	11.1	10.8	12.0	9.9	8.1	14.8	6.7	10.0
Return on Equity Before Income Taxes 47	28.5	•	104.8	73.0	60.6	25.4	35.0	50.5	34.1	28.1	26.2	21.8	27.3
Return on Equity After Income Taxes 48	20.0	•	104.2	69.3	59.5	22.4	33.7	45.5	32.9	23.9	21.8	16.0	17.8
Profit Margin (Before Income Tax) 49	27.3	15.6	14.3	25.7	25.4	12.8	18.1	20.2	20.8	11.8	21.6	19.0	31.8
Profit Margin (After Income Tax) 50	19.2	12.6	14.2	24.4	24.9	11.2	17.4	18.2	20.1	10.0	17.9	13.9	20.8

Table I

Corporations with and without Net Income

INVESTMENT BANKING AND SECURITIES DEALING

MONEY AMOUNTS AND SIZE OF ASSETS IN THOUSANDS OF DOLLARS

Item Description for Accounting Period 7/12 Through 6/13	Total	Zero Assets	Under 500	500 to 1,000	1,000 to 5,000	5,000 to 10,000	10,000 to 25,000	25,000 to 50,000	50,000 to 100,000	100,000 to 250,000	250,000 to 500,000	500,000 to 2,500,000	2,500,000 and over
Number of Enterprises **1**	3959	414	3111	121	167	19	34	38	18	10	6	10	12

Revenues ($ in Thousands)

	Total	Zero Assets	Under 500	500 to 1,000	1,000 to 5,000	5,000 to 10,000	10,000 to 25,000	25,000 to 50,000	50,000 to 100,000	100,000 to 250,000	250,000 to 500,000	500,000 to 2,500,000	2,500,000 and over
Net Sales **2**	124905135	358745	378391	200	380133	347244	87533	303463	458773	104047	1202901	1511431	119772274
Interest **3**	43749178	208583	5678	93	10402	3273	1104	23193	9525	25031	57834	173243	43231219
Rents **4**	558448	0	0	0	682	0	0	16	32	0	1813	0	555906
Royalties **5**	66979	0	0	0	117	0	0	0	11	6930	174	1	59747
Other Portfolio Income **6**	6098807	34043	19	0	5998	274	28844	6555	16851	14505	222	342492	5649002
Other Receipts **7**	74431723	116119	372694	107	362934	343697	57585	273699	432354	57581	1142858	995695	70276400
Total Receipts **8**	124905135	358745	378391	200	380133	347244	87533	303463	458773	104047	1202901	1511431	119772274
Average Total Receipts **9**	31550	867	122	2	2276	18276	2574	7986	25487	10405	200484	151143	9981023

Operating Costs/Operating Income (%)

	Total	Zero Assets	Under 500	500 to 1,000	1,000 to 5,000	5,000 to 10,000	10,000 to 25,000	25,000 to 50,000	50,000 to 100,000	100,000 to 250,000	250,000 to 500,000	500,000 to 2,500,000	2,500,000 and over
Cost of Operations **10**	12.5	•	•	•	•	•	•	•	•	•	1.6	•	13.0
Salaries and Wages **11**	16.8	8.0	2.2	3944.5	19.1	7.3	15.4	37.1	37.2	16.7	9.3	30.1	16.7
Taxes Paid **12**	1.5	4.8	2.8	204.0	2.9	1.1	8.2	3.7	3.0	2.2	1.0	2.4	1.4
Interest Paid **13**	26.1	18.4	0.0	•	0.1	0.8	0.3	4.0	2.8	9.4	1.3	8.8	27.0
Depreciation **14**	1.2	0.1	0.2	0.5	0.1	0.1	0.1	0.4	0.7	0.5	0.5	0.9	1.2
Amortization and Depletion **15**	0.7	0.0	0.6	45.0	0.5	•	0.1	0.1	0.1	0.0	26.6	4.4	0.4
Pensions and Other Deferred Comp. **16**	0.7	0.2	3.2	245.0	0.4	0.1	0.1	0.1	0.7	1.4	2.5	0.1	0.7
Employee Benefits **17**	0.7	0.3	1.0	98.5	1.7	0.9	1.6	0.6	2.3	0.9	0.7	1.2	0.7
Advertising **18**	0.2	0.0	8.6	57.0	0.1	0.2	0.1	1.9	0.2	0.0	0.7	0.1	0.1
Other Expenses **19**	26.9	96.5	35.6	22110.0	63.3	78.5	18.5	38.5	39.3	39.2	57.2	38.8	25.8
Officers' Compensation **20**	1.0	0.9	24.2	123.0	8.6	6.5	20.6	4.2	4.6	10.0	1.8	2.7	0.8
Operating Margin **21**	11.9	•	21.6	•	3.2	4.3	34.9	9.5	9.1	19.7	•	10.4	12.2
Operating Margin Before Officers' Comp. **22**	12.9	•	45.8	•	11.8	10.8	55.6	13.7	13.7	29.7	•	13.2	13.0

Selected Average Balance Sheet ($ in Thousands)													
Net Receivables 23	252927	0	7	0	9	3022	2740	6882	10185	31391	65388	80616	83267253
Inventories 24	•	•	•	•	•	•	•	•	•	•	•	•	•
Net Property, Plant and Equipment 25	3163	0	3	0	17	105	62	99	3660	1276	3565	6505	1028164
Total Assets 26	1073327	0	101	717	2692	7482	15774	33020	74050	145228	348384	1286317	352398447
Notes and Loans Payable 27	134374	0	0	0	275	2826	144	9198	21987	16297	73269	351806	43918160
All Other Liabilities 28	874844	0	12	0	225	2047	1539	8032	19333	34544	123951	614241	287954805
Net Worth 29	64109	0	89	717	2192	2609	14091	15790	32730	94387	151164	320270	20525482

Selected Financial Ratios (Times to 1)													
Current Ratio 30	1.1	•	5.0	22.6	2.5	2.6	10.0	3.7	1.6	1.1	1.3	1.1	1.1
Quick Ratio 31	0.6	•	3.9	22.3	2.4	2.5	6.4	3.0	1.2	0.9	1.1	0.3	0.6
Net Sales to Working Capital 32	0.7	•	2.7	1.3	7.0	5.3	0.3	0.7	1.8	3.5	4.1	3.2	0.7
Coverage Ratio 33	1.5	•	1511.8	•	45.7	6.4	99.7	3.4	3.5	2.9	•	2.1	1.5
Total Asset Turnover 34	0.0	•	1.2	0.0	0.8	2.4	0.2	0.2	0.3	0.1	0.6	0.1	0.0
Inventory Turnover 35	•	•	•	•	•	•	•	•	•	•	•	•	•
Receivables Turnover 36	•	•	•	•	•	•	•	•	•	•	•	•	•
Total Liabilities to Net Worth 37	15.7	•	0.1	0.0	0.2	1.9	0.1	1.1	1.3	0.5	1.3	3.0	16.2
Current Assets to Working Capital 38	16.1	•	1.3	1.0	1.7	1.6	1.1	1.4	2.7	14.8	4.1	13.2	16.3
Current Liabilities to Working Capital 39	15.1	•	0.3	0.0	0.7	0.6	0.1	0.4	1.7	13.8	3.1	12.2	15.3
Working Capital to Net Sales 40	1.3	•	0.4	0.8	0.1	0.2	4.0	1.4	0.6	0.3	0.2	0.3	1.4
Inventory to Working Capital 41	0.0	•	•	•	•	•	•	•	•	•	0.0	•	0.0
Total Receipts to Cash Flow 42	2.9	15.4	1.9	•	1.7	1.2	4.7	2.3	2.3	1.8	1.9	2.3	3.0
Cost of Goods to Cash Flow 43	0.4	•	•	•	•	•	•	•	•	0.0	•	0.4
Cash Flow to Total Debt 44	0.0	•	5.5	•	2.7	3.0	0.3	0.2	0.3	0.1	0.5	0.1	0.0

Selected Financial Factors (in Percentages)													
Debt Ratio 45	94.0	•	11.6	0.0	18.6	65.1	10.7	52.2	55.8	35.0	56.6	75.1	94.2
Return on Total Assets 46	1.2	•	26.0	•	2.5	12.4	5.4	3.2	3.4	2.0	•	2.2	1.2
Return on Equity Before Income Taxes 47	6.7	•	29.4	•	3.0	30.1	5.9	4.8	5.5	2.0	•	4.6	6.9
Return on Equity After Income Taxes 48	5.3	•	28.7	•	1.1	20.0	3.0	3.3	4.8	1.8	•	3.4	5.4
Profit Margin (Before Income Tax) 49	13.7	•	21.6	•	2.9	4.3	32.5	9.4	7.1	18.1	•	9.7	14.1
Profit Margin (After Income Tax) 50	10.8	•	21.0	•	1.1	2.9	16.3	6.5	6.1	16.0	•	7.3	11.2

Table II
Corporations with Net Income

INVESTMENT BANKING AND SECURITIES DEALING

MONEY AMOUNTS AND SIZE OF ASSETS IN THOUSANDS OF DOLLARS

Item Description for Accounting Period 7/12 Through 6/13	Total	Zero Assets	Under 500	500 to 1,000	1,000 to 5,000	5,000 to 10,000	10,000 to 25,000	25,000 to 50,000	50,000 to 100,000	100,000 to 250,000	250,000 to 500,000	500,000 to 2,500,000	2,500,000 and over
Number of Enterprises 1	1512	•	1275	54	94	•	•	22	11	6	3	7	8
Revenues ($ in Thousands)													
Net Sales 2	119563151	•	287165	59173	379034	•	•	217828	401991	91386	213042	1353233	115738510
Interest 3	42119539	•	5678	93	10402	•	•	23038	7967	24953	29641	129882	41678458
Rents 4	321798	•	0	0	682	•	•	16	32	0	0	0	321069
Royalties 5	66764	•	0	0	117	•	•	0	0	6900	0	1	59746
Other Portfolio Income 6	6051570	•	19	0	4970	•	•	4531	15318	4755	222	341856	5618622
Other Receipts 7	71003480	•	281468	59080	362863	•	•	190243	378674	54778	183179	881494	68060615
Total Receipts 8	119563151	•	287165	59173	379034	•	•	217828	401991	91386	213042	1353233	115738510
Average Total Receipts 9	79076	•	225	1096	4032	•	•	9901	36545	15231	71014	193319	14467314
Operating Costs/Operating Income (%)													
Cost of Operations 10	13.0	•	•	•	•	•	•	•	•	•	•	•	13.5
Salaries and Wages 11	16.9	•	2.1	13.3	14.2	•	•	34.3	33.8	18.6	39.6	30.5	16.7
Taxes Paid 12	1.4	•	2.7	0.7	2.9	•	•	3.5	2.6	2.4	3.6	2.5	1.3
Interest Paid 13	26.5	•	0.0	•	0.0	•	•	3.3	2.4	10.2	1.2	7.2	27.3
Depreciation 14	1.2	•	0.3	0.0	0.1	•	•	0.3	0.7	0.5	1.1	0.6	1.2
Amortization and Depletion 15	0.5	•	•	•	0.5	•	•	0.1	0.1	•	0.7	4.9	0.4
Pensions and Other Deferred Comp. 16	0.7	•	•	0.8	0.4	•	•	0.1	0.6	1.6	0.2	0.1	0.7
Employee Benefits 17	0.7	•	•	0.3	1.7	•	•	0.5	2.1	1.0	2.4	1.3	0.6
Advertising 18	0.1	•	11.3	0.2	0.1	•	•	0.0	0.2	0.0	0.2	0.1	0.1
Other Expenses 19	23.8	•	35.0	55.6	60.3	•	•	38.3	40.4	29.5	43.0	37.0	23.1
Officers' Compensation 20	0.9	•	13.7	0.4	7.8	•	•	3.2	4.9	11.4	3.0	2.7	0.8
Operating Margin 21	14.3	•	35.0	28.6	12.0	•	•	16.4	12.1	24.6	4.9	13.0	14.2
Operating Margin Before Officers' Comp. 22	15.2	•	48.6	29.0	19.8	•	•	19.5	17.0	36.0	7.9	15.7	15.0

Selected Average Balance Sheet ($ in Thousands)

Net Receivables	23	608121	•	0	0	16	•	•	6535	5851	31816	93979	115078 114745976
Inventories	24	•	•	•	•	•	•	•	•	•	•	•	•
Net Property, Plant and Equipment	25	6756	•	8	0	20	•	•	98	1846	2127	1270	4838 1265837
Total Assets	26	2621098	•	56	925	1588	•	•	33734	76499	146866	383619	1460537 493582916
Notes and Loans Payable	27	334064	•	0	0	10	•	•	3696	18457	21359	64472	301716 62797677
All Other Liabilities	28	1991452	•	18	0	399	•	•	11965	23784	31981	151797	781931 375535419
Net Worth	29	295583	•	38	925	1179	•	•	18074	34258	93526	167350	376890 55249820

Selected Financial Ratios (Times to 1)

Current Ratio	30	1.1	•	2.8	50.7	2.0	•	•	3.3	1.7	1.2	1.0	1.5	1.1
Quick Ratio	31	0.6	•	2.4	50.0	1.9	•	•	2.7	1.2	1.0	0.8	0.4	0.6
Net Sales to Working Capital	32	1.0	•	7.2	397.1	10.5	•	•	0.8	2.1	1.6	8.3	0.7	1.0
Coverage Ratio	33	1.6	•	1860.5	•	633.9	•	•	5.9	5.2	3.2	5.0	2.7	1.6
Total Asset Turnover	34	0.0	•	4.0	1.2	2.5	•	•	0.3	0.5	0.1	0.2	0.1	0.0
Inventory Turnover	35	•	•	•	•	•	•	•	•	•	•	•	•	•
Receivables Turnover	36	•	•	•	•	•	•	•	•	•	•	•	•	•
Total Liabilities to Net Worth	37	7.9	•	0.5	0.0	0.3	•	•	0.9	1.2	0.6	1.3	2.9	7.9
Current Assets to Working Capital	38	20.4	•	1.5	1.0	2.0	•	•	1.4	2.4	5.3	25.5	2.9	20.8
Current Liabilities to Working Capital	39	19.4	•	0.5	0.0	1.0	•	•	0.4	1.4	4.3	24.5	1.9	19.8
Working Capital to Net Sales	40	1.0	•	0.1	0.0	0.1	•	•	1.3	0.5	0.6	0.1	1.4	1.0
Inventory to Working Capital	41	0.0	•	•	•	•	•	•	•	•	•	•	•	0.0
Total Receipts to Cash Flow	42	3.0	•	1.5	1.2	1.5	•	•	2.0	2.1	2.0	2.5	2.3	3.0
Cost of Goods to Cash Flow	43	0.4	•	•	•	•	•	•	•	•	•	•	•	0.4
Cash Flow to Total Debt	44	0.0	•	8.3	12344.2	6.5	•	•	0.3	0.4	0.1	0.1	0.1	0.0

Selected Financial Factors (in Percentages)

Debt Ratio	45	88.7	•	31.9	0.0	25.7	•	•	46.4	55.2	36.3	56.4	74.2	88.8
Return on Total Assets	46	1.3	•	140.5	33.9	30.6	•	•	5.8	6.0	3.4	1.1	2.6	1.3
Return on Equity Before Income Taxes	47	4.3	•	206.3	33.9	41.1	•	•	9.0	10.9	3.7	2.1	6.2	4.2
Return on Equity After Income Taxes	48	3.5	•	201.9	33.9	34.7	•	•	6.7	9.7	3.3	1.6	4.9	3.4
Profit Margin (Before Income Tax)	49	16.1	•	35.0	28.6	12.0	•	•	16.4	10.2	22.8	4.9	12.2	16.1
Profit Margin (After Income Tax)	50	13.1	•	34.2	28.6	10.2	•	•	12.3	9.1	20.4	3.7	9.6	13.1

Table I

Corporations with and without Net Income

SECURITIES BROKERAGE

MONEY AMOUNTS AND SIZE OF ASSETS IN THOUSANDS OF DOLLARS

Item Description for Accounting Period 7/12 Through 6/13	Total	Zero Assets	Under 500	500 to 1,000	1,000 to 5,000	5,000 to 10,000	10,000 to 25,000	25,000 to 50,000	50,000 to 100,000	100,000 to 250,000	250,000 to 500,000	500,000 to 2,500,000	2,500,000 and over
Number of Enterprises **1**	6718	892	4460	370	732	54	78	31	22	17	15	17	28
Revenues ($ in Thousands)													
Net Sales **2**	79181378	575714	1895351	1283070	2287689	559250	2027143	887354	1030049	1532199	3635887	3401727	60065944
Interest **3**	19474845	55746	55	12336	2208	1832	9007	2225	10797	12549	17210	132252	19218629
Rents **4**	198864	0	0	0	967	2938	2017	178	0	0	603	35309	156852
Royalties **5**	6759	15	0	0	0	0	5534	0	0	0	653	277	281
Other Portfolio Income **6**	2354376	6039	0	0	6609	11754	6216	8466	50891	14150	16637	78665	2154947
Other Receipts **7**	57146534	513914	1895296	1270734	2277905	542726	2004369	876485	968361	1505500	3600784	3155224	38535235
Total Receipts **8**	79181378	575714	1895351	1283070	2287689	559250	2027143	887354	1030049	1532199	3635887	3401727	60065944
Average Total Receipts **9**	11786	645	425	3468	3125	10356	25989	28624	46820	90129	242392	200102	2145212
Operating Costs/Operating Income (%)													
Cost of Operations **10**	0.0	•	•	•	•	•	•	•	•	•	•	•	0.0
Salaries and Wages **11**	26.1	17.3	19.6	51.0	36.4	34.8	13.1	43.6	37.6	27.8	32.3	33.1	24.6
Taxes Paid **12**	2.2	4.2	3.2	2.2	3.5	3.0	1.8	4.2	3.1	2.0	2.2	2.8	2.0
Interest Paid **13**	13.8	7.3	1.0	•	0.7	0.2	0.8	0.4	0.9	1.6	1.9	5.8	17.5
Depreciation **14**	0.9	0.4	0.4	0.1	0.2	1.0	0.3	1.2	0.7	1.3	0.8	1.1	1.0
Amortization and Depletion **15**	0.8	2.7	0.2	•	0.0	0.2	0.2	0.3	1.2	1.6	0.8	1.8	0.8
Pensions and Other Deferred Comp. **16**	0.7	0.1	1.7	0.2	0.4	0.7	0.3	1.4	0.4	0.2	0.6	3.7	0.6
Employee Benefits **17**	1.6	0.9	0.5	1.4	1.5	2.2	1.4	2.0	2.1	0.9	1.5	1.6	1.6
Advertising **18**	1.1	0.2	1.4	0.0	0.1	0.4	0.3	1.0	0.7	1.5	0.4	0.5	1.2
Other Expenses **19**	35.7	46.0	38.4	33.7	39.3	38.4	76.6	37.4	40.7	58.7	57.0	42.2	31.6
Officers' Compensation **20**	5.3	7.3	19.0	10.6	12.2	11.8	3.5	6.5	5.8	1.5	2.1	1.3	5.0
Operating Margin **21**	11.8	13.6	14.7	0.8	5.6	7.4	1.7	2.0	6.9	2.8	0.4	6.0	14.0
Operating Margin Before Officers' Comp. **22**	17.1	21.0	33.7	11.4	17.8	19.1	5.3	8.5	12.7	4.3	2.5	7.3	19.0

Selected Average Balance Sheet ($ in Thousands)

Net Receivables 23	18220	0	1	217	61	403	1789	2726	6449	32560	62004	163228	4200903
Inventories 24	•	•	•	•	•	•	•	•	•	•	•	•	•
Net Property, Plant and Equipment 25	627	0	25	26	86	732	569	1662	1316	3954	7736	29196	113717
Total Assets 26	220447	0	105	649	2027	7829	15488	36926	69209	174788	356540	1242473	51608399
Notes and Loans Payable 27	22294	0	51	45	196	259	2459	2329	7826	28823	55892	171398	5167562
All Other Liabilities 28	183335	0	9	266	596	1883	5526	9812	21177	68299	167695	632643	43404747
Net Worth 29	14819	0	45	338	1235	5686	7502	24785	40205	77666	132953	438431	3036089

Selected Financial Ratios (Times to 1)

Current Ratio 30	0.9	•	1.6	2.2	3.1	2.6	2.1	2.1	2.1	1.4	1.3	1.2	0.9
Quick Ratio 31	0.2	•	1.3	1.9	2.1	1.9	1.5	1.6	1.3	0.9	1.0	0.9	0.2
Net Sales to Working Capital 32	•	•	43.8	11.3	3.7	3.4	4.4	2.5	2.3	3.1	4.6	2.0	•
Coverage Ratio 33	1.9	2.9	16.1	•	8.3	35.2	2.8	5.7	8.0	2.3	1.2	2.2	1.8
Total Asset Turnover 34	0.1	•	4.1	5.3	1.5	1.3	1.7	0.8	0.7	0.5	0.7	0.2	0.0
Inventory Turnover 35	•	•	•	•	•	•	•	•	•	•	•	•	•
Receivables Turnover 36	•	•	•	•	•	•	•	•	•	•	•	•	•
Total Liabilities to Net Worth 37	13.9	•	1.4	0.9	0.6	0.4	1.1	0.5	0.7	1.3	1.7	1.8	16.0
Current Assets to Working Capital 38	•	•	2.6	1.9	1.5	1.6	1.9	1.9	1.9	3.8	3.9	6.4	•
Current Liabilities to Working Capital 39	•	•	1.6	0.9	0.5	0.6	0.9	0.9	0.9	2.8	2.9	5.4	•
Working Capital to Net Sales 40	•	•	0.0	0.1	0.3	0.3	0.2	0.4	0.4	0.3	0.2	0.5	•
Inventory to Working Capital 41	•	•	•	•	•	•	•	0.0	•	0.0	0.0	•	•
Total Receipts to Cash Flow 42	2.3	1.8	2.4	3.2	2.5	2.5	1.3	2.9	2.2	1.7	1.8	2.3	2.4
Cost of Goods to Cash Flow 43	0.0	•	•	•	•	•	•	•	•	•	•	•	0.0
Cash Flow to Total Debt 44	0.0	•	2.9	3.5	1.6	1.9	2.5	0.8	0.7	0.5	0.6	0.1	0.0

Selected Financial Factors (in Percentages)

Debt Ratio 45	93.3	•	57.5	47.9	39.0	27.4	51.6	32.9	41.9	55.6	62.7	64.7	94.1
Return on Total Assets 46	1.4	•	63.5	4.5	9.5	9.8	3.8	1.8	4.9	1.9	1.5	2.1	1.3
Return on Equity Before Income Taxes 47	9.3	•	140.2	8.7	13.7	13.2	5.0	2.2	7.3	2.5	0.5	3.2	9.8
Return on Equity After Income Taxes 48	7.7	•	140.1	6.9	13.4	10.8	2.9	•	5.4	1.2	•	1.8	8.3
Profit Margin (Before Income Tax) 49	11.7	13.6	14.7	0.8	5.4	7.2	1.4	1.9	6.3	2.2	0.3	7.0	13.9
Profit Margin (After Income Tax) 50	9.7	8.0	14.7	0.7	5.3	5.9	0.8	•	4.6	1.1	•	3.8	11.7

Table II

Corporations with Net Income

SECURITIES BROKERAGE

MONEY AMOUNTS AND SIZE OF ASSETS IN THOUSANDS OF DOLLARS

Item Description for Accounting Period 7/12 Through 6/13	Total	Zero Assets	Under 500	500 to 1,000	1,000 to 5,000	5,000 to 10,000	10,000 to 25,000	25,000 to 50,000	50,000 to 100,000	100,000 to 250,000	250,000 to 500,000	500,000 to 2,500,000	2,500,000 and over
Number of Enterprises **1**	4372	403	3040	341	429	38	36	18	16	8	9	12	23
Revenues ($ in Thousands)													
Net Sales **2**	72073104	345109	1777989	1272363	933141	419613	1310045	637970	822522	1139467	2235000	2469079	58710806
Interest **3**	18738904	53994	1	3106	1379	1388	4418	1178	8766	8749	8299	45263	18602362
Rents **4**	197394	0	0	0	0	2938	1748	43	0	0	603	35309	156753
Royalties **5**	5815	0	0	0	0	0	5534	0	0	0	0	0	281
Other Portfolio Income **6**	2271985	4302	0	0	3720	11008	2243	1501	49064	13309	3423	53601	2129810
Other Receipts **7**	50859006	286813	1777988	1269257	928042	404279	1296102	635248	764692	1117409	2222675	2334906	37821600
Total Receipts **8**	72073104	345109	1777989	1272363	933141	419613	1310045	637970	822522	1139467	2235000	2469079	58710806
Average Total Receipts **9**	16485	856	585	3731	2175	11042	36390	35443	51408	142433	248333	205757	2552644
Operating Costs/Operating Income (%)													
Cost of Operations **10**	0.0	•	•	•	•	•	•	•	•	•	•	•	0.0
Salaries and Wages **11**	25.0	18.8	19.2	48.8	23.0	37.0	9.7	48.3	35.1	23.3	27.6	27.4	24.4
Taxes Paid **12**	2.1	4.0	3.2	2.2	3.8	3.9	1.5	4.2	2.9	1.9	2.2	2.9	2.0
Interest Paid **13**	14.5	10.0	1.0	•	0.4	0.2	0.6	0.5	0.9	0.5	1.0	5.7	17.4
Depreciation **14**	0.9	0.2	0.4	0.1	0.1	0.5	0.3	1.6	0.3	0.8	0.8	1.1	1.0
Amortization and Depletion **15**	0.7	2.2	0.0	•	•	0.2	0.2	0.3	0.8	0.8	0.2	2.0	0.7
Pensions and Other Deferred Comp. **16**	0.7	0.2	1.8	0.2	0.9	1.0	0.4	0.3	0.4	0.1	0.9	1.5	0.6
Employee Benefits **17**	1.5	1.2	0.3	1.4	0.8	2.4	1.2	1.8	2.2	0.5	1.7	1.2	1.6
Advertising **18**	1.1	0.1	1.0	0.0	0.2	0.5	0.5	0.7	0.6	1.4	0.5	0.2	1.3
Other Expenses **19**	33.7	27.5	36.5	32.9	23.0	23.4	76.1	25.2	38.9	57.9	57.5	42.1	31.2
Officers' Compensation **20**	5.4	6.6	19.1	10.5	22.0	15.0	3.6	4.7	6.1	1.6	0.9	0.8	5.0
Operating Margin **21**	14.4	29.2	17.5	3.9	25.7	16.0	6.0	12.5	11.8	11.2	6.6	15.1	14.9
Operating Margin Before Officers' Comp. **22**	19.8	35.8	36.6	14.4	47.8	31.0	9.5	17.2	17.8	12.8	7.5	15.9	19.9

Selected Average Balance Sheet ($ in Thousands)

Net Receivables 23	27301	0	1	235	61	534	2055	2322	7516	36914	64798	227870	5016636
Inventories 24	•	•	•	•	•	•	•	•	•	•	•	•	•
Net Property, Plant and Equipment 25	893	0	36	28	39	936	842	2082	1060	5420	7493	33182	136503
Total Assets 26	321488	0	130	656	1880	8095	17545	36230	68634	177555	334727	1193569	60116296
Notes and Loans Payable 27	32361	0	71	0	110	367	1492	3411	9477	30616	43728	185417	6003174
All Other Liabilities 28	267390	0	12	275	541	2378	6757	11334	22752	61711	167772	502161	50423225
Net Worth 29	21738	0	47	381	1228	5350	9296	21485	36406	85227	123227	505991	3689897

Selected Financial Ratios (Times to 1)

Current Ratio 30	0.9	•	1.7	2.1	5.3	2.0	2.2	2.5	2.1	1.3	1.6	1.3	0.9
Quick Ratio 31	0.2	•	1.3	1.9	3.6	1.4	1.6	1.7	1.2	1.0	1.2	1.1	0.2
Net Sales to Working Capital 32	•	•	42.6	12.5	1.8	4.3	4.7	2.0	2.3	6.5	3.0	1.6	•
Coverage Ratio 33	2.0	3.9	18.0	•	57.6	71.1	10.1	27.9	12.8	21.6	7.2	3.9	1.9
Total Asset Turnover 34	0.1	•	4.5	5.7	1.2	1.4	2.1	1.0	0.7	0.8	0.7	0.2	0.0
Inventory Turnover 35	•	•	•	•	•	•	•	•	•	•	•	•	•
Receivables Turnover 36	•	•	•	•	•	•	•	•	•	•	•	•	•
Total Liabilities to Net Worth 37	13.8	•	1.8	0.7	0.5	0.5	0.9	0.7	0.9	1.1	1.7	1.4	15.3
Current Assets to Working Capital 38	•	•	2.5	1.9	1.2	2.0	1.8	1.7	1.9	4.4	2.8	4.2	•
Current Liabilities to Working Capital 39	•	•	1.5	0.9	0.2	1.0	0.8	0.7	0.9	3.4	1.8	3.2	•
Working Capital to Net Sales 40	•	•	0.0	0.1	0.5	0.2	0.2	0.5	0.4	0.2	0.3	0.6	•
Inventory to Working Capital 41	•	•	•	•	•	•	•	•	•	•	•	•	•
Total Receipts to Cash Flow 42	2.3	1.9	2.4	2.9	2.2	3.1	1.2	3.0	2.1	1.5	1.6	1.9	2.3
Cost of Goods to Cash Flow 43	0.0	•	•	•	•	•	•	•	•	•	•	•	0.0
Cash Flow to Total Debt 44	0.0	•	3.0	4.6	1.5	1.3	3.6	0.8	0.8	1.0	0.7	0.2	0.0

Selected Financial Factors (in Percentages)

Debt Ratio 45	93.2	•	63.9	41.9	34.7	33.9	47.0	40.7	47.0	52.0	63.2	57.6	93.9
Return on Total Assets 46	1.5	•	83.6	22.2	29.8	21.9	13.4	12.5	8.9	8.7	5.6	3.8	1.4
Return on Equity Before Income Taxes 47	10.9	•	218.7	38.1	44.9	32.6	22.9	20.4	15.5	17.3	13.2	6.7	10.2
Return on Equity After Income Taxes 48	9.2	•	218.6	36.5	44.4	29.1	19.1	15.3	12.6	14.9	9.7	4.9	8.6
Profit Margin (Before Income Tax) 49	14.4	29.1	17.5	3.9	25.3	15.8	5.8	12.3	11.0	10.4	6.5	16.4	14.8
Profit Margin (After Income Tax) 50	12.1	19.8	17.5	3.7	25.1	14.1	4.9	9.3	8.9	8.9	4.8	12.1	12.5

Table I

Corporations with and without Net Income

COMMODITY CONTRACTS DEALING AND BROKERAGE

MONEY AMOUNTS AND SIZE OF ASSETS IN THOUSANDS OF DOLLARS

Item Description for Accounting Period 7/12 Through 6/13	Total	Zero Assets	Under 500	500 to 1,000	1,000 to 5,000	5,000 to 10,000	10,000 to 25,000	25,000 to 50,000	50,000 to 100,000	100,000 to 250,000	250,000 to 500,000	500,000 to 2,500,000	2,500,000 and over
Number of Enterprises **1**	2372	13	1668	451	133	14	44	16	11	5	7	4	6

Revenues ($ in Thousands)													
Net Sales **2**	4241622	184575	224255	46517	110399	46570	108864	164642	117330	20688	274889	171391	2771502
Interest **3**	309205	12355	411	6	15	115	49	1943	984	545	12716	16628	263438
Rents **4**	73083	0	0	0	0	0	0	0	0	168	176	0	72739
Royalties **5**	3510	0	0	0	0	0	0	0	0	0	3510	0	0
Other Portfolio Income **6**	191826	65073	0	53	0	15	10565	6098	1288	0	1210	1	107523
Other Receipts **7**	3663998	107147	223844	46458	110384	46440	98250	156601	115058	19975	257277	154762	2327802
Total Receipts **8**	4241622	184575	224255	46517	110399	46570	108864	164642	117330	20688	274889	171391	2771502
Average Total Receipts **9**	1788	14198	134	103	830	3326	2474	10290	10666	4138	39270	42848	461917

Operating Costs/Operating Income (%)													
Cost of Operations **10**	3.1	•	•	•	•	•	•	•	•	•	•	•	4.8
Salaries and Wages **11**	16.0	27.3	7.9	4.2	30.2	48.7	29.5	16.4	58.2	19.0	24.1	11.9	12.0
Taxes Paid **12**	2.7	1.0	1.3	6.5	3.5	3.9	5.6	5.7	4.1	7.8	2.9	1.8	2.5
Interest Paid **13**	8.5	35.8	1.6	4.1	0.0	0.1	3.2	2.9	3.8	25.6	5.2	10.3	8.7
Depreciation **14**	2.1	3.1	2.4	15.3	0.8	2.8	1.4	2.3	0.7	1.0	2.0	0.1	2.1
Amortization and Depletion **15**	2.0	1.0	•	23.9	0.4	•	0.0	0.0	4.6	0.0	6.0	2.9	1.5
Pensions and Other Deferred Comp. **16**	1.2	0.1	1.8	19.0	3.2	3.1	2.8	0.0	1.1	•	6.8	0.4	0.4
Employee Benefits **17**	1.3	•	1.8	0.9	1.1	1.9	1.9	2.5	2.5	3.3	2.7	1.0	1.1
Advertising **18**	0.3	•	0.3	1.0	0.6	•	0.1	3.2	1.0	0.1	0.9	0.0	0.1
Other Expenses **19**	52.6	27.5	39.3	47.0	43.3	57.3	50.3	59.3	32.6	54.0	39.0	52.0	57.7
Officers' Compensation **20**	5.2	0.7	13.9	114.4	22.8	9.6	4.6	4.1	7.3	12.9	8.4	9.0	1.5
Operating Margin **21**	4.9	3.6	29.7	•	•	•	0.5	3.5	•	•	2.0	10.5	7.6
Operating Margin Before Officers' Comp. **22**	10.1	4.3	43.7	•	16.8	•	5.1	7.7	•	•	10.4	19.5	9.2

Selected Average Balance Sheet ($ in Thousands)

Net Receivables 23	6316	0	8	12	904	9	4569	8917	20535	53177	11947	161803	2212526
Inventories 24	•	•	•	•	•	•	•	•	•	•	•	•	•
Net Property, Plant and Equipment 25	109	0	23	50	31	378	145	1174	281	796	5366	95	19532
Total Assets 26	26888	0	96	825	1826	7464	16633	31425	68088	157961	365609	698988	9128362
Notes and Loans Payable 27	3549	0	16	416	546	3139	2154	9648	9378	34630	100293	160170	1036461
All Other Liabilities 28	20966	0	4	134	1178	2284	9575	12471	29903	83584	169845	494176	7490577
Net Worth 29	2373	0	76	275	101	2041	4904	9306	28806	39747	95471	44642	601324

Selected Financial Ratios (Times to 1)

Current Ratio 30	1.6	•	9.5	1.0	1.5	1.8	2.8	1.6	1.1	1.0	0.8	0.9	1.8
Quick Ratio 31	1.0	•	9.2	0.9	1.4	1.7	1.7	1.4	0.7	0.6	0.5	0.6	1.1
Net Sales to Working Capital 32	0.2	•	2.4	•	2.4	1.9	0.3	1.5	2.3	•	•	•	0.1
Coverage Ratio 33	1.6	1.1	20.0	•	•	•	1.1	2.2	•	0.1	1.4	2.0	1.9
Total Asset Turnover 34	0.1	•	1.4	0.1	0.5	0.4	0.1	0.3	0.2	0.0	0.1	0.1	0.1
Inventory Turnover 35	•	•	•	•	•	•	•	•	•	•	•	•	•
Receivables Turnover 36	•	•	•	•	•	•	•	•	•	•	•	•	•
Total Liabilities to Net Worth 37	10.3	•	0.3	2.0	17.1	2.7	2.4	2.4	1.4	3.0	2.8	14.7	14.2
Current Assets to Working Capital 38	2.5	•	1.1	•	3.1	2.3	1.6	2.6	9.1	•	•	•	2.3
Current Liabilities to Working Capital 39	1.5	•	0.1	•	2.1	1.3	0.6	1.6	8.1	•	•	•	1.3
Working Capital to Net Sales 40	5.1	•	0.4	•	0.4	0.5	3.0	0.7	0.4	•	•	•	7.8
Inventory to Working Capital 41	0.0	•	•	•	•	•	•	•	0.0	•	•	•	•
Total Receipts to Cash Flow 42	2.1	•	1.6	•	4.3	4.4	3.1	2.0	9.7	3.6	2.8	1.6	1.8
Cost of Goods to Cash Flow 43	0.1	•	•	•	•	•	•	•	•	•	•	•	0.1
Cash Flow to Total Debt 44	0.0	•	4.3	•	0.1	0.1	0.1	0.2	0.0	0.0	0.1	0.0	0.0

Selected Financial Factors (in Percentages)

Debt Ratio 45	91.2	•	20.2	66.7	94.5	72.7	70.5	70.4	57.7	74.8	73.9	93.6	93.4
Return on Total Assets 46	0.9	•	44.0	•	•	•	0.6	2.1	•	0.0	0.8	1.3	0.8
Return on Equity Before Income Taxes 47	3.7	•	52.3	•	•	•	0.2	3.9	•	•	0.8	10.1	5.9
Return on Equity After Income Taxes 48	1.5	•	52.3	•	•	•	•	2.8	•	•	0.0	6.4	3.4
Profit Margin (Before Income Tax) 49	4.9	3.6	29.7	•	•	•	0.5	3.5	•	•	2.0	10.5	7.6
Profit Margin (After Income Tax) 50	2.0	•	29.7	•	•	•	•	2.5	•	•	0.1	6.7	4.4

Table II
Corporations with Net Income

COMMODITY CONTRACTS DEALING AND BROKERAGE

MONEY AMOUNTS AND SIZE OF ASSETS IN THOUSANDS OF DOLLARS

Item Description for Accounting Period 7/12 Through 6/13	Total	Zero Assets	Under 500	500 to 1,000	1,000 to 5,000	5,000 to 10,000	10,000 to 25,000	25,000 to 50,000	50,000 to 100,000	100,000 to 250,000	250,000 to 500,000	500,000 to 2,500,000	2,500,000 and over
Number of Enterprises 1	1447	•	1283	85	19	•	•	6	7	0	4	4	0
Revenues ($ in Thousands)													
Net Sales 2	2038527	•	224255	33187	61600	•	•	101653	139915	0	153713	998626	0
Interest 3	69369	•	411	6	0	•	•	1265	970	0	7259	46945	0
Rents 4	53642	•	0	0	0	•	•	0	168	0	0	53473	0
Royalties 5	0	•	0	0	0	•	•	0	0	0	0	0	0
Other Portfolio Income 6	144656	•	0	0	0	•	•	2	1288	0	1202	77091	0
Other Receipts 7	1770860	•	223844	33181	61600	•	•	100386	137489	0	145252	821117	0
Total Receipts 8	2038527	•	224255	33187	61600	•	•	101653	139915	0	153713	998626	0
Average Total Receipts 9	1409	•	175	390	3242	•	•	16942	19988	•	38428	249656	•
Operating Costs/Operating Income (%)													
Cost of Operations 10	6.5	•	•	•	•	•	•	•	•	•	•	13.2	•
Salaries and Wages 11	17.1	•	7.9	6.0	27.8	•	•	2.4	30.0	•	14.4	17.8	•
Taxes Paid 12	2.7	•	1.3	3.5	1.5	•	•	1.2	3.0	•	3.8	3.4	•
Interest Paid 13	8.4	•	1.6	3.6	•	•	•	3.4	6.0	•	5.2	8.0	•
Depreciation 14	2.1	•	2.4	•	•	•	•	0.3	0.5	•	1.9	2.8	•
Amortization and Depletion 15	2.2	•	•	33.5	•	•	•	•	1.6	•	3.1	2.5	•
Pensions and Other Deferred Comp. 16	0.9	•	1.8	•	0.7	•	•	•	0.8	•	0.6	1.1	•
Employee Benefits 17	0.5	•	1.8	1.2	0.7	•	•	0.1	1.5	•	0.6	0.2	•
Advertising 18	0.1	•	0.3	•	0.1	•	•	•	0.2	•	0.0	0.1	•
Other Expenses 19	25.9	•	38.8	13.2	34.3	•	•	60.1	24.2	•	33.3	19.3	•
Officers' Compensation 20	5.4	•	13.9	27.2	4.2	•	•	0.2	6.9	•	7.8	4.1	•
Operating Margin 21	28.1	•	30.2	11.8	30.8	•	•	32.3	25.2	•	29.3	27.4	•
Operating Margin Before Officers' Comp. 22	33.5	•	44.2	39.0	35.0	•	•	32.5	32.1	•	37.1	31.5	•

Selected Average Balance Sheet ($ in Thousands)

	C1	C2	C3	C4	C5	C6	C7	C8	C9	C10	C11	C12	C13
Net Receivables 23	5836	•	11	22	1934	•	•	8692	40347	•	14149	1999614	•
Inventories 24	•	•	•	•	•	•	•	•	•	•	•	•	•
Net Property, Plant and Equipment 25	96	•	30	0	0	•	•	84	779	•	4364	17934	•
Total Assets 26	10982	•	115	651	2865	•	•	31482	96504	•	398234	3181690	•
Notes and Loans Payable 27	4009	•	7	0	0	•	•	6636	38549	•	68889	1296264	•
All Other Liabilities 28	5250	•	5	535	1934	•	•	15296	36507	•	224915	1533942	•
Net Worth 29	1723	•	104	116	932	•	•	9550	21448	•	104431	351484	•

Selected Financial Ratios (Times to 1)

	C1	C2	C3	C4	C5	C6	C7	C8	C9	C10	C11	C12	C13
Current Ratio 30	1.6	•	8.5	30.0	1.5	•	•	1.6	0.9	•	0.8	1.7	•
Quick Ratio 31	1.4	•	8.1	29.8	1.4	•	•	1.2	0.6	•	0.4	1.6	•
Net Sales to Working Capital 32	0.5	•	2.8	1.1	3.5	•	•	2.5	•	•	•	0.2	•
Coverage Ratio 33	4.3	•	20.3	4.3	•	•	•	10.6	5.2	•	6.7	4.4	•
Total Asset Turnover 34	0.1	•	1.5	0.6	1.1	•	•	0.5	0.2	•	0.1	0.1	•
Inventory Turnover 35	•	•	•	•	•	•	•	•	•	•	•	•	•
Receivables Turnover 36	•	•	•	•	•	•	•	•	•	•	•	•	•
Total Liabilities to Net Worth 37	5.4	•	0.1	4.6	2.1	•	•	2.3	3.5	•	2.8	8.1	•
Current Assets to Working Capital 38	2.8	•	1.1	1.0	3.1	•	•	2.6	•	•	•	2.4	•
Current Liabilities to Working Capital 39	1.8	•	0.1	0.0	2.1	•	•	1.6	•	•	•	1.4	•
Working Capital to Net Sales 40	2.1	•	0.4	0.9	0.3	•	•	0.4	•	•	•	4.2	•
Inventory to Working Capital 41	0.0	•	•	•	•	•	•	•	•	•	•	•	•
Total Receipts to Cash Flow 42	2.0	•	1.6	4.0	1.5	•	•	1.1	2.1	•	1.6	2.2	•
Cost of Goods to Cash Flow 43	0.1	•	•	•	•	•	•	•	•	•	•	0.3	•
Cash Flow to Total Debt 44	0.1	•	9.3	0.2	1.1	•	•	0.7	0.1	•	0.1	0.0	•

Selected Financial Factors (in Percentages)

	C1	C2	C3	C4	C5	C6	C7	C8	C9	C10	C11	C12	C13
Debt Ratio 45	84.3	•	10.0	82.2	67.5	•	•	69.7	77.8	•	73.8	89.0	•
Return on Total Assets 46	4.7	•	48.1	9.2	34.8	•	•	19.2	6.5	•	3.3	2.8	•
Return on Equity Before Income Taxes 47	23.0	•	50.8	39.8	107.0	•	•	57.2	23.5	•	10.8	19.5	•
Return on Equity After Income Taxes 48	18.0	•	50.8	33.8	106.0	•	•	54.3	16.3	•	9.5	12.7	•
Profit Margin (Before Income Tax) 49	28.1	•	30.2	11.8	30.7	•	•	32.3	25.2	•	29.3	27.4	•
Profit Margin (After Income Tax) 50	22.0	•	30.2	10.0	30.5	•	•	30.6	17.5	•	25.9	17.8	•

Table I

Corporations with and without Net Income

SECURITIES & COMMODITY EXCHANGES, OTHER FINANCIAL INVESTMENT

MONEY AMOUNTS AND SIZE OF ASSETS IN THOUSANDS OF DOLLARS

Item Description for Accounting Period 7/12 Through 6/13	Total	Zero Assets	Under 500	500 to 1,000	1,000 to 5,000	5,000 to 10,000	10,000 to 25,000	25,000 to 50,000	50,000 to 100,000	100,000 to 250,000	250,000 to 500,000	500,000 to 2,500,000	2,500,000 and over
Number of Enterprises **1**	47578	10230	30368	2032	2906	871	534	254	138	112	47	53	34

Revenues ($ in Thousands)

	Total	Zero Assets	Under 500	500 to 1,000	1,000 to 5,000	5,000 to 10,000	10,000 to 25,000	25,000 to 50,000	50,000 to 100,000	100,000 to 250,000	250,000 to 500,000	500,000 to 2,500,000	2,500,000 and over
Net Sales **2**	119559632	2370856	8629708	1818823	6561364	5225972	3600591	3696176	3369067	7000987	5198632	13070831	59016625
Interest **3**	5009931	38949	5541	11853	34014	44019	26481	34343	98825	102295	126271	453161	4034181
Rents **4**	155782	448	2109	2049	134	3492	608	1647	164	14754	9750	32198	88428
Royalties **5**	209431	222	0	0	0	2278	10959	2627	15491	4369	16	126766	46703
Other Portfolio Income **6**	4252122	354855	62679	46040	152069	180462	187424	236067	228982	472783	324251	685254	1321252
Other Receipts **7**	109932366	1976382	8559379	1758881	6375147	4995721	3375119	3421492	3025605	6406786	4738344	11773452	53526061
Total Receipts **8**	119559632	2370856	8629708	1818823	6561364	5225972	3600591	3696176	3369067	7000987	5198632	13070831	59016625
Average Total Receipts **9**	2513	232	284	895	2258	6000	6743	14552	24414	62509	110609	246619	1735783

Operating Costs/Operating Income (%)

	Total	Zero Assets	Under 500	500 to 1,000	1,000 to 5,000	5,000 to 10,000	10,000 to 25,000	25,000 to 50,000	50,000 to 100,000	100,000 to 250,000	250,000 to 500,000	500,000 to 2,500,000	2,500,000 and over
Cost of Operations **10**	0.2	•	•	•	•	0.0	•	0.4	0.1	0.0	•	1.9	0.0
Salaries and Wages **11**	23.2	8.3	17.1	24.6	22.4	33.0	37.6	32.2	29.7	27.0	19.7	19.4	22.8
Taxes Paid **12**	2.5	2.4	3.0	2.4	2.7	2.9	5.2	3.1	3.0	2.4	2.4	2.1	2.2
Interest Paid **13**	6.3	2.6	0.7	1.1	1.0	1.3	1.9	1.8	5.5	3.7	4.2	7.0	9.3
Depreciation **14**	1.8	0.7	0.6	0.8	0.8	1.0	1.3	1.3	1.5	1.5	2.6	0.9	2.4
Amortization and Depletion **15**	1.9	3.0	0.1	0.5	0.4	0.6	0.7	1.0	1.4	1.7	6.2	4.5	1.7
Pensions and Other Deferred Comp. **16**	1.6	1.7	1.7	2.2	0.7	0.8	0.8	0.8	0.8	1.1	0.3	0.6	2.3
Employee Benefits **17**	1.8	1.3	2.0	1.3	2.1	2.7	1.7	2.7	1.8	1.4	1.9	1.4	1.8
Advertising **18**	1.2	0.1	1.1	0.2	1.0	0.3	0.5	0.3	0.5	1.9	0.6	0.5	1.6
Other Expenses **19**	36.3	87.4	33.1	28.7	30.1	36.7	30.6	28.6	43.2	35.2	43.3	49.8	32.6
Officers' Compensation **20**	7.1	7.4	21.3	22.0	20.7	7.9	6.9	11.6	9.3	9.1	3.2	5.7	3.0
Operating Margin **21**	16.1	•	19.3	16.1	18.2	12.7	12.7	16.3	3.3	14.8	15.7	6.1	20.3
Operating Margin Before Officers' Comp. **22**	23.2	•	40.6	38.1	38.8	20.6	19.6	27.8	12.6	23.9	18.9	11.8	23.3

Selected Average Balance Sheet ($ in Thousands)

Net Receivables 23	1211	0	4	181	257	1250	1536	3867	6335	18377	52106	87805	1277543
Inventories 24	•	•	•	•	•	•	•	•	•	•	•	•	•
Net Property, Plant and Equipment 25	321	0	9	49	273	411	531	1524	4407	8331	12118	30457	275051
Total Assets 26	14119	0	81	746	2490	7044	15410	35070	70139	153697	359388	964299	15952757
Notes and Loans Payable 27	3512	0	40	300	655	1532	4293	6331	22887	40829	91867	263055	3886007
All Other Liabilities 28	6079	0	19	63	261	1560	2666	6217	13019	41399	62659	264129	7647216
Net Worth 29	4529	0	22	383	1574	3952	8451	22522	34234	71469	204862	437114	4419534

Selected Financial Ratios (Times to 1)

Current Ratio 30	0.9	•	3.2	3.9	4.7	1.8	2.0	2.4	1.3	1.7	1.6	1.2	0.8
Quick Ratio 31	0.6	•	2.3	3.7	3.5	1.5	1.4	1.7	0.9	1.1	1.4	1.0	0.5
Net Sales to Working Capital 32	•	•	8.1	2.9	2.3	5.1	2.7	1.9	5.2	2.5	2.7	5.6	•
Coverage Ratio 33	3.7	•	27.6	15.7	20.0	10.8	7.6	10.2	1.6	5.0	4.9	2.0	3.3
Total Asset Turnover 34	0.2	•	3.5	1.2	0.9	0.9	0.4	0.4	0.3	0.4	0.3	0.3	0.1
Inventory Turnover 35	•	•	•	•	•	•	•	•	•	•	•	•	•
Receivables Turnover 36	•	•	•	•	•	•	•	•	•	•	•	•	•
Total Liabilities to Net Worth 37	2.1	•	2.7	0.9	0.6	0.8	0.8	0.6	1.0	1.2	0.8	1.2	2.6
Current Assets to Working Capital 38	•	•	1.5	1.3	1.3	2.3	2.0	1.7	4.5	2.4	2.7	5.8	•
Current Liabilities to Working Capital 39	•	•	0.5	0.3	0.3	1.3	1.0	0.7	3.5	1.4	1.7	4.8	•
Working Capital to Net Sales 40	•	•	0.1	0.3	0.4	0.2	0.4	0.5	0.2	0.4	0.4	0.2	•
Inventory to Working Capital 41	•	•	•	•	•	0.0	•	0.0	0.0	0.0	0.0	0.0	•
Total Receipts to Cash Flow 42	2.1	1.7	2.2	2.5	2.3	2.7	2.7	2.8	2.9	2.4	2.0	1.9	2.0
Cost of Goods to Cash Flow 43	0.0	•	•	•	•	0.0	•	0.0	0.0	0.0	•	0.0	0.0
Cash Flow to Total Debt 44	0.1	•	2.2	1.0	1.1	0.7	0.4	0.4	0.2	0.3	0.4	0.2	0.1

Selected Financial Factors (in Percentages)

Debt Ratio 45	67.9	•	72.7	48.6	36.8	43.9	45.2	35.8	51.2	53.5	43.0	54.7	72.3
Return on Total Assets 46	4.1	•	70.1	20.6	17.3	11.9	6.3	7.4	3.0	7.5	6.2	3.5	3.3
Return on Equity Before Income Taxes 47	9.3	•	247.5	37.5	26.1	19.3	10.0	10.5	2.3	12.9	8.7	3.7	8.4
Return on Equity After Income Taxes 48	6.6	•	245.7	35.6	23.4	17.8	8.4	8.4	•	11.1	6.0	0.0	5.8
Profit Margin (Before Income Tax) 49	16.7	•	19.3	16.1	18.2	12.7	12.6	16.2	3.2	14.8	16.1	6.6	21.3
Profit Margin (After Income Tax) 50	11.9	•	19.2	15.3	16.3	11.7	10.5	13.1	•	12.7	11.1	0.0	14.8

Table II
Corporations with Net Income

SECURITIES & COMMODITY EXCHANGES, OTHER FINANCIAL INVESTMENT

MONEY AMOUNTS AND SIZE OF ASSETS IN THOUSANDS OF DOLLARS

Item Description for Accounting Period 7/12 Through 6/13	Total	Zero Assets	Under 500	500 to 1,000	1,000 to 5,000	5,000 to 10,000	10,000 to 25,000	25,000 to 50,000	50,000 to 100,000	100,000 to 250,000	250,000 to 500,000	500,000 to 2,500,000	2,500,000 and over
Number of Enterprises 1	29798	4658	20465	1752	1776	522	274	140	64	56	28	37	27

Revenues ($ in Thousands)

Net Sales 2	108822868	1640179	7299500	1473404	5858618	4371713	2721523	3116705	2659275	5623904	4249379	12965312	56843357
Interest 3	3926870	23789	4676	11828	18246	26839	8089	25524	25151	88356	87862	308162	3298350
Rents 4	132463	21	1568	0	134	3492	596	1381	24	8153	2182	30840	84072
Royalties 5	191089	220	0	0	0	13	8	2589	14956	82	0	126766	46455
Other Portfolio Income 6	3928382	315322	59774	45932	147917	175101	118019	218842	219427	438486	250728	670454	1268378
Other Receipts 7	100644064	1300827	7233482	1415644	5692321	4166268	2594811	2868369	2399717	5088827	3908607	11829090	52146102
Total Receipts 8	108822868	1640179	7299500	1473404	5858618	4371713	2721523	3116705	2659275	5623904	4249379	12965312	56843357
Average Total Receipts 9	3652	352	357	841	3299	8375	9933	22262	41551	100427	151764	350414	2105310

Operating Costs/Operating Income (%)

Cost of Operations 10	0.1	•	•	•	•	0.0	•	0.1	0.1	0.0	•	1.2	0.0
Salaries and Wages 11	22.3	7.4	13.8	25.7	20.7	32.2	32.6	30.8	28.5	23.6	20.0	16.6	23.2
Taxes Paid 12	2.4	2.4	2.9	2.5	2.3	2.9	6.2	2.8	3.0	2.3	2.6	1.8	2.2
Interest Paid 13	5.0	0.3	0.6	1.2	0.4	0.8	0.8	0.9	1.8	2.5	1.8	4.0	8.0
Depreciation 14	1.7	0.4	0.5	0.8	0.7	0.7	0.7	0.7	0.9	0.8	1.6	0.7	2.5
Amortization and Depletion 15	1.3	4.2	0.1	0.5	0.3	0.3	0.1	0.4	0.7	0.8	1.8	2.2	1.6
Pensions and Other Deferred Comp. 16	1.6	1.7	2.0	2.8	0.7	0.8	1.0	0.9	0.7	1.1	0.3	0.6	2.2
Employee Benefits 17	1.7	1.4	1.6	1.2	1.8	2.4	1.7	2.7	1.6	0.9	2.0	1.1	1.8
Advertising 18	1.2	0.1	1.2	0.3	1.0	0.3	0.5	0.2	0.2	2.4	0.7	0.5	1.6
Other Expenses 19	31.6	19.2	27.1	20.8	22.9	30.2	18.7	20.8	28.9	29.5	41.8	44.5	31.6
Officers' Compensation 20	6.7	9.0	20.3	19.4	20.1	6.8	8.2	11.2	7.8	9.4	3.5	5.3	3.1
Operating Margin 21	24.3	53.9	29.8	25.0	29.1	22.5	29.6	28.6	25.9	26.7	24.0	21.5	22.3
Operating Margin Before Officers' Comp. 22	31.0	62.9	50.1	44.3	49.2	29.4	37.8	39.7	33.7	36.1	27.5	26.8	25.4

Selected Average Balance Sheet ($ in Thousands)

Net Receivables 23	1665	0	3	207	176	1810	2003	3656	9184	23385	65940	97520	1463739
Inventories 24	•	•	•	•	•	•	•	•	•	•	•	•	•
Net Property, Plant and Equipment 25	426	0	12	31	401	398	624	1390	3042	6200	12194	34630	331398
Total Assets 26	18795	0	72	727	2467	6833	15032	35394	70132	150977	364365	1034970	17734705
Notes and Loans Payable 27	3973	0	32	314	540	1471	3304	3912	13214	36558	78768	259072	3678250
All Other Liabilities 28	8833	0	21	46	180	1869	2663	6295	17986	35623	69554	318630	8996933
Net Worth 29	5989	0	19	368	1748	3493	9064	25187	38931	78795	216043	457268	5059521

Selected Financial Ratios (Times to 1)

Current Ratio 30	1.0	•	2.8	4.0	3.8	2.2	1.8	2.4	1.9	2.2	1.7	1.2	0.9
Quick Ratio 31	0.6	•	2.4	3.8	2.8	1.9	1.5	1.8	1.5	1.5	1.5	0.9	0.6
Net Sales to Working Capital 32	•	•	12.3	2.7	3.9	4.5	3.9	2.7	3.2	2.8	2.7	8.3	•
Coverage Ratio 33	5.9	171.2	51.6	21.4	65.9	29.0	38.3	32.9	15.6	11.7	14.8	6.5	3.9
Total Asset Turnover 34	0.2	•	4.9	1.2	1.3	1.2	0.7	0.6	0.6	0.7	0.4	0.3	0.1
Inventory Turnover 35	•	•	•	•	•	•	•	•	•	•	•	•	•
Receivables Turnover 36	•	•	•	•	•	•	•	•	•	•	•	•	•
Total Liabilities to Net Worth 37	2.1	•	2.7	1.0	0.4	1.0	0.7	0.4	0.8	0.9	0.7	1.3	2.5
Current Assets to Working Capital 38	•	•	1.5	1.3	1.4	1.8	2.2	1.7	2.1	1.9	2.3	6.8	•
Current Liabilities to Working Capital 39	•	•	0.5	0.3	0.4	0.8	1.2	0.7	1.1	0.9	1.3	5.8	•
Working Capital to Net Sales 40	•	•	0.1	0.4	0.3	0.2	0.3	0.4	0.3	0.4	0.4	0.1	•
Inventory to Working Capital 41	•	•	•	•	•	0.0	•	0.0	•	•	•	•	•
Total Receipts to Cash Flow 42	2.0	1.8	1.9	2.5	2.1	2.5	2.3	2.5	2.2	2.1	1.8	1.6	2.0
Cost of Goods to Cash Flow 43	0.0	•	•	•	•	0.0	•	0.0	0.0	0.0	•	0.0	0.0
Cash Flow to Total Debt 44	0.1	•	3.5	0.9	2.2	1.0	0.7	0.9	0.6	0.7	0.6	0.4	0.1

Selected Financial Factors (in Percentages)

Debt Ratio 45	68.1	•	73.3	49.4	29.1	48.9	39.7	28.8	44.5	47.8	40.7	55.8	71.5
Return on Total Assets 46	5.8	•	149.9	30.2	39.4	28.6	20.0	18.5	16.3	19.4	11.1	8.8	3.7
Return on Equity Before Income Taxes 47	15.2	•	551.0	56.9	54.8	54.0	32.3	25.2	27.5	34.0	17.4	16.9	9.7
Return on Equity After Income Taxes 48	12.0	•	547.9	54.6	52.5	51.2	29.3	22.0	22.8	30.7	13.1	11.8	6.8
Profit Margin (Before Income Tax) 49	24.9	53.9	29.8	24.9	29.0	22.5	29.5	28.5	25.8	26.7	24.8	22.1	23.2
Profit Margin (After Income Tax) 50	19.7	47.9	29.6	23.9	27.8	21.3	26.8	24.8	21.3	24.1	18.7	15.4	16.5

Table I

Corporations with and without Net Income

LIFE INSURANCE

MONEY AMOUNTS AND SIZE OF ASSETS IN THOUSANDS OF DOLLARS

Item Description for Accounting Period 7/12 Through 6/13	Total	Zero Assets	Under 500	500 to 1,000	1,000 to 5,000	5,000 to 10,000	10,000 to 25,000	25,000 to 50,000	50,000 to 100,000	100,000 to 250,000	250,000 to 500,000	500,000 to 2,500,000	2,500,000 and over
Number of Enterprises **1**	713	44	124	46	86	59	60	40	26	34	38	68	89
Revenues ($ in Thousands)													
Net Sales **2**	1149268634	6408261	12711	13899	58609	235059	406559	588027	556614	1720722	4935379	28796524	1105536270
Interest **3**	162825014	734755	337	150	3966	11092	20208	46606	41068	171096	666457	2897446	158231833
Rents **4**	2943248	2	0	0	45	392	3179	1747	10649	2503	11153	30726	2882852
Royalties **5**	5459	0	0	0	0	0	0	12	47	526	0	187	4687
Other Portfolio Income **6**	36049775	230862	199	260	3501	6212	9438	14878	18884	21105	122443	471893	35150099
Other Receipts **7**	947445138	5442642	12175	13489	51097	217363	373734	524784	485966	1525492	4135326	25396272	909266799
Total Receipts **8**	1149268634	6408261	12711	13899	58609	235059	406559	588027	556614	1720722	4935379	28796524	1105536270
Average Total Receipts **9**	1611877	145642	103	302	682	3984	6776	14701	21408	50609	129878	423478	12421756
Operating Costs/Operating Income (%)													
Cost of Operations **10**	46.7	71.4	24.3	22.4	31.1	15.7	41.8	52.2	52.8	41.2	50.2	53.8	46.4
Salaries and Wages **11**	1.9	0.0	•	•	•	•	0.2	•	0.4	3.0	0.8	0.5	1.9
Taxes Paid **12**	0.7	0.2	1.1	1.0	0.9	2.0	2.1	1.4	2.3	1.2	1.0	0.9	0.7
Interest Paid **13**	2.1	0.2	0.3	0.5	0.2	0.0	0.3	0.8	0.1	0.5	0.2	0.3	2.1
Depreciation **14**	0.5	0.0	•	0.0	0.0	0.1	0.5	0.5	0.7	0.2	0.3	0.2	0.6
Amortization and Depletion **15**	1.1	1.3	0.7	0.7	1.0	0.6	2.7	2.3	2.8	2.0	2.0	1.7	1.1
Pensions and Other Deferred Comp. **16**	0.4	0.0	•	0.0	0.0	0.2	0.8	0.5	0.6	0.8	0.6	0.5	0.4
Employee Benefits **17**	0.3	0.0	•	0.0	0.0	0.0	0.5	0.5	0.2	0.8	0.2	0.2	0.3
Advertising **18**	0.2	0.0	•	•	0.0	0.2	0.3	0.1	0.1	0.1	0.2	0.5	0.2
Other Expenses **19**	42.3	33.1	44.9	55.5	47.2	110.5	42.6	34.0	36.3	46.2	39.6	40.8	42.3
Officers' Compensation **20**	0.1	0.0	•	•	•	•	•	•	0.4	0.1	0.4	0.1	0.1
Operating Margin **21**	3.7	•	28.8	19.8	19.5	•	8.3	7.8	3.5	3.8	4.5	0.3	3.9
Operating Margin Before Officers' Comp. **22**	3.8	•	28.8	19.8	19.5	•	8.3	7.8	3.8	3.9	4.9	0.4	4.0

Selected Average Balance Sheet ($ in Thousands)

Net Receivables 23	186350	0	5	20	75	181	473	2001	389	5777	2730	14004	1477280
Inventories 24	•	•	•	•	•	•	•	•	•	•	•	•	•
Net Property, Plant and Equipment 25	69171	0	0	0	4	62	237	491	1400	832	1407	4700	548796
Total Assets 26	9712698	0	147	702	2476	7277	16663	36069	65239	161696	370032	1226291	76599727
Notes and Loans Payable 27	264821	0	0	0	0	0	84	8	79	372	3079	6362	2115141
All Other Liabilities 28	7998535	0	140	305	1315	4004	8745	23577	46944	137373	352413	1060612	63030364
Net Worth 29	1449343	0	6	397	1160	3274	7834	12485	18216	23952	14539	159316	11454223

Selected Financial Ratios (Times to 1)

Current Ratio 30	2.2	•	7.1	14.2	22.0	9.7	5.0	8.3	5.6	3.9	5.5	4.5	2.2
Quick Ratio 31	1.5	•	5.6	11.5	18.0	6.8	3.7	6.3	3.6	2.9	3.6	2.8	1.5
Net Sales to Working Capital 32	2.0	•	0.8	0.6	0.4	1.1	0.9	1.1	1.3	1.2	1.1	1.4	2.0
Coverage Ratio 33	2.8	•	114.2	37.7	113.1	•	28.0	11.3	55.4	8.4	26.6	1.9	2.8
Total Asset Turnover 34	0.2	•	0.7	0.4	0.3	0.5	0.4	0.4	0.3	0.3	0.4	0.3	0.2
Inventory Turnover 35	•	•	•	•	•	•	•	•	•	•	•	•	•
Receivables Turnover 36	•	•	•	•	•	•	•	•	•	•	•	•	•
Total Liabilities to Net Worth 37	5.7	•	21.9	0.8	1.1	1.2	1.1	1.9	2.6	5.8	24.5	6.7	5.7
Current Assets to Working Capital 38	1.8	•	1.2	1.1	1.0	1.1	1.2	1.1	1.2	1.3	1.2	1.3	1.9
Current Liabilities to Working Capital 39	0.8	•	0.2	0.1	0.0	0.1	0.2	0.1	0.2	0.3	0.2	0.3	0.9
Working Capital to Net Sales 40	0.5	•	1.2	1.6	2.2	0.9	1.2	0.9	0.8	0.9	0.9	0.7	0.5
Inventory to Working Capital 41	0.0	•	•	•	•	•	0.0	•	•	•	•	0.0	0.0
Total Receipts to Cash Flow 42	2.3	4.3	1.4	1.4	1.6	1.3	2.1	2.6	2.7	2.1	2.4	2.5	2.3
Cost of Goods to Cash Flow 43	1.1	3.1	0.3	0.3	0.5	0.2	0.9	1.3	1.4	0.8	1.2	1.4	1.1
Cash Flow to Total Debt 44	0.1	•	0.5	0.7	0.3	0.8	0.4	0.2	0.2	0.2	0.2	0.2	0.1

Selected Financial Factors (in Percentages)

Debt Ratio 45	85.1	•	95.6	43.5	53.1	55.0	53.0	65.4	72.1	85.2	96.1	87.0	85.0
Return on Total Assets 46	1.0	•	20.1	8.8	5.4	•	3.5	3.5	1.0	1.2	1.7	0.2	1.0
Return on Equity Before Income Taxes 47	4.2	•	455.3	15.1	11.3	•	7.1	9.1	3.6	7.3	40.5	0.8	4.3
Return on Equity After Income Taxes 48	3.2	•	429.6	13.7	9.8	•	5.5	6.9	0.7	5.8	28.2	•	3.3
Profit Margin (Before Income Tax) 49	3.8	•	28.5	19.8	19.3	•	8.2	7.8	3.0	3.5	4.5	0.3	3.9
Profit Margin (After Income Tax) 50	2.9	•	26.9	18.0	16.7	•	6.3	5.8	0.6	2.7	3.2	•	3.0

Table II

Corporations with Net Income

LIFE INSURANCE

MONEY AMOUNTS AND SIZE OF ASSETS IN THOUSANDS OF DOLLARS

Item Description for Accounting Period 7/12 Through 6/13	Total	Zero Assets	Under 500	500 to 1,000	1,000 to 5,000	5,000 to 10,000	10,000 to 25,000	25,000 to 50,000	50,000 to 100,000	100,000 to 250,000	250,000 to 500,000	500,000 to 2,500,000	2,500,000 and over
Number of Enterprises 1	525	25	88	37	70	48	42	28	14	22	27	50	74

Revenues ($ in Thousands)													
Net Sales 2	981571303	1148101	10827	13018	54583	90963	326548	713990	392716	1334411	3941239	14607362	958937544
Interest 3	139197952	12233	280	113	3070	8726	14884	53493	26527	95140	535066	2210099	136238321
Rents 4	2438721	2	0	0	45	332	2635	3785	2810	1033	6906	21803	2399370
Royalties 5	4726	0	0	0	0	0	0	0	0	0	0	185	4541
Other Portfolio Income 6	31176395	32840	153	174	3091	6002	7815	12154	12409	14341	103595	408420	30575400
Other Receipts 7	808753509	1103026	10394	12731	48377	75903	301214	644558	350970	1223897	3295672	11966855	789719912
Total Receipts 8	981571303	1148101	10827	13018	54583	90963	326548	713990	392716	1334411	3941239	14607362	958937544
Average Total Receipts 9	1869660	45924	123	352	780	1895	7775	25500	28051	60655	145972	292147	12958615

Operating Costs/Operating Income (%)													
Cost of Operations 10	44.0	7.8	23.3	21.8	29.2	32.7	45.7	37.1	52.4	38.6	47.5	42.2	44.0
Salaries and Wages 11	1.8	•	•	•	•	•	0.1	0.0	0.6	2.9	1.0	0.8	1.8
Taxes Paid 12	0.7	0.1	0.9	0.9	0.8	4.7	2.0	2.0	2.0	1.1	1.0	1.5	0.7
Interest Paid 13	2.3	•	0.3	0.6	0.2	0.0	0.4	0.1	0.1	0.6	0.2	0.3	2.3
Depreciation 14	0.6	0.0	•	0.0	0.0	0.1	0.3	0.3	0.3	0.2	0.3	0.4	0.6
Amortization and Depletion 15	1.2	0.6	0.5	0.6	1.0	0.8	1.7	2.6	1.3	1.8	2.0	2.7	1.2
Pensions and Other Deferred Comp. 16	0.4	0.1	•	0.0	•	0.4	0.6	0.7	0.3	0.7	0.7	0.9	0.4
Employee Benefits 17	0.3	0.0	•	•	0.0	0.1	0.6	0.4	0.1	0.9	0.2	0.4	0.3
Advertising 18	0.2	0.0	•	•	0.0	0.5	0.1	0.0	0.0	0.1	0.2	0.8	0.2
Other Expenses 19	43.6	85.6	39.5	53.1	46.3	34.9	35.4	47.4	29.6	47.1	39.5	42.5	43.6
Officers' Compensation 20	0.1	•	•	•	•	•	•	•	0.5	0.1	0.5	0.2	0.1
Operating Margin 21	4.8	5.8	35.6	23.0	22.5	25.7	13.0	9.4	12.8	5.9	7.1	7.4	4.8
Operating Margin Before Officers' Comp. 22	4.9	5.8	35.6	23.0	22.5	25.7	13.0	9.4	13.3	6.0	7.6	7.5	4.9

Selected Average Balance Sheet ($ in Thousands)

Net Receivables 23	242703	0	7	7	92	222	606	2490	39	7306	2689	5873	1713223
Inventories 24	•	•	•	•	•	•	•	•	•	•	•	•	•
Net Property, Plant and Equipment 25	90505	0	0	0	3	57	318	606	358	845	1911	2971	638625
Total Assets 26	11138527	0	146	699	2468	7289	16352	58834	67315	154339	368480	1230399	77959786
Notes and Loans Payable 27	338527	0	0	0	0	0	119	11	147	545	4334	3836	2397274
All Other Liabilities 28	8978315	0	154	357	1137	3733	7756	39526	46609	125086	359814	1012444	62812917
Net Worth 29	1821685	0	-8	342	1331	3556	8477	19298	20559	28708	4332	214119	12749595

Selected Financial Ratios (Times to 1)

Current Ratio 30	2.1	•	12.7	12.2	19.6	10.9	7.6	7.4	7.3	6.9	4.5	3.9	2.1
Quick Ratio 31	1.5	•	9.5	10.2	15.6	8.4	6.0	5.8	5.1	4.9	3.0	2.7	1.4
Net Sales to Working Capital 32	2.1	•	0.9	0.7	0.5	0.5	0.9	1.2	1.4	1.2	1.3	1.1	2.1
Coverage Ratio 33	3.2	•	121.3	40.9	121.7	11332.0	36.4	100.9	192.9	11.3	33.8	27.6	3.1
Total Asset Turnover 34	0.2	•	0.8	0.5	0.3	0.3	0.5	0.4	0.4	0.4	0.4	0.2	0.2
Inventory Turnover 35	•	•	•	•	•	•	•	•	•	•	•	•	•
Receivables Turnover 36	•	•	•	•	•	•	•	•	•	•	•	•	•
Total Liabilities to Net Worth 37	5.1	•	•	1.0	0.9	1.0	0.9	2.0	2.3	4.4	84.1	4.7	5.1
Current Assets to Working Capital 38	1.9	•	1.1	1.1	1.1	1.1	1.2	1.2	1.2	1.2	1.3	1.3	1.9
Current Liabilities to Working Capital 39	0.9	•	0.1	0.1	0.1	0.1	0.2	0.2	0.2	0.2	0.3	0.3	0.9
Working Capital to Net Sales 40	0.5	•	1.1	1.4	2.0	1.9	1.2	0.8	0.7	0.9	0.7	1.0	0.5
Inventory to Working Capital 41	0.0	•	•	•	•	•	0.0	•	•	•	•	0.0	0.0
Total Receipts to Cash Flow 42	2.2	1.1	1.3	1.3	1.5	1.8	2.2	1.8	2.5	1.9	2.3	2.1	2.2
Cost of Goods to Cash Flow 43	1.0	0.1	0.3	0.3	0.5	0.6	1.0	0.7	1.3	0.7	1.1	0.9	1.0
Cash Flow to Total Debt 44	0.1	•	0.6	0.7	0.4	0.3	0.5	0.4	0.2	0.2	0.2	0.1	0.1

Selected Financial Factors (in Percentages)

Debt Ratio 45	83.6	•	105.6	51.1	46.1	51.2	48.2	67.2	69.5	81.4	98.8	82.6	83.6
Return on Total Assets 46	1.2	•	30.3	11.8	7.1	6.5	6.3	4.1	5.1	2.4	2.9	1.8	1.2
Return on Equity Before Income Taxes 47	5.1	•	•	23.6	13.1	13.3	11.8	12.3	16.7	12.0	240.7	9.9	5.0
Return on Equity After Income Taxes 48	4.0	•	•	21.7	11.4	11.2	9.6	9.6	12.0	9.9	185.0	6.9	3.9
Profit Margin (Before Income Tax) 49	5.0	5.8	35.6	23.0	22.3	24.9	12.9	9.3	12.3	5.7	7.1	7.3	4.9
Profit Margin (After Income Tax) 50	3.9	3.8	33.7	21.1	19.5	21.0	10.5	7.3	8.8	4.7	5.5	5.1	3.9

Table I

Corporations with and without Net Income

LIFE INSURANCE, STOCK COMPANIES (FORM 1120L)

MONEY AMOUNTS AND SIZE OF ASSETS IN THOUSANDS OF DOLLARS

Item Description for Accounting Period 7/12 Through 6/13		Total	Zero Assets	Under 500	500 to 1,000	1,000 to 5,000	5,000 to 10,000	10,000 to 25,000	25,000 to 50,000	50,000 to 100,000	100,000 to 250,000	250,000 to 500,000	500,000 to 2,500,000	2,500,000 and over
Number of Enterprises	1	669	33	124	•	•	59	60	35	26	31	35	61	80

Revenues ($ in Thousands)

Net Sales	2	1017972008	6407116	12711	•	•	235059	406559	513522	556614	1615870	4585432	27000086	976568685
Interest	3	137246876	734739	337	•	•	11092	20208	38551	41068	145013	628099	2457187	133167219
Rents	4	2399575	2	0	•	•	392	3179	1100	10649	1587	8188	26377	2348101
Royalties	5	4626	0	0	•	•	0	0	12	47	0	0	166	4401
Other Portfolio Income	6	30990460	230862	199	•	•	6212	9438	14400	18884	19233	118649	449011	30120291
Other Receipts	7	847330471	5441513	12175	•	•	217363	373734	459459	485966	1450037	3830496	24067345	810928673
Total Receipts	8	1017972008	6407116	12711	•	•	235059	406559	513522	556614	1615870	4585432	27000086	976568685
Average Total Receipts	9	1521632	194155	103	•	•	3984	6776	14672	21408	52125	131012	442624	12207109

Operating Costs/Operating Income (%)

Cost of Operations	10	46.7	71.4	24.3	•	•	15.7	41.8	51.2	52.8	40.3	51.9	54.3	46.3
Salaries and Wages	11	2.0	0.0	•	•	•	•	0.2	•	0.4	3.2	0.8	0.5	2.0
Taxes Paid	12	0.7	0.2	1.1	•	•	2.0	2.1	1.3	2.3	1.2	0.9	0.9	0.7
Interest Paid	13	2.3	0.2	0.3	•	•	0.0	0.3	0.9	0.1	0.5	0.2	0.3	2.3
Depreciation	14	0.6	0.0	•	•	•	0.1	0.5	0.3	0.7	0.2	0.3	0.2	0.6
Amortization and Depletion	15	1.1	1.3	0.7	•	•	0.6	2.7	2.3	2.8	1.9	1.9	1.6	1.0
Pensions and Other Deferred Comp.	16	0.3	0.0	•	•	•	0.2	0.8	0.4	0.6	0.7	0.6	0.5	0.3
Employee Benefits	17	0.3	0.0	•	•	•	0.0	0.5	0.4	0.2	0.8	0.2	0.2	0.3
Advertising	18	0.2	0.0	•	•	•	0.2	0.3	0.1	0.1	0.1	0.2	0.6	0.2
Other Expenses	19	42.1	33.1	44.9	•	•	110.5	42.6	34.7	36.3	46.7	38.1	40.8	42.2
Officers' Compensation	20	0.1	•	•	•	•	•	•	•	0.4	0.1	0.4	0.1	0.1
Operating Margin	21	3.6	•	28.8	•	•	•	8.3	8.5	3.5	4.2	4.6	•	3.8
Operating Margin Before Officers' Comp.	22	3.7	•	28.8	•	•	•	8.3	8.5	3.8	4.3	5.0	0.1	3.9

Selected Average Balance Sheet ($ in Thousands)

Net Receivables 23	196360	0	5	•	•	181	473	2272	389	6210	2115	15494	1625206
Inventories 24	•	•	•	•	•	•	•	•	•	•	•	•	•
Net Property, Plant and Equipment 25	70767	0	0	•	•	62	237	477	1400	813	1496	4952	586149
Total Assets 26	9240680	0	147	•	•	7277	16663	35144	65239	157651	371556	1214415	76068090
Notes and Loans Payable 27	281045	0	0	•	•	0	84	9	79	408	3343	7092	2343117
All Other Liabilities 28	7540831	0	140	•	•	4004	8745	22250	46944	132535	358955	1044198	62019528
Net Worth 29	1418804	0	6	•	•	3274	7834	12885	18216	24708	9258	163125	11705444

Selected Financial Ratios (Times to 1)

Current Ratio 30	2.1	•	7.1	•	•	9.7	5.0	8.3	5.6	3.6	5.4	4.0	2.0
Quick Ratio 31	1.4	•	5.6	•	•	6.8	3.7	6.2	3.6	2.7	3.5	2.3	1.3
Net Sales to Working Capital 32	2.1	•	0.8	•	•	1.1	0.9	1.1	1.3	1.2	1.1	1.6	2.1
Coverage Ratio 33	2.6	•	114.2	•	•	•	28.0	10.8	55.4	8.7	25.5	0.9	2.7
Total Asset Turnover 34	0.2	•	0.7	•	•	0.5	0.4	0.4	0.3	0.3	0.4	0.4	0.2
Inventory Turnover 35	•	•	•	•	•	•	•	•	•	•	•	•	•
Receivables Turnover 36	•	•	•	•	•	•	•	•	•	•	•	•	•
Total Liabilities to Net Worth 37	5.5	•	21.9	•	•	1.2	1.1	1.7	2.6	5.4	39.1	6.4	5.5
Current Assets to Working Capital 38	1.9	•	1.2	•	•	1.1	1.2	1.1	1.2	1.4	1.2	1.3	2.0
Current Liabilities to Working Capital 39	0.9	•	0.2	•	•	0.1	0.2	0.1	0.2	0.4	0.2	0.3	1.0
Working Capital to Net Sales 40	0.5	•	1.2	•	•	0.9	1.2	0.9	0.8	0.8	0.9	0.6	0.5
Inventory to Working Capital 41	0.0	•	•	•	•	•	0.0	•	•	•	•	0.0	0.0
Total Receipts to Cash Flow 42	2.3	4.3	1.4	•	•	1.3	2.1	2.5	2.7	2.0	2.5	2.5	2.3
Cost of Goods to Cash Flow 43	1.1	3.1	0.3	•	•	0.2	0.9	1.3	1.4	0.8	1.3	1.4	1.1
Cash Flow to Total Debt 44	0.1	•	0.5	•	•	0.8	0.4	0.3	0.2	0.2	0.1	0.2	0.1

Selected Financial Factors (in Percentages)

Debt Ratio 45	84.6	•	95.6	•	•	55.0	53.0	63.3	72.1	84.3	97.5	86.6	84.6
Return on Total Assets 46	1.0	•	20.1	•	•	•	3.5	3.9	1.0	1.4	1.7	0.1	1.0
Return on Equity Before Income Taxes 47	4.0	•	455.3	•	•	•	7.1	9.7	3.6	8.1	65.6	•	4.0
Return on Equity After Income Taxes 48	3.1	•	429.6	•	•	•	5.5	7.2	0.7	6.4	45.5	•	3.2
Profit Margin (Before Income Tax) 49	3.7	•	28.5	•	•	•	8.2	8.5	3.0	3.8	4.6	•	3.9
Profit Margin (After Income Tax) 50	2.9	•	26.9	•	•	•	6.3	6.4	0.6	3.0	3.2	•	3.0

Table II

Corporations with Net Income

LIFE INSURANCE, STOCK COMPANIES (FORM 1120L)

MONEY AMOUNTS AND SIZE OF ASSETS IN THOUSANDS OF DOLLARS

Item Description for Accounting Period 7/12 Through 6/13	Total	Zero Assets	Under 500	500 to 1,000	1,000 to 5,000	5,000 to 10,000	10,000 to 25,000	25,000 to 50,000	50,000 to 100,000	100,000 to 250,000	250,000 to 500,000	500,000 to 2,500,000	2,500,000 and over
Number of Enterprises 1	497	19	88	34	•	48	42	•	14	22	27	•	•
Revenues ($ in Thousands)													
Net Sales 2	854320637	1148009	10827	12848	•	90963	326548	•	392716	1334411	3941239	•	•
Interest 3	114219084	12217	280	112	•	8726	14884	•	26527	95140	535066	•	•
Rents 4	1896833	2	0	0	•	332	2635	•	2810	1033	6906	•	•
Royalties 5	4420	0	0	0	•	0	0	•	0	0	0	•	•
Other Portfolio Income 6	26176198	32840	153	6	•	6002	7815	•	12409	14341	103595	•	•
Other Receipts 7	712024102	1102950	10394	12730	•	75903	301214	•	350970	1223897	3295672	•	•
Total Receipts 8	854320637	1148009	10827	12848	•	90963	326548	•	392716	1334411	3941239	•	•
Average Total Receipts 9	1718955	60422	123	378	•	1895	7775	•	28051	60655	145972	•	•
Operating Costs/Operating Income (%)													
Cost of Operations 10	43.4	7.8	23.3	22.0	•	32.7	45.7	•	52.4	38.6	47.5	•	•
Salaries and Wages 11	1.9	•	•	•	•	•	0.1	•	0.6	2.9	1.0	•	•
Taxes Paid 12	0.7	0.1	0.9	0.8	•	4.7	2.0	•	2.0	1.1	1.0	•	•
Interest Paid 13	2.5	•	0.3	0.0	•	0.0	0.4	•	0.1	0.6	0.2	•	•
Depreciation 14	0.6	0.0	•	0.0	•	0.1	0.3	•	0.3	0.2	0.3	•	•
Amortization and Depletion 15	1.2	0.6	0.5	0.6	•	0.8	1.7	•	1.3	1.8	2.0	•	•
Pensions and Other Deferred Comp. 16	0.4	0.1	•	0.0	•	0.4	0.6	•	0.3	0.7	0.7	•	•
Employee Benefits 17	0.3	0.0	•	•	•	0.1	0.6	•	0.1	0.9	0.2	•	•
Advertising 18	0.2	0.0	•	•	•	0.5	0.1	•	0.0	0.1	0.2	•	•
Other Expenses 19	43.7	85.6	39.5	53.5	•	34.9	35.4	•	29.6	47.1	39.5	•	•
Officers' Compensation 20	0.1	•	•	•	•	•	•	•	0.5	0.1	0.5	•	•
Operating Margin 21	4.9	5.8	35.6	23.0	•	25.7	13.0	•	12.8	5.9	7.1	•	•
Operating Margin Before Officers' Comp. 22	5.0	5.8	35.6	23.0	•	25.7	13.0	•	13.3	6.0	7.6	•	•

Selected Average Balance Sheet ($ in Thousands)

Net Receivables 23	253401	0	7	7	•	222	606	•	39	7306	2689	• •
Inventories 24	•	•	•	•	•	•	•	•	•	•	•	• •
Net Property, Plant and Equipment 25	91702	0	0	0	•	57	318	•	358	845	1911	• •
Total Assets 26	10309099	0	146	696	•	7289	16352	•	67315	154339	368480	• •
Notes and Loans Payable 27	355993	0	0	0	•	0	119	•	147	545	4334	• •
All Other Liabilities 28	8194186	0	154	380	•	3733	7756	•	46609	125086	359814	• •
Net Worth 29	1758920	0	-8	316	•	3556	8477	•	20559	28708	4332	• •

Selected Financial Ratios (Times to 1)

Current Ratio 30	1.9	•	12.7	12.2	•	10.9	7.6	•	7.3	6.9	4.5	• •
Quick Ratio 31	1.3	•	9.5	10.4	•	8.4	6.0	•	5.1	4.9	3.0	• •
Net Sales to Working Capital 32	2.3	•	0.9	0.7	•	0.5	0.9	•	1.4	1.2	1.3	• •
Coverage Ratio 33	3.0	•	121.3	1478.5	•	11332.0	36.4	•	192.9	11.3	33.8	• •
Total Asset Turnover 34	0.2	•	0.8	0.5	•	0.3	0.5	•	0.4	0.4	0.4	• •
Inventory Turnover 35	•	•	•	•	•	•	•	•	•	•	•	• •
Receivables Turnover 36	•	•	•	•	•	•	•	•	•	•	•	• •
Total Liabilities to Net Worth 37	4.9	•	•	1.2	•	1.0	0.9	•	2.3	4.4	84.1	• •
Current Assets to Working Capital 38	2.1	•	1.1	1.1	•	1.1	1.2	•	1.2	1.2	1.3	• •
Current Liabilities to Working Capital 39	1.1	•	0.1	0.1	•	0.1	0.2	•	0.2	0.2	0.3	• •
Working Capital to Net Sales 40	0.4	•	1.1	1.4	•	1.9	1.2	•	0.7	0.9	0.7	• •
Inventory to Working Capital 41	0.0	•	•	•	•	•	0.0	•	•	•	•	• •
Total Receipts to Cash Flow 42	2.2	1.1	1.3	1.3	•	1.8	2.2	•	2.5	1.9	2.3	• •
Cost of Goods to Cash Flow 43	0.9	0.1	0.3	0.3	•	0.6	1.0	•	1.3	0.7	1.1	• •
Cash Flow to Total Debt 44	0.1	•	0.6	0.8	•	0.3	0.5	•	0.2	0.2	0.2	• •

Selected Financial Factors (in Percentages)

Debt Ratio 45	82.9	•	105.6	54.6	•	51.2	48.2	•	69.5	81.4	98.8	• •
Return on Total Assets 46	1.3	•	30.3	12.5	•	6.5	6.3	•	5.1	2.4	2.9	• •
Return on Equity Before Income Taxes 47	4.9	•	•	27.5	•	13.3	11.8	•	16.7	12.0	240.7	• •
Return on Equity After Income Taxes 48	3.9	•	•	25.2	•	11.2	9.6	•	12.0	9.9	185.0	• •
Profit Margin (Before Income Tax) 49	5.0	5.8	35.6	23.0	•	24.9	12.9	•	12.3	5.7	7.1	• •
Profit Margin (After Income Tax) 50	4.0	3.8	33.7	21.1	•	21.0	10.5	•	8.8	4.7	5.5	• •

Table I

Corporations with and without Net Income

LIFE INSURANCE, MUTUAL COMPANIES (FORM 1120L)

MONEY AMOUNTS AND SIZE OF ASSETS IN THOUSANDS OF DOLLARS

Item Description for Accounting Period 7/12 Through 6/13		Total	Zero Assets	Under 500	500 to 1,000	1,000 to 5,000	5,000 to 10,000	10,000 to 25,000	25,000 to 50,000	50,000 to 100,000	100,000 to 250,000	250,000 to 500,000	500,000 to 2,500,000	2,500,000 and over
Number of Enterprises	1	44	11	0	•	•	0	0	5	0	3	3	7	9
Revenues ($ in Thousands)														
Net Sales	2	131296626	1146	0	•	•	0	0	74505	0	104852	349946	1796437	128967584
Interest	3	25578138	16	0	•	•	0	0	8055	0	26083	38358	440259	25064614
Rents	4	543673	0	0	•	•	0	0	647	0	916	2965	4349	534750
Royalties	5	832	0	0	•	•	0	0	0	0	526	0	21	286
Other Portfolio Income	6	5059313	0	0	•	•	0	0	478	0	1870	3794	22882	5029807
Other Receipts	7	100114670	1130	0	•	•	0	0	65325	0	75457	304829	1328926	98338127
Total Receipts	8	131296626	1146	0	•	•	0	0	74505	0	104852	349946	1796437	128967584
Average Total Receipts	9	2984014	104	•	•	•	•	•	14901	•	34951	116649	256634	14329732
Operating Costs/Operating Income (%)														
Cost of Operations	10	47.2	23.4	•	•	•	•	•	59.1	•	54.3	28.8	47.2	47.3
Salaries and Wages	11	1.1	•	•	•	•	•	•	•	•	•	0.0	•	1.1
Taxes Paid	12	0.7	45.6	•	•	•	•	•	2.2	•	2.0	2.6	1.7	0.7
Interest Paid	13	0.6	•	•	•	•	•	•	•	•	0.0	0.0	0.6	0.6
Depreciation	14	0.2	•	•	•	•	•	•	1.5	•	0.2	0.4	0.3	0.2
Amortization and Depletion	15	1.4	•	•	•	•	•	•	2.0	•	3.7	3.4	2.6	1.4
Pensions and Other Deferred Comp.	16	0.7	•	•	•	•	•	•	1.4	•	2.0	1.1	1.5	0.7
Employee Benefits	17	0.2	3.4	•	•	•	•	•	1.8	•	0.7	0.7	0.3	0.2
Advertising	18	0.2	•	•	•	•	•	•	0.0	•	0.1	0.1	0.0	0.2
Other Expenses	19	43.2	29.8	•	•	•	•	•	29.2	•	39.1	59.5	40.2	43.2
Officers' Compensation	20	0.1	0.3	•	•	•	•	•	•	•	•	•	•	0.1
Operating Margin	21	4.5	•	•	•	•	•	•	2.9	•	•	3.4	5.5	4.5
Operating Margin Before Officers' Comp.	22	4.5	•	•	•	•	•	•	2.9	•	•	3.4	5.5	4.5

Selected Average Balance Sheet ($ in Thousands)

Net Receivables **23**	34153	0	•	•	•	•	•	105	•	1302	9908	1020	162380
Inventories **24**	•	•	•	•	•	•	•	•	•	•	•	•	•
Net Property, Plant and Equipment **25**	44901	0	•	•	•	•	•	587	•	1026	369	2507	216774
Total Assets **26**	16889527	0	•	•	•	•	•	42549	•	203500	352257	1329778	81325393
Notes and Loans Payable **27**	18139	0	•	•	•	•	•	0	•	0	0	1	88680
All Other Liabilities **28**	14957723	0	•	•	•	•	•	32869	•	187362	276098	1203649	72015568
Net Worth **29**	1913664	0	•	•	•	•	•	9681	•	16139	76159	126128	9221145

Selected Financial Ratios (Times to 1)

Current Ratio **30**	5.0	•	•	•	•	•	•	7.9	•	23.8	7.2	19.6	4.9
Quick Ratio **31**	4.1	•	•	•	•	•	•	6.9	•	20.0	6.1	17.1	4.0
Net Sales to Working Capital **32**	1.3	•	•	•	•	•	•	0.8	•	0.6	1.1	0.5	1.3
Coverage Ratio **33**	8.0	•	•	•	•	•	•	•	•	•	194.8	9.4	7.9
Total Asset Turnover **34**	0.2	•	•	•	•	•	•	0.4	•	0.2	0.3	0.2	0.2
Inventory Turnover **35**	•	•	•	•	•	•	•	•	•	•	•	•	•
Receivables Turnover **36**	•	•	•	•	•	•	•	•	•	•	•	•	•
Total Liabilities to Net Worth **37**	7.8	•	•	•	•	•	•	3.4	•	11.6	3.6	9.5	7.8
Current Assets to Working Capital **38**	1.2	•	•	•	•	•	•	1.1	•	1.0	1.2	1.1	1.3
Current Liabilities to Working Capital **39**	0.2	•	•	•	•	•	•	0.1	•	0.0	0.2	0.1	0.3
Working Capital to Net Sales **40**	0.8	•	•	•	•	•	•	1.2	•	1.7	0.9	1.9	0.8
Inventory to Working Capital **41**	0.0	•	•	•	•	•	•	•	•	•	•	•	0.0
Total Receipts to Cash Flow **42**	2.3	3.7	•	•	•	•	•	3.2	•	3.0	1.6	2.3	2.3
Cost of Goods to Cash Flow **43**	1.1	0.9	•	•	•	•	•	1.9	•	1.7	0.5	1.1	1.1
Cash Flow to Total Debt **44**	0.1	•	•	•	•	•	•	0.1	•	0.1	0.3	0.1	0.1

Selected Financial Factors (in Percentages)

Debt Ratio **45**	88.7	•	•	•	•	•	•	77.2	•	92.1	78.4	90.5	88.7
Return on Total Assets **46**	0.9	•	•	•	•	•	•	1.0	•	•	1.1	1.2	0.9
Return on Equity Before Income Taxes **47**	6.9	•	•	•	•	•	•	4.3	•	•	5.0	10.9	6.8
Return on Equity After Income Taxes **48**	4.5	•	•	•	•	•	•	3.3	•	•	3.6	6.8	4.5
Profit Margin (Before Income Tax) **49**	4.4	•	•	•	•	•	•	2.8	•	•	3.3	5.4	4.4
Profit Margin (After Income Tax) **50**	2.9	•	•	•	•	•	•	2.1	•	•	2.4	3.3	2.9

Table II
Corporations with Net Income

LIFE INSURANCE, MUTUAL COMPANIES (FORM 1120L)

MONEY AMOUNTS AND SIZE OF ASSETS IN THOUSANDS OF DOLLARS

Item Description for Accounting Period 7/12 Through 6/13	Total	Zero Assets	Under 500	500 to 1000	1,000 to 5,000	5,000 to 10,000	10,000 to 25,000	25,000 to 50,000	50,000 to 100,000	100,000 to 250,000	250,000 to 500,000	500,000 to 2,500,000	2,500,000 and over
Number of Enterprises 1	29	5	0	3	•	0	0	•	0	0	0	•	•

Revenues ($ in Thousands)

	Total	Zero Assets	Under 500	500 to 1000	1,000 to 5,000	5,000 to 10,000	10,000 to 25,000	25,000 to 50,000	50,000 to 100,000	100,000 to 250,000	250,000 to 500,000	500,000 to 2,500,000	2,500,000 and over
Net Sales 2	127250666	92	0	170	•	0	0	•	0	0	0	•	•
Interest 3	24978868	16	0	1	•	0	0	•	0	0	0	•	•
Rents 4	541888	0	0	0	•	0	0	•	0	0	0	•	•
Royalties 5	307	0	0	0	•	0	0	•	0	0	0	•	•
Other Portfolio Income 6	5000197	0	0	168	•	0	0	•	0	0	0	•	•
Other Receipts 7	96729406	76	0	1	•	0	0	•	0	0	0	•	•
Total Receipts 8	127250666	92	0	170	•	0	0	•	0	0	0	•	•
Average Total Receipts 9	4387954	18	•	57	•	•	•	•	•	•	•	•	•

Operating Costs/Operating Income (%)

	Total	Zero Assets	Under 500	500 to 1000	1,000 to 5,000	5,000 to 10,000	10,000 to 25,000	25,000 to 50,000	50,000 to 100,000	100,000 to 250,000	250,000 to 500,000	500,000 to 2,500,000	2,500,000 and over
Cost of Operations 10	47.4	57.6	•	6.5	•	•	•	•	•	•	•	•	•
Salaries and Wages 11	1.1	•	•	•	•	•	•	•	•	•	•	•	•
Taxes Paid 12	0.7	2.2	•	7.6	•	•	•	•	•	•	•	•	•
Interest Paid 13	0.6	•	•	42.9	•	•	•	•	•	•	•	•	•
Depreciation 14	0.2	•	•	•	•	•	•	•	•	•	•	•	•
Amortization and Depletion 15	1.4	•	•	•	•	•	•	•	•	•	•	•	•
Pensions and Other Deferred Comp. 16	0.7	•	•	•	•	•	•	•	•	•	•	•	•
Employee Benefits 17	0.2	•	•	•	•	•	•	•	•	•	•	•	•
Advertising 18	0.2	•	•	•	•	•	•	•	•	•	•	•	•
Other Expenses 19	42.8	27.2	•	22.9	•	•	•	•	•	•	•	•	•
Officers' Compensation 20	0.1	•	•	•	•	•	•	•	•	•	•	•	•
Operating Margin 21	4.7	13.0	•	20.0	•	•	•	•	•	•	•	•	•
Operating Margin Before Officers' Comp. 22	4.7	13.0	•	20.0	•	•	•	•	•	•	•	•	•

Selected Average Balance Sheet ($ in Thousands)

Net Receivables 23	51000	0	•	0	•	•	•	•	•	•	•	•	•	•
Inventories 24	•	•	•	•	•	•	•	•	•	•	•	•	•	•
Net Property, Plant and Equipment 25	66882	0	•	0	•	•	•	•	•	•	•	•	•	•
Total Assets 26	24969111	0	•	737	•	•	•	•	•	•	•	•	•	•
Notes and Loans Payable 27	27522	0	•	0	•	•	•	•	•	•	•	•	•	•
All Other Liabilities 28	22107067	0	•	105	•	•	•	•	•	•	•	•	•	•
Net Worth 29	2834522	0	•	631	•	•	•	•	•	•	•	•	•	•

Selected Financial Ratios (Times to 1)

Current Ratio 30	4.9	•	•	12.4	•	•	•	•	•	•	•	•	•	•
Quick Ratio 31	4.0	•	•	•	•	•	•	•	•	•	•	•	•	•
Net Sales to Working Capital 32	1.3	•	•	0.6	•	•	•	•	•	•	•	•	•	•
Coverage Ratio 33	8.3	•	•	1.5	•	•	•	•	•	•	•	•	•	•
Total Asset Turnover 34	0.2	•	•	0.1	•	•	•	•	•	•	•	•	•	•
Inventory Turnover 35	•	•	•	•	•	•	•	•	•	•	•	•	•	•
Receivables Turnover 36	•	•	•	•	•	•	•	•	•	•	•	•	•	•
Total Liabilities to Net Worth 37	7.8	•	•	0.2	•	•	•	•	•	•	•	•	•	•
Current Assets to Working Capital 38	1.3	•	•	1.1	•	•	•	•	•	•	•	•	•	•
Current Liabilities to Working Capital 39	0.3	•	•	0.1	•	•	•	•	•	•	•	•	•	•
Working Capital to Net Sales 40	0.8	•	•	1.8	•	•	•	•	•	•	•	•	•	•
Inventory to Working Capital 41	0.0	•	•	•	•	•	•	•	•	•	•	•	•	•
Total Receipts to Cash Flow 42	2.3	2.7	•	•	•	•	•	•	•	•	•	•	•	•
Cost of Goods to Cash Flow 43	1.1	1.6	•	•	•	•	•	•	•	•	•	•	•	•
Cash Flow to Total Debt 44	0.1	•	•	•	•	•	•	•	•	•	•	•	•	•

Selected Financial Factors (in Percentages)

Debt Ratio 45	88.6	•	•	14.3	•	•	•	•	•	•	•	•	•	•
Return on Total Assets 46	0.9	•	•	4.8	•	•	•	•	•	•	•	•	•	•
Return on Equity Before Income Taxes 47	7.1	•	•	1.8	•	•	•	•	•	•	•	•	•	•
Return on Equity After Income Taxes 48	4.7	•	•	1.8	•	•	•	•	•	•	•	•	•	•
Profit Margin (Before Income Tax) 49	4.6	14.1	•	20.0	•	•	•	•	•	•	•	•	•	•
Profit Margin (After Income Tax) 50	3.0	12.0	•	20.0	•	•	•	•	•	•	•	•	•	•

Table I

Corporations with and without Net Income

MUTUAL PROPERTY AND CASUALTY COMPANIES (FORM 1120-PC)

MONEY AMOUNTS AND SIZE OF ASSETS IN THOUSANDS OF DOLLARS

Item Description for Accounting Period 7/12 Through 6/13		Total	Zero Assets	Under 500	500 to 1,000	1,000 to 5,000	5,000 to 10,000	10,000 to 25,000	25,000 to 50,000	50,000 to 100,000	100,000 to 250,000	250,000 to 500,000	500,000 to 2,500,000	2,500,000 and over
Number of Enterprises	1	1442	56	52	52	494	155	211	101	99	67	55	71	28

Revenues ($ in Thousands)

Net Sales	2	272783181	172054	794	12725	400744	418121	1261859	1090244	3097687	4843716	8675201	47363527	205446510
Interest	3	13126471	8258	17	87	22587	15850	48446	53597	118633	204536	340893	1497694	10815873
Rents	4	710983	0	25	0	1568	185	2215	573	4930	6464	15085	61547	618391
Royalties	5	932	0	0	0	0	0	0	0	0	1	0	237	693
Other Portfolio Income	6	9569540	5905	0	0	13113	12085	36532	43476	94341	199398	332107	1505859	7326725
Other Receipts	7	249375255	157891	752	12638	363476	390001	1174666	992598	2879783	4433317	7987116	44298190	186684828
Total Receipts	8	272783181	172054	794	12725	400744	418121	1261859	1090244	3097687	4843716	8675201	47363527	205446510
Average Total Receipts	9	189170	3072	15	245	811	2698	5980	10794	31290	72294	157731	667092	7337375

Operating Costs/Operating Income (%)

Cost of Operations	10	59.3	39.8	65.5	67.1	51.1	48.6	56.4	51.0	61.3	51.2	57.7	68.7	57.4
Salaries and Wages	11	14.3	13.2	0.4	31.6	15.8	11.1	10.0	13.3	14.4	18.6	15.2	13.4	14.4
Taxes Paid	12	2.5	1.9	0.1	4.3	3.5	1.7	3.9	2.9	2.4	2.9	2.6	1.9	2.6
Interest Paid	13	0.6	0.5	•	•	0.1	0.1	0.4	0.2	0.1	0.3	0.4	0.2	0.7
Depreciation	14	1.0	0.8	0.5	•	0.5	0.2	0.5	0.7	0.7	1.4	0.9	1.0	1.0
Amortization and Depletion	15	0.2	0.1	•	•	0.0	0.0	1.4	•	0.0	0.0	0.0	0.0	0.2
Pensions and Other Deferred Comp.	16	0.5	9.5	•	•	0.2	0.3	0.3	0.3	0.3	1.0	0.5	0.8	0.4
Employee Benefits	17	1.4	0.3	•	•	2.3	0.6	1.1	1.6	1.5	2.6	3.8	1.4	1.3
Advertising	18	1.0	0.4	•	•	0.5	0.3	0.3	0.4	0.5	0.8	0.4	0.4	1.2
Other Expenses	19	14.8	22.9	5.8	6.9	28.7	21.3	23.1	24.2	15.9	16.6	13.3	8.3	16.2
Officers' Compensation	20	0.3	•	•	•	3.3	1.7	0.8	1.1	1.1	0.8	0.9	0.4	0.2
Operating Margin	21	4.1	10.7	27.7	•	•	14.1	1.9	4.3	1.9	3.8	4.4	3.4	4.3
Operating Margin Before Officers' Comp.	22	4.4	10.7	27.7	•	•	15.9	2.8	5.5	3.0	4.6	5.2	3.8	4.5

Selected Average Balance Sheet ($ in Thousands)

Net Receivables 23	47610	0	3	92	92	187	1106	2432	6208	18079	39597	125844	1969852
Inventories 24	•	•	•	•	•	•	•	•	•	•	•	•	•
Net Property, Plant and Equipment 25	6484	0	2	2	55	80	171	285	975	2495	4440	22309	255473
Total Assets 26	527171	0	171	796	2781	7383	16231	34334	71699	166047	356498	1206401	22401245
Notes and Loans Payable 27	9962	0	28	40	1	6	229	23	182	940	5136	5653	483763
All Other Liabilities 28	303102	0	61	243	1069	4752	10769	22993	43937	103463	203037	707369	12804525
Net Worth 29	214107	0	82	513	1712	2625	5233	11318	27580	61644	148325	493380	9112958

Selected Financial Ratios (Times to 1)

Current Ratio 30	0.9	•	2.8	3.3	1.9	1.2	1.0	0.8	1.0	0.9	1.0	0.9	0.9
Quick Ratio 31	0.8	•	2.8	3.2	1.7	1.0	0.8	0.7	0.8	0.8	0.9	0.9	0.8
Net Sales to Working Capital 32	•	•	0.1	0.4	1.0	3.3	•	•	•	•	•	•	•
Coverage Ratio 33	5.2	19.7	•	•	•	208.0	4.1	14.6	8.4	9.3	9.1	12.2	4.6
Total Asset Turnover 34	0.4	•	0.1	0.3	0.3	0.4	0.4	0.3	0.4	0.4	0.4	0.6	0.3
Inventory Turnover 35	•	•	•	•	•	•	•	•	•	•	•	•	•
Receivables Turnover 36	•	•	•	•	•	•	•	•	•	•	•	•	•
Total Liabilities to Net Worth 37	1.5	•	1.1	0.6	0.6	1.8	2.1	2.0	1.6	1.7	1.4	1.4	1.5
Current Assets to Working Capital 38	•	•	1.6	1.4	2.1	6.3	•	•	•	•	•	•	•
Current Liabilities to Working Capital 39	•	•	0.6	0.4	1.1	5.3	•	•	•	•	•	•	•
Working Capital to Net Sales 40	•	•	7.1	2.3	1.0	0.3	•	•	•	•	•	•	•
Inventory to Working Capital 41	•	•	•	•	•	•	•	•	•	•	•	•	•
Total Receipts to Cash Flow 42	6.0	3.2	3.0	•	4.8	2.9	4.3	3.9	6.4	5.7	6.6	10.2	5.5
Cost of Goods to Cash Flow 43	3.5	1.3	2.0	•	2.4	1.4	2.4	2.0	3.9	2.9	3.8	7.0	3.1
Cash Flow to Total Debt 44	0.1	•	0.1	•	0.2	0.2	0.1	0.1	0.1	0.1	0.1	0.1	0.1

Selected Financial Factors (in Percentages)

Debt Ratio 45	59.4	•	52.2	35.5	38.4	64.4	67.8	67.0	61.5	62.9	58.4	59.1	59.3
Return on Total Assets 46	1.1	•	2.5	•	•	4.6	0.5	1.1	0.5	1.2	1.5	1.3	1.1
Return on Equity Before Income Taxes 47	2.2	•	5.2	•	•	13.0	1.3	3.1	1.1	2.9	3.3	3.0	2.1
Return on Equity After Income Taxes 48	1.3	•	5.2	•	•	10.6	•	1.8	•	1.4	1.8	1.6	1.3
Profit Margin (Before Income Tax) 49	2.5	9.7	27.7	•	•	12.6	1.1	3.2	0.9	2.5	3.1	2.2	2.6
Profit Margin (After Income Tax) 50	1.5	5.5	27.6	•	•	10.3	•	1.9	•	1.2	1.7	1.2	1.6

Table II

Corporations with Net Income

MUTUAL PROPERTY AND CASUALTY COMPANIES (FORM 1120-PC)

MONEY AMOUNTS AND SIZE OF ASSETS IN THOUSANDS OF DOLLARS

Item Description for Accounting Period 7/12 Through 6/13		Total	Zero Assets	Under 500	500 to 1,000	1,000 to 5,000	5,000 to 10,000	10,000 to 25,000	25,000 to 50,000	50,000 to 100,000	100,000 to 250,000	250,000 to 500,000	500,000 to 2,500,000	2,500,000 and over
Number of Enterprises	1	858	25	31	21	282	103	116	64	60	40	36	58	21

Revenues ($ in Thousands)

Net Sales	2	192866688	164358	794	87	218260	268983	692505	734670	1794380	2559746	5749378	40628632	140054896
Interest	3	9799273	8257	17	87	14978	10978	26107	36876	72308	125697	233778	1229979	8040212
Rents	4	593662	0	25	0	503	67	1929	313	4434	2064	13220	46587	524519
Royalties	5	924	0	0	0	0	0	0	0	0	1	0	237	685
Other Portfolio Income	6	7444418	5905	0	0	7415	7275	20336	29628	61388	109423	240915	1321461	5640671
Other Receipts	7	175028411	150196	752	0	195364	250663	644133	667853	1656250	2322561	5261465	38030368	125848809
Total Receipts	8	192866688	164358	794	87	218260	268983	692505	734670	1794380	2559746	5749378	40628632	140054896
Average Total Receipts	9	224786	6574	26	4	774	2611	5970	11479	29906	63994	159705	700494	6669281

Operating Costs/Operating Income (%)

Cost of Operations	10	58.2	36.3	65.5	•	33.4	38.3	42.1	44.6	52.0	41.3	51.9	68.3	56.1
Salaries and Wages	11	15.0	13.8	0.4	•	12.9	14.6	11.5	14.6	16.4	22.0	16.2	12.7	15.4
Taxes Paid	12	2.4	1.8	•	•	3.9	1.8	2.5	2.2	2.7	3.1	2.5	1.8	2.6
Interest Paid	13	0.4	0.5	•	•	0.1	0.1	0.4	0.1	0.1	0.3	0.2	0.2	0.5
Depreciation	14	1.1	0.8	0.5	•	0.4	0.3	0.7	0.5	0.9	1.6	1.0	1.0	1.2
Amortization and Depletion	15	0.1	•	•	•	0.0	•	0.0	0.0	0.0	0.0	0.0	0.0	0.2
Pensions and Other Deferred Comp.	16	0.5	9.9	•	•	0.1	0.4	0.2	0.4	0.3	1.6	0.6	0.8	0.4
Employee Benefits	17	1.5	0.3	•	•	1.1	0.7	1.5	1.8	1.8	3.2	2.8	1.2	1.5
Advertising	18	1.0	0.4	•	•	0.4	0.3	0.2	0.3	0.4	1.2	0.4	0.3	1.2
Other Expenses	19	12.5	21.4	3.0	20.7	23.1	12.0	22.1	20.9	14.2	14.2	14.1	7.9	13.7
Officers' Compensation	20	0.3	•	•	•	3.5	2.5	1.1	1.2	1.3	1.1	1.0	0.4	0.2
Operating Margin	21	7.0	14.8	30.6	79.3	21.1	28.9	17.7	13.5	10.1	10.5	9.3	5.4	7.1
Operating Margin Before Officers' Comp.	22	7.3	14.8	30.6	79.3	24.7	31.3	18.8	14.7	11.4	11.6	10.3	5.9	7.3

Selected Average Balance Sheet ($ in Thousands)

Net Receivables 23	58712	0	5	3	96	214	992	1887	7114	18417	33756	127015	1921157
Inventories 24	•	•	•	•	•	•	•	•	•	•	•	•	•
Net Property, Plant and Equipment 25	7875	0	4	5	50	108	174	297	1147	1640	4782	25414	233893
Total Assets 26	646772	0	255	929	2997	7095	16209	34169	73793	162965	357659	1251840	21563392
Notes and Loans Payable 27	9085	0	47	0	0	10	156	10	118	867	6069	6461	339946
All Other Liabilities 28	377545	0	59	275	839	4016	10020	21541	42120	101213	197671	715509	12644907
Net Worth 29	260142	0	148	654	2158	3069	6033	12618	31554	60886	153919	529869	8578539

Selected Financial Ratios (Times to 1)

Current Ratio 30	0.9	•	4.3	3.4	2.6	1.2	1.0	0.9	1.0	0.9	1.0	0.9	0.9
Quick Ratio 31	0.9	•	4.3	3.4	2.4	1.0	0.9	0.7	0.9	0.8	0.9	0.9	0.9
Net Sales to Working Capital 32	•	•	0.1	0.0	0.7	3.8	17.2	•	31.1	•	•	•	•
Coverage Ratio 33	13.2	26.4	•	•	285.7	289.1	42.7	97.4	180.0	33.7	51.1	26.4	10.7
Total Asset Turnover 34	0.3	•	0.1	0.0	0.3	0.4	0.4	0.3	0.4	0.4	0.4	0.6	0.3
Inventory Turnover 35	•	•	•	•	•	•	•	•	•	•	•	•	•
Receivables Turnover 36	•	•	•	•	•	•	•	•	•	•	•	•	•
Total Liabilities to Net Worth 37	1.5	•	0.7	0.4	0.4	1.3	1.7	1.7	1.3	1.7	1.3	1.4	1.5
Current Assets to Working Capital 38	•	•	1.3	1.4	1.6	6.6	27.8	•	42.2	•	•	•	•
Current Liabilities to Working Capital 39	•	•	0.3	0.4	0.6	5.6	26.8	•	41.2	•	•	•	•
Working Capital to Net Sales 40	•	•	7.5	156.4	1.5	0.3	0.1	•	0.0	•	•	•	•
Inventory to Working Capital 41	•	•	•	•	•	•	•	•	•	•	•	•	•
Total Receipts to Cash Flow 42	5.7	2.9	3.0	1.0	2.4	2.5	2.6	3.1	4.6	4.6	4.8	8.7	5.3
Cost of Goods to Cash Flow 43	3.3	1.1	1.9	•	0.8	1.0	1.1	1.4	2.4	1.9	2.5	5.9	3.0
Cash Flow to Total Debt 44	0.1	•	0.1	0.0	0.4	0.3	0.2	0.2	0.2	0.1	0.2	0.1	0.1

Selected Financial Factors (in Percentages)

Debt Ratio 45	59.8	•	41.8	29.6	28.0	56.7	62.8	63.1	57.2	62.6	57.0	57.7	60.2
Return on Total Assets 46	1.9	•	3.1	0.3	5.1	10.1	6.4	4.2	3.7	3.6	3.5	2.4	1.7
Return on Equity Before Income Taxes 47	4.4	•	5.3	0.5	7.1	23.2	16.7	11.2	8.6	9.4	8.0	5.5	3.9
Return on Equity After Income Taxes 48	3.3	•	5.3	0.4	5.5	20.2	14.0	9.4	6.3	6.9	5.8	4.0	2.9
Profit Margin (Before Income Tax) 49	5.1	13.7	30.6	78.2	19.7	27.3	16.9	12.3	9.0	9.0	7.8	4.2	5.0
Profit Margin (After Income Tax) 50	3.8	9.4	30.5	66.7	15.4	23.7	14.1	10.3	6.7	6.5	5.6	3.0	3.8

Table I

Corporations with and without Net Income

STOCK PROPERTY AND CASUALTY COMPANIES (FORM 1120-PC)

MONEY AMOUNTS AND SIZE OF ASSETS IN THOUSANDS OF DOLLARS

Item Description for Accounting Period 7/12 Through 6/13	Total	Zero Assets	Under 500	500 to 1,000	1,000 to 5,000	5,000 to 10,000	10,000 to 25,000	25,000 to 50,000	50,000 to 100,000	100,000 to 250,000	250,000 to 500,000	500,000 to 2,500,000	2,500,000 and over
Number of Enterprises 1	8019	441	2543	1311	2409	349	278	162	152	118	68	105	83

Revenues ($ in Thousands)

Net Sales 2	803629133	1480864	64699	79612	449108	637305	2573976	4059400	9011861	15719161	18873537	72058705	678620904
Interest 3	33526400	49769	6788	9759	52373	24818	124987	62580	127699	257359	403795	1867528	30538946
Rents 4	1143703	175	0	0	767	3070	1674	2000	4390	6857	16535	67148	1041089
Royalties 5	53141	0	0	0	15	2	6	0	0	0	15449	378	37291
Other Portfolio Income 6	17500152	49461	4457	8672	43425	41642	32690	59382	103459	181987	279325	1530244	15165408
Other Receipts 7	751405737	1381459	53454	61181	352528	567773	2414619	3935438	8776313	15272958	18158433	68593407	631838170
Total Receipts 8	803629133	1480864	64699	79612	449108	637305	2573976	4059400	9011861	15719161	18873537	72058705	678620904
Average Total Receipts 9	100216	3358	25	61	186	1826	9259	25058	59289	133213	277552	686273	8176155

Operating Costs/Operating Income (%)

Cost of Operations 10	59.4	44.9	57.0	69.1	46.0	52.8	62.1	64.5	67.8	69.0	65.9	64.2	58.3
Salaries and Wages 11	11.1	12.9	16.6	3.5	15.0	11.6	12.6	15.8	11.0	11.2	12.0	12.2	10.9
Taxes Paid 12	1.9	2.7	2.8	0.3	4.4	1.9	1.7	1.8	1.8	2.3	2.2	2.1	1.9
Interest Paid 13	1.2	1.1	0.3	1.4	0.3	0.1	0.6	0.1	0.3	0.2	0.4	0.9	1.3
Depreciation 14	0.7	0.3	0.1	0.0	0.5	0.3	0.2	0.6	0.5	0.7	0.7	0.8	0.7
Amortization and Depletion 15	0.3	0.0	0.6	0.0	0.1	0.1	0.3	0.2	0.3	0.1	0.3	0.3	0.3
Pensions and Other Deferred Comp. 16	0.4	0.2	•	•	0.0	0.1	0.0	0.1	0.1	0.1	0.3	0.6	0.4
Employee Benefits 17	1.4	1.0	0.8	0.3	0.8	0.5	0.4	1.3	0.8	0.5	1.0	1.0	1.4
Advertising 18	0.6	0.2	•	0.0	0.1	0.2	0.3	0.6	0.7	0.3	0.7	0.3	0.7
Other Expenses 19	19.2	40.0	15.2	20.2	24.0	29.2	24.7	12.7	15.3	11.6	61.0	13.1	18.8
Officers' Compensation 20	0.4	0.2	•	•	0.3	1.2	0.6	0.6	0.5	0.7	0.5	0.4	0.3
Operating Margin 21	3.6	•	6.7	5.1	8.5	1.9	•	1.6	0.9	3.3	•	4.0	5.0
Operating Margin Before Officers' Comp. 22	3.9	•	6.7	5.1	8.8	3.2	•	2.3	1.4	4.1	•	4.4	5.3

Selected Average Balance Sheet ($ in Thousands)

Net Receivables 23	15028	0	8	16	123	335	1293	3082	6570	12771	33721	99869	1251958
Inventories 24	•	•	•	•	•	•	•	•	•	•	•	•	•
Net Property, Plant and Equipment 25	3454	0	0	0	9	113	122	339	725	1494	6488	19183	298902
Total Assets 26	242170	0	218	715	2139	6819	15978	36251	72468	161625	341207	1125717	21097995
Notes and Loans Payable 27	19023	0	0	5	25	171	494	729	2982	6531	15449	64920	1723732
All Other Liabilities 28	132701	0	181	503	1841	4329	13153	69642	50891	125653	219387	727621	11183659
Net Worth 29	90446	0	36	207	273	2319	2330	-34120	18595	29441	106372	333177	8190604

Selected Financial Ratios (Times to 1)

Current Ratio 30	0.7	•	0.8	0.9	1.0	0.9	0.9	0.3	1.0	0.8	0.9	0.8	0.7
Quick Ratio 31	0.6	•	0.7	0.7	0.9	0.7	0.7	0.3	0.9	0.7	0.8	0.7	0.6
Net Sales to Working Capital 32	•	•	•	•	3.8	•	•	•	•	•	•	•	•
Coverage Ratio 33	3.5	•	25.9	3.4	26.0	6.8	•	10.8	3.3	13.2	•	4.5	4.4
Total Asset Turnover 34	0.4	•	0.1	0.1	0.1	0.3	0.6	0.7	0.8	0.8	0.8	0.6	0.4
Inventory Turnover 35	•	•	•	•	•	•	•	•	•	•	•	•	•
Receivables Turnover 36	•	•	•	•	•	•	•	•	•	•	•	•	•
Total Liabilities to Net Worth 37	1.7	•	5.0	2.4	6.8	1.9	5.9	•	2.9	4.5	2.2	2.4	1.6
Current Assets to Working Capital 38	•	•	•	•	25.7	•	•	•	•	•	•	•	•
Current Liabilities to Working Capital 39	•	•	•	•	24.7	•	•	•	•	•	•	•	•
Working Capital to Net Sales 40	•	•	•	•	0.3	•	•	•	•	•	•	•	•
Inventory to Working Capital 41	•	•	•	•	•	•	•	•	•	•	•	•	•
Total Receipts to Cash Flow 42	5.0	3.0	6.2	5.7	3.8	3.9	5.0	7.8	6.7	7.3	•	6.5	4.5
Cost of Goods to Cash Flow 43	3.0	1.3	3.6	4.0	1.7	2.0	3.1	5.0	4.6	5.0	•	4.2	2.6
Cash Flow to Total Debt 44	0.1	•	0.0	0.0	0.0	0.1	0.1	0.0	0.2	0.1	•	0.1	0.1

Selected Financial Factors (in Percentages)

Debt Ratio 45	62.7	•	83.5	71.0	87.2	66.0	85.4	194.1	74.3	81.8	68.8	70.4	61.2
Return on Total Assets 46	1.7	•	0.8	0.4	0.7	0.2	•	0.9	0.8	2.7	•	2.6	2.2
Return on Equity Before Income Taxes 47	3.2	•	4.6	1.0	5.4	0.5	•	•	2.1	13.7	•	6.8	4.3
Return on Equity After Income Taxes 48	1.7	•	2.0	•	1.2	•	•	0.2	•	8.2	•	5.0	2.8
Profit Margin (Before Income Tax) 49	2.9	•	6.6	3.3	7.8	0.6	•	1.2	0.7	3.0	•	3.3	4.3
Profit Margin (After Income Tax) 50	1.5	•	2.9	•	1.7	•	•	•	•	1.8	•	2.4	2.8

Table II

Corporations with Net Income

STOCK PROPERTY AND CASUALTY COMPANIES (FORM 1120-PC)

MONEY AMOUNTS AND SIZE OF ASSETS IN THOUSANDS OF DOLLARS

Item Description for Accounting Period 7/12 Through 6/13		Total	Zero Assets	Under 500	500 to 1,000	1,000 to 5,000	5,000 to 10,000	10,000 to 25,000	25,000 to 50,000	50,000 to 100,000	100,000 to 250,000	250,000 to 500,000	500,000 to 2,500,000	2,500,000 and over
Number of Enterprises	1	5908	241	1839	1028	1953	227	175	101	92	80	39	73	62

Revenues ($ in Thousands)														
Net Sales	2	717232682	582200	32874	32161	335907	331471	1434136	2859230	5848448	11345485	11698383	51897864	630834522
Interest	3	30060426	37244	6633	9442	48575	14886	108914	40509	74938	183828	165948	1272155	28097355
Rents	4	1095588	0	0	0	225	2822	1368	1585	2855	4106	12600	55805	1014222
Royalties	5	50843	0	0	0	15	2	0	0	0	0	13289	378	37159
Other Portfolio Income	6	15369120	47467	4444	8559	42411	31811	22817	38242	66467	136686	166375	1203605	13600234
Other Receipts	7	670656705	497489	21797	14160	244681	281950	1301037	2778894	5704188	11020865	11340171	49365921	588085552
Total Receipts	8	717232682	582200	32874	32161	335907	331471	1434136	2859230	5848448	11345485	11698383	51897864	630834522
Average Total Receipts	9	121400	2416	18	31	172	1460	8195	28309	63570	141819	299959	710930	10174750

Operating Costs/Operating Income (%)														
Cost of Operations	10	58.5	45.1	19.5	17.3	45.2	28.9	49.0	57.4	61.8	67.7	62.1	60.1	58.1
Salaries and Wages	11	10.4	13.3	23.5	0.1	3.2	12.0	15.1	18.5	11.1	10.4	10.3	12.6	10.2
Taxes Paid	12	1.9	2.7	3.9	•	0.8	1.6	2.1	1.7	1.9	2.2	2.1	2.3	1.9
Interest Paid	13	1.0	0.7	0.4	0.2	0.2	0.2	0.7	0.1	0.1	0.2	0.2	0.6	1.1
Depreciation	14	0.7	0.3	•	•	0.6	0.3	0.3	0.6	0.5	0.6	0.6	0.7	0.7
Amortization and Depletion	15	0.3	0.1	0.1	•	0.0	0.0	0.0	0.0	0.1	0.0	0.3	0.3	0.3
Pensions and Other Deferred Comp.	16	0.4	0.1	•	•	0.0	0.2	0.0	0.1	0.0	0.1	0.2	0.4	0.4
Employee Benefits	17	1.4	1.5	•	•	0.1	0.2	0.3	1.5	0.7	0.4	1.0	1.0	1.5
Advertising	18	0.6	0.3	•	•	0.0	0.1	0.2	0.8	0.8	0.3	0.3	0.2	0.7
Other Expenses	19	18.5	17.5	7.4	10.9	12.2	25.0	19.6	9.7	16.3	11.2	17.1	13.7	19.1
Officers' Compensation	20	0.3	0.5	•	•	0.2	1.3	0.7	0.7	0.4	0.8	0.4	0.5	0.3
Operating Margin	21	6.0	18.0	45.2	71.5	37.4	30.1	12.0	8.8	6.3	6.0	5.3	7.6	5.8
Operating Margin Before Officers' Comp.	22	6.3	18.4	45.2	71.5	37.7	31.4	12.6	9.5	6.7	6.8	5.7	8.1	6.1

Selected Average Balance Sheet ($ in Thousands)

Net Receivables 23	17368	0	7	15	114	351	1129	2864	5671	13506	31575	96670	1482303
Inventories 24	•	•	•	•	•	•	•	•	•	•	•	•	•
Net Property, Plant and Equipment 25	4365	0	0	0	6	119	142	429	481	1542	7991	18411	384782
Total Assets 26	288372	0	229	715	2107	6743	15682	36693	71463	167044	335918	1171809	25352759
Notes and Loans Payable 27	21526	0	0	0	27	142	431	770	1444	6065	11045	51683	1969601
All Other Liabilities 28	155793	0	186	503	1184	4178	8832	26429	44114	102214	187018	677324	13598644
Net Worth 29	111053	0	43	212	895	2423	6419	9494	25905	58766	137855	442802	9784514

Selected Financial Ratios (Times to 1)

Current Ratio 30	0.7	•	0.7	0.8	1.0	0.8	1.2	0.9	1.1	1.0	1.2	0.9	0.7
Quick Ratio 31	0.6	•	0.7	0.6	0.8	0.6	0.9	0.7	0.9	0.9	1.1	0.8	0.6
Net Sales to Working Capital 32	•	•	•	•	8.7	•	6.1	•	22.2	52.9	9.0	•	•
Coverage Ratio 33	6.4	23.4	121.9	289.3	223.4	155.9	17.5	109.5	52.1	25.2	21.1	13.2	5.8
Total Asset Turnover 34	0.4	•	0.1	0.0	0.1	0.2	0.5	0.8	0.9	0.8	0.9	0.6	0.4
Inventory Turnover 35	•	•	•	•	•	•	•	•	•	•	•	•	•
Receivables Turnover 36	•	•	•	•	•	•	•	•	•	•	•	•	•
Total Liabilities to Net Worth 37	1.6	•	4.3	2.4	1.4	1.8	1.4	2.9	1.8	1.8	1.4	1.6	1.6
Current Assets to Working Capital 38	•	•	•	•	60.3	•	7.3	•	15.4	34.8	5.9	•	•
Current Liabilities to Working Capital 39	•	•	•	•	59.3	•	6.3	•	14.4	33.8	4.9	•	•
Working Capital to Net Sales 40	•	•	•	•	0.1	•	0.2	•	0.0	0.0	0.1	•	•
Inventory to Working Capital 41	•	•	•	•	•	•	•	•	•	0.0	0.0	•	•
Total Receipts to Cash Flow 42	4.4	3.4	2.2	1.6	2.4	2.1	3.3	5.8	4.7	6.3	4.8	5.1	4.3
Cost of Goods to Cash Flow 43	2.6	1.6	0.4	0.3	1.1	0.6	1.6	3.3	2.9	4.2	3.0	3.1	2.5
Cash Flow to Total Debt 44	0.2	•	0.0	0.0	0.1	0.2	0.3	0.2	0.3	0.2	0.3	0.2	0.2

Selected Financial Factors (in Percentages)

Debt Ratio 45	61.5	•	81.3	70.3	57.5	64.1	59.1	74.1	63.8	64.8	59.0	62.2	61.4
Return on Total Assets 46	2.7	•	3.5	3.0	3.0	6.2	6.4	6.6	5.5	5.0	4.6	4.5	2.5
Return on Equity Before Income Taxes 47	5.9	•	18.7	9.9	7.1	17.1	14.7	25.1	14.8	13.6	10.7	11.0	5.4
Return on Equity After Income Taxes 48	4.1	•	15.7	8.6	5.5	12.6	10.4	18.5	10.6	9.6	7.1	9.1	3.7
Profit Margin (Before Income Tax) 49	5.4	15.6	44.9	67.2	36.7	28.5	11.5	8.4	6.0	5.6	4.9	6.8	5.2
Profit Margin (After Income Tax) 50	3.8	11.6	37.6	58.3	28.6	20.9	8.1	6.2	4.3	4.0	3.3	5.7	3.6

Table I

Corporations with and without Net Income

INSURANCE AGENCIES AND BROKERAGES

MONEY AMOUNTS AND SIZE OF ASSETS IN THOUSANDS OF DOLLARS

Item Description for Accounting Period 7/12 Through 6/13	Total	Zero Assets	Under 500	500 to 1,000	1,000 to 5,000	5,000 to 10,000	10,000 to 25,000	25,000 to 50,000	50,000 to 100,000	100,000 to 250,000	250,000 to 500,000	500,000 to 2,500,000	2,500,000 and over
Number of Enterprises **1**	91451	18777	63273	5460	3056	501	206	77	52	24	6	10	9

Revenues ($ in Thousands)													
Net Sales **2**	78892826	2531730	21149066	6016932	6573084	8537710	3634173	1764256	2525938	2427393	2093542	2716247	18922757
Interest **3**	333499	10871	9364	2768	5558	14303	4052	5043	7832	11166	8723	20345	233474
Rents **4**	59571	0	6449	1775	10256	12217	9373	52	1670	1086	18	6000	10675
Royalties **5**	199649	0	0	88	1550	0	0	0	30	0	0	439	197542
Other Portfolio Income **6**	1221271	51657	33302	14238	7445	15875	4519	2701	12591	5546	11018	96465	965916
Other Receipts **7**	77078836	2469202	21099951	5998063	6548275	8495315	3616229	1756460	2503815	2409595	2073783	2592998	17515150
Total Receipts **8**	78892826	2531730	21149066	6016932	6573084	8537710	3634173	1764256	2525938	2427393	2093542	2716247	18922757
Average Total Receipts **9**	863	135	334	1102	2151	17041	17642	22912	48576	101141	348924	271625	2102529

Operating Costs/Operating Income (%)													
Cost of Operations **10**	1.9	2.1	•	1.3	•	1.7	5.0	5.4	4.5	21.4	1.7	5.5	0.6
Salaries and Wages **11**	29.9	22.7	24.2	26.3	38.1	19.6	32.0	35.8	33.2	31.5	10.1	31.0	40.5
Taxes Paid **12**	3.4	2.8	3.6	3.8	3.9	1.5	3.0	3.8	4.4	3.1	3.0	2.7	3.8
Interest Paid **13**	2.5	5.5	0.8	1.6	1.0	0.4	0.7	2.8	0.9	1.7	1.1	4.0	6.3
Depreciation **14**	1.0	2.0	0.8	0.9	0.7	0.4	0.6	0.7	1.0	0.7	0.3	1.0	1.5
Amortization and Depletion **15**	1.6	1.7	0.7	2.4	1.0	0.4	0.9	1.2	1.5	2.3	0.4	4.9	2.7
Pensions and Other Deferred Comp. **16**	1.6	0.4	0.9	0.8	1.2	0.4	1.3	1.0	1.6	0.7	0.2	0.6	3.8
Employee Benefits **17**	2.1	1.5	1.8	2.2	2.6	1.3	2.3	2.6	2.8	2.8	1.0	2.2	2.5
Advertising **18**	1.5	2.7	2.4	1.3	0.8	0.5	1.2	3.0	0.8	2.4	1.3	4.8	0.5
Other Expenses **19**	34.0	42.9	30.4	30.1	24.7	63.2	33.0	24.4	33.5	25.8	77.0	34.5	25.5
Officers' Compensation **20**	10.6	8.5	18.8	14.5	16.4	6.0	11.9	12.6	7.5	3.9	0.6	1.8	3.8
Operating Margin **21**	10.1	7.5	15.5	14.8	9.6	4.5	8.1	6.7	8.3	3.7	3.4	6.9	8.6
Operating Margin Before Officers' Comp. **22**	20.7	15.9	34.3	29.3	26.0	10.6	20.0	19.3	15.8	7.5	4.0	8.7	12.4

Selected Average Balance Sheet ($ in Thousands)

Net Receivables 23	267	0	5	52	320	1548	3169	9797	13670	23330	26561	117634	1999540
Inventories 24	•	•	•	•	•	•	•	•	•	•	•	•	•
Net Property, Plant and Equipment 25	45	0	16	60	93	610	754	1317	3243	4710	7871	14339	158112
Total Assets 26	1413	0	87	670	1870	6872	15204	35301	68342	164591	347006	914030	9586847
Notes and Loans Payable 27	278	0	46	323	495	1301	2451	7615	12885	44839	78440	192658	1477714
All Other Liabilities 28	531	0	19	151	866	3755	8411	17803	37278	83085	199559	264629	3456717
Net Worth 29	604	0	22	196	508	1816	4342	9883	18178	36667	69006	456743	4652416

Selected Financial Ratios (Times to 1)

Current Ratio 30	1.1	•	1.6	1.3	1.4	1.2	1.3	1.3	1.1	0.9	1.2	1.0	1.0
Quick Ratio 31	0.9	•	1.4	1.1	1.2	1.2	1.2	1.2	0.9	0.7	1.1	0.8	0.8
Net Sales to Working Capital 32	21.4	•	22.8	14.9	6.9	18.2	6.9	4.2	11.8	•	13.9	•	•
Coverage Ratio 33	5.5	2.4	20.6	10.1	10.6	12.7	12.0	3.4	10.1	3.0	3.8	2.7	3.1
Total Asset Turnover 34	0.6	•	3.8	1.6	1.2	2.5	1.2	0.6	0.7	0.6	1.0	0.3	0.2
Inventory Turnover 35	•	•	•	•	•	•	•	•	•	•	•	•	•
Receivables Turnover 36	•	•	•	•	•	•	•	•	•	•	•	•	•
Total Liabilities to Net Worth 37	1.3	•	2.9	2.4	2.7	2.8	2.5	2.6	2.8	3.5	4.0	1.0	1.1
Current Assets to Working Capital 38	12.9	•	2.8	3.9	3.8	5.1	4.2	4.1	9.3	•	6.2	•	•
Current Liabilities to Working Capital 39	11.9	•	1.8	2.9	2.8	4.1	3.2	3.1	8.3	•	5.2	•	•
Working Capital to Net Sales 40	0.0	•	0.0	0.1	0.1	0.1	0.1	0.2	0.1	•	0.1	•	•
Inventory to Working Capital 41	0.0	•	•	•	•	•	0.0	0.0	0.0	•	•	•	•
Total Receipts to Cash Flow 42	2.5	2.4	2.5	2.6	3.4	1.5	2.7	3.6	2.6	3.9	1.3	2.7	3.3
Cost of Goods to Cash Flow 43	0.0	0.1	•	0.0	•	0.0	0.1	0.2	0.1	0.8	0.0	0.2	0.0
Cash Flow to Total Debt 44	0.4	•	2.0	0.9	0.5	2.2	0.6	0.3	0.4	0.2	1.0	0.2	0.1

Selected Financial Factors (in Percentages)

Debt Ratio 45	57.2	•	74.6	70.8	72.8	73.6	71.4	72.0	73.4	77.7	80.1	50.0	51.5
Return on Total Assets 46	8.4	•	62.5	27.0	12.2	12.2	10.3	6.1	6.5	3.3	4.3	3.3	4.3
Return on Equity Before Income Taxes 47	16.0	•	234.3	83.3	40.5	42.4	33.0	15.5	21.8	9.8	16.1	4.2	6.0
Return on Equity After Income Taxes 48	13.9	•	232.5	82.7	38.6	40.1	30.1	14.2	17.6	7.9	14.2	3.0	3.8
Profit Margin (Before Income Tax) 49	11.2	7.5	15.5	14.8	9.6	4.5	8.1	6.7	8.2	3.6	3.2	7.0	13.2
Profit Margin (After Income Tax) 50	9.8	6.9	15.4	14.7	9.1	4.3	7.4	6.1	6.6	2.8	2.8	5.0	8.5

Table II

Corporations with Net Income

INSURANCE AGENCIES AND BROKERAGES

MONEY AMOUNTS AND SIZE OF ASSETS IN THOUSANDS OF DOLLARS

Item Description for Accounting Period 7/12 Through 6/13		Total	Zero Assets	Under 500	500 to 1,000	1,000 to 5,000	5,000 to 10,000	10,000 to 25,000	25,000 to 50,000	50,000 to 100,000	100,000 to 250,000	250,000 to 500,000	500,000 to 2,500,000	2,500,000 and over
Number of Enterprises	1	68849	11209	49770	4637	2479	463	170	50	41	15	•	6	•

Revenues ($ in Thousands)

		Total	Zero Assets	Under 500	500 to 1,000	1,000 to 5,000	5,000 to 10,000	10,000 to 25,000	25,000 to 50,000	50,000 to 100,000	100,000 to 250,000	250,000 to 500,000	500,000 to 2,500,000	2,500,000 and over
Net Sales	2	68694713	1249217	19292935	5714013	5974759	8259288	3180490	1384153	2221389	1681239	•	2143943	•
Interest	3	254899	1711	8352	2164	4635	6429	3292	2326	7158	3976	•	17471	•
Rents	4	50665	0	6199	1775	10256	7610	9192	52	1668	1086	•	6000	•
Royalties	5	199647	0	0	87	1550	0	0	0	30	0	•	439	•
Other Portfolio Income	6	1176073	49633	28404	10844	7095	10440	4368	1449	12370	2426	•	96449	•
Other Receipts	7	67013429	1197873	19249980	5699143	5951223	8234809	3163638	1380326	2200163	1673751	•	2023584	•
Total Receipts	8	68694713	1249217	19292935	5714013	5974759	8259288	3180490	1384153	2221389	1681239	•	2143943	•
Average Total Receipts	9	998	111	388	1232	2410	17839	18709	27683	54180	112083	•	357324	•

Operating Costs/Operating Income (%)

		Total	Zero Assets	Under 500	500 to 1,000	1,000 to 5,000	5,000 to 10,000	10,000 to 25,000	25,000 to 50,000	50,000 to 100,000	100,000 to 250,000	250,000 to 500,000	500,000 to 2,500,000	2,500,000 and over
Cost of Operations	10	1.7	•	•	1.3	•	1.8	5.5	0.2	4.1	23.0	•	7.0	•
Salaries and Wages	11	29.5	9.8	23.7	26.5	38.0	18.0	30.8	35.5	33.2	29.8	•	25.0	•
Taxes Paid	12	3.3	2.6	3.5	3.6	3.8	1.4	2.9	4.0	3.9	3.0	•	2.5	•
Interest Paid	13	1.9	2.9	0.7	1.4	0.8	0.3	0.7	2.1	0.7	0.5	•	2.1	•
Depreciation	14	0.9	1.1	0.7	0.8	0.6	0.3	0.6	0.8	1.1	0.7	•	0.9	•
Amortization and Depletion	15	1.3	0.4	0.6	2.3	0.8	0.4	0.8	1.1	1.3	1.0	•	4.2	•
Pensions and Other Deferred Comp.	16	1.6	0.6	0.9	0.7	1.2	0.4	1.5	1.2	1.6	0.7	•	0.7	•
Employee Benefits	17	2.0	1.3	1.7	2.2	2.4	1.2	2.4	2.5	3.0	2.6	•	1.7	•
Advertising	18	1.4	1.1	2.3	1.3	0.6	0.4	0.9	3.5	0.6	2.9	•	6.0	•
Other Expenses	19	33.3	42.5	29.0	29.1	21.9	64.5	33.8	22.7	32.5	21.8	•	36.8	•
Officers' Compensation	20	10.2	14.2	18.5	14.2	16.5	6.0	9.6	14.8	7.6	3.7	•	2.2	•
Operating Margin	21	13.0	23.5	18.3	16.4	13.6	5.3	10.4	11.6	10.2	10.3	•	11.0	•
Operating Margin Before Officers' Comp.	22	23.1	37.7	36.8	30.6	30.1	11.2	20.0	26.4	17.9	14.0	•	13.2	•

Net Receivables 23	262	0	6	58	384	1526	3518	12112	13409	26156	•	127392	•
Inventories 24	•	•	•	•	•	•	•	•	•	•	•	•	•
Net Property, Plant and Equipment 25	50	0	17	59	98	607	817	1756	3654	5628	•	20455	•
Total Assets 26	1487	0	94	667	1982	6802	15108	35940	68687	151321	•	821426	•
Notes and Loans Payable 27	241	0	36	339	428	1202	2540	10958	12321	17259	•	149344	•
All Other Liabilities 28	515	0	20	117	949	3760	8518	16223	36105	87689	•	276571	•
Net Worth 29	731	0	37	211	605	1839	4050	8758	20261	46374	•	395512	•

Selected Financial Ratios (Times to 1)

Current Ratio 30	1.1	•	1.8	1.4	1.4	1.3	1.2	1.2	1.2	1.1	•	0.9	•
Quick Ratio 31	0.9	•	1.6	1.3	1.2	1.2	1.1	1.1	1.0	0.9	•	0.8	•
Net Sales to Working Capital 32	15.3	•	19.9	14.6	6.6	16.8	9.1	6.2	9.0	19.7	•	•	•
Coverage Ratio 33	8.5	9.2	26.2	12.4	18.6	17.7	14.9	6.5	14.8	20.3	•	6.4	•
Total Asset Turnover 34	0.7	•	4.1	1.8	1.2	2.6	1.2	0.8	0.8	0.7	•	0.4	•
Inventory Turnover 35	•	•	•	•	•	•	•	•	•	•	•	•	•
Receivables Turnover 36	•	•	•	•	•	•	•	•	•	•	•	•	•
Total Liabilities to Net Worth 37	1.0	•	1.5	2.2	2.3	2.7	2.7	3.1	2.4	2.3	•	1.1	•
Current Assets to Working Capital 38	8.3	•	2.3	3.3	3.6	4.5	5.2	5.3	6.7	14.0	•	•	•
Current Liabilities to Working Capital 39	7.3	•	1.3	2.3	2.6	3.5	4.2	4.3	5.7	13.0	•	•	•
Working Capital to Net Sales 40	0.1	•	0.1	0.1	0.2	0.1	0.1	0.2	0.1	0.1	•	•	•
Inventory to Working Capital 41	0.0	•	•	•	•	•	0.0	0.0	0.0	•	•	•	•
Total Receipts to Cash Flow 42	2.4	1.8	2.4	2.6	3.3	1.5	2.5	3.2	2.6	3.5	•	2.3	•
Cost of Goods to Cash Flow 43	0.0	•	•	0.0	•	0.0	0.1	0.0	0.1	0.8	•	0.2	•
Cash Flow to Total Debt 44	0.5	•	2.8	1.1	0.5	2.4	0.7	0.3	0.4	0.3	•	0.4	•

Selected Financial Factors (in Percentages)

Debt Ratio 45	50.9	•	60.1	68.3	69.5	73.0	73.2	75.6	70.5	69.4	•	51.9	•
Return on Total Assets 46	10.8	•	78.5	32.9	17.4	14.6	13.8	10.5	8.5	8.0	•	5.7	•
Return on Equity Before Income Taxes 47	19.4	•	189.3	95.6	54.0	51.0	48.0	36.6	27.0	24.8	•	10.0	•
Return on Equity After Income Taxes 48	17.1	•	188.0	94.9	52.1	48.5	44.3	34.3	22.2	22.4	•	7.7	•
Profit Margin (Before Income Tax) 49	14.2	23.5	18.3	16.4	13.6	5.3	10.4	11.6	10.1	10.3	•	11.0	•
Profit Margin (After Income Tax) 50	12.5	22.3	18.1	16.3	13.1	5.0	9.6	10.9	8.3	9.2	•	8.5	•

Table I

Corporations with and without Net Income

OTHER INSURANCE RELATED ACTIVITIES

MONEY AMOUNTS AND SIZE OF ASSETS IN THOUSANDS OF DOLLARS

Item Description for Accounting Period 7/12 Through 6/13	Total	Zero Assets	Under 500	500 to 1,000	1,000 to 5,000	5,000 to 10,000	10,000 to 25,000	25,000 to 50,000	50,000 to 100,000	100,000 to 250,000	250,000 to 500,000	500,000 to 2,500,000	2,500,000 and over
Number of Enterprises 1	16994	4198	11504	376	515	154	109	45	30	29	8	20	7

Revenues ($ in Thousands)													
Net Sales 2	53100360	166470	2992019	247284	3166138	2080567	1377610	1685917	1733280	3212418	1464779	8289340	26684538
Interest 3	659968	907	1879	1327	4105	5783	3350	7811	10651	31250	2867	133113	456925
Rents 4	108604	26	0	0	8033	1289	3151	0	6260	1773	20523	5955	61594
Royalties 5	18661	4	0	0	0	0	0	29	0	0	0	2490	16138
Other Portfolio Income 6	361203	5590	1833	12767	632	8040	32549	4591	10998	8880	56348	99257	119718
Other Receipts 7	51951924	159943	2988307	233190	3153368	2065455	1338560	1673486	1705371	3170515	1385041	8048525	26030163
Total Receipts 8	53100360	166470	2992019	247284	3166138	2080567	1377610	1685917	1733280	3212418	1464779	8289340	26684538
Average Total Receipts 9	3125	40	260	658	6148	13510	12639	37465	57776	110773	183097	414467	3812077

Operating Costs/Operating Income (%)													
Cost of Operations 10	11.7	•	•	•	4.7	0.7	0.2	8.0	11.2	0.8	9.7	20.9	14.3
Salaries and Wages 11	18.4	0.0	12.8	19.4	30.0	21.9	41.1	28.7	22.3	28.5	14.8	22.6	13.0
Taxes Paid 12	2.2	2.0	3.0	2.7	3.2	2.2	3.5	4.6	2.6	3.8	1.7	2.8	1.3
Interest Paid 13	2.5	0.9	1.1	0.6	0.5	0.4	0.9	0.5	0.5	2.2	3.4	3.1	3.2
Depreciation 14	0.8	0.1	0.4	0.2	0.6	0.8	0.9	1.1	1.3	1.4	1.1	1.1	0.7
Amortization and Depletion 15	1.0	0.6	0.0	1.6	0.0	0.3	1.2	2.3	0.9	1.1	3.8	1.5	0.9
Pensions and Other Deferred Comp. 16	1.2	•	6.9	1.9	0.7	0.7	0.6	1.6	0.6	1.1	0.4	0.7	0.8
Employee Benefits 17	2.0	2.8	1.2	1.9	3.2	2.8	3.8	5.4	2.6	2.1	2.7	3.5	1.1
Advertising 18	0.5	2.2	1.0	3.5	0.8	0.5	0.3	2.4	0.3	0.4	0.7	0.8	0.2
Other Expenses 19	51.0	82.1	47.3	57.9	42.8	60.0	31.5	43.9	48.1	50.5	51.4	37.1	57.4
Officers' Compensation 20	3.0	4.6	11.3	10.4	8.8	2.7	4.1	2.6	1.5	1.7	1.8	1.3	2.2
Operating Margin 21	5.7	4.7	15.0	0.0	4.8	7.2	11.9	•	8.1	6.4	8.6	4.6	4.7
Operating Margin Before Officers' Comp. 22	8.7	9.3	26.3	10.4	13.5	9.9	15.9	1.5	9.6	8.0	10.5	5.9	6.9

Selected Average Balance Sheet ($ in Thousands)

Net Receivables 23	543	0	15	32	271	989	3809	4139	7728	17772	131654	180336	391797
Inventories 24	•	•	•	•	•	•	•	•	•	•	•	•	•
Net Property, Plant and Equipment 25	142	0	8	8	221	498	1008	1389	4028	7076	14417	39843	101252
Total Assets 26	4754	0	63	672	2135	7027	15296	35240	71772	157756	388561	958406	6482559
Notes and Loans Payable 27	1256	0	39	369	517	898	2895	10708	8729	45244	123434	298187	1576210
All Other Liabilities 28	1951	0	10	37	1049	5673	6071	17768	31740	72337	193939	422943	2441025
Net Worth 29	1547	0	14	266	569	457	6330	6763	31304	40175	71189	237276	2465323

Selected Financial Ratios (Times to 1)

Current Ratio 30	1.3	•	1.3	3.7	1.3	1.2	1.5	1.6	1.3	1.4	1.3	1.0	1.8
Quick Ratio 31	1.0	•	1.2	2.2	0.9	1.0	1.3	1.3	0.8	1.1	1.0	0.8	1.3
Net Sales to Working Capital 32	8.6	•	32.0	3.3	19.9	20.2	4.4	5.7	6.9	6.4	4.5	•	6.6
Coverage Ratio 33	3.4	6.2	15.0	1.0	10.3	21.3	13.4	•	17.3	3.9	3.5	2.4	2.7
Total Asset Turnover 34	0.7	•	4.2	1.0	2.9	1.9	0.8	1.1	0.8	0.7	0.5	0.4	0.6
Inventory Turnover 35	•	•	•	•	•	•	•	•	•	•	•	•	•
Receivables Turnover 36	•	•	•	•	•	•	•	•	•	•	•	•	•
Total Liabilities to Net Worth 37	2.1	•	3.4	1.5	2.8	14.4	1.4	4.2	1.3	2.9	4.5	3.0	1.6
Current Assets to Working Capital 38	4.0	•	4.7	1.4	4.8	6.8	3.2	2.8	4.2	3.3	4.9	•	2.3
Current Liabilities to Working Capital 39	3.0	•	3.7	0.4	3.8	5.8	2.2	1.8	3.2	2.3	3.9	•	1.3
Working Capital to Net Sales 40	0.1	•	0.0	0.3	0.1	0.0	0.2	0.2	0.1	0.2	0.2	•	0.2
Inventory to Working Capital 41	0.0	•	•	•	•	0.0	•	0.0	0.0	0.0	0.0	•	0.0
Total Receipts to Cash Flow 42	1.8	1.6	1.7	2.0	2.2	1.5	2.6	2.5	1.9	1.8	1.7	2.6	1.6
Cost of Goods to Cash Flow 43	0.2	•	•	•	0.1	0.0	0.0	0.2	0.2	0.0	0.2	0.5	0.2
Cash Flow to Total Debt 44	0.5	•	3.1	0.8	1.8	1.3	0.5	0.5	0.8	0.5	0.3	0.2	0.6

Selected Financial Factors (in Percentages)

Debt Ratio 45	67.5	•	77.5	60.4	73.4	93.5	58.6	80.8	56.4	74.5	81.7	75.2	62.0
Return on Total Assets 46	5.6	•	66.9	0.6	15.2	14.4	10.5	•	6.9	6.0	5.6	3.2	5.2
Return on Equity Before Income Taxes 47	12.3	•	277.7	0.0	51.6	211.3	23.4	•	14.9	17.4	22.1	7.5	8.7
Return on Equity After Income Taxes 48	9.1	•	276.4	•	43.3	181.3	22.2	•	13.0	11.9	19.5	4.7	5.6
Profit Margin (Before Income Tax) 49	6.1	4.7	15.0	0.0	4.8	7.1	11.7	•	8.1	6.3	8.6	4.3	5.7
Profit Margin (After Income Tax) 50	4.5	1.8	14.9	•	4.0	6.1	11.1	•	7.0	4.3	7.6	2.7	3.6

Table II
Corporations with Net Income

OTHER INSURANCE RELATED ACTIVITIES

MONEY AMOUNTS AND SIZE OF ASSETS IN THOUSANDS OF DOLLARS

Item Description for Accounting Period 7/12 Through 6/13	Total	Zero Assets	Under 500	500 to 1,000	1,000 to 5,000	5,000 to 10,000	10,000 to 25,000	25,000 to 50,000	50,000 to 100,000	100,000 to 250,000	250,000 to 500,000	500,000 to 2,500,000	2,500,000 and over
Number of Enterprises 1	11270	2241	8380	60	296	107	85	31	22	21	•	15	•

Revenues ($ in Thousands)													
Net Sales 2	43811482	94914	1636863	110098	2806095	1912603	1220252	1143126	1496344	2745146	•	7464452	•
Interest 3	599565	907	1874	9	3795	5206	2760	3830	4466	28876	•	104319	•
Rents 4	80551	26	0	0	5700	842	2882	0	6260	1773	•	2535	•
Royalties 5	16245	4	0	0	0	0	0	0	0	0	•	103	•
Other Portfolio Income 6	309745	5514	1833	12767	612	7111	31867	4508	6893	3086	•	77619	•
Other Receipts 7	42805376	88463	1633156	97322	2795988	1899444	1182743	1134788	1478725	2711411	•	7279876	•
Total Receipts 8	43811482	94914	1636863	110098	2806095	1912603	1220252	1143126	1496344	2745146	•	7464452	•
Average Total Receipts 9	3887	42	195	1835	9480	17875	14356	36875	68016	130721	•	497630	•

Operating Costs/Operating Income (%)													
Cost of Operations 10	7.6	•	•	•	3.6	0.8	•	0.5	6.6	0.9	•	21.4	•
Salaries and Wages 11	18.1	•	8.9	28.4	28.8	20.3	43.0	30.6	22.6	28.4	•	21.3	•
Taxes Paid 12	2.2	2.9	3.7	3.5	3.0	2.0	3.6	4.4	2.5	3.6	•	2.6	•
Interest Paid 13	1.6	0.8	1.6	1.0	0.3	0.2	0.6	0.4	0.5	2.5	•	2.8	•
Depreciation 14	0.7	0.1	0.4	0.2	0.6	0.7	0.9	0.8	1.4	1.2	•	0.9	•
Amortization and Depletion 15	0.9	1.1	0.0	3.5	0.0	0.2	0.6	0.3	0.9	1.0	•	1.1	•
Pensions and Other Deferred Comp. 16	0.8	•	0.0	0.9	0.6	0.7	0.7	2.2	0.7	0.6	•	0.6	•
Employee Benefits 17	2.0	•	1.3	3.9	3.4	1.8	4.0	2.7	2.2	1.7	•	3.5	•
Advertising 18	0.5	3.0	1.6	7.5	0.8	0.5	0.4	2.7	0.3	0.3	•	0.8	•
Other Expenses 19	54.0	27.4	32.2	14.7	45.6	61.2	27.4	45.6	50.0	49.1	•	37.5	•
Officers' Compensation 20	2.3	8.1	15.5	4.6	5.3	2.7	4.5	1.8	1.5	1.3	•	1.0	•
Operating Margin 21	9.2	56.6	34.8	31.8	7.9	8.9	14.3	7.8	10.7	9.4	•	6.5	•
Operating Margin Before Officers' Comp. 22	11.4	64.7	50.3	36.4	13.2	11.6	18.8	9.7	12.2	10.7	•	7.5	•

Selected Average Balance Sheet ($ in Thousands)

Net Receivables 23	736	0	17	0	311	934	4748	4877	8835	22062	•	224079	•
Inventories 24	•	•	•	•	•	•	•	•	•	•	•	•	•
Net Property, Plant and Equipment 25	156	0	8	23	356	556	1252	1121	4788	4788	•	35030	•
Total Assets 26	5393	0	59	677	2362	6843	15531	34648	70587	155986	•	990641	•
Notes and Loans Payable 27	1151	0	28	386	559	947	2556	1966	6511	49778	•	321215	•
All Other Liabilities 28	2414	0	-14	20	1038	4823	6297	18444	32253	63095	•	442107	•
Net Worth 29	1828	0	45	271	765	1073	6678	14237	31824	43112	•	227320	•

Selected Financial Ratios (Times to 1)

Current Ratio 30	1.4	•	5.2	0.3	1.4	1.5	1.6	1.4	1.6	1.3	•	1.1	•
Quick Ratio 31	1.2	•	4.9	0.3	1.2	1.4	1.4	1.2	1.0	1.1	•	0.9	•
Net Sales to Working Capital 32	7.0	•	7.8	•	22.0	10.9	3.9	6.3	4.8	10.6	•	18.0	•
Coverage Ratio 33	6.5	74.6	23.3	34.3	24.2	47.8	23.3	21.6	21.9	4.8	•	3.2	•
Total Asset Turnover 34	0.7	•	3.3	2.7	4.0	2.6	0.9	1.1	1.0	0.8	•	0.5	•
Inventory Turnover 35	•	•	•	•	•	•	•	•	•	•	•	•	•
Receivables Turnover 36	•	•	•	•	•	•	•	•	•	•	•	•	•
Total Liabilities to Net Worth 37	2.0	•	0.3	1.5	2.1	5.4	1.3	1.4	1.2	2.6	•	3.4	•
Current Assets to Working Capital 38	3.3	•	1.2	•	3.5	2.8	2.8	3.3	2.6	4.5	•	14.6	•
Current Liabilities to Working Capital 39	2.3	•	0.2	•	2.5	1.8	1.8	2.3	1.6	3.5	•	13.6	•
Working Capital to Net Sales 40	0.1	•	0.1	•	0.0	0.1	0.3	0.2	0.2	0.1	•	0.1	•
Inventory to Working Capital 41	0.0	•	•	•	•	0.0	•	•	0.0	0.0	•	0.0	•
Total Receipts to Cash Flow 42	1.6	1.3	1.6	3.1	2.0	1.5	2.7	2.0	1.7	1.8	•	2.4	•
Cost of Goods to Cash Flow 43	0.1	•	•	•	0.1	0.0	•	0.0	0.1	0.0	•	0.5	•
Cash Flow to Total Debt 44	0.7	•	9.0	1.5	3.0	2.1	0.6	0.9	1.0	0.7	•	0.3	•

Selected Financial Factors (in Percentages)

Debt Ratio 45	66.1	•	22.9	60.0	67.6	84.3	57.0	58.9	54.9	72.4	•	77.1	•
Return on Total Assets 46	7.7	•	120.5	88.8	33.0	23.5	13.7	8.6	10.8	9.9	•	4.5	•
Return on Equity Before Income Taxes 47	19.1	•	149.6	215.4	97.8	146.9	30.5	19.9	22.9	28.4	•	13.4	•
Return on Equity After Income Taxes 48	15.0	•	149.0	184.5	87.1	128.6	29.0	17.3	20.3	21.4	•	9.7	•
Profit Margin (Before Income Tax) 49	9.0	56.6	34.8	31.8	7.9	8.8	14.2	7.7	10.7	9.4	•	6.1	•
Profit Margin (After Income Tax) 50	7.1	51.5	34.7	27.2	7.0	7.7	13.5	6.7	9.5	7.1	•	4.4	•

Table I

Corporations with and without Net Income

OPEN-END INVESTMENT FUNDS (FORM 1120-RIC)

MONEY AMOUNTS AND SIZE OF ASSETS IN THOUSANDS OF DOLLARS

Item Description for Accounting Period 7/12 Through 6/13		Total	Zero Assets	Under 500	500 to 1,000	1,000 to 5,000	5,000 to 10,000	10,000 to 25,000	25,000 to 50,000	50,000 to 100,000	100,000 to 250,000	250,000 to 500,000	500,000 to 2,500,000	2,500,000 and over
Number of Enterprises	1	15484	1080	115	108	955	1071	1875	1421	1306	1953	1622	2762	1217

Revenues ($ in Thousands)														
Net Sales	2	415919107	1942522	445	9824	128972	252598	1181029	1479010	2636733	9124623	17038129	87456268	294668955
Interest	3	142921178	336236	30	2311	39403	53179	248192	317040	510977	2154693	4888334	26095857	108274926
Rents	4	0	0	0	0	0	0	0	0	0	0	0	0	0
Royalties	5	0	0	0	0	0	0	0	0	0	0	0	0	0
Other Portfolio Income	6	58098166	565897	133	1588	40864	102932	400054	238112	637841	2290158	3658944	17624282	32537360
Other Receipts	7	214899763	1040389	282	5925	48705	96487	532783	923858	1487915	4679772	8490851	43736129	153856669
Total Receipts	8	415919107	1942522	445	9824	128972	252598	1181029	1479010	2636733	9124623	17038129	87456268	294668955
Average Total Receipts	9	26861	1799	4	91	135	236	630	1041	2019	4672	10504	31664	242127

Operating Costs/Operating Income (%)														
Cost of Operations	10	•	•	•	•	•	•	•	•	•	•	•	•	•
Salaries and Wages	11	0.0	0.0	0.2	0.0	0.1	0.1	0.1	0.1	0.1	0.1	0.1	0.1	0.0
Taxes Paid	12	0.4	0.5	•	3.9	1.2	0.3	0.5	0.5	0.6	0.6	0.6	0.5	0.3
Interest Paid	13	0.3	0.1	•	•	0.0	0.0	0.3	0.0	0.3	0.5	0.7	0.5	0.2
Depreciation	14	0.0	•	•	•	•	•	0.0	•	0.0	0.0	0.0	0.0	0.0
Amortization and Depletion	15	0.0	0.7	17.5	2.7	2.5	2.3	1.7	1.1	0.4	0.2	0.0	0.0	0.0
Pensions and Other Deferred Comp.	16	•	•	•	•	•	•	•	•	•	•	•	•	•
Employee Benefits	17	•	•	•	•	•	•	•	•	•	•	•	•	•
Advertising	18	0.0	•	•	•	•	•	•	0.0	•	0.0	0.0	0.0	0.0	0.0
Other Expenses	19	5.6	13.3	•	•	0.1	•	1.4	6.0	7.2	6.7	6.7	6.9	5.1
Officers' Compensation	20	0.0	0.0	2.2	•	•	•	0.1	0.2	0.1	0.0	0.0	0.0	0.0
Operating Margin	21	78.7	74.2	50.8	47.7	79.1	82.6	82.3	73.1	69.5	71.8	72.8	74.6	80.6
Operating Margin Before Officers' Comp.	22	78.7	74.2	53.0	47.7	79.1	82.6	82.3	73.3	69.6	71.8	72.8	74.6	80.6

Selected Average Balance Sheet ($ in Thousands)

Net Receivables 23	10291	0	0	3	13	28	155	231	842	1629	4077	12963	92025
Inventories 24	•	•	•	•	•	•	•	•	•	•	•	•	•
Net Property, Plant and Equipment 25	1	0	0	0	0	0	0	0	0	1	0	0	6
Total Assets 26	1076062	0	165	807	3070	7086	16610	35689	72314	165467	361466	1117574	10253590
Notes and Loans Payable 27	1415	0	0	0	1	0	54	0	111	624	1860	3972	5302
All Other Liabilities 28	45783	0	11	30	65	110	355	817	2764	7531	17996	55260	416396
Net Worth 29	1028864	0	154	778	3004	6976	16201	34872	69439	157311	341610	1058341	9831892

Selected Financial Ratios (Times to 1)

Current Ratio 30	3.7	•	3.8	3.4	6.6	13.3	14.9	12.2	5.5	4.0	3.4	3.3	3.8
Quick Ratio 31	3.4	•	2.9	0.2	1.4	1.6	2.5	3.4	3.3	3.3	3.0	3.0	3.6
Net Sales to Working Capital 32	0.2	•	0.1	1.3	0.4	0.2	0.1	0.1	0.2	0.2	0.2	0.3	0.2
Coverage Ratio 33	258.2	632.2	•	•	4793.2	2411.1	229.6	1479.4	164.0	111.8	88.5	138.5	383.7
Total Asset Turnover 34	0.0	•	0.0	0.1	0.0	0.0	0.0	0.0	0.0	0.0	0.0	0.0	0.0
Inventory Turnover 35	•	•	•	•	•	•	•	•	•	•	•	•	•
Receivables Turnover 36	•	•	•	•	•	•	•	•	•	•	•	•	•
Total Liabilities to Net Worth 37	0.0	•	0.1	0.0	0.0	0.0	0.0	0.0	0.0	0.1	0.1	0.1	0.0
Current Assets to Working Capital 38	1.4	•	1.4	1.4	1.2	1.1	1.1	1.1	1.2	1.3	1.4	1.4	1.4
Current Liabilities to Working Capital 39	0.4	•	0.4	0.4	0.2	0.1	0.1	0.1	0.2	0.3	0.4	0.4	0.4
Working Capital to Net Sales 40	4.7	•	7.6	0.8	2.7	5.7	8.3	8.3	5.8	4.7	4.1	4.0	4.9
Inventory to Working Capital 41	•	•	•	•	•	•	•	•	•	•	•	•	•
Total Receipts to Cash Flow 42	1.3	1.4	•	5.8	1.4	1.5	1.6	1.4	1.5	1.4	1.4	1.4	1.3
Cost of Goods to Cash Flow 43	•	•	•	•	•	•	•	•	•	•	•	•	•
Cash Flow to Total Debt 44	0.4	•	•	0.5	1.5	1.5	1.0	0.9	0.5	0.4	0.4	0.4	0.5

Selected Financial Factors (in Percentages)

Debt Ratio 45	4.4	•	6.4	3.7	2.1	1.5	2.5	2.3	4.0	4.9	5.5	5.3	4.1
Return on Total Assets 46	1.8	•	1.2	5.4	2.5	1.8	2.6	1.9	1.6	1.6	1.7	1.8	1.8
Return on Equity Before Income Taxes 47	1.9	•	1.3	5.6	2.5	1.8	2.7	1.9	1.6	1.7	1.8	1.9	1.9
Return on Equity After Income Taxes 48	1.9	•	1.3	5.6	2.5	1.8	2.7	1.9	1.6	1.7	1.8	1.9	1.9
Profit Margin (Before Income Tax) 49	71.9	61.7	50.8	47.7	55.7	54.4	68.4	63.9	55.8	55.9	59.3	63.0	76.1
Profit Margin (After Income Tax) 50	71.9	61.7	50.8	47.7	55.7	54.4	68.4	63.9	55.8	55.8	59.3	63.0	76.1

Table II
Corporations with Net Income

OPEN-END INVESTMENT FUNDS (FORM 1120-RIC)

MONEY AMOUNTS AND SIZE OF ASSETS IN THOUSANDS OF DOLLARS

Item Description for Accounting Period 7/12 Through 6/13		Total	Zero Assets	Under 500	500 to 1,000	1,000 to 5,000	5,000 to 10,000	10,000 to 25,000	25,000 to 50,000	50,000 to 100,000	100,000 to 250,000	250,000 to 500,000	500,000 to 2,500,000	2,500,000 and over
Number of Enterprises	1	13292	782	61	88	711	833	1600	1254	1105	1708	1472	2516	1163
Revenues ($ in Thousands)														
Net Sales	2	406083880	1802021	432	9075	105190	212144	1108611	1395264	2424379	8602472	16406573	83610082	290407637
Interest	3	142544977	331661	30	2309	39209	52817	244779	314164	491373	2136617	4862664	25950507	108118848
Rents	4	0	0	0	0	0	0	0	0	0	0	0	0	0
Royalties	5	0	0	0	0	0	0	0	0	0	0	0	0	0
Other Portfolio Income	6	52401085	476518	132	1548	24166	72201	357073	206741	536859	2054037	3394400	15549569	29727840
Other Receipts	7	211137818	993842	270	5218	41815	87126	506759	874359	1396147	4411818	8149509	42110006	152560949
Total Receipts	8	406083880	1802021	432	9075	105190	212144	1108611	1395264	2424379	8602472	16406573	83610082	290407637
Average Total Receipts	9	30551	2304	7	103	148	255	693	1113	2194	5037	11146	33231	249706
Operating Costs/Operating Income (%)														
Cost of Operations	10	•	•	•	•	•	•	•	•	•	•	•	•	•
Salaries and Wages	11	0.0	0.0	•	0.0	0.0	0.0	0.1	0.0	0.1	0.1	0.1	0.1	0.0
Taxes Paid	12	0.4	0.5	•	4.2	0.6	0.2	0.5	0.5	0.7	0.6	0.6	0.5	0.3
Interest Paid	13	0.3	0.1	•	•	0.0	0.0	0.3	0.0	0.1	0.5	0.7	0.4	0.2
Depreciation	14	0.0	•	•	•	•	•	•	•	0.0	0.0	0.0	0.0	0.0
Amortization and Depletion	15	0.0	0.7	16.9	2.5	3.1	2.7	1.7	1.1	0.4	0.2	0.0	0.0	0.0
Pensions and Other Deferred Comp.	16	•	•	•	•	•	•	•	•	•	•	•	•	•
Employee Benefits	17	•	•	•	•	•	•	•	•	•	•	•	•	•
Advertising	18	0.0	•	•	•	•	•	•	•	•	•	0.0	0.0	0.0	0.0
Other Expenses	19	5.4	11.7	•	•	•	•	0.6	4.3	5.3	5.8	6.2	6.5	5.0
Officers' Compensation	20	0.0	•	•	•	•	•	0.0	0.0	0.0	0.0	0.0	0.0	0.0
Operating Margin	21	79.6	77.2	66.7	53.2	82.9	85.7	86.0	77.4	74.5	74.9	75.1	76.2	81.0
Operating Margin Before Officers' Comp.	22	79.6	77.2	66.7	53.2	82.9	85.7	86.0	77.4	74.5	74.9	75.1	76.3	81.0

Selected Average Balance Sheet ($ in Thousands)

Net Receivables 23	11350	0	0	4	16	32	133	219	709	1674	4008	12307	94436
Inventories 24	•	•	•	•	•	•	•	•	•	•	•	•	•
Net Property, Plant and Equipment 25	1	0	0	0	0	0	1	0	0	1	0	0	6
Total Assets 26	1200491	0	234	829	3049	7120	16703	35576	72066	166336	362013	1117771	10463006
Notes and Loans Payable 27	1603	0	0	0	1	0	22	0	77	692	2030	4202	5546
All Other Liabilities 28	50805	0	4	30	56	118	340	738	2525	7572	17902	54030	426203
Net Worth 29	1148083	0	230	799	2992	7001	16341	34838	69464	158072	342082	1059540	10031257

Selected Financial Ratios (Times to 1)

Current Ratio 30	3.7	•	15.8	2.8	9.5	15.0	17.5	14.0	5.6	3.7	3.3	3.2	3.7
Quick Ratio 31	3.4	•	15.1	0.2	1.6	1.4	2.0	3.0	3.0	3.0	2.9	3.0	3.5
Net Sales to Working Capital 32	0.2	•	0.1	1.9	0.3	0.2	0.1	0.1	0.2	0.2	0.3	0.3	0.2
Coverage Ratio 33	276.6	1115.8	•	•	6709.4	2482.7	292.6	1941.9	447.0	126.1	96.9	152.3	397.8
Total Asset Turnover 34	0.0	•	0.0	0.1	0.0	0.0	0.0	0.0	0.0	0.0	0.0	0.0	0.0
Inventory Turnover 35	•	•	•	•	•	•	•	•	•	•	•	•	•
Receivables Turnover 36	•	•	•	•	•	•	•	•	•	•	•	•	•
Total Liabilities to Net Worth 37	0.0	•	0.0	0.0	0.0	0.0	0.0	0.0	0.0	0.1	0.1	0.1	0.0
Current Assets to Working Capital 38	1.4	•	1.1	1.6	1.1	1.1	1.1	1.1	1.2	1.4	1.4	1.4	1.4
Current Liabilities to Working Capital 39	0.4	•	0.1	0.6	0.1	0.1	0.1	0.1	0.2	0.4	0.4	0.4	0.4
Working Capital to Net Sales 40	4.4	•	8.0	0.5	3.2	6.5	8.1	8.1	5.0	4.0	3.7	3.6	4.7
Inventory to Working Capital 41	•	•	•	•	•	•	•	•	•	•	•	•	•
Total Receipts to Cash Flow 42	1.3	1.4	•	2.8	1.4	1.5	1.5	1.3	1.5	1.4	1.4	1.4	1.3
Cost of Goods to Cash Flow 43	•	•	•	•	•	•	•	•	•	•	•	•	•
Cash Flow to Total Debt 44	0.5	•	•	1.2	1.8	1.5	1.3	1.1	0.6	0.4	0.4	0.4	0.5

Selected Financial Factors (in Percentages)

Debt Ratio 45	4.4	•	1.6	3.6	1.9	1.7	2.2	2.1	3.6	5.0	5.5	5.2	4.1
Return on Total Assets 46	1.9	•	2.0	6.6	3.4	2.4	3.1	2.2	1.9	1.9	1.9	2.0	1.8
Return on Equity Before Income Taxes 47	2.0	•	2.1	6.9	3.5	2.4	3.2	2.2	2.0	1.9	2.0	2.1	1.9
Return on Equity After Income Taxes 48	2.0	•	2.1	6.9	3.5	2.4	3.2	2.2	2.0	1.9	2.0	2.1	1.9
Profit Margin (Before Income Tax) 49	74.0	68.6	66.7	53.2	70.2	66.7	75.0	69.7	63.6	60.7	62.5	66.5	77.3
Profit Margin (After Income Tax) 50	74.0	68.6	66.7	53.2	70.2	66.7	75.0	69.7	63.6	60.7	62.5	66.5	77.3

Table I

Corporations with and without Net Income

OTHER FINANCIAL VEHICLES

MONEY AMOUNTS AND SIZE OF ASSETS IN THOUSANDS OF DOLLARS

Item Description for Accounting Period 7/12 Through 6/13	Total	Zero Assets	Under 500	500 to 1,000	1,000 to 5,000	5,000 to 10,000	10,000 to 25,000	25,000 to 50,000	50,000 to 100,000	100,000 to 250,000	250,000 to 500,000	500,000 to 2,500,000	2,500,000 and over
Number of Enterprises 1	6983	1740	3192	161	966	174	174	109	98	100	71	124	74

Revenues ($ in Thousands)													
Net Sales 2	40455119	945634	233359	12843	95543	411732	407056	775619	936014	1465772	2106751	6485601	26579194
Interest 3	27968248	331211	1266	1043	53514	320938	52977	72508	393718	761688	1522480	4363680	20093225
Rents 4	1821038	3714	1	0	0	10018	1025	21621	42855	46297	55163	543669	1096674
Royalties 5	32048	403	0	39	2612	8	4056	20639	173	2478	1118	524	0
Other Portfolio Income 6	5214009	240832	553	763	22618	4397	38783	167369	118346	377742	119079	745340	3378189
Other Receipts 7	5419776	369474	231539	10998	16799	76371	310215	493482	380922	277567	408911	832388	2011106
Total Receipts 8	40455119	945634	233359	12843	95543	411732	407056	775619	936014	1465772	2106751	6485601	26579194
Average Total Receipts 9	5793	543	73	80	99	2366	2339	7116	9551	14658	29673	52303	359178

Operating Costs/Operating Income (%)													
Cost of Operations 10	0.3	•	3.2	•	•	•	21.6	0.2	•	2.3	•	•	•
Salaries and Wages 11	1.5	0.0	27.5	•	7.6	•	12.2	8.6	1.6	0.8	5.9	0.5	0.8
Taxes Paid 12	1.0	1.3	6.0	0.2	2.8	0.8	1.4	1.8	1.0	0.6	1.0	1.7	0.7
Interest Paid 13	20.2	6.3	6.8	26.4	36.0	20.8	6.9	6.0	19.0	17.4	47.9	23.9	18.5
Depreciation 14	1.1	0.2	0.1	0.2	0.1	0.0	0.7	0.4	0.4	0.1	0.9	2.0	1.0
Amortization and Depletion 15	0.5	0.5	0.0	0.4	6.6	0.6	1.0	0.2	1.5	1.0	1.9	0.6	0.3
Pensions and Other Deferred Comp. 16	0.1	0.0	0.0	•	1.1	0.0	0.4	2.8	0.1	0.0	0.1	0.0	•
Employee Benefits 17	0.4	•	1.2	•	0.8	•	1.0	2.1	0.2	0.1	0.6	0.0	0.5
Advertising 18	0.0	•	0.5	•	0.4	•	0.4	0.0	0.1	0.0	0.0	0.0	0.0
Other Expenses 19	29.5	38.0	54.6	78.7	187.1	109.0	45.3	35.0	58.2	26.4	50.7	40.5	21.5
Officers' Compensation 20	0.4	0.0	0.9	•	1.8	3.5	1.9	0.2	0.7	0.2	2.9	0.1	0.3
Operating Margin 21	45.0	53.7	•	•	•	•	7.2	42.6	17.1	51.1	•	30.7	56.3
Operating Margin Before Officers' Comp. 22	45.4	53.7	0.1	•	•	•	9.0	42.9	17.9	51.3	•	30.8	56.6

Selected Average Balance Sheet ($ in Thousands)

Net Receivables 23	11813	0	0	0	192	269	363	240	2723	7925	20695	86694	930904
Inventories 24	•	•	•	•	•	•	•	•	•	•	•	•	•
Net Property, Plant and Equipment 25	2878	0	2	0	32	164	622	1503	151	1520	6507	28777	210310
Total Assets 26	134670	0	95	678	2265	6718	15159	35102	71181	161787	350644	1183566	9937256
Notes and Loans Payable 27	32174	0	1	571	643	1868	2553	8003	14070	34386	79795	330030	2309501
All Other Liabilities 28	39506	0	18	0	971	1770	2276	5647	12391	22525	64965	119849	3386669
Net Worth 29	62991	0	76	107	651	3080	10330	21452	44720	104876	205884	733686	4241086

Selected Financial Ratios (Times to 1)

Current Ratio 30	0.7	•	7.1	•	2.3	1.7	1.6	2.0	1.7	0.9	1.3	1.1	0.7
Quick Ratio 31	0.6	•	6.3	•	2.0	1.2	1.4	1.5	1.3	0.8	1.0	0.8	0.5
Net Sales to Working Capital 32	•	•	1.3	0.3	0.3	4.8	1.7	2.8	1.5	•	1.7	2.0	•
Coverage Ratio 33	3.2	9.4	0.9	0.8	•	•	2.0	8.2	1.9	3.9	0.7	2.3	4.0
Total Asset Turnover 34	0.0	•	0.8	0.1	0.0	0.4	0.2	0.2	0.1	0.1	0.1	0.0	0.0
Inventory Turnover 35	•	•	•	•	•	•	•	•	•	•	•	•	•
Receivables Turnover 36	•	•	•	•	•	•	•	•	•	•	•	•	•
Total Liabilities to Net Worth 37	1.1	•	0.3	5.4	2.5	1.2	0.5	0.6	0.6	0.5	0.7	0.6	1.3
Current Assets to Working Capital 38	•	•	1.2	1.0	1.8	2.5	2.7	2.0	2.4	•	4.2	9.0	•
Current Liabilities to Working Capital 39	•	•	0.2	•	0.8	1.5	1.7	1.0	1.4	•	3.2	8.0	•
Working Capital to Net Sales 40	•	•	0.7	3.6	3.4	0.2	0.6	0.4	0.7	•	0.6	0.5	•
Inventory to Working Capital 41	•	•	0.0	•	•	•	•	•	•	•	•	•	•
Total Receipts to Cash Flow 42	1.6	1.5	2.0	1.8	•	1.4	2.3	1.9	1.7	1.9	3.1	1.6	1.5
Cost of Goods to Cash Flow 43	0.0	•	0.1	•	•	•	0.5	0.0	•	0.0	•	•	•
Cash Flow to Total Debt 44	0.1	•	1.9	0.1	•	0.5	0.2	0.3	0.2	0.1	0.1	0.1	0.0

Selected Financial Factors (in Percentages)

Debt Ratio 45	53.2	•	20.3	84.3	71.2	54.1	31.9	38.9	37.2	35.2	41.3	38.0	57.3
Return on Total Assets 46	2.8	•	4.7	2.4	•	•	2.1	10.0	4.8	6.2	3.0	2.4	2.7
Return on Equity Before Income Taxes 47	4.1	•	•	•	•	•	1.5	14.4	3.6	7.1	•	2.2	4.8
Return on Equity After Income Taxes 48	4.0	•	•	•	•	•	0.3	13.1	3.0	6.0	•	2.1	4.8
Profit Margin (Before Income Tax) 49	44.9	52.9	•	•	•	•	6.7	43.3	17.0	50.8	•	30.5	56.3
Profit Margin (After Income Tax) 50	43.9	40.3	•	•	•	•	1.2	39.5	13.9	42.8	•	29.7	56.2

Table II
Corporations with Net Income

OTHER FINANCIAL VEHICLES

MONEY AMOUNTS AND SIZE OF ASSETS IN THOUSANDS OF DOLLARS

Item Description for Accounting Period 7/12 Through 6/13	Total	Zero Assets	Under 500	500 to 1,000	1,000 to 5,000	5,000 to 10,000	10,000 to 25,000	25,000 to 50,000	50,000 to 100,000	100,000 to 250,000	250,000 to 500,000	500,000 to 2,500,000	2,500,000 and over
Number of Enterprises **1**	2174	346	1008	107	189	63	71	53	56	72	49	95	64

Revenues ($ in Thousands)													
Net Sales **2**	35413000	916943	227898	11933	48660	89808	242938	748622	529919	1315936	925488	5324094	25030759
Interest **3**	25548463	324221	661	1036	3019	7054	41774	55984	182019	661843	685411	4074896	19510544
Rents **4**	1060738	3688	1	0	0	10018	981	16328	29072	4043	61	122180	874366
Royalties **5**	26101	389	0	0	0	0	1141	20531	173	2478	1118	272	0
Other Portfolio Income **6**	4852169	218832	553	0	21622	4330	32667	163446	103347	370707	105095	518814	3312755
Other Receipts **7**	3925529	369813	226683	10897	24019	68406	166375	492333	215308	276865	133803	607932	1333094
Total Receipts **8**	35413000	916943	227898	11933	48660	89808	242938	748622	529919	1315936	925488	5324094	25030759
Average Total Receipts **9**	16289	2650	226	112	257	1426	3422	14125	9463	18277	18888	56043	391106

Operating Costs/Operating Income (%)													
Cost of Operations **10**	0.1	•	0.3	•	•	•	•	•	•	2.5	•	•	•
Salaries and Wages **11**	1.1	0.0	27.8	•	0.5	•	4.6	8.9	2.7	0.8	2.3	0.6	0.6
Taxes Paid **12**	0.7	1.3	2.2	0.3	2.4	1.9	1.0	1.7	1.5	0.7	0.4	0.8	0.6
Interest Paid **13**	16.4	2.5	0.2	11.0	3.4	3.0	3.3	1.3	9.4	11.8	17.6	18.9	17.5
Depreciation **14**	0.7	0.1	0.1	0.2	•	0.1	0.0	0.1	0.8	0.1	0.1	0.7	0.9
Amortization and Depletion **15**	0.2	0.5	0.0	•	•	0.0	0.4	0.2	1.9	1.0	1.2	0.3	0.1
Pensions and Other Deferred Comp. **16**	0.1	•	0.0	•	•	0.2	0.0	2.9	0.1	0.0	0.0	0.0	•
Employee Benefits **17**	0.1	•	1.2	•	•	•	1.1	2.2	0.3	0.1	0.3	0.0	•
Advertising **18**	0.0	•	0.5	•	•	•	0.7	•	0.1	0.0	0.0	0.0	0.0
Other Expenses **19**	18.5	12.8	25.4	76.5	24.0	22.9	27.1	13.7	24.9	17.2	16.2	19.4	18.5
Officers' Compensation **20**	0.2	0.0	0.7	•	•	16.2	2.8	0.3	1.2	0.2	0.3	0.1	0.2
Operating Margin **21**	61.8	82.8	41.5	12.0	69.7	55.7	59.0	68.7	57.0	65.5	61.5	59.1	61.6
Operating Margin Before Officers' Comp. **22**	62.1	82.8	42.2	12.0	69.7	71.9	61.8	69.0	58.2	65.7	61.8	59.2	61.8

Selected Average Balance Sheet ($ in Thousands)

Net Receivables 23	35557	0	0	0	31	35	317	489	3365	6631	25451	88650	1045463
Inventories 24	•	•	•	•	•	•	•	•	•	•	•	•	•
Net Property, Plant and Equipment 25	7259	0	5	0	0	0	49	250	254	2058	59	22712	209941
Total Assets 26	389168	0	105	677	2406	7513	16732	35440	72266	166584	343927	1185282	10880980
Notes and Loans Payable 27	81657	0	0	490	260	2385	1888	4362	12197	25921	43115	274844	2283334
All Other Liabilities 28	121050	0	5	0	267	1572	1729	5405	8042	18446	36890	126984	3858590
Net Worth 29	186460	0	99	187	1880	3556	13115	25673	52028	122217	263921	783454	4739056

Selected Financial Ratios (Times to 1)

Current Ratio 30	0.7	•	1.0	•	3.6	1.6	2.2	4.8	4.3	1.0	2.4	1.2	0.6
Quick Ratio 31	0.6	•	1.0	•	2.9	1.0	2.0	3.3	3.6	0.9	1.9	0.9	0.5
Net Sales to Working Capital 32	•	•	897.2	1.2	0.5	1.4	1.7	2.2	0.8	35.9	0.4	1.3	•
Coverage Ratio 33	4.8	33.8	186.2	2.1	21.2	19.5	18.8	53.6	7.1	6.5	4.5	4.1	4.5
Total Asset Turnover 34	0.0	•	2.2	0.2	0.1	0.2	0.2	0.4	0.1	0.1	0.1	0.0	0.0
Inventory Turnover 35	•	•	•	•	•	•	•	•	•	•	•	•	•
Receivables Turnover 36	•	•	•	•	•	•	•	•	•	•	•	•	•
Total Liabilities to Net Worth 37	1.1	•	0.1	2.6	0.3	1.1	0.3	0.4	0.4	0.4	0.3	0.5	1.3
Current Assets to Working Capital 38	•	•	22.7	1.0	1.4	2.5	1.8	1.3	1.3	34.4	1.7	5.7	•
Current Liabilities to Working Capital 39	•	•	21.7	•	0.4	1.5	0.8	0.3	0.3	33.4	0.7	4.7	•
Working Capital to Net Sales 40	•	•	0.0	0.8	2.1	0.7	0.6	0.5	1.3	0.0	2.4	0.8	•
Inventory to Working Capital 41	•	•	•	•	•	•	•	•	•	•	•	•	•
Total Receipts to Cash Flow 42	1.5	1.4	1.6	1.4	1.2	1.3	1.4	1.6	1.6	1.8	1.4	1.4	1.5
Cost of Goods to Cash Flow 43	0.0	•	0.0	•	•	•	•	•	•	0.0	•	•	•
Cash Flow to Total Debt 44	0.1	•	25.0	0.2	0.4	0.3	0.7	0.9	0.3	0.2	0.2	0.1	0.0

Selected Financial Factors (in Percentages)

Debt Ratio 45	52.1	•	5.4	72.3	21.9	52.7	21.6	27.6	28.0	26.6	23.3	33.9	56.4
Return on Total Assets 46	3.3	•	90.2	3.8	7.8	11.0	12.8	28.2	8.7	8.5	4.3	3.7	2.8
Return on Equity Before Income Taxes 47	5.4	•	94.9	7.1	9.5	22.0	15.4	38.2	10.4	9.8	4.4	4.2	5.1
Return on Equity After Income Taxes 48	5.3	•	94.4	6.3	8.6	18.7	13.0	36.0	9.4	8.5	4.3	4.1	5.1
Profit Margin (Before Income Tax) 49	61.8	82.6	41.5	12.0	69.6	54.9	59.1	69.4	57.0	65.5	61.5	58.9	61.6
Profit Margin (After Income Tax) 50	60.6	69.5	41.3	10.5	62.7	46.7	49.8	65.5	51.5	56.7	60.6	57.9	61.4

Table I

Corporations with and without Net Income

LESSORS OF BUILDINGS

MONEY AMOUNTS AND SIZE OF ASSETS IN THOUSANDS OF DOLLARS

Item Description for Accounting Period 7/12 Through 6/13	Total	Zero Assets	Under 500	500 to 1,000	1,000 to 5,000	5,000 to 10,000	10,000 to 25,000	25,000 to 50,000	50,000 to 100,000	100,000 to 250,000	250,000 to 500,000	500,000 to 2,500,000	2,500,000 and over
Number of Enterprises **1**	234415	27159	121060	37570	39949	4637	2315	719	395	281	107	157	65
Revenues ($ in Thousands)													
Net Sales **2**	92255296	2979786	2911456	2983033	6848535	2292735	3221484	2434053	3349071	5722693	4492851	18357114	36662486
Interest **3**	2517179	45008	10568	16794	52107	29832	36058	22020	66067	97976	162316	473146	1505287
Rents **4**	41693310	386586	22129	13354	177850	71121	316116	432198	721520	2061839	1883515	11339596	24267486
Royalties **5**	35411	63	9	255	10625	11398	1657	733	9996	81	391	79	125
Other Portfolio Income **6**	7980698	886731	262939	120875	550381	108630	377329	152853	226273	710735	270270	1693841	2619841
Other Receipts **7**	40028698	1661398	2615811	2831755	6057572	2071754	2490324	1826249	2325215	2852062	2176359	4850452	8269747
Total Receipts **8**	92255296	2979786	2911456	2983033	6848535	2292735	3221484	2434053	3349071	5722693	4492851	18357114	36662486
Average Total Receipts **9**	394	110	24	79	171	494	1392	3385	8479	20365	41989	116924	564038
Operating Costs/Operating Income (%)													
Cost of Operations **10**	4.5	5.0	4.8	10.1	16.9	4.5	9.2	8.3	12.2	6.9	17.7	0.7	0.2
Salaries and Wages **11**	5.2	0.8	7.3	8.0	7.8	14.2	7.3	12.4	8.4	5.7	2.9	4.2	3.8
Taxes Paid **12**	6.7	7.2	12.8	10.0	10.6	10.0	8.7	7.9	7.2	6.8	7.3	6.6	4.7
Interest Paid **13**	12.7	10.5	7.6	7.1	9.5	11.9	12.9	14.0	14.0	12.8	14.6	13.3	13.7
Depreciation **14**	12.1	10.0	11.2	7.3	9.5	10.6	10.2	13.2	12.3	10.8	10.8	12.3	13.6
Amortization and Depletion **15**	1.0	0.8	0.2	0.2	0.7	0.5	0.9	0.9	1.3	1.3	1.2	1.4	1.1
Pensions and Other Deferred Comp. **16**	0.1	0.0	0.1	0.3	0.4	0.7	0.3	0.4	0.7	0.1	0.2	0.0	0.0
Employee Benefits **17**	0.4	0.0	1.4	0.8	0.8	2.5	0.9	1.1	0.7	1.0	0.4	0.4	0.0
Advertising **18**	0.4	0.1	0.5	0.2	0.3	0.8	0.8	0.6	0.7	0.9	0.4	0.5	0.2
Other Expenses **19**	31.2	30.3	49.1	41.0	34.7	34.1	38.9	34.8	34.3	35.3	33.7	42.1	20.6
Officers' Compensation **20**	1.7	0.1	4.7	7.4	3.5	8.5	3.0	2.6	1.5	1.0	0.4	0.8	0.8
Operating Margin **21**	23.9	35.2	0.3	7.5	5.4	1.7	6.9	3.8	6.7	17.4	10.4	17.7	41.3
Operating Margin Before Officers' Comp. **22**	25.6	35.3	4.9	14.9	8.9	10.3	9.8	6.5	8.2	18.3	10.8	18.5	42.2

	Selected Average Balance Sheet ($ in Thousands)												
Net Receivables 23	63	0	4	13	37	273	424	628	1529	3798	7422	21103	59285
Inventories 24	•	•	•	•	•	•	•	•	•	•	•	•	•
Net Property, Plant and Equipment 25	2410	0	141	520	1457	4461	9122	21811	40266	85631	173411	588231	4027753
Total Assets 26	4010	0	190	707	2120	7008	14893	34872	68767	156341	355692	1133220	6564310
Notes and Loans Payable 27	1716	0	120	445	1406	4619	8883	19656	33213	60470	130187	409077	2314410
All Other Liabilities 28	324	0	11	32	229	536	1324	2648	4984	13088	16870	95705	529186
Net Worth 29	1970	0	59	230	486	1854	4687	12568	30571	82783	208635	628439	3720714

	Selected Financial Ratios (Times to 1)												
Current Ratio 30	1.3	•	2.7	2.6	1.9	2.4	2.0	2.1	1.6	2.3	1.1	1.2	0.9
Quick Ratio 31	0.9	•	2.2	1.8	1.2	1.7	1.4	1.4	1.1	1.6	0.9	0.9	0.6
Net Sales to Working Capital 32	4.7	•	1.3	1.4	1.1	0.8	1.4	1.4	2.9	2.1	20.2	12.1	•
Coverage Ratio 33	2.9	4.3	1.0	2.1	1.5	1.1	1.5	1.2	1.5	2.4	1.7	2.3	4.0
Total Asset Turnover 34	0.1	•	0.1	0.1	0.1	0.1	0.1	0.1	0.1	0.1	0.1	0.1	0.1
Inventory Turnover 35	•	•	•	•	•	•	•	•	•	•	•	•	•
Receivables Turnover 36	•	•	•	•	•	•	•	•	•	•	•	•	•
Total Liabilities to Net Worth 37	1.0	•	2.2	2.1	3.4	2.8	2.2	1.8	1.2	0.9	0.7	0.8	0.8
Current Assets to Working Capital 38	4.0	•	1.6	1.6	2.2	1.7	2.0	1.9	2.6	1.7	11.2	7.6	•
Current Liabilities to Working Capital 39	3.0	•	0.6	0.6	1.2	0.7	1.0	0.9	1.6	0.7	10.2	6.6	•
Working Capital to Net Sales 40	0.2	•	0.8	0.7	0.9	1.2	0.7	0.7	0.3	0.5	0.0	0.1	•
Inventory to Working Capital 41	0.0	•	•	•	0.0	0.0	0.0	0.0	0.0	0.0	0.1	0.0	•
Total Receipts to Cash Flow 42	2.5	2.8	4.0	2.7	3.8	3.9	3.8	3.5	3.7	3.1	3.0	2.4	2.0
Cost of Goods to Cash Flow 43	0.1	0.1	0.2	0.3	0.6	0.2	0.3	0.3	0.5	0.2	0.5	0.0	0.0
Cash Flow to Total Debt 44	0.1	•	0.0	0.1	0.0	0.0	0.0	0.0	0.1	0.1	0.1	0.1	0.1

	Selected Financial Factors (in Percentages)												
Debt Ratio 45	50.9	•	69.0	67.4	77.1	73.5	68.5	64.0	55.5	47.0	41.3	44.5	43.3
Return on Total Assets 46	3.6	•	1.0	1.6	1.2	0.9	1.8	1.7	2.5	3.9	3.0	3.2	4.7
Return on Equity Before Income Taxes 47	4.8	•	0.1	2.6	1.8	0.4	1.9	0.9	1.8	4.3	2.1	3.3	6.3
Return on Equity After Income Taxes 48	4.6	•	•	2.1	1.3	•	1.1	0.3	0.9	3.8	2.0	3.2	6.3
Profit Margin (Before Income Tax) 49	23.9	35.2	0.2	7.5	5.2	1.5	6.5	3.4	6.4	17.3	10.4	17.7	41.3
Profit Margin (After Income Tax) 50	23.0	31.0	•	6.2	3.6	•	3.8	1.2	3.1	15.4	9.9	17.3	41.3

Table II

Corporations with Net Income

LESSORS OF BUILDINGS

MONEY AMOUNTS AND SIZE OF ASSETS IN THOUSANDS OF DOLLARS

Item Description for Accounting Period 7/12 Through 6/13	Total	Zero Assets	Under 500	500 to 1,000	1,000 to 5,000	5,000 to 10,000	10,000 to 25,000	25,000 to 50,000	50,000 to 100,000	100,000 to 250,000	250,000 to 500,000	500,000 to 2,500,000	2,500,000 and over
Number of Enterprises **1**	48418	6688	22435	8132	8297	1279	761	268	178	154	•	103	•

Revenues ($ in Thousands)													
Net Sales **2**	74075822	2460838	2017110	2354293	4073312	1268497	1967167	1623564	2243525	3305480	•	14154781	•
Interest **3**	2250282	36597	8683	10847	35506	22838	27183	15831	54196	79426	•	398125	•
Rents **4**	35622946	376745	17484	7872	58932	26415	172541	201058	415668	1218409	•	8565096	•
Royalties **5**	14044	0	9	255	10265	2073	1	627	591	0	•	0	•
Other Portfolio Income **6**	7585094	879376	258751	105856	518372	85121	348501	131377	201024	686002	•	1558000	•
Other Receipts **7**	28603456	1168120	1732183	2229463	3450237	1132050	1418941	1274671	1572046	1321643	•	3633560	•
Total Receipts **8**	74075822	2460838	2017110	2354293	4073312	1268497	1967167	1623564	2243525	3305480	•	14154781	•
Average Total Receipts **9**	1530	368	90	290	491	992	2585	6058	12604	21464	•	137425	•

Operating Costs/Operating Income (%)													
Cost of Operations **10**	3.7	•	2.6	11.3	21.8	1.3	8.3	7.4	12.8	3.3	•	0.3	•
Salaries and Wages **11**	4.4	0.6	8.3	8.6	4.2	8.8	6.5	12.4	7.0	2.6	•	4.1	•
Taxes Paid **12**	5.9	5.7	8.9	7.5	7.6	8.8	7.6	7.3	6.5	7.0	•	6.8	•
Interest Paid **13**	11.2	9.0	6.5	5.4	6.8	9.1	8.7	9.0	9.4	10.7	•	10.7	•
Depreciation **14**	11.3	7.6	7.5	4.8	5.5	8.7	7.8	10.2	8.1	10.7	•	12.0	•
Amortization and Depletion **15**	0.9	0.8	0.1	0.2	0.6	0.4	0.6	0.7	0.9	1.3	•	1.1	•
Pensions and Other Deferred Comp. **16**	0.1	0.0	0.1	0.3	0.4	0.3	0.3	0.4	0.3	0.0	•	0.0	•
Employee Benefits **17**	0.2	0.0	0.5	0.6	0.4	0.7	0.7	0.7	0.5	0.1	•	0.2	•
Advertising **18**	0.3	0.1	0.7	0.2	0.2	0.9	0.2	0.4	0.4	0.2	•	0.5	•
Other Expenses **19**	23.0	23.5	32.1	34.0	22.3	25.7	24.4	26.7	25.8	21.2	•	28.6	•
Officers' Compensation **20**	1.4	0.1	4.9	7.7	3.0	4.0	3.0	2.5	1.1	0.9	•	0.7	•
Operating Margin **21**	37.7	52.6	27.9	19.3	27.3	31.4	32.1	22.3	27.3	42.0	•	34.8	•
Operating Margin Before Officers' Comp. **22**	39.1	52.7	32.8	27.0	30.3	35.4	35.1	24.8	28.3	42.9	•	35.5	•

Selected Average Balance Sheet ($ in Thousands)

Net Receivables 23	175	0	6	19	68	338	582	748	2156	3203	•	16713	•
Inventories 24	•	•	•	•	•	•	•	•	•	•	•	•	•
Net Property, Plant and Equipment 25	7531	0	108	478	1266	4156	8190	21573	36322	85548	•	611389	•
Total Assets 26	13115	0	169	708	2147	6711	15144	34803	70350	162241	•	1191771	•
Notes and Loans Payable 27	4540	0	113	419	1162	3276	7800	16372	27922	50616	•	362927	•
All Other Liabilities 28	1001	0	15	39	217	658	1363	2405	5307	12961	•	84278	•
Net Worth 29	7575	0	41	251	768	2778	5981	16027	37121	98664	•	744566	•

Selected Financial Ratios (Times to 1)

Current Ratio 30	1.2	•	3.1	2.9	2.9	3.3	2.7	1.6	1.7	2.4	•	1.2	•
Quick Ratio 31	0.8	•	2.8	2.3	2.1	2.5	1.8	1.1	1.2	1.7	•	0.9	•
Net Sales to Working Capital 32	12.1	•	3.4	3.5	1.6	1.1	1.4	3.6	3.9	2.3	•	13.3	•
Coverage Ratio 33	4.4	6.9	5.3	4.6	5.0	4.5	4.7	3.5	3.9	4.9	•	4.3	•
Total Asset Turnover 34	0.1	•	0.5	0.4	0.2	0.1	0.2	0.2	0.2	0.1	•	0.1	•
Inventory Turnover 35	•	•	•	•	•	•	•	•	•	•	•	•	•
Receivables Turnover 36	•	•	•	•	•	•	•	•	•	•	•	•	•
Total Liabilities to Net Worth 37	0.7	•	3.1	1.8	1.8	1.4	1.5	1.2	0.9	0.6	•	0.6	•
Current Assets to Working Capital 38	7.0	•	1.5	1.5	1.5	1.4	1.6	2.7	2.5	1.7	•	6.7	•
Current Liabilities to Working Capital 39	6.0	•	0.5	0.5	0.5	0.4	0.6	1.7	1.5	0.7	•	5.7	•
Working Capital to Net Sales 40	0.1	•	0.3	0.3	0.6	0.9	0.7	0.3	0.3	0.4	•	0.1	•
Inventory to Working Capital 41	0.0	•	•	•	0.0	0.0	0.0	0.0	0.0	0.0	•	0.0	•
Total Receipts to Cash Flow 42	2.1	2.2	2.4	2.4	2.5	2.1	2.8	2.6	2.6	2.5	•	2.2	•
Cost of Goods to Cash Flow 43	0.1	•	0.1	0.3	0.5	0.0	0.2	0.2	0.3	0.1	•	0.0	•
Cash Flow to Total Debt 44	0.1	•	0.3	0.3	0.1	0.1	0.1	0.1	0.1	0.1	•	0.1	•

Selected Financial Factors (in Percentages)

Debt Ratio 45	42.2	•	75.6	64.6	64.3	58.6	60.5	53.9	47.2	39.2	•	37.5	•
Return on Total Assets 46	5.7	•	18.2	10.1	7.8	6.0	6.9	5.4	6.5	7.0	•	5.2	•
Return on Equity Before Income Taxes 47	7.6	•	60.5	22.2	17.4	11.2	13.7	8.4	9.2	9.1	•	6.4	•
Return on Equity After Income Taxes 48	7.4	•	54.5	20.3	15.7	9.5	11.9	7.2	7.5	8.4	•	6.3	•
Profit Margin (Before Income Tax) 49	37.7	52.6	27.8	19.3	27.2	31.4	31.8	22.2	27.1	41.9	•	34.8	•
Profit Margin (After Income Tax) 50	36.5	47.5	25.1	17.6	24.5	26.5	27.5	18.9	22.2	38.6	•	34.4	•

Table I

Corporations with and without Net Income

LESSORS OF MINIWAREHOUSES, SELF-STORAGE, OTHER REAL ESTATE

MONEY AMOUNTS AND SIZE OF ASSETS IN THOUSANDS OF DOLLARS

Item Description for Accounting Period 7/12 Through 6/13	Total	Zero Assets	Under 500	500 to 1,000	1,000 to 5,000	5,000 to 10,000	10,000 to 25,000	25,000 to 50,000	50,000 to 100,000	100,000 to 250,000	250,000 to 500,000	500,000 to 2,500,000	2,500,000 and over
Number of Enterprises 1	76107	14187	37664	9660	11440	1296	879	355	222	211	86	89	18

Revenues ($ in Thousands)

Net Sales 2	38440306	1881906	3632828	1347357	2079473	812122	1508871	1246010	2167777	3816851	2448053	7817270	9681790
Interest 3	1368460	29489	17506	13089	39634	18632	53021	66236	49964	127243	179841	172332	601472
Rents 4	13707376	31797	39432	1110	27849	72711	330283	309973	910623	1597168	1347014	4189897	4849522
Royalties 5	87485	50	1086	8469	27616	1798	17708	2825	1486	6457	19986	3	0
Other Portfolio Income 6	6377220	597148	100998	42828	218357	123287	187331	290373	560301	844972	303578	1751219	1356824
Other Receipts 7	16899765	1223422	3473806	1281861	1766017	595694	920528	576603	645403	1241011	597634	1703819	2873972
Total Receipts 8	38440306	1881906	3632828	1347357	2079473	812122	1508871	1246010	2167777	3816851	2448053	7817270	9681790
Average Total Receipts 9	505	133	96	139	182	627	1717	3510	9765	18089	28466	87834	537877

Operating Costs/Operating Income (%)

Cost of Operations 10	0.9	0.0	•	0.2	6.6	2.9	0.8	0.0	0.2	0.3	4.9	0.3	•
Salaries and Wages 11	6.5	7.0	24.3	12.9	10.5	8.2	12.1	4.1	3.7	6.7	3.6	2.6	1.5
Taxes Paid 12	5.6	3.8	6.2	8.6	7.5	8.5	5.6	5.2	4.4	5.0	5.9	6.2	4.6
Interest Paid 13	11.3	15.6	1.3	4.6	8.1	15.3	13.2	12.3	15.7	14.6	14.1	13.0	10.6
Depreciation 14	8.7	4.0	2.0	3.4	7.5	12.8	7.6	7.6	8.4	10.9	10.8	12.9	8.4
Amortization and Depletion 15	1.1	0.2	0.0	0.2	0.5	0.5	0.7	0.7	1.2	1.2	2.1	1.4	1.5
Pensions and Other Deferred Comp. 16	0.1	0.0	0.2	0.3	0.3	0.1	0.1	0.1	0.0	0.2	0.0	0.0	•
Employee Benefits 17	0.6	0.6	3.6	0.6	0.9	0.9	0.6	0.4	0.3	0.2	0.4	0.1	•
Advertising 18	0.7	0.8	3.1	0.3	0.4	0.4	0.3	0.6	0.3	0.2	0.7	0.5	0.4
Other Expenses 19	46.5	61.8	42.9	56.0	41.9	46.9	57.6	44.9	54.1	51.3	62.3	41.7	39.1
Officers' Compensation 20	2.0	2.2	8.1	6.1	5.7	3.8	3.4	1.4	1.0	0.6	1.3	0.3	0.4
Operating Margin 21	16.2	4.0	8.2	6.9	10.2	•	•	22.6	10.6	8.9	•	21.2	33.4
Operating Margin Before Officers' Comp. 22	18.2	6.2	16.3	13.1	15.8	3.6	1.2	24.0	11.6	9.4	•	21.5	33.8

Selected Average Balance Sheet ($ in Thousands)

Net Receivables 23	97	0	6	37	84	251	646	1222	1741	4345	9690	3094	117479
Inventories 24	•	•	•	•	•	•	•	•	•	•	•	•	•
Net Property, Plant and Equipment 25	2277	0	76	354	1043	2826	5507	11021	21041	50506	142025	464622	4098476
Total Assets 26	4764	0	161	703	2049	6856	15382	35062	73639	160840	353523	975893	6882824
Notes and Loans Payable 27	1521	0	73	322	1129	3398	7217	12572	23692	45175	105473	288828	1786886
All Other Liabilities 28	642	0	24	64	245	742	2973	3803	4960	14089	15619	50517	1649602
Net Worth 29	2601	0	63	317	675	2716	5193	18687	44988	101576	232431	636548	3446335

Selected Financial Ratios (Times to 1)

Current Ratio 30	1.0	•	1.9	2.8	2.0	2.9	1.6	1.7	2.7	2.2	3.6	1.3	0.4
Quick Ratio 31	0.7	•	1.6	2.1	1.4	1.3	1.0	1.0	1.5	1.6	2.7	0.8	0.3
Net Sales to Working Capital 32	75.0	•	5.0	1.4	0.9	0.7	1.4	1.5	1.7	2.0	1.3	9.1	•
Coverage Ratio 33	2.4	1.3	7.3	2.5	2.3	0.9	0.8	2.8	1.7	1.6	0.6	2.6	4.1
Total Asset Turnover 34	0.1	•	0.6	0.2	0.1	0.1	0.1	0.1	0.1	0.1	0.1	0.1	0.1
Inventory Turnover 35	•	•	•	•	•	•	•	•	•	•	•	•	•
Receivables Turnover 36	•	•	•	•	•	•	•	•	•	•	•	•	•
Total Liabilities to Net Worth 37	0.8	•	1.5	1.2	2.0	1.5	2.0	0.9	0.6	0.6	0.5	0.5	1.0
Current Assets to Working Capital 38	66.6	•	2.1	1.6	2.0	1.5	2.6	2.4	1.6	1.8	1.4	4.5	•
Current Liabilities to Working Capital 39	65.6	•	1.1	0.6	1.0	0.5	1.6	1.4	0.6	0.8	0.4	3.5	•
Working Capital to Net Sales 40	0.0	•	0.2	0.7	1.1	1.5	0.7	0.6	0.6	0.5	0.7	0.1	•
Inventory to Working Capital 41	0.2	•	•	•	0.0	0.0	0.0	0.0	0.0	0.0	0.0	0.0	•
Total Receipts to Cash Flow 42	2.6	4.5	3.2	1.9	3.0	3.4	3.1	2.4	2.9	2.9	2.8	3.1	2.0
Cost of Goods to Cash Flow 43	0.0	0.0	•	0.0	0.2	0.1	0.0	0.0	0.0	0.0	0.1	0.0	•
Cash Flow to Total Debt 44	0.1	•	0.3	0.2	0.0	0.0	0.1	0.1	0.1	0.1	0.1	0.1	0.1

Selected Financial Factors (in Percentages)

Debt Ratio 45	45.4	•	60.5	54.9	67.1	60.4	66.2	46.7	38.9	36.8	34.3	34.8	49.9
Return on Total Assets 46	2.9	•	5.7	2.2	1.6	1.3	1.2	3.5	3.5	2.6	0.6	3.1	3.4
Return on Equity Before Income Taxes 47	3.1	•	12.5	3.0	2.7	•	•	4.2	2.3	1.6	•	2.9	5.2
Return on Equity After Income Taxes 48	2.9	•	11.8	2.5	1.9	•	•	3.5	2.1	1.4	•	2.9	5.2
Profit Margin (Before Income Tax) 49	16.2	3.9	8.2	6.7	10.1	•	•	22.4	10.5	8.8	•	21.2	33.4
Profit Margin (After Income Tax) 50	15.1	•	7.7	5.6	7.0	•	•	18.4	9.6	8.1	•	21.2	33.4

Table II

Corporations with Net Income

LESSORS OF MINIWAREHOUSES, SELF-STORAGE, OTHER REAL ESTATE

MONEY AMOUNTS AND SIZE OF ASSETS IN THOUSANDS OF DOLLARS

Item Description for Accounting Period 7/12 Through 6/13	Total	Zero Assets	Under 500	500 to 1,000	1,000 to 5,000	5,000 to 10,000	10,000 to 25,000	25,000 to 50,000	50,000 to 100,000	100,000 to 250,000	250,000 to 500,000	500,000 to 2,500,000	2,500,000 and over
Number of Enterprises **1**	21359	4132	9997	3303	2807	384	275	152	93	•	38	58	•

Revenues ($ in Thousands)

Net Sales **2**	30034011	1194469	3002937	897741	1654985	460704	1147610	928155	1582374	•	1299868	6057960	•
Interest **3**	1087515	2650	10506	10201	28589	14380	18989	58404	35312	•	70629	154010	•
Rents **4**	10240591	13969	5252	929	19196	36261	211240	215991	628739	•	826691	3077155	•
Royalties **5**	63486	0	1086	8466	27595	1798	16067	2683	1486	•	0	3	•
Other Portfolio Income **6**	5973109	560862	100028	39022	205159	101863	172139	254387	539818	•	231747	1706504	•
Other Receipts **7**	12669310	616988	2886065	839123	1374446	306402	729175	396690	377019	•	170801	1120288	•
Total Receipts **8**	30034011	1194469	3002937	897741	1654985	460704	1147610	928155	1582374	•	1299868	6057960	•
Average Total Receipts **9**	1406	289	300	272	590	1200	4173	6106	17015	•	34207	104448	•

Operating Costs/Operating Income (%)

Cost of Operations **10**	0.6	0.0	•	0.2	8.0	0.1	1.1	•	0.3	•	•	0.4	•
Salaries and Wages **11**	5.7	1.1	22.3	17.6	7.6	5.6	11.1	3.9	3.0	•	2.4	2.2	•
Taxes Paid **12**	4.6	2.2	5.0	9.1	5.9	5.3	3.9	4.2	3.3	•	5.2	5.3	•
Interest Paid **13**	7.9	11.6	0.8	4.0	5.8	7.0	5.2	8.2	8.9	•	11.8	10.3	•
Depreciation **14**	6.9	3.8	0.7	2.6	4.7	5.3	5.0	5.5	6.1	•	10.0	10.0	•
Amortization and Depletion **15**	0.9	0.0	0.0	0.2	0.6	0.6	0.4	0.5	1.0	•	0.9	1.2	•
Pensions and Other Deferred Comp. **16**	0.1	•	0.2	0.4	0.4	0.1	0.2	0.1	0.0	•	0.1	0.0	•
Employee Benefits **17**	0.5	0.4	3.4	0.5	0.5	0.6	0.5	0.3	0.2	•	•	0.1	•
Advertising **18**	0.7	0.9	3.8	0.5	0.3	0.2	0.3	0.6	0.3	•	0.3	0.4	•
Other Expenses **19**	34.8	23.5	40.3	32.1	24.6	38.1	35.8	26.6	38.6	•	39.8	30.8	•
Officers' Compensation **20**	1.7	0.6	5.9	7.7	5.6	2.8	2.3	1.2	0.9	•	1.0	0.4	•
Operating Margin **21**	35.5	56.0	17.8	25.2	36.0	34.5	34.4	49.0	37.6	•	28.5	39.1	•
Operating Margin Before Officers' Comp. **22**	37.2	56.6	23.7	32.9	41.6	37.3	36.7	50.2	38.5	•	29.5	39.5	•

		Selected Average Balance Sheet ($ in Thousands)											
Net Receivables	23	192	0	9	82	187	161	643	1610	953	•	1873	3237	•
Inventories	24	•	•	•	•	•	•	•	•	•	•	•	•	•
Net Property, Plant and Equipment	25	5641	0	48	304	1122	2358	5125	9920	22499	•	174638	490590	•
Total Assets	26	10952	0	149	701	2289	6336	15502	35160	75333	•	348107	994520	•
Notes and Loans Payable	27	2958	0	52	285	1281	2481	4566	11486	17512	•	120850	281777	•
All Other Liabilities	28	1799	0	32	91	296	727	3064	4454	3476	•	15792	51212	•
Net Worth	29	6196	0	65	325	713	3127	7872	19220	54345	•	211465	661531	•

		Selected Financial Ratios (Times to 1)											
Current Ratio	30	0.7	•	2.7	2.6	3.6	3.0	2.5	1.8	3.7	•	4.2	1.0	•
Quick Ratio	31	0.5	•	2.4	2.1	2.6	2.0	1.5	1.2	1.9	•	2.4	0.8	•
Net Sales to Working Capital	32	•	•	6.3	1.9	1.5	1.6	1.8	2.1	3.1	•	1.7	•	•
Coverage Ratio	33	5.5	5.8	24.4	7.2	7.2	5.9	7.6	7.0	5.2	•	3.4	4.8	•
Total Asset Turnover	34	0.1	•	2.0	0.4	0.3	0.2	0.3	0.2	0.2	•	0.1	0.1	•
Inventory Turnover	35	•	•	•	•	•	•	•	•	•	•	•	•	•
Receivables Turnover	36	•	•	•	•	•	•	•	•	•	•	•	•	•
Total Liabilities to Net Worth	37	0.8	•	1.3	1.2	2.2	1.0	1.0	0.8	0.4	•	0.6	0.5	•
Current Assets to Working Capital	38	•	•	1.6	1.6	1.4	1.5	1.7	2.2	1.4	•	1.3	•	•
Current Liabilities to Working Capital	39	•	•	0.6	0.6	0.4	0.5	0.7	1.2	0.4	•	0.3	•	•
Working Capital to Net Sales	40	•	•	0.2	0.5	0.7	0.6	0.6	0.5	0.3	•	0.6	•	•
Inventory to Working Capital	41	•	•	•	•	0.0	0.0	0.0	•	0.0	•	•	•	•
Total Receipts to Cash Flow	42	2.2	3.1	2.7	2.1	2.3	2.1	2.1	2.1	2.3	•	2.1	2.7	•
Cost of Goods to Cash Flow	43	0.0	0.0	•	0.0	0.2	0.0	0.0	•	0.0	•	•	0.0	•
Cash Flow to Total Debt	44	0.1	•	1.3	0.4	0.2	0.2	0.3	0.2	0.4	•	0.1	0.1	•

		Selected Financial Factors (in Percentages)											
Debt Ratio	45	43.4	•	56.1	53.7	68.9	50.6	49.2	45.3	27.9	•	39.3	33.5	•
Return on Total Assets	46	5.6	•	37.3	11.2	10.8	7.9	10.6	9.9	10.5	•	4.0	5.2	•
Return on Equity Before Income Taxes	47	8.1	•	81.6	20.9	29.8	13.2	18.2	15.5	11.8	•	4.6	6.2	•
Return on Equity After Income Taxes	48	7.8	•	78.7	19.5	26.5	10.9	15.8	13.8	11.4	•	4.6	6.2	•
Profit Margin (Before Income Tax)	49	35.5	56.0	17.8	25.0	36.0	34.4	34.3	48.7	37.5	•	28.5	39.1	•
Profit Margin (After Income Tax)	50	34.3	48.6	17.1	23.3	32.1	28.5	29.8	43.4	36.3	•	28.3	39.1	•

Table I

Corporations with and without Net Income

OFFICES OF REAL ESTATE AGENTS AND BROKERS

MONEY AMOUNTS AND SIZE OF ASSETS IN THOUSANDS OF DOLLARS

Item Description for Accounting Period 7/12 Through 6/13	Total	Zero Assets	Under 500	500 to 1,000	1,000 to 5,000	5,000 to 10,000	10,000 to 25,000	25,000 to 50,000	50,000 to 100,000	100,000 to 250,000	250,000 to 500,000	500,000 to 2,500,000	2,500,000 and over
Number of Enterprises 1	126106	35054	85311	3034	2272	239	133	23	16	10	4	5	3

Revenues ($ in Thousands)													
Net Sales 2	47267573	3730515	21966383	933631	5075900	1183607	1303401	347715	461075	577198	1909789	1498168	8280191
Interest 3	120036	6	11338	1197	15252	7371	2543	166	4773	6319	24562	35627	10882
Rents 4	141838	6219	20239	11632	15713	11539	2315	139	22908	12935	18204	11088	8905
Royalties 5	610804	0	0	0	2	23	53	0	0	0	217	30723	579786
Other Portfolio Income 6	199440	8910	16611	148	463	9750	2577	2506	36071	1304	16270	34938	69888
Other Receipts 7	46195455	3715380	21918195	920654	5044470	1154924	1295913	344904	397323	556640	1850536	1385792	7610730
Total Receipts 8	47267573	3730515	21966383	933631	5075900	1183607	1303401	347715	461075	577198	1909789	1498168	8280191
Average Total Receipts 9	375	106	257	308	2234	4952	9800	15118	28817	57720	477447	299634	2760064

Operating Costs/Operating Income (%)													
Cost of Operations 10	0.4	0.1	0.0	•	•	•	0.0	•	0.5	•	•	•	1.9
Salaries and Wages 11	33.4	7.9	27.9	16.1	47.6	51.5	38.1	23.7	23.5	25.1	8.4	51.3	53.3
Taxes Paid 12	2.7	2.0	2.4	4.9	1.6	3.4	2.5	4.2	4.6	3.2	1.0	2.7	4.7
Interest Paid 13	2.4	0.7	0.5	2.8	1.6	1.2	1.4	2.9	2.2	2.8	1.8	2.9	8.8
Depreciation 14	1.1	0.8	0.7	2.3	1.1	1.4	2.2	1.5	2.4	2.3	0.8	2.4	1.9
Amortization and Depletion 15	0.6	0.2	0.1	0.0	0.1	0.1	0.2	0.9	0.5	2.6	0.3	2.2	2.6
Pensions and Other Deferred Comp. 16	0.7	0.6	1.1	0.0	0.0	0.3	0.2	0.3	0.3	1.0	0.1	0.1	0.4
Employee Benefits 17	1.1	0.8	0.5	0.8	0.6	1.3	1.2	1.5	2.4	2.1	0.2	2.0	2.9
Advertising 18	2.7	2.1	3.1	7.2	1.9	6.7	3.2	6.3	3.8	2.5	0.5	2.4	1.9
Other Expenses 19	36.7	57.8	36.6	39.2	38.2	20.8	35.1	28.8	36.6	30.4	84.3	20.5	21.6
Officers' Compensation 20	7.9	14.7	12.3	11.7	1.7	3.4	4.6	9.7	5.2	8.3	0.4	5.9	0.1
Operating Margin 21	10.3	12.3	15.0	14.9	5.6	10.0	11.2	20.3	17.9	19.8	2.2	7.8	•
Operating Margin Before Officers' Comp. 22	18.2	27.0	27.3	26.6	7.3	13.3	15.8	30.0	23.1	28.0	2.6	13.6	0.1

Selected Average Balance Sheet ($ in Thousands)

Net Receivables 23	40	0	3	54	270	283	659	2572	7855	7627	60477	81873	998271
Inventories 24	•	•	•	•	•	•	•	•	•	•	•	•	•
Net Property, Plant and Equipment 25	59	0	15	377	578	868	4572	12976	25209	20230	50036	193695	285007
Total Assets 26	360	0	66	673	1939	6615	13951	34576	71580	161612	322328	925399	6788971
Notes and Loans Payable 27	169	0	39	538	1069	2864	6831	13497	25272	33758	150708	314788	3064420
All Other Liabilities 28	96	0	19	38	365	1764	2959	6649	14496	39596	110574	203298	2178741
Net Worth 29	94	0	9	96	505	1987	4160	14430	31813	88258	61045	407314	1545810

Selected Financial Ratios (Times to 1)

Current Ratio 30	1.3	•	1.6	2.2	1.8	1.4	1.5	2.0	2.5	1.2	3.2	1.1	1.0
Quick Ratio 31	1.0	•	1.3	1.4	1.2	1.0	0.8	1.4	2.1	0.7	2.8	0.9	0.8
Net Sales to Working Capital 32	13.8	•	19.9	2.3	6.6	7.1	6.8	2.3	2.4	5.6	7.2	19.0	•
Coverage Ratio 33	5.4	19.6	30.3	6.3	4.4	9.3	8.8	8.1	9.0	8.1	2.2	4.8	1.1
Total Asset Turnover 34	1.0	•	3.9	0.5	1.2	0.7	0.7	0.4	0.4	0.4	1.5	0.3	0.4
Inventory Turnover 35	•	•	•	•	•	•	•	•	•	•	•	•	•
Receivables Turnover 36	•	•	•	•	•	•	•	•	•	•	•	•	•
Total Liabilities to Net Worth 37	2.8	•	6.3	6.0	2.8	2.3	2.4	1.4	1.3	0.8	4.3	1.3	3.4
Current Assets to Working Capital 38	4.2	•	2.8	1.8	2.3	3.6	3.1	2.0	1.7	6.2	1.4	13.5	•
Current Liabilities to Working Capital 39	3.2	•	1.8	0.8	1.3	2.6	2.1	1.0	0.7	5.2	0.4	12.5	•
Working Capital to Net Sales 40	0.1	•	0.1	0.4	0.2	0.1	0.1	0.4	0.4	0.2	0.1	0.1	•
Inventory to Working Capital 41	0.0	•	•	•	•	0.0	0.0	•	0.0	•	•	•	•
Total Receipts to Cash Flow 42	2.7	1.5	2.3	2.1	2.8	4.4	2.5	2.7	2.5	2.6	7.4	4.6	6.5
Cost of Goods to Cash Flow 43	0.0	0.0	0.0	•	•	•	0.0	•	0.0	•	•	•	0.1
Cash Flow to Total Debt 44	0.5	•	2.0	0.3	0.6	0.2	0.4	0.3	0.3	0.3	0.2	0.1	0.1

Selected Financial Factors (in Percentages)

Debt Ratio 45	73.8	•	86.2	85.7	74.0	70.0	70.2	58.3	55.6	45.4	81.1	56.0	77.2
Return on Total Assets 46	13.4	•	60.2	8.1	8.4	8.4	8.9	10.1	8.1	8.1	5.9	4.5	3.8
Return on Equity Before Income Taxes 47	41.7	•	422.7	47.8	24.9	24.9	26.4	21.3	16.2	12.9	17.0	8.1	0.9
Return on Equity After Income Taxes 48	39.8	•	420.7	47.5	24.6	22.4	25.1	20.7	13.7	12.6	16.4	5.3	•
Profit Margin (Before Income Tax) 49	10.5	12.3	15.0	14.9	5.6	10.0	11.2	20.3	17.9	19.8	2.2	11.0	0.5
Profit Margin (After Income Tax) 50	10.0	12.3	14.9	14.8	5.6	9.0	10.7	19.7	15.1	19.3	2.1	7.2	•

Table II

Corporations with Net Income

OFFICES OF REAL ESTATE AGENTS AND BROKERS

MONEY AMOUNTS AND SIZE OF ASSETS IN THOUSANDS OF DOLLARS

Item Description for Accounting Period 7/12 Through 6/13	Total	Zero Assets	Under 500	500 to 1,000	1,000 to 5,000	5,000 to 10,000	10,000 to 25,000	25,000 to 50,000	50,000 to 100,000	100,000 to 250,000	250,000 to 500,000	500,000 to 2,500,000	2,500,000 and over
Number of Enterprises 1	85973	20243	62951	1551	946	147	91	19	10	•	•	5	0

Revenues ($ in Thousands)

	Total	Zero Assets	Under 500	500 to 1,000	1,000 to 5,000	5,000 to 10,000	10,000 to 25,000	25,000 to 50,000	50,000 to 100,000	100,000 to 250,000	250,000 to 500,000	500,000 to 2,500,000	2,500,000 and over
Net Sales 2	37128124	2234753	17168173	671096	4479382	1105176	1160297	350409	417947	•	•	7192819	0
Interest 3	50914	5	1131	650	7342	3200	2129	165	3932	•	•	13928	0
Rents 4	91039	4639	11251	10956	14916	7906	2315	0	19927	•	•	16063	0
Royalties 5	101192	0	0	0	0	23	53	0	0	•	•	101116	0
Other Portfolio Income 6	151931	7752	16611	147	339	6358	2575	2506	31276	•	•	78937	0
Other Receipts 7	36733048	2222357	17139180	659343	4456785	1087689	1153225	347738	362812	•	•	6982775	0
Total Receipts 8	37128124	2234753	17168173	671096	4479382	1105176	1160297	350409	417947	•	•	7192819	0
Average Total Receipts 9	432	110	273	433	4735	7518	12751	18443	41795	•	•	1438564	•

Operating Costs/Operating Income (%)

	Total	Zero Assets	Under 500	500 to 1,000	1,000 to 5,000	5,000 to 10,000	10,000 to 25,000	25,000 to 50,000	50,000 to 100,000	100,000 to 250,000	250,000 to 500,000	500,000 to 2,500,000	2,500,000 and over
Cost of Operations 10	0.4	•	0.0	•	•	•	0.1	•	•	•	•	2.1	•
Salaries and Wages 11	35.8	9.7	28.3	11.2	50.4	52.6	40.6	23.4	21.4	•	•	60.8	•
Taxes Paid 12	2.5	2.6	2.0	4.8	1.0	3.0	2.3	3.9	4.7	•	•	4.7	•
Interest Paid 13	1.2	0.4	0.5	2.8	0.4	0.5	1.0	2.1	1.6	•	•	3.2	•
Depreciation 14	1.0	0.9	0.6	1.1	0.9	1.0	2.0	1.5	2.5	•	•	2.0	•
Amortization and Depletion 15	0.4	0.4	0.0	0.0	0.0	0.0	0.2	0.9	0.4	•	•	1.5	•
Pensions and Other Deferred Comp. 16	0.7	1.0	1.3	0.0	0.0	0.3	0.2	0.3	0.3	•	•	0.2	•
Employee Benefits 17	1.0	0.8	0.4	0.8	0.6	1.0	1.0	1.5	2.5	•	•	2.8	•
Advertising 18	2.5	2.1	3.2	3.3	1.7	7.1	3.5	6.1	4.2	•	•	0.7	•
Other Expenses 19	29.7	33.8	29.2	32.3	33.7	17.6	28.5	27.6	30.0	•	•	15.0	•
Officers' Compensation 20	8.6	21.8	13.1	13.3	1.6	2.9	4.9	9.6	5.4	•	•	1.2	•
Operating Margin 21	16.1	26.5	21.2	30.4	9.6	13.9	15.6	23.1	26.9	•	•	5.8	•
Operating Margin Before Officers' Comp. 22	24.7	48.3	34.3	43.7	11.3	16.8	20.5	32.7	32.3	•	•	7.0	•

Selected Average Balance Sheet ($ in Thousands)

	1	2	3	4	5	6	7	8	9	10	11	12	13
Net Receivables 23	47	0	2	38	114	373	931	3113	10318	•	•	626249	•
Inventories 24	•	•	•	•	•	•	•	•	•	•	•	•	•
Net Property, Plant and Equipment 25	40	0	14	299	263	440	3482	5114	35457	•	•	146369	•
Total Assets 26	332	0	68	664	1839	6847	13258	31100	76154	•	•	3135841	•
Notes and Loans Payable 27	109	0	26	342	481	1036	4886	10546	32614	•	•	972604	•
All Other Liabilities 28	106	0	16	21	363	2710	3568	8034	11928	•	•	1203615	•
Net Worth 29	117	0	26	301	995	3101	4803	12521	31613	•	•	959621	•

Selected Financial Ratios (Times to 1)

	1	2	3	4	5	6	7	8	9	10	11	12	13
Current Ratio 30	1.4	•	2.2	2.5	2.5	1.5	1.8	2.0	2.6	•	•	1.0	•
Quick Ratio 31	1.1	•	1.9	1.5	1.4	1.1	0.9	1.4	2.4	•	•	0.9	•
Net Sales to Working Capital 32	11.3	•	12.8	2.3	9.4	6.4	4.8	2.3	2.5	•	•	49.3	•
Coverage Ratio 33	14.9	72.1	40.2	11.7	23.0	29.0	16.9	12.1	17.6	•	•	3.3	•
Total Asset Turnover 34	1.3	•	4.0	0.7	2.6	1.1	1.0	0.6	0.5	•	•	0.5	•
Inventory Turnover 35	•	•	•	•	•	•	•	•	•	•	•	•	•
Receivables Turnover 36	•	•	•	•	•	•	•	•	•	•	•	•	•
Total Liabilities to Net Worth 37	1.8	•	1.6	1.2	0.8	1.2	1.8	1.5	1.4	•	•	2.3	•
Current Assets to Working Capital 38	3.4	•	1.8	1.7	1.7	3.0	2.2	2.0	1.6	•	•	32.4	•
Current Liabilities to Working Capital 39	2.4	•	0.8	0.7	0.7	2.0	1.2	1.0	0.6	•	•	31.4	•
Working Capital to Net Sales 40	0.1	•	0.1	0.4	0.1	0.2	0.2	0.4	0.4	•	•	0.0	•
Inventory to Working Capital 41	0.0	•	•	•	•	•	0.0	•	0.0	•	•	•	•
Total Receipts to Cash Flow 42	2.7	1.8	2.2	1.7	2.6	4.0	2.7	2.6	2.5	•	•	5.8	•
Cost of Goods to Cash Flow 43	0.0	•	0.0	•	•	•	0.0	•	0.0	•	•	0.1	•
Cash Flow to Total Debt 44	0.7	•	3.0	0.7	2.2	0.5	0.6	0.4	0.4	•	•	0.1	•

Selected Financial Factors (in Percentages)

	1	2	3	4	5	6	7	8	9	10	11	12	13
Debt Ratio 45	64.9	•	62.1	54.7	45.9	54.7	63.8	59.7	58.5	•	•	69.4	•
Return on Total Assets 46	22.8	•	87.9	21.6	25.9	15.8	16.0	14.9	15.7	•	•	4.7	•
Return on Equity Before Income Taxes 47	60.6	•	226.0	43.6	45.7	33.7	41.4	34.0	35.6	•	•	10.8	•
Return on Equity After Income Taxes 48	58.3	•	225.0	43.5	45.3	31.2	39.8	33.1	31.5	•	•	7.3	•
Profit Margin (Before Income Tax) 49	16.4	26.5	21.2	30.4	9.6	13.9	15.6	23.1	26.9	•	•	7.2	•
Profit Margin (After Income Tax) 50	15.8	26.4	21.1	30.3	9.5	12.9	15.0	22.5	23.8	•	•	4.9	•

Table I

Corporations with and without Net Income

OTHER REAL ESTATE ACTIVITIES

MONEY AMOUNTS AND SIZE OF ASSETS IN THOUSANDS OF DOLLARS

Item Description for Accounting Period 7/12 Through 6/13	Total	Zero Assets	Under 500	500 to 1,000	1,000 to 5,000	5,000 to 10,000	10,000 to 25,000	25,000 to 50,000	50,000 to 100,000	100,000 to 250,000	250,000 to 500,000	500,000 to 2,500,000	2,500,000 and over
Number of Enterprises **1**	161714	38280	98180	10825	10901	1933	980	343	166	72	20	14	0

Revenues ($ in Thousands)

	Total	Zero Assets	Under 500	500 to 1,000	1,000 to 5,000	5,000 to 10,000	10,000 to 25,000	25,000 to 50,000	50,000 to 100,000	100,000 to 250,000	250,000 to 500,000	500,000 to 2,500,000	2,500,000 and over
Net Sales **2**	57254028	2465947	22773045	3732780	8742318	2897718	2292669	1421066	2435171	2261556	1024345	7207413	0
Interest **3**	1174093	13934	5683	13128	32752	53891	33694	68815	29681	59011	125853	737650	0
Rents **4**	1705931	183421	126816	61967	145510	147586	154292	122369	168848	114730	136278	344114	0
Royalties **5**	511091	6364	914	0	209	973	10656	70	54	452	11	491389	0
Other Portfolio Income **6**	3256212	345691	143277	88753	243087	120874	110057	33357	184953	92814	124657	1768693	0
Other Receipts **7**	50606701	1916537	22496355	3568932	8320760	2574394	1983970	1196455	2051635	1994549	637546	3865567	0
Total Receipts **8**	57254028	2465947	22773045	3732780	8742318	2897718	2292669	1421066	2435171	2261556	1024345	7207413	0
Average Total Receipts **9**	354	64	232	345	802	1499	2339	4143	14670	31410	51217	514815	•

Operating Costs/Operating Income (%)

	Total	Zero Assets	Under 500	500 to 1,000	1,000 to 5,000	5,000 to 10,000	10,000 to 25,000	25,000 to 50,000	50,000 to 100,000	100,000 to 250,000	250,000 to 500,000	500,000 to 2,500,000	2,500,000 and over
Cost of Operations **10**	0.4	1.2	0.6	•	0.0	0.0	0.9	0.8	0.2	0.8	•	0.0	•
Salaries and Wages **11**	33.2	10.1	37.8	28.5	43.2	31.8	30.6	22.0	14.6	38.0	11.8	28.7	•
Taxes Paid **12**	4.7	4.1	5.0	4.4	5.9	5.3	5.8	5.7	3.3	3.5	4.3	2.4	•
Interest Paid **13**	4.1	4.2	0.6	1.5	2.2	6.8	7.1	15.3	8.2	7.4	15.9	10.3	•
Depreciation **14**	2.1	3.0	0.7	1.8	1.8	3.0	4.6	5.0	3.8	5.4	4.8	3.0	•
Amortization and Depletion **15**	0.4	0.3	0.1	0.5	0.3	0.4	0.3	0.5	0.4	0.7	2.4	1.2	•
Pensions and Other Deferred Comp. **16**	0.6	0.7	0.6	0.6	0.8	0.2	0.6	0.3	0.4	0.3	0.6	0.8	•
Employee Benefits **17**	2.7	1.3	3.2	3.2	2.1	3.1	3.0	2.5	1.4	2.0	0.6	2.6	•
Advertising **18**	1.0	0.8	1.0	0.5	0.6	1.1	0.7	0.5	1.1	0.8	0.7	1.6	•
Other Expenses **19**	38.5	59.6	31.9	43.6	34.7	40.7	34.4	39.5	60.0	38.0	70.4	42.6	•
Officers' Compensation **20**	8.2	7.6	12.5	9.2	7.9	8.7	3.8	6.8	2.7	2.2	2.3	0.4	•
Operating Margin **21**	4.2	7.1	5.9	6.1	0.5	•	8.2	1.0	3.9	0.7	•	6.4	•
Operating Margin Before Officers' Comp. **22**	12.3	14.7	18.4	15.4	8.4	7.5	12.0	7.8	6.7	2.9	•	6.8	•

Selected Average Balance Sheet ($ in Thousands)

Net Receivables 23	69	0	3	35	128	535	1069	1769	3403	9241	44070	303330	•
Inventories 24	•	•	•	•	•	•	•	•	•	•	•	•	•
Net Property, Plant and Equipment 25	246	0	26	266	777	2167	5006	9820	19726	39097	83606	399251	•
Total Assets 26	839	0	85	685	2033	7161	15275	32836	68688	151073	347504	2031071	•
Notes and Loans Payable 27	424	0	54	466	1046	3536	7074	16885	25818	60663	162942	1094786	•
All Other Liabilities 28	159	0	15	83	295	1662	2652	6570	14175	27742	70608	447032	•
Net Worth 29	256	0	16	136	691	1964	5549	9381	28695	62668	113954	489253	•

Selected Financial Ratios (Times to 1)

Current Ratio 30	2.2	•	1.9	2.0	2.6	1.8	1.9	1.4	1.6	1.8	1.5	4.1	•
Quick Ratio 31	1.2	•	1.4	1.2	1.6	1.0	1.0	0.8	0.9	1.1	1.0	1.6	•
Net Sales to Working Capital 32	2.3	•	12.7	3.1	2.0	1.6	1.0	1.8	2.1	1.9	1.5	0.7	•
Coverage Ratio 33	2.0	2.7	10.4	5.1	1.2	0.8	2.1	1.1	1.5	1.1	0.2	1.7	•
Total Asset Turnover 34	0.4	•	2.7	0.5	0.4	0.2	0.2	0.1	0.2	0.2	0.1	0.3	•
Inventory Turnover 35	•	•	•	•	•	•	•	•	•	•	•	•	•
Receivables Turnover 36	•	•	•	•	•	•	•	•	•	•	•	•	•
Total Liabilities to Net Worth 37	2.3	•	4.4	4.0	1.9	2.6	1.8	2.5	1.4	1.4	2.0	3.2	•
Current Assets to Working Capital 38	1.8	•	2.2	2.0	1.6	2.3	2.1	3.4	2.8	2.3	2.9	1.3	•
Current Liabilities to Working Capital 39	0.8	•	1.2	1.0	0.6	1.3	1.1	2.4	1.8	1.3	1.9	0.3	•
Working Capital to Net Sales 40	0.4	•	0.1	0.3	0.5	0.6	1.0	0.6	0.5	0.5	0.7	1.4	•
Inventory to Working Capital 41	0.0	•	•	•	0.0	0.0	0.0	0.1	0.0	0.0	0.0	0.0	•
Total Receipts to Cash Flow 42	3.0	2.3	3.2	2.6	3.7	3.2	3.3	3.3	2.1	4.7	3.8	2.4	•
Cost of Goods to Cash Flow 43	0.0	0.0	0.0	•	0.0	0.0	0.0	0.0	0.0	0.0	•	0.0	•
Cash Flow to Total Debt 44	0.2	•	1.1	0.2	0.2	0.1	0.1	0.1	0.2	0.1	0.1	0.1	•

Selected Financial Factors (in Percentages)

Debt Ratio 45	69.5	•	81.5	80.1	66.0	72.6	63.7	71.4	58.2	58.5	67.2	75.9	•
Return on Total Assets 46	3.5	•	17.8	3.8	1.0	1.1	2.3	2.0	2.6	1.7	0.4	4.3	•
Return on Equity Before Income Taxes 47	5.8	•	86.8	15.2	0.5	•	3.4	0.4	1.9	0.3	•	7.1	•
Return on Equity After Income Taxes 48	4.6	•	85.5	14.2	•	•	2.6	•	1.2	•	•	5.1	•
Profit Margin (Before Income Tax) 49	4.2	7.1	5.9	6.0	0.4	•	8.1	0.8	3.7	0.6	•	6.8	•
Profit Margin (After Income Tax) 50	3.3	3.7	5.8	5.6	•	•	6.2	•	2.4	•	•	4.9	•

Table II

Corporations with Net Income

OTHER REAL ESTATE ACTIVITIES

MONEY AMOUNTS AND SIZE OF ASSETS IN THOUSANDS OF DOLLARS

Item Description for Accounting Period 7/12 Through 6/13	Total	Zero Assets	Under 500	500 to 1,000	1,000 to 5,000	5,000 to 10,000	10,000 to 25,000	25,000 to 50,000	50,000 to 100,000	100,000 to 250,000	250,000 to 500,000	500,000 to 2,500,000	2,500,000 and over
Number of Enterprises **1**	75675	16499	50430	4089	3358	698	355	116	76	36	7	10	0
Revenues ($ in Thousands)													
Net Sales **2**	38640556	1875705	13374750	2677448	5506251	1941245	1660795	981774	2002239	1667930	419898	6532519	0
Interest **3**	863098	9650	3216	8353	13450	49331	25953	55706	17071	30844	17138	632387	0
Rents **4**	911515	122396	67422	29406	66363	83353	81295	53338	121455	55356	44970	186159	0
Royalties **5**	502528	0	914	0	0	653	9013	51	54	452	11	491381	0
Other Portfolio Income **6**	2673526	309052	12453	51136	221579	100413	96346	26751	163719	85622	3649	1602807	0
Other Receipts **7**	33689889	1434607	13290745	2588553	5204859	1707495	1448188	845928	1699940	1495656	354130	3619785	0
Total Receipts **8**	38640556	1875705	13374750	2677448	5506251	1941245	1660795	981774	2002239	1667930	419898	6532519	0
Average Total Receipts **9**	511	114	265	655	1640	2781	4678	8464	26345	46331	59985	653252	•
Operating Costs/Operating Income (%)													
Cost of Operations **10**	0.2	•	0.3	•	0.0	0.1	1.2	0.0	0.3	1.0	•	0.0	•
Salaries and Wages **11**	27.4	8.2	27.6	27.3	40.2	24.9	22.0	17.9	13.7	32.8	7.8	29.2	•
Taxes Paid **12**	3.8	3.1	4.5	3.6	5.1	3.6	4.1	3.6	2.7	3.0	4.0	2.0	•
Interest Paid **13**	3.1	2.5	0.5	0.8	1.4	4.0	3.8	4.5	4.9	4.4	3.7	9.4	•
Depreciation **14**	1.5	1.8	0.7	0.9	1.2	2.1	2.6	2.8	2.5	2.4	1.5	2.6	•
Amortization and Depletion **15**	0.4	0.0	0.0	0.6	0.4	0.3	0.2	0.2	0.2	0.7	0.9	1.2	•
Pensions and Other Deferred Comp. **16**	0.7	1.0	0.7	0.7	1.0	0.2	0.4	0.3	0.1	0.3	1.2	0.9	•
Employee Benefits **17**	1.9	0.7	1.7	2.6	2.3	2.8	2.3	1.8	1.1	2.1	0.6	2.2	•
Advertising **18**	1.0	0.9	1.1	0.5	0.7	0.9	0.7	0.4	1.1	1.0	0.5	1.6	•
Other Expenses **19**	34.9	30.4	33.4	32.4	24.7	31.7	30.1	32.8	53.5	39.8	69.2	42.3	•
Officers' Compensation **20**	6.7	8.0	11.4	7.6	5.7	9.2	3.4	5.9	2.7	1.9	0.4	0.4	•
Operating Margin **21**	18.2	43.4	17.9	23.0	17.4	20.4	29.1	29.6	17.2	10.8	10.4	8.1	•
Operating Margin Before Officers' Comp. **22**	25.0	51.4	29.3	30.5	23.1	29.5	32.5	35.5	19.9	12.7	10.8	8.5	•

Selected Average Balance Sheet ($ in Thousands)

Net Receivables 23	90	0	3	35	166	809	1833	2549	3984	7989	25082	368936	•
Inventories 24	•	•	•	•	•	•	•	•	•	•	•	•	•
Net Property, Plant and Equipment 25	179	0	16	167	515	2015	4009	7688	19929	31795	71662	343182	•
Total Assets 26	816	0	77	671	2089	7029	15679	34038	69260	143877	333112	2093304	•
Notes and Loans Payable 27	379	0	33	265	948	3345	5586	12103	23279	52745	69967	1288874	•
All Other Liabilities 28	161	0	14	68	410	1467	3443	7240	13721	36289	110240	362234	•
Net Worth 29	276	0	31	338	732	2218	6650	14695	32260	54844	152905	442196	•

Selected Financial Ratios (Times to 1)

Current Ratio 30	2.8	•	2.7	2.8	2.2	1.8	2.1	1.7	1.9	1.3	1.1	6.2	•
Quick Ratio 31	1.5	•	2.3	2.0	1.7	1.1	1.1	1.1	1.1	0.7	0.8	2.3	•
Net Sales to Working Capital 32	2.1	•	10.1	3.3	3.4	2.2	1.2	1.8	2.4	5.0	11.9	0.6	•
Coverage Ratio 33	6.9	18.6	35.4	30.5	13.6	6.1	8.7	7.5	4.5	3.4	4.2	1.9	•
Total Asset Turnover 34	0.6	•	3.4	1.0	0.8	0.4	0.3	0.2	0.4	0.3	0.2	0.3	•
Inventory Turnover 35	•	•	•	•	•	•	•	•	•	•	•	•	•
Receivables Turnover 36	•	•	•	•	•	•	•	•	•	•	•	•	•
Total Liabilities to Net Worth 37	2.0	•	1.5	1.0	1.9	2.2	1.4	1.3	1.1	1.6	1.2	3.7	•
Current Assets to Working Capital 38	1.6	•	1.6	1.6	1.9	2.2	1.9	2.4	2.1	4.3	9.3	1.2	•
Current Liabilities to Working Capital 39	0.6	•	0.6	0.6	0.9	1.2	0.9	1.4	1.1	3.3	8.3	0.2	•
Working Capital to Net Sales 40	0.5	•	0.1	0.3	0.3	0.5	0.8	0.5	0.4	0.2	0.1	1.6	•
Inventory to Working Capital 41	0.0	•	•	•	0.0	0.0	0.0	0.0	0.0	0.0	0.0	0.0	•
Total Receipts to Cash Flow 42	2.2	1.8	2.2	2.3	2.9	2.3	2.0	1.9	1.8	3.3	1.4	2.2	•
Cost of Goods to Cash Flow 43	0.0	•	0.0	•	0.0	0.0	0.0	0.0	0.0	0.0	•	0.0	•
Cash Flow to Total Debt 44	0.4	•	2.6	0.9	0.4	0.3	0.3	0.2	0.4	0.2	0.2	0.2	•

Selected Financial Factors (in Percentages)

Debt Ratio 45	66.1	•	60.2	49.7	65.0	68.5	57.6	56.8	53.4	61.9	54.1	78.9	•
Return on Total Assets 46	13.4	•	63.2	23.2	14.6	9.6	9.8	8.4	8.4	4.9	2.8	5.6	•
Return on Equity Before Income Taxes 47	33.8	•	154.2	44.5	38.7	25.5	20.5	16.9	14.0	9.1	4.6	12.6	•
Return on Equity After Income Taxes 48	31.4	•	152.8	43.4	36.8	22.6	18.6	15.0	12.6	8.0	3.5	9.4	•
Profit Margin (Before Income Tax) 49	18.3	43.4	17.9	23.0	17.3	20.3	29.1	29.3	17.1	10.7	11.7	8.5	•
Profit Margin (After Income Tax) 50	17.0	38.9	17.7	22.4	16.4	18.0	26.4	26.1	15.4	9.5	9.0	6.4	•

Table I

Corporations with and without Net Income

AUTOMOTIVE EQUIPMENT RENTAL AND LEASING

MONEY AMOUNTS AND SIZE OF ASSETS IN THOUSANDS OF DOLLARS

Item Description for Accounting Period 7/12 Through 6/13	Total	Zero Assets	Under 500	500 to 1,000	1,000 to 5,000	5,000 to 10,000	10,000 to 25,000	25,000 to 50,000	50,000 to 100,000	100,000 to 250,000	250,000 to 500,000	500,000 to 2,500,000	2,500,000 and over
Number of Enterprises 1	6932	30	4510	944	1034	167	155	29	34	13	8	0	7

Revenues ($ in Thousands)

Net Sales 2	59501090	83826	1608811	379170	1336190	1255565	2483069	615250	1842654	1477131	2776006	0	45643419
Interest 3	523437	32	295	0	1648	1005	823	4061	926	1207	23410	0	490031
Rents 4	159587	0	0	0	0	0	41	21	1198	0	12	0	158315
Royalties 5	216850	0	0	0	241	0	27	0	0	0	0	0	216582
Other Portfolio Income 6	5865363	29636	34899	3182	158910	82805	260762	106705	265666	238166	146552	0	4538081
Other Receipts 7	52735853	54158	1573617	375988	1175391	1171755	2221416	504463	1574864	1237758	2606032	0	40240410
Total Receipts 8	59501090	83826	1608811	379170	1336190	1255565	2483069	615250	1842654	1477131	2776006	0	45643419
Average Total Receipts 9	8584	2794	357	402	1292	7518	16020	21216	54196	113625	347001	•	6520488

Operating Costs/Operating Income (%)

Cost of Operations 10	17.3	0.4	8.1	8.3	20.1	56.0	43.2	15.9	39.6	41.0	17.2	•	13.6
Salaries and Wages 11	12.1	14.2	5.3	4.8	5.4	7.2	6.8	5.9	6.9	7.8	6.1	•	13.8
Taxes Paid 12	3.1	2.1	2.3	4.2	2.6	1.7	1.7	1.2	1.6	2.6	0.9	•	3.5
Interest Paid 13	4.1	5.7	0.6	2.1	5.6	2.1	2.0	3.5	2.6	2.8	4.9	•	4.4
Depreciation 14	27.6	17.8	5.6	28.0	23.8	9.6	22.2	28.6	29.9	27.8	59.3	•	27.3
Amortization and Depletion 15	0.3	1.7	0.3	•	0.1	0.3	0.1	0.1	0.1	0.2	0.4	•	0.4
Pensions and Other Deferred Comp. 16	0.5	•	0.4	•	0.0	0.0	0.1	0.3	0.2	0.2	0.0	•	0.6
Employee Benefits 17	1.6	0.2	1.1	•	0.4	0.7	0.7	0.8	0.7	0.7	0.4	•	1.9
Advertising 18	1.2	0.9	0.4	0.8	0.6	0.6	0.6	0.2	0.5	0.5	0.2	•	1.5
Other Expenses 19	25.5	58.9	69.4	47.7	32.7	11.3	14.3	12.8	10.6	13.5	10.5	•	26.5
Officers' Compensation 20	1.3	4.1	5.1	4.8	2.7	1.1	1.3	1.8	1.2	0.7	0.3	•	1.1
Operating Margin 21	5.3	•	1.4	•	6.1	9.3	6.9	28.9	6.1	2.2	•	•	5.4
Operating Margin Before Officers' Comp. 22	6.6	•	6.5	4.2	8.8	10.4	8.2	30.7	7.3	2.9	0.2	•	6.5

Selected Average Balance Sheet ($ in Thousands)

Net Receivables 23	1174	0	6	77	348	918	1947	2730	4945	11776	32853	•	936912
Inventories 24	•	•	•	•	•	•	•	•	•	•	•	•	•
Net Property, Plant and Equipment 25	7712	0	28	422	1071	3146	8762	17214	37008	91448	359335	•	6303121
Total Assets 26	13267	0	107	740	2350	7145	15818	35690	64953	144731	738268	•	10525956
Notes and Loans Payable 27	7352	0	122	385	1816	3443	9767	21098	44968	96044	648888	•	5357233
All Other Liabilities 28	3587	0	3	31	233	504	2221	2943	6225	16357	138641	•	3219260
Net Worth 29	2328	0	-19	324	300	3198	3831	11649	13759	32330	-49261	•	1949463

Selected Financial Ratios (Times to 1)

Current Ratio 30	0.6	•	0.7	6.7	2.0	1.4	1.1	1.5	0.9	0.9	0.2	•	0.5
Quick Ratio 31	0.4	•	0.5	6.5	1.5	0.9	0.7	1.0	0.5	0.5	0.1	•	0.4
Net Sales to Working Capital 32	•	•	•	1.9	3.3	10.0	41.9	4.6	•	•	•	•	•
Coverage Ratio 33	2.3	•	3.3	0.7	2.1	5.4	4.4	9.2	3.4	1.8	1.0	•	2.2
Total Asset Turnover 34	0.6	•	3.3	0.5	0.5	1.1	1.0	0.6	0.8	0.8	0.5	•	0.6
Inventory Turnover 35	•	•	•	•	•	•	•	•	•	•	•	•	•
Receivables Turnover 36	•	•	•	•	•	•	•	•	•	•	•	•	•
Total Liabilities to Net Worth 37	4.7	•	•	1.3	6.8	1.2	3.1	2.1	3.7	3.5	•	•	4.4
Current Assets to Working Capital 38	•	•	•	1.2	2.0	3.3	11.8	2.9	•	•	•	•	•
Current Liabilities to Working Capital 39	•	•	•	0.2	1.0	2.3	10.8	1.9	•	•	•	•	•
Working Capital to Net Sales 40	•	•	•	0.5	0.3	0.1	0.0	0.2	•	•	•	•	•
Inventory to Working Capital 41	•	•	•	•	0.2	1.1	2.3	0.2	•	•	•	•	•
Total Receipts to Cash Flow 42	4.7	2.3	1.7	6.0	6.3	6.0	7.1	2.8	8.9	11.6	15.3	•	4.6
Cost of Goods to Cash Flow 43	0.8	0.0	0.1	0.5	1.3	3.4	3.1	0.4	3.5	4.7	2.6	•	0.6
Cash Flow to Total Debt 44	0.2	•	1.7	0.2	0.1	0.3	0.2	0.3	0.1	0.1	0.0	•	0.2

Selected Financial Factors (in Percentages)

Debt Ratio 45	82.5	•	117.9	56.2	87.2	55.2	75.8	67.4	78.8	77.7	106.7	•	81.5
Return on Total Assets 46	6.1	•	7.0	0.8	6.4	12.1	9.1	19.2	7.3	4.0	2.2	•	6.1
Return on Equity Before Income Taxes 47	19.7	•	•	•	26.0	21.9	28.9	52.5	24.1	7.9	0.8	•	18.1
Return on Equity After Income Taxes 48	18.6	•	•	•	23.9	21.8	28.5	52.2	23.9	7.5	0.8	•	16.9
Profit Margin (Before Income Tax) 49	5.3	•	1.4	•	6.0	9.3	6.9	28.8	6.1	2.2	•	•	5.4
Profit Margin (After Income Tax) 50	5.0	•	1.4	•	5.6	9.3	6.8	28.7	6.1	2.1	•	•	5.1

Table II
Corporations with Net Income

AUTOMOTIVE EQUIPMENT RENTAL AND LEASING

MONEY AMOUNTS AND SIZE OF ASSETS IN THOUSANDS OF DOLLARS

Item Description for Accounting Period 7/12 Through 6/13	Total	Zero Assets	Under 500	500 to 1,000	1,000 to 5,000	5,000 to 10,000	10,000 to 25,000	25,000 to 50,000	50,000 to 100,000	100,000 to 250,000	250,000 to 500,000	500,000 to 2,500,000	2,500,000 and over
Number of Enterprises 1	3956	•	2489	655	514	96	104	•	25	8	•	0	•
Revenues ($ in Thousands)													
Net Sales 2	53018637	•	548506	325903	1009361	1045463	2248011	•	1516409	1104502	•	0	•
Interest 3	502253	•	295	0	881	943	485	•	660	1207	•	0	•
Rents 4	159119	•	0	0	0	0	0	•	1198	0	•	0	•
Royalties 5	216823	•	0	0	241	0	0	•	0	0	•	0	•
Other Portfolio Income 6	5317300	•	24585	3182	145490	74738	220350	•	243645	186491	•	0	•
Other Receipts 7	46823142	•	523626	322721	862749	969782	2027176	•	1270906	916804	•	0	•
Total Receipts 8	53018637	•	548506	325903	1009361	1045463	2248011	•	1516409	1104502	•	0	•
Average Total Receipts 9	13402	•	220	498	1964	10890	21615	•	60656	138063	•	•	•
Operating Costs/Operating Income (%)													
Cost of Operations 10	15.9	•	18.5	9.6	25.7	59.2	45.6	•	45.0	46.3	•	•	•
Salaries and Wages 11	12.8	•	15.7	5.3	4.3	6.9	6.6	•	6.4	6.5	•	•	•
Taxes Paid 12	3.3	•	3.6	4.7	3.0	1.3	1.7	•	1.4	1.8	•	•	•
Interest Paid 13	4.1	•	1.3	1.9	2.1	1.7	1.7	•	2.0	2.6	•	•	•
Depreciation 14	26.5	•	5.4	15.3	13.7	5.9	19.0	•	26.0	16.3	•	•	•
Amortization and Depletion 15	0.4	•	0.8	•	0.1	0.2	0.0	•	0.1	0.3	•	•	•
Pensions and Other Deferred Comp. 16	0.6	•	0.7	•	0.0	0.0	0.1	•	0.1	0.2	•	•	•
Employee Benefits 17	1.8	•	2.9	•	0.4	0.8	0.7	•	0.5	0.7	•	•	•
Advertising 18	1.3	•	0.7	0.9	0.7	0.7	0.6	•	0.5	0.4	•	•	•
Other Expenses 19	25.4	•	28.0	47.2	35.5	9.6	13.4	•	8.5	11.9	•	•	•
Officers' Compensation 20	1.3	•	14.8	5.1	2.3	1.1	1.2	•	1.2	0.5	•	•	•
Operating Margin 21	6.6	•	7.7	10.1	12.2	12.6	9.3	•	8.2	12.5	•	•	•
Operating Margin Before Officers' Comp. 22	7.9	•	22.6	15.1	14.5	13.7	10.6	•	9.4	12.9	•	•	•

Selected Average Balance Sheet ($ in Thousands)

Net Receivables 23	1644	•	0	110	173	1006	2495	•	4327	15504	•	•	•
Inventories 24	•	•	•	•	•	•	•	•	•	•	•	•	•
Net Property, Plant and Equipment 25	11817	•	20	317	1097	2165	9140	•	37181	81199	•	•	•
Total Assets 26	20537	•	124	657	2139	7248	16209	•	64966	150745	•	•	•
Notes and Loans Payable 27	10804	•	64	181	1262	3691	9711	•	43148	90523	•	•	•
All Other Liabilities 28	5960	•	2	39	200	597	2385	•	5992	21861	•	•	•
Net Worth 29	3773	•	57	437	678	2961	4114	•	15826	38361	•	•	•

Selected Financial Ratios (Times to 1)

Current Ratio 30	0.5	•	0.4	5.3	2.1	2.0	1.2	•	1.0	1.0	•	•	•
Quick Ratio 31	0.3	•	0.4	5.2	1.6	1.0	0.8	•	0.5	0.6	•	•	•
Net Sales to Working Capital 32	•	•	•	2.4	5.3	6.7	24.2	•	•	157.8	•	•	•
Coverage Ratio 33	2.6	•	7.1	6.2	6.9	8.5	6.6	•	5.0	5.7	•	•	•
Total Asset Turnover 34	0.7	•	1.8	0.8	0.9	1.5	1.3	•	0.9	0.9	•	•	•
Inventory Turnover 35	•	•	•	•	•	•	•	•	•	•	•	•	•
Receivables Turnover 36	•	•	•	•	•	•	•	•	•	•	•	•	•
Total Liabilities to Net Worth 37	4.4	•	1.2	0.5	2.2	1.4	2.9	•	3.1	2.9	•	•	•
Current Assets to Working Capital 38	•	•	•	1.2	1.9	2.0	6.0	•	•	42.4	•	•	•
Current Liabilities to Working Capital 39	•	•	•	0.2	0.9	1.0	5.0	•	•	41.4	•	•	•
Working Capital to Net Sales 40	•	•	•	0.4	0.2	0.2	0.0	•	•	0.0	•	•	•
Inventory to Working Capital 41	•	•	•	•	0.4	0.9	1.4	•	•	12.9	•	•	•
Total Receipts to Cash Flow 42	4.6	•	4.5	4.6	4.6	5.3	6.5	•	7.7	5.4	•	•	•
Cost of Goods to Cash Flow 43	0.7	•	0.8	0.4	1.2	3.1	3.0	•	3.5	2.5	•	•	•
Cash Flow to Total Debt 44	0.2	•	0.7	0.5	0.3	0.5	0.3	•	0.2	0.2	•	•	•

Selected Financial Factors (in Percentages)

Debt Ratio 45	81.6	•	53.5	33.5	68.3	59.2	74.6	•	75.6	74.6	•	•	•
Return on Total Assets 46	7.0	•	16.1	9.1	13.1	21.5	14.7	•	9.6	13.9	•	•	•
Return on Equity Before Income Taxes 47	23.5	•	29.7	11.5	35.3	46.5	49.1	•	31.5	44.9	•	•	•
Return on Equity After Income Taxes 48	22.4	•	29.1	10.7	33.4	46.3	48.5	•	31.2	44.4	•	•	•
Profit Margin (Before Income Tax) 49	6.6	•	7.7	10.1	12.2	12.6	9.3	•	8.2	12.5	•	•	•
Profit Margin (After Income Tax) 50	6.3	•	7.6	9.4	11.5	12.6	9.2	•	8.1	12.3	•	•	•

Table I

Corporations with and without Net Income

OTHER CONSUMER GOODS AND GENERAL RENTAL CENTERS

MONEY AMOUNTS AND SIZE OF ASSETS IN THOUSANDS OF DOLLARS

Item Description for Accounting Period 7/12 Through 6/13	Total	Zero Assets	Under 500	500 to 1,000	1,000 to 5,000	5,000 to 10,000	10,000 to 25,000	25,000 to 50,000	50,000 to 100,000	100,000 to 250,000	250,000 to 500,000	500,000 to 2,500,000	2,500,000 and over
Number of Enterprises **1**	8745	407	7176	515	362	223	34	14	5	6	0	3	0
Revenues ($ in Thousands)													
Net Sales **2**	17605554	23424	2486677	729152	1028906	1873375	699315	718364	333384	989152	0	8723806	0
Interest **3**	31711	0	1	836	256	0	137	34	23	11375	0	19050	0
Rents **4**	3253	0	0	0	2217	0	0	0	1036	0	0	0	0
Royalties **5**	71291	0	0	0	0	0	0	0	0	0	0	71291	0
Other Portfolio Income **6**	241478	0	1083	6563	16841	21270	15372	798	3308	10635	0	165605	0
Other Receipts **7**	17257821	23424	2485593	721753	1009592	1852105	683806	717532	329017	967142	0	8467860	0
Total Receipts **8**	17605554	23424	2486677	729152	1028906	1873375	699315	718364	333384	989152	0	8723806	0
Average Total Receipts **9**	2013	58	347	1416	2842	8401	20568	51312	66677	164859	•	2907935	•
Operating Costs/Operating Income (%)													
Cost of Operations **10**	29.6	37.2	22.3	29.0	43.3	27.0	33.9	43.7	8.7	29.2	•	30.0	•
Salaries and Wages **11**	17.4	•	21.3	17.8	14.3	17.5	14.6	13.1	25.6	19.0	•	16.8	•
Taxes Paid **12**	3.2	1.2	4.8	3.7	3.7	3.4	2.6	2.6	3.0	3.9	•	2.6	•
Interest Paid **13**	1.1	•	0.8	0.9	2.3	0.3	1.1	1.3	1.9	5.6	•	0.7	•
Depreciation **14**	13.2	7.1	6.1	4.1	7.4	19.5	10.8	13.0	13.5	11.3	•	15.7	•
Amortization and Depletion **15**	1.0	•	0.4	•	0.3	0.1	0.0	0.4	1.1	9.2	•	0.8	•
Pensions and Other Deferred Comp. **16**	0.2	•	0.0	0.1	0.3	0.2	0.2	0.3	0.2	0.0	•	0.2	•
Employee Benefits **17**	1.2	•	0.6	0.7	0.7	1.4	0.7	1.7	3.3	1.1	•	1.4	•
Advertising **18**	3.7	0.1	1.4	1.3	1.6	2.3	1.3	2.5	10.1	0.6	•	5.4	•
Other Expenses **19**	20.2	65.7	36.1	27.9	19.8	15.0	19.6	15.1	25.7	20.9	•	16.3	•
Officers' Compensation **20**	2.1	•	3.9	3.1	6.8	3.4	7.6	0.9	1.3	1.0	•	0.5	•
Operating Margin **21**	7.0	•	2.3	11.5	•	9.8	7.6	5.5	5.7	•	•	9.5	•
Operating Margin Before Officers' Comp. **22**	9.2	•	6.2	14.6	6.3	13.3	15.3	6.4	7.0	•	•	10.1	•

Selected Average Balance Sheet ($ in Thousands)

Net Receivables 23	85	0	14	34	124	501	3791	3444	5796	10826	•	64888	•
Inventories 24	•	•	•	•	•	•	•	•	•	•	•	•	•
Net Property, Plant and Equipment 25	616	0	61	267	1149	3235	5257	12895	29161	80047	•	896586	•
Total Assets 26	1855	0	145	709	1868	7027	12328	32876	63876	191228	•	3409388	•
Notes and Loans Payable 27	590	0	137	233	1838	1140	6100	14625	20146	143567	•	585929	•
All Other Liabilities 28	676	0	17	201	265	714	2042	7358	17005	33942	•	1658409	•
Net Worth 29	589	0	-9	275	-236	5174	4185	10893	26726	13719	•	1165050	•

Selected Financial Ratios (Times to 1)

Current Ratio 30	0.7	•	1.8	2.0	2.1	2.2	1.8	1.4	0.7	0.7	•	0.3	•
Quick Ratio 31	0.4	•	1.0	0.9	1.4	0.9	1.4	1.0	0.6	0.6	•	0.2	•
Net Sales to Working Capital 32	•	•	13.8	7.3	9.0	6.9	6.8	16.3	•	•	•	•	•
Coverage Ratio 33	7.4	•	3.8	13.6	0.8	30.2	8.0	5.3	4.0	0.6	•	15.2	•
Total Asset Turnover 34	1.1	•	2.4	2.0	1.5	1.2	1.7	1.6	1.0	0.9	•	0.9	•
Inventory Turnover 35	•	•	•	•	•	•	•	•	•	•	•	•	•
Receivables Turnover 36	•	•	•	•	•	•	•	•	•	•	•	•	•
Total Liabilities to Net Worth 37	2.1	•	•	1.6	•	0.4	1.9	2.0	1.4	12.9	•	1.9	•
Current Assets to Working Capital 38	•	•	2.2	2.0	1.9	1.8	2.2	3.7	•	•	•	•	•
Current Liabilities to Working Capital 39	•	•	1.2	1.0	0.9	0.8	1.2	2.7	•	•	•	•	•
Working Capital to Net Sales 40	•	•	0.1	0.1	0.1	0.1	0.1	0.1	•	•	•	•	•
Inventory to Working Capital 41	•	•	0.9	1.0	0.4	0.7	0.2	0.7	•	•	•	•	•
Total Receipts to Cash Flow 42	4.9	2.2	3.8	4.1	8.2	4.9	5.4	6.9	3.7	9.0	•	4.8	•
Cost of Goods to Cash Flow 43	1.4	0.8	0.9	1.2	3.5	1.3	1.8	3.0	0.3	2.6	•	1.4	•
Cash Flow to Total Debt 44	0.3	•	0.6	0.8	0.2	0.9	0.5	0.3	0.5	0.1	•	0.3	•

Selected Financial Factors (in Percentages)

Debt Ratio 45	68.2	•	106.1	61.2	112.6	26.4	66.1	66.9	58.2	92.8	•	65.8	•
Return on Total Assets 46	8.8	•	7.3	24.8	2.8	12.2	14.5	10.5	7.9	3.1	•	8.7	•
Return on Equity Before Income Taxes 47	24.1	•	•	59.3	5.9	16.0	37.3	25.8	14.1	•	•	23.8	•
Return on Equity After Income Taxes 48	19.8	•	•	59.0	10.3	15.9	37.3	25.4	11.3	•	•	17.7	•
Profit Margin (Before Income Tax) 49	7.0	•	2.3	11.5	•	9.8	7.6	5.5	5.7	•	•	9.5	•
Profit Margin (After Income Tax) 50	5.8	•	2.2	11.4	•	9.8	7.6	5.4	4.5	•	•	7.1	•

Table II

Corporations with Net Income

OTHER CONSUMER GOODS AND GENERAL RENTAL CENTERS

MONEY AMOUNTS AND SIZE OF ASSETS IN THOUSANDS OF DOLLARS

Item Description for Accounting Period 7/12 Through 6/13	Total	Zero Assets	Under 500	500 to 1,000	1,000 to 5,000	5,000 to 10,000	10,000 to 25,000	25,000 to 50,000	50,000 to 100,000	100,000 to 250,000	250,000 to 500,000	500,000 to 2,500,000	2,500,000 and over
Number of Enterprises 1	4429	•	3719	397	88	181	15	•	•	3	0	•	0

Revenues ($ in Thousands)

	Total	Zero Assets	Under 500	500 to 1,000	1,000 to 5,000	5,000 to 10,000	10,000 to 25,000	25,000 to 50,000	50,000 to 100,000	100,000 to 250,000	250,000 to 500,000	500,000 to 2,500,000	2,500,000 and over
Net Sales 2	14953653	•	1463882	691604	245358	1896772	400319	•	•	556360	0	•	0
Interest 3	19586	•	1	503	1	0	5	•	•	0	0	•	0
Rents 4	3253	•	0	0	2217	0	0	•	•	0	0	•	0
Royalties 5	71291	•	0	0	0	0	0	•	•	0	0	•	0
Other Portfolio Income 6	214591	•	0	6537	14025	21270	1004	•	•	2776	0	•	0
Other Receipts 7	14644932	•	1463881	684564	229115	1875502	399310	•	•	553584	0	•	0
Total Receipts 8	14953653	•	1463882	691604	245358	1896772	400319	•	•	556360	0	•	0
Average Total Receipts 9	3376	•	394	1742	2788	10479	26688	•	•	185453	•	•	•

Operating Costs/Operating Income (%)

	Total	Zero Assets	Under 500	500 to 1,000	1,000 to 5,000	5,000 to 10,000	10,000 to 25,000	25,000 to 50,000	50,000 to 100,000	100,000 to 250,000	250,000 to 500,000	500,000 to 2,500,000	2,500,000 and over
Cost of Operations 10	29.0	•	22.5	29.9	40.5	26.6	38.8	•	•	20.1	•	•	•
Salaries and Wages 11	16.9	•	17.8	18.6	16.9	17.3	12.8	•	•	16.4	•	•	•
Taxes Paid 12	3.0	•	4.2	3.8	2.7	3.3	2.0	•	•	4.5	•	•	•
Interest Paid 13	0.8	•	0.8	0.4	0.7	0.3	0.8	•	•	3.9	•	•	•
Depreciation 14	13.5	•	3.3	3.0	2.4	19.2	2.6	•	•	11.2	•	•	•
Amortization and Depletion 15	1.1	•	0.5	•	0.1	0.1	0.0	•	•	14.6	•	•	•
Pensions and Other Deferred Comp. 16	0.2	•	0.0	0.1	0.1	0.2	0.3	•	•	0.1	•	•	•
Employee Benefits 17	1.3	•	0.2	0.7	0.8	1.4	0.9	•	•	1.6	•	•	•
Advertising 18	4.1	•	1.4	1.3	3.6	2.3	0.3	•	•	0.4	•	•	•
Other Expenses 19	18.5	•	33.4	26.5	24.9	14.6	15.1	•	•	19.3	•	•	•
Officers' Compensation 20	1.7	•	4.1	3.0	1.6	3.4	11.7	•	•	1.2	•	•	•
Operating Margin 21	10.0	•	11.8	12.6	5.7	11.2	14.8	•	•	6.6	•	•	•
Operating Margin Before Officers' Comp. 22	11.8	•	15.9	15.6	7.3	14.6	26.5	•	•	7.8	•	•	•

Selected Average Balance Sheet ($ in Thousands)

Net Receivables 23	122	•	0	44	16	617	7798	•	•	11161	•	•	•
Inventories 24	•	•	•	•	•	•	•	•	•	•	•	•	•
Net Property, Plant and Equipment 25	972	•	27	173	495	3986	1817	•	•	130034	•	•	•
Total Assets 26	3092	•	96	720	1414	6769	13264	•	•	223433	•	•	•
Notes and Loans Payable 27	685	•	88	211	233	1104	5727	•	•	121239	•	•	•
All Other Liabilities 28	1263	•	11	260	326	877	2305	•	•	34098	•	•	•
Net Worth 29	1144	•	-3	249	855	4788	5233	•	•	68096	•	•	•

Selected Financial Ratios (Times to 1)

Current Ratio 30	0.5	•	1.1	2.0	1.7	2.2	3.9	•	•	0.5	•	•	•
Quick Ratio 31	0.3	•	0.6	1.0	0.6	0.8	3.7	•	•	0.5	•	•	•
Net Sales to Working Capital 32	•	•	121.7	7.2	12.8	7.2	3.1	•	•	•	•	•	•
Coverage Ratio 33	13.8	•	15.2	31.9	9.4	34.7	20.6	•	•	2.7	•	•	•
Total Asset Turnover 34	1.1	•	4.1	2.4	2.0	1.5	2.0	•	•	0.8	•	•	•
Inventory Turnover 35	•	•	•	•	•	•	•	•	•	•	•	•	•
Receivables Turnover 36	•	•	•	•	•	•	•	•	•	•	•	•	•
Total Liabilities to Net Worth 37	1.7	•	•	1.9	0.7	0.4	1.5	•	•	2.3	•	•	•
Current Assets to Working Capital 38	•	•	8.1	2.0	2.5	1.8	1.3	•	•	•	•	•	•
Current Liabilities to Working Capital 39	•	•	7.1	1.0	1.5	0.8	0.3	•	•	•	•	•	•
Working Capital to Net Sales 40	•	•	0.0	0.1	0.1	0.1	0.3	•	•	•	•	•	•
Inventory to Working Capital 41	•	•	3.3	1.0	1.4	0.7	•	•	•	•	•	•	•
Total Receipts to Cash Flow 42	4.5	•	2.9	4.1	4.6	4.6	5.0	•	•	5.8	•	•	•
Cost of Goods to Cash Flow 43	1.3	•	0.7	1.2	1.9	1.2	1.9	•	•	1.2	•	•	•
Cash Flow to Total Debt 44	0.4	•	1.4	0.9	1.1	1.1	0.7	•	•	0.2	•	•	•

Selected Financial Factors (in Percentages)

Debt Ratio 45	63.0	•	103.0	65.4	39.5	29.3	60.6	•	•	69.5	•	•	•
Return on Total Assets 46	11.8	•	51.9	31.4	12.6	17.8	31.2	•	•	8.7	•	•	•
Return on Equity Before Income Taxes 47	29.6	•	•	88.0	18.7	24.5	75.2	•	•	18.0	•	•	•
Return on Equity After Income Taxes 48	25.2	•	•	87.5	13.7	24.5	75.2	•	•	17.6	•	•	•
Profit Margin (Before Income Tax) 49	10.0	•	11.8	12.6	5.7	11.2	14.7	•	•	6.6	•	•	•
Profit Margin (After Income Tax) 50	8.5	•	11.8	12.5	4.2	11.2	14.7	•	•	6.5	•	•	•

Table I

Corporations with and without Net Income

COMMERCIAL AND INDUSTRIAL MACHINERY AND EQUIPMENT RENTAL

MONEY AMOUNTS AND SIZE OF ASSETS IN THOUSANDS OF DOLLARS

Item Description for Accounting Period 7/12 Through 6/13	Total	Zero Assets	Under 500	500 to 1,000	1,000 to 5,000	5,000 to 10,000	10,000 to 25,000	25,000 to 50,000	50,000 to 100,000	100,000 to 250,000	250,000 to 500,000	500,000 to 2,500,000	2,500,000 and over
Number of Enterprises **1**	24647	2978	14724	2916	3076	278	394	103	67	50	22	30	8
Revenues ($ in Thousands)													
Net Sales **2**	51236879	1214625	4291841	1563640	4829254	2140618	4531617	2814443	3147687	3358124	3039690	8878911	11426430
Interest **3**	939969	2271	4044	2956	11434	8858	16063	13305	15836	88078	112577	221415	443132
Rents **4**	132866	6286	7727	6307	20724	0	642	3372	969	14379	1266	71193	0
Royalties **5**	1014	0	0	0	0	0	0	0	0	852	0	161	0
Other Portfolio Income **6**	2762019	556324	287186	22176	181643	30290	203438	131531	88690	225155	193137	245274	597174
Other Receipts **7**	47401011	649744	3992884	1532201	4615453	2101470	4311474	2666235	3042192	3029660	2732710	8340868	10386124
Total Receipts **8**	51236879	1214625	4291841	1563640	4829254	2140618	4531617	2814443	3147687	3358124	3039690	8878911	11426430
Average Total Receipts **9**	2079	408	291	536	1570	7700	11502	27325	46980	67162	138168	295964	1428304
Operating Costs/Operating Income (%)													
Cost of Operations **10**	27.6	14.3	31.7	20.2	24.7	42.2	37.7	47.7	41.7	28.7	22.2	31.0	12.6
Salaries and Wages **11**	10.9	3.3	8.6	19.2	10.1	13.3	10.7	9.9	9.9	11.5	12.6	12.4	10.1
Taxes Paid **12**	1.9	1.0	2.0	4.0	2.0	2.5	2.4	1.8	2.0	1.9	2.1	1.8	1.4
Interest Paid **13**	6.9	4.6	2.7	2.1	1.9	2.7	2.1	2.1	4.8	5.0	8.2	10.3	13.4
Depreciation **14**	22.2	16.4	7.0	15.4	16.8	11.6	16.7	14.1	18.4	21.6	26.5	25.8	34.9
Amortization and Depletion **15**	0.7	0.6	0.2	0.0	0.2	0.3	0.1	0.2	0.8	1.1	1.6	1.0	1.2
Pensions and Other Deferred Comp. **16**	0.2	0.0	0.1	0.5	0.2	0.3	0.2	0.3	0.5	0.2	0.4	0.2	0.2
Employee Benefits **17**	1.4	0.5	0.4	3.0	0.7	1.0	1.3	1.1	1.7	1.4	1.2	2.0	1.6
Advertising **18**	0.3	0.1	0.5	0.9	0.5	0.4	0.2	0.3	0.3	0.4	0.3	0.4	0.1
Other Expenses **19**	20.3	17.1	30.1	31.5	25.1	18.5	18.2	15.6	14.6	19.1	18.9	18.2	19.6
Officers' Compensation **20**	2.7	0.8	8.9	3.5	7.0	4.8	2.4	2.0	1.6	2.6	1.5	0.8	0.7
Operating Margin **21**	4.9	41.2	7.9	•	10.6	2.4	8.2	4.9	3.7	6.3	4.5	•	4.3
Operating Margin Before Officers' Comp. **22**	7.6	42.0	16.7	3.0	17.7	7.1	10.5	6.9	5.3	9.0	6.1	•	5.0

Selected Average Balance Sheet ($ in Thousands)

Net Receivables 23	750	0	11	36	238	1253	1807	5319	9266	31035	43266	90544	1255476
Inventories 24	•	•	•	•	•	•	•	•	•	•	•	•	•
Net Property, Plant and Equipment 25	2426	0	57	257	954	3083	7139	12646	31509	78870	173349	439620	3402730
Total Assets 26	5054	0	130	726	2042	7248	15331	34984	70093	159830	355396	1090884	6170718
Notes and Loans Payable 27	2901	0	123	402	1142	3397	6221	14402	34267	71911	185861	627593	3912650
All Other Liabilities 28	1018	0	39	48	346	2970	2323	7373	14471	24834	71200	229176	1268283
Net Worth 29	1136	0	-33	277	553	880	6788	13209	21355	63086	98335	234115	989784

Selected Financial Ratios (Times to 1)

Current Ratio 30	1.6	•	1.0	3.7	2.1	2.1	1.2	1.6	1.7	2.2	1.9	1.1	1.7
Quick Ratio 31	1.2	•	0.8	1.9	1.4	1.3	0.8	0.9	0.9	1.6	1.6	0.7	1.6
Net Sales to Working Capital 32	4.4	•	143.1	2.7	3.8	4.6	13.4	5.3	4.9	2.4	3.8	11.6	2.4
Coverage Ratio 33	1.7	10.3	3.9	0.8	6.6	1.9	5.0	3.3	1.8	2.3	1.6	0.6	1.3
Total Asset Turnover 34	0.4	•	2.2	0.7	0.8	1.1	0.8	0.8	0.7	0.4	0.4	0.3	0.2
Inventory Turnover 35	•	•	•	•	•	•	•	•	•	•	•	•	•
Receivables Turnover 36	•	•	•	•	•	•	•	•	•	•	•	•	•
Total Liabilities to Net Worth 37	3.4	•	•	1.6	2.7	7.2	1.3	1.6	2.3	1.5	2.6	3.7	5.2
Current Assets to Working Capital 38	2.7	•	21.8	1.4	1.9	1.9	5.4	2.6	2.5	1.9	2.2	8.1	2.4
Current Liabilities to Working Capital 39	1.7	•	20.8	0.4	0.9	0.9	4.4	1.6	1.5	0.9	1.2	7.1	1.4
Working Capital to Net Sales 40	0.2	•	0.0	0.4	0.3	0.2	0.1	0.2	0.2	0.4	0.3	0.1	0.4
Inventory to Working Capital 41	0.3	•	1.0	0.1	0.2	0.4	1.2	0.9	0.4	0.2	0.1	1.5	0.0
Total Receipts to Cash Flow 42	5.9	1.8	3.9	4.6	3.8	7.3	5.8	7.4	7.9	5.5	5.8	13.7	6.8
Cost of Goods to Cash Flow 43	1.6	0.3	1.2	0.9	0.9	3.1	2.2	3.5	3.3	1.6	1.3	4.2	0.8
Cash Flow to Total Debt 44	0.1	•	0.5	0.3	0.3	0.2	0.2	0.2	0.1	0.1	0.1	0.0	0.0

Selected Financial Factors (in Percentages)

Debt Ratio 45	77.5	•	125.1	61.9	72.9	87.9	55.7	62.2	69.5	60.5	72.3	78.5	84.0
Return on Total Assets 46	4.8	•	23.7	1.2	9.6	5.4	7.6	5.4	5.6	4.8	5.0	1.7	4.1
Return on Equity Before Income Taxes 47	9.0	•	•	•	30.2	20.6	13.8	10.1	8.0	6.8	6.4	•	6.1
Return on Equity After Income Taxes 48	7.9	•	•	•	28.9	15.8	12.8	7.9	6.3	5.5	2.3	•	5.9
Profit Margin (Before Income Tax) 49	4.9	42.3	7.9	•	10.6	2.3	8.1	4.9	3.7	6.4	4.6	•	4.2
Profit Margin (After Income Tax) 50	4.3	40.2	7.8	•	10.2	1.8	7.6	3.8	2.9	5.2	1.6	•	4.1

Table II
Corporations with Net Income

COMMERCIAL AND INDUSTRIAL MACHINERY AND EQUIPMENT RENTAL

MONEY AMOUNTS AND SIZE OF ASSETS IN THOUSANDS OF DOLLARS

Item Description for Accounting Period 7/12 Through 6/13	Total	Zero Assets	Under 500	500 to 1,000	1,000 to 5,000	5,000 to 10,000	10,000 to 25,000	25,000 to 50,000	50,000 to 100,000	100,000 to 250,000	250,000 to 500,000	500,000 to 2,500,000	2,500,000 and over
Number of Enterprises 1	12147	1347	6928	1497	1752	180	281	76	•	26	10	10	•

Revenues ($ in Thousands)													
Net Sales 2	36628492	877123	3074485	1063128	4169834	1842927	3789849	2196061	•	2316273	1935867	3258333	•
Interest 3	760438	1343	3977	724	9357	2673	15946	12546	•	27790	74910	156886	•
Rents 4	52906	0	7727	0	20724	0	642	3369	•	10161	1266	8967	•
Royalties 5	1014	0	0	0	0	0	0	0	•	852	0	161	•
Other Portfolio Income 6	2161019	553299	172819	22176	157364	23078	169211	108164	•	192212	133815	80234	•
Other Receipts 7	33653115	322481	2889962	1040228	3982389	1817176	3604050	2071982	•	2085258	1725876	3012085	•
Total Receipts 8	36628492	877123	3074485	1063128	4169834	1842927	3789849	2196061	•	2316273	1935867	3258333	•
Average Total Receipts 9	3015	651	444	710	2380	10238	13487	28896	•	89087	193587	325833	•

Operating Costs/Operating Income (%)													
Cost of Operations 10	27.0	7.1	27.0	29.6	25.0	44.8	39.4	49.6	•	27.8	20.4	28.7	•
Salaries and Wages 11	10.7	1.8	8.1	16.5	9.7	12.2	10.2	9.2	•	12.0	13.5	13.2	•
Taxes Paid 12	1.8	0.8	1.9	3.4	2.0	2.3	2.3	1.6	•	1.9	2.2	1.5	•
Interest Paid 13	5.6	3.9	3.5	1.5	1.3	1.3	1.9	1.5	•	2.8	5.0	5.3	•
Depreciation 14	18.6	11.3	5.1	13.0	13.8	9.2	14.9	10.9	•	16.6	19.0	23.8	•
Amortization and Depletion 15	0.6	0.8	0.2	0.0	0.1	0.1	0.0	0.1	•	0.5	0.8	1.2	•
Pensions and Other Deferred Comp. 16	0.2	0.0	•	0.7	0.1	0.3	0.2	0.3	•	0.2	0.2	0.3	•
Employee Benefits 17	1.3	0.2	0.4	3.1	0.7	0.9	1.3	0.9	•	1.4	1.1	1.5	•
Advertising 18	0.3	0.0	0.5	0.8	0.5	0.4	0.2	0.3	•	0.4	0.3	0.4	•
Other Expenses 19	18.4	7.6	31.7	19.8	21.2	13.8	15.3	13.4	•	17.2	17.7	11.3	•
Officers' Compensation 20	2.7	0.3	7.5	2.3	7.2	4.5	2.5	1.9	•	3.4	1.7	0.7	•
Operating Margin 21	12.8	66.1	13.9	9.4	18.3	10.2	11.7	10.2	•	15.8	18.2	12.1	•
Operating Margin Before Officers' Comp. 22	15.5	66.5	21.4	11.6	25.5	14.7	14.2	12.0	•	19.3	19.9	12.8	•

Selected Average Balance Sheet ($ in Thousands)

Net Receivables 23	1192	0	9	53	211	1333	1998	5533	•	35145	75843	143662	•
Inventories 24	•	•	•	•	•	•	•	•	•	•	•	•	•
Net Property, Plant and Equipment 25	2401	0	76	283	802	3352	7046	10602	•	61020	140835	186833	•
Total Assets 26	5869	0	162	755	2026	7411	15217	33701	•	160948	357542	895828	•
Notes and Loans Payable 27	3144	0	112	229	919	2789	5970	10203	•	47343	165852	397659	•
All Other Liabilities 28	1390	0	50	74	251	1608	2565	7051	•	32523	89209	319502	•
Net Worth 29	1335	0	-0	452	855	3014	6682	16447	•	81082	102480	178667	•

Selected Financial Ratios (Times to 1)

Current Ratio 30	1.7	•	1.2	3.1	2.7	2.2	1.6	1.5	•	1.9	2.8	1.2	•
Quick Ratio 31	1.3	•	0.8	1.4	1.8	1.3	1.0	0.8	•	1.4	2.5	0.9	•
Net Sales to Working Capital 32	4.1	•	54.6	2.8	4.1	5.6	6.9	6.5	•	3.1	2.3	8.4	•
Coverage Ratio 33	3.3	18.5	5.0	7.2	15.3	8.8	7.3	7.6	•	6.6	4.7	3.3	•
Total Asset Turnover 34	0.5	•	2.7	0.9	1.2	1.4	0.9	0.9	•	0.6	0.5	0.4	•
Inventory Turnover 35	•	•	•	•	•	•	•	•	•	•	•	•	•
Receivables Turnover 36	•	•	•	•	•	•	•	•	•	•	•	•	•
Total Liabilities to Net Worth 37	3.4	•	•	0.7	1.4	1.5	1.3	1.0	•	1.0	2.5	4.0	•
Current Assets to Working Capital 38	2.5	•	7.7	1.5	1.6	1.9	2.8	3.0	•	2.1	1.6	6.3	•
Current Liabilities to Working Capital 39	1.5	•	6.7	0.5	0.6	0.9	1.8	2.0	•	1.1	0.6	5.3	•
Working Capital to Net Sales 40	0.2	•	0.0	0.4	0.2	0.2	0.1	0.2	•	0.3	0.4	0.1	•
Inventory to Working Capital 41	0.2	•	0.0	0.0	0.2	0.5	0.6	1.1	•	0.3	0.1	1.1	•
Total Receipts to Cash Flow 42	4.2	1.4	3.1	4.6	3.1	5.4	5.0	5.8	•	3.8	3.2	4.9	•
Cost of Goods to Cash Flow 43	1.1	0.1	0.8	1.4	0.8	2.4	2.0	2.9	•	1.0	0.7	1.4	•
Cash Flow to Total Debt 44	0.2	•	0.9	0.5	0.6	0.4	0.3	0.3	•	0.3	0.2	0.1	•

Selected Financial Factors (in Percentages)

Debt Ratio 45	77.2	•	100.1	40.1	57.8	59.3	56.1	51.2	•	49.6	71.3	80.1	•
Return on Total Assets 46	9.5	•	47.6	10.2	23.0	15.8	12.0	10.0	•	10.4	12.6	6.3	•
Return on Equity Before Income Taxes 47	28.9	•	•	14.7	51.0	34.5	23.6	17.8	•	17.4	34.6	22.1	•
Return on Equity After Income Taxes 48	27.0	•	•	13.1	49.5	32.4	22.3	15.5	•	15.6	25.8	21.5	•
Profit Margin (Before Income Tax) 49	12.8	67.6	13.9	9.4	18.3	10.2	11.7	10.1	•	15.9	18.3	12.1	•
Profit Margin (After Income Tax) 50	12.0	64.8	13.9	8.3	17.8	9.5	11.1	8.8	•	14.2	13.7	11.8	•

Table I

Corporations with and without Net Income

LESSORS OF NONFINAN. INTANGIBLE ASSETS (EX. COPYRIGHTED WORKS)

MONEY AMOUNTS AND SIZE OF ASSETS IN THOUSANDS OF DOLLARS

Item Description for Accounting Period 7/12 Through 6/13	Total	Zero Assets	Under 500	500 to 1,000	1,000 to 5,000	5,000 to 10,000	10,000 to 25,000	25,000 to 50,000	50,000 to 100,000	100,000 to 250,000	250,000 to 500,000	500,000 to 2,500,000	2,500,000 and over
Number of Enterprises **1**	3390	391	2022	567	298	35	36	3	11	12	5	6	3

Revenues ($ in Thousands)

	Total	Zero Assets	Under 500	500 to 1,000	1,000 to 5,000	5,000 to 10,000	10,000 to 25,000	25,000 to 50,000	50,000 to 100,000	100,000 to 250,000	250,000 to 500,000	500,000 to 2,500,000	2,500,000 and over
Net Sales **2**	9339906	377637	443139	283237	720434	104134	422848	164845	194979	897907	909756	2754987	2066003
Interest **3**	142889	276	2	0	126	1673	179	18	2072	17316	29239	14319	77669
Rents **4**	15796	0	0	0	18	0	0	0	350	4851	0	10577	0
Royalties **5**	2706774	222971	38494	0	27117	36057	21069	0	49792	119372	598429	1176217	417256
Other Portfolio Income **6**	462766	0	0	0	2426	0	93	0	1427	578	889	391714	65639
Other Receipts **7**	6011681	154390	404643	283237	690747	66404	401507	164827	141338	755790	281199	1162160	1505439
Total Receipts **8**	9339906	377637	443139	283237	720434	104134	422848	164845	194979	897907	909756	2754987	2066003
Average Total Receipts **9**	2755	966	219	500	2418	2975	11746	54948	17725	74826	181951	459164	688668

Operating Costs/Operating Income (%)

	Total	Zero Assets	Under 500	500 to 1,000	1,000 to 5,000	5,000 to 10,000	10,000 to 25,000	25,000 to 50,000	50,000 to 100,000	100,000 to 250,000	250,000 to 500,000	500,000 to 2,500,000	2,500,000 and over
Cost of Operations **10**	11.5	0.0	•	0.2	13.6	1.9	18.7	16.8	37.3	13.8	3.3	17.6	7.5
Salaries and Wages **11**	16.9	0.6	11.4	23.3	30.4	18.9	19.3	2.0	9.1	21.1	5.8	13.5	24.4
Taxes Paid **12**	2.2	0.1	0.8	2.9	1.8	2.8	2.4	0.4	2.9	5.0	0.5	1.8	2.8
Interest Paid **13**	5.0	4.0	0.1	5.5	0.3	0.6	4.3	0.2	4.5	2.7	4.7	2.7	12.8
Depreciation **14**	2.8	3.9	0.4	0.9	0.6	1.2	2.0	0.3	1.3	3.0	11.0	1.9	2.2
Amortization and Depletion **15**	3.4	•	0.5	2.8	1.8	3.0	2.3	1.1	4.0	2.1	1.9	5.5	4.1
Pensions and Other Deferred Comp. **16**	0.4	•	•	•	0.4	1.5	0.6	0.6	0.1	0.7	0.0	0.4	0.5
Employee Benefits **17**	1.1	0.0	0.5	2.3	0.4	1.1	1.4	0.3	0.4	1.5	0.2	1.2	1.8
Advertising **18**	2.1	2.3	1.0	0.0	6.0	6.0	2.9	0.4	1.3	3.2	1.4	2.6	0.4
Other Expenses **19**	28.2	58.3	33.1	45.7	26.6	57.7	25.8	8.8	15.1	32.9	15.2	26.8	26.9
Officers' Compensation **20**	2.7	0.2	1.0	9.0	2.4	9.4	3.2	6.6	5.3	4.4	1.5	2.0	2.7
Operating Margin **21**	23.7	30.5	51.1	7.4	15.8	•	17.0	62.5	18.8	9.5	54.4	23.9	13.9
Operating Margin Before Officers' Comp. **22**	26.4	30.7	52.1	16.5	18.2	5.2	20.2	69.0	24.1	14.0	55.9	25.9	16.5

Selected Average Balance Sheet ($ in Thousands)

Net Receivables 23	477	0	3	2	382	846	1135	9562	4425	10416	99578	83058	75109
Inventories 24	•	•	•	•	•	•	•	•	•	•	•	•	•
Net Property, Plant and Equipment 25	413	0	14	13	164	76	1496	321	4827	17664	4503	120656	82676
Total Assets 26	8244	0	109	736	1400	7553	13747	35843	71854	159182	413252	1330654	4424914
Notes and Loans Payable 27	2737	0	44	533	295	2516	8012	4417	15131	34730	141986	378008	1616491
All Other Liabilities 28	1419	0	8	34	177	1730	1187	7536	13559	69092	113726	210654	594699
Net Worth 29	4088	0	57	169	927	3308	4548	23890	43164	55360	157539	741992	2213723

Selected Financial Ratios (Times to 1)

Current Ratio 30	1.8	•	1.0	6.4	3.5	2.7	1.5	1.9	3.5	1.1	2.3	3.5	1.1
Quick Ratio 31	1.0	•	0.3	6.4	3.2	1.6	0.9	1.8	1.5	0.9	2.0	2.3	0.3
Net Sales to Working Capital 32	2.7	•	•	3.6	3.4	1.1	5.2	8.1	0.8	32.3	1.9	1.4	11.8
Coverage Ratio 33	5.8	8.6	445.7	2.4	52.6	•	5.0	262.4	5.1	4.5	12.7	9.9	2.1
Total Asset Turnover 34	0.3	•	2.0	0.7	1.7	0.4	0.9	1.5	0.2	0.5	0.4	0.3	0.2
Inventory Turnover 35	•	•	•	•	•	•	•	•	•	•	•	•	•
Receivables Turnover 36	•	•	•	•	•	•	•	•	•	•	•	•	•
Total Liabilities to Net Worth 37	1.0	•	0.9	3.4	0.5	1.3	2.0	0.5	0.7	1.9	1.6	0.8	1.0
Current Assets to Working Capital 38	2.2	•	•	1.2	1.4	1.6	3.0	2.1	1.4	13.5	1.8	1.4	13.4
Current Liabilities to Working Capital 39	1.2	•	•	0.2	0.4	0.6	2.0	1.1	0.4	12.5	0.8	0.4	12.4
Working Capital to Net Sales 40	0.4	•	•	0.3	0.3	0.9	0.2	0.1	1.2	0.0	0.5	0.7	0.1
Inventory to Working Capital 41	0.0	•	•	•	0.0	0.1	0.1	•	0.0	0.1	0.0	0.0	0.0
Total Receipts to Cash Flow 42	2.3	1.2	1.2	2.2	2.5	1.9	2.6	1.4	3.4	2.6	1.5	3.0	2.9
Cost of Goods to Cash Flow 43	0.3	0.0	•	0.0	0.3	0.0	0.5	0.2	1.3	0.4	0.0	0.5	0.2
Cash Flow to Total Debt 44	0.3	•	3.6	0.4	2.0	0.4	0.5	3.3	0.2	0.3	0.5	0.3	0.1

Selected Financial Factors (in Percentages)

Debt Ratio 45	50.4	•	47.5	77.0	33.8	56.2	66.9	33.3	39.9	65.2	61.9	44.2	50.0
Return on Total Assets 46	9.6	•	103.2	8.8	27.9	•	18.2	96.1	5.8	5.8	26.3	9.2	4.2
Return on Equity Before Income Taxes 47	16.1	•	196.2	22.0	41.3	•	43.8	143.7	7.7	13.0	63.6	14.9	4.4
Return on Equity After Income Taxes 48	12.0	•	193.7	22.0	38.8	•	42.2	138.4	6.4	8.1	41.6	9.6	3.2
Profit Margin (Before Income Tax) 49	23.8	30.5	51.1	7.4	15.8	•	17.0	62.5	18.8	9.6	55.0	24.1	14.1
Profit Margin (After Income Tax) 50	17.8	26.6	50.4	7.4	14.9	•	16.3	60.2	15.6	6.0	36.0	15.5	10.3

Table II

Corporations with Net Income

LESSORS OF NONFINAN. INTANGIBLE ASSETS (EX. COPYRIGHTED WORKS)

MONEY AMOUNTS AND SIZE OF ASSETS IN THOUSANDS OF DOLLARS

Item Description for Accounting Period 7/12 Through 6/13	Total	Zero Assets	Under 500	500 to 1,000	1,000 to 5,000	5,000 to 10,000	10,000 to 25,000	25,000 to 50,000	50,000 to 100,000	100,000 to 250,000	250,000 to 500,000	500,000 to 2,500,000	2,500,000 and over
Number of Enterprises 1	2431	391	1178	549	241	19	24	3	6	9	•	•	3
Revenues ($ in Thousands)													
Net Sales 2	8453693	377637	440541	261360	717100	90908	281019	164845	144460	895222	•	•	2066003
Interest 3	137926	276	2	0	88	1533	26	18	1477	17201	•	•	77669
Rents 4	15796	0	0	0	18	0	0	0	350	4851	•	•	0
Royalties 5	2479648	222971	38494	0	26074	36057	19993	0	33167	117156	•	•	417256
Other Portfolio Income 6	461313	0	0	0	2426	0	43	0	1336	578	•	•	65639
Other Receipts 7	5359010	154390	402045	261360	688494	53318	260957	164827	108130	755436	•	•	1505439
Total Receipts 8	8453693	377637	440541	261360	717100	90908	281019	164845	144460	895222	•	•	2066003
Average Total Receipts 9	3477	966	374	476	2976	4785	11709	54948	24077	99469	•	•	688668
Operating Costs/Operating Income (%)													
Cost of Operations 10	9.3	0.0	•	•	13.7	0.6	2.4	16.8	38.2	13.9	•	•	7.5
Salaries and Wages 11	17.2	0.6	11.5	24.6	30.5	19.8	20.9	2.0	4.2	20.9	•	•	24.4
Taxes Paid 12	2.2	0.1	0.7	2.9	1.8	3.0	2.1	0.4	2.9	4.9	•	•	2.8
Interest Paid 13	5.2	4.0	0.1	4.6	0.3	0.1	1.5	0.2	0.9	2.7	•	•	12.8
Depreciation 14	2.9	3.9	0.3	0.4	0.6	1.4	1.5	0.3	1.2	3.0	•	•	2.2
Amortization and Depletion 15	2.9	•	0.5	2.9	0.5	1.1	0.3	1.1	0.9	1.1	•	•	4.1
Pensions and Other Deferred Comp. 16	0.4	•	•	•	0.4	1.8	0.9	0.6	0.0	0.7	•	•	0.5
Employee Benefits 17	1.1	0.0	0.5	2.2	0.4	1.2	1.3	0.3	0.2	1.5	•	•	1.8
Advertising 18	1.9	2.3	1.0	•	6.0	6.6	3.4	0.4	1.0	3.2	•	•	0.4
Other Expenses 19	26.4	58.3	31.7	34.6	26.3	44.4	21.7	8.8	11.5	32.4	•	•	26.9
Officers' Compensation 20	2.7	0.2	0.6	9.8	2.4	10.7	3.7	6.6	2.3	4.4	•	•	2.7
Operating Margin 21	27.9	30.5	53.1	18.0	17.3	9.2	40.2	62.5	36.8	11.4	•	•	13.9
Operating Margin Before Officers' Comp. 22	30.6	30.7	53.7	27.8	19.7	19.9	43.9	69.0	39.1	15.8	•	•	16.5

Selected Average Balance Sheet ($ in Thousands)

Net Receivables 23	595	0	5	2	217	1524	1072	9562	6488	12880	•	•	75109
Inventories 24	•	•	•	•	•	•	•	•	•	•	•	•	•
Net Property, Plant and Equipment 25	496	0	1	1	154	139	1285	321	7781	23543	•	•	82676
Total Assets 26	10022	0	· 158	732	1342	7949	13679	35843	69826	164874	•	•	4424914
Notes and Loans Payable 27	3303	0	66	466	350	2045	4711	4417	6923	46306	•	•	1616491
All Other Liabilities 28	1592	0	8	12	216	1898	2577	7536	14484	72074	•	•	594699
Net Worth 29	5127	0	84	254	776	4006	6391	23890	48419	46493	•	•	2213723

Selected Financial Ratios (Times to 1)

Current Ratio 30	1.8	•	1.0	49.5	2.8	2.7	2.0	1.9	3.0	1.0	•	•	1.1
Quick Ratio 31	1.1	•	0.3	49.5	2.5	1.5	1.3	1.8	1.6	0.9	•	•	0.3
Net Sales to Working Capital 32	2.8	•	•	2.9	4.8	1.3	4.8	8.1	1.0	114.5	•	•	11.8
Coverage Ratio 33	6.5	8.6	460.6	4.9	61.1	152.8	27.9	262.4	44.0	5.2	•	•	2.1
Total Asset Turnover 34	0.3	•	2.4	0.7	2.2	0.6	0.9	1.5	0.3	0.6	•	•	0.2
Inventory Turnover 35	•	•	•	•	•	•	•	•	•	•	•	•	•
Receivables Turnover 36	•	•	•	•	•	•	•	•	•	•	•	•	•
Total Liabilities to Net Worth 37	1.0	•	0.9	1.9	0.7	1.0	1.1	0.5	0.4	2.5	•	•	1.0
Current Assets to Working Capital 38	2.2	•	•	1.0	1.6	1.6	2.0	2.1	1.5	45.4	•	•	13.4
Current Liabilities to Working Capital 39	1.2	•	•	0.0	0.6	0.6	1.0	1.1	0.5	44.4	•	•	12.4
Working Capital to Net Sales 40	0.4	•	•	0.3	0.2	0.8	0.2	0.1	1.0	0.0	•	•	0.1
Inventory to Working Capital 41	0.0	•	•	•	0.1	0.2	0.0	•	0.0	0.5	•	•	0.0
Total Receipts to Cash Flow 42	2.2	1.2	1.2	2.2	2.5	1.9	1.7	1.4	2.1	2.5	•	•	2.9
Cost of Goods to Cash Flow 43	0.2	0.0	•	•	0.3	0.0	0.0	0.2	0.8	0.3	•	•	0.2
Cash Flow to Total Debt 44	0.3	•	4.2	0.5	2.1	0.6	1.0	3.3	0.5	0.3	•	•	0.1

Selected Financial Factors (in Percentages)

Debt Ratio 45	48.8	•	47.1	65.3	42.2	49.6	53.3	33.3	30.7	71.8	•	•	50.0
Return on Total Assets 46	11.5	•	125.8	14.7	39.0	5.6	35.7	96.1	13.0	8.5	•	•	4.2
Return on Equity Before Income Taxes 47	19.1	•	237.2	33.8	66.3	11.0	73.6	143.7	18.3	24.4	•	•	4.4
Return on Equity After Income Taxes 48	14.6	•	234.2	33.8	62.6	8.5	71.9	138.4	16.2	16.8	•	•	3.2
Profit Margin (Before Income Tax) 49	28.1	30.5	53.1	18.0	17.3	9.2	40.2	62.5	36.8	11.4	•	•	14.1
Profit Margin (After Income Tax) 50	21.5	26.6	52.4	18.0	16.3	7.1	39.2	60.2	32.5	7.8	•	•	10.3

Table I

Corporations with and without Net Income

LEGAL SERVICES

MONEY AMOUNTS AND SIZE OF ASSETS IN THOUSANDS OF DOLLARS

Item Description for Accounting Period 7/12 Through 6/13	Total	Zero Assets	Under 500	500 to 1,000	1,000 to 5,000	5,000 to 10,000	10,000 to 25,000	25,000 to 50,000	50,000 to 100,000	100,000 to 250,000	250,000 to 500,000	500,000 to 2,500,000	2,500,000 and over
Number of Enterprises 1	125468	23256	93470	4685	3539	295	155	37	22	4	0	4	0

Revenues ($ in Thousands)													
Net Sales 2	107327228	2742689	48715071	12374769	19311805	6156038	6485071	4465371	3376543	520229	0	3179642	0
Interest 3	34266	2439	3557	8203	3968	897	1002	1563	3227	165	0	9246	0
Rents 4	43436	0	6570	12996	921	4037	1989	7278	1598	264	0	7783	0
Royalties 5	22319	21730	536	0	0	0	0	0	54	0	0	0	0
Other Portfolio Income 6	51345	5065	2842	620	1979	133	979	3462	7728	0	0	28535	0
Other Receipts 7	3613760	68148	1698213	622294	769803	17095	230725	64450	48028	74446	0	20558	0
Total Receipts 8	111092354	2840071	50426789	13018882	20088476	6178200	6719766	4542124	3437178	595104	0	3245764	0
Average Total Receipts 9	885	122	539	2779	5676	20943	43353	122760	156235	148776	•	811441	•

Operating Costs/Operating Income (%)													
Cost of Operations 10	4.8	2.0	3.9	8.9	5.8	1.0	2.8	•	3.8	8.0	•	17.2	•
Salaries and Wages 11	30.7	17.9	22.4	29.5	33.0	45.5	51.5	52.3	58.2	62.6	•	23.2	•
Taxes Paid 12	3.5	4.0	3.6	3.5	3.6	3.9	3.6	3.2	3.6	3.5	•	1.5	•
Interest Paid 13	0.5	0.3	0.4	0.7	0.3	0.5	0.5	0.5	0.7	2.0	•	4.2	•
Depreciation 14	0.6	0.4	0.4	0.6	0.5	0.7	0.9	1.0	1.4	1.6	•	1.5	•
Amortization and Depletion 15	0.2	0.0	0.0	0.0	0.0	0.0	0.1	0.0	0.5	2.1	•	4.1	•
Pensions and Other Deferred Comp. 16	1.7	0.9	1.9	1.4	1.3	1.4	2.4	2.3	2.3	0.5	•	0.5	•
Employee Benefits 17	2.0	2.0	1.6	1.5	2.4	3.3	2.7	2.1	2.7	2.6	•	2.1	•
Advertising 18	2.6	5.0	2.5	1.5	4.7	1.3	1.4	1.2	0.9	0.1	•	0.6	•
Other Expenses 19	26.8	41.2	29.3	25.5	21.9	21.1	20.7	28.8	23.3	32.0	•	34.5	•
Officers' Compensation 20	18.2	16.3	23.3	20.0	16.4	16.9	9.0	8.2	2.1	1.5	•	0.8	•
Operating Margin 21	8.4	10.0	10.7	6.8	9.9	4.6	4.4	0.3	0.3	•	•	9.9	•
Operating Margin Before Officers' Comp. 22	26.6	26.3	34.0	26.9	26.3	21.4	13.4	8.5	2.5	•	•	10.7	•

Selected Average Balance Sheet ($ in Thousands)

Net Receivables 23	18	0	4	16	183	271	1828	3507	9790	5648	•	102190	•
Inventories 24	1	0	0	12	7	0	175	6	821	0	•	42	•
Net Property, Plant and Equipment 25	30	0	9	115	315	786	2272	5602	9351	5742	•	55239	•
Total Assets 26	239	0	79	692	1903	7107	15884	35481	66968	155330	•	1152740	•
Notes and Loans Payable 27	79	0	31	238	497	1408	3142	13191	16736	54021	•	530799	•
All Other Liabilities 28	99	0	34	276	826	4722	7065	15277	18642	81340	•	322670	•
Net Worth 29	60	0	14	179	580	977	5678	7013	31590	19969	•	299270	•

Selected Financial Ratios (Times to 1)

Current Ratio 30	1.4	•	1.5	1.3	1.5	1.3	1.6	1.3	2.2	0.9	•	1.1	•
Quick Ratio 31	1.0	•	1.2	0.8	1.0	0.8	0.9	0.8	1.5	0.2	•	0.8	•
Net Sales to Working Capital 32	19.8	•	27.6	33.0	11.9	16.1	11.0	20.1	7.7	•	•	49.6	•
Coverage Ratio 33	23.0	42.9	41.3	18.4	41.4	11.3	18.4	5.3	3.8	•	•	3.8	•
Total Asset Turnover 34	3.6	•	6.6	3.8	2.9	2.9	2.6	3.4	2.3	0.8	•	0.7	•
Inventory Turnover 35	52.8	•	•	19.4	48.1	•	6.8	•	7.2	•	•	3251.8	•
Receivables Turnover 36	50.3	•	•	69.4	36.1	85.4	29.4	28.1	17.0	•	•	7.3	•
Total Liabilities to Net Worth 37	3.0	•	4.8	2.9	2.3	6.3	1.8	4.1	1.1	6.8	•	2.9	•
Current Assets to Working Capital 38	3.3	•	3.0	4.9	2.8	4.2	2.7	4.1	1.8	•	•	15.0	•
Current Liabilities to Working Capital 39	2.3	•	2.0	3.9	1.8	3.2	1.7	3.1	0.8	•	•	14.0	•
Working Capital to Net Sales 40	0.1	•	0.0	0.0	0.1	0.1	0.1	0.0	0.1	•	•	0.0	•
Inventory to Working Capital 41	0.0	•	•	0.2	0.0	•	0.0	•	0.1	•	•	0.0	•
Total Receipts to Cash Flow 42	3.1	2.2	2.7	3.2	3.2	5.2	4.3	4.2	5.5	4.2	•	2.3	•
Cost of Goods to Cash Flow 43	0.1	0.0	0.1	0.3	0.2	0.0	0.1	•	0.2	0.3	•	0.4	•
Cash Flow to Total Debt 44	1.6	•	2.9	1.6	1.3	0.7	1.0	1.0	0.8	0.2	•	0.4	•

Selected Financial Factors (in Percentages)

Debt Ratio 45	74.8	•	82.8	74.2	69.5	86.3	64.3	80.2	52.8	87.1	•	74.0	•
Return on Total Assets 46	44.8	•	96.0	48.6	40.9	15.9	22.3	8.6	6.6	•	•	11.2	•
Return on Equity Before Income Taxes 47	169.6	•	545.6	178.0	131.0	105.1	59.1	35.2	10.3	•	•	31.7	•
Return on Equity After Income Taxes 48	166.0	•	541.2	176.0	129.8	100.0	56.6	28.2	6.9	•	•	23.8	•
Profit Margin (Before Income Tax) 49	11.9	13.6	14.2	12.0	13.9	4.9	8.0	2.0	2.1	•	•	11.9	•
Profit Margin (After Income Tax) 50	11.7	13.6	14.1	11.9	13.8	4.7	7.7	1.6	1.4	•	•	9.0	•

Table II
Corporations with Net Income

LEGAL SERVICES

MONEY AMOUNTS AND SIZE OF ASSETS IN THOUSANDS OF DOLLARS

Item Description for Accounting Period 7/12 Through 6/13	Total	Zero Assets	Under 500	500 to 1,000	1,000 to 5,000	5,000 to 10,000	10,000 to 25,000	25,000 to 50,000	50,000 to 100,000	100,000 to 250,000	250,000 to 500,000	500,000 to 2,500,000	2,500,000 and over
Number of Enterprises 1	95651	15351	73430	3633	2836	211	142	•	19	0	0	•	0

Revenues ($ in Thousands)

	Total	Zero Assets	Under 500	500 to 1,000	1,000 to 5,000	5,000 to 10,000	10,000 to 25,000	25,000 to 50,000	50,000 to 100,000	100,000 to 250,000	250,000 to 500,000	500,000 to 2,500,000	2,500,000 and over
Net Sales 2	92524977	2306053	42803507	9122386	16947646	5070559	6148320	•	2822766	0	0	•	0
Interest 3	22795	2366	2429	7510	2998	668	778	•	3226	0	0	•	0
Rents 4	31153	0	4897	6069	918	2506	104	•	1598	0	0	•	0
Royalties 5	21731	21730	0	0	0	0	0	•	1	0	0	•	0
Other Portfolio Income 6	50679	5060	2674	561	1809	94	954	•	7528	0	0	•	0
Other Receipts 7	3247901	39572	1488435	586558	766799	13646	227338	•	45720	0	0	•	0
Total Receipts 8	95899236	2374781	44301942	9723084	17720170	5087473	6377494	•	2880839	0	0	•	0
Average Total Receipts 9	1003	155	603	2676	6248	24111	44912	•	151623	•	•	•	•

Operating Costs/Operating Income (%)

	Total	Zero Assets	Under 500	500 to 1,000	1,000 to 5,000	5,000 to 10,000	10,000 to 25,000	25,000 to 50,000	50,000 to 100,000	100,000 to 250,000	250,000 to 500,000	500,000 to 2,500,000	2,500,000 and over
Cost of Operations 10	4.6	1.7	3.4	10.6	5.8	1.0	3.0	•	2.7	•	•	•	•
Salaries and Wages 11	30.3	18.8	22.5	28.2	32.1	43.3	50.7	•	58.3	•	•	•	•
Taxes Paid 12	3.4	3.5	3.5	3.3	3.4	3.9	3.6	•	3.6	•	•	•	•
Interest Paid 13	0.5	0.3	0.3	0.7	0.3	0.3	0.4	•	0.5	•	•	•	•
Depreciation 14	0.6	0.3	0.4	0.7	0.4	0.6	0.9	•	1.3	•	•	•	•
Amortization and Depletion 15	0.2	•	0.0	0.0	0.0	0.0	0.1	•	0.3	•	•	•	•
Pensions and Other Deferred Comp. 16	1.6	0.3	1.7	1.0	1.3	1.3	2.3	•	2.2	•	•	•	•
Employee Benefits 17	1.9	1.7	1.5	1.1	2.4	3.6	2.7	•	2.5	•	•	•	•
Advertising 18	2.1	5.6	2.0	1.7	3.5	0.9	1.4	•	1.0	•	•	•	•
Other Expenses 19	26.6	41.1	29.2	24.3	22.6	20.6	20.7	•	22.2	•	•	•	•
Officers' Compensation 20	17.1	10.7	21.7	18.2	16.5	17.7	9.1	•	2.3	•	•	•	•
Operating Margin 21	11.2	16.0	13.9	10.3	11.7	6.8	5.1	•	3.0	•	•	•	•
Operating Margin Before Officers' Comp. 22	28.4	26.7	35.6	28.4	28.2	24.5	14.1	•	5.3	•	•	•	•

Selected Average Balance Sheet ($ in Thousands)

Net Receivables 23	19	0	5	21	173	203	1831	•	9211	•	•	•	•
Inventories 24	1	0	0	16	5	0	175	•	1519	•	•	•	•
Net Property, Plant and Equipment 25	32	0	11	121	280	805	2048	•	8116	•	•	•	•
Total Assets 26	256	0	87	695	1989	6650	15613	•	70551	•	•	•	•
Notes and Loans Payable 27	78	0	28	229	506	1132	3056	•	12028	•	•	•	•
All Other Liabilities 28	104	0	34	286	834	4150	6861	•	25577	•	•	•	•
Net Worth 29	74	0	24	180	650	1368	5696	•	32947	•	•	•	•

Selected Financial Ratios (Times to 1)

Current Ratio 30	1.5	•	1.6	1.1	1.6	1.3	1.6	•	2.1	•	•	•	•
Quick Ratio 31	1.0	•	1.2	0.8	1.0	1.0	0.9	•	1.0	•	•	•	•
Net Sales to Working Capital 32	19.9	•	25.9	53.2	11.4	22.3	11.5	•	6.2	•	•	•	•
Coverage Ratio 33	32.1	58.6	60.9	26.2	57.7	22.5	21.1	•	11.3	•	•	•	•
Total Asset Turnover 34	3.8	•	6.7	3.6	3.0	3.6	2.8	•	2.1	•	•	•	•
Inventory Turnover 35	50.2	•	•	17.1	71.7	•	7.4	•	2.6	•	•	•	•
Receivables Turnover 36	52.8	•	148.1	51.3	41.8	168.2	29.4	•	•	•	•	•	•
Total Liabilities to Net Worth 37	2.5	•	2.6	2.9	2.1	3.9	1.7	•	1.1	•	•	•	•
Current Assets to Working Capital 38	3.2	•	2.7	8.1	2.6	4.4	2.7	•	2.0	•	•	•	•
Current Liabilities to Working Capital 39	2.2	•	1.7	7.1	1.6	3.4	1.7	•	1.0	•	•	•	•
Working Capital to Net Sales 40	0.1	•	0.0	0.0	0.1	0.0	0.1	•	0.2	•	•	•	•
Inventory to Working Capital 41	0.0	•	•	0.3	•	•	0.0	•	0.1	•	•	•	•
Total Receipts to Cash Flow 42	2.8	1.9	2.5	2.9	2.9	4.7	4.1	•	5.0	•	•	•	•
Cost of Goods to Cash Flow 43	0.1	0.0	0.1	0.3	0.2	0.0	0.1	•	0.1	•	•	•	•
Cash Flow to Total Debt 44	1.9	•	3.7	1.7	1.5	1.0	1.1	•	0.8	•	•	•	•

Selected Financial Factors (in Percentages)

Debt Ratio 45	71.1	•	72.2	74.1	67.3	79.4	63.5	•	53.3	•	•	•	•
Return on Total Assets 46	57.9	•	119.1	63.3	49.7	26.9	25.6	•	11.7	•	•	•	•
Return on Equity Before Income Taxes 47	194.3	•	421.1	235.3	149.4	125.1	66.8	•	22.8	•	•	•	•
Return on Equity After Income Taxes 48	190.4	•	418.0	232.8	148.1	120.0	64.0	•	19.1	•	•	•	•
Profit Margin (Before Income Tax) 49	14.9	18.9	17.4	16.9	16.2	7.1	8.8	•	5.1	•	•	•	•
Profit Margin (After Income Tax) 50	14.6	18.9	17.3	16.7	16.1	6.8	8.4	•	4.2	•	•	•	•

Table I

Corporations with and without Net Income

ACCOUNTING, TAX PREPARATION, BOOKKEEPING, AND PAYROLL SERVICES

MONEY AMOUNTS AND SIZE OF ASSETS IN THOUSANDS OF DOLLARS

Item Description for Accounting Period 7/12 Through 6/13	Total	Zero Assets	Under 500	500 to 1,000	1,000 to 5,000	5,000 to 10,000	10,000 to 25,000	25,000 to 50,000	50,000 to 100,000	100,000 to 250,000	250,000 to 500,000	500,000 to 2,500,000	2,500,000 and over
Number of Enterprises 1	85320	21109	62036	1417	606	43	61	24	10	6	5	0	3

Revenues ($ in Thousands)													
Net Sales 2	51641254	2449158	19026791	5337063	6413772	933486	1017035	778325	1646285	353983	594734	0	13090623
Interest 3	602117	118	17606	9024	642	501	421	660	2801	3410	5086	0	561849
Rents 4	53773	0	559	11414	0	0	1185	124	238	0	0	0	40254
Royalties 5	339834	0	0	0	0	0	450	210	57	0	55133	0	283983
Other Portfolio Income 6	539481	41511	52158	655	3370	906	931	39	467	0	7	0	439433
Other Receipts 7	1821223	10506	355186	63360	76517	79568	20929	36965	9768	2783	3763	0	1161880
Total Receipts 8	54997682	2501293	19452300	5421516	6494301	1014461	1040951	816323	1659616	360176	658723	0	15578022
Average Total Receipts 9	645	118	314	3826	10717	23592	17065	34013	165962	60029	131745	•	5192674

Operating Costs/Operating Income (%)													
Cost of Operations 10	10.2	4.0	4.0	6.8	33.7	27.6	8.7	0.5	74.4	1.9	18.4	•	1.5
Salaries and Wages 11	32.4	14.9	29.5	36.0	47.2	33.5	37.1	30.4	15.3	31.8	30.6	•	32.9
Taxes Paid 12	4.3	4.0	4.8	3.8	4.9	2.9	4.0	4.5	0.8	3.7	3.8	•	4.3
Interest Paid 13	1.2	1.3	0.4	0.4	0.2	0.3	1.0	1.2	0.7	2.5	9.8	•	2.9
Depreciation 14	1.1	0.9	0.7	0.9	0.3	0.5	2.1	0.7	0.3	0.9	3.1	•	2.1
Amortization and Depletion 15	0.8	0.6	0.2	0.3	0.3	0.2	0.7	1.0	0.4	4.9	7.6	•	1.7
Pensions and Other Deferred Comp. 16	0.9	0.6	1.4	1.1	0.5	0.7	2.8	0.3	0.0	0.2	0.4	•	0.5
Employee Benefits 17	2.3	2.8	1.8	3.0	1.0	2.3	3.6	2.8	0.5	3.4	2.4	•	3.2
Advertising 18	1.0	1.1	0.8	0.6	0.2	1.2	0.8	0.2	0.3	0.9	0.2	•	1.8
Other Expenses 19	29.4	35.0	25.4	25.6	6.5	20.1	22.1	65.0	5.2	36.3	29.5	•	48.8
Officers' Compensation 20	11.2	21.3	20.5	17.1	2.5	4.5	14.3	0.6	0.3	15.3	1.2	•	0.2
Operating Margin 21	5.3	13.5	10.4	4.3	2.6	6.1	2.9	•	1.8	•	•	•	0.1
Operating Margin Before Officers' Comp. 22	16.5	34.8	30.9	21.4	5.1	10.6	17.1	•	2.1	13.7	•	•	0.3

Selected Average Balance Sheet ($ in Thousands)

Net Receivables 23	46	0	3	68	366	1666	2552	1966	22348	24391	16102	• 897485
Inventories 24	0	0	0	0	7	22	10	45	216	0	67	• 2683
Net Property, Plant and Equipment 25	26	0	11	215	172	372	1252	1759	1746	3902	17840	• 308213
Total Assets 26	994	0	55	688	2148	7780	13713	36185	73308	172662	524756	• 24233696
Notes and Loans Payable 27	107	0	18	311	820	1028	5186	6368	21884	43486	208482	• 1689480
All Other Liabilities 28	655	0	15	200	680	1411	7193	29038	31329	91121	191583	• 17093211
Net Worth 29	231	0	22	177	648	5341	1334	779	20094	38054	124691	• 5451005

Selected Financial Ratios (Times to 1)

Current Ratio 30	1.1	•	2.0	0.8	0.8	2.3	1.2	1.3	1.3	1.0	2.0	• 1.1
Quick Ratio 31	0.3	•	1.5	0.7	0.6	1.9	0.9	0.6	1.0	0.3	0.4	• 0.2
Net Sales to Working Capital 32	12.4	•	19.9	•	•	8.6	10.5	4.8	16.6	18.5	1.3	• 5.3
Coverage Ratio 33	10.9	12.7	30.3	15.2	20.2	48.2	6.2	•	4.9	1.0	1.4	• 8.1
Total Asset Turnover 34	0.6	•	5.6	5.5	4.9	2.8	1.2	0.9	2.2	0.3	0.2	• 0.2
Inventory Turnover 35	264.7	•	1123.6	2289.0	484.4	273.0	145.2	3.4	566.7	•	327.1	• 24.4
Receivables Turnover 36	12.8	•	88.6	33.2	41.2	18.0	5.8	6.0	10.6	•	•	• 4.6
Total Liabilities to Net Worth 37	3.3	•	1.5	2.9	2.3	0.5	9.3	45.4	2.6	3.5	3.2	• 3.4
Current Assets to Working Capital 38	7.9	•	2.0	•	•	1.8	5.7	4.2	4.1	33.4	2.0	• 10.9
Current Liabilities to Working Capital 39	6.9	•	1.0	•	•	0.8	4.7	3.2	3.1	32.4	1.0	• 9.9
Working Capital to Net Sales 40	0.1	•	0.1	•	•	0.1	0.1	0.2	0.1	0.1	0.8	• 0.2
Inventory to Working Capital 41	0.0	•	0.0	•	•	0.0	0.0	0.0	0.0	•	0.0	• 0.0
Total Receipts to Cash Flow 42	2.8	2.3	3.1	3.8	11.0	3.2	4.5	1.7	13.8	3.1	3.6	• 1.6
Cost of Goods to Cash Flow 43	0.3	0.1	0.1	0.3	3.7	0.9	0.4	0.0	10.3	0.1	0.7	• 0.0
Cash Flow to Total Debt 44	0.3	•	3.0	1.9	0.6	2.8	0.3	0.5	0.2	0.1	0.1	• 0.1

Selected Financial Factors (in Percentages)

Debt Ratio 45	76.7	•	60.2	74.3	69.8	31.4	90.3	97.8	72.6	78.0	76.2	• 77.5
Return on Total Assets 46	8.2	•	73.0	34.5	20.1	42.1	7.5	•	7.2	0.9	3.1	• 4.2
Return on Equity Before Income Taxes 47	31.8	•	177.3	125.2	63.3	60.1	65.1	•	20.8	0.1	3.6	• 16.5
Return on Equity After Income Taxes 48	26.7	•	176.3	124.4	62.1	58.5	49.0	•	20.3	•	2.2	• 10.8
Profit Margin (Before Income Tax) 49	12.2	15.6	12.6	5.9	3.9	14.8	5.2	•	2.5	0.1	3.8	• 20.6
Profit Margin (After Income Tax) 50	10.2	15.3	12.5	5.8	3.8	14.4	3.9	•	2.5	•	2.3	• 13.5

Table II

Corporations with Net Income

ACCOUNTING, TAX PREPARATION, BOOKKEEPING, AND PAYROLL SERVICES

MONEY AMOUNTS AND SIZE OF ASSETS IN THOUSANDS OF DOLLARS

Item Description for Accounting Period 7/12 Through 6/13	Total	Zero Assets	Under 500	500 to 1,000	1,000 to 5,000	5,000 to 10,000	10,000 to 25,000	25,000 to 50,000	50,000 to 100,000	100,000 to 250,000	250,000 to 500,000	500,000 to 2,500,000	2,500,000 and over
Number of Enterprises 1	63232	13193	48201	1241	493	31	37	•	7	•	•	3	0
Revenues ($ in Thousands)													
Net Sales 2	41705381	1997081	15023205	4760023	3566019	917309	863390	•	1411765	•	•	12088164	0
Interest 3	592510	12	16377	8178	638	235	323	•	2800	•	•	556224	0
Rents 4	53650	0	559	11414	0	0	1185	•	238	•	•	40254	0
Royalties 5	333177	0	0	0	0	0	450	•	57	•	•	277536	0
Other Portfolio Income 6	531318	41477	45097	481	3369	54	930	•	467	•	•	439433	0
Other Receipts 7	1790166	10349	323512	61198	74588	77272	20760	•	9769	•	•	1171029	0
Total Receipts 8	45006202	2048919	15408750	4841294	3644614	994870	887038	•	1425096	•	•	14572640	0
Average Total Receipts 9	712	155	320	3901	7393	32093	23974	•	203585	•	•	4857547	•
Operating Costs/Operating Income (%)													
Cost of Operations 10	10.9	0.4	1.6	7.7	60.2	28.1	4.4	•	86.8	•	•	1.8	•
Salaries and Wages 11	28.0	16.8	27.4	35.3	14.7	32.4	40.3	•	3.2	•	•	33.4	•
Taxes Paid 12	4.1	3.4	4.5	3.7	4.5	2.7	4.3	•	0.5	•	•	4.4	•
Interest Paid 13	0.7	1.2	0.4	0.4	0.4	0.3	0.7	•	0.6	•	•	1.0	•
Depreciation 14	1.1	0.7	0.8	1.0	0.2	0.5	1.9	•	0.3	•	•	2.1	•
Amortization and Depletion 15	0.8	0.5	0.3	0.2	0.5	0.2	0.3	•	0.0	•	•	1.8	•
Pensions and Other Deferred Comp. 16	0.9	0.7	1.3	1.0	0.3	0.7	2.4	•	0.0	•	•	0.5	•
Employee Benefits 17	2.3	2.5	1.8	3.1	0.9	1.8	4.0	•	0.4	•	•	2.9	•
Advertising 18	1.0	0.8	0.7	0.5	0.3	1.2	0.8	•	0.3	•	•	2.0	•
Other Expenses 19	31.0	30.0	25.1	25.6	8.3	19.7	19.1	•	5.0	•	•	49.8	•
Officers' Compensation 20	11.9	23.3	22.1	16.2	4.1	4.6	15.3	•	0.3	•	•	0.1	•
Operating Margin 21	7.4	19.6	14.0	5.2	5.7	7.7	6.4	•	2.6	•	•	0.1	•
Operating Margin Before Officers' Comp. 22	19.3	42.9	36.1	21.4	9.8	12.3	21.8	•	2.9	•	•	0.3	•

Selected Average Balance Sheet ($ in Thousands)

Net Receivables 23	47	0	4	78	435	2299	3460	•	30458	•	•	641802	•
Inventories 24	0	0	0	0	9	30	7	•	242	•	•	1026	•
Net Property, Plant and Equipment 25	32	0	12	234	138	513	1787	•	2113	•	•	295877	•
Total Assets 26	1169	0	62	710	2219	7903	14277	•	73530	•	•	21705428	•
Notes and Loans Payable 27	68	0	14	332	665	1426	4062	•	24859	•	•	665046	•
All Other Liabilities 28	806	0	16	187	589	1941	6328	•	29534	•	•	15832334	•
Net Worth 29	295	0	32	190	965	4536	3887	•	19137	•	•	5208047	•

Selected Financial Ratios (Times to 1)

Current Ratio 30	1.1	•	2.1	0.8	0.9	2.3	1.3	•	1.6	•	•	1.1	•
Quick Ratio 31	0.3	•	1.6	0.7	0.8	1.9	0.8	•	1.5	•	•	0.2	•
Net Sales to Working Capital 32	11.0	•	17.0	•	•	8.6	12.3	•	12.0	•	•	5.6	•
Coverage Ratio 33	23.6	19.4	39.5	17.4	23.4	53.0	14.3	•	7.0	•	•	22.7	•
Total Asset Turnover 34	0.6	•	5.0	5.4	3.3	3.7	1.6	•	2.7	•	•	0.2	•
Inventory Turnover 35	283.9	•	24583.8	2289.0	485.3	273.0	137.1	•	722.7	•	•	69.5	•
Receivables Turnover 36	13.8	•	80.0	33.5	24.3	18.5	6.1	•	•	•	•	12.6	•
Total Liabilities to Net Worth 37	3.0	•	0.9	2.7	1.3	0.7	2.7	•	2.8	•	•	3.2	•
Current Assets to Working Capital 38	8.1	•	1.9	•	•	1.8	4.5	•	2.7	•	•	11.9	•
Current Liabilities to Working Capital 39	7.1	•	0.9	•	•	0.8	3.5	•	1.7	•	•	10.9	•
Working Capital to Net Sales 40	0.1	•	0.1	•	•	0.1	0.1	•	0.1	•	•	0.2	•
Inventory to Working Capital 41	0.0	•	•	•	•	0.0	0.0	•	0.0	•	•	0.0	•
Total Receipts to Cash Flow 42	2.5	2.2	2.8	3.7	7.0	3.1	4.3	•	12.2	•	•	1.6	•
Cost of Goods to Cash Flow 43	0.3	0.0	0.0	0.3	4.2	0.9	0.2	•	10.6	•	•	0.0	•
Cash Flow to Total Debt 44	0.3	•	3.7	2.0	0.8	2.8	0.5	•	0.3	•	•	0.2	•

Selected Financial Factors (in Percentages)

Debt Ratio 45	74.8	•	48.2	73.2	56.5	42.6	72.8	•	74.0	•	•	76.0	•
Return on Total Assets 46	9.3	•	84.9	39.6	26.9	61.8	16.1	•	11.3	•	•	4.3	•
Return on Equity Before Income Taxes 47	35.4	•	159.8	139.1	59.3	105.7	54.9	•	37.3	•	•	17.3	•
Return on Equity After Income Taxes 48	30.0	•	158.9	138.2	58.3	103.0	45.8	•	36.6	•	•	11.3	•
Profit Margin (Before Income Tax) 49	15.8	22.2	16.5	6.9	7.9	16.2	9.2	•	3.5	•	•	22.4	•
Profit Margin (After Income Tax) 50	13.4	21.9	16.4	6.9	7.8	15.8	7.6	•	3.5	•	•	14.6	•

Table I

Corporations with and without Net Income

ARCHITECTURAL, ENGINEERING, AND RELATED SERVICES

MONEY AMOUNTS AND SIZE OF ASSETS IN THOUSANDS OF DOLLARS

Item Description for Accounting Period 7/12 Through 6/13	Total	Zero Assets	Under 500	500 to 1,000	1,000 to 5,000	5,000 to 10,000	10,000 to 25,000	25,000 to 50,000	50,000 to 100,000	100,000 to 250,000	250,000 to 500,000	500,000 to 2,500,000	2,500,000 and over
Number of Enterprises 1	103079	20354	73735	3454	4091	599	497	130	85	58	31	35	11

Revenues ($ in Thousands)

	Total	Zero Assets	Under 500	500 to 1,000	1,000 to 5,000	5,000 to 10,000	10,000 to 25,000	25,000 to 50,000	50,000 to 100,000	100,000 to 250,000	250,000 to 500,000	500,000 to 2,500,000	2,500,000 and over
Net Sales 2	223422878	2153588	40079990	9578063	21774318	9771437	15085515	7751172	9683389	11963074	9741917	34322958	51517458
Interest 3	333497	1298	5384	2113	8015	3184	11346	7886	9110	10189	43265	136661	95046
Rents 4	216152	205	1153	10152	3715	4245	2833	3529	9671	8108	5106	36244	131190
Royalties 5	78489	0	0	0	3176	3859	1110	394	6917	5549	12303	7369	37813
Other Portfolio Income 6	633542	7273	18481	41626	45531	11704	10539	20309	17401	57332	63746	105681	233914
Other Receipts 7	2783356	58755	105870	188751	236394	118969	227626	219114	153835	182858	146686	496646	647857
Total Receipts 8	227467914	2221119	40210878	9820705	22071149	9913398	15338969	8002404	9880323	12227110	10013023	35105559	52663278
Average Total Receipts 9	2207	109	545	2843	5395	16550	30863	61557	116239	210812	323001	1003016	4787571

Operating Costs/Operating Income (%)

	Total	Zero Assets	Under 500	500 to 1,000	1,000 to 5,000	5,000 to 10,000	10,000 to 25,000	25,000 to 50,000	50,000 to 100,000	100,000 to 250,000	250,000 to 500,000	500,000 to 2,500,000	2,500,000 and over
Cost of Operations 10	45.7	24.8	22.6	23.5	33.9	37.8	38.1	43.7	46.5	47.4	48.4	48.0	75.1
Salaries and Wages 11	19.0	22.3	21.0	24.9	23.7	21.1	24.1	22.8	20.7	18.2	20.8	17.7	12.3
Taxes Paid 12	2.9	3.3	4.2	3.7	3.7	3.5	3.2	3.3	3.1	2.7	2.8	2.2	1.8
Interest Paid 13	0.9	3.0	0.6	0.3	0.6	0.3	0.5	0.5	0.6	1.0	2.2	1.8	0.7
Depreciation 14	1.5	3.1	1.0	0.9	1.4	1.5	1.4	1.6	1.9	1.5	2.2	2.4	1.1
Amortization and Depletion 15	0.5	0.9	0.1	0.0	0.2	0.2	0.2	0.3	0.5	0.5	1.4	1.2	0.6
Pensions and Other Deferred Comp. 16	1.1	1.1	1.1	1.0	1.1	1.4	1.3	1.4	1.2	1.0	1.1	1.0	1.1
Employee Benefits 17	2.4	1.5	2.2	1.8	2.1	2.8	2.9	2.9	3.2	2.5	3.2	2.5	2.3
Advertising 18	0.3	0.5	0.5	0.3	0.4	0.4	0.3	0.4	0.3	0.2	0.2	0.3	0.0
Other Expenses 19	17.6	38.1	26.2	28.4	19.8	19.0	20.0	18.1	18.7	21.3	16.9	19.8	3.8
Officers' Compensation 20	4.8	9.1	12.6	9.5	6.5	7.3	4.7	3.7	2.8	2.2	1.2	1.1	0.9
Operating Margin 21	3.1	•	8.0	5.6	6.6	4.6	3.4	1.3	0.5	1.6	•	2.0	0.1
Operating Margin Before Officers' Comp. 22	7.9	1.4	20.6	15.1	13.0	11.9	8.1	5.0	3.2	3.8	1.0	3.1	1.0

	Selected Average Balance Sheet ($ in Thousands)												
Net Receivables 23	354	0	8	138	727	3014	5526	12965	22536	46052	78126	266753	901340
Inventories 24	44	0	1	8	117	436	790	1246	1489	7006	19233	24710	102795
Net Property, Plant and Equipment 25	155	0	18	174	426	956	2272	5524	8934	15369	34762	115123	279884
Total Assets 26	1447	0	77	693	2383	7058	15733	35317	70807	148643	347420	1088381	4653679
Notes and Loans Payable 27	389	0	62	328	712	1549	3142	8935	16230	37815	108221	299929	948005
All Other Liabilities 28	521	0	19	201	689	2563	6114	13117	29668	59803	112321	400234	1734100
Net Worth 29	536	0	-4	165	982	2946	6477	13265	24909	51025	126878	388218	1971574

	Selected Financial Ratios (Times to 1)												
Current Ratio 30	1.5	•	1.5	1.5	1.9	1.8	1.6	1.6	1.4	1.5	1.6	1.6	1.3
Quick Ratio 31	1.1	•	1.4	1.2	1.6	1.6	1.2	1.3	1.1	1.1	1.1	1.3	0.7
Net Sales to Working Capital 32	9.4	•	37.6	22.4	7.5	7.0	8.2	7.3	8.8	7.0	5.5	6.1	10.4
Coverage Ratio 33	6.7	•	15.2	31.8	14.5	20.3	11.2	10.3	5.0	5.5	2.3	3.5	4.4
Total Asset Turnover 34	1.5	•	7.0	4.0	2.2	2.3	1.9	1.7	1.6	1.4	0.9	0.9	1.0
Inventory Turnover 35	22.6	•	134.2	82.1	15.4	14.2	14.6	20.9	35.6	13.9	7.9	19.1	34.2
Receivables Turnover 36	6.6	•	65.0	21.6	7.7	5.6	5.5	5.0	5.3	4.8	4.1	4.1	5.7
Total Liabilities to Net Worth 37	1.7	•	•	3.2	1.4	1.4	1.4	1.7	1.8	1.9	1.7	1.8	1.4
Current Assets to Working Capital 38	3.1	•	3.0	3.2	2.1	2.2	2.8	2.8	3.5	3.0	2.8	2.7	4.8
Current Liabilities to Working Capital 39	2.1	•	2.0	2.2	1.1	1.2	1.8	1.8	2.5	2.0	1.8	1.7	3.8
Working Capital to Net Sales 40	0.1	•	0.0	0.0	0.1	0.1	0.1	0.1	0.1	0.1	0.2	0.2	0.1
Inventory to Working Capital 41	0.2	•	0.1	0.0	0.2	0.2	0.2	0.1	0.1	0.2	0.3	0.1	0.3
Total Receipts to Cash Flow 42	5.3	3.4	3.3	3.1	4.3	4.7	4.7	5.3	5.8	4.6	6.4	4.8	36.4
Cost of Goods to Cash Flow 43	2.4	0.8	0.8	0.7	1.5	1.8	1.8	2.3	2.7	2.2	3.1	2.3	27.4
Cash Flow to Total Debt 44	0.4	•	2.0	1.7	0.9	0.8	0.7	0.5	0.4	0.5	0.2	0.3	0.0

	Selected Financial Factors (in Percentages)												
Debt Ratio 45	62.9	•	105.0	76.2	58.8	58.3	58.8	62.4	64.8	65.7	63.5	64.3	57.6
Return on Total Assets 46	8.9	•	62.6	33.8	19.0	14.7	10.7	8.5	5.0	7.3	4.5	5.7	3.3
Return on Equity Before Income Taxes 47	20.5	•	•	137.4	42.8	33.5	23.8	20.5	11.4	17.4	6.9	11.4	6.1
Return on Equity After Income Taxes 48	17.9	•	•	133.5	40.9	30.4	21.1	18.5	7.7	12.5	3.4	9.4	3.8
Profit Margin (Before Income Tax) 49	5.1	•	8.3	8.2	7.9	6.0	5.1	4.5	2.5	4.3	2.8	4.5	2.6
Profit Margin (After Income Tax) 50	4.4	•	8.2	7.9	7.5	5.5	4.5	4.1	1.7	3.1	1.4	3.7	1.6

Table II
Corporations with Net Income

ARCHITECTURAL, ENGINEERING, AND RELATED SERVICES

MONEY AMOUNTS AND SIZE OF ASSETS IN THOUSANDS OF DOLLARS

Item Description for Accounting Period 7/12 Through 6/13	Total	Zero Assets	Under 500	500 to 1,000	1,000 to 5,000	5,000 to 10,000	10,000 to 25,000	25,000 to 50,000	50,000 to 100,000	100,000 to 250,000	250,000 to 500,000	500,000 to 2,500,000	2,500,000 and over
Number of Enterprises 1	67729	9749	51184	2808	2937	396	393	100	60	46	20	27	8

Revenues ($ in Thousands)													
Net Sales 2	183284051	1324073	35570185	8038534	17007376	6896504	12602693	5777682	7616457	10228115	7167969	29629197	41425267
Interest 3	216979	36	2423	1943	3735	934	4579	3287	5702	7425	9005	116011	61899
Rents 4	122837	35	598	10152	2130	3509	2708	3507	2650	8108	3469	32351	53618
Royalties 5	50262	0	0	0	3176	0	11	394	232	5446	3813	6120	31070
Other Portfolio Income 6	500739	7257	8818	18227	41063	9563	7525	12330	12274	56273	32318	71714	223376
Other Receipts 7	2356376	11410	95191	184778	191030	106470	205732	206542	98287	154804	74706	453743	573687
Total Receipts 8	186531244	1342811	35677215	8253634	17248510	7016980	12823248	6003742	7735602	10460171	7291280	30309136	42368917
Average Total Receipts 9	2754	138	697	2939	5873	17720	32629	60037	128927	227395	364564	1122561	5296115

Operating Costs/Operating Income (%)													
Cost of Operations 10	44.3	19.0	22.7	20.8	35.2	33.4	36.6	45.6	48.5	42.9	45.9	46.4	73.6
Salaries and Wages 11	18.8	21.2	20.7	24.0	21.1	21.2	23.9	21.3	18.2	19.4	21.0	18.5	12.6
Taxes Paid 12	2.8	2.8	4.1	3.8	3.5	3.2	3.1	3.4	3.0	2.7	2.9	2.1	1.5
Interest Paid 13	0.7	0.7	0.6	0.2	0.5	0.2	0.4	0.5	0.4	0.7	0.7	1.5	0.8
Depreciation 14	1.3	3.3	0.9	0.8	1.3	1.0	1.2	1.6	1.5	1.4	2.2	1.8	1.0
Amortization and Depletion 15	0.4	0.1	0.1	0.0	0.1	0.2	0.2	0.3	0.3	0.4	0.8	0.8	0.7
Pensions and Other Deferred Comp. 16	1.1	1.3	1.1	0.9	1.1	1.2	1.3	1.5	1.3	1.1	1.2	1.1	0.8
Employee Benefits 17	2.4	1.0	2.1	1.9	1.6	2.0	2.7	3.2	3.0	2.6	3.6	2.1	2.8
Advertising 18	0.3	0.4	0.5	0.2	0.4	0.4	0.2	0.4	0.3	0.2	0.1	0.3	0.0
Other Expenses 19	17.5	30.0	24.7	29.7	18.2	19.1	19.9	15.8	15.6	22.8	16.9	21.0	4.4
Officers' Compensation 20	4.7	8.0	11.8	9.5	5.7	8.9	4.8	3.1	2.7	2.4	1.0	1.2	0.9
Operating Margin 21	5.7	12.3	10.8	8.2	11.2	9.2	5.8	3.3	5.2	3.4	3.8	3.4	0.9
Operating Margin Before Officers' Comp. 22	10.5	20.3	22.6	17.7	17.0	18.1	10.6	6.4	7.9	5.8	4.7	4.5	1.8

Selected Average Balance Sheet ($ in Thousands)

Net Receivables 23	413	0	8	140	768	3370	5669	12686	22789	49226	89300	271240	921657
Inventories 24	39	0	1	8	81	328	718	1226	1327	7666	17767	15044	73584
Net Property, Plant and Equipment 25	173	0	21	178	434	650	2170	5922	8131	14761	36484	120161	255013
Total Assets 26	1649	0	92	686	2377	7366	15521	34787	69783	147683	333946	1076610	4851742
Notes and Loans Payable 27	435	0	67	253	611	1460	2644	8235	12899	29165	77702	302986	1155206
All Other Liabilities 28	551	0	23	214	508	2405	5465	13901	29265	59675	127006	352464	1623252
Net Worth 29	663	0	3	219	1258	3501	7411	12652	27619	58843	129239	421160	2073284

Selected Financial Ratios (Times to 1)

Current Ratio 30	1.6	•	1.6	1.4	2.7	2.1	1.8	1.5	1.4	1.6	1.5	1.6	1.3
Quick Ratio 31	1.2	•	1.5	1.2	2.4	2.0	1.5	1.2	1.2	1.2	1.1	1.3	0.8
Net Sales to Working Capital 32	8.8	•	33.3	24.0	6.0	5.8	6.8	7.4	9.1	6.6	6.5	6.7	8.4
Coverage Ratio 33	11.6	22.0	20.4	51.8	28.5	57.0	21.1	15.2	16.3	9.6	9.1	4.9	5.5
Total Asset Turnover 34	1.6	•	7.6	4.2	2.4	2.4	2.1	1.7	1.8	1.5	1.1	1.0	1.1
Inventory Turnover 35	30.8	•	139.4	70.7	25.3	17.7	16.3	21.5	46.4	12.4	9.3	33.8	51.8
Receivables Turnover 36	7.1	•	79.3	23.1	8.1	5.0	5.9	5.5	5.6	5.2	3.8	4.6	6.2
Total Liabilities to Net Worth 37	1.5	•	34.8	2.1	0.9	1.1	1.1	1.7	1.5	1.5	1.6	1.6	1.3
Current Assets to Working Capital 38	2.8	•	2.6	3.4	1.6	1.9	2.2	2.9	3.3	2.7	3.0	2.6	3.9
Current Liabilities to Working Capital 39	1.8	•	1.6	2.4	0.6	0.9	1.2	1.9	2.3	1.7	2.0	1.6	2.9
Working Capital to Net Sales 40	0.1	•	0.0	0.0	0.2	0.2	0.1	0.1	0.1	0.2	0.2	0.1	0.1
Inventory to Working Capital 41	0.1	•	0.1	0.0	0.1	0.0	0.1	0.2	0.1	0.2	0.3	0.1	0.1
Total Receipts to Cash Flow 42	4.7	2.5	3.2	2.7	3.8	3.8	4.2	5.2	5.4	4.0	5.4	4.3	25.1
Cost of Goods to Cash Flow 43	2.1	0.5	0.7	0.6	1.3	1.3	1.5	2.4	2.6	1.7	2.5	2.0	18.5
Cash Flow to Total Debt 44	0.6	•	2.5	2.2	1.4	1.2	0.9	0.5	0.6	0.6	0.3	0.4	0.1

Selected Financial Factors (in Percentages)

Debt Ratio 45	59.8	•	97.2	68.1	47.1	52.5	52.3	63.6	60.4	60.2	61.3	60.9	57.3
Return on Total Assets 46	13.7	•	88.0	46.5	31.9	26.4	16.3	12.7	13.1	10.2	7.0	7.6	4.5
Return on Equity Before Income Taxes 47	31.2	•	2999.7	143.1	58.2	54.5	32.5	32.7	31.0	23.0	16.0	15.4	8.6
Return on Equity After Income Taxes 48	28.0	•	2984.1	139.5	56.1	50.6	29.5	30.1	26.3	17.6	10.7	13.1	5.6
Profit Margin (Before Income Tax) 49	7.6	13.7	11.1	10.9	12.6	11.0	7.5	7.2	6.8	6.1	5.8	5.9	3.4
Profit Margin (After Income Tax) 50	6.9	13.2	11.0	10.7	12.2	10.2	6.8	6.6	5.7	4.7	3.9	5.0	2.2

336

Table I

Corporations with and without Net Income

SPECIALIZED DESIGN SERVICES

MONEY AMOUNTS AND SIZE OF ASSETS IN THOUSANDS OF DOLLARS

Item Description for Accounting Period 7/12 Through 6/13	Total	Zero Assets	Under 500	500 to 1,000	1,000 to 5,000	5,000 to 10,000	10,000 to 25,000	25,000 to 50,000	50,000 to 100,000	100,000 to 250,000	250,000 to 500,000	500,000 to 2,500,000	2,500,000 and over
Number of Enterprises 1	39818	7674	30462	872	684	73	36	•	•	•	0	3	0
Revenues ($ in Thousands)													
Net Sales 2	22188676	646598	12355077	1383505	2778114	259545	684479	•	•	•	0	3482412	0
Interest 3	2854	23	1011	161	193	155	87	•	•	•	0	1165	0
Rents 4	226	0	0	177	49	0	0	•	•	•	0	0	0
Royalties 5	113372	0	0	0	0	525	0	•	•	•	0	112847	0
Other Portfolio Income 6	11566	798	1446	585	237	299	5370	•	•	•	0	0	0
Other Receipts 7	76262	885	14201	2578	1490	15836	-331	•	•	•	0	40036	0
Total Receipts 8	22392956	648304	12371735	1387006	2780083	276360	689605	•	•	•	0	3636460	0
Average Total Receipts 9	562	84	406	1591	4064	3786	19156	•	•	•	•	1212153	•
Operating Costs/Operating Income (%)													
Cost of Operations 10	38.6	30.3	38.4	59.9	43.6	61.8	53.8	•	•	•	•	21.5	•
Salaries and Wages 11	15.0	9.7	10.0	18.7	14.1	11.0	10.1	•	•	•	•	34.2	•
Taxes Paid 12	2.4	2.1	2.5	1.8	2.2	2.4	2.1	•	•	•	•	2.8	•
Interest Paid 13	0.6	0.6	0.3	0.2	0.7	0.8	0.3	•	•	•	•	1.5	•
Depreciation 14	1.1	1.0	0.7	0.5	2.4	1.5	2.4	•	•	•	•	1.7	•
Amortization and Depletion 15	0.2	0.1	0.0	0.2	0.2	0.3	0.2	•	•	•	•	0.8	•
Pensions and Other Deferred Comp. 16	0.5	0.8	0.5	0.0	0.5	1.3	0.5	•	•	•	•	0.4	•
Employee Benefits 17	1.3	0.1	1.1	0.5	0.9	1.8	1.4	•	•	•	•	3.0	•
Advertising 18	1.1	0.9	0.8	2.6	1.4	0.4	0.4	•	•	•	•	1.8	•
Other Expenses 19	26.9	39.5	28.1	20.0	27.1	15.0	16.2	•	•	•	•	27.4	•
Officers' Compensation 20	8.3	12.0	11.3	4.3	5.2	7.5	7.3	•	•	•	•	2.1	•
Operating Margin 21	3.9	2.9	6.4	•	1.8	•	5.3	•	•	•	•	2.8	•
Operating Margin Before Officers' Comp. 22	12.2	14.8	17.7	•	7.0	3.6	12.6	•	•	•	•	4.9	•

Selected Average Balance Sheet ($ in Thousands)

	C1	C2	C3	C4	C5	C6	C7	C8	C9	C10	C11	C12	C13
Net Receivables 23	33	0	11	328	208	636	2696	•	•	•	•	92626	•
Inventories 24	16	0	2	100	169	589	217	•	•	•	•	65041	•
Net Property, Plant and Equipment 25	48	0	13	95	419	286	2364	•	•	•	•	324769	•
Total Assets 26	209	0	80	621	1678	7927	13857	•	•	•	•	796407	•
Notes and Loans Payable 27	93	0	43	1137	709	563	3886	•	•	•	•	166872	•
All Other Liabilities 28	95	0	20	605	994	5348	3894	•	•	•	•	388338	•
Net Worth 29	21	0	17	-1121	-25	2016	6077	•	•	•	•	241197	•

Selected Financial Ratios (Times to 1)

	C1	C2	C3	C4	C5	C6	C7	C8	C9	C10	C11	C12	C13
Current Ratio 30	1.7	•	2.0	1.4	0.7	1.8	2.3	•	•	•	•	3.0	•
Quick Ratio 31	1.3	•	1.8	1.2	0.4	1.2	1.7	•	•	•	•	2.0	•
Net Sales to Working Capital 32	12.1	•	14.4	10.4	•	3.7	4.2	•	•	•	•	4.9	•
Coverage Ratio 33	9.7	6.1	21.9	•	3.8	4.1	20.2	•	•	•	•	5.9	•
Total Asset Turnover 34	2.7	•	5.1	2.6	2.4	0.4	1.4	•	•	•	•	1.5	•
Inventory Turnover 35	13.4	•	66.7	9.5	10.5	3.7	47.2	•	•	•	•	3.8	•
Receivables Turnover 36	20.3	•	40.8	7.6	17.8	11.2	10.7	•	•	•	•	14.4	•
Total Liabilities to Net Worth 37	9.1	•	3.7	•	•	2.9	1.3	•	•	•	•	2.3	•
Current Assets to Working Capital 38	2.5	•	2.0	3.3	•	2.2	1.7	•	•	•	•	1.5	•
Current Liabilities to Working Capital 39	1.5	•	1.0	2.3	•	1.2	0.7	•	•	•	•	0.5	•
Working Capital to Net Sales 40	0.1	•	0.1	0.1	•	0.3	0.2	•	•	•	•	0.2	•
Inventory to Working Capital 41	0.4	•	0.1	0.5	•	0.6	0.1	•	•	•	•	0.3	•
Total Receipts to Cash Flow 42	3.8	2.7	3.5	91.3	3.7	7.6	5.3	•	•	•	•	3.4	•
Cost of Goods to Cash Flow 43	1.5	0.8	1.4	54.6	1.6	4.7	2.9	•	•	•	•	0.7	•
Cash Flow to Total Debt 44	0.8	•	1.8	0.0	0.6	0.1	0.5	•	•	•	•	0.6	•

Selected Financial Factors (in Percentages)

	C1	C2	C3	C4	C5	C6	C7	C8	C9	C10	C11	C12	C13
Debt Ratio 45	90.1	•	78.6	280.6	101.5	74.6	56.1	•	•	•	•	69.7	•
Return on Total Assets 46	14.5	•	34.7	•	6.0	1.5	9.2	•	•	•	•	12.7	•
Return on Equity Before Income Taxes 47	131.1	•	155.0	11.9	•	4.4	19.9	•	•	•	•	34.8	•
Return on Equity After Income Taxes 48	122.5	•	153.9	12.1	•	2.9	19.2	•	•	•	•	27.0	•
Profit Margin (Before Income Tax) 49	4.9	3.1	6.5	•	1.8	2.5	6.4	•	•	•	•	7.2	•
Profit Margin (After Income Tax) 50	4.6	2.9	6.5	•	1.8	1.6	6.1	•	•	•	•	5.6	•

Table II

Corporations with Net Income

SPECIALIZED DESIGN SERVICES

MONEY AMOUNTS AND SIZE OF ASSETS IN THOUSANDS OF DOLLARS

Item Description for Accounting Period 7/12 Through 6/13		Total	Zero Assets	Under 500	500 to 1,000	1,000 to 5,000	5,000 to 10,000	10,000 to 25,000	25,000 to 50,000	50,000 to 100,000	100,000 to 250,000	250,000 to 500,000	500,000 to 2,500,000	2,500,000 and over
Number of Enterprises	1	24669	3486	20465	194	465	18	27	11	0	0	0	3	0

Revenues ($ in Thousands)

Net Sales	2	16618469	287097	9440973	585329	1619779	171865	552823	478190	0	0	0	3482412	0
Interest	3	2435	1	894	93	17	142	65	58	0	0	0	1165	0
Rents	4	49	0	0	0	49	0	0	0	0	0	0	0	0
Royalties	5	112847	0	0	0	0	0	0	0	0	0	0	112847	0
Other Portfolio Income	6	3061	798	1446	509	2	299	7	0	0	0	0	0	0
Other Receipts	7	66117	2136	9274	296	780	13504	-1198	1288	0	0	0	40036	0
Total Receipts	8	16802978	290032	9452587	586227	1620627	185810	551697	479536	0	0	0	3636460	0
Average Total Receipts	9	681	83	462	3022	3485	10323	20433	43594	•	•	•	1212153	•

Operating Costs/Operating Income (%)

Cost of Operations	10	35.5	10.1	37.7	62.4	36.4	53.9	49.8	51.8	•	•	•	21.5	•
Salaries and Wages	11	13.9	2.2	7.4	16.8	9.5	7.9	11.8	16.8	•	•	•	34.2	•
Taxes Paid	12	2.2	2.7	2.1	1.3	2.1	2.5	2.3	1.9	•	•	•	2.8	•
Interest Paid	13	0.6	0.6	0.2	0.0	1.0	0.9	0.3	0.6	•	•	•	1.5	•
Depreciation	14	1.0	0.9	0.6	0.5	0.8	1.8	2.4	1.2	•	•	•	1.7	•
Amortization and Depletion	15	0.2	•	0.0	0.4	0.1	0.1	0.3	0.1	•	•	•	0.8	•
Pensions and Other Deferred Comp.	16	0.5	1.9	0.6	0.1	0.4	2.0	0.4	0.6	•	•	•	0.4	•
Employee Benefits	17	1.4	0.1	0.9	0.4	1.1	1.7	1.6	3.8	•	•	•	3.0	•
Advertising	18	1.0	1.0	0.8	2.4	0.6	0.0	0.5	0.4	•	•	•	1.8	•
Other Expenses	19	26.4	35.3	26.6	12.0	35.9	14.3	15.4	13.7	•	•	•	27.4	•
Officers' Compensation	20	8.6	22.2	11.8	2.0	5.6	10.0	6.8	2.9	•	•	•	2.1	•
Operating Margin	21	8.6	23.1	11.3	1.8	6.5	4.9	8.4	6.2	•	•	•	2.8	•
Operating Margin Before Officers' Comp.	22	17.2	45.3	23.1	3.7	12.1	14.9	15.2	9.1	•	•	•	4.9	•

	Selected Average Balance Sheet ($ in Thousands)												
Net Receivables 23	34	0	11	410	159	1700	2498	7896	•	•	•	92626	•
Inventories 24	14	0	2	182	183	42	205	6873	•	•	•	74168	•
Net Property, Plant and Equipment 25	62	0	13	80	317	1016	2756	3321	•	•	•	324769	•
Total Assets 26	245	0	92	741	1606	6152	12826	37666	•	•	•	796407	•
Notes and Loans Payable 27	68	0	29	19	832	1695	4047	5806	•	•	•	166872	•
All Other Liabilities 28	86	0	19	278	474	1035	1806	19941	•	•	•	388338	•
Net Worth 29	90	0	44	444	300	3422	6972	11919	•	•	•	241197	•

	Selected Financial Ratios (Times to 1)												
Current Ratio 30	2.2	•	3.1	2.2	0.8	3.9	3.3	1.3	•	•	•	3.0	•
Quick Ratio 31	1.6	•	2.7	2.0	0.5	3.8	2.5	0.6	•	•	•	2.0	•
Net Sales to Working Capital 32	8.8	•	10.4	8.7	•	3.3	3.9	6.9	•	•	•	4.9	•
Coverage Ratio 33	18.5	39.5	64.5	77.8	7.6	15.7	28.1	11.8	•	•	•	5.9	•
Total Asset Turnover 34	2.8	•	5.0	4.1	2.2	1.6	1.6	1.2	•	•	•	1.5	•
Inventory Turnover 35	16.6	•	85.3	10.4	6.9	124.0	49.9	3.3	•	•	•	3.4	•
Receivables Turnover 36	23.6	•	45.0	10.0	16.6	11.2	11.3	3.5	•	•	•	25.1	•
Total Liabilities to Net Worth 37	1.7	•	1.1	0.7	4.4	0.8	0.8	2.2	•	•	•	2.3	•
Current Assets to Working Capital 38	1.8	•	1.5	1.8	•	1.3	1.4	4.2	•	•	•	1.5	•
Current Liabilities to Working Capital 39	0.8	•	0.5	0.8	•	0.3	0.4	3.2	•	•	•	0.5	•
Working Capital to Net Sales 40	0.1	•	0.1	0.1	•	0.3	0.3	0.1	•	•	•	0.2	•
Inventory to Working Capital 41	0.3	•	0.1	0.0	•	0.0	0.1	1.9	•	•	•	0.3	•
Total Receipts to Cash Flow 42	3.2	1.8	3.1	10.2	2.4	4.5	5.0	5.9	•	•	•	3.4	•
Cost of Goods to Cash Flow 43	1.1	0.2	1.2	6.4	0.9	2.4	2.5	3.0	•	•	•	0.7	•
Cash Flow to Total Debt 44	1.4	•	3.1	1.0	1.1	0.8	0.7	0.3	•	•	•	0.6	•

	Selected Financial Factors (in Percentages)												
Debt Ratio 45	63.1	•	52.5	40.1	81.3	44.4	45.6	68.4	•	•	•	69.7	•
Return on Total Assets 46	28.3	•	58.2	8.0	16.4	21.4	13.6	8.2	•	•	•	12.7	•
Return on Equity Before Income Taxes 47	72.6	•	120.5	13.1	76.3	36.0	24.2	23.8	•	•	•	34.8	•
Return on Equity After Income Taxes 48	69.4	•	119.9	11.0	76.1	32.3	23.4	22.1	•	•	•	27.0	•
Profit Margin (Before Income Tax) 49	9.7	24.1	11.4	1.9	6.6	12.9	8.2	6.5	•	•	•	7.2	•
Profit Margin (After Income Tax) 50	9.3	23.6	11.4	1.6	6.6	11.6	8.0	6.1	•	•	•	5.6	•

Table I

Corporations with and without Net Income

COMPUTER SYSTEMS DESIGN AND RELATED SERVICES

MONEY AMOUNTS AND SIZE OF ASSETS IN THOUSANDS OF DOLLARS

Item Description for Accounting Period 7/12 Through 6/13	Total	Zero Assets	Under 500	500 to 1,000	1,000 to 5,000	5,000 to 10,000	10,000 to 25,000	25,000 to 50,000	50,000 to 100,000	100,000 to 250,000	250,000 to 500,000	500,000 to 2,500,000	2,500,000 and over
Number of Enterprises **1**	142799	35274	92625	5371	6749	1281	836	275	163	121	39	54	12

Revenues ($ in Thousands)													
Net Sales **2**	280819498	13954751	36805231	12354403	33850433	20331604	21631590	12357977	12702144	16381856	10570772	45539229	44339507
Interest **3**	875978	3234	4281	3168	15791	6524	16639	9536	9837	26626	17499	108572	654272
Rents **4**	136616	111	41383	63	269	1217	1065	52	5109	3410	4963	74283	4693
Royalties **5**	1320980	11043	1781	2559	113	9828	17663	54601	21608	2377	166695	404331	628383
Other Portfolio Income **6**	2847819	45185	150419	39023	117404	53710	75725	43941	121847	43890	104572	337716	1714384
Other Receipts **7**	3988952	236914	485133	200403	526902	148721	377003	152773	418711	187990	69635	675308	509457
Total Receipts **8**	289989843	14251238	37488228	12599619	34510912	20551604	22119685	12618880	13279256	16646149	10934136	47139439	47850696
Average Total Receipts **9**	2031	404	405	2346	5113	16043	26459	45887	81468	137571	280362	872953	3987558

Operating Costs/Operating Income (%)													
Cost of Operations **10**	31.1	22.2	34.3	23.6	30.6	39.3	44.3	36.7	49.7	33.5	39.0	39.1	5.6
Salaries and Wages **11**	25.6	34.7	19.0	25.3	28.9	25.1	26.4	28.5	21.6	28.5	26.8	17.2	33.4
Taxes Paid **12**	3.6	3.7	2.9	3.0	3.3	2.6	3.0	3.2	3.2	2.7	2.1	2.1	7.9
Interest Paid **13**	1.9	0.6	0.4	0.6	0.6	0.6	0.7	0.7	0.9	1.0	1.4	3.0	5.9
Depreciation **14**	1.4	0.5	0.6	0.6	0.7	0.8	1.4	1.4	1.8	1.8	1.4	1.7	2.8
Amortization and Depletion **15**	1.0	0.5	0.1	0.3	0.4	0.2	0.8	0.9	1.0	1.8	1.4	2.2	1.4
Pensions and Other Deferred Comp. **16**	0.8	0.6	0.6	0.7	0.7	0.5	0.6	0.5	0.4	0.2	0.3	0.5	1.9
Employee Benefits **17**	2.5	1.5	1.2	1.9	2.5	1.9	2.4	2.5	2.0	2.4	2.2	2.9	4.2
Advertising **18**	0.9	0.7	0.6	0.6	0.8	1.3	1.3	2.4	2.1	1.0	1.1	0.7	0.2
Other Expenses **19**	26.4	28.9	22.4	34.8	23.2	24.2	19.3	23.7	19.7	26.8	23.2	25.8	37.4
Officers' Compensation **20**	4.3	5.7	12.2	6.9	7.3	3.7	3.3	2.8	1.6	2.7	2.7	0.9	0.6
Operating Margin **21**	0.5	0.5	5.5	1.5	1.1	•	•	•	•	•	•	3.8	•
Operating Margin Before Officers' Comp. **22**	4.8	6.2	17.7	8.4	8.3	3.5	•	•	•	0.3	1.1	4.7	•

Selected Average Balance Sheet ($ in Thousands)

	1	2	3	4	5	6	7	8	9	10	11	12	13
Net Receivables 23	394	0	10	203	677	2435	4849	9661	16377	30199	68034	174617	1782676
Inventories 24	16	0	1	25	57	155	261	538	876	1751	4220	7269	18389
Net Property, Plant and Equipment 25	100	0	7	40	102	386	1251	2138	5080	7305	12454	68927	391321
Total Assets 26	1843	0	66	712	2056	6859	15740	33568	70317	158370	350073	1170005	8392024
Notes and Loans Payable 27	612	0	42	680	693	1815	2945	5919	14036	31193	57500	358656	3423609
All Other Liabilities 28	614	0	27	254	930	3438	8432	16817	28285	52182	129155	321668	2343527
Net Worth 29	617	0	-2	-222	434	1606	4362	10832	27996	74995	163418	489681	2624888

Selected Financial Ratios (Times to 1)

	1	2	3	4	5	6	7	8	9	10	11	12	13
Current Ratio 30	1.3	•	1.8	1.7	1.7	1.6	1.4	1.3	1.5	1.6	1.3	1.4	0.9
Quick Ratio 31	1.1	•	1.6	1.4	1.5	1.4	1.2	1.1	1.1	1.2	1.1	1.1	0.8
Net Sales to Working Capital 32	12.3	•	19.8	11.0	8.0	7.9	9.5	8.5	6.5	5.2	7.5	9.6	•
Coverage Ratio 33	3.2	5.6	18.9	6.5	5.9	2.5	•	•	1.7	0.7	2.4	3.5	2.3
Total Asset Turnover 34	1.1	•	6.0	3.2	2.4	2.3	1.6	1.3	1.1	0.9	0.8	0.7	0.4
Inventory Turnover 35	37.2	•	97.4	22.0	26.8	40.2	43.9	30.7	44.3	25.9	25.0	45.4	11.2
Receivables Turnover 36	4.7	•	38.9	12.0	7.5	7.7	5.2	4.5	4.6	4.4	3.8	5.2	1.7
Total Liabilities to Net Worth 37	2.0	•	•	•	3.7	3.3	2.6	2.1	1.5	1.1	1.1	1.4	2.2
Current Assets to Working Capital 38	4.7	•	2.3	2.5	2.4	2.7	3.9	3.9	3.1	2.7	4.1	3.7	•
Current Liabilities to Working Capital 39	3.7	•	1.3	1.5	1.4	1.7	2.9	2.9	2.1	1.7	3.1	2.7	•
Working Capital to Net Sales 40	0.1	•	0.1	0.1	0.1	0.1	0.1	0.1	0.2	0.2	0.1	0.1	•
Inventory to Working Capital 41	0.1	•	0.1	0.2	0.1	0.1	0.1	0.1	0.1	0.1	0.1	0.1	•
Total Receipts to Cash Flow 42	3.7	3.5	3.7	2.8	4.2	4.3	6.4	4.9	5.7	4.4	4.4	3.2	2.6
Cost of Goods to Cash Flow 43	1.1	0.8	1.3	0.7	1.3	1.7	2.8	1.8	2.8	1.5	1.7	1.3	0.1
Cash Flow to Total Debt 44	0.4	•	1.6	0.9	0.7	0.7	0.4	0.4	0.3	0.4	0.3	0.4	0.2

Selected Financial Factors (in Percentages)

	1	2	3	4	5	6	7	8	9	10	11	12	13
Debt Ratio 45	66.5	•	103.8	131.1	78.9	76.6	72.3	67.7	60.2	52.6	53.3	58.1	68.7
Return on Total Assets 46	6.4	•	47.1	13.2	8.8	3.4	•	•	1.8	0.6	2.7	7.6	6.0
Return on Equity Before Income Taxes 47	13.0	•	•	•	34.7	8.9	•	•	2.0	•	3.3	13.0	10.9
Return on Equity After Income Taxes 48	9.4	•	•	•	31.2	3.2	•	•	•	•	1.4	9.0	7.5
Profit Margin (Before Income Tax) 49	4.1	2.6	7.4	3.5	3.0	0.9	•	•	0.7	•	2.0	7.6	7.8
Profit Margin (After Income Tax) 50	3.0	1.8	7.3	3.3	2.7	0.3	•	•	•	•	0.8	5.2	5.3

Table II

Corporations with Net Income

COMPUTER SYSTEMS DESIGN AND RELATED SERVICES

MONEY AMOUNTS AND SIZE OF ASSETS IN THOUSANDS OF DOLLARS

Item Description for Accounting Period 7/12 Through 6/13	Total	Zero Assets	Under 500	500 to 1,000	1,000 to 5,000	5,000 to 10,000	10,000 to 25,000	25,000 to 50,000	50,000 to 100,000	100,000 to 250,000	250,000 to 500,000	500,000 to 2,500,000	2,500,000 and over
Number of Enterprises **1**	90329	19629	60848	4115	4017	860	479	147	84	69	30	42	9

Revenues ($ in Thousands)													
Net Sales **2**	230128274	12034894	31634290	10734010	26913886	16176672	15363371	8177363	8183425	12087763	9080546	39542081	40199973
Interest **3**	476598	595	1867	2738	7931	3704	6931	5232	6489	19191	13440	92962	315517
Rents **4**	93273	15	818	0	89	1217	155	52	4979	2715	4963	74283	3988
Royalties **5**	983194	9103	0	2540	0	9454	5157	28615	9731	1634	159965	386753	370243
Other Portfolio Income **6**	2716021	44026	146098	31930	78494	43371	51183	36155	113351	40258	104570	337577	1689010
Other Receipts **7**	3412124	258328	453861	171139	460597	126272	310380	116403	398476	123640	58276	541934	392815
Total Receipts **8**	237809484	12346961	32236934	10942357	27460997	16360690	15737177	8363820	8716451	12275201	9421760	40975590	42971546
Average Total Receipts **9**	2633	629	530	2659	6836	19024	32854	56897	103767	177901	314059	975609	4774616

Operating Costs/Operating Income (%)													
Cost of Operations **10**	30.4	20.9	35.1	23.4	32.3	43.9	47.6	42.8	49.5	34.9	43.6	35.3	2.8
Salaries and Wages **11**	24.1	33.2	18.1	24.5	25.2	23.0	20.5	22.5	19.8	26.1	22.2	17.8	34.2
Taxes Paid **12**	3.7	3.6	2.7	2.9	3.1	2.5	2.9	2.5	3.5	2.6	1.9	2.3	8.4
Interest Paid **13**	1.7	0.3	0.3	0.2	0.2	0.5	0.4	0.4	0.7	0.6	1.5	2.7	5.4
Depreciation **14**	1.3	0.3	0.5	0.6	0.5	0.6	1.0	0.7	1.6	1.2	1.2	1.7	2.9
Amortization and Depletion **15**	0.7	0.4	0.0	0.1	0.2	0.1	0.4	0.7	0.6	1.1	1.4	1.8	1.1
Pensions and Other Deferred Comp. **16**	0.8	0.3	0.7	0.2	0.8	0.6	0.6	0.6	0.5	0.2	0.4	0.6	1.7
Employee Benefits **17**	2.3	1.4	0.9	1.6	2.0	1.7	1.9	2.0	1.8	2.1	2.1	2.7	4.4
Advertising **18**	0.5	0.2	0.5	0.5	0.5	0.9	0.8	1.8	0.7	0.6	0.7	0.5	0.2
Other Expenses **19**	24.6	27.6	19.2	33.3	19.3	14.9	15.0	18.3	16.8	24.1	21.9	28.0	37.1
Officers' Compensation **20**	3.8	4.3	11.2	5.8	6.6	3.8	3.0	2.1	1.6	1.8	1.0	1.0	0.6
Operating Margin **21**	6.0	7.5	10.9	6.9	9.5	7.3	6.0	5.5	3.0	4.7	2.3	5.5	1.2
Operating Margin Before Officers' Comp. **22**	9.8	11.8	22.0	12.6	16.0	11.1	9.0	7.6	4.5	6.5	3.3	6.5	1.8

Selected Average Balance Sheet ($ in Thousands)

Net Receivables 23	437	0	11	220	731	3047	5975	10375	19844	36861	72698	204528	1445647
Inventories 24	19	0	2	29	76	151	220	630	1043	2318	4183	6723	18785
Net Property, Plant and Equipment 25	123	0	8	41	88	381	1059	1742	5794	5127	11695	81351	493390
Total Assets 26	2141	0	78	704	2070	6754	15394	34049	70839	166147	348147	1227244	8867788
Notes and Loans Payable 27	625	0	29	243	281	1247	2305	5357	12903	29669	61271	309796	3519394
All Other Liabilities 28	733	0	20	193	795	3379	7989	15464	28726	56437	129975	365574	2937009
Net Worth 29	783	0	30	269	994	2129	5100	13228	29209	80041	156901	551873	2411384

Selected Financial Ratios (Times to 1)

Current Ratio 30	1.3	•	2.9	2.2	2.3	1.7	1.5	1.5	1.5	1.7	1.2	1.5	0.9
Quick Ratio 31	1.1	•	2.7	1.8	2.0	1.4	1.3	1.3	1.1	1.3	1.0	1.2	0.7
Net Sales to Working Capital 32	12.3	•	13.3	9.0	6.9	8.3	8.7	7.8	8.0	5.5	15.1	7.9	•
Coverage Ratio 33	6.7	38.2	50.5	39.7	61.2	19.0	22.1	19.3	15.1	12.6	5.3	4.5	2.7
Total Asset Turnover 34	1.2	•	6.6	3.7	3.2	2.8	2.1	1.6	1.4	1.1	0.9	0.8	0.5
Inventory Turnover 35	41.5	•	101.6	20.9	28.4	54.9	69.5	37.8	46.2	26.3	31.5	49.5	6.6
Receivables Turnover 36	5.5	•	49.1	13.6	8.9	7.5	5.4	4.9	4.6	5.1	4.1	5.3	2.4
Total Liabilities to Net Worth 37	1.7	•	1.6	1.6	1.1	2.2	2.0	1.6	1.4	1.1	1.2	1.2	2.7
Current Assets to Working Capital 38	4.0	•	1.5	1.9	1.8	2.5	3.0	2.8	3.2	2.5	6.6	3.0	•
Current Liabilities to Working Capital 39	3.0	•	0.5	0.9	0.8	1.5	2.0	1.8	2.2	1.5	5.6	2.0	•
Working Capital to Net Sales 40	0.1	•	0.1	0.1	0.1	0.1	0.1	0.1	0.1	0.2	0.1	0.1	•
Inventory to Working Capital 41	0.1	•	0.0	0.1	0.1	0.1	0.0	0.1	0.1	0.1	0.2	0.1	•
Total Receipts to Cash Flow 42	3.2	2.9	3.4	2.5	3.5	4.6	4.7	4.1	4.3	3.6	3.9	2.9	2.5
Cost of Goods to Cash Flow 43	1.0	0.6	1.2	0.6	1.1	2.0	2.2	1.8	2.1	1.2	1.7	1.0	0.1
Cash Flow to Total Debt 44	0.6	•	3.2	2.4	1.8	0.9	0.7	0.7	0.5	0.6	0.4	0.5	0.3

Selected Financial Factors (in Percentages)

Debt Ratio 45	63.4	•	62.1	61.8	52.0	68.5	66.9	61.1	58.8	51.8	54.9	55.0	72.8
Return on Total Assets 46	13.5	•	86.6	33.6	37.8	24.9	18.3	13.6	14.3	7.9	6.7	9.3	7.4
Return on Equity Before Income Taxes 47	31.5	•	223.7	85.8	77.4	74.9	52.8	33.2	32.4	15.1	12.0	16.2	17.1
Return on Equity After Income Taxes 48	27.0	•	221.2	84.5	74.9	68.5	47.5	31.1	27.9	11.7	9.4	11.6	12.0
Profit Margin (Before Income Tax) 49	9.7	10.1	12.8	8.8	11.5	8.5	8.4	7.9	9.7	6.9	6.2	9.5	9.2
Profit Margin (After Income Tax) 50	8.3	9.1	12.6	8.7	11.1	7.7	7.6	7.4	8.4	5.3	4.9	6.8	6.5

Table I

Corporations with and without Net Income

MANAGEMENT, SCIENTIFIC, AND TECHNICAL CONSULTING SERVICES

MONEY AMOUNTS AND SIZE OF ASSETS IN THOUSANDS OF DOLLARS

Item Description for Accounting Period 7/12 Through 6/13		Total	Zero Assets	Under 500	500 to 1,000	1,000 to 5,000	5,000 to 10,000	10,000 to 25,000	25,000 to 50,000	50,000 to 100,000	100,000 to 250,000	250,000 to 500,000	500,000 to 2,500,000	2,500,000 and over
Number of Enterprises	1	225730	57054	154590	6274	5958	857	515	217	111	83	33	31	6

Revenues ($ in Thousands)														
Net Sales	2	212570808	6015527	50686374	15053994	25708775	10676972	11238234	8868082	6822114	10863865	8249954	31288630	27098287
Interest	3	370795	3519	11421	4780	17041	9529	29191	7990	17734	26420	22475	126963	93732
Rents	4	61345	0	2588	0	6407	1996	1633	1398	8181	12831	3987	3743	18581
Royalties	5	160014	0	3216	0	30	123	5381	172	394	58947	34038	28749	28965
Other Portfolio Income	6	1679333	492191	11646	25610	63691	26989	62170	82772	7027	23085	564179	64087	255885
Other Receipts	7	4225531	287113	742583	77363	822598	141514	403538	243662	349865	549388	157099	137310	313497
Total Receipts	8	219067826	6798350	51457828	15161747	26618542	10857123	11740147	9204076	7205315	11534536	9031732	31649482	27808947
Average Total Receipts	9	970	119	333	2417	4468	12669	22796	42415	64913	138970	273689	1020951	4634824

Operating Costs/Operating Income (%)														
Cost of Operations	10	30.8	6.0	17.6	28.7	23.8	35.6	43.2	31.2	25.7	37.2	33.2	48.0	39.7
Salaries and Wages	11	23.8	13.5	17.6	19.9	28.6	26.1	24.3	26.2	26.6	25.3	36.5	21.8	30.5
Taxes Paid	12	3.0	3.1	2.5	3.5	3.1	3.2	3.1	2.7	2.3	2.5	3.2	3.9	2.7
Interest Paid	13	0.8	0.7	0.4	0.3	0.5	0.4	0.8	1.0	1.8	1.6	1.3	1.6	0.8
Depreciation	14	0.9	0.8	0.8	0.5	0.5	0.6	0.9	1.6	1.7	1.9	2.1	0.9	1.0
Amortization and Depletion	15	0.5	0.7	0.1	0.0	0.4	0.2	0.4	1.0	0.8	1.2	1.4	1.0	0.3
Pensions and Other Deferred Comp.	16	1.3	0.9	1.7	1.3	0.9	0.9	1.0	0.7	0.9	1.2	0.9	0.8	2.5
Employee Benefits	17	2.2	4.0	1.8	1.0	1.4	2.4	2.3	2.7	2.3	2.9	1.9	4.1	1.4
Advertising	18	0.5	0.6	0.5	0.5	0.6	0.5	0.4	1.8	0.8	0.6	0.2	0.3	0.1
Other Expenses	19	23.8	42.3	30.8	28.2	24.8	18.9	17.0	17.4	34.8	24.0	20.5	15.7	17.5
Officers' Compensation	20	7.3	18.0	16.2	7.1	10.3	7.1	4.6	4.1	3.1	2.2	1.7	0.6	0.5
Operating Margin	21	5.0	9.5	9.9	9.1	5.2	4.2	1.9	9.5	•	•	•	1.4	3.0
Operating Margin Before Officers' Comp.	22	12.4	27.4	26.1	16.2	15.4	11.3	6.5	13.6	2.4	1.7	•	2.0	3.5

Selected Average Balance Sheet ($ in Thousands)

	C1	C2	C3	C4	C5	C6	C7	C8	C9	C10	C11	C12	C13
Net Receivables 23	117	0	5	91	490	1887	3783	7224	15408	31668	54471	181959	892721
Inventories 24	12	0	1	7	43	50	400	321	1258	1815	5909	38189	29948
Net Property, Plant and Equipment 25	52	0	9	137	281	741	1447	3551	6617	16183	28329	50804	165916
Total Assets 26	611	0	58	690	2155	7268	15385	33874	71083	157003	341838	1028327	4375541
Notes and Loans Payable 27	175	0	46	242	939	2482	3672	8890	24490	40641	53992	258036	582554
All Other Liabilities 28	244	0	15	163	453	3628	5727	9972	21061	60022	114420	385924	2956924
Net Worth 29	192	0	-3	284	763	1157	5986	15012	25533	56340	173426	384367	836063

Selected Financial Ratios (Times to 1)

	C1	C2	C3	C4	C5	C6	C7	C8	C9	C10	C11	C12	C13
Current Ratio 30	1.5	•	2.3	1.4	2.1	1.9	1.5	1.8	1.5	1.3	1.7	1.4	1.0
Quick Ratio 31	1.1	•	2.0	1.2	1.7	1.4	1.2	1.4	1.1	1.0	1.0	0.9	0.8
Net Sales to Working Capital 32	10.5	•	15.4	21.9	6.5	6.1	7.7	5.6	5.5	8.3	4.2	9.5	•
Coverage Ratio 33	11.1	37.9	29.3	38.1	18.5	17.0	8.5	14.6	3.8	4.6	6.1	2.7	8.5
Total Asset Turnover 34	1.5	•	5.6	3.5	2.0	1.7	1.4	1.2	0.9	0.8	0.7	1.0	1.0
Inventory Turnover 35	24.6	•	46.4	101.2	24.1	89.0	23.5	39.7	12.6	26.8	14.0	12.7	59.9
Receivables Turnover 36	7.8	•	60.7	27.0	8.1	6.8	6.0	5.3	4.8	4.1	4.7	5.5	4.5
Total Liabilities to Net Worth 37	2.2	•	•	1.4	1.8	5.3	1.6	1.3	1.8	1.8	1.0	1.7	4.2
Current Assets to Working Capital 38	3.1	•	1.8	3.4	1.9	2.2	2.9	2.3	3.1	4.5	2.5	3.5	•
Current Liabilities to Working Capital 39	2.1	•	0.8	2.4	0.9	1.2	1.9	1.3	2.1	3.5	1.5	2.5	•
Working Capital to Net Sales 40	0.1	•	0.1	0.0	0.2	0.2	0.1	0.2	0.2	0.1	0.2	0.1	•
Inventory to Working Capital 41	0.1	•	0.1	0.0	0.1	0.0	0.1	0.0	0.2	0.1	0.2	0.3	•
Total Receipts to Cash Flow 42	3.5	1.7	2.5	3.0	3.3	4.7	4.9	3.5	2.8	3.8	5.7	6.3	4.8
Cost of Goods to Cash Flow 43	1.1	0.1	0.4	0.9	0.8	1.7	2.1	1.1	0.7	1.4	1.9	3.0	1.9
Cash Flow to Total Debt 44	0.6	•	2.1	2.0	0.9	0.4	0.5	0.6	0.5	0.3	0.3	0.2	0.3

Selected Financial Factors (in Percentages)

	C1	C2	C3	C4	C5	C6	C7	C8	C9	C10	C11	C12	C13
Debt Ratio 45	68.6	•	104.8	58.8	64.6	84.1	61.1	55.7	64.1	64.1	49.3	62.6	80.9
Return on Total Assets 46	14.0	•	66.6	34.9	18.4	10.7	10.2	17.3	5.9	6.2	5.8	4.2	6.9
Return on Equity Before Income Taxes 47	40.6	•	•	82.5	49.1	63.3	23.1	36.3	12.0	13.5	9.6	7.1	32.0
Return on Equity After Income Taxes 48	36.6	•	•	81.1	47.7	58.5	21.5	34.7	9.8	11.5	6.6	4.8	20.9
Profit Margin (Before Income Tax) 49	8.3	27.2	11.4	9.8	8.7	5.9	6.3	13.3	5.0	5.8	6.7	2.7	5.9
Profit Margin (After Income Tax) 50	7.5	22.4	11.3	9.6	8.4	5.4	5.9	12.7	4.1	4.9	4.6	1.8	3.9

Table II

Corporations with Net Income

MANAGEMENT, SCIENTIFIC, AND TECHNICAL CONSULTING SERVICES

MONEY AMOUNTS AND SIZE OF ASSETS IN THOUSANDS OF DOLLARS

Item Description for Accounting Period 7/12 Through 6/13	Total	Zero Assets	Under 500	500 to 1,000	1,000 to 5,000	5,000 to 10,000	10,000 to 25,000	25,000 to 50,000	50,000 to 100,000	100,000 to 250,000	250,000 to 500,000	500,000 to 2,500,000	2,500,000 and over
Number of Enterprises 1	147231	30403	107104	4396	4136	554	332	128	70	•	20	25	•

Revenues ($ in Thousands)

	Total	Zero Assets	Under 500	500 to 1,000	1,000 to 5,000	5,000 to 10,000	10,000 to 25,000	25,000 to 50,000	50,000 to 100,000	100,000 to 250,000	250,000 to 500,000	500,000 to 2,500,000	2,500,000 and over
Net Sales 2	184546537	5131082	43204077	13886555	20822854	9260815	9263146	6752782	5154998	•	6534145	29351776	•
Interest 3	257530	2199	6739	3563	6707	8914	19363	3489	10178	•	6132	125111	•
Rents 4	48979	0	12	0	5017	1269	1357	265	2472	•	3987	3249	•
Royalties 5	131579	0	3216	0	0	123	5381	81	0	•	26832	27704	•
Other Portfolio Income 6	1486562	485636	8961	24566	40561	26988	24155	80152	3421	•	540643	44287	•
Other Receipts 7	3642091	279695	547141	89402	783429	129713	290426	193013	293257	•	100228	158183	•
Total Receipts 8	190113278	5898612	43770146	14004086	21658568	9427822	9603828	7029782	5464326	•	7211967	29710310	•
Average Total Receipts 9	1291	194	409	3186	5237	17018	28927	54920	78062	•	360598	1188412	•

Operating Costs/Operating Income (%)

	Total	Zero Assets	Under 500	500 to 1,000	1,000 to 5,000	5,000 to 10,000	10,000 to 25,000	25,000 to 50,000	50,000 to 100,000	100,000 to 250,000	250,000 to 500,000	500,000 to 2,500,000	2,500,000 and over
Cost of Operations 10	31.3	4.8	17.4	28.1	22.7	36.0	42.2	31.7	25.1	•	39.2	49.4	•
Salaries and Wages 11	23.0	13.0	16.4	19.8	28.9	26.4	23.2	21.6	24.9	•	33.7	21.1	•
Taxes Paid 12	2.9	2.3	2.3	3.6	3.1	3.3	2.9	2.5	2.2	•	2.8	3.9	•
Interest Paid 13	0.6	0.8	0.2	0.2	0.4	0.2	0.4	0.7	1.0	•	0.9	1.2	•
Depreciation 14	0.8	0.7	0.6	0.4	0.5	0.5	0.7	1.6	1.3	•	1.1	0.8	•
Amortization and Depletion 15	0.3	0.6	0.1	0.0	0.2	0.0	0.3	0.6	0.5	•	0.9	0.7	•
Pensions and Other Deferred Comp. 16	1.3	0.9	1.5	1.3	0.9	0.9	1.0	0.7	0.8	•	0.9	0.8	•
Employee Benefits 17	2.2	4.5	1.7	0.9	1.3	2.2	2.2	2.6	2.1	•	1.7	4.2	•
Advertising 18	0.4	0.5	0.5	0.5	0.4	0.5	0.4	1.9	0.7	•	0.2	0.3	•
Other Expenses 19	21.7	37.9	28.0	27.1	23.5	13.8	14.1	14.9	33.9	•	17.8	15.0	•
Officers' Compensation 20	6.7	13.8	15.9	7.0	8.4	7.7	4.7	3.2	3.4	•	1.3	0.5	•
Operating Margin 21	8.6	20.2	15.4	11.0	9.6	8.5	7.9	18.0	4.1	•	•	2.1	•
Operating Margin Before Officers' Comp. 22	15.4	34.1	31.4	18.1	18.1	16.2	12.7	21.2	7.5	•	0.7	2.5	•

Selected Average Balance Sheet ($ in Thousands)

Net Receivables 23	147	0	4	104	597	2296	4648	8116	17791	•	63305	192798	•
Inventories 24	15	0	1	8	45	44	339	308	711	•	12641	47020	•
Net Property, Plant and Equipment 25	53	0	9	95	227	600	1466	3511	7128	•	25680	46309	•
Total Assets 26	678	0	60	688	2246	7262	15387	33876	69585	•	317170	1021575	•
Notes and Loans Payable 27	153	0	20	236	612	1184	3078	8822	20200	•	45359	236177	•
All Other Liabilities 28	239	0	10	149	458	2408	5206	9195	22876	•	108648	416743	•
Net Worth 29	285	0	29	303	1176	3670	7103	15859	26509	•	163162	368655	•

Selected Financial Ratios (Times to 1)

Current Ratio 30	1.7	•	2.9	1.4	2.7	2.0	1.9	2.1	1.8	•	1.7	1.5	•
Quick Ratio 31	1.4	•	2.6	1.2	2.2	1.6	1.5	1.7	1.4	•	1.1	0.9	•
Net Sales to Working Capital 32	8.9	•	15.6	27.5	5.7	6.3	6.4	5.9	4.5	•	4.9	9.6	•
Coverage Ratio 33	19.9	52.3	72.8	59.0	35.2	47.6	29.2	32.3	10.7	•	11.8	3.9	•
Total Asset Turnover 34	1.8	•	6.7	4.6	2.2	2.3	1.8	1.6	1.1	•	1.0	1.1	•
Inventory Turnover 35	26.2	•	67.4	105.9	25.6	138.4	34.7	54.3	26.0	•	10.1	12.3	•
Receivables Turnover 36	8.2	•	87.5	32.0	8.2	7.7	6.6	6.2	5.1	•	•	5.7	•
Total Liabilities to Net Worth 37	1.4	•	1.0	1.3	0.9	1.0	1.2	1.1	1.6	•	0.9	1.8	•
Current Assets to Working Capital 38	2.4	•	1.5	3.7	1.6	2.0	2.2	2.0	2.2	•	2.4	3.2	•
Current Liabilities to Working Capital 39	1.4	•	0.5	2.7	0.6	1.0	1.2	1.0	1.2	•	1.4	2.2	•
Working Capital to Net Sales 40	0.1	•	0.1	0.0	0.2	0.2	0.2	0.2	0.2	•	0.2	0.1	•
Inventory to Working Capital 41	0.1	•	0.1	0.0	0.1	0.0	0.1	0.0	0.1	•	0.2	0.4	•
Total Receipts to Cash Flow 42	3.3	1.5	2.4	2.9	2.9	4.8	4.3	2.9	2.5	•	5.9	6.2	•
Cost of Goods to Cash Flow 43	1.0	0.1	0.4	0.8	0.7	1.7	1.8	0.9	0.6	•	2.3	3.1	•
Cash Flow to Total Debt 44	1.0	•	5.6	2.8	1.6	1.0	0.8	1.0	0.7	•	0.4	0.3	•

Selected Financial Factors (in Percentages)

Debt Ratio 45	57.9	•	51.2	56.0	47.6	49.5	53.8	53.2	61.9	•	48.6	63.9	•
Return on Total Assets 46	23.2	•	114.3	55.4	31.5	24.2	21.8	35.5	11.8	•	11.2	5.3	•
Return on Equity Before Income Taxes 47	52.3	•	231.0	123.9	58.4	47.0	45.5	73.5	28.2	•	19.9	10.9	•
Return on Equity After Income Taxes 48	48.2	•	229.6	122.0	57.1	44.6	43.4	70.9	24.7	•	14.5	8.0	•
Profit Margin (Before Income Tax) 49	11.9	40.8	16.8	11.9	13.6	10.3	11.6	22.1	10.1	•	9.9	3.4	•
Profit Margin (After Income Tax) 50	11.0	35.2	16.7	11.7	13.3	9.8	11.0	21.3	8.9	•	7.2	2.5	•

Table I

Corporations with and without Net Income

SCIENTIFIC RESEARCH AND DEVELOPMENT SERVICES

MONEY AMOUNTS AND SIZE OF ASSETS IN THOUSANDS OF DOLLARS

Item Description for Accounting Period 7/12 Through 6/13	Total	Zero Assets	Under 500	500 to 1,000	1,000 to 5,000	5,000 to 10,000	10,000 to 25,000	25,000 to 50,000	50,000 to 100,000	100,000 to 250,000	250,000 to 500,000	500,000 to 2,500,000	2,500,000 and over
Number of Enterprises **1**	16841	3282	9360	1111	1774	500	426	135	118	78	25	27	5

Revenues ($ in Thousands)

	Total	Zero Assets	Under 500	500 to 1,000	1,000 to 5,000	5,000 to 10,000	10,000 to 25,000	25,000 to 50,000	50,000 to 100,000	100,000 to 250,000	250,000 to 500,000	500,000 to 2,500,000	2,500,000 and over
Net Sales **2**	51584427	636020	4170457	2065046	3628974	2385275	3181706	2741593	2969443	4289358	2633804	15664243	7218509
Interest **3**	224036	7899	388	893	8363	3395	33963	6117	22673	28115	22312	72740	17178
Rents **4**	25865	0	6493	145	3075	213	3454	125	1900	3535	2099	4231	595
Royalties **5**	2582588	3837	0	0	3450	46228	11491	1938	134504	288893	95825	543736	1452685
Other Portfolio Income **6**	1085695	73417	16837	12	1440	2531	111559	18237	70367	193283	142370	396946	58696
Other Receipts **7**	4683217	22918	143631	129386	152467	280631	348378	272980	293079	357495	20779	1748024	913448
Total Receipts **8**	60185828	744091	4337806	2195482	3797769	2718273	3690551	3040990	3491966	5160679	2917189	18429920	9661111
Average Total Receipts **9**	3574	227	463	1976	2141	5437	8663	22526	29593	66163	116688	682590	1932222

Operating Costs/Operating Income (%)

	Total	Zero Assets	Under 500	500 to 1,000	1,000 to 5,000	5,000 to 10,000	10,000 to 25,000	25,000 to 50,000	50,000 to 100,000	100,000 to 250,000	250,000 to 500,000	500,000 to 2,500,000	2,500,000 and over
Cost of Operations **10**	29.7	30.1	6.9	10.8	34.7	45.9	33.1	30.5	23.5	27.9	16.2	27.4	52.4
Salaries and Wages **11**	33.4	82.8	27.5	32.1	35.5	33.5	43.5	37.9	43.1	38.3	51.3	24.1	32.1
Taxes Paid **12**	3.3	5.4	3.4	3.6	4.5	5.0	5.0	4.2	4.6	3.9	3.9	2.0	2.3
Interest Paid **13**	3.3	6.3	0.6	1.6	2.4	3.5	3.9	1.6	3.6	2.8	4.2	4.1	4.2
Depreciation **14**	3.2	2.7	1.0	1.4	4.0	3.4	6.0	4.8	4.8	3.5	4.1	2.6	3.2
Amortization and Depletion **15**	2.5	6.4	0.5	0.3	2.4	3.3	3.7	1.9	5.5	6.2	5.6	1.4	1.1
Pensions and Other Deferred Comp. **16**	0.8	0.8	2.9	0.4	1.0	0.9	0.7	1.6	0.5	0.9	0.7	0.5	0.4
Employee Benefits **17**	3.6	5.7	2.6	4.6	4.7	3.9	5.7	3.6	4.9	3.6	4.6	3.2	2.3
Advertising **18**	2.0	3.1	3.2	0.9	1.0	1.0	1.4	1.0	2.8	3.7	1.6	1.9	1.8
Other Expenses **19**	51.4	253.0	49.8	48.2	52.8	61.8	77.1	57.9	76.6	61.8	60.5	43.2	15.7
Officers' Compensation **20**	5.3	23.2	11.4	6.2	12.1	9.0	8.6	6.3	7.1	5.9	5.6	1.4	0.7
Operating Margin **21**	•	•	•	•	•	•	•	•	•	•	•	•	•
Operating Margin Before Officers' Comp. **22**	•	•	1.6	•	•	•	•	•	•	•	•	•	•

Selected Average Balance Sheet ($ in Thousands)

Net Receivables 23	722	0	21	246	309	756	1573	4350	5838	12790	33203	104917	830770
Inventories 24	208	0	3	21	82	460	553	1425	2068	3592	10409	39138	162598
Net Property, Plant and Equipment 25	579	0	24	73	303	742	1979	4463	6457	12974	31868	108279	317576
Total Assets 26	6184	0	115	715	2144	6871	15769	33528	70915	154710	349452	997527	5538774
Notes and Loans Payable 27	1790	0	137	592	1029	2054	5128	5993	12182	17932	83406	362814	1529059
All Other Liabilities 28	2027	0	96	247	918	2577	5669	12535	23533	40762	102084	270123	2028691
Net Worth 29	2367	0	-118	-124	197	2239	4973	15001	35200	96016	163963	364590	1981024

Selected Financial Ratios (Times to 1)

Current Ratio 30	1.9	•	0.6	2.6	1.6	2.0	2.1	2.2	2.5	3.3	3.2	1.4	1.5
Quick Ratio 31	1.4	•	0.5	2.5	1.3	1.6	1.7	1.8	1.8	2.2	2.2	0.9	1.1
Net Sales to Working Capital 32	2.2	•	•	5.4	3.9	2.0	1.4	1.6	0.9	0.8	0.8	5.5	3.0
Coverage Ratio 33	•	•	•	•	•	•	•	•	•	•	•	2.7	5.8
Total Asset Turnover 34	0.5	•	3.9	2.6	1.0	0.7	0.5	0.6	0.4	0.4	0.3	0.6	0.3
Inventory Turnover 35	4.4	•	11.5	9.4	8.6	4.8	4.5	4.3	2.9	4.3	1.6	4.1	4.7
Receivables Turnover 36	4.4	•	19.9	11.1	6.5	6.3	5.0	5.6	4.4	4.0	2.8	4.1	2.6
Total Liabilities to Net Worth 37	1.6	•	•	•	9.9	2.1	2.2	1.2	1.0	0.6	1.1	1.7	1.8
Current Assets to Working Capital 38	2.1	•	•	1.6	2.7	2.0	1.9	1.8	1.7	1.4	1.4	3.4	3.2
Current Liabilities to Working Capital 39	1.1	•	•	0.6	1.7	1.0	0.9	0.8	0.7	0.4	0.4	2.4	2.2
Working Capital to Net Sales 40	0.4	•	•	0.2	0.3	0.5	0.7	0.6	1.1	1.2	1.2	0.2	0.3
Inventory to Working Capital 41	0.2	•	•	0.0	0.2	0.2	0.1	0.1	0.1	0.1	0.1	0.4	0.4
Total Receipts to Cash Flow 42	4.3	•	3.0	2.6	•	•	•	9.6	12.9	6.8	17.3	2.2	3.3
Cost of Goods to Cash Flow 43	1.3	•	0.2	0.3	•	•	•	2.9	3.0	1.9	2.8	0.6	1.7
Cash Flow to Total Debt 44	0.2	•	0.6	0.8	•	•	•	0.1	0.1	0.1	0.0	0.4	0.1

Selected Financial Factors (in Percentages)

Debt Ratio 45	61.7	•	202.7	117.4	90.8	67.4	68.5	55.3	50.4	37.9	53.1	63.5	64.2
Return on Total Assets 46	•	•	•	•	•	•	•	•	•	•	•	6.6	6.2
Return on Equity Before Income Taxes 47	•	•	21.9	54.8	•	•	•	•	•	•	•	11.4	14.4
Return on Equity After Income Taxes 48	•	•	22.1	55.6	•	•	•	•	•	•	•	6.3	11.0
Profit Margin (Before Income Tax) 49	•	•	•	•	•	•	•	•	•	•	•	7.2	19.8
Profit Margin (After Income Tax) 50	•	•	•	•	•	•	•	•	•	•	•	4.0	15.1

Table II

Corporations with Net Income

SCIENTIFIC RESEARCH AND DEVELOPMENT SERVICES

MONEY AMOUNTS AND SIZE OF ASSETS IN THOUSANDS OF DOLLARS

Item Description for Accounting Period 7/12 Through 6/13	Total	Zero Assets	Under 500	500 to 1,000	1,000 to 5,000	5,000 to 10,000	10,000 to 25,000	25,000 to 50,000	50,000 to 100,000	100,000 to 250,000	250,000 to 500,000	500,000 to 2,500,000	2,500,000 and over
Number of Enterprises 1	6612	869	4100	800	457	154	107	43	28	26	6	17	5
Revenues ($ in Thousands)													
Net Sales 2	38133156	160080	2606162	1931240	2271467	1696221	2107994	2028969	1594629	2917961	1160191	12439732	7218509
Interest 3	90381	127	140	615	731	398	1985	1580	3855	5430	8113	50229	17178
Rents 4	12821	0	0	145	3050	0	2143	0	0	2656	0	4231	595
Royalties 5	2265961	0	0	0	109	43924	4975	989	51060	108388	76027	527802	1452685
Other Portfolio Income 6	933571	65787	16573	10	369	815	98289	12167	32229	118434	135387	394813	58696
Other Receipts 7	3105805	26656	8087	128411	25632	25556	135124	131544	197640	197981	6841	1308891	913448
Total Receipts 8	44541695	252650	2630962	2060421	2301358	1766914	2350510	2175249	1879413	3350850	1386559	14725698	9661111
Average Total Receipts 9	6736	291	642	2576	5036	11473	21967	50587	67122	128879	231093	866218	1932222
Operating Costs/Operating Income (%)													
Cost of Operations 10	31.0	1.1	7.7	9.3	39.5	51.3	31.4	27.7	20.2	31.9	11.5	26.5	52.4
Salaries and Wages 11	24.7	6.8	18.1	28.4	16.8	15.3	22.8	30.1	26.4	23.3	46.2	21.6	32.1
Taxes Paid 12	2.6	1.1	3.5	3.3	2.7	3.3	3.0	3.2	2.9	2.8	4.7	1.8	2.3
Interest Paid 13	2.2	0.3	0.2	1.2	0.4	0.8	0.6	0.2	1.5	0.7	4.0	3.0	4.2
Depreciation 14	2.2	1.1	0.8	0.9	1.7	0.8	3.0	2.1	2.9	1.7	2.2	2.2	3.2
Amortization and Depletion 15	0.9	0.0	0.1	0.0	0.1	0.9	0.3	0.3	0.6	1.9	3.3	1.0	1.1
Pensions and Other Deferred Comp. 16	0.9	0.3	3.7	0.4	0.8	1.1	0.8	2.1	0.6	1.2	1.2	0.6	0.4
Employee Benefits 17	2.8	0.4	1.5	4.3	2.1	2.3	3.8	2.3	3.5	2.3	4.0	3.1	2.3
Advertising 18	1.6	0.3	0.3	0.9	0.9	0.3	0.5	0.2	0.7	4.2	0.3	2.1	1.8
Other Expenses 19	29.9	41.7	38.0	39.0	16.0	8.5	24.6	24.4	40.1	26.3	31.6	41.7	15.7
Officers' Compensation 20	2.9	20.3	11.3	5.1	7.7	3.2	3.4	3.5	2.0	2.2	2.2	1.1	0.7
Operating Margin 21	•	26.6	15.0	7.1	11.3	12.2	5.6	4.0	•	1.6	•	•	•
Operating Margin Before Officers' Comp. 22	1.3	46.9	26.3	12.2	19.0	15.4	9.0	7.5	0.6	3.7	•	•	•

Selected Average Balance Sheet ($ in Thousands)

Net Receivables 23	1393	0	34	335	775	1394	3423	8641	9962	27156	53194	119919	830770
Inventories 24	330	0	6	0	107	1004	705	1879	3585	5453	7596	60989	191044
Net Property, Plant and Equipment 25	847	0	24	65	333	1080	2899	5287	8654	20030	25212	123106	317576
Total Assets 26	9080	0	141	736	2291	6776	16393	32710	66611	160348	407467	1026164	5538774
Notes and Loans Payable 27	2406	0	25	366	301	788	1756	3950	8504	17025	104912	349516	1529059
All Other Liabilities 28	2968	0	23	158	512	1546	6187	11228	25168	41301	123188	301601	2028691
Net Worth 29	3705	0	93	212	1478	4442	8451	17532	32939	102022	179367	375047	1981024

Selected Financial Ratios (Times to 1)

Current Ratio 30	1.8	•	3.9	3.8	3.5	2.8	2.4	2.0	2.6	2.6	2.9	1.5	1.5
Quick Ratio 31	1.3	•	3.6	3.8	3.1	2.0	1.9	1.7	2.0	1.9	2.3	0.9	1.1
Net Sales to Working Capital 32	3.8	•	8.2	5.5	4.5	3.7	3.4	4.7	2.2	2.2	1.6	6.0	3.0
Coverage Ratio 33	8.3	303.5	97.6	12.3	32.4	21.4	28.9	49.8	12.7	23.6	3.1	5.9	5.8
Total Asset Turnover 34	0.6	•	4.5	3.3	2.2	1.6	1.2	1.4	0.9	0.7	0.5	0.7	0.3
Inventory Turnover 35	5.4	•	8.6	1059.0	18.4	5.6	8.8	6.9	3.2	6.6	2.9	3.2	4.0
Receivables Turnover 36	4.8	•	16.7	13.4	6.6	7.9	6.3	6.2	5.9	5.0	2.9	4.1	3.5
Total Liabilities to Net Worth 37	1.5	•	0.5	2.5	0.5	0.5	0.9	0.9	1.0	0.6	1.3	1.7	1.8
Current Assets to Working Capital 38	2.3	•	1.3	1.4	1.4	1.6	1.7	2.0	1.6	1.6	1.5	3.1	3.2
Current Liabilities to Working Capital 39	1.3	•	0.3	0.4	0.4	0.6	0.7	1.0	0.6	0.6	0.5	2.1	2.2
Working Capital to Net Sales 40	0.3	•	0.1	0.2	0.2	0.3	0.3	0.2	0.5	0.5	0.6	0.2	0.3
Inventory to Working Capital 41	0.2	•	0.1	0.0	0.1	0.3	0.2	0.2	0.1	0.1	0.1	0.4	0.4
Total Receipts to Cash Flow 42	2.4	1.2	2.0	2.1	3.9	4.9	3.0	3.2	2.0	2.6	2.8	1.9	3.3
Cost of Goods to Cash Flow 43	0.8	0.0	0.2	0.2	1.6	2.5	0.9	0.9	0.4	0.8	0.3	0.5	1.7
Cash Flow to Total Debt 44	0.4	•	6.6	2.2	1.6	1.0	0.8	1.0	0.8	0.7	0.3	0.6	0.1

Selected Financial Factors (in Percentages)

Debt Ratio 45	59.2	•	34.4	71.2	35.5	34.4	48.5	46.4	50.6	36.4	56.0	63.5	64.2
Return on Total Assets 46	11.6	•	72.9	49.3	28.3	27.9	21.3	16.4	15.8	12.1	5.9	12.8	6.2
Return on Equity Before Income Taxes 47	24.9	•	110.0	157.3	42.5	40.5	39.9	30.0	29.5	18.1	9.0	29.2	14.4
Return on Equity After Income Taxes 48	20.6	•	109.3	156.7	40.0	36.9	34.1	28.3	25.2	16.0	7.1	21.3	11.0
Profit Margin (Before Income Tax) 49	16.0	84.5	16.0	13.8	12.6	16.3	17.1	11.2	17.0	16.5	8.3	14.9	19.8
Profit Margin (After Income Tax) 50	13.2	80.2	15.9	13.8	11.9	14.9	14.6	10.5	14.6	14.6	6.6	10.9	15.1

Table I
Corporations with and without Net Income

ADVERTISING AND RELATED SERVICES

MONEY AMOUNTS AND SIZE OF ASSETS IN THOUSANDS OF DOLLARS

Item Description for Accounting Period 7/12 Through 6/13	Total	Zero Assets	Under 500	500 to 1,000	1,000 to 5,000	5,000 to 10,000	10,000 to 25,000	25,000 to 50,000	50,000 to 100,000	100,000 to 250,000	250,000 to 500,000	500,000 to 2,500,000	2,500,000 and over
Number of Enterprises **1**	49260	12975	32382	1179	1970	348	218	85	37	33	11	16	5

Revenues ($ in Thousands)													
Net Sales **2**	98299399	2132990	20048150	2332726	10656046	6979695	5728694	4579630	2670615	9216167	2734925	10713021	20506740
Interest **3**	768345	713	2699	27	2920	1408	2319	6915	1590	12427	739	59591	676997
Rents **4**	123247	0	137	30	3296	594	0	659	661	239	283	8983	108365
Royalties **5**	124066	0	0	0	7	0	0	39861	48801	270	6319	28516	292
Other Portfolio Income **6**	426337	56645	13571	0	8057	615	2551	3364	4372	3708	645	42187	290619
Other Receipts **7**	2476455	35324	307442	2374	64722	350137	271452	21491	37977	71163	75984	575812	662578
Total Receipts **8**	102217849	2225672	20371999	2335157	10735048	7332449	6005016	4651920	2764016	9303974	2818895	11428110	22245591
Average Total Receipts **9**	2075	172	629	1981	5449	21070	27546	54728	74703	281939	256263	714257	4449118

Operating Costs/Operating Income (%)													
Cost of Operations **10**	38.8	24.7	44.7	35.7	29.9	66.4	65.7	62.0	59.1	62.6	43.4	35.5	5.3
Salaries and Wages **11**	20.7	16.0	9.5	14.7	19.7	9.7	13.5	17.1	17.7	12.1	23.9	21.1	43.6
Taxes Paid **12**	2.4	2.4	1.7	2.4	2.2	1.2	1.5	1.7	1.9	1.4	2.3	3.3	4.2
Interest Paid **13**	3.2	1.1	0.2	1.8	0.4	0.5	0.4	0.8	1.5	1.0	2.3	8.4	9.0
Depreciation **14**	1.3	1.6	0.6	1.6	0.5	0.6	0.5	0.8	1.6	1.2	1.0	2.2	2.6
Amortization and Depletion **15**	1.3	0.9	0.0	0.2	0.3	0.3	0.3	0.5	1.7	1.1	1.0	4.4	2.7
Pensions and Other Deferred Comp. **16**	0.6	2.0	0.3	0.5	0.4	0.2	0.2	1.2	0.2	0.2	0.6	0.2	1.2
Employee Benefits **17**	1.4	1.9	0.6	1.2	1.3	0.5	0.9	1.3	1.3	1.0	2.3	3.0	2.1
Advertising **18**	4.3	4.5	6.8	1.0	11.1	9.6	4.0	0.4	1.8	1.4	2.6	3.8	0.2
Other Expenses **19**	22.1	38.5	22.3	32.6	24.3	11.8	10.9	12.6	16.9	17.8	20.6	21.6	29.6
Officers' Compensation **20**	4.2	9.4	7.3	7.8	6.4	2.4	5.6	2.5	2.1	0.8	1.5	0.8	3.8
Operating Margin **21**	•	•	5.9	0.4	3.5	•	•	•	•	•	•	•	•
Operating Margin Before Officers' Comp. **22**	3.7	6.4	13.2	8.2	9.9	•	2.2	1.5	•	0.4	0.1	•	•

Selected Average Balance Sheet ($ in Thousands)

Net Receivables 23	481	0	15	246	675	2420	5734	10913	21359	40736	66130	189604	2535963
Inventories 24	34	0	1	20	181	204	365	557	594	2267	3485	10503	152639
Net Property, Plant and Equipment 25	136	0	18	241	230	378	1215	4672	3944	10789	15159	75588	546069
Total Assets 26	2672	0	78	768	2166	7232	15407	35556	72005	165734	327728	1332076	16396940
Notes and Loans Payable 27	687	0	72	611	1487	1161	1723	6863	14895	39817	66706	705856	2515409
All Other Liabilities 28	1183	0	30	309	1319	4778	8965	14988	32947	67929	144394	411188	7564055
Net Worth 29	802	0	-24	-152	-640	1294	4719	13704	24163	57989	116627	215032	6317476

Selected Financial Ratios (Times to 1)

Current Ratio 30	1.0	•	1.6	1.0	1.5	1.5	1.2	1.6	1.4	1.2	1.0	0.9	0.8
Quick Ratio 31	0.7	•	1.4	0.9	1.3	1.4	1.1	1.4	1.1	1.0	0.8	0.7	0.6
Net Sales to Working Capital 32	•	•	34.5	•	9.6	10.2	12.3	6.5	5.8	19.7	71.9	•	•
Coverage Ratio 33	2.1	2.3	38.2	1.3	11.3	4.9	4.8	1.7	•	1.6	1.7	1.3	1.5
Total Asset Turnover 34	0.7	•	7.9	2.6	2.5	2.8	1.7	1.5	1.0	1.7	0.8	0.5	0.3
Inventory Turnover 35	22.6	•	224.4	34.5	8.9	65.2	47.2	60.0	71.7	77.1	30.9	22.6	1.4
Receivables Turnover 36	4.4	•	45.4	9.2	7.1	7.7	4.6	5.8	3.2	7.8	3.9	3.8	1.7
Total Liabilities to Net Worth 37	2.3	•	•	•	•	4.6	2.3	1.6	2.0	1.9	1.8	5.2	1.6
Current Assets to Working Capital 38	•	•	2.8	•	2.9	3.0	5.3	2.8	3.6	5.5	36.7	•	•
Current Liabilities to Working Capital 39	•	•	1.8	•	1.9	2.0	4.3	1.8	2.6	4.5	35.7	•	•
Working Capital to Net Sales 40	•	•	0.0	•	0.1	0.1	0.1	0.2	0.2	0.1	0.0	•	•
Inventory to Working Capital 41	•	•	0.1	•	0.4	0.0	0.1	0.1	0.0	0.1	1.1	•	•
Total Receipts to Cash Flow 42	4.6	3.1	3.7	4.0	4.0	8.6	9.9	9.6	8.6	5.8	5.1	4.7	3.7
Cost of Goods to Cash Flow 43	1.8	0.8	1.7	1.4	1.2	5.7	6.5	5.9	5.1	3.6	2.2	1.7	0.2
Cash Flow to Total Debt 44	0.2	•	1.6	0.5	0.5	0.4	0.2	0.3	0.2	0.4	0.2	0.1	0.1

Selected Financial Factors (in Percentages)

Debt Ratio 45	70.0	•	131.2	119.8	129.5	82.1	69.4	61.5	66.4	65.0	64.4	83.9	61.5
Return on Total Assets 46	5.1	•	61.3	6.0	11.5	6.6	3.0	2.1	•	2.6	3.0	5.5	3.5
Return on Equity Before Income Taxes 47	9.0	•	•	•	•	29.2	7.8	2.2	•	2.9	3.6	8.0	3.1
Return on Equity After Income Taxes 48	7.4	•	•	•	•	24.6	6.8	0.3	•	•	1.6	3.3	2.3
Profit Margin (Before Income Tax) 49	3.6	1.4	7.6	0.5	4.2	1.9	1.4	0.6	•	0.6	1.7	2.6	4.8
Profit Margin (After Income Tax) 50	3.0	1.2	7.5	0.0	4.0	1.6	1.2	0.1	•	•	0.7	1.1	3.6

Table II
Corporations with Net Income

ADVERTISING AND RELATED SERVICES

MONEY AMOUNTS AND SIZE OF ASSETS IN THOUSANDS OF DOLLARS

Item Description for Accounting Period 7/12 Through 6/13	Total	Zero Assets	Under 500	500 to 1,000	1,000 to 5,000	5,000 to 10,000	10,000 to 25,000	25,000 to 50,000	50,000 to 100,000	100,000 to 250,000	250,000 to 500,000	500,000 to 2,500,000	2,500,000 and over
Number of Enterprises **1**	29957	4047	23497	515	1377	251	150	51	21	23	•	11	•

Revenues ($ in Thousands)													
Net Sales **2**	80005368	1092175	17998921	1054573	8790991	6252938	4500027	3182393	1614986	7973191	•	5916620	•
Interest **3**	710542	13	33	3	1696	372	1926	996	684	5507	•	22193	•
Rents **4**	114976	0	137	30	1707	0	0	48	0	239	•	4562	•
Royalties **5**	122457	0	0	0	7	0	0	39861	48801	270	•	27026	•
Other Portfolio Income **6**	360648	4762	9497	0	6755	409	2551	1465	550	2459	•	41266	•
Other Receipts **7**	1898806	34432	172818	3	65338	59060	254106	20518	37279	68524	•	453047	•
Total Receipts **8**	83212797	1131382	18181406	1054609	8866494	6312779	4758610	3245281	1702300	8050190	•	6464714	•
Average Total Receipts **9**	2778	280	774	2048	6439	25151	31724	63633	81062	350008	•	587701	•

Operating Costs/Operating Income (%)													
Cost of Operations **10**	38.3	5.0	46.8	31.9	23.1	70.2	63.7	68.4	63.6	69.0	•	32.2	•
Salaries and Wages **11**	21.6	13.1	9.7	17.4	19.0	8.1	13.1	13.2	13.6	10.1	•	28.8	•
Taxes Paid **12**	2.4	2.5	1.7	2.6	2.2	1.0	1.5	1.3	1.8	1.3	•	3.6	•
Interest Paid **13**	2.9	0.5	0.2	0.7	0.3	0.1	0.3	0.6	1.7	0.7	•	6.2	•
Depreciation **14**	1.0	1.0	0.4	0.3	0.4	0.2	0.4	0.5	1.2	0.7	•	2.5	•
Amortization and Depletion **15**	1.0	0.3	0.0	0.1	0.0	0.1	0.2	0.4	1.1	0.8	•	3.3	•
Pensions and Other Deferred Comp. **16**	0.6	3.9	0.3	0.8	0.4	0.2	0.3	0.4	0.3	0.2	•	0.4	•
Employee Benefits **17**	1.3	2.2	0.5	0.5	1.1	0.3	0.8	1.0	1.1	0.9	•	3.1	•
Advertising **18**	3.5	2.7	4.6	0.4	13.3	2.9	5.0	0.5	1.7	0.3	•	2.6	•
Other Expenses **19**	19.9	33.0	20.4	22.0	25.0	9.6	8.0	7.8	10.7	12.9	•	14.6	•
Officers' Compensation **20**	4.4	13.9	7.0	8.2	6.6	2.4	6.2	2.1	2.2	0.6	•	0.9	•
Operating Margin **21**	3.2	21.9	8.5	15.1	8.5	5.0	0.5	3.8	1.0	2.6	•	1.8	•
Operating Margin Before Officers' Comp. **22**	7.6	35.8	15.5	23.4	15.1	7.3	6.7	5.9	3.2	3.2	•	2.7	•

Selected Average Balance Sheet ($ in Thousands)

Net Receivables 23	667	0	12	337	693	2805	5825	12117	25501	41870	•	169066	•
Inventories 24	42	0	1	3	97	272	259	865	869	3226	•	10385	•
Net Property, Plant and Equipment 25	122	0	15	14	145	247	1058	4785	3089	9279	•	54786	•
Total Assets 26	3712	0	79	656	1910	7096	14728	36014	70825	161540	•	1279831	•
Notes and Loans Payable 27	695	0	66	75	262	350	1907	6572	18076	35172	•	531051	
All Other Liabilities 28	1665	0	30	301	874	4636	9079	16724	43211	77434	•	303466	•
Net Worth 29	1352	0	-17	280	774	2109	3742	12718	9538	48934	•	445313	•

Selected Financial Ratios (Times to 1)

Current Ratio 30	0.9	•	1.6	1.6	1.6	1.5	1.2	1.5	1.2	1.1	•	1.0	•
Quick Ratio 31	0.7	•	1.4	1.6	1.4	1.4	1.0	1.3	0.9	0.8	•	0.7	•
Net Sales to Working Capital 32	•	•	39.1	9.6	11.7	12.2	17.0	8.0	10.8	76.9	•	116.7	•
Coverage Ratio 33	3.6	48.3	46.8	23.5	33.6	70.0	21.1	11.3	4.9	6.1	•	2.8	•
Total Asset Turnover 34	0.7	•	9.7	3.1	3.3	3.5	2.0	1.7	1.1	2.1	•	0.4	•
Inventory Turnover 35	24.2	•	594.5	199.7	15.3	64.2	73.9	49.4	56.3	74.1	•	16.7	•
Receivables Turnover 36	4.3	•	78.9	6.1	8.2	8.2	5.9	6.4	3.1	10.2	•	3.2	•
Total Liabilities to Net Worth 37	1.7	•	•	1.3	1.5	2.4	2.9	1.8	6.4	2.3	•	1.9	•
Current Assets to Working Capital 38	•	•	2.7	2.6	2.7	2.8	6.4	3.2	6.8	17.2	•	68.7	•
Current Liabilities to Working Capital 39	•	•	1.7	1.6	1.7	1.8	5.4	2.2	5.8	16.2	•	67.7	•
Working Capital to Net Sales 40	•	•	0.0	0.1	0.1	0.1	0.1	0.1	0.1	0.0	•	0.0	•
Inventory to Working Capital 41	•	•	0.0	0.0	0.2	0.0	0.3	0.1	0.1	0.7	•	3.1	•
Total Receipts to Cash Flow 42	4.2	1.9	3.7	3.4	3.2	7.4	8.4	8.7	6.6	6.5	•	4.4	•
Cost of Goods to Cash Flow 43	1.6	0.1	1.7	1.1	0.7	5.2	5.3	5.9	4.2	4.5	•	1.4	•
Cash Flow to Total Debt 44	0.3	•	2.2	1.6	1.8	0.7	0.3	0.3	0.2	0.5	•	0.1	•

Selected Financial Factors (in Percentages)

Debt Ratio 45	63.6	•	121.2	57.3	59.5	70.3	74.6	64.7	86.5	69.7	•	65.2	•
Return on Total Assets 46	7.5	•	94.4	49.4	32.4	21.1	13.4	11.0	8.8	9.0	•	7.4	•
Return on Equity Before Income Taxes 47	14.8	•	•	110.8	77.5	69.9	50.1	28.5	51.6	24.8	•	13.7	•
Return on Equity After Income Taxes 48	13.2	•	•	103.0	75.8	66.0	48.3	25.0	43.6	19.5	•	10.4	•
Profit Margin (Before Income Tax) 49	7.5	25.5	9.5	15.1	9.4	5.9	6.3	5.8	6.4	3.5	•	11.4	•
Profit Margin (After Income Tax) 50	6.7	25.1	9.5	14.1	9.2	5.6	6.0	5.1	5.4	2.7	•	8.6	•

Table I

Corporations with and without Net Income

OTHER PROFESSIONAL, SCIENTIFIC, AND TECHNICAL SERVICES

MONEY AMOUNTS AND SIZE OF ASSETS IN THOUSANDS OF DOLLARS

Item Description for Accounting Period 7/12 Through 6/13	Total	Zero Assets	Under 500	500 to 1,000	1,000 to 5,000	5,000 to 10,000	10,000 to 25,000	25,000 to 50,000	50,000 to 100,000	100,000 to 250,000	250,000 to 500,000	500,000 to 2,500,000	2,500,000 and over
Number of Enterprises 1	104261	21994	74160	4290	2910	477	238	•	•	•	12	19	0
Revenues ($ in Thousands)													
Net Sales 2	105205542	2395598	35078694	8486164	11631976	5495523	6773558	•	•	•	3465633	19696692	0
Interest 3	137496	16595	7916	983	6228	3476	2435	•	•	•	1078	55257	0
Rents 4	45156	0	3994	885	351	0	53	•	•	•	0	38762	0
Royalties 5	918247	2242	15679	0	0	20938	0	•	•	•	239	822420	0
Other Portfolio Income 6	405413	34644	130428	20701	19577	18437	39038	•	•	•	13675	115190	0
Other Receipts 7	1232163	150074	178772	24602	114058	143128	124413	•	•	•	18819	229364	0
Total Receipts 8	107944017	2599153	35415483	8533335	11772190	5681502	6939497	•	•	•	3499444	20957685	0
Average Total Receipts 9	1035	118	478	1989	4045	11911	29158	•	•	•	291620	1103036	•
Operating Costs/Operating Income (%)													
Cost of Operations 10	27.0	7.0	22.9	21.4	27.4	54.4	45.1	•	•	•	24.2	16.5	•
Salaries and Wages 11	22.9	16.4	19.8	28.0	30.0	17.5	19.4	•	•	•	21.7	26.9	•
Taxes Paid 12	3.1	2.3	3.3	4.1	3.6	2.4	2.7	•	•	•	2.4	2.7	•
Interest Paid 13	1.9	2.6	0.6	0.8	0.8	0.3	0.5	•	•	•	1.4	6.2	•
Depreciation 14	1.3	1.4	0.8	1.3	0.9	1.0	1.3	•	•	•	1.3	2.1	•
Amortization and Depletion 15	1.2	1.4	0.3	0.6	0.4	0.2	0.3	•	•	•	2.3	3.4	•
Pensions and Other Deferred Comp. 16	0.9	0.3	1.1	1.0	0.8	0.7	0.4	•	•	•	0.9	1.1	•
Employee Benefits 17	2.5	2.3	1.4	3.2	1.0	1.6	1.6	•	•	•	3.0	5.9	•
Advertising 18	0.6	1.1	0.7	0.4	0.6	0.6	0.7	•	•	•	0.3	0.4	•
Other Expenses 19	28.2	50.1	28.4	23.8	22.8	15.2	24.4	•	•	•	34.9	36.1	•
Officers' Compensation 20	6.4	9.8	11.3	7.8	8.7	3.1	2.9	•	•	•	1.5	1.4	•
Operating Margin 21	4.0	5.1	9.5	7.8	3.0	2.9	0.8	•	•	•	6.0	•	•
Operating Margin Before Officers' Comp. 22	10.4	14.9	20.8	15.5	11.7	6.1	3.7	•	•	•	7.5	•	•

Selected Average Balance Sheet ($ in Thousands)

	C1	C2	C3	C4	C5	C6	C7	C8	C9	C10	C11	C12	C13
Net Receivables 23	99	0	10	92	294	1947	3635	•	•	•	77826	188821	•
Inventories 24	12	0	4	23	26	106	786	•	•	•	4810	9356	•
Net Property, Plant and Equipment 25	68	0	20	191	293	685	1546	•	•	•	17303	93791	•
Total Assets 26	738	0	96	670	1789	6845	14823	•	•	•	353574	2082036	•
Notes and Loans Payable 27	241	0	45	309	753	1827	3535	•	•	•	94873	640777	•
All Other Liabilities 28	278	0	25	162	645	2253	4692	•	•	•	90903	943301	•
Net Worth 29	219	0	26	199	391	2766	6597	•	•	•	167799	497959	•

Selected Financial Ratios (Times to 1)

	C1	C2	C3	C4	C5	C6	C7	C8	C9	C10	C11	C12	C13
Current Ratio 30	1.4	•	2.1	1.7	1.5	2.5	1.9	•	•	•	1.4	1.0	•
Quick Ratio 31	1.0	•	1.8	1.5	1.3	2.1	1.4	•	•	•	1.1	0.6	•
Net Sales to Working Capital 32	15.5	•	16.7	17.7	15.8	5.1	6.8	•	•	•	7.0	•	•
Coverage Ratio 33	4.6	6.1	19.8	11.5	6.2	22.5	7.5	•	•	•	5.9	1.7	•
Total Asset Turnover 34	1.4	•	4.9	3.0	2.2	1.7	1.9	•	•	•	0.8	0.5	•
Inventory Turnover 35	22.9	•	24.7	18.6	41.7	59.1	16.3	•	•	•	14.5	18.3	•
Receivables Turnover 36	9.9	•	50.4	19.3	12.8	8.5	8.3	•	•	•	3.6	6.1	•
Total Liabilities to Net Worth 37	2.4	•	2.7	2.4	3.6	1.5	1.2	•	•	•	1.1	3.2	•
Current Assets to Working Capital 38	3.8	•	1.9	2.5	3.1	1.7	2.1	•	•	•	3.8	•	•
Current Liabilities to Working Capital 39	2.8	•	0.9	1.5	2.1	0.7	1.1	•	•	•	2.8	•	•
Working Capital to Net Sales 40	0.1	•	0.1	0.1	0.1	0.2	0.1	•	•	•	0.1	•	•
Inventory to Working Capital 41	0.2	•	0.1	0.2	0.1	0.1	0.2	•	•	•	0.0	•	•
Total Receipts to Cash Flow 42	3.3	1.7	3.0	3.9	4.5	5.6	4.7	•	•	•	2.6	2.8	•
Cost of Goods to Cash Flow 43	0.9	0.1	0.7	0.8	1.2	3.0	2.1	•	•	•	0.6	0.5	•
Cash Flow to Total Debt 44	0.6	•	2.2	1.1	0.6	0.5	0.7	•	•	•	0.6	0.2	•

Selected Financial Factors (in Percentages)

	C1	C2	C3	C4	C5	C6	C7	C8	C9	C10	C11	C12	C13
Debt Ratio 45	70.3	•	72.8	70.3	78.2	59.6	55.5	•	•	•	52.5	76.1	•
Return on Total Assets 46	11.7	•	54.0	27.1	11.1	11.1	7.4	•	•	•	6.8	5.2	•
Return on Equity Before Income Taxes 47	30.8	•	188.4	83.5	42.7	26.2	14.4	•	•	•	12.0	8.7	•
Return on Equity After Income Taxes 48	28.4	•	187.2	81.9	41.4	24.6	12.3	•	•	•	9.8	6.5	•
Profit Margin (Before Income Tax) 49	6.7	13.6	10.4	8.4	4.2	6.3	3.3	•	•	•	6.9	4.2	•
Profit Margin (After Income Tax) 50	6.2	10.4	10.4	8.2	4.0	5.9	2.9	•	•	•	5.7	3.1	•

Table II
Corporations with Net Income

OTHER PROFESSIONAL, SCIENTIFIC, AND TECHNICAL SERVICES

MONEY AMOUNTS AND SIZE OF ASSETS IN THOUSANDS OF DOLLARS

Item Description for Accounting Period 7/12 Through 6/13	Total	Zero Assets	Under 500	500 to 1,000	1,000 to 5,000	5,000 to 10,000	10,000 to 25,000	25,000 to 50,000	50,000 to 100,000	100,000 to 250,000	250,000 to 500,000	500,000 to 2,500,000	2,500,000 and over
Number of Enterprises 1	69858	10306	54110	3251	1573	330	167	47	34	16	•	•	0

Revenues ($ in Thousands)

Net Sales 2	84636582	1455414	29584135	7113661	8372609	5202382	6101824	3148515	2808048	2091269	•	•	0
Interest 3	88727	385	3066	215	3330	3126	1106	1678	30465	3257	•	•	0
Rents 4	42263	0	3013	885	334	0	23	0	936	43	•	•	0
Royalties 5	266167	1157	0	0	0	20938	0	0	35	418	•	•	0
Other Portfolio Income 6	363053	20244	125391	20701	18311	14016	29271	12637	385	642	•	•	0
Other Receipts 7	936684	128499	169133	22373	107012	142145	106162	31982	65992	23908	•	•	0
Total Receipts 8	86333476	1605699	29884738	7157835	8501596	5382607	6238386	3194812	2905861	2119537	•	•	0
Average Total Receipts 9	1236	156	552	2202	5405	16311	37356	67975	85466	132471	•	•	•

Operating Costs/Operating Income (%)

Cost of Operations 10	25.5	4.1	20.9	22.1	27.4	55.4	47.4	48.0	39.5	32.1	•	•	•
Salaries and Wages 11	22.4	8.5	18.6	28.9	32.6	15.7	17.4	19.8	22.0	25.6	•	•	•
Taxes Paid 12	3.0	1.7	3.0	4.2	3.5	2.2	2.1	2.6	3.2	3.6	•	•	•
Interest Paid 13	1.4	0.7	0.5	0.6	0.4	0.3	0.4	0.4	1.7	2.2	•	•	•
Depreciation 14	1.2	1.5	0.6	1.2	0.6	0.8	1.1	1.0	1.6	1.9	•	•	•
Amortization and Depletion 15	0.7	0.3	0.3	0.2	0.2	0.2	0.2	0.3	1.2	2.0	•	•	•
Pensions and Other Deferred Comp. 16	0.9	0.2	1.1	1.2	0.3	0.7	0.4	1.1	0.6	0.9	•	•	•
Employee Benefits 17	2.6	2.5	1.3	3.6	1.0	1.2	1.0	1.8	2.3	2.2	•	•	•
Advertising 18	0.6	0.5	0.8	0.3	0.6	0.5	0.6	0.3	1.7	0.5	•	•	•
Other Expenses 19	26.4	37.1	28.4	18.5	19.7	13.0	21.5	16.0	20.7	19.8	•	•	•
Officers' Compensation 20	6.1	11.2	11.4	8.1	4.6	2.9	2.2	1.8	1.7	2.7	•	•	•
Operating Margin 21	9.2	31.9	13.2	11.2	9.3	7.1	5.6	6.8	4.0	6.6	•	•	•
Operating Margin Before Officers' Comp. 22	15.3	43.1	24.5	19.2	13.9	10.0	7.8	8.6	5.7	9.3	•	•	•

Selected Average Balance Sheet ($ in Thousands)

Net Receivables 23	116	0	10	107	334	2461	4543	9220	14975	23944	•	•	•
Inventories 24	13	0	5	27	33	137	960	717	1375	1042	•	•	•
Net Property, Plant and Equipment 25	68	0	19	198	169	818	1830	4170	5997	13793	•	•	•
Total Assets 26	701	0	102	648	1722	6986	15245	35901	68870	164461	•	•	•
Notes and Loans Payable 27	190	0	41	233	426	1467	3005	5403	21537	49159	•	•	•
All Other Liabilities 28	272	0	22	161	656	2101	4946	11689	19179	41461	•	•	•
Net Worth 29	240	0	39	254	641	3418	7295	18809	28154	73841	•	•	•

Selected Financial Ratios (Times to 1)

Current Ratio 30	1.6	•	2.5	1.7	1.8	2.5	1.9	2.0	1.6	0.8	•	•	•
Quick Ratio 31	1.3	•	2.1	1.5	1.6	2.1	1.4	1.5	1.3	0.6	•	•	•
Net Sales to Working Capital 32	11.4	•	15.6	19.9	12.6	5.9	7.1	5.4	6.6	•	•	•	•
Coverage Ratio 33	8.8	61.2	28.3	21.8	30.3	41.0	18.6	19.9	5.5	4.7	•	•	•
Total Asset Turnover 34	1.7	•	5.3	3.4	3.1	2.3	2.4	1.9	1.2	0.8	•	•	•
Inventory Turnover 35	24.5	•	24.2	17.7	44.4	63.9	18.0	44.9	23.7	40.3	•	•	•
Receivables Turnover 36	11.3	•	58.2	17.7	15.7	10.8	8.9	6.5	5.6	•	•	•	•
Total Liabilities to Net Worth 37	1.9	•	1.6	1.5	1.7	1.0	1.1	0.9	1.4	1.2	•	•	•
Current Assets to Working Capital 38	2.6	•	1.7	2.5	2.3	1.7	2.1	2.0	2.6	•	•	•	•
Current Liabilities to Working Capital 39	1.6	•	0.7	1.5	1.3	0.7	1.1	1.0	1.6	•	•	•	•
Working Capital to Net Sales 40	0.1	•	0.1	0.1	0.1	0.2	0.1	0.2	0.2	•	•	•	•
Inventory to Working Capital 41	0.1	•	0.1	0.2	0.1	0.1	0.3	0.0	0.1	•	•	•	•
Total Receipts to Cash Flow 42	3.0	1.3	2.7	4.0	3.8	4.9	4.4	4.6	3.9	4.0	•	•	•
Cost of Goods to Cash Flow 43	0.8	0.1	0.6	0.9	1.0	2.7	2.1	2.2	1.5	1.3	•	•	•
Cash Flow to Total Debt 44	0.9	•	3.2	1.4	1.3	0.9	1.0	0.9	0.5	0.4	•	•	•

Selected Financial Factors (in Percentages)

Debt Ratio 45	65.8	•	61.4	60.8	62.8	51.1	52.2	47.6	59.1	55.1	•	•	•
Return on Total Assets 46	22.0	•	78.7	42.0	34.6	24.5	19.9	16.1	11.0	8.1	•	•	•
Return on Equity Before Income Taxes 47	57.0	•	196.6	102.2	90.0	48.9	39.3	29.1	21.9	14.1	•	•	•
Return on Equity After Income Taxes 48	53.7	•	195.6	100.6	88.5	47.0	36.6	24.8	19.1	9.9	•	•	•
Profit Margin (Before Income Tax) 49	11.3	42.2	14.2	11.9	10.8	10.6	7.9	8.2	7.5	8.0	•	•	•
Profit Margin (After Income Tax) 50	10.6	37.0	14.1	11.7	10.7	10.2	7.3	7.0	6.5	5.6	•	•	•

Table I

Corporations with and without Net Income

OFFICES OF BANK HOLDING COMPANIES

MONEY AMOUNTS AND SIZE OF ASSETS IN THOUSANDS OF DOLLARS

Item Description for Accounting Period 7/12 Through 6/13	Total	Zero Assets	Under 500	500 to 1,000	1,000 to 5,000	5,000 to 10,000	10,000 to 25,000	25,000 to 50,000	50,000 to 100,000	100,000 to 250,000	250,000 to 500,000	500,000 to 2,500,000	2,500,000 and over
Number of Enterprises 1	4767	145	9	7	150	3	108	371	795	1444	840	719	176

Revenues ($ in Thousands)													
Net Sales 2	177917499	468976	21983	0	223677	1315	11214	179266	755267	3373799	3357528	8338216	161186257
Interest 3	379451859	1069345	46507	80	13632	401	46093	189436	1023685	4829233	7092999	19719665	345420784
Rents 4	18376979	12882	381	0	357	0	381	915	7649	30279	39853	279513	18004769
Royalties 5	252298	0	0	0	0	0	0	0	36	156	209	4001	247896
Other Portfolio Income 6	35411609	594500	50380	0	7433	2252	8222	40644	178311	790981	964490	2465731	30308666
Other Receipts 7	115836455	342205	6851	36269	15213	596	85302	460546	1564603	3557463	3655903	6919445	99192058
Total Receipts 8	727246699	2487908	126102	36349	260312	4564	151212	870807	3529551	12581911	15110982	37726571	654360430
Average Total Receipts 9	152559	17158	14011	5193	1735	1521	1400	2347	4440	8713	17989	52471	3717957

Operating Costs/Operating Income (%)													
Cost of Operations 10	1.2	•	•	•	•	•	•	•	0.3	0.0	0.0	0.0	1.4
Salaries and Wages 11	78.8	148.1	175.3	•	38.0	32.3	102.7	55.5	60.9	61.9	84.9	95.9	78.1
Taxes Paid 12	9.4	14.9	10.2	•	5.1	5.6	28.3	12.4	13.0	12.0	15.0	15.0	8.9
Interest Paid 13	50.5	67.8	65.0	•	5.3	17.1	94.2	47.0	50.7	48.4	61.1	57.3	50.0
Depreciation 14	13.8	9.3	7.6	•	8.5	1.9	23.9	7.1	8.9	9.9	11.1	13.3	14.1
Amortization and Depletion 15	5.8	1.2	0.8	•	0.0	0.2	2.7	0.8	1.2	1.4	1.7	2.7	6.2
Pensions and Other Deferred Comp. 16	4.1	7.1	1.2	•	1.7	•	3.0	4.1	3.8	3.9	4.7	5.5	4.0
Employee Benefits 17	10.4	15.7	9.4	•	3.4	5.4	40.1	14.3	13.8	11.5	13.2	12.0	10.2
Advertising 18	6.1	2.8	2.1	•	1.4	1.1	5.2	3.7	3.5	4.5	4.4	4.7	6.3
Other Expenses 19	171.0	243.7	536.2	•	46.9	134.4	1035.4	297.2	228.9	132.6	160.0	154.6	172.3
Officers' Compensation 20	4.9	24.2	14.7	•	7.0	25.9	146.1	49.3	43.9	31.3	29.8	20.7	2.7
Operating Margin 21	•	•	•	•	•	•	•	•	•	•	•	•	•
Operating Margin Before Officers' Comp. 22	•	•	•	•	•	•	•	•	•	•	•	•	•

Selected Average Balance Sheet ($ in Thousands)

Net Receivables 23	1227283	0	0	0	179	111	7997	19288	40577	93118	200344	532029	29118592
Inventories 24	11	0	0	0	28	0	0	0	0	0	7	14	187
Net Property, Plant and Equipment 25	24285	0	0	0	703	11	263	468	1279	3247	6720	19084	513559
Total Assets 26	3060123	0	156	583	1471	6747	18708	38429	74234	164175	349913	987849	75402326
Notes and Loans Payable 27	411723	0	1918	3679	641	6956	4513	758	2370	5836	13783	41205	10853631
All Other Liabilities 28	2148904	0	5839	17825	1828	76141	19189	37859	68802	146402	309431	850009	51646868
Net Worth 29	499496	0	-7601	-20921	-998	-76351	-4994	-188	3061	11937	26699	96635	12901826

Selected Financial Ratios (Times to 1)

Current Ratio 30	0.9	•	0.0	0.0	0.3	0.5	0.8	1.0	1.0	1.0	1.0	0.9	0.9
Quick Ratio 31	0.8	•	0.0	0.0	0.3	0.4	0.7	1.0	1.0	1.0	0.9	0.9	0.8
Net Sales to Working Capital 32	•	•	•	•	•	•	•	•	•	•	•	•	•
Coverage Ratio 33	2.1	0.8	•	1.9	0.6	5.7	•	0.5	1.5	1.9	1.8	2.0	2.1
Total Asset Turnover 34	0.0	•	15.7	•	1.0	0.1	0.0	0.0	0.0	0.0	0.0	0.0	0.0
Inventory Turnover 35	41.3	•	•	•	•	•	•	•	24.8	2.9	0.1	0.0	67.0
Receivables Turnover 36	0.0	•	•	•	2.6	7.9	0.0	0.0	0.0	0.0	0.0	0.0	0.0
Total Liabilities to Net Worth 37	5.1	•	•	•	•	•	•	•	23.2	12.8	12.1	9.2	4.8
Current Assets to Working Capital 38	•	•	•	•	•	•	•	•	•	•	•	•	•
Current Liabilities to Working Capital 39	•	•	•	•	•	•	•	•	•	•	•	•	•
Working Capital to Net Sales 40	•	•	•	•	•	•	•	•	•	•	•	•	•
Inventory to Working Capital 41	•	•	•	•	•	•	•	•	•	•	•	•	•
Total Receipts to Cash Flow 42	0.5	0.5	2.4	•	2.9	0.4	0.1	0.5	0.5	0.6	0.5	0.5	0.5
Cost of Goods to Cash Flow 43	0.0	•	•	•	•	•	•	•	0.0	0.0	0.0	0.0	0.0
Cash Flow to Total Debt 44	0.0	•	0.1	0.2	0.2	0.0	0.0	0.0	0.0	0.0	0.0	0.0	0.0

Selected Financial Factors (in Percentages)

Debt Ratio 45	83.7	•	4982.7	3690.3	167.8	1231.7	126.7	100.5	95.9	92.7	92.4	90.2	82.9
Return on Total Assets 46	1.3	•	•	106.1	3.3	6.4	•	0.3	0.9	1.3	1.2	1.3	1.3
Return on Equity Before Income Taxes 47	4.0	•	81.3	•	3.0	•	3.1	58.0	7.1	8.1	7.1	6.9	3.8
Return on Equity After Income Taxes 48	2.7	•	81.3	•	3.0	•	3.4	70.3	5.3	6.6	5.2	4.9	2.6
Profit Margin (Before Income Tax) 49	53.1	•	•	•	•	81.1	•	•	23.0	41.6	47.5	57.4	53.8
Profit Margin (After Income Tax) 50	36.2	•	•	•	•	81.1	•	•	17.1	33.8	34.7	40.8	36.4

Table II

Corporations with Net Income

OFFICES OF BANK HOLDING COMPANIES

MONEY AMOUNTS AND SIZE OF ASSETS IN THOUSANDS OF DOLLARS

Item Description for Accounting Period 7/12 Through 6/13	Total	Zero Assets	Under 500	500 to 1,000	1,000 to 5,000	5,000 to 10,000	10,000 to 25,000	25,000 to 50,000	50,000 to 100,000	100,000 to 250,000	250,000 to 500,000	500,000 to 2,500,000	2,500,000 and over
Number of Enterprises 1	3788	50	•	•	•	0	67	277	620	1168	698	609	154
Revenues ($ in Thousands)													
Net Sales 2	169648659	248091	•	•	•	0	5425	147643	628632	2977861	2948541	7327421	155151971
Interest 3	356361654	377113	•	•	•	0	28848	148981	755992	3715026	5799408	16350733	329184331
Rents 4	17279300	4468	•	•	•	0	244	681	3862	22351	25470	242224	16980001
Royalties 5	249747	0	•	•	•	0	0	0	28	143	206	1474	247896
Other Portfolio Income 6	33492431	503907	•	•	•	0	7618	30925	148764	673349	816460	2205625	29096141
Other Receipts 7	109991441	85457	•	•	•	0	26912	199479	811462	2576582	2953536	5950759	97364938
Total Receipts 8	687023232	1219036	•	•	•	0	69047	527709	2348740	9965312	12543621	32078236	628025278
Average Total Receipts 9	181368	24381	•	•	•	•	1031	1905	3788	8532	17971	52674	4078086
Operating Costs/Operating Income (%)													
Cost of Operations 10	1.3	•	•	•	•	•	•	•	0.3	0.0	0.0	0.0	1.4
Salaries and Wages 11	77.4	168.4	•	•	•	•	136.0	50.1	55.9	55.6	79.5	91.0	77.2
Taxes Paid 12	9.1	15.1	•	•	•	•	44.4	11.7	12.2	11.2	14.4	14.5	8.7
Interest Paid 13	49.8	38.8	•	•	•	•	136.0	43.0	46.2	42.8	55.3	53.1	49.7
Depreciation 14	13.2	8.9	•	•	•	•	18.0	6.4	8.2	9.3	10.6	13.2	13.3
Amortization and Depletion 15	5.7	0.3	•	•	•	•	•	0.6	0.9	1.2	1.6	2.5	6.1
Pensions and Other Deferred Comp. 16	4.0	5.2	•	•	•	•	5.3	3.4	3.8	3.8	4.8	5.5	4.0
Employee Benefits 17	10.2	15.1	•	•	•	•	63.0	13.9	13.3	10.7	12.6	11.5	10.1
Advertising 18	6.2	2.7	•	•	•	•	8.9	3.5	3.6	4.5	4.4	4.6	6.3
Other Expenses 19	165.3	146.5	•	•	•	•	351.4	107.4	105.5	90.4	114.0	122.5	170.2
Officers' Compensation 20	4.5	24.6	•	•	•	•	227.4	47.3	41.3	29.4	29.0	20.1	2.5
Operating Margin 21	•	•	•	•	•	•	•	•	•	•	•	•	•
Operating Margin Before Officers' Comp. 22	•	•	•	•	•	•	•	•	•	•	•	•	•

Net Receivables 23	1483678	0	•	•	•	•	9337	20704	41699	94913	202846	546346 32485487
Inventories 24	11	0	•	•	•	•	0	0	0	0	0	17 204
Net Property, Plant and Equipment 25	27138	0	•	•	•	•	152	453	1199	3127	6499	18892 533261
Total Assets 26	3628598	0	•	•	•	•	19184	38716	74060	164661	350442	988272 82131223
Notes and Loans Payable 27	505145	0	•	•	•	•	246	628	1505	5296	12279	39518 12165574
All Other Liabilities 28	2513716	0	•	•	•	•	17271	35369	64842	143940	305386	847640 55670282
Net Worth 29	609737	0	•	•	•	•	1667	2719	7714	15424	32777	101114 14295367

Selected Financial Ratios (Times to 1)

Current Ratio 30	0.9	•	•	•	•	•	0.9	1.0	1.0	1.0	1.0	0.9	0.9
Quick Ratio 31	0.8	•	•	•	•	•	0.9	1.0	1.0	1.0	1.0	0.9	0.8
Net Sales to Working Capital 32	•	•	•	•	•	•	•	•	0.9	•	•	•	•
Coverage Ratio 33	2.2	2.6	•	•	•	•	2.8	2.3	2.4	2.4	2.5	2.6	2.1
Total Asset Turnover 34	0.0	•	•	•	•	•	0.0	0.0	0.0	0.0	0.0	0.0	0.0
Inventory Turnover 35	52.8	•	•	•	•	•	•	•	24.9	2.9	4.9	0.0	70.2
Receivables Turnover 36	0.0	•	•	•	•	•	0.0	0.0	0.0	0.0	0.0	0.0	0.0
Total Liabilities to Net Worth 37	5.0	•	•	•	•	•	10.5	13.2	8.6	9.7	9.7	8.8	4.7
Current Assets to Working Capital 38	•	•	•	•	•	•	•	•	55.2	•	•	•	•
Current Liabilities to Working Capital 39	•	•	•	•	•	•	•	•	54.2	•	•	•	•
Working Capital to Net Sales 40	•	•	•	•	•	•	•	•	1.2	•	•	•	•
Inventory to Working Capital 41	•	•	•	•	•	•	•	•	0.0	•	•	•	•
Total Receipts to Cash Flow 42	0.5	0.5	•	•	•	•	0.2	0.7	0.6	0.6	0.5	0.5	0.5
Cost of Goods to Cash Flow 43	0.0	•	•	•	•	•	•	•	0.0	0.0	0.0	0.0	0.0
Cash Flow to Total Debt 44	0.0	•	•	•	•	•	0.0	0.0	0.0	0.0	0.0	0.0	0.0

Selected Financial Factors (in Percentages)

Debt Ratio 45	83.2	•	•	•	•	•	91.3	93.0	89.6	90.6	90.6	89.8	82.6
Return on Total Assets 46	1.3	•	•	•	•	•	1.6	1.4	1.5	1.6	1.7	1.7	1.3
Return on Equity Before Income Taxes 47	4.3	•	•	•	•	•	12.1	10.9	8.8	10.2	10.6	10.1	4.0
Return on Equity After Income Taxes 48	3.0	•	•	•	•	•	10.9	9.8	7.8	8.8	8.7	7.9	2.8
Profit Margin (Before Income Tax) 49	58.9	60.2	•	•	•	•	249.6	55.6	66.7	61.9	82.2	85.2	57.2
Profit Margin (After Income Tax) 50	41.2	44.0	•	•	•	•	225.0	49.8	59.6	53.1	67.6	66.3	39.2

Table I

Corporations with and without Net Income

OFFICES OF OTHER HOLDING COMPANIES

MONEY AMOUNTS AND SIZE OF ASSETS IN THOUSANDS OF DOLLARS

Item Description for Accounting Period 7/12 Through 6/13	Total	Zero Assets	Under 500	500 to 1,000	1,000 to 5,000	5,000 to 10,000	10,000 to 25,000	25,000 to 50,000	50,000 to 100,000	100,000 to 250,000	250,000 to 500,000	500,000 to 2,500,000	2,500,000 and over
Number of Enterprises 1	48011	10063	22717	3815	6248	1660	1647	747	481	377	118	105	33
Revenues ($ in Thousands)													
Net Sales 2	2646639	27534	22028	27971	200730	61781	19386	15161	36825	62621	248551	94226	1829825
Interest 3	5738615	174209	9430	16874	69083	49259	136968	159582	151413	327561	296591	1319605	3028040
Rents 4	496256	219891	2596	1400	42242	16078	22496	19889	55227	43577	24248	39804	8807
Royalties 5	2296337	103463	2324	15245	368	8205	21189	10573	14106	38193	18124	66598	1997948
Other Portfolio Income 6	14289025	1025129	866667	110761	586832	292060	916701	586821	1005693	1027832	473081	1619452	5777998
Other Receipts 7	33137597	2958054	631233	-6088	1608995	959977	1723691	1312017	1600606	2537483	1952083	6588167	11271378
Total Receipts 8	58604469	4508280	1534278	166163	2508250	1387360	2840431	2104043	2863870	4037267	3012678	9727852	23913996
Average Total Receipts 9	1221	448	68	44	401	836	1725	2817	5954	10709	25531	92646	724667
Operating Costs/Operating Income (%)													
Cost of Operations 10	25.4	61.0	•	•	0.1	28.4	18.4	46.2	12.7	45.7	0.3	32.1	30.8
Salaries and Wages 11	61.3	801.2	45.8	25.6	292.8	37.1	447.7	264.9	141.4	73.6	47.0	158.9	15.5
Taxes Paid 12	62.3	367.5	78.0	43.6	24.7	44.5	401.5	300.1	168.7	145.5	55.4	215.3	45.0
Interest Paid 13	418.1	1630.7	468.5	66.7	49.0	798.1	1068.0	1355.4	1131.2	1099.3	285.1	1664.5	333.8
Depreciation 14	14.2	113.2	12.1	3.2	9.2	5.7	117.5	178.6	38.0	48.2	20.4	67.3	6.0
Amortization and Depletion 15	45.6	359.2	54.5	1.8	4.0	18.9	470.4	107.8	190.4	203.8	11.0	613.4	9.0
Pensions and Other Deferred Comp. 16	13.9	5.0	137.6	3.0	113.7	12.4	7.0	9.8	3.8	9.5	3.2	4.5	4.2
Employee Benefits 17	28.2	58.4	177.5	5.4	10.3	4.6	94.6	28.8	7.4	8.0	1.6	30.7	32.9
Advertising 18	7.0	0.3	0.4	0.3	0.3	0.2	4.3	15.5	7.4	1.8	0.2	2.2	9.5
Other Expenses 19	665.3	9596.0	2350.4	640.9	74.6	1001.9	6003.8	5683.3	3812.7	2998.7	440.1	3495.8	207.9
Officers' Compensation 20	23.8	113.4	390.3	46.5	44.9	52.0	243.5	222.1	82.1	37.6	15.8	44.8	8.8
Operating Margin 21	•	•	•	•	•	•	•	•	•	•	•	•	•
Operating Margin Before Officers' Comp. 22	•	•	•	•	•	•	•	•	•	•	•	•	•

Selected Average Balance Sheet ($ in Thousands)

	C1	C2	C3	C4	C5	C6	C7	C8	C9	C10	C11	C12	C13
Net Receivables 23	571	0	4	10	84	162	416	688	2094	2668	7886	57098	496282
Inventories 24	6	0	3	0	0	3	1	22	37	150	551	497	1672
Net Property, Plant and Equipment 25	123	0	5	56	79	201	518	855	1076	2560	6719	3828	17371
Total Assets 26	14491	0	119	720	2220	7021	15897	35108	70269	155217	332030	1011182	11353761
Notes and Loans Payable 27	5013	0	66	727	637	1894	2864	6299	12603	29865	76290	314390	4863446
All Other Liabilities 28	2306	0	43	72	356	814	2168	3209	10749	18819	52144	141714	2018663
Net Worth 29	7172	0	9	-79	1227	4314	10864	25599	46917	106533	203597	555078	4471652

Selected Financial Ratios (Times to 1)

	C1	C2	C3	C4	C5	C6	C7	C8	C9	C10	C11	C12	C13
Current Ratio 30	0.8	•	1.3	1.2	1.8	1.6	1.4	2.0	2.2	1.4	2.2	1.2	0.6
Quick Ratio 31	0.5	•	0.8	0.6	1.1	0.9	0.9	0.9	1.2	0.8	1.3	0.8	0.3
Net Sales to Working Capital 32	•	•	0.1	0.3	0.1	0.1	0.0	0.0	0.0	0.0	0.1	0.0	•
Coverage Ratio 33	3.9	2.9	7.9	•	13.9	1.3	6.8	5.4	2.9	2.6	2.7	3.5	4.3
Total Asset Turnover 34	0.0	•	0.0	0.0	0.0	0.0	0.0	0.0	0.0	0.0	0.0	0.0	0.0
Inventory Turnover 35	2.2	•	•	•	0.3	3.2	3.0	0.4	0.3	0.5	0.0	0.6	10.2
Receivables Turnover 36	0.1	•	0.3	0.6	0.4	0.2	0.0	0.0	0.0	0.1	0.2	0.0	0.1
Total Liabilities to Net Worth 37	1.0	•	11.6	•	0.8	0.6	0.5	0.4	0.5	0.5	0.6	0.8	1.5
Current Assets to Working Capital 38	•	•	4.2	6.0	2.2	2.8	3.5	2.0	1.9	3.7	1.8	5.0	•
Current Liabilities to Working Capital 39	•	•	3.2	5.0	1.2	1.8	2.5	1.0	0.9	2.7	0.8	4.0	•
Working Capital to Net Sales 40	•	•	10.4	3.3	7.2	12.9	62.8	152.1	77.9	35.0	12.9	38.6	•
Inventory to Working Capital 41	•	•	0.3	0.0	•	0.0	0.0	0.0	0.0	0.0	0.0	0.0	•
Total Receipts to Cash Flow 42	0.1	0.0	0.1	0.6	0.2	0.1	0.0	0.0	0.0	0.0	0.1	0.0	0.1
Cost of Goods to Cash Flow 43	0.0	0.0	•	•	0.0	0.0	0.0	0.0	0.0	0.0	0.0	0.0	0.0
Cash Flow to Total Debt 44	0.1	•	0.1	0.0	0.1	0.1	0.2	0.2	0.1	0.1	0.1	0.1	0.1

Selected Financial Factors (in Percentages)

	C1	C2	C3	C4	C5	C6	C7	C8	C9	C10	C11	C12	C13
Debt Ratio 45	50.5	•	92.1	111.0	44.7	38.6	31.7	27.1	33.2	31.4	38.7	45.1	60.6
Return on Total Assets 46	6.3	•	30.3	•	9.9	5.5	5.4	4.3	3.6	3.1	4.8	5.1	7.1
Return on Equity Before Income Taxes 47	9.4	•	334.6	23.1	16.6	2.0	6.7	4.8	3.5	2.8	5.0	6.7	13.8
Return on Equity After Income Taxes 48	6.3	•	235.8	25.3	13.9	0.5	4.9	3.4	1.8	1.7	2.8	5.1	9.2
Profit Margin (Before Income Tax) 49	1226.0	3142.5	3253.7	•	633.7	237.1	6180.5	6011.1	2136.5	1811.2	478.7	4136.8	1114.8
Profit Margin (After Income Tax) 50	818.1	959.8	2292.3	•	530.3	59.4	4490.5	4317.3	1074.4	1097.8	272.7	3136.2	744.2

Table II
Corporations with Net Income

OFFICES OF OTHER HOLDING COMPANIES

MONEY AMOUNTS AND SIZE OF ASSETS IN THOUSANDS OF DOLLARS

Item Description for Accounting Period 7/12 Through 6/13		Total	Zero Assets	Under 500	500 to 1000	1,000 to 5,000	5,000 to 10,000	10,000 to 25,000	25,000 to 50,000	50,000 to 100,000	100,000 to 250,000	250,000 to 500,000	500,000 to 2,500,000	2,500,000 and over
Number of Enterprises	1	18025	4128	•	•	•	783	711	353	207	185	59	58	24
Revenues ($ in Thousands)														
Net Sales	2	2498101	4673	•	•	•	58602	16587	326	27178	56364	245149	55027	1814038
Interest	3	4097601	74491	•	•	•	28154	98151	104714	90774	201561	151913	991241	2285707
Rents	4	399423	185328	•	•	•	8277	19248	17722	47890	33529	2554	36953	8807
Royalties	5	2163719	1081	•	•	•	8203	20911	8818	12905	32282	16797	61145	1997948
Other Portfolio Income	6	13479909	972335	•	•	•	222199	869330	559115	930890	889392	293386	1482645	5735619
Other Receipts	7	32900560	2757863	•	•	•	975296	1805996	1422589	1672922	2982968	1824374	5727348	11275129
Total Receipts	8	55539313	3995771	•	•	•	1300731	2830223	2113284	2782559	4196096	2534173	8354359	23117248
Average Total Receipts	9	3081	968	•	•	•	1661	3981	5987	13442	22682	42952	144041	963219
Operating Costs/Operating Income (%)														
Cost of Operations	10	25.1	•	•	•	•	•	14.0	•	13.6	50.3	0.3	54.0	31.0
Salaries and Wages	11	47.6	157.1	•	•	•	20.8	482.3	1467.5	74.0	29.8	41.1	185.9	15.3
Taxes Paid	12	56.4	1546.2	•	•	•	36.2	313.6	9949.4	196.6	119.3	44.2	241.3	45.1
Interest Paid	13	300.1	2940.6	•	•	•	80.0	460.7	20590.8	626.1	593.6	94.2	1856.6	294.8
Depreciation	14	10.2	110.3	•	•	•	4.2	114.4	3649.1	35.3	2.2	9.7	106.0	6.0
Amortization and Depletion	15	28.6	598.9	•	•	•	14.6	78.4	2854.3	132.4	106.7	3.3	695.8	9.0
Pensions and Other Deferred Comp.	16	12.4	3.4	•	•	•	2.4	4.7	278.8	3.7	2.5	0.1	3.8	4.2
Employee Benefits	17	26.1	0.4	•	•	•	4.4	105.4	215.3	3.5	3.8	0.7	7.8	33.2
Advertising	18	7.1	1.1	•	•	•	0.1	1.5	245.7	2.3	1.4	0.1	0.8	9.6
Other Expenses	19	213.3	5039.7	•	•	•	218.7	2133.6	51313.8	1925.9	849.9	105.5	884.4	168.2
Officers' Compensation	20	17.2	537.9	•	•	•	25.5	249.8	5006.1	53.1	13.2	13.7	22.6	8.8
Operating Margin	21	•	•	•	•	•	•	•	•	•	•	•	•	•
Operating Margin Before Officers' Comp.	22	•	•	•	•	•	•	•	•	•	•	•	•	•

Selected Average Balance Sheet ($ in Thousands)

Net Receivables 23	776	0	•	•	•	124	408	508	2278	2554	8093	75917	312674
Inventories 24	10	0	•	•	•	0	1	0	60	78	332	758	2297
Net Property, Plant and Equipment 25	125	0	•	•	•	131	487	444	1547	2125	2965	1943	23811
Total Assets 26	27244	0	•	•	•	7120	15935	35195	72191	151526	324975	1130558	13581416
Notes and Loans Payable 27	10273	0	•	•	•	1231	1984	4178	11660	20604	56514	355034	6253896
All Other Liabilities 28	3361	0	•	•	•	798	1720	2645	10201	21150	40811	156812	1649535
Net Worth 29	13610	0	•	•	•	5091	12231	28372	50330	109772	227650	618713	5677986

Selected Financial Ratios (Times to 1)

Current Ratio 30	0.8	•	•	•	•	1.6	1.8	2.5	1.9	1.7	2.3	1.8	0.6
Quick Ratio 31	0.4	•	•	•	•	1.1	1.2	1.2	1.2	1.0	1.3	1.1	0.3
Net Sales to Working Capital 32	•	•	•	•	•	0.1	0.0	0.0	0.0	0.0	0.1	0.0	•
Coverage Ratio 33	7.3	26.1	•	•	•	23.6	30.7	28.7	12.4	10.6	10.2	7.1	5.0
Total Asset Turnover 34	0.0	•	•	•	•	0.0	0.0	0.0	0.0	0.0	0.0	0.0	0.0
Inventory Turnover 35	3.5	•	•	•	•	•	2.5	•	0.3	2.0	0.0	0.7	10.2
Receivables Turnover 36	0.1	•	•	•	•	•	0.1	0.0	0.1	0.1	0.3	0.0	0.1
Total Liabilities to Net Worth 37	1.0	•	•	•	•	0.4	0.3	0.2	0.4	0.4	0.4	0.8	1.4
Current Assets to Working Capital 38	•	•	•	•	•	2.6	2.2	1.6	2.1	2.4	1.8	2.3	•
Current Liabilities to Working Capital 39	•	•	•	•	•	1.6	1.2	0.6	1.1	1.4	0.8	1.3	•
Working Capital to Net Sales 40	•	•	•	•	•	6.7	51.0	3670.9	44.2	29.3	8.3	99.8	•
Inventory to Working Capital 41	•	•	•	•	•	•	0.0	•	0.0	0.0	0.0	0.0	•
Total Receipts to Cash Flow 42	0.1	0.0	•	•	•	0.1	0.0	0.0	0.0	0.0	0.1	0.0	0.1
Cost of Goods to Cash Flow 43	0.0	•	•	•	•	•	0.0	•	0.0	0.0	0.0	0.0	0.0
Cash Flow to Total Debt 44	0.1	•	•	•	•	0.6	0.7	0.7	0.3	0.4	0.3	0.2	0.1

Selected Financial Factors (in Percentages)

Debt Ratio 45	50.0	•	•	•	•	28.5	23.2	19.4	30.3	27.6	29.9	45.3	58.2
Return on Total Assets 46	11.1	•	•	•	•	19.9	20.7	15.5	14.1	12.6	12.3	11.0	8.1
Return on Equity Before Income Taxes 47	19.1	•	•	•	•	26.6	26.1	18.6	18.7	15.7	15.9	17.3	15.5
Return on Equity After Income Taxes 48	14.7	•	•	•	•	23.8	22.4	16.0	14.9	13.5	12.1	14.7	10.5
Profit Margin (Before Income Tax) 49	1877.7	73868.3	•	•	•	1808.5	13695.6	570416.6	7150.3	5672.8	869.3	11299.1	1164.9
Profit Margin (After Income Tax) 50	1446.6	61347.1	•	•	•	1621.2	11759.7	491648.8	5715.1	4880.2	660.8	9585.7	791.0

Table I

Corporations with and without Net Income

EMPLOYMENT SERVICES

MONEY AMOUNTS AND SIZE OF ASSETS IN THOUSANDS OF DOLLARS

Item Description for Accounting Period 7/12 Through 6/13		Total	Zero Assets	Under 500	500 to 1,000	1,000 to 5,000	5,000 to 10,000	10,000 to 25,000	25,000 to 50,000	50,000 to 100,000	100,000 to 250,000	250,000 to 500,000	500,000 to 2,500,000	2,500,000 and over
Number of Enterprises	1	23363	3524	17071	896	1554	87	112	51	19	17	10	18	3

Revenues ($ in Thousands)														
Net Sales	2	163644484	7598716	27506757	5924170	20749181	4319337	7953494	10564198	6314804	6314139	8064149	47197306	11138233
Interest	3	113142	1013	787	65	1958	1898	489	768	369	8243	5729	89083	2742
Rents	4	19517	782	0	11469	480	0	0	1520	0	2044	609	2613	0
Royalties	5	293505	17459	0	0	0	0	0	0	0	0	23745	52586	199716
Other Portfolio Income	6	217877	35543	455	31	10376	22	16559	2408	436	1708	68660	24648	57032
Other Receipts	7	1173970	3351	90079	12808	27389	5642	19084	23551	-22033	3160	24170	921199	65566
Total Receipts	8	165462495	7656864	27598078	5948543	20789384	4326899	7989626	10592445	6293576	6329294	8187062	48287435	11463289
Average Total Receipts	9	7082	2173	1617	6639	13378	49734	71336	207695	331241	372311	818706	2682635	3821096

Operating Costs/Operating Income (%)														
Cost of Operations	10	49.5	57.9	24.3	51.1	36.5	62.8	63.0	42.6	76.1	24.3	68.3	70.4	18.1
Salaries and Wages	11	24.6	19.9	24.8	24.6	38.2	18.4	17.6	39.9	7.2	60.1	13.7	9.8	55.8
Taxes Paid	12	7.2	5.8	10.5	9.4	7.2	3.3	5.6	7.2	6.1	7.9	4.8	6.0	7.8
Interest Paid	13	0.4	0.6	0.2	0.1	0.3	0.5	0.3	0.4	0.4	0.4	0.5	0.7	0.4
Depreciation	14	0.2	0.3	0.1	0.2	0.2	0.2	0.3	0.2	0.2	0.2	0.3	0.3	0.3
Amortization and Depletion	15	0.4	0.5	0.0	0.1	0.0	0.1	0.4	0.2	0.3	0.7	1.0	0.6	0.5
Pensions and Other Deferred Comp.	16	0.2	0.1	0.3	1.9	0.2	0.1	0.0	0.0	0.1	0.0	0.2	0.1	0.2
Employee Benefits	17	3.0	3.6	1.1	1.0	2.4	2.3	2.5	1.9	2.6	2.2	1.6	5.5	1.8
Advertising	18	0.2	0.2	0.2	0.3	0.2	0.7	0.3	0.1	0.1	0.2	0.5	0.2	0.2
Other Expenses	19	11.3	11.3	32.8	4.8	10.7	7.8	8.3	6.3	5.3	3.3	6.4	5.1	9.4
Officers' Compensation	20	1.6	0.5	4.8	4.1	1.7	1.5	1.4	0.5	0.4	0.2	1.3	0.4	0.6
Operating Margin	21	1.4	•	0.9	2.4	2.5	2.3	0.5	0.7	1.3	0.4	1.4	0.8	4.9
Operating Margin Before Officers' Comp.	22	2.9	•	5.7	6.5	4.2	3.9	1.9	1.2	1.7	0.6	2.7	1.2	5.5

Selected Average Balance Sheet ($ in Thousands)

Net Receivables	23	544	0	15	227	857	3043	6455	11896	28681	51791	105902	238286	848240
Inventories	24	2	0	0	0	1	7	7	0	51	1806	266	244	237
Net Property, Plant and Equipment	25	72	0	10	54	132	493	769	1243	2008	6099	13134	35985	50429
Total Assets	26	1970	0	92	703	2121	7646	15906	33663	67336	171276	356245	936764	3919098
Notes and Loans Payable	27	454	0	40	98	608	2534	5143	12093	25191	32980	68931	208507	664565
All Other Liabilities	28	695	0	19	397	663	4497	9166	14759	25455	96635	110405	336242	1021855
Net Worth	29	822	0	33	208	850	615	1598	6811	16690	41662	176909	392015	2232678

Selected Financial Ratios (Times to 1)

Current Ratio	30	1.4	•	1.8	2.1	1.7	1.2	1.2	1.3	1.2	1.1	1.8	1.3	1.7
Quick Ratio	31	1.2	•	1.6	1.7	1.5	0.9	1.1	1.1	1.0	0.7	1.6	1.1	1.6
Net Sales to Working Capital	32	26.2	•	64.0	23.0	19.7	58.6	39.5	36.4	52.7	30.2	10.9	33.2	7.7
Coverage Ratio	33	6.8	1.2	8.5	46.5	9.8	6.0	4.7	3.7	3.7	2.4	6.4	5.5	21.6
Total Asset Turnover	34	3.6	•	17.5	9.4	6.3	6.5	4.5	6.2	4.9	2.2	2.3	2.8	0.9
Inventory Turnover	35	1931.9	•	2227219.3	•	5540.0	4328.5	6041.2	225245.4	4934.7	50.0	2069.1	7563.7	2829.1
Receivables Turnover	36	12.6	•	137.8	18.3	16.6	10.9	9.0	18.0	13.2	8.2	6.3	8.5	8.8
Total Liabilities to Net Worth	37	1.4	•	1.8	2.4	1.5	11.4	9.0	3.9	3.0	3.1	1.0	1.4	0.8
Current Assets to Working Capital	38	3.5	•	2.2	1.9	2.4	7.3	5.9	4.0	7.4	9.3	2.3	5.0	2.4
Current Liabilities to Working Capital	39	2.5	•	1.2	0.9	1.4	6.3	4.9	3.0	6.4	8.3	1.3	4.0	1.4
Working Capital to Net Sales	40	0.0	•	0.0	0.0	0.1	0.0	0.0	0.0	0.0	0.0	0.1	0.0	0.1
Inventory to Working Capital	41	0.0	•	0.0	•	0.0	•	0.0	•	0.0	0.2	0.0	0.0	0.0
Total Receipts to Cash Flow	42	7.8	9.8	3.1	15.3	8.0	10.8	12.3	14.9	17.7	28.6	13.6	13.8	6.2
Cost of Goods to Cash Flow	43	3.9	5.7	0.7	7.8	2.9	6.8	7.8	6.4	13.5	7.0	9.3	9.7	1.1
Cash Flow to Total Debt	44	0.8	•	9.0	0.9	1.3	0.7	0.4	0.5	0.4	0.1	0.3	0.3	0.4

Selected Financial Factors (in Percentages)

Debt Ratio	45	58.3	•	63.7	70.4	59.9	92.0	90.0	79.8	75.2	75.7	50.3	58.2	43.0
Return on Total Assets	46	10.6	•	24.6	27.0	18.8	19.6	5.3	8.3	6.4	2.2	7.9	11.0	8.6
Return on Equity Before Income Taxes	47	21.7	•	59.7	89.1	42.2	203.5	42.0	29.7	18.9	5.3	13.4	21.4	14.3
Return on Equity After Income Taxes	48	17.5	•	58.9	84.2	40.7	191.9	35.5	24.6	17.2	2.7	10.2	13.8	13.3
Profit Margin (Before Income Tax)	49	2.5	0.1	1.2	2.8	2.7	2.5	0.9	1.0	0.9	0.6	2.9	3.2	8.6
Profit Margin (After Income Tax)	50	2.1	•	1.2	2.6	2.6	2.4	0.8	0.8	0.9	0.3	2.2	2.1	8.0

Table II

Corporations with Net Income

EMPLOYMENT SERVICES

MONEY AMOUNTS AND SIZE OF ASSETS IN THOUSANDS OF DOLLARS

Item Description for Accounting Period 7/12 Through 6/13		Total	Zero Assets	Under 500	500 to 1,000	1,000 to 5,000	5,000 to 10,000	10,000 to 25,000	25,000 to 50,000	50,000 to 100,000	100,000 to 250,000	250,000 to 500,000	500,000 to 2,500,000	2,500,000 and over
Number of Enterprises	1	14707	1911	10825	580	1173	57	83	33	9	10	7	•	•
Revenues ($ in Thousands)														
Net Sales	2	132817958	3827978	24002153	2558350	15189659	3526766	7173718	8755969	2997033	3842790	7153438	•	•
Interest	3	80111	52	18	20	1803	1730	220	608	197	2057	992	•	•
Rents	4	16180	782	0	11469	409	0	0	1520	0	723	609	•	•
Royalties	5	285688	17459	0	0	0	0	0	0	0	0	20917	•	•
Other Portfolio Income	6	208942	35543	455	0	10324	7	15743	745	175	237	68643	•	•
Other Receipts	7	971424	1463	84937	12801	20021	4813	12304	16336	-7072	2864	5280	•	•
Total Receipts	8	134380303	3883277	24087563	2582640	15222216	3533316	7201985	8775178	2990333	3848671	7249879	•	•
Average Total Receipts	9	9137	2032	2225	4453	12977	61988	86771	265914	332259	384867	1035697	•	•
Operating Costs/Operating Income (%)														
Cost of Operations	10	49.2	62.9	25.5	7.8	39.8	62.4	67.9	38.9	68.8	28.6	76.4	•	•
Salaries and Wages	11	23.5	10.4	21.9	55.9	32.1	19.1	13.7	43.3	11.8	55.2	8.5	•	•
Taxes Paid	12	7.2	2.6	11.3	8.1	7.4	3.8	5.7	7.2	6.7	8.4	4.9	•	•
Interest Paid	13	0.3	0.9	0.2	0.1	0.1	0.1	0.2	0.3	0.4	0.4	0.4	•	•
Depreciation	14	0.2	0.4	0.1	0.3	0.1	0.1	0.2	0.1	0.2	0.2	0.3	•	•
Amortization and Depletion	15	0.3	0.8	0.0	0.1	0.0	0.0	0.2	0.1	0.4	0.3	0.5	•	•
Pensions and Other Deferred Comp.	16	0.1	0.0	0.1	0.3	0.2	0.1	0.0	0.0	0.1	0.0	0.1	•	•
Employee Benefits	17	2.9	0.8	1.0	2.2	1.8	2.0	2.4	1.5	1.8	1.7	1.4	•	•
Advertising	18	0.2	0.3	0.2	0.6	0.2	0.8	0.2	0.1	0.2	0.2	0.5	•	•
Other Expenses	19	11.8	18.1	32.8	9.4	12.2	6.6	6.0	6.4	6.7	3.0	3.3	•	•
Officers' Compensation	20	1.7	0.6	5.1	7.9	1.8	1.0	1.3	0.5	0.3	0.1	1.2	•	•
Operating Margin	21	2.5	2.1	1.8	7.3	4.2	3.9	2.2	1.6	2.6	1.9	2.6	•	•
Operating Margin Before Officers' Comp.	22	4.2	2.8	6.9	15.2	6.1	4.9	3.6	2.1	2.9	2.0	3.8	•	•

Selected Average Balance Sheet ($ in Thousands)

Net Receivables 23	697	0	17	324	753	3571	7366	11205	28217	74552	131191	•	•
Inventories 24	1	0	0	0	1	11	8	0	27	706	380	•	•
Net Property, Plant and Equipment 25	92	0	12	75	144	391	728	1356	3000	3905	12731	•	•
Total Assets 26	2514	0	107	706	1989	7840	16444	34260	64457	185518	377977	•	•
Notes and Loans Payable 27	404	0	25	28	386	1678	3378	9761	17495	41289	69643	•	•
All Other Liabilities 28	856	0	18	226	592	3081	6884	14909	26288	112448	120948	•	•
Net Worth 29	1253	0	64	452	1011	3080	6183	9590	20674	31780	187386	•	•

Selected Financial Ratios (Times to 1)

Current Ratio 30	1.5	•	1.5	3.7	2.1	1.8	1.6	1.5	1.2	1.1	1.9	•	•
Quick Ratio 31	1.3	•	1.3	3.4	1.8	1.3	1.4	1.1	1.1	0.8	1.7	•	•
Net Sales to Working Capital 32	22.0	•	118.6	10.7	16.5	19.9	18.4	36.3	62.0	40.1	11.1	•	•
Coverage Ratio 33	13.6	5.1	15.2	70.9	32.0	41.3	11.7	7.6	7.3	6.6	12.1	•	•
Total Asset Turnover 34	3.6	•	20.8	6.2	6.5	7.9	5.3	7.7	5.2	2.1	2.7	•	•
Inventory Turnover 35	4426.2	•	2043964.0	•	4418.8	3509.7	7124.0	234843.9	8344.4	155.8	2053.2	•	•
Receivables Turnover 36	13.5	•	177.0	•	20.5	9.7	10.9	22.3	12.0	6.5	6.4	•	•
Total Liabilities to Net Worth 37	1.0	•	0.7	0.6	1.0	1.5	1.7	2.6	2.1	4.8	1.0	•	•
Current Assets to Working Capital 38	2.8	•	3.2	1.4	1.9	2.2	2.6	3.1	6.5	13.6	2.1	•	•
Current Liabilities to Working Capital 39	1.8	•	2.2	0.4	0.9	1.2	1.6	2.1	5.5	12.6	1.1	•	•
Working Capital to Net Sales 40	0.0	•	0.0	0.1	0.1	0.1	0.1	0.0	0.0	0.0	0.1	•	•
Inventory to Working Capital 41	0.0	•	0.0	•	0.0	•	0.0	•	0.0	0.0	0.0	•	•
Total Receipts to Cash Flow 42	6.9	5.0	3.0	6.5	6.4	10.2	13.1	12.9	12.2	21.6	17.0	•	•
Cost of Goods to Cash Flow 43	3.4	3.2	0.8	0.5	2.5	6.4	8.9	5.0	8.4	6.2	12.9	•	•
Cash Flow to Total Debt 44	1.0	•	17.6	2.7	2.1	1.3	0.6	0.8	0.6	0.1	0.3	•	•

Selected Financial Factors (in Percentages)

Debt Ratio 45	50.2	•	39.8	36.0	49.1	60.7	62.4	72.0	67.9	82.9	50.4	•	•
Return on Total Assets 46	14.6	•	48.2	52.2	29.8	32.9	15.0	15.9	14.3	5.0	11.8	•	•
Return on Equity Before Income Taxes 47	27.1	•	74.8	80.4	56.8	81.6	36.5	49.2	38.3	24.9	21.8	•	•
Return on Equity After Income Taxes 48	22.7	•	74.1	76.9	55.1	78.1	34.2	43.6	35.4	19.2	17.4	•	•
Profit Margin (Before Income Tax) 49	3.8	3.6	2.2	8.2	4.4	4.1	2.6	1.8	2.4	2.1	4.0	•	•
Profit Margin (After Income Tax) 50	3.2	2.5	2.1	7.9	4.3	3.9	2.4	1.6	2.2	1.6	3.2	•	•

Table I

Corporations with and without Net Income

TRAVEL ARRANGEMENT AND RESERVATION SERVICES

MONEY AMOUNTS AND SIZE OF ASSETS IN THOUSANDS OF DOLLARS

Item Description for Accounting Period 7/12 Through 6/13		Total	Zero Assets	Under 500	500 to 1,000	1,000 to 5,000	5,000 to 10,000	10,000 to 25,000	25,000 to 50,000	50,000 to 100,000	100,000 to 250,000	250,000 to 500,000	500,000 to 2,500,000	2,500,000 and over
Number of Enterprises	1	16585	2419	12336	1094	435	118	77	38	28	16	13	11	0
Revenues ($ in Thousands)														
Net Sales	2	40027920	220422	6014834	5675601	3410830	1814137	2951992	1391856	3046141	2780052	3625254	9096800	0
Interest	3	165954	281	149	0	316	68	1699	10775	5560	4710	14268	128128	0
Rents	4	67821	0	0	0	0	17	160	2259	2262	3407	4206	55508	0
Royalties	5	189786	0	0	0	0	0	0	0	624	0	0	189162	0
Other Portfolio Income	6	154260	900	0	392	113	342	1806	25283	11016	45967	44173	24273	0
Other Receipts	7	1981606	1855	21607	58655	97385	2753	28342	45225	267437	224743	485556	748045	0
Total Receipts	8	42587347	223458	6036590	5734648	3508644	1817317	2983999	1475398	3333040	3058879	4173457	10241916	0
Average Total Receipts	9	2568	92	489	5242	8066	15401	38753	38826	119037	191180	321035	931083	•
Operating Costs/Operating Income (%)														
Cost of Operations	10	47.8	33.2	74.5	70.2	63.0	6.8	59.1	60.8	61.8	45.8	45.5	10.3	•
Salaries and Wages	11	15.4	6.3	5.5	6.8	10.9	13.1	18.4	13.9	16.1	16.4	16.7	27.8	•
Taxes Paid	12	1.9	1.8	0.8	1.0	1.9	1.2	1.6	1.6	1.8	2.1	1.7	3.6	•
Interest Paid	13	0.9	0.2	0.1	0.1	0.0	0.0	0.0	0.4	0.8	1.1	1.3	2.8	•
Depreciation	14	0.8	0.4	0.2	0.4	0.6	0.6	0.4	0.7	1.3	2.1	1.7	1.0	•
Amortization and Depletion	15	0.6	0.8	0.1	0.0	0.2	0.0	0.3	0.4	0.6	0.8	0.8	1.7	•
Pensions and Other Deferred Comp.	16	0.5	0.2	0.1	0.3	0.3	0.1	0.3	0.5	0.5	0.8	0.8	1.1	•
Employee Benefits	17	1.6	2.7	0.6	0.8	0.2	0.5	1.6	1.2	1.7	1.7	2.0	3.3	•
Advertising	18	4.5	10.2	0.9	0.3	0.9	0.7	5.0	1.8	3.6	1.2	3.2	13.6	•
Other Expenses	19	27.2	24.7	14.5	14.3	19.4	72.5	13.2	21.6	16.5	31.9	38.4	40.6	•
Officers' Compensation	20	1.9	10.5	1.9	3.1	2.0	1.8	1.6	1.1	1.9	0.7	0.7	2.0	•
Operating Margin	21	•	8.9	0.8	2.8	0.6	2.6	•	•	•	•	•	•	•
Operating Margin Before Officers' Comp.	22	•	19.5	2.7	5.8	2.6	4.4	0.1	•	•	•	•	•	•

Selected Average Balance Sheet ($ in Thousands)

Net Receivables 23	211	0	3	56	403	1987	3239	5294	10996	15620	52687	118150	•
Inventories 24	24	0	0	0	175	2	868	1272	431	1491	1373	13986	•
Net Property, Plant and Equipment 25	135	0	7	93	94	317	758	1544	10773	23141	24105	79688	•
Total Assets 26	1757	0	52	697	2076	5613	14836	37841	73182	148095	350916	1327803	•
Notes and Loans Payable 27	354	0	33	90	204	427	748	20212	10833	30041	38901	282835	•
All Other Liabilities 28	881	0	25	262	1361	4506	9068	17494	42097	59405	179290	642060	•
Net Worth 29	522	0	-6	345	511	680	5019	135	20252	58648	132725	402907	•

Selected Financial Ratios (Times to 1)

Current Ratio 30	1.0	•	2.0	1.9	1.3	5.5	1.2	0.5	1.2	1.2	0.9	0.9	•
Quick Ratio 31	0.7	•	1.8	1.8	0.9	4.0	0.8	0.4	0.8	0.7	0.6	0.5	•
Net Sales to Working Capital 32	1303.3	•	24.7	20.5	17.3	3.7	21.5	•	15.0	22.1	•	•	•
Coverage Ratio 33	4.4	53.0	19.3	27.2	189.0	98.2	•	6.9	4.7	6.1	2.8	2.8	•
Total Asset Turnover 34	1.4	•	9.4	7.4	3.8	2.7	2.6	1.0	1.5	1.2	0.8	0.6	•
Inventory Turnover 35	47.8	•	3357.0	•	28.2	424.4	26.1	17.5	156.0	53.4	92.4	6.1	•
Receivables Turnover 36	11.1	•	213.4	98.2	13.0	10.2	12.9	5.2	11.0	11.0	5.3	6.6	•
Total Liabilities to Net Worth 37	2.4	•	•	1.0	3.1	7.3	2.0	278.5	2.6	1.5	1.6	2.3	•
Current Assets to Working Capital 38	392.1	•	2.0	2.1	4.0	1.2	6.2	•	5.4	7.6	•	•	•
Current Liabilities to Working Capital 39	391.1	•	1.0	1.1	3.0	0.2	5.2	•	4.4	6.6	•	•	•
Working Capital to Net Sales 40	0.0	•	0.0	0.0	0.1	0.3	0.0	•	0.1	0.0	•	•	•
Inventory to Working Capital 41	17.8	•	0.0	•	0.4	0.0	0.7	•	0.1	0.2	•	•	•
Total Receipts to Cash Flow 42	3.6	3.6	8.1	5.8	4.8	1.3	9.1	4.7	5.9	2.9	2.7	2.4	•
Cost of Goods to Cash Flow 43	1.7	1.2	6.0	4.1	3.0	0.1	5.4	2.8	3.6	1.3	1.2	0.2	•
Cash Flow to Total Debt 44	0.5	•	1.0	2.5	1.1	2.3	0.4	0.2	0.4	0.7	0.5	0.4	•

Selected Financial Factors (in Percentages)

Debt Ratio 45	70.3	•	111.8	50.4	75.4	87.9	66.2	99.6	72.3	60.4	62.2	69.7	•
Return on Total Assets 46	5.7	•	11.6	29.4	13.3	7.6	•	2.5	5.5	7.5	2.8	5.0	•
Return on Equity Before Income Taxes 47	14.9	•	•	57.2	53.8	61.8	•	594.5	15.5	15.9	4.9	10.6	•
Return on Equity After Income Taxes 48	11.9	•	•	56.1	49.3	57.9	•	323.4	10.5	13.1	3.5	7.4	•
Profit Margin (Before Income Tax) 49	3.2	10.3	1.2	3.8	3.5	2.7	•	2.2	2.9	5.4	2.3	5.2	•
Profit Margin (After Income Tax) 50	2.6	9.9	1.1	3.7	3.2	2.6	•	1.2	2.0	4.4	1.6	3.6	•

Table II

Corporations with Net Income

TRAVEL ARRANGEMENT AND RESERVATION SERVICES

MONEY AMOUNTS AND SIZE OF ASSETS IN THOUSANDS OF DOLLARS

Item Description for Accounting Period 7/12 Through 6/13	Total	Zero Assets	Under 500	500 to 1,000	1,000 to 5,000	5,000 to 10,000	10,000 to 25,000	25,000 to 50,000	50,000 to 100,000	100,000 to 250,000	250,000 to 500,000	500,000 to 2,500,000	2,500,000 and over
Number of Enterprises **1**	10128	1988	6410	1094	405	•	43	24	17	11	9	•	0

Revenues ($ in Thousands)

Net Sales **2**	32175213	158920	2198639	5675601	3366432	•	2174018	1187898	2016279	2047216	2890602	•	0
Interest **3**	78628	278	36	0	308	•	1474	10438	4052	3611	5841	•	0
Rents **4**	39538	0	0	0	0	•	160	2167	1592	3089	4162	•	0
Royalties **5**	189162	0	0	0	0	•	0	0	0	0	0	•	0
Other Portfolio Income **6**	108355	900	0	392	113	•	1393	24502	9731	11143	35569	•	0
Other Receipts **7**	1436638	1855	21539	58655	97386	•	23486	72257	190653	162738	67552	•	0
Total Receipts **8**	34027534	161953	2220214	5734648	3464239	•	2200531	1297262	2222307	2227797	3003726	•	0
Average Total Receipts **9**	3360	81	346	5242	8554	•	51175	54053	130724	202527	333747	•	•

Operating Costs/Operating Income (%)

Cost of Operations **10**	42.5	15.9	54.7	70.2	63.8	•	67.4	62.6	62.4	39.8	36.1	•	•
Salaries and Wages **11**	15.7	6.5	6.6	6.8	10.4	•	15.0	12.2	14.7	16.8	15.4	•	•
Taxes Paid **12**	2.0	2.4	1.2	1.0	1.8	•	1.2	1.4	2.0	2.2	1.6	•	•
Interest Paid **13**	0.9	0.3	0.1	0.1	0.0	•	0.0	0.4	0.5	0.3	1.6	•	•
Depreciation **14**	0.8	0.6	0.5	0.4	0.6	•	0.3	0.6	0.9	2.3	1.0	•	•
Amortization and Depletion **15**	0.6	•	0.1	0.0	0.2	•	0.1	0.3	0.2	0.1	0.7	•	•
Pensions and Other Deferred Comp. **16**	0.6	0.3	•	0.3	0.3	•	0.3	0.4	0.6	0.6	0.9	•	•
Employee Benefits **17**	1.6	3.7	0.9	0.8	0.2	•	1.4	0.7	1.4	1.9	1.7	•	•
Advertising **18**	5.1	8.0	1.2	0.3	0.9	•	4.3	1.8	4.2	1.1	2.8	•	•
Other Expenses **19**	29.1	31.1	25.3	14.3	19.0	•	7.1	21.2	15.6	34.5	38.1	•	•
Officers' Compensation **20**	1.9	14.0	2.5	3.1	1.7	•	1.6	1.0	1.4	0.7	0.6	•	•
Operating Margin **21**	•	17.1	7.1	2.8	1.0	•	1.3	•	•	•	•	•	•
Operating Margin Before Officers' Comp. **22**	1.2	31.2	9.6	5.8	2.8	•	2.9	•	•	0.4	0.3	•	•

Selected Average Balance Sheet ($ in Thousands)

Net Receivables 23	254	0	2	56	433	•	4052	7530	11418	12520	13770	•	•
Inventories 24	23	0	0	0	177	•	1475	2006	421	536	832	•	•
Net Property, Plant and Equipment 25	166	0	6	93	101	•	815	2003	8280	20583	23547	•	•
Total Assets 26	2329	0	51	697	2105	•	15392	37978	71348	155345	322934	•	•
Notes and Loans Payable 27	367	0	28	90	207	•	994	1490	8321	4064	50078	•	•
All Other Liabilities 28	1165	0	18	262	1351	•	10492	23528	38186	66527	116350	•	•
Net Worth 29	797	0	5	345	547	•	3907	12960	24841	84754	156505	•	•

Selected Financial Ratios (Times to 1)

Current Ratio 30	1.0	•	2.1	1.9	1.3	•	1.1	1.1	1.1	1.0	0.8	•	•
Quick Ratio 31	0.7	•	1.7	1.8	0.9	•	0.7	0.7	0.7	0.7	0.5	•	•
Net Sales to Working Capital 32	2604.0	•	16.7	20.5	17.6	•	44.9	25.6	24.7	123.1	•	•	•
Coverage Ratio 33	6.5	70.5	154.4	27.2	224.7	•	66.1	19.3	14.1	28.2	3.3	•	•
Total Asset Turnover 34	1.4	•	6.8	7.4	3.9	•	3.3	1.3	1.7	1.2	1.0	•	•
Inventory Turnover 35	57.8	•	1419.1	•	30.0	•	23.1	15.5	175.8	138.1	139.4	•	•
Receivables Turnover 36	11.9	•	325.1	•	17.1	•	12.7	4.7	11.1	14.8	13.8	•	•
Total Liabilities to Net Worth 37	1.9	•	9.9	1.0	2.8	•	2.9	1.9	1.9	0.8	1.1	•	•
Current Assets to Working Capital 38	754.6	•	1.9	2.1	3.9	•	10.5	10.9	8.1	41.2	•	•	•
Current Liabilities to Working Capital 39	753.6	•	0.9	1.1	2.9	•	9.5	9.9	7.1	40.2	•	•	•
Working Capital to Net Sales 40	0.0	•	0.1	0.0	0.1	•	0.0	0.0	0.0	0.0	•	•	•
Inventory to Working Capital 41	22.6	•	•	•	0.4	•	1.9	1.2	0.1	0.4	•	•	•
Total Receipts to Cash Flow 42	3.2	2.5	3.6	5.8	4.7	•	11.6	3.9	5.0	2.4	2.6	•	•
Cost of Goods to Cash Flow 43	1.3	0.4	2.0	4.1	3.0	•	7.8	2.5	3.1	1.0	0.9	•	•
Cash Flow to Total Debt 44	0.7	•	2.1	2.5	1.1	•	0.4	0.5	0.5	1.1	0.8	•	•

Selected Financial Factors (in Percentages)

Debt Ratio 45	65.8	•	90.9	50.4	74.0	•	74.6	65.9	65.2	45.4	51.5	•	•
Return on Total Assets 46	8.2	•	54.8	29.4	15.7	•	8.5	9.0	11.2	10.6	5.1	•	•
Return on Equity Before Income Taxes 47	20.3	•	595.9	57.2	60.1	•	33.1	25.0	29.8	18.7	7.4	•	•
Return on Equity After Income Taxes 48	17.2	•	593.0	56.1	55.6	•	30.7	20.5	23.1	15.8	5.6	•	•
Profit Margin (Before Income Tax) 49	5.1	19.0	8.1	3.8	4.0	•	2.6	6.5	6.2	8.5	3.6	•	•
Profit Margin (After Income Tax) 50	4.3	18.4	8.0	3.7	3.7	•	2.4	5.4	4.8	7.2	2.7	•	•

Table I

Corporations with and without Net Income

OTHER ADMINISTRATIVE AND SUPPORT SERVICES

MONEY AMOUNTS AND SIZE OF ASSETS IN THOUSANDS OF DOLLARS

Item Description for Accounting Period 7/12 Through 6/13		Total	Zero Assets	Under 500	500 to 1,000	1,000 to 5,000	5,000 to 10,000	10,000 to 25,000	25,000 to 50,000	50,000 to 100,000	100,000 to 250,000	250,000 to 500,000	500,000 to 2,500,000	2,500,000 and over
Number of Enterprises	1	225497	55620	155316	7602	5315	831	397	173	102	59	29	45	8

Revenues ($ in Thousands)

Net Sales	2	241038856	15129849	68945127	16556441	25243064	13691900	11336174	8058364	8916683	8339278	9828192	42800198	12193587
Interest	3	583273	93291	5329	5911	7986	4455	7220	11024	9730	5671	27105	239479	166071
Rents	4	50273	965	2545	5902	6923	900	2811	301	4983	68	2684	18596	3594
Royalties	5	443443	12576	0	0	0	87871	3553	3008	32515	751	14035	120269	168865
Other Portfolio Income	6	1683815	55999	126320	34069	110158	12173	48802	27055	16504	54258	240509	656879	301085
Other Receipts	7	4625965	258694	252456	93557	389923	547334	301366	123047	584722	168581	57299	2065197	-216207
Total Receipts	8	248425625	15551374	69331777	16695880	25758054	14344633	11699926	8222799	9565137	8568607	10169824	45900618	12616995
Average Total Receipts	9	1102	280	446	2196	4846	17262	29471	47531	93776	145231	350684	1020014	1577124

Operating Costs/Operating Income (%)

Cost of Operations	10	35.6	33.2	32.9	46.0	46.7	52.2	46.1	32.1	40.8	34.7	38.8	31.0	1.2
Salaries and Wages	11	22.3	19.0	20.2	17.4	18.7	17.0	22.1	25.8	25.9	17.4	23.2	29.4	32.2
Taxes Paid	12	3.8	2.6	3.9	3.0	4.0	3.2	3.8	3.7	3.8	3.1	3.0	4.4	4.5
Interest Paid	13	2.3	7.1	0.5	0.5	0.6	0.7	0.7	1.1	1.3	2.6	3.6	3.0	13.2
Depreciation	14	2.0	3.0	1.6	2.5	1.6	1.5	1.2	2.3	1.9	1.9	2.0	2.0	4.0
Amortization and Depletion	15	1.2	3.6	0.2	0.1	0.2	0.2	0.4	0.8	1.0	3.3	1.7	2.4	3.1
Pensions and Other Deferred Comp.	16	0.5	0.4	0.4	0.3	0.5	0.4	0.3	0.4	0.6	0.4	0.3	0.8	0.9
Employee Benefits	17	2.2	3.0	1.1	1.0	1.3	2.6	2.5	2.8	4.0	1.9	3.6	3.4	3.0
Advertising	18	1.3	1.9	1.7	0.9	0.9	0.5	0.3	3.3	2.5	1.6	1.0	0.7	1.2
Other Expenses	19	23.0	27.0	23.6	20.7	15.5	18.4	19.2	23.9	19.6	31.4	23.1	23.9	33.8
Officers' Compensation	20	4.1	3.1	8.4	4.9	4.8	2.5	2.1	3.1	2.3	1.3	0.8	0.8	1.0
Operating Margin	21	1.8	•	5.4	2.7	5.2	0.9	1.4	0.7	•	0.5	•	•	1.9
Operating Margin Before Officers' Comp.	22	5.9	•	13.9	7.6	10.0	3.3	3.5	3.8	•	1.8	•	•	2.9

Selected Average Balance Sheet ($ in Thousands)

Net Receivables 23	116	0	7	147	432	1628	4558	7290	18150	27779	69942	214139	246990
Inventories 24	10	0	2	37	41	347	474	749	1965	2599	4366	6506	13728
Net Property, Plant and Equipment 25	111	0	24	202	393	1553	1995	5873	10705	13798	29064	107449	878148
Total Assets 26	724	0	77	722	2011	6999	14634	35068	71412	154609	360058	1063785	5356796
Notes and Loans Payable 27	306	0	57	353	733	2590	4218	11750	21265	57716	151926	406105	2424396
All Other Liabilities 28	175	0	16	212	539	2203	5518	8529	27034	43334	105285	235130	1017331
Net Worth 29	243	0	4	157	739	2206	4898	14789	23113	53559	102846	422549	1915069

Selected Financial Ratios (Times to 1)

Current Ratio 30	1.6	•	1.4	1.7	1.8	1.2	1.4	1.7	1.3	1.5	1.5	1.7	1.7
Quick Ratio 31	1.2	•	1.2	1.3	1.4	0.8	1.1	1.3	1.0	1.1	1.1	1.4	0.9
Net Sales to Working Capital 32	12.0	•	42.4	13.8	10.3	26.3	11.9	6.2	12.2	6.8	8.1	6.8	4.7
Coverage Ratio 33	3.2	0.8	12.0	7.6	12.8	8.9	7.9	3.5	3.9	2.2	1.6	3.0	1.5
Total Asset Turnover 34	1.5	•	5.8	3.0	2.4	2.4	2.0	1.3	1.2	0.9	0.9	0.9	0.3
Inventory Turnover 35	36.5	•	61.9	26.9	54.5	24.8	27.8	19.9	18.1	18.9	30.2	45.4	1.3
Receivables Turnover 36	9.4	•	55.8	17.2	10.1	10.8	6.6	6.9	4.6	5.3	5.9	4.5	5.6
Total Liabilities to Net Worth 37	2.0	•	19.1	3.6	1.7	2.2	2.0	1.4	2.1	1.9	2.5	1.5	1.8
Current Assets to Working Capital 38	2.8	•	3.4	2.5	2.3	6.7	3.5	2.3	4.6	3.0	3.2	2.4	2.4
Current Liabilities to Working Capital 39	1.8	•	2.4	1.5	1.3	5.7	2.5	1.3	3.6	2.0	2.2	1.4	1.4
Working Capital to Net Sales 40	0.1	•	0.0	0.1	0.1	0.0	0.1	0.2	0.1	0.1	0.1	0.1	0.2
Inventory to Working Capital 41	0.1	•	0.2	0.2	0.1	0.6	0.2	0.1	0.3	0.1	0.1	0.0	0.0
Total Receipts to Cash Flow 42	4.2	4.6	4.0	5.1	5.3	4.8	4.9	4.3	5.3	3.1	4.9	4.0	2.9
Cost of Goods to Cash Flow 43	1.5	1.5	1.3	2.3	2.5	2.5	2.2	1.4	2.2	1.1	1.9	1.3	0.0
Cash Flow to Total Debt 44	0.5	•	1.5	0.8	0.7	0.7	0.6	0.5	0.3	0.4	0.3	0.4	0.2

Selected Financial Factors (in Percentages)

Debt Ratio 45	66.4	•	95.0	78.2	63.3	68.5	66.5	57.8	67.6	65.4	71.4	60.3	64.2
Return on Total Assets 46	10.8	•	37.9	12.3	18.5	14.9	10.2	5.2	6.0	5.3	5.6	8.0	5.7
Return on Equity Before Income Taxes 47	22.1	•	697.3	49.0	46.4	42.0	26.6	8.7	13.9	8.4	7.6	13.4	5.6
Return on Equity After Income Taxes 48	18.9	•	692.2	46.8	44.7	40.8	24.0	7.7	11.3	5.5	4.1	9.7	2.2
Profit Margin (Before Income Tax) 49	5.0	•	6.0	3.5	7.2	5.6	4.6	2.8	3.7	3.2	2.3	6.0	7.0
Profit Margin (After Income Tax) 50	4.3	•	6.0	3.4	7.0	5.5	4.1	2.4	3.0	2.1	1.2	4.3	2.8

Table II

Corporations with Net Income

OTHER ADMINISTRATIVE AND SUPPORT SERVICES

MONEY AMOUNTS AND SIZE OF ASSETS IN THOUSANDS OF DOLLARS

Item Description for Accounting Period 7/12 Through 6/13	Total	Zero Assets	Under 500	500 to 1,000	1,000 to 5,000	5,000 to 10,000	10,000 to 25,000	25,000 to 50,000	50,000 to 100,000	100,000 to 250,000	250,000 to 500,000	500,000 to 2,500,000	2,500,000 and over
Number of Enterprises 1	142075	30717	100716	5407	4070	607	308	102	67	32	13	32	5

Revenues ($ in Thousands)

	Total	Zero Assets	Under 500	500 to 1,000	1,000 to 5,000	5,000 to 10,000	10,000 to 25,000	25,000 to 50,000	50,000 to 100,000	100,000 to 250,000	250,000 to 500,000	500,000 to 2,500,000	2,500,000 and over
Net Sales 2	176363161	7547638	50969188	11905706	20989225	10817926	10085509	5373454	6323883	5667998	4980957	33215266	8486410
Interest 3	335518	33518	3082	3230	4984	1123	6736	8754	4190	4763	23867	218991	22281
Rents 4	35865	965	5	5902	5510	838	1961	301	4574	68	65	12767	2910
Royalties 5	367936	7633	0	0	0	87871	2742	2	30946	750	579	88629	148783
Other Portfolio Income 6	1557131	44405	103344	32917	98100	9516	46383	20655	13676	49502	232547	618590	287492
Other Receipts 7	4629333	182255	199487	86715	367230	528866	289795	85547	556101	157468	36248	1961981	177644
Total Receipts 8	183288944	7816414	51275106	12034470	21465049	11446140	10433126	5488713	6933370	5880549	5274263	36116224	9125520
Average Total Receipts 9	1290	254	509	2226	5274	18857	33874	53811	103483	183767	405713	1128632	1825104

Operating Costs/Operating Income (%)

	Total	Zero Assets	Under 500	500 to 1,000	1,000 to 5,000	5,000 to 10,000	10,000 to 25,000	25,000 to 50,000	50,000 to 100,000	100,000 to 250,000	250,000 to 500,000	500,000 to 2,500,000	2,500,000 and over
Cost of Operations 10	35.5	36.4	31.7	43.1	42.0	51.8	45.8	35.6	39.0	35.1	28.7	35.4	0.3
Salaries and Wages 11	22.3	16.1	19.7	15.9	20.4	16.8	22.1	26.8	25.2	14.3	30.2	28.3	36.2
Taxes Paid 12	3.9	1.9	3.7	3.1	4.3	3.4	3.6	4.1	3.9	3.0	3.9	4.6	5.5
Interest Paid 13	1.3	3.3	0.5	0.4	0.6	0.5	0.4	0.8	1.2	1.4	1.5	1.9	7.4
Depreciation 14	1.6	1.2	1.4	1.7	1.4	1.4	1.2	1.6	1.7	1.8	1.8	1.8	4.1
Amortization and Depletion 15	0.6	1.2	0.2	0.1	0.3	0.1	0.2	0.5	0.9	0.7	1.2	1.2	1.6
Pensions and Other Deferred Comp. 16	0.5	0.4	0.3	0.4	0.4	0.3	0.4	0.5	0.7	0.5	0.3	0.8	1.1
Employee Benefits 17	2.1	2.6	1.1	1.0	1.3	2.5	2.4	3.2	3.3	1.7	3.3	3.5	3.0
Advertising 18	1.0	0.5	1.5	0.9	1.0	0.5	0.3	0.5	1.7	2.0	1.6	0.8	0.7
Other Expenses 19	21.3	26.4	22.4	21.1	15.1	17.6	17.6	17.2	22.0	32.6	24.5	20.2	31.3
Officers' Compensation 20	4.1	2.8	8.0	5.4	5.0	2.2	2.1	2.5	2.3	1.3	0.7	0.7	1.0
Operating Margin 21	5.9	7.3	9.7	6.9	8.2	2.9	3.9	6.7	•	5.6	2.4	0.8	7.9
Operating Margin Before Officers' Comp. 22	9.9	10.1	17.7	12.3	13.2	5.1	6.0	9.2	0.5	6.9	3.1	1.5	8.9

Selected Average Balance Sheet ($ in Thousands)

Net Receivables 23	133	0	6	144	434	1530	5013	7771	20088	29876	90246	235027	298387
Inventories 24	11	0	2	36	43	190	500	811	2261	3659	5209	6000	17827
Net Property, Plant and Equipment 25	124	0	24	200	419	1558	2160	4044	10470	17147	27223	119329	979481
Total Assets 26	716	0	83	724	2051	7197	14542	34414	71369	154786	355010	1031022	4293650
Notes and Loans Payable 27	261	0	50	184	789	2691	3213	11035	22288	50490	77251	317635	1977274
All Other Liabilities 28	166	0	13	213	471	1915	5660	7858	23806	45739	107832	217700	817795
Net Worth 29	289	0	20	326	792	2591	5669	15522	25275	58556	169927	495687	1498580

Selected Financial Ratios (Times to 1)

Current Ratio 30	1.7	•	1.7	1.8	2.2	1.2	1.6	1.9	1.5	1.6	1.8	2.0	1.6
Quick Ratio 31	1.4	•	1.5	1.4	1.7	0.9	1.3	1.4	1.2	1.0	1.5	1.6	1.0
Net Sales to Working Capital 32	10.1	•	31.1	12.1	8.6	22.0	9.4	5.7	7.7	6.9	6.0	5.8	5.2
Coverage Ratio 33	8.7	4.3	21.5	21.1	18.4	17.9	18.7	12.8	7.6	7.8	6.7	6.2	3.4
Total Asset Turnover 34	1.7	•	6.1	3.0	2.5	2.5	2.3	1.5	1.3	1.1	1.1	1.0	0.4
Inventory Turnover 35	40.8	•	82.2	26.5	50.5	48.5	30.0	23.1	16.3	17.0	21.1	61.3	0.3
Receivables Turnover 36	9.3	•	69.7	17.9	10.8	14.3	7.2	8.5	5.0	5.5	4.7	4.4	4.4
Total Liabilities to Net Worth 37	1.5	•	3.2	1.2	1.6	1.8	1.6	1.2	1.8	1.6	1.1	1.1	1.9
Current Assets to Working Capital 38	2.3	•	2.4	2.3	1.9	5.4	2.7	2.1	3.0	2.8	2.3	2.0	2.6
Current Liabilities to Working Capital 39	1.3	•	1.4	1.3	0.9	4.4	1.7	1.1	2.0	1.8	1.3	1.0	1.6
Working Capital to Net Sales 40	0.1	•	0.0	0.1	0.1	0.0	0.1	0.2	0.1	0.1	0.2	0.2	0.2
Inventory to Working Capital 41	0.1	•	0.1	0.2	0.1	0.3	0.2	0.1	0.2	0.2	0.1	0.0	0.0
Total Receipts to Cash Flow 42	3.7	3.0	3.5	3.9	4.7	4.3	4.6	4.4	4.0	2.6	3.7	4.0	2.3
Cost of Goods to Cash Flow 43	1.3	1.1	1.1	1.7	2.0	2.2	2.1	1.5	1.5	0.9	1.1	1.4	0.0
Cash Flow to Total Debt 44	0.8	•	2.3	1.4	0.9	0.9	0.8	0.6	0.5	0.7	0.6	0.5	0.3

Selected Financial Factors (in Percentages)

Debt Ratio 45	59.7	•	76.3	54.9	61.4	64.0	61.0	54.9	64.6	62.2	52.1	51.9	65.1
Return on Total Assets 46	19.6	•	66.2	25.4	27.8	22.8	17.4	14.7	12.0	12.3	10.5	11.8	9.9
Return on Equity Before Income Taxes 47	42.9	•	266.0	53.7	68.2	59.8	42.4	30.1	29.3	28.3	18.7	20.7	20.1
Return on Equity After Income Taxes 48	38.7	•	264.5	52.2	66.2	58.4	39.4	28.3	25.8	23.4	13.9	16.2	13.2
Profit Margin (Before Income Tax) 49	10.0	10.9	10.3	8.0	10.5	8.7	7.3	8.9	7.9	9.4	8.3	9.9	17.7
Profit Margin (After Income Tax) 50	9.0	10.6	10.2	7.7	10.2	8.5	6.8	8.4	6.9	7.7	6.2	7.7	11.7

Table I

Corporations with and without Net Income

WASTE MANAGEMENT AND REMEDIATION SERVICES

MONEY AMOUNTS AND SIZE OF ASSETS IN THOUSANDS OF DOLLARS

Item Description for Accounting Period 7/12 Through 6/13		Total	Zero Assets	Under 500	500 to 1,000	1,000 to 5,000	5,000 to 10,000	10,000 to 25,000	25,000 to 50,000	50,000 to 100,000	100,000 to 250,000	250,000 to 500,000	500,000 to 2,500,000	2,500,000 and over
Number of Enterprises	1	13947	1833	8662	1232	1452	417	205	51	38	26	12	9	9
Revenues ($ in Thousands)														
Net Sales	2	75214977	979154	4810300	2780766	8272432	6371515	4642520	2239134	2640438	3880216	3290002	5180331	30128169
Interest	3	101338	2506	758	661	1762	395	5343	1147	1232	1151	3937	8684	73762
Rents	4	71530	527	763	0	187	0	4511	703	651	2217	4941	7758	49272
Royalties	5	28444	0	0	0	0	0	15	13	523	9	2	7900	19982
Other Portfolio Income	6	1160600	245863	28682	29907	42870	8336	213149	15040	5022	11047	14984	48072	497630
Other Receipts	7	616093	-11569	18945	9521	18536	-19220	90556	48599	23066	35446	29109	26514	346588
Total Receipts	8	77192982	1216481	4859448	2820855	8335787	6361026	4956094	2304636	2670932	3930086	3342975	5279259	31115403
Average Total Receipts	9	5535	664	561	2290	5741	15254	24176	45189	70288	151157	278581	586584	3457267
Operating Costs/Operating Income (%)														
Cost of Operations	10	39.6	32.5	36.2	39.7	40.5	64.2	45.3	55.1	56.2	44.7	38.6	20.6	34.2
Salaries and Wages	11	16.5	20.1	13.7	13.5	11.2	10.3	14.3	8.3	8.8	14.2	19.8	19.3	20.9
Taxes Paid	12	3.5	3.2	2.8	3.4	3.1	2.2	2.6	1.7	2.2	2.7	2.2	4.1	4.5
Interest Paid	13	2.7	7.4	0.5	1.0	0.7	1.2	1.7	1.2	2.5	2.7	2.2	4.0	4.1
Depreciation	14	5.3	3.0	1.8	5.4	3.0	1.7	5.5	5.2	4.8	5.7	7.2	8.5	6.5
Amortization and Depletion	15	2.2	4.6	0.0	0.1	0.0	0.2	0.5	0.8	0.9	1.6	2.6	3.6	4.0
Pensions and Other Deferred Comp.	16	0.4	0.2	0.3	0.2	0.3	0.3	0.6	0.3	0.3	0.4	0.3	1.8	0.2
Employee Benefits	17	2.3	4.0	2.4	1.5	1.5	1.5	1.9	7.6	2.0	2.8	2.6	3.4	2.0
Advertising	18	0.3	0.4	0.5	0.8	0.5	0.4	0.4	0.2	0.3	0.2	0.2	0.3	0.3
Other Expenses	19	23.2	61.2	28.9	25.6	31.4	13.9	22.6	19.2	20.9	23.7	26.7	37.0	18.3
Officers' Compensation	20	1.7	5.0	5.8	6.8	1.9	1.9	2.5	1.8	1.8	1.5	0.8	0.9	0.4
Operating Margin	21	2.4	•	7.0	2.0	5.9	2.4	2.1	•	•	•	•	•	4.7
Operating Margin Before Officers' Comp.	22	4.1	•	12.8	8.8	7.8	4.4	4.7	0.3	1.1	1.3	•	•	5.1

Selected Average Balance Sheet ($ in Thousands)

Net Receivables 23	656	0	22	98	549	2115	2847	4975	12214	24967	42256	60672	462298
Inventories 24	89	0	4	57	26	499	271	1346	1462	3533	18683	16697	25984
Net Property, Plant and Equipment 25	2562	0	33	291	1062	2024	6629	12720	21856	43566	125500	368220	2656949
Total Assets 26	6936	0	118	674	2290	7266	15618	34683	71230	158976	340959	937345	7131823
Notes and Loans Payable 27	2844	0	48	492	837	3139	7004	12864	29019	57618	115944	448901	2888891
All Other Liabilities 28	1945	0	20	73	942	1620	3521	10917	19640	43683	84812	200817	2093845
Net Worth 29	2146	0	50	109	511	2507	5092	10902	22571	57676	140203	287627	2149088

Selected Financial Ratios (Times to 1)

Current Ratio 30	1.2	•	2.3	2.6	1.4	1.8	1.6	1.4	1.5	1.4	1.7	0.8	1.0
Quick Ratio 31	0.9	•	1.9	1.9	1.2	1.1	1.4	0.9	1.1	1.0	1.0	0.5	0.7
Net Sales to Working Capital 32	20.8	•	13.4	11.8	21.8	7.3	8.8	12.4	8.9	10.8	7.3	•	99.7
Coverage Ratio 33	2.9	•	18.0	4.4	10.2	2.9	6.2	2.2	1.2	1.4	0.3	0.6	3.0
Total Asset Turnover 34	0.8	•	4.7	3.3	2.5	2.1	1.5	1.3	1.0	0.9	0.8	0.6	0.5
Inventory Turnover 35	24.1	•	45.1	15.8	88.6	19.6	37.8	18.0	26.7	18.9	5.7	7.1	44.0
Receivables Turnover 36	8.1	•	23.6	30.8	9.2	7.8	8.9	7.7	5.9	5.1	6.4	7.7	7.5
Total Liabilities to Net Worth 37	2.2	•	1.3	5.2	3.5	1.9	2.1	2.2	2.2	1.8	1.4	2.3	2.3
Current Assets to Working Capital 38	5.2	•	1.8	1.6	3.8	2.2	2.6	3.3	3.1	3.5	2.5	•	26.6
Current Liabilities to Working Capital 39	4.2	•	0.8	0.6	2.8	1.2	1.6	2.3	2.1	2.5	1.5	•	25.6
Working Capital to Net Sales 40	0.0	•	0.1	0.1	0.0	0.1	0.1	0.1	0.1	0.1	0.1	•	0.0
Inventory to Working Capital 41	0.4	•	0.1	0.3	0.1	0.3	0.1	0.4	0.2	0.3	0.6	•	0.9
Total Receipts to Cash Flow 42	4.7	•	3.4	5.0	3.0	8.1	4.3	6.0	6.0	5.1	4.7	3.3	5.2
Cost of Goods to Cash Flow 43	1.8	•	1.2	2.0	1.2	5.2	1.9	3.3	3.3	2.3	1.8	0.7	1.8
Cash Flow to Total Debt 44	0.2	•	2.4	0.8	1.1	0.4	0.5	0.3	0.2	0.3	0.3	0.3	0.1

Selected Financial Factors (in Percentages)

Debt Ratio 45	69.1	•	57.4	83.8	77.7	65.5	67.4	68.6	68.3	63.7	58.9	69.3	69.9
Return on Total Assets 46	6.0	•	40.2	14.8	18.4	7.2	15.3	3.4	2.8	3.5	0.5	1.5	5.7
Return on Equity Before Income Taxes 47	12.7	•	89.1	70.7	74.5	13.8	39.4	5.8	1.2	2.6	•	•	12.6
Return on Equity After Income Taxes 48	9.7	•	88.4	67.7	69.7	12.7	32.6	5.7	0.4	1.1	•	•	9.0
Profit Margin (Before Income Tax) 49	5.1	•	8.0	3.4	6.7	2.3	8.9	1.4	0.4	1.0	•	•	8.1
Profit Margin (After Income Tax) 50	3.9	•	8.0	3.3	6.2	2.1	7.3	1.4	0.1	0.4	•	•	5.8

Table II

Corporations with Net Income

WASTE MANAGEMENT AND REMEDIATION SERVICES

MONEY AMOUNTS AND SIZE OF ASSETS IN THOUSANDS OF DOLLARS

Item Description for Accounting Period 7/12 Through 6/13	Total	Zero Assets	Under 500	500 to 1,000	1,000 to 5,000	5,000 to 10,000	10,000 to 25,000	25,000 to 50,000	50,000 to 100,000	100,000 to 250,000	250,000 to 500,000	500,000 to 2,500,000	2,500,000 and over
Number of Enterprises 1	9426	1516	5808	582	1057	•	152	27	21	15	5	3	•

Revenues ($ in Thousands)

	Total	Zero Assets	Under 500	500 to 1,000	1,000 to 5,000	5,000 to 10,000	10,000 to 25,000	25,000 to 50,000	50,000 to 100,000	100,000 to 250,000	250,000 to 500,000	500,000 to 2,500,000	2,500,000 and over
Net Sales 2	58943945	326489	3770101	1474812	6991638	•	3717279	1555765	1714248	2245624	1424506	2140760	•
Interest 3	83813	268	254	431	1488	•	5193	474	923	492	19	427	•
Rents 4	54391	0	763	0	15	•	3974	0	504	147	0	0	•
Royalties 5	19998	0	0	0	0	•	15	0	0	0	0	0	•
Other Portfolio Income 6	929284	66939	28682	29907	41834	•	212746	4448	4134	3985	858	37685	•
Other Receipts 7	564315	57127	16253	9497	17679	•	85559	24246	12612	2883	21105	-5574	•
Total Receipts 8	60595746	450823	3816053	1514647	7052654	•	4024766	1584933	1732421	2253131	1446488	2173298	•
Average Total Receipts 9	6429	297	657	2602	6672	•	26479	58701	82496	150209	289298	724433	•

Operating Costs/Operating Income (%)

	Total	Zero Assets	Under 500	500 to 1,000	1,000 to 5,000	5,000 to 10,000	10,000 to 25,000	25,000 to 50,000	50,000 to 100,000	100,000 to 250,000	250,000 to 500,000	500,000 to 2,500,000	2,500,000 and over
Cost of Operations 10	39.0	3.9	33.4	53.0	38.0	•	46.9	65.5	63.2	48.1	32.4	13.9	•
Salaries and Wages 11	16.6	30.0	13.0	8.1	11.3	•	13.1	6.3	6.9	13.6	22.7	18.2	•
Taxes Paid 12	3.5	5.1	2.6	3.2	3.0	•	2.6	1.2	1.9	3.0	2.5	3.3	•
Interest Paid 13	2.6	9.1	0.5	0.3	0.6	•	1.6	0.5	1.0	1.5	2.1	5.0	•
Depreciation 14	5.0	2.3	1.7	3.4	3.0	•	4.8	3.3	4.0	4.9	5.7	9.4	•
Amortization and Depletion 15	2.2	3.8	0.0	0.0	0.1	•	0.4	0.4	0.3	1.2	2.0	6.3	•
Pensions and Other Deferred Comp. 16	0.3	•	0.3	0.4	0.3	•	0.7	0.2	0.4	0.5	0.5	0.4	•
Employee Benefits 17	2.0	8.2	2.4	1.5	1.6	•	1.9	1.2	1.4	2.1	3.1	2.9	•
Advertising 18	0.3	0.5	0.3	0.5	0.5	•	0.2	0.2	0.2	0.2	0.2	0.1	•
Other Expenses 19	21.2	52.5	27.9	15.8	32.0	•	21.0	14.7	12.8	18.2	27.0	37.8	•
Officers' Compensation 20	1.5	12.8	5.9	8.6	1.6	•	2.7	1.8	1.7	1.4	1.0	0.6	•
Operating Margin 21	5.7	•	11.9	5.2	8.0	•	4.1	4.5	6.3	5.3	0.8	2.2	•
Operating Margin Before Officers' Comp. 22	7.2	•	17.8	13.8	9.7	•	6.7	6.3	7.9	6.7	1.9	2.8	•

Selected Average Balance Sheet ($ in Thousands)

Net Receivables 23	755	0	27	87	614	•	2766	4764	13545	23659	43614	65205	•
Inventories 24	87	0	5	120	19	•	278	2140	1537	3136	15703	4055	•
Net Property, Plant and Equipment 25	3021	0	31	190	957	•	6761	11302	20086	36559	139710	578088	•
Total Assets 26	8330	0	135	677	2356	•	15779	35023	66602	155368	346484	1335958	•
Notes and Loans Payable 27	3266	0	40	355	758	•	6438	8601	15622	50395	151180	786607	•
All Other Liabilities 28	2378	0	16	36	923	•	3084	12301	14956	38075	76139	269624	•
Net Worth 29	2686	0	79	287	675	•	6257	14122	36024	66898	119165	279727	•

Selected Financial Ratios (Times to 1)

Current Ratio 30	1.3	•	4.2	10.9	1.4	•	2.0	1.9	1.7	1.4	1.0	0.6	•
Quick Ratio 31	0.9	•	3.5	7.9	1.2	•	1.7	1.1	1.3	1.0	0.7	0.5	•
Net Sales to Working Capital 32	20.2	•	9.4	6.6	20.2	•	7.1	8.3	7.6	10.1	83.7	•	•
Coverage Ratio 33	4.2	2.1	26.7	27.8	14.9	•	8.5	12.8	8.5	4.9	2.2	1.7	•
Total Asset Turnover 34	0.8	•	4.8	3.7	2.8	•	1.5	1.6	1.2	1.0	0.8	0.5	•
Inventory Turnover 35	28.0	•	45.2	11.2	133.1	•	41.2	17.6	33.6	23.0	5.9	24.4	•
Receivables Turnover 36	8.1	•	24.1	37.5	10.2	•	9.6	8.8	5.8	4.5	6.2	•	•
Total Liabilities to Net Worth 37	2.1	•	0.7	1.4	2.5	•	1.5	1.5	0.8	1.3	1.9	3.8	•
Current Assets to Working Capital 38	4.9	•	1.3	1.1	3.5	•	2.0	2.1	2.4	3.5	21.9	•	•
Current Liabilities to Working Capital 39	3.9	•	0.3	0.1	2.5	•	1.0	1.1	1.4	2.5	20.9	•	•
Working Capital to Net Sales 40	0.0	•	0.1	0.2	0.0	•	0.1	0.1	0.1	0.1	0.0	•	•
Inventory to Working Capital 41	0.3	•	0.1	0.3	0.1	•	0.1	0.4	0.2	0.3	3.9	•	•
Total Receipts to Cash Flow 42	4.3	1.7	3.0	5.7	2.8	•	4.1	5.5	5.7	5.3	3.9	2.8	•
Cost of Goods to Cash Flow 43	1.7	0.1	1.0	3.0	1.1	•	1.9	3.6	3.6	2.6	1.3	0.4	•
Cash Flow to Total Debt 44	0.3	•	3.9	1.1	1.4	•	0.6	0.5	0.5	0.3	0.3	0.2	•

Selected Financial Factors (in Percentages)

Debt Ratio 45	67.7	•	41.8	57.7	71.3	•	60.3	59.7	45.9	56.9	65.6	79.1	•
Return on Total Assets 46	8.3	•	65.5	30.8	26.7	•	21.6	11.2	10.1	6.9	3.7	4.6	•
Return on Equity Before Income Taxes 47	19.7	•	108.3	70.1	87.1	•	48.0	25.5	16.4	12.7	5.9	9.4	•
Return on Equity After Income Taxes 48	16.3	•	107.7	67.7	82.1	•	40.6	25.3	15.5	10.4	5.4	6.8	•
Profit Margin (Before Income Tax) 49	8.5	9.7	13.1	7.9	8.9	•	12.3	6.3	7.3	5.7	2.5	3.7	•
Profit Margin (After Income Tax) 50	7.0	9.6	13.0	7.7	8.4	•	10.4	6.2	6.8	4.7	2.3	2.7	•

Table I

Corporations with and without Net Income

EDUCATIONAL SERVICES

MONEY AMOUNTS AND SIZE OF ASSETS IN THOUSANDS OF DOLLARS

Item Description for Accounting Period 7/12 Through 6/13	Total	Zero Assets	Under 500	500 to 1,000	1,000 to 5,000	5,000 to 10,000	10,000 to 25,000	25,000 to 50,000	50,000 to 100,000	100,000 to 250,000	250,000 to 500,000	500,000 to 2,500,000	2,500,000 and over
Number of Enterprises 1	56523	16662	35670	1822	1766	279	159	65	38	38	11	11	3

Revenues ($ in Thousands)

Net Sales 2	67075520	2458840	11194916	4299415	8113076	3158776	3259564	3373592	2806544	5938632	3119345	11210849	8141971
Interest 3	129164	2981	362	459	3059	3981	3687	2684	5839	8386	5349	14046	78330
Rents 4	57344	344	1	0	915	37	2654	3257	5955	25428	8814	3660	6278
Royalties 5	112563	101	0	0	137	20671	39	3911	376	25983	4578	52661	4106
Other Portfolio Income 6	213436	55916	22342	2302	13969	4782	20559	6320	1563	11591	6270	60369	7455
Other Receipts 7	642216	25060	122313	16995	35764	23679	8612	32319	43842	155637	39129	82102	56763
Total Receipts 8	68230243	2543242	11339934	4319171	8166920	3211926	3295115	3422083	2864119	6165657	3183485	11423687	8294903
Average Total Receipts 9	1207	153	318	2371	4625	11512	20724	52647	75372	162254	289408	1038517	2764968

Operating Costs/Operating Income (%)

Cost of Operations 10	12.1	29.6	11.6	20.1	9.4	13.5	16.1	25.1	12.3	11.9	6.3	10.4	3.1
Salaries and Wages 11	30.6	17.9	24.1	32.6	30.5	31.4	30.2	30.2	33.6	32.3	34.4	31.0	38.2
Taxes Paid 12	3.3	2.4	4.1	3.0	3.6	3.8	4.2	3.1	4.0	3.8	4.7	2.1	2.8
Interest Paid 13	1.7	0.7	0.7	0.5	0.7	0.4	0.8	1.9	2.5	2.6	2.7	2.4	3.5
Depreciation 14	2.3	1.9	1.4	0.8	1.5	1.4	1.6	2.9	3.3	2.7	4.3	2.7	3.5
Amortization and Depletion 15	0.8	0.2	0.1	0.2	0.3	0.2	0.9	0.9	1.3	2.2	1.6	1.3	0.8
Pensions and Other Deferred Comp. 16	0.4	0.1	0.4	0.4	0.7	0.4	0.3	0.4	0.7	0.3	0.4	0.4	0.2
Employee Benefits 17	2.4	0.9	1.4	2.2	0.9	2.2	2.3	2.7	3.1	2.4	4.5	5.1	1.6
Advertising 18	5.8	6.6	2.0	1.4	1.7	3.4	7.3	5.6	5.9	7.3	5.9	11.3	8.9
Other Expenses 19	32.6	38.0	41.4	28.2	37.0	35.3	31.8	22.0	28.8	31.2	28.7	27.1	31.9
Officers' Compensation 20	3.9	2.9	9.6	5.5	8.0	2.4	2.9	1.5	1.6	1.9	1.0	0.9	1.0
Operating Margin 21	4.0	•	3.3	5.2	5.7	5.6	1.7	3.7	2.7	1.5	5.6	5.2	4.6
Operating Margin Before Officers' Comp. 22	7.9	1.8	12.9	10.7	13.6	8.0	4.6	5.2	4.3	3.4	6.6	6.1	5.6

Selected Average Balance Sheet ($ in Thousands)

Net Receivables 23	107	0	5	128	520	1569	2778	7466	8597	18622	32741	103359	262456
Inventories 24	10	0	2	8	63	38	292	1644	604	1505	938	8765	6730
Net Property, Plant and Equipment 25	192	0	20	183	605	1560	2971	8174	17731	32119	133439	216228	514173
Total Assets 26	925	0	80	668	2256	6913	15336	36924	70843	159342	370144	1072722	4280166
Notes and Loans Payable 27	301	0	59	189	522	1128	2364	19323	24871	50484	105975	295081	1467666
All Other Liabilities 28	301	0	36	213	774	3526	6033	13713	20961	48111	87086	353027	1226783
Net Worth 29	323	0	-15	266	960	2259	6938	3888	25011	60747	177083	424615	1585718

Selected Financial Ratios (Times to 1)

Current Ratio 30	1.4	•	1.1	1.7	1.7	1.7	1.5	1.1	1.3	1.3	1.3	1.5	1.3
Quick Ratio 31	1.1	•	0.8	1.4	1.4	1.5	1.2	0.9	1.1	1.1	1.1	1.1	1.0
Net Sales to Working Capital 32	12.6	•	71.0	13.7	7.8	7.3	7.1	42.0	12.1	13.3	13.8	9.9	10.0
Coverage Ratio 33	4.4	4.0	7.8	12.1	9.5	18.8	4.6	3.7	2.9	3.1	4.0	4.0	2.9
Total Asset Turnover 34	1.3	•	3.9	3.5	2.0	1.6	1.3	1.4	1.0	1.0	0.8	1.0	0.6
Inventory Turnover 35	14.0	•	17.9	57.7	6.9	39.8	11.3	7.9	15.1	12.4	19.1	12.1	12.7
Receivables Turnover 36	11.5	•	61.0	24.2	9.3	7.2	6.2	8.4	8.6	8.3	8.5	•	•
Total Liabilities to Net Worth 37	1.9	•	•	1.5	1.3	2.1	1.2	8.5	1.8	1.6	1.1	1.5	1.7
Current Assets to Working Capital 38	3.6	•	9.2	2.5	2.4	2.5	2.9	15.9	3.9	4.2	4.3	3.1	4.5
Current Liabilities to Working Capital 39	2.6	•	8.2	1.5	1.4	1.5	1.9	14.9	2.9	3.2	3.3	2.1	3.5
Working Capital to Net Sales 40	0.1	•	0.0	0.1	0.1	0.1	0.1	0.0	0.1	0.1	0.1	0.1	0.1
Inventory to Working Capital 41	0.1	•	0.6	0.1	0.1	0.0	0.1	1.5	0.1	0.1	0.0	0.1	0.0
Total Receipts to Cash Flow 42	3.4	3.2	2.9	4.4	2.9	3.1	3.6	4.7	3.8	3.6	3.5	3.7	3.1
Cost of Goods to Cash Flow 43	0.4	0.9	0.3	0.9	0.3	0.4	0.6	1.2	0.5	0.4	0.2	0.4	0.1
Cash Flow to Total Debt 44	0.6	•	1.1	1.3	1.2	0.8	0.7	0.3	0.4	0.4	0.4	0.4	0.3

Selected Financial Factors (in Percentages)

Debt Ratio 45	65.1	•	119.0	60.2	57.4	67.3	54.8	89.5	64.7	61.9	52.2	60.4	63.0
Return on Total Assets 46	9.6	•	20.8	21.7	14.4	12.6	4.7	9.9	7.6	7.8	8.3	9.3	6.4
Return on Equity Before Income Taxes 47	21.3	•	•	50.1	30.4	36.6	8.2	68.4	14.1	13.8	13.0	17.6	11.4
Return on Equity After Income Taxes 48	16.3	•	•	49.4	29.6	35.7	7.1	56.2	9.0	8.7	8.7	11.1	5.9
Profit Margin (Before Income Tax) 49	5.8	2.3	4.6	5.6	6.3	7.3	2.8	5.1	4.8	5.4	8.1	7.3	6.6
Profit Margin (After Income Tax) 50	4.4	1.6	4.5	5.6	6.2	7.1	2.4	4.2	3.0	3.4	5.5	4.6	3.4

Table II

Corporations with Net Income

EDUCATIONAL SERVICES

MONEY AMOUNTS AND SIZE OF ASSETS IN THOUSANDS OF DOLLARS

Item Description for Accounting Period 7/12 Through 6/13	Total	Zero Assets	Under 500	500 to 1,000	1,000 to 5,000	5,000 to 10,000	10,000 to 25,000	25,000 to 50,000	50,000 to 100,000	100,000 to 250,000	250,000 to 500,000	500,000 to 2,500,000	2,500,000 and over
Number of Enterprises 1	36819	9592	24013	1385	1458	155	102	51	18	•	8	•	0
Revenues ($ in Thousands)													
Net Sales 2	53663469	2095453	8498179	3261828	6862067	2532570	2386898	2999334	1906921	•	2613348	•	0
Interest 3	46605	565	106	451	2651	3647	2290	2543	3639	•	5347	•	0
Rents 4	44650	344	0	0	398	37	2654	1713	754	•	8767	•	0
Royalties 5	86701	101	0	0	137	20671	39	2487	100	•	4578	•	0
Other Portfolio Income 6	159784	55916	22185	2302	13969	4782	17049	6316	567	•	5638	•	0
Other Receipts 7	511357	24834	130246	1809	32462	16851	2449	27426	20280	•	38693	•	0
Total Receipts 8	54512566	2177213	8650716	3266390	6911684	2578558	2411379	3039819	1932261	•	2676371	•	0
Average Total Receipts 9	1481	227	360	2358	4741	16636	23641	59604	107348	•	334546	•	•
Operating Costs/Operating Income (%)													
Cost of Operations 10	12.5	30.0	11.5	18.8	9.9	9.4	17.9	25.3	11.1	•	6.7	•	•
Salaries and Wages 11	28.9	17.9	20.3	29.5	29.7	32.1	26.9	29.2	31.4	•	34.2	•	•
Taxes Paid 12	3.2	2.2	3.7	2.6	3.8	3.7	3.6	3.1	4.2	•	4.7	•	•
Interest Paid 13	1.1	0.5	0.6	0.5	0.6	0.2	0.5	1.2	0.9	•	1.8	•	•
Depreciation 14	2.3	1.8	1.3	0.9	1.5	1.2	1.3	2.9	2.5	•	4.0	•	•
Amortization and Depletion 15	0.6	0.2	0.0	0.2	0.2	0.0	0.4	0.3	0.4	•	1.7	•	•
Pensions and Other Deferred Comp. 16	0.4	0.0	0.5	0.4	0.6	0.3	0.3	0.4	0.7	•	0.4	•	•
Employee Benefits 17	2.1	1.0	1.0	1.7	0.8	2.0	2.0	2.5	2.3	•	4.5	•	•
Advertising 18	5.4	6.5	1.5	1.8	1.5	3.1	4.7	5.8	6.6	•	5.6	•	•
Other Expenses 19	30.6	30.1	39.6	28.1	34.1	35.7	30.6	19.9	26.2	•	28.1	•	•
Officers' Compensation 20	4.2	3.3	11.0	5.4	8.7	2.3	3.4	1.5	1.3	•	0.8	•	•
Operating Margin 21	8.7	6.5	8.9	10.0	8.7	9.9	8.5	7.8	12.3	•	7.5	•	•
Operating Margin Before Officers' Comp. 22	12.9	9.8	19.9	15.4	17.3	12.3	11.9	9.3	13.6	•	8.4	•	•

Selected Average Balance Sheet ($ in Thousands)

	C1	C2	C3	C4	C5	C6	C7	C8	C9	C10	C11	C12	C13
Net Receivables 23	132	0	6	127	593	1956	2387	7825	7974	•	39880	•	•
Inventories 24	13	0	2	10	68	46	411	2019	768	•	805	•	•
Net Property, Plant and Equipment 25	230	0	16	203	586	1647	3860	9242	23121	•	128857	•	•
Total Assets 26	993	0	82	682	2244	7340	15244	36974	72061	•	381168	•	•
Notes and Loans Payable 27	259	0	41	156	499	905	2215	15742	17661	•	97047	•	•
All Other Liabilities 28	337	0	36	182	705	3083	5487	13478	22375	•	111123	•	•
Net Worth 29	396	0	5	345	1040	3352	7543	7754	32025	•	172998	•	•

Selected Financial Ratios (Times to 1)

	C1	C2	C3	C4	C5	C6	C7	C8	C9	C10	C11	C12	C13
Current Ratio 30	1.5	•	1.4	2.0	1.8	1.9	1.6	1.6	1.6	•	1.2	•	•
Quick Ratio 31	1.2	•	1.0	1.8	1.4	1.7	1.2	1.2	1.3	•	1.0	•	•
Net Sales to Working Capital 32	10.0	•	25.9	11.2	7.3	6.9	6.9	7.6	10.2	•	20.8	•	•
Coverage Ratio 33	10.2	20.8	17.5	19.9	18.0	74.2	19.3	8.4	15.5	•	6.8	•	•
Total Asset Turnover 34	1.5	•	4.3	3.5	2.1	2.2	1.5	1.6	1.5	•	0.9	•	•
Inventory Turnover 35	14.2	•	20.8	45.1	6.9	33.6	10.2	7.4	15.3	•	27.4	•	•
Receivables Turnover 36	11.6	•	91.6	30.5	8.6	7.9	7.2	9.6	9.7	•	•	•	•
Total Liabilities to Net Worth 37	1.5	•	15.0	1.0	1.2	1.2	1.0	3.8	1.3	•	1.2	•	•
Current Assets to Working Capital 38	2.9	•	3.7	2.0	2.2	2.1	2.6	2.8	2.7	•	6.4	•	•
Current Liabilities to Working Capital 39	1.9	•	2.7	1.0	1.2	1.1	1.6	1.8	1.7	•	5.4	•	•
Working Capital to Net Sales 40	0.1	•	0.0	0.1	0.1	0.1	0.1	0.1	0.1	•	0.0	•	•
Inventory to Working Capital 41	0.1	•	0.2	0.1	0.1	0.0	0.1	0.3	0.1	•	0.1	•	•
Total Receipts to Cash Flow 42	3.0	2.9	2.6	3.9	2.7	2.7	3.1	4.3	3.0	•	3.2	•	•
Cost of Goods to Cash Flow 43	0.4	0.9	0.3	0.7	0.3	0.3	0.5	1.1	0.3	•	0.2	•	•
Cash Flow to Total Debt 44	0.8	•	1.8	1.8	1.4	1.5	1.0	0.5	0.9	•	0.5	•	•

Selected Financial Factors (in Percentages)

	C1	C2	C3	C4	C5	C6	C7	C8	C9	C10	C11	C12	C13
Debt Ratio 45	60.1	•	93.7	49.5	53.6	54.3	50.5	79.0	55.6	•	54.6	•	•
Return on Total Assets 46	16.9	•	49.0	36.8	20.9	26.5	15.3	16.5	21.4	•	10.6	•	•
Return on Equity Before Income Taxes 47	38.1	•	737.3	69.1	42.5	57.3	29.3	69.3	45.1	•	19.9	•	•
Return on Equity After Income Taxes 48	31.8	•	722.0	68.4	41.6	56.2	27.8	61.6	36.6	•	13.9	•	•
Profit Margin (Before Income Tax) 49	10.4	10.4	10.7	10.1	9.4	11.8	9.5	9.1	13.6	•	10.5	•	•
Profit Margin (After Income Tax) 50	8.7	9.7	10.5	10.0	9.2	11.5	9.0	8.1	11.1	•	7.4	•	•

Table I

Corporations with and without Net Income

OFFICES OF PHYSICIANS

MONEY AMOUNTS AND SIZE OF ASSETS IN THOUSANDS OF DOLLARS

Item Description for Accounting Period 7/12 Through 6/13	Total	Zero Assets	Under 500	500 to 1,000	1,000 to 5,000	5,000 to 10,000	10,000 to 25,000	25,000 to 50,000	50,000 to 100,000	100,000 to 250,000	250,000 to 500,000	500,000 to 2,500,000	2,500,000 and over
Number of Enterprises **1**	158672	17104	131317	5221	4245	492	167	54	35	27	6	4	0

Revenues ($ in Thousands)

	Total	Zero Assets	Under 500	500 to 1,000	1,000 to 5,000	5,000 to 10,000	10,000 to 25,000	25,000 to 50,000	50,000 to 100,000	100,000 to 250,000	250,000 to 500,000	500,000 to 2,500,000	2,500,000 and over
Net Sales **2**	251826450	8677797	134944588	18686936	38457382	14367693	8731867	5689608	4224756	4323443	1957206	11765176	0
Interest **3**	59521	1433	11636	1696	6918	2515	1357	3743	2144	6951	7944	13184	0
Rents **4**	135962	5207	57894	59	23884	4189	2843	20793	8809	6261	6023	0	0
Royalties **5**	32281	0	0	0	0	0	0	0	0	0	0	32281	0
Other Portfolio Income **6**	687842	40266	336463	93648	57078	36361	60907	11862	1518	32583	4763	12392	0
Other Receipts **7**	7646540	311426	4732910	442624	715572	524702	180328	114630	124878	194198	50802	254469	0
Total Receipts **8**	260388596	9036129	140083491	19224963	39260834	14935460	8977302	5840636	4362105	4563436	2026738	12077502	0
Average Total Receipts **9**	1641	528	1067	3682	9249	30357	53756	108160	124632	169016	337790	3019376	•

Operating Costs/Operating Income (%)

	Total	Zero Assets	Under 500	500 to 1,000	1,000 to 5,000	5,000 to 10,000	10,000 to 25,000	25,000 to 50,000	50,000 to 100,000	100,000 to 250,000	250,000 to 500,000	500,000 to 2,500,000	2,500,000 and over
Cost of Operations **10**	3.9	1.4	3.3	3.1	3.3	7.9	8.3	4.8	3.1	6.5	23.4	3.7	•
Salaries and Wages **11**	31.5	53.2	25.7	22.5	32.9	41.2	43.6	50.4	54.5	47.2	34.8	46.6	•
Taxes Paid **12**	3.2	3.6	3.2	2.9	3.2	3.1	3.6	3.0	3.0	3.8	2.6	2.8	•
Interest Paid **13**	0.4	0.2	0.2	0.4	0.4	0.4	0.3	0.4	1.0	1.7	0.8	1.0	•
Depreciation **14**	0.9	0.3	0.7	1.2	1.3	1.5	1.2	1.3	1.5	1.9	1.3	0.7	•
Amortization and Depletion **15**	0.1	0.1	0.0	0.0	0.1	0.1	0.1	0.2	0.4	0.8	0.3	0.4	•
Pensions and Other Deferred Comp. **16**	3.7	2.1	3.8	4.2	3.1	2.9	2.6	3.9	2.5	2.3	1.1	7.9	•
Employee Benefits **17**	2.5	4.7	1.9	1.1	2.1	2.6	3.1	12.2	3.7	4.1	3.2	6.3	•
Advertising **18**	0.5	0.3	0.4	0.7	0.8	0.3	0.4	0.7	0.4	0.3	0.2	0.1	•
Other Expenses **19**	31.2	25.0	30.3	33.5	32.8	32.2	35.3	26.7	31.8	36.1	32.5	32.4	•
Officers' Compensation **20**	19.9	12.1	26.5	23.8	17.8	10.3	3.0	1.4	1.1	3.6	0.8	0.3	•
Operating Margin **21**	2.2	•	3.9	6.5	2.4	•	•	•	•	•	•	•	•
Operating Margin Before Officers' Comp. **22**	22.2	9.1	30.4	30.3	20.1	7.8	1.3	•	•	•	•	•	•

Selected Average Balance Sheet ($ in Thousands)

Net Receivables 23	31	0	3	83	149	1632	3311	5645	13109	17494	72293	122526	•
Inventories 24	2	0	0	7	5	35	100	238	213	607	1294	30173	•
Net Property, Plant and Equipment 25	67	0	23	168	658	1946	3853	10666	15328	24326	32244	98912	•
Total Assets 26	302	0	92	686	1855	6885	15569	37644	69069	161924	295030	1971844	•
Notes and Loans Payable 27	132	0	49	281	1011	3008	7292	11682	27618	69910	102122	487516	•
All Other Liabilities 28	152	0	37	184	607	3288	7143	14554	18067	47719	113878	2409924	•
Net Worth 29	18	0	7	221	237	588	1135	11408	23385	44295	79030	-925596	•

Selected Financial Ratios (Times to 1)

Current Ratio 30	1.2	•	1.1	2.0	1.2	1.2	1.0	1.4	1.2	1.3	1.4	1.4	•
Quick Ratio 31	1.0	•	1.0	1.6	1.0	0.8	0.8	0.9	0.9	0.9	0.9	1.1	•
Net Sales to Working Capital 32	59.4	•	183.1	16.8	68.6	47.9	230.2	21.0	23.3	17.7	7.2	22.2	•
Coverage Ratio 33	17.0	6.5	37.6	24.1	11.4	5.0	4.6	•	1.5	•	3.8	1.5	•
Total Asset Turnover 34	5.2	•	11.2	5.2	4.9	4.2	3.4	2.8	1.7	1.0	1.1	1.5	•
Inventory Turnover 35	32.9	•	91.1	16.2	63.9	65.9	43.6	21.2	17.4	17.0	59.1	3.6	•
Receivables Turnover 36	54.1	•	418.3	49.3	55.8	25.2	15.3	16.2	9.3	7.1	9.0	23.5	•
Total Liabilities to Net Worth 37	15.5	•	12.8	2.1	6.8	10.7	12.7	2.3	2.0	2.7	2.7	•	•
Current Assets to Working Capital 38	5.0	•	9.0	2.0	5.9	6.7	31.5	3.7	5.5	4.7	3.7	3.5	•
Current Liabilities to Working Capital 39	4.0	•	8.0	1.0	4.9	5.7	30.5	2.7	4.5	3.7	2.7	2.5	•
Working Capital to Net Sales 40	0.0	•	0.0	0.1	0.0	0.0	0.0	0.0	0.0	0.1	0.1	0.0	•
Inventory to Working Capital 41	0.1	•	0.1	0.0	0.0	0.1	0.4	0.0	0.0	0.1	0.0	0.2	•
Total Receipts to Cash Flow 42	3.2	4.3	3.1	2.6	3.2	3.5	3.3	4.8	3.5	3.4	3.1	3.5	•
Cost of Goods to Cash Flow 43	0.1	0.1	0.1	0.1	0.1	0.3	0.3	0.2	0.1	0.2	0.7	0.1	•
Cash Flow to Total Debt 44	1.8	•	3.9	2.9	1.7	1.3	1.1	0.8	0.8	0.4	0.5	0.3	•

Selected Financial Factors (in Percentages)

Debt Ratio 45	93.9	•	92.8	67.8	87.2	91.5	92.7	69.7	66.1	72.6	73.2	146.9	•
Return on Total Assets 46	31.4	•	89.1	50.9	23.9	7.7	4.7	•	2.6	•	3.5	2.1	•
Return on Equity Before Income Taxes 47	487.4	•	1196.9	151.3	170.6	72.0	50.3	•	2.5	•	9.8	•	•
Return on Equity After Income Taxes 48	477.7	•	1189.7	149.8	168.1	67.8	38.2	•	0.5	•	4.7	•	•
Profit Margin (Before Income Tax) 49	5.6	1.2	7.8	9.3	4.5	1.5	1.1	•	0.5	•	2.4	0.4	•
Profit Margin (After Income Tax) 50	5.5	1.1	7.7	9.2	4.4	1.4	0.8	•	0.1	•	1.1	0.0	•

Table II

Corporations with Net Income

OFFICES OF PHYSICIANS

MONEY AMOUNTS AND SIZE OF ASSETS IN THOUSANDS OF DOLLARS

Item Description for Accounting Period 7/12 Through 6/13	Total	Zero Assets	Under 500	500 to 1,000	1,000 to 5,000	5,000 to 10,000	10,000 to 25,000	25,000 to 50,000	50,000 to 100,000	100,000 to 250,000	250,000 to 500,000	500,000 to 2,500,000	2,500,000 and over
Number of Enterprises 1	110177	8935	93849	3881	2998	343	106	21	21	•	•	•	0

Revenues ($ in Thousands)

Net Sales 2	168768049	2297181	93088391	10188318	26021163	9407877	5593256	2401379	3458431	•	•	•	0
Interest 3	36681	70	8128	783	3164	1164	653	357	1447	•	•	•	0
Rents 4	89427	4903	45949	0	15639	2806	842	11759	3206	•	•	•	0
Royalties 5	0	0	0	0	0	0	0	0	0	•	•	•	0
Other Portfolio Income 6	634966	31093	327937	92989	45491	33039	60539	41	592	•	•	•	0
Other Receipts 7	6186576	352012	3927035	277572	669097	358615	140298	19997	81496	•	•	•	0
Total Receipts 8	175715699	2685259	97397440	10559662	26754554	9803501	5795588	2433533	3545172	•	•	•	0
Average Total Receipts 9	1595	301	1038	2721	8924	28582	54675	115883	168818	•	•	•	

Operating Costs/Operating Income (%)

Cost of Operations 10	3.9	4.2	2.7	5.6	3.8	5.5	9.1	4.0	3.3	•	•	•	•
Salaries and Wages 11	28.2	22.4	22.3	25.1	29.1	39.2	40.1	53.4	54.0	•	•	•	•
Taxes Paid 12	3.2	4.2	3.2	3.0	3.1	3.3	3.8	3.2	2.8	•	•	•	•
Interest Paid 13	0.3	0.7	0.2	0.6	0.4	0.5	0.3	0.4	0.6	•	•	•	•
Depreciation 14	0.8	0.8	0.6	1.4	1.1	1.6	1.2	1.6	1.2	•	•	•	•
Amortization and Depletion 15	0.1	0.2	0.1	0.1	0.0	0.1	0.0	0.2	0.2	•	•	•	•
Pensions and Other Deferred Comp. 16	3.8	2.3	3.9	2.6	3.2	2.8	3.0	2.4	2.9	•	•	•	•
Employee Benefits 17	2.2	1.4	1.7	1.0	1.9	2.7	2.2	2.9	3.5	•	•	•	•
Advertising 18	0.5	0.8	0.4	1.1	0.9	0.3	0.5	0.4	0.4	•	•	•	•
Other Expenses 19	30.1	41.4	29.2	27.3	30.8	32.8	32.2	29.2	29.7	•	•	•	•
Officers' Compensation 20	20.4	21.4	27.8	15.9	19.8	10.3	4.1	1.6	1.1	•	•	•	•
Operating Margin 21	6.5	0.2	8.1	16.2	6.0	0.9	3.4	0.7	0.3	•	•	•	•
Operating Margin Before Officers' Comp. 22	26.9	21.6	35.9	32.1	25.7	11.2	7.4	2.3	1.4	•	•	•	•

Selected Average Balance Sheet ($ in Thousands)

	C1	C2	C3	C4	C5	C6	C7	C8	C9	C10	C11	C12	C13
Net Receivables 23	30	0	3	84	82	1717	2803	4931	16352	•	•	•	•
Inventories 24	2	0	0	9	3	27	112	175	236	•	•	•	•
Net Property, Plant and Equipment 25	66	0	22	173	616	2259	3561	13910	17876	•	•	•	•
Total Assets 26	309	0	100	692	1868	7052	15568	36669	70153	•	•	•	•
Notes and Loans Payable 27	99	0	38	264	736	2686	4851	17836	24669	•	•	•	•
All Other Liabilities 28	164	0	34	114	544	2140	4846	13474	21238	•	•	•	•
Net Worth 29	46	0	27	315	588	2225	5871	5359	24247	•	•	•	•

Selected Financial Ratios (Times to 1)

	C1	C2	C3	C4	C5	C6	C7	C8	C9	C10	C11	C12	C13
Current Ratio 30	1.6	•	1.4	3.2	1.5	2.0	1.2	1.1	1.3	•	•	•	•
Quick Ratio 31	1.3	•	1.3	2.6	1.3	1.5	1.0	0.9	1.0	•	•	•	•
Net Sales to Working Capital 32	30.7	•	61.4	9.3	31.3	13.2	50.4	64.6	21.3	•	•	•	•
Coverage Ratio 33	33.7	26.1	59.8	32.2	24.1	12.0	24.6	5.6	5.7	•	•	•	•
Total Asset Turnover 34	5.0	•	10.0	3.8	4.6	3.9	3.4	3.1	2.3	•	•	•	•
Inventory Turnover 35	27.2	•	70.5	16.0	113.5	55.5	42.9	26.2	23.3	•	•	•	•
Receivables Turnover 36	57.9	•	364.2	37.7	87.2	25.0	•	17.2	10.7	•	•	•	•
Total Liabilities to Net Worth 37	5.7	•	2.7	1.2	2.2	2.2	1.7	5.8	1.9	•	•	•	•
Current Assets to Working Capital 38	2.8	•	3.4	1.5	2.9	2.0	6.3	8.0	4.3	•	•	•	•
Current Liabilities to Working Capital 39	1.8	•	2.4	0.5	1.9	1.0	5.3	7.0	3.3	•	•	•	•
Working Capital to Net Sales 40	0.0	•	0.0	0.1	0.0	0.1	0.0	0.0	0.0	•	•	•	•
Inventory to Working Capital 41	0.0	•	0.0	0.0	0.0	0.0	0.1	0.0	0.0	•	•	•	•
Total Receipts to Cash Flow 42	2.8	2.0	2.8	2.5	3.0	3.2	3.1	3.9	3.4	•	•	•	•
Cost of Goods to Cash Flow 43	0.1	0.1	0.1	0.1	0.1	0.2	0.3	0.2	0.1	•	•	•	•
Cash Flow to Total Debt 44	2.0	•	5.0	2.8	2.3	1.8	1.7	0.9	1.1	•	•	•	•

Selected Financial Factors (in Percentages)

	C1	C2	C3	C4	C5	C6	C7	C8	C9	C10	C11	C12	C13
Debt Ratio 45	85.0	•	72.7	54.5	68.5	68.4	62.3	85.4	65.4	•	•	•	•
Return on Total Assets 46	54.2	•	128.7	77.6	42.5	21.7	24.7	7.6	8.0	•	•	•	•
Return on Equity Before Income Taxes 47	350.3	•	463.8	165.2	129.6	63.0	62.9	42.8	19.1	•	•	•	•
Return on Equity After Income Taxes 48	344.8	•	461.3	163.8	128.2	61.3	59.2	37.5	15.8	•	•	•	•
Profit Margin (Before Income Tax) 49	10.6	17.1	12.7	19.8	8.8	5.1	7.0	2.0	2.8	•	•	•	•
Profit Margin (After Income Tax) 50	10.4	16.7	12.6	19.7	8.7	5.0	6.6	1.8	2.3	•	•	•	•

Table I

Corporations with and without Net Income

OFFICES OF DENTISTS

MONEY AMOUNTS AND SIZE OF ASSETS IN THOUSANDS OF DOLLARS

Item Description for Accounting Period 7/12 Through 6/13		Total	Zero Assets	Under 500	500 to 1,000	1,000 to 5,000	5,000 to 10,000	10,000 to 25,000	25,000 to 50,000	50,000 to 100,000	100,000 to 250,000	250,000 to 500,000	500,000 to 2,500,000	2,500,000 and over
Number of Enterprises	1	77546	4890	63363	7600	1661	13	12	0	4	0	3	0	0

Revenues ($ in Thousands)

Net Sales	2	68359528	4280451	45270354	12621247	4375399	184516	492479	0	228090	0	906994	0	0
Interest	3	8496	534	2046	2501	83	63	139	0	30	0	3099	0	0
Rents	4	143	0	0	0	0	0	0	0	143	0	0	0	0
Royalties	5	0	0	0	0	0	0	0	0	0	0	0	0	0
Other Portfolio Income	6	84995	25639	56701	2030	418	0	18	0	186	0	3	0	0
Other Receipts	7	1879186	234114	1500731	41073	92641	1621	2220	0	509	0	6277	0	0
Total Receipts	8	70332348	4540738	46829832	12666851	4468541	186200	494856	0	228958	0	916373	0	0
Average Total Receipts	9	907	929	739	1667	2690	14323	41238	•	57240	•	305458	•	•

Operating Costs/Operating Income (%)

Cost of Operations	10	5.6	1.5	5.4	5.8	10.1	•	7.5	•	40.5	•	0.1	•	•
Salaries and Wages	11	25.0	47.2	22.6	26.6	20.9	20.1	21.9	•	17.2	•	42.4	•	•
Taxes Paid	12	3.8	4.7	3.9	3.5	2.9	1.8	1.5	•	3.9	•	3.6	•	•
Interest Paid	13	1.2	1.0	0.9	1.7	1.7	0.2	0.0	•	7.9	•	7.3	•	•
Depreciation	14	1.9	1.4	1.7	2.3	2.5	0.2	0.1	•	4.0	•	4.1	•	•
Amortization and Depletion	15	0.6	1.1	0.4	0.8	0.9	0.4	0.3	•	4.5	•	3.2	•	•
Pensions and Other Deferred Comp.	16	2.1	0.6	2.2	2.7	1.1	•	2.3	•	0.0	•	0.2	•	•
Employee Benefits	17	1.2	1.7	1.1	1.4	0.6	1.4	1.7	•	2.0	•	1.1	•	•
Advertising	18	1.6	4.2	1.4	1.2	1.4	2.7	0.2	•	1.8	•	2.2	•	•
Other Expenses	19	31.8	36.7	32.3	25.4	35.0	63.4	61.3	•	16.4	•	37.8	•	•
Officers' Compensation	20	17.9	5.8	20.7	17.3	9.5	9.9	0.5	•	1.1	•	1.9	•	•
Operating Margin	21	7.4	•	7.4	11.2	13.4	•	2.9	•	0.6	•	•	•	•
Operating Margin Before Officers' Comp.	22	25.3	•	28.1	28.5	22.9	9.6	3.4	•	1.7	•	•	•	•

Selected Average Balance Sheet ($ in Thousands)

Net Receivables 23	10	0	4	26	80	2878	3762	•	7629	•	34637	•	•
Inventories 24	1	0	0	0	0	0	19	•	526	•	354	•	•
Net Property, Plant and Equipment 25	83	0	55	242	485	198	227	•	9824	•	70445	•	•
Total Assets 26	252	0	151	655	1523	5985	16133	•	159413	•	535166	•	•
Notes and Loans Payable 27	152	0	90	456	923	2797	6526	•	56916	•	251958	•	•
All Other Liabilities 28	51	0	32	142	244	2379	5948	•	19210	•	104018	•	•
Net Worth 29	49	0	29	57	356	809	3659	•	83286	•	179189	•	•

Selected Financial Ratios (Times to 1)

Current Ratio 30	1.2	•	1.3	0.9	2.1	0.7	0.6	•	2.2	•	1.1	•	•
Quick Ratio 31	1.1	•	1.2	0.8	1.9	0.6	0.6	•	0.8	•	0.9	•	•
Net Sales to Working Capital 32	60.7	•	61.8	•	8.9	•	•	•	3.7	•	67.7	•	•
Coverage Ratio 33	9.6	1.2	13.1	7.9	10.1	4.8	133.5	•	1.1	•	0.6	•	•
Total Asset Turnover 34	3.5	•	4.7	2.5	1.7	2.4	2.5	•	0.4	•	0.6	•	•
Inventory Turnover 35	98.0	•	83.9	220.0	•	•	159.9	•	44.0	•	0.7	•	•
Receivables Turnover 36	83.6	•	225.1	67.9	31.6	3.2	12.4	•	8.9	•	5.8	•	•
Total Liabilities to Net Worth 37	4.2	•	4.2	10.5	3.3	6.4	3.4	•	0.9	•	2.0	•	•
Current Assets to Working Capital 38	5.0	•	4.2	•	1.9	•	•	•	1.8	•	10.9	•	•
Current Liabilities to Working Capital 39	4.0	•	3.2	•	0.9	•	•	•	0.8	•	9.9	•	•
Working Capital to Net Sales 40	0.0	•	0.0	•	0.1	•	•	•	0.3	•	0.0	•	•
Inventory to Working Capital 41	0.0	•	0.0	•	•	•	•	•	0.0	•	•	•	•
Total Receipts to Cash Flow 42	2.9	3.4	2.8	3.3	2.2	1.6	1.6	•	8.1	•	4.0	•	•
Cost of Goods to Cash Flow 43	0.2	0.1	0.2	0.2	0.2	•	0.1	•	3.3	•	0.0	•	•
Cash Flow to Total Debt 44	1.5	•	2.1	0.9	1.0	1.7	2.1	•	0.1	•	0.2	•	•

Selected Financial Factors (in Percentages)

Debt Ratio 45	80.6	•	80.7	91.3	76.6	86.5	77.3	•	47.8	•	66.5	•	•
Return on Total Assets 46	40.2	•	55.5	33.7	29.8	2.0	8.6	•	3.2	•	2.5	•	•
Return on Equity Before Income Taxes 47	185.6	•	265.3	339.5	114.7	11.9	37.4	•	0.7	•	•	•	•
Return on Equity After Income Taxes 48	184.4	•	263.9	338.2	114.7	7.8	36.4	•	0.2	•	•	•	•
Profit Margin (Before Income Tax) 49	10.3	0.2	10.8	11.6	15.5	0.7	3.3	•	1.0	•	•	•	•
Profit Margin (After Income Tax) 50	10.2	•	10.7	11.6	15.5	0.4	3.2	•	0.3	•	•	•	•

Table II

Corporations with Net Income

OFFICES OF DENTISTS

MONEY AMOUNTS AND SIZE OF ASSETS IN THOUSANDS OF DOLLARS

Item Description for Accounting Period 7/12 Through 6/13		Total	Zero Assets	Under 500	500 to 1,000	1,000 to 5,000	5,000 to 10,000	10,000 to 25,000	25,000 to 50,000	50,000 to 100,000	100,000 to 250,000	250,000 to 500,000	500,000 to 2,500,000	2,500,000 and over
Number of Enterprises	1	59750	1618	50184	6580	1344	•	8	•	0	0	0	0	0

Revenues ($ in Thousands)														
Net Sales	2	54827437	2961244	36686656	11143693	3336640	•	316310	•	0	0	0	0	0
Interest	3	3370	98	656	2409	8	•	129	•	0	0	0	0	0
Rents	4	143	0	0	0	0	•	0	•	0	0	0	0	0
Royalties	5	0	0	0	0	0	•	0	•	0	0	0	0	0
Other Portfolio Income	6	49027	21361	26378	711	375	•	0	•	0	0	0	0	0
Other Receipts	7	1646986	157055	1355504	40210	90482	•	1418	•	0	0	0	0	0
Total Receipts	8	56526963	3139758	38069194	11187023	3427505	•	317857	•	0	0	0	0	0
Average Total Receipts	9	946	1941	759	1700	2550	•	39732	•	•	•	•	•	•

Operating Costs/Operating Income (%)														
Cost of Operations	10	5.6	0.7	5.8	5.3	7.6	•	•	•	•	•	•	•	•
Salaries and Wages	11	23.6	51.2	21.6	24.4	19.1	•	26.0	•	•	•	•	•	•
Taxes Paid	12	3.7	4.8	3.9	3.2	2.9	•	1.5	•	•	•	•	•	•
Interest Paid	13	1.1	0.4	0.9	1.5	1.7	•	0.0	•	•	•	•	•	•
Depreciation	14	1.6	0.6	1.5	2.1	2.5	•	0.0	•	•	•	•	•	•
Amortization and Depletion	15	0.5	0.6	0.4	0.7	0.9	•	0.1	•	•	•	•	•	•
Pensions and Other Deferred Comp.	16	2.2	0.8	2.1	2.9	1.1	•	3.5	•	•	•	•	•	•
Employee Benefits	17	1.1	1.1	1.1	1.1	0.3	•	2.4	•	•	•	•	•	•
Advertising	18	1.6	5.2	1.4	1.1	1.5	•	0.0	•	•	•	•	•	•
Other Expenses	19	30.4	32.8	30.8	25.8	35.2	•	64.8	•	•	•	•	•	•
Officers' Compensation	20	17.9	4.7	20.1	18.1	8.3	•	0.4	•	•	•	•	•	•
Operating Margin	21	10.7	•	10.3	13.6	18.9	•	1.1	•	•	•	•	•	•
Operating Margin Before Officers' Comp.	22	28.7	1.9	30.4	31.7	27.2	•	1.5	•	•	•	•	•	•

Selected Average Balance Sheet ($ in Thousands)

Net Receivables 23	10	0	5	27	51	•	3476	•	•	•	•	•	•	•
Inventories 24	1	0	1	1	0	•	0	•	•	•	•	•	•	•
Net Property, Plant and Equipment 25	87	0	57	248	477	•	72	•	•	•	•	•	•	•
Total Assets 26	254	0	161	664	1526	•	15411	•	•	•	•	•	•	•
Notes and Loans Payable 27	140	0	84	436	772	•	6653	•	•	•	•	•	•	•
All Other Liabilities 28	38	0	29	83	131	•	6589	•	•	•	•	•	•	•
Net Worth 29	76	0	48	146	624	•	2169	•	•	•	•	•	•	•

Selected Financial Ratios (Times to 1)

Current Ratio 30	1.5	•	1.5	1.4	2.6	•	0.5	•	•	•	•	•	•	•
Quick Ratio 31	1.4	•	1.4	1.2	2.3	•	0.5	•	•	•	•	•	•	•
Net Sales to Working Capital 32	32.3	•	41.1	33.6	6.5	•	•	•	•	•	•	•	•	•
Coverage Ratio 33	13.8	9.0	16.2	10.3	13.5	•	423.8	•	•	•	•	•	•	•
Total Asset Turnover 34	3.6	•	4.6	2.6	1.6	•	2.6	•	•	•	•	•	•	•
Inventory Turnover 35	96.9	•	75.9	176.3	•	•	•	•	•	•	•	•	•	•
Receivables Turnover 36	107.8	•	193.9	80.5	42.4	•	•	•	•	•	•	•	•	•
Total Liabilities to Net Worth 37	2.4	•	2.3	3.6	1.4	•	6.1	•	•	•	•	•	•	•
Current Assets to Working Capital 38	2.8	•	3.0	3.4	1.6	•	•	•	•	•	•	•	•	•
Current Liabilities to Working Capital 39	1.8	•	2.0	2.4	0.6	•	•	•	•	•	•	•	•	•
Working Capital to Net Sales 40	0.0	•	0.0	0.0	0.2	•	•	•	•	•	•	•	•	•
Inventory to Working Capital 41	0.0	•	0.0	0.0	•	•	•	•	•	•	•	•	•	•
Total Receipts to Cash Flow 42	2.7	3.5	2.7	3.0	1.9	•	1.5	•	•	•	•	•	•	•
Cost of Goods to Cash Flow 43	0.2	0.0	0.2	0.2	0.1	•	•	•	•	•	•	•	•	•
Cash Flow to Total Debt 44	1.9	•	2.5	1.1	1.4	•	2.0	•	•	•	•	•	•	•

Selected Financial Factors (in Percentages)

Debt Ratio 45	70.3	•	69.9	78.1	59.1	•	85.9	•	•	•	•	•	•	•
Return on Total Assets 46	53.8	•	68.3	39.6	38.1	•	4.1	•	•	•	•	•	•	•
Return on Equity Before Income Taxes 47	167.7	•	213.0	163.3	86.2	•	29.2	•	•	•	•	•	•	•
Return on Equity After Income Taxes 48	166.7	•	212.0	162.8	86.2	•	26.6	•	•	•	•	•	•	•
Profit Margin (Before Income Tax) 49	13.8	3.2	14.1	14.0	21.7	•	1.6	•	•	•	•	•	•	•
Profit Margin (After Income Tax) 50	13.7	2.8	14.0	14.0	21.7	•	1.5	•	•	•	•	•	•	•

Table I

Corporations with and without Net Income

OFFICES OF OTHER HEALTH PRACTITIONERS

MONEY AMOUNTS AND SIZE OF ASSETS IN THOUSANDS OF DOLLARS

Item Description for Accounting Period 7/12 Through 6/13	Total	Zero Assets	Under 500	500 to 1,000	1,000 to 5,000	5,000 to 10,000	10,000 to 25,000	25,000 to 50,000	50,000 to 100,000	100,000 to 250,000	250,000 to 500,000	500,000 to 2,500,000	2,500,000 and over
Number of Enterprises **1**	120662	25348	91253	2679	1192	35	89	29	18	9	4	6	0

Revenues ($ in Thousands)

Net Sales **2**	72544323	3126261	41663647	3771280	5019059	1186739	2754556	1407664	1740204	2620789	558207	8695917	0
Interest **3**	85437	96	1636	353	46	77	348	2631	2069	8106	17303	52770	0
Rents **4**	30762	0	16162	0	17	0	102	0	5836	2266	6379	0	0
Royalties **5**	0	0	0	0	0	0	0	0	0	0	0	0	0
Other Portfolio Income **6**	41708	1655	8	0	497	294	392	23	13168	4338	14227	7107	0
Other Receipts **7**	2766035	16047	277222	62907	80718	42165	158124	14520	564224	165022	49113	1335976	0
Total Receipts **8**	75468265	3144059	41958675	3834540	5100337	1229275	2913522	1424838	2325501	2800521	645229	10091770	0
Average Total Receipts **9**	625	124	460	1431	4279	35122	32736	49132	129194	311169	161307	1681962	•

Operating Costs/Operating Income (%)

Cost of Operations **10**	14.9	4.5	11.2	8.1	12.1	2.6	44.8	1.3	51.4	66.6	18.2	11.9	•
Salaries and Wages **11**	22.6	12.6	20.1	34.1	30.8	56.4	30.5	26.8	21.3	21.2	39.1	19.9	•
Taxes Paid **12**	3.0	2.6	3.1	4.2	3.9	3.3	2.8	2.1	2.7	1.8	3.2	1.8	•
Interest Paid **13**	0.8	0.6	0.4	1.0	0.5	0.3	0.6	1.2	1.4	0.3	10.3	1.9	•
Depreciation **14**	0.9	0.9	0.9	0.8	0.6	0.9	1.4	1.1	0.9	0.8	1.7	0.9	•
Amortization and Depletion **15**	0.4	0.2	0.2	1.1	0.4	•	0.3	0.5	0.7	0.2	1.9	1.4	•
Pensions and Other Deferred Comp. **16**	0.8	1.0	1.0	0.9	1.0	0.4	0.5	0.2	0.3	0.3	•	0.4	•
Employee Benefits **17**	1.6	1.0	1.1	1.3	1.6	3.3	2.7	1.8	2.3	2.1	3.4	3.5	•
Advertising **18**	1.2	1.1	1.4	1.1	1.4	0.4	1.1	0.1	0.3	0.5	2.9	0.4	•
Other Expenses **19**	40.7	46.7	38.4	25.0	37.1	27.7	17.6	62.1	52.7	12.0	37.9	70.4	•
Officers' Compensation **20**	9.0	13.2	12.6	11.1	6.1	3.7	2.0	0.8	0.4	0.2	0.9	0.3	•
Operating Margin **21**	4.3	15.7	9.6	11.3	4.6	1.0	•	2.0	•	•	•	•	•
Operating Margin Before Officers' Comp. **22**	13.3	28.9	22.2	22.4	10.6	4.7	•	2.8	•	•	•	•	•

Selected Average Balance Sheet ($ in Thousands)

Net Receivables 23	26	0	2	62	293	1338	3695	5713	11630	24953	29258	211290	•
Inventories 24	4	0	2	13	48	179	307	262	702	742	782	13742	•
Net Property, Plant and Equipment 25	36	0	24	136	363	1520	2072	4892	9677	19563	30465	67834	•
Total Assets 26	193	0	78	646	1695	7516	15260	35761	69685	143068	328916	988704	•
Notes and Loans Payable 27	79	0	37	269	664	2313	7145	14581	34632	18014	181690	337761	•
All Other Liabilities 28	54	0	14	94	451	2580	5544	10406	15947	55253	269808	286485	•
Net Worth 29	60	0	28	283	579	2623	2572	10774	19106	69801	-122582	364459	•

Selected Financial Ratios (Times to 1)

Current Ratio 30	1.5	•	1.8	2.8	2.1	1.5	0.9	1.4	0.8	1.4	0.5	2.1	•
Quick Ratio 31	1.1	•	1.5	2.2	1.5	1.3	0.8	0.9	0.6	1.0	0.2	1.7	•
Net Sales to Working Capital 32	21.7	•	30.1	7.7	7.7	31.4	•	9.6	•	15.2	•	7.5	•
Coverage Ratio 33	11.8	29.7	24.2	14.3	14.0	15.5	3.7	3.6	0.4	4.6	0.6	2.7	•
Total Asset Turnover 34	3.1	•	5.9	2.2	2.5	4.5	2.0	1.4	1.4	2.0	0.4	1.5	•
Inventory Turnover 35	24.0	•	22.2	8.6	10.7	5.0	45.0	2.4	70.8	261.3	32.4	12.6	•
Receivables Turnover 36	23.9	•	163.4	24.6	18.1	14.7	9.8	8.5	9.1	12.3	3.3	6.9	•
Total Liabilities to Net Worth 37	2.2	•	1.8	1.3	1.9	1.9	4.9	2.3	2.6	1.0	•	1.7	•
Current Assets to Working Capital 38	3.0	•	2.2	1.6	1.9	3.2	•	3.6	•	3.5	•	1.9	•
Current Liabilities to Working Capital 39	2.0	•	1.2	0.6	0.9	2.2	•	2.6	•	2.5	•	0.9	•
Working Capital to Net Sales 40	0.0	•	0.0	0.1	0.1	0.0	•	0.1	•	0.1	•	0.1	•
Inventory to Working Capital 41	0.1	•	0.2	0.1	0.1	0.1	•	0.1	•	0.0	•	0.1	•
Total Receipts to Cash Flow 42	2.3	1.8	2.4	3.2	2.6	3.9	6.5	1.6	2.1	9.3	4.1	1.4	•
Cost of Goods to Cash Flow 43	0.3	0.1	0.3	0.3	0.3	0.1	2.9	0.0	1.1	6.2	0.7	0.2	•
Cash Flow to Total Debt 44	1.9	•	3.8	1.2	1.4	1.8	0.4	1.2	0.9	0.4	0.1	1.7	•

Selected Financial Factors (in Percentages)

Debt Ratio 45	68.8	•	64.5	56.2	65.8	65.1	83.1	69.9	72.6	51.2	137.3	63.1	•
Return on Total Assets 46	28.2	•	62.8	30.5	16.6	22.2	4.6	6.0	0.9	2.5	2.7	7.6	•
Return on Equity Before Income Taxes 47	82.6	•	169.6	64.8	45.0	59.5	19.8	14.4	•	4.0	4.4	13.0	•
Return on Equity After Income Taxes 48	79.7	•	168.8	64.8	44.9	50.3	12.6	10.8	•	2.4	7.0	9.0	•
Profit Margin (Before Income Tax) 49	8.3	16.2	10.3	13.0	6.2	4.6	1.6	3.2	•	1.0	•	3.3	•
Profit Margin (After Income Tax) 50	8.0	14.9	10.2	13.0	6.2	3.9	1.0	2.4	•	0.6	•	2.3	•

Table II
Corporations with Net Income

OFFICES OF OTHER HEALTH PRACTITIONERS

MONEY AMOUNTS AND SIZE OF ASSETS IN THOUSANDS OF DOLLARS

Item Description for Accounting Period 7/12 Through 6/13	Total	Zero Assets	Under 500	500 to 1,000	1,000 to 5,000	5,000 to 10,000	10,000 to 25,000	25,000 to 50,000	50,000 to 100,000	100,000 to 250,000	250,000 to 500,000	500,000 to 2,500,000	2,500,000 and over
Number of Enterprises 1	91601	17415	70537	2428	1079	32	71	•	10	•	0	•	0

Revenues ($ in Thousands)

	Total	Zero Assets	Under 500	500 to 1,000	1,000 to 5,000	5,000 to 10,000	10,000 to 25,000	25,000 to 50,000	50,000 to 100,000	100,000 to 250,000	250,000 to 500,000	500,000 to 2,500,000	2,500,000 and over
Net Sales 2	56171164	2704855	29405535	3653659	3923435	1186739	2400622	•	712736	•	0	•	0
Interest 3	79458	13	153	346	4	77	275	•	1789	•	0	•	0
Rents 4	20212	0	12893	0	0	0	74	•	3673	•	0	•	0
Royalties 5	0	0	0	0	0	0	0	•	0	•	0	•	0
Other Portfolio Income 6	38255	1344	8	0	497	294	363	•	12653	•	0	•	0
Other Receipts 7	2648319	12335	229612	62921	77488	28322	142354	•	543615	•	0	•	0
Total Receipts 8	58957408	2718547	29648201	3716926	4001424	1215432	2543688	•	1274466	•	0	•	0
Average Total Receipts 9	644	156	420	1531	3708	37982	35827	•	127447	•	•	•	•

Operating Costs/Operating Income (%)

	Total	Zero Assets	Under 500	500 to 1,000	1,000 to 5,000	5,000 to 10,000	10,000 to 25,000	25,000 to 50,000	50,000 to 100,000	100,000 to 250,000	250,000 to 500,000	500,000 to 2,500,000	2,500,000 and over
Cost of Operations 10	14.5	3.3	10.2	8.1	15.3	2.6	50.5	•	7.6	•	•	•	•
Salaries and Wages 11	21.6	11.2	19.0	32.8	30.1	55.3	23.8	•	37.7	•	•	•	•
Taxes Paid 12	3.0	2.4	3.3	4.2	4.7	3.2	2.6	•	3.3	•	•	•	•
Interest Paid 13	0.8	0.6	0.6	0.9	0.6	0.3	0.4	•	1.4	•	•	•	•
Depreciation 14	0.9	0.4	1.0	0.9	0.8	0.9	1.3	•	1.7	•	•	•	•
Amortization and Depletion 15	0.4	0.1	0.2	1.1	0.4	•	0.3	•	1.1	•	•	•	•
Pensions and Other Deferred Comp. 16	0.7	0.4	0.8	0.9	1.2	0.4	0.3	•	0.6	•	•	•	•
Employee Benefits 17	1.6	0.6	1.0	1.2	1.7	3.3	2.0	•	3.9	•	•	•	•
Advertising 18	1.3	1.0	1.8	1.1	1.7	0.4	1.2	•	0.6	•	•	•	•
Other Expenses 19	39.1	45.3	34.2	24.6	28.9	26.8	14.9	•	115.6	•	•	•	•
Officers' Compensation 20	8.9	12.5	13.2	11.4	6.2	3.7	1.8	•	0.6	•	•	•	•
Operating Margin 21	7.2	22.2	14.8	12.8	8.4	3.1	0.8	•	•	•	•	•	•
Operating Margin Before Officers' Comp. 22	16.1	34.7	27.9	24.2	14.6	6.7	2.7	•	•	•	•	•	•

Selected Average Balance Sheet ($ in Thousands)

Net Receivables 23	27	0	2	28	210	1463	4069	•	13266	•	•	•	•
Inventories 24	4	0	3	10	53	157	371	•	303	•	•	•	•
Net Property, Plant and Equipment 25	39	0	27	146	389	1663	2090	•	9768	•	•	•	•
Total Assets 26	202	0	86	653	1614	7573	15059	•	69156	•	•	•	•
Notes and Loans Payable 27	72	0	36	280	582	2530	3209	•	36209	•	•	•	•
All Other Liabilities 28	52	0	13	45	384	2822	5558	•	16430	•	•	•	•
Net Worth 29	78	0	37	328	647	2222	6292	•	16518	•	•	•	•

Selected Financial Ratios (Times to 1)

Current Ratio 30	1.9	•	2.2	4.0	2.7	1.4	1.6	•	0.7	•	•	•	•
Quick Ratio 31	1.5	•	1.7	3.0	1.8	1.3	1.4	•	0.6	•	•	•	•
Net Sales to Working Capital 32	14.5	•	20.4	7.8	6.3	31.9	11.3	•	•	•	•	•	•
Coverage Ratio 33	16.6	42.2	28.9	17.4	19.1	18.3	18.1	•	4.2	•	•	•	•
Total Asset Turnover 34	3.0	•	4.8	2.3	2.3	4.9	2.2	•	1.0	•	•	•	•
Inventory Turnover 35	23.1	•	15.7	11.7	10.5	6.2	46.0	•	18.0	•	•	•	•
Receivables Turnover 36	24.8	•	236.6	45.4	21.5	•	10.3	•	7.2	•	•	•	•
Total Liabilities to Net Worth 37	1.6	•	1.3	1.0	1.5	2.4	1.4	•	3.2	•	•	•	•
Current Assets to Working Capital 38	2.1	•	1.9	1.3	1.6	3.2	2.8	•	•	•	•	•	•
Current Liabilities to Working Capital 39	1.1	•	0.9	0.3	0.6	2.2	1.8	•	•	•	•	•	•
Working Capital to Net Sales 40	0.1	•	0.0	0.1	0.2	0.0	0.1	•	•	•	•	•	•
Inventory to Working Capital 41	0.1	•	0.1	0.1	0.1	0.1	0.1	•	•	•	•	•	•
Total Receipts to Cash Flow 42	2.2	1.6	2.4	3.1	3.1	4.0	5.6	•	0.9	•	•	•	•
Cost of Goods to Cash Flow 43	0.3	0.1	0.2	0.3	0.5	0.1	2.8	•	0.1	•	•	•	•
Cash Flow to Total Debt 44	2.2	•	3.5	1.5	1.2	1.8	0.7	•	1.5	•	•	•	•

Selected Financial Factors (in Percentages)

Debt Ratio 45	61.3	•	56.9	49.8	59.9	70.7	58.2	•	76.1	•	•	•	•
Return on Total Assets 46	39.2	•	78.1	35.5	24.7	28.5	16.1	•	6.3	•	•	•	•
Return on Equity Before Income Taxes 47	95.3	•	174.8	66.5	58.3	91.9	36.5	•	20.3	•	•	•	•
Return on Equity After Income Taxes 48	92.3	•	174.0	66.5	58.2	80.0	32.8	•	17.5	•	•	•	•
Profit Margin (Before Income Tax) 49	12.1	22.8	15.6	14.5	10.4	5.5	6.8	•	4.7	•	•	•	•
Profit Margin (After Income Tax) 50	11.7	21.3	15.5	14.5	10.4	4.8	6.1	•	4.1	•	•	•	•

Table I

Corporations with and without Net Income

OUTPATIENT CARE CENTERS

MONEY AMOUNTS AND SIZE OF ASSETS IN THOUSANDS OF DOLLARS

Item Description for Accounting Period 7/12 Through 6/13		Total	Zero Assets	Under 500	500 to 1,000	1,000 to 5,000	5,000 to 10,000	10,000 to 25,000	25,000 to 50,000	50,000 to 100,000	100,000 to 250,000	250,000 to 500,000	500,000 to 2,500,000	2,500,000 and over
Number of Enterprises	1	7655	1027	5399	659	372	87	43	26	18	9	5	11	0
Revenues ($ in Thousands)														
Net Sales	2	34396011	714968	2918484	1499210	1704617	1934559	1512459	2385328	2430677	1695694	1276106	16323910	0
Interest	3	179135	965	2	747	2445	107	7049	329	4103	2345	3718	157326	0
Rents	4	9507	146	0	0	53	0	879	0	0	3076	208	5144	0
Royalties	5	0	0	0	0	0	0	0	0	0	0	0	0	0
Other Portfolio Income	6	148197	11	0	1791	7879	2183	842	5	7935	7913	289	119347	0
Other Receipts	7	2762106	86314	22037	1575	77693	12661	24002	14421	35684	-5714	113506	2379926	0
Total Receipts	8	37494956	802404	2940523	1503323	1792687	1949510	1545231	2400083	2478399	1703314	1393827	18985653	0
Average Total Receipts	9	4898	781	545	2281	4819	22408	35936	92311	137689	189257	278765	1725968	•
Operating Costs/Operating Income (%)														
Cost of Operations	10	23.7	6.3	8.2	13.9	13.7	22.6	0.7	31.5	32.4	23.6	3.7	30.6	•
Salaries and Wages	11	21.6	31.7	21.4	18.7	29.0	22.3	19.2	19.6	7.4	23.6	21.1	23.0	•
Taxes Paid	12	3.1	3.5	4.5	2.6	2.3	3.3	1.7	2.0	0.9	2.0	2.1	3.7	•
Interest Paid	13	3.7	5.9	0.3	0.2	0.7	0.1	0.7	0.6	0.9	1.6	9.6	6.1	•
Depreciation	14	2.1	3.6	0.5	0.5	0.6	0.4	1.0	0.5	0.5	1.1	1.9	3.6	•
Amortization and Depletion	15	1.9	2.8	0.0	0.1	1.3	0.1	0.1	0.6	0.5	1.1	3.2	3.1	•
Pensions and Other Deferred Comp.	16	0.6	0.4	0.6	0.1	1.7	1.7	0.4	0.4	0.0	0.4	0.2	0.7	•
Employee Benefits	17	3.3	1.6	1.2	1.0	3.9	6.6	1.8	1.8	0.8	1.7	1.7	4.5	•
Advertising	18	0.6	5.3	0.6	0.7	2.5	0.3	0.1	1.3	0.4	0.5	0.2	0.3	•
Other Expenses	19	38.7	45.7	43.0	41.5	24.3	38.5	71.9	37.1	57.6	42.6	66.3	30.7	•
Officers' Compensation	20	3.0	3.0	12.5	3.4	18.4	1.8	2.3	1.1	0.5	0.6	1.1	0.8	•
Operating Margin	21	•	•	7.1	17.2	1.7	2.4	0.0	3.4	•	1.1	•	•	•
Operating Margin Before Officers' Comp.	22	0.7	•	19.6	20.7	20.0	4.1	2.3	4.5	•	1.7	•	•	•

Selected Average Balance Sheet ($ in Thousands)

Net Receivables 23	663	0	27	0	382	1864	2614	9472	6123	13898	32891	351656	•
Inventories 24	66	0	5	4	8	7	11	80	306	1641	2501	39888	•
Net Property, Plant and Equipment 25	570	0	9	131	280	343	2182	1780	6308	39027	19761	308159	•
Total Assets 26	5885	0	78	695	2277	6029	15900	36105	66918	148890	396747	3331363	•
Notes and Loans Payable 27	2986	0	42	61	649	2349	5457	6445	21080	49200	271729	1778390	•
All Other Liabilities 28	1325	0	76	231	739	2634	6091	17752	26328	58111	23545	657761	•
Net Worth 29	1574	0	-40	402	889	1046	4352	11909	19509	41579	101475	895213	•

Selected Financial Ratios (Times to 1)

Current Ratio 30	1.4	•	0.9	24.9	1.2	1.3	1.4	1.3	1.3	1.0	2.0	1.5	•
Quick Ratio 31	1.1	•	0.7	6.4	0.7	1.0	1.0	1.1	0.9	0.8	1.6	1.1	•
Net Sales to Working Capital 32	12.1	•	•	5.7	20.4	22.3	13.9	16.2	17.8	1505.9	10.5	8.3	•
Coverage Ratio 33	2.8	1.4	23.7	84.8	11.0	24.7	3.9	7.8	1.3	1.9	0.8	2.5	•
Total Asset Turnover 34	0.8	•	6.9	3.3	2.0	3.7	2.2	2.5	2.0	1.3	0.6	0.4	•
Inventory Turnover 35	16.1	•	9.4	86.3	74.1	694.4	21.2	360.1	142.9	27.1	3.8	11.4	•
Receivables Turnover 36	6.1	•	26.3	204.4	5.7	19.6	10.8	9.6	19.9	12.3	7.6	3.8	•
Total Liabilities to Net Worth 37	2.7	•	•	0.7	1.6	4.8	2.7	2.0	2.4	2.6	2.9	2.7	•
Current Assets to Working Capital 38	3.4	•	•	1.0	6.4	4.8	3.4	4.3	4.0	332.3	2.0	3.1	•
Current Liabilities to Working Capital 39	2.4	•	•	0.0	5.4	3.8	2.4	3.3	3.0	331.3	1.0	2.1	•
Working Capital to Net Sales 40	0.1	•	•	0.2	0.0	0.0	0.1	0.1	0.1	0.0	0.1	0.1	•
Inventory to Working Capital 41	0.2	•	•	•	0.0	0.0	0.0	0.0	0.0	11.9	0.1	0.2	•
Total Receipts to Cash Flow 42	2.5	2.4	2.4	1.9	3.7	2.5	1.4	2.6	1.8	2.5	1.6	3.0	•
Cost of Goods to Cash Flow 43	0.6	0.2	0.2	0.3	0.5	0.6	0.0	0.8	0.6	0.6	0.1	0.9	•
Cash Flow to Total Debt 44	0.4	•	1.9	4.2	0.9	1.8	2.1	1.5	1.6	0.7	0.5	0.2	•

Selected Financial Factors (in Percentages)

Debt Ratio 45	73.3	•	150.7	42.1	61.0	82.7	72.6	67.0	70.8	72.1	74.4	73.1	•
Return on Total Assets 46	8.0	•	56.5	57.9	15.0	12.1	6.5	11.8	2.3	4.0	4.9	6.8	•
Return on Equity Before Income Taxes 47	19.3	•	•	98.9	35.0	66.7	17.6	31.2	1.6	6.9	•	15.3	•
Return on Equity After Income Taxes 48	14.6	•	•	98.5	29.9	64.1	15.8	26.4	0.8	6.0	•	10.2	•
Profit Margin (Before Income Tax) 49	6.8	2.5	7.8	17.5	6.8	3.1	2.2	4.1	0.2	1.5	•	9.2	•
Profit Margin (After Income Tax) 50	5.1	•	7.8	17.4	5.8	3.0	2.0	3.4	0.1	1.3	•	6.2	•

Table II

Corporations with Net Income

OUTPATIENT CARE CENTERS

MONEY AMOUNTS AND SIZE OF ASSETS IN THOUSANDS OF DOLLARS

Item Description for Accounting Period 7/12 Through 6/13	Total	Zero Assets	Under 500	500 to 1,000	1,000 to 5,000	5,000 to 10,000	10,000 to 25,000	25,000 to 50,000	50,000 to 100,000	100,000 to 250,000	250,000 to 500,000	500,000 to 2,500,000	2,500,000 and over
Number of Enterprises 1	6193	643	4574	659	183	•	36	22	9	5	•	•	0

Revenues ($ in Thousands)

	Total	Zero Assets	Under 500	500 to 1,000	1,000 to 5,000	5,000 to 10,000	10,000 to 25,000	25,000 to 50,000	50,000 to 100,000	100,000 to 250,000	250,000 to 500,000	500,000 to 2,500,000	2,500,000 and over
Net Sales 2	27310467	475772	2676058	1499210	743462	•	1177969	2170746	1634108	791601	•	•	0
Interest 3	151054	560	0	747	1247	•	6997	319	65	70	•	•	0
Rents 4	1813	131	0	0	53	•	854	0	0	0	•	•	0
Royalties 5	0	0	0	0	0	•	0	0	0	0	•	•	0
Other Portfolio Income 6	135569	0	0	1791	7879	•	839	5	477	7856	•	•	0
Other Receipts 7	2470384	59710	5479	1575	75740	•	23818	12129	26578	3921	•	•	0
Total Receipts 8	30069287	536173	2681537	1503323	828381	•	1210477	2183199	1661228	803448	•	•	0
Average Total Receipts 9	4855	834	586	2281	4527	•	33624	99236	184581	160690	•	•	•

Operating Costs/Operating Income (%)

	Total	Zero Assets	Under 500	500 to 1,000	1,000 to 5,000	5,000 to 10,000	10,000 to 25,000	25,000 to 50,000	50,000 to 100,000	100,000 to 250,000	250,000 to 500,000	500,000 to 2,500,000	2,500,000 and over
Cost of Operations 10	27.1	8.1	6.2	13.9	4.2	•	0.9	34.6	26.3	41.3	•	•	•
Salaries and Wages 11	19.6	31.8	18.9	18.7	24.6	•	20.4	20.1	2.7	18.7	•	•	•
Taxes Paid 12	3.2	3.4	4.1	2.6	1.9	•	2.0	2.1	0.3	2.0	•	•	•
Interest Paid 13	3.5	4.9	0.3	0.2	0.5	•	0.9	0.6	0.5	1.4	•	•	•
Depreciation 14	2.3	4.4	0.4	0.5	1.0	•	1.0	0.5	0.2	2.1	•	•	•
Amortization and Depletion 15	2.0	1.9	0.0	0.1	2.9	•	0.1	0.5	0.1	1.2	•	•	•
Pensions and Other Deferred Comp. 16	0.5	0.3	0.7	0.1	0.2	•	0.5	0.4	0.0	0.2	•	•	•
Employee Benefits 17	3.4	1.4	0.9	1.0	1.3	•	1.5	1.8	0.1	0.8	•	•	•
Advertising 18	0.5	1.3	0.6	0.7	4.8	•	0.1	1.4	0.3	0.7	•	•	•
Other Expenses 19	34.9	38.2	41.1	41.5	36.2	•	64.0	32.6	68.5	23.5	•	•	•
Officers' Compensation 20	2.7	4.2	12.8	3.4	12.1	•	2.8	1.0	0.1	0.9	•	•	•
Operating Margin 21	0.4	0.2	14.0	17.2	10.2	•	5.9	4.5	0.9	7.2	•	•	•
Operating Margin Before Officers' Comp. 22	3.0	4.4	26.8	20.7	22.3	•	8.7	5.5	1.0	8.1	•	•	•

Selected Average Balance Sheet ($ in Thousands)

Net Receivables 23	715	0	25	0	637	•	2307	10025	2677	5563	•	•	•
Inventories 24	76	0	5	0	17	•	13	76	170	1902	•	•	•
Net Property, Plant and Equipment 25	619	0	10	131	204	•	2212	1283	7706	63158	•	•	•
Total Assets 26	6226	0	80	695	2631	•	15238	34878	66353	158818	•	•	•
Notes and Loans Payable 27	3209	0	45	61	487	•	5957	6514	15116	49194	•	•	•
All Other Liabilities 28	1191	0	48	231	561	•	3830	19547	24018	50927	•	•	•
Net Worth 29	1826	0	-13	402	1582	•	5450	8817	27219	58697	•	•	•

Selected Financial Ratios (Times to 1)

Current Ratio 30	1.5	•	1.3	24.9	1.7	•	2.3	1.2	1.4	0.9	•	•	•
Quick Ratio 31	1.2	•	1.2	6.4	1.4	•	1.6	1.0	0.9	0.7	•	•	•
Net Sales to Working Capital 32	9.7	•	40.2	5.7	7.6	•	6.6	22.3	19.1	•	•	•	•
Coverage Ratio 33	4.0	3.7	49.7	84.8	41.9	•	10.8	9.9	6.3	7.4	•	•	•
Total Asset Turnover 34	0.7	•	7.3	3.3	1.5	•	2.1	2.8	2.7	1.0	•	•	•
Inventory Turnover 35	15.7	•	8.0	•	9.9	•	21.2	446.7	280.6	34.4	•	•	•
Receivables Turnover 36	5.6	•	29.6	11314.8	2.6	•	12.1	11.4	52.3	13.0	•	•	•
Total Liabilities to Net Worth 37	2.4	•	•	0.7	0.7	•	1.8	3.0	1.4	1.7	•	•	•
Current Assets to Working Capital 38	2.9	•	4.0	1.0	2.5	•	1.8	5.7	3.5	•	•	•	•
Current Liabilities to Working Capital 39	1.9	•	3.0	0.0	1.5	•	0.8	4.7	2.5	•	•	•	•
Working Capital to Net Sales 40	0.1	•	0.0	0.2	0.1	•	0.2	0.0	0.1	•	•	•	•
Inventory to Working Capital 41	0.2	•	0.5	•	0.0	•	0.0	0.0	0.0	•	•	•	•
Total Receipts to Cash Flow 42	2.5	2.2	2.2	1.9	2.0	•	1.5	2.8	1.4	3.6	•	•	•
Cost of Goods to Cash Flow 43	0.7	0.2	0.1	0.3	0.1	•	0.0	1.0	0.4	1.5	•	•	•
Cash Flow to Total Debt 44	0.4	•	2.9	4.2	2.0	•	2.3	1.3	3.3	0.4	•	•	•

Selected Financial Factors (in Percentages)

Debt Ratio 45	70.7	•	116.0	42.1	39.9	•	64.2	74.7	59.0	63.0	•	•	•
Return on Total Assets 46	9.9	•	105.5	57.9	33.9	•	20.4	16.0	8.3	10.0	•	•	•
Return on Equity Before Income Taxes 47	25.2	•	•	98.9	55.0	•	51.8	56.9	17.0	23.4	•	•	•
Return on Equity After Income Taxes 48	20.2	•	•	98.5	49.1	•	50.1	49.2	15.9	22.2	•	•	•
Profit Margin (Before Income Tax) 49	10.4	12.9	14.2	17.5	21.4	•	8.6	5.1	2.5	8.7	•	•	•
Profit Margin (After Income Tax) 50	8.4	9.0	14.2	17.4	19.1	•	8.4	4.4	2.4	8.2	•	•	•

Table I

Corporations with and without Net Income

MISC. HEALTH CARE AND SOCIAL ASSISTANCE

MONEY AMOUNTS AND SIZE OF ASSETS IN THOUSANDS OF DOLLARS

Item Description for Accounting Period 7/12 Through 6/13	Total	Zero Assets	Under 500	500 to 1,000	1,000 to 5,000	5,000 to 10,000	10,000 to 25,000	25,000 to 50,000	50,000 to 100,000	100,000 to 250,000	250,000 to 500,000	500,000 to 2,500,000	2,500,000 and over
Number of Enterprises **1**	69298	13111	51180	2560	1771	290	193	63	51	37	18	20	3

Revenues ($ in Thousands)													
Net Sales **2**	112228272	3203046	32270371	6188960	5896324	3888618	5599555	3062581	3688579	8372097	7178472	17788536	15091134
Interest **3**	125604	21662	1724	1225	3202	759	3797	2225	3442	3247	1016	18648	64656
Rents **4**	33654	336	2087	3045	6242	213	4347	678	1148	9971	426	4902	261
Royalties **5**	89112	0	0	0	0	0	52	0	34429	30981	15	6160	17475
Other Portfolio Income **6**	247517	1305	5003	2431	62286	803	29295	5605	5102	5228	781	46696	82981
Other Receipts **7**	1776136	18606	629103	51323	207096	77603	86257	37699	15455	21292	97594	435168	98939
Total Receipts **8**	114500295	3244955	32908288	6246984	6175150	3967996	5723303	3108788	3748155	8442816	7278304	18300110	15355446
Average Total Receipts **9**	1652	247	643	2440	3487	13683	29654	49346	73493	228184	404350	915006	5118482

Operating Costs/Operating Income (%)													
Cost of Operations **10**	15.1	27.7	7.6	8.9	16.2	13.1	28.8	26.3	26.3	24.2	14.1	13.7	18.4
Salaries and Wages **11**	34.2	20.7	40.0	45.7	36.0	36.8	28.3	33.8	30.4	24.4	41.5	35.4	22.7
Taxes Paid **12**	4.1	3.4	4.7	4.4	4.3	4.1	3.3	5.3	4.0	4.0	4.8	4.4	2.5
Interest Paid **13**	2.1	2.6	0.3	0.7	1.5	1.3	1.1	1.7	2.6	2.4	3.0	5.0	3.4
Depreciation **14**	1.7	2.5	0.8	0.9	1.9	1.2	1.2	2.6	1.8	2.3	2.0	3.0	2.0
Amortization and Depletion **15**	0.9	2.1	0.2	0.2	0.2	0.4	0.7	0.7	1.5	1.5	1.6	1.5	1.5
Pensions and Other Deferred Comp. **16**	0.3	0.3	0.3	0.5	0.6	0.3	0.4	0.6	0.2	0.2	0.1	0.2	0.5
Employee Benefits **17**	2.6	1.0	1.6	1.2	2.0	2.8	2.2	3.3	3.2	2.4	3.0	3.1	5.1
Advertising **18**	0.5	0.8	0.7	0.4	0.5	0.6	0.8	0.4	0.5	0.6	0.3	0.5	0.2
Other Expenses **19**	32.1	33.6	32.6	26.8	30.6	39.0	32.5	22.9	28.6	35.6	27.3	34.5	32.0
Officers' Compensation **20**	4.1	7.5	9.0	6.3	4.4	2.3	2.8	2.0	1.6	0.9	0.6	0.7	1.3
Operating Margin **21**	2.0	•	2.2	4.2	1.8	•	•	0.4	•	1.7	1.9	•	10.4
Operating Margin Before Officers' Comp. **22**	6.1	5.4	11.2	10.4	6.2	0.5	0.8	2.3	0.7	2.6	2.5	•	11.7

Selected Average Balance Sheet ($ in Thousands)

Net Receivables 23	151	0	11	40	249	1492	3769	6927	13028	33080	69603	133297	655618
Inventories 24	10	0	1	3	12	91	297	614	1128	2146	4042	11227	29527
Net Property, Plant and Equipment 25	164	0	27	262	811	1542	1863	7355	8463	19074	42407	160659	497892
Total Assets 26	1064	0	84	685	2078	6914	15331	36211	70132	159475	330376	1025342	6931376
Notes and Loans Payable 27	527	0	57	347	1029	2792	4341	11917	27708	73338	168160	580529	3246893
All Other Liabilities 28	265	0	20	172	520	1481	6136	12108	20092	46060	126072	214788	1425642
Net Worth 29	272	0	7	167	530	2641	4854	12186	22332	40078	36144	230026	2258841

Selected Financial Ratios (Times to 1)

Current Ratio 30	1.4	•	1.4	1.4	1.3	2.3	1.3	1.6	1.4	1.5	1.7	1.5	1.0
Quick Ratio 31	1.0	•	1.2	1.1	1.1	2.0	1.1	1.1	0.9	1.3	1.3	1.1	0.6
Net Sales to Working Capital 32	18.2	•	53.9	33.7	15.9	6.1	13.9	7.3	10.4	11.2	7.7	11.8	916.3
Coverage Ratio 33	2.9	0.7	13.4	8.3	5.5	1.2	1.3	2.1	1.3	2.1	2.1	1.2	4.6
Total Asset Turnover 34	1.5	•	7.5	3.5	1.6	1.9	1.9	1.3	1.0	1.4	1.2	0.9	0.7
Inventory Turnover 35	23.7	•	56.9	68.9	46.3	19.1	28.1	20.8	16.9	25.5	13.9	10.9	31.3
Receivables Turnover 36	10.4	•	62.6	36.6	9.6	11.0	8.4	5.2	5.2	7.8	5.6	6.3	7.7
Total Liabilities to Net Worth 37	2.9	•	11.3	3.1	2.9	1.6	2.2	2.0	2.1	3.0	8.1	3.5	2.1
Current Assets to Working Capital 38	3.6	•	3.4	3.6	4.1	1.8	4.1	2.7	3.8	2.8	2.5	3.2	228.1
Current Liabilities to Working Capital 39	2.6	•	2.4	2.6	3.1	0.8	3.1	1.7	2.8	1.8	1.5	2.2	227.1
Working Capital to Net Sales 40	0.1	•	0.0	0.0	0.1	0.2	0.1	0.1	0.1	0.1	0.1	0.1	0.0
Inventory to Working Capital 41	0.1	•	0.1	0.0	0.0	0.1	0.2	0.1	0.2	0.1	0.1	0.1	5.7
Total Receipts to Cash Flow 42	3.2	3.7	3.2	3.8	3.1	3.0	3.6	4.8	3.8	2.8	3.7	3.5	2.5
Cost of Goods to Cash Flow 43	0.5	1.0	0.2	0.3	0.5	0.4	1.0	1.3	1.0	0.7	0.5	0.5	0.5
Cash Flow to Total Debt 44	0.6	•	2.5	1.2	0.7	1.1	0.8	0.4	0.4	0.7	0.4	0.3	0.4

Selected Financial Factors (in Percentages)

Debt Ratio 45	74.4	•	91.9	75.7	74.5	61.8	68.3	66.3	68.2	74.9	89.1	77.6	67.4
Return on Total Assets 46	9.5	•	34.0	20.5	12.8	2.9	2.7	4.9	3.5	6.9	7.6	5.1	11.3
Return on Equity Before Income Taxes 47	24.3	•	387.5	74.0	40.9	1.0	2.0	7.7	2.4	14.2	36.2	3.3	27.0
Return on Equity After Income Taxes 48	19.0	•	383.2	73.6	38.9	•	•	4.9	•	9.8	27.1	0.7	17.9
Profit Margin (Before Income Tax) 49	4.1	•	4.2	5.1	6.5	0.2	0.3	1.9	0.7	2.5	3.3	0.8	12.1
Profit Margin (After Income Tax) 50	3.2	•	4.2	5.1	6.2	•	•	1.2	•	1.7	2.5	0.2	8.0

Table II
Corporations with Net Income

MISC. HEALTH CARE AND SOCIAL ASSISTANCE

MONEY AMOUNTS AND SIZE OF ASSETS IN THOUSANDS OF DOLLARS

Item Description for Accounting Period 7/12 Through 6/13	Total	Zero Assets	Under 500	500 to 1,000	1,000 to 5,000	5,000 to 10,000	10,000 to 25,000	25,000 to 50,000	50,000 to 100,000	100,000 to 250,000	250,000 to 500,000	500,000 to 2,500,000	2,500,000 and over
Number of Enterprises **1**	42145	6005	32790	1724	1201	186	120	48	27	•	9	9	•
Revenues ($ in Thousands)													
Net Sales **2**	82428265	2291947	25346730	4971732	4463020	2340302	3640076	2586850	2361800	•	3783320	9143446	•
Interest **3**	113073	21542	1202	1214	2734	391	2866	1162	1135	•	377	14320	•
Rents **4**	26178	0	2077	358	6241	213	2977	207	0	•	51	3842	•
Royalties **5**	75554	0	0	0	0	0	0	0	27093	•	0	5	•
Other Portfolio Income **6**	207676	721	4906	2138	53681	711	9219	5413	71	•	433	42429	•
Other Receipts **7**	997905	9429	151160	50438	184357	67805	66361	35310	19093	•	25942	272036	•
Total Receipts **8**	83848651	2323639	25506075	5025880	4710033	2409422	3721499	2628942	2409192	•	3810123	9476078	•
Average Total Receipts **9**	1990	387	778	2915	3922	12954	31012	54770	89229	•	423347	1052898	•
Operating Costs/Operating Income (%)													
Cost of Operations **10**	15.0	32.6	7.8	10.0	13.6	14.5	18.0	21.6	27.3	•	21.8	15.0	•
Salaries and Wages **11**	32.2	17.2	39.1	41.8	36.8	39.4	29.0	36.1	31.8	•	24.7	32.0	•
Taxes Paid **12**	3.7	2.7	4.2	4.0	4.2	4.2	3.7	5.8	4.1	•	3.2	3.6	•
Interest Paid **13**	1.7	3.0	0.2	0.6	1.2	0.8	0.4	1.3	2.4	•	2.1	4.7	•
Depreciation **14**	1.5	3.1	0.8	0.6	1.9	1.1	1.0	2.7	1.6	•	1.9	2.6	•
Amortization and Depletion **15**	0.7	2.1	0.1	0.0	0.1	0.1	0.4	0.4	1.1	•	1.5	1.3	•
Pensions and Other Deferred Comp. **16**	0.4	0.3	0.2	0.6	0.7	0.3	0.5	0.6	0.2	•	0.0	0.3	•
Employee Benefits **17**	2.5	0.9	1.5	1.2	1.8	1.7	2.1	3.4	3.2	•	2.1	2.7	•
Advertising **18**	0.5	0.9	0.7	0.4	0.5	0.7	0.9	0.3	0.4	•	0.2	0.6	•
Other Expenses **19**	30.7	25.7	30.2	25.2	27.0	28.5	33.9	20.4	18.8	•	31.0	35.4	•
Officers' Compensation **20**	3.9	5.8	7.8	7.1	4.7	1.5	3.5	1.9	1.4	•	0.5	0.6	•
Operating Margin **21**	7.1	5.7	7.2	8.5	7.6	7.0	6.5	5.5	7.6	•	10.8	1.1	•
Operating Margin Before Officers' Comp. **22**	11.1	11.5	15.0	15.6	12.3	8.5	10.1	7.4	9.0	•	11.3	1.7	•

Selected Average Balance Sheet ($ in Thousands)

Net Receivables **23**	170	0	6	25	211	1343	3641	7736	14779	•	83431	191020	•
Inventories **24**	11	0	1	5	9	118	260	423	1426	•	5928	18537	•
Net Property, Plant and Equipment **25**	182	0	26	271	903	2071	2040	8153	10100	•	29186	207681	•
Total Assets **26**	1233	0	84	706	2091	6660	15038	36198	69885	•	331503	1266171	•
Notes and Loans Payable **27**	545	0	33	192	965	2314	3285	11932	31824	•	153299	669569	•
All Other Liabilities **28**	286	0	21	166	249	1195	4427	11907	18234	•	156012	259183	•
Net Worth **29**	402	0	31	348	877	3150	7326	12359	19828	•	22192	337419	•

Selected Financial Ratios (Times to 1)

Current Ratio **30**	1.5	•	1.7	1.7	3.0	2.2	1.6	1.5	1.4	•	2.0	1.6	•
Quick Ratio **31**	1.1	•	1.3	1.5	2.5	1.8	1.3	1.1	1.0	•	1.6	1.2	•
Net Sales to Working Capital **32**	16.6	•	48.8	23.4	6.8	7.9	9.5	8.4	12.3	•	6.0	8.6	•
Coverage Ratio **33**	6.1	3.4	33.2	17.9	11.8	12.9	21.7	6.4	5.0	•	6.4	2.0	•
Total Asset Turnover **34**	1.6	•	9.2	4.1	1.8	1.9	2.0	1.5	1.3	•	1.3	0.8	•
Inventory Turnover **35**	26.5	•	49.9	62.5	53.9	15.4	21.0	27.4	16.7	•	15.4	8.2	•
Receivables Turnover **36**	11.7	•	100.7	40.8	14.6	10.7	9.1	6.7	6.0	•	5.3	3.6	•
Total Liabilities to Net Worth **37**	2.1	•	1.7	1.0	1.4	1.1	1.1	1.9	2.5	•	13.9	2.8	•
Current Assets to Working Capital **38**	3.1	•	2.5	2.3	1.5	1.8	2.6	2.8	3.7	•	2.0	2.7	•
Current Liabilities to Working Capital **39**	2.1	•	1.5	1.3	0.5	0.8	1.6	1.8	2.7	•	1.0	1.7	•
Working Capital to Net Sales **40**	0.1	•	0.0	0.0	0.1	0.1	0.1	0.1	0.1	•	0.2	0.1	•
Inventory to Working Capital **41**	0.1	•	0.1	0.0	0.0	0.1	0.1	0.0	0.2	•	0.1	0.1	•
Total Receipts to Cash Flow **42**	2.9	3.5	3.1	3.4	2.8	3.1	2.6	4.3	3.9	•	2.5	2.8	•
Cost of Goods to Cash Flow **43**	0.4	1.1	0.2	0.3	0.4	0.4	0.5	0.9	1.1	•	0.5	0.4	•
Cash Flow to Total Debt **44**	0.8	•	4.6	2.4	1.1	1.2	1.5	0.5	0.4	•	0.5	0.4	•

Selected Financial Factors (in Percentages)

Debt Ratio **45**	67.4	•	63.4	50.7	58.0	52.7	51.3	65.9	71.6	•	93.3	73.4	•
Return on Total Assets **46**	16.8	•	74.5	41.3	25.5	20.4	18.7	12.5	15.2	•	17.3	7.6	•
Return on Equity Before Income Taxes **47**	43.1	•	197.5	79.1	55.6	39.7	36.7	31.0	42.7	•	218.0	14.3	•
Return on Equity After Income Taxes **48**	37.2	•	196.0	78.8	53.8	37.7	33.4	27.5	37.5	•	188.4	10.4	•
Profit Margin (Before Income Tax) **49**	8.9	7.1	7.9	9.6	13.1	9.9	8.9	7.1	9.7	•	11.5	4.8	•
Profit Margin (After Income Tax) **50**	7.6	6.4	7.8	9.5	12.7	9.4	8.1	6.3	8.5	•	9.9	3.5	•

Table I

Corporations with and without Net Income

HOSPITALS, NURSING, AND RESIDENTIAL CARE FACILITIES

MONEY AMOUNTS AND SIZE OF ASSETS IN THOUSANDS OF DOLLARS

Item Description for Accounting Period 7/12 Through 6/13	Total	Zero Assets	Under 500	500 to 1,000	1,000 to 5,000	5,000 to 10,000	10,000 to 25,000	25,000 to 50,000	50,000 to 100,000	100,000 to 250,000	250,000 to 500,000	500,000 to 2,500,000	2,500,000 and over
Number of Enterprises 1	18126	1580	12006	1656	2139	357	185	79	46	35	9	22	13
Revenues ($ in Thousands)													
Net Sales 2	152051805	2272849	10800854	3728501	11686169	5131938	4390562	4368349	5286655	8304821	3617774	15719252	76744079
Interest 3	1352784	136	43	462	2980	1530	1388	5325	5938	8090	7940	28452	1290500
Rents 4	565089	55	0	468	646	68	8079	4167	4794	29110	18866	34340	464497
Royalties 5	462	0	0	0	3	0	0	0	0	460	0	0	0
Other Portfolio Income 6	700748	0	18581	2411	2287	313	13709	19161	16936	32925	110265	232104	252053
Other Receipts 7	10993715	33331	23040	17234	561253	101600	54735	83789	170277	661398	18587	655671	8612803
Total Receipts 8	165664603	2306371	10842518	3749076	12253338	5235449	4468473	4480791	5484600	9036804	3773432	16669819	87363932
Average Total Receipts 9	9140	1460	903	2264	5729	14665	24154	56719	119230	258194	419270	757719	6720302
Operating Costs/Operating Income (%)													
Cost of Operations 10	4.5	•	8.6	8.4	2.8	15.6	13.3	10.0	3.4	6.6	4.6	3.2	2.8
Salaries and Wages 11	41.5	42.1	39.4	41.9	46.0	28.4	29.3	39.1	40.1	41.0	50.6	42.0	42.3
Taxes Paid 12	5.5	5.6	5.6	5.3	6.2	6.6	5.8	6.5	6.1	6.8	6.5	5.7	4.9
Interest Paid 13	4.2	0.5	0.5	1.1	0.8	1.3	1.1	1.4	1.5	1.4	4.1	4.2	6.5
Depreciation 14	2.7	2.7	0.9	1.2	1.0	1.0	1.3	2.0	2.3	2.0	2.3	3.5	3.5
Amortization and Depletion 15	0.6	0.2	0.1	0.2	0.1	0.3	0.3	0.3	0.5	0.4	0.9	1.1	0.8
Pensions and Other Deferred Comp. 16	0.4	0.6	0.1	0.1	0.2	0.4	0.4	0.1	0.2	0.3	0.3	0.1	0.6
Employee Benefits 17	4.8	4.2	1.9	1.6	3.3	4.1	4.7	3.9	6.3	3.2	3.0	6.0	5.6
Advertising 18	0.4	0.3	0.7	0.7	0.2	0.2	0.3	0.3	0.4	0.5	0.4	0.2	0.3
Other Expenses 19	38.6	46.4	34.2	27.2	37.8	38.4	42.2	34.9	41.7	43.8	29.1	35.4	40.1
Officers' Compensation 20	1.1	1.7	5.2	6.2	1.2	0.5	1.3	0.7	1.0	0.6	0.6	0.8	0.4
Operating Margin 21	•	•	2.7	6.2	0.4	3.2	0.0	0.7	•	•	•	•	•
Operating Margin Before Officers' Comp. 22	•	•	7.9	12.4	1.5	3.7	1.4	1.4	•	•	•	•	•

Selected Average Balance Sheet ($ in Thousands)

	23												
Net Receivables 23	916	0	9	151	497	1314	3026	7570	13636	30291	55468	65665	764324
Inventories 24	13	0	0	1	3	13	47	209	430	1055	896	2399	5771
Net Property, Plant and Equipment 25	3117	0	63	255	701	1966	4142	14723	26779	58286	164301	467247	2780984
Total Assets 26	8690	0	124	749	2133	6656	14226	33634	70442	158399	397864	1082794	8182061
Notes and Loans Payable 27	5492	0	195	377	859	5118	6523	17992	32473	64701	264004	484036	5653571
All Other Liabilities 28	2210	0	33	181	612	3857	5704	10857	20793	52425	64385	372024	1784715
Net Worth 29	988	0	-105	191	662	-2319	1998	4785	17176	41274	69476	226733	743776

Selected Financial Ratios (Times to 1)

Current Ratio 30	1.3	•	0.4	2.1	1.9	1.4	1.1	1.3	1.4	1.4	1.3	1.5	1.3
Quick Ratio 31	1.0	•	0.3	1.9	1.5	0.9	0.9	1.0	1.1	1.2	1.1	0.9	1.0
Net Sales to Working Capital 32	18.7	•	•	10.9	10.2	14.4	47.7	18.1	15.1	14.5	21.3	10.4	18.3
Coverage Ratio 33	2.1	•	6.8	7.2	7.3	5.1	2.6	3.3	1.1	2.6	1.5	2.0	1.9
Total Asset Turnover 34	1.0	•	7.3	3.0	2.6	2.2	1.7	1.6	1.6	1.5	1.0	0.7	0.7
Inventory Turnover 35	30.0	•	917.0	218.0	59.7	176.8	66.3	26.3	9.2	14.8	20.6	9.4	28.3
Receivables Turnover 36	9.3	•	77.1	16.1	9.1	11.5	6.9	7.6	8.8	8.3	6.9	11.0	8.1
Total Liabilities to Net Worth 37	7.8	•	•	2.9	2.2	•	6.1	6.0	3.1	2.8	4.7	3.8	10.0
Current Assets to Working Capital 38	4.1	•	•	1.9	2.1	3.8	11.8	4.6	3.7	3.6	4.8	3.1	4.1
Current Liabilities to Working Capital 39	3.1	•	•	0.9	1.1	2.8	10.8	3.6	2.7	2.6	3.8	2.1	3.1
Working Capital to Net Sales 40	0.1	•	•	0.1	0.1	0.1	0.0	0.1	0.1	0.1	0.0	0.1	0.1
Inventory to Working Capital 41	0.0	•	•	0.0	0.0	0.0	0.1	0.1	0.0	0.1	0.1	0.0	0.0
Total Receipts to Cash Flow 42	2.8	3.4	4.1	3.7	2.7	3.0	2.9	3.1	2.8	2.7	4.5	3.1	2.5
Cost of Goods to Cash Flow 43	0.1	•	0.4	0.3	0.1	0.5	0.4	0.3	0.1	0.2	0.2	0.1	0.1
Cash Flow to Total Debt 44	0.4	•	1.0	1.1	1.4	0.5	0.7	0.6	0.8	0.7	0.3	0.3	0.3

Selected Financial Factors (in Percentages)

Debt Ratio 45	88.6	•	184.6	74.5	69.0	134.8	86.0	85.8	75.6	73.9	82.5	79.1	90.9
Return on Total Assets 46	8.6	•	25.9	23.7	15.5	13.9	4.8	7.8	2.6	5.3	6.2	5.5	9.0
Return on Equity Before Income Taxes 47	39.9	•	•	80.1	43.3	•	21.3	38.0	0.7	12.5	11.9	13.1	47.7
Return on Equity After Income Taxes 48	30.1	•	•	77.8	43.0	•	17.7	35.6	•	10.8	8.8	9.6	32.7
Profit Margin (Before Income Tax) 49	4.7	•	3.0	6.8	5.2	5.2	1.8	3.3	0.1	2.2	2.1	4.1	6.0
Profit Margin (After Income Tax) 50	3.6	•	3.0	6.6	5.2	4.9	1.5	3.1	•	1.9	1.5	3.1	4.1

Table II

Corporations with Net Income

HOSPITALS, NURSING, AND RESIDENTIAL CARE FACILITIES

MONEY AMOUNTS AND SIZE OF ASSETS IN THOUSANDS OF DOLLARS

Item Description for Accounting Period 7/12 Through 6/13		Total	Zero Assets	Under 500	500 to 1,000	1,000 to 5,000	5,000 to 10,000	10,000 to 25,000	25,000 to 50,000	50,000 to 100,000	100,000 to 250,000	250,000 to 500,000	500,000 to 2,500,000	2,500,000 and over
Number of Enterprises	1	11807	410	7862	1403	1619	260	112	59	24	25	4	16	13
Revenues ($ in Thousands)														
Net Sales	2	131499804	568089	8017955	3356714	8874101	4347009	2532876	2927373	2765651	5669110	2251870	13444978	76744079
Interest	3	1327732	69	16	84	1748	943	1175	207	4507	7829	3967	16687	1290500
Rents	4	520798	1	0	0	646	40	0	2473	3377	15022	3724	31018	464497
Royalties	5	460	0	0	0	0	0	0	0	0	460	0	0	0
Other Portfolio Income	6	661299	0	18581	2411	1221	6	13105	18739	12743	30349	95958	216127	252053
Other Receipts	7	10787283	30780	20795	14950	552613	96505	11123	60590	150888	600528	22571	613141	8612803
Total Receipts	8	144797376	598939	8057347	3374159	9430329	4444503	2558279	3009382	2937166	6323298	2378090	14321951	87363932
Average Total Receipts	9	12264	1461	1025	2405	5825	17094	22842	51006	122382	252932	594522	895122	6720302
Operating Costs/Operating Income (%)														
Cost of Operations	10	4.3	•	10.7	7.3	2.2	15.5	17.5	10.6	4.0	5.2	4.4	2.4	2.8
Salaries and Wages	11	41.4	46.6	35.0	41.4	47.6	26.5	19.1	35.3	36.4	45.2	56.6	43.0	42.3
Taxes Paid	12	5.4	8.2	6.4	5.2	6.4	6.7	5.5	6.0	5.3	6.7	6.7	5.7	4.9
Interest Paid	13	4.5	0.4	0.6	1.1	1.0	0.4	1.0	1.5	1.2	1.5	2.5	3.7	6.5
Depreciation	14	2.8	0.8	0.9	0.9	1.2	0.7	1.3	2.0	1.9	2.0	1.6	3.0	3.5
Amortization and Depletion	15	0.7	•	0.0	0.2	0.1	0.2	0.2	0.3	0.5	0.5	0.8	1.0	0.8
Pensions and Other Deferred Comp.	16	0.5	0.6	0.1	0.1	0.2	0.4	0.1	0.1	0.3	0.4	0.1	0.1	0.6
Employee Benefits	17	4.8	3.3	2.1	1.7	3.3	4.1	4.5	3.2	3.1	3.3	3.5	6.2	5.6
Advertising	18	0.4	0.3	0.7	0.7	0.2	0.2	0.3	0.3	0.5	0.7	0.4	0.2	0.3
Other Expenses	19	38.0	32.3	30.7	27.6	34.7	39.3	42.8	35.3	47.9	40.5	22.3	34.5	40.1
Officers' Compensation	20	1.1	4.8	6.1	6.0	1.2	0.6	1.8	0.8	0.9	0.7	0.7	0.5	0.4
Operating Margin	21	•	2.6	6.7	7.7	2.0	5.4	5.9	4.6	•	•	0.5	•	•
Operating Margin Before Officers' Comp.	22	•	7.4	12.8	13.7	3.2	6.0	7.7	5.4	•	•	1.2	0.2	•

Selected Average Balance Sheet ($ in Thousands)

Net Receivables 23	1256	0	13	134	460	1436	3081	7398	15011	32856	73095	77252	764324
Inventories 24	14	0	0	1	2	12	50	165	363	1024	673	1565	6915
Net Property, Plant and Equipment 25	4232	0	74	271	770	1258	4045	15253	24257	54912	152770	459705	2780984
Total Assets 26	12047	0	140	732	2190	6105	13958	33417	71871	162772	404526	1103925	8182061
Notes and Loans Payable 27	7682	0	277	384	818	3000	5630	18405	26176	65058	278118	456530	5653571
All Other Liabilities 28	2968	0	23	131	511	3746	4658	9221	17115	47643	77891	418191	1784715
Net Worth 29	1397	0	-161	218	861	-642	3671	5791	28580	50071	48516	229204	743776

Selected Financial Ratios (Times to 1)

Current Ratio 30	1.4	•	0.3	2.8	2.2	1.2	1.4	1.8	1.6	1.7	1.4	1.8	1.3
Quick Ratio 31	1.0	•	0.3	2.7	1.6	0.8	1.3	1.5	1.4	1.5	1.2	1.0	1.0
Net Sales to Working Capital 32	15.9	•	•	9.5	8.8	21.7	12.4	7.5	11.1	8.5	20.3	8.1	18.3
Coverage Ratio 33	2.4	19.8	13.5	8.3	9.6	22.5	8.1	5.9	4.7	4.3	3.5	2.7	1.9
Total Asset Turnover 34	0.9	•	7.3	3.3	2.5	2.7	1.6	1.5	1.6	1.4	1.4	0.8	0.7
Inventory Turnover 35	35.4	•	6244.4	275.3	53.6	222.6	79.1	31.7	12.6	11.6	36.8	12.7	23.6
Receivables Turnover 36	10.9	•	68.8	20.8	11.2	14.9	6.2	7.7	8.4	7.4	•	•	•
Total Liabilities to Net Worth 37	7.6	•	•	2.4	1.5	•	2.8	4.8	1.5	2.3	7.3	3.8	10.0
Current Assets to Working Capital 38	3.5	•	•	1.5	1.9	5.3	3.2	2.2	2.7	2.4	3.5	2.3	4.1
Current Liabilities to Working Capital 39	2.5	•	•	0.5	0.9	4.3	2.2	1.2	1.7	1.4	2.5	1.3	3.1
Working Capital to Net Sales 40	0.1	•	•	0.1	0.1	0.0	0.1	0.1	0.1	0.1	0.0	0.1	0.1
Inventory to Working Capital 41	0.0	•	•	0.0	0.0	0.0	0.0	0.0	0.0	0.0	0.0	0.0	0.0
Total Receipts to Cash Flow 42	2.7	3.1	3.9	3.4	2.8	2.9	2.4	2.7	2.2	2.6	4.8	3.0	2.5
Cost of Goods to Cash Flow 43	0.1	•	0.4	0.3	0.1	0.4	0.4	0.3	0.1	0.1	0.2	0.1	0.1
Cash Flow to Total Debt 44	0.4	•	0.9	1.4	1.5	0.9	0.9	0.7	1.2	0.8	0.3	0.3	0.3

Selected Financial Factors (in Percentages)

Debt Ratio 45	88.4	•	215.1	70.3	60.7	110.5	73.7	82.7	60.2	69.2	88.0	79.2	90.9
Return on Total Assets 46	10.0	•	56.9	30.6	23.1	21.8	12.7	13.2	8.7	9.1	11.9	7.7	9.0
Return on Equity Before Income Taxes 47	50.7	•	•	90.3	52.5	•	42.3	63.3	17.1	22.7	70.5	23.4	47.7
Return on Equity After Income Taxes 48	40.2	•	•	87.9	52.2	•	39.1	60.6	16.3	20.7	60.5	18.8	32.7
Profit Margin (Before Income Tax) 49	6.4	8.0	7.2	8.2	8.2	7.6	6.9	7.4	4.3	5.0	6.1	6.4	6.0
Profit Margin (After Income Tax) 50	5.0	6.6	7.1	8.0	8.2	7.2	6.3	7.1	4.0	4.6	5.2	5.1	4.1

Table I

Corporations with and without Net Income

OTHER ARTS, ENTERTAINMENT, AND RECREATION

MONEY AMOUNTS AND SIZE OF ASSETS IN THOUSANDS OF DOLLARS

Item Description for Accounting Period 7/12 Through 6/13	Total	Zero Assets	Under 500	500 to 1,000	1,000 to 5,000	5,000 to 10,000	10,000 to 25,000	25,000 to 50,000	50,000 to 100,000	100,000 to 250,000	250,000 to 500,000	500,000 to 2,500,000	2,500,000 and over
Number of Enterprises 1	77117	17406	54996	2502	1819	174	110	30	28	19	16	17	0
Revenues ($ in Thousands)													
Net Sales 2	58831167	1014086	20744170	6265588	6838303	2384682	1839244	691568	921854	2447942	3895708	11788022	0
Interest 3	171444	922	1105	158	2066	1411	1189	5638	1116	1249	7988	148602	0
Rents 4	100836	2480	5288	0	3420	13	844	625	0	2325	28861	56978	0
Royalties 5	66433	307	0	0	0	898	5264	3190	22	33278	20514	2959	0
Other Portfolio Income 6	169831	35538	10097	360	30977	4890	33723	9363	539	4669	13127	26548	0
Other Receipts 7	2812691	155048	155956	60896	55702	36745	268931	180433	180874	334354	761713	622043	0
Total Receipts 8	62152402	1208381	20916616	6327002	6930468	2428639	2149195	890817	1104405	2823817	4727911	12645152	0
Average Total Receipts 9	806	69	380	2529	3810	13958	19538	29694	39443	148622	295494	743832	•
Operating Costs/Operating Income (%)													
Cost of Operations 10	24.6	17.0	24.9	8.8	12.3	33.8	30.5	17.6	29.4	18.3	22.9	39.3	•
Salaries and Wages 11	15.3	4.3	10.3	7.7	15.5	15.6	27.2	42.4	29.7	42.8	32.0	13.3	•
Taxes Paid 12	3.3	2.5	1.9	1.8	3.2	1.7	3.2	3.5	5.0	3.2	3.1	7.1	•
Interest Paid 13	1.5	2.2	0.2	0.2	0.8	0.2	0.4	1.5	2.6	2.1	2.6	4.7	•
Depreciation 14	1.7	1.1	0.6	0.4	1.1	0.7	2.3	5.2	3.7	2.5	2.3	4.1	•
Amortization and Depletion 15	1.4	0.8	0.0	0.0	0.2	0.3	0.4	1.2	2.4	1.2	5.7	4.0	•
Pensions and Other Deferred Comp. 16	1.4	1.4	2.3	0.6	0.5	0.0	0.5	0.6	0.6	2.0	2.4	0.7	•
Employee Benefits 17	1.0	0.6	0.6	0.2	0.5	0.3	1.8	2.1	1.5	2.7	3.5	1.2	•
Advertising 18	1.8	2.2	0.6	1.9	1.9	1.8	1.8	1.7	3.1	2.5	3.1	3.0	•
Other Expenses 19	29.7	72.9	29.9	21.0	30.9	38.1	28.3	49.4	33.7	34.5	32.0	24.8	•
Officers' Compensation 20	17.4	14.2	22.4	55.0	20.4	6.0	4.8	4.4	5.4	1.2	3.5	0.9	•
Operating Margin 21	0.9	•	6.3	2.3	12.6	1.4	•	•	•	•	•	•	•
Operating Margin Before Officers' Comp. 22	18.3	•	28.7	57.3	33.0	7.5	3.7	•	•	•	•	•	•

Selected Average Balance Sheet ($ in Thousands)

Net Receivables 23	39	0	1	22	93	416	1165	4716	5153	23327	27099	78891	•
Inventories 24	11	0	1	29	194	74	61	64	843	2498	2827	15494	•
Net Property, Plant and Equipment 25	142	0	7	184	427	840	2005	8949	14357	45147	80476	359768	•
Total Assets 26	581	0	51	669	1938	7449	15181	37073	72039	157052	355483	1296447	•
Notes and Loans Payable 27	229	0	44	219	870	2071	2598	16063	22678	52406	117016	498028	•
All Other Liabilities 28	203	0	17	117	763	2470	4795	15036	33580	75421	142625	410707	•
Net Worth 29	149	0	-10	333	304	2909	7788	5974	15781	29225	95843	387711	•

Selected Financial Ratios (Times to 1)

Current Ratio 30	1.3	•	2.2	3.6	1.4	1.2	2.1	1.6	1.5	1.0	1.1	1.0	•
Quick Ratio 31	0.8	•	1.9	2.8	1.0	0.7	1.6	1.2	0.8	0.8	0.6	0.6	•
Net Sales to Working Capital 32	15.9	•	18.9	8.8	12.1	24.2	4.4	3.5	4.6	74.2	40.1	41.0	•
Coverage Ratio 33	5.4	0.9	38.9	14.7	17.4	15.2	38.0	0.4	2.0	2.1	4.2	1.9	•
Total Asset Turnover 34	1.3	•	7.4	3.7	1.9	1.8	1.1	0.6	0.5	0.8	0.7	0.5	•
Inventory Turnover 35	16.6	•	124.3	7.5	2.4	62.5	84.0	63.4	11.5	9.5	19.7	17.6	•
Receivables Turnover 36	19.4	•	257.3	119.9	43.4	32.7	15.2	4.9	4.8	6.4	9.5	8.3	•
Total Liabilities to Net Worth 37	2.9	•	•	1.0	5.4	1.6	0.9	5.2	3.6	4.4	2.7	2.3	•
Current Assets to Working Capital 38	4.8	•	1.8	1.4	3.6	5.6	1.9	2.6	3.1	28.7	18.9	26.0	•
Current Liabilities to Working Capital 39	3.8	•	0.8	0.4	2.6	4.6	0.9	1.6	2.1	27.7	17.9	25.0	•
Working Capital to Net Sales 40	0.1	•	0.1	0.1	0.1	0.0	0.2	0.3	0.2	0.0	0.0	0.0	•
Inventory to Working Capital 41	0.2	•	0.0	0.1	0.6	0.1	0.0	0.0	0.0	1.6	0.6	0.8	•
Total Receipts to Cash Flow 42	3.1	1.6	3.0	4.5	2.5	2.6	2.6	2.3	3.0	3.2	2.8	4.3	•
Cost of Goods to Cash Flow 43	0.8	0.3	0.7	0.4	0.3	0.9	0.8	0.4	0.9	0.6	0.7	1.7	•
Cash Flow to Total Debt 44	0.6	•	2.1	1.7	0.9	1.2	0.9	0.3	0.2	0.3	0.3	0.2	•

Selected Financial Factors (in Percentages)

Debt Ratio 45	74.3	•	119.8	50.2	84.3	61.0	48.7	83.9	78.1	81.4	73.0	70.1	•
Return on Total Assets 46	10.7	•	54.1	13.1	28.5	6.4	17.8	0.4	2.4	3.7	7.4	4.8	•
Return on Equity Before Income Taxes 47	33.9	•	•	24.4	171.1	15.4	33.7	•	5.5	10.4	20.9	7.8	•
Return on Equity After Income Taxes 48	31.5	•	•	23.9	170.2	14.0	32.8	•	3.7	9.7	17.1	5.5	•
Profit Margin (Before Income Tax) 49	6.6	•	7.1	3.2	13.8	3.3	15.7	•	2.6	2.4	8.2	4.3	•
Profit Margin (After Income Tax) 50	6.2	•	7.0	3.2	13.8	3.0	15.3	•	1.8	2.2	6.7	3.1	•

Table II
Corporations with Net Income

OTHER ARTS, ENTERTAINMENT, AND RECREATION

MONEY AMOUNTS AND SIZE OF ASSETS IN THOUSANDS OF DOLLARS

Item Description for Accounting Period 7/12 Through 6/13	Total	Zero Assets	Under 500	500 to 1,000	1,000 to 5,000	5,000 to 10,000	10,000 to 25,000	25,000 to 50,000	50,000 to 100,000	100,000 to 250,000	250,000 to 500,000	500,000 to 2,500,000	2,500,000 and over
Number of Enterprises 1	45384	7454	34845	1893	965	91	75	11	18	10	11	12	0

Revenues ($ in Thousands)

	Total	Zero Assets	Under 500	500 to 1,000	1,000 to 5,000	5,000 to 10,000	10,000 to 25,000	25,000 to 50,000	50,000 to 100,000	100,000 to 250,000	250,000 to 500,000	500,000 to 2,500,000	2,500,000 and over
Net Sales 2	45170577	744392	18174237	5926181	4965987	2144613	1557859	384436	659898	1546047	3190992	5875936	0
Interest 3	140597	265	617	158	1538	360	865	101	1101	870	7576	127146	0
Rents 4	70408	2480	1006	0	3155	0	844	0	0	2325	17268	43329	0
Royalties 5	30957	0	0	0	0	0	5264	3190	22	20817	33	1631	0
Other Portfolio Income 6	158152	31859	8853	360	30872	4626	33664	9358	503	4144	12688	21225	0
Other Receipts 7	2171167	149596	78294	38710	71725	55671	247923	124358	130877	286638	417971	569405	0
Total Receipts 8	47741858	928592	18263007	5965409	5073277	2205270	1846419	521443	792401	1860841	3646528	6638672	0
Average Total Receipts 9	1052	125	524	3151	5257	24234	24619	47404	44022	186084	331503	553223	•

Operating Costs/Operating Income (%)

	Total	Zero Assets	Under 500	500 to 1,000	1,000 to 5,000	5,000 to 10,000	10,000 to 25,000	25,000 to 50,000	50,000 to 100,000	100,000 to 250,000	250,000 to 500,000	500,000 to 2,500,000	2,500,000 and over
Cost of Operations 10	22.3	16.5	27.6	5.9	11.5	35.3	32.9	0.5	20.1	10.9	22.1	29.8	•
Salaries and Wages 11	15.0	3.3	9.7	7.4	14.7	13.8	24.2	41.5	32.7	46.7	31.1	17.7	•
Taxes Paid 12	3.3	2.5	1.6	1.7	2.6	1.4	2.9	2.6	4.9	3.7	3.2	11.0	•
Interest Paid 13	1.0	0.9	0.1	0.3	0.2	0.0	0.4	0.6	2.2	1.5	1.7	5.4	•
Depreciation 14	1.3	0.3	0.4	0.4	0.4	0.3	2.2	0.9	2.3	2.9	1.8	5.3	•
Amortization and Depletion 15	0.8	0.1	0.0	0.0	0.0	0.1	0.1	0.7	1.1	0.1	5.0	3.4	•
Pensions and Other Deferred Comp. 16	1.5	2.0	2.3	0.7	0.5	0.0	0.5	0.7	0.7	2.3	2.7	1.1	•
Employee Benefits 17	0.9	0.5	0.5	0.2	0.4	0.1	1.7	0.7	1.9	3.1	2.9	1.4	•
Advertising 18	1.0	1.4	0.5	0.2	0.8	1.6	0.9	0.2	4.3	1.5	2.9	1.8	•
Other Expenses 19	25.6	52.3	26.5	19.2	21.3	35.6	22.9	55.3	24.2	39.3	23.0	22.4	•
Officers' Compensation 20	19.9	16.7	20.3	58.0	25.0	6.3	5.0	6.5	6.4	1.0	4.0	1.1	•
Operating Margin 21	7.4	3.7	10.5	6.0	22.7	5.4	6.3	•	•	•	•	•	•
Operating Margin Before Officers' Comp. 22	27.3	20.4	30.8	64.0	47.7	11.7	11.3	•	5.6	•	3.6	0.6	•

Selected Average Balance Sheet ($ in Thousands)

	1	2	3	4	5	6	7	8	9	10	11	12	13
Net Receivables 23	37	0	1	27	119	615	1159	3492	5896	20992	27728	55184	•
Inventories 24	9	0	1	1	62	116	34	4	635	2356	4028	19003	•
Net Property, Plant and Equipment 25	152	0	5	188	205	516	1930	3538	12261	64085	63186	365063	•
Total Assets 26	624	0	56	697	1972	7003	14714	39338	71693	156146	351095	1189069	•
Notes and Loans Payable 27	213	0	24	277	217	515	3045	9166	18130	59822	89087	485923	•
All Other Liabilities 28	192	0	16	80	331	4308	4123	14280	44666	75572	140416	307472	•
Net Worth 29	219	0	15	340	1424	2181	7546	15892	8897	20752	121593	395674	•

Selected Financial Ratios (Times to 1)

	1	2	3	4	5	6	7	8	9	10	11	12	13
Current Ratio 30	1.5	•	2.4	5.7	4.0	1.3	2.7	2.1	2.0	0.9	1.4	1.1	•
Quick Ratio 31	0.9	•	2.2	5.1	3.3	0.7	2.2	1.4	1.0	0.7	0.8	0.4	•
Net Sales to Working Capital 32	11.0	•	21.1	9.3	5.1	19.8	4.2	3.2	2.5	•	6.3	19.8	•
Coverage Ratio 33	13.7	34.1	124.6	27.8	159.2	627.2	68.3	43.6	9.8	5.8	9.2	3.3	•
Total Asset Turnover 34	1.6	•	9.4	4.5	2.6	3.4	1.4	0.9	0.5	1.0	0.8	0.4	•
Inventory Turnover 35	24.5	•	167.8	187.4	9.5	71.4	203.9	36.9	11.6	7.1	15.9	7.7	•
Receivables Turnover 36	24.9	•	356.0	140.5	46.2	34.8	18.0	8.1	6.5	9.1	10.7	6.9	•
Total Liabilities to Net Worth 37	1.8	•	2.7	1.0	0.4	2.2	0.9	1.5	7.1	6.5	1.9	2.0	•
Current Assets to Working Capital 38	3.0	•	1.7	1.2	1.3	4.5	1.6	1.9	2.0	•	3.3	16.7	•
Current Liabilities to Working Capital 39	2.0	•	0.7	0.2	0.3	3.5	0.6	0.9	1.0	•	2.3	15.7	•
Working Capital to Net Sales 40	0.1	•	0.0	0.1	0.2	0.1	0.2	0.3	0.4	•	0.2	0.1	•
Inventory to Working Capital 41	0.1	•	0.0	0.0	0.0	0.0	0.0	•	0.0	•	0.1	0.6	•
Total Receipts to Cash Flow 42	2.8	1.3	2.9	4.1	2.3	2.4	2.3	1.3	2.5	2.4	3.1	3.2	•
Cost of Goods to Cash Flow 43	0.6	0.2	0.8	0.2	0.3	0.8	0.8	0.0	0.5	0.3	0.7	1.0	•
Cash Flow to Total Debt 44	0.9	•	4.4	2.1	4.1	2.0	1.2	1.1	0.2	0.5	0.4	0.2	•

Selected Financial Factors (in Percentages)

	1	2	3	4	5	6	7	8	9	10	11	12	13
Debt Ratio 45	64.9	•	72.8	51.2	27.8	68.9	48.7	59.6	87.6	86.7	65.4	66.7	•
Return on Total Assets 46	22.6	•	104.3	31.2	65.1	27.7	35.5	23.1	11.0	8.9	12.8	7.5	•
Return on Equity Before Income Taxes 47	59.7	•	380.9	61.7	89.6	88.7	68.3	56.0	79.5	55.5	32.9	15.7	•
Return on Equity After Income Taxes 48	56.9	•	376.7	61.0	89.3	85.1	66.8	55.6	74.4	53.5	28.5	12.7	•
Profit Margin (Before Income Tax) 49	13.1	28.2	11.0	6.7	24.8	8.2	24.8	25.5	19.3	7.5	13.8	12.7	•
Profit Margin (After Income Tax) 50	12.5	26.9	10.9	6.6	24.7	7.9	24.3	25.3	18.1	7.2	11.9	10.2	•

Table I

Corporations with and without Net Income

AMUSEMENT, GAMBLING, AND RECREATION INDUSTRIES

MONEY AMOUNTS AND SIZE OF ASSETS IN THOUSANDS OF DOLLARS

Item Description for Accounting Period 7/12 Through 6/13		Total	Zero Assets	Under 500	500 to 1,000	1,000 to 5,000	5,000 to 10,000	10,000 to 25,000	25,000 to 50,000	50,000 to 100,000	100,000 to 250,000	250,000 to 500,000	500,000 to 2,500,000	2,500,000 and over
Number of Enterprises	1	46435	9466	29783	2762	3252	606	321	138	51	28	13	12	4
Revenues ($ in Thousands)														
Net Sales	2	51968853	486877	13530694	2448456	7193675	2807174	3396384	2127704	1875104	2278443	2852510	7027385	5944449
Interest	3	400766	280	868	1176	3930	2525	6104	7491	9970	7226	7026	17077	337092
Rents	4	141791	25	8325	5124	5500	14708	7353	10413	2210	7308	22427	30648	27750
Royalties	5	106132	0	0	39	24	628	264	0	748	14087	19549	0	70794
Other Portfolio Income	6	345584	81607	13300	1819	28525	12010	2162	46237	21841	30439	924	8514	98208
Other Receipts	7	3042393	71498	54268	161948	408555	182498	357163	185264	176768	6707	360287	893945	183487
Total Receipts	8	56005519	640287	13607455	2618562	7640209	3019543	3769430	2377109	2086641	2344210	3262723	7977569	6661780
Average Total Receipts	9	1206	68	457	948	2349	4983	11743	17225	40915	83722	250979	664797	1665445
Operating Costs/Operating Income (%)														
Cost of Operations	10	21.2	9.5	29.5	13.1	29.9	20.3	27.7	23.2	15.8	13.7	15.4	7.2	15.9
Salaries and Wages	11	22.4	26.4	15.7	24.4	20.1	31.2	25.9	30.9	23.4	25.8	25.9	27.8	20.6
Taxes Paid	12	8.4	7.1	4.3	5.8	7.9	6.2	5.6	6.0	8.8	6.8	9.1	13.8	16.7
Interest Paid	13	4.0	6.0	0.6	1.8	2.1	3.9	2.6	3.6	2.7	2.1	6.7	9.0	9.2
Depreciation	14	6.9	5.3	2.6	5.1	4.8	6.7	6.8	7.7	8.4	7.7	8.1	9.9	15.1
Amortization and Depletion	15	0.8	3.9	0.1	0.0	0.3	0.2	0.8	1.1	0.8	1.3	1.6	1.5	2.0
Pensions and Other Deferred Comp.	16	0.2	0.3	0.1	0.8	0.1	0.6	0.2	0.2	0.3	0.3	0.5	0.1	0.3
Employee Benefits	17	1.5	0.9	1.0	1.0	1.0	1.8	2.7	2.0	2.3	2.6	2.2	1.4	1.3
Advertising	18	2.7	3.2	1.9	2.4	2.0	2.9	2.8	1.9	2.7	5.4	3.5	3.3	3.8
Other Expenses	19	34.9	89.1	37.2	41.0	33.2	30.1	32.5	31.1	43.6	46.1	33.7	38.8	19.1
Officers' Compensation	20	3.2	10.2	6.4	3.1	2.6	3.8	1.7	1.0	1.2	1.7	0.9	1.2	2.3
Operating Margin	21	•	•	0.4	1.5	•	•	•	•	•	•	•	•	•
Operating Margin Before Officers' Comp.	22	•	•	6.8	4.6	•	•	•	•	•	•	•	•	•

Selected Average Balance Sheet ($ in Thousands)

Net Receivables 23	57	0	3	15	96	487	773	2065	3775	10065	14375	33226	73328
Inventories 24	26	0	5	10	60	234	322	1023	1370	2405	2315	17274	21236
Net Property, Plant and Equipment 25	817	0	60	489	1327	4376	10949	18826	41398	65178	156005	802153	1532200
Total Assets 26	1464	0	114	695	2130	6951	15701	34421	71352	151262	360386	1213629	3651382
Notes and Loans Payable 27	787	0	91	301	1431	4554	7094	8771	30323	59842	217584	788110	1646983
All Other Liabilities 28	353	0	25	153	377	786	5915	13296	19897	58932	85862	318187	554926
Net Worth 29	324	0	-2	241	322	1610	2692	12353	21132	32487	56939	107332	1449473

Selected Financial Ratios (Times to 1)

Current Ratio 30	1.0	•	0.9	0.9	1.3	1.0	0.9	1.1	1.3	1.3	0.7	0.7	1.4
Quick Ratio 31	0.7	•	0.7	0.8	1.0	0.8	0.6	0.7	1.0	0.9	0.5	0.5	1.0
Net Sales to Working Capital 32	2445.1	•	•	•	17.1	•	•	23.0	10.0	9.5	•	•	12.8
Coverage Ratio 33	1.4	•	2.6	5.8	2.0	0.9	1.7	1.9	1.4	•	2.0	1.0	1.6
Total Asset Turnover 34	0.8	•	4.0	1.3	1.0	0.7	0.7	0.4	0.5	0.5	0.6	0.5	0.4
Inventory Turnover 35	9.1	•	28.6	11.4	11.1	4.0	9.1	3.5	4.2	4.6	14.6	2.4	11.1
Receivables Turnover 36	21.1	•	159.0	39.4	21.1	10.8	15.1	10.1	8.6	9.3	16.3	19.0	21.8
Total Liabilities to Net Worth 37	3.5	•	•	1.9	5.6	3.3	4.8	1.8	2.4	3.7	5.3	10.3	1.5
Current Assets to Working Capital 38	556.5	•	•	•	4.2	•	•	10.4	4.0	4.7	•	•	3.5
Current Liabilities to Working Capital 39	555.5	•	•	•	3.2	•	•	9.4	3.0	3.7	•	•	2.5
Working Capital to Net Sales 40	0.0	•	•	•	0.1	•	•	0.0	0.1	0.1	•	•	0.1
Inventory to Working Capital 41	49.8	•	•	•	0.5	•	•	1.6	0.4	0.3	•	•	0.2
Total Receipts to Cash Flow 42	4.2	4.4	4.1	2.6	4.4	5.0	3.7	4.2	3.3	7.1	3.5	4.2	5.2
Cost of Goods to Cash Flow 43	0.9	0.4	1.2	0.3	1.3	1.0	1.0	1.0	0.5	1.0	0.5	0.3	0.8
Cash Flow to Total Debt 44	0.2	•	1.0	0.7	0.3	0.2	0.2	0.2	0.2	0.1	0.2	0.1	0.1

Selected Financial Factors (in Percentages)

Debt Ratio 45	77.9	•	101.4	65.3	84.9	76.8	82.9	64.1	70.4	78.5	84.2	91.2	60.3
Return on Total Assets 46	4.1	•	6.5	13.0	4.3	2.4	2.9	3.0	2.0	•	8.1	4.1	6.2
Return on Equity Before Income Taxes 47	4.9	•	•	30.9	13.9	•	6.7	3.9	2.0	•	25.3	•	6.1
Return on Equity After Income Taxes 48	3.1	•	•	30.6	13.7	•	6.4	3.5	0.7	•	18.9	•	4.3
Profit Margin (Before Income Tax) 49	1.4	•	1.0	8.4	2.0	•	1.7	3.2	1.2	•	6.6	•	5.9
Profit Margin (After Income Tax) 50	0.9	•	1.0	8.3	2.0	•	1.6	2.8	0.4	•	4.9	•	4.2

Table II
Corporations with Net Income

AMUSEMENT, GAMBLING, AND RECREATION INDUSTRIES

MONEY AMOUNTS AND SIZE OF ASSETS IN THOUSANDS OF DOLLARS

Item Description for Accounting Period 7/12 Through 6/13	Total	Zero Assets	Under 500	500 to 1,000	1,000 to 5,000	5,000 to 10,000	10,000 to 25,000	25,000 to 50,000	50,000 to 100,000	100,000 to 250,000	250,000 to 500,000	500,000 to 2,500,000	2,500,000 and over
Number of Enterprises **1**	22869	1852	17198	1899	1428	199	163	71	29	11	10	•	•

Revenues ($ in Thousands)

Net Sales **2**	30181453	138465	7201257	2099200	4681096	1295398	2111813	1264082	1411717	1143337	1945254	•	•
Interest **3**	361939	226	492	877	3315	965	1605	2524	2201	3598	1016	•	•
Rents **4**	105861	25	912	4591	3741	12663	3940	9367	1370	2761	12735	•	•
Royalties **5**	102893	0	0	0	0	628	0	0	748	13206	17518	•	•
Other Portfolio Income **6**	291956	66394	9095	1488	23654	8460	1233	44101	11884	25916	888	•	•
Other Receipts **7**	2365854	23609	40934	158040	308809	105092	217495	78865	62495	21994	318703	•	•
Total Receipts **8**	33409956	228719	7252690	2264196	5020615	1423206	2336086	1398939	1490415	1210812	2296114	•	•
Average Total Receipts **9**	1461	123	422	1192	3516	7152	14332	19703	51394	110074	229611	•	•

Operating Costs/Operating Income (%)

Cost of Operations **10**	19.7	2.9	15.3	10.8	34.1	32.8	35.3	16.2	14.2	9.1	10.4	•	•
Salaries and Wages **11**	21.2	16.7	16.8	23.2	15.9	24.7	20.3	33.6	22.6	25.1	26.0	•	•
Taxes Paid **12**	8.8	5.2	4.8	5.7	7.7	5.0	5.7	5.9	9.3	9.0	9.7	•	•
Interest Paid **13**	3.7	11.7	0.6	1.1	1.6	1.7	2.1	2.1	2.4	1.3	6.8	•	•
Depreciation **14**	6.5	4.4	2.6	4.7	2.8	4.3	4.9	6.6	7.7	8.1	9.3	•	•
Amortization and Depletion **15**	0.8	0.4	0.1	0.0	0.2	0.2	0.5	0.8	0.8	1.3	1.7	•	•
Pensions and Other Deferred Comp. **16**	0.3	•	0.1	0.9	0.1	1.1	0.2	0.2	0.4	0.5	0.5	•	•
Employee Benefits **17**	1.4	0.3	1.3	0.8	0.8	1.3	2.0	1.8	2.1	3.3	2.3	•	•
Advertising **18**	2.5	2.5	1.6	2.5	1.7	1.8	3.2	2.6	2.9	2.1	4.1	•	•
Other Expenses **19**	31.7	39.4	42.0	42.4	27.5	22.6	24.0	29.5	31.2	29.7	35.2	•	•
Officers' Compensation **20**	3.7	5.6	8.2	2.6	2.6	3.7	1.4	0.9	1.4	2.7	0.9	•	•
Operating Margin **21**	•	10.9	6.5	5.4	4.9	0.8	0.5	•	4.9	7.9	•	•	•
Operating Margin Before Officers' Comp. **22**	3.4	16.5	14.8	8.1	7.5	4.5	1.9	0.8	6.3	10.7	•	•	•

Selected Average Balance Sheet ($ in Thousands)

Net Receivables 23	64	0	3	18	135	398	666	3211	3298	8722	5188	•	•
Inventories 24	28	0	5	8	81	586	373	1015	1328	1454	1784	•	•
Net Property, Plant and Equipment 25	889	0	60	467	1442	3400	8951	16521	42026	56195	146055	•	•
Total Assets 26	1751	0	115	672	2543	6938	15161	35036	73697	134149	356856	•	•
Notes and Loans Payable 27	767	0	53	180	1161	3433	5202	7437	19305	45674	204259	•	•
All Other Liabilities 28	346	0	21	154	333	1275	3420	8338	29485	40632	56345	•	•
Net Worth 29	638	0	40	338	1049	2230	6538	19261	24907	47844	96252	•	•

Selected Financial Ratios (Times to 1)

Current Ratio 30	1.4	•	1.6	1.2	1.6	2.0	1.4	1.3	1.3	1.5	1.0	•	•
Quick Ratio 31	1.1	•	1.3	1.1	1.2	1.7	1.0	0.9	1.0	1.2	0.7	•	•
Net Sales to Working Capital 32	14.1	•	27.9	36.1	11.4	7.0	13.0	10.5	13.0	7.7	597.6	•	•
Coverage Ratio 33	3.8	7.5	12.4	13.5	8.6	7.4	6.4	5.9	5.3	11.6	2.6	•	•
Total Asset Turnover 34	0.8	•	3.7	1.6	1.3	0.9	0.9	0.5	0.7	0.8	0.5	•	•
Inventory Turnover 35	9.3	•	14.1	15.4	13.9	3.6	12.3	2.8	5.2	6.5	11.3	•	•
Receivables Turnover 36	26.8	•	131.8	89.5	26.5	15.6	19.0	9.0	17.1	14.6	48.8	•	•
Total Liabilities to Net Worth 37	1.7	•	1.9	1.0	1.4	2.1	1.3	0.8	2.0	1.8	2.7	•	•
Current Assets to Working Capital 38	3.4	•	2.8	5.6	2.6	2.0	3.7	5.0	4.3	3.2	172.9	•	•
Current Liabilities to Working Capital 39	2.4	•	1.8	4.6	1.6	1.0	2.7	4.0	3.3	2.2	171.9	•	•
Working Capital to Net Sales 40	0.1	•	0.0	0.0	0.1	0.1	0.1	0.1	0.1	0.1	0.0	•	•
Inventory to Working Capital 41	0.3	•	0.3	0.2	0.3	0.2	0.3	0.5	0.3	0.1	6.5	•	•
Total Receipts to Cash Flow 42	3.1	1.3	2.8	2.3	3.2	3.9	3.3	3.2	2.9	2.9	2.9	•	•
Cost of Goods to Cash Flow 43	0.6	0.0	0.4	0.2	1.1	1.3	1.2	0.5	0.4	0.3	0.3	•	•
Cash Flow to Total Debt 44	0.4	•	2.0	1.5	0.7	0.4	0.5	0.4	0.3	0.4	0.3	•	•

Selected Financial Factors (in Percentages)

Debt Ratio 45	63.6	•	65.0	49.8	58.7	67.9	56.9	45.0	66.2	64.3	73.0	•	•
Return on Total Assets 46	10.6	•	28.8	23.6	17.7	11.5	11.3	6.4	8.5	11.7	9.8	•	•
Return on Equity Before Income Taxes 47	21.5	•	75.7	43.5	37.9	30.9	22.1	9.7	20.5	30.0	22.4	•	•
Return on Equity After Income Taxes 48	19.7	•	75.3	43.2	37.7	28.1	21.8	9.1	18.5	27.8	17.5	•	•
Profit Margin (Before Income Tax) 49	10.4	76.1	7.3	13.3	12.1	10.6	11.1	10.5	10.5	13.8	11.1	•	•
Profit Margin (After Income Tax) 50	9.5	70.5	7.2	13.2	12.1	9.6	11.0	9.9	9.4	12.8	8.7	•	•

Table I

Corporations with and without Net Income

ACCOMMODATION

MONEY AMOUNTS AND SIZE OF ASSETS IN THOUSANDS OF DOLLARS

Item Description for Accounting Period 7/12 Through 6/13	Total	Zero Assets	Under 500	500 to 1,000	1,000 to 5,000	5,000 to 10,000	10,000 to 25,000	25,000 to 50,000	50,000 to 100,000	100,000 to 250,000	250,000 to 500,000	500,000 to 2,500,000	2,500,000 and over
Number of Enterprises **1**	32784	3971	15986	3506	7553	987	475	133	64	51	21	24	13

Revenues ($ in Thousands)

	Total	Zero Assets	Under 500	500 to 1,000	1,000 to 5,000	5,000 to 10,000	10,000 to 25,000	25,000 to 50,000	50,000 to 100,000	100,000 to 250,000	250,000 to 500,000	500,000 to 2,500,000	2,500,000 and over
Net Sales **2**	86642788	2001817	4376739	1344111	8105392	3744375	4063286	4070079	2406753	9722980	3840044	7567183	35400029
Interest **3**	1126107	8709	2095	72	8202	1795	6307	9904	8112	17293	15792	128862	918964
Rents **4**	530228	47901	10627	7833	324	1255	4973	16088	15519	18036	18695	108003	280975
Royalties **5**	2893024	12691	0	0	0	0	1117	0	26557	3672	255645	243	2593100
Other Portfolio Income **6**	5020091	47053	164079	232	17567	8861	56390	11075	7021	71131	15892	1119424	3501364
Other Receipts **7**	11253880	171206	60663	7446	721528	347450	62056	109253	45758	418378	110379	354986	8844779
Total Receipts **8**	107466118	2289377	4614203	1359694	8853013	4103736	4194129	4216399	2509720	10251490	4256447	9278701	51539211
Average Total Receipts **9**	3278	577	289	388	1172	4158	8830	31702	39214	201010	202688	386613	3964555

Operating Costs/Operating Income (%)

	Total	Zero Assets	Under 500	500 to 1,000	1,000 to 5,000	5,000 to 10,000	10,000 to 25,000	25,000 to 50,000	50,000 to 100,000	100,000 to 250,000	250,000 to 500,000	500,000 to 2,500,000	2,500,000 and over
Cost of Operations **10**	17.0	5.1	15.3	10.1	15.3	15.3	32.6	26.1	21.1	23.3	18.2	18.1	13.4
Salaries and Wages **11**	27.1	9.2	14.7	15.4	16.0	16.5	13.8	14.3	16.6	12.3	16.4	24.1	43.4
Taxes Paid **12**	7.1	4.5	6.4	9.3	6.5	6.6	5.1	5.1	4.9	3.5	3.4	11.8	8.5
Interest Paid **13**	9.1	8.7	2.5	7.4	7.4	6.8	4.7	2.9	4.0	1.2	2.6	9.5	15.1
Depreciation **14**	5.9	4.4	2.9	6.0	7.4	8.5	6.5	4.5	7.0	1.9	7.3	10.2	5.7
Amortization and Depletion **15**	0.9	0.5	0.4	0.3	0.9	0.4	0.2	0.5	0.4	0.3	0.4	1.2	1.2
Pensions and Other Deferred Comp. **16**	0.6	0.4	0.0	0.0	0.0	0.2	0.1	0.1	0.3	0.1	0.2	0.9	1.1
Employee Benefits **17**	2.9	0.3	0.5	0.6	1.4	1.7	0.8	1.8	2.6	1.3	3.1	2.5	4.9
Advertising **18**	2.9	0.9	1.5	1.4	5.0	2.5	1.7	1.8	3.1	2.7	3.0	3.1	3.0
Other Expenses **19**	44.0	90.9	57.6	41.9	41.3	45.7	34.4	43.8	41.8	56.2	52.0	27.3	40.8
Officers' Compensation **20**	1.5	0.7	2.3	3.3	2.3	2.4	1.6	0.9	1.1	0.3	2.2	1.1	1.4
Operating Margin **21**	•	•	•	4.3	•	•	•	•	•	•	•	•	•
Operating Margin Before Officers' Comp. **22**	•	•	•	7.5	•	•	0.0	•	•	•	•	•	•

Selected Average Balance Sheet ($ in Thousands)

Net Receivables **23**	301	0	2	6	61	110	1008	1767	3284	9988	25356	36378	491251
Inventories **24**	87	0	1	1	15	28	141	182	551	1552	3349	17700	153171
Net Property, Plant and Equipment **25**	3152	0	114	588	1668	5060	10186	20226	46059	70368	189164	481686	4021050
Total Assets **26**	7328	0	159	725	2147	6673	14708	34730	70251	163396	339791	918573	12210263
Notes and Loans Payable **27**	3886	0	114	497	1683	5336	9628	20484	35389	52780	141977	443026	6152139
All Other Liabilities **28**	2118	0	19	23	222	642	1641	5844	10765	52547	67830	134707	4396676
Net Worth **29**	1324	0	26	205	242	695	3438	8403	24097	58069	129985	340840	1661448

Selected Financial Ratios (Times to 1)

Current Ratio **30**	1.2	•	1.1	2.2	1.3	0.9	1.5	1.5	1.5	1.0	1.8	1.1	1.2
Quick Ratio **31**	0.8	•	0.9	1.6	1.1	0.6	1.1	1.1	1.1	0.7	1.3	0.5	0.8
Net Sales to Working Capital **32**	15.5	•	155.5	9.4	20.6	•	9.0	11.1	8.1	•	5.4	19.7	11.9
Coverage Ratio **33**	2.1	•	1.6	1.7	1.7	1.5	1.3	1.6	1.3	3.0	1.8	2.4	2.3
Total Asset Turnover **34**	0.4	•	1.7	0.5	0.5	0.6	0.6	0.9	0.5	1.2	0.5	0.3	0.2
Inventory Turnover **35**	5.2	•	49.7	48.3	11.3	20.4	19.7	43.8	14.4	28.7	9.9	3.2	2.4
Receivables Turnover **36**	9.0	•	118.2	44.8	16.9	31.7	9.8	21.8	12.4	20.1	8.3	6.0	6.0
Total Liabilities to Net Worth **37**	4.5	•	5.1	2.5	7.9	8.6	3.3	3.1	1.9	1.8	1.6	1.7	6.3
Current Assets to Working Capital **38**	5.9	•	12.3	1.8	4.5	•	3.0	2.9	3.1	•	2.3	10.7	6.3
Current Liabilities to Working Capital **39**	4.9	•	11.3	0.8	3.5	•	2.0	1.9	2.1	•	1.3	9.7	5.3
Working Capital to Net Sales **40**	0.1	•	0.0	0.1	0.0	•	0.1	0.1	0.1	•	0.2	0.1	0.1
Inventory to Working Capital **41**	0.5	•	0.4	0.0	0.3	•	0.2	0.1	0.1	•	0.1	1.4	0.6
Total Receipts to Cash Flow **42**	2.8	1.9	3.1	2.5	2.7	3.0	3.8	4.1	3.3	3.2	2.8	4.1	2.4
Cost of Goods to Cash Flow **43**	0.5	0.1	0.5	0.3	0.4	0.5	1.2	1.1	0.7	0.8	0.5	0.7	0.3
Cash Flow to Total Debt **44**	0.2	•	0.7	0.3	0.2	0.2	0.2	0.3	0.2	0.6	0.3	0.1	0.1

Selected Financial Factors (in Percentages)

Debt Ratio **45**	81.9	•	83.6	71.7	88.7	89.6	76.6	75.8	65.7	64.5	61.7	62.9	86.4
Return on Total Assets **46**	6.9	•	6.7	6.8	6.5	5.6	3.7	4.1	2.8	4.2	2.5	7.7	7.7
Return on Equity Before Income Taxes **47**	20.2	•	14.6	10.1	24.6	16.9	4.0	6.1	1.8	7.9	2.8	11.9	31.7
Return on Equity After Income Taxes **48**	12.9	•	10.0	10.0	23.7	15.1	3.2	4.5	0.7	6.2	0.5	7.8	19.7
Profit Margin (Before Income Tax) **49**	10.1	•	1.4	5.4	5.6	3.1	1.6	1.7	1.2	2.4	2.0	12.9	19.3
Profit Margin (After Income Tax) **50**	6.5	•	0.9	5.4	5.4	2.8	1.3	1.2	0.4	1.9	0.4	8.5	12.0

Table II
Corporations with Net Income

ACCOMMODATION

MONEY AMOUNTS AND SIZE OF ASSETS IN THOUSANDS OF DOLLARS

Item Description for Accounting Period 7/12 Through 6/13	Total	Zero Assets	Under 500	500 to 1,000	1,000 to 5,000	5,000 to 10,000	10,000 to 25,000	25,000 to 50,000	50,000 to 100,000	100,000 to 250,000	250,000 to 500,000	500,000 to 2,500,000	2,500,000 and over
Number of Enterprises **1**	16441	1554	7063	1896	4849	671	239	76	32	30	8	14	9

Revenues ($ in Thousands)

Net Sales **2**	53564695	677204	2308452	872261	5973171	2426320	2595052	2287709	1609246	6376845	2047913	6023519	20367004
Interest **3**	876701	7600	166	14	8070	1001	2693	6030	7092	15214	9758	25214	793849
Rents **4**	346840	0	10616	969	324	1086	4737	14279	8762	17235	6332	102283	180217
Royalties **5**	2858553	12691	0	0	0	0	342	0	26557	295	255645	242	2562781
Other Portfolio Income **6**	4704217	11537	156504	177	12864	8568	44301	9729	6155	57792	7649	1109285	3279656
Other Receipts **7**	8677495	222808	54014	3551	165566	334763	50234	90903	34401	355858	54325	276810	7034260
Total Receipts **8**	71028501	931840	2529752	876972	6159995	2771738	2697359	2408650	1692213	6823239	2381622	7537353	34217767
Average Total Receipts **9**	4320	600	358	463	1270	4131	11286	31693	52882	227441	297703	538382	3801974

Operating Costs/Operating Income (%)

Cost of Operations **10**	17.0	4.1	23.4	2.3	14.1	12.2	39.6	27.2	23.1	14.6	12.0	12.8	16.8
Salaries and Wages **11**	31.0	14.1	11.1	14.2	12.7	16.8	11.6	15.6	14.2	13.9	15.0	26.1	55.5
Taxes Paid **12**	5.8	4.5	6.3	10.5	5.9	7.3	4.8	5.8	3.7	2.7	2.7	12.6	4.9
Interest Paid **13**	6.5	3.3	3.3	7.0	6.8	7.1	3.8	2.4	3.5	0.9	3.1	7.5	9.7
Depreciation **14**	5.1	3.8	3.0	5.1	6.6	6.9	4.1	4.8	4.6	1.5	5.7	9.3	4.7
Amortization and Depletion **15**	0.8	0.3	0.6	0.3	0.4	0.5	0.2	0.1	0.2	0.2	0.5	1.3	1.1
Pensions and Other Deferred Comp. **16**	0.8	0.0	0.0	•	0.1	0.3	0.1	0.2	0.2	0.1	0.2	1.1	1.6
Employee Benefits **17**	2.8	0.0	0.2	0.8	0.9	1.3	0.7	2.9	2.3	1.3	1.9	2.8	4.9
Advertising **18**	2.8	0.7	1.5	1.4	1.3	1.7	1.3	1.6	3.3	3.6	3.9	2.9	3.6
Other Expenses **19**	41.4	75.0	42.6	42.4	38.1	45.5	26.9	36.0	41.3	61.9	58.4	25.3	39.6
Officers' Compensation **20**	1.9	1.9	2.9	3.1	2.6	3.0	1.9	1.1	0.6	0.3	3.4	1.0	2.1
Operating Margin **21**	•	•	5.1	12.8	10.5	•	5.1	2.3	3.1	•	•	•	•
Operating Margin Before Officers' Comp. **22**	•	•	8.0	15.9	13.1	0.3	7.0	3.5	3.7	•	•	•	•

Selected Average Balance Sheet ($ in Thousands)

Net Receivables 23	383	0	4	4	75	112	1707	1686	3945	11492	47176	22382	458074
Inventories 24	142	0	0	0	18	35	159	186	414	924	4956	21465	168011
Net Property, Plant and Equipment 25	3160	0	151	600	1626	4975	9617	23417	39828	64730	158712	475697	2589642
Total Assets 26	8152	0	195	707	2177	6836	15087	35498	71086	166997	358286	1019004	9495065
Notes and Loans Payable 27	4122	0	142	541	1625	5312	9433	21401	33059	48640	172274	456000	4459413
All Other Liabilities 28	2245	0	18	22	157	343	1195	4644	12769	45298	86675	146599	3400270
Net Worth 29	1786	0	35	144	394	1182	4458	9453	25258	73060	99337	416405	1635383

Selected Financial Ratios (Times to 1)

Current Ratio 30	1.4	•	1.7	2.2	2.3	1.2	1.9	1.4	1.8	1.3	2.2	1.9	1.2
Quick Ratio 31	0.9	•	1.4	1.2	1.9	0.9	1.4	1.0	1.2	0.9	1.6	0.7	0.8
Net Sales to Working Capital 32	8.7	•	26.3	10.8	7.3	29.8	6.2	13.4	6.4	21.1	3.8	4.5	9.8
Coverage Ratio 33	4.6	9.9	5.4	2.9	3.0	2.6	3.4	4.2	3.4	8.1	4.1	4.0	5.2
Total Asset Turnover 34	0.4	•	1.7	0.7	0.6	0.5	0.7	0.8	0.7	1.3	0.7	0.4	0.2
Inventory Turnover 35	3.9	•	352.8	139.2	9.6	12.6	27.0	44.0	28.0	33.5	6.2	2.6	2.3
Receivables Turnover 36	9.9	•	100.2	55.4	16.8	33.6	7.6	19.5	14.8	20.8	•	23.3	•
Total Liabilities to Net Worth 37	3.6	•	4.5	3.9	4.5	4.8	2.4	2.8	1.8	1.3	2.6	1.4	4.8
Current Assets to Working Capital 38	3.6	•	2.4	1.9	1.8	6.3	2.2	3.6	2.3	4.8	1.8	2.2	5.9
Current Liabilities to Working Capital 39	2.6	•	1.4	0.9	0.8	5.3	1.2	2.6	1.3	3.8	0.8	1.2	4.9
Working Capital to Net Sales 40	0.1	•	0.0	0.1	0.1	0.0	0.2	0.1	0.2	0.0	0.3	0.2	0.1
Inventory to Working Capital 41	0.4	•	0.0	•	0.1	0.4	0.1	0.1	0.1	0.1	0.1	0.3	0.7
Total Receipts to Cash Flow 42	2.2	1.4	2.8	2.0	2.3	2.3	3.5	3.7	2.9	2.6	1.9	3.5	1.7
Cost of Goods to Cash Flow 43	0.4	0.1	0.7	0.0	0.3	0.3	1.4	1.0	0.7	0.4	0.2	0.4	0.3
Cash Flow to Total Debt 44	0.2	•	0.7	0.4	0.3	0.3	0.3	0.3	0.4	0.9	0.5	0.2	0.2

Selected Financial Factors (in Percentages)

Debt Ratio 45	78.1	•	81.8	79.6	81.9	82.7	70.4	73.4	64.5	56.3	72.3	59.1	82.8
Return on Total Assets 46	12.0	•	30.1	13.2	11.6	9.9	9.2	8.5	8.2	8.9	9.0	12.6	12.1
Return on Equity Before Income Taxes 47	42.9	•	135.1	42.6	42.5	35.3	22.0	24.3	16.3	17.9	24.7	23.2	56.9
Return on Equity After Income Taxes 48	32.2	•	127.4	42.3	41.6	33.8	20.8	21.7	14.2	15.6	16.9	17.5	39.2
Profit Margin (Before Income Tax) 49	23.5	29.8	14.6	13.3	13.6	11.5	9.0	7.6	8.2	6.2	9.6	22.4	41.1
Profit Margin (After Income Tax) 50	17.6	27.5	13.8	13.3	13.3	11.1	8.5	6.8	7.1	5.4	6.6	16.9	28.4

Table I

Corporations with and without Net Income

FOOD SERVICES AND DRINKING PLACES

MONEY AMOUNTS AND SIZE OF ASSETS IN THOUSANDS OF DOLLARS

Item Description for Accounting Period 7/12 Through 6/13	Total	Zero Assets	Under 500	500 to 1,000	1,000 to 5,000	5,000 to 10,000	10,000 to 25,000	25,000 to 50,000	50,000 to 100,000	100,000 to 250,000	250,000 to 500,000	500,000 to 2,500,000	2,500,000 and over
Number of Enterprises **1**	269939	46844	197366	13772	10134	1023	481	130	64	54	21	36	13

Revenues ($ in Thousands)													
Net Sales **2**	381339528	8540075	119399062	27651218	46602974	15896311	13332317	7785680	8115811	12576530	10067759	37443057	73928733
Interest **3**	445345	978	5891	5259	7337	6367	2224	4783	859	2563	24168	111466	273450
Rents **4**	382837	893	9954	1032	14688	3589	3082	10515	3310	35865	10705	174413	114790
Royalties **5**	5018434	0	186	331	0	3961	55202	46952	78624	227631	648491	1066460	2890595
Other Portfolio Income **6**	2405501	208055	160312	36795	124848	32034	17290	12755	19226	22653	12919	476447	1282168
Other Receipts **7**	8437565	168336	617425	196445	397932	174984	280269	154447	107183	137377	147898	1263980	4791292
Total Receipts **8**	398029210	8918337	120192830	27891080	47147779	16117246	13690384	8015132	8325013	13002619	10911940	40535823	83281028
Average Total Receipts **9**	1475	190	609	2025	4652	15755	28462	61655	130078	240789	519616	1125995	6406233

Operating Costs/Operating Income (%)													
Cost of Operations **10**	42.2	42.8	42.4	39.5	43.9	36.9	42.1	44.3	37.2	38.1	42.2	40.8	44.7
Salaries and Wages **11**	19.0	17.1	17.7	19.9	16.2	22.3	19.5	18.2	16.0	23.0	25.4	22.4	18.9
Taxes Paid **12**	4.2	5.0	4.5	4.2	3.5	3.9	4.1	4.0	3.5	4.2	3.7	3.8	4.6
Interest Paid **13**	1.6	1.3	0.5	0.8	0.9	1.1	1.2	1.4	1.1	2.2	3.0	2.4	3.9
Depreciation **14**	2.6	2.2	1.6	2.3	2.3	2.5	3.0	2.9	3.0	3.7	3.4	4.4	3.3
Amortization and Depletion **15**	0.6	0.8	0.3	0.5	0.5	0.5	0.7	0.4	0.4	0.8	1.3	0.7	0.9
Pensions and Other Deferred Comp. **16**	0.2	0.0	0.0	0.1	0.1	0.0	0.2	0.2	0.1	0.2	0.3	0.4	0.5
Employee Benefits **17**	1.1	0.5	0.5	0.5	0.8	0.8	1.1	1.5	0.9	1.6	2.2	1.2	2.5
Advertising **18**	2.3	1.0	1.7	2.3	2.8	3.8	3.0	2.4	2.6	2.4	2.1	3.1	2.0
Other Expenses **19**	23.4	33.9	24.5	24.3	22.9	24.2	21.9	22.0	33.6	24.5	21.7	21.7	20.5
Officers' Compensation **20**	2.3	3.9	4.2	3.1	2.3	0.9	1.3	1.3	0.9	1.0	0.7	1.2	0.6
Operating Margin **21**	0.5	•	2.1	2.6	3.9	3.1	1.8	1.4	0.7	•	•	•	•
Operating Margin Before Officers' Comp. **22**	2.8	•	6.3	5.7	6.2	4.0	3.2	2.7	1.6	•	•	•	•

Selected Average Balance Sheet ($ in Thousands)

Net Receivables 23	45	0	4	20	90	336	1024	2140	3040	7943	16494	45486	488961
Inventories 24	23	0	8	27	45	216	463	808	1826	3840	9442	18613	178914
Net Property, Plant and Equipment 25	294	0	58	306	874	3410	6624	15545	32536	70183	123766	441710	1674791
Total Assets 26	897	0	125	697	1947	7084	15264	35057	70063	158262	365216	1000492	8635118
Notes and Loans Payable 27	404	0	93	435	1036	3972	7479	13948	28659	73135	213214	319446	3312548
All Other Liabilities 28	282	0	25	136	349	1515	3443	8525	19865	47303	114573	330329	3338044
Net Worth 29	211	0	7	126	562	1597	4342	12584	21539	37825	37428	350717	1984525

Selected Financial Ratios (Times to 1)

Current Ratio 30	1.1	•	1.5	1.1	1.5	1.2	1.3	1.1	0.9	0.7	0.9	0.9	0.9
Quick Ratio 31	0.7	•	0.9	0.7	1.0	0.7	0.9	0.8	0.6	0.4	0.6	0.6	0.6
Net Sales to Working Capital 32	126.3	•	48.5	105.0	22.5	50.1	25.8	65.3	•	•	•	•	•
Coverage Ratio 33	4.1	•	6.8	5.6	6.7	5.1	4.7	4.2	4.0	1.7	1.8	3.8	3.9
Total Asset Turnover 34	1.6	•	4.8	2.9	2.4	2.2	1.8	1.7	1.8	1.5	1.3	1.0	0.7
Inventory Turnover 35	26.0	•	33.9	29.7	45.2	26.5	25.2	32.8	25.8	23.1	21.4	22.8	14.2
Receivables Turnover 36	31.6	•	165.7	91.1	46.7	53.6	28.7	29.7	39.4	26.9	33.4	23.8	•
Total Liabilities to Net Worth 37	3.3	•	15.7	4.5	2.5	3.4	2.5	1.8	2.3	3.2	8.8	1.9	3.4
Current Assets to Working Capital 38	15.5	•	3.2	10.6	3.1	6.9	4.3	10.2	•	•	•	•	•
Current Liabilities to Working Capital 39	14.5	•	2.2	9.6	2.1	5.9	3.3	9.2	•	•	•	•	•
Working Capital to Net Sales 40	0.0	•	0.0	0.0	0.0	0.0	0.0	0.0	•	•	•	•	•
Inventory to Working Capital 41	2.1	•	0.6	1.4	0.2	0.7	0.4	1.0	•	•	•	•	•
Total Receipts to Cash Flow 42	5.3	6.3	5.9	5.3	5.2	5.2	5.5	5.3	3.4	6.0	6.0	5.4	4.7
Cost of Goods to Cash Flow 43	2.2	2.7	2.5	2.1	2.3	1.9	2.3	2.4	1.3	2.3	2.5	2.2	2.1
Cash Flow to Total Debt 44	0.4	•	0.9	0.7	0.6	0.5	0.5	0.5	0.8	0.3	0.2	0.3	0.2

Selected Financial Factors (in Percentages)

Debt Ratio 45	76.5	•	94.0	81.9	71.1	77.5	71.6	64.1	69.3	76.1	89.8	64.9	77.0
Return on Total Assets 46	10.5	•	15.5	12.3	14.2	12.2	10.4	9.7	7.8	5.6	7.0	9.3	9.8
Return on Equity Before Income Taxes 47	33.7	•	220.5	55.5	41.8	43.4	28.8	20.5	19.1	9.9	29.3	19.6	31.6
Return on Equity After Income Taxes 48	26.7	•	215.8	54.4	41.2	42.1	28.2	18.2	17.3	6.6	14.0	13.9	20.5
Profit Margin (Before Income Tax) 49	5.0	•	2.7	3.5	5.1	4.5	4.5	4.3	3.2	1.6	2.3	6.6	11.0
Profit Margin (After Income Tax) 50	4.0	•	2.7	3.4	5.0	4.3	4.4	3.8	2.9	1.1	1.1	4.7	7.1

Table II

Corporations with Net Income

FOOD SERVICES AND DRINKING PLACES

MONEY AMOUNTS AND SIZE OF ASSETS IN THOUSANDS OF DOLLARS

Item Description for Accounting Period 7/12 Through 6/13	Total	Zero Assets	Under 500	500 to 1,000	1,000 to 5,000	5,000 to 10,000	10,000 to 25,000	25,000 to 50,000	50,000 to 100,000	100,000 to 250,000	250,000 to 500,000	500,000 to 2,500,000	2,500,000 and over
Number of Enterprises **1**	159625	19153	120704	10457	7768	913	395	98	48	36	15	28	10

Revenues ($ in Thousands)													
Net Sales **2**	310595020	3515820	88203868	22763605	39645458	15061692	11288181	6102352	6507294	8404578	7914152	32198767	68989254
Interest **3**	320515	697	2250	1841	5567	3811	1938	3437	793	1560	22678	36045	239897
Rents **4**	319825	887	4513	1032	14296	1867	1835	9965	3215	31140	5548	153592	91933
Royalties **5**	3874992	0	186	331	0	14	47903	38470	74640	188208	526269	847881	2151090
Other Portfolio Income **6**	2234735	194323	154881	34831	106924	25687	15260	5574	19223	21988	12919	453834	1189293
Other Receipts **7**	7729887	78017	419489	183475	329374	174162	263753	112315	100537	116046	89154	1034422	4829142
Total Receipts **8**	325074974	3789744	88785187	22985115	40101619	15267233	11618870	6272113	6705702	8763520	8570720	34724541	77490609
Average Total Receipts **9**	2036	198	736	2198	5162	16722	29415	64001	139702	243431	571381	1240162	7749061

Operating Costs/Operating Income (%)													
Cost of Operations **10**	42.1	41.1	42.0	39.6	43.5	36.4	42.8	45.0	36.7	39.4	43.9	42.5	43.5
Salaries and Wages **11**	18.5	14.2	16.8	19.2	15.8	22.5	18.3	16.8	14.6	22.0	24.4	20.8	19.6
Taxes Paid **12**	4.1	5.4	4.2	4.0	3.6	3.9	4.1	3.8	3.2	4.0	3.6	3.7	4.7
Interest Paid **13**	1.4	0.7	0.4	0.8	0.8	1.1	1.1	1.0	1.0	1.6	2.4	1.9	3.2
Depreciation **14**	2.4	1.4	1.2	1.8	1.7	2.5	2.7	2.7	2.6	3.6	3.5	4.7	3.1
Amortization and Depletion **15**	0.5	0.3	0.2	0.5	0.4	0.5	0.7	0.4	0.3	0.8	1.1	0.4	0.8
Pensions and Other Deferred Comp. **16**	0.2	0.0	0.1	0.1	0.1	0.0	0.1	0.2	0.1	0.3	0.3	0.4	0.5
Employee Benefits **17**	1.2	0.2	0.5	0.5	0.8	0.8	1.1	0.9	0.7	1.7	2.3	1.2	2.7
Advertising **18**	2.3	1.0	1.7	2.4	2.7	3.7	3.1	2.7	2.8	2.5	1.8	2.9	2.0
Other Expenses **19**	22.1	28.8	22.7	23.0	21.9	24.1	20.9	21.0	35.3	22.8	19.0	20.1	20.7
Officers' Compensation **20**	2.3	4.1	4.4	3.0	2.5	0.9	1.3	1.4	0.9	1.0	0.7	1.1	0.6
Operating Margin **21**	2.9	2.9	5.8	5.1	6.2	3.6	3.8	4.0	1.8	0.1	•	0.2	•
Operating Margin Before Officers' Comp. **22**	5.2	7.0	10.2	8.1	8.7	4.5	5.1	5.4	2.7	1.1	•	1.3	•

Selected Average Balance Sheet ($ in Thousands)

Net Receivables 23	61	0	5	18	106	356	727	1933	2902	7710	20678	45372	531827
Inventories 24	34	0	8	25	43	227	381	713	1800	3775	10946	20601	225324
Net Property, Plant and Equipment 25	393	0	57	301	852	3531	6823	15995	32803	74723	134890	510013	1812290
Total Assets 26	1226	0	136	707	1958	7027	14952	34727	68850	162309	358264	1037418	9741237
Notes and Loans Payable 27	492	0	63	402	941	3746	7803	14602	27184	58892	203337	316319	3616697
All Other Liabilities 28	385	0	22	133	294	1235	2867	6204	19053	45984	124855	341796	3823711
Net Worth 29	349	0	50	172	723	2047	4282	13921	22613	57433	30071	379303	2300829

Selected Financial Ratios (Times to 1)

Current Ratio 30	1.1	•	1.8	1.2	1.7	1.2	1.2	1.0	1.0	0.8	0.9	0.9	0.8
Quick Ratio 31	0.7	•	1.3	0.8	1.2	0.9	0.9	0.7	0.7	0.5	0.6	0.6	0.5
Net Sales to Working Capital 32	102.4	•	33.0	57.1	17.4	46.2	37.8	292.1	325.9	•	•	•	•
Coverage Ratio 33	6.5	16.3	17.8	8.6	10.6	5.7	7.0	7.9	5.8	3.7	3.2	5.4	4.7
Total Asset Turnover 34	1.6	•	5.4	3.1	2.6	2.3	1.9	1.8	2.0	1.4	1.5	1.1	0.7
Inventory Turnover 35	24.3	•	39.2	34.0	52.2	26.4	32.1	39.3	27.6	24.4	21.2	23.7	13.3
Receivables Turnover 36	•	•	179.2	102.1	44.4	55.4	36.2	32.4	51.1	27.8	•	28.2	•
Total Liabilities to Net Worth 37	2.5	•	1.7	3.1	1.7	2.4	2.5	1.5	2.0	1.8	10.9	1.7	3.2
Current Assets to Working Capital 38	12.3	•	2.2	5.8	2.4	5.5	5.1	41.6	36.7	•	•	•	•
Current Liabilities to Working Capital 39	11.3	•	1.2	4.8	1.4	4.5	4.1	40.6	35.7	•	•	•	•
Working Capital to Net Sales 40	0.0	•	0.0	0.0	0.1	0.0	0.0	0.0	0.0	•	•	•	•
Inventory to Working Capital 41	1.8	•	0.4	0.7	0.2	0.7	0.5	4.1	4.7	•	•	•	•
Total Receipts to Cash Flow 42	4.8	3.7	5.1	4.8	4.8	5.1	5.0	4.9	3.0	5.1	5.6	5.4	4.5
Cost of Goods to Cash Flow 43	2.0	1.5	2.1	1.9	2.1	1.9	2.1	2.2	1.1	2.0	2.5	2.3	1.9
Cash Flow to Total Debt 44	0.5	•	1.7	0.8	0.9	0.6	0.5	0.6	1.0	0.4	0.3	0.3	0.2

Selected Financial Factors (in Percentages)

Debt Ratio 45	71.6	•	62.8	75.7	63.1	70.9	71.4	59.9	67.2	64.6	91.6	63.4	76.4
Return on Total Assets 46	14.7	•	37.1	21.1	21.2	14.3	15.0	13.9	11.5	8.6	11.3	11.5	10.7
Return on Equity Before Income Taxes 47	43.8	•	94.1	76.6	52.0	40.3	45.1	30.4	29.0	17.8	92.7	25.5	35.8
Return on Equity After Income Taxes 48	36.6	•	93.0	75.5	51.4	39.1	44.3	27.6	26.6	14.5	66.0	18.7	23.4
Profit Margin (Before Income Tax) 49	7.9	10.7	6.5	6.0	7.4	5.0	6.8	6.8	4.8	4.4	5.3	8.4	11.9
Profit Margin (After Income Tax) 50	6.6	10.3	6.4	6.0	7.3	4.9	6.6	6.2	4.4	3.6	3.8	6.2	7.8

Table I

Corporations with and without Net Income

AUTOMOTIVE REPAIR AND MAINTENANCE

MONEY AMOUNTS AND SIZE OF ASSETS IN THOUSANDS OF DOLLARS

Item Description for Accounting Period 7/12 Through 6/13		Total	Zero Assets	Under 500	500 to 1,000	1,000 to 5,000	5,000 to 10,000	10,000 to 25,000	25,000 to 50,000	50,000 to 100,000	100,000 to 250,000	250,000 to 500,000	500,000 to 2,500,000	2,500,000 and over
Number of Enterprises	1	114735	19287	86008	6344	2871	130	63	•	0	11	•	•	0

Revenues ($ in Thousands)

Net Sales	2	74577213	3113205	43396039	9347194	9814857	1394890	2059569	•	0	1934775	•	•	0
Interest	3	16710	194	2476	2541	917	7705	949	•	0	318	•	•	0
Rents	4	22577	5336	3451	1559	3851	87	117	•	0	173	•	•	0
Royalties	5	32320	27605	0	0	92	0	1285	•	0	3338	•	•	0
Other Portfolio Income	6	177751	41467	40616	7604	47755	2790	11797	•	0	13545	•	•	0
Other Receipts	7	372795	11520	191027	14555	50774	19278	56241	•	0	5589	•	•	0
Total Receipts	8	75199366	3199327	43633609	9373453	9918246	1424750	2129958	•	0	1957738	•	•	0
Average Total Receipts	9	655	166	507	1478	3455	10960	33809	•	•	177976	•	•	•

Operating Costs/Operating Income (%)

Cost of Operations	10	50.2	43.4	46.9	54.5	58.7	56.0	64.8	•	•	56.7	•	•	•
Salaries and Wages	11	13.8	16.4	14.5	10.2	12.0	8.9	12.1	•	•	15.4	•	•	•
Taxes Paid	12	3.6	4.7	3.6	3.6	3.4	2.6	2.3	•	•	2.4	•	•	•
Interest Paid	13	1.0	1.8	0.7	2.1	1.3	0.8	0.4	•	•	2.5	•	•	•
Depreciation	14	1.6	1.4	1.1	2.5	2.1	1.5	2.1	•	•	2.3	•	•	•
Amortization and Depletion	15	0.3	0.7	0.2	0.3	0.5	0.0	0.3	•	•	1.5	•	•	•
Pensions and Other Deferred Comp.	16	0.2	0.1	0.1	0.0	0.1	0.2	0.1	•	•	0.2	•	•	•
Employee Benefits	17	1.3	0.5	1.3	1.4	1.0	0.9	1.2	•	•	2.0	•	•	•
Advertising	18	1.2	1.1	1.3	1.1	1.1	0.8	1.0	•	•	0.5	•	•	•
Other Expenses	19	18.7	31.1	20.4	15.0	13.6	16.2	13.5	•	•	15.1	•	•	•
Officers' Compensation	20	5.7	4.8	7.0	5.1	3.9	3.4	1.5	•	•	0.8	•	•	•
Operating Margin	21	2.5	•	2.7	4.2	2.4	8.7	0.6	•	•	0.4	•	•	•
Operating Margin Before Officers' Comp.	22	8.2	•	9.8	9.2	6.3	12.1	2.1	•	•	1.3	•	•	•

Selected Average Balance Sheet ($ in Thousands)

	C1	C2	C3	C4	C5	C6	C7	C8	C9	C10	C11	C12	C13
Net Receivables 23	16	0	8	38	134	1077	2353	•	•	12983	•	•	•
Inventories 24	21	0	13	54	176	784	1476	•	•	3321	•	•	•
Net Property, Plant and Equipment 25	80	0	34	341	823	1028	4927	•	•	29343	•	•	•
Total Assets 26	205	0	96	678	1711	6562	14686	•	•	145774	•	•	•
Notes and Loans Payable 27	128	0	75	526	911	1610	3797	•	•	62116	•	•	•
All Other Liabilities 28	44	0	25	99	336	940	3060	•	•	38301	•	•	•
Net Worth 29	34	0	-4	53	465	4012	7828	•	•	45357	•	•	•

Selected Financial Ratios (Times to 1)

	C1	C2	C3	C4	C5	C6	C7	C8	C9	C10	C11	C12	C13
Current Ratio 30	1.6	•	1.6	1.9	1.8	2.8	1.1	•	•	0.9	•	•	•
Quick Ratio 31	1.0	•	1.0	1.1	1.2	2.2	0.6	•	•	0.7	•	•	•
Net Sales to Working Capital 32	24.1	•	30.5	14.6	12.8	4.7	62.7	•	•	•	•	•	•
Coverage Ratio 33	4.2	•	5.9	3.2	3.7	14.5	10.2	•	•	1.7	•	•	•
Total Asset Turnover 34	3.2	•	5.3	2.2	2.0	1.6	2.2	•	•	1.2	•	•	•
Inventory Turnover 35	15.2	•	18.5	14.9	11.4	7.7	14.4	•	•	30.0	•	•	•
Receivables Turnover 36	40.6	•	62.9	33.3	27.3	10.7	18.9	•	•	•	•	•	•
Total Liabilities to Net Worth 37	5.1	•	•	11.8	2.7	0.6	0.9	•	•	2.2	•	•	•
Current Assets to Working Capital 38	2.8	•	2.8	2.1	2.2	1.6	12.0	•	•	•	•	•	•
Current Liabilities to Working Capital 39	1.8	•	1.8	1.1	1.2	0.6	11.0	•	•	•	•	•	•
Working Capital to Net Sales 40	0.0	•	0.0	0.1	0.1	0.2	0.0	•	•	•	•	•	•
Inventory to Working Capital 41	0.8	•	0.9	0.5	0.6	0.3	3.7	•	•	•	•	•	•
Total Receipts to Cash Flow 42	6.5	5.9	6.1	6.8	7.9	4.3	8.3	•	•	8.9	•	•	•
Cost of Goods to Cash Flow 43	3.3	2.6	2.9	3.7	4.6	2.4	5.4	•	•	5.0	•	•	•
Cash Flow to Total Debt 44	0.6	•	0.8	0.3	0.3	1.0	0.6	•	•	0.2	•	•	•

Selected Financial Factors (in Percentages)

	C1	C2	C3	C4	C5	C6	C7	C8	C9	C10	C11	C12	C13
Debt Ratio 45	83.7	•	104.3	92.2	72.8	38.9	46.7	•	•	68.9	•	•	•
Return on Total Assets 46	13.7	•	20.8	14.1	9.5	19.1	9.8	•	•	5.3	•	•	•
Return on Equity Before Income Taxes 47	63.9	•	•	123.3	25.5	29.1	16.6	•	•	7.1	•	•	•
Return on Equity After Income Taxes 48	62.0	•	•	120.1	25.0	28.7	16.0	•	•	5.0	•	•	•
Profit Margin (Before Income Tax) 49	3.3	•	3.3	4.4	3.5	10.9	4.0	•	•	1.8	•	•	•
Profit Margin (After Income Tax) 50	3.2	•	3.3	4.3	3.4	10.7	3.8	•	•	1.3	•	•	•

Table II

Corporations with Net Income

AUTOMOTIVE REPAIR AND MAINTENANCE

MONEY AMOUNTS AND SIZE OF ASSETS IN THOUSANDS OF DOLLARS

Item Description for Accounting Period 7/12 Through 6/13	Total	Zero Assets	Under 500	500 to 1,000	1,000 to 5,000	5,000 to 10,000	10,000 to 25,000	25,000 to 50,000	50,000 to 100,000	100,000 to 250,000	250,000 to 500,000	500,000 to 2,500,000	2,500,000 and over
Number of Enterprises 1	68636	9447	52558	4503	1932	123	52	•	0	•	•	•	0

Revenues ($ in Thousands)													
Net Sales 2	56818374	1403741	31967236	7404157	9018527	1325071	2018392	•	0	•	•	•	0
Interest 3	12367	0	172	2515	832	7702	902	•	0	•	•	•	0
Rents 4	6597	43	3	1559	3851	87	4	•	0	•	•	•	0
Royalties 5	4118	0	0	0	92	0	1285	•	0	•	•	•	0
Other Portfolio Income 6	154251	41333	36507	7509	44543	2652	11797	•	0	•	•	•	0
Other Receipts 7	300364	7010	149207	10286	48077	18990	53591	•	0	•	•	•	0
Total Receipts 8	57296071	1452127	32153125	7426026	9115922	1354502	2085971	•	0	•	•	•	0
Average Total Receipts 9	835	154	612	1649	4718	11012	40115	•	•	•	•	•	•

Operating Costs/Operating Income (%)													
Cost of Operations 10	50.9	33.0	47.1	55.6	61.3	55.8	65.2	•	•	•	•	•	•
Salaries and Wages 11	13.2	16.6	13.9	9.0	11.2	9.0	12.1	•	•	•	•	•	•
Taxes Paid 12	3.4	3.4	3.4	3.6	3.2	2.6	2.3	•	•	•	•	•	•
Interest Paid 13	0.8	1.3	0.5	1.5	0.9	0.8	0.3	•	•	•	•	•	•
Depreciation 14	1.1	0.9	0.8	1.3	1.5	0.9	1.9	•	•	•	•	•	•
Amortization and Depletion 15	0.2	0.4	0.1	0.3	0.3	0.0	0.3	•	•	•	•	•	•
Pensions and Other Deferred Comp. 16	0.1	0.1	0.1	0.0	0.2	0.2	0.1	•	•	•	•	•	•
Employee Benefits 17	1.3	0.6	1.4	1.6	0.9	0.8	1.2	•	•	•	•	•	•
Advertising 18	1.1	0.9	1.1	1.1	1.0	0.8	1.0	•	•	•	•	•	•
Other Expenses 19	16.7	31.0	18.6	14.1	12.0	16.5	13.0	•	•	•	•	•	•
Officers' Compensation 20	5.6	5.0	6.8	5.3	3.9	3.3	1.5	•	•	•	•	•	•
Operating Margin 21	5.6	6.7	6.2	6.4	3.6	9.3	1.0	•	•	•	•	•	•
Operating Margin Before Officers' Comp. 22	11.2	11.7	13.0	11.7	7.6	12.6	2.5	•	•	•	•	•	•

Selected Average Balance Sheet ($ in Thousands)

Net Receivables 23	22	0	10	46	190	1089	2825	•	•	•	•	•	•
Inventories 24	24	0	13	52	214	570	1696	•	•	•	•	•	•
Net Property, Plant and Equipment 25	74	0	26	301	697	902	4171	•	•	•	•	•	•
Total Assets 26	222	0	94	677	1716	6518	14632	•	•	•	•	•	•
Notes and Loans Payable 27	106	0	53	383	799	1414	3791	•	•	•	•	•	•
All Other Liabilities 28	52	0	27	110	346	945	5896	•	•	•	•	•	•
Net Worth 29	65	0	15	184	571	4160	4944	•	•	•	•	•	•

Selected Financial Ratios (Times to 1)

Current Ratio 30	1.7	•	1.8	1.9	1.8	3.5	1.0	•	•	•	•	•	•
Quick Ratio 31	1.1	•	1.2	1.1	1.2	2.9	0.6	•	•	•	•	•	•
Net Sales to Working Capital 32	20.7	•	26.3	13.4	14.0	4.3	133.4	•	•	•	•	•	•
Coverage Ratio 33	9.2	8.7	13.6	5.4	6.3	15.7	14.2	•	•	•	•	•	•
Total Asset Turnover 34	3.7	•	6.4	2.4	2.7	1.7	2.7	•	•	•	•	•	•
Inventory Turnover 35	17.5	•	22.2	17.4	13.4	10.5	14.9	•	•	•	•	•	•
Receivables Turnover 36	39.6	•	64.7	31.8	26.1	12.2	19.3	•	•	•	•	•	•
Total Liabilities to Net Worth 37	2.4	•	5.5	2.7	2.0	0.6	2.0	•	•	•	•	•	•
Current Assets to Working Capital 38	2.4	•	2.3	2.1	2.2	1.4	24.4	•	•	•	•	•	•
Current Liabilities to Working Capital 39	1.4	•	1.3	1.1	1.2	0.4	23.4	•	•	•	•	•	•
Working Capital to Net Sales 40	0.0	•	0.0	0.1	0.1	0.2	0.0	•	•	•	•	•	•
Inventory to Working Capital 41	0.6	•	0.7	0.4	0.6	0.2	8.0	•	•	•	•	•	•
Total Receipts to Cash Flow 42	5.8	3.2	5.4	6.1	7.8	4.1	8.4	•	•	•	•	•	•
Cost of Goods to Cash Flow 43	3.0	1.1	2.5	3.4	4.8	2.3	5.5	•	•	•	•	•	•
Cash Flow to Total Debt 44	0.9	•	1.4	0.6	0.5	1.1	0.5	•	•	•	•	•	•

Selected Financial Factors (in Percentages)

Debt Ratio 45	70.9	•	84.6	72.8	66.7	36.2	66.2	•	•	•	•	•	•
Return on Total Assets 46	26.9	•	47.3	20.0	15.2	20.3	12.3	•	•	•	•	•	•
Return on Equity Before Income Taxes 47	82.6	•	284.9	59.9	38.4	29.8	33.8	•	•	•	•	•	•
Return on Equity After Income Taxes 48	80.9	•	283.5	58.6	37.9	29.4	32.6	•	•	•	•	•	•
Profit Margin (Before Income Tax) 49	6.4	10.2	6.8	6.7	4.7	11.5	4.3	•	•	•	•	•	•
Profit Margin (After Income Tax) 50	6.3	10.1	6.8	6.6	4.6	11.4	4.2	•	•	•	•	•	•

Table I

Corporations with and without Net Income

OTHER REPAIR AND MAINTENANCE

MONEY AMOUNTS AND SIZE OF ASSETS IN THOUSANDS OF DOLLARS

Item Description for Accounting Period 7/12 Through 6/13		Total	Zero Assets	Under 500	500 to 1,000	1,000 to 5,000	5,000 to 10,000	10,000 to 25,000	25,000 to 50,000	50,000 to 100,000	100,000 to 250,000	250,000 to 500,000	500,000 to 2,500,000	2,500,000 and over
Number of Enterprises	1	58676	13092	40083	3213	1844	239	128	•	•	3	4	0	0
Revenues ($ in Thousands)														
Net Sales	2	44355799	1752261	12900759	7288588	8010589	3104839	3190243	•	•	554755	1873467	0	0
Interest	3	107744	2473	261	4185	6252	958	1328	•	•	8	90993	0	0
Rents	4	24497	0	1292	0	4006	5574	6009	•	•	140	7254	0	0
Royalties	5	164358	0	0	0	101	0	96	•	•	0	163845	0	0
Other Portfolio Income	6	177482	27084	7019	3139	32351	46363	32289	•	•	4337	2499	0	0
Other Receipts	7	581560	11485	182187	41010	11855	46610	75250	•	•	1046	163208	0	0
Total Receipts	8	45411440	1793303	13091518	7336922	8065154	3204344	3305215	•	•	560286	2301266	0	0
Average Total Receipts	9	774	137	327	2284	4374	13407	25822	•	•	186762	575316	•	•
Operating Costs/Operating Income (%)														
Cost of Operations	10	53.8	38.6	42.7	57.8	51.4	64.6	60.1	•	•	40.9	69.1	•	•
Salaries and Wages	11	12.2	8.9	14.8	12.0	13.2	11.3	9.8	•	•	28.1	8.2	•	•
Taxes Paid	12	2.6	2.1	3.0	2.6	2.8	2.5	2.4	•	•	4.3	2.7	•	•
Interest Paid	13	1.4	1.4	0.5	0.5	0.8	0.6	0.5	•	•	1.2	16.6	•	•
Depreciation	14	1.7	2.3	1.7	1.5	1.5	1.0	2.5	•	•	3.6	1.6	•	•
Amortization and Depletion	15	0.3	0.6	0.0	0.2	0.3	0.0	0.1	•	•	0.4	2.2	•	•
Pensions and Other Deferred Comp.	16	0.3	0.1	0.3	0.1	0.3	0.4	0.4	•	•	0.6	0.1	•	•
Employee Benefits	17	1.8	0.9	0.9	2.0	1.9	1.9	2.6	•	•	3.6	0.9	•	•
Advertising	18	0.6	0.7	0.8	0.5	0.7	0.2	0.3	•	•	0.1	1.5	•	•
Other Expenses	19	17.2	32.1	21.7	16.0	15.9	9.4	16.2	•	•	9.6	18.6	•	•
Officers' Compensation	20	5.2	7.1	9.1	4.2	5.0	3.2	2.7	•	•	0.3	1.6	•	•
Operating Margin	21	2.9	5.3	4.6	2.7	6.2	4.9	2.5	•	•	7.3	•	•	•
Operating Margin Before Officers' Comp.	22	8.1	12.3	13.7	6.9	11.3	8.1	5.2	•	•	7.6	•	•	•

Selected Average Balance Sheet ($ in Thousands)

Net Receivables 23	73	0	9	200	544	1724	2895	•	•	27758	152319	•	•
Inventories 24	47	0	12	97	286	1115	3184	•	•	9990	8644	•	•
Net Property, Plant and Equipment 25	50	0	17	106	272	874	3237	•	•	43453	51998	•	•
Total Assets 26	384	0	62	679	1833	7283	14276	•	•	161552	1793349	•	•
Notes and Loans Payable 27	170	0	29	364	664	2235	4116	•	•	51803	1037284	•	•
All Other Liabilities 28	107	0	20	184	470	1726	3251	•	•	52513	476921	•	•
Net Worth 29	107	0	14	131	700	3322	6908	•	•	57236	279144	•	•

Selected Financial Ratios (Times to 1)

Current Ratio 30	2.0	•	1.7	2.2	2.6	2.1	2.2	•	•	1.7	1.6	•	•
Quick Ratio 31	1.3	•	1.2	1.3	1.8	1.5	1.3	•	•	1.0	1.2	•	•
Net Sales to Working Capital 32	7.7	•	19.6	8.1	5.5	4.4	5.2	•	•	6.9	3.5	•	•
Coverage Ratio 33	4.7	6.6	12.6	7.3	10.0	14.6	12.7	•	•	8.3	1.0	•	•
Total Asset Turnover 34	2.0	•	5.2	3.3	2.4	1.8	1.7	•	•	1.1	0.3	•	•
Inventory Turnover 35	8.6	•	11.7	13.5	7.8	7.5	4.7	•	•	7.6	37.4	•	•
Receivables Turnover 36	9.6	•	26.5	12.5	8.6	8.1	8.1	•	•	•	•	•	•
Total Liabilities to Net Worth 37	2.6	•	3.5	4.2	1.6	1.2	1.1	•	•	1.8	5.4	•	•
Current Assets to Working Capital 38	2.0	•	2.3	1.8	1.6	1.9	1.8	•	•	2.4	2.6	•	•
Current Liabilities to Working Capital 39	1.0	•	1.3	0.8	0.6	0.9	0.8	•	•	1.4	1.6	•	•
Working Capital to Net Sales 40	0.1	•	0.1	0.1	0.2	0.2	0.2	•	•	0.1	0.3	•	•
Inventory to Working Capital 41	0.5	•	0.6	0.5	0.4	0.5	0.6	•	•	0.4	0.1	•	•
Total Receipts to Cash Flow 42	5.5	2.9	4.3	7.8	5.1	7.0	5.4	•	•	6.2	6.0	•	•
Cost of Goods to Cash Flow 43	2.9	1.1	1.9	4.5	2.6	4.5	3.2	•	•	2.6	4.2	•	•
Cash Flow to Total Debt 44	0.5	•	1.5	0.5	0.8	0.5	0.6	•	•	0.3	0.1	•	•

Selected Financial Factors (in Percentages)

Debt Ratio 45	72.0	•	77.9	80.7	61.8	54.4	51.6	•	•	64.6	84.4	•	•
Return on Total Assets 46	13.2	•	34.4	13.0	18.2	15.5	11.7	•	•	11.0	4.3	•	•
Return on Equity Before Income Taxes 47	37.2	•	143.6	58.3	42.8	31.7	22.2	•	•	27.2	•	•	•
Return on Equity After Income Taxes 48	35.3	•	142.4	56.0	42.0	30.0	20.9	•	•	20.5	•	•	•
Profit Margin (Before Income Tax) 49	5.3	7.6	6.1	3.4	6.9	8.1	6.2	•	•	8.4	•	•	•
Profit Margin (After Income Tax) 50	5.0	7.1	6.1	3.2	6.8	7.7	5.8	•	•	6.3	•	•	•

Table II
Corporations with Net Income

OTHER REPAIR AND MAINTENANCE

MONEY AMOUNTS AND SIZE OF ASSETS IN THOUSANDS OF DOLLARS

Item Description for Accounting Period 7/12 Through 6/13	Total	Zero Assets	Under 500	500 to 1,000	1,000 to 5,000	5,000 to 10,000	10,000 to 25,000	25,000 to 50,000	50,000 to 100,000	100,000 to 250,000	250,000 to 500,000	500,000 to 2,500,000	2,500,000 and over
Number of Enterprises **1**	39364	8236	27013	2371	1391	200	94	•	13	•	0	0	0

Revenues ($ in Thousands)													
Net Sales **2**	35742790	1228749	10658100	6234766	6750641	2602847	2472205	•	1427813	•	0	0	0
Interest **3**	12675	134	77	4004	5900	864	1050	•	337	•	0	0	0
Rents **4**	24297	0	1292	0	4006	5452	5963	•	0	•	0	0	0
Royalties **5**	197	0	0	0	101	0	96	•	0	•	0	0	0
Other Portfolio Income **6**	167175	27049	6121	3100	30871	46276	30831	•	812	•	0	0	0
Other Receipts **7**	229554	3632	53961	38346	10488	26061	72001	•	2690	•	0	0	0
Total Receipts **8**	36176688	1259564	10719551	6280216	6802007	2681500	2582146	•	1431652	•	0	0	0
Average Total Receipts **9**	919	153	397	2649	4890	13408	27470	•	110127	•	•	•	•

Operating Costs/Operating Income (%)													
Cost of Operations **10**	52.6	32.6	41.0	59.1	49.9	63.7	60.4	•	69.2	•	•	•	•
Salaries and Wages **11**	11.6	5.4	14.3	9.7	14.1	11.7	7.9	•	5.8	•	•	•	•
Taxes Paid **12**	2.5	1.9	2.7	2.3	2.5	2.5	2.5	•	2.1	•	•	•	•
Interest Paid **13**	0.6	1.0	0.5	0.3	0.6	0.6	0.4	•	1.0	•	•	•	•
Depreciation **14**	1.6	1.7	1.5	1.4	1.5	0.7	2.4	•	2.0	•	•	•	•
Amortization and Depletion **15**	0.2	0.2	0.0	0.2	0.3	0.0	0.1	•	0.5	•	•	•	•
Pensions and Other Deferred Comp. **16**	0.3	0.0	0.4	0.1	0.2	0.2	0.4	•	0.2	•	•	•	•
Employee Benefits **17**	1.7	0.4	1.0	2.1	1.6	1.6	2.4	•	6.7	•	•	•	•
Advertising **18**	0.5	0.3	0.7	0.5	0.9	0.2	0.3	•	0.2	•	•	•	•
Other Expenses **19**	16.2	33.3	20.8	15.6	15.3	8.8	15.1	•	7.0	•	•	•	•
Officers' Compensation **20**	5.1	8.1	8.8	3.9	4.8	3.2	2.6	•	1.3	•	•	•	•
Operating Margin **21**	7.0	15.1	8.2	4.7	8.2	6.7	5.7	•	4.0	•	•	•	•
Operating Margin Before Officers' Comp. **22**	12.1	23.2	17.1	8.6	13.0	9.9	8.3	•	5.3	•	•	•	•

Selected Average Balance Sheet ($ in Thousands)

Net Receivables 23	73	0	8	212	530	1599	2784	•	21092	•	•	•	•
Inventories 24	52	0	12	59	302	1144	3393	•	11476	•	•	•	•
Net Property, Plant and Equipment 25	58	0	18	114	322	708	3400	•	9544	•	•	•	•
Total Assets 26	311	0	66	703	1855	7279	14128	•	68386	•	•	•	•
Notes and Loans Payable 27	106	0	26	275	621	2214	4142	•	28947	•	•	•	•
All Other Liabilities 28	78	0	23	162	406	1486	2654	•	18169	•	•	•	•
Net Worth 29	127	0	17	267	828	3579	7332	•	21270	•	•	•	•

Selected Financial Ratios (Times to 1)

Current Ratio 30	2.3	•	1.8	2.8	2.7	2.4	2.3	•	1.6	•	•	•	•
Quick Ratio 31	1.5	•	1.3	1.8	1.9	1.6	1.4	•	1.0	•	•	•	•
Net Sales to Working Capital 32	8.0	•	21.4	8.1	5.9	4.0	5.7	•	6.6	•	•	•	•
Coverage Ratio 33	15.1	18.5	19.6	17.3	15.1	16.2	28.6	•	5.2	•	•	•	•
Total Asset Turnover 34	2.9	•	6.0	3.7	2.6	1.8	1.9	•	1.6	•	•	•	•
Inventory Turnover 35	9.1	•	13.0	26.2	8.0	7.3	4.7	•	6.6	•	•	•	•
Receivables Turnover 36	10.6	•	38.4	14.0	10.1	7.8	9.0	•	6.5	•	•	•	•
Total Liabilities to Net Worth 37	1.4	•	2.9	1.6	1.2	1.0	0.9	•	2.2	•	•	•	•
Current Assets to Working Capital 38	1.8	•	2.2	1.6	1.6	1.7	1.8	•	2.6	•	•	•	•
Current Liabilities to Working Capital 39	0.8	•	1.2	0.6	0.6	0.7	0.8	•	1.6	•	•	•	•
Working Capital to Net Sales 40	0.1	•	0.0	0.1	0.2	0.3	0.2	•	0.2	•	•	•	•
Inventory to Working Capital 41	0.5	•	0.6	0.3	0.4	0.4	0.6	•	0.8	•	•	•	•
Total Receipts to Cash Flow 42	4.9	2.2	4.0	7.0	4.7	6.5	4.4	•	10.7	•	•	•	•
Cost of Goods to Cash Flow 43	2.6	0.7	1.6	4.1	2.4	4.1	2.7	•	7.4	•	•	•	•
Cash Flow to Total Debt 44	1.0	•	2.0	0.9	1.0	0.5	0.9	•	0.2	•	•	•	•

Selected Financial Factors (in Percentages)

Debt Ratio 45	59.1	•	74.5	62.1	55.4	50.8	48.1	•	68.9	•	•	•	•
Return on Total Assets 46	25.7	•	55.5	21.7	25.2	18.5	19.6	•	8.5	•	•	•	•
Return on Equity Before Income Taxes 47	58.6	•	206.9	53.8	52.8	35.4	36.4	•	22.2	•	•	•	•
Return on Equity After Income Taxes 48	56.2	•	205.4	52.3	51.8	33.5	34.7	•	19.3	•	•	•	•
Profit Margin (Before Income Tax) 49	8.2	17.6	8.8	5.5	9.0	9.7	10.1	•	4.3	•	•	•	•
Profit Margin (After Income Tax) 50	7.9	16.9	8.8	5.3	8.8	9.2	9.7	•	3.7	•	•	•	•

Table I

Corporations with and without Net Income

PERSONAL AND LAUNDRY SERVICES

MONEY AMOUNTS AND SIZE OF ASSETS IN THOUSANDS OF DOLLARS

Item Description for Accounting Period 7/12 Through 6/13	Total	Zero Assets	Under 500	500 to 1,000	1,000 to 5,000	5,000 to 10,000	10,000 to 25,000	25,000 to 50,000	50,000 to 100,000	100,000 to 250,000	250,000 to 500,000	500,000 to 2,500,000	2,500,000 and over
Number of Enterprises 1	169056	41288	116550	6077	4582	341	132	37	•	11	•	•	0

Revenues ($ in Thousands)

Net Sales 2	79288002	2929586	32012568	7991537	8884800	5543301	2081798	1300495	•	1072292	•	•	0
Interest 3	103147	1252	2327	1693	14737	3312	1584	5109	•	3543	•	•	0
Rents 4	64885	1	2324	7099	1470	4854	3603	2209	•	2660	•	•	0
Royalties 5	230444	0	53009	0	0	3669	49	1465	•	0	•	•	0
Other Portfolio Income 6	364657	59785	17542	29543	67309	6350	28602	5264	•	1146	•	•	0
Other Receipts 7	2439989	3751	621343	1118739	146508	70111	64061	64151	•	7174	•	•	0
Total Receipts 8	82491124	2994375	32709113	9148611	9114824	5631597	2179697	1378693	•	1086815	•	•	0
Average Total Receipts 9	488	73	281	1505	1989	16515	16513	37262	•	98801	•	•	•

Operating Costs/Operating Income (%)

Cost of Operations 10	29.0	13.1	25.7	24.5	33.4	53.7	25.8	23.1	•	29.8	•	•	•
Salaries and Wages 11	20.6	15.8	19.6	27.4	21.5	15.4	21.3	18.8	•	22.3	•	•	•
Taxes Paid 12	4.1	3.6	3.9	4.7	4.5	3.8	3.5	2.2	•	4.2	•	•	•
Interest Paid 13	1.6	0.5	0.7	1.3	1.8	0.6	1.4	1.9	•	1.4	•	•	•
Depreciation 14	2.9	2.3	2.0	2.8	3.1	2.3	3.6	4.5	•	3.7	•	•	•
Amortization and Depletion 15	1.3	0.5	0.4	0.7	0.8	0.3	0.5	0.7	•	1.1	•	•	•
Pensions and Other Deferred Comp. 16	0.4	0.3	0.1	0.4	0.5	0.3	0.5	0.6	•	0.7	•	•	•
Employee Benefits 17	1.2	0.2	0.7	1.0	1.3	0.7	2.8	4.0	•	4.4	•	•	•
Advertising 18	1.4	1.9	1.3	1.3	1.4	1.3	2.1	0.5	•	1.9	•	•	•
Other Expenses 19	31.0	52.9	34.4	38.0	24.5	18.2	33.6	38.8	•	24.9	•	•	•
Officers' Compensation 20	5.7	10.5	8.4	7.4	5.8	1.3	2.7	1.7	•	1.3	•	•	•
Operating Margin 21	0.9	•	2.8	•	1.4	2.1	2.3	3.2	•	4.2	•	•	•
Operating Margin Before Officers' Comp. 22	6.6	8.8	11.2	•	7.2	3.5	5.0	4.9	•	5.5	•	•	•

Selected Average Balance Sheet ($ in Thousands)

Net Receivables 23	24	0	3	44	201	1122	1485	4051	•	11881	•	•	•
Inventories 24	14	0	2	32	57	459	341	1665	•	2910	•	•	•
Net Property, Plant and Equipment 25	107	0	28	328	741	2119	4368	9603	•	30984	•	•	•
Total Assets 26	340	0	71	707	1688	6766	14373	34532	•	148186	•	•	•
Notes and Loans Payable 27	150	0	59	337	1002	2029	5744	10405	•	28847	•	•	•
All Other Liabilities 28	119	0	13	95	400	1897	4442	12391	•	56395	•	•	•
Net Worth 29	71	0	-0	274	286	2840	4187	11737	•	62945	•	•	•

Selected Financial Ratios (Times to 1)

Current Ratio 30	1.5	•	1.3	2.1	1.7	1.5	1.3	1.9	•	1.4	•	•	•
Quick Ratio 31	1.0	•	1.0	1.7	1.3	1.0	0.8	1.0	•	1.0	•	•	•
Net Sales to Working Capital 32	16.0	•	50.8	11.2	8.9	14.7	15.5	4.3	•	12.1	•	•	•
Coverage Ratio 33	4.2	2.2	7.9	4.9	3.2	7.7	6.0	6.0	•	4.9	•	•	•
Total Asset Turnover 34	1.4	•	3.9	1.9	1.1	2.4	1.1	1.0	•	0.7	•	•	•
Inventory Turnover 35	9.7	•	31.2	10.0	11.4	19.0	11.9	4.9	•	10.0	•	•	•
Receivables Turnover 36	19.4	•	105.6	26.6	9.1	17.1	8.7	9.3	•	•	•	•	•
Total Liabilities to Net Worth 37	3.8	•	•	1.6	4.9	1.4	2.4	1.9	•	1.4	•	•	•
Current Assets to Working Capital 38	3.0	•	4.2	1.9	2.5	3.1	5.0	2.1	•	3.4	•	•	•
Current Liabilities to Working Capital 39	2.0	•	3.2	0.9	1.5	2.1	4.0	1.1	•	2.4	•	•	•
Working Capital to Net Sales 40	0.1	•	0.0	0.1	0.1	0.1	0.1	0.2	•	0.1	•	•	•
Inventory to Working Capital 41	0.5	•	0.5	0.2	0.2	0.4	0.4	0.2	•	0.4	•	•	•
Total Receipts to Cash Flow 42	4.1	2.8	3.8	3.5	4.9	5.7	4.1	3.4	•	5.1	•	•	•
Cost of Goods to Cash Flow 43	1.2	0.4	1.0	0.9	1.6	3.1	1.1	0.8	•	1.5	•	•	•
Cash Flow to Total Debt 44	0.4	•	1.0	0.9	0.3	0.7	0.4	0.5	•	0.2	•	•	•

Selected Financial Factors (in Percentages)

Debt Ratio 45	79.2	•	100.6	61.2	83.1	58.0	70.9	66.0	•	57.5	•	•	•
Return on Total Assets 46	9.1	•	22.1	11.7	6.6	10.2	9.1	11.3	•	4.6	•	•	•
Return on Equity Before Income Taxes 47	33.5	•	•	23.9	26.6	21.2	26.0	27.7	•	8.6	•	•	•
Return on Equity After Income Taxes 48	29.9	•	•	23.4	24.8	19.0	23.3	24.6	•	7.8	•	•	•
Profit Margin (Before Income Tax) 49	5.0	0.6	5.0	5.0	3.9	3.7	6.9	9.2	•	5.5	•	•	•
Profit Margin (After Income Tax) 50	4.5	0.4	4.9	4.9	3.6	3.3	6.2	8.2	•	5.1	•	•	•

Table II

Corporations with Net Income

PERSONAL AND LAUNDRY SERVICES

MONEY AMOUNTS AND SIZE OF ASSETS IN THOUSANDS OF DOLLARS

Item Description for Accounting Period 7/12 Through 6/13	Total	Zero Assets	Under 500	500 to 1,000	1,000 to 5,000	5,000 to 10,000	10,000 to 25,000	25,000 to 50,000	50,000 to 100,000	100,000 to 250,000	250,000 to 500,000	500,000 to 2,500,000	2,500,000 and over
Number of Enterprises 1	99683	19683	71925	4512	3143	270	87	31	11	•	•	•	0

Revenues ($ in Thousands)													
Net Sales 2	60094386	2058383	22108765	6046855	7146688	5102619	1736710	1239654	1363959	•	•	•	0
Interest 3	62207	522	1575	1620	12490	2367	913	5031	534	•	•	•	0
Rents 4	53676	1	2314	5499	697	4854	3445	2209	84	•	•	•	0
Royalties 5	141186	0	0	0	0	3669	49	1465	371	•	•	•	0
Other Portfolio Income 6	336813	56803	15162	18386	64685	6292	26305	5264	723	•	•	•	0
Other Receipts 7	1910502	6828	230307	1105774	104425	53960	55867	59887	14204	•	•	•	0
Total Receipts 8	62598770	2122537	22358123	7178134	7328985	5173761	1823289	1313510	1379875	•	•	•	0
Average Total Receipts 9	628	108	311	1591	2332	19162	20957	42371	125443	•	•	•	•

Operating Costs/Operating Income (%)													
Cost of Operations 10	26.6	10.9	19.4	28.6	32.5	54.1	25.0	23.4	44.4	•	•	•	•
Salaries and Wages 11	21.2	14.1	19.3	29.2	21.2	15.5	20.1	17.5	16.4	•	•	•	•
Taxes Paid 12	3.9	3.2	4.0	4.1	4.4	3.8	3.3	2.0	2.8	•	•	•	•
Interest Paid 13	1.4	0.4	0.6	1.0	1.6	0.3	1.2	1.9	1.2	•	•	•	•
Depreciation 14	2.7	1.9	1.8	2.5	2.5	2.1	3.4	4.6	2.2	•	•	•	•
Amortization and Depletion 15	1.2	0.2	0.4	0.5	0.8	0.3	0.2	0.6	0.9	•	•	•	•
Pensions and Other Deferred Comp. 16	0.5	0.5	0.2	0.5	0.6	0.3	0.5	0.7	0.2	•	•	•	•
Employee Benefits 17	1.1	0.3	0.6	0.8	1.2	0.6	2.4	4.0	1.3	•	•	•	•
Advertising 18	1.3	1.9	1.3	1.4	1.3	0.8	2.0	0.5	1.2	•	•	•	•
Other Expenses 19	29.4	42.9	33.9	34.9	22.3	17.8	35.4	38.9	21.6	•	•	•	•
Officers' Compensation 20	5.6	11.0	8.9	7.8	5.7	1.1	2.1	1.5	2.6	•	•	•	•
Operating Margin 21	5.1	12.6	9.7	•	6.0	3.4	4.5	4.3	5.3	•	•	•	•
Operating Margin Before Officers' Comp. 22	10.7	23.6	18.5	•	11.6	4.5	6.6	5.8	7.9	•	•	•	•

Selected Average Balance Sheet ($ in Thousands)

Net Receivables 23	30	0	2	41	209	1200	1674	3899	9651	•	•	•	•
Inventories 24	19	0	2	34	44	535	377	1418	2546	•	•	•	•
Net Property, Plant and Equipment 25	130	0	28	318	710	1691	4950	10991	17524	•	•	•	•
Total Assets 26	421	0	75	702	1653	6686	14134	35055	75343	•	•	•	•
Notes and Loans Payable 27	175	0	49	260	999	2011	5520	11502	26734	•	•	•	•
All Other Liabilities 28	145	0	10	89	353	1807	4229	11185	25390	•	•	•	•
Net Worth 29	101	0	16	353	302	2869	4384	12369	23220	•	•	•	•

Selected Financial Ratios (Times to 1)

Current Ratio 30	1.7	•	2.0	2.7	1.7	1.5	1.3	2.0	1.2	•	•	•	•
Quick Ratio 31	1.1	•	1.5	2.2	1.3	1.0	0.9	1.0	0.9	•	•	•	•
Net Sales to Working Capital 32	13.6	•	25.9	8.5	9.5	14.3	14.5	5.0	29.6	•	•	•	•
Coverage Ratio 33	7.6	37.1	18.4	8.6	6.2	16.1	8.7	6.5	6.5	•	•	•	•
Total Asset Turnover 34	1.4	•	4.1	1.9	1.4	2.8	1.4	1.1	1.6	•	•	•	•
Inventory Turnover 35	8.6	•	24.2	11.3	16.9	19.1	13.2	6.6	21.6	•	•	•	•
Receivables Turnover 36	20.7	•	126.6	28.6	11.6	18.2	12.6	11.6	•	•	•	•	•
Total Liabilities to Net Worth 37	3.2	•	3.7	1.0	4.5	1.3	2.2	1.8	2.2	•	•	•	•
Current Assets to Working Capital 38	2.5	•	2.0	1.6	2.5	2.8	3.9	2.0	5.8	•	•	•	•
Current Liabilities to Working Capital 39	1.5	•	1.0	0.6	1.5	1.8	2.9	1.0	4.8	•	•	•	•
Working Capital to Net Sales 40	0.1	•	0.0	0.1	0.1	0.1	0.1	0.2	0.0	•	•	•	•
Inventory to Working Capital 41	0.4	•	0.2	0.2	0.2	0.4	0.4	0.2	0.6	•	•	•	•
Total Receipts to Cash Flow 42	3.6	2.2	3.3	2.9	4.3	5.4	3.8	3.3	4.8	•	•	•	•
Cost of Goods to Cash Flow 43	1.0	0.2	0.6	0.8	1.4	2.9	1.0	0.8	2.1	•	•	•	•
Cash Flow to Total Debt 44	0.5	•	1.6	1.3	0.4	0.9	0.5	0.5	0.5	•	•	•	•

Selected Financial Factors (in Percentages)

Debt Ratio 45	75.9	•	78.9	49.7	81.8	57.1	69.0	64.7	69.2	•	•	•	•
Return on Total Assets 46	15.4	•	46.8	16.1	13.9	14.3	15.1	13.9	12.6	•	•	•	•
Return on Equity Before Income Taxes 47	55.6	•	209.7	28.3	63.8	31.3	43.0	33.2	34.7	•	•	•	•
Return on Equity After Income Taxes 48	51.3	•	208.0	27.8	61.3	28.5	39.1	29.7	29.2	•	•	•	•
Profit Margin (Before Income Tax) 49	9.4	15.7	10.8	7.5	8.5	4.7	9.4	10.3	6.5	•	•	•	•
Profit Margin (After Income Tax) 50	8.6	15.4	10.7	7.3	8.1	4.3	8.6	9.2	5.5	•	•	•	•

Table I

Corporations with and without Net Income

RELIGIOUS, GRANTMAKING, CIVIC AND PROFESSIONAL ORGANIZATIONS

MONEY AMOUNTS AND SIZE OF ASSETS IN THOUSANDS OF DOLLARS

Item Description for Accounting Period 7/12 Through 6/13	Total	Zero Assets	Under 500	500 to 1,000	1,000 to 5,000	5,000 to 10,000	10,000 to 25,000	25,000 to 50,000	50,000 to 100,000	100,000 to 250,000	250,000 to 500,000	500,000 to 2,500,000	2,500,000 and over
Number of Enterprises 1	45797	9742	29760	3340	2621	213	91	11	14	3	3	0	0

Revenues ($ in Thousands)

Net Sales 2	9335650	430857	2849451	1330688	2512724	495884	854879	294684	341294	208851	16339	0	0
Interest 3	63274	447	9246	10244	30309	5162	3150	1081	2701	919	14	0	0
Rents 4	48639	0	23475	6374	9427	3244	210	0	310	5600	0	0	0
Royalties 5	23055	0	0	1847	0	304	0	0	2	18247	2655	0	0
Other Portfolio Income 6	29609	176	3897	2751	11014	2570	1150	467	5440	1947	200	0	0
Other Receipts 7	3253306	2105	858094	351817	520729	157974	170974	49712	92861	5099	1043936	0	0
Total Receipts 8	12753533	433585	3744163	1703721	3084203	665138	1030363	345944	442608	240663	1063144	0	0
Average Total Receipts 9	278	45	126	510	1177	3123	11323	31449	31615	80221	354381	•	•

Operating Costs/Operating Income (%)

Cost of Operations 10	14.6	6.0	11.9	7.8	16.2	10.8	6.6	48.8	36.9	49.9	22.6	•	•
Salaries and Wages 11	13.2	8.6	7.1	11.2	16.0	24.1	12.7	23.8	26.9	11.2	174.1	•	•
Taxes Paid 12	2.5	1.7	2.3	1.8	2.5	4.8	1.9	4.7	3.0	3.6	18.2	•	•
Interest Paid 13	0.9	0.7	0.7	0.5	0.9	1.3	1.3	0.9	0.5	0.5	29.2	•	•
Depreciation 14	2.2	1.3	1.1	1.1	2.4	4.9	3.9	4.9	4.9	2.3	12.4	•	•
Amortization and Depletion 15	0.1	•	0.0	0.0	0.1	0.0	0.2	0.2	0.0	1.9	18.5	•	•
Pensions and Other Deferred Comp. 16	0.4	•	0.6	•	0.1	1.3	0.1	0.3	0.6	0.4	15.6	•	•
Employee Benefits 17	1.6	•	0.6	0.8	2.2	3.2	1.8	3.2	3.1	5.9	29.9	•	•
Advertising 18	2.7	6.0	0.3	6.5	0.4	2.7	11.4	0.1	3.0	0.1	1.6	•	•
Other Expenses 19	94.3	71.0	102.3	96.6	78.9	71.9	80.5	22.0	40.8	25.9	6185.9	•	•
Officers' Compensation 20	1.3	5.9	1.5	•	0.7	2.9	0.1	1.5	1.9	1.5	37.0	•	•
Operating Margin 21	•	•	•	•	•	•	•	•	•	•	•	•	•
Operating Margin Before Officers' Comp. 22	•	4.8	•	•	•	•	•	•	•	•	•	•	•

Selected Average Balance Sheet ($ in Thousands)

Net Receivables 23	22	0	6	31	71	318	692	4692	8003	40421	39089	•	•
Inventories 24	1	0	0	1	9	26	79	192	422	2035	1205	•	•
Net Property, Plant and Equipment 25	73	0	8	70	372	2301	9026	17708	18827	11495	28649	•	•
Total Assets 26	504	0	95	693	1978	6532	16443	35192	65708	139218	2715886	•	•
Notes and Loans Payable 27	35	0	13	35	195	599	2283	3586	4606	6841	43225	•	•
All Other Liabilities 28	235	0	15	135	332	1313	3341	6747	22224	45884	2635832	•	•
Net Worth 29	234	0	68	524	1451	4621	10820	24859	38878	86493	36829	•	•

Selected Financial Ratios (Times to 1)

Current Ratio 30	1.9	•	5.1	6.7	4.6	3.0	2.0	2.9	1.2	1.7	1.0	•	•
Quick Ratio 31	1.2	•	4.7	6.3	4.2	2.6	1.4	2.8	0.9	1.5	0.0	•	•
Net Sales to Working Capital 32	1.3	•	1.5	0.9	0.9	1.0	3.9	2.5	6.1	2.2	•	•	•
Coverage Ratio 33	4.1	0.3	5.1	5.0	3.1	5.9	0.9	9.1	18.0	24.0	•	•	•
Total Asset Turnover 34	0.4	•	1.0	0.6	0.5	0.4	0.6	0.8	0.4	0.5	0.0	•	•
Inventory Turnover 35	23.8	•	196.3	33.6	16.9	9.7	7.9	68.2	21.3	17.1	1.0	•	•
Receivables Turnover 36	8.9	•	17.3	12.5	12.4	7.3	9.8	3.4	2.4	•	•	•	•
Total Liabilities to Net Worth 37	1.2	•	0.4	0.3	0.4	0.4	0.5	0.4	0.7	0.6	72.7	•	•
Current Assets to Working Capital 38	2.1	•	1.2	1.2	1.3	1.5	2.0	1.5	5.1	2.4	•	•	•
Current Liabilities to Working Capital 39	1.1	•	0.2	0.2	0.3	0.5	1.0	0.5	4.1	1.4	•	•	•
Working Capital to Net Sales 40	0.8	•	0.7	1.2	1.1	1.0	0.3	0.4	0.2	0.4	•	•	•
Inventory to Working Capital 41	0.0	•	0.0	0.0	0.0	0.0	0.0	0.0	0.1	0.1	•	•	•
Total Receipts to Cash Flow 42	1.2	1.9	1.2	1.2	1.4	1.4	1.4	4.5	2.5	2.7	0.0	•	•
Cost of Goods to Cash Flow 43	0.2	0.1	0.1	0.1	0.2	0.2	0.1	2.2	0.9	1.4	0.0	•	•
Cash Flow to Total Debt 44	0.6	•	2.9	2.0	1.3	0.9	1.2	0.6	0.4	0.5	0.1	•	•

Selected Financial Factors (in Percentages)

Debt Ratio 45	53.5	•	28.7	24.4	26.6	29.3	34.2	29.4	40.8	37.9	98.6	•	•
Return on Total Assets 46	1.4	•	3.5	1.3	1.4	2.7	0.7	6.0	3.1	6.3	•	•	•
Return on Equity Before Income Taxes 47	2.3	•	4.0	1.4	1.3	3.2	•	7.6	4.9	9.8	•	•	•
Return on Equity After Income Taxes 48	1.8	•	3.6	1.2	0.9	2.5	•	4.7	4.0	7.3	•	•	•
Profit Margin (Before Income Tax) 49	2.7	•	2.8	1.8	2.0	6.3	•	7.0	7.9	12.1	•	•	•
Profit Margin (After Income Tax) 50	2.1	•	2.6	1.6	1.4	4.9	•	4.4	6.4	9.1	•	•	•

Table II

Corporations with Net Income

RELIGIOUS, GRANTMAKING, CIVIC AND PROFESSIONAL ORGANIZATIONS

MONEY AMOUNTS AND SIZE OF ASSETS IN THOUSANDS OF DOLLARS

Item Description for Accounting Period 7/12 Through 6/13	Total	Zero Assets	Under 500	500 to 1,000	1,000 to 5,000	5,000 to 10,000	10,000 to 25,000	25,000 to 50,000	50,000 to 100,000	100,000 to 250,000	250,000 to 500,000	500,000 to 2,500,000	2,500,000 and over
Number of Enterprises 1	21671	4868	12694	2045	1889	119	38	5	8	•	•	0	•

Revenues ($ in Thousands)

	Total	Zero Assets	Under 500	500 to 1,000	1,000 to 5,000	5,000 to 10,000	10,000 to 25,000	25,000 to 50,000	50,000 to 100,000	100,000 to 250,000	250,000 to 500,000	500,000 to 2,500,000	2,500,000 and over
Net Sales 2	5753536	255663	1251346	879317	2003051	312964	328163	207770	306411	•	•	0	•
Interest 3	51022	309	6979	8838	25254	4617	1603	426	2065	•	•	0	•
Rents 4	25059	0	4958	5835	7132	1067	210	0	257	•	•	0	•
Royalties 5	18247	0	0	0	0	0	0	0	0	•	•	0	•
Other Portfolio Income 6	23267	0	1638	2751	8900	2019	522	467	5021	•	•	0	•
Other Receipts 7	2144194	-239	421733	206565	212012	69875	89101	17778	78353	•	•	0	•
Total Receipts 8	8015325	255733	1686654	1103306	2256349	390542	419599	226441	392107	•	•	0	•
Average Total Receipts 9	370	53	133	540	1194	3282	11042	45288	49013	•	•	•	•

Operating Costs/Operating Income (%)

	Total	Zero Assets	Under 500	500 to 1,000	1,000 to 5,000	5,000 to 10,000	10,000 to 25,000	25,000 to 50,000	50,000 to 100,000	100,000 to 250,000	250,000 to 500,000	500,000 to 2,500,000	2,500,000 and over
Cost of Operations 10	18.7	0.4	12.8	11.8	19.7	11.0	5.1	64.0	41.1	•	•	•	•
Salaries and Wages 11	12.5	13.5	8.2	9.6	10.6	21.1	14.7	15.0	29.6	•	•	•	•
Taxes Paid 12	2.5	2.4	3.6	1.8	1.8	3.0	1.8	3.7	3.1	•	•	•	•
Interest Paid 13	0.4	•	0.2	0.2	0.5	0.3	0.4	0.1	0.5	•	•	•	•
Depreciation 14	1.7	0.0	1.2	0.8	1.9	1.6	3.2	1.6	4.1	•	•	•	•
Amortization and Depletion 15	0.2	•	•	•	0.1	0.0	0.0	0.3	0.0	•	•	•	•
Pensions and Other Deferred Comp. 16	0.2	•	0.1	•	0.1	1.5	•	0.4	0.7	•	•	•	•
Employee Benefits 17	1.6	•	0.1	1.1	1.7	2.0	2.4	2.5	3.4	•	•	•	•
Advertising 18	1.0	9.1	0.0	0.0	0.5	4.1	0.1	0.0	3.3	•	•	•	•
Other Expenses 19	91.2	55.4	93.4	95.2	71.0	63.1	97.2	8.2	29.3	•	•	•	•
Officers' Compensation 20	1.4	9.9	0.8	•	0.7	4.6	•	2.1	2.1	•	•	•	•
Operating Margin 21	•	9.3	•	•	•	•	•	2.0	•	•	•	•	•
Operating Margin Before Officers' Comp. 22	•	19.2	•	•	•	•	•	4.1	•	•	•	•	•

Selected Average Balance Sheet ($ in Thousands)

Net Receivables 23	35	0	8	33	64	379	608	9132	13836	•	•	•	•
Inventories 24	2	0	0	1	11	26	113	82	581	•	•	•	•
Net Property, Plant and Equipment 25	73	0	9	63	321	1410	8006	7088	13050	•	•	•	•
Total Assets 26	786	0	118	693	1962	6687	17798	33814	63975	•	•	•	•
Notes and Loans Payable 27	29	0	9	26	180	314	822	765	3296	•	•	•	•
All Other Liabilities 28	439	0	12	117	294	1571	3209	7235	28594	•	•	•	•
Net Worth 29	319	0	98	550	1488	4803	13767	25814	32085	•	•	•	•

Selected Financial Ratios (Times to 1)

Current Ratio 30	1.8	•	7.8	6.6	5.5	3.3	2.9	3.4	1.5	•	•	•	•
Quick Ratio 31	0.9	•	7.4	6.3	5.1	2.8	1.7	3.3	1.3	•	•	•	•
Net Sales to Working Capital 32	1.1	•	1.1	0.9	0.9	0.8	2.1	2.5	4.0	•	•	•	•
Coverage Ratio 33	23.3	•	66.0	32.9	8.0	38.9	8.3	101.9	21.9	•	•	•	•
Total Asset Turnover 34	0.3	•	0.8	0.6	0.5	0.4	0.5	1.2	0.6	•	•	•	•
Inventory Turnover 35	28.1	•	313.6	66.5	19.2	10.9	3.9	325.5	27.1	•	•	•	•
Receivables Turnover 36	7.7	•	13.9	18.1	15.4	7.3	5.4	3.2	1.6	•	•	•	•
Total Liabilities to Net Worth 37	1.5	•	0.2	0.3	0.3	0.4	0.3	0.3	1.0	•	•	•	•
Current Assets to Working Capital 38	2.3	•	1.1	1.2	1.2	1.4	1.5	1.4	2.9	•	•	•	•
Current Liabilities to Working Capital 39	1.3	•	0.1	0.2	0.2	0.4	0.5	0.4	1.9	•	•	•	•
Working Capital to Net Sales 40	0.9	•	0.9	1.2	1.1	1.2	0.5	0.4	0.2	•	•	•	•
Inventory to Working Capital 41	0.0	•	0.0	0.0	0.0	0.0	0.0	0.0	0.1	•	•	•	•
Total Receipts to Cash Flow 42	1.1	2.0	1.2	1.1	1.5	1.5	1.1	5.9	2.9	•	•	•	•
Cost of Goods to Cash Flow 43	0.2	0.0	0.2	0.1	0.3	0.2	0.1	3.8	1.2	•	•	•	•
Cash Flow to Total Debt 44	0.5	•	4.1	2.7	1.5	1.0	1.9	0.9	0.4	•	•	•	•

Selected Financial Factors (in Percentages)

Debt Ratio 45	59.5	•	17.4	20.6	24.2	28.2	22.6	23.7	49.8	•	•	•	•
Return on Total Assets 46	2.8	•	12.1	3.2	2.4	5.0	1.5	13.6	6.6	•	•	•	•
Return on Equity Before Income Taxes 47	6.6	•	14.4	3.9	2.7	6.8	1.8	17.7	12.6	•	•	•	•
Return on Equity After Income Taxes 48	5.8	•	13.9	3.7	2.2	5.7	1.2	11.7	10.6	•	•	•	•
Profit Margin (Before Income Tax) 49	7.9	9.3	14.3	5.0	3.8	12.5	2.8	11.0	10.5	•	•	•	•
Profit Margin (After Income Tax) 50	6.9	8.9	13.8	4.7	3.1	10.3	2.0	7.3	8.9	•	•	•	•

APPENDIX

APPENDIX

Naics To Published Industry Codes

SOI Published Code	PBA Code	NAICS Code	Industry

AGRICULTURE, FORESTRY, FISHING AND HUNTING

Crop Production

111005	111100		**Oilseed and Grain Farming**
		111150	Corn Farming
		111130	Dry Pea and Bean Farming
		111199	Grain Farming, NEC
		111120	Oilseed (except Soybean) Farming
		111191	Oilseed and Grain Comination Farming
		111160	Rice Farming
		111110	Soybean Farming
		111140	Wheat Farming

111005	111210		**Vegetable and Melon Farming**
		111211	Potato Farming
		111219	Vegetable (except Potato) and Melon Farming

111005	111300		**Fruit & Tree Nut Farming**
		111331	Apple Orchards
		111334	Berry (except Strawberry) Farming
		111320	Citrus (except Orange) Groves
		111336	Fruit and Nut Combination Farming
		111332	Grape Vineyards
		111310	Orange Groves
		111339	Other Noncitrus Fruit Farming
		111333	Strawberry Farming
		111335	Tree Nut Farming

SOI PUBLISHED CODE	PBA CODE	NAICS CODE	INDUSTRY
111005	111400		**Greenhouse, Nursery & Floriculture Production**
		111422	Floriculture Production
		111411	Mushroom Production
		111421	Nursery and Tree Production
		111419	Other Food Crops Grown Under Cover
111005	111900		**Other Crop Farming**
		111920	Cotton Farming
		111998	Crop Farming, NEC
		111940	Hay Farming
		111992	Peanut Farming
		111991	Sugar Beet Farming
		111930	Sugarcane Farming
		111910	Tobacco Farming

Animal Production

SOI PUBLISHED CODE	PBA CODE	NAICS CODE	INDUSTRY
111005	112111		**Beef Cattle Ranching and Farming**
111005	112112		**Cattle Feedlots**
111005	112120		**Dairy Cattle and Milk Production**
111005	112210		**Hog and Pig Farming**
111005	112300		**Poultry and Egg Production**
		112320	Broilers & Other Meat Type Chicken Production
		112310	Chicken Egg Production
		112340	Poultry Hatcheries
		112390	Poultry Production, NEC
		112330	Turkey Production

SOI Published Code	PBA Code	NAICS Code	Industry
111005	112400		**Sheep and Goat Farming**
		112420	Goat Farming
		112410	Sheep Farming
111005	112510		**Animal Aquaculture (including shellfish, finfish farms & hatcheries)**
		112511	Finfish Farming and Fish Hatcheries
		112519	Other Animal Aquaculture
		112512	Shellfish Farming
111005	112900		**Other Animal Production**
		112990	Animal Production, NEC
		112910	Apiculture
		112390	Fur-Bearing Animal and Rabbit Production
		112920	Horse and Other Equine Production (breeding horses)

Forestry and Logging

SOI Published Code	PBA Code	NAICS Code	Industry
113005	113110		**Timber Tract Operations**
113005	113210		**Forest Nuseries and Gathering of Forest Products**
113005	113310		**Logging**

Fishing and Trapping

SOI Published Code	PBA Code	NAICS Code	Industry
114005	114110		**Fishing**
		114111	Finfish Fishing
		114119	Marine Fishing, NEC
		114112	Shellfish Fishing

SOI PUBLISHED CODE	PBA CODE	NAICS CODE	INDUSTRY
114005	114210		**Hunting and Trapping**

Support Activities for Agricultre and Forestry

114005	115110		**Support Activities for Crop Production**
		115111	Cotton Ginning
		115113	Crop Harvesting, Primarily by Machine
		115115	Garm Labor Contractors and Crew Leaders
		115116	Farm Management Services
		115114	Postharvest Crop Activities (except Cotton Ginning)
		115112	Soil Preparation, Planting and Cultivating
114005	115210		**Support Activities for Animal Production**
114005	115310		**Support Activities for Forestry**

MINING

Mining

211110	211110		**Oil and Gas Extraction**
		211111	Crude Petroleum and Natural Gas Extraction
		211112	Natural Gas Liquid Extraction
212110	212110		**Coal Mining**
		212113	Anthracite Mining
		212112	Bituminous Coal Underground Mining
		212111	Bituminous Coal and Lignite Surface Mining
212200	212200		**Metal Ore Mining**
		212234	Copper Ore and Nickel Ore Mining
		212221	Gold Ore Mining

SOI PUBLISHED CODE	PBA CODE	NAICS CODE	INDUSTRY
		212210	Iron Ore Mining
		212231	Lead Ore and Zinc Ore Mining
		212299	Metal Ore Mining, NEC
		212222	Silver Ore Mining
		212291	Uranium-Radium-Vanadium Ore Mining
212315	**212310**		**Stone Mining and Quarrying**
		212313	Crushed and Broken Granite Mining and Quarrying
		212312	Crushed and Broken Limestone Mining and Quarrying
		212319	Crushed and Broken Stone Mining and Quarrying, NEC
		212311	Dimension Stone Mining and Quarrying
212315	**212320**		**Sand, Gravel, Clay & Ceramic & Refactory Minerals, Mining & Quarrying**
		212325	Clay and Ceramic and Refactory Minerals Mining
		212321	Construction Sand and Gravel Mining
		212322	Industrial Sand Mining
		212324	Kaolin and Ball Clay Mining
212315	**212390**		**Other Nonmetallic Mineral Mining and Quarrying**
		212399	Nonmetallic Mineral Mining, NEC
		212393	Other Chemical and Fertilizer Mineral Mining
		212392	Phosphate Rock Mining
		212391	Potash, Soda, and Borate Mineral Mining
213110	**213110**		**Support Activities for Mining**
		213111	Driling Oil and Gas Wells
		213113	Support Activities for Coal Mining
		213114	Support Activities for Metal Mining
		213115	Support Activities for Nonmetallic Minerals (except Fuels)
		213112	support Activities for Oil and Gas Operations

SOI Published Code	PBA Code	NAICS Code	Industry

UTILITIES

Utilities

SOI Published Code	PBA Code	NAICS Code	Industry
221100	221100		**Electric Power Generation, Transmission & Distribution**
		221121	Electric Bulk Power Transmission and Control
		221122	Electric Power Distribution
		221112	Fossil Fuel Electric Power Generation
		221111	Hydroelectric Power Generation
		221113	Nuclear Electric Power Generation
		221119	Other Electric Power Generation
221210	221210		**Natural Gas Distribution**
221300	221300		**Water, Sewage, & Other Systems**
		221320	Sewage Treatment Facilities
		221330	Steam and Air-Conditioning Supply
		221310	Water Supply and Irrigation Systems
221500	221500		**Combination Electric and Gas Services**

CONSTRUCTION

Construction

SOI Published Code	PBA Code	NAICS Code	Industry
236115	236110		**Residential Building Construction**
		236115	New Sinlge-Family Housing Construction (except Operative Builders)
		236116	New Multifamily Housing Construction (except Operative Builders)
		236117	New Housing Operative Builders
		236118	Residential Remodelers
236115	236200		**Nonresidential Building Construction**
		236210	Industrial Building Construction
		236220	Commerical and Industrial Building Contruction

SOI Published Code	PBA Code	NAICS Code	Industry
Heavy and Civil Engineering Construction			
237105	237100		**Utility System Construction**
		237110	Water and Sewer Line and Related Structure Construction
		237120	Oil and Gas Pipeline and Structures Construction
		237130	Power & Communication Line and Related Structure Construction
237210	237210		**Land Subdivision**
237105	237310		**Highway, Street, and Bridge Construction**
237105	237990		**Other Heavy and Civil Engineering Construction**
Specialty Trade Contractors			
238905	238100		**Foundation, Structure & Building Exterior Contractors (including framing, carpentry, masonry, glass, roofing, and siding)**
		238110	Poured Concrete Foundation and Structure Contractors
		238120	Structural Steel and Precast Concrete Contractors
		238130	Framing Contractors
		238140	Masonry Contractors
		238150	Glass and Glazing Contractors
		238160	Roofing Contractors
		238170	Siding Contractors
		238190	Other Foundation, Structure, and Building Exterior Contractors
238210	238210		**Electrical Contractors**
238220	238220		**Plumbing, Heating, and Air-Conditioning Contractors**
238905	238290		**Other Building Equipment Contractors**

SOI PUBLISHED CODE	PBA CODE	NAICS CODE	INDUSTRY
238905	238300		**Building Finishing Contractors (including drywall, insulation, paiting, wallcovering, flooring, tile and finish carpentry)**
		238310	Drywall and Insulation Contractors
		238320	Painting and Wall Covering Contractors
		238330	Floor Contractors
		238340	Tile and Terrazzo Contractors
		238350	Finish Carpentry Contractors
		238390	Other Building Finishing Contractors
238905	238900		**Other Specialty Trade Contractors (including site preparation)**
		238910	Site Preparation Contractors
		238990	All Other Specialty Trade Contractors

MANUFACTURING

Food Manufacturing

SOI PUBLISHED CODE	PBA CODE	NAICS CODE	INDUSTRY
311115	311110		**Animal Food Manufacturing**
		311111	Dog and Cat Food Manufacturing
		311119	Other Animal Food Manufacturing
311115	311200		**Grain and Oilseed Milling**
		311230	Breakfast Cereal Manufacturing
		311225	Fats and Oils Refining and Blending
		311211	Flour Milling
		311213	Malt Manufacturing
		311212	Rice Milling
		311222	Soybean Processing
		311221	West Corn Milling
311300	311300		**Sugar & Confectionery Product Manufacturing**
		311313	Beet Sugar Manufacturing
		311312	Cane Sugar Refining

SOI PUBLISHED CODE	PBA CODE	NAICS CODE	INDUSTRY
		311320	Chocolate and Confectionery Manufacturing from Cacao Beans
		311330	Confectionery Manufacturing from Purchased Chocolate
		311340	Noncholocate Confectionary Manufacturing
		311311	Sugarcane Mills
311400	**311400**		**Fruit & Vegetable Preserving & Specialty Food Manufacturing**
		311423	Dried and Dehydrated Food Manufacturing
		311411	Frozen Fruit, Juice and Vegetable Manufacturing
		311412	Frozen Specialty Food Manufacturing
		311421	Fruit and Vegetable Canning
		311422	Specialty Canning
311500	**311500**		**Dairy Product Manufacturing**
		311513	Cheese Manufacturing
		311512	Creamery Butter Manufacturing
		311514	Dry, Condensed, and Evaporated Dairy Product Manufacturing
		311511	Fluid Milk Manufacturing
		311520	Ice Cream and Frozen Dessert Manufacturing
311615	**311610**		**Animal Slaughtering & Processing**
		311611	Animal (except Poultry) Slaughtering
		311612	Meat Processed for Carcasses
		311615	Poultry Processing
		311613	Rendering and Meat Byproduct Processing
311615	**311710**		**Seafood Product Preparation & Packaging**
		311712	Fresh and Frozen Seafood Processing
		311711	Seafood Canning
311800	**311800**		**Bakeries & Tortilla Manufacturing**
		311812	Commerical Bakeries

SOI PUBLISHED CODE	PBA CODE	NAICS CODE	INDUSTRY
		311821	Cookie and Cracker Manufacturing
		311823	Dry Pasta Manufacturing
		311822	Flour Mixes and Dough Manufacturing from Purchased Flour
		311813	Frozen Cakes, Pies, and other Pastries Manufacturing
		311811	Retail Bakeries
		311830	Toritilla Manufacturing
311900	**311900**		**Other Food Manufacturing (including coffee, tea, flavorings & seasonings)**
		311920	Coffee and Tea Manufacturing
		311930	Flavoring Syrup and Concentrate Manufacturing
		311999	Flood Manufacturing, NEC
		311941	Mayonnaise, Dressing and Other Prepared Sauce Manufacturing
		311919	Other Snack Food Manufacturing
		311991	Perishable Prepared Food Manufacturing
		311911	Roasted Nuts and Peanut Butter Manufacturing
		311942	Spice and Extract Manufacturing

Beverage & Tobacco Product Manufacturing

SOI PUBLISHED CODE	PBA CODE	NAICS CODE	INDUSTRY
312110	**312110**		**Soft Drink & Ice Manufacturing**
		312112	Bottled Water Manufacturing
		312113	Ice Manufacuring
		312111	Soft Drink Manufacturing
312120	**312120**		**Breweries**
312135	**312130**		**Wineries**
312135	**312140**		**Distilleries**

SOI PUBLISHED CODE	PBA CODE	NAICS CODE	INDUSTRY
312200	312200		**Tobacco Manufacturing**
		312221	Cigarette Manufacturing
		312229	Tobacco Product Manufacturing, NEC
		312210	Tobacco Stemming and Redrying

Textile Mills & Textile Product Mills

313000	313000		**Textile Mills**
		313311	Broadwoven Fabric Finishing Mills
		313210	Broadwoven Fabric Mills
		313320	Fabric Coating Mills
		313221	Narrow Fabric Mills
		313230	Nonwoven Fabric Mills
		313249	Other Knit Fabric and Lace Mills
		313222	Schiffli Machine Embroidery
		313312	Textile and Fabric Finishing (except Broadwoven Fabric) Mills
		313113	Thread Mills
		313241	Weft Knit Fabric Mills
		313111	Yarn Spinning Mills
		313112	Yarn Texturing, Throwing, and Twisting Mills
314000	314000		**Textile Product Mills**
		314912	Canvas and Related Product Mills
		314110	Carpet and Rug Mills
		314121	Curtain and Drapery Mills
		314129	Other Household Textile Product Mills
		314991	Rope, Cordage, and Twine Mills
		314911	Textile Bag Mills
		314999	Textile Product Mills, NEC
		314992	Tire Cord and Tire Fabric Mills

SOI Published Code	PBA Code	NAICS Code	Industry
			Apparel Manufacturing
315100	315100		**Apparel Knitting Mills**
			315119 Other Hosiery and Sock Mills
			315191 Outerwear Knitting Mills
			315111 Sheer Hosiery Mills
			315192 Underwear and Nightwear Knitting Mills
315215	315210		**Cut and Sew Apparel Contractors**
			315211 Men's and Boy's Cut and Sew Apparel Contractors
			315212 Women's, Girls and Infants Cuts and Sew Apparel Contractors
315215	315220		**Men's and Boy's Cut and Sew Apparel Manufacturing**
			315228 Men's and Boys' Cut and Sew Other Outerwear Manufacturing
			315223 Men's and Boys' Cut and Sew Shirt (except Work Shirt) Manufacturing
			315222 Men's and Boys' Cut and Sew Suit, Coat, and Overcoat Manufacturing
			315224 Men's and Boys' Cut and Sew Trouser, Slack and Jean Manufacturing
			315221 Men's and Boys' Cut and Sew Underwear and Nightware
			315225 Men's and Boys' Cut and Sew Work Clothing Manufacturing
315215	315230		**Women's and Girls' Cut and Sew Apparel Manufacturing**
			315232 Women's and Girls' Cut and Sew Blouse and Shirt Manufacturing
			315233 Women's and Girls' Cut and Sew Dress Manufacturing
			315231 Women's and Girls' Cut and Sew Lingerie, Loungwear, & Nightgown Manufacturing
			315239 Women's and Girls' Cut and Sew Other Outerwear Manufacturing
			315234 Women's and Girls' Cut and Sew Suit, Coat, Tailored Jackt and Skirt Manufacturing
315215	315290		**Other Cut and Sew Apparel**
			315299 All Other Cut and Sew Apparel Manufacturing
			315292 Fur and Leather Apparel Manufacturing
			315291 Infants' Cut and Sew Apparel Manufacturing

SOI PUBLISHED CODE	PBA CODE	NAICS CODE	INDUSTRY
315990	315990		**Apparel Accessories and Other Apparel Manufacturing**
			315992 Glove and Mitten Manufacturing
			315991 Hat, Cap, and Millinery Manufacturing
			315993 Men's and Boy's Neckwear Manufacturing
			315999 Other Apparel Accessories and Other Apparel Manufacturing

Leather and Allied Products Manufacturing

SOI PUBLISHED CODE	PBA CODE	NAICS CODE	INDUSTRY
316115	316110		**Leather and Hide Tanning and Finishing**
316115	316210		**Footwear Manufacturing (including Rubber and Plastics)**
			316212 House Slipper Manufacturing
			316213 Men's Footwear (except Athletic) Manufacturing
			316219 Other Footwear Manufacturing
			316211 Rubber and Plastics Footwear Manufacturing
			316214 Women's Footwear (except Athletic) Manufacturing
316115	316990		**Other Leather & Allied Product Manufacturing**
			316999 Leather Good Manufacturing, NEC
			316991 Luggage Manufacturing
			316993 Personal Leather Good (except Women's Handbag and Purse) Manufacturing
			316992 Women's Handbag and Purse Manufacturing

Wood Product Manufacturing

SOI PUBLISHED CODE	PBA CODE	NAICS CODE	INDUSTRY
321115	321110		**Sawmills and Wood Preservation**
			321113 Sawmills
			321114 Wood Preservation
32115	321210		**Veneer, Plywood & Engineered Wood Product Manufacturing**
			321213 Engineered Wood Member (except Truss) Manufacturing
			321211 Hardwood Veneer and Plywood Manufacturing
			321219 Reconstituted Wood Product Manufacturing

SOI Published Code	PBA Code	NAICS Code	Industry
		321212	Softwood Veneer and Plywood Manufacturing
		321214	Truss Manufacturing
321115	**321900**		**Other Wood Product Manufacturing**
		321999	All Other Miscellaneous Wood Product Manufacturing
		321912	Cut Stock, Resawing Lumber, and Planing
		321991	Manufactured Home (Mobile Home) Manufacturing
		321918	Other Millwork (including Flooring)
		321992	Prefabricated Wood Building Manufacturing
		321920	Wood Container and Pallet Manufacturing
		321911	Wood Window and Door Manufacturing

Paper Manufacturing

SOI Published Code	PBA Code	NAICS Code	Industry
322100	**322100**		**Pulp, Paper and Paperboard Mills**
		322122	Newsprint Mills
		322121	Paper (except Newsprint) Mills
		322130	Paperboard Mills
		322110	Pulp Mills
322200	**322200**		**Converted Paper Product Manufacturing**
		322299	All Other Converted Paper Product Manufacturing
		322221	Coated and Laminated Packaging Paper and Plastics Film Manufacturing
		322222	Coated and Laminated Paper Manufacturing
		322211	Corrugated and Solid Fiber Box Manufacturing
		322231	Die-Cut Paper and Paperboard Office Supplies Manufacturing
		322232	Envelope Manufacturing
		322214	Fiber Can, Tube, Drum, and Similar Products Manufacturing
		322212	Folding Paperboard Box Manufacturing
		322225	Laminated Aluminum Foil Manufacturing for Felxible Pacakaging Uses
		322215	Nonfolding Sanitary Food Container Manufacturing
		322223	Plastics, Foil and Coated Paper Bag Manufacturing
		322291	Sanitary Paper Product Manufacturing
		322213	Setup Paperboard Box Manufacturing

SOI PUBLISHED CODE	PBA CODE	NAICS CODE	INDUSTRY
		322233	Satationery, Tablet, and Related Product Manufacturing
		322226	Surface-Coated Paperboard Manufacturing
		322224	Uncoated Paper and Multiwall Bag Manufacturing

Printing and Related Support Activites

323100	**323100**		**Printing and Related Support Activites**
		323118	Blankbood, Looseleaf Binders, and Devices Manufacturing
		323117	Books Printing
		323112	Commerical Flexographic Printing
		323111	Commerical Gravure Printing
		323110	Commercial Lithographic Printing
		323113	Commerical Screen Printing
		323115	Digital Printing
		323116	Manifold Business Forms Printing
		323119	Other Commerical Printing
		323122	Prepress Services
		323114	Quick Printing
		323121	Tradebinding and Related Work

Petroleum and Coal Products Manufacturing

324110	**324110**		**Petroleum Refineries (including Integrated)**
324115	**324120**		**Asphalt Paving, Roofing & Saturated Materials Manufacturing**
		324121	Asphalt Paving, Mixture and Block Manufacturing
		324122	Asphalt Shingle and Coating Materials Manufacturing
324125	**324190**		**Other Petroleum and Coal Products**
		324199	All Other Petroleum and Coal Products Manufacturing
		324191	Petroleum Lubricating Oil and Grease Manufacturing

SOI Published Code	PBA Code	NAICS Code	Industry
Chemical Manufacturing			
325100	325100		**Basic Chemical Manufacturing**
		325181	Alkalies and Chlorine Manufacturing
		325188	All Other Basic Inorganic Chemical Manufacturing
		325199	All Other Basic Organic Chemical Manufacturing
		325182	Carbon Black Manufacturing
		325192	Cyclic Crude and Intermediate Manufacturing
		325193	Ethyl Alcohol Manufacturing
		325191	Gum and Wood Chemical Manufacturing
		325120	Industrial Gas Manufacturing
		325131	Inorganic Dye and Pigment Manufacturing
		325110	Petrochemical Manufacturing
		325132	Synthetic Organic Dye and Pigment Manufacturing
325200	325200		**Resin, Synthetic Rubber & Artificial & Synthetic Fibers & Filaments Manufacturing**
		325221	Cellulosic Organic Fiber Manufacturing
		325222	Noncellulosic Organic Fiber Manufacturing
		325211	Plastics Material and Resin Manufacturing
		325212	Synthetic Rubber Manufacturing
325905	325300		**Pesticide, Fertilizer, & Other Agricultural Chemical Manufacturing**
		325314	Fertilizer (Mixing Only) Manufacturing
		325311	Nitrogenous Fetilizer Manufacturing
		325320	Pesticide and Other Agricultural Chemical Manufacturing
		325312	Phosphatic Fertilizer Manufacturing
325410	325410		**Pharmaceutical & Medicine Manufacturing**
		325414	Biological Product (except Diagnostic) Manufacturing
		325413	In-Vitro Diagnostic Sustance Manufacturing
		325411	Medicinal and Botanical Manufacturing
		325412	Pharmaceutical Preparation Manufacturing

SOI PUBLISHED CODE	PBA CODE	NAICS CODE	INDUSTRY
325500	325500		**Paint, Coating and Adhesive Manufacturing**
		325520	Adhesive Manufacturing
		325510	Paint and Coating Manufacturing
325600	325600		**Soap, Cleaning Compound & Toilet Preparation Manufacturing**
		325612	Polish and Other Sanitation Good Manufacturing
		325611	Soap and Other Detergent Manufacturing
		325613	Surface Active Agent Manufacturing
		325620	Toilet Preparation Manufacturing
325905	325900		**Other Chemical Products & Preparation Manufacturing**
		325998	Chemical Product and Preparation Manufacturing, NEC
		325991	Custom Compounding of Purchased Resins
		325920	Explosives Manufacturing
		325992	Photographic Film, Paper, Plate, and Chemical Manufacturing
		325910	Printing Ink Manufacturing

Plastics and Rubber Products Manufacturing

SOI PUBLISHED CODE	PBA CODE	NAICS CODE	INDUSTRY
326100	326100		**Plastics Product Manufacturing**
		326130	Laminated Plastics Plate, Sheet and Shape Manufacturing
		326160	Plastics Bottle Manufacturing
		326122	Plastics Pipe and Pipe Fitting Manufacturing
		326191	Plastics Plumbing Fixture Manufacturing
		326199	Plastics Product Manufacturing, NEC
		326140	Polystyrene Foam Product Manufacturing
		326192	Resilient Floor Covering Manufacturing
		326111	Unsupported Plastics Bag Manufacturing
		326113	Unsupported Plastics Film and Sheet (except Packaging) Manufacturing
		326112	Unsupported Plastics Packaging Film and Sheet Manufacturing
		326121	Unsupported Plastics Profile Shape Manufacturing
		326150	Urethane and Other Foam Product (except Polystyrene) Manufacturing

SOI Published Code	PBA Code	NAICS Code	Industry
326200	326200		**Rubber Product Manufacturing**
		326299	All Other Rubber Product Manufacturing
		326291	Rubber Product Manufacturing for Mechanical Use
		326220	Rubber and Plastics Hoses and Belting Manufacturing
		326211	Tire Manufacturing (except Retreading)
		326212	Tire Retreading

Nonmetallic Mineral Product Manufacturing

327105	327100		**Clay Product & Refactory Manufacturing**
		327121	Brick and Structural Clay Tile Manufacturing
		327122	Ceramic Wall and Floor Tile Manufacturing
		327124	Clay Refactory Manufacturing
		327125	Nonclay Refactory Manufacturing
		327123	Other Structual Clay Product Manufacturing
		327113	Porcelain Electrical Supply Manufacturing
		327111	Vitreous China Plumbing Fixture and China and Earthenware Bathroom Accessories Manufacturing
		321112	Vitreous China, Fine Earthenware, and Other Pottery Product Manufacturing
327210	327210		**Glass and Glass Product Manufacturing**
		327211	Flat Glass Manufacturing
		327213	Glass Container Manufacturing
		327215	Glass Product Manufactuing Made of Purchased Glass
		327212	Other Pressed and Blown Glass and Glassware Manufacturing
327305	327300		**Cement and Concrete Products Manufacturing**
		327310	Cement Manufacturing
		328331	Concrete Block and Brick Manufacturing
		327332	Concrete Pipe Manufacturing
		327390	Other Concrete Product Manufacturing
		327320	Ready-Mix Concrete Manufacturing

SOI Published Code	PBA Code	NAICS Code	Industry
327305	327400		**Lime & Gypsum Product Manufacturing**
		327420	Gypsum Product Manufacturing
		327410	Lime Manufacturing
327105	327900		**Other Nonmetallic Mineral Product Manufacturing**
		327910	Abrasive Product Manufacturing
		327991	Cut Stone and Stone Product Manufacturing
		327992	Ground or Treated Mineral and Earth Manufacturing
		327993	Mineral Wood Manufacturing
		327999	Nonmetallic Mineral Product Manufacturing, NEC

Primary Metal Manufacturing

SOI Published Code	PBA Code	NAICS Code	Industry
331115	331110		**Iron and Steel Mills and Ferroalloy Manufacturing**
		331112	Electometallurgical Ferroalloy Product Manufacturing
		331111	Iron and Steel Mills
331115	331200		**Steel Product Manufacturing from Purchased Steel**
		331210	Iron and Steel Pipe Tube Manufacturing from Purchased Steel
		331221	Rolled Steel Shape Manufacturing
		331222	Steel Wire Drawing
331315	331310		**Alumina & Aluminum Production and Processing**
		331311	Alumina Refining
		331316	Aluminum Extruded Product Manufacturing
		331315	Aluminum Sheet, Plate, and Foil Manufacturing
		331319	Other Aluminum Rolling and Drawing
		331312	Primary Aluminum Production
		331314	Secondary Smelting and Alloying of Aluminum

SOI Published Code	PBA Code	NAICS Code	Industry
331315	331400		**Nonferrous Metal (except Aluminum) Production and Processing**
		331421	Copper Rolling, Drawing and Extruding
		331422	Copper Wire (except Mechanical) Drawing
		331491	Nonferrous Metal (except Copper and Aluminum) Rolling, Drawing Extrudinga and Alloying
		331411	Primary Smelting and Refining of Copper
		331419	Primary Smelting and Refining of Nonferrous Metal (except Copper and Aluminum)
		331423	Secondary Smelting and Refining, and Alloying of Copper
		331492	Secondary Smelting and Refining, and Alloying of Nonferrous Metal (except copper and aluminum)
331500	331500		**Foundries**
		331521	Aluminum Die-Casting Foundries
		331524	Aluminum Foundries (except Die-Casting)
		331525	Copper Foundries (except Die-Casting)
		331511	Iron Foundries
		331522	Nonferrous (except Aluminum) Die-Casting Foundries
		331528	Other Nonferrous Foundries (except Die-Casting)
		331513	Steel Foundries (except Investment)
		331512	Steel Investment Foundries

Fabricated Metal Product Manufacturing

SOI Published Code	PBA Code	NAICS Code	Industry
332110	332110		**Forging and Stamping**
		332115	Crown and Closure Manufacturing
		332114	Custom Roll Forming
		332111	Iron and Steel Forging
		332116	Metal Stamping
		332112	Nonferrous Forging
		332117	Powder Metallurgy Part Manufacturing
332215	332210		**Cutlery and Handtool Manufacturing**
		332211	Cutlery and Flatware (except Precious) Manufacturing

SOI PUBLISHED CODE	PBA CODE	NAICS CODE	INDUSTRY
		332212	Hand and Edge Tool Manufacturing
		332214	Kitchen Utensil, Pot and Pan Manufacturing
		332213	Saw Blade and Handsaw Manufacturing
332300	**332300**		**Architectural and Structural Metals Manufacturing**
		332312	Fabricated Structural Metal Manufacturing
		332321	Metal Window and Door Manufacturing
		332323	Ornamental and Architectural Metal Work Manufacturing
		332313	Plate Work Manufacturing
		332311	Prefabricated Metal Building and Component Manufacturing
		332322	Sheet Metal Work Manufacturing
332400	**332400**		**Boiler, Tank and Shipping Container Manufacturing**
		332431	Metal Can Manufacturing
		332420	Metal Tank (Heavy Gauge) Manufacturing
		332439	Other Metal Container Manufacturing
		332410	Power Boiler and Heat Exchanger Manufacturing
332215	**332510**		**Hardware Manufacturing**
332215	**332610**		**Spring and Wire Product Manufacturing**
		332618	Other Fabricated Wire Product Manufacturing
		332611	Spring (Heavy Gauge) Manufacturing
		332612	Spring (Light Gauge) Manufacturing
332215	**332700**		**Machine Shops, Turned Product, and Sew, Nut and Bold Manufacturing**
		332722	Bolt, Nut, Screw, Rivet and Washer Manufacturing
		332710	Machine Shops
		332721	Precision Turned Product Manufacturing

SOI Published Code	PBA Code	NAICS Code	Industry
332810	332810		**Coating, Engraving, Heat Treating and Allied Activites**
		332813	Electoplating, Plating, Polishing, Anodizing and Coloring
		332812	Metal Coating, Engraving (except Jewelry and Silverware), and Allied Services to Manufacturers
		332811	Metal Head Treating
332900	332900		**Other Fabricated Metal Product Manufacturing**
		332999	All Other Miscellaneous Fabricated Metal Product Manufacturing
		332993	Ammunition (except Small Arms) Manufacturing
		332991	Ball and Roller Bearing Manufacturing
		332998	Enameled Iron and Metal Sanitary Ware Manufacturing
		332996	Fabricated Pipe and Pipe Fitting Manufacturing
		332912	Fluid Power Valve and Hose Fitting Manufacturing
		332997	Industrial Pattern Manufacturing
		332911	Industrial Valve Manufacturing
		332919	Other Metal Valve and Pipe Fitting Manufacturing
		332995	Other Ordnance and Accessories Manufacturing
		332913	Plumbing Fixture Fitting and Trim Manufacturing
		332992	Small Arms Ammunition Manufacturing
		332994	Small Arms Manufacturing

Machinery Manufacturing

SOI Published Code	PBA Code	NAICS Code	Industry
333100	333100		**Agriculture, Construction and Mining Machinery Manufacturing**
		333120	Construction Machinery Manufacturing
		333111	Farm Machinery and Equipmetn Manufacturing
		333112	Lawn and Garden Tractor and Home Lawn and Garden Equipment Manufacturing
		333131	Mining Machinery and Equipment Manufacturing
		333132	Oil and Gas Field Machinery and Equipment Manufacturing
333200	333200		**Industrial Machinery Manufacturing**
		333298	All Other Industrial Machinery Manufacturing
		333294	Food Product Machinery Manufacturing

SOI PUBLISHED CODE	PBA CODE	NAICS CODE	INDUSTRY
		333291	Paper Industry Machinery Manufacturing
		333220	Plastics and Rubber Industry Machinery Manufacturing
		333293	Printing Machinery and Equipment Manufacturing
		333210	Sawmill and Woodworking Machinery Manufacturing
		333295	Semiconductor Machinery Manufacturing
		333292	Textile Machinery Manufacturing
333310	**333310**		**Commerical and Service Industry Machinery Manufacturing**
		333311	Automatic Vending Machine Manufacturing
		333312	Commerical Laundry, Drycleaning, and Pressing Machine Manufacturing
		333313	Office Machinery Manufacturing
		333314	Optical Instrument and Lens Manufacturing
		333319	Other Commerical and Service Industry Machinery Manufacturing
		333315	Photographic and Photocopying Equipment Manufacturing
333410	**333410**		**Ventilation, Heating, Air Conditioning, and Commerical Refrigeration Equipment Manufacturing**
		333411	Air Purification Equipment Manufacturing
		333415	Air-Conditiong and warm Air Heating Equipment and Commerical Industrial Refrigeration Equipment Manufacturing
		333414	Heating Equipment (except Warm Air Furnaces) Manufacturing
		333412	Industrial and Commerical Fan and Blower Manufacturing
333510	**333510**		**Metalworking Machinery Manufacturing**
		333511	Industrial Mold Manufacturing
		333512	Machine Tool (Metal Cutting Types) Manufacturing
		333513	Machine Tool (Metal Forming Types) Manufacturing
		333518	Other Metalworking Machinery Manufacturing
		333516	Rolling Mill Machinery and Equipment Manufacturing
		333514	Special Die and Tool, Die Set, Jig and Fixture Manufacturing
		333515	Cutting Tool and Machine Tool Accessory Manufacturing

SOI PUBLISHED CODE	PBA CODE	NAICS CODE	INDUSTRY
333610	333610		**Engine, Turbine and Power Transmission Equipment Manufacturing**
		333613	Mechanical Power Transmission Equipment Manufacturing
		333618	Other Engine Equipment Manufacturing
		333612	Speed Changer, Industrial High-Speed Drive, and Gear Manufacturing
		333611	Turbine and Turbine Generator Set Units Manufacturing
333900	333900		**Other General Purpose Machinery Manufacturing**
		333912	Air and Gas Compressor Manufacturing
		333999	All Other Miscellaneous General Purpose Machinery Manufacturing
		333922	Conveyor and Conveying Equipment Manufacturing
		333921	Elevator and Moving Stairway Manufacturing
		333995	Fluid Power Cylinder and Actuator Manufacturing
		333996	Fluid Power Pump and Motor Manufacturing
		333994	Industrial Process Furnace and Oven Manufacturing
		333924	Industrial Truck, Tractor, Trailer and Stacker Machinery Manufacturing
		333913	Measuring and Dispensing Pump Manufacturing
		333923	Overhead Traveling Crane, Hoist, and Monorail System Maufacturing
		333993	Packaging Machinery Manufacturing
		333991	Power-Driven Handtool Manufacturing
		333911	Pump and Pumping Equipment Manufacturing
		333997	Scale and Balance (except Laboratory) Manufacturing
		333992	Welding and Soldering Equipment Manufacturing

Computer & Electronic Product Manufacturing

SOI PUBLISHED CODE	PBA CODE	NAICS CODE	INDUSTRY
334110	334110		**Computer and Periphery Equipment Manufacturing**
		334112	Computer Storage Device Manufacturing
		334113	Computer Terminal Manufacturing
		334111	Electronic Computer Manufacturing
		334119	Other Computer Peripheral Equipmemt Manufacturing
334200	334200		**Communications Equipment Manufacturing**
		334290	Communcations Equipment Manufacturing, NEC

SOI Published Code	PBA Code	NAICS Code	Industry
		334220	Radio and Television Broadcasting and Wireless Communication Equipment Manufacturing
		334210	Telephone Apparatus Manufacturing
334315	**334310**		**Audio and Visual Equipment Manufacturing**
334410	**334410**		**Semiconductor & Other Electronic Components Manufacturing**
		334412	Bare Printed Circuit Board Manufacturing
		334411	Electorn Tube Manufacturing
		334414	Electronic Capacitor Manufacturing
		334416	Electronic Coil, Transformer, and Other Inductor Manufacturing
		334417	Electronic Connector Manufacturing
		334415	Electronic Resistor Manufacturing
		334419	Other Electric Component Manufacturing
		334418	Printed Circuit Assembly (Electronic Aseembly) Manufacturing
		334413	Semiconductor and Related Device Manufacturing
334500	**334500**		**Navigational, Measuring, Electromedical & Control Instruments Manufacturing**
		334516	Analytical Laboratory Instrument Manufacturing
		334512	Automatic Enviromental Control Manufacturing for Residential, Commerical and Appliance Use
		334510	Electromedical and Electrotherapeutic Apparatus Manufacturing
		334515	Instrument Manufacturing for Measuring and Testing Electricity and Electrical Signals
		334513	Instruments and Related Prodcuts Manufacturing for Measuring, Displaying and Controlling Industrial Process Variables
		334517	Irradiation Apparatus Manufacturing
		334519	Other Measuring and Controlling Device Manufacturing
		334511	Search, Detection, Navigationk Guidance, Aeronautical, and Nautical System and Instrument Manufacturing
		334514	Totalizing Fluid Meter and Counting Device Manufacturing
		334518	Watch, Clock and Part Manufacturing

SOI Published Code	PBA Code	NAICS Code	Industry
334315	334610		**Manufactuing and Reproducing Magnetic and Optical Media**
		334613	Magnetic and Optical Recording Media Manufacturing
		334612	Prerecorded Compact Disc (except Software) Tape, and Record Reproduction
		334611	Software Reproducing

Electrical Equipment, Appliance and Component Manufacturing

335105	335100		**Electical Lighting Equipment Manufacturing**
		335122	Commercial, Industrial, and Institutional Electric Lighting Fixture Manufacturing
		335110	Electric Lamp Bulb and Part Manufacturing
		335129	Other Lighting Equipment Manufacturing
		335121	Residential Electric Lighting Fixture Manufacturing
335105	335200		**Household Appliance Manufacturing**
		335211	Electric Housewares and Household Fan Manufacturing
		335221	Household Cooking Appliance Manufacturing
		335224	Household Laundry Equipment Manufacturing
		335222	Household Refrigerator and Home Freezer Manufacturing
		335212	Household Vacuum Cleaner Manufacturing
		335228	Other Major Household Appliance Manufacturing
335310	335310		**Electrical Equipment Manufacturing**
		335312	Motor and Genrator Manufacturing
		335311	Power, Distribution, and Specialty Transformer Manufacturing
		335314	Relay and Industrial Control Manufacturing
		335313	Switchgear and Switchboard Apparatus Manufacturing
335900	335900		**Other Electrical Equipment and Component Manufacturing**
		335991	Carbon and Graphite Product Manufacturing
		335931	Current-Carrying Wiring Device Manufacturing
		335999	All Other Miscellaneous Electrical Equipment and Component Manufacturing

SOI PUBLISHED CODE	PBA CODE	NAICS CODE	INDUSTRY
		335921	Fiber Optic Cable Manufacturing
		335932	Noncurrent-Carrying Wiring Device Manufacturing
		335929	Other Communication and Energy Wire Manufacturing
		335912	Primary Battery Manufacturing
		335911	Storage Battery Manufacturing

Transportation Equipment Manufacturing

336105	336100		**Motor Vehicle Manufacturing**
		336111	Automobile Manufacturing
		336120	Heavy Duty Truck Manufacturing
		336112	Light Truck and Utility Vehicle Manufacturing

336105	336210		**Motor Vehicle Body and Trailer Manufacturing**
		336213	Motor Home Manufacturing
		336211	Motor Vehicle Body Manufacturing
		336214	Travel Trailer and Camper Manufacturing
		336212	Truck Trailer Manufacturing

336105	336300		**Motor Vehicle Parts Manufacturing**
		336399	All Other Motor Vehicle Parts Manufacturing
		336311	Carburetor, Piston, Piston Ring and Valve Manufacturing
		336312	Gasoline Engine and Engine Parts Manufacturing
		336391	Motor Vehicle Air-Conditioning Manufacturing
		336340	Motor Vehicle Brake System Manufacturing
		336370	Motor Vehicle Metal Stamping
		336360	Motor Vehicle Seating and Interior Trim Manufacturing
		336330	Motor Vehicle Steering and Suspension Component (except Spring) Manufacturing
		336350	Motor Vehicle Transmission and Power Train Parts Manufacturing
		336322	Other Motor Vehicle Electrical and Electronic Equipment Manufacturing
		336321	Vehicular Lighting Equipment Manufacturing

SOI PUBLISHED CODE	PBA CODE	NAICS CODE	INDUSTRY
336410	336410		**Aerospace Product and Parts Manufacturing**
			336412 Aircraft Engine and Engine Parts Manufacturing
			336411 Aircraft Manufacturing
			336414 Guided Missile and Space Vehicle Manufacturing
			336415 Guided Missile and Space Vehicle Propulsion Unit and Propulsion Unit Parts Manufacturing
			336413 Other Aircraft Parts and Auxillary Equipment Manufacturing
			336419 Other Guided Missile and Space Vehicle Parts and Auxillary Equipment Manufacturing
336995	336510		**Railroad Rolling Stock Manufacturing**
336610	336610		**Ship and Boat Building**
			336612 Boat Building
			336611 Ship Building and Repairing
336995	336990		**Other Transportation Equipment Manufacturing**
			336992 Military Armored Vehicle, Tank and Tank Component Manufacturing
			336991 Motorcycle, Bicycle and Parts Manufacturing
			336999 Transportation Equipment Manufacturing, NEC

Furniture and Related Product Manufacturing

SOI PUBLISHED CODE	PBA CODE	NAICS CODE	INDUSTRY
337000	337000		**Furniture and Related Product Manufacturing**
			337920 Blind and Shade Manufacturing
			337212 Custom Architectural Woodwork and Millwork Manufacturing
			337125 Household Furniture (except Wood and Metal) Manufacturing
			337127 Institutional Furniture Manufacturing
			337910 Mattress Manufacturing
			337124 Metal Household Furniture Manufacturing
			337122 Nonupholstered Wood Household Furniture Manufacturing
			337214 Office Furniture (Except Wood) Manufacturing
			337215 Showcase, Partition, Shelving, and Locker Manufacturing

SOI PUBLISHED CODE	PBA CODE	NAICS CODE	INDUSTRY
		337121	Upholstered Household Furniture Manufacturing
		337110	Wood Kitchen Cabinet and Countertop Manufacturing
		337211	Wood Office Furniture Manufacturing
		337129	Wood Television, Radio and Sewing Machine Cabinet Manufacturing

Miscellaneous Manufacturing

339110	339110		**Medical Equipment and Supplies Manufacturing**
		339114	Dental Equipment and Supplies Manufacturing
		339116	Dental Laboratories
		339111	Laboratory Apparatus and Furniture Manufacturing
		339115	Ophthalmic Goods Manufacturing
		339113	Surgical Appliance and Supplies Manufacturing
		339112	Surgical and Medical Instrument Manufacturing

339900	339900		**Other Miscellaneous Manufacturing**
		339994	Broom, Brush and Mop Manufacturing
		339995	Burial Casket Manufacturing
		339944	Carbon Paper and Inked Ribbon Manufacturing
		339914	Costume Jewelry and Novelty Manufacturing
		339931	Doll and Stuff Toy manufacturing
		339993	Fastener, Button, Needle, and Pin Manufacturing
		339932	Game, Toy, and Children's Vehicle Manufacturing
		339991	Gasket, Packing, and Sealing Device Manufacturing
		339913	Jewelers' Material and Lapidary Work Manufacturing
		339911	Jewelry (except Costume) Manufacturing
		339942	Lead Pencil and Art Good Manufacturing
		339943	Marking Device Manufacturing
		339999	Miscellaneous Manufacturing, NEC
		339992	Musical Instrument Manufacturing
		339941	Pen and Mechanical Pencil Manufacturing
		339950	Sign Manufacturing
		339912	Silverware and Holloware Manufacturing
		339920	Sporting and Athletic Goods Manufacturing

SOI PUBLISHED CODE	PBA CODE	NAICS CODE	INDUSTRY

WHOLESALE TRADE

Merchant Wholesalers, Durable Goods

| 423100 | 423100 | | **Motor Vehicle & Motor Vehicle Parts & Supplies** |

423110 Automobile and Other Motor Vehicle Merchant Wholesalers

423120 Motor Vehicle Supplies and New Parts Merchant Wholesalers

423130 Tire and Tube Merchant Wholesalers

423140 Motor Vehicle Parts (Used) Merchant Wholesalers

| 423905 | 423200 | | **Furniture and Home Furninshings** |

423210 Furniture Merchant Wholesalers

423220 Home Funishings Merchant Wholesalers

| 423300 | 423300 | | **Lumber and Other Construction Materials** |

423310 Lumber, Plywood, Millwork, and Wood Panel Merchant Wholesalers

423320 Brick, Stone, and Related Construction Material Merchant Wholesalers

423330 Roofing, siding and Insulation Material Merchant Wholesalers

423390 Other Construction Material Merchant Wholesalers

| 423400 | 423400 | | **Professional and Commerical Equipment and Supplies** |

423410 Photographic Equipment and Supplies Merchant Wholesalers

423420 Office Equipment Merchant Wholesalers

423430 Computer and Computer Peripheral Equipment and Software Merchant Wholesalers

423440 Other Commerical Equipment Merchant Wholesalers

423450 Medical, Dental, and Hospital Equipment and Supplies Merchant Wholesalers

423460 Ophthalmic Goods Merchant Wholesalers

423490 Other Professional Equipment and Supplies Merchant Wholesaler

| 423500 | 423500 | | **Metal and Mineral (Except Petroleum)** |

423510 Metal Service Centers and Other Metal Merchant Wholesalers

423520 Coal and Other Minearl and Ore Merchant Wholesalers

SOI Published Code	PBA Code	NAICS Code	Industry
423600	423600		**Electrical and Electronic Goods**
		423610	Electrical Apparatus and Equipment, Wiring Supplies, and Related Equipment Merchant Wholesalers
		423620	Electrical and Electronic Appliance, Television and Radio Set Merchant Wholesalers
		423690	Other Electronic Parts and Equipment Merchant Wholesalers
423700	423700		**Hardware & Plumbing & Heating Equipment & Supplies**
		423710	Hardware Merchant Wholesales
		423720	Plumbing and Heating Equipment and Supplies (Hydronics) Merchant Wholesalers
		423730	Warm Air Heating and Air-Conditioning Equipment and Supplies Merchant Wholesalers
		423740	Refrigeration Equipment and Supplies Merchant Wholesalers
423800	423800		**Machinery, Equipment and Supplies Wholesalers**
		423810	Construction and Mining (except Oil Well) Machinery and Merchant Equipment
		423820	Farm and Garden Machinery and Equipment Merchant Wholesalers
		423890	Industrial Machinery and Equipment Merchant Wholesalers
		423840	Industrial Supplies Merchant Wholesalers
		423850	Service Establishment Equipment and Supplies Merchant Wholesalers
		423860	Transporation Equipment and Supplies (except Motor Vehicles) Merchant Wholesalers
423905	423910		**Sporting and Recreational Goods and Supplies**
423905	423920		**Toy and Hobby Goods and Supplies**
423905	423930		**Recyclable Materials**

SOI PUBLISHED CODE	PBA CODE	NAICS CODE	INDUSTRY
423905	423940		**Jewelry, Watch, Precious Stone, and Precious Metals**
423905	423990		**Other Miscellaneous Durable Goods**

Merchant Wholesalers, Nondurable Goods

424100	424100		**Paper and Paper Products**
		424110	Printing and Writing Paper Merchant Wholesalers
		424120	Stationery and Office Supplies Merchant Wholesalers
		424130	Industrial and Personal Service Paper Merchant Wholesalers
424210	424210		**Drug and Druggists' Sundries**
424300	424300		**Apparel, Piece Goods and Notions**
		424310	Piece Goods, Notions, and Other Dry Goods Merchant Wholesalers
		424320	Men's and Boys' Clothing and Furnishings Merchant Wholesalers
		424330	Women's Children's and Infant's Clothing and Accessories Merchant Wholesalers
		424340	Footwear Wholesalers
424400	424400		**Grocery and Related Products**
		424450	Confectionary Merchant Wholesalers
		424430	Dairy Product (except Dried or Canned) Merchant Wholesalers
		424460	Fish and Seafood Merchant Wholesalers
		424480	Fresh Fruit and Vegetable Merchant Wholesalers (tomatoes, produce)
		424410	General Line Grocery Merchant Wholesalers
		424470	Meat and Meat Product Merchant Wholesalers
		424490	Other Grocery and Related Products Merchant Wholesalers
		424420	Packaged Frozen Food Merchant Wholesalers
		424440	Poultry and Poultry Product Merchant Wholesalers

SOI Published Code	PBA Code	NAICS Code	INDUSTRY
424500	424500		**Farm Product Raw Materials**
			424510 Grain and Field Bean Merchant Wholesalers
			424520 Livestock Merchant Wholesalers
			424590 Other Farm Product Raw Material Merchant Wholesalers
424600	424600		**Chemical and Allied Products**
			424690 Other Chemical and Allied Products Merchant Wholesalers
			424610 Plastics Materials and Basic Forms and Shapes Merchant Wholesalers
424700	424700		**Petroleum and Petroleum Products**
			424710 Petroleum Bulk Stations and Terminals
			424720 Petroleum and Petroleum Products Merchant Wholesalers (except Bulk Stations and Terminals)
424800	424800		**Beer, Wine and Distilled Alcoholic Beverages**
			424810 Beer and Ale Merchant Wholesalers
			424820 Wine and Distilled Alcoholic Beverage Merchant Wholesalers
424915	424910		**Farm Supplies**
424915	424920		**Book, Periodical, and Newspapers**
424915	424930		**Flower, Nursery Stock, Florists' Supplies**
424915	424940		**Tobacco and Tobacco Products**
424915	424950		**Paint, Varnish and Supplies**

SOI Published Code	PBA Code	NAICS Code	Industry
424915	424990		Other Miscellaneous Nondurable Goods

Wholesale Electronic Markets & Agents & Brokers

425115	425110		Busines to Business Electronic Markets
425115	425120		Wholesale Trade Agents and Brokers

RETAIL TRADE

Motor Vehicle and Parts Dealers

441115	441110		New Car Dealers
441115	441120		Used Car Dealers
441215	441210		Recrational Vehicle Dealers
441215	441221		Motorcycle Dealers
441215	441222		Boat Dealers
441215	441229		All Other Motor Vehicle Dealers
441215	441300		Automotive Parts, Accessories

441310 Automotive Parts and Accessories Stores
441320 Tire Dealers

SOI PUBLISHED CODE	PBA CODE	NAICS CODE	INDUSTRY
Furniture and Home Furnishings Stores			
442115	442110		Furniture Stores
442115	442210		Floor Covering Stores
442115	442291		Window Treatment Stores
442115	442299		All Other Home Furnishings Stores
Electronics and Appliance Stores			
443115	443111		Household Appliance Stores
443115	443112		Radio, Television, and Other Electronics Stores
443115	443120		Computer and Software Stores
443115	443130		Camera and Photographic Supplies Store
444115	444110		Home Centers
444115	444120		Paint and Wallpaper Stores
444130	444130		Hardware Stores
444190	444190		Other Building Material Dealers

SOI PUBLISHED CODE	PBA CODE	NAICS CODE	INDUSTRY
444200	444200		**Law and Garden Equipment and Supplies Stores**
			444210 Outdoor Power Equipment Stores

Food and Beverage Stores

445115	445110		**Supermarkets and Other Grocery (except Convience) Stores**
445115	445120		**Convience Stores**
445115	445210		**Meat Markets**
445115	445220		**Fish and Seafood Markets**
445115	445230		**Fruit and Vegetables Markets**
445115	445291		**Baked Good Stores**
445115	445292		**Confectionery and Nut Store**
445115	445299		**All Other Specialty Food Stores**
445310	445310		**Beer, Wine and Liquor Stores**

Health and Personal Care Stores

446115	446110		**Pharmacies and Drug Stores**

SOI PUBLISHED CODE	PBA CODE	NAICS CODE	INDUSTRY
446115	446120		Cosmetics, Beauty Supplies and Perfume Stores
446115	446130		Optical Goods Stores
446115	446190		Other Health and Person Care Stores
		446199	All Other Health and Personal Care Stores
		446191	Food (Health) Supplement Stores
447100	447100		Gasoline Stations
		447110	Gasoline Stations with Convience Stores
		447190	Other Gasoline Stations

Clothing and Clothing Acessories Stores

448115	448110		Men's Clothing Stores
448115	448120		Women's Clothing Stores
448115	448130		Children's and Infant's Clothing Stores
448115	448140		Family Clothing Stores
448115	448150		Clothing Acessories Stores
448115	448190		Other Clothing Stores
448115	448210		Shoe Stores

SOI Published Code	PBA Code	NAICS Code	Industry
448115	448310		Jewelry Stores
448115	448320		Luggage and Leather Goods Stores

Sporting Goods, Hobby, Book & Music Stores

SOI Published Code	PBA Code	NAICS Code	Industry
451115	451110		Sporting Goods Stores
451115	451120		Hobby, Toy, and Game Stores
451115	451130		Sewing, Needlework, and Piece Goods Stores
451115	451140		Musical Instrument and Supplies Stores
451115	451211		Book Stores
451115	451212		News Dealers and Newsstands
451115	451220		Prerecorded Tape, Compact Disc, and Record Stores

General Merchandise Stores

SOI Published Code	PBA Code	NAICS Code	Industry
452115	452110		Department Stores
452115	452900		General Merchandise Stores

452990 All Other General Merchandise Stores

452910 Warehouse Clubs and Superstores

SOI Published Code	PBA Code	NAICS Code	Industry
Miscellaneous Store Retailers			
453115	453110		Florists
453115	453210		Office Supplies and Stationary Stores
453115	453220		Gift, Novelty and Souvenir Stores
453115	453310		Used Merchandise Stores
453115	453910		Pet and Pet Supplies Stores
453115	453920		Art Dealers
453115	453930		Manufactured (Mobile) Home Dealers
453115	453990		All Other Miscellaneous Store Retailers (including Tobacco, Candle & Trophy Shops) 453998 Miscellaneous Store Retailers (except Tobacco Stores) 453991 Tobacco Stores
Nonstore Retailers			
454115	454110		Electronic Shopping and Mail-Order Houses
454115	454210		Vending Machine Operators

SOI PUBLISHED CODE	PBA CODE	NAICS CODE	INDUSTRY
454115	454311		**Heating Oil Dealers**
454115	454312		**Liquified Petroleum Gas (Bottled Gas) Dealers**
454115	454319		**Other Fuel Dealers**
454115	454390		**Other Direct Selling Establishments**

WHOLESALE/RETAIL NON-ALLOCABLE

460000	460000		**Wholesale/Retail Non-Allocable**

TRANSPORTATION AND WAREHOUSING

Air, Rail and Water Transportation

481000	481000		**Air Transportation**
		481212	Nonscheduled Chartered Freight Air Transportation
		481211	Nonscheduled Chartered Passenger Air Transportation
		481219	Other Nonscheduled Air Transportation
		481112	Scheduled Freight Air Transportation
		481111	Scheduled Passenger Air Transportation
482110	482110		**Rail Transportation**
		482111	Line-Haul Railroads
		482112	Short Line Railroads
483000	483000		**Water Transportation**
		483113	Coastal and Great Lakes Freight Transportation
		483114	Coastal and Great Lakes Passenger Transportation

SOI PUBLISHED CODE	PBA CODE	NAICS CODE	INDUSTRY
		483111	Deep Sea Freight Transportation
		483112	Deep Sea Passenger Transportation
		483211	Inland Water Freight Transportation
		483212	Inland Water Passenger Transportation

Truck Transportation

484115	484110		**General Freight Trucking, Local**
484115	484120		**General Freight Trucking, Long Distance**
		484122	General Freight Trucking, Long Distance, Less Than Truckload
		484121	General Freight Trucking, Long Distance, Truckload
484115	484190		**General Freight Trucking Non Allocable**
484200	484200		**Specialized Freight Trucking**
		484220	Specialized Freight (except Used Goods) Trucking, Local
		484230	Specialized Freight (except Used Goods) Trucking, Long-Distance
		484210	Used Household and Office Goods Moving

Transit and Ground Passenger Transportation

485115	485110		**Urban Transit Systems**
		485113	Bus and Other Motor Vehicle Transit Systems
		485112	Commuter Rail Systems
		485111	Mixed Mode Transit Systems
		485119	Other Urban Transit Systems
485115	485210		**Interurban & Rural Bus Transportation**
485115	485310		**Taxi Service**

SOI PUBLISHED CODE	PBA CODE	NAICS CODE	INDUSTRY
485115	485320		**Limousine Service**
485115	485410		**School and Employee Bus Transportation**
485115	485510		**Charter Bus Industry**
485115	485990		**Other Transit & Ground Passenger Transportation**
			485991 Special Needs Transportation
			485999 Transit and Ground Passenger Transportation, NEC

Pipeline Transportation

SOI PUBLISHED CODE	PBA CODE	NAICS CODE	INDUSTRY
486000	486000		**Pipeline Transportation**
			486990 All Other Pipeline Transportation
			486110 Pipeline Transportation of Cruide Oil
			486210 Pipeline Transportation of Natural Gas
			486910 Pipeline Transportation of Refined Petroleum Products

Scenic & Sightseeing Transportation

SOI PUBLISHED CODE	PBA CODE	NAICS CODE	INDUSTRY
487005	487000		**Scenic & Sightseeing Transportation**
			487110 Scenic & Sightseeing Transportation, Land
			487990 Scenic & Sightseeing Transportation, Other
			487210 Scenic & Sightseeing Transportation, Water

Support Activities for Transportation

SOI PUBLISHED CODE	PBA CODE	NAICS CODE	INDUSTRY
487005	488100		**Support Activities for Air Transportation**
			488111 Air Traffic Control
			488119 Other Airport Operations
			488190 Support Activities for Air Transportation, NEC

SOI Published Code	PBA Code	NAICS Code	Industry
487005	488210		**Support Activities for Rail Transportation**
487005	488300		**Support Activities for Water Transportation**
		488330	Navigational Services to Shipping
		488310	Port and Harbor Operations
		488390	Support Activities for Water Transportation, NEC
487005	488410		**Motor Vehicle Towing**
487005	488490		**Other Support Activities for Road Transportation**
487005	488510		**Freight Transportation Arrangement**
487005	488990		**Other Support Activities for Transportation**
		488991	Packing and Crating
		488999	Support Activities for Transportation, NEC

Couriers and Messengers

SOI Published Code	PBA Code	NAICS Code	Industry
487005	492110		**Couriers**
487005	492210		**Local Messengers and Local Delivery**

Warehousing and Storage

SOI Published Code	PBA Code	NAICS Code	Industry
493100	493100		**Warehousign & Storage (excluding lessor or miniwarehouses & Self Storage)**
		493130	Farm Product Warehousing and Storage
		493110	General Warehousing and Storage
		493190	Other Warehousing and Storage
		493120	Refigerated Warehousing and Storage

SOI PUBLISHED CODE	PBA CODE	NAICS CODE	INDUSTRY

INFORMATION

Publishing Industries (except Internet)

511110	511110		**Newspaper Publishing**
511120	511120		**Periodical Publishers**
511130	511130		**Book Publishers**
511145	511140		**Directory & Mailing List Publishers**
511145	511190		**Other Publishers**

511191 Greeting Card Publishers
511199 All Other Publishers

511210	511210		**Software Publishers**

Motion Picture & Sound Recording Industries

512100	512100		**Motion Picture & Video Industries (except Video Rental)**

512132 Drive-In Motion Picture Theaters
512131 Motion Picture Teathers (except Drive-Ins)
512120 Motion Picture and Video Distribution
512199 Other Motion Picture and Video Industries
512110 Motion Picture and Video Production
512191 Teleproduction and Other Postproduction Services

512200	512200		**Sound Recording Industries**

512220 Integrated Record Production/Distribution
512230 Music Publishers

SOI PUBLISHED CODE	PBA CODE	NAICS CODE	INDUSTRY
		512290	Other Sound Recoring Industries
		512210	Record Production
		512240	Sound Recording Studios

Broadcasting (except Internet)

515105	515100		**Radio & Television Broadcasting**
		513111	Radio Networks
		513112	Radio Stations
		513120	Television Broadcasting

515105	515210		**Cable & Other Subscription Programming**

Telecommunications

517000	517000		**Telecommunications (including paging, cellular, satellite, cable & other program distribution, resellers & other telecommunications**
		517110	Wired Telecommunications Carriers
		517210	Wireless Telecommunication Carriers (except Satellite)
		517410	Statelitte Telecommunications
		517911	Telecommunication Resellers
		517919	All Other Telecommunications

Internet Service Providers, Web Search Portals & Data Processing Services

518210	518210		**Data Processing, Hosting & Related Services**

Other Information Services

519100	519100		**Other Information Services (including new syndicates & libraries)**
		519110	News Syndicates
		519130	Internet Publishing and Broadcasting and Web Search Portals
		519120	Libraries and Archives
		519190	All Other Information Services

SOI Published Code	PBA Code	NAICS Code	Industry
			FINANCE & INSURANCE
Depository Credit Intermediation			
522110	522110		Commerical Banking
522125	522120		Savings Institutions
522125	522130		Credit Unions
522125	522190		Other Depository Credit Intermediation
Nondepository Credit Intermediation			
522215	522210		Credit Card Issuing
522215	522220		Sales Financing
522215	522291		Consumer Lending
522292	522292		Real Estate Credit (including Mortgage Bankers, and Originators)
522295	522293		International Trade Financing
522295	522294		Secondary Market Financing
522295	522298		All Other Nondepository Credit Intermediation

SOI PUBLISHED CODE	PBA CODE	NAICS CODE	INDUSTRY

Activities Related to Credit Intermediation

522300	522300		**Activities Related to Credit Intermediation (including loan brokers, check clearing & money transmitting)**
		522320	Financial Transactions Processing, Reserve and Clearinghouse Activities (AutomatedClearinghouse, Electronic Funds Transfer Services)
		522310	Mortgage and Nonmortgage Loan Brokers
		522390	Other Activities Related to Credit Intermediation

Securities, Commodity Contracts, and Other Finanical Investment Activities

523110	523110		**Investment Banking and Securities Dealing**
523120	523120		**Securities Brokerage**
523135	523130		**Commodity Contracts Dealings**
523135	523140		**Commodity Contracts Brokerage**
523905	523210		**Securities and Commodity Exchanges**
523905	523900		**Other Financial Investment Activities (including portfolio management & investment advice)**
		523999	Finanical Investment Advice (Securities/Commodities Exchange Clearinghouses, Stock Quotation Services)
		523930	Investment Advice (Finanical Advice, Advisory, Counseling, or Investment Services, Finanical Planner/Consultant, Management Group)
		523910	Miscellaneous Intermediation (Investment Clubs, Venture Capital Cos.)
		523920	Portfolio Management (Investment or Financial Management, Commodity Trading Advisor (CTA)
		523991	Trust, Fiduciary and Custody Activities

SOI Published Code	PBA Code	NAICS Code	Industry
Insurance Carriers & Related Activities			
524142	524142		**Life Insurance, Stock Companies (Form 1120L)**
524143	524143		**Life Insurance, Mutual Companies (Form 1120L)**
524156	524156		**Mutual Property and Casualty Companies (Form 1120PC)**
524159	524159		**Stock Property and Casualty Companies (Form 1120PC)**
524210	524210		**Insurance Agencies and Brokerages**
524290	524290		**Other Insurance Realted Activities (including third-party administration or insurance and pension funds)**
		524298	All Other Insurance Related Activities
		524291	Claims Adjusting
		524292	Third Party Adminstration of Insurance and Pension Funds
Funds, Trusts & Other Finanical Variables			
525995	525100		**Insurance & Other Employee Benefits**
		525120	Health and Welfare Funds
		525190	Other Insurance Funds
		525110	Pension Funds
525910	525910		**Open-End Investment Funds (Form 1120-RIC)**
525995	525920		**Trust, Estates, and Agency Accounts**
525995	525990		**Other Financial Vehicles**

SOI PUBLISHED CODE	PBA CODE	NAICS CODE	INDUSTRY

REAL ESTATE AND RENTAL AND LEASING

Real Estate

SOI PUBLISHED CODE	PBA CODE	NAICS CODE	INDUSTRY
531115	531110		**Lessor of Residential Buildings and Dwellings (Form 1120-REIT, Equity Only)**
531115	531114		**Cooperative Housing (Form 1120-REIT, Equity Only)**
531115	531120		**Lessor of Nonresidential Buildings (except Miniwarehouses) (Form 1120-REIT Equity Only)**
531135	531130		**Lessor of Miniwarehouses & Self-Storage Units (Form 1120-REIT Equity Only)**
531135	531190		**Lessor of Other Real Estate Property (Form 1120-REIT Equity Only)**
531210	531210		**Offices of Real Estate Agents and Brokers**
531315	531310		**Real Estate Property Managers** 531312 Nonresidential Property Managers 531311 Residential Property Managers (condominium management)
531315	531320		**Offics of Real Estate Appraisers**
531315	531390		**Other Activities Related to Real Estate**

SOI PUBLISHED CODE	PBA CODE	NAICS CODE	INDUSTRY
Rental and Leasing Services			
532100	**532100**		**Automotive Equipment Rental and Leasing**
		532112	Passenger Car Leasing
		532111	Passenger Car Rental
		532120	Truck, Utility Trailer and RV (Recreation Vehicle) Rental and Leasing
532215	**532210**		**Consumer Electronics & Appliances Rental**
532215	**532220**		**Formal Wear and Costume Rental**
532215	**532230**		**Video Tape and Disc Rental**
532215	**532290**		**Other Consumer Goods Rental**
		532299	Consumer Goods Rental, NEC
		532291	Home Health Equipment Rental
		532292	Recreational Goods Rental
532215	**532310**		**General Rental Centers**
532400	**532400**		**Commerical and Industrial Machinery & Equipment Rental**
		532411	Commerical Air, Rail and Water Transportation Equipment Rental & Leasing
		532412	Construction, Mining and Forestry Machinery & Equipment Rental & Leasing
		532420	Office Machinery and Equipment Rental & Leasing
		432490	Other Commerical and Industrial Machinery & Equipment Rental & Leasing

SOI PUBLISHED CODE	PBA CODE	NAICS CODE	INDUSTRY

Lessor of Nonfinanical Intangible Assets (except copyrighted work)

533110	533110		Lessor of Nonfinanical Intangible Assets (except Copyrighted Work)

PROFESSIONAL, SCIENTIFIC AND TECHNICAL SERVICES

Legal Services

541115	541110		Office of Lawyers
541115	541190		Other Legal Services

541199 Legal Services, NEC

541191 Title Abstract and Settlement Offices

Accounting, Tax Preparation, Bookkeping & Payroll Services

541215	541211		Offices of Certified Public Accoutants
541215	541213		Tax Preparation Services
541215	541214		Payroll Services
541215	541219		Other Accounting Services

Architectual, Engineering & Related Services

541315	541310		Architectural Services
541315	541320		Landscape Architectural Services

SOI Published Code	PBA Code	NAICS Code	Industry
541315	541330		Engineering Services
541315	541340		Drafting Services
541315	541350		Building Inspection Services
541315	541360		Geophysical Surveying and Mapping Services
541315	541370		Surveying and Mapping (except Geophysical) Services
541315	541380		Testing Laboratories

Specialized Design Services

SOI Published Code	PBA Code	NAICS Code	Industry
541400	541400		Specialied Design Services (including interior, industrial, graphic & fashion design)
		541430	Graphic Design Services
		541420	Industrial Design Services
		541410	Inerior Design Services
		541490	Other Specialized Design Services

Computer Systems Design & Related Services

SOI Published Code	PBA Code	NAICS Code	Industry
541515	541511		Custom Computer Programming Services
541515	541512		Computer Systems Design Services
541515	541513		Computer Facilities Management Services

SOI PUBLISHED CODE	PBA CODE	NAICS CODE	INDUSTRY
541515	541519		**Other Computer Related Services**

Other Professional, Scientific & Technical Services

541600	541600		**Management, Scientific & Technical Consulting Services**

541611 Administrative Management and General Management Consulting Services

541620 Environmental Consulting Services

541612 Human Resources Consulting Services

541613 Marketing Consulting Services

541618 Other Management Consulting Services

541690 Other Scientific and Technical Consulting Services

541614 Process, Physical Distribution and Logistics Consulting Services

541700	541700		**Scientific Research & Development Services**

541711 Research and Development in Biotechnology

541712 Research and Development in Physical, Engineering & Life Sciences (except Biotechnology)

541720 Research and Development in the Social Sciences and Humanities

541800	541800		**Advertising & Related Services**

541810 Advertising Agencies

541870 Advertising Material Distribution Services

541860 Direct Mail Advertising

541850 Display Advertising

541830 Media Buying Agencies

541840 Media Representatives

541890 Other Services Related to Advertising

541820 Public Relations Agencies

541915	541910		**Marketing Research & Public Opinion Polling**

SOI PUBLISHED CODE	PBA CODE	NAICS CODE	INDUSTRY
541915	541920		**Photographic Services**
		541922	Commercial Photography
		541921	Photography Studios, Portrait
541915	541930		**Translation and Interpretation Services**
541915	541940		**Veterinary Services**
541915	541990		**All Other Professional, Scientific, and Technical Services**

MANAGEMENT OF COMPANIES (HOLDING COMPANIES)

551111	551111		**Offices of Bank Holding Companies**
551112	551112		**Office of Other Holding Companies (personal holding companies, investments)**

ADMINISTRATIVE AND SUPPORT & WASTE MANAGEMENT & REMEDIATION SERVICES

Administrative and Support Services

561905	561110		**Office Administrative Services**
561905	561210		**Facilities Support Services**
561300	561300		**Employment Services**
		561330	Professional Employer Organizations
		561311	Employment Placement Agencies

SOI Published Code	PBA Code	NAICS Code	Industry
		561312	Executive Search Services
		561320	Temporary Help Services
561905	561410		**Document Preparation Services**
561905	561420		**Telephone Call Centers**
		561421	Telephone Answering Services
		561422	Telemarketing Bureaus and Other Contact Centers
561905	561430		**Business Services Centers (including private mail centers & copy shops)**
		561439	Other Business Service Centers (including Copy Shops)
		461431	Private Mail Centers
561905	561430		**Business Services Centers (Including private mail center & copy shops)**
		561439	Other Business Service Centers (including Copy Shops)
		461431	Private Mail Centers
561905	561440		**Collection Agencies**
561905	561450		**Credit Bureaus**
561905	561490		**Other Business Support Services (including repossession services, court reporting & stenotype services)**
		561492	Court Reporting and Stenotype Services
		561499	Business Support Services, NEC
		561491	Repossession Services

SOI PUBLISHED CODE	PBA CODE	NAICS CODE	INDUSTRY
561500	561500		**Travel Arrangement and Reservation Services**
		561591	Convention and Visitors Bureaus
		561520	Tour Operators
		561510	Travel Agencies
		561599	Travel Arrangement and Reservation Services, NEC
561905	561600		**Investigation & Sercurity Services**
		561613	Armored Car Services
		561611	Investigation Services
		561622	Locksmiths
		561612	Security Guards and Patrol Services
		561621	Security Systems Services (except Locksmiths)
561905	561710		**Extermination & Pest Control Services**
561905	561720		**Janitorial Services**
561905	561730		**Landscaping Services**
561905	561740		**Carpet & Upholstery Cleaning Services**
561905	561790		**Other Services to Buildings and Dwellings**
561905	561900		**Other Support Services**
		561920	Convention and Trade Show Organizers
		561910	Packaging and Labeling Services
		561990	All Other Support Services

SOI PUBLISHED CODE	PBA CODE	NAICS CODE	INDUSTRY

Waste Management & Remediation Services

| 562000 | 562000 | | **Waste Management & Remediation Services** |

562998 All other Miscellaneous Waste Management Services

562112 Hazardous Waste Collection

562211 Hazardous Waste Treatment and Disposal

562920 Materials Recovery Facilities

562219 Other Nonhazardous Waste Treatment and Disposal

562119 Other Waste Collection

562910 Remediation Services

562991 Spetic Tank and Related Services

562111 Solid Waste Collection

562213 Solid Waste Combustors and Incinerators

562212 Solid Waste Landfill

EDUCATIONAL SERVICES

| 611000 | 611000 | | **Educational Services (including schools, colleges & universities)** |

611699 All Other Miscellaneous Schools and Instruction

611513 Apprenticeship Training

611692 Automobile Driving Schools

611410 Business and Secretarial Schools

611310 Colleges, Universities and Professional Schools

611420 Computer Training

611511 Cosmetology and Barber Schools

611710 Educational Support Services

611110 Elementary and Secondary Schools

611691 Exam Preparation and Tutoring

611610 Fine Arts Schools

611512 Flight Training

611210 Junior Colleges

611630 Language Schools

611519 Other Technical and Trade Schools

611430 Professional and Management Development Training

611620 Sports and Recreation Instruction

SOI Published Code	PBA Code	NAICS Code	Industry

HEALTH CARE AND SOCIAL ASSISTANCE

Offices & Physicians & Dentists

621115	621111		Offices of Physicians (except Mental Health Specialist)
621115	621112		Offices of Physicians, Mental Health Specialist
621210	621210		Offices of Dentists

Offices of Other Health Practitioners

621315	621310		Offices of Chiropractors
621315	621320		Offices of Optometrists
621315	621330		Office of Mental Health Practitioners (except Physicians)
621315	621340		Offices of Physical, Occupational and Speech Therapists & Audiologist
621315	621391		Offices of Podiatrists
621315	621399		Offices of All Other Miscellaneous Health Practitioners

Outpatient Care Centers

621415	621410		Family Planning Centers

SOI Published Code	PBA Code	NAICS Code	Industry
621415	621420		**Outpatient Mental Health and Substance Abuse Centers**
621415	621491		**HMO Medical Centers**
621415	621492		**Kidney Dialysis Centers**
621415	621493		**Freestanding Ambulatory Surgical & Emergency Centers**
621415	621498		**All Other Outpatient Care Centers**

Medical and Diagnostic Laboratories

621515	621510		**Medical and Diagnostic Laboratories**

621512 Diagnostic Imaging Centers

621511 Medical Laboratories

Home Health Care Services

621515	621610		**Home Health Care Services**

Other Ambulatory Health Care Services

621515	621900		**All Other Miscellaneous Ambulatory Health Care Services**

621910 Ambulance Services

621991 Blood and Organ Banks

Hospitals

622005	622000		**Hospitals**

622110 General Medical and Surgical Hospitals

622210 Psychiatric and Substance Abuse Hospitals

622310 Specialty (except Psychiatric and Substance Abuse) Hosptials

SOI PUBLISHED CODE	PBA CODE	NAICS CODE	INDUSTRY

Nursing & Residential Care Facilities

622005	623000		**Nursing & Residential Care Facilities**
		623311	Continuing Care Retirement Communities
		623312	Homes for the Elderly
		623110	Nursing Care Facilities
		623990	Other Residential Care Facilities
		623220	Residential Mental Health and Substance Abuse Facilities
		623210	Residential Mental Health Retardation Facilities

Social Assistance

621515	624100		**Individual and Family**
		624110	Child and Youth Services
		624190	Other Individual and Family Services
		624120	Service for the Elderly and Persons with Disabilities

621515	624200		**Community Food & Housing & Emergency & Other Relief Services**
		624210	Community Food Services
		624230	Emergency and Other Relief Services
		624229	Other Community Housing Services
		624221	Temporary Services

| 621515 | 624310 | | **Vocational Rehibilitation Services** |

| 621515 | 624410 | | **Child Day Care Services** |

ARTS, ENTERTAINMENT AND RECREATION

Performing Arts, Spectator Sports & Related Industries

| 711105 | 711100 | | **Performing Arts Companies** |
| | | 711120 | Dance Companies |

SOI Published Code	PBA Code	NAICS Code	Industry
			711130 Musical Groups and Artists
			711190 Other Performing Arts Companies
			711110 Theater Companies and Dinner Theaters
711105	711210		**Spectator Sports (Including Sports Clubs and Racetracks)**
			711219 Other Spectator Sports
			711212 Racetracks
			711211 Sports Teams and Clubs
711105	711300		**Promoters of Performing Arts, Sports, and Similar Events**
			711310 Promoters of Performing Arts, Sports, and Similar Events with Facilities
			711320 Promoters of Performing Arts, Sports, and Similar Events without Facilities
711105	711410		**Agents & Managers for Artists, Athletes, Entertainers & Other Public Figures**
711105	711510		**Independent Artists, Writers and Performers**

Museums, Historical Sites & Similar Institutions

SOI Published Code	PBA Code	NAICS Code	Industry
711105	712100		**Museums, Historical Sites & Other Similar Institutions**
			712120 Historical Sites
			712110 Museums, Historical Sites & Other Similar Institutions
			712190 Nature Parks and Other Similar Institutions
			712130 Zoos and Botanical Gardens

Amusement, Gambling and Recreational Activities

SOI Published Code	PBA Code	NAICS Code	Industry
713105	713100		**Amusement Parks and Arcades**
			713120 Amusement Arcades
			713110 Amusement and Theme Parks

SOI Published Code	PBA Code	NAICS Code	Industry
713105	713200		**Gambling Industry**
		713210	Casinos (except Casino Hotels)
		713290	Other Gambling Industries
713105	713900		**Other Amusement & Recreation Industries (including golf courses, skiing facilities, marinas, fitness centers & bowling centers)**
		713990	All Other Amusement and Recreation Industries
		713950	Bowling Centers
		713940	Fitness and Recreational Sports Centers
		713910	Gold Courses and Country Clubs
		713930	Marinas
		713920	Skiing Facilities

ACCOMMODATION & FOOD SERVICES

Accommodation

SOI Published Code	PBA Code	NAICS Code	Industry
721115	721110		**Hotels (except Casino Hotels) and Motels**
721115	721120		**Casino Hotels**
721115	721191		**Bed-and-Breakfast Inns**
721115	721199		**All Other Traveler Accomodation**
721115	721210		**RV (Recreational Vehicle) Parks and Recreational Parks**
		721211	RV (Recreational Vehicle) Parks and Campgrounds
		721214	Recreational and Vacation Camps (except Campgrounds)

SOI PUBLISHED CODE	PBA CODE	NAICS CODE	INDUSTRY
721115	721310		**Rooming and Boarding Houses**

Food Services and Drinking Places

SOI PUBLISHED CODE	PBA CODE	NAICS CODE	INDUSTRY
722115	722110		**Full-Service Restaurants**
722115	722210		**Limited Service Eating Place**
		722212	Cafeterias
		722211	Limited-Service Restaurants
		722213	Snack and Nonalcoholic Beverage Bars
722115	722300		**Special Food Services (including food service contractors & caterers)**
		722320	Caterers
		722310	Food Service Contractors
		722330	Mobile Food Services
722115	722410		**Drinking Places (Alcoholic Beverages)**

OTHER SERVICES

Repair and Maintenance

SOI PUBLISHED CODE	PBA CODE	NAICS CODE	INDUSTRY
811115	811110		**Automotive Mechanical and Electrical Repair and Maintenance**
		811112	Automotive Exhaust System Repair
		811113	Automotive Transmission Repair
		811111	General Automotive Repair Maintenance
		811118	Other Automotive Mechanical and Electrical Repair and Maintenance
811115	811120		**Automotive Body, Paint, Interior & Glass Repair**
		811121	Automotive Body, Paint, and Interior Repair and Maintenance
		811122	Automotive Glass Replacement Shops

SOI PUBLISHED CODE	PBA CODE	NAICS CODE	INDUSTRY
811115	811190		**Other Automotive Repair & Maintenance (including oil change & lubrication shops & car washes)**
			811198 All Other Automotive Repair and Maintenance
			811191 Automotive Oil Change and Lubrication Shops
			811192 Car Washes
811215	811210		**Electronic & Precision Equipment Repair & Maintenance**
			811213 Communication Equipment Repair and Maintenance
			811212 Computer and Office Machine Repair and Maintenance
			811211 Consumer Electronics Repair and Maintenance
			811219 Other Electronic & Precision Equipment Repair & Maintenance except Automotive
811215	811310		**Commerical & Industrial Machinery & Equipment (except Automotive & Electronic) Repair & Maintenance**
811215	811410		**Home & Garden Equipment & Appliance Repair & Maintenance**
			811412 Appliance Repair and Maintenance
			811411 Home and Garden Equipment Repair and Maintenance
811215	811420		**Reupholstery & Furniture Repair**
811215	811430		**Footware and Leather Goods Repair**
811215	811490		**Other Personal and Household Goods Repair & Maintenance**

Personal and Laundry Services

SOI PUBLISHED CODE	PBA CODE	NAICS CODE	INDUSTRY
812115	812111		**Barber Shops**

SOI Published Code	PBA Code	NAICS Code	Industry
812115	812112		**Beauty Salons**
812115	812113		**Nail Salons**
812115	812190		**Other Personal Care Services (including diet & weight reducing centers)**
		812191	Diet and Weight Reducing Centers
		812199	Other Personal Care Services
812115	812210		**Funeral Homes and Funeral Services**
812115	812220		**Cemeteries and Crematories**
812115	812310		**Coin-Operated Laundries and Drycleaners**
812115	812320		**Drycleaning and Laundry Services (except Coin-Operated)**
812115	812330		**Linen and Uniform Supply**
		812332	Industrial Launderers
		812331	Linen Supply
812115	812910		**Pet Care (except Veterinary) Services**
812115	812920		**Photofinishing**
		812992	One-Hour Photofinishing
		812921	Photofinishing Laboratories (except One-Hour)

SOI PUBLISHED CODE	PBA CODE	NAICS CODE	INDUSTRY
812115	812930		**Parking Lots and Garages**
812115	812990		**All Other Personal Services**

Religious, Grantmaking, Civic, Professional and Similar Organizations

SOI PUBLISHED CODE	PBA CODE	NAICS CODE	INDUSTRY
813000	813000		**Religious, Grantmaking, Civic, Professional and Similar Organizations**

813910 Business Activities

813410 Civic and Social Organizations

813312 Environment, Conservation and Wildlife Organizations

813211 Grantmaking Foundations

813311 Human Rights Organization

813930 Labor Unions and Similar Labor Organizations

813219 Other Grantmaking and Giving Services

813990 Other Similar Organizations
(except Business, Professional, Labor and Political Organizations)

813319 Other Social Advocacy Organizations

813940 Political Organizations

813920 Professional Organizations

813110 Religious Oraganizations

813212 Voluntary Health Organizations

NATURE OF BUSINESS NOT ALLOCABLE

SOI PUBLISHED CODE	PBA CODE	NAICS CODE	INDUSTRY
900000	900000		**Nature of Business Not Allocable**

INDEX

INDEX